WHITE'S 1844 SUFFOLK

WHITE'S
1844 SUFFOLK

A Reprint of the 1844 issue of
*History, Gazetteer, and Directory of
Suffolk*

By

WILLIAM WHITE

DAVID & CHARLES REPRINTS

7153 4714 4

This book was first published in 1844

This edition published 1970

PUBLISHER'S NOTE: This is one of a series of William White's Directories and Gazetteers being reprinted by the present publishers using an enlarged page size for easier reading. The Suffolk volume was first published in 1844 and this is a new impression of that edition. The works, invaluable source material for the historian, have become increasingly scarce and expensive on the secondhand market, and will clearly remain in use for generations to come. Though the title pages of the original volumes mention maps these were not usually included in the books themselves, and will not therefore appear in the current reprints. The reprint of the first edition of the one-inch Ordnance Survey of England and Wales, published by David & Charles in 97 sheets, covers substantially the same period as White was at work.

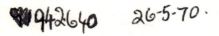
Printed in Great Britain by
Clarke Doble & Brendon Limited Plymouth Devon
for David & Charles (Publishers) Limited
South Devon House Railway Station
Newton Abbot Devon

HISTORY,
GAZETTEER, AND DIRECTORY,
OF
SUFFOLK,
AND THE TOWNS NEAR ITS BORDERS;
COMPRISING,

UNDER A LUCID ARRANGEMENT OF SUBJECTS,

A GENERAL SURVEY OF THE COUNTY,
AND SEPARATE

Histories, & Statistical & Topographical
DESCRIPTIONS OF ALL THE

HUNDREDS, LIBERTIES, UNIONS,
𝔅𝔬𝔯𝔬𝔲𝔤𝔥𝔰, 𝔗𝔬𝔴𝔫𝔰, 𝔓𝔬𝔯𝔱𝔰,
PARISHES, TOWNSHIPS, VILLAGES, & HAMLETS;
SHEWING THEIR EXTENT AND POPULATION;

Their Agriculture, Manufactures, Fisheries, Markets, Fairs, Trade and Commerce; their Charities and Public Institutions; their Churches and Chapels; the Annual Value, and Patrons and Incumbents of the Benefices; the Lords of the Manors and Owners of the Soil and Tithes; the Civil and Ecclesiastical Jurisdictions; the Addresses of the Inhabitants; the Mediums of Public Conveyance, by Land and Water; the

𝔖𝔢𝔞𝔱𝔰 𝔬𝔣 𝔑𝔬𝔟𝔦𝔩𝔦𝔱𝔶 𝔞𝔫𝔡 𝔊𝔢𝔫𝔱𝔯𝔶;

MAGISTRATES AND PUBLIC OFFICERS;
And a Variety of other
AGRICULTURAL, STATISTICAL, & BIOGRAPHICAL
INFORMATION.

In ONE VOLUME, with a MAP of the County.

BY WILLIAM WHITE,
AUTHOR OF SIMILAR WORKS FOR NORFOLK, LINCOLNSHIRE, YORKSHIRE, AND OTHER COUNTIES.

PRINTED FOR THE AUTHOR,
BY R. LEADER, INDEPENDENT OFFICE, SHEFFIELD;
And Sold by W. WHITE, 200, *Brook Hill, Sheffield;*
BY HIS AGENTS, AND THE BOOKSELLERS.
Price to Subscribers, 13s. 6d. in Calf Binding, or 12s. in Boards.
1844.

PREFACE.

Though SUFFOLK is one of the most important Agricultural and Maritime Counties in England, no General History and Topography of it, on a satisfactory scale, has hitherto been published ; and the printed information relating to its principal Towns is rather scanty, loose, and indigested, except the "Guide to Ipswich," published by Mr. Wodderspoon, in 1842. "*The Suffolk Traveller*," published by John Kirby, in one small volume, in 1735, and of which a new edition was published in 1764, as noticed at page 76, is the only distinct work that has hitherto appeared on the topography of the county in general. *Messrs. Davy and Jermyn* commenced collecting materials for a voluminous history of the county more than thirty years ago, and their manuscript labours are now in the hands of D. E. Davy, Esq., of Ufford, who is making extensive additions, with the view of publishing the Work at some future period.

In presenting to an indulgent public, the following essay towards a *popular History* and *complete Topography of Suffolk*, with a *Directory* of its principal inhabitants, the Author has to tender his grateful acknowledgments to many literary and official gentlemen of the county, for their valuable assistance, and also to *three thousand Subscribers*, who have honoured him with their patronage. Authenticity being the grand requisite of topography, all possible care has been taken to avoid errors ; every parish, and almost every house in the county, has been visited, and the information either collected or verified on the spot ; it is therefore hoped that the following pages will be found as free from inaccuracies as is compatible with the vast body of information, and the great variety of subjects compressed within their ample limits.

The PLAN OF THE WORK embraces a *General Historical and Descriptive Survey of the County*, shewing its Extent and Population, its Civil, Ecclesiastical, and other Divisions and Liberties ; its Soil, Agriculture, Trade, Commerce, Manufactures, Produce, Rivers, Navigations, Fisheries, &c. ; the Seats of its Nobility, Gentry, and Clergy ; the Magistrates and Public Officers, and a variety of other information ; followed by separate Statistical Descriptions of its *twenty-one HUNDREDS*, and Histories and Directories of all the *Boroughs, Towns, Parishes, Villages,* and *Hamlets,* in each of these divisons ; shewing the Poor Law Unions, Deaneries, Archdeaconries, and Manors, in which they are respectively comprised. This arrangement, proceeding *en route* from Ipswich on the east, and Bury St. Edmund's on the west, presents in a readable form, a connected Topography of a whole Division or Hundred ; and the copious *Index of Places* gives the volume all the advantages of an Alphabetical Gazetteer.

The *Parochial Histories* shew the situation, extent, and population of the Boroughs, Towns, Villages, &c. ; the Owners of the Soil and Lords of the Manors ; the Churches, Chapels, Charities, and Public Institutions ; and th substance of all that relates to Suffolk in the works of ancient and modern Authors, and in the voluminous Parliamentary Reports on Population, Charities, Church Revenues, Agriculture, Poor Law Unions, &c. The value of the benefices in the *King's Books,* or *Liber Regis,* according to a valuation made in 1535, is distinguished by the contraction K.B., but in all cases, their present value, or that in 1835, is added, together with an account of glebe lands and tithe commutations. The *Directory* of each place follows its History, presenting in an easy classification for reference, the Addresses and Occupations of the principal Inhabitants ; the Post Office Regulations ; and the Arrival and Departure of Coaches, Carriers, Steam Packets, and Trading Vessels.

Sheffield, February 1st, 1844. W. WHITE.

TABLE,

Shewing the Distances of the Market Towns in Suffolk, from each other, and from London. With the Market Days.

EXPLANATION.

The figures in each column shew the Distances from the Places opposite them, to the Place at the head of each column.

The Towns marked * have Corn Markets. Where no days are named, the Markets are obsolete.

There are also Corn Markets at Laxfield on Monday; and at Stradbroke on Tuesday.

MARKET TOWNS.	LONDON		
Aldborough Wed. & Fri	94	Aldborough
*Beccles ....Saturday ..	108	22 Beccles
Bildeston	63	36 46 Bildeston
Botesdale ..Thursday ..	98	38 28 20 Botesdale
*Brandon ..Thursday ..	78	59 49 30 21 Brandon
*Bungay ....Thursday..	108	25 6 41 21 38 Bungay
Bury ......Wed. & Sat.	72	50 43 15 16 15 38 Bury St. Edmund's
Clare ......Monday ..	56	55 10 30 31 51 18 Clare
Debenham	83	25 31 20 15 33 20 22 29 Debenham
*Eye ......Monday	90	30 23 8 29 17 19 31 7 Eye
*Framlingham Saturday	87	16 23 25 21 41 22 30 35 8 14 Framlingham
*Hadleigh ..Monday	64	34 48 5 28 36 43 20 19 27 28 Hadleigh
*Halesworth Tuesday	100	16 10 38 26 47 9 42 50 20 19 13 39 Halesworth
Haverhill ..Friday	59	58 62 22 33 32 55 18 7 37 40 43 25 56 Haverhill
*Ipswich ...Tues. & Sat.	69	24 40 11 27 41 40 26 26 13 20 19 10 31 34 Ipswich
Ixworth	79	37 16 9 15 30 7 23 18 16 30 20 36 25 24 Ixworth
Lavenham	63	40 5 22 26 49 10 10 24 26 30 43 17 16 16 Lavenham
Lowestoft ..Wednesday	114	31 11 54 37 59 16 52 64 33 30 54 18 72 45 46 59 Lowestoft
Mendlesham	81	32 31 13 9 30 24 18 27 6 7 13 18 20 33 15 11 20 38 Mendlesham
Mildenhall ..Friday.....	72	52 27 24 9 45 12 22 35 31 41 32 50 22 38 16 22 61 30 Mildenhall
Nayland	57	42 56 11 32 38 47 22 16 28 33 8 46 22 16 28 12 60 26 41 Nayland
*Needham-mkt...Saturday	71	43 8 16 30 31 21 16 20 21 18 15 29 9 15 12 44 8 29 18 Needham-market
Orford	88	8 33 51 31 43 44 11 25 44 29 21 52 19 37 36 34 24 55 36 25 Orford
*Saxmundham, Thursday,	89	20 31 28 48 19 37 44 12 20 7 14 29 11 51 21 35 24 18 48 37 21 10 Saxmundham
Southwold ..Thursday..	105	18 12 46 33 53 18 46 52 25 27 21 46 10 60 36 42 48 13 32 57 50 34 24 14 Southwold
Stowmarket *Thursday,	80	36 36 9 14 26 31 14 20 10 12 13 26 12 30 12 18 46 12 13 46 7 26 22 3 30 Stowmarket
*Sudbury ....Thursday..	55	46 60 12 29 32 54 17 7 27 32 35 12 47 13 14 30 8 65 24 27 9 15 40 42 55 19 Sudbury
*Woodbridge, Wednesday	77	16 32 19 28 49 31 34 13 21 11 19 24 41 8 31 25 37 18 46 24 16 12 13 28 20 29 Woodbridge

INDEX OF PLACES,

Containing, in Alphabetical Order, the Names of all the Hundreds, Parishes, Towns, Townships, Villages, Hamlets, Manors, and Seats in Suffolk.

(FAIRS are held at those places marked thus *.)

☞ *See also Indexes at Page* 48.

INDEX OF SUBJECTS.

GENERAL HISTORY

AND

DESCRIPTION

OF THE

COUNTY OF SUFFOLK.

SUFFOLK, one of the most eastern counties of England, and one of the most interesting agricultural and maritime divisions of the kingdom, comprises an *area* of 1,515 *square statute miles*, or about 969,600 *acres* of land, watered by many navigable rivers and smaller streams, and possessing all the varieties of soil from a light steril sand to a rich loam. It lies between the parallels of 51 deg. 57 min. and 52 deg. 35 min. North Latitude; and between 24 minutes and one deg. 45 min. East Longitude; but it is of an irregular figure, extending only about 56 miles in a direct line from east to west, and 32 from north to south ; though its eastern side occupies about 50 miles of sea coast, sweeping in a curved line from the estuary of the Orwell and Stour, near Harwich, northward to Yarmouth, where it terminates in a narrow apex ; from whence, a line drawn across the county, in a south-westerly direction to Haverhill, at its south-western angle, is more than 70 miles in length. It is *bounded on the north* by Norfolk, from which it is separated by the Waveney and Little Ouse rivers, rising near Redgrave, and flowing in opposite directions; *on the west*, by Cambridgeshire, where it is only about 26 miles in breadth ; *on the south*, by Essex, from which it is separated by the river Stour, in a winding course of about 48 miles ; and *on the east*, by the German Ocean, on which it has some fine *bays*, *havens*, and *creeks*, and a bold range of *cliffs* and *headlands*, of which, that at Lowestoft is the most easterly point of England. It increased its *Population* from 210,431 souls in 1801, to 315,073 in 1841. Compared with the other counties in England, it ranks as the eighth in agricultural, and the fifteenth in total population. It is in the *Norfolk Circuit;* in the *Province of Canterbury ;* and in the *Sees of Norwich and Ely.* Till a few years ago, it was wholly in the Diocese of Norwich; but the greater part of the *Arehdeaconry of Sudbury*, forming the western part of the county, has been added to the Diocese of Ely; and the rest of the county forms the *Archdeaconry of Suffolk*, in the See of Norwich, as will be seen at a subsequent page. *Quarter Sessions* are held at Beccles, Woodbridge, Ipswich, and Bury, for the four divisions of the county. At Beccles, is a small House of Correction; and there

are large *Shire Halls and County Gaols and Houses of Correction* at
Bury St. Edmund's and Ipswich; and since 1839, the *Lent
Assizes* have been held at the former, and *Summer Assizes* at the
latter town; but before that year, both the yearly Assizes and Gaol
Deliveries for this county, were held at Bury, which may be called
the *western*, and Ipswich the *eastern capital* of Suffolk. The latter has
25,384 inhabitants, and the former 12,538. There are in the county
28 other MARKET TOWNS, of which *Sudbury, Woodbridge,* and *Lowestoft*, have each about 5,000 souls; *Bungay* and *Beccles* each
upwards of 4,000; and *Hadleigh* and *Stowmarket* each upwards of
3,000; but the remainder have smaller populations, many of them
numbering less than 2,000 souls.

Before the passing of the PARLIAMENTARY REFORM ACT, of 1832,
two members were returned for the *county*, and two each for its seven
boroughs of Ipswich, Bury St. Edmund's, Sudbury, Eye, Orford,
Dunwich, and Aldeburgh. By this act, the three last named
boroughs were disfranchised, and the county was divided into *two
divisions*, each sending two knights of the shire to parliament. The
EASTERN DIVISION comprises the largest and most populous
part of the county, and its *Polling Places* are Ipswich, Needham,
Woodbridge, Framlingham, Saxmundham, Halesworth, and Bec-
les. Ipswich is the principal place of election for this division, which
had 6,278 *registered voters* in 1837; of whom, 3,780 were *freeholders*,
750 *copyholders*, 1,624 *tenants-at-will*, and 34 *leaseholders* The WES-
TERN DIVISION comprises Hartismere and Stow Hundreds, and
the *Liberty of Bury St. Edmund's,* which consists of the Borough of
Bury St. Edmund's and the seven Hundreds of Babergh, Blackbourn, Cosford, Lackford, Risbridge, Thedwestry, and Thingoe. This
division had 4,958 *registered voters* in 1837; of whom, 3,139 were
freeholders, 539 *copyholders*, 1,196 *tenants-at-will*, and 15 *leaseholders*.
Its principal place of election is Bury, and its other *Polling Places* are
Wickhambrook, Lavenham, Stowmarket, Botesdale, Mildenhall, and
Hadleigh. The county now sends only seven BOROUGH MEMBERS
to parliament, viz: two each for *Ipswich, Bury St. Edmund's,* and
Sudbury, and one for *Eye.* The latter being much below the population standard of the Reform Act, was (from some influence) saved
from total disfranchisement, by extending the limits of its parliamentary borough to a wide extent of surrounding parishes. On the
ground of bribery and corruption, Sudbury has now no representatives in parliament, and proceedings have been some time in progress for its disfranchisement.

The High Sheriff, for the time being, is at the head of the *civil government* of the county, which, in this respect, is divided into the *Geldable and
Franchises.* In the former, the issues and forfeitures are paid to the
Crown; and in the latter, to the lords of the liberties. The eight GELDA-
BLE HUNDREDS are—Samford, Bosmere-and-Claydon, Stow, Hartismere,
Hoxne, Blything, Wangford, and Mutford-and-Lothingland. For these
the Quarter Sessions are held at *Ipswich and Beccles,*—that is, at Beccles
for Wangford, Blything, and Mutford-and-Lothingland;—and at Ipswich
for the other five. The FRANCHISE, OR LIBERTY OF ST. ETHELRED,
formerly belonged to the prior and convent, and now to the Dean and
Chapter of Ely, and comprises the six Hundreds of Carlford, Colneis, Wilford, Plomesgate, Loes, and Thredling, for which the Quarter Sessions are

held at Woodbridge. The prior and convent of Ely possessed this liberty in the time of Edward the Confessor; and when they were changed, in 1541, into a dean and chapter, it was reputed to be of the yearly value of £20. The FRANCHISE, OR LIBERTY OF ST. EDMUND, sometimes called the *Liberty of Bury St. Edmund's*, was given to Bury Abbey, by Edward the Confessor, and comprehends the seven Hundreds of Cosford, Babergh, Risbridge, Lackford, Blackbourn, Thedwestry, and Thingoe, for which the Quarter Sessions are held at Bury. The Marquis of Bristol is now lord of this liberty. The DUKE OF NORFOLK'S LIBERTY comprises only the manors of Bungay, Kelsale, Carlton, Peasenhall, Dennington, Brundish, Cratfield, the three Stonhams, and the four Ilketshalls. It was granted by letters patent of Edward IV., in 1468, and has a separate coroner. The Duke has all fines and amercements, and John Muskett, Esq. of Fornham-St.-Genevieve, is steward of the courts. At the assizes, *two grand juries* are appointed,—one for the Liberty of St. Edmund, and the other for the rest of the county. Suffolk and Norfolk had formerly only one High Sheriff; but since 1576, a distinct officer has been appointed for each. Suffolk contains about 500 *parishes*, several *Extra-parochial places*, thirty *towns*, (of which the markets of seven are obsolete,) and about 1,000 *villages and hamlets*. It is divided into *twenty-one Hundreds*, each having *chief constables* and *petty sessions*; but three of its boroughs—Ipswich, Bury, and Sudbury, are distinct jurisdictions, and have separate commissions of the peace and courts of Quarter Sessions. Of these Hundreds and Boroughs, the following is an enumeration, shewing their *territorial extent*, and their *population* in 1801 and 1841:—

☞ Those marked thus * are in the WESTERN DIVISION, and all the others are in the EASTERN DIVISION of the County. The whole of the former, except Stow and Hartismere Hundred, is in the *Liberty of Bury St. Edmund's*.

HUNDREDS.	Acres	Population in 1801.	1841.	HUNDREDS.	Acres.	Population in 1801.	1841.
*Babergh	70,632	18,685	24,069	Samford	44,940	8,556	11,797
*Blackbourn	66,272	10,803	14,658	*Stow	22,710	5,899	9,025
Blything	87,631	18,010	25,769	*Thedwestry	40,362	7,259	10,947
Bosmere-and-Claydon	45,773	10,042	13,136	*Thingoe	31,850	4,982	6,656
Carlford	25,461	4,500	6,229	Thredling	10,000	2,616	3,504
Colneis	16,712	2,946	4,587	Wangford	34,679	9,972	14,153
*Cosford	30,712	7,384	10,806	Wilford	31,500	5,279	7,857
*Hartismere	53,479	13,897	18,530				
Hoxne	55,648	13,185	16,798	BOROUGHS.			
*Lackford	83,712	8,985	14,504	*Bury St. Edmund's	3,040	7,655	12,538
Loes	31,321	9,578	13,894	Ipswich	8,450	10,402	25,384
Mutford & Lothingland	33,368	9,409	16,392	Sudbury	1,250	3,283	5,085
Plomesgate	41,579	8,478	11,262				
*Risbridge	58,468	11,987	17,493	TOTAL	932,549	213,792	315,073

From the above, it appears that the POPULATION of the county increased more than one-third from 1801 to 1841; amounting in the former year to 213,792; in 1811 to 234,211; in 1821 to 270,540; in 1831 to 296,304; and in 1841 to 315,073 *souls*; comprising 154,095 *males*, and 160,978 *females*; and of whom, 287,446 were ascertained to have been *born in* the county, and 27,627 elsewhere. Of this population, 79,558 *males*, and 86,733 *females*, were *above 20 years of age*:—Of these, 9,054 persons were from 70 to 80; 2,654 from 80 to 90; and 204 from 90 to 100 years of age. There were also in the county, in 1841, three females *above* 100 *years of age* !! The number of *births registered* in the county, in 1840, was 9,831; *deaths*, 5,960; and *marriages*, 2,297. The CLIMATE of Suffolk is unquestionably one of the driest in the kingdom; but the frosts are severe, and the north-east winds, in spring, are sharp and prevalent. It appears to be highly salubrious, as the average mortality of all parts of the county has been found

not to exceed one in 54; while the number of births is as one to thirty. The AREA OF SUFFOLK is 1,515 *square miles,* or about 969,600 *statute acres;* of which, nearly 40,000A. of waste, water, and roads, are not calculated in the contents of the Hundreds, as stated in the preceding Table. The ANNUAL VALUE of the land and buildings, in the county, as assessed to the Property Tax in 1815, was £1,127,404.

The OCCUPATIONS of the inhabitants, as returned to the census of 1841, are not yet published. In 1831, the population of the county was divided into 61,533 FAMILIES; of which 31,491 were employed in *agriculture;* 18,116 in *trade, manufacture, or handicraft;* and 11,926 were either engaged in professional pursuits, or unemployed. In the same year, (1831) the number of *farmers* in the county, employing labourers, was 4,526; and the number not employing labourers 1,121: the number of capitalists, bankers, professional, or other educated men, was 2,228; and the number of *labouring men* was as follows:— 33,040 employed in *agriculture;* 5,336 in *handicraft;* and 676 in *manufactures,* or in making *machinery.* The number of *domestic servants,* in the county, in 1831, was, males above 20 years of age, 1,342; males under 20 years of age, 690; and females, of all ages, 11,483. There are about 600 looms, and about 300 men, at and near *Sudbury,* employed in the manufacture of *silk, velvet, satin, bunting, &c.* At and near *Haverhill,* more than 170 men, and a considerable number of women and children are employed in making silk fabrics, for parasols, umbrellas, &c., *drabbetts* for *smock-frocks,* and *Tuscan Straw-plat* for ladies' bonnets. Straw-plat is also made at Clare, Lavenham, and at some other places in the south-western parts of the county. There are a few *silk and worsted mills* at or near Bungay, Hadleigh, Glemsford, Nayland, and Lavenham. At the latter place, *worsted and poplin yarns* of the finest descriptions are made. (See page 543.) At Leiston, Ipswich, and a few other places in the county, are extensive manufactories of *agricultural implements and machinery;* and at Ipswich, Thetford, and Bungay, are large *paper mills. Malting* is extensively carried on in various parts of the county; but its ancient staple manufacture of "*Suffolk Hempen Cloth,*" is now nearly obsolete, except in the vale of the Waveney, on the borders of Norfolk and Suffolk, where there are a few *flax mills,* and a number of looms, &c., employed in producing this useful fabric for shirts, sheets, &c., at and near Hoxne, Syleham, Diss, and Harleston. The *spinning of fine worsted yarn,* on the domestic wheel and distaff, for the manufacture of Norwich crape and other worsted stuffs, formerly gave employment to a large portion of the female population of Suffolk and Norfolk, and there was scarcely a cottage, or a farm-house in either county, where the *spinning-wheel* was not to be found. The introduction of machine spinning in Yorkshire and Lancashire, annihilated this primitive branch of industry in the early part of the present century; and with it the valuable trade of *wool combing* left this part of the kingdom, where it had given employment to a considerable number of men. Hadleigh, Lavenham, Sudbury, Ipswich, and some other places in Suffolk, were formerly celebrated for the manufacture of *woollen cloths;* but the trade declined in the 16th and 17th, and became extinct in the early part of the 18th century. (See pages 64, 553, 573). At Brandon, about 60 men are employed in getting and dressing *gun-flints;* and the HERRING AND MACKEREL FISHERIES of *Lowestoft, Pakefield, and Yarmouth,* give employment to many hundred men and boys of Suffolk, as well as Norfolk. (See page 499.)

The following enumeration of the two *Incorporated Hundreds,* and the seventeen *Unions,* into which Suffolk has been divided by the *New Poor Law Commissioners,* shews the number of *parishes, persons,* and *houses,* in each; and the number of paupers which their *Workhouses* are capable of accommodating, with the number of inmates, at the time of the Census, in July 1841:—

UNIONS, and Superintendent Registrars' Districts.	No. of Parishes	Population in 1841	Houses, in 1841.	Workhouses. will hold	inmates, in 1841.
Blything	49	27,319	5,827	560	215
Bosmere-and-Claydon	39	16,521	3,443	500	183
Bury St. Edmund's	2	12,544	2,702	200	93
Cosford	28	18,237	3,945	500	108
‡Hartismere	32	18,529	3,756	‡500	153
Hoxne	24	15,546	3,190	300	120
Ipswich	14	25,254	5,782	400	191
Mildenhall	13	9.184	1,897	110	29
*Mutford-and-Lothingland ..	25	16,391	3,617	350	141
Newmarket, (part of)	§7	6,029	1,136	380	182
Plomesgate	40	21,059	4,581	370	100
Risbridge, (part of)	§20	13,565	2,819	280	106
*Samford	28	11,818	2,432	500	191
Stow	3ɫ	19,675	4,072	350	91
Sudbury, (part of)	§26	22.061	4,833	350	196
Thetford, (part of)	§16	6,491	1,337	300	169
Thingoe	16	18,031	3,717	250	106
Wangford	26	13,860	2,920	450	133
Woodbridge	48	23,015	4,969	350	187
Total	847	315,129	66,975	7,000	2,694

§ *Sudbury Union* comprises 18 other parishes in Essex ; *Newmarket Union* has 22 other parishes in Cambridgeshire ; *Risbridge* has also 6 parishes in Essex ; and *Thetford Union* has also 18 parishes in *Norfolk*.

Of the 66,975 HOUSES, 64,081 were *inhabited* ; 2,317 *uninhabited* ; and 577 *building*, when the Census was taken in July 1841. The number of houses in the County, in 1801, was only 30,805, and 552 were returned as unoccupied. In 1831, they had increased to 50,139 ; of which, 1,141 were empty, and 259 building, when the Census was taken in that year.

‡ *Hartismere* has two old Workhouses, which have been greatly enlarged, since the formation of the Union. *Hartismere, Hoxne,* and *Thredling Hundreds* were *incorporated* for the support of their poor, in 1779 ; but the incorporation was never carried into effect. (See page 322.) *Loes and Wilford Hundreds* were incorporated for the same purpose in 1765 ; but were dis-incorporated in 1827, when their *Workhouse;* at Melton, was converted into the Suffolk Lunatic Asylum. *Colneis and Carlford Hundreds* were incorporated in 1756, but were added to Woodbridge Union, in 1835. *Blything, Bosmere-and-Claydon, Cosford, Stow,* and *Wangford Hundreds,* were each incorporated for the support of their poor in the latter part of last century, but were formed into Unions under the New Poor Law, in 1835.

* The large *Incorporated Houses of Industry* for *Mutford-and-Lothingland* and *Samford Hundreds*, built under acts passed in 1763, are still independent of the New Poor Law Commissioners ; and the incorporation of the former was amended by another act passed in 1833.

In the preceding Table and Notes, it has been seen that there are in Suffolk twenty large WORKHOUSES, having accommodations for 7,000 paupers ; but in summer, they have seldom as many as 3,000, and in winter, rarely more than 5,000 inmates. Eight of the largest are old incorporated

"*Houses of Industry,*" built in the latter part of last century, under Gilbert's and local Acts; but six of them are now under the New Poor Law Commissioners, by whom the whole county, except the two incorporations of Mutford-and-Lothingland and Samford Hundreds, was divided into large Unions, in 1835, since which, ten large new workhouses have been erected, and the old ones have been enlarged or altered, so as to adapt them to the new system of classification, inspection, and control. Though the old workhouses seldom contained more than half the number of inmates for which they had accommodation, the out-door able bodied paupers were very numerous in all parts of this, and other agricultural counties, owing to the long continued mal-administration of the old poor law, which was eating, like a canker, into the heart of the nation, pauperising the labourers, taking away the motive and the reward of industry, and oppressing that capital which should employ and remunerate labour.

The POOR RATES collected in Suffolk, during the three years ending Easter 1750, averaged £28,063 per annum. In 1803, they amounted to £124,658; in 1823 to £259,748; in 1833 to £266,157; in 1839 to £145,871; and in 1840 to £141,536. Of the assessment, in 1823, £214,667 was levied on *land;* £38,965 on *dwelling-houses;* £5,286 on *mills and factories,* and £829 on *manorial profits.* Of the dwelling-houses in that year, only 58 were assessed at the annual value of from £50 to £100. Out of the Poor Rates are paid the COUNTY RATES, which amounted in 1805 to £25,557; in 1823 to £13,759; and in 1838 to £17,765. The principal items of *expenditure,* in the latter year, were—Constables and Vagrants, £1,001; Gaols, £346; Prosecutions, £3,567; Prisoners' maintenance, &c., £3,959; and Bridges, £1,113. The number of offenders committed for CRIME to the assizes and quarter sessions of Suffolk, in 1838, was 505, of whom 342 were convicted; and of these 9 were transported for life; 74 were transported for shorter periods; 254 were imprisoned chiefly for six months, and under; and five were fined, &c. Of the cases, 27 were offences against the person; 49 offences against property; 3 malicious offences against property; 10 were cases of forgery and offences against the currency; and 9 were other offences. The SUFFOLK CONSTABULARY FORCE, established a few years ago, under the *rural police act,* has no doubt been highly useful both in detecting offenders, and preventing crime, but many of the inhabitants complain of the increase which it has entailed upon the County Rates. Mr. J. Hatton, of Ipswich, is *Chief Constable* of this force, which has a separate establishment for the two parliamentary divisions of the county. That for the *Eastern Division,* comprising the largest and most populous portion of the county, consists of a Deputy-chief Constable, two Superintendents, four Inspectors, eight Sub-inspectors, and fifty-two Constables, located in *forty Sub-districts,* in many of which are *Station Houses.* The expense of this force, for this division of the county, amounted for the year, ending March, 1842, to £4,332; and in the following year, to £4,441. SUFFOLK LUNATIC ASYLUM is at Melton, near Woodbridge, as noticed at page 146, and was established by the County Magistrates, in 1827, chiefly for *pauper lunatics.* It has now upwards of 200 inmates, and is about to be enlarged. In 1836, the number of pauper lunatics in the county, was 166, and idiots 179, more than half of whom were females.

ANCIENT HISTORY:---Suffolk, so called from the Saxon appellation of *Sudfolk,* or southern folk, in contra-distinction to the *Nordfolk,* (Norfolk) or northern people, constituted at the time of the invasion of the Romans, part of the district belonging to the *Cenomanni, or Ceniomagni,* a numerous tribe of that division of the *ancient Britons,* called the *Iceni,* who originally came from Gaul, and occupied Suffolk, Norfolk, Cambridgeshire, Lincolnshire, Hunting-

donshire, and parts of Bedfordshire and Northamptonshire. They are supposed to have settled here about a thousand years before the Christian era. Prior to the Roman conquest, the aboriginal inhabitants of the southern parts of Britain had made some progress towards civilization ; but those in the north were as wild and uncultivated as their native hills. Their religion was *Druidism,* which is supposed to have been introduced into England by the Phœnicians of Cadiz, who were the first merchants that discovered and traded to this Island, and for a considerable time monopolized its commerce, by carefully concealing their traffic from other nations ; but the lucrative trade in tin, and other useful metals, with which Britain abounds, was ultimately traced to its source, and brought the Roman and other adventurers to our shores. The civil jurisdiction and religion of the *Druids* prevailed in every part of the Island. They dispensed justice, not under any written code of laws, but on what they professed to be equitable principles,---all their verdicts being determined by such sense as the assembled delegates entertained of impartial justice ; and on discordance of opinion in the congress, appeal was made to the *Arch-Druid,* whose sentence was decisive. Their religious ceremonies were few, and nearly in unison with those of the ancient Hebrews. They worshipped on high places, and in deep groves; and were not addicted to idolatry, as some authors have asserted, but adored the God of Nature, and rendered him praise on the yearly succession of the seasons, which they kept as solemn festivals. Their maxims of justice were taught orally, and the sons of chief personages were disciples in their ethic schools, where the rules of moral life were inculcated as the foundation of human wisdom. They studied medicine and the virtue of plants, of which the *misletoe* was their chief specific. In their civil government, capital offenders were sentenced to death, and publicly sacrificed on the altars of their temples; whilst those convicted of minor crimes, were excommunicated from all civil and religious benefits, till they had redeemed their character by penitence and good behaviour. The Druids exercised their utmost authority in opposing the invasion and usurpation of the Romans, who, fired with equal resentment, determined to secure their conquest, by exterminating the Druidic Order, which, after many massacres, and the defeat of Queen Boadicea, rapidly disappeared. There is no evidence in history that Suffolk was the scene of any of the sanguinary conflicts between the Britons and the Romans; the more southern district of Essex and Middlesex, inhabited by the *Trinovantes,* being the chief theatre on which British valour was displayed, with such zeal, as excited the admiration of the victors. Traces of the *Iceni* are yet discoverable in the names of various places in this county, as *Iken, Iksning,* (now Exning) &c., and in *Icnield-street,*--- the Roman road which extended from Caistor in Norfolk, through Colchester to London, in the line of an ancient British track-way.

The ROMANS having overrun Gaul, invaded Britain 55 years before the birth of Christ, under the command of Julius Cæsar, who, after a sanguinary struggle renewed in the following year, succeeded in establishing a Roman government, unsettled in its nature, and transient in its duration ; for, the conquerors being distracted by civil war, were obliged to return home, to preserve the seat of empire.

After their departure, the Britons remained unmolested till A. D. 43, when the Emperor Claudius sent over an army under Plautius, who was succeeded by Ostorius Scapula, and he by the cruel general Suetonius Paulinus, who completed the conquest of a great part of Britain, and exterminated many thousands of the Druids. After the death of Constantine the Great, at York, in 337, Britain was divided into two Roman Provinces, called *Maxima Cæsariensis* and *Valentia*. Suffolk, with the rest of the country of the Iceni, was included in a præsidial district of the latter province, called *Flavia Cæsariensis*. To keep the conquered tribes in subjection, as well as to guard the coasts against the frequent attempts of the northern hordes, the Roman generals established a number of military posts in this part of their newly acquired territory. The principal ROMAN STATIONS in Suffolk, are supposed to have been---*Combretonium*, at Brettenham or Icklingham ; *Ad-Ansam*, at Stratford St. Mary ; *Sitomagus* at Haughley or Woolpit ; *Garianonum*, at Burgh Castle ; *Extensium*, at Easton Ness; and *Villa Faustini*, at Bury. The Roman garrisons, on the eastern coast, were placed under the command of an officer called *Comes litoris Saxonicis*, that is, Count of the Saxon Shore, so called from the Saxons having there made frequent descents upon the Roman territories. In the early part of the fifth century, dissensions from within, and assaults from without, were fast hastening the overthrow of the mighty empire of Rome ; and in 448, the Romans finally relinquished all possession, power, and authority in Britain.

SAXONS :---After the Romans had abandoned Britain, the country sunk into a state of anarchy. Under the Romans, England and Wales contained thirty *civitates*, governed by their own magistrates, and it is supposed that the Britons, when left to themselves, established the same number of republics. Civil discord terminated in the establishment of military tyrannies, and to aggravate these maladies, the Picts and Scots again renewed their marauding irruptions into England. The Saxons were at length introduced as auxiliaries against these invaders, whom they had no sooner overthrown, than, in their greedy concupiscence to possess the fertile country for which they had been fighting, they turned their swords upon the Britons, who made an obstinate resistance, in which they fought many great battles under Vortigern and the renowned King Arthur, who, in 520, expelled the Saxons almost from the kingdom ; but after the death of that monarch, they again prevailed, and by a slow progression of conquest, at length obtained possession of the whole of that part of the island, which from them obtained the name of England. They were confederated tribes, consisting of the *Angles*, (hence the term *Anglo-Saxons*,) the *Jutes*, and the genuine Saxons, who had long been settled on the shores of the German Ocean, and extended from the Eyder to the Rhine. The Britons yielded to them no part of the country until it had been dearly purchased with blood ; and 111 years elapsed from their invasion, under Hengist and Horsa, before they established the northern part of the *Heptarchy*, or *seven kingdoms* of Kent, East-Anglia, Essex, Sussex, Wessex, Northumbria, and Mercia, into which England was divided. In 495, *Cerdic*, a Saxon prince, with Cenric his son, and a considerable body of soldiers, whom he had transported in five ships, effected

a landing on the sand bank, which was afterwards called *Cerdic Sand*, and upon which Yarmouth was built at a much later period. After gaining some advantages over the inhabitants, Cerdic departed for the western part of the island. After this, Suffolk was gradually overrun by other Saxon adventurers; and in 475, *Uffa* established himself king of EAST ANGLIA, which comprised Suffolk, Norfolk, and Cambridgeshire. To this petty kingdom the German Ocean formed a natural boundary on the east and north; the river Stour, on the south, divided it from Essex; and on the west it bordered upon Mercia, and was defended by several extensive entrenchments, one of which is the "*Devil's Ditch*," running seven miles in a direct line from near Newmarket to the fens of Ely. Some authors say that *Grecca*, father of Uffa, was the first sovereign of East Anglia. Uffa died in 578, and was succeeded by his son Titul, who died about 599, and was succeeded by his son *Redwald*, who embraced *Christianity;* but the influence of his queen caused him to relapse into the doctrines of paganism. His son *Erpwald*, or Erpenwald, who ascended the throne in 624, also professed the Christian religion, although the greater part of his subjects still continued in the rudest state of idolatry. After a short reign of six years, he was basely murdered by the hand of a relation. The honour of giving Christianity a permanent footing in East-Anglia, was reserved for *Sigbrecht*, or *Sigebert*, the successor of Erpwald. This prince was the son by a former marriage of Redwald's second queen; and finding that the popularity which his amiable qualities and accomplishments obtained for him, had excited the jealousy of his step-father, he retired to France. There he became a proficient in the literature of the age, and a zealous professor of the Christian faith. From this voluntary exile Sigebert was recalled on the death of his half-brother, for the purpose of being placed on the vacant throne. He brought over with him *Felix*, a learned and pious Burgundian priest, whom he appointed *bishop of Dunwich*. (Vide page 366.) In consequence of the indefatigable exertions of this prelate, and the judicious assistance of the sovereign, the latter soon had the satisfaction of witnessing the general conversion of his subjects to the Christian faith. To this monarch the town of Bury was indebted for the germ of the ecclesiastical distinction to which it afterwards attained: for here Sigebert founded a monastery, and built a church, which he dedicated to the Blessed Virgin. (See page 605.) After a reign of seven years, motives of mistaken piety impelled this prince to resign the cares of a crown to his kinsman *Egric*, and to become a monk in his own convent. The royal recluse was not destined long to enjoy the pleasures of retirement. Penda, king of Mercia, having turned his arms against the East-Angles, Sigebert was prevailed upon to quit his monastery, and to assume the command of their army. His attempt to oppose the invader, proved unsuccessful, both himself and Egric being slain in 644. The crown now devolved to *Anna*, the nephew of Redwald, a prince distinguished for wisdom and valor. Notwithstanding these qualities, he was unable to cope with the superior power of Penda; and after an unequal contest of ten years, he bravely fell with his son Firminus, in an obstinate battle fought at Bulcamp, near Blythburgh, in 654. (See page 357.) Their remains were interred

in Blythburgh church; but afterwards removed to the abbey church at Bury. The assistance afforded to Penda, by *Ethelred*, the natural brother of Anna, procured his elevation to the throne of East-Anglia, which continued to be governed by its own princes, till *Offa*, King of Mercia, about the year 792, basely assassinated *Ethelbert*, and seized his kingdom. Ravaged by contending armies, East-Anglia was now converted into a scene of bloodshed and desolation; and in 828, it was obliged to submit to the preponderating power of Egbert, King of Wessex. That monarch, instead of incorporating it with his own kingdom, suffered it to remain as a tributary state, under its own sovereigns, the last of whom was the unfortunate *Edmund*, who was killed by the Danes, in 870, and dignifed after his death, with the titles of *Saint and Martyr*.

Of St. Edmund, and the cause of the *Danish Invasion*, there are many *legendary* tales, as noticed at pages 605 to 608. (See also Hoxne, page 458.) The Danish marauders, under *Inguar* and *Hubba*, having slain King Edmund, and sacked Thetford, his capital, overrun the whole of East Anglia, sparing neither towns nor churches, unless redeemed by the inhabitants with large sums of money. But they were repeatedly checked by the sons and successors of Egbert, king of Wessex, especially the youngest, who obtained the name of *Alfred the Great*, and constrained them to abandon East Anglia entirely. The Danes afterwards concentrated their forces in Wessex, and were again defeated by Alfred, who assigned them East Anglia for their limited residence, after compelling them to receive Christian baptism. *Guthrum*, their leader, was to hold East Anglia in capite, as a feudatory prince, and he received a code of laws from Alfred. The restless spirit of the Danes could not long brook restraint. Encouraged by rumours of fresh arrivals of their countrymen, they revolted, but were again subdued. The Anglo-Saxon monarch, Ethelred II., having gained additional strength and confidence, by marrying the daughter of Richard, Duke of Normandy, secretly ordered a general *massacre of the Danes* to take place on Nov. 13th, 1002. To revenge this outrage, *Sweyn, King of Denmark*, assembled a numerous army, invaded England, burnt Norwich, Thetford, &c., and, after ravaging the country at various intervals, during the succeeding eleven years, was proclaimed King of England in 1013, but died at Gainsborough in the following year. His son, *Canute*, returned with fresh levies of troops, in 1016, and, after several battles, the kingdom was divided between him and Edmund Ironside. In the following year, Canute obtained dominion over the whole kingdom, and committed East Anglia to the government of the Danish Earl, Turketel, or Turkill. On the death of Hardicanute, the fourth and last Danish King of England, in 1041, *Edward the Confessor*, by general consent, ascended the throne of his Saxon ancestors. He expelled the Danes from the kingdom, abolished the oppressive tax, called *Danegelt*, and firmly united East Anglia to his other dominions. He died in 1066, and with him ended both the Saxon and Danish rule in Britain.

NORMAN CONQUEST:—After the death of Edward, Harold, the son of Godwin, ascended the throne, but was opposed by his brother Tosti, at whose instance, Harfrager, King of Norway, entered the

Humber with a mighty armament, embarked on board a kind of Norwegian armada, and landed his forces in Yorkshire, where they were completely overthrown by Harold, who left his brother and his royal confederate dead on the field. Harold's triumph was, however, of short duration; for, whilst rejoicing over his victory at York, he received information that *William, Duke of Normandy,* (nephew of Edward the Confessor, and whom that monarch is said with his dying breath to have nominated as his successor,) had landed at Pavensey, in Sussex, with a numerous and well disciplined army. To meet this foe, Harold marched his forces to Hastings, where, in a sanguinary battle, he lost both his life and his kingdom. No sooner was William the Conqueror seated on the English throne, in the year 1066, than he showed that his policy was to root out the ancient nobility, by dividing their estates among his followers, and to degrade the native inhabitants of the humbler classes to the rank of miserable slaves; though in this work he was obstinately, but unsuccessfully, opposed in the north of England, where he burnt York and many other places, and swore, " by the splendour of God," (his favourite oath,) that he would not leave a soul of his enemies alive. Conscious of the detestation in which he was held, he entertained a perpetual jealousy of the English. He built and garrisoned strong castles to keep them in awe; and in the wantonness of his power, he obliged them to extinguish their fires and candles every evening at the ring of a bell, called " *the Curfew.*" He also caused a survey to be made of all the lands in the kingdom; the register of which is called DOMESDAY BOOK, and was finished in 1081, after a labour of six years, on the model of the Book of Winchester, compiled by order of Alfred the Great. Through all time, this " Book of Judicial Verdict" will be held in estimation, not merely for its antiquity, but also for its intrinsic value. It afforded the Conqueror an exact knowledge of his own land and revenue, while the rights of his subjects, in disputed cases, were settled by it; and to this day it serves to show what manor is, and what is not, *ancient demesne.* It specifies the extent of the land in each district; the state it was in, whether meadow, pasture, wood, or arable; the name of the proprietor; the tenure by which it was held; and the value at which it was estimated. That nothing might be wanting to render this document complete, and its authority perpetual, commissioners were appointed to superintend the survey, and the returns were made under the sanction of juries of all orders of freemen, in each district, empannelled for the purpose. This best monument to the memory of the Conqueror, written in Roman, with a mixture of Saxon, is still preserved in the chapterhouse, at Westminster, amongst the national archives. This valuable manuscript, which had for so many centuries remained unpublished, was printed in the 40th of George III., for the use of the members of both Houses of Parliament, and the public libraries in the kingdom.

In parcelling out the lands of the kingdom among his followers, the Conqueror gave 629 *manors,* in Suffolk, as follows :---to Hugh de Albrincis, Earl of Chester, 32; Robert, Earl of Morton and Cornwall, 10; Odo of Champagne, Earl of Albemarle, 14; Wm. Warren, Earl of Surrey, 18; Endo de Rye, steward of his household, 10; Wm. Mallet, lord of Eye, 221; Robt. de Todenei, 4; Robt. de Stafford, 2;

Alberic de Vere, Earl of Oxford, 9; Jeffery de Magnavil, or Man-
devill, 26; Richd. de Tonebruge, or de Clare, 95; Roger Bigod, Earl
of Norfolk, 117; Ralph de Limesi, 11; Hugh de Grentmaisnell, 1;
Peter de Valoines, 6; Ralph Baynard, 17; Swene de Essex, 9;
Roger de Aubervil, 14; and Robert Blound, or Blunt, 13.   At the
same time Ralph de Waher, or Guader, was by the Conqueror constituted *Earl*, or chief governor of Suffolk and Norfolk; but having
conspired against the king, he was obliged to quit the country in 1075,
and histitles were conferred on Roger Bigod.   Of the great proprietary
usurpers established here by the Norman Conqueror, but few of their
descendents held their estates for any great length of time; and since
the abolition of the feudal system, there has been as great a diffusion
of real property in Suffolk, as in most other parts of the kingdom.
There are now in the county upwards of 7,000 freeholders, and more
than 2,000 copyholders.   The principal BARONIAL CASTLES, erected
in Suffolk, by its early Norman lords, some of them on the sites of
Saxon fortresses, were at Framlingham, Bungay, Clare, Felixstow,
Haughley, Ipswich, Mettingham, Offton, Ousden, Wingfield, Walton,
Orford, and Burgh.   Of some of them, there are still interesting
ruins, as will be seen at subsequent pages.

After the Norman Conquest, this county was often the scene of tu-
mult and bloodshed.   In 1153, Ipswich and Bungay were besieged
by king Stephen; and his son Eustace committed great ravages at
the same time, in the neighbourhood of Bury, at which town he died
the same year.   During the reign of Henry II., in 1173, the Earl of
Leicester, supporting the claims of the King's eldest son, landed at
Walton, in Suffolk, with an army of Flemings, and being joined by
Hugh Bigod, Earl of Lancaster, overran and laid waste many parts
of the county; but being met near Bury, by the royal troops, under
Richd. de Lucie, the lord chief justice, they were routed with great
slaughter.   (Vide pages 51, 426, and 622.)   During the first *war
between the barons and King John*, Hugh de Boves, a French knight,
not less remarkable for his valor than for his arrogance, promised to
bring over a strong army to the assistance of the latter.   In consideration of this intended service, he obtained of the king a charter, granting him the counties of Norfolk and Suffolk, from which he designed,
as it was reported, to expel the inhabitants, and to re-people them
with foreigners.   With this view, he assembled a formidable army
at Calais.   These troops, with their wives and children, being there
embarked, with an intent to land at Dover, were overtaken by a violent tempest, in which Hugh himself and all his followers perished.
The number of lives lost was estimated at 40,000.   The king was
thus disappointed of the expected succour; but the inhabitants of
Suffolk were not a little rejoiced at their escape from the destruction
intended them.   Though the county was saved by this providential
interference from the rapacity of the King's confederates, it was destined to suffer severely from the allies of the barons; for Louis, the
dauphin of France, in conjunction with the nobles, who were in arms
against John, made incursions into it, and having ravaged the towns
and villages, reduced it into complete subjection to themselves.   As
noticed at page 623, King John met them at Bury, and there bound
himself by a public oath, to establish that palladium of the liberties

of Englishmen—*Magna Charta.* In 1267, the insurgent barons having taken post in the Isle of Ely, Henry III. assembled his forces at Bury, which was again made royal head quarters by the queen of Edward II. in 1326. Several *parliaments* were held at Bury in the fifteenth century, and the town received many royal visits. Many of the Suffolk men, during the rebellion of *Wat Tyler*, joined the Norfolk insurgents in their formidable revolt, which was suppressed by the Bishop of Norwich. (Vide p. 545 and 624.) In the 15th of Henry VII., one Patrick, an Augustine friar of this county, having a scholar, named Ralph Wilford, the son of a shoemaker, instructed him to assume the character of the Earl of the Warwick, nephew of Edward IV. and Richard III., at that time confined in the tower, whence the impostor pretended to have escaped by the aid of the friar. This story gained credit from many people, as soon as it was divulged, which encouraged the friar to assert its authenticity from the pulpit. The king being informed of these transactions, caused both master and scholar to be apprehended: the latter was hanged, and the friar condemned to perpetual imprisonment. It does not appear that the people of Suffolk had any share in *Kett's rebellion* in the reign of Edward VI., which arose in Norfolk, and like several others, had for its object the re-establishment of the monastic institutions, and the prevention of the enclosure of the open lands of the dissolved houses, on which the poor had previously exercised the right of commonage.

On Edward's decease, the inhabitants of Suffolk, though as sincere Protestants as any part of the nation, zealously supported the title of his sister *Mary*, against the pretensions of Lady Jane Grey's adherents. When the princess repaired on this occasion from Norfolk to Framlingham Castle, in this county, the nobility and gentry resorted to her, offering their services to vindicate her rightful claim to the crown, on condition that they might enjoy their religion as established in the reign of her predecessor. Mary assured them that no alteration should be made in that point by her consent, and still less by her authority; but no sooner was she firmly seated on the throne, than the people of Suffolk found themselves as much the victims of the misguided system of this princess, as the rest of their fellow subjects. They ventured to remonstrate with her majesty, and humbly entreated her to be mindful of her promise to them, but were answered, contrary to their expectation, that " it was not the place of members to govern the head, nor subjects their prince, as they should hereafter know." The threat conveyed in the concluding words was fulfilled in the rigorous persecution to which many of the inhabitants of this county fell a sacrifice. In 1578, the nobility and gentry of Suffolk magnificently entertained *Queen Elizabeth* in her progress; for though they had but short notice of her intended visit, they prepared so well for it, that on her entering the county, she was received by two hundred young gentlemen clad in white velvet, three hundred of the graver sort in black, and 1500 attendants on horseback, under the conduct of the high-sheriff, Sir William Spring. When her majesty, highly pleased with her entertainment, left the county on her return, she was attended to the confines by the like escort.

During the *Civil Wars* between Charles I. and the Parliament, this was one of those counties that associated for the maintenance of the

cause of the latter, and were placed under the command of the Earl of Manchester. Sir Edward Barker, Sir John Petty, and other loyal gentlemen of Suffolk, endeavoured to raise a force to secure the county for the king, but Cromwell surprised and reduced them to obedience. (See page 502.) In 1782, when England was involved in a war with France, Spain, Holland, and America, the principal inhabitants of Suffolk, at a meeting held at Stowmarket, agreed upon a subscription, in order to raise a sum sufficient to build a 74 gun ship, to be presented to Government; but at the close the year, it was found that only £20,000 had been subscribed; and a general peace following soon after, the subscribers were never called upon for the various sums for which they had pledged themselves. At the breaking out of this war, Lowestoft and other places on the coast were fortified. In the Dutch war, in the reign of Charles II., a memorable *naval engagement* took place off Lowestoft; and in 1672, a sanguinary engagement between the French and English fleets on the one side, and the Dutch fleet on the other, occurred in Southwold Bay. (See pages 389 and 502.)

As already noticed, William the Conqueror created Ralph Waher or Guader, *Earl of Norfolk and Suffolk*, and after his death, the title was held by the *Bigods*, till the death of Roger Bigod, in 1307, without issue, after which the earldom of Norfolk was conferred on Thomas Plantagenet, and passed to the *Mowbrays and Howards*, as stated at pages 188 and '9. Robert de Ufford, in 1337, was created EARL OF SUFFOLK, and was succeeded by his son *Wm. de Ufford*, who died on the steps of the House of Lords, in 1382, without issue. (See page 149.) Michael de la Pole, the first Baron de la Pole, was created *Earl of Suffolk*, in 1385, and his second son, William, was created *Marquis* in 1444, and *Duke of Suffolk* in 1448. As noticed at page 476, the *De la Poles* were seated at Wingfield Castle, and became extinct in 1525. Edmund, the third duke, was beheaded in 1513, and being attainted, his honors became extinct. In 1514, *Charles Brandon*, son of Sir Thos. Brandon, was created by Henry VIII., Viscount Lisle and Duke of Suffolk; but these titles became extinct on the death of his son Henry, without issue, in 1551. His first wife was Mary Tudor, dowager *Queen of France*, and sister to Henry VIII. They often visited Bury, and she was interred there, as noticed at page 630. In 1551, *Henry Grey*, Marquis of Dorset, having married the daughter of Chas. Brandon and Mary Tudor, was created Duke of Suffolk, but was beheaded in 1554. The dukedom has never been revived, but the title of *Earl of Suffolk* was conferred on *Thomas Howard*, younger son of Thomas Duke of Norfolk, in 1603. In his family, it has ever since remained. Thomas Howard, the present *Earl of Suffolk and Berkshire*, *Viscount Andover*, and *Baron Howard of Charleton*, has his seats at Charleton, in Wiltshire, and at *Suffolk House*, near Cheltenham, Gloucestershire. Many places in Suffolk confer titles in the *peerage*, and there are in the county about twenty *baronets*, and many other persons of wealth and distinction.

ECCLESIASTICAL HISTORY.— The Christian religion, which had gained a small footing in the kingdom of the East Angles, in the reigns of Redwald and Erpenwald, was not established in that country till Sigebert was invested with the government. Redwald, while viceroy of Kent under King Ethelbert, was converted to Christianity, and

baptised; but succeeding his father Titul in the kingdom of the East Angles, he was persuaded by his wife to return to his former idolatry; yet that he might not seem wholly to renounce christianity, he erected in the same temple an altar for the service of Christ, and another for sacrifices to idols, which, as Bede informs us, were standing in his time. Thus christianity was banished from his kingdom during his reign. The queen, however, who had thus excluded the true religion, was the means of its establishment in the sequel. Being the widow of a nobleman, by whom she had a son named *Sigebert*, she introduced him at the court of Redwald. By Redwald, she had two sons, Reynhere and Erpenwald, who being brought up with Sigbert, were so far surpassed by him both in person and behaviour, that Redwald took umbrage at the youth, and banished him to France, where he continued during the remainder of Redwald's reign, and that of Earpenwald, who succeeded his father, because Reynhere had been killed in battle with Ethelfred, King of Northumbria, in Nottinghamshire. Erpenwald having been convinced of the truth of Christianity, by Edwin, King of Northumbria, while residing as an exile at his father's court, had embraced that religion; and on his ascension to the throne, he openly professed it, hoping that his subjects would follow his example; but, contrary to his expectations, they were so dissatisfied, that a conspiracy was formed against his life, and he fell by the hand of an assassin, leaving no issue. The East Angles being now destitute of an heir to the throne, and considering none so well qualified to fill it as *Sigebert*, made him an offer of the crown. Having accepted it, he returned to his native country, and brought with him *Felix*, a pious Burgundian ecclesiastic, to preach the gospel to his subjects. Felix, on his arrival, was constituted *Bishop of East Anglia*, and fixed his seat at *Dunwich*, on the sea coast, in Suffolk. (Vide p. 366.) Charmed by the impressive eloquence of this evangelist, and incited by the royal example, numerous converts were soon made, and schools were instituted and churches erected for public worship. Felix was consecrated to the pastoral office in 630, by Honorius, the second Archbishop of Canterbury. After his death, in 647, he was canonized as a saint, and his festival appointed to be held yearly on the 8th of March. The second Bishop of East Anglia, was *Thomas*, who had been deacon to Felix, and died in 653. He was succeeded by *Boniface*, or *Bregilsus* on whose death, in 669, *Bisa*, or *Bosa*, became the fourth bishop. In consequence of its great extent, and his own infirmities, Bisa, in his declining years, divided East Anglia into two bishoprics, the seat of one of which remained at *Dunwich*, and the other was fixed at *North Elmham*, in Norfolk. He was present at the council of Hertford, in 673, and died the same year. He was succeeded, in the see of Dunwich, by *Etta*, or *Æcca*, who, about two years afterwards, embraced the monastic life in the abbey of St. Osyth, in Essex. *Astulfus*, or *Easculphus*, was the next bishop, and was succeeded, in 731, by *Eadrid*, or *Edrid*, who was present at the council of Clovesho, and subscribed himself *Heardelfus Episcopus Dummocencis*. The eight succeeding *Bishops of Dunwich* were Eadrid, Guthwin, Albrith, Eglaf, Hardred, Alsinus, Titefertus, or Widfrith; and Weremundus, or Wermund. The latter died in 870, about the same time with Humbert, bishop of North Elmham, whose successor, *Wybred*, again united

that see with Dunwich, and fixed the episcopal seat at the former place, whence it was removed to *Thetford*, in 1070, but it was translated to *Norwich*, in 1094.

Until 1837, the whole of Suffolk was in the *Diocese of Norwich*, except four parishes, viz., Hadleigh, Monks Eleigh, and Moulton, which are *peculiars* to the Archbishop of Canterbury; and Freckenham, which is a peculiar to the Bishop of Rochester. The Bishop of Norwich had but one archdeacon, in Suffolk, till 1126, when Richard, archdeacon of the whole county, being elevated to an episcopal see in France, Eborard, the then diocesan, divided Suffolk into two archdeaconries, making the western part of it, together with such parishes in Cambridgeshire as belonged to his diocese, subject to the Archdeacon of Sudbury, and the eastern portion subject to the Archdeacon of Suffolk. The *Ecclesiastical Commissioners of England*, appointed and incorporated by an act of parliament passed in the 6th and 7th of Wm. IV., to carry into effect the Reports of the Commissioners appointed by Letters Patent in 1832, to consider the state of the Established Church in England and Wales, obtained, in 1836, the sanction of his Majesty in Council, to certain schemes and decrees, of which the following is the substance :—" That all parishes which are locally situated in one diocese, and are under the jurisdiction of another, be made subject to that See within which they are locally situated ;—that certain new dioceses should be created, that such apportionment or exchange of ecclesiastical patronage should be made among the archbishops and bishops, as should be consistent with the relative magnitude and importance of their Sees, so as to leave an average yearly income of £15,000 to the Archbishop of Canterbury ; £10,000 to the Archbishop of York ; £10,000 to the Bishop of London ; £8000 to the Bishop of Durham ; £7000 to the Bishop of Winchester ; £5000 to the Bishops of Ely, Worcester, and Bath and Wells, respectively ; £5200 to the Bishop of St. Asaph and Bangor ; and that out of the funds arising from the said dioceses over and above the said incomes, the commissioners should grant such stipends to the other bishops as should make their average annual incomes not less than £4000, nor more than £5000." By this parliamentary commission, the whole of the ARCHDEACONRY OF SUDBURY has been added to the Diocese of Ely, except the deaneries of Stow and Hartismere, which have been added to the ARCHDEACONRY OF SUFFOLK, which is still in the *Diocese of Norwich*, and comprises the greater part of the county, divided into the sixteen DEANERIES of Ipswich, Carlford, Claydon, Bosmere, Colneis, Samford, Wilford, Loes, Orford, Dunwich, Wangford, Lothingland, Hoxne, Southelmham, Stow, and Hartismere. The *Archdeaconry of Sudbury* now comprises the *six Deaneries* of Thingoe, Thedwestry, Clare, Blackbourn, Sudbury, and Fordham, the latter of which is partly in Cambridgeshire. These six Deaneries comprise all the Liberty of Bury St. Edmund's.

The *Venerable Henry Denny Berners, LL.B.*, of Woolverstone Hall, is ARCHDEACON of SUFFOLK, and holds *visitations* at Ipswich, Wickham-Market, Yoxford, Beccles, and Stradbroke. The officers of the archdeaconry are the Rev. C. N. Wodehouse, A.M., of Norwich, *official;* the Rev. John Hy. Steward, of East Carlton, Norfolk, *registrar;* and Chas. Steward, Esq., of Ipswich, *deputy registrar.* The RURAL DEANS appointed for the Archdeaconry of Suffolk are as follows :—*Bosmere*, Revds. R. Longe

and C. Shorting; *Carlford*, W. Potter and E. J. Moor ; *Claydon*, J. Bedingfeld and W. Kirby ; *Colneis*, W. J. Edge and H. Edgell ; *Dunwich*, S. Clissold ; *South Elmham*, E. A. Holmes; *Hartismere*, Lord Bayning and R. Cobbold; *Hoxne*, E. Barlee ; *Ipswich*, S. Croft ; *Loes*, Lord T. Hay and G. Attwood ; *Lothingland*, F. Cunningham and C. Greene ; *Orford*, H. T. Dowler and J. D. Money ; *Samford*, R. Berners and E. Gould ; *Stow*, A. G. Hollingsworth and C. Bridges ; *Wangford*, A. J. Suckling; *Wilford*, W. P. Larken and E. Walford.

The *Ven. Geo. Glover*, *M.A.*, of South Repps, Norfolk, is ARCHDEACON OF SUDBURY ; and the officers of the Archdeaconry are the Rev. C. N. Wodehouse, M.A., *commissary ;* the Ven. H. D. Berners, LL.B., *official ;* Henry Younge, Esq., *commissary's registrar;* Rev. J. Lewis Gooch, *archdeacon's registrar ;* Philip James Case, Esq., of Bury, *deputy registrar;* and James Borton, Esq., *proctor.* The office is at 87, Whiting st., Bury.

From a statistical table, pul lished in 1829, it appears that there were in Suffolk, in that year, 486 *church livings*, of which 54 were in the gift of the Crown, 277 in the gift of laymen, 34 in the patronage of University Colleges, 4 in the gift of corporations, 4 in the gift of parishioners, and 113 in the gift of clergy, &c. The total number of CHAPELS in the county were stated, in the same year, to be 127, namely,— 4 Roman Catholic, 2 Presbyterian, 33 Independent, 35 Particular Baptist, 2 General Baptist, 10 Society of Friends, 40 Wesleyan, and 1 Calvinistic Methodist ; but they now amount to more than 160. The *Church Rates*, levied in the county in the year 1839, amounted to £15,182. The *Church and Poor's Lands*, and various *Charitable Funds and Estates*, in Suffolk, produce considerably more than £30,000 per annum, and are to be found in nearly every parish, in many of which are school endowments, and in some of them *almshouses* for aged poor. The late *Parliamentary Commissioners* for inquiring into the *Public Charities of England and Wales*, commenced their labours in 1817, but did not finish them till 1837. Their copious *Reports* occupy about 30 large folio volumes. From these, the substance of all that relates to the Suffolk Charities will be found in the following pages, where it will be seen that there are also in the county numerous *National and other Day and Sunday Schools*, and various charitable institutions, supported by annual subscriptions and donations. In 1839, there were in the county 182 *Friendly Societies*, to which the contributions for the mutual benefit of the members amounted to nearly £20,000. In the same year, here were 180 *Charitable Institutions*, with an income of nearly £8000 ; and 13 *Savings' Banks*, the deposits in which amounted to £255,789, belonging to 8503 depositors. The *Suffolk General Hospital*, noticed at page 642 ; and the *East Suffolk and Ipswich Hospital and Dispensary*, noticed at page 84, are extensive and valuable charities for the relief of lame, sick, and infirm poor, and are liberally supported by the wealthier portion of the inhabitants of all parts of the county. *Mutford and Lothingland Infirmary and Dispensary*, at Lowestoft ; and *Risbridge Infirmary*, at Haverhill, are similar institutions for those divisions of the county.

The *Ecclesiastical Architecture of Suffolk* presents a great variety of styles and orders, and many venerable relics of antiquity. The Gothic *Abbey Gate*, and the fine *Norman Tower*, at Bury St. Ed-

mund's, are two of the finest specimens of ancient architecture in the kingdom. (See p. 618 and 619.) Some of the parish churches present fine specimens of *flint work*, intermixed with stone; and many of them, in the northern parts of the county, where flint abounds and stone is scarce, are built almost entirely of the former material. The churches with *round towers* are numerous in all parts of the county, and are generally attributed to the Saxons and Danes; but some of these towers are surmounted by octagonal turrets, raised after the Norman Conquest. The churches in many of the parishes have undergone extensive repairs during the present century, and some of them have handsome square towers, crowned by elegant spires.

MONASTIC INSTITUTIONS were as numerous here as in most other parts of the kingdom. There were *abbeys* at Bury, Leiston, and Sibton; *priories* at Blythburgh, Butley, Clare, Stoke, Dodnash, Ipswich, Eye, Felixstow, Bricett, Herringfleet, Hoxne, Ixworth, Kersey, Letheringham, Mendham, Snape, Wangford, Woodbridge, and Bury; *nunneries*, at Bruisyard, Bungay, Campsey, Flixton, and Redlingfield; and *collegiate churches* at Ipswich, Mettingham, Stoke, Sudbury, and Wingfield. There were also, at some of these, and at various other places in the county, *hospitals for lepers*, endowed *chantries*, and other inferior institutions of a monastic character.

SOIL.—No county in England contains a greater variety of soil, or more clearly discriminated than Suffolk. A *strong loam* on a clay-marl bottom, predominates through the greater part of it, extending from its southwestern extremity near Sudbury, Clare, and Haverhill, to Halesworth and North Cove, near Beccles. The northern boundary of this tract of loam extends from Dalham, by Barrow, Little Saxham, near Bury, Rougham, Pakenham, Ixworth, Bonnington, Knettishall, and then in a line near the Waveney to Beccles; but every where leaving a slope and vale of rich friable loam of various breadths, along the side of the river. It then turns southward to Wrentham, Wangford, Blythford, Holton, Yoxford, Saxmundham, Woodbridge, Culpho, Hadleigh, and following the high lands on the west side of the Brett, to the Stour, it is thence bounded by the latter river to its source, leaving along it a very rich tract of vale and slope. This district is crossed by many rivers and rivulets, and the slopes and bottoms of the vales through which they run, are generally composed of rich friable loams, as also are the valleys extending southward from Woodbridge, Ipswich, and Hadleigh, to the Stour, and the mouths of the Orwell and Deben. In this southern part of the county, is a vein of friable, putrid, vegetable mould, more inclined to sand than clay, and of extraordinary fertility. The best is about Walton, Trimley, and Felixstow, where for depth and richness, much of it can scarcely be exceeded by any soils in England. In the line from Ipswich to Hadleigh the soil varies considerably, in many places approaching sand, and in others clay. With the exception of the small portion at the southern extremity, near the estuaries of the Orwell and Deben, the whole of the extensive *maritime district* of Suffolk is sandy, but the soil is of various qualities, and has generally a fertile mixture of loam, distinguished according to the various proportions, by the names of *sandy loams* and *loamy sands*. That eminent agriculturist, the late *Arthur Young, Esq.*, was a native of Suffolk (vide p. 304,) and in his "General View of the Agriculture of the County," published in 1804, he considers the district now under consideration, as one of the best cultivated in England, and one of the most profitable to the cultivator. It abounds in wealthy farmers, and contains a large proportion of occupying proprietors, possessing from one hundred to three or four hundred a pounds a year. The inferior

stratum in this maritime district varies considerably, but in general consists of sand, chalk, and crag, and in some parts of marl and loam. The *Crag* is a singular mixture of cockle and other shells, found in great masses, in most of the parishes extending from Dunwich to the Orwell and Woolverstone park : it is both red and white, but mostly of the former colour, and the shells are so broken as to resemble sand. In 1718, Mr. E. Edwards, of Levington, discovered the fertilizing effect of this marine deposit, as noticed at page 125. There are pits of it to be seen at various places, from which it has been got to the depth of from 15 to 20 feet, for improving heaths ; but on lands long in tillage, it is not much used, and upon light lands it has been found to make the sands blow more. The *Western Sand District* comprehends the whole north-western angle of the county, except the western corner, which consists of about 15,000 acres of *low fen*, now well drained and cultivated, and forming part of the great *Bedford Level.* (See page 581.) The chief part of this district, lying east of the fen and extending from Mildenhall and Lakenheath, to Brandon, Thetford, and Euston, is a light blowing sand, in which are extensive *open heaths* and *rabbit warrens*, rising in bold undulations. The under stratum is a more or less perfect *chalk*, under which are extensive beds of *flint*, in some places in large blocks, of which gun-flints are made at Brandon, as noticed at page 583. Santon Downham, near Brandon, was nearly buried by an *inundation of sand*, in the 17th century. (Vide p. 599.) Many large open *sheep walks*, and some rabbit-warrens, are to be seen in other parts of the country, especially between Woodbridge, Orford, and Saxmundham, though many thousand acres of heath and open fields have been enclosed during the present century. There are also several small narrow tracts of fens or low marshes, on the eastern side of the county, which have been improved by systems of drainage, viz., the *Level of Iken*, near Aldeburgh, the *Levels of Sudbourn and Orford*, and the *Minsmere Level*, (see p. 397 ;) and there are other tracts of low lands near Beccles, and in other parts of the vale of the Waveney. In 1804, Mr. Young estimated the total annual value of the county, according to its different soils, at £538,664; viz. 30,000A. of fen at 4s.; 46,600A. of rich loam, at 18s.; 156,600A. of sandy land, at 12s.; 113,300A. of light sandy lands and heaths, at 6s.; and 453,300A. of strong loam, at 16s. per acre. But since his time, the land in most parts of the country has been greatly improved, and the fens, which he estimates at 4s., are now worth upwards of 20s. per acre. The present annual value of the land and buildings in the county is more than £1,500,000.

AGRICULTURE:—Suffolk is one of the most skilfully tilled and most productive counties in England, and its husbandry is similar to that of Norfolk. The old custom of letting the land lie *idle* one year in every three, for the advantages of what are called *fallowing*, has here been long exploded, the necessity for it being superseded by a judicious *course of cropping*, so that one crop may fertilize as another exhausts. The mode of cropping most generally practised about 15 years ago, was what is termed a *six course* shift, viz., first year, wheat; second, barley, with or without clover ; third, turnips ; fourth, barley or oats, with or without clover ; fifth, clover mown for hay ; sixth, grazed and ploughed up for wheat again; but this mode is now generally varied by a four, and sometimes a five course shift. Wheat is a general crop all over the county, but thrives best on the stiff loamy lands, the sandy soils being more favourable to barley, vast quantities of which are raised and malted in the county for London and other markets. Both wheat and barley are either drilled, (for which several kinds of ingeniously

contrived *barrow drills* are used,) or else planted with the hand by women and children, called *dibbling*. The quantities produced according
to the seed sown, vary with the nature of the soil, some of the strong
loams and mixed soils yielding five or six quarters of wheat, or from
nine to ten of oats per acre ; while the farmers of the light sands rarely
obtain more than two of oats, or three of barley. The other occasional
crops are, rye, buck-wheat, peas, beans, vetches or tares, cole-seed,
rye and other artificial grasses, burnet, cocks-foot, chickery, cabbage,
mangel-wurzel, lucerne, carrots, and potatoes. There are a few small
hop grounds near Stowmarket, Dagworth, and Foxhall. *Flax and
hemp* were formerly grown extensively in the vale of the Waveney, and
in other parts of the county ; but since the decline of the manufacture
of " Suffolk hempen cloth," very little has been cultivated. (See p. 16.)
Efforts are now making by various Agricultural Societies and Farmers'
Clubs, for the revival and extension of the cultivation of flax in this
and the neighbouring counties, both as a means of profit to the farmer,
and of finding ample employment for the poor. The advantages of cultivating this plant for the double purposes of fibre and seed, are very
great, and have been fully proved in Ireland by the Belfast Flax Society, and by the recent experiments of the flax-growers in Norfolk, who
had nearly £10,000 worth of flax and seed for sale in 1843. In the
same year, many acres of flax were grown, and many bullocks fattened
with linseed compound, in the neighbourhood of Ipswich, where, at the
anniversary meeting of the Ipswich and Ashbocking Farmers' Club, an
Association was formed for the cultivation of flax, and it was recommended that one hundred farmers should each grow one acre, by way
of experiment, in 1844. At this meeting, John Warnes, jun., Esq., of
Trimingham, Norfolk, exhibited a variety of specimens of flax and linseed, grown in Suffolk, Norfolk, Essex, and other counties ; explained
the mode of cultivation, and showed the flax in all its stages, the various processes connected with its preparation for the market, and the
method of forming the seed into cattle food. From nine to twelve millions
sterling are annually sent out of the kingdom, for the purchase of flax, linseed, oil, and cake, the whole of which, it is confidently asserted, might
be produced from our own soil, and would furnish abundant employment for the redundant population of the agricultural districts. Flax
is worth more per acre, and affords more employment, than any other
production of the earth. A good crop is worth to the grower from £20
to £30 per acre ; and on the present improved system of management
and rotation crops, it improves, instead of impoverishing the soil. *Saf-
fron*, when an article of cookery, as well as medicine, was extensively
grown in Suffolk, Norfolk, Essex, and Cambridgeshire ; but what little
is now grown of it, is confined chiefly to the latter county.

Suffolk has made considerable improvement in its *live stock*, since
the general introduction of turnip husbandry; and like Norfolk, it fur-
nishes great quantities of sheep and oxen for the London and other
markets. The Suffolk cows have long been celebrated for the abundance of their milk ; and in some parts of the county, are extensive
dairies, from which, it is said, about 40,000 firkins of butter are sent
annually to London. In some parts of the county, it is a common practice of the farmers to buy Scotch and other lean cattle about Michaelmas, and fatten them for the metropolis and other places. The Nor-

folk, or, as it might with greater propriety be denominated, the *Suffolk breed of sheep*, since the finest flocks are found about Bury, is still to be seen in most parts of the county. For the quality of the mutton in cold weather ; for fatting at an early age ; for the fineness of the wool, which is the third in price in England ; for endurance of hard driving ; and for hardiness and success as nurses, this indigenous race is highly esteemed ; but these excellencies are counterbalanced by several bad qualities, among which are, a restless disposition, a loose, ragged habit of wool, and ill-formed carcases. Consequently, this breed has been nearly changed during the last forty years by crossing, and the introduction of the *South-down*, *Lincolnshire*, and *Leicestershire breeds*, which are larger and more prolific in wool. These breeds are now everywhere prevalent in the county. The Suffolk breed of *horses* are a bony, active, hardy race, from 14 to 15 hands high, admirably adapted for purposes of husbandry and the road. They were formerly rough and ill formed, and could " trot no more than a cow ;" but they were greatly improved, more than thirty years ago, by being crossed with horses of better blood and symmetry. Hogs and poultry are very abundant here, and turkeys are reared in nearly as large quantities as in Norfolk. At Fritton, and a few other places, are *wild-fowl decoys*, (see p. 489 ;) and in the sand districts, are prolific *rabbit warrens*, one of which, near Brandon, is said to yield upwards of 40,000 a year. Having a great extent of sea coast, and many rivers and smaller streams, some of them swelling out into large *broads*, or lakes, Suffolk is well supplied with *fresh and salt water-fish.* Among the former, are pike, tench, trout, perch, smelts, &c. Sea water fish, of nearly every description, are taken in great plenty on the coast; but the most lucrative of the piscatory concerns are the *Herring and Mackerel Fisheries* (see p. 499.)

Agricultural Societies and *Farmers' Clubs*, which have been productive of extensive improvements, are now very numerous in Suffolk, though, in 1811, there was only one in the county, which met alternately at Melford and Bury. The principal of these *associations* are the *Central Suffolk*, the *East Suffolk*, the *West Suffolk*, and the *North Suffolk and South Norfolk*. They are patronised by the nobility and other principal landowners of the county. At their annual general meetings, which are busy and animating scenes, premiums are awarded to deserving labourers and servants in husbandry, and prizes to farmers and graziers for improvements in live stock, and the cultivation of the soil ; and also to mechanics for improvements in ploughs, drills, and other agricultural implements and machines, of which there are in the county several extensive manufactories, at Leiston, Ipswich, &c. As already noticed, there are in the county about 7000 freeholders and 2000 copyholders, most of whom are occupiers. These *yeomen*, as Mr. Young emphatically remarked, " are a most valuable set of men, who, having the means, and the most powerful inducements to good husbandry, carry agriculture to a high degree of perfection." The *farms* in Suffolk, though some of them are extensive, are not generally so large as in Norfolk. In the district of strong wet loams, there are many small farms from £30 to £100 a year; but these are intermixed with others, rising from £150 to £300, and even higher. In the sand districts they are much larger, rising from £300 to £900, and are occupied by a wealthy tenantry, who carry agriculture to great

perfection. The *Woodland Districts* of Suffolk are not extensive, and are confined chiefly to the central and south-western parts of the county. Here are but few ancient woods, though, in the *Parks* of some of the nobility and gentry, there are still to be seen many large oak and other timber trees, especially at Ickworth, Euston, Livermere, Heveningham, and Oakley. Framlingham Park, now divided into farms, was celebrated for the largest oaks in England, and produced the enormous tree which afforded the beams of the " Royal Sovereign." (See page 188.) During the last fifty years, large *Plantations* have been made in various parts of the county, especially in the sand districts, where, through the encouragement of leases of from 7 to 21 years, many extensive tracts have been converted from warren and sheep-walks into productive enclosures. The silk, worsted, linen, and other *manufactures* of Suffolk, are trivial compared with its agricultural importance, and are already noticed at page 16. The *imports* of the county are coal, timber, iron, groceries, wine, spirits, and such other produce as are wanted for internal consumption ; and its *exports* consist chiefly of corn and malt, for which the principal *Ports* are Ipswich, Woodbridge, Southwold, Lowestoft, and Yarmouth. The *mineral productions* of the county are few and unimportant, except chalk, lime, flint, and the fertilizing marine deposit called *crag*. (See page 31.) Stone, suitable for building purposes, is scarce); but the beds of *clay* in various places make excellent bricks, and here are a few coarse earthenware manufactories. The *Woolpit bricks* are white, and nearly as beautiful and durable as stone. The botanical productions of Suffolk are as various as those of any county in England, and among them are a great number of *rare plants*, found in various parts of the county, especially near the sea-coast.

RIVERS.—Suffolk is a well-watered county. Its boundaries on the north and south are rivers navigable to a considerable extent ; and it is everywhere intersected with streams, which, if the practice of irrigation was more generally adopted, would be productive of incalculable benefit. The STOUR, which rises in Cambridgeshire, and forms the boundary of Suffolk and Essex, flows eastward to the sea at Harwich, and during the last ten miles of its course, forms a broad estuary, which, in the lower part, is about two miles across. It was made navigable as high as Sudbury in 1706. In its course from that town it receives the Brett from Hadleigh, and many smaller streams. The tide flows up it to Manningtree, whence it presents a broad expansive sheet of the briny element at high water, but the effect is considerably diminished by its muddy channel and contracted stream during the ebb. It meets the *Orwell* from Ipswich, and their united waters fall into the German Ocean, between Harwich and Landguard Fort. The GIPPING has its sources in the centre of the county, near Stowmarket, up to which town it was made navigable in 1793. Running southward to *Ipswich*, it takes the name of ORWELL, and part of it, on the south side of that town, has recently been formed into the largest *Wet Dock* in the kingdom, comprising no less than 32 acres, as noticed at pages 62 and 63. From Ipswich, the Orwell flows in a noble tide stream (in many places nearly a mile in breadth,) to Harwich, where it falls, with the Stour, into the ocean. It is navigable for ships of considerable burthen, and its banks rise into pleasing elevations, beau-

tifully fringed with wood, and adorned with several fine seats. The
Deben, which has its source in a central part of the county, near
Debenham, is supposed to have been anciently navigable for barges up
to that town, though it is now only a small stream, till it reaches *Melton and Woodbridge*, nearly 20 miles below, where it becomes a fine
tide stream, navigable for vessels of 120 tons burthen, and extending
ten miles southward, where it falls into the sea between Bawdsey
and Walton, where it is sometimes called Bawdsey Haven. The
Alde rises near Framlingham, and runs south-east nearly to Aldeburgh, on the coast, where, having approached within a short distance
of the ocean, it suddenly takes a southerly direction, and passing
Orford, receives the Butley, and falls with the latter into *Hollesley Bay*,
about 9 miles S.S.W. of Aldeburgh. (See p. 155.) It is navigable
for small craft to *Snape Bridge*, 5 miles above Aldeburgh. The small
river Ore, which falls into the Alde at Snape Bridge, is supposed to
have been anciently navigable to Framlingham. (See p. 186.) The
river Butley, which falls into the Alde below Orford, is another tide
river, but is navigable only for small craft from Orford Haven to Butley, a distance of about three miles. The Blythe, which rises near
Laxfield, runs thence east-north-east to Halesworth, and from that
town proceeds almost due east to Blythburgh and Southwold, where it
falls into the sea. Though it receives many tributary streams, it is
but a small river. It was, however, made navigable for small craft to
Halesworth, by an act passed in 1756, and there are upon it several
wharfs and quays, where much business is done in corn, coal, &c.
(Vide p. 371.) The small river *Yox*, or *Minsmere*, flows eastward
from Yoxford to *Minsmere Haven*, on the coast, about 2 miles S. of
Dunwich. The *Norwich and Lowestoft Navigation*, for sea-borne
vessels, and the *Beccles Navigation* with which it communicates, are
described at pages 412 and 498. They were completed in 1833, but
have recently undergone considerable improvements. The Waveney, which forms more than half of the boundary line between Norfolk and Suffolk, rises from a copious spring in the swampy grounds
near Lopham and Redgrave, (vide page 342,) and after running about
forty miles in an easterly direction, to the vicinity of Oulton Broad
and Lake Lothing, within five miles of the sea, it is opposed by rising
grounds, which give it a direction due north, and cause it to flow to
the Yare, near Burgh Castle, three miles west of Yarmouth, where
the united streams take the name of Breydon Water, but do not enter
the ocean till they have passed, three miles southward, through *Yarmouth Haven*, to the termination of the narrow tongue of land upon
which Yarmouth is built. (See p. 515.) The meadows through which
the Waveney passes, in an even and gentle course, are supposed to be
among the richest in England, and upon them are fattened yearly numerous herds of starved cattle, from the highlands of Scotland. The
Yare is properly a Norfolk river, and is navigable to Norwich for large
keels and small steamers. The Little Ouse, which has its source
from a copious spring near that which gives rise to the Waveney, flows
westward in a winding course along the northern boundary of Suffolk,
past Thetford and Brandon, to the fens of Lakenheath, where, turning
northward, it enters Norfolk, and is soon lost in the *Great Ouse*, which
runs to the sea below Lynn. It is navigable for boats to Thetford.

The LARK, or *Burn*, is a small river which rises from several rivulets, south of Bury St. Edmund's, and flows past that town to Mildenhall, and the north-west angle of the county, where it enters Cambridgeshire, and is soon lost in the Great Ouse, which communicates with Lynn and several of the Midland Counties, by means of collateral rivers and canals. The Lark was made navigable for small craft, to Fornham, near Bury, under acts passed in 1698 and 1817, as noticed at page 603.

The *Turnpike Roads* in every part of the county are excellent, and so are most of the cross-roads, but many of the bye-lanes are narrow and miry, especially in the marshy and clayey districts. The *highway rates*, for three years ending 1814, show an average annual expenditure of £42,833, on 322 miles of paved streets and turnpike roads, and 2962 miles of other highways used for wheeled carriages, in this county. The amount of highway rates, in 1827, was £24,848. The returns of turnpike trusts for 1839, shew a total expenditure of £10,583, by 14 trusts. In thirteen of these trusts, the roads were reported in 1840 to be in good repair, and the other was said to be in tolerable repair. Suffolk is not yet connected with the great chain of *Railways* which now traverse the kingdom from north to south. Though the act for the EASTERN COUNTIES' RAILWAY received the royal assent on the 4th of July, 1836, it was only opened as far as *Colchester*, in March, 1843, and no progress has been made in the remainder of the line, which was to have entered Suffolk between Stratford St. Mary and Manningtree, about nine miles north of Colchester, and have passed northward through the centre of the county, by Ipswich, Ashbocking, Yaxley, Eye, and Scole, to Norwich and Yarmouth. The compulsory powers for completing this line expired some time ago, and the company of proprietors have determined not to carry it beyond Colchester, but to apply to Parliament for powers to make a railway from the terminus at Colchester, by way of Hadleigh, Bury, and Thetford, and thence to Norwich by a line to be made from Brandon to that city. They also propose to make a branch from Hadleigh to Ipswich, but with this arrangement, the inhabitants of Ipswich and the eastern parts of Suffolk are not satisfied, and they are now taking active measures to induce the Eastern Counties Railway Company to adhere to the original line; and in the event of their refusal, a new company is to be formed with the intention of completing the line under the name of the *Eastern Union Railway*. That part of the line extending from *Norwich to Yarmouth*, was intrusted some time ago to another company, who are vigorously proceeding with the undertaking. By means of a line from Scole or Diss, through Thetford or Brandon, to join the *Peterborough Railway*, it is in contemplation to form a junction with the *Birmingham and Midland Counties Railways*, which will be of great advantage to Norfolk and Suffolk, as it will connect them with the midland, western, and northern parts of the kingdom, with which their present channels of communication are circuitous and expensive. It is very probable that both lines now contemplated in Suffolk will ultimately be made, and that branches will be extended from the eastern line to Harwich, Woodbridge, Bungay, and some other towns, as well as one from Ipswich to Bury.

OPENING OF A ROMAN TUMULUS: The antiquities of Suffolk will be described

at subsequent pages in the histories of the parishes where they are situated, and have been briefly noticed in the preceding outline of the General History of the County, in the Roman, Saxon, Danish, and Norman eras. Near Nacton, Barrow, Barnham, and Rougham, and in other parts of Suffolk, are to be seen many *tumuli* or *barrows*, covering the ashes of Roman, Saxon, or Danish chieftains. On September 30th, 1843, Professor Henslow superintended the opening of a tumulus at *Rougham*, and the following is abridged from his account of the investigation, communicated to the editor of the *Bury Post*. "The Barrow explored on this occasion, covered a space 82 feet in diameter, but was of low elevation, not being raised more than six feet above the general level of the soil. When I arrived at the spot, the workmen had already dug a trench about four feet wide, directly opposite the middle of the Barrow, and nearly down to a level with the surface of the field. This trench ranged nearly N.E. and S.W., its direction being a little more than this to the E. and W. Upon digging a little deeper, about the middle part of the trench, we struck upon some masonry, and on clearing away the soil, we laid bare a sort of low dome covered with a thin layer of mortar, and not very unlike the top of a cottager's oven, but of larger dimensions and flatter. The mortar was spread over a layer of pounded brick about one inch and a half thick, which had been reduced to a coarse powder, intermixed with small fragments. Under this was a layer of light brown loamy clay, which was probably some of the very brick earth from which the bricks had been fabricated. The three layers together averaged about two and a half or three inches in thickness, and formed a crust which had been spread over an irregular layer of broken tiles and bricks, which lay confusedly piled round the sides and over the top of a regular piece of masonry within them. Had time permitted, we might have levelled the Barrow, or at least have dug fairly round the brickwork, and thus have exposed it entirely, before we proceeded to examine the contents; but the public having been invited to attend by three o'clock, it became impossible for us to proceed otherwise than by immediately penetrating from above. The result of this part of the investigation was the discovery of a chamber of brickwork, covered by broad tiles seventeen inches long, twelve broad, and two thick. The general character of the masonry was the same as that which is described in the Archæologia, vol. 25, and figured at plate 3, by the late excellent antiquary, and greatly regretted John Gage Rokewode, Esq., in his first paper on the Barrows at Bartlow. The floor of the chamber was two feet two and a half inches from N.E. to S.W., extending (singularly enough) in the very direction of the trench which crossed the Barrow; and it was nearly square. The walls were composed of five courses of brickwork, cemented by rather thick layers of mortar. The roof was formed by four ranges of tiles laid horizontally, so that each range lapped over and projected on every side by about 1½ to 2 inches more inwardly than the one beneath it, until the opening was finally closed by two narrow strips of tile, filling in the space left in the last range. The height of the chamber from the floor to the top was 2 feet 3 inches. The whole was covered by an additional layer of four broad tiles; and a bed of mortar and clay between each layer had received the impressions from the tiles above it in a manner which at first conveyed a notion that they had been painted. On removing one of the smaller tiles in the upper range, I had the satisfaction of peeping into a chamber, with its furniture as beautifully arranged as that in the one described by Mr Rokewode; with the unlucky exception, that a large glass vase, owing to the joint effects of time and corruption, had fallen to pieces, and its fragments were now lying towards the north corner, in a confused heap, intermixed with the burnt human bones it had contained. Upon the heap was lying a beautiful glass lachrymatory, slightly injured in its projecting rim. Everything else was entire, and eight pieces of pottery appeared still to retain the very positions in which they had been placed by the sorrowing friends and attendants of the deceased, 16 or 17 centuries before."

Among the societies and institutions which have references to the county at large, and are not previously noticed, are the *Suffolk Humane Society*, of which Sir T. S. Gooch, Bart., is president, (see p. 500 ;) the *Suffolk Benevolent Medical Society*, of which Mr. C. C. Smith is honorary secretary; the *Suffolk Clergy Charity*, of which the Revs. H. Hasted and S. Croft are secretaries; the *Diocesan Societies*, for promoting the education of the poor in the Archdeaconries of Suffolk and Sudbury; the *Suffolk and General Country Amicable Insurance Company*; and the *Suffolk Banking Company*, which has establishments at Bury and Ipswich.

SEATS

OF THE

NOBILITY, GENTRY, AND CLERGY

Of Suffolk.

☞ *There are above* 200 *ACTING MAGISTRATES in Suffolk ; and they are distinguished by Asterisks (*) appended to their names, in the following pages; except those not resident in the County, who will be found, at page* 46 .

Acton, 3 miles N. by E. of Sudbury, Rev. L. Ottley, M. A., *vicar.*

Akenham Hall, 3½ miles N. of Ipswich, Rt. B. Orford, Esq.

Aldeburgh, 5 miles N. E. of Orford, Rt. Shafto Adair, Esq., *Little Cassino;* Hon. Arthur Thellusson, *Cassino ;* and W. T. F. V. Wentworth, Esq., *Marine Villa,* and Wentworth Castle, Yorkshire.

Alderton Rectory, 7½ m. S. E. of Woodbridge, Rev. Wm. A. Norton, M. A.*

Aldringham, 2 miles N. by W. of Aldeburgh, Fras. Hayle, Esq.

Alton Hall, (Stutton,) 7 miles S. of Ipswich, William Deane, Esq.

Ampton Hall, 5 miles N. of Bury, Lord Calthorpe, and Hon. Frederick Calthorpe, (brothers.)

Ashfield Lodge, 5 miles E.S.E. of Ixworth, Lord Thurlow.

Ashmans, (Barsham,) 1 mile W. of Beccles, Rev. Rede Rede.

Aspall House, 2 miles N. of Debenham, Rev. John Chevallier, M. D.* ; and Charles Chevallier, Esq.

Assington Hall, 4½ miles N. W. of Nayland, John Gurdon, Esq.*

Bacton Rectory, 5½ miles N. of Stowmarket, Rev. Edw. B. Barker.

Badingham, 3½ miles N. N. E. of Framlingham, Rev. Robt. Gorton.*

Bardwell Rectory, 2½ miles N. of Ixworth, Rev. Henry Adams, B. D.

Barking Rectory, 1 m. S. W. of Needham Market, Rev. F. Steward, M. A.*

Barningham Rectory, 6 miles N. N. E. of Ixworth, Rev. G. Hunt, M. A.

Barrow Rectory, 6 miles W. of Bury, Rev. A. J. Carrighan, B. D.

Barsham House, 3 miles W. by S. of Beccles, C. R. Bewicke, Esq.; and Rev. A. I. Suckling, *Rectory.*

Barton Hall, 3 miles N. E. of Bury, Sir H. E. Bunbury, Bart., K. C. B.*; C.J.F. Bunbury, Esq ; & Sir Hy. Chas. Blake*, & Rev. W. Blake, *Vicarage*

Barton Mere House, (Pakenham,) 3 miles N. E. of Bury, Thomas* and William Quayle, Esqrs.

Barton Mills, 1 mile S. E. of Mildenhall, Capt William T. Squire; and Rev. J. Fox, B. A.

Baylham, 6 miles N. W. of Ipswich, Rev. W. Colvile, M. A.*

Beacon Hill House, 2 miles S.W. of Woodbridge, Edw. S. Gooch, Esq.*

Bealings House, 2½ miles W. of Woodbridge, Major Edward Moor*; Hon. and Rev. W. C. Henniker*, *Rectory ;* & Jas. Colvin, Esq. *Bealings Grove.*

Beccles, Edw. P. Montague, Esq.* ; and Rev. Hugh Owen, L.L.D.*

Belton Rectory, 5 miles S. W. of Yarmouth, Rev. T. G. F. Howes.

Benacre Hall, 7 miles S. E. of Beccles, Sir Thos. Sherlock Gooch, Bart.*

Benhall Lodge, 2 miles S. W. of Saxmundham, Rev. Edmund Hollond.

Bergholt East, 6 miles S. S. E. of Hadleigh; Sir Rd. Hughes, Bart., & Dowager Lady Sar. Hughes, *Lodge ;* Dowager Countess Morton, *Old Hall ;* C. Rowley, Esq., *West-Lodge ;* Rev. J. Rowley, M. A., *Rectory;* and C T. Oakes, Esq.*, *Highlands.*

Berghersh House, 4½ miles N. of Ipswich, D. R. Meadows, Esq.

Beyton Hall, 5⅝ miles E. by S. of Bury, Henry Cocksedge, Esq.; and Wm. Walpole, Esq., *Beyton Lodge.*

Bildeston Rectory, 5 miles N. by W. of Hadleigh, Rev. Charles Johnson.

Birkfield Lodge, 1 mile S. of Ipswich, Fdk. William Campbell, Esq.*

Blaxhall, 6 miles S. S. W. of Saxmundham, Rev. Ellis Wade, M. A.

Bloomville Hall, 4 miles S. by E. of Framlingham, Edw. Hanbury, Esq.

Blundeston, 3 miles N. N. W. of Lowestoft, Chas. Steward, Esq.*

Bosmere Hall, 1 mile S. E. of Needham-Market, Major Genl. C. Turner.

Bougle Hall, 3½ miles N. E. of Woodbridge, John Fitz-Gerald, Esq.*

Boxford, 5 miles N. W. of Nayland, Hon. & Rev. F. A. Phipps.*

Boxted Hall, 6 miles N. E. by E. of Clare, G. W. Poley, Esq.*

Boyton Rectory, 4 miles S. W. of Orford. Rev. Wm. W. Aldrich, B. C. L.

Bradfield-St.-George, 4½ miles S. E. of Bury, Rev. Rt. Davers.*

Bradfield Combust, 5 miles S. by E. of Bury, Miss Mary Young, *Hall ;* and Rev. Henry J. Hasted, M. A., *Rectory.*

Bradfield Lodge, 5 miles S. S. E. of Bury, Thomas Walton, Esq.

Bradley, (Little) 5 miles N. by E. of Haverhill, C. & W. Lamprell, Esqrs.

Bradwell Rectory, 3 miles S. W. of Yarmouth, Rev, Wm. Trivett, M. A.

Bramfield Hall, 2 miles S. of Halesworth, Rev. Reginald Rabett.

Bramford Hall, 2½ miles N. W. of Ipswich, Dowager Lady Middleton.

Brampton Hall, 4½ miles N. E. of Halesworth, Rev. G. O. Leman.

Brandon, 6 miles W. N. W. of Thetford, Edw. Bliss, Esq., *Park ;* Rev. Rd. Ward, *Rectory* ; and——Rogers, Esq., *Brandon Hall.*

Bredfield Hall, 3 miles N. of Woodbridge, (unoccupied)

Bricett Hall, 5 miles S. W. of Needham-Market, George Mumford, Esq.

Brockford, 3½ miles N. W. of Debenham, Tobias Revett, Esq.

Brockley Rectory, 6½ miles S. by W. of Bury, Rev. Jas. D. Sprigge, B. C.L.

Broke Hall, *(Nacton,)* 4½ miles S. E. of Ipswich, Sir P. Broke, Bart.

Brook Hall, 2 miles S. of Halesworth, Capt. Thos. Page.

Brook House, 2 miles S. W. of Bury, A. J. Brooke, Esq.

Browston Hall, 5 miles S. W. of Yarmouth, J Baker, Esq.

Brundish Hall, 4½ miles N. by W. of Framlingham, John N. Gooch, Esq.; and Chas. Chaston, Esq., *Lodge.*

Bungay, *(Olland House, Ditchingham House, &c.—(See page* 431.)

Bures, 5½ miles S. S. E. of Sudbury, Rev. A. Hanbury, M. A.

Burgh Castle, 4 miles W. S. W. of Yarmouth, Rev. C. Green, *Rectory.*

Bury St. Edmund's, Hon. Chas. Petre; Vice Admiral Chas. Wollaston; F. G. Probart, M. D.*; and T. Robinson, Esq.* (See. also p. 646 to 650)

Butley Priory, 3 miles W. of Orford, Rev. Saml. Hobson, L.L.B.

Buxhall, 3½ miles W. by S. of Stowmarket, Rev. C. Hill, M. A.*, *Lodge;* Rev. Chas. Green, B.A.,*Rectory;* and John, Garnham, Esq. *Buxhall Vale.*

Campsey Ash Rectory, 2 miles E. of Wickham Market, Rev. Jermyn Pratt*; and Hon. and Rev. R. Wilson.*

Carlton-Colville, 3½ miles S, W. of Lowestoft, Rev. Edw. Jermyn, M. A.

Carlton Hall, 1 mile N. of Saxmundham, Hon. Chas. Andrew Vanneck; (Edw. Fuller, Esq.*, *abroad.*)

Cavendish, 3 miles E. by N. of Clare, Rev. Thos. Castley, M. A.

Cavenham Hall, 4½ miles S. E. of Mildenhall, H. S. Waddington, Esq. M.P.*

Chadacre Park, 8 miles N. of Sudbury, Thos. Hallifax, Esq.

Chauntry, 2 miles W. of Ipswich, Chas. Lillingstone, Esq.

Chediston Park, 1 mile W. of Halesworth, Geo. Parkyns, Esq.

Chellesworth House, 5 miles N. N. W. of Hadleigh, Sir Hy. E. Austin., Kt.

Chevington Rectory, 6 miles S. W. of Bury, Rev. John. White, M. A.

Chilton Lodge, 1 mile N. of Sudbury, T. F. Addison, Esq.*

Christ Church Park, Ipswich, Wm. Chas. Fonnereau, Esq.*

Clare Priory, 8 miles E. of Haverhill, Mrs. Barker; and Col. Baker.

Claydon, 4 miles N. N. W. of Ipswich, Capt. Chas. Phillipps, R. N.*

Cockfield Hall, 4 miles N. by E. of Saxmundham, Sir C. Blois, Bart.*
Cockfield Rectory, 4½ miles N. by W. of Lavenham, Rev. Rd. Jeffreys.
Coddenham, 3 miles E. S. E of Needham Market, Rev. Rt. Longe, M. A.
Codenham Hall, (Boxford,) 5 miles N. W. of Nayland, Wm. Green, Esq.
Coldham Hall, 5½ miles S. by E. of Bury, Rt. C. Taylor, Esq.
Combs Rectory, 1 mile S. of Stowmarket, Rev. Rd. Daniel, M. A., F. S. A.*
Copdock, 3½ miles S.W. of Ipswich, Lieut.-Gen. Sir S. T. Dickens, K.C.H.,
    Copdock House; Jas. Josselyn, Esq.; and Hen. and Rev. Frederick De
    Grey, Rectory.
Cornard Little, (Rectory,) 1 mile S. E. of Sudbury, Rev. Wm. Pochin,
Cotton Rectory, 6½ miles N. by W. of Stowmarket, Rev. Peter Eade, B.A.
Cove, (North) 3 miles E. by S. of Beccles, J. Cooper, Esq., Hall.
Cransford Lodge, 2 miles E. by N. of Framlingham, W. A. Shuldham, Esq.
Creeting Rectory, 2 miles N. E. of Needham Market, Rev. J. G. Dupuis.
Cretingham, 5 miles W. S. W. of Framlingham, Nathl. Barthropp, Esq.,
    Rookery; Rev. R. B. Exton*, Parsonage.
Cross Green, (Capel,) 5½ miles S. E. of Hadleigh, C. W. Brooke, Esq.
Crow Hall, 7½ miles S. of Ipswich, John Page Reade, Esq.
Culford Hall, 4 miles N. N. W. of Bury, Rev. E. R. Benyon, M. A.*
Dalham Hall, 6 miles E. S. E. of Newmarket, Rev. Sir Rt. Affleck, Bart.* ;
    and Rev. Jas. D. Affleck, Rectory.
Dallinghoo Rectory, 4½ miles N. of Woodbridge, Rev. Ellis Walford.
Darsham, 5½ m. N. N. E. of Saxmundham, C. Purvis ; & F. Stanford, Esqrs.
Debach Rectory, 5 miles N.N.W. of Woodbridge, Rev. O. S. Reynolds, M.A.
Debenham, 7½ miles S. of Eye, Very Rev. Jas. Bedingfeld*, Vicarage ;
    Geo. Mordant, Esq., Gosling's Hall; and Mark Wade, Esq., White Hall.
Dennington, 2½ m. N. of Framlingham, Hon. & Rev. Fdk. Hotham, M.A.*
Denston Hall, 6 miles N. of Clare, Samuel Yate Benyon, Esq.*
Drinkstone, 8 miles E. by S. of Bury, Rev. E. Rust* ; J. H. Powell, Esq.* ;
    Mrs. Grigby, (Park ;) and H. Franklyn, Esq.
Dunwich, (Shrubbery Hall,) Frederick Barne, Esq.*
Earl-Soham, 3½ miles W. of Framlingham, Rev. J. H. Groome,* M.A.; and
    Rev. W. W. Henchman.
Easton Park, 3½ miles S.E. of Framlingham, Duke of Hamilton, (here only
    occasionally ; generally in Scotland.)
Edgar House, (Combs) 1 mile S. of Stowmarket, Thos. R. Daniel, Esq.
Edwardstone Hall, 5 miles E. of Sudbury, Charles Dawson, Esq.*
Eldo House, (Rougham) 4 miles E. by S. of Bury, Col. Philip Ray.
Elmsett Rectory, 4 miles N. of Hadleigh, Rev. J. Speare, M.A.
Elmswell Rectory, 4 miles N.W. of Stowmarket, Rev. J. T. Lawton.
Elvedon Hall, 4 miles S.W. of Thetford, William Newton, Esq.*
Ereswell, 3 miles N. of Mildenhall, Alexander Murray, Esq.
Erwarton Rectory, 9 miles S.E. of Ipswich, Rev. Ralph Berners, M.A.
Euston Hall, 4 miles S.E. of Thetford, Duke of Grafton ; Earl of Euston* ;
    Lord Chas. Fitzroy, M.P.* ; and Rev Jas. D. Hustler, M.A., Rectory.
Exning Lodge, 2 miles N.W. of Newmarket, R. W. Bryant, Esq.
Eye, 5½ miles S.S.E. of Diss.   (See page 333.)
Felsham Rectory, 8 miles S.E. of Bury, Rev. T. Anderson.*
Felixstow, 10 miles S. by E. of Woodbridge, Rev. J. R. Edgar.
Fen Hall, 4 miles S.E. of Woodbridge, Burrell Edwards, Esq.
Fern-Villa, 1 mile N.E. of Woodbridge, Rolla Rouse, Esq.
Finborough (Great) Hall, 3 miles W. by S. of Stowmarket, Rt., and Rt.
    John Bussell, Esqrs.
Finningham, 7 miles S.W. of Eye, Rev. William Hepworth, M.A.
Fidget Hall, (Moulton) 3 miles E. of Newmarket, Wm. Webber, Esq.
Flempton Rectory, 5 miles N.W. of Bury St. Edmund's, Rev. Rd. S. Dixon.
Flixton Hall, 2½ miles S.W. of Bungay, Sir Robt. Shafto Adair, Bart.* ;
    Alexander Shafto Adair, Esq.* ; and Hugh A. Adair, Esq.

Fornham All Saints, 2½ miles N.W. of Bury, Rev. Rd. Haggitt, M.A.

Fornham House, 2 miles N. of Bury, John Thomas Ord, Esq.

Fornham Park, 2½ miles N.E. by N. of Bury, Lord Manners.

Fornham Priory, 2½ miles N.W. of Bury, Jas. Drage Merest, Esq.*

Foxburgh Hall, 1 mile N.E. of Woodbridge, Chas. Walford, Esq.

Foxhall, (*Temple*) 4 miles E. of Ipswich, W. T. Cobbold, gentleman.

Framlingham, Rev. John W. Darby, B.A.*; Rev. Geo. Attwood, M.A.; and J. Pierson, Esq.

Freckenham Rectory, 4 miles S.W. of Mildenhall, Rev. G. B. Paley.*

Fressingfield, 3½ miles N.N.E. of Stradbroke, Rev. T. Alsopp.

Freston Lodge, 3½ miles S. of Ipswich, Edward B. Venn, Esq.

Fritton Hall, 6 miles S.W. of Yarmouth, D.Dunnell, Esq.; & Rev.F.W.Cubitt.

Frostenden Grove, 4½ miles N. by W. of Southwold, Rev. Jas. Carlos.

Gifford's Hall, 2 miles N.E. of Nayland, P. P. Mannock, Esq.

Gipping Hall, 4 miles N.N.E. of Stowmarket, Richard Dalton, Esq.* (*sporting seat.*)

Gisleham Rectory, 5 miles S.W. by S. of Lowestoft, Rev. Robt. Collyer, M.A.

Gislingham Rectory, 5 miles W.S.W. of Eye, Rev. Thomas Collyer.

Glemham Hall, 5 miles S.W. of Saxmundham, Hon. Mrs. Sophia North.

Glemham House, 4 miles W. by S. of Saxmundham, John Moseley, Esq.*

Glemsford Rectory, 4½ miles E.N.E. of Clare, Rev. Geo. Coldham, M.A.

Glevering Hall, 6 miles N.N.W. of Woodbridge, Andrew Arcedeckne, Esq.*

Goldroyd, 1 mile S. of Ipswich, Mrs. Rebecca Alexander.

Gorleston, 2 miles S. of Yarmouth, J.S., J. P., and Rd. Bell, Esqrs.; Jas. Barber, Esq.; M. Goody, gent.; Rev. Fras. Upjohn, M.A.; R. M. Rope, gent.; and others. (See page 518.)

Groton, 6 miles E. of Sudbury, Isaac Strutt, Esq.; & Rev. G.A. Dawson, M.A.*

Grove House near Yoxford, (*unoccupied.*)

Grove, (The) 1 mile S. of Bungay, Robert Butcher, Esq.*

Grundisburgh, 3½ miles W.N.W. of Woodbridge, Rev. Geo. E. Webster; and B. Gurdon, Esq.*

Gunton, 2 miles N. by W. of Lowestoft, Mrs. Fowler, R. C. Fowler, Esq.; and Rev. Frederick Cooke Fowler.

Hacheston. (See Glevering Hall and Bloomville Hall.)

Hadleigh, Very Rev. Hy. Barry Knox, M.A.*; Rev. W. R. Lyall*; and Hy. Offord, Esq. (See page 291.)

Halesworth, Rev. Jph. Chas. Badeley, LL.B.; Rev. Lomb Atthill; Jno. Crabtree, Esq.; and Harry White, Esq. (See page 374.)

Hardwick House, 1½ mile S. of Bury, Rev. Sir T. G. Cullum, Bart.

Hasketon, 2 miles N.W. of Woodbridge, E. Jenny, Esq.; & Rev. H. Freeland.

Haughley Park, 3 miles N.N.W. of Stowmarket, Rev. Wm.Hy.Crawford,M.A.*

Hawkedon, 6 miles N.N.E. of Clare, J.Frost,Esq.; & Rev. A.Hanbury,D.C.L.*

Hawstead House, 3 miles S. of Bury, Henry Metcalf, Esq.

Helmingham, 4 miles S. of Debenham, John Tollemache, Esq. *Hall*; and Rev. Edmund Bellman, M.A., *Rectory.*

Hemingstone, 5½ miles N. by W. of Ipswich, Rd. B. Martin, Esq., *Hall*; & Rev. Thos. Brown, B.A.,* *Rectory.*

Hengrave Hall, 4 miles W. of Bury, Henry Browning, Esq.

Henham Hall, 4 miles E. by N. of Halesworth, Earl of Stradbroke.*

Henley Hall, 4 miles N. of Ipswich, Miss H. Ibbitson.

Henstead, 5½ miles S.E. of Beccles, Rev. Thos. Sherriffe*, *Hall*; and Rev. Chas. Clarke, *Parsonage.*

Hepworth Rectory, 5 miles N.E. by N. of Ixworth, Rev. Edw. R. Payne.

Herringfleet Hall, 7 miles S.W. of Yarmouth, John Fras. Leathes, Esq.*

Herringswell, 6 miles N.E. by E. of Newmarket, G. Mure, Esq.*; & J. T. Hales, Esq.*

Heveningham Hall, 5 miles S.W. of Halesworth, Lord Huntingfield* ; and Rev. Harry Owen, M.A*., *Rectory.*

Higham Cottage, 5 miles S. of Hadleigh, Sir Chas. Witham, Kt. ; and Mrs. Eliz. Stutter, *Hall.*

High House, 2 miles E. of Wickham Market, John Sheppard, Esq.

Highlands, 6 miles S.E. of Hadleigh, Chas. Tyrell Oakes, Esq.

Hill House, 10 miles S.E. of Ipswich, Edwin Julian, Esq.

Hinderclay Rectory, 2½ miles W. by N. of Botesdale, Rev. Thos. Wilson.

Hintlesham Hall, 5½ miles W. of Ipswich, Jas. H. L. Anstruther, Esq.*

Hitcham, 7 miles S.W. of Stowmarket, Rev. J. S. Henslow, M.A., F.L.S.*

Holbecks, ½ a mile S. of Hadleigh, Lady Susan Edith Rowley.

Holbrook House, 6 miles S. of Ipswich, Mrs. Reade ; and J. Berners, Esq.* *Reade Hall.*

Hollesley, 6 miles S.W. of Orford, John Barthorp, Esq. ; and Mrs. Walker.

Holton Hall, 1 mile E. of Halesworth, Rev. Rd. Day, M.A.

Homersfield Rectory, 5 miles S.W. of Bungay, Rev. C. B. Bruce.*

Horham Rectory, 5 miles S.E. of Eye, Rev. Wm. Bumpstead Mack.*

Horsecroft, 2 miles S. by W. of Bury, Wm. Bacon Wigson, Esq.

Hoxne Hall.   (*See Oakley Park.*)

Hoxne, 3½ miles N.E. of Eye, Rev. John Hodgson, M.A., *Vicarage;* Nathl. Scott, Esq., *Reading-Green ;* and C. Smithies, Esq., *Oak-Farm.*

Hunston Hall, 3 miles S.E. of Ixworth, John Henry Heigham, Esq.*

Hurts Hall, ½ a mile S.E. of Saxmundham, Wm. Long, Esq.*

Icklingham Rectory, 4 miles E.S.E. of Mildenhall, Rev. D. Gwilt, M.A.

Ickworth Park, 4 miles S.W. of Bury, *Marquis of Bristol ;* Earl Jermyn ; Hon. & Rev. Lord Arthur Hervey ; & Hon. & Rev. Chas. Hervey.

Ingham, 4 miles N. of Bury, John Worlledge, Esq.

Ipswich, Rd. Dykes Alexander, Esq. ; Thos. D'Eye Burroughs, Esq.; J. C. Cobbold, Esq* ; Admiral B. W. Page ; J. B. Smyth, Esq., *Orwell Lodge ;* W. F. Shreiber, Esq.,* *Round-Wood ;* J. Orford, gent., *Broke's Hall ;* Rev. M. G. Edgar, *Red House ;* Rev. Fras. Cobbold, *Groves House ;* Hon. Lyndsey Burrell, *Stoke Park ;* H. Phillipps, Esq., *Stoke Hall ;* F. W Campfield,* *Birkfield Lodge ;* Mrs. & G. F. Alexander, Esq., *Goldroyd ;* and W. C. Fonnereau, Esq.,* *Christ Church Park.*

Ixworth Abbey, 6 miles N.E. of Bury, Rd. N. Cartwright, Esq.*

Kedington Rectory, 5 miles W.N.W. of Clare, Rev. B. B. Syer.*

Kelsale, 1½ mile N. of Saxmundham, Rev. L. R. Brown, M.A.,* *Rectory;* S. Capon, Esq., *Kelsale House ;* and John Lee Farr, Esq.,* *Maple House.*

Kentwell Hall, 3 miles N. of Sudbury, Edw. Sarkie Bence, Esq.

Kersey Priory, 2¼ miles N.W. Hadleigh, Richard Newman, Esq.

Kesgrave Hall, 4½ miles E. by N. of Ipswich, R. N. Shawe, Esq.*

Kessingland Vicarage, 5 miles S.S.W. of Lowestoft, Rev. D. G. Norris.

Kettlebaston Rectory, 7 miles N.N.W. of Hadleigh, Rev. John Rt. Fiske.

Kettleburgh, 2½ miles S.S.W. of Framlingham, Mrs. S. Garrett, *Hall ;* and Rev. Geo. Thos. Turner, M.A.,* *Rectory.*

Knodishall Rectory, 4 miles S.E. of Saxmundham, Rev. Geo. Ayton Whitaker, M.A.

Lakenheath Cottage, 5 miles N. of Mildenhall, Wm. Eagle, Esq.

Lavenham Rectory, 7 miles N. of Sudbury, Rev. Rd. Johnson, M.A.*

Langham Hall, 3 miles E. of Ixworth.   (*unoccupied.*)

Lawshall Rectory, 6 miles S. of Bury, Rev. Nathl. Colvile, D.D.*

Layham Rectory, 1½ mile S. of Hadleigh, Rev. Hy. H. Hughes, B.D.*

Leiston, 4 miles E. by S. of Saxmundham, Rt. E. Curwen, & T. Theobald, Esq., *Cupola ;* and Rev. J. C. Blathwayt, M.A., *Rectory.*

Levington Hall, 6 miles S.E. of Ipswich, Major Charles Walker.

Little Haugh Hall, 3 miles S.S.E. of Ixworth, Peter Huddleston, Esq.

Little Redisham Hall, 4 miles S.S.W. of Beccles, John Garden, Esq.*

Livermere Park, 5 miles N.N.E. of Bury, Sir Wm. F. Fowle-Middleton, Bart. (mostly at *Shrubland Park*.)

Loudham Hall, 3 miles N.N.E. of Woodbridge, Frederick Corance, Esq.*

Lound, 4 miles N.N.W. of Lowestoft, T. Morse, Esq., *Hall*; & Rev. E. Thurlow.

Lowestoft, W. Jones, Esq.*; E. Leathes,* Esq.; and Rev. F. Cunningham.

Marlesford, 2 miles N.E. of Wickham Market, Wm. Abm. Shuldham, Esq., *Hall*; and Rev. George Henry Porter, M.A., *Rectory*.

Martlesham, 2 miles S.W. of Woodbridge. Rev. Thos. D'Eye Betts,* *Rectory*; Edw. Sherlock Gooch, Esq.*, *Beacon-Hill*.

Melford, (Long) 3 miles N. by W. of Sudbury, Sir Hyde Parker, Bart.*, *Melford Hall*; Chas. Westropp, Esq., *Melford Place*; Rt. Gordon, Esq., *Hill Cottage*; and Thos. Castley, Esq., *Rose Cottage*.

Melton, 1 mile N.E. of Woodbridge, Capt. Rd. Aplin,* *Melton Lodge*; and Thos. Bland, M.D.*, *Melton Grange*.

Mendlesham, 7 miles S.S.W. of Eye, Rev. Hy. Thos. Day, L.L.D.*

Mettingham Castle, 2 miles E. by S. of Bungay, Rev. Chas. C. Safford, A.B.

Mildenhall, 9½ miles N.E. of Newmarket, G. Gataker, Esq.*

Monk's Eleigh Rectory, 2 miles S.W. of Bildeston, Rev. Hy. Carrington, M.A.

Moulton, 3½ miles E. of Newmarket, Rev. Geo. H. Greenall, M.A.*

Nacton. (See Orwell Park and Broke Hall.)

Nedging Rectory, 4 miles N. of Hadleigh, Rev. William Edge.

Newmarket, C. E. Hammond, Wm. Bryant, E. Wetherby, S. Piper, G. Ford, W. Edwards, C. Lushington, & W. Crockford, Esqrs. (See p.717.)

Newton Rectory, 3 miles E. of Sudbury, Rev. C. Smith, B.D.

Normanstone House, 1 mile S.W. of Lowestoft, Edw. Leathes, Esq.*

North Court Lodge, 6 miles W.N.W. of Thetford, Thos. C. Kenyon, Esq.

Norton Rectory, 3 miles S.S.E. of Ixworth, Rev. Aldersey Dicken, D.D.

Nowton Court, 2 miles S. by E. of Bury, Henry James Oakes, Esq.*

Oakley House, 3 miles N.N.E. of Eye, Mrs. Bacon Frank.

Oakley Park, 3 miles N.E. of Eye, Lieut.-Genl, Sir E. Kerrison, Bart., M.P.*; and E. C. Kerrison, Esq.

Offton, 4½ miles S. by W. of Needham Market, Rev. N. J. Stubbin.

Orford, 5 miles S.S.W. of Aldeburgh, Rev. John Maynard, M.A.

Orwell Lodge, 1 mile S. of Ipswich, Joseph Burch Smyth, Esq.

Orwell Park, 4 miles S.S.E. of Ipswich, Sir Robt. Harland, Bart.*

Otley Rectory, 6 miles N.W. of Woodbridge, Rev. Francis Storr, M.A.

Oulton Rectory, 3 miles W. of Lowestoft, Rev. E. P. Dennis, B.C.L.

Ousden, 7 miles S.E. of Newmarket, T. J. Ireland, Esq.*

Pakenham, 2 miles S. of Ixworth, Thos. Thornhill, jun., Esq.,* *Lodge*; W. C. Bassett, Esq., *NetherHall*; Rev. W. J. S. Casborne, M.A.,* *NewHouse*; and Thos.*, and Wm. Quayle, Esqrs., *Barton Mere House*.

Plashwood, (Haughley) 3 miles N.N.W. of Stowmarket, Rev. Sir Augustus Brydges Henniker, Bart.*, (and Newton Hall, Essex.)

Petistree Lodge, 4 miles N.N.E. of Woodbridge, Richard Brook, Esq.

Playford Hall, 4 miles N.E. of Ipswich, Thomas Clarkson, Esq.

Plumpstead House, 4½ miles S. by W. of Bury, Sir Thos. Hammond, Bart.

Polstead Hall, 4½ miles S.W. of Hadleigh, Chas. Tyrell, Esq.*; and Rev. James Coyte, M.A., *Rectory*.

Poslingford Park, 3½ miles N. of Clare, Lieut.-Col. Thos. Weston.

Preston Rectory, 2 miles E. by N. of Lavenham, Rev. Wm. H. Shelford, M.A.

Rattlesden, 5 miles W. of Stowmarket, Windsor Parker, Esq.*

Raydon Rectory, 3½ miles S.E. of Hadleigh, Rev. Thomas Reeve.

Raydons, near Orford, Fras. Keer, and Samuel Toller, gentlemen.

Redgrave, 5 miles W.S.W. of Diss, Geo. St. Vincent Wilson, Esq.,* *Hall*; and Rev. Marmaduke Wilkinson, *Rectory*.

Red House, 1 mile N. by E. of Ipswich, Rev. Mileson G. Edgar, M.A.

Reade Hall, 6 miles S. of Ipswich, John Berners, Esq.*

Rendlesham Hall, 3 miles S.E. of Wickham Market, Lord Rendlesham, M.P.*

Reydon Hall, 2 miles N.N.W. of Southwold, Mrs. and Misses Strickland.

Rice Hall, 3 miles N. by W. of Ipswich, Robert Woodward, Esq.

Ringshall, 4½ miles S. of Stowmarket, Rev. Chas. Fdk Parker, M.A.

Risby Rectory, 4 miles W. by N. of Bury, Rev. Saml. Hy. Alderson, M.A.*

Rookery, 1 mile N. of Saxmundham, Rt. Knipe Cobbold, Esq.

Rookery Hall, 3½ miles E. by S. of Bury, Robert Bevan, Esq.*

Rougham Hall, 3½ miles E. of Bury, Philip Bennet, Esq.*; and Capt. Philip Bennet, *New Hall.*

Round-Wood, 2 miles E. by N. of Ipswich, W. F. Shreiber, Esq.*

Rushbrooke Hall, 3 miles S.E. of Bury, Lieut.-Col. Rt. Rushbrooke, M.P.*

Rushmere Hall, 6 miles E.S.E. of Beccles, Wm. Tallent, Esq.

Santon Downham, 2 miles E. of Brandon, Lord William Powlett.*

Saxham Hall, 5 miles W. by S. of Bury, William Mills, Esq.*

Semer, 3 miles N. by W. of Hadleigh, Jph. Archer, Esq., *Lodge;* and Rev. James Young Cooke, M.A.,* *Rectory.*

Shadingfield Hall, 4½ miles S. of Beccles, Rev. C. T., & Thos. Chas. Scott, Esq.

Shimpling, 4½ miles W.N.W. of Lavenham, Rev. M. C. Bolton, *Rectory;* & Thos. Hallifax, sen. and jun., Esqrs.*, *Chadacre Hall.*

Shrubbery Hall, 4½ miles S.W. of Southwold, Frederick Barne, Esq.*

Shrubland Park, 6 miles N.N.W. of Ipswich, Sir W. F. F. Middleton, Bart.

Sibton Park, 2½ miles W. of Yoxford, Robt. Sayer, Esq.; and John E. E. Spink, Esq., *Abbey House.*

Soham Lodge, 3 miles W. of Framlingham, J. Clubbe, Esq.,

Somerleyton, 4½ miles N.W. of Lowestoft, Lord Sydney G. Osborne, *Hall;* and Rev. Edw. Missenden Love,* *Rectory.*

Somerton, 7 miles N.E. of Clare, Jph. E. Hale, Esq.,; & Rev. J. Maddy, D.D.*

Sotterley Hall, 4½ miles S.S.E. of Beccles, Fdk. Barne, Esq.*; Mrs. Mary Barne; and Major General Sir Edward Bowater, G. C. H.

Southelmham, 5 miles S.W. by W. of Bungay, Rev. Courtenay Boyle Bruce, B.A*.; and Rev. Adolphus Holmes, M.A., F.L.S.

South Town, (Yarmouth) Admiral Sir Geo. Parker, K.C.B.; W. D. Palmer, Esq.; J. Garnham, Esq.; R. P. Kemp, Esq. (See page 518.)

Southwold, 9 miles E. of Halesworth, Alfred Lillingstone, Esq.*

Spring Hall, 7 miles N. of Sudbury, Rt. Mapletoft, Esq.*

Spexhall, 2½ miles N. by W. of Halesworth, Rev. Rd. Crutwell, L.L.D.

Sproughton, 2 miles W. by N. of Ipswich, G. J. Gunnell, Esq.; & Rev. Edw. Gould, M. A.

Stanton Rectory, 3 miles N.E. of Ixworth, Rev. Geo. Bidwell.*

Sternfield, 1½ mile S. of Saxmundham, Rev. Jas. D. Money.

Stoke College, 2½ m. W. of Clare, C. Gonne, Esq.; & Jno. P. Elwes, Esq.*

Stoke Park, 1½ mile S. of Ipswich, Hon. Lyndsey Burrell.

Stoke Priory, 2 miles N. E. by N. of Nayland, Isaac Hoy, Esq.

Stoke Ash, 3½ miles S. W. of Eye, Rev. J. Ward.*

Stonham Aspall, 5 m. N.E. of Needham Market, Rev Chas. Shorting, M.A.

Stonham-Earl, 5 miles E. of Stowmarket, Rev. John Phear.*

Stowlangtoft Hall, 2½ miles S. S. E. of Ixworth, Henry Wilson, Esq.*

Stowmarket Vicarage, Rev. A. G. H. Hollingsworth, M. A.

Stradbroke, 7 miles E. S. E of Eye, Rev. John Taylor Allen, M. A.; and C. Bradfield, Esq.

Stradishall, 5½ miles N. by W. of Clare, W. Rayner, Esq.; and Rev. C. Jenkin, D. D.

Stratford Rectory, 6 miles S. by E. of Hadleigh, Rev. C. Golding.*

Stutton, 7½ miles S. of Ipswich, Rev. Thos. Mills, M. A.*, *Rectory;* J. P. Reade, Esq.*, *Crow Hall;* and W. Deane, Esq., *Alton Hall.*

Sudborne Hall, 1 mile N. W. of Orford, Marquis of Hertford.

Sudbury, Lady Lachlam Maclean, W. R. Bevan, Esq., &c. (See p. 577.)

Sutton, 3 miles S.E. of Woodbridge, T. Waller, Esq.; and Rev. Rt. Field, M.A.

Syleham Hall, 3½ miles N. by W. of Stradbrook, Rev. A. Cooper, B. A.*

Tattingstone, $5\frac{1}{2}$ miles S. S. W. of Ipswich, Thos. Burch Western, Esq. *; and Rev. Charles Boileau Elliott, M. A., F. R. S.*

Tendring Hall, (Stoke) $1\frac{1}{2}$ m. W.N.W. of Nayland, Sir J. R. Rowley, Bart.*

Theberton, 3 miles N. E. of Saxmundham, Rev. C. M. Doughty, B. A., *Hall;* Rev. H. Hardinge, B.A., *Rectory;* T. M. Gibson, Esq., M.P., *House.*

Thetford, L. S. Bidwell, Esq.*; H. Best, Esq., &c. (See p. 712.)

Thorington Hall, $6\frac{1}{2}$ miles N. N. E. of Saxmundham, Col. H. Bence Bence.*

Thornham Park, 3 miles S. W. of Eye, Lord Henniker, M.P.*

Thorpe Morieux, $3\frac{1}{2}$ miles N. by E. of Lavenham, Rev. Thos. T. Harrison.*

Thorpe Hall, $2\frac{1}{2}$ miles N. W. of Woodbridge, Cha. Baldry, Esq.

Thrandeston Rectory, 3 miles N. W. of Eye, Rev. Nathl. D' Eye, M. A.*

Thurlow, (Great) 4 miles N. N. E. of Haverhill, Rev. W. Wayman, M. A., *Vicarage;* and J. A. Hardcastle, Esq., *Hall,* (and London.)

Thurlow Little, $4\frac{1}{2}$ miles N. by E. of Haverhill, Capt. Dench.

Thurston House, 5 miles E. by N. of Bury, Jas. Bunbury Blake, Esq.

Troston Hall, $2\frac{1}{2}$ miles N. W. of Ixworth, Evelyn Lofft, Esq.

Tunstall Rectory, 7 miles N. E. of Woodbridge, Rev. T. G. Ferrand.

Ufford, $2\frac{1}{2}$ miles N. N. E. of Woodbridge, Fras. C. Brooke Esq.; and Rev. Wm. Pochin Larkin.

Uggeshall Rectory, $5\frac{1}{2}$ m. E.N.E. of Halesworth, Rev. Wm. C. Edgell, M.A.

Uplands, $3\frac{1}{2}$ miles S. W. of Lowestoft, Wm. Woodthorpe, Esq.

Undley Hall, 5 miles N. of Mildenhall, Thos. Waddelow, Esq.

Waldingfield Rectory, 3 miles N.E. of Sudbury, Rev. H. Kirby, M. A.

Waldringfield Rectory, 4 miles S. of Woodbridge, Rev. W. J. Edge.*

Walsham House, 5 miles E. of Ixworth, Hooper John Wilkinson, Esq.*

Wattisfield, 3 miles W. S. W. of Botesdale, Geo. Mallows, Esq.

Whenham Rectory, $4\frac{1}{2}$ miles S.E. of Hadleigh, Rev. D. C. Whalley.

Westhorpe Rectory, 8 miles N. of Stowmarket, Rev. R. Hewitt, D. D.

Westleton, 5 miles N.E. of Saxmundham, Rev. H. Packard, M. A.

Wetheringsett, 4 miles N. W. of Debenham, Rev. Robt. Moore, B. A.

Weston Market, $4\frac{1}{4}$ m. W.N.W. of Botesdale, John Thurston, Esq.,* *Lodge;* and John Josselyn, Esq., *Hall.*

Wetherden, 4 miles N.W. of Stowmarket, Hon. & Rev. Sir Henry Leslie, Bart.*

Whalebone Cottage, $3\frac{1}{2}$ miles W. S. of Stowmarket, Rt. O. Fuller, Esq.

Whatfield, 3 miles N. E. of Hadleigh, Rev. Fdk. Calvert.*

Whepstead, $4\frac{1}{2}$ miles S. of Bury, Sir Thos. Hammond, Bart.*

White House, $3\frac{1}{2}$ miles N. N. E. of Framlingham, W. A. Stanford, Esq.

Wherstead, $2\frac{1}{2}$ miles S. of Ipswich, Wm. Scrope, Esq., *Lodge;* and Rev. Geo. Capper, M. A.,* *Vicarage.*

Wickhambrook, 7 miles N. of Clare, Rev. C. Borton.*

Withersfield Rectory, 2 miles N. W. of Haverhill, Rev. Wm. Mayd, M. A.*

Witnesham Rectory, $4\frac{1}{2}$ miles N. of Ipswich, Rev. Wm. Potter, M. A.

Woodbridge, 8 miles E.N.E. of Ipswich, F. Doughty, Esq.*; Geo. Thomas, Esq.*; Chas. S. Sharpe, Esq.; Rev. T. S. Bomford; and Rev. C. G. Watson. (See page 209.)

Wood Hall, 4 miles S. E. of Woodbridge, Hy. and Thos. Edwards, Esqrs.

Woolverstone Hall, 4 miles S. of Ipswich, Ven. Hy. Denny Berners, L.L.B.*

Worlingham Hall, 2 m. E.b.S. of Beccles, Earl of Gosford; & Viscount Acheson.

Worlingham Rectory, $1\frac{1}{2}$ mile S. E. of Beccles, Rev. David H. Leighton.

Worlingworth, 5 miles N. W. of Framlingham, Rev. Edw. Barlee*

Wortham, 3 miles S. W. of Diss, J. J. Tuck, Esq.*; & Rev. R. Cobbold.

Wratting, (Great) $2\frac{1}{2}$ miles N. E. of Haverhill, Rev. T. B. Syer, B. A.*

Wrentham Rectory, 5 miles N. of Southwold, Rev. S. Clissold, M. A.*

Yarmouth, (Norfolk) John Penrice, Esq.*; Sir E. H. K. Lacon, Bart.*; and Dawson Turner, Esq.*

Yaxley Hall, $1\frac{1}{2}$ mile W. of Eye, Mrs. Leeke; & P. R. Welch, Esq.

Yoxford, 4 miles N. by E. of Saxmundham, Sir Chas. Blois, Bart.*; Misses Colmer; Rev. H. Packard; and Rev. W. Weddell.

THE SUFFOLK MAGISTRATES, residing in the County, are marked* in the prece ding list of Seats. There are upwards of thirty others, who do not reside in Suffolk, of whom, the following is an enumeration. They mostly reside in Norfolk, Essex, and Cambridgeshire,—near the borders of Suffolk.

Albemarle Earl of, Quiddenham
Bacon Sir E., Bart., Raveningham
Barclay Charles, Esq.
Barker Rev. Jas., Hildersham
Beddingfeld J. J., Esq., Ditchingham
Bennett Rev. J. T., Cheveley
Brise J. R., Esq., Finchingfield
Cadogan Earl of, Downham, &c.,
Chafy Dr. Wm., Cambridge
De Horsey Spencer, Esq.
Dixon John, Esq.
Fitzroy Rev. Augustus
Frere Rev. Temple, Roydon
Hemley, Rev. B., Bures, (Essex.)
Havers Thos., Esq., Thelveton
Hooper John Wilkinson, Esq.
Hunt Rev George
Hill Rev. N. J., Snailswell

Kerrich J., Esq., Geldestone Hall
Kett G. S., Esq., Brooke
Lacon SirEdm.H.K.,Bart.,Yarmouth
Mackworth, Lieut.Col.SirDigby,Bart.
Manning Rev. Wm., Diss
Matthews Rev. J. S.
Matthews Wm., Esq., Pentlow
Meyrick W. H., Esq., Bulmer
Munro John Hector, Esq.
Montgomery T. Molineux, Esq.
Mure George, Esq.
Neville Hon. and Rev. Lord
Ord John Thomas, Esq.
Proctor Sir W. B. Bart., *Langley*
Slapp Rev. T. P. Old Buckenham
Wilson John, Esq., and Hon. R.
Wright John, Esq., Kilvestone

MEMBERS OF PARLIAMENT.

SUFFOLK, Lord Henniker, *Major House*, Thornham, and Lord Rendle sham, Rendlesham Hall, for the *Eastern Division;* and Robt. Rushbrooke, Esq., Rushbrooke Hall, and Harry Spencer Waddington, Esq., Cavenham Hall, for the *Western Division.*

Bury St. Edmund's, *Lord Charles Fitzroy,* second son of the Duke of Grafton, and Fredk. Wm. Hervey, *Earl Jermyn,* eldest son of the Marquis of Bristol.

Ipswich, John Neilstone Gladstone, Esq., and Sackville Lane Fox, Esq.

EYE, Lieut General Sir Edward Kerrison, Bart., *Oakley Park.*

SUDBURY. (*None Sitting. Vide page 572.*)

PUBLIC OFFICERS OF THE COUNTY.

Lord Lieutenant, His Grace the Duke of Grafton, Euston Hall.
Magistrates. (See pages 38 to 46.)
High Sheriff, in 1843, Wm. Long, Esq., Hurts Hall.
(The others nominated were, Sir P. Broke and H. Wilson, Esq.)
Under Sheriff, J. Crabtree, Esq., Halesworth.
Clerk of the Peace, Henry Borton, Esq., Bury St. Edmund's.
County Court Clerk, Wm. Hammond, Esq., Ipswich.
Distributor of Stamps, W. W. Humphreys, Esq., Sudbury.
Inspecting Reviewer of Taxes, Henry Vie, Esq., Colchester.
Surveyor of County Bridges, Mr. J. Whiting, Ipswich.
Coronors :—J. E. Sparrowe, and Chas. Gross, Esqrs., of Ipswich, *for the County ;* John Wood, jun., Esq., of Woodbridge, for the *Liberty of St. Ethelred ;* H. Wayman, Esq., of Bury, for the *Liberty of St. Edmund ;* and Eleazer Lawrence, Esq., of Ipswich, for the *Duke of Norfolk's Liberty.*
County Treasurers :—Wm. Hammond, Esq., *Ipswich ;* Henry James Oakes, Esq., *Bury ;* Charles Moor, Esq., *Woodbridge ;* and E. C. Sharpin, Esq., *Beccles.*
*County Gaolers, and Keepers of the Houses of Correction :—*Mr. Edward. Amond Johnson, *Ipswich ;* and Mr. John Orridge, Bury St. Edmund's.
Bridewell Keeper at Beccles, Mr. S. Drewell.

The **Chief Constables** are named with the general descriptions of the Hundreds, at subsequent pages.

Chief Constable of the Suffolk Constabulary Force,—Mr. J. Hatton.

PEERS, BARONETS, &c.

Who have seats in Suffolk, or are otherwise connected with the County.

☞ *The figures shew the dates of the Creations.*

PEERS OF PARLIAMENT.

1483 Duke of Norfolk, (See p. 308.)
1675 Duke of Grafton, Euston Hall.
1694 Duke of Devonshire, (see p. 544.)
1711 Duke of Brandon & Hamilton, *Easton Park*, (and Scotland.)
1793 Marquis of Hertford, Sudborne Hall
1826 Marquis of Bristol, Ickworth Park.
1603 Earl of Suffolk & Berkshire, Suffolk House, *Cheltenham.*
1753 Earl Cornwallis & Viscount Brome, (see page 326.)
1806 Earl of Orford, Wolterton Park, *Norfolk.*
1821 Earl of Stradbroke, Henham Hall
1792 Lord Thurlow, Ashfield Lodge.
1796 Lord Calthorpe, Ampton Park
1797 Rt. Hon. & Rev. Lord Bayning, Brome Rectory.
1807 Lord Manners, Fornham Park.
1835 Lord Worlingham, Worlingham Hall (also *Earl of Gosford*, in Ireland.)

PEERS OF IRELAND.

1796 Lord Hutingfield, Heveningham Hall.
1800 Lord Henniker, M.P. Thornham
1806 Lord Rendlesham, M. P. Rendlesham Hall

BARONETS.

1838 Adair Robt. Shafto, Flixton Hall.
1782 Affleck Rev. Robt., Dalham.
1772 Blake Hy. Cha., Great Barton.
1686 Blois Chas., Cockfield Hall.
1813 Broke Philip, Broke Hall
1681 Bunbury Lieut. Gen. H.E. Barton
1660 Cullum Rev. Thos. Gery, Hardwick House.
1759 Fludyer Saml., Felixstow.
1662 Gage Thomas, Hengrave Hall.
1746 Gooch Thos. S., Benacre Hall
— Hammond Sir Thos., Whepstead.
1813 Henniker Rev., A.B., Plashwood.
1773 Hughes Richard, East Bergholt
1821 Kerrison Lieut. Genl. Edward, K. C. B., G. C. H., and M.P., Oakley Park.
1818 Lacon E. H. K., Yarmouth.

1784 Leslie Hon. & Rev. H., rector of Wetherden, (*Boxhill Surrey.*)
1804 Middleton Wm. F. Fowle, Shrubland Park.
1681 Parker Hyde, Melford Hall.
1791 Rich Chas. Hy., Rose Hall near Beccles (*does not reside there*)
1836 Rowley J. R. Tendring Hall.
1836 Roe Fdk. Adair, Brundish, (does not reside there.)

KNIGHTS.

1832 Austin, H. E., Chellesworth.
1812 M'Lean Lachlan, Sudbury, (died in 1843.)
1830 Witham, Chas., L.L.I., Higham.

ADMIRALS.

Page B. W., Ipswich.
Parker Sir Geo., K.C.B., South Town.

GENERALS.

Lieut. Genl. Sir H.E. Bunbury, Barton.
Lieut. Genl. Sir E. Kerrison, Oakley.
Lieut. Genl. Sir S.T. Dickens, K.C.H., Copdock.
Major Genl. C. Turner, Bosmere Hall.
Major Genl. Sir E. Bowater, G.C.H., Sotterley Hall.

HONORABLES. (*Sons of Peers, &c.*)

Viscount Acheson, M.P., Worlingham Hall.
Earl Jermyn, M P.; Rev. Lord A. Hervey, and Rev. C. Hervey, *Ickworth Hall.*
Earl of Euston, and Lord Chas. Fitzroy, M.P., *Euston Hall.*
Lord Wm. Powlett, Santon Downham.
Rev. Lord Thomas Hay.
Lord S. G. Osborne, Somerleyton.
Hon. F. Calthorpe, Ampton.
Hon. C. A. Vanneck, Carlton.
Hon. and Rev. F. De Grey, Copdock.
Hon. & Rev. W.C. Henniker, Bealings.
Hon. & Rev. F. A. Phipps, Boxford.
Hon. & Rev. Fdk. Hotham, Dennington.
Hon. & Rev. R. Wilson, Campsey Ash.
Hon. Arthur Thellusson, Aldeburgh.
Hon. Lyndsey Burrell, *Stoke Park.*
Hon. Charles Petre, Bury.
Dowager Countess Morton, East Bergholt.
Dowager Lady Middleton, Bramford

48

INDEX TO THE HISTORY OF IPSWICH.

INDEX TO BURY ST. EDMUND'S.

HISTORY

OF THE

BOROUGH AND LIBERTY

OF

IPSWICH.

IPSWICH, the capital of Suffolk, and the largest market-town and port in the county, is an ancient borough and liberty, holding a pleasant and salubrious situation, mostly on the north-east side of the *Gipping*, at the point where that navigable river assumes the name of *Orwell*, and begins to expand into a broad estuary, which terminates in the German Ocean, at Harwich, about 13 miles S.E. of the town, which is distant 69 miles N.E. of London, 20 miles N.E. of Colchester, 25 miles S.E. by E. of Bury St. Edmunds, 54 miles S.S.W. of Yarmouth, 8½ miles W.S.W. of Woodbridge, and 43 miles S. of Norwich; being in 52 deg. 3 min. north latitude, and in 1 deg. 9 min. east longitude. It is in the line of the *Eastern Counties Railway*, which is completed from London to Colchester, and is to be extended to Norwich. It suffered considerably during the greater part of last century, from the loss of its ancient staple manufacture of woollen cloth and canvass; but being favourably seated for commerce, it has risen rapidly in wealth, population, and importance, during the present century, in which it has increased its population from 10,402, to upwards of 25,000 souls. In 1793, the *Gipping* was made navigable for barges to Stowmarket, and the commerce of Ipswich has since been facilitated by various improvements in the navigation of the *Orwell*, and in 1842, by the completion of a *Wet Dock*, formed in the old channel of the river, and presenting a floating surface of 32 acres, with a depth of 14 feet of water; a *Lock*, 140 feet in length, and 45 feet in breadth; and a line of *Quay*, 2780 feet long, and 30 broad.

The *Borough of Ipswich*, anciently called *Gyppeswic*, from its situation at the confluence of the river Gipping with the Orwell, sends two representatives to Parliament, and is a *polling place*, and the principal place of election for the Eastern Division of Suffolk. It forms an *Union* under the new poor law, and gives name to a *Deanery* in the *Archdeaconry of Suffolk* and *Diocese of Norwich*. It has a separate commission of the peace, a recorder, courts of record, requests, &c., quarter and petty sessions, and a gaol for felons, misdemeanors, and debtors, distinct from those of the county and hundreds; and it also claims an *admiralty jurisdiction* over the whole extent of the Orwell, from the town to Pollshead, on the Andrews Sand, in the Ocean, beyond the cliffs of Walton and Felixstow. Though Ipswich has always been considered the capital of the county of Suffolk, the *Assizes* were held at Bury St. Edmunds, till 1839, since which year the Summer Assize has been held here, and the Spring Assize at Bury. Except Stoke, and some other small suburbs on the opposite banks, Ipswich is situated on a declivity, with a southern aspect, declining by an easy descent

to the Orwell and the Gipping, and sheltered on the north-east *by* gently-rising grounds and verdant hills, picturesquely studded with neat villas, gardens, and pleasure grounds, among which, close to the north side of the town, is *Christ Church Park*, well clothed with wood and stocked with deer. The sub-soil being sand, crag, or gravel, the *town* is dry and healthy, but it is well supplied with water, from about 50 copious springs, in the neighbouring hills. It contains *twelve parish churches;* and within the limits of the borough are the villages and churches of Whitton and Westerfield, distant about two miles north of the town. The *Liberty of Ipswich* is co-extensive with the *Borough*, and comprises about 8450 acres, bounded by the Hundreds of Bosmere-and-Claydon, Samford, Colneis, and Carlford, and extending about five miles in length, and four in breadth; with the town nearly in the centre. Besides the twelve parishes into which the town extends, the borough comprises nearly the whole of Whitton and Westerfield, some small portions of four other parishes, and five extra-parochial places, as will be seen in the following Table and Notes, shewing the *annual value* of the lands and buildings in each parish, as assessed to the property tax in 1815, and the *population* of each at the five decennial periods of the parliamentary census :—

BOROUGH & LIBERTY of IPSWICH. PARISHES.	ANNUAL VALUE, in 1815.	POPULATION IN				
		1801.	1811.	1821.	1831.	1841.
St. Clement*	£4879	1584	3305	4424	4779	5973
St. Helen	2184	327	848	781	961	1352
St. Lawrence	1890	469	494	503	565	570
St. Margaret*	8681	1923	2705	3214	4300	4512
St. Mary at Elms	771	447	441	634	778	856
St. Mary at Quay	2135	810	573	773	1039	1082
St. Mary at Stoke	3615	385	568	752	789	992
St. Mary at Tower	3033	688	810	914	951	985
St. Matthew§	3903	1206	1353	1722	2204	3458
St. Nicholas	2529	758	832	1086	1313	1693
St. Peter	3791	986	1125	1567	1646	2410
St. Stephen	1446	422	416	561	530	509
Westerfield†	1538	187	248	289	327	324
Whitton†	2117	210	200	255	346	538
Total ‡	42,512	10,402	13,918	17,475	20,528	25,254

☞ The *annual value* of the town, in 1837, was £55,979. 10s.

* St. Clement's includes *Fore Hamlet, Back Hamlet, Wykes Bishop,* and *Warren House.* The latter is EXTRA-PAROCHIAL; as also are, *Cold Dunghills* and *Felaw's Houses*, in St. Margaret's; the *Shire Hall yard*, in St. Mary's at Quay; and several houses in *Globe lane*, included with St. Mary at Tower.

§ St. Matthew's population, in 1841, included 308 in the *Queen's Barracks;* St. Peter's, 191 in the *Union Workhouse;* and Whitton, 116 in the *County Gaol;* but the latter is mostly in St. Helen's, St. Margaret's, and St. Stephen's parishes.

† *Westerfield* and *Whitton* parishes are in the country, but mostly within the liberty of the borough, which also includes some small portions of the parishes of *Sproughton, Bramford, Rushmere,* and *Belstead.*

‡ The number of *houses* in the borough, in 1841, was 5776; of which 322 were uninhabited, and 241 were building, when the census was taken. The number of *males* was 11,824, and *females*, 13,430.

IPSWICH UNION comprises the fourteen parishes enumerated in the foregoing table, and forms a REGISTRATION DISTRICT, of which Mr. Thos. Grimsey is *superintendent registrar;* Mr. Jas. O. Francis, *registrar of marriages;* and

Messrs. Wm. Hutchinson. Henry Watson, and Geo. J. Harmer, are *registrars of births and deaths*. Mr. Grimsey is also clerk to the Board of Guardians. The UNION WORKHOUSE, on the Wherstead road, near the west bank of the Orwell, is an extensive brick building, erected about five years ago, on the radiating plan, with the governor's house in the centre, commanding a view of all the wards. It cost upwards of £6000, and has accommodations for 400 paupers. Mr. Robert Clamp is the governor, and Mrs. Clamp the matron. The total *expenditure* of the fourteen parishes, for the *relief of the poor*, during the three years before they were united, averaged about £13,000 per annum, but it has since averaged only about £10,000 per annum. In March, 1843, there were 330 paupers in the workhouse, who were fed and clothed at the average weekly cost of 2s. 9¼d. per head ; and during the preceding three months, no fewer than 2090 out-door paupers were relieved, at the cost of £1675. 16s. 1d. The *Borough Rates* paid by the fourteen parishes, in the same *quarter* of the year 1843, amounted to £1215. 12s. 7d.

ANCIENT HISTORY.—As already noticed, Ipswich derives its name from its situation at the point where the river Gipping discharges itself into the Orwell. It is variously written in Domesday Book *Gyppeswik*, *Gyppeswiz*, *Gyppewicus*, and *Gyppewic*, which mode of spelling was gradually changed into *Yppyswyche* and *Ipswich*. It was of small extent in the Saxon era, and was encompassed by a *rampart* or wall, which was defended on the outside by a ditch, and was broken down by the Danes when they pillaged the town, in the years 991 and 1000. This fortification was afterwards renewed and repaired in the fifth of King John. A *castle* is said to have been erected here by William the Conqueror, and to have been destroyed in the reign of Henry II. In the rampart or wall which encompassed the town, were four *gates*, called from their situation after the four cardinal points of the compass ; and we also read of a fifth, called *Losegate*, which stood on the bank of the Orwell, at the spot where there once was a ford. All vestiges of the wall, gates, and castle disappeared many years ago ; but there are still some traces of the ditch and the earthen rampart on which the wall stood, from which it appears that the parishes of St. Clement, St. Helen, and St. Mary Stoke, with part of those of St. Margaret and St. Matthew, were not included within the gates, and are, accordingly, in old writings, denominated the suburbs of Ipswich. The castle was perhaps merely a bastion tower, which stood in the place still called the *Tower Ditches*. As early as A.D. 964, money was coined here, and specimens are extant of *coins* struck at a mint here, from that period to the reign of Henry III. Being remotely situated from the great lines of communication through the kingdom, Ipswich did not suffer much from the intestine wars which so frequently ravaged England from the eleventh to the fifteenth century. The town, in conjunction with the neighbouring country, espoused the cause of the sons of Henry II. ; and during the contest between these rebels and their royal father, a large army of *Flemings*, in 1173, headed by Robert de Bellomont, Earl of Leicester, sailed up the Orwell, and landed at this port, whence they passed to Framlingham castle, the stronghold of Hugh Bigod, Earl of Norfolk, who had joined the rebel princes. The feeble garrison of Ipswich vainly opposed the entrance of the Flemings, who demolished the fortifications. They afterwards attacked the castle of Haughley, near Stowmarket, then commanded by Ralph Broc, for the king, and razed it to the earth. Flushed with victory, they passed westward to Fornham St. Genevieve, where they were completely routed by the king's forces, under Henry de Bohun, and ten thousand of them slain. This battle completely destroyed the

hopes of the rebels, and it has been conjectured that some of the Flemings, spared from the wreck of Leicester's army, purchased their lives and subsistence by locating in this part of the kingdom, and instructing the inhabitants in the manufacture of *jersey*, or worsted stuffs, which had been introduced at Norwich, by some of their countrymen, in the preceding reign.

Before, and for many years after the Norman Conquest, Ipswich was in the same condition as all other boroughs that were in the demense of the crown. For some time anterior to the *Domesday survey*, it appears to have been rapidly declining. " In the time of King Edward," (the Confessor,) says that document, " there were 538 burgesses who paid custom to the king, and they had forty acres of land. But now there are 110 burgesses who pay custom, and 100 poor burgesses, who can pay no more than one penny a head to the king's geld. Thus, upon the whole, they have forty acres of land, and 328 houses now empty, and which, in the time of King Edward, scotted to the king's geld. Roger, the vice-earl, let the whole for £40 ; afterwards he could could not have that rent, and abated sixty shillings of it, so that it now pays £37, and the earl always hath the third part." We are also informed by the same ancient record, that during the reign of Edward the Confessor, his queen Edith, the daughter of Earl Godwin, had two-thirds of this borough, and Earl Guert, the sixth son of the same nobleman, possessed the remaining third. The queen had a grange, to which belonged four carucates of land, and the earl another, valued at one hundred shillings, besides the third penny of the borough. In the reign of Richard I., the inhabitants had so much increased in numbers and wealth, that they purchased their freedom from that monarch. The *first charter* obtained by the town, was granted by King John, in 1190, and conferred on the inhabitants important privileges, some of which strikingly illustrate the oppressions under which the mass of the people must, in those early ages, have groaned. By this charter, the king granted to the burgesses, the borough of Ipswich, with all its appurtenances, liberties, &c., to be held of him and his heirs, by the payment of the usual annual farm of £35, and one hundred shillings more at the exchequer. He exempted them from the payment of all taxes, under the denominations of *tholl*, *lestage*, *stallage*, *passage*, *pontage*, and all other customs throughout his land and sea-ports. The other privileges granted to the people of Ipswich by this charter were as follows :—That they should have a *merchants' guild and hanse* of their own ; that no person should be quartered upon them without their consent, or take anything from them by force ; that they might hold their lands, and recover their just dues, from whomsoever they were owing ; that none of them should be fined or amerced but according to the laws of the free borough ; and that they might choose *two bailiffs* and four *coroners* out of the principal men of the town. As early as 1254, a *court of pleas* was established here for the trial of disputed debts, without the king's writ.

Ipswich was not the theatre of any of the violent commotions which arose from the quarrels between King John and his barons ; but it passively contributed about £300 to the tax or " *quinzieme*," which he levied in the seventh year of his reign. In 1215, the duty levied on *woad*, (used in dyeing,) amounted in Suffolk, to £50 ; Yorkshire,

to £96; Lincolnshire, to £47; and Southamptonshire, to £79: thus it appears that Ipswich then enjoyed a considerable share of the *woollen manufacture*, which was introduced by the Flemings, and fostered by royal charters, and the *monasteries* founded in the town and neighbourhood.

Edward I., in 1285, for some offence committed by the burgesses, seized the borough into his own hands, and kept it till 1291, when, being pleased with the service performed by some ships from Ipswich, in his expedition against Scotland, he re granted the borough and its liberties to the burgesses, and confirmed the charters of his predecessors, John and Henry III.; but he advanced the *fee farm rent* from £40 to £60 per annum. In 1317, Edward II. granted a charter, confirming the former privileges of the borough, but reducing the number of coroners from four to two. The oppressive levies made by Edward II. to assist him in his wars against Scotland, and in the defence of his favourites, the De Spencers, caused much dissension in the kingdom; and, in 1324, a great riot broke out in Ipswich, headed by the representatives of the borough, and many of the principal inhabitants. In 1328, a powerful fleet was collected on the coast of Suffolk, to assist *Edward III.* in his designs upon France, for which kingdom Sir John Howard embarked 500 men, at Ipswich, in 1337. Edward III. being on a visit at Walton, in 1339, confirmed the charters of Ipswich, and granted further immunities; but, in 1345, for some time disfranchised the borough, on account of an insult received here, at the assizes, by a judge named Sharford, from some sailors, who thinking his lordship staid too long at dinner, one of them, in a frolic, took his seat upon the bench, and caused another to make proclamation, requiring William Sharford to come into court and save his fine; and as he did not appear, ordered him to be fined. The judge, who was a morose man, so highly resented this joke, that because the magistrates refused to apprehend the sailors, he prevailed upon the king to seize the borough, and to place it under the government of the sheriff of Norfolk and Suffolk; but before the end of the year, it was again under the control of the bailiffs.

Henry VI., by a charter in the 24th year of his reign, (1445,) incorporated the town by the style of the burgesses of Ipswich. He authorised them annually to elect two burgesses as bailiffs, at the accustomed time and place, to hold that office for one whole year. He granted to the bailiffs, and four such other burgesses as the bailiffs should appoint from among the *twelve portmen*, the office of *justice of the peace* within the town, together with all fines, forfeitures, and amercements arising from that office, and the assize of bread, wine, and ale. He appointed such one of the bailiffs, as should be chosen by the burgesses at the time of election, to be escheator, and expressly granted the *admiralty* and clerkship of the market, although the bailiffs had always exercised these offices by the custom of the town. No notice was taken of this charter in that of Edward IV., but that monarch granted all the privileges mentioned in it, with these alterations and additions:—He incorporated the town by the name of the *bailiffs, burgesses, and commonalty*, of the town of Ipswich; he confined the election of bailiffs expressly to the 8th of September, in the Guildhall, to serve for one year; and he expressly exempted the burgesses from

serving on juries out of the borough. The most interesting charter granted by succeeding monarchs for insuring these privileges, was that of *Charles II.*, who, in the 17th year of his reign, ratified the ancient privileges of the borough, and confirmed the *high steward*, the *twelve portmen*, the 24 *chief-constables*, the recorder, and *town clerk* for the time being, by thair names, and directed, that upon the death or removal of any of the portmen, or twenty-four chief constables, the vacancies should be filled up by the rest of those respective bodies. Though the burgesses, towards the close of the same reign, surrendered their charter, and received another, by which the number of chief constables (or council-men) was reduced to eighteen; yet, as neither the surrender was enrolled, nor any judgment entered upon record, the officers who had acted under the former charter, resumed their functions, on the proclamation of James II., who, in 1688, confirmed all the privileges of the borough granted by the charters of Edward IV., Henry VIII., and Charles II., which were considered as governing charters till the passing of the Municipal Reform Act, in 1835. According to these charters, the *corporate body* consisted of two bailiffs, a high-steward, a recorder, twelve portmen, of whom four were justices of the peace; and twenty-four chief-constables, two of whom were coroners, and the twelve seniors were head-boroughs. The *officers* comprised a town-clerk, treasurer, two chamberlains, a water bailiff, four serjeants-at-mace, &c. Besides the privileges already named, the bailiffs were port admirals, and claimed all waifs, estrays, and goods cast on shore within their *admiralty jurisdiction*, which extended down the Orwell to the sea, below Harwich and Languard Fort. By a solemn decision in their favour in the 14th of Edward III., the bailiffs and burgesses had confirmed to them the right of taking custom-duties for goods entering the port of Harwich; and in a trial with the city of London, they established their claim to exemption from tolls and duties in all the ports of the kingdom.

The Municipal Commissioner, who enquired into the state of the Ipswich Corporation, in 1834, says, at the close of his voluminous and elaborate *Report*, " It is a constitution which still presents the appearance of a popular government, but it is in reality no such thing. Considered with reference to the corporate body only, it is an ill-regulated republic :—considered with reference to the local community, it is an oligarchy of the worst description. It is a government which excludes from municipal rights the most considerable portion of the inhabitants, whether considered with reference to number, property, or taxation ; and which disqualifies for municipal office the most respectable, intelligent, and independent classes of the community. Nor has it even secured the subordinate end of its existence—self-preservation ; for, in consequence of the party feuds of the two self-elected bodies which share its official power, the Corporation is now fast approaching to a legal dissolution." The Commissioner also found that the police was very inefficient; that the bailiffs were sometimes insulted by freemen, even when sitting on the magisterial bench; that the Corporation monopolised the right of supplying the town with water, but that the supply was greatly inadequate to the wants of the inhabitants; that the Corporation property was charged with a debt of £14,300; that various alienations of property had been made, and the proceeds applied

to the general purposes of the Corporation ; and that the *corporate revenues* amounted to upwards of £2000 per annum, of which about £700 arose from the water-works, and about £250 from a duty of 2d. per chaldron on all *coals, coke, cinders,* and *culm,* imported by non-freemen. This duty was originally granted to the Corporation, as conservators of the river Orwell, but they so shamefully neglected the *navigation,* that in 1805 it was taken out of their hands by an Act of Parliament, which placed it under the control of a body of gentlemen, called the River Commissioners, who, in their turn, gave place, in 1837, to the Dock Commissioners, as will be seen at a subsequent page.

Under the Act for the regulation of Municipal Corporations in England and Wales, passed in 1835, the borough of Ipswich is divided into *five wards,* and is governed by a *mayor, ten aldermen, and thirty councillors,* with a commission of the peace, a recorder, quarter sessions, &c. *Charities* to the amount of more than £2000 per annum were vested with the old Corporation ; but, under this Act, they are now vested with 21 trustees. The *Income of the Corporation,* or as it is now called, the Town Council, amounted to about £4800 in 1839, of which £2414 arose from *borough rates ;* £1783 from *land, buildings* and *water rents ;* and £415 from *tolls and dues.* Their *expenditure,* in the same year, amounted to nearly £4600, of which the principal items were,—salaries and allowances to officers, £772 ; police and constables, £885 ; prosecutions, &c., £358 ; gaol and maintenance of prisoners, £699, coroner, £83 ; public works, repairs, &c., £387 ; charities, £235 ; *debts paid off and interest, &c.,* £883 ; municipal elections, £43 ; and law expenses, £39.

Ipswich has sent *two members to Parliament* since the 25th of Henry VI., and in the court books of the borough are many curious memoranda, respecting the *wages* paid at different periods to its representatives. In 1462, they each had from 12d. to 20d. a day ; in 1472, from 3s. 4d. to 5s. per week, and in the reigns of Charles 1st and 2nd, they had in some years from £20 to upwards of £100. The right of election previous to the Parliamentary Reform Act of 1832, was in the *freemen* not receiving alms, of whom 1003 voted in 1826, but only about 400 of them were resident in the borough. The *number of electors* registered in 1837 was 1418, of whom 368 were freemen, and 1058 occupiers of houses of the yearly value of £10 or upwards. The representatives returned by the borough, at the general election in July, 1841, being petitioned against, a new writ was issued in August, 1842, and the *poll* was taken on the 16th of that month, when the five candidates and the number of votes received by each were as follows :— *Capt. John N. Gladstone,* 651 ; *Sackville Lane Fox, Esq.,* 641 ; D. Thornbory, Esq., 548 ; Mr. Henry Vincent, (sent by the Sturgites,) 473 ; and J. Nicholson, Esq., 2. The Ipswich elections have often been severely contested, and the candidates returned have several times been unseated on the petition of the opposing party, or have resigned rather than undergo the ordeal of a scrutiny.

As will be seen in the accounts of the churches, parishes, and charities of Ipswich, at subsequent pages, the town had formerly *twenty-one churches, five priories and several hospitals, guilds,* and other *religious fraternities.* The *priories* were large and richly endowed, and were founded in the 12th and 13th centuries. Two of them belonged

to *Black canons*, and the other three to *Black, Grey, and White friars.*
From the year 1390 to 1515, several religious houses in various parts
of the kingdom were dissolved, and their revenues settled on different
colleges in Oxford and Cambridge.   In 1525, *Cardinal Wolsey*, by
license of the King and Pope, dissolved above thirty religious houses
for the founding and endowing of his colleges at Oxford and Ipswich.
About the same time, a papal bull was granted to Wolsey, to suppress
monasteries, in which there were not above six monks, to the value of
8000 ducats a year, for endowing Windsor and King's colleges, in
Cambridge.   The erection of WOLSEY'S COLLEGE, at Ipswich,
(his native town,) was commenced on the 15th of June, 1528, upon
the site of the *Priory of St. Peter and St. Paul*, the last prior of which,
Wm. Brown, surrendered to the Cardinal, on the 6th of March, 1527.
The building rapidly progressed, and to augment its endowment the
Corporation gave the property which Richard Felaw had bequeathed
to them for the support of a free school and hospital.   Wolsey intended this collegiate academy as a nursery for his new college at Oxford.   It was dedicated to the Blessed Virgin, and was endowed with
the possessions of the monasteries of Snape, Dodnash, Wykes, Felixstow, Rumburgh, Montjoy, Bromhill, Bliburgh, Horkesley, and Tip-
tree, as well as with St. Peter's and Trinity priories, in Ipswich.   The
establishment consisted of a dean, eight clerks, twelve secular canons,
eight choristers, fourteen bedesmen, and a considerable number of scholars.   From its munificent endowment, and the extent and grandeur
of the building, it is evident that Wolsey intended this college to be a
lasting monument of his greatness, but it was scarcely completed, when
he fell into disgrace, and died in 1530 ; and Henry VIII. revenged
himself by seizing both it and the college, which the Cardinal had
founded at Oxford.   The latter was re-established after a lapse of three
years, but Ipswich College was granted to Thomas Alverde, and its
possessions to various other persons in royal favour ; and all that now
remains of it is a *Gateway* of decorated brick-work, flanked by octagonal turrets, and having over the entrance a stone tablet, bearing
the arms of Henry VIII.   This gate adjoins St. Peter's church-yard,
and is supposed to have been an outlet from one of the college wings.
The site of the college comprises about six acres, and now belongs to
the Alexander family.

THOMAS WOLSEY, the haughty *cardinal* of the reign of that lascivious monarch Henry VIII., was born in 1471, at Ipswich, where his
father (Robert Wolsey or Wuley) is supposed to have been in easy
circumstances, and not a butcher, as has been stated by many writers.
He was related to the Daundy family, who ranked among the most
respectable inhabitants of the town.   By his distinguished abilities and
a fortunate concurrence of circumstances, Wolsey raised himself to the
highest offices in church and state.   After being some time at school
in Ipswich, he was sent to Magdalen College, Oxford, of which he
became a fellow.   Having embraced the ecclesiastical profession, he
was presented, in 1500, to the rectory of Lymington, by the Marquis
of Dorset, whose three sons were under his tuition.   Probably through
the recommendation of this nobleman, he was sent by Henry VII.
on a mission to the Emperor Maximilian, and acquitted himself so
much to the satisfaction of the king, that, on his return, he was re-

warded with the deanery of Lincoln, and a prebend in that cathedral. His introduction to the court of Henry VIII. he owed to Fox, bishop of Winchester, whom he soon supplanted in royal favour, and became himself sole and absolute minister. He successively rose to the offices of bishop of Tournay in Flanders, (which city the king had just taken,) bishop of Bath and Wells, bishop of Lincoln, Durham, and Winchester; archbishop of York, and cardinal and lord-high-chancellor of England. The revenues derived from his various offices equalled those of the sovereign, and he expended them in a manner not less magnificent; having in his retinue 800 persons, many of whom were knights and gentlemen. He built the palace of Hampton-Court; and York-place in London, which afterwards received the name of Whitehall. Naturally ambitious, Wolsey aspired even to the papal tiara, and being disappointed in his hopes of attaining that honour by the emperor Charles V., who had promised to support him, he revenged himself by promoting the divorce of Henry VIII. from Catharine of Arragon, aunt to his imperial majesty. This affair, however, proved the occasion of the cardinal's downfal. The obstacles to the accomplishment of Henry's wishes being too powerful for even Wolsey to remove so speedily as the king desired, he incurred Henry's displeasure, and being at the same time undermined by his enemies, he was suddenly stripped of all his employments, banished from the court, and arrested for high treason. He was taken at Cawood, near York, and from thence escorted to Sheffield Manor, where he remained sixteen days in the custody of the Earl of Shrewsbury. Though he was here seized with a violent dysentery which his physician predicted would terminate in death in a few days, he was hurried towards London, to take his trial, mounted upon a mule, but he could proceed no further than Leicester Abbey, where he said, on his arrival, to the head of the convent—"Father Abbot, I am come to leave my bones among you." He died Nov. 30th, 1530, the second day after his arrival at Leicester, and was thus saved from farther humiliation. He was a man of extraordinary talent and industry ; but his good qualities were overshadowed by the poison of ambition, and the arrogance of pride. He governed England for the space of twenty years, during which time he knew all the cabals of foreign courts, and had spies on every prince in Europe, by which he rendered himself truly formidable. He was courted, bribed, and caressed by the greatest potentates in Christendom. In virtue of his authority as *pope's legate*, he instituted an inquisitorial court, in which he exercised a power not known before in England. He so absolutely governed the king " that he turned him which way he pleased ; but managed so artfully, that the king always fancied he took his own course." On many occasions of the utmost importance, he displayed his contempt of the laws and constitution of his country, when they stood between him and his ambition. He was charged with great immoralities and a lascivious life, though in public he kept up much show of solemnity and religion. Cavendish, his gentleman usher, said, in all his proceedings, he was the haughtiest man alive, and had more respect to the honour of his own person than he had to his spiritual profession. He was capricious, haughty, and insolent, even to the ancient nobles of the land, who could ill brook such conduct from one who, by his talent and learning, had raised himself from a humble sphere to be se-

cond only to his sovereign in splendour and authority; and they therefore used all their influence to bring about his humuliation. With his last breath, he said—"Had I but served my God as diligently as I served the king, he would not have given me over in my gray hairs."

The *general Dissolution of the Monasteries* and the *Reformation of the Church*, did not commence till after the death of Wolsey, in whose time Henry VIII. had written a work in favour of the Romish church, which so pleased the Pope that he conferred on him the title of "Defender of the Faith," which has ever since been attached to the crowned head of England. In 1533, an act of parliament was passed requiring the Lord's prayer, the creed, &c., to be read in English; and in the following year, Henry VIII. sanctioned the *Protestants*,—a name which originated in the Diet of Spiers, (in 1529,) in Germany, where Martin Luther began that great reform which Wickliffe, nearly a centery and a half before, had laboured to effect in England. An act for the suppression of the lesser monasteries was passed in 1535; another for the suppression of the larger abbeys, priories, &c., in 1540; and one for the dissolving all colleges, free chapels, hospitals, chantries, &c., in 1545. The latter act was further enforced by one of the 1st of Edward VI. The number of monastic institutions suppressed in England by these acts amounted to about 3200, and their total clear yearly revenue to upwards of £150,000, which was immense, as the value of money at that period was at least six times as much as at present. The suppression of these houses and the consequent dispersion of many thousand monks and nuns, occasioned much discontent, which in many parts of the kingdom broke out into open rebellion, in which, however, Ipswich does not appear to have been concerned, though it was greatly affected by the change, which transferred the revenues of its monasteries to the coffers of the king, or to the use of those who pandered to his lasciviousness and extravagance. In the time of Wolsey, Henry VIII. persecuted the Protestants with as much cruelty as he afterwards did the adherents to the Romish faith. *Thomas Bilney*, one of the earliest promulgators of the doctrines of Wickliffe and Luther, in Norfolk and Suffolk, often preached here in St. George's chapel, which stood near St. Matthew's church, where Cardinal Wolsey set spies upon him, and after being twice dragged from his pulpit by the monks, he was taken to London, where, after undergoing much privation, he was induced by his friends to recant; but this so troubled his conscience that shortly after his return, he boldly offered himself as a martyr to the reformed religion, and suffered at the stake, in Norwich. In 1548, there were three *printers* in Ipswich, though the typographical art was then in its infancy. In the reign of Mary, the Roman Catholic religion was again established, and this town became the scene of several burnings and sacrifices, for the rights of conscience, and many of the protestants were obliged to leave the town or "lurk in secret places." Among those *burnt at the stake*, in Ipswich, were the Rev. Robt. Samuel, of East Bergholt, in 1555; Nicholas Peke, of Earl Stonham; and Ann Potter and Joan Trunchfield, in or about the same year; one Kerby, in 1556; and Alexander Gooch and Alice Driver, in 1558. In the latter part of the latter year, the cruelties of Mary ended in her death, and the protestant Elizabeth commenced her long and glorious reign. When the faggots were blazing about

Peke, Dr. Reading called out—" Peke, recant thy opinion, and I have thy pardon in my hand ;" but he answered, " I defy it and thee, and withal spit out a mouthful of blood." Hearing this answer, Dr. Reading promised in the name of the bishop of Norwich, 40 days' pardon for sins, to all who would cast a stick into the fire. " Whereupon Sir John Audley, kt., Mr. Barnes, Mr. Curson, and divers others of reputation, there present, cut down boughs from the trees with their swords, and threw them into the fire."

In 1561, *Queen Elizabeth* visited the town, and taxed the inhabitants with the expenses of her journey, ordering that all the burgesses who refused to contribute thereto should be disfranchised. She again visited the town in 1565, and finding that the parochial clergy were poor, caused an act to be passed for the augmentation of their benefices, and the support of the churches, by yearly assessments to be levied on the parishioners at the discretion of the Corporation, proof being first given by the officers of the several parishes that such assessments are needed. In the 13th of Elizabeth, the first *act for paving the town* was passed, and it appears to be the earliest act obtained by any borough in England for the same purpose. An " *Act for paving, lighting, cleansing, and otherwise improving the town of Ipswich,*" was obtained in the 33rd of George III., and was amended by four other acts, passed in 1797, 1815, 1821, and 1837. In the 30th and 39th of Elizabeth, Ipswich furnished two ships for the general defence of the nation. During this and the following reign, the town greatly increased, though it suffered much from a visitation of the *plague* in 1603, when upwards of 30,000 persons died in London of that dreadful malady. In 1654, the town suffered considerably by *fire ;* and it had another fatal visitation of the plague in 1666, the year of the great plague and fire in London. During the *civil wars* between Charles I. and the Parliament, which commenced in 1642, and terminated in the decapitation of the misguided and unfortunate monarch in 1648, Ipswich was not the scene of any of those sanguinary conflicts which so frequently distracted various parts of the kingdom. At the commencement of this long-continued struggle, the inhabitants of both Suffolk and Norfolk generally declared for the Parliament, and at no period were the Royalists able to make much impression in either county. In these troublesome times, numerous instances of fraud and credulity occurred here and at other places, under the delusion of *witchcraft and demonology ;* and so ignorant were the magistrates of many towns, that they actually employed designing villains, who styled themselves *witchfinders*, and pricked harmless persons with pins, or ducked them in rivers, under the pretence of deciding whether they were witches or not ; and being paid a certain sum per head for each conviction, they did not often let their victims escape. A poor fanatical old woman, called *Mother Lakeland*, was arraigned, condemned, and burnt for a witch at Ipswich, on the 9th of September, 1645 ; and in a pamphlet published after her death, she is represented as having confessed that she had sold herself to the devil twenty years before, and had been furnished with three imps, in the forms of two little dogs and a mole, by means of which she grievously afflicted Mr. Lawrence, Mr. Beal, a maid of Mrs. Jennings, and other persons in the town. Many are said to have suffered, in various parts of Suffolk, under the belief in this

kind of supernatural agency, which ceased to prevail many years ago, except amongst the most ignorant of the vulgar ; and the repeal of all the statutes relating to witchcraft has removed from our criminal code the reproach cast upon it by such ridiculous enactments.

The *restoration of monarchy and episcopacy*, in 1660, appears to have been hailed with gladness in Ipswich, for immediately after Charles II. had ascended the long-vacant throne, the Corporation voted him £300 out of their revenue ; and in addition to this gift, the inhabitants raised a voluntary subscription. The grateful, but gay and extravagant monarch, granted the town a new charter in 1678, as already noticed. In 1693, the Corporation entered into an engagement with fifty families of French Protestants, skilled in the manufacture of *lutestring*, to settle in the town, promising to support them liberally, and to erect and endow a church for their accommodation ; but after remaining here for some time, they appear to have removed to Norwich. In 1704, a *nightly watch* was established in the town, and it was agreed that every person who refused to take his turn as watchman should be fined. In 1709, some German weavers, &c., applied to be allowed to settle in the town, but were answered, that by " reason of decay of trade, and having no manufactory to employ poor people, and the great burden and increase of its own poor inhabitants," they could not possibly be accommodated in the town. In 1787, it was found, that though the Corporation possessed a large estate, their debts and mortgages were so heavy, as to leave only a clear income of £132 per ann. In 1794, Ipswich determined to follow the example of many other towns, which had formed *corps of volunteers*, for internal defence against insurrection, or the threatened invasion of the French. But some time elapsed before the " *Loyal Ipswich Volunteers*" were properly organised. They numbered about 200, and were bound, in case of invasion, to march to any part of the kingdom. Many of the inhabitants belonged to the *East Suffolk Militia* (which still has its staff here,) and the loyalty of the town and county stood pre-eminent during the fear-exciting period of the French Revolution. Being situated conveniently for the embarkation of troops to Holland, &c., Ipswich was generally crowded with soldiers during the late wars, and barracks were erected on the old dock side, on the Woodbridge road, and near St. Matthew's street, for the accommodation of more than 12,000 men, chiefly infantry ; but these buildings have been taken down or appropriated to other uses, except the *Queen's Barracks* (as they are now called,) which occupy an airy situation near the end of St. Matthew's street, and were built by Government in 1795, for the accommodation of three troops of cavalry. In the location of troops, a regiment of horse is generally apportioned between Norwich and Ipswich, and the head-quarters are usually here. At the close of the war, Ipswich lost its military character, and became absorbed in the less-exciting, but more pleasing and profitable pursuits of commerce, for which it is so well adapted.

During the last twenty years, the *town* has greatly increased in wealth and population, as already noticed at page 50 ; and many new streets, neat mansions, and public edifices have been erected, some of them presenting handsome fronts of white brick. The *streets* in the old parts of the town are rather narrow and irregular, but the princi-

pal thoroughfares have been widened and straightened, since 1821,
under the powers of the two last of five successive acts of Parliament
for paving, lighting, and improving the town. (See page 59.) The
Water-works belong to the Corporation, as noticed at page 55, and
afford an abundant supply of the pure beverage of nature, brought in
pipes from about fifty springs in the neighbouring hills. The *Gas-
works* were finished, in 1821, by a company of proprietors, holding
1400 shares of £10 each, and have two gasometers, each of the capacity of 1400 cubic feet. Tavern street, Westgate street, Cornhill,
Butter market, and the other principal streets, contain many handsome and well-stocked shops and commodious inns; but the largest
and perhaps the most valuable premises are the warehouses, &c., situated near the common quay, and along the banks of the Orwell. A
handsome and substantial cast-iron bridge, called STOKE BRIDGE,
connects the town with the parish of Stoke, and was erected at the
cost of £7000, in lieu of the old stone bridge, which was destroyed by
a flood on the 12th of April, 1818.

Handford Bridge, which crosses the Gipping on the London road,
was erected about 1795, at a considerable expense, being carried for
some distance across the head of the *marshes*, which form a small
island on the west side of the town, encompassed by two channels of
the river, which diverge and re-unite between the two bridges, after a
separation of more than a mile. The old channel skirts the western
side of the town, where it is crossed by a smaller bridge, leading to the
marshes, which belong to the Corporation.

Ancient Houses.—Though the hand of modern improvement has
considerably reduced them, the town still retains a considerable number of ancient *half-timbered houses*, of the Elizabethan and other ages,
having their many-gabled fronts ornamented with carvings, and some
of them projecting their upper stories two or more feet into the street.
MR. SPARROWE'S HOUSE, the largest and most interesting of these
antique dwellings, is very extensive. It fronts the Butter market, and
was built in 1567, by George Copping, Esq., but has been occupied
more than two centuries and a half by the Sparrowe family, and is now
the property and residence of J. E. Sparrowe, Esq. The basement
front is finely carved in pendant fruit, and extends about 70 feet in
length, and above it are four large bay windows, on the base of which
are sculptured emblematical figures of Europe, Asia, Africa, and America, with their peculiar attributes. Above these windows, is a considerable projection, or pediment, forming a promenade, on the outside,
nearly round the house, and in front of the attic windows, which are
crowned by ornamented gables. Indeed, the whole exterior of this
unique dwelling is profusely ornamented with carvings of animals,
fruit, flowers, wreaths of roses, and other devices. The interior contains many fine apartments. The dining room is 22 feet by 21, and is
closely panneled in dark oak, carved in a manner which would do
honour even to the great genius of Grinling Gibbon. Upon the first
floor, fronting the street, is a noble apartment, 46 feet by 21, having
its ceiling traversed by heavy oak beams, and divided into compartments, ornamented by ponderous wreaths of fruit. There are in the
house many fine old paintings, and among them is a portrait, by Vandyke, of Charles II., who is said to have been some time concealed

here during the Commonwealth, but this tradition is not supported by history. The Tankard public-house, in Tacket street, taken down in 1843, was the last-remaining portion of an extensive and highly ornamented mansion, which was the residence of *Sir Anthony Wingfield,* a distinguished courtier of the days of Henry VIII. The house in which *Cardinal Wolsey* was born stands in St. Nicholas street, on the south side of the passage leading to the churchyard. The old timber carvings still existing upon the corner posts of many other houses, shew that they were built by wealthy families. Indeed, in the Elizabethan age, the town was distinguished for the " fair and goodly residences" of its merchants. In front of the Half-Moon public-house, appears, well carved, the old story of the fox preaching to the geese, supposed to have had a satirical reference to the condition of the townspeople and the monks before the suppression of the monasteries. In a yard behind the quay, are the remains of a house, exhibiting the framework of a fine Tudor window, and having on one of its corner posts a carved effigy of Queen Elizabeth. Among the numerous old buildings on the banks of the Orwell, were several quaint in character, but they were removed a few years ago to make room for the new quay, and their sites are now occupied by a long line of lofty warehouses, granaries, &c.

The RIVER GIPPING, which gave name to the town, as noticed at page 51, is a small stream, but it was made navigable for barges, at the cost of about £27,000, in 1793, up to Stowmarket, which lies in the centre of Suffolk, about 14 miles N.N.W. of Ipswich. It takes its rise from three rivulets, which have their sources near the villages of Gipping, Rattlesden, and Wetherden, and unite at Stowmarket, whence it flows to Ipswich by a winding course of sixteen miles, through a fertile country, which has been considerably benefitted by the navigation. Below Stoke bridge, at Ipswich, the Gipping assumes the name of ORWELL, and becomes a broad estuary, in which the tide rises about twelve feet. The Orwell extends S.S.E. from Ipswich to the North Sea, or German Ocean, at Harwich (distant about twelve miles,) in a bed varying from half a mile to upwards of a mile in breadth at high water. At Harwich, it unites with the Stour, which is the boundary of Suffolk and Essex, and is navigable to Sudbury for barges. The channel of the Orwell has been straightened, deepened,[*] and very much improved since 1805, when an *Act* was obtained "*for improving and rendering more commodious the Port of Ipswich,*" so that vessels of 200 tons burthen, or drawing 12 feet water, might come up to the quays, instead of receiving and discharging their cargoes by means of lighters, at *Downham Reach,* about three miles below, where there is at all times of the tide water sufficient for ships of the greatest draught. For effecting these improvements, the act incorporated a body of gentlemen under the name of the *River Commissioners,* who thus became the conservators of the Orwell, which had been so long neglected by

---

[*] *Submerged Forest :*—In deepening various parts of the Orwell, and particularly the creek leading up to Halifax ship-yard, such immense quantities of vegetable remains have been found, as to render it probable that, at a remote period a *forest* existed in what is now the bed of the Orwell. Large quantities of hazel-nuts, brush-wood, and timber-trees, have been raised from what might be termed the natural bed of the river. On becoming dry, after exposure to the air, they crumbled into dust.

the Corporation. (See page 55.) Though these commissioners did essential service in facilitating the passage of large vessels to and from the town, the Orwell was still left nearly dry at low water, when broad and constantly accumulating banks of silt presented themselves opposite the quays. This injury to the trade and shipping of the port was proposed to be removed about fifty years ago by damming up the river at Downham Reach, or by making a large basin and lock close to the town, so as to pen up the water at flood-tide opposite the quays ; but no decisive measures were taken till November, 1836, when it was resolved, at a large public meeting of the gentry and merchants of the town and neighbourhood, that an act of Parliament should be obtained to enable a new body of commissioners to deepen the old channel next the town ; to form it, by means of stupendous embankments, into a *Wet Dock* of 32 acres ; and to cut a *new channel*, about 2500 feet long, on the opposite side of the river, for the free motion of the tidal water, and the discharge of the Gipping. After much opposition, the act for accomplishing his grand *desideratum* was obtained in June, 1837, and H. R. Palmer, Esq., was appointed engineer, and D. Thornbory, Esq., became chief contractor for the works. The duties of the River Commissioners now became absorbed in the " *Dock Commission*," and they paid over to the latter £25,000 three per cent. consols, which had accumulated from the careful administration of their trust. In addition to this sum, the dock commissioners were empowered to borrow £60,000, to complete the works, but, in 1840, they were under the necessity of applying to Parliament for power to borrow £25,000 more ; and this not being found sufficient, they obtained another act in May, 1843, enabling them to borrow a further sum of £20,000, and to levy an extra sixpence per ton on all coals imported. The foundation stone of the *lock* was laid June 6th, 1839, and the work proceeded, with few interruptions, till January, 1842, when the gates of the lock being closed at high water, the harbour of Ipswich became the largest WET DOCK in the kingdom, presenting the ample surface of 32 acres, with a depth of 14 feet of water, laving the walls of a new line of *Quay*, 2780 feet in length, and 30 in breadth. The dimensions of this noble dock are nine acres more than the whole area of the Hull docks, and three acres more than the London docks. The excavations from the dock and the new channel furnished earth for the broad embankments which rise several feet above high-water mark. The lock chamber is 140 feet long, 45 feet broad, and 20 feet 6 inches deep, from the surface of the quay. Among other improvements intended to be made in the river, below the dock, are a new cut through the *Black Ooze*, and the removal of the shoal from the *Cliff Reach* to the " *Lower Hearth Point*," by means of the dredging machine. The DOCK COMMISSIONERS consist of a number of the principal inhabitants, and one-third of them are changed annually. For the support of the dock and the improvement of the navigation, they levy certain *dues* on vessels according to their tonnage, and 1s. 6d. per ton on coals, which also pay 1½d. per ton for town dues. They have also the exclusive privilege of supplying *ballast*, for which they charge 1s. per ton, besides 5d. for the labour of putting it on board. The navigation dues from 1820 to 1834, averaged £2630 a year, but, including the dock dues, they now average more than twice that amount. D., Alexander

Esq., is *treasurer* to the Dock Commissioners ; P. B. Long, *clerk ;* G. H. Potter, *collector and accountant ;* George Hurwood, *engineer ;* Samuel Smith, *harbour master ;* and James Barber, *lock master.* Mr. Smith is also *pilot master*, and has under his control 13 pilots, licensed by the Trinity House, London.

In June, 1843, the Corporation commenced the erection of a com- modious *public building* upon the Common Quay, (from a design by Mr. Clark, the architect,) to be used as the Custom House,* Excise Office, Dock Office, &c. The cost of this erection will be about £4000. The *Custom House Officers* are Wm. Lane, Esq., *collector ;* Abraham Cook, Esq., *comptroller ;* Saml. Christopherson, *clerk ;* Wm. Hooper, *tide surveyor ;* G. T. Soley, *searcher and landing waiter ;* and Jph. Frost, Lilly Pattison, E. Bird, S. Ford, and G. Scrutton, tide waiters. The Excise Officers are John Wild, Esq., *collector ;* E. Dobson, *clerk ;* J. Morson, *supervisor ;* and T. R. Leath, *permit writer.* The jurisdiction of the port extends to Liv- ington Creek. The gross amount of *customs duty* received here aver- ages about £40,000 per annum ; and the *number of vessels*, belonging to the port, is upwards of 300, though it had not more than 150 in 1830.

Trade and Commerce.—As already noticed, Ipswich was dis- tinguished for the wealth and commercial enterprise of its merchants, in the 15th and 16th centuries ; and it had then many large ships em- ployed by the merchants of London in the coal and Baltic trades. De Foe, in his history of the Plague, says that dreadful malady was car- ried to Ipswich, by those large vessels called the *Ipswich Cats.* But, during the middle of the 17th century, the manufactures of *woollen cloth and sail cloth*, for which the town had long been famous, began to decline, and gradually disappeared, together with most of the fami- lies, to whom they had given employment. This loss was so severely felt, that Ipswich had for some time the character of being "a town without people." Favourably seated for commercial speculation, it recovered from this shock in the latter part of last century, and has since encreased rapidly in consequence and population. (See page 50.) It has now two extensive *iron foundries ;* the largest agricultural im- plement manufactory in England ; a large *soap boiling* establishment ; *Roman cement works ;* a large *paper mill ;* two extensive *ship yards*, with patent slips ; a large *oil-cake* manufactory ; about fifteen *corn mills ;* and a considerable number of *malt-kilns ;* indeed, there is, perhaps, no town of the same magnitude where the process which con- verts Sir John Barley Corn into his sacchrine antetype, is carried on to so great an extent as at Ipswich. Besides malt and flour, about 250,000 *quarters of corn* are exported annually to London and other markets, and more than 40,000 chaldrons of *coal* are imported yearly, for the supply of the town, and the central parts of Suffolk, to which the river Gipping, or Stowmarket canal, affords a direct navigation for numerous barges employed in bringing down vast quantities of agricultural produce, and returning with coal, timber, groceries, &c., &c. A general foreign trade of some extent is also carried on here.

* A *Ducking Stool* was preserved in the old Custom House, some years ago, and in the chamberlain's books are various entries of money paid to porters for taking down and fixing this ancient machine in the river, where it was used for the purpose of cooling the inflammable passions of scolding women.

The trade with the Baltic is encreasing, and a few years ago the Lords of the Treasury made this a bonded port for foreign timber. The *bonded warehouses* here have hitherto been limited to wine and spirits, wood-goods, barilla, and corn ; but it is expected that the port will, ere long, be privileged for the direct importation of East India and all other foreign goods, for which its extensive dock, quay, wharfs, and warehouses, afford ample accommodation.

Two fine *steam packets* ply twice a week to and from Ipswich and London, and make the voyage in about seven hours ; and another plies daily to and from Ipswich and Harwich, calling at the various ferries on the *Orwell*, which, for its extent (about 12 miles) may be pronounced one of the finest salt rivers in the kingdom ; and is bounded on either side with gently rising hills, enriched with gentlemen's seats, neat villages, umbrageous woods, verdant avenues, and beautiful deer parks, extending to the water's edge. In the passage from Ipswich, the view is terminated in front by the ocean ; on the right, with the prospect of Harwich, the banks of the Stour, and the high coast of Essex ; and on the left, by the high land of Walton and the cliffs of Felixstow. On the return to Ipswich, the scene closes with a view of the town and the capacious new dock, where hundreds of vessels may be accommodated with floating berths, secure from the violence of storms, and freed from the danger of having their keels-laid bare and dry at low water, as was formerly the case with all vessels lying in the harbour at low water, to the great injury of their timbers. Ships of large tonnage now ride here at all times of the tide, as redolent of the briny element as the ocean itself, and may float out daily without harm or impediment.

MARKETS AND FAIRS.—The weekly markets held here on Tuesday and Saturday, are well supplied with provisions, and the former is an extensive corn and cattle mart. Two large *stock fairs* are held here yearly on the first Tuesday in May, and on the 22nd of August. The former, called *St. George's Fair*, is held in two fields, near the Barracks, and is also noted for toys, pedlery, and shows ; and the latter is the largest *lamb fair* in England, upwards of 100,000 lambs being generally sold at it. The lambs are shown on the Handford Hall estate. *St. Margaret's Fair*, held on September 25th, was formerly a large cheese and butter mart, but is now only noted for sausages and sweetmeats. Here was also a pleasure fair on July 25th, but it is now obsolete. CORN HILL, the largest open market place in Ipswich, was rendered very commodious in 1811 and '12, by the removal of a pile of old buildings, called the Rotunda, and the demolition of the old Shambles and Market Cross, which were built in 1510 by Edmund Daundy. In 1810, five gentlemen of the town commenced the erection of the *New Market*, which they finished in the following year at the cost of about £10,000. This market occupies nearly an acre of ground, and is composed of an outer and inner quadrangle, round each of which runs a range of butchers' and other shops, and a covered colonnade, affording to the market people protection from the weather. In the centre is a fountain, the pedestal of which is surmounted with a pyramid of Portland stone, 20 feet in height. Round the pedestal, a basin is cut in the solid stone, and supplied with water from a lion's head above. Adjoining is an enclosed *cattle market* belonging to

the same proprietors. The *Corn Exchange*, built in 1812, by the corporation, is a neat and commodious building, standing on part of the site of the Rotunda. A small *Fishmarket* has recently been erected by Mr. George Doust, at the foot of Orwell street.

The Town Hall, on the Corn-hill, was anciently the church of St. Mildred, and remained with little alteration till 1818, when the antique front, which had a stair-case outside, was taken down, and a new one erected. At the same time, the interior underwent great alterations, but the basement story was left unfinished till 1841, when it was converted into a commodious *Sessions' Hall*, in which the borough courts have been held since the demolition of the Old Shire Hall. A stair-case from the right of the seat of justice leads to the *Council Chamber*, which has recently been remodelled out of the old apartment in a very handsome style, and is of noble dimensions, having room for more than 1200 persons. The Police Station is within the building, and on the ground level is a range of strong cells. The upper story is appropriated to the use of the library and museum of the Ipswich Literary Institution. The Borough Gaol, in the Borough road, was originally a house of correction belonging to the county, but was purchased and altered for its present use about fifty years ago at the cost of nearly £3000, including the purchase of the land which extends beyond the boundary walls, and adjoins those of the county gaol. By alterations made some years ago, pursuant to the recommendations of the government commission for inspecting prisons, it has been rendered as safe and convenient as its confined space will allow. It is encircled by a brick wall forming an irregular hexagon. On each side of the entrance are two stacks of buildings appropriated to debtors and persons convicted of misdemeanors. The governor's house is in the centre, between the two felons' wards. The debtors are confined here upon *writs of capias*, issuing out of the *Court of Small Pleas*, now called the Court of Requests; having been extended by act of parliament to debts amounting to £5. This and the other borough courts are already noticed with the charters, privileges, and jurisdiction of the borough, at pages 51 to 55, and the following is a list of the corporate body, and the borough magistrates and officers.

Members of Parliament, Sackville Lane Fox and John Neilson Gladstone. Esqrs. (See page 55.)
Recorder, Sir Charles Frederick Williams, Knt., (appointed 1842.)
Mayor, George Josselyn, Esq. (1843.)

ALDERMEN (1843.)

P. B. Long, Esq.	Wm. Bullar, Esq.	A. K. Cowell, Esq.
J. D. Harmer, Esq.	Wm. May, Esq.	S. Footman, Esq.
S. Abbot, Esq.	Geo. Bullen, Esq.	W.T.Cobbold&J.Head,Esq.

COUNCILLORS (1843.)

St. Clement's Ward.	Mr. Wm. Brooks,	Mr. Robert Bowman,
Mr. H. G. Bristo,	,, T. Shuttleworth.	,, Wm. Read,
,, T. B. Ross,	*Middle Ward.*	,, J. L. Ensor,
,, D. Thornbory,	Mr. Charles Steward,	,, J. B. Batley,
,, J. Cobbold,	,, George Josselyn,	*Westgate Ward.*
,, W. Bayley,	,, C. Meadows,	Mr. Wm. Churchman,
,, G. G. Sampson.	,, R. Burrows,	,, Jas. Haill,
St. Margaret's Ward.	,, Walton Turner,	,, John Orford,
Mr. Francis Fisk,	,, A. B. Cook.	,, J. C. Cobbold,
,, John Barker,	*Bridge Ward.*	,, Wm. Rodwell,
,, Henry Bond,	Mr. Thomas Conder,	,, R. S. Cole.
,, J. May,	,, W. Colchester,	

BOROUGH MAGISTRATES.— G. Josselyn, Shepherd Ray, John Ridley, R. N. Shawe, Benj. Braine, Jas. Ram, Lawrence Squire, Thos. D'Eye Burroughes, F. W. Campbell, and W. C. Fonnerau, Esqrs.

Town Clerk and Clerk of the Peace, S. A. Notcutt, jun. Esq.

Magistrates' Clerk, Eleazar Lawrence, Esq.

Treasurer, R. W. Porter, Esq. || Coroner, S. B. Jackaman, Esq.
Gaoler, Rt. Fletcher || Crier, Jas. Nunn.

Water Bailiff, Joseph Jobson.

Town Sergeants, George Baxter and Thomas Robinson.

BOROUGH POLICE.— James Smith, superintendent; Geo. Cole, W. C. Mason, and Fredk. Hewes, sergeants; and sixteen policemen.

[The SUFFOLK POLICE FORCE consists of Mr. John Hatton, chief constable; a deputy chief constable, three superintendents, and 64 men, stationed in 34 districts.]

The COURT OF REQUESTS is held at the Town-Hall, every Tuesday, at ten o'clock. Wm. Hammond, Esq., is clerk; and Mr. Wm. Clark, sergeant. Mr. Hammond is also clerk of the County Court.

The Paving and Lighting Commissioners, under the improvement act noticed at page 59, appoint, out of their own body, a committee of 24, who meet at the Town-Hall, on the first Friday of every month. Dykes Alexander, Esq. is treasurer; Chas. Gross, Esq., clerk; Mr. G. Mason, surveyor; and Mr. Shepherd Dunningham, collector of rates.

The COUNTY COURTS were erected in 1836-7, in front of the County Gaol, in lieu of the Old Shire Hall, which had become dilapidated, and was used both by the county and the borough, but was taken down a few years ago. These Courts, constituting the New Shire Hall, form a handsome building, in the Tudor style, 250 feet long, and 50 feet broad, erected of white brick, with stone dressings, at the cost of £6149. The front has four towers. In the centre is the chief entrance to the prison, and in the wings are the Criminal and Nisi-Prius Courts, each about 45 feet long, 30 broad, and 20 high. Attached are commodious rooms for the magistrates, grand jury, counsel, witnesses, &c. The Suffolk Assizes were both held at Bury St. Edmund's, till 1839, since which year the Summer Assize has been held here, in satisfaction of the long-reiterated complaints of the inhabitants of the eastern and most populous part of the county. Quarter Sessions for the county are held here on the Fridays of the usual Session weeks, in January, April, June, and October. The COUNTY GAOL and HOUSE OF CORRECTION were erected in 1790, on the plan of the celebrated Mr. Howard, and consisted originally of a central building and four radiating wings, to which four other ranges of buildings have been added. The outer wall, built in a sunken fosse, is crowned by an iron chevaux de frise, and encloses an area 260 feet square, which was anciently a burial ground. There are six tread-wheels in one of the yards, employed in grinding corn, &c. On the 4th of April, 1843, there were 149 prisoners here, of whom 16 were debtors. The Rev. J. R. Tunney, LL.B., is the chaplain; Mr. E. A. Johnson, governor; Mrs. Johnson, matron; Mr. A. H. Bartlett, surgeon; and Wm. Glandfield, turnkey.

CHURCHES AND PARISHES.

Domesday Book only enumerates nine churches, as standing in Ipswich and its liberty, viz., Holy Trinity, St. Austin, St. Michael, St. Mary, St. Lawrence, St. Peter, St. Stephen, and those at Whitton and Thurlston. The three first-named are supposed to have been destroyed in a dreadful tempest, on New Year's day, 1287, when Stowe

informs us many other churches and buildings were beaten down by the jarring elements, at Yarmouth, Dunwich, &c.   At a later period, it is said here were no fewer than 21 churches, but no doubt this number included those which were attached to the monastic institutions, and were not parochial.   There are now *twelve parish churches*, and a chapel of ease in the town ; and the two churches of Whitton and Westerfield parishes are within the liberty of the borough.   They are mostly ancient fabrics, which have undergone many repairs, and some of them considerable alterations.   St. Mary's-at-the-Tower has about 1200 sittings, and each of the others from 700 to 1000, except St. Mary's-at-the-Quay, which has only 500.

St. Clement's Church, erected about 1500, is a plain structure, consisting of a nave, two spacious side-aisles, and a fine tower, in which are a good clock and six musical bells.   Among the monuments in the interior is one to the memory of *Thomas Eldred*, who accompanied Cavendish in his circumnavigation of the globe, during the years 1586, '7, and '8.   The benefice is a *rectory*, consolidated with that of St. Helen's, and now valued at £326 per annum.   In monastic times, it was appropriated to the priory of St. Peter.   The Rev. J. T. Nottidge, A.M., is both *patron* and *rector;* the Rev. W. W. Woodhouse, M.A., *curate;* Mr. R. N. Cade, *clerk;* and J. A. Parker, *sexton*.   The Parish of St. Clements includes a large portion of the town, and about 1209 acres of land, extending more than two miles southward along the east bank of the Orwell.   It increased its population from 1584 souls, in 1801, to 5973, in 1841, including 892 in *Fore Hamlet*, 270 in *Back Hamlet*, and 123 in *Wykes-Bishop Hamlet*, which are now connected parts of the town.   This parish also comprises part of *Cold Dunhills Hamlet*, which is partly in St. Margaret's ; and within its limits is *Warren House*, which is extra-parochial, and is now divided into six tenements, belonging to Sir P. B. V. Broke, who owns a great part of the freehold land in the parish.   The copyhold lands are held of the *manor of Wykes-Bishop*, of which John Cobbold, Esq., is lord and principal owner.   Richard I. gave this manor to John Oxenford, bishop of Norwich, and the succeeding bishops held it till 1535, and frequently resided here, in a house near the Nacton road, of which nothing now remains.   Part of the manor of *Wykes-Ufford* extends into this parish, but it is mostly in Westerfield and Rushmere.   This manor belonged to the Ufford family, Earls of Suffolk ; but since the reign of Elizabeth, it has belonged to the owners of Christchurch estate.   There was anciently a chapel dedicated to *St. James*, at Wykes, but all vestiges of it are gone.   TRINITY CHURCH, situated in that now populous part of St. Clement's parish between the Back and Fore Hamlets, is a neat *chapel of ease*, or *district church*, which was erected at the cost of £2000, in 1835, by the Rev. J. T. Nottidge, the present patron and incumbent of St. Clements and St. Helens, who also endowed it with £1230 three per cent. consolidated bank annuities, and £1103 reduced bank annuities, for the support of the minister and the reparation of the building.   It is surrounded on three sides with a gallery, under which are the free seats.   A portico shadows the entrance, above which is a small belfry, surmounted by a cupola.   The founder is the patron, and the Rev. J. W. Reeve, M.A., is the incumbent curate.   St. Clement's is supposed to have been

erected in lieu of the *Church of Osterbolt*, which anciently stood near the East gate.

St. Helen's Church, on the east side of the town, is of very ancient foundation, but it has lately undergone considerable repairs and alterations, the chancel being rebuilt in 1835, and neat brick transepts added in 1837. It was anciently impropriated to the *Leprous hospital of St. James*, or Mary Magdalen, which stood near it; but it is now a rectory, which, ever since the Reformation, has been consolidated with that of St. Clement's, and is valued in K.B. at £8. 13s. 9d. Its parish increased its inhabitants from 327 in 1801, to 1352 in 1841; but it contains only about 300 acres of land, besides the building sites, gardens, &c. N. Byles and J. Cobbold, Esqs., are the principal landowners, but *Groves House*, on a bold acclivity, embowered in wood, belongs to the Rev. J. T. Nottidge. In a field near Caldwell Hall, stood the church of *St. John the Baptist*, which was in the appropriation of Trinity Priory, but all traces of it disappeared many years ago. At the south-west corner of Rosemary lane, stood a chapel dedicated to *St. Edmund-a-Pountney*, which was appropriated to St. Peter's Priory, but no vestiges of it are now extant. A portion of corn tithes from certain lands in Hoxne, formerly belonged to this chapel, but are now attached to the rectory. The Borough Gaol and Belle Vue Asylum are in St. Helen's parish.

St. Lawrence's Church is a plain but ancient fabric, which is mentioned in Domesday Book, but is said to have been rebuilt in 1431 by John Bottold, who was buried in it, as also was Edmund Daundy, one of the benefactors of the town, who died in 1515. Upon the wall, behind the western gallery, is a painting of Christ disputing with the doctors, executed by Sir R. K. Porter, a military officer, during his sojourn at the barracks here. The benefice was appropriated to Trinity Priory, and is now a perpetual curacy, valued at £175. The parishioners are *patrons ;* the Rev. J. C. Aldrich, *incumbent ;* and Mr. Wm. Scarlett, clerk and sexton. The parish is small, and has only 570 inhabitants.

St. Margaret's Church, on the green to which it gives name, is a large and ancient structure of mixed architecture, consisting of a chancel, nave, aisles, and transepts, with a fine tower and south porch. It has a curious antique font, and a singularly painted ceiling, with several grotesque carvings standing out from the walls. The Parliamentary Commissioners, who came to Ipswich in 1643, removed from this church the twelve apostles in stone, and desired that 20 or 30 pictures, which decorated the walls, should be taken away and destroyed. The *benefice* is a perpetual curacy, valued at £115, in the gift of W. C. Fonnereau, Esq., and incumbency of the Rev. George Murray. Mr. B. Bugg is the clerk and sexton. *The parish* increased its population from 1923 in 1801, to 4513 in 1841, including 66 in Cold *Dunghills*, and 24 in *Felaw's Houses*, which are extra-parochial. East Suffolk Hospital, Christ Church Park, the *Folly*, and *Bolton hamlet*, are in St. Margaret's parish, which contains, besides the building sites, about 1260 acres of land, extending northward from the town, and mostly copyhold of the *manor of Christ Church*, of which W. C. Fonnereau, Esq., is lord and principal owner. Part of the soil belongs to the Rev. M. G. Edgar, J. E. Todd, Esq., and others, and the fines paid by the copyholders are arbitrary. In this parish stood Trinity Priory, which was founded before 1177 by Norman Gastrode, for black canons of the Order of St. Augustine, to whom Henry II. granted a fair on Sept. 14th, and the two following days. Not long after the foundation of this monastery, its church and offices were consumed by fire, but they were rebuilt by John of Oxford, bishop of Norwich. *Trinity, or Christ Church*, noticed in Domesday book as having 26 acres of land, is supposed to have been the parish church, and being appropriated to the priory, St. Margaret's, was afterwards erected for the use of the parishioners. King John granted to the priory all the

land and rents formerly belonging to the churches of *St. Michael and St. Saviour*, which had then gone to decay, and are supposed to have stood, the former near that of St. Nicholas, and the latter behind St. Mary-at-Elms. At the dissolution, in the 26th of Henry VIII., Trinity Priory was valued at £88. 6s. 9d. per annum, and the site was granted ten years afterwards to Sir Thomas Pope, from whom it passed to the families of Withipol, Cornwallis, and Hereford, of the latter of whom it was purchased by Claude Fonnereau, Esq. Upon the site of the priory, Sir Edmund Withipol, in 1550, erected in the highly picturesque Tudor style, the extensive mansion called CHRIST CHURCH, which stands in a well-wooded *deer park*, extending northward from St. Margaret's church, and is now the seat and property of W. C. Fonnereau, Esq., who liberally allows the inhabitants to promenade in the park, in which the last remains of the foundations of the old priory church were blown up with gunpowder in 1674. The mansion is of brick, with stone dressings and ornaments, and contains some fine family portraits.

ST. MARY-AT-ELMS is an ancient church, with a brick tower, supposed to stand near or upon the site of St. Saviour's, as already noticed. In front of it is a row of fine elms, and near it are Smyth's almshouses, and several old dwellings, bearing marks of former grandeur. This church was appropriated to Trinity Priory, and is now a perpetual curacy, valued at £80, in the gift of the parishioners, and incumbency of the Rev. W. Aldrich, B.D. Mr. J. Whistle is clerk and sexton. The parish is small, and has only 851 souls.

ST. MARY-AT-THE-QUAY is a plain structure, with a tower curiously built of flint, and containing six bells. It must have been rebuilt after 1448, when Richard Gowty ordered his body to be buried in the churchyard, and gave Calyon stone " for the whole new church, which was to be erected." The church spoliator, Dowsing, paid a visit to this edifice, in 1643, and tore down nine superstitious pictures, and destroyed many inscriptions. The roof is supported by light clustered columns; and in a small transept is the tomb of Henry Tooley, the founder of the almshouses bearing his name. The living is a perpetual *curacy*, valued at £103, in the gift of the parishioners, and incumbency of the Rev. Wm. Harbur. Mr. J. Harvey is clerk and sexton. The parish contains 1082 inhabitants, including 94 residing in the *Shirehall yard*, which is extra-parochial, being the site of an extensive monastery of *Black Friars*, of which there are still some remains of the cloisters. This house of Black Dominican Friars, commonly called *Preachers*, was founded in the reign of Henry III., by Henry Mansby, Henry Redhead, and Henry Loudham, and afterwards enlarged by John Harys. It was richly endowed, and was granted in the 33rd of Henry VIII. to Wm. Sabyn, but was afterwards purchased by the Corporation, who converted the greater part of the building into the Grammar School, Christ's Hospital, the Bridewell, and the old Shirehall, which have recently been taken down, and their sites offered on building leases.

ST. MARY-AT-STOKE, commonly called *Stoke Church*, is picturesquely seated on the south bank of the river Gipping, opposite the rest of the town, and consists of a nave, chancel, north aisle, a fine tower, and a brick porch. It is of ancient foundation, but has undergone so many repairs and renovations, that little of the original fabric remains. It was given by King Edgar, in 970, to the prior and convent of Ely ; and their successors, the Dean and Chapter of Ely, are now patrons of the *rectory*, which is valued in K.B. at £12, and is now worth about £500 per annum, the tithes having recently been commuted for a yearly modus of £475. The Rev. Stephen Croft, M.A., is the present incumbent, and Mr. James Morfey is clerk and sexton. The *Parish of Stoke* increased its inhabitants from 385 in 1801, to 992 souls in 1841, and contains several neat mansions, and about 1500 acres

of land, rising boldly from the Gipping and the Orwell, and extending about 1½ mile southward along the western bank of the latter river. P. P. Long, Esq., does not own much land here, but is lessee lord of the *Manor of Stoke*, which he holds under the Dean and Chapter of Ely. The soil is mostly freehold, and the principal owners are the Hon. Lyndsey Burrell, of *Stoke Park*, a neat mansion with pleasant grounds, 1½ mile S. of Ipswich ; F. W. Campbell, Esq., of *Birkfield Lodge*, one mile S. of Ipswich ; J. B. Smyth, Esq., of *Orwell Lodge ;* Mr. W. Waspe, of *Gusford Hall ;* and the family of Alexander, the owners of *Goldroyd*, anciently called *Golden-rood*, from a celebrated cross which stood near it in monastic times. Gusford Hall, anciently called *Godlesford*, gives name to a small manor, which belonged to Leigh priory, in Devonshire, and was granted by Henry VIII. to Sir John Raineforth ; but it appears to have been for a long period a seat of the Andrews family, one of whom became Baron Windsor, in 1529. The manor of Stoke is described in *Domesday Book* as of the yearly value of £10, and as having had in the Confessor's time five carucates, nine villains, 15 bordars, a church with 40A. of free land, a mill, 20A. of meadow, and a mediety of a *loche* beyond the bridge, then of the value of 100 shillings.

St. Mary at the Tower is the largest, and is considered the principal church in the town, though only a *perpetual curacy*, valued at £103, in the gift of the parishioners, and incumbency of the Rev. Wm. Nassau Leger, B.A. Mr. T. Wilkinson is the *clerk*, and James Day, *sexton*. The corporation attend this church on Sunday mornings. It was given by Norman, the son of Eadnoth, to Trinity Priory, and is a spacious and commodious fabric, consisting of a nave, chancel, porch, side aisles, and a fine tower, containing a peal of ten bells, and formerly surmounted by a spire, towards rebuilding which, Wm. Edgar, about 1730, left £200, which was all expended in a chancery suit. The interior is handsomely fitted up, and has an excellent organ and several handsome monuments,— one in memory of Wm. Smart, and another bearing kneeling effigies of John and Elizabeth Robinson. Upon the pavement of the middle aisle, is a fine old brass. It was in this church that the *Guild of Corpus Christi** (instituted about 1325) used to deposit the tabernacle in which the host was carried, and in which their money and valuables were kept. The *parish* occupies the central part of the town, and was, no doubt, anciently defended on the north by a strongly fortified *tower*, which stood near the spot still called the *Tower Ditches*. It increased its population from 688 in 1801, to 986 in 1841, including 18 residing in several extra-parochial houses in Globe lane. Kirby says *Ipswich Castle* was entirely demolished by Henry the Second, in 1176, after the defection of Roger Bigod, Earl of Norfolk.

St. Matthew's Church, at the west entrance to the town, stands in a large burial ground, and is a plain, unassuming structure, consisting of a nave, chancel, side aisles, tower, and south porch. It was re-pewed a few

* *Corpus Christi Guilds* were founded in most of the boroughs in England, in the 14th and 15th centuries, and it was their custom to walk in procession, and perform plays and dirges on the festival of Corpus Christi. In these pageantries they were joined by other guilds and free companies, and their theatrical representations were often very indelicate, especially their plays of " Adam and Eve," and " Noah's Ark." The ancient play of " *King Johan*," written by Bale, Bishop of Ossory, for the use of these guilds, is supposed to have been first performed at Ipswich, as the author was a native of Suffolk, and represents King John as having favoured Ipswich, Dunwich, and Bury. *Guilds* were confederations for mutual benefit in trade, and for the purpose of aiding charity and religion. To the Guild of Corpus Christi at Ipswich, every burgess was required to pay 16d. yearly, or forfeit his freedom ; and 3d. a fortnight to the master of the Grammar School, who was chaplain to the guild, and celebrated 30 days' mass for every deceased brother or sister.

years ago, and has three galleries and a small organ. It has only about 700 sittings. In the churchyard, beneath an altar tomb, lie the remains of the Rt. Hon. John Howe, *Lord Chedworth*, who died in 1804, and left most of his large property to persons not at all related to him. Having a strong predilection for the drama, the performers on the Ipswich stage shared largely in his bequests. The churchyard is open, but is about to be enclosed. The *rectory* was appropriated to St. Peter's Priory; but was granted by Edward VI. to persons named Webb and Bretton. The great tithes now belong to the Fonnereau family, though the benefice is still called a rectory, and is valued in K.B. at £5. The Crown is patron, the Rev. G. P. G. Cosserath, *incumbent;* and Mr. Wm. Hadcraft, *clerk and sexton.* The *parish* increased its population from 1206 in 1801, to 3458 souls in 1841, including 308 in the Queen's Barracks. It contains about 500A. of farming and garden land, and several modern suburbs on and near the London and Norwich road; and extends about $1\frac{1}{2}$ mile westward to *Boss Hall*, the property of Thos. Kersey, Esq.; and one mile N. to *Brokes Hall*, the property of Mr. John Orford. It anciently contained four other churches or chapels, viz., *All Saints*, the site of which is unknown; *St. George's*, of which some remains may be seen in a barn in George lane; *St. Mildred's*, which was converted into the Town-hall, as already noticed; and *St. Mary's Chapel*, which stood at the north-west corner of Lady lane, and was famous for an image of the Blessed Virgin, called by the numerous pilgrims who visited it, "*Our Lady of Ipswich;*" but after the Reformation, it was taken to London, and there publicly burnt. The site of this chapel is covered with modern buildings. *St. Matthew's*, or the *West Gate*, was rebuilt in the time of Henry VI., and was for a long period used as the Borough Goal, but was demolished many years ago.

St. Nicholas's Church, in the lower part of the town, near the river, is supposed to have been built upon the site, and partly with the materials of St. Michael's, which is mentioned in Domesday Book. It is built partly of flint, and has a cemented tower, containing four bells. A rudely carved stone at the west end of the south aisle, represents St. Michael encountering a dragon. During the progress of some repairs, in 1827, five large *urns* were found embedded in one of the walls, but they contained no ashes or bones. Behind one of the tombs, is a curious specimen of ancient painting, supposed to represent the Archangel St. Michael, towards the execution of which Wolsey's father left 40s. From the floor of this church, the parliamentary visitors in 1643, took up three sepulchral brasses; and they also destroyed six pictures on the walls. It was appropriated to St. Peter's Priory, and is now a *perpetual curacy*, valued at £150, in the gift of the parishioners, and incumbency of the Rev. M. G. Edgar, M.A. Mr. Jas. West is clerk and sexton. Westward of the church, on the banks of the Gipping, stood a convent of *Franciscan or Grey Friars*, founded in the reign of Edward I., by Lord Tibtoth, of Nettlestead, and a small portion of it may still be seen in the garden ground occupying the site. The *White or Carmelite Friary*, founded in 1279, by Sir Thomas Loudham and other benefactors, stood partly in this parish, and partly in that of St. Lawrence, and extended from St. Nicholas' street to St. Stephen's lane. Of this extensive monastery, which produced many persons eminent for learning, no remains are now extant, though, as late as the latter part of the seventeenth century, part of it served as the county gaol. The parish of St. Nicholas increased its population from 758 in 1801, to 1698 souls in 1841.

St. Peter's is one of the largest and most ancient churches in the town, standing close to the site of Wolsey's College. It is a plain structure, consisting of a chancel, nave, aisles, south porch, and a tower containing six bells. The tower is a good specimen of the flint work so frequently observed in Suffolk and Norfolk. A few years ago, the church was much

improved, and the burial ground enclosed. It contains an ancient font, covered with carvings of animals, and is a *perpetual curacy*, valued at £138, in the gift of the trustees of the Rev. C. Simeon. The Rev. H. T. Lumsden is the *incumbent*; S. Stokes, *clerk*; and Wm. Hall, *sexton*. This church had large possessions in Edward the Confessor's time, but was afterwards appropriated to *St. Peter's Priory*, which stood contiguous to the churchyard, and was founded in the reign of Henry II. by the Lacy family, and dedicated to St. Peter and St. Paul. This convent of black canons of the order of St. Augustine, was richly endowed, and on its suppression in 1527, it was given to Cardinal Wolsey, who founded upon its site the splendid but shortlived College already noticed at page 56. In 1643, the parliamentary visitors broke to pieces the crown of thorns, the sponge and nails, and the Trinity, which were represented in stone in the porch of St. Peter's church. The *Parish of St. Peter* increased its population from 986 in 1801, to 2420 souls in 1841, including 191 in the Union Workhouse. It is mostly on the north side of the Gipping, but includes on the south side of that river, West Bridge street, Dock street, Great Whip street, part of Bell lane, and about 60A. of marhes, which anciently formed a separate parish, with a church dedicated to *St. Austin*, which was in use till the close of the 15th century, and stood near *St. Leonard's Hospital*, now a farm house belonging to Christ's Hospital. Near Silent street, is a malt kiln said to be the remains of a mansion which was granted by Edward VI. to the Bishop of Norwich, after the decease of Thomas Manning, prior of Butley, who was created *suffragan bishop of Ipswich* in 1525, and had the said house for his residence.

St. Stephen's is one of the churches mentioned in Domesday Book, and is mostly built of flint, except the tower, which is of brick, cemented. It contains a monument, with kneeling effigies of Wm. Leeman and his wife. The *rectory*, valued in K.B. at £4. 12s. 8½d., and now at £82, is in the gift of W. C. Fonnereau, Esq., and incumbency of the Rev. Edward Harston. Mr. E. Harvey is *clerk*. The parish is small, and has only 509 inhabitants. The Coach and Horses Inn, in Brook street, occupies the site of a house which was occupied by Charles Brandon, Duke of Suffolk; and near it was the Tankard public-house, in Tacket street, which was taken down and rebuilt in 1843, and was supposed to have formed part of the extensive mansion of *Sir Anthony Wingfield*, one of the executors of Henry VIII. One of the rooms had its oak wainscot richly carved in festoons of flowers; and over the fireplace, was a bass-relievo, representing the judgment of Paris and its consequences, in five compartments.

CHAPELS.—The twelve parish churches, and the chapel of ease just described, have seat-room for about 9000 persons; and there is accommodation for nearly as many more in the fourteen other places of worship in the town, of which twelve belong to Dissenters and Methodists, one to the Roman Catholics, and one to the Jews. *Tacket Street Independent Chapel* was erected in 1720, by the Presbyterian congregation, who had previously, for more than forty years, occupied a small chapel in the Green yard, St. Peter's, and were the successors of the *Nonconformists*, who were so called from their refusing to subscribe to every thing contained in the Book of Common Prayer, as required by the Act of Uniformity, passed soon after the restoration of Charles II. This chapel will seat about 850 nearers, and has a good organ and a burial ground. Near it is a house for the minister, the Rev. William Notcutt, whose grandfather officiated here till his death, in 1756, in his 84th year. The *Independent Chapel*, in St. Nicholas street, is a neat Gothic structure, which was opened in 1829. It nas about 1000 sittings, including the gallery erected in 1842, and is under the ministry of the Rev. J. Whitby. The *Unitarian Chapel*, in St. Nicholas street, is one of the oldest chapels in the town, and has a beautifully carved

pulpit, and about 900 sittings. The Rev. T. F. Thomas is the pastor. The *Quakers' Meeting House*, in Lower Brook street, was built in 1706, and will seat about 800 hearers. The CATHOLIC CHAPEL, on the Woodbridge road, was erected in 1825, and enlarged in 1839, chiefly at the expense of its first priest, the Rev. P. L. Simon, one of the refugees who left France at the commencement of the Revolution, and resided here till his death, in September, 1839. It is a small building in the early English style, and is now under the pastoral care of the Rev. James O'Neill. The *Baptist Chapel*, in Dairy lane, was built by a congregation of Baptists formed in 1758. It has 800 sittings, and is under the ministry of the Rev. James Nunn. *Zoar Chapel*, in David street, was built in 1841, by the Baptists who seceded from Mr. Nunn's ministry, in 1829. It cost about £900, and has 500 sittings, but no pews. The Rev. J. Bateman is the minister. *Salem Chapel*, in Globe lane, built in 1812, and *Turret Green Chapel*, erected in 1842, are both small meeting houses belonging to the Baptists. The latter is under the ministry of the Rev. J. Sprigg, who, with part of the congregation, lately separated from *Stoke Chapel*, which is the largest of the five Baptist Chapels in Ipswich, and was erected in 1774, but has since been rebuilt and several times enlarged, so that it will now seat about 900 hearers. It is an octangular building, and is now under the ministry of the Rev. J. Webb. The *Wesleyan Chapel*, in New Market lane, was erected in 1816, and is a neat brick building, containing about 1000 sittings. The *Association Methodist Chapel*, in Friar street, was built in 1837, for about 600 hearers; and the *Primitive Methodist Chapel*, in Rope lane, was built in 1839, and has about 500 sittings. The *Jews Synagogue*, in Rope lane, is a small brick building with pointed windows. The Jews have a small burial ground behind the Green Man Inn, and Harris Isaacs is their rabbi. *Bible, Tract, Missionary, and other Societies* for promoting Christian knowledge, are liberally supported both by the church and disseuting congregations in Ipswich.

THE IPSWICH LITERARY INSTITUTION, established in 1818, has its library and museum, and holds its meetings in the Town Hall. It was instituted by shareholders, but is supported also by a number of annual subscribers, those residing in the town paying £2. 2s., and those in the country £1. 10s. per annum. Besides the extensive *library* belonging to the society, a large collection of old books belonging to the corporation are deposited in the rooms. This collection was derived from the gifts of Wm. Smart, Mrs. Walter, and other donors, and was formerly deposited in Christ's Hospital. The *museum* contains many curious and rare specimens of natural history, and some interesting pieces of antiquity. The *Public Library*, at Mr. Pawsey's, in the Butter Market, is extensive and well selected. There is a *Law Library*, and also several circulating libraries in the town. The MECHANICS' INSTITUTION, in Tavern street, was established in 1824, and has now a valuable library of upwards of 3000 volumes. It occupies a building containing a spacious lecture room, library, museum, committee rooms, and other apartments. The great utility of this institution, for the diffusion of knowledge among the lower classes, is duly appreciated by the wealthier inhabitants of the town and neighbourhood, many of whom support it by donations, annual subscriptions, and literary services. The building which it now occupies was purchased in 1833, at the cost of £1000, raised in £5 shares; and the sum of £300, given by J. Morrison and R. Wason, Esqrs., the borough members, was laid out in making the necessary alterations and repairs. The members are from 300 to 400 in number, and contribute 10s. each

per annum, for which they have the use of the library, reading room, &c., and the privilege of introducing two friends to the lectures. Mr. Webster is the honorary secretary; Mr. Ormond, the paid secretary; and Mr. Franklin, the librarian. A *Society for Mental Improvement* was founded in 1836, by the numerous workmen and youths employed at the extensive foundry of Messrs. J. R. and A. Ransome, who contribute liberally towards its support. It numbers about 140 members, and has a library of more than 600 volumes. The *Ipswich Horticultural Society* is supported by many of the principal gentry of the town and neighbourhood. Sir W. F. F. Middleton is its president; and Mr. Wm. Woollard, secretary.

Three weekly NEWSPAPERS are published here, viz., the *Ipswich Journal*, which was commenced as early as 1739; the *Suffolk Chronicle*, which was established in 1810; and the *Ipswich Express*, commenced in 1839. The *Journal* advocates tory, and the two latter whig or liberal politics. The *Journal* and *Chronicle* are published on Saturday, the former by Mr. Postle Jackson, and the latter by Mr. John King. The *Express* is published every Tuesday, by Mr. Stpn. Piper. Two small monthly periodicals are published in the town, viz., the *Suffolk Temperance Recorder*, commenced in 1840, and the *Independent Magazine*, established in 1842.

The THEATRE, in Tacket street, is a small but neat building, which was erected by a number of shareholders in 1803, and is occupied several weeks during the summer. Ipswich enjoys the honour of having first witnessed and acknowledged the inimitable powers of *David Garrick*, who, under the assumed name of Lyddal, is said to have made his first dramatic essay here in 1739, in Dunstal's company, from London, in the part of *Dick*, in the Lying Valet. The new ASSEMBLY ROOMS form a neat white brick building, in Northgate street, erected in 1820, and containing a spacious and elegant ball room, supper rooms, orchestra, &c. An *Amateur Musical Society* was established here in 1839. IPSWICH RACES, held in or about July, were formerly very numerously attended, but their attraction has rapidly declined of late years, as also has the taste for dramatic performances. The *Race Course* is about half a mile east of the town. In Quay street, is a commodious suite of PUBLIC BATHS, embracing plunging and shower salt water baths, either cold or warm, as well as vapour and sulphur-vapour baths. They belong to several proprietors. In June, 1843, the Corporation completed a large and convenient *Bathing Place*, near the bank of the Orwell, for the use of the inhabitants. It is connected with the river by a covered sluice and flood-gates, so that the water may be changed every tide.

WORTHIES.—The most elevated, but not the most honourable niche in the Ipswich temple of fame, is occupied by *Cardinal Wolsey*, already noticed at page 56. Among other distinguished men who were born or flourished here, are the following:—RALPH BROWNRIG, son of a merchant of Ipswich, was born in 1592, and became bishop of Exeter in 1641. He was deprived of his preferments at the commencement of the Commonwealth; but, notwithstanding his loyalty, Cromwell consulted him on a subject of considerable importance, and he is said to have returned this answer:—"My lord, the best advice I can give you is, Render unto Cæsar the things that are Cæsar's, and unto God the things that are God's." He was chosen preacher at the Temple in 1657, and died at London in 1659.

Two folio volumes of his sermons were published in 1661 and 1664. BENJ. LANY was born here towards the close of the 16th century. He was successively bishop of Peterborough, Lincoln, and Ely, and died in 1674. Dr. WM. BUTLER was born here, and died in 1621, aged 83. He was many years an eminent physician in London, and was distinguished for wit and slovenliness, as well as physic. *Sir Nicholas Bacon*, keeper of the great seal in the reign of Elizabeth, deeply interested himself in the well-being of the charities of Ipswich; and his third son, *Nathaniel Bacon*, was recorder of Ipswich, and compiled the annals of the town; but they were never printed, owing, it is said, to their containing many gross mistakes, and strong political prejudices. He successively held the offices of town-clerk and recorder of Ipswich, and from 1654 to 1660, was one of the representatives of the borough in Parliament. *Sir Edward Coke*, the celebrated lawyer, though not a native of Ipswich, resided frequently within it, and generally at Wherstead. *Sir Cphr. Hatton*, who is said to have *danced* himself so far into the favour of Queen Elizabeth, as to reach one of the highest offices of state, resided here for some time, in a house in the street now called Hatton court. *Thomas Green, Esq.*, who was born in 1760, and resided many years in Lower Brook street, where he died in 1825, was the author of many well-written essays, and of " Extracts from the Diary of a Lover of Literature." He was a great encourager of the fine arts, and possessed a valuable collection of paintings, which was always open to the inspection and study of artists. *George Frost*, an excellent landscape painter, who died here in 1821, availed himself of this opportunity, to correct the crudity of his genius. *Joshua Kirby*, a well-known topographical draughtsman, and designer in perspective to George III., died here in 1774. He was the son of JOHN KIRBY, of Wickham Market, who published the " *Suffolk Traveller*, from an actual survey of the county in the years 1732, '33, and '34," and died here in 1753. A second edition of this work was published in 1764, with additions and alterations, by the *Rev. Richard Canning, M.A.*, who was 40 years minister of St. Lawrence church, and published a translation of the principal charters, and an account of the charities of Ipswich, in 1747 and 1754. He died in 1775. The *Rev. Jas. Ford*, late incumbent of St. Lawrence's, published several works in religion and biography. *Clara Reeve*, author of that pleasing fiction, " *The Old English Baron*," resided at Ipswich, where her father was perpetual curate of the parish of St. Nicholas. She commenced her literary career in 1772, and died in 1807. *Sarah Trimmer*, daughter of the before-named Joshua Kirby, wrote many valuable works for the religious instruction of young people and the poor, and died here in 1810, in her 70th year. *Mr. Henry Davy*, a highly talented artist, now living here, has drawn, etched, and published a considerable number of views of churches, seats, and ancient buildings in the county of Suffolk. *Mr. John Wodderspoon*, another resident, has recently published an interesting." *Guide to Ipswich*," and another work on the "Historic Sites, and other Remarkable and Interesting Places in Suffolk," with prefatory verses by *Bernard Barton*, the Woodbridge poet, who was educated here, and whose daughter Lucy has published several useful books for young people, both in prose and verse.

CHARITY TRUSTEES.—Until the passing of the Municipal Reform Act, the Corporation of Ipswich were trustees of the following charities, which yield an annual income of more than £2000, viz., the *Grammar School, Christ's Hospital, Tooley's and Smart's Almshouses*, and *Tyler's, Allen's, Scrivener's, Burrough's, Martin's, Cutler's, Osmond's, Snow's, Crane's*, and *Sir Thos. White's charities;* but since 1836, they have been placed under the management of 21 trustees, appointed for life by the Town Council, with the sanction of the Lord

Chancellor. The present trustees are the Rev. J. C. Ebden, W. C. Fonnereau, Jeremiah Head, Hy. Bond, Chas. Colchester, Hy. Aldrich, P. B. Long, Robt. Bowman, John Footman, Walton Turner, Shepherd Ray, and Wm. Rodwell, Esqs.; Rev. J. T. Nottidge, and Michael Turner, Benj. Brame, Chas. C. Hammond, Geo. Josselyn, John Cobbold, G. C. E. Bacon, H. G. Bristo, and John Bond, Esqs. The last five were elected in June, 1843. Mr. Rodwell is the *treasurer*.

The GRAMMAR SCHOOL is free to fifty boys for instruction in classical learning, but for commercial and other branches of education, they are charged one guinea each per quarter. By Letters Patent of the 8th Elizabeth, (1565,) reciting that there had for a long time been a free grammar school, founded by Henry VIII. in Ipswich, consisting of a master and usher, who had for their wages £38. 13s. 4d. per annum, out of her Majesty's manors, lands, and hereditaments in Suffolk; her Majesty ratified and confirmed the said foundation ; and further ordained that the bailiffs, burgesses, and commonalty of Ipswich, and their successors, should thenceforth have the appointment of the head master, with the sanction of the Bishop of Norwich ; and should also appoint such a proper person to be usher, as the master should adjudge fit for that office. Her Majesty also granted that the above-named annuity of £38. 13s. 4d. should be paid out of the fee farm of the borough of Ipswich, as follows :—£24. 6s. 8d. to the master, and £14. 6s. 8d. to the usher. Since 1771, the offices of master and usher have been consolidated, and held together by the master for the time being, who has also the yearly sum of £11 out of the revenues of Christ's Hospital, under Felaw's gift; £6. 13s. 4d. from Smart's charity; and other payments from the corporation, swelling his yearly salary to £116 per annum. He has also the use of a large and commodious house, (purchased by the corporation in 1610,) and is allowed to take from 30 to 40 boarders, and also a number of day scholars, not on the foundation. The school was kept in the refectory of the Black Friars, until about a year ago, when a new school room was erected by the corporation. In 1643, *Wm. Tyler* left £300 for schooling, clothing, and apprenticing poor children. It was laid out in the purchase of *one-third* part of a farm of 142A. at Creeting, now let for £150. For many years, the yearly proceeds of Tyler's charity (£50,) have been expended in providing books, &c., for the free scholars, and in giving apprentices fees of £5 with the poorest of them, after being four years at school. There are *two exhibitions*, one of £14 and the other of £6 a year, for two students at Cambridge, who have been scholars at this school. (See Martin's charity.) A *lending library* (chiefly of Greek and Latin classics) has been attached to the school by various donations. The Mayor and Town Council appoint the free scholars, and also the master, who must be a graduate of one of the universities, and in holy orders. The Rev. J. Fenwick, the present master, was elected in May, 1843.

CHRIST'S HOSPITAL, where forty poor boys are now maintained and educated, was established by the corporation of Ipswich, in 1569, for the purpose of making provision for poor persons, orphans, and such as were unable from age, sickness, or infirmity, to support themselves, and for a workhouse for vagrants. With this design, the corporation ordered that part of the premises, called the *Black Friars*, which they had recently become possessed of, should thenceforth be an hospital for the poor of Ipswich ; and a subscription was raised for fitting them up for that purpose. For the support of the hospital, the corporation imposed a *tonnage duty* on ships belonging to the port, and a payment of 1s. by every person on taking out his freedom of the borough, but they have not been collected during the last twenty years. In 1672, a *charter* was granted, empowering the corporation to grant and hold lands, &c., for the support of the hospital ; to make rules

and ordinances for its government; and to appoint yearly four burgesses to be governors. The endowment has been derived from various sources, and some portions of it were originally destined for other charitable uses. For some time, the hospital was conducted as a general poor-house, but after the establishment of poor laws, it was confined to the purpose of *maintaining, educating, bringing up, and apprenticing of poor boys.* The premises, formerly the *Black Friars*, comprised the old hospital; the old Bridewell; the old grammar school, and other buildings in the *Shire Hall Yard,* most of which have been taken down, and the remainder will shortly be removed, and the sites let on building leases, except those portions which have long formed Tooley's Alms-houses. In 1482, RICHARD FELAW left property for the foundation and support of a free-school and hospital, but on the establishment of a college and grammar school at Ipswich, by Cardinal Wolsey, it was given to the dean and canons of that college, with whom it remained till their dissolution, when the corporation resumed possession of it, and appropriated it to the use of this hospital, with some exceptions noticed in the following particulars of the property derived under FELAW'S GIFT :— viz., a house in Foundation street; a stable and several ground-rents, &c., near the said house, let for £4. 0s. 6d. per annum ; the fourth part of a farm of 158 acres, at Whitton, let for the yearly rent of £120 ; the ninth-part of a farm of 91 acres, at Whitton and Bramford, let for £118, as noticed with Tooley's charity ; and two fields in the parish of St. Mary Stoke. The last mentioned land is now included in a farm of 26A. 2R. 4P., let for £93 per annum, the other part of which was purchased in 1722, with £340 left to the hospital by *Thos. Bright and Richard Philipps.* The other possessions of the hospital are — the third-part of a farm of 142A. at Creeting, (let for £150,) purchased with Smart's and Tyler's charities, and money arising from the sale of two houses, given by *Daniel Snow and Rd. Felaw;* a farm of 84A. at Debenham, let for £120, and bequeathed, in 1670 by *Nicholas Philipps;* a meadow of 3A. in St. Mary Stoke, purchased for £250; one-third part of a farm of 103A. at Otley, let for £118, and purchased with £300 belonging to the hospital and Tooley's and Smart's charities ; a yearly rent charge of £19. 13s. 4d., out of a house and land in Ipswich and Bramford, purchased with £280 in the 7th James I.; £7. 10s. yearly from the corporation, as interest of £250, left by Eliz. Robinson, Cath. Baxter, and Thos. Goodwin ; £1 yearly out of a house in Knight lane; and £7. 4s. from £240 three per cent. consols, left by *Amy Kemp* in 1745. The yearly income from the sources above-named is about £500. Since the passing of the Municipal Reform Act, the charities, formerly under the management of the corporation, have been placed under the care of a board of 21 trustees, who, in 1841, removed Christ's Hospital to Chenery farm, pleasantly situated in Great Whip street, where an ancient but commodious house, belonging to the charity, has been altered, repaired, and enlarged for the purpose, at the cost of about £1500, and now affords accommodation for the master, and 40 poor boys, who are clothed, maintained, and educated, at the expense of the charity till the age of 14, when the trustees give small apprentice fees with such as are bound to trades. Besides his victuals and lodgings, the master has a yearly salary of £100. The boys are instructed in reading, writing, and arithmetic, and are occasionally employed in cultivating the extensive gardens attached to the hospital, in the west front of which is a statue of one of the scholars, removed from the old hospital, where only sixteen boys were victualled under the care of the bridewell keeper, and instructed by a master who received only a small salary, and did not reside on the premises.

The SCHOOLS OF GREY-COAT BOYS AND BLUE-COAT GIRLS, in Curriers' lane, were established by subscription in 1709, since which year they have received many benefactions and bequests, which, with the surplus in-

come, have been invested for their endowment. They receive about £300 yearly from *Pemberton's Charity* for educating and apprenticing poor boys and girls, and are also supported by a long list of annual subscribers. Seventy boys and fifty girls are clothed and educated in these schools, and many of the former are apprenticed to trades at the expense of the charity. The LANCASTERIAN SCHOOL, in Crown street, was established in 1811 for the education of 200 boys, but it is now attended only by about 160, including 40 *Red Sleeve* and 12 *Green Sleeve Boys*, who are also partly clothed by subscription, and were formerly taught in separate schools. The Girls' Lancasterian School, or *School of Industry*, was established a few years afterwards, and is attended by 120 poor girls. The NATIONAL SCHOOLS were established in 1825, and are attended by 150 boys and 70 girls. *St. Clement's Schools* are supported chiefly by the rector of that parish, and are attended by about 130 boys and 80 girls. *St. Helen's School*, held in the parsonage house of that parish, is supported by the rector and other contributors, for the education of about 60 girls. The *Green Gown Charity School* is supported by the minister and congregation of Tacket street Chapel, for clothing and educating 16 poor girls. The *Infant School*, on St. Margaret's Green, was erected in 1839 by W. C. Fonnereau, Esq. It is a neat Gothic building, and is attended by about 100 children. There are several other day schools supported partly by subscription, and partly by small weekly payments received from the scholars. *Sunday Schools* are attached to most of the places of worship, and are numerously attended. The *Diocesan Society*, of the Archdeaconry of Suffolk, has for its principal object the establishment and support of National Schools, in the Eastern Division of the county. The Bishop of Norwich is its patron, and the Rev. R. J. C. Alderson and Messrs. W. Potter and W. Rodwell are joint secrearies.

The *Almshouses, near Shirehall yard*, are supported by TOOLEY'S and SMART'S CHARITIES, the former of which relieves about 24 *in*, and 55 *out* pensioners, and the latter about 10 *in*, and 40 *out* pensioners, besides three families in the almshouses at Stoke. Each *in*-pensioner has 3s. 6d., and each *out*-pensioner 2s. 6d. weekly, and they have all an allowance of coal and clothing yearly ; and £50 per annum is paid to a surgeon for medical assistance to such of them as require it. TOOLEY'S FOUNDATION produces about £916 a year, arising from the following property, derived from the will of *Henry Tooley*, (dated Nov. 4th, 1550 ;) viz., the manors of Ulverston and Sackvylls, in Debenham, yielding about £35 yearly ;—Ulverston Hall farm, 305A., let for £352 ; Limekiln farm, at Claydon, 93A., let for £150 ; Walnut Tree Farm, 160A. near Claydon, let for £190 ; half of a farm of 190A. at Whitton, let for £210 ; one-fifth part of a farm of 91A. at Whitton and Brandon, let for £118 ; two-thirds of a farm of 104A. at Otley, let for £118 ; two rent charges of 10s. each out of houses in St. Helen's parish ; and the interest of £650 vested on mortgage. SMART'S FOUNDATION produces about £480 per annum, arising from the following property, under the will of *Wm. Smart*, in 1598 ; viz., a farm of 372A., and a piece of water of 5½A. at Fakenham and Kirton, let for £420; a third part of a farm of 91A. at Creeting, let for £150 ; and a fifth-part of the above-named farm of 190A. at Whitton and Brandon. The buildings occupied by Smart's almspeople, were purchased with £120, in 1764, but have since been enlarged and repaired. They adjoin Tooley's Almshouses, which formed part of the Black Friary, but have undergone many alterations and repairs.

SMYTH'S ALMSHOUSES :—In 1729, *Ann Smyth*, widow, left £5000 in trust to the Drapers' Company, for the foundation of twelve almshouses for twelve poor women of the age of 50 or upwards, being communicants of the Church of England, and inhabitants of the *parish of St. Mary Elms,*

but her relations of the families of Lynch, Penel, Smyth, and Purplet, wherever they should inhabit, to be preferred ; and for want of a competent number of such poor, she directed the number wanting to be made up out of the other parishes of Ipswich. After building the almshouses, the foundress ordered the residue of the legacy to be laid out in land, and the rents to be applied for the relief of the almswomen, except £10 to a minister for reading prayers to them every Wednesday and Friday, and £3 to the clerk. The Drapers' Company (London,) refused to accept the trust, which was conferred by the Court of Chancery on the perpetual curates of St. Peter and St. Mary-Elms, and their successors. The site of the almshouses was not purchased till 1757. The endowment is £132. 19s. 4d. per annum, arising from £4432. 5s. 2d., Old South Sea Annuities. Each almswoman receives 3s. 6d. per week.

There are 15 ALMSHOUSES in St. Matthew's parish, five in St. Clement's, two in St. Margaret's, and two in St. Mary at Stoke, for the residence of poor persons of those parishes, but they have no endowments. Several other buildings, bequeathed for the residence of poor families, were used as *parish workhouses*, till the new poor law came into operation, as will be seen in the account of the parochial charities, at a subsequent page.

Allen's, Scrivener's, Burrough's, and Martin's Charities, are in some measure consolidated, in consequence of an order of the corporation, in 1744, directing that one person only should be yearly appointed receiver and dispenser of them. *John Allen*, about 1750, gave £60 to provide a yearly distribution of clothing for the most needy poor of Ipswich, and it is vested in a yearly rent-charge of £4. 10s. out of the Bull Inn. *Ralph Scrivener*, in the 32nd of Elizabeth, gave a yearly rent-charge of £7 for the same purpose, and it was settled in the 7th of James I. on a farm of 120A. in Ipswich and Bramford. In 1613, *John Burroughs* left £100 to purchase land, the rent thereof to be distributed yearly on Good Friday at the Church of St. Lawrence, among 40 poor men and women of Ipswich. This legacy was laid out in the purchase of land at Westerfield, which has been added to a farm in that parish, given by *Richard Martin*, in 1621, in trust to the corporation, to pay £20 yearly to two students at Cambridge, who have been scholars at Ipswich Free School ; to distribute £10 yearly in clothing, and to *lend* the surplus profits upon good security, freely to poor clothiers and shearmen, or other poor freemen of Ipswich. This farm is let for about £123 per annum.

WM. CUTLER, in 1620, left £100 to be laid out in land, of the yearly value of £6, to be divided among three poor persons. The corporation laid out this legacy in the purchase of a meadow, which they have added to the Handford Hall farm, out of which they pay the annuity of £6. In 1619, BENJ. OSMOND left £350 to be bestowed as follows :—£100 to buy or build tenements for four aged poor men to dwell in ; £200 to be laid out in land for their weekly relief ; and £50 towards building a new Cornhill cross. The corporation only received £250 of this legacy, and all that now remains of the charity is a building comprising four cottages, three of which are occupied rent-free by poor persons, and the other is let for £6 a year.

JOHN CRANE, by will in 1651, directed his executors to purchase lands of the yearly value of £62, and to convey them to feoffees, in trust, to give the first year's rent to Cambridge University, the second to the town of Wisbech ; the third to the town of Cambridge ; the fourth to Lynn Regis ; and the fifth to Ipswich, for charitable loans and gifts ; and the subsequent years' rent to the University and the four towns, in the same order successively. The estate purchased comprises 132 acres in Fleet and Holbeach, Lincolnshire, and it is now let for about £430 per annum. The Ipswich Charity Trustees receive the rents every fifth year, and distribute them in relieving the poor of the town, especially honest and indigent poor men who

are imprisoned for debt. Agreeable to the donor's will, a *loan fund* of £200 was accumulated by the corporation in 1713, and added to the fund noticed below.

LENDING CASH FUND:—*Sir Thos. White, Kt.*, Alderman of London, in 1566, gave £2000 to the corporation of Bristol, on condition that they should purchase an estate, and out of the rents thereof pay yearly the sum of £104, in succession, to one of the 24 cities and towns named in the deed, and of which Ipswich is one. Of each annual payment, the donor directed £100 *to be lent in sums of* £25, to four young men, " of honest fame," free of interest for ten years, and £4 to be divided among the trustees, for their trouble. For these uses the corporation of Ipswich have received £104 every 24 years, and ought now to have a loan fund of £1000, but it has mostly been lost or applied to other uses. An expensive suit in Chancery, instituted against the corporation for the recovery of part of this fund was terminated in 1843, by their agreeing to pay the costs of the suit, (about £500,) and also £150, the amount of six bonds of £25 each, which appeared upon the books to have been repaid to them.

PEMBERTON'S CHARITY:—In 1718, *John Pemberton* bequeathed his rectories of Pettistree, Wickham, and Bing, with the tithes and profits thereto belonging, and the tithe barn at Wickham, to Edw. Spencer, John Revet, John Sparrowe, Benj. Crocker, and Michael Beaumont, in trust, to divide yearly out of the rents and profits, £25 among the indigent *widows and orphans of clergymen*, inhabiting within 15 miles of Ipswich, and within the county of Suffolk ; and to pay the residue to the treasurer of the *charity schools for Grey-coat boys and Blue-coat girls*, towards educating and apprenticing poor boys and girls. And after giving several legacies, the testator bequeathed the residue of his personal estate to the same trustees, to be laid out in the purchase of lands, the rents thereof to be applied towards the relief of poor *insolvent debtors* imprisoned in any of the gaols in Suffolk ; either for delivering them out of prison, or relieving them whilst there, as the trustees should see fit ; provided such debtors should be persons born in Suffolk, and not indebted to any of the trustees. The testator directed that when any of the trustees die or become incapacitated, the survivors, or the major part of them, shall forthwith elect others. The rectorial tithes and barn produce a clear yearly rent of about £300, after deducting land tax, a customary tithe dinner, &c. Of this income, £25 is applied to the relief of widows and orphans of clergymen, and the remainder (about £275,) is paid to the treasurer of the above-named charity schools. The other branch of this charity consists of a farm of 103A. 0R. 19P. at Cranswick, purchased with £1823, which was the clear residue of the testator's personal estate. This farm was let from 1831 to 1835, for £120 per annum. The rent has been advanced, and is applied (after payment of £2 to each of the trustees,) in providing bread, meat, and beer, every week for the *debtors in Ipswich and Bury gaols*. The trustees in 1828, were Sir Philip Bowes Vere Broke, Bart., Wm. Pearson, Esq., Rev. G. Drury, Rev. Wm. Aldrich, and Wm. Rodwell, Esq.

The *Charity for Widows and Orphans of poor Clergymen of Suffolk* was commenced in 1704, by a few gentlemen of Ipswich and Woodbridge, and is now supported by a numerous list of subscribers residing in various parts of the county.

PAROCHIAL CHARITIES.

ST. CLEMENT'S PARISH.—The *Parish Almshouses* consist of five tenements, occupied by poor persons, and were built in the 26th of Elizabeth, on land given by the corporation. In 1680, *Eliz. Robinson* gave £100 to the corporation, for a distribution of 1s. worth of bread, at the church,

every Sunday, to twelve aged poor parishioners. In 1698, *Mary Wright* conveyed to trustees 5 messuages in this parish, to be by them and the church-wardens fitted up for the residence of needy poor, partly as a workhouse for children, who should be taught to read one hour every day. The deed conveying these houses requires that the churchwardens shall distribute 40s. yearly out of the poor rates, among 40 poor persons. The houses were occupied as the parish workhouse, but were taken down about two years ago. In 1685, SAMUEL GREEN left £50, to be laid out in land, for the relief of the widows and children of *seamen* of this parish. With this legacy, and £10 given by the testator's widow, 5A. of land was purchased at Westerfield, and it was augmented at the enclosure with an allotment of 3 rods. The rent, £17 a year, is distributed on the 28th of November. In 1719, *Robert Cole* left £50, to provide for a distribution of bread, once a fortnight, at the church, among poor widows of seamen. This legacy was used in repairing the church, but 2s. worth of bread is distributed once a fortnight, and paid for out of the church-rates. In 1722, *Edward Larke* charged his house here with the yearly payment of 10s., for a sermon on Oct. 22nd ; 2s. for the clerk ; and 20s., to be given in bread to the working poor. JOHN DORKING, in 1727, left £100 to be laid out in land, the profits thereof to be distributed yearly as follows :—10s. to the minister, for reading prayers on the 14th of September ; and the remainder among poor seamen's widows and children, and other poor not receiving parochial relief. The land purchased with this legacy consists of 2A. 2R. 2P., in St. Helen's parish, let for £15 a year, which is distributed by the minister and churchwardens.

PARISH OF ST. LAWRENCE.—In 1630, *Tobias Bloss* bequeathed four marks (£2. 13s. 4d.) a year, to be paid out of his lands called Apostle's Esher, in St. Margaret's parish, and distributed as follows, four times a-year : viz., 10s. for a sermon, 1s. to the sexton, and 2s. 4d. in bread among the poor. In 1680, *Wm. Sayer* left £100 to the corporation, in trust, to distribute the yearly interest (£5,) in doles of bread, every Sunday, in the church of St. Lawrence, or that of St. Mary Tower. In 1729, *Fras. Coleman* gave the corporation 6A. of land, in St. Helen's parish, subject to the yearly payment of £8. 2s. for the poor not receiving parochial aid, namely, £5. 2s. to be distributed in weekly doles of bread, and the remainder in shirts and shifts. The trustees are appointed by the parishioners.

ST. MARGARET'S.—The *Parish Land*, comprising 8A., has for a long period been vested in trustees, for the benefit of the parishioners and the reparation of the church. It is let for about £16 a-year, which is added to the church-rate. *Two cottages*, in St. Margaret street, are occupied by two poor persons, placed therein by the minister and churchwardens, but the donor is unknown. The BREAD CHARITIES produce about £57 a-year, which is distributed in weekly doles of bread every Sunday, and arises as follows : about £20, from 4A. 3R. 31P. of land, on the Westerfield road, given by *Richd.* and *John Philipps; £4*, from 3A. at Copdike, purchased with the gifts of *Sarah Philipps* and *Thomas Bunning ; £8*, from a building site in St. Margaret street, purchased with £50 given by *Leicester Martin ; £15*, as half the rent of a house in Carr street, left by the *Rev. Thos. Rederich*, in 1628, to the poor of this parish, and to Jesus College, Oxford, in equal shares ; £19. 6s. 4d., from £483 new four per cent. annuities, purchased with £500 left by *Benj. Palmer Green*, in 1814 ; and £5. 4s. from the corporation, as interest of £100 left by *James Caston*, in 1660. The poor parishioners have also a yearly rent-charge of 10s., left by *Henry Dade*, out of a house at Earl-Soham, belonging to Mr. Bellman.

The *Parish of St. Mary Elms* enjoys most of *Smyth's Almshouses*, noticed at page 79 ; and its poor have an annuity of 40s., left by *Nicholas Kerrington*, in 1687, out of a house in St. Matthew's, for distributions of bread. In 1635, *John Hunt* left £100, to be lent to five poor tradesmen, at

four per cent., and he directed the interest to be distributed in shirts and shifts, among the poor of this parish.

Parish of St. Mary at Quay.—The POOR'S ESTATE consists of 23A. of land, at Lindsey ; and 2A. 28P. at Monks Illeigh ; the former purchased in 1647, with £116 benefactions to the poor, and the latter in 1813, with £40 subscribed by the parishioners. The estate is vested in 14 trustees, and is let for £20 per annum, which is distributed in money and bread, at vestry meetings on the 1st of January and 2nd of February. The overseers and churchwardens distribute 1s. worth of bread weekly, as interest of £50, left by *John Rycroft*, in 1708; and they also distribute in coals, on the 5th of November, a rent-charge of £2, left by *Sir Emanuel Sorrel*, in 1665, out of property now belonging to the Crawley family.

Parish of St. Mary Stoke.—In 1724, NATHANIEL THURSTON left £100 to be laid out in land by the churchwardens and overseers of this parish, for a distribution of bread every Sunday, at the church. The house and stable, purchased with this legacy, in Little King street, were sold in 1816, to the commissioners of the Improvement Act, for £350, which lay many years unproductive in the Bank of England, in the name of the Accountant-General, for want of trustees. In 1734, *Chpr. Thorne* charged his house here with the yearly payment of £2. 12s. for a weekly distribution of 1s. worth of bread, to the poor of St. Mary Stoke and St. Peter's. In 1680, *Edward Sheppard* left two cottages, for the residence of four poor widows of St. Mary Stoke and St. Matthew's.

Parish of St. Mary Tower.—The corporation distribute among the poor 3s. 6d. worth of bread, at the church, every Sunday, and 2s. 6d. worth on the 9th of March, as the proceeds of £200 left by *Leonard Caston*, in 1617, and *Eliz. Robinson*, in 1680. The yearly rent-charges of £2, out of the Swan Inn, left by *John Parker*, in 1664, and £5 out of Mr. Ridley's house, bequeathed by *Wm. Neave*, are distributed in coals among the poor, on Saint Thomas's day, by the churchwardens. In 1680, *John Rednall* gave for the residence of poor parishioners a house and four small tenements, near the Tower-ditches, with the gardens belonging thereto. These premises were the parish workhouse, but are now let to various tenants.

Parish of St. Matthew.—DAUNDY'S ALMSHOUSES consist of 15 small tenements, erected in 1515, by Edward Daundy, for the use of poor parishioners. They are repaired at the expense of the parish. In 1698, *Henry Skynner* gave £100 to provide for a weekly distribution of bread, and it was laid out in the purchase of 6A. 2R. 20P. of land, in this parish, let in 1804, on a 99 years' lease, to Dykes Alexander, Esq., at the rent of £21 per annum. As the proceeds of this charity, the churchwardens distribute 8s. worth of bread every Sunday. They also distribute in bread the yearly sum of £2, left by *Nicholas Kerrington*, in 1687, out of a house now belonging to Mr. Leverett. In 1717, JOHN GIBBON left a house, to be sold, and the produce thereof to be laid out in land, to be vested in five or seven trustees, to apply the yearly rents as follows: 20s. for a sermon on Aug. 2nd ; £4 to the charity schools of Grey-coat Boys and Blue-coat Girls ; and the remainder to be laid out in coats and gowns, for the most aged and helpless poor men and women of the parish frequenting the church, to be given on the feast of St. John the Evangelist. The house sold for £190, which was laid out in the purchase of a house, barn, and 16A. of land at Shotley, now let for £18 a-year, which is distributed by the vicar as directed by the donor.

The poor of *St. Nicholas' parish* have two yearly rent-charges, viz., £5 for coals, left by *John Cutler*, in 1645, and £5 for weekly doles of bread, left by *Nicholas Kerrington*, in 1647. Those of *St. Stephen's parish* have £10 a-year from a cottage and 4A. 7P. of land, at Grundisburgh, purchased with £100, left by John Reynolds, in 1647.

St. Peter's Parish.—In 1665, *Sir Emanuel Sorrel* left a yearly rent-

charge of £2. 10s., out of two houses now belonging to the Crawley family. It is distributed in coals, together with £4 a-year paid out of the poor-rates, as an acknowledgment for the premises left by *Isaac Blomfield*, in 1772, and long used as the parish workhouse.   In 1723, *Mary Chapple* left a house, yard, &c. for the benefit of the poor.   The house was rebuilt by the parish, at the cost of £100, and converted into two cottages, now occupied by paupers.   The poor parishioners have also a yearly rent-charge of £1. 6s., left by *John Blythe*, in 1756, and one-half of Thorne's rent-charge of £2. 12s., as noticed with the parish of St. Mary Stoke.   The poor of *St. Stephen's parish* have distributed among them, on New Year's day, £10, as the rent of 4A. 7P. of land, at Grundisburgh, purchased with £100, left by John Reynolds, in 1647.

EAST SUFFOLK AND IPSWICH HOSPITAL AND DISPENSARY is a handsome structure, of white brick and stone, and was erected in 1835 and '6, at the cost of about £2500, upon a bold eminence, overlooking the town and a wide extent of the surrounding country. It stands near the centre of about two acres of land, which was purchased by the trustees of the Rev. W. C. Fonnereau, and is now tastefully laid out in lawns, gardens, and shrubberies. It is approached through a lofty portico, of the Ionic order, and affords accommodation for upwards of 50 in-patients. The wards and passages are spacious, and well ventilated, and the interior arrangement is highly creditable to the skill of the architect, Mr. B. Backhouse. R. D. Alexander, Esq., and a few other gentlemen, first called the attention of the inhabitants of East Suffolk to the establishment of this house of mercy, for the relief of the sick, lame, and infirm poor; and the generous flame spread so rapidly, that before the opening of the hospital, on August 3rd, 1836, no less than £5000 had been raised by voluntary contribution, and a list of annual subscribers showed a yearly revenue of more than £800. The charity has since received many legacies and benefactions, and its income is now about £1000 per annum, nearly £600 of which is derived from yearly subscriptions, about £200 from the dividends of stock and the interest of money vested with the Dock Commissioners, and the remainder from donations and other irregular contributions. Patients are admitted on the recommendation of subscribers or benefactors; but in cases not admitting of delay, no recommendation is necessary. The number admitted yearly is upwards of 200 *in*, and 450 *out* patients, but seldom more than 30 are fed and lodged in the hospital at one time. Sir Wm. F. F. Middleton, Bart. is *president ;* and he and Sir Robert Harland, and Andrew Archedeckne and F. W. Campbell, Esqrs. are *trustees* of the charity. The Rev. J. C. Aldrich, M.A., is *chaplain ;* A. W. Baird and E. Beck are the *physicians ;* and A. H. Bartlett, G. Bullen, C. C. Hammond, and G. G. Sampson, are the *surgeons.*

BELLE VUE ASYLUM, pleasantly situated on the Woodbridge road, is a private establishment, for the reception of persons afflicted with insanity. It was commenced in 1835, by its present proprietor, Mr. Jas. Shaw, surgeon, and has accommodations for 40 patients.

Besides those already noticed, here are several other charitable institutions, supported by the contributions of the benevolent, for the solace of poverty; and among them is a " Society for Clothing the Infant Poor," of which Mrs. J. Cobbold is president. Here are also many *Friendly Societies* and *Secret Orders*, in which the members, by small monthly or other contributions, make provision for sickness, superan-

nuation, and death; and one of them is the *Seamen's Shipwreck Benevolent Society*, established in 1825, and held at the White Elm Inn. Here are three *Lodges of Free Masons*, viz., the British Union Lodge, held at the Assembly Rooms, on the Monday on or before full-moon; St. Luke's Lodge, at the Coach and Horses, on the second Wednesday of every month; and the Lodge of Perfect Friendship, at the Bee Hive, on the third Wednesday of every month. There are in the town two SAVINGS' BANKS, both established in 1818, viz., the *Ipswich Provident Bank*, in Queen street; and the *Ipswich and Suffolk Savings' Bank*, on Cornhill. In November, 1842, the former had deposits amounting to £70,696, belonging to 2048 individuals, 37 charitable institutions, and 15 friendly societies. The *Suffolk and General Country Fire Office* was established here and at Bury St. Edmunds, in 1802, for securing houses, buildings, farming stock, goods, merchandise, and ships in harbour, against loss or damage by fire. During the last few years, the temperance cause has made as much progress here as in most other parts of the kingdom, and has wrought a great improvement in the morals and habits of a large portion of the inhabitants. The *Ipswich Total Abstinence Society* now numbers several hundred members, who hold their meetings in the *Temperance Hall*, a large and handsome building, of Doric architecture, erected in 1840, at the sole expense of R. D. Alexander, Esq. This Hall will accommodate 800 persons, being 68 feet long, and 40½ feet wide, and having a spacious gallery and platform.

HAMLETS, &c., IN THE BOROUGH.
(See pages 50, 68, and 87.)

WESTERFIELD, a small village, pleasantly situated, 2 miles N. by E. of Ipswich, has in its parish 1070 acres of land, and 324 souls. About 464 acres of land, and 70 of the inhabitants, are in Bosmere and Claydon Hundred, and all the rest of the parish is within the jurisdiction of the borough of Ipswich. The soil belongs to the Rev. M. G. Edgar, and several smaller proprietors, and is partly in the manor of Wykes-Ufford. The *Church* (St. Mary) is a rectory, valued in K.B. at £11. 10s. 7½d. The Bishop of Ely is patron, and the Rev. Chas. Drage, M.A., is the incumbent. The tithes have lately been commuted for a yearly modus of £350. The *National School* was built by subscription, in 1840; and the mistress receives the rent of a cottage and four acres of land, at Claydon, left in 1662, by *Bridget Collet*, for schooling poor children, and now let for £10 per annum. In 1775, *James Brooks* left £300, and directed half of the yearly proceeds to be expended in providing clothes and religious books for poor scholars of Westerfield, and the remainder to be laid out in coals for the industrious poor not receiving parochial relief. This legacy was vested in the purchase of £323 old South Sea Annuities. The *Poors' Houses* are two tenements, let for £6 a year, which is applied in clothing poor children.

Ablett Adolphus, gentleman	Drage Rev Charles, M.A., rector,
Cade Wm. blacksmith	*Rectory*
Davy John, shoemaker	Foulger Wm. gardener
Davy Robt. beer and swine dealer	Garrod John, gardener

Hammond Jeremiah, shoemaker
Mallett John, vict. Swan
Norman Nathan, joiner, shopkeeper, and parish clerk
Owen James, M.D.
Salter Susanna, schoolmistress
Salter Wm. corn miller, *Follymill*

Threadkell Wm. Barrett, corn miller

FARMERS.

Bird Samuel || Bird Thomas
Edwards Edw. *Westerfield hall*
Hunt Wm. || Payne Ann
Salter Henry || Salmon Wm.
Waller Stephen, *Westerfield house*

WHITTON is a small, well-built village, on the Norwich road, 2 miles N. by W. of Ipswich. Adjoining it, on the west, are the Crown Inn, the White House, and a few other buildings, which are in the parish of Bramford, but in the borough of Ipswich, which includes all the parish of Whitton, except a few houses at the northern extremity, which are in Blything Hundred. *Whitton parish* contains 1437A. of land, and includes the ancient hamlet of *Thurlston*. It had 422 inhabitants, in 1841, exclusive of the County Gaol and House of Correction, which had 116 inmates, and is partly in this parish, but mostly in those of St. Margaret, St. Helen, and St. Stephen. The principal owners of the soil are the Rev. Edward Woolnough, the Ipswich Charity Trustees, W.C. Fonnereau, Esq., and Mr. J. O. Flindell. *Whitton Church* (St. Mary) is a small ancient structure, without a tower, and is a rectory, valued in K.B. at £6. 11s. 5½d., and now at £250. The Bishop of Ely is patron, and the Rev. Wm. Howorth, M.A., incumbent. *Thurlston Church* (St. Botolph) was parochial, and is no doubt the church mentioned in Domesday Book, under the name of *Thurlweston*. It was appropriated to St. Peter's Priory, and was granted by Henry VIII., with the manor, to Cardinal Wolsey, and by Queen Elizabeth to Thomas Seckford, Esq. It was in use in 1500, but the vicarage being consolidated with the rectory of Whitton, it was neglected after that period, and has long been used as a barn. The great tithes of *Whitton-cum-Thurlston* were recently commuted for a yearly modus of £440, of which one-half belongs to the Rev. E. Woolnough, the impropriator of Thurlston, and lord of the manor. The *Poor's Land*, about 4A., let for £5 a-year, was purchased with 20 marks, left by John Reynolds, in 1647.

WHITTON DIRECTORY.
Clarke Rd. joiner||Codd Mr Thos.
Cross John, vict. May Pole
Day Edward, shoemaker
Field Edw. corn miller
Goldsmith John, parish clerk
Hunt Chas. gent||Hallam Mrs Maria
Harvey Thos. K. gardener
Kembell Thomas, poulterer
King Henry, blacksmith
Knight Thomas, baker
Lovely Wm. nurseryman and vict. Crown
Nunn John, cattle dealer & drover
Perry Wm. shopkeeper
Rogers Miss Martha Maria
Rowell John, coach proprietor

Smith Richard, shoemaker
Scutcheon Wm. shopkeeper
Sparrow Miss Sarah
Steward Rev Ambrose, White house
Woolnough Rev Edw. Thurlston hall
Wood John, whitesmith
Woollard Edw. shoemaker
Woollard Thomas, wheelwright

FARMERS.—(* *are Owners.*)

Allen Wm. Ely, Glebe farm
Bowman Robert, junior
*Catt Samuel, Whitton cottage
Clark Henry, Dale hall
*Flindell John Orford
Green Benj. P. (and Blakenham)
Howard Stephen||Kersey Thomas
Knights John || Rowland Saml.

LIST OF STREETS,

COURTS, LANES, HAMLETS, VILLAS, FARMS, &c.,
IN THE BOROUGH OF IPSWICH,

WITH REFERENCES TO THEIR RESPECTIVE SITUATIONS.

Adelphi place, Lower Brook street
Albert terrace, Norwich road
Albion street, Fore Hamlet
Albion wharf, Quay street
Anchor yard, Duke street
Anglesey mills, Back street
Angel lane, Fore street
Asylum yard, Lower Orwell street
Back Hamlet, St Clement's street
Back road, Crown lane
Back street, Eagle street
Bank place, Woodbridge road
Bank street, Foundation street
Barclay street, Cox lane
Barrack lane, St Matthew's street
Bath yard, Duke street
Bell lane, Bridge street West
Belle vue, Woodbridge road
Belstead road, Stoke street
Belvedere terrace, Norwich road
Berners street, St Matthew's street
Birkfield Lodge, Belstead road
Bird's gardens, Priory street
Black Horse lane, Westgate street
Bolton lane & farm, Tuddenham road
Borough road, Rope lane
Boos Hall, Bramford road
Bourn bridge, Halifax
Bramford road, Norwich road
Bridge street, St. Peter's street
Brook st.(Upper & Lower) Tavern st
Brooks Hall, Norwich road
Butter market, King street
Caldwell Hall, Woodbridge road
Carr street, Tavern street
Cattle market, Falcon street
Christie's yard, Back street
Christ Church Park, St Margaret's
Church lane, Church street
Church street, Back Hamlet
Clay lane, Woodbridge road
Cliff, Wykes Bishop
Cold Dunghills, Eagle street
Coleman street, Northgate street
Coleman's villas, Norwich road
College street, St Peter's street
Common quay, Quay street
Cook row, Tavern street
Corn hill, Market place

Cottage place, Orford street
Cox lane, Carr street
Coyte's gardens, Friars' street
Crane hall, London road
Cross yard, Corn hill
Crown lane, Westgate & Bridge st
Curriers' lane, Friars' street
Dairy lane, St Margaret's plane
Dale Hall, 2 miles N.N.W.
David street, Victoria street
Denny's passage, Corn hill
Dial place, Currier's lane
Dock street, Bridge street West
Dog's Head lane, St Stephen's lane
Dove lane, Rope lane
Downham Reach, Cliff
Duke street, St Clement's street
Eagle street, Upper Orwell street
East st. St Helen's st. and Rope ln
Elm street, King street
Falcon street, Queen street
Felaw's Houses, Foundation street
Folly, Tuddenham road
Fore Hamlet, St Clement's street
Fore street, St Clement's
Foundation street, Tacket street
Foundry road, Carr street
Friar's street and road, Queen st
Gipping street, Tanner's lane
Globe lane, Hyde Park corner
Goldroyd, Belstead road
Goodwin's gardens, Providence st
Great Whip street, Dock street
Green yard lane, Turret lane
Green yard, Duke street
Greenwich, Cliff road
Groves House, St Helen's street
Gusford Hall, Stoke street
Haill's road and ter. London road
Halifax, Wherstead road
Handford Hall, London road
Handford street, Mount
Hatton court, Tavern street
High street, Back road
Hill House, Back Hamlet
Hyde Park Corner, St Matthew's st
Holywells, 1 mile S. by E.
John street, Duke street
Key street, Bank street

King street, Corn hill
Lady lane, Westgate street
Lawrence place, Currier's lane
Little Barclay street, Barclay street
Little Coleman street, Carr street
Little Whip street, Great Whip st
Lock road, College street
London road, St Matthew's street
Long lane, New street
Major's Corner, Carr street
Mile End, London road
Mill street, Victoria street
Mount pleasant, Woodbridge road, and Globe lane
Mount, and Mount street, Elm st
Neptune quay, Quay street
New bank, Stoke
New Market street, Falcon street
New Market lane, Butter market
New street, Church street
New Town, Haill's road
Northgate street, Tavern street
Norwich road, St Matthew's street
Oak lane, Northgate street
Orchard lane, Gipping street
Orford street, Norwich road
Orwell court, Lower Orwell street
Orwell Lodge, Belstead road
Orwell place, Tacket street
Orwell street, (Upper and Lower) Orwell place
Orwell Works, Duke street
Page's court, Star lane
Panorama, Norwich road
Pleasant row, Shirehall yard
Portman street, Priory street
Portman's walk, Friar's road
Potter's street, Victoria street
Princes street, Back street
Priory place, Friar's street
Priory street, Friar's road
Providence street, Westgate street
Quay street, College street
Queen street, King street
Race Ground, Rose hill
Red House, (1½ m.) Tuddenham rd
Regent street, St Helen's street
Revitt's yard, Duke street
Rope lane, Eagle street
Roper's yard, Duke street
Rose hill, Fore Hamlet
Rose lane, St Peter's street
Rosemary lane, Lower Brook street
Round Wood, (2 m.) Woodbridge rd
Salthouse lane, Quay street
Sand pit, Globe lane
St Clement's street, Fore street

St. George's terrace, Globe lane
St Helen's street, Carr street
St James' street, Portman street
St John street, Portman street
St Lawrence street, Tavern street
St Margaret's green, St Margt's. st
St Margaret's plane, Northgate
St Margaret's street, Coleman street
St Margaret's ter. Woodbridge road
St Mary Elms, King street
St Mary Quay, Bank street
St Mary Tower, Tower street
St Matthew's street, Westgate st
St Matthew's terrace, Norwich rd
St Nicholas street, Queen street
St Peter's quay, College street
St Peter's street, St Nicholas street
St Stephen's lane, Butter market
School street, Back road
Shirehall yard, Foundation street
Short lane, New street
Silent St. or New Market street, St Stephen's lane
Smart's wharf, Quay street
Soane street, St Margaret's plane
Star lane, Bank street
Steam mill place, Rope lane
Stoke green, Great Whip street
Stoke Park, Belstead road
Stoke street, Bridge street, *West*
Tacket street, Brook street
Tanner's lane, Friar's street
Tavern street, Corn hill
Thoroughfare, Corn hill
Thurlston, 2 m. N.N.W. Henley rd
Thursby's lane, Elm street
Tower ditches, Northgate street
Tower lane and st., Tavern street
Trafalgar buildings, Shirehall yard
Tuddenham road, St Margaret's grn
Turret lane, St Stephen's lane
Union street, Cox lane
Upper Orwell street, Carr street
Victoria street, Back street
Victoria terrace, Woodbridge road
Warren House, 1½ mile S. by E.
Westerfield, 2 miles N.
Westgate street, Cornhill
Westrow cottages, Woodbridge rd
Wherry quay, Quay street
Wherstead road, Halifax
Whitnesham road, Tuddenham road
Whitton (2 m. N.) Norwich road
Williams' place, Orchard street
Woodbridge road, St Margaret's st
Wykes Bishop, Duke street
Wykes Bishop street, Fore Hamlet

IPSWICH DIRECTORY.

The POST-OFFICE is in the Thoroughfare, and Mr. Wm. Stevenson Fitch is the *postmaster;* Mr. Wm. Collins, *clerk;* and George Brame, Edgar Boar, James Cooper, and Sarah Jennings are the *letter carriers.* The office *opens* at 7 morning, and closes at half-past nine night. *London, Norwich,* and *Yarmouth Letters* are received and despatched in the night, or early in the morning, during the time the office is closed. Letters for *Manchester, Liverpool, Bury St. Edmund's,* and the *North of England,* arrive at nine morning, and are despatched thither at five afternoon. *Stowmarket Letters* are received at nine night, and despatched at six morning.

MISCELLANY *of Gentry, Clergy, Partners in Firms and others, not arranged under the Classification of Trades and Professions.*

Abbott Abm. foreman, 38 Boro.' road
Ablitt Mrs Sarah, St Nicholas street
Ablitt Edward, gent. Foundation st
Ablitt Mrs Elizabeth, Foundation 'st
Ainge Mrs Elizabeth, St Peter's st
Alderson Rev Robert Jarvis Cook, rector of Kirton, Lower Brook st
Aldrich Rev John Cobbold, M.A. incumbent of St Lawrence, St Matthew's stre
Aldrich Rev Wm. B. D. incumbent of St Mary Elms, Stoke street
Alexander Mrs Ann, Quay street
Alexander Dykes, Esq. banker, Norwich road
Alexander Mrs Eliz. 14 Victoria ter
Alexander Mrs E. 5 St George's ter
Alexander Geo. Frederick, banker, *Goldroyd*
Alexander Mrs Rebecca, *Goldroyd*
Alexander Richard Dykes, Esq. St Matthew's street
Alexander Saml. porter, Union Wks
Alexander Wm. Hy. Esq., banker, Bank street
Allen John, coach maker; h Mount
Allen Wm. sweep, Currier's lane
Andrews John, butler, Stoke street
Andrews Samuel, bookpr. Bridge st
Anniss Richard, gent. Bell lane
Archer Mr Francis, Handford st
Archer Mrs Lydia, St Clement's st
Archer Robert, clerk, Borough road
Bacon Edw. Esq. banker, Tavern st
Bacon Mrs Eliz. St Peter's street
Bacon George Constantine Edgar, solicitor; h Tavern street
Baillie John, town missionary, St Nicholas street
Baker Simon, gent. Westgate street
Baldick John, serjeant major, East Suffolk militia, Norwich road
Bampton Mrs My. St Margaret's gn

Bantoft Rd. shopman, 11 Victoria ter
Barchard Michl. clerk, 1 Globe lane
Bardwell Henry, printer, Tanner's ln
Barker Chas. jun. grocer; h Back st
Barber James, lock master, Lock rd
Barfield Wm. Edward, bookkeeper, Great Whip street
Barker Mrs Ann, Orwell place
Barton Mr John Gibson, 5 Boro.' rd
Basket Miss, Lower Brook street
Bateman Rev John (Baptist,) 40 Borough road
Batley Henry, clerk, 9 Berners st
Batterby Ptr. travlr. 10 Victoria ter
Bayley Mrs Ann, Lower Brook st
Bayley Lieut Charles Bisset, R.N. Berners street
Bayley Wm. shipwright, Fore Hamlt
Bayley Wm. Villiers, gent. London rd
Baylis Philip, gent. New town
Beaumont Geo. pilot, Fore Hamlet
Bedwell Mr John, Woodbridge rd
Bedwell Mrs Sophia, St Matthew's st
Bennett John, gent. Upr. Brook st
Benneworth, James, excise, Woodbridge road
Bentley Thomas Fuller, bookkeeper, Duke street
Benyon Fredk. gent. Berners street
Berry Lady Louisa, Providence st
Bird Edw. tide waiter, Foundation st
Bird Wm. bookkeeper, Foundation st
Birkitt George, gent. Carr street
Bishop Richard, clerk, Silent street
Blaxall Mrs Marian, Belvedere ter
Bloomfield Miss Harriet, Potter st
Bloomfield Mrs Sarah, Asylum yard
Bloss Robert, sawyer; h St Peter's st
Boar Edgar, letter car. 4 Priory st
Bolton Lieut Chas. R.N. Berners st
Bolton Miss Harriet, London road
Bond John, tanner, St Margaret's street, and *Woodbridge*

Booty Mr Edward, Upper Orwell st
Borrett Thomas, clerk, St John st
Boulter Joseph, sweep, Cook row
Bowman Mrs Tamer, Green yard ln
Box Mrs Elizabeth, 31 Borough rd
Bradley Jonathan Bell, gent. 3 Victoria terrace
Brame George, letter carrier, St Matthew's lane
Bray Jacob Peele, gent. Friar's rd
Brewer Mrs Sarah, 9 Belvedere ter
Brightwell Wm. bookpr. Mill place
Bristo Henry Gallant, wine mercht.; h Tacket street
Bromley Mrs Mary, High street
Bromley Mr John, Upper Orwell st
Brook James, clerk, Silent street
Brookes Wm. gent. Northgate street
Brown James, timber merchant; h St John street
Brown Robert, gent. London road
Brown Mrs Sarah, Norwich road
Bruce Mrs Mary, Little Coleman st
Bruce Rd. bookkeeper, Foundation st
Bryan Miss Maria, Woodbridge rd
Bryant Mrs Sarah, Silent street
Buck George, gent. Woodbridge rd
Buck Philip, draper ; h Butter mkt
Buck Mrs Ann, Berners street
Bull Miss Margaret, Woodbridge rd
Buller Mrs Sarah, Eagle street
Buller Wm, Esq. banker, Duke st
Bunniss Mr Benjamin, Halifax
Burbage Mrs Eliz. Victoria street
Burch Mrs Mary, 9 Albert terrace
Burrell Hon. Lyndsey, *Stoke Park*
Burroughes Thomas D'Eye, Esq. 1 Albert terrace
Burrows Sl. plumber ; h Orwell pl
Burton Rt. gent. 7 St Margaret's ter
Bush Mrs Elizabeth, Tower ditches
Butcher Rt. gent. 3 St. Margt's. ter
Buxton Mrs Martha, Black Horse ln
Byles Nathl. merchant; h *Hillhouse*
Calthorpe John, pilot, Duke street
Campbell Frederick William, Esq. *Birkfield Lodge*
Cardew James, gent. Globe lane
Carr Serjt. Major Jas. Handford st
Carter Mrs Jane, Friary
Castle Wm. Gt White Horse Hotel
Caston MrsAnn Maria, St Helen's st
Caston Mrs Rhoda, St Helen's st
Caston Mrs Sarah, Woodbridge rd
Catt Benj. Butley, gent. London road
Cavell Mrs Eliz. Foundation street
Chamberlain Mrs Eliz. Globe lane

Chaplin Mrs Ann, 8 Belvidere ter
Chaplin Edward, pilot, John street
ChapmanEdw. gardnr. St Matthew's street
Cheselden Mr Wm. College street
Chevalier Miss Emma, Church st
Church Clement Rutland, gentleman, Norwich road
Clamp Rt. governor, Union Workhs
Clark Mrs Sarah, Cox lane
Clark Thomas, gent. Norwich road
Clark Mr Thomas, Victoria street
Clark Mr Wm. St Helen's street
Clarke Mrs Elizabeth, Eagle street
Clarke John, gent. St John street
Clarke Mrs Mary Ann, New Town
Clarke Mrs Susan, Silent street
Clarke Mrs Sarah, 5 Halifax
Clarke Welham, gent. Back Hamlet
Clarkson Thomas, paver, Fore st
Cobbold Jno.Chevalier,Esq.Tower st
Cobbold Mrs Elizabeth, Carr street
Cobbold Rev Francis, *Groves House*
Cobbold Lieut.Frdk. 5Albert terrace
Cobbold Miss, Tacket street
Cobbold Mrs Mary Ann Fearnley, Northgate street
Cobbold Mrs Mercy, St Matthew's st
Cockerell Mrs Hannah, Norwich rd
Cochrane James, compositor, Mount
Codd Lucy, weighing machine keeper, Crown court
CoeChs.Kersey, shipownr.London rd
Colchester Charles, soap manufacturer ; house, St Peter's street
Colchester Mrs Eliz. Berners street
Cole Geo. police serjt. Tower ditches
Cole John, sawyer, Bird's gardens
Collett Miss Charlotte, Berners st
Collins William, post office clerk, St John street
Coleman Thomas, gent. Berners st
Conder Geo. gent. St Peter's street
Conder Mr John Garwood, Brook st
Conder Thos. gent. St Nicholas st
Cook Abraham, Esq. comptroller of customs, St Helen's street
Cook Edward, gent. Stoke green
Cook Miss Emma, 4 St Matthew's ter
Cook Miss Mary, Norwich road
Cooper Jas. letter carrier, Barclay st
Cooper John, lecturer on astronomy, Rose lane
Cooper Mr Joseph, Berners street
Cooper Mrs My. Ann, Providence st
Cooper Rev Richard (Wesleyan) St Margaret's plane

Corder Henry Shewell, draper; house, Berners street

Corder James, gent. Berners street

Cordingley Mrs Eliz. Norwich rd

Cosserat Rev Geo. Pelaquin Graham, rect. of St Matthew's, Handford st

Cousins Mr John, Norwich road

Cowey Mrs Sarah, St Matthew's st

Cox Mrs Frances, Norwich road

Cox Mrs Har. 5 St Margaret's ter

Cranmer Mrs Mary Ann, 32 Borough road

Crawley Thos. gent. 7 Albert terrace

Creasey Wm. musician, Crown lane

Crisp Thos. clothier; h London road

Crispin John, tailor; h Silent street

Christopherson Sml. clerk in customs, Bank buildings

Croft Rev Stephen, M.A. rural dean, and rector of *Stoke*

Cross Mr Wm. College street

Cunningham Miss Laura, 5 Victoria terrace

Cuthbert Chas. slater, *Cold Dunghills*

Cutting Mrs Ann, Lower Orwell st

Cutting Chas. gent. Woodbridge rd

Daking George, wharfinger; house Stoke street

Dalby James, clerk, Woodbridge rd

Davey Mrs Mary, Berners street

Davie J. surgeon; house Fore street

Davy Mrs Ann. Woodbridge road

Dawson Miss Jane, Foundation st

Death Mrs Elizabeth, Falcon street

Denham Mrs Elizabeth, Crown st

Dennant James, gent. Short lane

Denny Henry, paper hanging dealer, Norwich road

Denny Mrs Mary Ann, Cross yard

Denny Thomas, gent. Berners street

Dewell Mr Stokes, Bramford road

Dewey Mr Edmund Johnson, St Nicholas street

Dickson Mrs Emily, *Cliff cottage*

Dobson Edw. excise clerk, College st

Dothie Jas. tobacco mfr; h Orwell pl

Drake James Roper, R.N. Woodbridge road

Drew Mr Thomas, Victoria street

Dunningham Joseph, gent. Woodbridge road

Dunningham Shepherd, gent. Falcon street

Durrant Hy. clerk, 34 Borough rd

Eade Charles, wine merchant; house 4 Albert terrace

Eade Rt. coachman, Woodbridge rd

Edgar Rev Mileson Gery, M.A. incumbent of St Nicholas, and rector of Trimley, *Red House*

Edmonds Rt. missionary, Globe lane

Edwards Bennett, ratcatcher, Lower Orwell street

Edwards Mrs Harriet, Foundation st

Ehn George, furrier, Globe lane

Ellis Michl. bookpr. St Nicholas st

Elliston Wm. wine merchant; house St Nicholas street

Elmer Mr Samuel, Queen street

Elmer Mrs Rose, Lower Orwell st

Elvins Mr Edward, St Matthew's st

Emerson Thos. coachman, Friars st

Ennew Robt. Clamp, tallow chandler; house Queen street

Ethersey Mrs Eliz. Norwich road

Faiers Wm. Bransby, gent. Berners st

Farman Mr Jas. 18 Victoria terrace

Farrow Benj. Baldry, clerk, Lock rd

Fenn Thos. sen. gent. Tacket street

Fenning Miss Mary, 9 Friars street

Fenny Mrs Elizabeth, Foundry rd

Fisher Mrs Eliz. 4 Belvidere terrace

Fitch Mrs Elizabeth, Queen street

Fitch Wm. Stevenson, postmaster, Thoroughfare

Fletcher Rt. governor of Borough gaol

Fonnereau William Charles, Esq. *Christ Church Park*

Ford Simon, tide waiter, Custom house

Forth Mrs Mary Ann, Priory lane

Fosdyke Mrs Elizabeth, Tacket st

Frankland Rev Chas. Wm. curate of St Helen's, Albion hill

Franklin Mrs Ann, Friars street

Franklin Rd. gent. Westgate street

Fraser Wm. draper; h Woodbridge rd

Frewer Isaac, gent. Coleman street

Frost Jph. tide waiter, Fore Hamlet

Fruer John, gent. Tacket street

Fryatt Mrs Sar. Lower Orwell street

Fuller John, gent. Church street

Gardiner George, bookkeeper, Halifax ship-yard

Garnham Hy. wine mert; h Berners st

Garrett Garrett, merchant; house Victoria terrace

Garrod Mrs. Providence street

Garrod Wm. printer; h Friars st

Gee Mrs. Lower Brook street

Garwood Mr Wm. Draper, 7 Halifax

Giddy Wm. bookr. St Margaret's grn

Giles Mrs Sar. 6 Belvidere terrace

Gill Geo. & Hy. H. bookps. High st

Gill Stn. bookkeeper, Woodbridge rd

Gill Wm. fire office clerk, Bank st
Gilligan John, clerk of the works, Barracks
Girling James, pilot, John street
GladingIsaac, cooper, St Nicholas st
GlandfieldWm.turnkey, County gaol
Goddard Ebenr. clerk, Gas works
Godbold Mrs Maria, 4 Berners st
Gooch Lieut Geo. Woodbridge road
Gooch Jas.gent. 11 St Margaret's ter
Good Rev Alex. 8 Adelphi place
Goodchild Mrs Han. Upper Brook st
Goodchild Wm. gent. St Helen's st
Gooding Mrs Ann, St Peter's street
Gooding Mrs Constantia, Cox lane
Gooding Nathl. gent. Back Hamlet
GoodingMrsRebecca,Woodbridge rd
Gooding Mrs. Short lane
Gooding Samuel Ralph, relieving officer, New street
Goose Mrs Eliz. Mary, Queen street
Goose Mrs & Miss Sarah, Berners st
GoslingWm.whitesmith; h St John st
Gower Charles Foote, soap manfr. and Miss Mary Ann, *Nova Scotia*
Gowing Thos. Shave, gent. Mount
Graham Miss My. 4 St George's ter
Graves Rt. gent. 3 Belvidere terrace
Griffiths Capt. 3 St George's terrace
Groome David, bookkeeper, Quay st
Gross Charles, junior, surveyor of taxes, Lower Brook street
Gunn Mrs My. Ann, Victoria street
Hadcraft William, parish clerk, St Matthew's lane
Hagg Wm. clothes dealer; house Upper Brook street
Haill Mrs Susan, Norwich road
Haines Major John, Berners street
Hamblin Mr Benj. Garway, Wykes Bishop street
Hamilton Mrs My Ann, Low hill hs
HanbyHoward,shopmn.St Helen's st
Hanmer MrsCharlotte, 12 Albert ter
Harbur Charles A. agent ; house Foundation street
Harbur Rev Wm. incumbent of St Mary Quay, Foundation street
Harcourt John, gent. Coleman st
Hardy Theophilus, plumber ; house Orwell place
Harmer John Dalton, druggist ; house Carr street
Harmer George Joseph, registrar of births and deaths, and collector of rates, New street
Harrison Jas lockkeeper, Lock rd

Harrison Miss Sarah, St Nicholas st
Hart Mr John, *Cold Dunghills*
Harvey Edwd. clerk of St Stephen's, Turret lane
Hatch Mr James, St Margaret's st
Hatton John, chief constable of the Suffolk police, Tanner's lane
Hawkins Jno. paver, Tower ditches
Hawke George, coachman, 1 St Matthew's terrace
HaywardHy.Daines,gent.Berners st
Hayward Mrs Lucy, midwife,Cox ln
Head Mrs Hannah Maria, 12 St Margaret's street
Head Jeremiah, Esq. *Hill house*
Head John, gent. 2 Adelphi place
Heath Benjamin, gent. Stoke street
Hewes Mr Edmund, Coyte's garden
Hewes Frdk. police, Tower ditches
Hewes Mr James, St Matthew's st
Hill James, gent. St Nicholas st
Hockley Major Thomas Henry, St Matthew's street
Hodges Mr James, Cottage place
Hodgson Alfred Gowing, pawn-broker ; house Fore street
Holden Mrs Catherine, High street
Holker Mr Ralph, StMatthew's lane
Hooper Wm. tide surveyor, Bell lane
Hopkins Thomas, clerk, West row
Howard MrsEliz.4 St Margaret's ter
Howard Miss Mary, Norwich road
Howes Mrs Ann, Trafalgar buildings
Howlett Mrs Hannah, Norwich rd
Howorth Rev Wm. Westgate street
Hudson Rd. Sl. law stationer, Elm st
Hughes Mrs Jane, Coleman street
Hunt Mrs Ann, Berners street
Hunt Mrs Mary, St Helen's street
Hunt Mrs Mary, Norwich road
Hunt Chas. North, solicitor ; house 11 Albert terrace
Hutchinson Wm. regr. & poor rate collr. for St Margaret's District, and assessor and collector of taxes, St Helen's street
Isaacs Harris, rabbi, Fore street
Innes Misses Catherine & Charlotte, Westgate street
Jackson Rev Stephen, Halifax
Jacobs Mrs Sarah, Friar's street
Jaques Mrs My. Ann, St Peter's st
Jay Mrs Philippa, Norwich road
Jeckell Mr Robt. Woodbridge road
Jennings Mrs Sarah, Foundation st
JobsonJph.water bailiff,St Clement's

Johnson Edward Amond, governor, County gaol
Johuson Mr James, Norwich road
Johnson Mr Stephen, 30 Borough rd
Joiner Wm. shopman, High street
Jones Mrs Jane, 7 Globe lane
Josselyn Mrs Sarah, St Matthew's st
Julian Mr Ezekiel, 9 Victoria ter
Kemball Hammond, mert. Norwich rd
Kemball Mr John, 4 St Matthew's ter
Kemball Richd. gent. 5 Globe lane
Kemball Wm. glass agent, Upper Brook street
Kemp Mrs Sophia, Norwich road
Kerridge Mr George, Corn hill
Kerridge Mrs Sarah, St John street
Kewell John, bank clerk, Priory st
Kilburn Miss Eliz. Falcon street
Kimble Benj. compositor, Cox lane
King Mrs Ann, *The Folly*
King Mrs Mary, Friar's cottage
King Robert, gent. 2 Halifax row
King Wm. clerk, Lower Brook st
Kingsbury Wm. gent. 8 Albert ter
Klopfer Mrs Alethea, Friar's road
Knight Mr John, Handford street
Lacey Robert, gent. Albion hill
Lake Mrs Mary, Soane street
Lane Wm. Esq. collector of customs, and Swedish and Norwegian vice-consul, St Peter's street
Last Benj. shopman, St John st
Lay Mrs Eliz. Foundation street
Lay Mr Thomas, 16 Victoria terrace
Layton Mrs Mary Ann, Elm street
Leach John Dennington, gent. *Rose hill cottage*
Leath Thomas Rand, permit writer, Woodbridge road
Lee Mrs Hannah, Upper Orwell st
Leger Rev Wm. Nassau, B.A. incumbent of St Mary Tower, Albert cottage, Panorama
Leggett Wm. gent. Berners street
Lester Miss My. Ann, Berners st
Leverett Hy. gent. St Matthew's st
Levett Nelson Trafalgar, librarian, Providence street
Ling Wm. gent. Bramford road
Littlewood Mrs Chtte. 10 St Mgt's. ter
Lloyd John, sweep, St Mgt.'s ditches
Long Robert, relieving officer, Black Horse lane
Lott Mr John, Friars street
Lucock Fras. gent. New town
Lumsden Rev Hy. Thos. B.A. incumbent of St Peter's, Bell lane

Maitland Adam, travlr. St Helen's st
Manning John, relvng. officer, Carr st
Margets Mr Thos. Barclay street
Marriott Mrs M. D., Woodbridge rd
Marston Mrs My. Ann, Berners st
Marten Robt. sweep, Fore hamlet
Martin Misses, Coleman's villas
Mason Rev Thomas, incumbent of Culpho; house Carr street
Mason Mrs Mary, Lwr. Orwell st
Mason Mrs Sarah, Victoria street
Mason Wm. pawnbroker, Fore st
Mason Wm. gent. 7 Priory place
Mason Wm. Carrington, police sergeant, Tower ditches
Matthews Mrs Sarah, New street
Maw John, gent. St Margaret's ter
May Benj. excise, Bird's gardens
May Wm. gent. Lower Brook street
McDougall Lieut. Thos. 6 Albert ter
McFarlane Mrs My. A. 2 St Mary's ter
McKenzie John, gent. 11 Albert ter
Miller John, sen. gent. Butter mkt
Minter Mrs Eliza, High street
Mitchinson Mrs Margt. Woodbdg. rd
Molyneaux Mr Geo. Barclay street
Moor Mrs Eliz. Fore street
Morson John, supervisor, Duke st
Moyse Mrs Sarah, 2 Globe lane
Mudd Geo. collector of water rent, Berners street
Mulley Mrs Eliz. Friar street
Mulliner Mrs Eliz. Woodbridge rd
Munro Robt. barrack serjeant, Bks
Murray Rev George, A.M. incbt. of St Margt's; h St Margaret's pl
Musgrave Miss Charlte. London rd
Naunton Geo. prntr. Gooding's gdn
Neale Jas. Esq. post office surveyor, Carr street
Neeve Mrs Eliz. St Nicholas street
Newson Mr Samuel, Fore street
Nicolson Alex. Fras. draper; house Norwich road
Notcutt Rev Wm. (Indpt.) Tacket st
Nottidge Rev John Thos. A.M. rector of St Clement's, St Helen's st
Nunn Rev Jas. (Baptist.) Halifax
Nunn Jas. town crier, Victoria st
Nunn Jph. sweep, St Helen's st
Nunn Wm. Henry, Green yard lane
O'Neil Rev Jas. (Cath.) 7 Vict. ter
Orford Rev Jas. M.A. chaplain to the Ipswich Union, Queen street
Orford John, gent. *Brokes Hall*
Ottywill Zach. coachmaker, St Matthew's street

Owen Jph. bank clerk, Coleman st

Page Benj. Wm. Admiral of the Blue, Tower street

Page Enos, ship bldr. St Clement's st

Parish Frdk. musician, Church lane

Parkington Miss Sar. Globe lane

Parkhirst Miss Alice, Back Hamlet

Parkyn Rev Nathl. Assn. Meth.) St Helen's street

Pattison Lilly, tide waiter, 3 Foundation street

Paston Benj. musician, School st

Patteson Mrs. Tower Church yard

Paul Rt. wharfinger; h Woodbdg. rd

Payne Mrs Frances, St Peter's st

Payne Horace, gent. 3 Adelphi pl

Peacock Jno. gent. St. Margaret's gr

Pearce Robt. R. editor, St George's ter

Pennington Mrs Amy, Berners street

Pepper Mr Jno. 2 St Matthew's ter

Perry Robert, gent. Berners street

Phillips Henry, Esq. *Stoke Park*

Pigg Charles, excise, Victoria street

Pinkney Jno. coachmn. St Peter's st

Pipe Mr William, Tavern street

Pitcairn Miss Sus. 2 Albert terrace

Pitcher John, surgeon, h. Fore street

Pitts Wm. T. traveller, 5 Priory pl

Pollard Wm. miller, Green yard

Poppey Mrs Sarah, Tower ditches

Porter Richd. gent. Lower Brook st

Posford Mrs Eliz. 1 St Matthew's ter

Potter Geo. Hall, collector of dock dues, College street

Powell Mrs Ann, Upper Brook st

Pratt Mr Joseph, Rope lane

Prentice Mrs Pamela, Woodbdg. rd

Quilter John, gent. 2 Belvidere ter

Quinten, J. A. printer, 12 Vict. ter

Ram James, Esq. barrister, Silent st

Ramplen Stepn. gent. Gt. Whip st

Ramsay, Capt. Rt. R.N. Berners st

Rance Mrs My. Ann, Handford st

Randall Ts. Garwood, compr. Mount

Ransome Allen, ironfounder; house St Peter's street

Ransome Fredk. ironfounder; house Carr street

Ransome Geo. druggist; h Northgate street

Ransome Jas. ironfndr; h *Rushmere*

Ransome Rt. ironfndr; h Norwich rd

Ranson Robt. paper manufacturer, Anglesey mills

Ranson Mrs Sarah, Berners street

Ray Shepherd, Esq. St Helen's st

Ray Wm. Jarrold, draper; house Tavern street

Raynham Ambrose, cattle salesman, Woodbridge road

Read John, traveller, Orford street

Read Mr Thomas, Norwich road

Read Wm. shipbuilder; h Halifax

Reedman Wm. excise officer, St Margaret's green

Reeve Rev John Wm. M.A., incumbent of Trinity Church, Church st

Reeve Mrs Sophia, Lower Brook st

Reeve Mrs. Foundation street

Revett John, coachman, 12 Berners st

Revett John, gentleman, Fore street

Ridley Geo. wine mert; h Fore st

Ridley Hy. wine mert; h London rd

Ridley John, gent. St Peter's street

Ridley Wm. wine mert; h Fore st

Ringrose Mrs Sarah, Rope lane

Rist Robert, gent. 10 Adelphi place

Rivers Mrs Ann Maria, *Caldwell hs*

Rivis Mrs Ann, St Clement's st

Roberts Wm. accompt. College st

Roberts Mr Wm. Currier's lane

Robinson Mr John, Halifax row

Roddam Mrs My. St Clement's st

Rodwell Wm. solr; h Westgate st

Roope George, barrack master, St Matthew's street

Roper Sophia, nurse, Cox lane

Rust Mr John, College street

Sage Mrs & Miss Ann, St Peter's st

Sampson John, gent. 7 Belvidere ter

Samson Ths. book agt. St Matt's ter

Saul Tom, coachman, Woodbdg. rd

Saxe F. gent. 1 Belvidere terrace

Sayer Mrs Harriet, Friars st

Scarlett Robt. gent. College street

Scroggins Mr Wm. Norwich road

Scotchmer Hy. whsman. Bk. Hamlet

Scott Eliz. plumber; h Fore street

Scott Capt Thomas, 6 Belvidere ter

Scrutton George, tide waiter

Seagrave G. coachman, Woodbdg. rd

Seaman John, naturalist, Carr st

Seekamp Mrs F. Norwich road

Selsby Mrs Chas. Providence street

Sewell Jas. clerk, Woodbridge road

Sharman Mrs Mary, Berners street

Shaw Jas. surgn. Belle vue Asylum

Sheldrake Mrs Mary, matron, East Suffolk Hospital

Sheppard Thos. clerk, Norwich road

Sheppard Nelson, model maker, Woodbridge road

Shriber Wm. Fdk. Esq. *Round Wood*

Shreve Wm. Henry, excise officer, Tower Churchyard

SibleyMiss Urania, medicine vendor, Globe lane

Silbourne Miss Sar. 11 Halifax

Simpson Lieut Jas. Currier's lane

Simpson Mrs Susanna, Berners st

Singleton Mr Thomas, St Helen's st

Smart Misses, 8 St Margaret's ter

Smart Mrs Mary Ann, Handford st

Smith Edw. sweep, Black Horse in

Smith Mrs Eliz. Westrow cottages

Smith Geo. Jno. clothier, Butter mkt

Smith Miss Hannah Maria, Lower Brook street

Smith James, gent. Berners street

Smith James, superintendent of police, Victoria street

Smith John, clerk, Victoria street

Smith Samuel, harbour and pilot master, Duke street

Smyth James, bank clerk, London rd

Smyth Jph Burch, Esq. *Orwell lodge*

Smyth Wm. clerk, High street

Snowling Mr Wm. 13 Borough road

Soley Geo. Thomas, landing waiter, Woodbridge road

Soundy Josiah, tobacco manufactr; house Orwell place

Sparks Miss Hannah, Falcon st

Sparrowe Jno. Newman, gent. London road

Sporle Mr George, Handford street

Sporle Mr Joseph, Albion hill

Sporle Saml. mate, Gt. Whip street

Sprigg Rev James, (Bapt.) Tuddenham road

Squire Lwnce. Esq. Woodbridge rd

St Felix Mons de, teacher of French, 5 High street

Stannard Sophia, upholsteress, Portman street

Stearn Thos. plumber, Barclay st

Stebbing Miss Susan, Orwell place

Stevens Mrs My. Ann, Tower lodge

Strahan Miss Eliz. 6 Priory place

Strait George, bath keeper, Quay st

Stuart Charles, printer, Elm street

Sutton Mrs Eliz. Gt. Whip street

Symonds Saml. sweep, Angel lane

Taylor Robinson, reporter, Berners st

Taylor Saml. coachmn. Woodbdg. rd

Temple Mrs Amelia, Handford st

Thacker John, R.N. Woodbridge rd

Thomas Mrs Rebecca, Friars st

Thomas Rev Thomas Felix, (Unit.) St Nicholas street

Thompson Mrs Eliza, West row

Thornbory David, civil engineer, &c. 13 Albert terrace

Tovell Mrs Judith, Tacket street

Trall Mr. 7 Adelphi place

Tunmer Chas. turnkey, Boro' Gaol

Tunney Mrs Jane, Berners street

Tunney Rev John Robert, L.L.B. chaplain to County Goal, Foundation street

Turner Miss Eliz. London road

Turner Major Michael, Westgate st

Vachell Mrs Cath. 6 Adelphi place

Vertue Edw. clerk, Handford road

Vesey Mrs Sarah, Norwich road

Wade Mrs Martha, 6 Borough road

Ward Ebzr. shopman, Cox lane

Ward Mrs Eliza, 11 Berners street

Ward Mrs Eliz. St Nicholas street

Ward Mrs Mary, 4 Victoria ter

Warn Jph. postman, Tower ditches

Waspe Mrs Eliz. Woodbridge road

Watson Alex. gent. 1 Haills ter

Watson Henry, registrar, and poor rate collector, Norwich road

Webb Rev Jas. (Bapt.) Stoke green

Webster Mrs Sarah, 4 Halifax

Weeding Nathl. harness polishing paste, &c. manfr. Woodbridge rd

Welch Robt. R.N. 8 Globe lane

Wenn Mrs Hannah, Berners street

Wenn Percy Jno. clerk, Norwich rd

West Edward, gent. Norwich road

West Mrs Sarah, Elm street

West Mr Wm. West row cottages

White Mr Samuel, Church street

White Mrs Sarah, Globe lane

Whitehead Rev Rt. 6 St Margt.'s ter

Whitehead Mr Wm. Globe lane

Whitby Rev John, Friars road

Williams John, gent. Norwich road

Williams Thos. excise, St Helen's st

Wilson Mrs My.Ann, 5 Belvidere ter

Wilson Miss My. Ann, College st

Windsor Edw. Chas. gent. Stoke gn

Wodderspoon John, reporter, 9 Adelphi place

Wood Mrs Mary, Woodbridge rd

Woodgate Mrs Eliz. 4 Adelphi pl

Woodhouse Rev Walter Webb, M.A. Short lane

Woods Mrs Miriam, Orford street

Worby Wm. engineer, Duke street

Worthey Mrs Sar. 6 Victoria ter

Wright David, pilot, Fore hamlet

Wright John, gent. Norwich road

Wright Mrs Lucy, St Helen's st

Wright Saml. John, millwright; h St Helen's street
Wroth Mr John, Lower Brook street
Young Rev Benj. incumbent of Tuddenham, Woodbridge road

ACADEMIES.
*Marked * take Boarders.*

Andrews Maria, Stoke street
Archer Rebecca, Woodbridge road
Bacon Amy, Tanners lane
*Batchelor Sarah, Berners street
Barton Mary Ann, 5 Borough road
Beal Mary Ann, St Margaret's gn
*Blagrove Mrs Ruth, Northgate st
* Bowman Mrs Edmund Burkitt, Lower Brook street
Brady Miss, Upper Brook street
Bradlaugh Lewis, Duke street
Brothers Mary Ann, Lawrence st
*Buck Joseph, Berners street
*Buck Mary, St Helen's st
Buck Jph. Smith, Norwich road
Burman Hannah, Church street
Burrage Mrs & Miss My. Silent st
Bushby Sarah, Quay street
*Buxton Henry, Carr street
Chapman Hannah, St Matthew st
Chisnall Sarah, Gooding's gardens
*Christ's Hospital,*Thos.Potter Howe, Great Whip street
*Codd Elizabeth, Soane street
Cooper Elizabeth, 8 Princes street
Cork Daniel S. Rose ln; h Queen st
Cundy Martha, Portman street
Cutting Eliz. St Nicholas street
*Doughty Sophia, Lower Brook st
Ennew Julia, Silent street
Fell Mary, Back hamlet
*Foster Louisa, Elm street
Franks Jas. *(navigation,)* Elm st
Giles Jacob, Mount
Garrod Susan, Cox lane
Girls' Free, My. Clarke, St Helen's
Godbold Jno. Friars st; h College st
Gooding Elizabeth, Turret lane
Grammar School, Foundation street, *Rev John Fenwick, B.A.
Green Gown, (girls',) Fore street; Lydia Smith
Grey Coat Boys' & Blue Coat Girls', James Franks and Mary Leggett, Currier's lane
*Groom Ann, London road
*Harston Rev Edw. St Stephen's
Hempson Jph. Benj. Victoria street
Humfrey Eliz. St Nicholas street
Hutchins Susanna, St John street

Jacob Eleanor, Norwich road
Kedgley Robert, Potter st; h Fore st
Kingsford John, Foundry road
Kitton Mary, St Matthew's street
Lancasterian, (Boys',) Crown street, Jas. Lankester; *Girls',* Foundation street, Harriet Bennett
Limmer Ann, Back street
Long Daniel, St Helen's street
Middleditch Hanh. Eliz. Berners street
Moscroft Lucy (French,) Orwell pl
National School (Boys',) Thursby's ln Henry Morley; *(Girls',)* Currier's lane, Mrs Franks
Orriss John, New street
Otzman Anna Maria, 7 Boro.' road
*Paglar Charles, Elm street
Paxman Wm. St Nicholas st; house 2 Priory place
*Payne My. Ann, St Peter's street
Pite Eliz. St Nicholas street
*Powell Sar. Ann, St Peter's street
St Clement's Schools, David st, Rt. Nottidge Cade & Emma Wedgery
St Peter's Boys, Saml. Stokes, St Peter's street
St Stephen's Girls, Sus. Bird, St Stephen's Church yard
Seaman Eliz. and Mahew Frances, 5 Adelphi place
*Smart Misses, Church street
*Smith Caroline & Sisters, Church st
Stannard Tryphena, St Nicholas st
Stead Charles, Fore street
Tempany Misses, Adelphi place
Thurlow My. Ann, Woodbridge rd
Thrower Robert, Barclay street
Trinity Church School, Fore Hamlet, Jp. Pardoe & Emily Scotchmer
Walford Jane, Black Horse lane
*Watson Charles, Berner's street
Wolton My. Ann, St Helen's street
* Woodcock Ann Sus. Elm street

AGENTS.
*Marked * are Estate, † Commission, and ‡ Ship Agents.*

†Akers Lieut. Thos. R.N. (Patent Marine Glue,) St Peter's street
†Bailey Rt., St Nicholas street
†‡Baldock Stephen, Salthouse lane; house St Clement's street
*Chamberlain Thos. Handford st
†Cornell Benjamin, Quay street
*Doust George, Carr street
†Ensor John Lott, Thoroughfare
*Garrod Robert, Butter market
*Haill Jas. St Matthew's street

*Parkes Saml. Wyatt, Corn hill
†‡Wilkinson Wm. & Co. Dockside ;
  house Victoria street
    Agricultural Implement Mfrs.
Ransome T. R. & A. Orwell works
  and St Margaret's

ARCHITECTS.
(And Land & Building Surveyors.)
Backhouse Benj. Norwich road
Clark John Medland, Upr. Brook st ;
  house Orwell cottage
Harvey Fredk. Hatton court
Mason Geo. jun. Lower Brook st ;
  house Coleman's villas
RibbansWm.Parkes, St Matthew's st
White Edward, 15 Berners street
Whiting John *(county surveyor,)*
  Crown street

ARTISTS
(And Teachers of Drawing.)
Davy Hy. (author of Architectural
  Antiquities,) Globe lane
Nursey Claude Lorraine, Berners st
Smart John, Elm street
Smith Edward, New Town
Wallis Joshua (landscape,) Halifax
Williams Wm. (photographic por-
  trait,) Berners street

ATTORNEYS.
Brame Benjamin, Bank street
Bunn Henry, Elm street
Bunn Reeve and Son, Westgate st
Burton Charles, Berners street
Cobbold Alfred (& notary) Tower st
Daniel Woodroofe, Elm street
Dunnington John, Lower Brook st
  (master in Chancery and comssr.
  for taking acknowledgments of
  married women, and affidavits in
  Courts of Queen's Bench, &c.)
Ewington Sir Wm., Thoroughfare ;
  h *Woodbridge*, (coroner for Lib. of
  Duchy of Lancaster)
Galsworthy Robert, Carr street
Grimsey Thos. St Nicholas street
  (union clerk and sup. regr.)
Gross Chas. Lower Brook st (county
  coroner and clerk to Comssrs. of
  taxes, &c)
Gross John, Silent street
HammondWm. Hatton court, (coun-
  ty court clerk, &c)
Hunt Wm. Powell, St Matthew's st
Jackaman Simon Batley, Silent st.
  (coroner for the borough)
Josselyn George, Tower street
Lawrance Eleazar, Coleman street,

  (clerk to the magistrates, and co-
  roner for Dk. of Norfolk's Liberty)
Long Peter Bartw. Queen st. (comssr.
  for taking ackmts. of married wo-
  men, and clerk to dock comssrs.)
Notcutt Stephen Abbott, sen. West-
  gate street
Notcutt Stephen Abbott, jun. (town
  clerk,) Westgate street
Porter Rd. Wm. Fore street
Pownall Edward, Lower Brook st
Pretyman Charles, Silent street
Rodwell, Steward, and Bacon, Pro-
  vidence street
Sparrowe John Eddowes, (county
  coroner,) Butter market
Steward Chas. (dep. registrar of the
  Archdeaconry of Suffolk,) Provi-
  dence street ; house *Wherstead*
Walford Desborough, 2 Mattw's. ter

AUCTIONEERS.
Berryman Thomas, King street
Bransby Hy. Knevett, Carr street
Colchester Benj. & Son, Westgate st
Garrod Robt. Butter market
Haill Jas. (and comssr. for taking
  special bail) St Matthew's street
McPherson Donald, Green yard
Randall Wm. Upper Orwell street
Ross Thos. Baldock, St. Clement's
  street and Westgate street

BAKERS & FLOUR DLRS.
*Marked * are Confectioners also.*
Bailey Thos. (army baker) Lady ln
Black Edmund, St Nicholas street
Bloomfield James, Duke street
Bruce Westhorp C., Dog's head ln
Carter Jonathan, Stoke street
Cattermole Wm. Victoria street
Chaplin Thomas, Norwich road
Church John, St Helen's street
*Clarke James, Eagle street
Double John, New Town
Elliston Edward, Turret lane
Ellison Wm. Mount street
Feek John, Friars' road
Feek Michael, Upper Orwell street
*Fulcher Joseph, Fore hamlet
Funnel James, Lower Orwell street
Garnham Wm. Halifax
Girling James, Upper Orwell street
Girling Robert, East street
Goreham Edward, New street
Green Elijah, Wykes Bishop street
Greenleaf James, St Clement's st
Greenleaf James, Fore street

Hancock Timy. Thos., and Son, 4
　Carr street & 1 St Nicholas street
Hewes James, St Matthew's street
Howgego Jermh. St Margaret's plane
Hunt John, St Peter's street
Kent Susanna, Norwich road
Kitton Harvey Rd. Norwich road
Mann Louisa, Bell lane
Matham Robert, Rope lane
Mayhew James, 27 Borough road
*Mixer Robert, Westgate st
Norman Henry, Handford street
Oxborrow Edmund, St Margaret's st
*Oxborrow James, Lawrence street
Page Robert, Quay street
Parish John, St Margaret's street
Parker Joseph, St Matthew's street
Perryman Thos. St Matthew's st
Platt Frances, Elm street
Rose George, Friars' street
Scarlett Charles, St Helen's street
Shreeve Thomas, Fore street
Snell Daniel, Mount
Snell John, Back Hamlet
Snell John, jun. Fore Hamlet
Snell Robert, Barclay street
Studd Hy. Ralph, Black horse lane
*Thompson Robert, Tavern street
Todd Edwin, Stoke street
*Ward John, Corn hill
Whitehead Wm. Rope lane and St
　Margaret's plane
*Wilkinson Thomas, Fore street
Wood James, Woodbridge road

BANKERS.

Alexanders & Co. Bank st & Need-
　ham market (draw on Barnetts,
　Hoare, and Co.)
Bacon, Cobbold, Rodwell, and Cob-
　bold, Tavern street, (draw on Sir
　R. C. Glyn and Co.)
National Provincial Bank of Eng-
　land, Butter market, (draw on Lon-
　don Joint Stock Bank.)　Mr. Hy.
　Miller, *agent*
Suffolk Banking Co. Elm st. (draw
　on London and Westminster Bank.)
　Mr. Wm. Ingelow, manager
Ipswich Provident Savings' Bank,
　(open Friday from 10 to 1.)　Mr.
　Jeremiah Head, *cashier*, and Mr.
　Wm. Cheselden, *actuary*
Ipswich & Suffolk Savings' Bank,
　Corn hill, (open Wed. from 11 to 1
　o'clock.　R. W. Porter and S. B.
　Chapman, *secretaries*

BASKET MAKERS.

Barns Eliza, St Peter's street
Jackson Wm. Bridge street, West
Noble James, Woodbridge road
Osborne Samuel, Fore street
Smith Eleanor, St Matthew's street
Symonds John, Currier's lane
Tooke John, Norwich road

BLACKSMITHS.

Archer George, Upper Orwell st
Avis Thomas, Eagle street
Bacon Chas. Read, St Margaret's pln
Barton Richard, Stoke street
Betts Lott, Westgate street
Blomfield Nimrod, St Margaret's st
Bradbrook James, Carr street
Chaplin Joseph, Back street
Cooper and Hurwood, Salthouse ln
Durrant Henry, Tower ditches
Garwood Sl. & Michl. Norwich rd
Garwood Ths. Bull yard; h Quay st
Harvey Saml. Dove yd. St Helen's st
Hayward Edward, Fore street
Kent Thomas, Friars' road
Knights Jas. (shipsmith) Salthouse ln
Oxborrow Edward, Dog's head lane
Page John, Great Whip street
Tydeman Wm. Bell lane
Webb Saml. jun. Fore Hamlet

BOOKBINDERS.

Dowsing Daniel, Queen street
Parker Joseph, St Stephen's lane

BOOKSELLERS, STATION-ERS, PRINTERS, & BINDERS.
*Marked * are Printers only.*

Burton Jph. Mumford, Tavern st
Conder James, Butter market
Cowell Saml. Harrison, Butter mkt
Deck Robert, Corn hill
Dorkin Anthony, Upper Brook st
Hunt Robt. (music dlr.) Tavern st
*Jackson Postle, *Journal Office*, But-
　ter market
*King John, *Chronicle Office*, Ta-
　vern street
Morley Dd. Queen st & Butter mkt
Page Joshua, Fore street
Pask Chas. Alfred, (stationer & peri-
　odical agent) Norwich road
Pawsey Fredk. Butter market
*Piper Stph. *Express Office*, Butter mkt
Read Jas. (old and new) Corn hill
Rainer John Smith, (stationer and
　machine ruler,) Tacket street
Root Robt. Westgate street
Scoggins John, Orwell place
Shalders James, Westgate street

BOOT & SHOE MAKERS.

Bacon John, Cox lane
Bailey Wm. Woodbridge road
Baker Robt. Louis, Rope lane
Barker James, Rope lane
Bennett Wm. Church street
Bennett Wm. Lower Brook street
Blake Henry, Fore street
Blasby Wm. St Matthew's street
Brett Michl. Geo. Tavern street
Bristo James, Carr street
Brummit Geo. St Helen's street
Buckingham Jonathan, Tavern st
Burch Jeremiah, College street
Carr John, Lawrence street
Choat John, Butter market
Clarke Henry, King street
Clarke John Stanford, Fore street
Clarke Joseph, Butter market
Clarke Joseph, 16 Mill street
Clarke Robt. St Stephen's street
Clarke Robert, College street
Clarke Wm. Upper Orwell street
Clarke Wm. jun. Fore street
Cole Benj. Upper Orwell street
Cook Edw. Wm. Rope lane
Cook George, Back street
Cook Jonathan, Rope lane
Cook Robert, Cox lane
Cooper Thos. Lower Orwell street
Cooper Jas. Little Barclay street
Cooper John, Carr street
Cooper Rt. Lavender, Woodbdg. rd
Crapnell Jas. Tower Church yard
Creswell James, Queen street
Damant James, Westgate street
Day Edward, Whitton
Day Robt. Handford street
Day Thos. St Stephen's lane
Dennis Saml. Fras. College street
Dobson Daniel, Cold Dunghills
Emmett Peter, Stoke street
Felby James, East street
Finney Robert, Albion place
Fox Philip, Green yard lane
Fox Salter, St Nicholas street
Fox Salter, jun. Woodbridge road
Freeman Wm. St Helen's street
Fulcher Wm. Orford street
Fuller Wm. Bell lane
Garrard Wm. Back Hamlet
Goodchild Charles, Fore street
Goslin John, Black horse lane
Green Daniel, Halifax row
Hall Wm. College street
Harrison Henry, St Nicholas street
Harrison Wm. Palmer, Upr. Brook st

Holden John, Norwich road
Howitt James, Cottage place
Hibbard Thos. (list shoe,) New st
Johnson Robt. Tacket street
Johnson Wm. Fore street
King Richard, Oak lane
Mayhew Wm. St Helen's street
Moore John, John street
Osborn Henry, Falcon street
Osborn Roger, Tavern street
Osborn Samuel, Church lane
Parker James, Rope lane
Rayner John, Fore Hamlet
Reeve Edward, Black horse lane
Richmond Jas. Upper Orwell street
Rivers Benj. Coytes' gardens
Robinson James, Lady lane
Robinson Thomas, Rope lane
Russell John, Foundry road
Scrutton Edmund, King street
Sewell James, Fore street
Sheldrake John, Carr street
Sheldrake Wm. Hy. Tavern street
Ship John, St James's street
Simpson James, St Lawrence street
Smith John, Coytes' gardens
Smyth George, St. Peter's street
Sporle George, Gt Whip street
Sporle Jabez, Tavern street
Sporle Joseph, Stoke street
Stannard Saml. Lower Orwell st
Stearn Thomas, Handford street
Stevens Robt. Carr st. and Back st
Stokes Samuel, Back Hamlet
Taylor Thomas, East street
Turner Wm. Stoke street
Tye James, Victoria street
Upson Thomas, Bramford road
Ward Jonth. St Margaret's green
Websdale Wm. St Margaret's green
Wiles Samuel, Duke street
Wells Chas. Lucas, Stoke green
Wilkinson Thos. Tower Church yd
Wilson John, Cook row
Wright George, St Helen's street
Youngs George, Barclay street
Youngs Samuel, Cox lane

BRAZIERS & TINNERS.
See also Ironmongers.

Barker Wm. St Margaret's street
Barnard Wm. Salthouse street
Baxter Joseph, Rope lane
Bevan Geo. Wm. St Helen's street
Cook Isaac, Fore Hamlet
Harvey Joseph, Lower Orwell st
Thurston John, Upper Orwell st

BREWERS.
Bowman Bobert Falcon street
Chaplin Wm. Jackson, Crown lane
Cobbold John, Cliff Brewery
Fisk Robert, Quay street
Ridley H. G. & W. Fore st & Mill pl
Whimper Nathl. St Margaret's grn

BRICKLAYERS & PLASTRS.
Bennett John and Son, Back street
Bird Bloss, Norwich road
Bird Joseph, Orford street
Blasby Benjamin, Globe lane
Borrett Wm. Currier's lane
Butcher Thos. 12 Princes street
Canham Simon, Back Hamlet
Dale Samuel, Bell lane
Dale Samuel, jun. Tanner's lane
Denham Daniel, Crown street
Ellis George, Friars' street
Fisk Henry, Rope lane
Fisk Wm. 5 Princes street
Fisk Wm. Cox lane
Garnham Wm. New Town
Goddard John, Wykes Bishop street
Green Thos. jun. Northgate street
Green Thomas, Globe lane
Grimwood Charles, Tuddenham rd
Hurricks Henry, Friars' road
Jenkines Wm. St Peter's street
Lawrence Joshua, Star lane
Lawrence Josiah, Woodbridge road
Morfey James, Stoke street
Morfey Wm. Norwich road
Mulley George, Back street
Neale Thomas, Rope lane
Parker Wm. Silent street
Pells John, Borough road
Rowland John, Duke street
Roy John, Fore Hamlet
Scarlett Henry, Rose lane
Trew John, Tower ditches
Trew Robert, Fore Hamlet
Trew Samuel, Asylum yard
Trew Thomas, Little King street
Trott Henry, Coytes' gardens

BRICKMAKERS.
Canham Noah Clark, Long lane
Cobbold John, Duke street
Fisk Francis, St Helen's street
Mason Geo. (Suffolk white,) Wood-
    bridge rd; house Coleman's villas
Thorndike Jas. Stoke; h Silent street
Wells Lepper Harry, St Helen's st

BRUSH MAKERS.
Bishop Edward Wilmott, Falcon st
Bullett Frederick, Upper Orwell st

BUTCHERS.
*Marked * are Pork Butchers.*
(Nkt. signifies New Market.)
Andrews Alfd. 7 Nkt.; h Crown st
*Andrews Jacob, St. Peter's street
Andrews John, 4 Nkt. & Butter mkt
Baker Eliza, Bridge street
Baker John, Queen street
Baker Rd. Wm. St. Margaret's st
Baker Thos. Nkt.; h Friars' street
*Bass Isaac, Back Hamlet
Beard Isaac, 2 Nkt.; h Northgate
Beard Mary Ann, Tavern street
Beard Philip, St Peter's street
Bevan Edward, Major's corner
Bevan Jas. 3 Nkt. & Butter market
Bush John, 9 Nkt.; h Tanner's lane
Canham Wm. 15 Upper Brook street
Capon James, Wykes Bishop street
Chenery John, Westgate street
Clarke Joseph, New Town
Cockerell John, Salthouse street
*Cocksedge Robert, Cox lane
*Cox John, Handford street
*Cox Samuel, St Matthew's street
Curtis Wm. Thoroughfare
Death Wm. Nkt.; h 3 St John st
Farthing Geo. 14 Nkt.; h Carr st
Farthing James, Carr street
Forman Saml. St Helen's street
Gilbert Stephen, Norwich road
Glading Geo. 70 Nkt. and Rope ln
Glading James, Fore Hamlet
Glading Wm. 78 Nkt. and Rope ln
*Herbert Samuel, Fore street
Holder Wm. 77 Nkt. & Currier's ln
Howland Sar. Ann, Fore street
Kent Wm. Henry, Mount street
King Martha, Queen street
King Stephen, Tacket street
King Stph. Burdett, Fore street
Leech Elizabeth, King street
*Lloyd James, Fore Hamlet
Lorking Jas. 47 Nkt.; h Currier's ln
*Mallow's Thos. Woodbridge road
Marshall Edmund, Tacket street
*Mudd John, Bell lane
Orvis Robert, Bell lane
Osborne Alfred, 17 Nkt.; h Lower
    Orwell street
*Pratt Charles, Queen street
Pratt Geo. 10 Nkt.; h Upr. Orwell st
Prentice Stephen, Elm street
*Scrivener John, St Helen's street
*Scrivener Henry, Black horse lane
Scott John, Fore Hamlet
Serjeant Charlotte, Victoria street

'Seager Thos. St Peter's street
Siggers Charles, Silent street
*Smith Edward, Upper Orwell st
Smith Wm. Upper Orwell street
Stevenson Rt. and Alfred, Crown st
Sturgeon Chtte. Nkt. and Victoria st
Suckermore John, Elm street
*Sutterfield John, Fore street
Symonds Robt. Lower Orwell street
Taylor Saml 82 Nkt. and Quay st
Turner James, St Margaret's plane
Upson Michl. 16 New market
Welham David, St Matthew's street
Wolsey Abraham W. Fore street
*Wood Thomas, St Stephen's lane
Woodsell Henry, Handford street

CABINET MAKERS AND
UPHOLSTERERS.

Chapman John, John street
Chilver Robt. 4 St John street
Collins James, Queen street
Doole Wm. St Stephen's lane
Downing James, Priory street
Dowsing James Frederick (chair,)
  Thurby's lane
Greenleaf Richard, Fore street
Hill Isaac, Cox lane
Howard Wm. St Helen's street
Iron Mark Oliver, Fore street
Jeffries Joseph, Queen street
Keningale Robt. Butter market
Kersey Rt. Saml. Upper Orwell st
Lambert Stephen, Friars' road
Last Joshua, Globe lane
Leverett James, Mount street
Leverett Richard, Globe lane
Leverett Wm. St Matthew's street
Maplestone Chas. Westgate street ;
  house Providence street
Mulley John, Upper Brook street
Newson John, St Peter's street
Phillips John, St Peter's street
Setterfield Thomas, Falcon street
Stannard Wm. Friars' street
Thorn Edward, Tower ditches
Thurston Joseph, Queen street
Tidman Thos. Northgate street
Tunmer James Robt. Orwell place

CARVERS & GILDERS.
*Marked * are Carvers only.*
*Constantine Henry, Norwich road
Jennings Thomas, Tacket street
Noble John, Eagle street
*Ringham Henry, Upr. Orwell st
Roe Owen, (looking glass mfr. and
  picture dlr.) Upper Brook street

Whittle Wm. St Matthew's street
CHEESE, &c., FACTORS.
See also Grocers.
Clark Peter, New mkt. ; h Green yd
Hannah John, St Stephen's lane ; h
  Silent street
May John, Common Quay ; house St
  Peter's street
May Wm. and Co. St Peter's wharf,
  (and *Yarmouth*)
Thorndike James, Common Quay ;
  house Silent street

CHEMISTS & DRUGGISTS.
*Marked * are Oil and Colourmen.*
Alderson Frederick, Westgate street
Chapman Samuel Belcher, Corn hill
Cole Wm. Tavern street
Cook Arthur Bott, 18 Upr. Brook st
Cornell Philip James, Tavern street
Eyre Alfred Benjamin, Tacket st
Fitch Wm. Stevenson, Butter mkt
*Harmer and Ransome, Carr street
Hooker Francis James, Butter mkt
Lambert Alfred (and British wine
  dealer,) St Matthew's street
*Ridley Henry, Fore street
Savage Charles, St Matthew's st
Sawer Wm. Fore street
Silverston Jas. Wm. St Nicholas st

CLOTHES BROKERS.
Ashford Alfred, Fore street
Barker Margaret, New street
Barker Sarah, Tacket street
Cook George & Co. Dog's head lane
Crisp and Smith, Butter market
Bugg Buckingham, St Margaret's gn
Goldsby Wm. New market lane
Goose Robert, St Helen's street
Goodwin Eliza, Lower Orwell street
Gray John, Rope lane
Holmes Thomas, Dog's head lane
Marsh Obadiah, Upper Orwell st
Mills Amy, Mount
Samuel Simon, Fore street

COACH BUILDERS.
Alderton John, St Nicholas street
Bennett Henry, St Clement's street
Catt Wm. St Matthew's street
Huunibell Timothy, Fore Hamlet
Hood Thomas, Friars' street
Kent Abraham, Tanners' lane ; h
  St James s reet
Manning John, Tower ditches
Ottywill and Allen, Mount
Quadling Edwin P. St Margaret's
Quadling Edwin, Bell lane

COACH PROPRIETORS.
Haxell James, Lower Brook street
Rowell John ; house *Whitton*
Waterhouse John, Tavern street

COAL MERCHANTS.
Aldrich Henry, Albion wharf
Alexanders and Co. Quay street
Bailey Robt. Crown & Sceptre wharf ; house St Nicholas street
Baldock Stephen, Salthouse street
Beaumont Wm. St Clement's street
Brook Timothy Sherwin, Friars' rd
Burman Edward, Turret lane
Byles Jeremiah & Co. College street
Chenery James, Great Whip street
Cobbold John, Fore street
Cowell Abraham Kersey, Fore st ; house Church street
Christie John, Salthouse street ; h Fore street
Fisk Robert, Quay street
Garrett Eliz. & Son, Salthouse st
Hardee James and Co. Quay street ; house Back street
Harrington Wm. Walter, Salthouse street ; house Back street
Hill John, Quay ; h Lower Orwell st
Pollard William, Fore street ; house Foundation street
Prentice Thos. & Co. Neptune Quay
Sheppard Alfred, Fore street
Stammers Samuel, Lady lane
Waspe Jonathan, Bridge street
Webster Joseph, Bell lane
Whitehead James, Tanner's lane ; house Globe lane

CONFECTIONERS, &c.
(See also Bakers.)
Collett Elizabeth, Carr street
Feck Wm. Tavern street
Fuller Wm. King street
Hancock Chas. & Son, Carr street
Jackson Wm. Falcon street
Marshall John (fruiterer,) 18 New market ; house Friars' street
McCredie Wm. Westgate street
Moore Samuel, Barclay street
Moyse Margaret, Tacket street
Phillips Mary, St Matthew's street
Pooley Wm. Upper Orwell street
Skoulding Joseph, Tavern street
Squires John, Carr street
Ward John, Corn hill
Wild Thos. (fruiterer,) Tavern st

COOPERS.
Alexander Henry, St Helen's st

Barns Eliza, (and hoop manfr.) St Peter's street and Westgate st
Fisk Wm. Tuddenham road
Howe Stephen, Foundry road
Ludbrook John, Gooding's gardens
Matt Jonathan, King street
Paternoster Henry, St Matthew's st
Peck Henry, Rose lane
Smith James, Back Hamlet
Warner Isc. Fore st. & Salthouse ln
Warner Wm. Long lane
Whybrew Wm. Tacket street

CORK CUTTERS.
Chaplin Wm. Jackson, Westgate st
Peck Shadrach, Cook row

CORN & FLOUR DEALERS.
Andrews Charles, Bell lane
Bailey Robert, St Nicholas street
Bantoft John, St Matthew's street
Bass(Isaac) & Bennett (Jno.) Quay st
Bradlaugh Wm. Friars' road
Bruce James, Back street
Buckingham John, Tanners' lane
Cook James, Fore street
Denny Samuel, 3 St Nicholas street
Fisher Benjamin, Currier's lane
Folkard John, St Clement's street
Fox Marjoram, Silent street
Giles Robert, Rope lane
Harris George, Upper Orwell st
Haywood Jas. Cooper, 18 Borough rd
Limmer John, Upper Brook street
Roper James, St Margaret's street
Sadler Andrew, Fore street
Sallows Robert, Corn hill ; house Bramford road
Scarle Robert Stephen, Carr street
Squirrell Wm. Obadiah, Silent st
Sykes John, St Margaret's green
Wallis —, St Mary Elms
Wooltorton Robert, St Matthew's st

CORN MERCHANTS.
Abbott Abraham, Park Cottage
Aldrich Henry, Albion wharf ; house St Matthew's street
Baldock Stephen, Salthouse lane
Byles Jeremiah and Co. College st
Cobbold John, Fore street ; house *Holywells*
Cowell Abraham Kersey, Fore st ; house Church street
Emerson Wm. Fore street
Pollard Wm. Fore st ; h Foundation st
Prentice Thos. & Co. Neptune quay
Sheppard Alfred, Fore street
Waspe Jonathan, Bridge street
Webster Joseph, Bell lane

CORN MILLERS.

Archer Wm. Woodbridge road
Bird Wm. Woodbridge road
Bruce Wm. Stoke green
Buckingham John (oatmeal manufacturer,) Tanners' lane
Buttrum Samuel, Halifax
Coleby Kincy, Mill place ; house St Margaret's plane
Dalton Ezra, Stoke street
Fison Jph. Tide Mill, Bridge street
Goodchild Jno. Stoke st ; h Bell lane
Haken and Ship, Woodbridge road
Moore Fenn, Bolton
Mudd George, Woodbridge road
Sallows Robert, Bramford road
Salter Wm. Folly mill

CURRIERS & LTHER. CUTRS.

Bond (Henry) and Shuttleworth (Thomas,) St Helen's street
Conder Thomas, jun. Butter market
Firth Wm. *(fancy leather cutter,)* Woodbridge road
Garrard Wm. Back Hamlet
Turner Walton, Elm street

CUTLERS.

Bird James, St Nicholas street
Smith Wm. St Matthew's street

DENTISTS.

Gaches Daniel, Northgate street
Tracey John, Tacket street

DYERS AND SCOURERS.

Batley John, Fore street
Haxell Wm. Carr street
Hayward Stephen, St Nicholas st
Spearman James, St Matthew's st
Talbot John, St Matthew's street
White Ann, Church street

EARTHENWARE MFRS.

Schulen Mary Ann, Rope lane
Schulen Jno. Wm., Mill pl. & Back st

EATING HOUSES.

Chenery James, Carr street
Cutting Henry, Queen street
Daniell Brett, Queen street
Parker Wm. Silent street
Ringham Wm. Major's corner
White Wm. Crown street

ENGRAVERS, &c.
(* are only Copperplate Printers.)

Ashford Henry, Tacket street
Dallinger Wm. Henry, Silent st
*Lamb Wray Palliser, Tower street
*Manning Wm. Tower street

FARMERS, &c.

Marked * are Cow keepers, and † Cart owners only.
(See also Whitton and Westerfield.)
Ashford Robert, *Sproughton*
†Balls John, Globe lane
†Banyard John, Handford street
†Batley Zebediah, Salthouse lane
Bell John, Upper Orwell street
Borrett Thomas, *Caldwell Hall*
Borsley John, *Folly farm*
Canham Wm. (bailiff,) Norwich rd
†Chisnell John, Stoke street
Clarke Robert, St Helen's street
Cooper Wm. Rose hill
†Durrant James, Norwich road
*Edwards George, Friars' road
†Freeston Simon, Friars' road
Goss My. (drill owner,) Black Horse ln
Grimwood Joseph, St Helen's street
Hare George and G. F. *Freston*
Hervey Jph. & Ernest, Bolton farm
Hicks Henry (sandpit,) Bolton
Howard Thomas, *Sproughton*
Hill Francis, Carr street
Howes James, *Washbrook*
Lacey Robert, Woodbridge road
†Last Robert and Wm. Pleasant row
Last Thomas, Fore Hamlet
†Lloyd Wm. Bell lane
*Mabson Wm. & Chas. Tower ditches
Masters Wm. 9 St Margaret's ter
*Mayhew Harriet, Barclay street
Newson Wm. *Rushmere*
Norman Wm. Bramford road
Orford John, Norwich road
*Pollard Fras. St Margaret's street
*Ratcliffe James, Norwich road
Roe Joseph, Woodbridge road
†Rogers Wm. Salthouse lane
Sawer John, Greenwich farm
†Sharman David, Black Horse lane
Stevenson Elizabeth, Back road
Wake Thomas, *Downham Reach*
Waller Henry, Handford Hall
Waspe Wm. Bonner, *Gusford Hall*
†Whitehead James, Lower Orwell st
Wilson Pettit, *Rushmere*

FELLMONGERS.

Corley John, Portman's walk
Pugh Hugh, London road
Pulfer Wm. Currier's lane

FILE MANUFACTURER.

Fuller John, Friars' road

FIRE AND LIFE OFFICES.

Active (Life,) C. Barker, Fore st
Albion (Life,) R. W. Porter, Fore st

Alliance, Richard Dykes Alexander, Esq. St Matthew's street

Clerical, Medical, & General (Life,) S. B. Chapman, Corn hill, and W. S. Fitch, Butter market

County (Fire) and Provident (Life,) S. H. Cowell, Butter market

Dissenters' (and General,) George Christopherson, Fore street

Family Endowment, Thos. Grimsey, St Nicholas street

Freemasons' and General (Life,) Thomas Fenn, jun.

Guardian, Henry Miller, Butter mkt

London Assurance, Burrows & Son, Butter market

Mutual Insurance, John Choat, Butter market

National Endowment, Harmer and Ransome, Carr street

National Provident Institution, Rt. Miller, Butter market

New Equitable(Fire,) John Duningham, Lower Brook street

Norwich Union, H. G. & W. Ridley, Fore street

London, Edinburgh,& Dublin (Life,) W. P. Mills, Mount

Pelican (Life,) Charles Pretyman, Silent street

Phœnix (Fire,) Rd.Wm. Porter,Fore st & Chas. Gross, jun. Lr. Brook st

Promoter (Life,) Eliz. Lawrance, Coleman street

Protector (Fire,) Robert Garrod, Butter market

Royal Exchange, Frederick Pawsey, Butter market

Suffolk&GeneralCountry(Fire,)Wm. Bullar, *secretary*, Bank street; house St Clement's

Sun, Thos. Grimsey, St Nicholas st

FISHMONGERS.
*(Marked * are Game dealers.)*

*Bare Joseph Hall, Butter market

Bird Wm. St Matthew's street

Brady Wm. Lower Orwell street

*Daniell Joseph, Queen street

*Holland Robert, New street

Lunn John, Bell lane

Manning Benj. Corn hill ; h Friars st

Moye Henry, Woodbridge road

Roper Richard, Cook row

Townsend Wm. *(and clerk of market,)* New market

Wisby Henry, Fore street

FRUITERERS.
(See Confectioners)

FURNITURE BROKERS.

Alexander James, Fore street

Barker Jno. Butter mkt. & Eagle st

Broom John, 106 New market; house St Helen's

Brown Robert, Upper Orwell street

Chapman Samuel, New market lane

Christie John, Fore street

Cole Edward, 102 New market ; house Woodbridge road

Fisk Wm. Tuddenham road

Miller John, New market lane

Moss Wm. Henry, St Helen's street

Randall Wm. Chenery, Fore street

Roe Joseph, Upper Brook street

Samuel Moses, Upper Brook street

Warden Joseph, New market lane

Wright John, Falcon street

FURRIERS.

Gooch Wm. Upper Brook street

Pearce Joseph, Tacket street

GAME DLRS. *(See Poulterers.)*

GARDENERS,SEEDSMEN,&c.
*Marked * are Green Grocers only.*

Adams Wm. Portman's walk

Allen George, St Helen's street

Austin John, 1 Stoke green

*Baker Hannah, Duke street

Barnard Charles, Norwich road

Barney John, Mount

*Baxter Martha, Rope lane

Bird John, Friars' road

Blomfield Henry, Handford street

Bolton John, Albion street

Bradbrook Samuel, Handford street

*Brasby James, Short lane

*Brighten Susan, Fore street

Brunning Robert, 8 Halifax

Canham James, Back Hamlet

Cant George, Bell lane

*Chaplin Richard, St Matthew's st

Clements Robert, Bourn bridge

*Church Thos. Lewis, St Helen's st

Cook Jasper, Portman's walk

Cooper John, St Margaret's street

Crick John, King street

*Driver Levi, Stoke street

*Drake John, Silent street

*Eaton Charles, Currier's lane

Edwards Edward, St Peter's street

Farthing Wm. Friar's road

Gardiner Wm. Duke street

*Gislingham George, Handford st

Godbold Jasper, Norwich road

Hewke Henry, St Helen's street

Jeffries Robt. and Jas. (nurserymen,) Corn hill and London road; house St Matthew's street
*Keeley Francis, Quay street
Lawrence Thomas, Gt. Whip street
Loom John, Friars' street
*Marshall John, 18 New market
Milbourn Robert, Black Horse lane
Orman Robert, Friary gardens
Paterson Letitia, St Nicholas street
*Plantin Edward, 89 New market; house Bell lane
Pratt Stephen, Handford street
Ramsden Eliz. Ann, (public gdns.) Fore Hamlet
Regent Ann, Norwich road
Revett Jas. Green yd. Duke street
*Scopes Wm. Queen street & Fore st
Seagriff Wm. Duke street
Smith John, *(florist,)* Norwich road
Soar Wm. Norwich road
*Tilley George, Bridge street
Turner Wm. Fore Hamlet
*Wallerton Thos. Upper Orwell st
Woollard Wm. *(florist,)* Ranelagh gardens

GLASS, CHINA, & EARTHENWARE DEALERS.

Alderton Abm. Upper Brook street
Barrett Thomas & Co. Upr Brook street and Colchester
Bowers Enoch, King street
Burrows Robert and Son, (glass) Butter market
Everett Wm. Tavern street
Greaves Wm. Butter market
Jacob Robert, Norwich road
Johnson Sarah, Upper Orwell st
Ritchie Jas. 30 New mkt & Tacket st
Smith John, St Helen's street
Suthers Wm. Butter market
Taylor Robert, St Clement's street

GLOVERS.

Carter Mary, (stock mfr.) Tavern st
Carter Mary, Black Horse lane
Chisnall Thomas, Currier's lane
Dennington Eliz. 121 New market
Grimwade Rd. (& hosier,) Corn hill
Smith John, New market lane

GROCERS & TEA DEALERS.

*Marked * are also Cheesemongers, and †Tallow Chandlers.— See also Tea Dealers and Shopkeepers.*
*Abbott Charles, Tavern street
*Abbott Samuel, Corn hill
*Andrews John, Mount
*Ashford Charles, Westgate street

Aston Jph. (seedsman,) Butter mkt
†*Baker Isaac, St Clement's street
*Barker Charles, Fore street
*Brook Edward, King street
Burton Charles & Son, (wholesale,) Tavern street
Clark John S. Upper Brook street
Clements Thos. Talmash, Major's corner
*Colbourn Charles, Fore street
Conder James, Butter market
Crispin J. 2 Mount
†Delf Harriet, St Matthew's street
Denny Arthur Good, Norwich road
*Denny Thomas Wm. Orwell place
Denny Samuel, 3 St Nicholas st
*Goldsbury George, St Peter's st
*Goodwin Edgar, Upper Brook st
*Goodwin Edward, Fore street
*Goss Charles, Northgate street
†Hacker Wm. St Matthew's street
*Harmer Robert, Westgate street
*Kimble George, Bridge street
*Last Henry, Fore Hamlet
*Limmer John, Upper Brook street
*Lot Wm. Quay street
Manistre George, St Matthew's st
*Manistre Robert, Fore street
Miller Robert, Butter market
*Sallows George, Tacket street
*Setterfield George, Fore Hamlet
Silburn Charles, (Italian warehouse,) Tavern street
*Spurling Samuel, Westgate street
Stiff John, Carr street
*Tallent Alfred, Fore street
Taylor Joseph, St Matthew's street
*Turner Charles, Butter market
*Wainwright Saml. Butter market
*Waller Thomas, King street
*West Philip, St Matthew's street
*Wretts John, Quay street

GUN MAKERS.

Backhouse Noah, St Matthew's st
Bales George Wm. Corn hill
Bird James, St Nicholas street
Jaye Daniel, Orwell street
Robinson Henry, Tower street

HABERDASHERS.

Conder James, Butter market
Dickerson Thomas, Upper Brook st
Dorling Edward, Upper Brook st
Grimwade Richard, Corn hill
Lambert John, St Matthew's street
Suthers Wm. Butter market

HAIR DSSRS. & PERFUMERS.

Billinge Samuel Waller, Tavern st

Day John, Friars' road
Death John, Friars' road
Demuth Frederick, Crown lane
Drane Wm. St Margaret's street
English Henry, Lower Orwell st
Faiers Samuel Howe, Tavern street
Frost John, Carr street
Glading George, Mount street
Glide John, Eagle street
Graves Henry, Dove lane
Hazel Joseph, Duke street
Hatcher Henry, Mount street
Licence Paul, Bell lane
Mulley George, (register office,) Tacket street
Naunton Wm. King street
Parsons Charles, Westgate street
Read Charles, Fore street
Roberts Thomas, Tavern street
Rowlson Wm. St Matthew's street
Smith Wm. Angel lane
Stannard John, St Nicholas street
Wade Wm. Fore street
Woolner George, Fore Hamlet
Woolner John Bridge street
Woolnough Wm. Lower Orwell st

HARDWARE & TOY DLRS.

Alexander Wm. 28 New market; h Priory place
Barber Benj. 41 New mkt; h Rope ln
Barnes Thomas, St John street
Dorling Edward, Upper Brook st
Lambert John, St Matthew's street
Levi Moses, St Matthew's street
Rands Emanuel, Fore street
Suthers Wm. Butter market

HATTERS.

*Marked * are Hat Manufacturers.*

Batley John, Butter market
Brook Timy. Sherwin, Friars' street
*Brothers Gilbert, Tavern street
Butcher John, Butter market
*Croyden John Fredk. Fore street
Footman John & Co. Westgate st
*Francis Saml. George, Globe ln
Girling Henry Wm. Cox lane
Grimwade Rd. (out-fitter,) Corn hill
Jennings John, Tavern street
Parkes Saml. Wyatt & Co. Corn hill
Raphael Abraham, Fore street
Sewell James, Northgate street

HAY & STRAW DEALERS.

Boar Edward, Crown lane
Chenery James, Great Whip street
Foulger Wm. Crown lane
Grimwood Joseph, St Helen's st
Mayhew Lionel, 3 Berners street

Scrivener Henry, Black Horse lane

HORSE DEALERS.

Shorten Thos. St Matthew's street
Smith John, St Matthew's street

HOSIERS.

See Linen Drapers & Haberdashers.

James Solomon, *(hosiery and calico manufacturer,)* Fore Hamlet

HOTELS, INNS, & TAVNS.

Admiral's Head, Richard Caston, St Margaret's street
Anchor, John Cornwell, Duke street
Angel, John Hazalton, Angel lane
Bee Hive, Jph. Miller, Butter mkt
Bell, Samuel Smith, Dock street
Black Bell, Rt. Smith Baxter, Elm st
Black Horse, Christopher Goss, Black Horse lane
Blue Bell, Samuel Mullett, Corn hill
Blue Coat Boy, John Wells, Cattle market
Boar's Head, John Rivers, Bell ln
Buck's Head, Jared Hill, Upper Orwell street
Bull, Martha Brooks, Quay
Bull & Dog, Edw. Hayward, Fore st
Bull's Head, Ts. Gooding, Orwell pl
Canteen, Saml. Norman, Barrack yd
Castle, John Roper, Orwell street
Chaise and Pair, Samuel Wilson, Woodbridge road
Coach and Horses, Wm. Brooks, jun. Upper Brook street
Cock and Pye, Wm. Lamb, Upper Brook street
Corn Exchange Coffee House, Hy. Horrobin, Corn hill
Cow & Gate, Samuel Webb, Quay st
Cow and Pail, Jno. Newby, Rope ln
Crooked Billet, Hy. Waller, Handford hall
Cross Keys, Chas. Lewis Robinson, Carr street
Crown, Ths. Middleditch, Bridge st
Crown and Anchor, Thos. Harrison, Westgate street
Crown and Anchor, John Shulver, Lock road
Crown and Sceptre, Chas. Garrard, Quay street
Curriers' Arms, Wm. Holder, Curriers' lane
Defiance, Jph. Laws, Stoke street
Dove, Obadiah Lucas, St Helen's st
Duke of York, Wm. Hines, Albion hill

Elephant and Castle, Hannah Bowman, Mount

Falcon, Robert Bowman, Falcon st

Feathers, Lott Betts, Westgate st

Fleece, Ts. Shorten, St Matthew's st

Fox, Henry Haken, Upr. Brook st

Friars' Head, Samuel Farritt, Friars' street

Gardeners' Arms, Samuel Webb, Fore Hamlet

Globe, David Lyons, Globe lane

Golden Lion, (posting,) Sml. Smyth, Corn hill; *tapster*, W. M. Garwood

Good Hope, Robt. Golding Osborn, Tower street

Great White Horse, (posting hs.) Chaplin & Castle, Tavern st

Green Man, Thos. Cowles, Quay st

Greyhound, John Snelling, Globe ln

Griffin, Geo. Adcock, New bank

Gun, John M. Runnacles, Quay st

Halberd, Mary Pilch, Northgate st

Half Moon, John Allen, Foundtn. st

Half Moon and Star, John Bantoft, St Matthew's street

Horse and Groom, James Smith, Woodbridge road

Ipswich Arms, Philip Stevens, Lwr. Brook street

Joiners' Arms, Jas. Wevers, Upper Orwell street

King's Arms, Wm. Bacon, Corn hill

King's Head, John Ling, King st; *tapster*, Wm. Scott

Leopard, Thos. Trew, Tower ditches

Life Boat, Wm. Batley, Halifax row

Lord Chancellor, William Foulger, Crown lane

Lord Nelson, Saml. Nelson, Fore st

Marquis Cornwallis, John Stevens, St Margaret's street

May Pole, Jas. Cook, St Helen's st

Neptune, Geo. Jackson, Fore street

New Inn, Anthy. Breckles, Duke st

Orwell, Jas. Adams, Lwr. Orwell st

Partridge, David John Hamblin, St Margaret's plane

Pilot, My. Ann Crabb, Ridley's quay

Plough, John Burrell, Turret lane

Porto-Bello, Wm. Mortimer, Upper Orwell street

Post Chaise, John Serjeant, Woodbridge road

Prince of Wales, John Setterfield, Fore street

Queen's Head, Wright Hunt, St Matthew's street

Queen's Head, J. Lord, Fore Hamlet

Ram, Dudley Smith, Quay street

Rose Inn, Rachel Spalding, St Peter's street

Rose and Crown, Westrop William Waller, Norwich road

Royal Oak, John Robinson, Northgate street

Royal William, Wm. Woollard, Ranelagh gardens & Bowling green

Running Buck, Wm. Jannings, St Margaret's plane

Safe Harbour, John Head, Boro' rd

Sailors' Home, Jas. Mills, Gt Whip st

Salutation, Jas. Bradbrook, Carr st

Saracen's Head, Robt. Bedwell, St Margaret's green

Sea Horse, David Worby, Bank st

Ship, John Stearn, Back Hamlet

Shipwrights' Arms, James Chenery, Great Whip street

Smack, Eliz. Birkitt, Quay street

Sorrel Horse, Tampion Brownsmith, St Clement's street

Spread Eagle, Abm. Wolsey, Fore st

Steam Packet, John Allen, Fore st

Steam Packet, Geo. Potto, Duke st

Suffolk Hotel, (posting,) Jas. Cherinton, Westgate street

Sun, James Shorten, St Stephen's ln

Unicorn, W. Rudland

Union Jack, Henry Jenkines, New quay

Victoria, John Bacon, Berners st

Vine, John Garrod, Church street

Waggon and Horses, Jas. Frewin, Butter market

Welcome Sailor, Cornelius Perryman, Fore Hamlet

Wellington, Robt. Naunton, Carr st

Wherry, Edw. Swan, Wherry quay

White Elm, Eliz. Ann Ramsden, Fore Hamlet

White Hart, Robt. George Boby, St Lawrence street

White Lion, George Ponder, St Margaret's street

White Lion, Noah Hambling, Bridge street West

White Swan, Thomas Dale, King. t

Woolpack, Samuel Taylor, Tuddenham road

BEER HOUSES.

Austin John, Stoke green

Baker Wm. New quay

Barnard Charles, Norwich road

Baxter Mary, Curriers' lane

Bird John, Friars' road
Bird John, Woodbridge road
Bishop Richard, Quay street
Blasby Benj. Globe lane
Blomfield Henry, Handford street
Bond Benj. Albion street
Bradbrook Samuel, Bell lane
Bruce Wm. Cox lane
Calver Thomas, Grent Whip street
Cattermole Jonth. Potter street
Chamberlain Wm. Crown lane
Clarke Hannah, Handford street
Clarke John, Silent street
Crickmore Anna Linsey, New st
Dennant Benj. Back street
Doole Wm. St Stephen's lane
Dynes Samuel, Woodbridge road
Ellis Wm. Winter, Friars' road
Elmer John, Lady lane
Esling Robert, Tower ditches
Emmett Peter, Stoke street
Farritt George, St James' street
Francis Edward, Lady lane
Freston James, Albion street
Gardiner James, East street
Glading James, Fore street
Gross Philip, Victoria street
Hales John, Mount
Harvey Wm. Mount
Hines Robert, New Bank
Huckman Joseph, Rope lane
Hunt John, St Peter's street
Jackson Charles, Friars' road
Last Daniel, Lower Orwell s
Maple John, Mount street
Olive John Thomas, Norwich road
Osborn Robert, Upper Orwell st
Palmer Peter, Fore Hamlet
Parker Thomas, Rope lane
Parker Wm. Silent street
Phillips John, Rose lane
Pizey Wm. Fore Hamlet
Powling John, Borough road
Pulham Charles, Bramford road
Ramplen Richd. Hyde Park corner
Read Wm. London road
Reynolds John, Tower ditches
Ringham Wm. Major's corner
Robinson Thomas, Rope lane
Seagriff Wm. Duke street
Small Lucy, Lower Barclay street
Smith Thomas, Halifax beach
Steward Mary Ann, New town
Steward Samuel, Tanners' lane
Thurston John, Rope lane
Todd Edwin, Stoke street
Turner Wm. Fore Hamlet

Worth Elizabeth, Duke street

IRONFOUNDERS, &c.

Bond, Turner, and Hurwood, (and
machine makers, &c.) College st
Ransome J. R. & A. (and agricultural implement, &c. manufactrs.)
Orwell Works and St Margaret's

IRON MERCHANTS.

Alexander and Co, Queen street
Garrett Elizabeth and Son, St Margaret's green

IRONMONGERS.

*Marked * are also Braziers, &c.*

Archer Thomas, (and stamp office,)
Tavern street
Christopherson Geo. (and appraiser,)
Fore street
*Cook Samuel, Westgate street
Harcourt Fredk. Butter market
*Meadows Charles, Tavern street
and Fore street
Ridley John, jun., Corn hill
Rose James, (and oil & colourman,)
Westgate street
Scrivener John, Queen street
*Singleton John, Butter market
*Singleton Wm. Upper Brook st

JEWELLERS (WORKING.)

(See also Watchmakers.)

Robertson Alexander, Silent street
Warren John, Queen st; h Berners st

JOINERS & BUILDERS.

Aldous James, Back road
Aldred George, St Helen's street
Bacon Samuel, 11 Berners street
Baldistone Samuel, Stoke street
Beaumont Charles, St Matthew's ln
Bloomfield William, Stoke street
Catchpole John Nathl. Borough road
Catchpole Robert, Tavern street
Chisnall Thomas, Salthouse street
Clarke Richard, Whitton
Cornish Charles, New town
Davy Henry, Cock and Pye yard;
house Carr street
Day James, Tower ditches
Day Thomas, Tuddenham road
Dennant Wm. Tacket street
Farman George, Upper Orwell st
Farman Robert, St Helen's street
Fayers Wm. Notcutt, Carr street
Franklin Rt. Howe, Coyte's gardens
Girling John, Stoke st; h Friars' rd
Goldsmith Thomas, Cox lane
Groom John, Providence street
Hales John, Mount
Hearsum John, Crown street

Hunt Samuel, St Margaret's street
Jackson James, St Margaret's st
Kimble John, St Peter's street
Lawrence James, Mount
Mason George, Lower Brook street
Minter Matthew, Orford street
Newson Richard Revitt, Back st
Nichols Wm. Mount street
Pettit John, Elm street
Pettit Joseph Ablett, Star lane
Pulfer Wm. St. Peter's street
Redgrave James, Norwich road
Ribbans Wm. Parkes, St Matthew's st
Roper John, Lower Orwell street
Rudland Wm. Woodbridge road
Runicles Henry, Norwich road
Scrivener Wm. Woodbridge road
Seager Joseph, Friars' street
Shribbs Wm. London road
Smith Hy. Baring, St Lawrence st
Smith Thomas, Victoria street
Tillett Wm. Handford street
Ward John, High street
Watts James, St Margaret's street
Webb John Davy, Upper Orwell st
Welham Edward, Crown street
Whight John, St Stephen's lane

LIBRARIES.

Law Library, Butter market; Fdk.
  Pawsey, librarian
Literary Institution, Corn hill; Nel-
  son Trafalgar Levett, librarian
Public Library, Butter market; Fdk.
  Pawsey, librarian
Mechanics' Institution, Tavern st;
  R. H. Franklin, librarian
Dallinger Wm. Henry, Silent st
Page Joshua, Fore street
Pawsey Frederick, Butter market
Shalders James, Westgate street

LINEN & WLN. DRAPERS.

Balfour Ebenezer, Upper Brook st
Bloxsome Samuel, Upper Brook st
Burrows Rt. & Son (woollen) Buttermkt
Buck and Fraser, Butter market
Butcher Thomas, Westgate street
Corder Edw. and Henry Shewell,
  Tavern street
Footman John and Co. Westgate st;
  house Norwich road
Gower Geo. & Arthur, Upr. Brook st
Leavold Thomas, Tavern street
Litchfield Fredk. John, Salthouse st
Lodge James, Tavern street
Messent George, St Matthew's st
Miller Henry, Butter market
Pearce Jph. jun. St Matthew's st

Prentice John, Butter market
Ray Shepherd & Son, Tavern street;
  house Saint Helen's
Roberts John, Fore street
Tunmer Joseph, Tacket street

DRAPERY & TEA DEALERS.
(Travelling.)

Campbell Robt. 5 Berners street
Ferguson John, 1 Gt Coleman street
Hunter Wm. St Nicholas street
McDowell John & Robert, 1 Great
  Coleman street
Robinson Joseph, Little King street
Taylor John, Poplar house, Short ln

LODGING HOUSES.

Alexander Richard, Tanners' lane
Blyes Mrs Mary Ann, Handford st
Childs Harriet, St Margaret's lane
Clarke Henry, St Helen's street
Daldry Wm. Coleman street
Felgate Mrs Mary, St Helen's st
Hill John, 3 Globe lane
Howard Elizabeth, 8 Berners street
Kemble Susanna, Stoke street
Levett Lucy Eliz. Foundation st
Messent Charles, Woodbridge road
Moor Mrs Ann, 33 Borough road
Mower Edward, Friars' street
Naunton John, Tower churchyard
Rogers James, Friars' road
Rose Robert, Foundation street
Taylor Ann, St Peter's street
Wilson Thomas, Mount
Woodcock Mrs Elizabeth, Globe ln

MALTSTERS.

Abbott Abram, Saint Matthew's st;
  house Park cottage
Aldrich Henry, Albion wharf; house
  Saint Matthew street
Alexanders and Co. Quay street
Baldock Stephen, Salthouse lane
Bowman Robert, Falcon street
Byles Nathaniel Byles, Green yard;
  house Back Hamlet
Cobbold John, Fore st; house *Cliff*
Cowell Marianne, Quay st; h Fore st
Gardiner Edward, New street
Neeve Hy. Currier's ln; h*Sproughton*
Pollard Wm. Foundation street
Prentice Thos. & Co. Neptune quay
Ridley H. G. and W., Fore street
Sheppard Alfred, Fore street
Ship Edward, College street
Waspe Jonathan, Bridge street
Webster Joseph, Bell lane
Wollard John, Curriers' lane

Marine Insurance Offices.
Ipswich, Alfred Cobbold, Tower st
" *Lloyds*," Wm. Mulley, Quay st
MAST, *Block, and Pump Maker.*
Garrard Wm. Neptune quay

MASTER MARINERS.
*Those marked * are Shipowners.*

Askew James, Back Hamlet
Askew Thomas, Fore Hamlet
*Barfield Wm. Great Whip street
Barker Joseph, Fore street
Barnes Thomas, Victoria street
Bennett Joseph, Duke street
Bines Joseph, Fore Hamlet
Bousfield Isaac, Long lane
Breukley Thomas, Victoria street
Burns Chas. Carman, Victoria st
Caston Peter, Trafalgar buildings
Charlton Joseph, Rope lane
Christie Samuel, 23 Princes street
Christie Wm. Angel lane
*Cloyd Charles, Church street
Cole James, Foundation street
Cole John, Quay street
Cook John, Fore Hamlet
Cook Robert Denton, 24 Boro' road
*Cooper Thomas, Foundation street
Cousins Wm. Dock street
Cracknell John, Trafalgar buildings
Day George, Reve's yard, Fore st
*Derward George, Upper Brook st
Dowse Thomas, Duke street
*Finch Samuel, Fore street
Garrod Jeremiah, John street
Garrod Wm. 39 Borough road
Garwood Edward, Victoria street
Girling Charles, Fore Hamlet
Goddard Richard, 17 Victoria street
Hadcraft Wm. 18 Victoria street
Hadcraft Wm. Fore Hamlet
*Hadcraft Wm. 10 Halifax
Hadman Benjamin, Fore Hamlet
*Harris Jonathan, 12 Halifax
*Jenkins Henry, Cox lane
Johnson George, Lower Orwell st
Kemp James, Victoria street
Leggett Abraham, Fore Hamlet
Lester Wm. Victoria street
Lord Wm. Back street
Matthews Wm. Lower Orwell street
Moore John, Foundation street
Noy Wm. Robert, Church street
Parker John, Fore Hamlet
Pear Wm. Victoria street
Peck Edward, Long lane
Pratt Isaac, Victoria street
Proom Thomas, 22 Princes street

Quilter John, John street
Rackham Sl. Richardson,GtWhip st
Raymer John, Bridge street West
Riches Thomas, Long lane
Risker Robert, Fore Hamlet
Ruggles George, Victoria street
Skeet Wm. Rope lane
Southgate Robert, St Peter's street
Stevens James, St Peter's street
Swaffer Wm. 8 Priory place
Thompson Thos. 41 Borough road
Tunmer Abraham, Victoria street
Webster Wm. New bank
Wells Joseph, Great Whip street
*White John, Tacket street
*White Wm. 8 Borough road
Wilkinson John Field, Star lane
Williams James, Back street
Wood Wm. New street
Woods Robert, Lower Orwell street
Wright John, Lower Orwell street
Wright Wm. Foundation street

MILLINERS, &c.
(See also Straw Hat Makers.)

Aldred Elizabeth, Queen street
Balfour Mrs Ebenezer, Upr.Brook st
Baldry Emily, Tavern street
Beeston Susanna, Church lane
Bird Ann and Rebecca, Silent st
Bird Mary, Lower Orwell street
Block and Dalinger, Northgate st
Blythe Elizabeth, St Helen's street
Bonner Susan, Northgate street
Bristo Harriet, Carr street
Butcher Emily, East street
Butcher Sarah, Westgate street
Catlin Emma, SaintStephen's lane
Chapman Maria, Portman street
Clark Elizabeth, Coleman street
Clarke Eliz. & Eliza, Upr.Orwell s
Clarke Mary Ann, Elm street
Cleveland Susanna, Friars' road
Cole Eliz. (lace dealer) Tacket st
Collins Emily, Saint John street
Cork and Bird, Queen street
Cudding Harriet Hannah, King st
Dawson Harriet, St James street
Dring Emma & Jane, St Nicholas st
Edwards Mary, Lower Orwell st
Ethersey Eliza, Westgate street
Evans Eliza, Duke street
Fairweather Mary, Cox lane
Finch Mary, Berners street
Fisher Mary, Tavern street
Garrod Frances, Barclay street
Green Sarah, Potter street
Green Mary Ann, Northgate street

Groom Har. & Ellen, Friars' street
Garwood Mary Ann, St James st
HammondHan.Mar. 5 StMatw.'s ter
Howes Charlotte, Friars' street
Kent Sarah, Silent street
Lamb Mary Ann, St Peter's street
Lambert Martha, Potter street
Last Rachel, St Matthew's street
Lock Mary, Fore street
Matthews Jane and Emily (baby linen) Carr street
Mayhew Betsy & Ann, Tanners' ln
Milnes Eliz.Harriet, St Matthew's st
Neal Elizabeth, Fore street
Pizey Mary, Crown street
Read Mary Ann, Black Horse lane
Russell Sarah, Norwich road
SamsonEln.&Emma, 3StMatw.'s ter
Sawer Eliz. Saint Peter's street
Smart Mary Ann, Elm street
Smith Mary, St Matthew's street
Smith Sarah, Tavern street
Smith Susanna, Foundation street
Spall Harriet & Rebecca, Cook row
White Jane, Tacket street
Wright Harriet, Fore street
Whybrew Harriet, Tacket street
Woods Jane, Upper Orwell street
Yeoman Sarah, College street

MILLWRIGHTS.

Collins John, Woodbridge road
Wright Samuel & Son, St Helen's st

MUSIC DEALERS, &c.

* are Teachers, and † Tuners only.

Ball Eliz. & Son, 17 Upr. Brook st
*Ball John Henry George, (& dancing) Orford street
†*Ball Squire, Upper Brook street
Bianchi George Henry, Tavern st
*Bianchi Misses Maria & Amelia, Tavern street
†Clarke Thos. Cansdale (piano and organ manufacturer) St Helen's st
*FosterRt.W.(&dancing)Norwich rd
*Godball James, Foundation street
*Godball Wm. St Margaret's green
Humfress George, Carr street
†Last Alfred, Cook row
*Loyd Robert, Carr street
†Milnes Benj. Geo. (instrument mfr) Saint Matthew's street
Walker Charles, Corn hill
*Walker Ellen, Corn hill

NEWSPAPERS.

Ipswich Express (Tuesday,) Stephen Piper, Butter market

Ipswich Journal (Saturday,) Postle Jackson, Butter market
Suffolk Chronicle (Saturday,) John King, Tavern street; h Carr st

NEWS AGENTS.

Cook John, Upper Orwell street
Garrod Wm. Falcon street
Root Robert, Westgate street
Seward Wm. (correspondent to Bury & Suffolk Herald) Norwich road

OIL MILLER & CAKE MFR.

Webber Samuel, Handford street; house Stone Lodge

OPTICIANS.

Bianchi Geo. Henry, Tavern street
Jennings Thomas, Tacket street

PAINTERS.

(See also Plumbers and Glaziers.)

Andrews James, St James's street
Andrews Wm. Handford street
Booth Robert, John street
Cuthbert John, Carr street
Harvey Daniel, Lower Orwell st
Manning George, St Nicholas st
Miller Thomas, Fore Hamlet
Salmon Richard, New Town

PAPER MAKER.

(By patent machinery.)

Ranson Elizabeth, Anglesey mills, Back street

PATTEN & CLOG MAKERS.

(Marked * are also Last Makers.)

*Garlic James Smith, Tavern st
*Hill Arnold, Carr street
Pepper Sl.Hy.,Ch.yd. St Mary Elms

PAWNBROKERS.

Burrows Robert & Son, Silent st
Christie Ann, Fore street
Christie George, Fore street
Fraser Roderick Donald, Elm st
Mason and King, Fore street

PHYSICIANS.

Baird Andrew Wood, Lwr. Brook st
Beck Edward, Northgate street
Drummond Hy. Pilkington, Silent st
Durrant Chpr. Mercer, Northgate st

PLUMBERS, PAINTERS, & GLAZIERS.

Austin Henry, Back Hamlet
Bacon Wm. Corn hill
Bass Isaac, Saint Clement's street
Batley Henry Baring, Carr street
Beard Joseph, Silent street
Bird Wm. & Buckingham, Queen st
Burrows & Hardy, Orwell place
Chaplin Wm. Princes street
Coleman John, Mile end

Cook Wm. Foundation street
Cuthbert Wm. Bridge street
Day Joseph, Falcon street
Gregory Alfred, Upper Orwell st
Hagger Edward, King street
Keeble George, Quay street
King Robert & Son, Upper Brook st
Manning George, Norwich road
Miller Thomas, Victoria street
Minter John, Saint Margaret's st
Osbaldston John, St Peter's street
Patrick Orlando, St Nicholas street
Ramplen Richd. Hyde park corner
Ribbans John, St Matthew's street
Root Wm. Lower Brook street
Scarlett Wm. Cook row
Scott and Stearn, Fore street
Watcham Wm. College street; h
  Tower terrace
Woods James Devereaux, St Margaret's street

POST MASTERS.
(Horses, Gigs, and Chaise for hire.)
Burman Edward, Turret lane
Cullum John, Lady ln; h High st
Catlin John, St Stephen's lane
Crisp Joseph, St Margaret's ditches
Dennent James, jun. East street
Foulger William, Crown lane
Garwood Wm. Minter, Black Horse
  lane; h Golden Lion Tap
Lyons David, Globe lane
Norbrook Wm. Tower ditches
Page John, Great Whip street
Rouse James, St Helen's street
Scott Thomas, Black Horse lane
Shorten James, St Stephen's lane
Smith Samuel, St Stephen's lane
Wells John, Cattle market

POULTERERS.
(Marked * are Game dealers.—See
also Fishmongers.)
*Bales George Wm. Corn hill
*Daniell Brett, Queen street
Mudd John, Bell lane
*Seaman John, Tacket street

PRINTERS *(See Booksellers.)*
Rag and Marine Store dealers.
Cowell Sl. Harrison, New market ln
Dorling Edward, Upper Brook st
Lambert John, St Matthew's street
ROMAN CEMENT, &c. MFR.
Tovell George, Lock road

ROPE & TWINE MAKERS.
Rands Edmund, Bridge street
Rands Emanuel, Fore street
Rands Nathaniel, Quay street

Runting James (and sack maker,)
  Butter market
Woods James, Norwich road

SADDLERS, &c.
Blasby Barnes, St Matthew's street
Dawson John, Woodbridge road
Debenham Thos. St Margaret's pln
Emmerson Thomas, St Matthew's st
Hamilton Andrew, Great Whip st
Howes John, St Matthew's street
King Henry, Curriers' lane
Leigh Thos. Corn hill & Westgt. st
Norbrook James, Fore street
Poole Edward, Back road
Payne William, St Peter's street; h
  Norwich road
Redgrave Joseph, Northgate street
Ringe Wm. Carr street
Stockins Wm. Dock street
Terry Wm. Bridge street, West
Wade Samuel, Corn hill

SAIL MAKERS.
Pickles Jonth. Quay and Fore street
Horn Wm. Bell, Quay street
Mulley Wm. Robinson, Quay street
Sharman Wm. Lower Orwell street

SALT MERCHANTS.
Christie John, Salthouse street
Harrington Wm. Walter, Salths. st
Saw Manufacturer.
Roberts John *(and dealer in Tools,)*
  Upper Orwell street

SAWERS *(Hackney.)*
Bloss and Cole, Duke street
Finch Joseph and Benjamin, Friars'
  street; h St James' street
Hart Henry, Handford street
Smith James and Alfred, Back st

SHERIFFS' OFFICERS.
Clarke John, Eagle street
Collins Wm. 4 St Nicholas street

SHIP BUILDERS.
Bayley Wm. & Co. Cliff Ship yard
Read and Page, Halifax Ship yard

SHIP CHANDLERS.
Barker Charles, Fore street
Christopherson George, Fore street
Horn Wm. Bell, Quay street
Lott Wm. Quay street
Mulley Wm. Robinson, surveyor to
  Lloyds, Quay street

SHOPKEEPERS.
(Grocery, Flour, &c. dealers.)
Ahlitt Sarah Julia, Duke street
Andrews James, Friars' street
Bailey Edward, Silent street
Benham Samuel, Upper Orwell st

Birch Robert, Lower Orwell street
Bird Bloss, Norwich road
Bird John, Woodbridge road
Blomfield Mahala, Norwich road
Boston Susan, 21 Princes street
Bristo Isaac, Mount street
Burch Robert, Tower ditches
Buxton David, Tower ditches
Calver Thomas, Bell lane
Calver Wm. Great Whip street
Catchpole Edmund, Lower Orwell st
Cattermole James, Cox lane
Chaplin Wm. 28 Princes street
Chaplin Wm. Bell lane
Church Henry, St Helen's street
Clarke Hannah, Handford street
Collins Henry, Duke street
Collins Jeremiah, Woodbridge road
Cook George, Albion street
Cresswell James, St Margaret's grn
Dennis Samuel Francis, College st
Ditchham Henry, Barclay street
Dodd James, St James' street
Driver John, Tanners' lane
Dunnett Thomas, Fore street
Earnshaw Markham, Long lane
English James, New street
Evatt Mary, Green yard, Duke st
Everett Wm. Back street
Fisk Francis, 13 Princes street
Francis Edward, Lady lane
Freeman Wm. St Helen's street
Frost John Winter, St Margaret's st
Gibborn John, Albion hill
Goddard John, Wykes, Bishop st
Gooderham Lydia, Elm street
Green Henry, Bell lane
Greir Robert, St Helen's street
Gross Philip, Victoria street
Hamblin Hannah, John street
Hawes James, Priory street
Haywood Wm. St Matthew's street
Hempson Joseph Benj. Victoria st
Herries Jane, Duke street
Hill Isaac, St Margaret's green
Hopson (Edward) & Wright (Wm.)
   Rope lane
Howell Wm. Stoke street
King Henry, New street
Lankester Charles, Tuddenham rd
Leggett Philip, Friars' road
Lloyd Francis, New street
Manning George, Norwich road
Marsh Obadiah, Upper Orwell st
Martin Joshua, Great Whip street
Mason Sarah, Victoria street
Miller Jthn. Branham, 37 Boro.' rd

Mollison Sarah, Albion street
Moss Wm. Henry, St Helen's st
Norman Thomas, Woodbridge road
Paine Sarah Page, Borough road
Payne John, East street
Payne Wm. Norwich road
Perry Wm. *Whitton*
Powling John, Borough road
Proctor Sarah, Bramford road
Robinson James, Barrack lane
Roper Sarah, Duke street
Rose Hannah, Tower ditches
Sage John, Stoke street
Seager Joseph, Friars' street
Searle Robert Stephen, Rope lane
Sheldrake John, Albion place
Ship John, St James' street
Singleton George, St Margaret's grn
Singleton Wm. Upper Orwell street
Smart Wm. Luke, Curriers' lane
Smith John, Portman street
Smith Paul, Rope lane
Stanton James, King street
Stevens Wm. Bridge street, West
Steward Mary Ann, New Town
Taylor Samuel, Regent street
Thrower Henry, Foundation street
Thurlow James, Fore Hamlet
Webb Robert, Fore street
Williams James, St Margaret's grn
Woods James D., St Margaret's st
Whittle Francis, Friars' road
Wright Jabez, Little Barclay street

SHOT MANUFACTURER.

Wright John, Falcon street

SLATE MERTS. *(See Timber.)*

SOAP MANUFACTURERS.

Colchester & Co. Friars' road

STAY MAKERS.

Clarke Harriet, Friars' road
Clarke My. & Lucy, St Nicholas st
Clements Frances, Eagle street
Cook Sarah Ann, Upper Orwell st
Edwards Eliz. Crown street cottage
Edwards Sarah, Upper Brook street
Edwards Wm. Silent street
Fagan Susanna, St Helen's street
Newson Emily, Back street
Ribbans Mary, St Matthew's street
Waspe Elizabeth, Crown street
Wroth Caroline, Falcon street

Stone (Artificial) & Scagliola mfr.

Sparrow Charles, Norwich road

STONE & MARBLE MASONS.

Backhouse Benj. Norwich road
Frewer James, St Margaret's green
Hutchins John Wm. St John street

Ireland Robert, Lower Brook street
Tovell George Singleton, Carr street and Lock road
Wells Joseph, Great Whip street

STRAW HAT MAKERS.
*(Marked * are Milliners also.)*

Archer Jonathan, Mount
Barker Elizabeth, Rope lane
Boss Eliza, Rope lane
Belcher Martha, Victoria street
Boston John, Carr street
Burrage Elizabeth, Falcon street
Chaplin Robert, Butter market
Dennant Hannah, Barclay street
*Deward and Cook, Upr. Brook st
*Ellis Sarah, St James' street
Gooch Wm. Upper Brook street
*Juby Eliz. and Sophia, Butter mkt
Kersey Sarah Ann, Black Horse ln
King Sarah, Fore street
Manning Sarah, Tower street
Nunn Hannah, Victoria street
Pearce Joseph, Tacket street
*Pegg Mary Ann, Black Horse ln
Ringe Caroline, Carr street
Robinson Eliza, Major's corner
Squirrell Lydia, Silent street
Thrower Han. Maria, Foundation st
Watcham Maria, Bridge street
*Webb Celia & Sarah Ann, Coytes gardens
Wright Elizabeth, Cox lane

SURGEONS.

Adams Webster, Elm street
Angier Jas. Hague, 1 St Geo.'s ter
Atthill Robert, Fore street
Bartlett Alexander, Lower Brook st
Bartlett Alex. Henry, Lwr. Brook st
Bullen George, Carr street
Colchester Edmund, *East Suffolk Hospital*
Cowell Geo. Kersey, St Nicholas st
Davie and Pitcher, Fore street
Edwards George, Northgate
Elliston Wm. St Stephen's street
Francis James Ougham, (registrar of marriages,) Bank street
Hamilton Wm. Westgate
Hammond Charles, Lower Brook st
Hammond H. K. Berner's street
Johnson Fredk. Wm. 1 Priory place
Lambert John, M.D. Berners street
Lloyd Robert, Foundation street
Mills Wm. Partridge, Mount
Mumford Wm. Tower cottage
Prentice Alfd. M.D. St Matthew's st
Ranson John, Westgate street

Sampson Geo.Green, St Matthew's st
Sanderson Wm. Bell, Westgate st
Scott Walter, Lower Brook street
Shaw James, *Belle Vue Asylum*
Webster Wm. H. B. Carr street

SURVEYORS (LAND, &c.)
(See also Architects, &c.)

Doust George, Carr street
Fleury Christopher, Panorama
Gower Stephen S. Soane street
Groom Samuel German, Orford st
Hearsum John, Crown street
Orman Robert, Friars' road
Parkes Samuel Wyatt, Corn hill
Seward Wm. Norwich road
Whiting John *(county surveyor,)* Crown street

TAILORS.
*Marked * are Woollen Drapers also.*

Austin Samuel, Short lane
*Balls Edward, Queen street
Balls Robt. and Son, Queen street
*Bare Fredk. Upper Brook street
Barker Thomas, Tacket street
Bell Robt. Corbyn, Norwich road
Berry Chas. Upper Orwell street
*Blomfield Wm. Lawrence,Tavern st
Borrett Jas. (and clothes cleaner,) Handford street
Brackenridge John, Carr street
Chenery Richd. Great Whip street
Chisnall John, Upper Orwell street
*Clarke James, King street
*Clarke Wm. Upper Brook st. and St Stephen's lane
*Corbyn Jonathan, Carr street
Corbyn Wm. 2 Berners street
Creasy Lionel, Victoria street
*Cudding Wm. King street
*Cunnold George, Butter market
Dowsing Thos. St Nicholas street
Edgley Alfred, Norwich road
Edgley George, St Peter's street
Edgley Thomas, Bell lane
Elvin George, Norwich road
*Fisher Theophilus, Victoria street
Frost John Winter, St Margaret's st
*Fuller George, East street
Garnham John, Handford street
Garrod Wm. School street
*Gill Edward, Carr street
Gosling Edward, St Helen's street
Goss Ebenjer Turrell, Coleman st
Gowing Richard, Victoria street
Grimwood Wm. Stoke street
*Hagg & Son, Upper Brook street
Harvey Charles, Tower ditches

Harvey Robt. St Margaret's street
*Hillyard John, Fore street
Howes Wm. Church street
Humphreys James, Fore street
James Rt. Ellis, Dog's head lane
Keary Robert, 6 Priory street
Keeble Wm. Globe lane
Lake John, Silent street
Lawrance Hy. 14 Upr. Brook street
*Leeks John Thos. Carr street
*Lovewell Henry, Carr street
Maddocks John, Providence street
*Mallett Francis, Upr. Brook st
Manning George, St Stephen's st
*Nunn, Brothers, & Co. Tavern st
*Pearson James, Tacket street
Read Edward, Fore Hamlet
*Read Edw. Thos. Silent street
Read Samuel, Coleman street
Robertson John, Dog's head lane
*Rogers John, Fore street
Roper Thomas, Turret lane
*Rush Wm. Upper Brook street
*Seccull Arthur, Silent street
*Shewell and Smith, Tavern street
Smith John, Lawrence street
Smith Joseph, Fore street
*Stephens Philip, Lower Brook st
*Titlow Robt. St Margaret's street
*Tunmer George, Tavern street
*Tunmer Geo. & Sons, Tacket st
Vesey Wm. Friars' street
Welham John, Westgate street
*Whistle John, Elm street
*Worts Fredk. St Nicholas street

TALLOW CHANDLERS.
See also Grocers.
Clarke Joshua, Crown ln; h Friars' rd
Ennew and Porter, Queen street
Limmer John, Upper Brook street

TEA & COFFEE DEALERS.
See also Grocers, &c.
Brewster Rd. St Margaret's street
Cook Elizabeth, Tower street
Cowell Saml. Harrison, New mkt. ln
Dobson Geo. 17 Victoria terrace
Kerr James, Oak lane
Ritchie James, Tacket street
Studd Hannah, Berners street
Walker Charles, Corn hill

TIMBER MERCHANTS.
*Marked * are also Slate Merchants.*
*Brown Wm. & Co. St Nicholas st
Byles Jerh. & Co. College st; h Hill hs
*Colchester Wm. & Co. College st
Everett Joseph David, St Margaret's
street; house Church street

Groom John, Providence street
Lenton James, Handford street
Orman Rt. & Co. (and mahogany,)
Friars' road

TOBACCONISTS.
*Marked * are Manufacturers.*
*Churchman Wm. Hyde Park corner
Clark John G. Upper Brook street
Cole Edward & Co. St Helen's st
*Dothie and Soundy, Orwell place
*Giles Edwin, Tavern street
Porter Hy. (cigar dealer,) Queen st

TOBACCO PIPE MAKERS.
Adams Webster, Curriers' lane and
Needham market
Miller and Goodwin, Fore street

TOY DLRS. & FANCY WHS.
Barber Benjamin, Rope lane
Dorling Edward, Upr. Brook street
Durrant and Hammond, Tavern st
Lambert John, St Matthew's street
Levi Moses, St Matthew's street
Morley David, Butter market
Samuel Moses, Upr. Brook street
Suthers Wm. Butter market
Taylor James, Quay street
Warren Wm. Barker, Tacket street

TRUSS MAKER.
Smith John, New market lane

TURNERS (WOOD, &c.)
Alderton Thomas, Falcon street
Hayward Rt. Upper Orwell street
Hughes John, Friars' street; house
Handford road
Miller Matthew, Cox lane
Milnes Benjamin George, *(ivory)* St
Matthew's street
Senton Jas. Carr st. & Handford st
Turner Thomas, Short lane

UMBRELLA MAKERS.
Durrant & Hammond, Tavern street
Kemp Simon, St Margaret's green
Spinks Margaret, Friars' road

VETERINARY SURGEONS.
Cage Thomas, St Margaret's green
Girling Robt. H. Norwich road
Long John, King street
Shorten Chas. Thos. Crown street
Smith Robert Trafalgar buildings
Vincent Nathl. Handford street
Warner John, Mount

WATCH & CLOCK MAKERS.
*Marked * are Silversmiths, &c.*
Ablitt Frederick, Tavern street
*Ashford Wm. Fore street
*Bennett George, Fore street
*Burgess Chas. Smith, Tavern st

Cade Robert, Borough road
*Cansdale Solomon, Upr. Brook st
*Cole Richard Stinton, King street
Grayston Joseph, Lwr. Orwell st
*Levi Moses, St Matthew's street
*Read Daniel, Westgate street
Robertson Ebenezer, Lwr. Brook st
Roe Joseph, Tacket st ; h Brook st
*Schulen Charles, Tacket street
Squirrell Samuel, Upr. Orwell st
Weston James, Cook row

WHEELWRIGHTS.

Dunnet Thos. Upper Orwell street
Page John, Great Whip street
Planten Wm. Luis, Back street
Pulham Charles, Bramford road
Quadling Edwin, Bell lane
Robinson John, Major's corner
Singleton George, jun. and Wm. St
  Margaret's green

WHITESMITHS, &c.
*Marked * are Gas Fitters.*

*Avis Thomas, Queen street
*Bird John, Northgate street
Brown John, Tower ditches
Cooper & Hurwood, (ship & anchor,)
  Salthouse street
Cooper and Noble, (coach spring and
  hurdle mfrs.) St Margaret's green
Edwards Solomon, Crown street
Gosling John and Son, (& stove mfr.)
  St Nicholas street
Osborn Robt. Upper Orwell street
Robinson Charles, King street
Smith James, Curriers' lane
*Teager John, Little King street
Wright John, (edge tool manufac-
  turer,) Fore Hamlet

WHITING MANUFACTRS.

Fisk James, Rope lane
Turner Wm. Back road

WINE & SPIRIT MERCHTS.

Bowman Robert, Falcon street
Bristo Thos. and Son, Tacket street
Chaplin Wm. Jackson, Westgate st
Churchman John & Co. Hyde Park
  corner
Cobbold Jno. & Son, Lower Brook st
Doggett Francis, Newmarket lane ;
  house Silent street
Elliston and Eade, St Nicholas st
Flory George, St Peter's street
Garnham Wm. & Hy. Butter market
Garrod George, Tower street
Manning John Spooner, Corn hill
Miller Robert (wine,) Butter mkt
Rabett Charles Edward, King st

Ridley Henry, George, & Wm. Fore st
Whimper Nathl. St Margaret's green

WIRE WORKERS.

Hill Joseph, St Matthew's street
Keeble Jeremiah, Butter market

WOOLSTAPLER.

Alexander Edward, Tanners' lane ;
  house St John street

COACHES.

*From the Great White Horse Hotel,
the White Hart, and the Suffolk
Hotel.*
Mails to London, at ½-past 11 night,
and to Norwich and Yarmouth, at
½ past 3 morning
From the Suffolk Hotel.
The Original Blue, to *London*, at ¼
past 1 afternoon, and to Yarmouth,
at ½ past 1 aft. daily, except Sund
To Bury St Edmunds & Cambridge,
at 11 morning and 4 afternoon,
daily, except Sunday, through
Needham-market and Stowmarket
From Haxell's office, Brook street.
To meet the *Eastern Counties' Railway Trains at Colchester,* the
QUICKSILVER, at 7 morning ; the
RETALIATOR (from Woodbridge)
at 20 min. before 9 morning ; the
SHANNON (from Halesworth) at
½ past 11 mg ; and the NORWICH
DAY COACH, at ½ past one, daily,
except Sunday. By these con-
veyances, passengers go from *Ips-
wich to London* in 4½ hours ; and
persons going by the Quicksilver,
and returning the same day, have
five hours in London
The Shannon, *to Halesworth,* through
Woodbridge, Wickham - market,
Saxmundham, and Yoxford, at 4
afternoon
The Retaliator, *to Woodbridge,* at 8
evening
The Day Coach, *to Norwich,* through
Scole, Bungay, &c. at half-past
one afternoon (except Sunday)
From the Coach and Horses.
The Regulator, *to Bury St Edmunds,*
&c. at 4 afternoon
From the Crown and Anchor.
The *Union,* to London and Norwich,
(*via* Framlingham,) at ½ past 3
afternoon

From the Rose Inn.

To Manningtree, Wm. Blyth's coach, every Tues. Thurs. & Sat. at 5 aft

OMNIBUSES.

To Hadleigh (John Warren) daily, at 5 aft. and Thos. Howard's, to *Sudbury,* Wed. & Sat. at 11 morn. from the Waggon and Horses

To Walton and Felixstow (Edmund Chapman) every Monday, Tuesday, Thursday, & Sat. at 5 aftn

To Colchester (James Rouse) from St Helen's street, Tuesday, Thursday, and Saturday, at 12 noon

STEAM PACKETS.

To London, calling at Harwich and Walton-on-the-Naze.

The ORWELL (Capt. S. Rackham,) from the Ipswich Steam Navigation Company's Wharf, every Monday and Thursday, at 8 morn. to Nicholson's Wharf, Lower Thames street, London. *(Returns Tuesday and Friday)*

The ORION (Capt. R. Wheeler,) from Wm. May's wharf, opposite St. Peter's church, every Tuesday and Friday mornings, at 8, to the Old Swan Pier, Upper Thames street, London. *(Returns Thursday and Saturday)*

☞ *Omnibuses* convey passengers to and from Woodbridge, Saxmundham, Yoxford, Stowmarket, &c. on the arrival and departure of the London steamers

STEAM PACKET TO HARWICH, the River Queen, from the Ipswich Steam Navigation Co.'s Wharf, daily in summer, and three times a week in winter, according to tide. George Daking, *wharfinger*

CARRIERS.

(By Waggon, Van, &c.)

NOLLER'S SPRING VANS convey goods from the Queen's Head Inn to Norwich, Eye, Debenham, &c. every Wednesday and Saturday nights, at 10 ; and to London (*by Railway from Colchester,*) every Tuesday & Friday mornings at 6

Henry, Robert, and John Smith's waggons, from Carr street to *London,* every Sunday, Tuesday, and Thursday, and to Yarmouth, Norwich, Bungay, and all the

towns in Suffolk and Norfolk, every Mon. Thurs. and Sat. aft

James Rouse, from St Helen's street, to Colchester, &c., every Tuesday, Thursday, and Saturday, at 12 noon, with goods for London, &c.

John Warren's Van, from the Waggon and Horses, to *London* and *Hadleigh* daily

CARRIERS FROM THE INNS.

Those marked 1, attend the Admiral's Head ; 2, Angel ; 3, Bell ; 4, Black Horse ; 5, Bull ; 6, Cow and Gate ; 7, Curriers' Arms ; 8, Feathers ; 9, Green Man ; 10, Gun ; 11, Halberd ; 12, Ipswich Arms ; 13, Plough ; 14, Post Chaise ; 15, Queen's Head, St. Matthew's street ; 16, Rose Inn ; 17, Royal Oak ; 18, Salutation ; 19, Sea Horse ; 20, Ship ; 21, Sorrel Horse ; 22, Sun ; 23, Waggon & Horses ; 24, White Swan ; and 25, from the White Lion, St. Margaret's street.

☞ When not otherwise expressed, they arrive on Tuesday and Saturday mornings, and depart about 4 afternoon.

Places.	Carriers.

11 Aldborough, James Smith, Tue. Thu. and Sat. 11 morning

Ash Bocking, (Globe,) Henry Robinson

11 Ashfield, Wm. Osborn

Beccles and Bungay, (see Smith's waggons)

19 Bentley, J. Reynolds, Wed. & Sat ; 13 Rouse, Tues ; and 23 Joseph Peck, Wednesday and Friday

Bergholt, (King's Head,) W. Church

19 Bildeston, Jas. Gosling, Monday, Wed. and Thu ; & 10 Webb, daily

13 Blaxhall, Thomas Cooper

6 Botesdale, R. Barham ; and 19 Minter

23 Boxford, T. Howard, Wed. & Sat

10 Branston, John Bonn

6 Brundish, Reeve and Steggall, Monday and Thursday

2 Bucklesham, — Syer, Saturday

23 Burgh, David Baxter

19 Bury St Edmunds, Garrod's waggons, Mon. Tues. Thu. and Fri ; & 23 *Mail Cart,* daily, at 5 evng

25 Cambridge, Isle of Ely, &c. Jas. Bradman, Friday morning

23 Charsfield, Mary Smith, Sat

3 Chelmondiston, Wright, M. Wed. & Fri ; & 23 Scaff, Tue. Thu. & S

19 Chellesworth, Snell, M. W. & Sat

5 Clackton, G. Townsend, W. & Sat

6 Cockfield, Osborn, Tue. and Fri
8 Coddenham, Wm. Wells, Mon.
  Wednesday and Saturday
Colchester, (see Noller's, Smiths's,
  Rouse's, and Warren's vans,) 11 S.
  Garwood ; and T. Harbur, from
  Cross Keys, Mon. Wed. & Fri ;
  also, Sheldrake, from the Cock
  and Pye, Tuesday and Thursday
23 Copdock, J. Peck, Wed. and Fri
12 Cretingham, Stockings, Wed. and
  Sat ; and 23 W. Kettle, Saturday
8 Crowfield, Dale, Durrant, & Carter
5 Debenham, M. and R. Page; 6 J.
  Alexander ; 10 Abbott and Son :
  22 A. Page ; and 23 Edw. Page,
  Tuesday, Thurday, and Saturday
Diss, 19 Cutting ; and 5 Webster
11 Earl Soham, James Rodgers
Easton, (Blue Coat Boy,) T. Airey
13 & 23 Elmsett, Wm. Podd, W. & S
23 Erwarton, S. Scruton, Tuesday,
  Thursday, and Saturday
Eye, 6 Gosling ; and 19 Robt. Dade
21 Fakenham, J. Parker
11 Framlingham, Whiteman, Fri ;
  19 S. Ixworth, Mon. & Thu. mng
19 Fressingfield, Alfred Hart, Tue
Framsden, (Saracen's Head,) Brown
  and Talmash
5 Gislingham, T. Talbot ; & 19 Davey
11 Grundisburgh, Bedingfield, Mon.
  Thu. and Sat ; and 23 D. Baxter
23 Hadleigh, John Warren, daily
5 Halesworth, Coates, Tue. & Sat ;
  and 14 Jas. Sawyer, Tue. & S. noon
23 Harwich, Rt. Salter, Tue. & Fri
8 Helmingstone, W. Adamson
20 Hemley, Page and Balls
16 Holbrook and Harkstead, Wm.
  Holden, Mon. Wed. & Sat ; 23
  Jas. Alderson, Tue. Thu. & Sat ;
  & Michl. Holden, (King's Head,)
  Tuesday and Saturday
21 Kirton, Hy. Wright, Tue. & Thu
6 Lavenham, Rushbrook and Springett, Tue. and Sat ; 10 T. Smith,
  Wednesday and Sat ; and 19 John
  Dakin, Tue. and Fri. mornings
12 Letheringham, Borlden, Sat
21 Levington, J. Chapman, Tues.
  Thursday, and Saturday
10 Manningtree, Wm. Blyth, daily,
  half-past four
23 Manningtree, Rt. Salter, Tue. & F
19 Melford, (Long,) Dakin, M. & Thu
6 Mendlesham, E. Woodscar, Tue

19 Middleton, J. Free
12 Nacton, J. Wheatley, M. W. & S
23 Nayland, Samuel Parker, Tue
11 Needham-market, T. Theobald,
  Tue. and Sat ; and 10 and 15 R.
  Kerridge, Mon. Tu. W. Thu. & S
23 Newton, Robt. Cramp, Sat
18 Norwich, Benj. Beart, Mon. 6
  evening ; (see Noller's vans, &c.)
23 Oakley, Robt. Salter, Tue. & F ;
  and 19 Bagley, Tue. and Sat
14 Orford, Hy. Pead, Sat ; and Wm.
  Mason, (chaise and pair,) Sat
12 Otley, J. Bumpstead & G. Smith,
  from Saracen's Head, Tue. & Sat
11 Saxmundham, Joseph Rouse
3 Shotley, G. Glading ; 16 William
  Grimwood, & Wm. Jackson, Tue.
  and Sat ; and 23 mail cart, daily,
  6 morning
Shottisham, (Chaise and Pair,) Benj.
  Kemp, Saturday
16 Stonham, Gilbert, Tue. and Sat ;
  23 Jph. Bridges, Tues. Thu. & S ;
  and 18 Higgins, Tuesday and Sat
10 Stowmarket, R. Kerridge ; 9 and
  15 Miller ; and 23 J. Syrett, Mon.
  Tue. Wed. Thu. and Sat ; also 23
  Mail Cart, daily, 6 morning
5 Stradbroke, W. Mann ; & 6 J. Smith
23 Stutton, John Askew, Tue. and
  Sat ; & *Mail Cart*, daily, 6 mrng
5 Sudbury, Wm. Man, Mon. and F ;
  and 23 Wm. Ruggall, Tues. mg ;
  and Howard's Omnibus, Wed. and
  Saturday, 11 morning
23 Tattingstone, Wm. Smith and Rt.
  Salter, Tuesday and Friday
19 Thetford, George Lambert, Fri.
19 Thorpe-le-Soken, Jas. Bagaley,
  Wednesday and Saturday
9 Thwaite, J. Robinson ; and Annis,
  from Half-Moon and Star, Sat
21 Trimley, Baxter, Tue. and Sat
14 Tunstall, — Stevenson, Sat
19 Walsham, Forman, Thursday
21 Walton and Felixstow, J. Page,
  & J. Charrington, M. Tue. Thu. & S
24 Wenham, Wm. Molton, Tuesday,
  Thursday and Saturday
19 Wetheringsett, J. Chapman
Wickham Market, (see Halesworth)
19 Wickham Skeeth, Rt. Davy ; and
  9 J. Ford, Saturday
23 Witnesham, Amor Shepherd
23 Woodbridge, Robt. Green ; and 1
  Thomas Newton, Mon. Tue. Thu.

Fri. and Sat; also 23 *Mail Cart*, daily, 9 morning

6 Woolpit, J. Wilden, Tue. & F. mg

Worlingworth, Wm. Youngs, Tue. and Sat; and 6 Steward, Sat. mg

TRADING VESSELS.

The *Suffolk and Norfolk Shipping Company's Vessels*, sail from Smart's Wharf, Quay street, every Tuesday, Thu. and Sat. to *Hay's Wharf, London*; J. B. Ross, *sec*; and Chas. Harbur, *wharfinger*

The *Ipswich and London United Shipping Company's Vessels*, from Wherry Quay, every Wednesday and Sat. to *Wool Quay, London*; Robert Paul, *Wharfinger*

Mulley, Bayley, and Co.'s Vessels, from the Quay, weekly, to Hull & Gainsborough; W. R. Mulley, acting partner

STEAM PACKETS, *(See Page* 117.*)*

COLNEIS HUNDRED

Is in the *Deanery* to which it gives name, in the *Archdeaconry of Suffolk*, and in *Woodbridge Union*. It is one of the smallest divisions of Suffolk, being only from four to five miles in breadth, but extending about ten miles S.E. from the Liberty of Ipswich, along the north-east bank of the river Orwell, to the Ocean, where it terminates in the cliffs of Felixstow, Walton, and Landguard Fort. It is bounded on the east by the river Deben, and on the north by Carlford Hundred, and comprises 4587 inhabitants, and about 17,000 acres of land, mostly a sandy but fertile loam, encompassed on three sides by the tides of the Ocean, the Orwell, and the Deben. It has an *Association for the Prosecution of Felons*, of which Mr. R. W. Porter is secretary; and has two *chief constables*, viz., Mr. Wm. Harper, of Falkenham, and Mr. Geo. Cobbold, of Trimley. Exclusive of several small extra-parochial places, it is divided into *ten parishes*, of which the following is an enumeration, shewing their territorial extent, the annual value of their land and buildings, as assessed to the property tax in 1815, and their population in 1801 and 1841.

PARISHES.	Acrs.	Rental.	Populatn. 1801.	Populatn. 1841.	PARISHES.	Acres.	Rental. £.	Populatn. 1801.	Populatn. 1841.
Bucklesham	1800	1713	186	255	Trimley Saint Martin	1200	3338	256	486
Falkenham	1550	2697	219	290					10
Felixstow*	1170	1670	259	552	Stratton Hall§				
Hemley	1155	504	66	71	Trimley St. Mary	1868	2100	330	430
Kirton..........	1929	1558	376	607	Walton	2000	2957	628	907
Levingion	1660	686	165	214					
Nacton†	2380	2065	461	765	Total ‡ ..	16,712	19,288	2946	4587

‡ In 1841, Colneis Hundred had 2285 *males*, 2302 *females*, and 964 *houses*, of which 34 were unoccupied. Of the males, 1166 were upwards of 20 years of age, and 201 of the inhabitants were not born in Suffolk.

* *Felixstow* includes 47 persons in *Landguard Fort*, of whom 8 are soldiers.

§ *Stratton Hall* is extra-parochial, and adjoins Levington.

† *Nacton* includes *Alnesbourn Priory* and *Purdies Farm*, which are *extra-parochial*, and comprise 8 houses and 39 souls.

† WOODBRIDGE UNION WORKHOUSE, which had 187 inmates, in 1841, and 157 in 1831, is in Nacton parish, and was built in 1756, at the cost of £4800, as a Workhouse for the paupers of the 28 parishes of *Colneis & Carlford Hundreds*, which were incorporated for the maintenance of their poor, by an act of the 29th of George II. To these 28 parishes, 18 others have been added by

the New Poor Law Commissioners, viz., Woodbridge and Charsfield, in *Loes Hundred ;* and 16 of the 17 parishes of *Wilford Hundred*, which see. The 46 united parishes now bear the name of WOODBRIDGE UNION, though the Workhouse is 8 miles S.S.W. of the town of Woodbridge, which returns four *guardians*, but each of the other parishes only one. The *population* of the Union, in 1841, was 23,015. The number of *paupers relieved* during the quarter ending March 17th, 1843, was 575 in-door, and 2431 out-door, of whom about 1100 were children. The *expenditure* for the relief of the poor, during the same quarter, was £3072. The average *weekly cost*, per head, of each pauper in the Workhouse, is 2s. 0½d. for food, and 5¼d. for clothing. Mr. John Constable is *master of the Workhouse*, which stands in a healthy situation, and has accommodations for 350 inmates. Mrs. Constable is the *matron*, and the Rev. W. Elston chaplain. The *Guardians* meet at the *Board Room, in Woodbridge*, every Monday morning ; and Mr. Benj. Moulton is their *clerk*. Mr. Thos. Carthew is SUPERINTENDENT REGISTRAR for this Union ; and Mr. Wm. Kemp is *Registrar of Marriages*. The REGISTRARS OF BIRTHS & DEATHS are Mr. J. Thurton, for *Woodbridge and Wilford Town District ;* Mr. Isaac Kent, of Dallinghoo, for *Woodbridge Out-District ;* Mr. J. Sheppard, of Rushmere, for *Carlford District ;* and Mr. T. Miles, of Trimley, for *Colneis District.*

BUCKLESHAM, a village, nearly 5 miles E.S.E. of Ipswich, has in its parish 255 souls, and about 1800 acres of land, of which 1525 acres are arable, 53A. woodland, and 41A. heath. Many curious petrifactions are found in this parish, which was anciently called *Bulechamp*, and was the demesne of Wm. de Kerdeston, in the reign of Edward III. The Rev. John Cartwright is now lord of the manor of Bucklesham, and owner of a great part of the soil ; but the hamlet of *Kembroke*, 1½ mile S.E. of the village, is the lordship of Sir Philip Broke ; and other portions of the parish belong to Sir Robt. Harland, the families of Garrod, Daniel, and Grimwood ; and a few smaller proprietors. The *Church* (St. Mary) is a small ancient fabric, which was re-pewed in 1842, and is a discharged *rectory*, valued in K.B. at £9. 1s. 7d., and in 1835, at £560. The tithes have recently been commuted for a yearly rent-charge of £524. The Rev. Ellis Walford, of Dallinghoo, is patron and incumbent. DIRECTORY : Rev. Benj. Lucas Cubitt, *curate ;* Wm. Ablett, *shoemaker ;* John Bennett, shopkeeper & vict., *Shannon ;* Jas. Collington, *blacksmith ;* Wm. Daniel, *corn miller ;* Henry Gowing, *mill manager ;* John Steel, *farrier ;* and Nathaniel Thurston Codd, Barnabas Collings, John Cross, Joseph Dawson, Hy. and Thos. Garrod, George Read, and Edward Robinson, *farmers.*

FALKENHAM, a scattered village, about a mile west of the river Deben, nearly 10 miles E.S.E. of Ipswich, and 7 miles S. of Woodbridge, has in its parish 290 souls, and 1550 acres of land, partly in rich marshes, extending southward to *King's Fleet*, a large sheet of water, stretching eastward from Trimley to the Deben, and serving as a drain for the low lands in this neighbourhood. The Duke of Hamilton is lord of the manor, but a great part of the soil (both freehold and copyhold) belongs to other proprietors. The *Church* (St. Ethelbert) is a discharged *vicarage*, endowed with all the tithes except those of barley, which were appropriated to the priory of Dodnash, and now belong to the manor of Falkenham-Dodnash. The benefice is valued in K.B. at £7. 11s., but is now worth about £300 per annum. The Crown is patron, and the Rev. Wm. Jackaman incumbent. Here is an Independent Chapel, erected some years ago, by Mr. Deane, at the cost of £500, and recently enlarged at the expense of £200, raised by subscription. In 1625, the *Rev. John Webb* left three copyhold cot-

tages, and 4A. 1R. of land, for the relief of the poor of this parish not receiving parochial aid. They are now let for £15. 6s. per annum. DIRECTORY:—Rev. Wm. Jackaman, *Vicarage;* Edwd. Kersey, gent. *Falkenham Hall;* Thomas Dains, gent.; Thos. Cornish, vict. *Dog;* Thos. Cooper, *blacksmith;* Harriet Jones, *schoolmistress;* Rev. H.H. Scullard, *Independent minister;* Samuel Block and John Stannard, *shopkeepers;* Thomas Smith and Wm. Thompson, *joiners;* Robert Daniel and Wm. Harper, *farmers;* and John Ruffles, *corn miller,* &c.

FELIXSTOW is a delightfully situated village and *bathing place,* on the sea coast, a little south of the mouth of the river Deben, 5 miles E.N.E. of Harwich, 12 miles S.E. by E. of Ipswich, and 10 miles S. by E. of Woodbridge. Its parish has 552 souls, and about 1170 acres of land, forming a narrow tract, terminating in bold *cliffs* on the sea-shore, along which it extends nearly five miles, from the mouth of the estuary of the Orwell and Stour, to that of the Deben or Bawdsey Haven. It is said to have been called Felix-stow, from *Felix,* the Burgundian, who converted the East Anglians to Christianity, and became the first bishop of Dunwich, in 630. It has been conjectured that this saint landed, and for some time resided here, on his arrival in this country; but the place was no doubt a part of the parish of Walton, and did not receive its present name till a *Priory of Black Monks,* dedicated to St. Felix, was founded here by Roger Bigod, Earl of Norfolk, who gave it as a cell to the priory at Rochester, about A.D. 1105. He endowed it with the lands taken out of his manor of Walton, and it was afterwards called the manor of Felixstow Priory. It was one of the monasteries which Henry VIII. suppressed, and gave to Cardinal Wolsey, towards the endowment of his college at Ipswich, in 1525, when it was valued at £6. 16s. 1d. per annum. It was granted in the 29th of Elizabeth to Thomas Seckford, and became annexed to Seckford Hall estate, in Bealings. No traces of the priory are now extant, though many carved stones, and " littled mitred images," are said to have been found upon its site about a century ago. WALTON CASTLE stood in Felixstow parish, upon the high cliff, nearly a mile south of the village, where its western foundations, about 187 yards in length, were remaining in 1740, but were, some years afterwards, washed away by the ocean, which is slowly but constantly encroaching on this part of the coast. This castle occupied the site of a *Roman fortification,* supposed to have been built by Constantine the Great, when he withdrew his legions from the frontier towns in the east of Britain. Many *Roman urns, rings,* and *coins,* of the Vespasian and Antonine families; of Severus and his successors, to Gordian the Third; and of Gallienus and his successors, to Arcadius and Honorius, have been found here, together with several dies that had been used for coining money. This was one of the castles of Hugh Bigod, Earl of Norfolk, which were destroyed in 1174, by order of Henry II., in consequence of that nobleman having joined the rebel princes, as already noticed at page 51. The demolition of Walton Castle is said to have been so complete, that " to prevent its ever rising again, the stones of it were carried into all parts of Felixstow, Walton, and Trimley; and footpaths were paved with them, on both sides of the roads." About a quarter of a mile west of Felixstow village, are the ruins of an extensive mansion, long known by the name of the *Old Hall,* and supposed to have been erected as the

manor-house of Walton, after the destruction of the castle. In this house, Edward III. lodged several nights, when on a visit to his manor of Walton, in 1339. (See p. 53.) The ruins now standing are about 73 feet in length, and 32 in breadth, and vary from 6 to 24 feet in height.

LANDGUARD FORT, or *Languard Fort*, at the southern extremity of Felixstow parish, stands upon a narrow tongue of land, which projects into the ocean, at the mouth of the Orwell, opposite Harwich, and forms the south-eastern point of Suffolk. Camden, who wrote before the first fort was erected here, says, that " the shore is very well defended by a vast ridge, called *Langerston*, which, for about two miles, lies all along out of the sea, not without great danger and terror to mariners. 'Tis, however, of use to fishermen for drying of their fish, and does in a manner fence the spacious harbour of Orwell." Its name is a corruption of *Langer Fort*, and the tongue of land, on the point of which it stands, consists of a common and marshes, which have been called *Langer* from time immemorial, and are supposed to have been recovered from the ocean at some remote period, as it is evident that the estuary of the Orwell and Stour once extended about two miles more northward than it does now, to the cliffs of Walton and Felixstow. It is about two miles across the estuary from the fort to Harwich ; but the only safe entrance for shipping, is by a deep but narrow channel on the Suffolk side, near the fort. The *first fort* had four bastions, called the King's, Queen's, Warwick's, and Holland's, and each mounting fifteen large guns. It was built about the beginning of the reign of Charles I., and its chapel was consecrated by the Bishop of Norwich, in 1628. It was demolished by order of parliament, and its site is now a burial ground for the use of the garrison. The present fort was erected in 1718, about a quarter of a mile further to the south, at the termination of the tongue of land, so that it is encompassed on three sides by the ocean, and on the north by a deep fosse, across which is a drawbridge, opposite the entrance gate. Considerable labour and expense were required in laying the foundations of the walls and batteries, upon which there are 23 *thirty-two-pounders*, and 21 smaller pieces of cannon. During the late war, this fort had a numerous garrison, and the yearly salary paid to its governor was £365, and that to the lieutenant-governor, £182. 10s. It has now only a *lieutenant-governor* (viz., Lieut.-Colonel Charles Augustus West,) and a resident garrison, consisting of a sergeant-major, a master-gunner, a sergeant, three men of the royal artillery, and two invalids. About the year 1806, eight small towers, each mounting three guns, were erected on the coast near this fort, but three of them being undermined by the sea, were taken down in 1826 and 1838. The Dutch, in 1667, landed 3000 men at the foot of Felixstow cliff, and marching under cover of some sandhills towards the fort, lodged themselves within musket-shot on two sides of it. After an hour's incessant firing with their small arms, they were put to flight by the discharge of two or three guns from a galliot lying off the shingle, which scattered the pebbles among them, and so alarmed them, that they fled to their ships and left the coast.

The VILLAGE OF FELIXSTOW has been much improved of late years, by the erection of many neat houses for the accommodation of

visitors, and it is now in high celebrity as a bathing place. It is situated more than three miles north of Languard Fort, on the crown and side of a bold acclivity, commanding extensive views of the ocean and the shores of Suffolk and Essex, and descending to a beautiful beach, where some of the houses stand within a few yards of the high-watermark at spring tides. At the mouth of the Deben, or Bawdsey Haven, about a mile north of the village, is the hamlet of *Felixstow Ferry*. On the cliff, a little west of the village, is *Felixstow Cottage*, originally a fishmonger's hut, which the taste of the eccentric Philip Thicknesse, when lieutenant-governor of Languard Fort, converted into a charming retreat, which is described at considerable length by Mrs. Thicknesse, in her Memoirs, but has since undergone many alterations. The arch which she mentions as being formed of hugh stones in front of the cottage, has been removed, for the purpose of opening out a more extensive marine prospect from the terrace that winds round the edge of the cliff. This retreat is now a handsome mansion, with beautiful grounds, and is occupied by J. C. Cobbold, Esq., of Ipswich, but belongs to *Sir Samuel Brudenell Fludyer, Bart.*, whose grandfather was created a baronet in 1759. The spring tides now approach within about twenty yards of the house, though in 1800 its pleasure grounds extended more than 200 yards between it and the beach. Sir Robert Harland, of Orwell Park, erected a handsome villa here for his occasional residence, in 1843. Mr. C. Meadows, of Ipswich, and other speculators, have within the last few years erected here neat houses and cottages, which are let to visitors during the bathing season. The Hotel was built by J. C. Cobbold, Esq., in 1839. Human bones have occasionally been washed up here by the tides; and, in 1828, an arm bone was found on the beach, with a gold bracelet upon it. The coast in this neighbourhood abounds in *septaria*, of which great quantities are collected for the Roman cement works at Ipswich, and other places. Felixstow, except the small priory manor, is in the manor of Walton-with-Trimley, of which the Duke of Hamilton is lord; but the soil belongs to various freeholders and copyholders. The *Church* (St. Peter and St. Paul) is a small ancient structure, and is a *vicarage*, valued in K.B. at £5. 9s. 7d., and united with Walton, in the same patronage, impropriation, and incumbency.—(See Walton.) The *Poor's Estate*, anciently left for the benefit of poor widows, is copyhold of the manor of Walton-with-Trimley, and consists of two cottages, a blacksmith's shop, a garden, and 1A. 3R. of land, let for £16. 19s. 6d. per annum, to which is added a yearly rent-charge of 7s. out of the Town Piece. Mr. Chandler and others are trustees.

FELIXSTOW DIRECTORY.

Cobbold J. C. Esq. (and *Ipswich*)
Dobson Mr Daniel, (lodgings)
Edgar Rev John Rt. *Felixstow Hs*
Goram James, grocer and draper
Hall George, sen. shoemaker
Hall Hannah, shopkeeper
Harland Sir Robt. (& *Orwell Park*)
Hopkins Rev Thomas Mattw. *curate*, (and boarding school)
Rend Mrs Mary, *High row House*
Sawyer Henry, (lodgs.) Myrtle pl
Smith Wm. (lodgings,) Verandas
Whayman Benj. blacksmith

INNS AND TAVERNS.
Ferry Boat, Edward Pasifull, *Ferry*
Fludyer's Arms, Wm. Smith, (machine and bath owner)
Hotel, Mary Ann Mahew
Queen Victoria, Wm. Clark, *Ferry*
White Horse, George Hall, jun. (& shoemaker)

FARMERS AND GRAZIERS.
Bugg Joseph, Laurel farm

Cobbold Henry||Chandler John | Hyem Richard||Hyem Thomas
Cooke James P.||Horne Daniel | Pipe John Wroot||Lee Daniel

HEMLEY, a small village on the west bank of the river Deben, 5 miles S. of Woodbridge, and 8 miles E.S.E. of Ipswich, has in its parish 71 souls, and 1155 acres of land, belonging to the Chaplin, Meadows, and other families. At the Domesday survey, it was called *Hemele*, and was the lordship of Odo de Campania. The *Church* (All Saints) is a discharged *rectory*, valued in K.B. at £4. 19s. 1d., and in 1835, at £150. The Crown is patron, and the Rev. Fras. Cobbold, of Ipswich, is incumbent. The *farmers* are, James Cooper, William Kersey, *High House ;* and Pearl Cross, *Hemley Hall.*

KIRTON, a pleasant village 9 miles E.S.E. of Ipswich, and 6 miles S. of Woodbridge, has in its parish 607 inhabitants, and 1929 acres of fertile land, including 23A. of wood, and extending 1½ mile eastward to the river Deben and *Kirton Sluice,* where it has some rich salt marshes; and nearly 1 mile N.W. to the hamlet of *Kirton-Brook-Green.* It is in two manors, of which the Duke of Hamilton and the Rev. J. Cartwright are lords, but a great part of the soil belongs to the Executors of William Hawkins, Esq., Wm. Goodchild, Esq., Mr. G. Cook, the Ipswich Charity Trustees, and several smaller owners. The *Church* (St. Mary) is a rectory, valued in K.B. at £10. 13s. 4d., and in 1835, at £400. The Crown is patron, and the Rev. J. C. Alderson, M.A., incumbent. The glebe is 7A., and a handsome new Rectory House was built in 1843, at the cost of about £1500. Here is a neat Wesleyan Chapel, built in 1827. The *Poor's Allotment*, more than 4A., was awarded at an enclosure, in the 45th of George III., to provide fuel for the poor parishioners.

Alderson Rev J. C. rector
Alderton George, gent. *Manor Hs*
Catt John, butcher
Cook George, gent. *Kirton Hall*
Dardry John, parish clerk
Lanham Miss Sarah
Rivers Jas. O. vict. *Greyhound*
Smith John, schoolmaster
Smith S. blacksmith
   Collar & Harness Makers.
Fenton Danl.||Hudson Daniel
   Boot and Shoe Makers.
Baldwin Stephen||Fenton Philip
Page John||Ward Henry

   Bricklayers, &c.
Brooks Wm.||Simpson James
   Shopkeepers.
Ansell John, (grocer and draper)
Baldwin Stephen||Gooding Joseph
   Wheelwrights.
Durrant Charles||Hacon Henry
FARMERS. *(Marked * are Owners.)*
*Alderton George||Ansell Thomas
Ashwell John, (and grazier)
Burch Wm.||*Cook George
*Clark Wm.||Cross Henry
Marriott Thomas, (and corn mert.)
Sewell Francis||Spraggons Joseph

LEVINGTON, 6 miles S.E. of Ipswich, is a village and parish pleasantly situated on the north-east bank of the Orwell. It contains 214 souls, and 1660 acres of land, exclusive of *Stratton Hall*, (a farmhouse,) which, with 600A. of land, is extra-parochial, and belongs to Major Walker. Stratton was anciently a separate parish, and had a lazar-house and a church, and the foundations of the latter may still be seen, overgrown with trees and bushes. Sir Robert Harland and Sir Philip Broke are lords of Levington manor, and owners of most of the soil. *Levington Hall* is a small manor, belonging to Major Walker. The *Church* (St. Peter) is a rectory, valued in K.B. at £6. 1s. 8d., and united with Nacton. The steeple is said to have been erected by

Sir Robert Hitcham, who, in 1654, founded *six almshouses* here, for three poor women of Levington and three of Nacton, with an endowment, now affording to each inmate about 5s. per week, and a yearly allowance of clothing and fuel, as will be noticed with the founder's other charities at Framlingham. The *Church Estate,* comprising a house, and 2½A. of land, at Trinley St. Martin, let for £15 a year, has for a long period been appropriated to the use of Levington church. In 1718, Edmund Edwards, a farmer of this parish, discovered the fertilizing effects of the *Crag or Shell,* now so extensively used in Suffolk for manuring the land. Being short of dung, he carried several loads of crag, and spread it over part of a field, which, to his surprise, yielded a much better crop than those parts which he had covered with dung. This crag is a sandy stratum, full of small shells, and other marine deposits, and is in many places of considerable thickness. It is said to have been used in the west of England as a fertilizer of the soil, long before it was used for that purpose in Suffolk. DIRECTORY: Major Charles Walker, *Levington Hall;* Wm. Bryant, John Cook, John Dawson, L. Kersey (Stratton Hall,) and Rt. Woodrow, *farmers;* Wm. Franks, *shoemaker ;* Charles Pierce, vict., *Ship ;* and Mary Simpson, *shopkeeper.*

NACTON, on the north-east bank of the broad river Orwell, 4 miles S.E. of Ipswich, is a pleasant scattered village and parish, comprising 2380 acres of land, and 765 inhabitants, including *Woodbridge Union Workhouse,* (noticed at page 119;) the extra-parochial places called *Alnesbourn Priory* and *Purdies Farm ;* and the beautiful seats of *Orwell Park* and *Broke Hall,* which have extensive pleasure-grounds descending to the water's edge. *Nacton Heath,* on the north side of the parish, was mostly enclosed under an act passed in 1810. Sir Philip Broke is lord of the *manors* called Cow Haugh, Nacton, and Kembroke, but part of the soil belongs to Sir Robert Harland and Major Walker. These manors were anciently held by the Fastolf family, and passed in marriage with their heiress to the Brokes. *Sir Richard Broke,* Lord Chief Baron in the reign of Henry VIII., is supposed to have built *Cow Haugh,* or BROKE HALL (as it is now called,) about the year 1526, but it was mostly rebuilt, and considerably enlarged, by Philip Bowes Broke, Esq., in 1767. Robert Broke, of Nacton, was created a baronet in 1661 ; but on his death without male issue, the title became extinct. His daughter and heiress married his nephew, who left issue only by his second wife, daughter of Sir John Hewet. The late gallant *Admiral Sir Philip Bowes Vere Broke,* son of the late Philip Broke, Esq., of Broke Hall, was created a *baronet* in 1813, and died in 1841, when he was succeeded by his eldest son, the present baronet. His brother, the late *Major-General Charles Broke Vere,* K.C.B., was a highly distinguished officer, in active service from 1799 till the battle of Waterloo, in 1815 ; and was one of the Parliamentary representatives of the Eastern Division of Suffolk from 1834, till his death in April, 1843. The late celebrated ADMIRAL VERNON, the captor of Porto Bello, fixed his residence at Nacton. His nephew, to whom he left most of his fortune, rebuilt the house, and surrounded it with the extensive and beautiful grounds called ORWELL PARK, from the noble river which bounds them on the south. This gentleman was created a peer of Ireland, in 1776, by the title of *Vis-*

count Orwell, and in the following year was raised to the dignity of *Earl of Shipbrooke;* but on his death, in 1783, both these titles became extinct, and his estates passed to his nephew, the late John Vernon, Esq., whose heiress carried them in marriage to their present owner, *Sir Robert Harland, Bart.*, now of Orwell Park, and formerly of Wherstead Lodge, whose father was created a baronet, in 1771, by the title of *Sir Robert Harland of Sproughton*, and sailed in the same year as commander-in-chief of his Majesty's fleet to the East Indies, —was second in command to Admiral Keppel, in 1778, and was appointed one of the Lords of the Admiralty in 1782, but died in 1784. The present worthy baronet was born in 1765. ALNESBOURN PRIORY and PURDIES FARM form an extra-parochial district on the north side of Nacton, about 3 miles S.E. of Ipswich, and contain about 777A. of land, (belonging to Sir Philip Broke,) eight houses, and 39 inhabitants. This district is said to have had three churches, viz., *Hallowtree, St. Petronille*, and *Bixley*, but their sites are unknown. *Alnesbourn Priory* was a small house of Augustine monks, which was added as a cell to Woodbridge in 1452. The site of this priory is occupied by a farm-house, and that of its chapel by a barn, near which many human bones were lately found. On the heath, near the Union Workhouse, are a number of mounds or *barrows*, commonly called *Seven Hills*, and supposed to occupy the spot where *Earl Ulfketel* engaged the Danes in 1010. In these *tumuli*, human bones have occasionally been found. NACTON CHURCH is dedicated to St. Martin, and is a rectory, valued in K.B. at £8. 7s. 1d., and having that of Levington annexed to it. The tithes of the two parishes were commuted, in 1839, for a yearly modus of £513. Lady Harland is patroness, and the Rev. Henry Edgell, M.A., incumbent. Here is a small Wesleyan Chapel, built in 1839.

NACTON DIRECTORY.

Broke Sir Philip, Bart. (also Colonel G. H. and Lieutenants G. N. and C. A. Broke,) *Broke Hall*
Harland Sir Rt. Bart. *Orwell Park*
Browne Mr., Flewell Enefer
Cooke Wm. shopkeeper
Cooper Jno. farmer, *Purdies Farm*
Cooper Charles Thomas, farmer, *Alnesbourn Priory*
Constable John, governor of Woodbridge Union Workhs. (See p. 119)
Edgell Rev. Henry, M.A. *Rectory*
Elston Mrs Sarah

Field Wm. shopkpr. & schoolmaster
Fish Mr Js. (& Ann, boarding school)
Fuller John, joiner
Grimwade John, *Park Farm*
Hamond Wm. shoemaker
Herbert Joseph, butcher
Keen Robert, vict. Anchor
Mellor Joshua, blacksmith
Page Miles. corn miller & overseer
Roughhead George, shoemaker
Stephens Frederick, tailor
Webb Hy. farmer, *Manbrook Farm*
Webster Jas. wheelwright and shopr
Wheatley Mary, shopkeeper

TRIMLEY ST. MARTIN and ST. MARY, 9 miles S.E. by E. of Ipswich, form a large village and two adjoining parishes, having their churches standing in the same churchyard, and their lands extending more than a mile westward, to the shores of the Orwell, and eastward to the King's Fleet, which drains the marshes, and extends three miles eastward to the river Deben. Trimley heath was enclosed about 1804 and 1808. *Trimley St. Martin* has 1200A. of land, and had 486 inhabitants, in 1841, including the family occupying an extra-parochial estate, called *Stratton Hall*, which adjoins Levington, and with which

it is described at page 124. *Trimley St. Mary* has 430 inhabitants, and 1868 acres of land, including *Blowfield Hall, Searson*, and other farms, near the Orwell, from one to two miles S.W. of the village. Both parishes are in the Duke of Hamilton's *manor* of Walton with-Trimley, but part of the soil belongs to Edwin Julian, Esq., Mr. G. Cobbold, Mr. B. Ashwell, and several smaller proprietors. *St. Martin's Church* is a discharged rectory, valued in K.B. at £12. 0s. 6d., and in 1835, at £423. It is in the patronage of Thomas Waller, Esq., and incumbency of the Rev. Dr. Kilderbee. *St. Mary's Church* is a venerable fabric, with a steeple, which has long been in ruins, and is supposed to have been built by Thomas de Brotherton, son of Edward I., whose arms are over the door. The living is a discharged rectory, valued in K.B. at £16. 13s. 4d., and in 1835 at £355; but the tithes were commuted in 1840 for a yearly modus of £480. 6s. 9d. to the rector, and £3. 13s. to the impropriator and vicar of Walton. The patronage is in the Crown; and the Rev. M. G. Edgar, M.A., of Ipswich, is the incumbent. *Alteston*, formerly a parish and rectory, was consolidated with Trimley, in 1362, and its church is supposed to have stood near Grimston Hall, where many human bones were dug up in 1720. In the village is a *Wesleyan Chapel*, built in 1839. The *Church School* was established in 1832, and is supported by subscription, for the education of the poor of both parishes. The *poor of St. Mary's* have a copyhold estate, left by ELLIS KINDGE, in 1669, and consisting of two cottages, a garden, and 10A. 1R. 14P. of land, let for £20 a year, which is distributed by Mr. Ashwell, one of the trustees. They have also an allotment of 4A., awarded in 1804, and let for £8. 17s.; and another allotment of 4A., awarded in 1808, and now let for £10 a year. The rents are distributed by the churchwardens and overseers. The poor of St. Martin's have an allotment of 4A., awarded in 1808, and now let for £10, which is distributed in coals at Christmas. *Grimston Hall*, now a farm-house, was the residence of the Barker family, now extinct, one of whom was created a baronet in 1621. It was previously the seat of THOMAS CAVENDISH, Esq., who was born here, and was the second Englishman that circumnavigated the globe. At his own expense, he fitted out three small vessels, of 120, 60, and 40 tons, manned by 123 men and boys, for the purpose of annoying the Spaniards in their American possessions. Sailing from Plymouth, in July, 1586, he passed through the straits of Magellan, and entered the South Seas, where he plundered several towns on the coasts of Chili and Peru, and took many valuable prizes. He returned home by way of the Cape of Good Hope, and reached Plymouth in Sept. 1588. The success of this voyage encouraged him to make a second attempt, with a stronger force; and in Aug. 1591, he sailed from Plymouth with five ships, but having passed the straits of Magellan, in May, 1592, he was parted from his fleet in the night, and never heard of afterwards.

TRIMLEY DIRECTORY.

*Those marked * are in St. Martin's, and the others in St. Mary's.*

*Cockle John, Esq.
Edgar Rev Edward R. curate
Glanfield Mrs Hannah
Miles Thos. regr. & relieving officer
Moore Thomas, schoolmaster
Norton Saml. brick & tile maker
Pearce Thomas, farrier
*Pooley James, corn miller
*Redgrave Wm. parish clerk
ScarlettD. btchr.&vict. Mariners'Inn
Sparling Wm. parish clerk

Woods Jas. plumber, glazier, and painter, *Post Office.* Letters despatched ½ past 4 afternoon

Blacksmiths.	Carpenters.
Green James	Copping Wm.
*Winks James	Kent Aaron
Boot &Shoe Mkrs.	FARMERS.
Gorham Wm.	Ashwell Benj.
*James Joseph	ChurchmanMary
ParkerWm.Sturgeon	*Churchman Wm

*Cobbold George, (chief constable) CordyChas. *Searson Farm*
Dawson John
*Everitt Samuel
*LastWm. *Grimston Hall*
Pipe Jas. *Blowfield Hall*
*Williams John

Shopkeepers.
Baxter David
*Cook Abm.
*James Joseph
Parker Thomas
Tailors.
Jacobs John
Smith Wm.
CARRIER TO IPSWICH.
Baxter David

WALTON, a large and well-built village, with several good shops and neat houses, was anciently a market-town, and is pleasantly situated about a mile from the cliffs of Felixstow, nearly two miles from the estuaries of the Deben and Orwell, 2¼ miles N. by E. of Landguard Fort, and 10 miles S.E. of Ipswich. Its parish contains 907 inhabitants, and about 2000 acres of fertile land, extending two miles westward, to *Walton Ferry,* and the small hamlet of *Wadgate,* on the east bank of the estuary of the Orwell and Stour, nearly opposite Harwich. The Duke of Hamilton is lord of the *manor of Walton-with-Trimley,* which includes nearly all the parish of *Felixstow,* within the bounds of which stood *Walton Castle,* already noticed at page 121. A great part of the soil belongs to E. Julian, Esq., J. Morrison, Esq., Mr. W. Fulcher, and other free and copyholders. It has been seen, in the history of Felixstow, that the noble family of Bigod, Earls of Norfolk, were anciently lords of Walton ; and one of them, Roger Bigod, obtained a charter for a market here, in 1288, but it has long been obsolete. The *Market Cross* is still standing, and is now used as a lock-up, for the temporary confinement of prisoners. The *Church* (St. Mary) is an ancient structure, and that portion used for divine worship is kept in good repair; but the tower is nearly demolished, and nothing remains of one of the aisles except the wall, to the height of about a foot from the ground. The benefice is a discharged *vicarage,* valued in K. B. at £4. 6s. 8d., and in 1839 at £290, with the vicarage of Felixstow annexed to it. — Richards, Esq., and others, are patrons and impropriators; and the Rev. F. Nairn is the incumbent. Here is a *Baptist Chapel,* erected in 1812, at the cost of £500, by a congregation formed in 1808.

Post Office, at Frdk. Parker's. Letters arrive at 11 A.M., and are despatched at 4 P. M.
Barnes Stephen, cooper
Breeze Wm. coach maker
Charlton James, baker, &c
Chenery Cyrius, schoolmaster
Clifford Peter, hair dresser
Coghlan RevJohnArmstrong, curate
Durrant Stpn. collar & harness mkr
DurrantHy.cabinet mkr&paper hngr
Elphick Captain James
Fulcher Mr Wm. sen. and jun
Green Mrs Deborah
Harnby Mrs S. ‖ Green Mrs Debh.

Hodeley RevThos. Baptist minister
Julian Edwin, Esq. *Hill House*
Linch Captain William
Pearson Robt. plumber & glazier
Quilter John, gent. and Mrs Sarah
Smith Robert, gardener
Smith Jonathan, lodgings
Young John, parish clerk
INNS AND PUBLIC HOUSES.
Angel, Edmund Palmer
Ferry Boat, Richd. Hyem, jun. (& coal merchant) *Walton Ferry*
Feathers, James Chattin
Half Moon, Thomas Farnley

Blacksmiths.
Chaplin John
Whiteman John
Vincent Henry
Bricklayers.
Woolner Samuel
Woolner W.
Butchers.
Last George
Warren Charles
Corn Millers.
Denny Robert
Hughes Robert
Mower Wm.
FARMERS.
* *are Owners.*
Abbott Abm.
*Ashwood Joshua

Boby Wm.
Chapman Wm.
*Fulcher Wm.
*Julian Edwin
*Page Rd. Miles
Last George
*Steel John J.,
Wadgate
Woodgate Thos.
Joiners, &c.
Jackson Isaac (&
ironmonger)
Jackson George
Smith Edward,
(wheelwright)
Policemen.
Larter James

May George
Pork&SwineDlrs
BloomfieldEphm.
Horn James
Shoemakers.
Horne Robert
Hunting Wm.
Parker Fredk.
Thurston Wm.
SHOPKEEPERS.
† *are Grocers &*
Drapers.
Brook Wm.
†Capon Robert
Horne Wm.
†Page Wm.

†Stannard James
†TaylorJohnBur-
wood
Surgeons.
Grimwood Thos.
Wilkin Henry
Tailors.
Everitt Henry
Lovett Wm.
Scrutton Wm.
CARRIERS
To Ipswich and
Woodbridge.
Chapman James
Charrington Jno.
ChurchmanEdm.
Page John

CARLFORD HUNDRED

Is of an irregular figure, about ten miles in length, from north to south, and from 4 to 6 miles in breadth. It is bounded on the south by Col-neis Hundred; on the west, by Woodbridge, the river Deben, and Wilford Hundred; on the north, by Loes and Debenham Hundreds; and on the west, by Bosmere-and-Claydon Hundred, and the borough of Ipswich. It is in the *Deanery of Carlford*, Archdeaconry of Suf-folk, and Woodbridge Union. (See page 119.) The southern part of it, extending from the bounds of Ipswich to Woodbridge and the river Deben, has generally a light sandy soil, and several open heaths; but in its northern parts a rich loam prevails, and there is a strip of rich marsh land, and a few small *hop-yards*, on its southern boundary, in the valley extending eastward from *Bixley Decoy Ponds*, near Ipswich, *to Kirton Sluice*, on the river Deben. It contains *eighteen parishes*, of which the following is an enumeration, shewing their territorial extent, the annual value of their lands and buildings, as assessed to the pro-perty tax in 1815, and their population in 1801 and 1841.

PARISHES.	Acrs.	Ren-tal.	Populatn. 1801.	1841	PARISHES.	Acres.	Rental. £.	Populatn. 1801.	1841.
Bealings Great..	1100	1659	218	377	Newbourn	840	882	150	163
Bealings Little ..	755	842	277	322	Otley	2157	3097	415	647
Brightwell	510	486	50	81	Playford	650	1710	216	253
Burgh	1200	2182	222	266	Rushmere(part-				
Clopton*........	2034	3310	389	389	ly in Ipswich	2720	2301	287	564
Culpho	704	559	73	70	borough†) ..}				
Foxhall	1060	1385	150	200	Tuddenham	1232	2424	205	423
Grundisburgh ..	1897	2844	641	874	Waldringfield ..	834	764	118	174
Hasketon	1600	2783	360	508	Witnesham	2000	2993	387	543
Kesgrave*......	1610	965	73	88					
Martlesham	2558	1975	269	510	Total†....	25,461	33,761	4500	6452

* Clopton had 468 inhabitants, and Kesgrave, 101, in 1831.

† Of the 564 souls in *Rushmere*, in 1841, 223 were within the Liberty of the Borough of Ipswich.

‡ The number of HOUSES in 1841, was 1305 *inhabited*, 31 *empty, & 4 building*.

☞ The *Chief Constables* are, Mr. Arthur Biddell, of Playford; and Mr. John Spurling, of Burgh.

BEALINGS (GREAT,) a pleasant village and parish, 2¼ miles W. of Woodbridge, has 377 souls and about 1100 acres of land. It was successively the Lordship of the families of Petches, Tuddenham, Clynch, Pitts, Bridges, and Major, who resided at *Bealing's Hall*, which stood near the church, and was taken down about 60 years ago. The heiress of the Major family married an ancestor of Lord Henniker, the present Lord of the manor, who resides at Worlingworth Hall. A great part of the soil belongs to George Moor, Esq., of Bury St. Edmunds, Major E. Moor, of *Bealings House*, and other proprietors. G. Moor, Esq., owns the estate attached to SECKFORD HALL, which stands about 1¼ mile W. of Woodbridge, and has been farmed during the last 60 years by the Heard family. This hall was the seat of the Seckford family from the time of Edward I. to that of Charles I., and was rebuilt, or considerably improved in the reign of Elizabeth, by *Thomas Seckford, Esq.*, the munificent founder of the almshouses at Woodbridge, as noticed at a subsequent page. The last of the Seckfords married Dorothy, daughter of Sir Henry North, and settled the estate upon her. At her death, in 1673, she bequeathed it to Seckford Cage, the heir-general of the Seckford family, by whom it was sold to the Atkinsons. The house, now the seat of Major Edward Moor, was the residence of the Rev. — Evanson, author of " *The Dissonance of the Evangelists ;*" and was occupied by Admiral Sir Joshua Rowley, about the year 1806, when the Major purchased it, with the contiguous estate. Several *urns*, supposed to be Roman, have been found in the parish. The *Church* (St. Mary) is a rectory, valued in K.B. at £10. 4s. 7d., and in 1835 at £250, but is now worth £300 per annum. Lord Henniker, M.P., is patron, and the Hon. and Rev. W. C. Henniker, M.A., incumbent.

Baldry Samuel, vict. *Boot Inn*
Boon Thos. brick and tile maker
Booth Wm. hurdle maker
Broom Thomas, shoemaker
Carr Edward, joiner
Flory Wm. wheelwright and machine maker
Garrod Charles, gardener
Henniker Hon.& Rev.W.C.*Rectory*,
Hinde Wm. shoemaker
Kersey Mr George
Kersey George, jun. bricklayer
Leggett Jerh. blacksmith&drill mkr.
London F. boarding & day school

Luccock Mr Wm John
Mayhew John, gentleman
Meadows Daniel Charles, solicitor, (office Woodbridge)
Mickelbright James, gentleman
Moor Major Edwd. F.R.S., F.A.S., &c. Bealings House
Moor Rev Edw. Jas. B.A. incumbent of Brightwell

FARMERS.

Rivers, Joseph, corn miller.
Brundley Wm. *Bealings Hall*
Heard Thos. & Jerh. *Seckford Hall*
Flory John || Loom Frederick
Rose David || Smith John

BEALINGS (LITTLE,) 3 miles W. by S. of Woodbridge, is a village and parish, containing 322 souls and 755 acres of land, watered on the north by a small rivulet. Lord Henniker is Lord of the manor, but the greater part of the soil belongs to Jas. Colvin, Esq., R. N. Shawe, Esq., and a few smaller proprietors. The *Church* (All Saints) is a rectory valued in K.B. at £6. 7s. 3d., and in 1835 at £140, but the tithes have recently been commuted for a yearly modus of £204. F. Smythies, Esq., is patron, and the Rev. F. Nairn incumbent. The principal inhabitants are James Colvin, Esq., of *Bealings Grove*, (a handsome mansion mostly erected in 1830.) Robt. Adams, parish

clerk ; David Baldwin, *shoemaker ;* Wm. Finch, and Eliz. Weeding, *shopkeepers ;* John Hagger, blacksmith ; John Hullis, gardener ; Jas. Last, *tailor ;* Edward Pells, vict., *Admiral's Head ;* and Thos. Smith Flory and Jeremiah Heard, *farmers.*

BRIGHTWELL, a parish of only 510 acres and 81 souls, has a few scattered houses on a pleasant acclivity, 5½ miles E. by S. of Ipswich, on the north side of the rivulet, running from Bixley Decoy to Kirton Sluice. It was successively the lordship of the families of Lamput, Jermy, Hewett, Wingfield, Essington, and Barnardiston. In 1663, Sir Samuel Barnardiston was created a baronet, and rebuilt the hall at a great expense, but it was taken down about 1760, except a portion occupied by a farmer. The manor passed with the heiress of the Barnardistons to an ancestor of its present owner, Sir John Kenward Shaw, of Eltham, Kent, who is also patron of the church (St. John) which is a perpetual curacy, with that of Foxhall annexed to it, valued at only £54, and enjoyed (together with Kesgrave) by the Rev. E. J. Moor, B.A., of Great Bealings. *Directory :*—Wm. Everitt, farmer, *Brightwell Hall ;* Thos. Garrod, farmer, *Derry Farm ;* Wm. Gault, blacksmith ; and Thos. Ward, wheelwright.

BURGH, a village on the Debenham road, 3½ miles N. W. of Woodbridge, has in its parish 266 souls and 1200 acres of land. The manor belonged to Odo, Earl of Albemarle, at the Domesday survey, and afterwards passed to the Uffords. Maude de Lancaster, relict of Wm. de Burgh, gave it to the chantry which she founded at Campesse, but soon afterwards transferred to the nuns of Bruisyard. John Fitzgerald, Esq., is now lord of the manor, but a great part of the soil belongs to W. W. Page, Esq., J. Brand, Esq., the trustees of W. Rouse, Esq., and several smaller owners. *Thistleton Hall,* about a mile east of the village, is an ancient mansion occupied by a farmer, and surrounded by a moat. One of its rooms has a richly carved chimney-piece and wainscot. The *Church* (St. Botolph) is a small ancient structure, and near it there is supposed to have been a castle or encampment, either of the Romans or Saxons. The *rectory*, valued in K.B. at £8. 3s. 4d., and in 1835 at £247, is in the gift of M. Barnes, Esq., and incumbency of the Rev. G. F. Barlow, M.A., who has a neat residence half a mile from the church. The glebe is 7a. 3r., and the tithes have recently been commuted for a yearly modus of £356. The *Town Lands, &c.,* partly free and partly copyhold, are appropriated to the repairs of the church, the payment of public charges, and other public uses, and have from an early period been vested in trustees, chosen from time to time by the surviving trustees and the parishioners. They comprise three cottages occupied by poor persons rent free ; 12a. 7p. in Burgh, let for about £10 a year ; and 1a. 2r. in Grundisburgh, let for £2 a year.

Barlow Rev. G. F., M.A., *Rectory*
Buttrum John, corn miller
Spurling John, gent. (chief constable,) *White House*

    Boot and Shoe Makers.
Broom Rt. || Baxter David (carrier)

FARMERS.
Baxter David || Smith James
Button Robert || Ellis Benjamin
Jasper George || Rudkin T.
Buttrum Fras. || Spurling Benjamin
Symonds Nathaniel, *Thistleton Hall*
Woods John || Wright Wm. (owner)

CLOPTON, a village and parish, on the Debenham road, 4 miles N.W. of Woodbridge, has 389 inhabitants and 2034 acres of land, including Clopton Green and several scattered houses and farms, extending two miles N. of the village. It is in the *manors* of Kingshall, Brendhall, Rousehall, and Wascolies, of which Major-General Felix Vincent Raper is lord, and holds a general *customary court* in the court-house yearly in July. Mr. Wm. Whiteside is steward. A great part of the soil is held by Lord Rendlesham, Mr. Wm. Steel, and other freeholders and customary tenants. In the 31st of Edward I., John de Weyland obtained a charter for a market and fair here, but they have long been obsolete. The Sackvilles, Weylands, and Bardolfs, were successively Lords of Clopton from the reign of Henry I. till after that of Edward III. The *Church* (St. Mary) is a small ancient fabric, and is a rectory valued in K.B. at £16. 13s. 4d., and in 1835 at £538, but the tithes were commuted in 1843 for £694 per annum. The Rev. Geo. Taylor is patron, and the Rev. Charles Taylor, B.A., is the incumbent, and has a neat *Rectory House*, which was much improved in 1831. The TOWN ESTATE comprises four tenements occupied rent-free by poor families; 14A. of land, held since 1489, for the repairs of the church and the relief of the poor, and let in 1828 for £32 a year; and the *Bell Pightle*, 1½A. let for £2. 5s. a year, which is applied in the service of the church bells. *Directory :—* Rev. Charles Taylor, B.A., *Rectory ;* James Crapnall and John Day, *shoemakers ;* John Crapnall, blacksmith; Richard Grayston, *wheelwright ;* and Wm. Barker, Eunice Baldry, James Bolton, Jph. Burch, Henry Broom, John Buckingham, Joshua Catt, *(Hall ;)* Wm. Catt, Samuel May. Wm. Smith, Wm. Steel, (and owner,) Wm. Steel, jun., and George Watkins, *farmers.*

CULPHO, a small parish, 4 miles west of Woodbridge, has only 70 souls and 704 acres of land. It was given by Wm. de Valoines, to Leiston Abbey, but was granted by Queen Elizabeth to Edward Grimstone. In 1764, it belonged to Sir John Blois, Bart.; but T. B. Gurdon, Esq., is now lord of the manor, impropriator of the tithes, and patron of the Church (St. Botolph,) which is a small ancient structure. The living is a perpetual curacy, valued at £54, and now enjoyed by the Rev. Thomas Mason. The poor parishioners have £4. 14s. 2½d. yearly from Sir M. Stanhope's charity, (see Sutton.) The *farmers* are Robert Harrison, Wm. Hunt, and James Thompson.

FOXHALL, a scattered village upon a gentle acclivity on the north side of the stream flowing from Bixley Decoy, 4 miles E. by S. of Ipswich, has in its parish 200 souls and 1060 acres of land, including a portion of the sandy heath on the north, and some rich marsh land on the south. Sir Robert Harland is lord of the manor and impropriator; but J. C. Cobbold, Esq., has an estate and a *hop garden* of 23A. here, and other portions of the parish belong to several smaller owners. The *Church* (All Saints,) was appropriated by Hughe de Darnford to Trinity Priory, Ipswich, but was granted by Henry VIII. to Sir Thomas Pope. It was much decayed in 1530, and for want of repairs, it soon afterwards became unfit for Divine service. Part of it is now standing, and used as one of the out-houses of the old *hall*, now a farmhouse. The living is a perpetual curacy, which has long been consolidated with that of the adjacent parish of Brightwell. In a small

planting of firs is a monument in memory of the Rev. George Routh, erected by his widow, in 1831. *Directory :*—William Brown, *beerhouse ;* Walter T. Cobbold, gent. *Temple ;* John Rout, blacksmith; John Rout, jun., and Bennett Skippin, *shoemakers ;* David Skippin, shopkeeper ; and John Burch, Robert Goodall, Mark Major *(Hall,)* James Salter and John Steel, *farmers.*

GRUNDISBURGH, a large village on a pleasant acclivity, 3½ miles W.N.W. of Woodbridge, and 7 miles N.E. by N. of Ipswich, has in its parish 874 souls and 1897A. of land. In 1285, Hugh Peche claimed a market here every Tuesday, and a fair during the whole of Whitsun-week, but both were obsolete some centuries ago. The *manor* was for many years the seat and property of the family of Blois, one of whom was created a baronet in 1668, and removed his residence to Cockfield Hall. (See Yoxford.) B. G. Dillingham, Esq., was seated here in 1811, but T. B. Gurdon, Esq., is now Lord of the manor ; and a great part of the soil belongs to the families of Sharpe, Dawson, Rouse, Catt, Barker, Stearn, Read, and Iveson. The *Church* (St. Mary) is a fine ancient structure, but the tower, which had fallen down, was rebuilt about 1731, by the executors of Mr. Robert Thinge, who left an estate to be sold for that purpose. It was repewed and thoroughly repaired in 1841 ; and the organ, which is of a novel construction, by Pilcher, of London, was erected in March, 1843, at the cost of about £100. The *rectory*, valued in K.B. at £17. 11s. 3d., and in 1835 at £472, is in the patronage of Trinity College, Cambridge, and incumbency of the Rev. G. E. Webster. The tithes have recently been commuted for a yearly modus of £542. 13s. 4d. Here is a neat *Baptist Chapel*, which was built in 1798, at the cost of £400, by the late Mr. John Thompson, of Culpho, and was enlarged, in 1810, at the cost of £600. It will seat 1000 hearers, and its congregation are scattered over about 36 parishes, and have two ministers. The TOWN ESTATE, comprising several cottages, and about 28A. of land, is let for about £40 a year, and was given at an early period by the *Rev. John Yate*, and was vested in feoffees in the reign of Henry VIII., for th use and benefit of the town, " in such manner and form as the same had been anciently used and employed." The rents are applied by the churchwardens, mostly in the service of the church, and partly in distributions to the poor. In 1730, *Robert Thinge* left a yearly rentcharge of 52s., to provide for a weekly distribution of 1s. worth of bread among the poor, and it is paid out of a farm belonging to the Stearn family. *John Lucock*, some years ago, left funds for the purchase of £284, four per cent. annuities, the dividends thereof to be applied yearly as follows : £5 for a weekly distribution of three penny loaves, £5 for the support of a Sunday-school, and the residue for an annual distribution of bread and coals among poor parishioners.

Post Office at Mr George Manby's.
Letters despatched at 9 morning, (except Sunday)
Acton Edward, surgeon
Braham Edward, grocer and draper
Collins Rev Saml. Baptist minister
Cresswell Mrs. tailor
Forsdick Henry, corn miller
Groom Sarah, schoolmistress
Gurdon Brampton, gent. *Hall*
Henrys Wm. gent||Jackson Mr Postle
Knights Wm. corn dealer and shopr
Lambert John, beerhouse
Lovell Isaac, chimney sweeper

Parker Maria, beerhouse
Pipe John Wilgress, basket maker, cooper, &c
Pyke John, vict. *Dog Inn*
Ridley John, seedsman and corn dlr
Robinson Edward, day & bdg. school
Stearn Charles, vict. Half Moon
Steggall Wm. surgeon
Syret Lieutenant James
Taylor Robert, plumber and glazier
Webster Rev George E. *Rectory*
Wilson Rev Daniel, Baptist minister

Blacksmiths.
Groom Jonathan
Motum J.

Boot & Shoe Mkrs.
Smith John
Woolnough Jas.

Bricklayers.
Parker James
Woolnough Wm.

Butchers.
Groom Joseph
Loomb Eli
Warren James

FARMERS.
Ablitt Robert
Bedwell Benjmn.
Catt Joshua
Harris Philip
Harris John
Manby Henry

Manby John
Newson John
ReadThs.(ownr.)
Spurling John

Joiners, &c.
Groom Herman
Hayward Wm.
(wheelwright)
Tillett Henry,
(constable)
Waley Nathaniel
Tailors.
Cresswell Mrs
Last James

HASKETON, a straggling village, 2 miles N.W. of Woodbridge, has in its parish 508 souls, and about 1600 acres of land, including *Thorpe Hall* estate, which forms a separate manor, about a mile W. of the village. The rest of the parish is in the manor of Hasketon Hall, except a small manor belonging to the rectory. R. Rouse, Esq., is lord of the two former, but a great part of the soil belongs to Edmd. Jenny, Esq., Charles Baldry, Esq., and several smaller owners. The *Church* (St. Andrew) is an ancient fabric, with a tower, round at the base, and octangular at the top. The *rectory*, valued in K.B. at £13. 6s. 8d., and in 1835 at £290, is in the patronage and incumbency of the Rev. H. Freeland. The tithes have been commuted for a yearly modus of £570, of which £195, paid out of Thorpe Hall estate, belongs to J. Jenny, Esq., the impropriator of that part of the parish which was formerly in the appropriation of Letheringham priory. A cottage and 5A. of land, left by *Agnes Emme*, in 1488, for repairing the church, are let for £13 a year. In 1614, *Thos. Tymme* bequeathed to 18 trustees, a house, barn, and 18A. of land, in trust for the maintenance of two of the most impotent, poor, and aged persons of Hasketon; and they are now let for £31 a year. There is also belonging to this charity two tenements, a blacksmith's shop, and half an acre of copyhold ground, purchased many years ago with money arising from the sale of timber, and now let for £9; so that the two pensioners have each about £20 per annum, subject to deductions for repairs. In 1678, *Alice Osborne* charged the Angel Inn, in Woodbridge, with the yearly payment of 20s. for the most needy poor of Hasketon. In 1776, *John Rutland* left a yearly rent-charge of £3 out of his estate here (now belonging to Mr. Salkeld,) to provide coats for three poor men of this prrish. In 1820, *Mary Brown* left the dividends of £100 three per cent. consols, to be divided yearly among the poor of Hasketon.

Baldry Charles, Esq. *Thorpe Hall*
Freeland Rev Henry, rector
Jenny Edmund, Esq.
Moor Mr Walter, solicitor
Lyons Richard, cattle jobber
Richardson Rt. collar & harness mkr
Shimmen Robert, blacksmith
Smith Rev Jno. Independent minister

Tillett Wm. joiner
Walker Simon, vict. Turk's Head
Corn Millers.
Buttrum Charles
Forsdick John
FARMERS.
Butcher Robert
Kerridge Samuel

Newson John
Plant Edward,
Manor House
Phillips Francis
Runnacles Geo.
Richardson Fras.

Ward Robert	Ellis Francis Rt.	Tye James	Tye Wm.
Boot&ShoeMkrs.	(and shopkpr.)	Tye David	Wright James
Buckels George			

KESGRAVE parish has a few houses near the church, on the Woodbridge road, 4 miles E. by N. of Ipswich, and contains 88 inhabitants, and 1610 acres of land, belonging to several proprietors, the largest of whom is Robert Newton Shawe, Esq., of *Kesgrave Hall*, pleasantly situated about a mile E. by N. of the church, and rebuilt in 1812. It is a large and handsome mansion, and has commodious out-offices, which were built in 1832. The *Church* is an ancient structure, and has a beautiful octagonal font, which was given by W. Wood, Esq., in 1843. It was appropriated to Butley priory. Sir J. K. Shaw is now impropriator, and patron of the perpetual curacy, which is valued at £58, and enjoyed, together with Brightwell and Foxhall, by the Rev. E. J. Moor, B.A., of Great Bealings. The principal inhabitants are R. N. Shawe, Esq., Kesgrave Hall; Edward Trafford, cattle dealer and vict., *Bell ;* Jordan Unwin, *farmer, overseer, &c. ;* and Samuel Walton, *farmer.*

MARTLESHAM, a neat village, near the confluence of a rivulet with the Deben, 2 miles S.S.W. of Woodbridge, and 7 miles E. by N. of Ipswich, has in its parish 510 inhabitants, and 2558 acres of land, partly in rich marshes washed by the tides of the Deben, and partly a large, sandy, and unenclosed *heath*, extending about 2 miles S.W., and affording pasturage for numerous herds of sheep and cattle. About 60 acres, called the Lamb and Street farms, belong to the church and poor of Woodbridge, and the rest of the parish belongs chiefly to F. G. Doughty, Esq., R. N. Shawe, Esq., and the Rev. George Capper. Sir John Verdun was seated here in 1328, and his estate afterwards passed to the Noons and Goodwins, who occupied the hall, now a farm-house. The *Church* (St. Mary) is an ancient structure, except the chancel, which was rebuilt in 1837. The *rectory*, valued in K.B. at £10. 18s. 9d., and in 1835 at £370, is in the gift of F. G. Doughty, Esq., and incumbency of the Rev. Thomas D'Eye Betts, B.A. The tithes have recently been commuted for a yearly modus of £423. 10s.

Balls Zdkh. blacksmith; h *Ufford*
Betts Rev T. D'Eye, B.A. *Rectory*
Chapman John, gentleman
Fletcher Charles, carpenter
Fletcher Wm. bricklayer
Gooch Edward Sherlock, Esq. *Beacon Hill House*
Groom Frederick, butcher
Groom Ann, vict. Red Lion
Groom Wm. & Brothers, brewers
Hills Wm. cattle dealer
Hudson Wm. shoemaker
Jay Henry, wheelwright
Kent Catherine, shopkeeper
Kidby Joseph, shoemaker
Runnacles Robert, cattle dealer

FARMERS & GRAZIERS.
Ashford Thomas || Barrell Wm.
Brighten Thomas
Cobb Wm. (and *corn miller*)
Cooke John (and *owner*)
Garrod Henry || Groom Wm.
Mills James, *High Red House*
Pollard John || Ramplen Charles
Sheppard Edw. || Sheppard John
White Samuel, (and *owner*)

NEWBOURN, a small village and parish, 7 miles E. by S. of Ipswich, has 163 inhabitants and 840 acres, extending about a mile southward to the *bourn* or rivulet, which falls into the Deben at Kirton Sluice. The *crag-pits* here, at the depth of 20 feet, are full of shells, fish-teeth, &c. Through this marine deposit several springs boil up

copious streams, even in the driest seasons.   Sir J. R. Rowley is lord
of the manor of Haspley in Newbourn, owner of most of the soil, and
patron of the *Church* (St. Mary,) which is a rectory, valued in K.B.
at £7. 4s. 2d., and in 1835 at £192, but the tithes have recently been
commuted for a yearly modus of £220.   The Rev. John Gale Dobree,
M.A., of Holton, is the incumbent.   Near the *hall*, now a farm house, are
two venerable *yews*, supposed to have braved the storms of several centuries.   *Directory :*—John Dorkin, shopkeeper ; Jonathan Clark, shoemaker ; James Neale, farmer, *Street-farm ;* Stephen Jackson, vict.,
Fox ; Samuel Walton, farmer, *Newbourn Hall* ; and Richard Ward,
blacksmith.

OTLEY, a large, scattered and pleasant village, on the Debenham
road, 6 miles N.W. of Woodbridge, and 8 miles N. by E. of Ipswich,
has in its parish 2157A. 2R. 8P. of land, extending 2 miles N. and W.
of the village.   The Earl of Abergavenny is lord of the manor, but a
great part of the soil belongs to Lord Rendlesham, J. Tollemach, Esq.,
General Revow, and a few smaller proprietors.   The manor has been
held by the Earls of Abergavenny since the reign of Edward III., together with the patronage of the *rectory*, valued in K.B. at £16. 6s. 5¼d.
and in 1835, at £510.   The Rev. Fras. Storr is the incumbent, and
has a handsome *Rectory House*, built in 1839 at the cost of £1400,
borrowed of the Governors of Queen Anne's Bounty.   The glebe is
72A. 2R. 9P., and the tithes have recently been commuted for a yearly
modus of £670.   The *Church* (St. Mary) has a tower and five bells,
and was thoroughly repaired, furnished with a good organ and new gallery, and decorated with a stained glass window in 1839, at the cost of
£600, mostly contributed by the rector, who also erected in the same
year a commodious school, with a dwelling for the master and mistress,
at the cost of £500.   In the church is the monument of *John Gosnold,*
whose family were long seated here in the old hall, and suffered so
much for their loyalty to Charles I., that the Rev. Lionel Gosnold,
who was rector here, was obliged to sell his estate.   Here is a *Baptist
Chapel*, erected in 1800, and enlarged in 1837.   *Otley Green*, which
comprised about 25A., was enclosed about 1809.   A yearly rent-charge
of 20s., left for the poor of Otley by *Geoffry Pleasants*, is paid out of
the third part of a farm here, belonging to Christ's Hospital, in Ipswich.

Barker Saml. vict. *White Horse*
Bennett Thos. postman to Ipswich,
    daily
Bigsby Thomas, parish clerk
Burch Jermh. grocer and draper
Bloomfield Captain Edwin
Costerton Misses E. H. and M.
Glanville Rev. Wm. Bapt. minister
Gander Joseph and Sarah, *school*
Hill Mary Ann, grocer
Moor Hy. L. gent||Last John, *tailor*
Ralph Wm. bricklayer & plasterer
Reeve Hannah, vict. *White Hart*
Storr Rev Frs. M.A. *Rectory*
Wightman George, shopkeeper
Wightman Wm. seedsman
Wilson Wm. collar & harness maker

Blacksmiths.
Miller John
Ward Cs. Welton
Boot&ShoeMkrs.
Batho Wm.
Bennett Wm.
    (beerhouse)
Monser Lionel
Roper John
Corn Millers.
Dawson N. W.
Miller John
    FARMERS.
Barker Charles
Burch Robert
Catt Alfred
Cutting Philip

Cutting Samuel
Garnham Wm.
King James
Last John
Last James
Last Jas. Wade
Ling Saml. *Hall*
McClure David
Miller Thomas
Moor Pearl
Pipe Thomas
Pipe Keeble
Scase Harper
Simons Robert
Todd Charles
Todd Wm.

Joiners.	Wheelwrights.	CARRIERS	Smith George
Forsdick Jeffry	Barker W. F.	To Ipswich.	Tues. and Sat.
Forsdick Jerh.	Wightman Jas.	Bumpstead Wm.	

PLAYFORD, a pleasant village 4 miles N.E. of Ipswich, has in its parish 253 souls and 650 acres of land. The Marquis of Bristol is lord of the manor, owner of most of the soil, impropriator, and patron of the *Church* (St. Mary) which is a perpetual curacy, valued at £53, and enjoyed by the Rev. T. D. West, B.A., of Rushmere. The venerable *Thomas Clarkson, Esq., M.A.*, to whose exertions the abolition of negro slavery is as much indebted as to Wilberforce, resides at *Playford Hall*, which was long the seat of the *Felton family*, one of whom, (Lieutenant Felton,) assassinated the Duke of Buckingham in 1629. Robert Playford obtained Playford by marrying the heiress of Sir Thos. Sampson, Kt. Anthony Felton was knighted at the coronation of James I., and his son Henry was created a baronet in 1621. The title became extinct on the death of Sir Compton Felton without male issue, and his estates passed to the first Earl of Bristol, in right of his wife. *Directory:*—Arthur Biddell, land valuer and chief constable; Thos. Clarkson, Esq., *Playford Hall*; Rev. W. Dickinson, curate; Wm. Field, farmer; Sarah Garrod, shopkeeper; and Wm. Mann, shoemaker.

RUSHMERE, a scattered village with many neat houses, 2 miles E. by N. of Ipswich, has in its parish 564 souls and 2720 acres of land, including a large sandy *heath*, on which each of the farmers and others having common-right, depasture as many sheep and cattle as they think proper. Part of the soil and about 230 of the inhabitants are within the limits of the Borough of Ipswich. (See page 50.) For a long period, it was the lordship of the Feltons of Playford. The Marquis of Bristol is now lord of the manor, impropriator of the rectorial tithes, and owner of part of the parish; and the remainder belongs to Sir Philip Broke, (about 1000A. ;) J. Cobbold, Esq. ; J. D. Everitt, R. W. Porter, N. Ablitt, W. F. Schrieber, and several smaller owners. The *Church* (St. Andrew) is an ancient structure, with a tower, which was erected in 1521, with money left for that purpose by Catharine Cadye. A new gallery was erected in 1838. Rushmere was appropriated to the priory of Christ's Church, Ipswich. The vicarage, valued in K.B. at £4. 6s. 8d., and in 1835, at £156, is in the gift of the Marquis of Bristol, and incumbency of the Rev. Thos. Dennent West, B.A., who has a neat residence. The tithes are about to be commuted for a yearly modus. BIXLEY, now only a farm in Rushmere, is nearly 2 miles E. of Ipswich, and was anciently a separate parish, with a church dedicated to St. Petronville, and was in some way connected with the adjacent extra-parochial places, called Alnesbourn Priory and Purdies Farm. (See page 126.) From *Bixley Decoy Ponds*, on the south side of the parish, a rivulet flows eastward to the Deben, and has near it some rich marsh land. These ponds or *meres*, anciently abounding in rushes, gave name to the parish of Rushmere *Round Wood*, the pleasant seat of W. F. Schrieber, Esq., is in the liberty of Ipswich.

Marked * are in the Borough of Ipswich.	*Baker Thomas, vict. Greyhound
Ablitt Mr John, *Coffee house*	Betts Hy. corn miller, Tower mill
	Clark Joseph, farmer, *Poplar Farm*

Fox Mr Thos. || Crisp Jno. wheelgt
Gale Sarah, farmer, *Rushmere hall*
Grimsey John, shoemaker
Hall Jas. shopkpr. & horse breaker
Kennett Nathan, beerhouse
Newson Samuel, vict. *Britannia*
*Newson Wm. farmer
Parish Joshua, beerhs. *Hop garden*
*Perry Stn. gent. || Palmer Mrs Eliz.
Potter Frederick, shoemaker
Ransome James, *Reed cottage*, (and ironfounder, &c. at Ipswich)

*Schrieber Wm. Fredk. Esq. *Round Wood*
Ledger John and Php. blacksmiths
Shewell John T. gentleman
Shepherd John, regr. & relvg. officer
Skeet Rt. farmer, *Rushmere House*
Skeet Robert, jun. farmer
Stannard John, farmer, *Bixley*
West Rev Thos. D., B.A., *Vicarage*
Wilson Pettit, farmer and beerhouse
Wrattislaw J. T. gentleman, *Rushmere cottage*

TUDDENHAM, a pleasant village and parish, 3 miles N. by E. of Ipswich, contains 423 souls, and 1232 acres of land. Major Michael Turner and J. Wrattislaw, Esqrs., are lords of the manor, but part of the soil belongs to the Rodwell and other families. The latter is also impropriator of the rectory and patron of the vicarage, valued in K.B. at £10. 13s. 4d., and now enjoyed by the Rev. Mesac Thomas. The rectorial tithes have recently been commuted for £220. 12s., and the vicarial tithes for £110. 6s. per annum. The *Church* (St. Martin) is an ancient structure, formerly in the appropriation of Trinity Priory, Ipswich. In 1672, *George Knapp* left an annuity of £5 for the repairs of the church. Pursuant to a decree in Chancery, £100 was received in lieu of this annuity, and was vested, in 1718, in the purchase of a yearly rent-charge of £5, out of 19A. of land at Grundisburgh. In 1738, *Wm. Minter*, whose family, long lords of the manor, left the residue of the rent of this land to be distributed yearly in clothing among the poor of Tuddenham. It is now let for about £27 per annum.

Cook Mrs My. || Chaplin Jno. shopr
Garnham James, vict. Fountain
Garnham James & Wm. maltsters
Hammond Wm. shoemaker
Kell George, blacksmith
Luff Henry, joiner
Luff Jas. & John, brick & tile mkrs
Maple Elizabeth, *(Post to Ipswich)*
Neeve John, corn miller
Thomas Rev Mesac, *Vicarage*

Thompson Wm. shopkeeper
Thompson James, beerhouse
Waspe Mary, butcher
Watts Philip, corn miller
Wright Rev J. B., M.A. curate
FARMERS.
Betts Ann || Ling Samuel. *Hall*
Luff James, jun. || Rush David
Smith George [] Neeve John
Waspe Jonathan || Woolnough Wm.

WALDRINGFIELD, a small parish and scattered village, on the western bank of the river Deben, 4 miles S. of Woodbridge, contains 174 souls, and 831 acres of land. The Rev. W. J. Edge owns most of the soil, and is lord of the manor, and patron and incumbent of the *rectory*, which is valued in K.B. at £4. 17s. 11d., and in 1835, at £187. The *Church* (All Saints) is an ancient fabric, and near it is a good Rectory House. *Directory:*—Rev. W. J. Edge, rector; Geo. David Badham, farmer, *White Hall;* Daniel Button, *Bush;* Wm. Lewes, shoemaker; Joseph Linstead, shopkeeper; Jonathan Mallett, tailor; Fras. Orford, blacksmith and wheelwright; and Wm. Stannard, *farmer.*

WITNESHAM, 4½ miles N. by E. of Ipswich, is a large straggling village and parish, containing 543 souls and 2022 acres of land, belonging to the Meadows family and a few smaller proprietors. In the reign of Edward III., *Sir Bartholomew Berghersh* had a charter for a free

warren here. The Berghersh family were long seated here in a moated mansion, of which there were some traces in Kirby's time.   The mansion, now called *Berghersh House,* is the seat of Daniel Rust Meadows, Esq., and *Witnesham Hall* is the residence of Mr. Thos. Meadows, whose family has been seated here since the time of Edward III. The *Church* (St. Mary) stands near the source of the Fynn rivulet, and is a rectory, valued in K.B. at £18. 13s. 4d., and in 1835, at £498.   The patronage is in St. Peter's College, and the Rev. Wm. Potter, M.A., is the incumbent.   Here is the National school, built chiefly at the expense of the rector, in 1840; and a small Baptist chapel, erected in 1838.   In Berghersh Meadow, there was anciently a free chapel, dedicated to *St. Thomas,* but all traces of it are gone.

Barker John, vict. Barley mow
Barnes Wm. plumber and glazier
Cooper John, corn miller & maltster
Garnham Jno. collar & harness mkr
Kersey Thomas, bricklayer
Meadows Daniel Rust, Esq. Rev J.
    B.; and G. F. surgeon, *Berghersh House*
Meadows Thomas, gentleman, *Witnesham Hall*
Parker Henry, schoolmaster
Potter Rev Wm., M.A. *Rectory*
Steggall My. & Sar. boardg. school
Woodley M. W. gentleman

FARMERS.
Amos John
Butcher George
Catt Joseph
Cooper John
Gooding J.
Gooding Wm.
    Red House
Harris Wm.
Poppey Charles
Reynold Isaac
Roe Joseph
    Blacksmiths.
Barker John
Cage Wm.

Oxborrow Ephm.
    Joiners, &c.
    * *are Wheelgts.*
*Damant Temple
*Dowsing Temple
*Dowsing Richd.
Wood Wm.
    Shoemakers.
Cullum John
Emerson John
    Shopheepers.
Meeking Ann
Pyett Wm.
Saddler Mary
Sheppard Edw.

WILFORD HUNDRED

Extends about 12 miles southward from Debach to Woodbridge, and along the eastern shores of the Deben, to Bawdsey Haven and Hollesley Bay, in the German Ocean.   It stretches about 8 miles along the sea coast, between the mouths of the Deben and Orford Haven, but its northern parts decrease to less than five miles in breadth, and are bounded by Carlford and Loes Hundreds.   In the vale of the Deben, from Wickham Market to Woodbridge and the sea, it has some rich arable and marsh lands; but its central parts, about Sutton, are sandy, and comprise some large open heaths, affording tolerable pasturage for sheep and cattle, and rising in bold undulations.   It is in the *Deanery of Wilford,* and *Archdeaconry of Suffolk,* and comprises *seventeen parishes,* of which the following is an enumeration, shewing their territorial extent, the annual value of their land and buildings, as assessed to the property tax in 1815, and their population in 1801 and 1841.   All of them are in *Woodbridge Union,* (see page 119,) except Wickham Market, which is in Plomesgate Union.

PARISHES.	Acrs.	Rental.	Populatn. 1801.	Populatn. 1841.	PARISHES.	Acres.	Rental. £.	Populatn. 1801.	Populatn. 1841.
Alderton........	2600	3418	425	620	Melton*	1408	2649	501	98
Bawdsey	2640	2014	344	468	Petistree	1768	2583	241	30
Boulge	545	988	39	45	Ramsholt	1990	2113	152	192
Boyton	1890	1648	201	239	Shottisham......	1033	1035	161	283
Bredfield‡	1067	2078	334	468	Sutton..........	5789	2479	406	707
Bromeswell	1442	887	143	200	Ufford..........	1555	2065	450	673
Capel St. Andrew	2000	1121	162	222	Wickham Market	1178	3014	896	1400
Dallinghoo‡	1495	2331	246	346					
Debach	500	807	117	121	Total § ..	31,500	34,956	5279	7857
Hollesley	2600	3726	461	590					

* Melton includes 217 persons in *Suffolk Lunatic Asylum.*
† Wickham Market includes 100 persons in *Plomesgate Union Workhouse.* (See Plomesgate Hundred.)
§ The number of HOUSES, in 1841, was 1627, of which 55 were unoccupied, and 5 building. The number of *males* was 3889, and *females*, 3968 ; and of the former, 2024, and the latter, 2184, were upwards of 20 years of age.
‡ Bredfield and Dallinghoo are partly in Loes Hundred.
☞ The Chief Constables are Mr. Philip Dykes, jun., of Petistree; and Mr. Samuel Chilton Gross, of Alderton.

ALDERTON, a remarkably neat and pleasant village, about a mile from the sea, and 7½ miles S.E. by S. of Woodbridge, has in its parish 620 souls, and 2,600 acres of land, extending in rich marshes, &c., to the sea, and rising in bold undulations on the north. The soil belongs to the late Peter Thellusson's trustees, (represented by Lord Rendlesham,) the Hon. George Andrew Vanneck, Mrs. Goodwyn, Mrs. Plaiston, Colonel Raper, and a few smaller owners. It is in four *manors*, called *Naunton*, or *Alderton Hall, Boviles, Pechys*, and *Alderton Comitis* or *Earls Alderton*. The Bishop of Norwich is lord of the latter. Each of these manors had the advowson of the rectory in turn, but it has lately been vested with the family of the Rev. William Addington Norton, M.A., the present incumbent, subject to the fourth turn of presentation by the Bishop of Norwich. The rectory, valued in K.B. at £14. 18s. 4d., and in 1835, at £563, is now worth £733 a year. The tithes have recently been commuted, and a large handsome *Rectory House* was built by the late Rev. Richard Frank, D.D., who held the living more than forty years, and died in 1813. The *Church* (St. Andrew,) being much dilapidated, was repaired in 1840, but its tower is still a detached ruin. The Rev. Giles Fletcher, a former rector, who died here in 1623, was author of " *Christ's Victorie,*" and was distinguished for the elegance of his manners ; as well as for his attainments as a scholar and poet. He was cousin to *John Fletcher*, who, in conjunction with his literary partner, *Beaumont*, was an eminent dramatic writer. The ancient family of Naunton were seated here, and owned most of the parish, for a long period before *Sir Robt. Naunton* removed to Letheringham, in the reign of James I. A *school* for the education of poor children was established here in 1839, by subscription and a grant from the British and Foreign School Society. The rents of a house, garden, and 2A. of land, let for £19. 10s. per annum, have, from an early period, been applied to charitable purposes, by the rector and parish officers. In 1687, *Thomas Trusson* left a yearly rent-charge of £3 out of an estate here, to provide for a weekly distribution of bread among the poor parishioners.

Balls Wm. veterinary surgeon
Beeton Samuel, plumber and glazier
Brown John, joiner, wheelwright and cabinet maker
Buck Joseph and Son, tailors
Cole Jacob, butcher
Cullum Hy. grocer and draper, *Post Office*, (letters desp ½ past 4 aft)
Cullum James, baker
Fletcher Frederick Wm. corn miller and merchant
Garrod Thos. brick and tile makers
Gorham Richard, surgeon
Gross Samuel Chilton, gent. (chief constable)
Hartridge Wm. M. grocer and draper
May Joseph Chaplin, schoolmaster
Mayhew James, vict. & blacksmith, *Swan*
Norton Rev. Wm. Addington, M.A. rector of Alderton & Eyke, *Rectory House*

Rodwell Joshua, gentleman
Smith James, beerhouse
Thompson Wm. & John, collar and harness makers
Thompson Wm. blacksmith
Wesbroom John, tailor
Woods Mary, wheelwright

BOOT AND SHOE MAKERS.
Dun George || Kay George
Mann Robert || Olding Wm.

FARMERS AND GRAZIERS.
Ablitt George || Ablitt John
Broom Thomas || Hiller Wm.
Hiller Wm. || Roberts Thomas
Roberts Robert

CARRIERS.
Abraham Hill, to Woodbridge, Monday & Wed. return Tuesday & Sat.
Wm. G. Turrall, to Woodbridge, Mon. Wed. & Sat. & Ipswich Thursday

BAWDSEY, a compact and well-built village on the coast opposite Hollesley Bay, 8 miles S. by E. of Woodbridge, has in its parish 468 souls, and 2,640 acres of land, extending nearly three miles S.W. to the mouth of the broad river Deben, sometimes called *Bawdsey Haven;* and nearly 2 miles E.N.E., to the hamlet of *Shingle Street*, on the fine beach of Hollesley Bay, where the *Life Boat Inn*, and several other houses were erected in 1810, for the accommodation of sea bathers. The shingle thrown upon the beach in this neighbourhood abounds in *gold stones*, of which great quantities are gathered for the manufacture of *copperas*. In the 11th of Edward I., *Robert de Ufford*, who was twice chief justice of Ireland, obtained a license for a weekly market, on Fridays; and a fair on the eve, day, and morrow of the nativity of the Virgin Mary, at his manor of *Bawdresey*, or Bawdsey; but the market was discontinued in 1797, and the fair in 1835. The Willoughby family held the manor from the reign of Henry IV. to that of Edward IV., and it afterwards passed to the Tollemaches, Earls of Dysart. The parish now belongs chiefly to John Tollemache, Esq., John Wilson Shepherd, Esq., and the Trustees of the late Peter Thellusson, Esq. The *Church* (St. Mary,) was appropriated to Butley Priory, by Ranulph Glanvile. Its venerable tower, though it has lost much of its pristine altitude, is still a conspicuous sea-mark. When undergoing repairs in 1841, some boys got upon it to exhibit fireworks, and accidentally set fire to the church, which was completely gutted and the roof destroyed before the flames could be extinguished. It was repaired and new roofed in 1843. The *vicarage*, valued in K.B. at £6. 13s. 4d., and in 1835, at £170, is in the patronage of the Crown. Here is a small Wesleyan Chapel, erected in 1810.

Branch George, parish clerk
Broom James, overseer, *East lane*
Cooper Edward, grocer and draper
Ford Isaac, joiner, &c

Lennard Daniel, brricklayer
Mannell Wm. victualler, *Life Boat*, *Shingle street*
Mann Daniel, shopkeeper

Moor George, butcher
Robinson Fras. thatcher & vict. *Star*
BOOT AND SHOE MAKERS.
Dossor Charles || Ransby Saml.
FARMERS AND GRAZIERS.
Borrows Saml. || Robinson Francis
Cavell Edward, *Bawdsey Hall*

Felgate My. Ann, Emma, & Sarah, *Manor House*
Utting Gardner, *High House*
CARRIER.
Philip Cutting, to Ipswich,Mon. and Woodbridge,Wednesday & Friday

BOULGE, 3½ miles N. of Woodbridge, is a small parish containing only 45 inhabitants and 545 acres. John Fitzgerald, Esq., of *Boulge Hall*, a neat mansion with pleasant grounds, is lord of the manor and owner of a great part of the soil. The *Church* (St. Michael) is a rectory, valued in K.B. at £3. 12s. 1d., and in 1835, at £222, with the rectory of Debach annexed to it. The two rectories were consolidated by the Rev. Sir William Bunbury, about 1730. The Rev. Osborne Shribb Reynolds, M.A., is patron and incumbent, and has 4A. 1R. 31P. of glebe. The tithes of Boulge have recently been commuted for a yearly modus of £134. Messrs. Charles Moor & Son, of Woodbridge, are stewards of the *manors of Boulge Hall, Bast Struttings, and Debach-Burgh*. Robert Todd is the parish clerk, and the *farmers* are Charles Bugg, Joseph Smith, and Samuel Smith.

BOYTON, a pleasant village, 4 miles S.W. of Orford, and 7½ miles E.S.E. of Woodbridge, has in its parish 247 souls and 1890 acres of land, extending more than a mile eastward of Butley river and Orford Haven, and westward to a tract of open heath. The *Church* (St. Andrew) is a *rectory*, valued in K.B. at £5. 12s. 1d., and in 1835 at £365. The Rev. Wm. Wogan Aldrich, B.C.L., is the incumbent. The *advowson and the manor* were held by Butley Priory, but were granted by Henry VIII. to Wm. Forthe and Richard Moryson. They afterwards passed to the family of *Warner*, and are now vested in the trustees of Mrs. Mary Warner, as will be seen in the following account of her munificient charitable bequest. The *principal inhabitants* are the Rev. W. W. Aldrich, B.C.L., *Rectory ;* Samuel Arnold, *butcher ;* Robert Bloomfield, *joiner ;* Wm. Cloughton, *blacksmith ;* Sarah Ann Flory, *shopkeeper ;* Hy. Francis Summers, vict. *Bell Inn ;* and Chas. and Edward Bennington, Robert Johnson, and Wm. Miller, *farmers* and *graziers*.

WARNER'S CHARITY :—In 1736, *Mary Warner* gave the undermentioned valuable estates, &c., for the erection and endowment of an ALMSHOUSE at BOYTON, for six poor men and six poor women, and for other charitable uses. After the erection of the Almshouse, she directed the trustees to apply the yearly income of the trust property as follows ; viz. 4s. a week to each of the 12 almspeople ; 50s. yearly to each, to buy them suits of brown warm clothes ; £40 a year to the minister of Boyton, or any other persons who should be appointed to look after the almspeople, and read prayers to them daily ; £10 a year to the master of *Stradroke School*, for teaching 12 poor children ; £5 every Christmas to each of the parishes of *Dennington* and *Parham*, for the poor ; and to apply the residue of the income at their discretion, towards releasing *insolvent debtors*, in the county of Suffolk, whose debts should not amount to more than £10. This charity did not come into operation till 1757, after the death of Mrs. Warner, when an almshouse for 12 poor people was erected by the trustees at Boyton. The income being much greater than the expenditure, various schemes and orders have been sanctioned by the Court of Chancery since 1790, for extending the various branches of the charity. In 1802, it was ordered that four new apartments should be added to the Almshouse, so as to encrease the number of the *almspeople* from 12 to 16, and that each of them should have a weekly stipend of 7s., and a yearly allowance of £2. 15s. for clothing; £2.5s. for firing, and £1. 1s. towards the expense of their washing. It was also

ordered that the *nurse*, (who occupies a house near the almshouse, and acts as servant to the almspeople,) should also have 7s. a week, and the same allowance for clothes and firing, as well as 1s. 6d. per week for heating the common-oven; that £12. 12s. a year should be paid to a surgeon for attending the almspeople, and supplying them with medicines; and that the annuity paid to the master of Stradbroke School should be encreased to £15. These and the other branches of the charity have been considerably extended since 1829, when the *charity estates* were let for £1129. 11s. 5d. *per annum,* besides which the trustees receive yearly £202 from the dividends of £1000 Navy five per cents, and £4000 new four per cent. annuities, purchased with the savings of former years. The perpetual advowson of the rectory of Boyton also belongs to this charity; and its other property given by Mrs. Warner, comprises the manor and quit rents of Boyton, (worth about £15 a year,) Boyton Wood, 7A. 3R. 3P.; two farms in Boyton, containing 1012 acres; two cottages and a farm of 162A. 3R. 3P., at Stradbroke, and a farm of 69A. 17P. at Dennington. The *Almshouse* contains 16 sets of rooms, with a small garden to each. Sir T. S. Gooch, the Earl of Stradbroke, Sir Chas. Blois, Charles Tyrell, Esq., and others are the *trustees.*

BREDFIELD, a scattered village 3 miles N. of Woodbridge, has in its parish 468 inhabitants and 1067 acres of land, partly in Loes Hundred. Edward Jenny, Esq., is lord of the manor, but a great part of the soil belongs to John Wood, and Francis C. Brooke, Esqrs. The *Church* (St. Andrew) is a fine ancient structure, with a flint tower, containing four bells. The nave and chancel have a beautifully carved ceiling. A small gallery was erected in 1838, at the cost of E. Jenny, Esq. The *vicarage,* valued in K.B. at £4. 4s., and in 1835 at £249, is in the patronage of the Crown, and incumbency of the Rev. Geo. Crabbe, M.A., who erected a new Vicarage House in 1836, at the cost of £1400. The glebe is 30A., and the tithes have recently been commuted for a yearly modus of £325. Six acres of copyhold land, let for £7. 10s. a year, have been held by the parishioners from an early period for charitable and public uses, but the rent is all expended in the service of the Church. Here is a small *Independent Chapel,* erected in 1813. *Bredfield Hall,* still the property and formerly a seat of the Jenny family, is now unoccupied. From several urns and other antiquities discovered in 1843, it is supposed there was a *Roman Encampment* about a mile north of the Church. *High House* is a fine specimen of ancient brick work, with ornamental chimneys.

Atkins Edw. grocer, draper & tailor
Crane James, bricklayer
Cone Saml. harness maker & shopkr
Crabbe Rev George, M.A., *vicar*
Diggins Charles, tailor
Lyons John, parish clerk
Martin John, vict. *Castle*
Snell James, hurdle mkr & beerhs
Wainwright Emma, schoolmistress
Boot & Shoe makers. — Godbold Wm.
Williams John || Wright Wm.

FARMERS.
Burrows David || Garrod Mary
Grimwood T. (owner) *Bredfield Place*
Grimwood Thomas, *High House*
Oxborrow Edward, (and *corn miller*)
Randall Saml. || Martin Samuel
Seammen Wm. || Seammen George
Smith George || Welton Nathl.
JOINERS AND WHEELWRIGHTS.
Clark John, jun. (and blacksmith)
Pemberton John || Clark John, sen.

BROMESWELL, a straggling village on the east side of the river Deben, 2 miles N.E. of Woodbridge, has in its parish 200 souls and 1442 acres of land, mostly the property of the Marquis of Bristol, and Sir Charles E. Kent. The former is patron of the rectory, valued in K.B. at £4. 15s. 7½d., and now at £150, in the incumbency of the Rev. Thomas Simons. The *Church* (St Edmund) is a small ancient edifice, which was new-roofed in 1820. The parish is in the manor of Staver-

ton-with-Bromswell. (See Eyke.) The *Town Lands*, let for £5. 2s., comprise 3A. 2R., in this parish, and 1A. in Ufford, and have been vested from an early period, for the relief of the poor, but the rents have for many years been applied with the Church-rates. The poor of Bromeswell have £4. 14s. 8d. yearly, from Sir M. Stanhope's charity. (See Sutton.) *Directory*: Robert Goodchild, parish clerk; Robert Parker, vict. *Cherry Tree;* and Samuel Burrows, Thos. Gross, John King, Joseph King, and Noah Patrick, *farmers.*

CAPEL ST. ANDREW is a small scattered village and churchless parish, nearly 4 miles W.S.W. of Orford, and 7½ miles E.S.E. of Woodbridge, containing 222 inhabitants, and about 2000 acres of land, belonging to Lord Rendlesham, and extending a mile eastward to Butley river, and westward to the sandy heath, near *Tangham Farm* and *Capel Folly.* The church was standing in 1529, and was appropriated to Butley Priory, but all vestiges of it are gone. It stood on the site of the farm house occupied by Mr. Oxborrow, where many human bones have been dug up. The parish has for a long period been connected ecclesiastically with Butley. A cottage and 1A. 3R. of land at Butley, have from an early period belonged to the poor of Capel, and are let for £6 year, which is added to the poor rates. The *farmers* are James Button (and shopkeeper,) John Luccock, My. May, & Stn. Oxborrow.

DALLINGHOO, a scattered village, on an eminence, 4½ miles N. of Woodbridge, has in its parish 346 souls, and 1495 acres of land, partly in Loes Hundred. Here was a handsome *hall*, built by Wm. Churchill, and for some time the seat of his son-in-law, Fras. Negus, Esq., but it was burnt down in 1729. Here are two manors, of which John Wood and Andrew Archdeckne, Esqrs. are lords, but part of the soil belongs to the Wade, Jarrold, Reeve, and other families. The *Church* (St. Mary) is a rectory, valued in K.B. at £13. 6s. 8d., but now having 32A. of glebe, and a yearly modus of £427. 1s. 11d. The Rev. Ellis Walford is patron and incumbent.

Jacobs Benjamin, shopkeeper
Kent Isaac, schoolmaster and regr
Last John, blacksmith
Leggett Wm. shoemaker
Motum Jn. wheelgt. & machine mkr
Wainwright Emma, schoolmistress
Walford Rev Ellis, *Rectory*
Wright Henry, tailor and shopkpr

FARMERS.
Bendall Arthur || Blake Arthur
Buxton Robert || Cole Mary
Elliott James || Jarrold John
Reeve Wm. || Runnacles George
Tye Edm. *Brook* || Tye Wm. *Moat*
Walker Dd. *Hall* || Woolnough Sl.
CARRIER, John Shepherd, to Woodbridge, Wednesday and Sat.

DEBACH, 5 miles N.N.W. of Woodbridge, is a small scattered village and parish, containing only 121 inhabitants and about 500 acres of land, mostly the property of the Rev. Osborne Shribb Reynolds, M.A., who is also patron and incumbent of the *rectory*, which is consolidated with that of Boulge. (See page 142. The *Church* (All Saints,) is a small ancient fabric, and near it is a neat Rectory House, which was much improved in 1813. The *" Town Lands,"* comprise about 27A., including the site and gardens of four cottages, belonging to the same trust. The cottages are occupied by poor families at small rents, and the land is let for about £40 a year. From old deeds, it appears that part of the land was anciently held in trust for payment of tenths and fifteenths for the parish of Debach, and for the relief of

the poor, and the reparation of the church ; and that the other part thereof was purchased with money arising from the sale of the eighth-part of a ship, left for the poor, by *Richard Francis*. About one-third of the rent is distributed among poor parishioners in coals, &c., and the remainder is mostly applied to the use of the church. *Directory :*—George Mannall, *corn miller ;* Stephen Marjoram, shopkr. and wheelwright ; Rev. O. S. Reynolds, M.A., *Rectory ;* and Samuel Copling, James and Christopher Marjoram, John Newby, John Reynolds, Daniel Stammers, and John Ward, *farmers*.

HOLLESLEY is a well-built village, pleasantly situated on the banks of a rivulet, about a mile and a half from Orford Haven and *Hollesley Bay*, 6 miles S.W. of Orford, and 7 miles S.E. of Woodbridge. Its parish contains 590 souls, and 2600 acres of land, extending southward to the sea, and northward to a large, sandy, unenclosed heath, of which it comprises about 440 acres. Sir Charles E. Kent is lord of the manor, but part of the soil belongs to J. Barthorp, Esq., R. Brook, Esq., C. Walker, H. Balls, and several smaller owners. The *Church*, (All Saints,) has a lofty steeple, which is a conspicuous sea-mark. The *rectory*, valued in K.B. at £12. 16s. 8d., is in the patronage of W. Bolton, Esq. The tithes have recently been commuted for a yearly modus of £943. The poor have have £4. 16s. 8d. yearly from *Sir M. Stanhope's Charity*. (See Sutton.) During the late war, Hollesley Bay was often visited by ships of war. In 1804, two very ancient and curious pieces of cannon were found here.

Barthorp John, Esq.
Burrell Geo. sieve & basket maker
Burch Stephen, gardener
Capon Mr John||John jun. *mariner*
Carver Henry, gardener
Cooper Elizabeth, vict. *Fox*
Field James, corn miller
Fisher Rev Charles James, curate
Kemp Wm. shopkeeper
Kett Wm. K. surgeon
Osborn John, schoolmaster
Waller Mrs Mary Ann, *Hollesley Grove*
Warnett Charles, bricklayer
Wilmhurst Wm. grocer, draper, and tailor. *Post office*, letters desp. at half-past 3 afternoon

Blacksmiths.
Levitt John
Manthorp Wm.
Pamifer John
Boot & Shoe Mkrs.
Cook Wm.
Hudson Wm.
Last Robert

FARMERS.
Barthorp John
Capon Samuel
Hayward John
Kemp Benjamin
Kemp Wm.
Lewin John

Rouse Thomas
Smith Edgar
Stephens Thos.
Turtle Benj. (& corn miller)
Joiners, &c.
Broom Thomas
Broom Simon
Burrows John
Wright Wm. *wheelwright*

CARRIER.
Richard Clark to Woodbridge, Wed. & Sat.

MELTON is a large, pleasant, and well-built village, on the western side of the river Deben, about a mile N.E. of Woodbridge. Its parish increased its population from 501, in 1801, to 980 souls, in 1841, including 217 in Suffolk Lunatic Asylum. It comprises about 1410 acres of land, stretching southward to the suburbs of Woodbridge, from which the navigation of the Deben has been extended up to a *new quay* here, constructed a few years ago by Mr. R. W. Burleigh. The soil belongs chiefly to J. H. Buckingham, F. C. and T. Brooke, E. Jenney, T. Pytches, and J. Jeaffreson, Esqrs., and several smaller owners, some of whom have neat mansions here. The Dean and Chapter of Ely are lords of the manor and patrons of the *Church* (St. Andrew)

which is a *rectory*, valued in K.B. at £9. 6s. 8d., and now enjoyed by the Rev. Christopher George Walton. The tithes have recently been commuted for a yearly modus of £395. 3s. 5d. *Wilford Bridge*, which here crosses the Deben, was rebuilt by the county about 1539, when several small legacies were left by Richd. Cook and other donors, towards the expense of its renovation.

Melton Church and Poor's Estate is partly freehold and partly copyhold, and consists of seven cottages let at low rents; 2A. 1R. 12P. of land, called Green Man Meadow, let for about £10 a year, and given to the poor many years ago by one *John Jenner;* two cottages and 28A. 1R. 4P. of land in several enclosures, appropriated at an early period to the repairs of the *church*, and now let for about £35 a year; and 15A. 6P., worth about £19 a year, and given at some remote period by persons named *Halifax*, *Cook*, and *Histed*, for providing fuel, &c., for the poor.

SUFFOLK LUNATIC ASYLUM, which stands in a healthy and airy situation, near Woodbridge, but in Melton parish, was originally erected as a House of Industry for the parishes of Loes and Wilford Hundreds, which were incorporated for the maintenance of their poor in 1765, but disincorporated in 1827, when the building was purchased by the county magistrates, chiefly for the reception of pauper lunatics. Whilst a workhouse, it had sometimes as many as 250 inmates, and there are now within its walls upwards of 200 persons labouring under that worst of all human maladies—insanity. They are nearly all Suffolk paupers, for whom their respective parishes pay at the rate of about six shillings per week per head; but there are a few boarders paying from 9s. 4d. to 21s. each per week.. This useful and well-regulated establishment, including the purchase of the grounds and the original buildings, and the subsequent alterations, enlargements, and improvements, with the furniture, &c., has cost about £30,000. It is now so crowded, and the applications for admission have been so numerous, that it is in contemplation to make considerable additions to the present buildings, which are well ventilated, and are provided with warm and cold baths, and are aired by Arnott's stoves. The grounds are very extensive, and are partly laid out in gardens, lawns, and shrubberies, affording pleasing recreation and healthy employment to the inmates, who are managed with such skill and tenderness that personal restraint is seldom necessary. Dr. Kirkman, the *resident physician*, in his report of the Asylum for 1842, says, " We have found great advantage this year by the additional piece of ground (nearly 2A.) at the back of the house, retained in cultivation by the patients. We have generally as many as 15 or 20 employed on this piece of ground, and they work very much under the direction of a very insane man, who fancies himself a *king*, but who never appears to suppose that his monarchial dignity can be compromised by the use of the spade. We have a *queen* too, in our laundry, who bears great sway, and though hers is not quite so mild a government, as that of the aforesaid king, yet she labours effectually herself for the general good, and keeps her subjects in due order." Mr. Head is *house steward;* Dr. Lynn, of Woodbridge, *consulting physician;* the Rev. T. W. Hughes, *chaplain;* and Mr. Pizey, *auditor.*

ANCISCO

MELTON DIRECTORY.

Post Office, at Mr Wm. Elvis's. Letters received at 7 morning, and despatched at 8 evening

Aplin Capt. Richd. *Melton Lodge*
Armstrong Samuel, surgeon
Ashford Geo. grocer and draper
Baker Mr James || Barret Mr C.
Barrell George, parish clerk
Bilby Wm. sen. builder & surveyor
Bilby & Last, joiners & builders
Bennington Nathl. maltster, &c
Bland Thos. M.D. *Melton Grange*
Brook Thomas, Esq.
Bryant Joshua, ironfounder and machine maker
Burleigh Robt. & Wm. corn & coal merchants & maltsters, New quay
Capon Francis, butcher
Churchyard Mrs Ann
Collins Henry, millwright
Cook Wm. brick and tile maker
Cook Lydia, beerhouse
Cullum Wm. gardener and seedsman
Dorling George, brick and tike mkr
Durrant Maria, milliner
Fisher Henry, hay and straw dlr
Hayward Alfred, corn miller
Head Wm. John, steward, *Asylum*
Kirkman, John, M.D. supt. *Lunatic Asylum*
Leech Mary, midwife
Lister Isaac, blacksmith & wheelgt
Levett Wm. Richd. hay & straw dlr
Provart Philip, constable, &c.
Pulham Ann, collar & harness mkr

Pytches Thomas, Esq.
Riches Martha, baker
Rouse Rolla, Esq. (barrister.) *Fern Villa*
Sawyer Edw. baker and brewer
Schrieber Mrs Ann, *Hill House*
Shuldham Lieut. Molineux, R.N.
Styles John, gentleman
Thompson & Bennington, corn and coal merchants and maltsters
Walford Chas. Esq. *Foxburgh Hall*
Whayman Mrs Jane
Wolton Rev Chas. George, *rector*
Wood John, sen. gent. *Melton Hall*
Woodley Wm. Matthew, gentleman

INNS & TAVERNS.

Coach & Horses, Bilby Smith
Horse & Groom, George Ward
Lion, Wm. Tuffield

BOOT & SHOE MAKERS.

Godbold Charles || Osborn Jerh.

FARMERS.

Aston Eliz. || Hunt John
Rout Wm. || Smith Bilby
Seammen Charles W.
Studd Jonathan Abbott, *(owner)*
Trott John || Ward George

TAILORS.

Booth George || Crane Joseph

CARRIERS.

From Woodbridge to Alderton, Bawdsey, &c. call at the Horse and Groom. An *Omnibus* runs to meet the London Steamers at Ipswich from the Coach and Horses

PETISTREE, or *Pettistree*, a small pleasant village, 4 miles N.N.E. of Woodbridge, has in its parish 303 souls, and 1767A. 3R. 7P. of fertile land, including the small hamlets and manors of *Loudham* and *Bing*. The latter (now only a farm) claimed a market in the 14th of Edward I., and was afterwards given with Petistree, to Campsey Priory. The Duke of Hamilton is now lord of these manors, but Loudham belongs to Jacob W. C. Whitbread, Esq.; and Lord Rendlesham, R. Brook, Esq., P. Dykes, Esq., and some smaller owners, have estates in the parish. *Loudham Hall*, occupied by Fredk. Corrance, Esq., is a handsome mansion, in a beautiful park, 3 miles N.E. of Woodbridge, and was rebuilt by Charles Wood, Esq., a descendant of Sir Henry Wood, Knt., to whom the estate passed from the Loudhams and Blenherhaysetts. The rectorial tithes of Petistree and Bing belong to Pemberton's Charity, as noticed at page 81. The Church (St. Peter and St. Paul) is a small ancient structure. The *vicarage*, valued in K.B. at £6. 10s., and now at £96. 15s., is in the patronage of the Crown, and incumbency of the Rev. George Crabbe. In the Liber Regis, it is called Loudham-cum-Petistree. The *Town Estate* comprises a house occupied by paupers, and 17A. of land, let for £25

a-year, which is applied, conformably to old usage, in the service of the church. For a distribution of bread, every other Sunday, the poor have a yearly rent-charge of £5, left by John Jessup, in 1717, out of land now belonging to the Dykes family. They have also 5s. quarterly, in bread, from *Mills' Charity.* (See Framlingham.) *Directory :—* Richd. Brook, Esq., *Petistree Lodge ;* Fredk. Corrance, Esq., *Loudham Hall ;* Philip Dykes, gent. ; Wm. Smith, joiner and vict. *Greyhound ;* Mrs. Studd ; Henry Turrall, vict. *Three Tuns ;* and Wm. Clark, Isaac and Jas. Churchyard, *Bing Hall ;* Wm. Walker, *(Loudham,)* Mrs. Threadkell, and Henry Jeffries, *farmers.*

RAMSHOLT, on the east bank of the river Deben, opposite Kirton Sluice, 5 miles S. by E. of Woodbridge, is a village and parish, containing 192 souls and 1990 acres, including an old farm house, more than a mile east of the village, called *Peyton Hall,* anciently a seat of the Peytons, who, in the reign of Henry III., assumed the name of Ufford. The trustees of the late Peter Thellusson, Esq., are lords of the manor, but part of the soil belongs to the Wyse and other families. The *Church* (All Saints) is a perpetual curacy, which has been augmented with Queen Anne's Bounty, and is now worth £70 per annum. C. Pennington, Esq., is impropriator and patron, and the Rev. Robt. Field, M.A., of Sutton, is the incumbent. The tithes have been commuted for £456 per annum. *Directory :—*Samuel Banks, vict., *Dock Inn ;* George Cracknell, master mariner ; Lieut. George Prettyman, R. N. ; and Charles French, John Prettyman *(Lodge,)* Thomas Roberts, Dendy Sharwood *(Peyton Hall)* and John Vertue, *(*Vale Cottage,*) farmers.*

SHOTTISHAM, a scattered village, 4½ miles S.E. of Woodbridge, on the banks of a rivulet flowing eastward to the Deben, has in its parish 283 souls, and 1040 acres of sandy land, including part of an open heath. Mrs. E. Darby and Miss Mary Kett own the manor and most of the soil, and have the patronage of the *Church* (St. Margaret,) which is a rectory, valued in K.B. at £4. 16s. ½d., and now at £250. The Rev. John Darby, B.A., is the incumbent. The Glanviles and Wingfields were anciently lords of the manor. A cottage and an acre of land have from an early period been vested for the repairs of the church. The poor have £2 yearly out of an estate belonging to T. Waller, Esq., left by Sarah Clarke, in 1708.

Archer Eliza, schoolmistress
Bird Wm. blacksmith
Cullum James, collar & harness mkr
Edwards Geo. gent. *Shottisham Hall*
Fairhead John, wheelwright
Fletcher Frederick, corn miller
Hudson Wm. shoemaker
Kemp Thomas, butcher
Kett Mrs Charlotte and Miss Mary
Lawrence Wm. farrier
Manthorpe Saml. vict. Sorrel Horse
Pallant Thomas, veterinary surgeon
Stimpson Rev John Henry, curate
Skipper Charles, land agent
Stollery John, shopkeeper
Squirrel Rev Samuel, Baptist min
Squirrel Asaph, shopkeeper
Symonds Wm. shoemaker

SUTTON, a scattered village, from 3 to 4 miles S.E. of Woodbridge, has in its parish 707 inhabitants, and 5789A. of land, including nearly a thousand acres of open sandy heath, called *Sutton Walks,* on the north ; *Wood Hall* and *Fen Hall,* about one mile south, and the small hamlets of *Methers-gate, Little Hough,* &c., on the east bank of the river Deben, from 1 to 3 miles S.S.E. of Woodbridge. Thomas

Waller, Esq., is lord of the manor of Sutton; H. Edwards, Esq., of Wood Hall, and B. Edwards, Esq., of Fen Hall; but part of the soil belongs to R. Cobbold, Thellusson's Trustees, and a few smaller proprietors. The Bacons and Chapmans were formerly lords of the two first-named manors, and the Burrells were seated at Fen Hall, from the reign of Elizabeth till about 1730. The *Church* (All Saints,) is a small fabric, and the living is a vicarage, valued in K.B. at £8. 2s. 1d., and now at £310. The Rev. Robert Field, M.A., is patron and incumbent. The vicarage house was burnt to the ground by an accidental fire in 1831, and has not yet been rebuilt. Here is a small *Baptist Chapel*, erected in 1813. *Sir Michael Stanhope*, in the 16th of James I., granted to trustees, in fee, certain yearly rents, amounting to £48, out of the demesne lands of the manor of Valence, in Blaxhall; upon trust for the relief of the poor of this and about nine other parishes. The portion belonging to Sutton is £4 per annum. In 1687, *Susannah Burrell* left a yearly rent charge of £5. 4s. out of her lands in the manor of Staverton-with-Bromeswell, for a distribution of 2s. worth of bread every Sunday at Sutton church, among the poor of the parish. The vicar receives 20s. yearly for sermons on St. Thomas's day and Good Friday, and the poor 2s. 6d. on each of those days, in bread, from Sir Robert Harland, pursuant to the bequest of a Mr. Bloss.

Archer Henry, shopr. *Post-Office*
Barrett Robert, farmer, *Hough*
Colchester Benjamin, farmer
Edwards Henry & Thomas, Esqrs. *Wood Hall*
Edwards Burrell, Esq. *Fen Hall*
Easter John, steward
Field Rev Robert, M.A. vicar
Fairhead Tyrrel, joiner & builder
Freston George, blacksmith
Gooch Thomas, tailor
Hillen Robert, farmer, *Ferry*
Howe Simon, boot and shoemaker
Knappit Richard, boot and shoemkr
Nichols James, corn miller
Paternoster Thomas, collar & harness maker
Pleasance Charles, maltster & brickmaker, *Methers gate*
Roper Charles, farmer
Simpson James, farmer
Solomon Rt. vict. *Plough and Horses*
Trusson Wm. boot and shoemaker
Waller Thomas Esq. *Sutton Hall*
Wolton Robert, shopkeeper

UFFORD is a well-built village, in two parts, called *Upper and Lower Streets*, distant nearly half a mile from each other, and 2½ miles N.N.E. of Woodbridge, near the Deben, but above the point to which that river is navigable. Its parish contains 673 souls, and 1155 acres of land, under which is an abundance of that fertilizing marine deposit called cragg. The principal owners of the soil and lords of the manors are, J. W. C. Whitbread, Esq., Rev. Jas. Worsley, and F. C. Brooke, Esq., of *Ufford Place*, a handsome mansion, with pleasant grounds, formerly the seat of the Hammonds. The Peytons, when they removed here from Peyton Hall, in Ramsholt, assumed the name of Ufford. *Robert de Ufford* was made Chief Justice of Ireland in 1269, and his son, of the same name, was created *Baron Ufford* in 1308. Robert, the second Baron, was created *Earl of Suffolk* in 1337, but on the death of his son William, without issue, in 1382, both titles became extinct. At one period, the Uffords were possessed of the castles of Orford, Eye, Framlingham, Bungay, Mettingham, and Haughley. Their seat in this parish stood about two furlongs north of the church, near the farmhouse belonging to Mills' Charity. Part of Ufford forms

the manor of *Sogenhoe*, where there was anciently a chapel, near an acre and a half of land, which is encompassed by a moat or ditch, and is supposed to be the site of a castellated mansion. The Ottley s had a seat and estate here, and one of them, Wm. Ottley, was Lord Mayor of London in 1434. The *Church* (St. Mary) is a neat structure, with a lofty tower, built of flint. It was re-pewed and thoroughly repaired in 1840 and '41, and has an organ, which was purchased in 1837. The interior was once highly ornamented, but suffered much from the puritanical Vandals of the 17th century. The visitors sent here by parliament, in January, 1648, took up six inscriptions in brass, broke thirty pictures, and gave directions for the destruction of 37 more pictures, and 40 cherubims of wood. Their instructions not being obeyed, they returned again in August following, to finish their work with their own hands, which they did after some obstruction from the churchwardens, but they appear to have spared what they described as a " glorious cover over the font, like a pope's triple crown, with a pelican on the top picking its breast, all gilt over with gold." This cover still remains, and was repaired some years ago, at the expense of the Antiquarian Socieiy. It is elaborately executed, and rises pyramidically to the roof. The *rectory*, valued in K.B. at £8. 5s., and now at £340, is in the patronage of Fras. Capper Brooke, Esq., and incumbency of the Rev. Wm. P. Larkin, who has a neat residence near the church. The *Rev. Richard Lovekin* was rector here from 1621 till 1678, when he died in his 111th year. This venerable divine did all the duties of his function, even to the Sunday before his death. During the civil wars, he was plundered of everything he possessed, except one silver spoon, which he hid in his sleeve. *D. E. Davy, Esq.*, of Ufford, is well known to the literary world, and is now making collections for a general history of Suffolk. The TOWN ESTATE consists of a double cottage, occupied by paupers, and a cottage and 41A. of land in Ufford and Melton, let for £55 a year, which is applied in the service of the church. The *Almshouse*, for four poor men of Ufford, was erected by the Rt. Rev. Thomas Wood, Bishop of Lichfield and Coventry, who, in 1690, endowed it with a yearly rent-charge of £15, out of his manor of Barham, which he also charged with the repairs of the almshouse, and with providing a coat once in two years, for each of the almsmen. *Smock Meadow*, 3A. 3R., was given to the poor by a Mr. Sayer, and is let for £8 a year, which is distributed partly in bread and partly in shifts for poor women. For distributions of bread, the poor parishioners have 40s. yearly from *Mills' Charity*, (see Framlingham,) and an annual rent-charge of £3, left by one *Ballett*, out of three meadows, now belonging to Mr. Gross.

Baker James, mason
Barrell Robert, sawyer
Beecroft Mrs. vict. *Crown Inn*
Bloomfield Charles, tailor
Brooke Francis Capper, Esq. *Ufford Place*
Dale Geo. stone and marble mason
Davy David Elisha, Esquire
Doughty Miss Mary
Dove Charles, bricklayer
Garrett Charles, blacksmith

Haywood Rebecca, vict. *Lion*
Haywood Wm. broker
Johnson Edw. day and bdg. school
Kemp Kemble, butcher
Larkin Rev Wm. Pochin, *Rectory*
Manning Stephen, sawyer
May John, corn, &c. merchant
Noy Jas. survyr; & Mrs My. Ann
Olding James, brick and tile maker
Patrick Jonathan, bricklayer
Simpson Mrs Martha Elizabeth

Stephenson Henry, corn miller
Warby Rebecca, schoolmistress
Woolnough Miss Mary
Wright Thos. schoolmaster

Boot&ShoeMkrs.
Bond James
Bond Thomas
Garrett Wm.
Lambert Isaac
Nichols Samuel

Trusson Wm.
FARMERS.
Balls Zedekiah
Betts George, &
    coal dealer)
Bickers Thos.

Burrows Richd.
Churchyard Hy.
Crow Edward
Kemp Henry
Turner May
Joiners.
Carr John
Downing Jph.
Shopkeepers.
Fuller Ann

Kell Herbert
Lambert Issac
Smith Isaac

Wheelwrights.
Forsdick Thos.
Garrett Edw.
Margham Geo.

WICKHAM-MARKET, on a^{n} eminence near the river Deben,
5 miles N.N.E. of Woodbridge, and 8 miles S.W. of Saxmundham, is
a small ancient town, which has still a *fair* on the 24th of June, and
had a weekly market, but it has been disused more than a century.
The market, and two fairs, were granted by Henry VI. in 1440. The
parish contains 1174A. 3R. 4P. of land, and had 1400 inhabitants in
1841, including 100 in *Plomesgate Union Workhouse,* which was
erected here in 1836-7. (See Plomesgate Hundred.) Wickham-
Market was formerly of such consequence, that it had a Shire Hall, in
which quarter sessions were held; but they were removed to Woodbridge many years ago, and the hall was taken down by the lord of the
manor, and the materials used in the erection of a farmhouse at Letheringham. The Archdeacon of Suffolk still holds his visitations here
for the Deanery of Wilford. The Duke of Hamilton is lord of the
manor, but a great part of the soil belongs to A. Archdeckne, Esq.,
and several smaller owners. The Ufford family gave the manor and
church to Campsey priory, and Henry VIII. granted the former to
Anthony Wingfield. The *Church* (All Saints) is a handsome structure, with an octagonal tower, surmounted by a leaded spire, and containing six bells, a clock, and chimes. It stands upon a hill, and its
steeple is a conspicuous sea mark, though only about 70 feet high. From
the top of the tower, nearly 50 churches may be seen. The aisle or
chapel on the north side, was built by Walter Fulburn, who was
buried there in 1489. The *Vicarage,* valued in K.B. at £6. 16s. 8d.,
is in the patronage of the Crown, and incumbency of the Rev. W.
Butler, who has a good residence. The *Rectory* belongs to Pemberton's Charity, as noticed at page 81. The tithes have been commuted
for yearly moduses, viz., £105 to the vicar, and £195 to the impropriate rectory. The *Independents* have a small chapel here. The TOWN
LANDS comprise one acre of freehold land in Hacheston, and 38A.
29P. of copyhold land, in this parish, let for about £135 per annum.
About 17 acres, called the *Old Town Lands,* have for a very long period been appropriated to charitable and public uses. The remainder
of the estate, (about 21A.) called the *New Town Lands,* was purchased with £320, of which £300 was left by *Mrs. Ann Barker,* in
1730, to be laid out by the minister and churchwardens in the purchase of lands, upon trust, that two-thirds of the rents thereof should
be applied towards the benefit of the poor, either in a workhouse or
otherwise ; and that the other third should be applied to the teaching
poor children to read and write. The rents of the whole are applied
in repairing the church; in the payment of charges incidental to the
offices of churchwarden and constable; in occasionally apprenticing one
or two boys; in repairing the town pump, and some cottages belonging

to the parish; and in paying £26 a-year to the *schoolmaster*, for teach
ing 13 poor children to read and write. Here is a school, connected
with the British and Foreign School Society ; and a *National School*
was built here in 1842. In 1690, the RIGHT REV. THOS. WOOD,
Bishop of Lichfield and Coventry, by his will, after reciting other charitable bequests, charged his manor of Barham with the payment of
£15 per annum, for equal division among four poor men of Wickham-
Market, and with providing each of them with a gown once in two
years, marked with the letters H.W. The testator's heir, Henry
Webb, neglected to pay these charges till 1705, when it was ordered,
by a decree of the Court of Exchequer, that the estate of Barham
Hall should be charged with the further yearly sum of £6, as interest
of the arrears, so that the four pensioners each receive £5. 5s. per annum, and a gown once in two years. The poor parishioners have 5s.
worth of bread every three months from *Mills' Charity*. (See Framlingham.) *John Kirby*, who wrote the "*Suffolk Traveller*," resided
here, as noticed at page 76.

WICKHAM MARKET.

Marked 1, *are in High street ; 2,
Low street ; & 3, Market hill.*
Post Office, at Mr Edward Tice's.
Letters arrive at 7 morning, and
are despatched at 7 evening.
1 Barclay Jas. Pringle, solicitor, &
sec. to Wickham Market Association for the Prosecution of Felons,
and to the Farmers' Club
1 Bird John, tinner and brazier
Bunn Nathaniel, bricklayer
Burrell Mrs M. *Belle vue*
Butcher Mr Wm. *Church cottage*
Butler Rev Weeden, *Vicarage*
3 Catton Jno. plumber, paper hanger,
and builder
2 Clark Reeve, & 1 Wm. gentlemen
2 Cochrane George, surgeon
2 Coleman Wm. marble & stone msn
2 Dale Geo. marble & stone mason
Dallenger John, clerk to Plomesgate
Union, supt. registrar, agent to the
Free Masons' Life Assurance Co.,
and auctioneer
2 Deane Mr Geo.||Edwards Mrs Ann
Drew Rev J. curate, *Belle vue*
2 Edwards Benjamin, cooper
2 Garrod Fredk. register office
2 Gowing Wm. corn chandler
1 Grayston J., bricklayer
2 Griffiths Lieutenant James
3 Harsant Thomas, gentleman
2 Hawke Chas. clock & watch mkr
3 Hill David, cabinet maker
3 Hill Jesse, parish clerk & whtsmith
2 Knevett Wm. gardener

2 Leek Stephen, basket maker and
game dealer
1 Marjarom Richard, gun maker
3 Marsingall Anthony, police officer
1 Minter M.A. fancy repository
1 Minter Chas. Churchyard, registrar and auctioneer
1 Minter Robt. wine & spirit mercht.
& agent to the Suffolk Fire Office
Moor Chas. & George, solicitors, (&
Woodbridge)
2 Moor Mrs Rebecca
Moore John, governor of *Plomesgate
Union Workhouse*
3 Motum Wm. Ferdinando, ironmonger, & agent to Sun Fire Office
2 Muriel Wm. surgeon
2 Newson Geo. fishmonger
1 Oxborrow Robert, coach builder
2 Olding Wm. glover
3 Rackham John, harness maker
2 Rouse Wm. cabinet maker
2 Roe Wm. collar & harness mkr
Smith Jas. brick and tile maker
2 Smith Wm. plumber & glazier
2 Starling A. lodgings
2 Thurlow Mrs Susanna
3 Tice (Edw.) & Dallenger (John,)
auctioneeers, &c
1 Walton Mrs Sophia
2 Walker Mrs Hannah
3 Watkins John, straw hat maker
2 White James, clock & watch mkr.
and agent to the Norwich Equitable Assurance Company
2 Whitmore John, engineer, millwright, and iron founder

Wigg Richard, relieving officer
1 Woodhead Mr Thomas
2 Yates Thos. chemist & druggist

INNS AND TAVERNS.

2 Chaise and Pair, James Foreman
2 Chequers, Wm. Nickles
2 Crown, James Woods
2 George, Francis Richardson
White Hart, Edw. Tice (posting)

Academies.
take Boarders.
2 Brown Mrs M.
*2 Downes Geo.
(classical)
1*Kemp Benoni
1 Olding Wm.
2 Squires Emily
and Emma
2 Tyler Sarah
Watling John

Bakers.
2 Flory Jonathan
2 Wade Joseph
3 Wade Wm.

Blacksmiths.
1 Burch Wm.

Leggett Geo. (&
farrier)
3 Hill Jesse
Boot & Shoe Mkrs.
2 Carr Wm.
1 Cattermole Jtn.
2 Dennison John
2 Kerridge Geo.
2 Knevett Wm.
3 Tyler John
3 Tyler Samuel
Butchers.
Reeve Thomas
2 Sherwood Wm.
Corn Millers.
2 Cadman Saml.
Lewin John

2 Woolnough Chs.

FARMERS.

Blake John
Brook Jacob
2 Churchyard Jas.
(& farrier)
Reeve Thomas
Threadkell Sarah
2 Welton Cornls.
Whitmore Nathl.
Grocers & Drprs.
2 Churchyard Chs
2 Coleman John
1 Cattermole Jtn.
1 Fish George
2 Mayhew Robt.
2 Shave Nancy
3 Thurston Jas.

CARRIERS.

Thos. Tyler and Robt. Mayhew, to
Woodbridge, &c. daily.

COACHES AND CARRIERS,

From Ipswich and Woobridge, to
Halesworth, Saxmundham, Yarmouth, &c. call at the inns daily.
(See page 116)

White James
Hair Dressers.
Lay David
2 Licence Isaac
Joiners.
Blackham Wm.
2 Welton Robert
Milliners, &c.
2 Churchyard Elz.
2 Coleman Sarah
2 Smith Jane
Tailors.
* are Drapers.
2*Balls John
2 Brown George
2 Garrord Fred.
2*Leek Isaac

PLOMESGATE HUNDRED

Comprises the small ancient boroughs and ports of *Aldeburgh* and *Orford*, the market town of *Saxmundham*, and twenty other parishes. It extends about 14 miles S.S.E. from the neighbourhood of Framlingham and Bruisyard, to the German Ocean, where it is about nine miles in breadth. It is watered by the river Alde and its tributary streams, and is generally a fertile, loamy district, rising in bold undulations from the valleys and the coast; but in its southern parts are some sandy heaths and commons, still unenclosed, but affording good pasturage for sheep and cattle. It is in the *Deanery of Orford*, Archdeaconry of Suffolk, and *Plomesgate Union*, and is bounded on the east by the sea; on the north, by Blything Hundred, and a detached part of Hoxne Hundred; on the west, by Hoxne and Loes Hundreds; and on the south, by the latter and Butley river, which joins the Alde in Orford Haven. The following is an enumeration of its 23 *parishes*, shewing their territorial extent, the annual value of their lands and buildings, as assessed to the property tax in 1815, and their population in 1801 and 1841.

PARISHES.	Acrs.	Rental.	Populatn. 1801	1841.	PARISHES.	Acres.	Rental. £.	Population. 1801.	1841.
Aldeburgh*	1710	2005	804	1557	Parham	1970	2407	399	514
Benhall	2154	2621	533	749	Rendham	1687	2247	367	412
Blaxhall	1975	2203	373	576	Saxmundham	1400	2580	855	1097
Bruisyard	1127	1266	225	296	Snape	1700	1191	402	542
Chillesford	1693	1514	154	220	Sternfield	1107	1309	170	193
Cransford	1174	1523	210	303	Stratford St. ⎱	638	847	203	201
Farnham	1154	960	216	186	Andrew .. ⎰				
Friston	1851	1233	299	455	Sudborne ..	5000	3295	441	623
Glemham Great	1801	2378	384	370	Swefling	1120	1529	333	308
Glemham Little	1160	1545	319	333	Tunstall§	2642	2448	586	658
Haselwood*	1897	785	93	108	Wantisden....	1300	956	79	110
Iken	2579	1305	282	342					
Orford borough †	2740	3906	751	1109	Total‡..	41,579	42,053	8478	11,262

☞ *Aldeburgh* and *Orford* are ancient *boroughs*, but lost their parliamentary franchise by the Reform Bill of 1832.

* *Haselwood* is connected with and sometimes deemed a hamlet of the parish of Aldeburgh. From the latter, 197 *seamen* were deducted in 1831.

† *Orford* includes the hamlets of *Raydon, Gedgrave,* and *Havergate Island,* which had 95 inhabitants, in 1841. The two latter are *extra parochial.*

§ Tunstall includes the hamlet of *Dunningworth,* which had 25 souls, in 1841.

‡ The number of HOUSES in 1841, was 2413 *inhabited,* 91 *empty,* & 12 *building.* The number of MALES was 5506 ; and FEMALES, 5756.

☞ The *Chief Constables* are, Mr. James Newson, of Great Glemham ; and Mr. John Flatt, of Dunningworth Hall.

PLOMESGATE UNION comprises about 21,000 inhabitants, and *forty parishes,* consisting of all the 23 parishes in Plomesgate Hundred, 16 of the 18 parishes of Loes Hundred, and Wickham Market, in Wilford Hundred. Framlingham returns two *guardians,* but each of the other parishes only one. The UNION WORKHOUSE is at Wickham Market, and was erected in 1836-7, at the cost of about £7000. It is handsomely built of brick, in the Elizabethan style, and has room for 370 inmates, and had as many as 278 in January, 1843, though it had only 100 in July, 1841. They are maintained at the weekly cost per head of 1s. 10¾d. for food, and 7d. for clothing. The total sum expended for the relief of the *in* and *out-*door poor, during the first quarter of 1843, was £2595. 12s. 1¾d., which was £175 less than the cost of the preceding quarter. The Union is divided into six Registration Districts, under Mr. John Dallenger, the *Superintendent Registrar* and *Clerk to the Board of Guardians.* Mr. John and Mrs. Susan Moore are *master and matron of the Workhouse,* and the Rev. William B. Bransby is the *chaplain.* The other principal officers are John Cottingham, Richard Wigg, and John Garrod, *relieving officers ;* Messrs. Wm. Muriel, Wm. Jeaffreson, Edward Gross, Robt. Freeman, Saml. Randall, and Fredk. Bell, *surgeons ;* Fras. W. Ellis, *auditor ;* Mr. Robert Welham, of Framlingham, *Registrar of Marriages ;* and the following REGISTRARS OF BIRTHS AND DEATHS, viz., Mr. Edward Gross, for *Earl Soham District ;* Mr. H. L. Freeman, *Saxmundham District ;* Mr. John Garrod, *Aldeburgh District ;* Mr. Richd. Wigg, *Orford District ;* Mr. C. C. Minter, *Wickham Market District ;* and Mr. John Cottingham, for *Framlingham District.*

ALDEBURGH, or *Aldborough,* a small but ancient *borough,* is a *seaport, fishing town,* and delightful *bathing place,* pleasantly situated

on the side of a picturesque acclivity, rising boldly from the German Ocean, 23 miles E.N.E. of Ipswich, 15 miles E.N.E. of Woodbridge, 7 miles S.E. of Saxmundham, 5 miles N.N.E. of Orford, and 92 miles N.E. of London. Its parish increased its population from 804 souls in 1801, to 1557 in 1841, and contains 1710 acres of land, of which Wm. Frederick Thomas Vernon Wentworth, Esq., is principal owner, and lord of the *manor*, which passed to his family after the death of the last Earl of Strafford in 1799. Wm. Martel, in 1155, gave this manor to Snape priory, and it was granted with the other possessions of that monastery to Cardinal Wolsey, for the endowment of his college at Ipswich, in 1527, but was soon afterwards given by Henry VIII. to Thomas Duke of Norfolk. The *River Alde*, from which the borough has its name, rises near Brundish, 17 miles N.W. by W. of Aldeburgh, but it is only navigable as high as Snape bridge, five miles above the town, where it begins to expand into a broad tide stream. After pursuing an easterly course to the south side of Aldeburgh, and within a few hundred yards of the sea, the Alde suddenly turns to the south, and runs in that direction more than nine miles, parallel with the coast, before it empties itself (with the river Butley) into the ocean at Hollesley Bay, below Orford, up to which town it is sometimes called Orford Haven. The valley through which it flows southward from Aldeburgh is called *Slaughden*, and anciently extended much further to the north ; but the eastern side, opposite the town, has been washed away by the ocean, which, in the whole course of the Alde below the town, is only separated from that river by a sandy strip of land, called the Beach and the *Lantern Marshes*, from two light-houses at *Orford Ness*, a small promontory, in the broadest part of this singular peninsula, which varies from one to less than a quarter of a mile in breadth, though it is more than nine miles in length, and has, on the river side of it, the small island of Havergate. (See Orford.) Two centuries and a half ago, Aldeburgh was a place of considerable importance, but repeated encroachments of the sea reduced it to the rank of a small fishing town. During the last century, the ocean made great ravages, overthrowing many houses, together with the market-place and cross. A plan of the town in 1559 proves it to have been at that time of considerable magnitude, and represents the church as being at more than ten times its present distance from the shore. From the same plan, it also appears that there were " *denes*" of some extent, similar to those at Yarmouth, between the town and the sea. The former importance of Aldeburgh induced many monarchs to grant it extensive charters. The last of these, renewed by Charles II., entrusts the *government of the town* to two bailiffs, ten capital, and twenty-four inferior burgesses, giving also a power to the majority of the capital burgesses, one of them being a bailiff, to elect an unlimited number of freemen, either resident or not. By the bailiffs and burgesses resident in the borough, and not receiving alms, (about forty in number,) two members were returned to Parliament, till the borough lost this privilege by the Reform Act of 1832, which disfranchised all the other small boroughs in this kingdom. It first sent representatives in the 13th of Elizabeth, and as Willis supposes, obtained the elective franchise in the tenth year of that Queen's reign, when she granted the Duke of Norfolk a weekly market on Saturday, at his manor of Aldeburgh. It is not

included in any of the schedules of the Municipal Reform Act of 1835, therefore its *Corporation* still exists in its pristine form, but many of its members reside at a distance.   The two bailiffs are annually elected from the freemen, and are coroners and justices of the peace *ex officio ;* but in addition to them, two other *magistrates* are appointed for the borough, viz., H. Muller, Esq., of Aldeburgh, and W. O'Grady, Esq., of Orford.   The present bailiffs are S. Randall, Esq., of Orford, and J. Osborne, Esq., of Aldeburgh.   P. B. Long, Esq., of Ipswich, is *town clerk ;* H. Southwell, of Saxmundham, *clerk to the magistrates ;* Wm. Hunt, *chief constable ;* Horatio Salton, *inspector of weights and measures ;* and J. Rust and J. Richardson, *mace bearers.*   The corporate body hold a *court of sessions* yearly in September, and are possessed of 198A. 1R. 8P. of marshes, let for about £240 a year.   The *Town Hall* is an ancient half-timbered building, with a prison in the ground story. Small *markets* for provisions are held here on Wednesdays and Fridays, and *fairs* for toys, &c., on March 1st and May 3rd.

The *Custom-House* is a small building, at the south end of the town, near the *Slaughden Quay,* on the river Alde, where vessels as large as 200 tons receive and discharge their cargoes, and where there is also a yard in which ships are built.   Thos. Underwood, Esq., is *collector of customs,* and Edward Leigh, Esq., *comptroller.*   Orford is a creek under their jurisdiction, and the former is also superintendent of the *pilots,* of whom here are about twenty.   The customs duty collected here averages only about £200 per annum.   The trade of the port consists chiefly in the exportation of corn and wool, and the importation of coal and timber.   There are about 40 vessels belonging to it, employing about 147 men, and averaging about 60 tons each.   Here are also about 200 licensed *fishing boats.*   Soles and lobsters are taken in great abundance ; also herrings and sprats, which are salted and dried for Holland, London, and other markets.   Within the limits of the port are two *coast-guard stations,* and a cruiser.   The fishing boats use the sea-beach, near which, at the north end of the town, is a large but shallow lake, called *Aldeburgh Mere,* sometimes called the Haven. At the southern extremity of the main street, overlooking the river and the sea, is a massive *tower battery,* erected about 1806, and presenting four semicircular fronts.   This tower was intended as a garrison for 100 men, but is now under the care of one.   On the beach, about three quarters of a mile farther to the south, is a small martello tower, and there were formerly batteries on the heights north of the town.   On the terrace above the town, is one of *Watson's General Telegraphic Stations.*   An account of all vessels seen from this ob servatory is sent daily by post to London.

Till the commencement of the present century, Aldeburgh, impoverished and depopulated by the encroachments of the ocean, was hastening to decay ; but several families of distinction, wishing for a greater degree of privacy and retirement than can be enjoyed in a fashionable watering-place, having made it their summer residence, its appearance has, since that period, been totally changed.   The deep sands which formerly led to it have given place to excellent turnpike roads ; and instead of the clay-built cottages, which gave the place a mean and squalid appearance, are now seen neat and comfortable dwellings, and several large and handsome mansions, which are the

occasional retreat of persons of rank and fortune. Near the church is an elegant *marine villa*, built after an Italian plan, by the late L. Vernon, Esq., and now the property and occasional residence of W. F. T. Vernon Wentworth, Esq., the present lord of the manor. On the brow of the hill, is *Wyndham House*, built by the Hon. Mr. Wyndham about 40 years ago, and near it is a romantic " *Cassino*," which was the favourite summer residence of the Earl of Salisbury, and is now the seat of the Hon. Arthur Thellusson. At the opposite end of the terrace, is the Little Cassino, which was the seat of W. C. Crespigny, Esq., but is now the residence of R. S. Adair, Esq. Here are also several other neat villas, of more recent erection. For invalids, Aldeburgh possesses advantages scarcely equalled, and certainly not excelled, by any which the most fashionable places of resort can boast. The *beach*, to which the descent is remarkably easy, is not more than about 50 yards from most of the lodging-houses; and during the ebb of the tide, and frequently for weeks together, it is peculiarly adapted for both bathing and walking, the sand being hard and firm. Here are several convenient bathing machines, and a suite of warm, cold, and shower baths. The magnificent terrace on the summit of the hill behind the town commands a most extensive prospect of Aldeburgh and Hollesley Bays, richly studded with their moving treasures, and separated by the promontory of Orford-ness; and also of the fertile country through which flows the capacious Alde, which, as if loth to lose itself in the ocean, makes a sudden turn below the terrace, and runs nine miles southward, parallel with the shore, before it gives up its waters. Here are two large and commodious hotels, and many of the inhabitants have furnished lodgings for the accommodation of visitors. Most of the houses are built on *copyhold tenures*, subject to small certain fines; but those above the terrace pay arbitrary fines.

The Magna Britannia notices a *miraculous appearance of peas* on the sea coast, near Aldeburgh, during a famine, in the reign of Queen Mary, by which the lives of many of the neighbouring poor were saved. These peas, as well as the coleworts found growing on the south part of the mere-shingles, are met with in several similar situations on the English coast. The former are the fruit of the *Pisum marinum*, which bears a purple blossom in June, and is a prostrate plant, perennial, with a very deep root; and though it must have grown here before, distress probably first brought it into notice on the occasion above alluded to. The *Church*, dedicated to St. Peter and St. Paul, stands on the summit of the hill, above the town, and is an ancient structure of flint and freestone, much intermixed with modern repairs of brick. The tower is a well-known sea-mark, and contains five bells and a clock. The living is a discharged *vicarage*, with Haselwood annexed to it, valued in K.B. at £33. 6s. 8d., and in 1835, at £220. W. F. T. Vernon Wentworth, Esq., is patron and impropriator, and the Rev. H. T. Dowler, M.A., is the incumbent, and has a neat residence finely embowered in trees, and nearly 15A. of glebe. The *Baptists*, *Congregationalists*, and the *Wesleyans* have chapels here. The *National School* was built by subscription in 1839, and is attended by about 60 boys and 50 girls. A charitable society for the relief of the poor was established in 1843, and there is a branch of the Woodbridge *Savings' Bank*, at Mr. Robt. Miller's, open every Monday from 9 till 12 o'clock

The *Slaughden Quay Trust Estate* consists of a quay, or wharf, with certain coal-yards, saltings, and other premises, on the river Alde, held of the manor of Aldeburgh, under the gift of one of the Earls of Strafford. The premises were surrendered to new trustees in 1754, and again in 1808, in trust for the general use of the inhabitants. The trustees let the premises to a wharfinger for about £50 a year, which is expended in repairing the quay, &c., and in schooling poor children. The vicar and others are trustees. The *Poor's Land*, 1A., is let for £3 a year, which is distributed among the poor. A yearly rent-charge of £11 is paid out of the Town Marsh (belonging to the Corporation,) in respect of £200 left by *Capt. Wm. Lawes* and *Capt. Thos. Chenery,* and an annuity of £2, given by *Capt. Wm. Covell.* This annuity was settled on the Town Marsh by a decree of the Court of Chancery, in 1736; and, agreeable to the wills of the three donors, £5 is applied in apprenticing poor children, £1 is paid to the minister for a sermon on Good Friday, and the remainder, £6, is distributed in bread and money among the poor, on the same day. *Crabbe, the Poet,* was born here in 1754.

ALDEBURGH DIRECTORY.

Post Office at Mr Robt. Lee's. Letters received at 8 morn. and desp. at ¼ past 6 evening

Adair Rt. Shafto, Esq. *Little Cassino*
Barnes Edgar, wine and spirit and ale and porter merchant
Barrett Mrs Amy||Bedwell Mrs My.
Bromley Lieut. Samuel, R.N.
Cole Julia, shopwoman
Davis Mrs Frances, *Pavilion*
Dodds Wm. Tower-keeper and collector of wharfage
Dowler Rev Henry Turner, M.A. *Vicarage*
Easter Mrs Alice
Eminey John, bricklayer
Fielden John, gardener
Fisher Mrs Mary
Fleming Rev John, B.A. curate
Ferrand Rev T. G. *rector of Tunstall*
Garrod John, cooper
Hunt Edward, ship builder
Hunt Wm. chief constable & par. clerk
Hunt Wm. jun. ship builder
James Mrs Caroline, *Wyndham Hs*
Kendall Peter, Esq., *Marine Villa*
Kersey Thomas, bricklayer & builder
Lincoln Benj. Carbould, watchmaker, jeweller, and stationer (circulating library)
Mann Stephen, basket maker
Mapleston Wm. fruiterer
Marjoram John, saddler
Mayhew Mr Jas.||Meyer Miss Rose
Muller Henry, Esq
Mathews Rev John, Baptist minister
Osborne Capt. John, R.N.

Ramsey Lieut. Frederick, R.N. commander of Coast Guard
Richardson John, mace bearer
Rust Jacob, mace bearer
Smith Wm. lapidary & bath keeper
Southwell Henry and James, solicitors (and Saxmundham)
Squires Mrs My. || Stevens Miss P.
Thellusson Honble. Arthur, *Cassino*
Wade Mrs Mary Ann
Wentwworth Wm. Fredk. Thomas Vernon, Esq. Marine Villa, and *Wentworth Castle, Yorkshire*
Whitaker Rev George Ayton, M.A. rector of Knodishall

HOTELS, INNS, AND TAVERNS.
Cross, Joseph Revett
Cross Keys, Jane Winslow
King's Head, Mary Riches
Mill, John Kemp
New Inn and Commercial Hotel, Benjamin Thompson (posting)
Three Mariners, Ann Easter, Wharf
White Hart, Mary Thurrell
White Lion Inn and Family Hotel, Frances Nunn (posting)

Academies.
Dance Ann
Everett Robert
Taylor Wm.

Bakers and Confectioners.
Neeve Jane
Snare Robert
Todd James
Woods Wm.

Blacksmiths.
Felgate Henry

Felgate Thomas
Podd Wm. (and ironmonger)
Beer Houses.
Lee Robert
Lockwood John
Boot & Shoe Mkrs.
Broodbank Thos.
Collis James
Fisher Frederick
Knevett Abrm.
Salton Horatio

Smith James
Woods Wm.
Butchers.
Bush James
Bush Timothy
Downing Wm.
Chemists&Drgts.
Miller Robert
Rudland Charles
Coal&CornMerts
Garrett Newson
Garrett Rd. and
  Son (and iron)
Leigh Edw.Leon.
Osborne Js.&Son
Ralph Robert
Tyrrell Geo. M.
Corn Millers.
Geater Frederick
Woods Wm.
FARMERS.
Bedingfield Wm.
Cable Charles
Easter John
Gayford Wm.
Last Wm. *Hall*
Self Robert
Fishermen and
Smack Owners.
Burwood Charles
Burwood Edward
BurwoodEdw.jun
Cable John
Cable Thomas
Cable Thos. jun
Filby Samuel
Finnery Henry
Green John
Self George
Skeet Samuel
Walford Henry
Ward Samuel

Wilson Robert
Gardeners.
Page John
Read Wm.
Glass,&c.Dealrs.
Downing Wm.
Sparling John
Grocers & Drprs.
Beart James
Beart John
Fielder Wm.
Fox Wm.
JohnsonWm&Co
Sawyer Henry
Hair Dressers,&c
Starkweather Jas
Turner Robert
Joiners, &c.
Block Roht. (and
  cabinet maker)
Smyth James
WrightWm.(and
  timber dealer)
Lime Burners.
Osborne Js.& Son
Tyrrell Geo. M.
Lodging Houses.
BroodbankMrsA.
Butcher Joshua
Butcher Susanna
Cable Sarah
Curtis Mary Ann
Easter Thomas
Groome Sarah
Hale Mary
Hunt Wm.
McNab Mary
Neeve Elizabeth
Pallant Charles
Podd Wm.
Rabett Wm. Hy.
Self Robert

Storey James
Turner Abigail
Walker James
Ward Thomas
Maltsters.
Garrard John (&
  brewer)
Garrard Wm.

MasterMariners.
Bramham Bdgfd.
Dance John
Dance Wm.
Howsagoe John
Moor Thomas
Nunn George
Pallant John
Parker James
Parker Wm.
Roberts Richard
Sparling John
Storey James
Milliners, &c.
Levitt Sarah
Murrow Mary
Reeder Mary
SparrowMy.&Co.
  (haberdashers)
Welton Margaret

Painters, Plum-
bers,&Glaziers.
Calver Henry
Clodd Wm.
PILOTS.
Cable Wm.
Catmore Daniel
Gibson James
Thorp Wm.
Ship Builders.
HuntWm.& Sons
Shipping Agents.
Garrett Newson,
  (to Lloyds)
LeighEdw.Leon.
Straw Hat Mkrs.
Baxter Amelia
Hindes Emily
Surgeons.
Barker John
Bell Frederic
Tailors&Draprs
Chapman Wm.
Haken Joseph
Hindes Wm.
Redgrave Wm.
Revett Joseph
Simpson Henry
Thurrell George

COACH from the New Inn, to meet
the coaches at Saxmundham, every
morning at eight during summer

CARRIERS.
James Smith's *Van* to *Ipswich*, every
Monday, Wednesday, and Friday
Benjamin Baxter, to Ipswich, every
Tuesday and Friday morning
Mail Cart, from the Mill Inn to Sax-
mundham, at ½ past 6 evening

BENHALL, a scattered village, from 1 to 2 miles S.W. of Saxmundham, has in its parish 749 souls, and 2154A. of land, mostly a
rich but sandy loam. The Rev. Edmund Hollond, of *Benhall Lodge*,
(a handsome mansion in a well wooded park,) owns a great part of the
soil, and is lord of the manor, which was given by Henry II. to Ra-
nulfe Glanville. It was afterwards sold to Guido Kerr, who obtained a
charter for a fair here in the 20th of Edward I. Sir Edward Duke,
who built old Benhall Lodge, in 1638, was created a baronet in 1661,
but his grandson dying without issue, the estate went to his nephew, Edmund Tyrrel, Esq., who sold it to John Rush, Esq. It was
afterwards the seat of the late Admiral Sir Hyde Parker. The *Church*
(St. Mary,) has a tower and six bells, and was thoroughly repaired in
1842, at the expense of the patron. Two of the bells were erected in

May, 1843. On the chancel floor is a fine brass, on which is graven the effigy of Edward Duke, Esq., who died in 1598. The *vicarage*, valued in K.B. at £7. 1s. 3d., and in 1835, at £173, is enjoyed by the Rev. John Mitford, M.A. The Rev. E. Hollond is patron and impropriator, and has lately erected a *National School* on Benhall green, now attended by 60 boys and 55 girls. An estate, called *Benhall Sir Robert*, forms a small manor, belonging to the trustees of J. W. Sheppard, Esq. Mrs. Mary Toller and J. Moseley, Esq., have estates in the parish. In 1731, *Sir Edward Duke* left £1000, to be settled for the support of a *schoolmaster*, to teach poor children of this parish to read and write. Part of this legacy was laid out in purchasing and building the master's house, school, play-ground, and garden ; and the remainder was laid out in the purchase of £761. 1s. 10d., Old South Sea Annuities. The yearly dividend, £22. 16s. 8d., is paid to the schoolmaster, for teaching reading, writing, and arithmetic to all the poor children of the parish. He has also a yearly rent-charge of £5, left by *Wm. Corbold*, in 1746, for teaching four boys of Saxmundham parish. In 1829, the late Edward Hollond, Esq., of Benhall Lodge, left £500 for repairing the school premises and increasing the master's salary. After paying the legacy duty, the remainder was vested on mortgage, and now yields £18 a year, half of which is paid to the master.

Hollond Rev Edm. *Benhall Lodge*
Batho Wm. shoemaker
Bloomfield Wm. tailor and draper
Brightwell Rt. Free School master
Chase Rd. joiner and parish clerk
Cox John, agent to Sun Fire office
Howard John, hurdle maker
Leggett Robert, blacksmith
Marjoram James, joiner
Mills Robert, shoemaker
Mitford Rev John, M.A. *Vicarage*
Newby James, shoemaker
Newman Benjamin, gardener
Newson John, shopkeeper
Orford Saml. vict. Horse & Groom
Rackham Peter, shopkeeper
Reynolds David, corn miller
Robinson Wm. wheelwright

Sugden Rev Frank, curate
Thurlow John, brickmaker ; house *Saxmundham*
Toller Mrs My. ‖ Rous Mrs Sarah
Wilson John, gentleman
Wood Peter & Emma, National schl
FARMERS.
Andrews Wm. ‖ Capon Samuel
Easter Robert, *Benhall Sir Robert*
Mills Simon, *Old Lodge*
Neeve James ‖ Gray George
Plant John ‖ Robinson Wm.
Skeet Joseph ‖ Smith Charles
Toller James ‖ Stanford Samuel
CARRIERS.
James Rous's *omnibus* to Ipswich, Wednesday & Friday, 5 morning. (See also Saxmundham.)

BLAXHALL, a straggling village, 6 miles S.S.W. of Saxmundham, and 8 miles N.E. of Woodbridge, has in its parish 576 souls, and 1975 acres of land, partly in the manor of Valence, and mostly the property of the Hon. Mrs. Sophia North, and the trustees of J. W. Sheppard, Esq. The *Church* (St. Peter,) has several neat mural monuments, a very ancient font, and five bells. The *rectory*, valued in K.B. at £20, and in 1835 at £498, is in the gift of Agnes Ingleby, and incumbency of the Rev. Ellis Wade, M.A., who has a neat residence and 80 acres of glebe. The tithes have been commuted for about £500 per annum. Several *Roman urns* were found in a mound in this parish, in 1827. To provide clothing for the poor of Blaxhall, *Thos. Garthwaite* left the Red Cross House, in Woodbridge, now let for £18 a year.

Alexander Henry, joiner
Block John, blacksmith
Brightwell John, vict. Ship
Clark John, cooper
Daniels Robert, parish clerk and shoemaker
Gibson John, shoemaker
Leggett Wm. blacksmith
Pope Miss Mary || Watts Miss E.
Richardson Wm. postman
Sparrow Mr Jno. || Smith Jas. tailor

Wade Rev Ellis, M.A. *Rectory*
Whitehead Wm. shopkeeper
Wilson Samuel, shopkeeper

FARMERS AND GRAZIERS.

Bates George, *Blaxhall Hall*
Burrell Samuel || Hillen Benjamin
Hillen James, land agent to Lord Rendlesham, *Limetree Hall*
Keer John, (farm bailiff)
Pope Ann || Pizey Samuel
Toller Henry, *Stones Farm*

BRUISYARD, a small scattered village, on an acclivity above the river Alde, nearly 4 miles N.E. by E. of Framlingham, has in its parish 296 souls, and 1127 acres of land, including 140 acres of woodland. The soil is a rich strong loam, and the Earl of Stradbroke is the principal owner and lord of the manor. The hall, now a farm house, occupies the site of a collegiate chantry of a warden and four secular priests, which was translated hither from Campsey Ash, in 1354, and was, about 11 years afterwards, changed into a *nunnery* of the order of St. Clare. At the dissolution, this nunnery was of the yearly value of £56. 2s. 1d., and was granted to Nicholas Hare, from whose family it passed to that of Rous. The *Church* (St. Peter,) is an ancient structure, with a round tower. The living is a perpetual curacy, valued at £39, and enjoyed by the Rev. — Mason, of Bramfield. The Earl of Stradbroke is patron and impropriator, and receives a yearly modus of £92, in lieu of tithes from the farms here, which belong to Mr. N. Edwards, Mrs. Cooper, and Catherine Hall, Cambridge.

Cook Wm. shoemaker
Daniels John, shoemaker
Daniels Wm. parish clerk
Edwards Nathaniel, gentleman
Girling Edw. Horatio, shopkeeper
Grayston Robert, vict. and butcher, Butchers' Arms
Hayward James, shoemaker
Howard Rt. chimney sweep & shopr

Kell Edward, corn miller
Row James Green, hurdle maker

FARMERS.

Burrows Nathl || Greenwood Saml.
Row James (and shopkeeper)
Row James, jun. || Heffer James
Row John || Sherwood John
Wase Jeremiah, *Bruisyard Hall*

CHILLESFORD, near the river Butley, 3 miles N.W. by W. of Orford, has in its parish 220 souls, and 1693 acres of land, belonging to the Marquis of Hertford, the lord of the manor, which was given to Butley priory by John Staverton. The *Church* (St. Peter,) is a rectory, valued in K.B. at £5. 3s. 4d., and in 1835 at £295. The Rev. James Dewing, B.A., of Orford, is patron and incumbent. The poor have £5 yearly from Sir M. Stanhope's Charity. (See Sutton.) The houses are scattered, and the principal inhabitants are Mrs. M. Catlin, Thomas Crisp, farmer; Sophia Dykes, *boarding school;* Robert Hayward, farm bailiff; and James Pallant, shoemaker.

CRANSFORD, a scattered village, 2 m. E. by N. of Framlingham, has in its parish 303 souls, and 1174 acres of strong loamy land. Lady Tuthill is lady of the manor, and owns the hall and a great part of the soil, and the remainder belongs to Spencer de Horsey, Pemberton's Charity, J. Moseley, Esq., W. A. Shuldham, Esq., Miss Ashford, Mr. T. Harris, and the Meadows family. The *Church* (St. Peter) was appropriated to Sibton Abbey, but the *vicarage*, valued in K.B. at £6.

13s. 4d., and in 1835 at £305, was endowed by A. Dammant, Esq., with the rectorial tithes, and 48 acres of glebe, in 1713. G. Pooley, Esq., of Sandbach, Cheshire, is patron, and the Rev. Dr. John Chevallier, of Aspall Hall, is the incumbent. The tithes have been commuted for a yearly modus of £330. The Baptists have a neat chapel here, erected in 1841. In 1729, *A. Dammant, Esq.*, charged his lands at Bruisford, with the payment of 10s. a year to the vicar of Cransford, for a sermon on Good Friday, and 6s. 8d. quarterly for a distribution of bread among the poor.

Alston Rev Edw. Constable, M.A. curate, *Cransford Hall*
Daniels Wm. shoemaker
Elvin Robert, blacksmith
Howard John, blacksmith
Knights Mr Francis, parish clerk
Norris Rev Joseph, Baptist minister
Pipe Silvanus, wheelwright
Shuldham William Abraham, Esq. *Cransford Lodge*
Smith Benjamin, schoolmaster
Smith Joseph, wheelwright
Watts Samuel, joiner & shopkeeper
Winter Robert, corn miller; house *Chediston*

FARMERS.

Beaumont Jacob, *Parsonage*
Fisk Robert || Garrod Thomas
Harris Thomas || Hart Newson
Mayhew Daniel, *Fiddlers' Hall*
Spalding George || Steptoe Nathl.
Wightman John, *West House*

FARNHAM, a small neat village, on the east bank of the Alde, 3 miles S.W. of Saxmundham, and 9 miles N.E. of Woodbridge, has in its parish 186 souls, and 1154A. of land. Wm. Long, Esq., is lord of the manor, and owner of a great part of the soil, and the rest belongs to Miss Ann Pope, Miss E. Plant, (owner of *Rose Hill,*) and W. Hollond, Esq. The *Church* (St. Mary) is a perpetual curacy, valued at £78, and enjoyed by the Rev. S. F. Page, for whom a neat parsonage-house was built in 1842, at the cost of £1200, of which £200 was obtained from Queen Anne's Bounty, and £600, with 8A. of land, was given by Wm. Long, Esq., the patron and impropriator. The tithes have been commuted for a yearly modus of £240.

Barber Thos. farmer, *FarnhamHall*
Chaplin Wm. gent. *Rose Hill*
Deacon Mrs Eliz.||Garrett Mrs E.
Gooding Rt. and Stpn. blacksmiths
Howard Wm. shopr. *Post Office*
Heffer Henry, machine maker and wheelwright
Page Rev. Saml. Flood, incumbent
Pearse Thos. vict. George Inn
Plant Crisp, farmer, *High House*
Tibnam Edw. boot and shoe maker

FRISTON, a pleasant village on the Aldeburgh road, 2¼ miles S.S.E. of Saxmundham, has adjoining it several houses belonging to Knodishall. Its parish contains 455 souls, and 1851 acres of land, including an open moor of 60 acres. Colonel Thomas Howard Vyse is lord of the manor, which is mostly copyhold, subject to arbitrary fines. The other principal landowners are, Mrs. Whitaker, of Scole Lodge, Norfolk; Capt. Bagnold, and the Vernon-Wentworth family, whose ancestor, Thomas Earl of Strafford, married the heiress of Sir Henry Johnson, who built Friston Hall, now a farm-house. The *Church* (St. Mary) is a vicarage, united with Snape, and valued in K.B. at £5, and in 1835, at £194. The Rev. Robert Baker, A.M., is the incumbent, and Col. T. H. Vyse is patron and impropriator of the rectory, which was given to Butley priory by Ranulph Glanville. There is no parsonage house, and only two acres of glebe. In 1802, the *Rev. John Lambert* left £200, the yearly proceeds thereof to be

divided at Christmas among poor housekeepers. This legacy is vested in £250 three per cent. consols. Here is a small Baptist chapel, erected about eleven years ago.

FRISTON DIRECTORY.
(See also Knodishall.)

Baker Rev Robt. A.M. *Friston Hs*
Barrett Mr Wm.||Buck Rt. tailor
Broom Benj. blacksmith
Brown Rev Wm. Baptist minister
Davy Henry, schoolmaster
Moulton Joseph, wheelwright
Reynolds Robert, corn miller
Salter Robert, shoemaker

Sharman Wm. vict. Chequers
Smith John, blacksmith
Woolnough Frederick, shoemaker

FARMERS.

Cooper Charles||Moss John
Hammond Robt. *Friston Hall*
Jaye Samuel, Park Farm
Orford Wm.||Orford Bridget
Wainwright Jno.||Pettit James

GLEMHAM (GREAT) is a village and parish, 4 miles W. by S. of Saxmundham, containing 370 souls, and 1801A. of well wooded land, rising in bold undulations, and generally having a light but rich loamy soil. The manor is all freehold, and did belong, with the rectorial tithes, to Butley priory, and afterwards to the Edgar family. Spencer de Horsey, Esq., owns the Hall and Poads farms, and is considered lord of the manor; and the rest of the parish belongs chiefly to John Moseley, Esq., of *Glemhall House,* (a handsome mansion, in a small park,) Lady North, W. A. Shuldham, Esq., Rev. G. Crabbe, and the executors of the late John Newson. The small tithes have been commuted for £95. 3s., and the rectorial tithes for £352. 14s. per annum. The latter belong to the landowners. The *Church* (All Saints) has a fine tower, containing a clock and five bells, and is a curacy, consolidated with the rectory of Little Glemham. About 22A. of land has, from an early period, been appropriated to the repairs of the church and the relief of the poor, and is now let for £28 per annum, with some cottages, formerly the parish workhouse.

Benstead Thomas, saddler
Hurren Davy, schoolmaster
Matten Wm. thatcher
Moseley John, Esq. *Glemham Hs*
Muttit Mrs My.||Payne Wm. tailor
Robinson Benjamin, butler
Robinson Wm. vict. Crown Inn

Blacksmiths.
Ellenger Geo.
Goldsmith John

Boot & Shoe Mkrs.
Johnson George
Nichols George

FARMERS.
Benham Wm.
Chapman Edw.
Poads
Cook James
Cooper Wm.
Frost John
Frost Wm.
Kemp James
Matten Wm.
Newson Mrs J.

Newson John,
(Executors of)
Read Thos. *Hall*
Tacon Robert
Shopkeepers.
Benstead J.
Cone Joseph
Levitt John
Wheelwrights.
Dale Emanuel
Dale Michael

GLEMHAM (LITTLE,) a village and parish 5 miles S.W. of Saxmundham, and 7½ miles N.E. by N. of Woodbridge, has 333 souls, and 1160A. of fertile land, all the property and manor of the Hon. Sophia North, of *Glemham Hall,* a large and handsome brick mansion, pleasantly situated in a richly wooded park of about 376 acres. The ancient *family of Glemham* flourished here till the middle of the 17th century, when two of them raised themselves to great eminence in their respective professions. *Sir Thomas Glemham* took the part of his majesty in the civil wars between Charles I. and his parliament, and having reduced York, which had declared for the parliament, he was appointed governor of that city, and defended it for eighteen weeks against the united forces of the English and Scotch, till the defeat of

the king, at Marston Moor, compelled him to capitulate, upon terms honourable to himself and advantageous to the citizens. He was then sent to command the garrison at Carlisle, which, assisted by his gallant countrymen, Col. Gosnold, of Otley, and Major Naunton, of Letheringham, he defended nine months, in spite of pestilence and famine, and on his surrender, obtained terms no less honourable than those on which he had capitulated at York. At the close of the war, he was for some time imprisoned, and on his release, fled to Holland, where he died in 1649, but his remains were brought to England, and interred in Glemham church, by his brother, the *Rev. Henry Glemham*, who, on the restoration of Charles II., was rewarded for his loyalty with the bishopric of St. Asaph, but died in 1669, two years after his installation. In the grandson of Sir Thomas, the family of Glemham became extinct. The estate was purchased by Dudley North, Esq., who made great improvements in the Hall, where his son, of the same name, died in 1829, leaving no issue, and bequeathing the estate to his relict, the present Hon. Mrs. North, for her life, and afterwards to the Earl of Guilford, who represents the elder branch of the noble family of North. The *Church* (St. Andrew) is a neat fabric, on a bold eminence, shaded by lofty trees. It contains many handsome mural tablets; and in a chapel or transept on the north side, rebuilt for the purpose, is an elegant monument, bearing a full length statue of the late Dudley North, Esq., erected at the expense of his relict. This fine piece of statuary was executed in Italy, and is a second production, the first being lost by shipwreck in its passage to England. The Hon. Mrs. North (sister to the Earl of Yarborough) is patroness of the *rectory*, which is valued in K.B. at £6, and in 1835 at £329, with the curacy of Great Glemham annexed to it. The Rev. Robert Meadows White, M.A., is the incumbent, for whom a new Rectory House has been built. The glebe is 6A., and the tithes of Little Glemham have been commuted for £305 per annum.

North Hon. Mrs Spha. *GlemhamHall*
Arnett John, house steward
Bicker James, butcher
Brightwell Charlotte, schoolmistress
Garrett Abraham, blacksmith
Garrett Lewis, wine, spirit, & porter merchant
Garrett Sarah, grocer and draper
Geater George, corn miller
Jordan Simon, boot and shoe maker

Ledgett Thomas, wheelwright
Pipe Wm. tailor
White Rev Robert Meadows, M.A. *Rectory*
Woolnough Charles, vict. Red Lion
Farmers : — Robert Cand, Edgar Hammod, and Wm. Salmon
Coach and Carriers to Ipswich, Yarmouth, &c. call at Red Lion

HASELWOOD or *Hazelwood*, 1½ mile N. W. of Aldeburgh, is a churchless parish, containing 108 souls, and 1897 acres of land, including 44A. of plantations, and about 200A. called the *Flatts*, lying on the north side of the Alde, and mostly inundated at high water. W. T. F. V. Wentworth, Esq., is lord of the manor, impropriator, and owner of most of the soil. There are still some traces of the church, though it was in ruins several centuries ago, when the parish was united ecclesiastically with Aldeburgh, where it is said the inhabitants used to marry and bury, as early as the reign of king John, though Kirby says the churchyard here was used occasionally till the latter part of last century. The *farmers* are James Barnes, James Cole, John Cole,

Samuel Studd, *Ballingford Hall;* Wm.Wainwright, *Haselwood Hall;* and Robert Easter, *shopkeeper.*

IKEN, on the south side of the broadest part of the river Alde, from 3 to 4 miles W. of Aldeburgh, is a parish of scattered houses, containing 343 souls and 2579A. of land, including about 1000A. of the large heath which extends south-west to Chillesford and Wantisden. On the river is a corn and coal wharf, and in the adjacent marshes was formerly a *decoy* for wild fowl. The Marquis of Hertford is lord of the manor, and owner of most of the soil. The *Church* (St. Botolph) is an ancient structure, with a tower and four bells. The rectory, valued in K.B. at £6. 13s. 4d., and in 1835 at £311, is in the patronage and incumbency of the Rev. C. J. Baldrey. The *Town Estate* consisted of the parish workhouse, and about 29A. of land, but in 1814, the land was given to the Marquis of Hertford, in exchange for a yearly rent-charge of £36 out of a farm of 300A. This annuity is applied with the poor-rates. *Directory:*—Philip French, vict., *Anchor,* and agent to Mingay and Rope, of Orford, *corn and coal merchants;* David Mayhew, shopkeeper and tailor; L. Panifer, *blacksmith;* and David Barnes, Eliz. Barnes, Robt. Cullum, *Decoy;* John Gobbitt, *Iken Hall,* and Wm. Clark, *farmers.*

ORFORD, a small *town, port,* and *ancient borough,* which had formerly a weekly market, is seated on the west bank of the Alde, 5 miles above the mouth of that river; 5 miles S.S.W. of Aldeburgh; 19 miles E.N.E. of Ipswich; 11 miles E. of Woodbridge; 10 miles S. by E. of Saxmundham; and 88 miles N.E. of London. The river Alde, and the singular manner in which it turns southward at Aldeburgh, and runs past Orford, parallel with the sea coast, is already noticed at page 155. *Orfordness* and the *Lantern Marshes,* which lay opposite Orford, are only about a mile in breadth, but form the broadest part of the long but narrow peninsula which separates the town and the river from the sea. The *parish of Orford* had 1302 inhabitants in 1831, but only 1109 in 1841, including 12 in *Raydons,* (an estate and two houses near a mile N.E. of the town,) 69 in *Gedgrave,* a tithe-free lordship of about 1500 acres, extending three miles southward to the confluence of the rivers *Butley and Alde;* and 12 in HAVERGATE, an *extra-parochial Island* of about 260 acres, in the river Alde, from 1½ to 3½ miles S. of Orford, where the estuary is commonly called *Orford Haven.* This island belongs to H. Edwards, Esq., of Sutton. The Marquis of Hertford is lord of the manors of Orford, Gedgrave, and Raydons, and owns most of the parish, which comprises about 3400 acres of land. Upon the summit of the hill, on the west side of the town, are the massive remains of ORFORD CASTLE, consisting of the keep, which, though of Norman origin, is still in good preservation. Its figure is a polygon of eighteen sides, described within a circle whose radius is 27 feet. It is flanked by three square towers, placed at equal distances, on the west, north-east, and south-east sides; each tower measures in front about 22 feet, and overlooks the polygon which is ninety feet high. The walls at the base are 20 feet thick; at the lower part they are solid, but galleries and small apartments are formed in them above. Round this building ran two circular ditches, one 15 and the other 38 feet distant from the walls. Between these ditches was a circular wall, part of which, opposite the south-east tower, was lately

remaining. This wall was 40 feet high, and had a parapet and battlements at the top. The entrance to the castle was through a square building, adjoining the west side of the keep, to which a bridge conducted over the two ditches. The interior of the keep contained one room in each of its four stories, but the original floors and roof went to decay many years ago. A new floor was laid in one of the upper stories in 1831, by the late Marquis of Hertford, who also put on a new roof, inserted several new windows, and furnished the apartment with a table, chairs, &c., for the accommodation of visitors. A spiral staircase leads to the top of the building, which commands extensive prospects both of sea and land. Francis, the second Marquis of Hertford, purposed to take down the keep of this once-formidable castle about the year 1805, but as it was considered a necessary sea-mark, especially for ships coming from Holland, which, by steering so as to make the castle cover, or hide the church, avoided a dangerous sand-bank, called the Whiting, government interfered and prevented its demolition. An incredible story relates that in the sixth of king John, some fishermen of Orford took in their nets a sea monster, resembling a man in size and figure, which was given to the governor of the castle, who kept it several days; after which, the fishermen took it out to sea again, where it made its escape by diving under three rows of nets placed for its security. On returning home, however, the fishermen are said to have been followed by the monster, which lived with them for some time, but at length, being weary of the land, "stole away to sea," and was never seen afterwards. It is said that the monster had a long and ragged beard, and a bald head, and that it ate fish and flesh, and lay down on its couch at sun-set and rose at sun-rise. The story is quoted by Camden from Ralph de Goggeshall, an ancient writer, and is gravely related by several more modern writers.

In 1215, Hugh Bigod and John Fitz-Robert were made governors of Norwich and Orford Castles; and after them Hubert de Burgh was appointed governor of both. In the 48th of Henry III., after that monarch had been taken prisoner at the battle of Lewes, by his barons, they conferred this post, which seems to have been considered an important one, on Hugh le Despenser. By one of Henry's successors, Orford Castle was given to the descendants of *Peter de Valoines*, who made it the chief seat of their barony. In the 4th of Edward III., *Robert de Ufford*, having married the daughter and co-heiress of Robert de Valoines, obtained a grant of this town and castle, which afterwards passed to the Willoughby de Eresby family, and from them to the Stanhope and Devereux families. In 1754, this and the adjoining manor of Sudborne, was sold by the executors of the late Viscount Hereford to the Earl, afterwards Marquis of Hertford. The *town of Orford* is said to have been once of considerable extent, and to have had the castle in its centre. Great quantities of old bricks, stones, and other remains of buildings have frequently been turned up by the plough, in the fields to the west and south of the castle, where several enclosures still retain the name of street annexed to their denomination of field, in allusion to streets formerly situated there. Its *market*, formerly held on Monday, was established in king Stephen's reign, but is now obsolete. It had two *fairs*, but has now only one, held on the 24th of June. The *Borough* was incorporated at an early period,

and sent two members to Parliament, until it lost that privilege by being placed in schedule A. among the other small boroughs, in the Reform Act of 1832. It was represented as early as the reign of Edward I., but neglecting, for a long series of years, to avail itself of the elective franchise, it lost this right, which is supposed to have been restored to it by Richard III., who, in the first year of his reign, granted the town a charter, under which it is still governed by a mayor, eight portmen, twelve capital burgesses, and a recorder, who hold a *court of sessions* on the Monday before the feast of St. John, or oftener if necessary. Having but a small and unimportant jurisdiction, the corporation of Orford was left untouched by the Municipal Reform Act of 1835, like that at Aldeburgh, which it much resembles ; indeed several persons are members and officers of both corporations, and many of them reside at a distance. The Orford *corporate body and officers* are Chpr. Churchill, Esq., *mayor ;* Geo. Capron, Esq., *recorder ;* Jno. Wood, Esq., of Woodbridge, *deputy-recorder ;* Marquis of Hertford, Geo. Mingay, Rt. Hon. J. W. Croker, Capt. R. Meynell, Geo. Randall, S. Randall, Wm. O'Grady, and Sir Horace B. Seymour, *portmen ;* Henry Muller, Robt. Freeman, Benj. Bunnip, Fredk. Steele, Geo. Capron, P. B. Long, Chas. Webber, Geo. Roper, and Fras. Keer, *burgesses ;* P. B. Long, Esq., *town clerk ;* and S. Randall, Esq., *chamberlain.* The *Town Hall* is a small mean building ; and here is a plain brick structure called the Assembly House, erected by a late Marquis of Hertford about seventy years ago, but very little used. In 1359, Orford sent three ships and 62 men to the siege of Calais. The town is now small and indifferently built, but was once much larger, and had a considerable trade, said to have been ruined by the harbour becoming blocked up by a dangerous bar, which prevented the passage of large vessels. It is now a *creek* under Aldeburgh. (See page 156.) A few vessels are employed here in the corn and coal trade, and there was formerly in the river a considerable *oyster fishery.* In 1810, the Marquis of Hertford granted licences at one guinea each to eighty vessels, to dredge for oysters in the Alde, but none have been found of late years. Here is a coast guard station, and at *Orfordness,* on the sea coast, about 1½ mile E. of the town, and a mile from each other, are two Light Houses, called the *High and Low Lights.* The latter was erected in 1792, and has a new patent light with 220 plate glass reflectors, put up in 1841 ; and the former was built more than a century ago, and has 14 burners.

Orford gave the title of *Earl* to Admiral Russell, who was elevated to the peerage by William III., for his eminent services; but it became extinct on his death without issue, in 1727, but was revived again in the person of Sir Robert Walpole, in 1742. It again became extinct on the death of Horatio, the fourth earl, in 1797; but in 1806, it was conferred on Horatio, the second Baron Walpole, of Wolterton, and is now held by his grandson, *Horatio Walpole,* M.A., the present *Earl of Orford,* Baron Walpole of Walpole, and Baron Walpole of Wolterton, in Norfolk. He resides at the latter place, and is colonel of the West Norfolk Militia, and High Steward of the borough of Lynn. *Herbert de Losinga,* the first Bishop of Norwich, is said to have been born here. He became so rich, from the numerous preferments given him by William Rufus, that he purchased the abbacy of Winchester,

and the see of Thetford, but removed the latter to Norwich, where he founded the cathedral, and died in 1119. *Orford Church* (St. Bartholomew) was, when entire, a large and handsome structure. The nave and its two side-aisles are entire, but the chancel, having fallen to ruin, was excluded by a wall built across the east end of the nave, many years ago ; and the remains of it consist of a double row of five thick columns, supporting circular arches, decorated with the zig-zag ornament. This chancel is supposed to have been built long before the nave, and appears to have been in a very ruinous condition in 1720, when a marble monument, bearing the kneeling effigy of the *Rev. Frs. Mason*, was removed from it to the nave. This learned divine was incumbent here many years, and died in 1621. He was chaplain to James I., and wrote many works in defence of the Church of England. There are in the church several brass inscriptions, an ancient but elegant font, and a coffin-shaped stone, bearing a cross fleury. The upper part of the tower fell down in 1829, and has not been rebuilt. The benefice is a *curacy*, which has from an early period been consolidated with the *rectory* of the adjoining parish of *Sudborne*, in the patronage of the Crown, and now in the incumbency of the Rev. John Maynard, M.A., who has a neat parsonage here. (See Sudborne.) Besides this church, Orford had formerly two chapels, dedicated to *St. John* and *St. Leonard*, both of which were standing in 1500, and the former stood on the land still called St. John's Chapel Field. Here were also a Benedictine Nunnery, founded by Ralph de Albini, an hospital of St. Leonard, and a chantry—valued at the dissolution at £6. 13s. 11½d. per annum. Here are two small chapels, belonging to the Independents and the Primitive Methodists. The TOWN ESTATE comprises the old Workhouse and garden, occupied by paupers ; a building site, 234 feet by 94, let for £2 a year ; about 7A. of land, let for £24 a year ; and an annuity of £30, paid by the Marquis of Hertford, in respect (as is supposed) of land in his possession, formerly belonging to the hospital of St. Leonard. The income derived from these sources is applied with the poor rates. About £9. 10s., received yearly from *Sir M. Stanhope's Charity*, (vide Sutton,) is distributed in small sums among the poor of Orford.

ORFORD DIRECTORY.

Post Office, at Mrs Jane Langmaid's. Letters despatched at 9 evg.
Billing Robert, saddler
Chandler Mr Thomas
Crisp Mr Thomas and Mrs Mary, farmers, *Gedgrave Hall*
Cullum Henry, farmer
Dewing Rev James, B.A. rector of Chillesford, &c
Field Wm. corn miller & merchant
Finch John, *Low Light house*
Gibbs Wm. sail maker
Hunt Edward, tide surveyor
Keer Fras. gent. *Raydon Hall*
Longmaid Thomas, coast guard
Last John, professor of music
Ling Jas. glove and breeches maker

Makin S. A., shopkeeper
Martin Robert, corn miller
Mills Robert, accoucheur
Maynard Rev John, M.A. Rectory
Mingay Miss Mary Ann
Mingay George, shipowner
Mingay & Rope, corn & coal merts
Moss Jane, straw hat maker
Pope John, farmer
O'Grady Capt. Wm. land agent to the Marquis of Hertford
Randall Samuel, surgeon
Randall Mrs Mary & Miss Harriet
Read Geo. Wm. joiner
Read George, boat builder
Roberts Joseph, beer house
Rope S. & G., agents for Truman, Hanbury, & Co.'s London porter, &c

Rope Geo. agent to Suffolk Fire Offc
Rope Samuel, grocer, draper, news agent, &c
Sewell Chas. plumber, glzr. & paintr
Simpson Charlotte, milliner
Steele Mrs Mary Ann
Till Joseph, shopkeeper
Toller Saml. gent. *Raydon House*
Turner John, hair dresser
Wade Mrs Eliz. *Raydon Cottage*
Whayman John, *High Light house*
HOTELS, INNS, AND TAVERNS.
Crown & Castle, Michael Cundy
Jolly Sailor, Elizabeth Fuller
King's Head, Robt. Martin (& corn miller)
White Hart, James Worn

Academies.
Brown Robert
Howard Hannah
Smith Ann

Bakers.
Field Wm.
Thredkell John

Blacksmiths.
Barnard Thomas
Dowsing Samuel
Newson Henry
Pettit John
Boot&Shoe Mkrs.
Dennington John
Peck Wm.
Wade Barnabas
Butchers.
Brinkley Wm.
Kindred Mattw.
Master Mariners.
Buckman John
Butcher John
Burrows James
Burrows Wm.
Glanfield John

Green John
Hamby Thomas
Hunt James
Ling Edward
Lucock George
Nichols Wm.
Nottage James
Wade George
Tailors & Drprs.
Butcher Thomas
Grimwood John
Grimwood Thos.
Harris Thomas
Turner Robert
Wheelwrights.
French James
Hammond John
CARRIERS—

Hy. Pead and W. Mason, to *Ipswich*, Sat; and *Mail Cart,* daily, 9 evening, from the King's Head

PARHAM, a pleasant, scattered village, in the vale of the small river Ore, 2½ miles S.S.E. of Framlingham, has in its parish 514 souls, and 1970A. 3R. 11P. of land, including the hamlets of *North, Cuttles,* and *Silverlace Greens,* and mostly belonging to F. Corrance, Esq., the lord of the manor, in which the copyholds are subject to arbitrary fines. It was the lordship of the Uffords, one of whom, Wm. de Ufford, second Earl of Suffolk, built the church in the reign of Edward III. but, dying without issue, the estate passed to his sister, who married Sir Robert Willoughby, whose descendants became *Lords Willoughby, of Eresby,* and younger branches of them, *Lords Willoughby de Broke,* and *Lords Willoughby of Parham.* William Willoughby, whose father made Parham his seat, was created Baron Willoughby of Parham, in 1547; but on the death of George, the seventeenth lord, without issue, in 1779, the barony became extinct. *Parham Hall,* where the Willoughbys resided, is a large Elizabethan mansion, now occupied by a farmer. It stands on a bold eminence, and is still encompassed by a moat. *Parham Lodge,* a neat modern mansion, belongs to the Rev. G. Crabbe, and was the seat of the late Mr. Crabbe. *High House* is the pleasant seat of Mr. Henry Clarke; and other portions of the parish belong to Mills' Charity, W. Cann, and a few smaller owners. In 1734, the bones of a man, an urn, and the head of a spear, were found here, in a gravel pit, and were supposed to have belonged to some Danish chieftain. *Joshua Kirby, F.R.S., A.S.,* the celebrated designer in perspective, already noticed at page 76, was born here, in 1717. The *Church* (St. Mary) is a lofty, ancient structure, consisting of a nave, chancel, porch, and tower. The vicarage, certified in K.B. at £20, was valued in 1835 at £299, with the vicarage of Hacheston annexed to it. The Rev. J. G. Haggett, M.A., of Bury St. Edmunds, is the incumbent; and F. Corrance, Esq., is patron and impropriator. The rectorial tithes of Parham have been commuted for £205. 18s., and the vicarial tithes for £177 per annum. The poor parishioners have £1. 14s. worth of bread, and the minister 6s. 8d., for a sermon on

Good Friday, left by *Mrs. Warner ;* and the former have also 20s. a-year, left by *Thomas Mills,* in 1703, for distributions of bread. In 1736, *Mary Warner* left an annuity of £5, for ten poor families of Parham, not receiving parochial relief; and it is paid by the trustees of her charity, noticed with Boyton. Mr. Corrance has built and supports a *school* here, for the education of about 40 poor children.

Marked 1, reside at Cuttles Green ; 2, North Green ; 3, Silverlace Green ; & the rest in Parham.

Bennington Mrs Mary||Cooper Mrs
3 Burrows James, shopkeeper
Capon Robert, shoemaker
Clarke Hy. gent. *High House*
Durrant John, shopkeeper
Evans Rev Fredk. B.A. curate
Folkard Wm. bricklayer
Frost James, joiner
2 Girling Wm. shoemaker
1 Gray Edward, corn miller

Gray James, vict. and wheelwright, Willoughby Arms
Howell John, blacksmith
Howell Mary, schoolmistress

FARMERS.

1 Chandler Wm. ||3 Frost Wm.
Gray John || Hart Anthony
Heffer Robert, *Parham House*
Keer Henry, *Parham Hall*
Precious John || Pattle Robert
2 Teager John || Turner Wm.
2 Williams Benjamin

RENDHAM, a pleasant village in the vale of the Alde, 4½ miles E. of Framlingham, and 3 miles W. of Saxmundham, has in its parish 412 souls, and 1687A. of rich, loamy land, belonging to the Thellusson, Collett, Page, Webber, Williams, Eade, and other families, some of whom have neat houses here. J. Crabtree, Esq., is lord of the manor of *Barnies,* in which the copyholds pay arbitrary fines. The Earl of Stradbroke's manor of Bruisyard Hall extends into this parish. The *Church* (St. Michael) is a vicarage, which was certified at £36, but has now a yearly modus of £101, in lieu of small tithes. The trustees of the late Rev. C. Simeon are patrons, and the Rev. Rowland Morgan is the incumbent. The impropriate rectory was sold to the landowners, about thirty years ago. Here is a neat *Independent Chapel,* (with a house for the minister,) erected in 1750, in lieu of a smaller one at Swefling, which was built in 1650. The poor have three cottages, built on waste land, given by the lord of the manor ; and about 3A. of land, purchased in 1646. The cottages are occupied nearly rent free, and the land is let for £4. 10s. a year, which is added to the poor rates. In 1704, *Thos. Neal, Esq.* left a yearly rent-charge of £2. 10s., out of land in Bramfield, for the support of a *free school,* at Rendham, for poor children, and 10s. a-year to provide them with books. This charity is applied in aid of the National School, which was built by subscription, in 1841.

Barham Henry, bricklayer
Bicker Samuel, butcher
Cooper Wm. blacksmith
Daniels Hy. & Andrews J. shoemkrs
Easter Charles, wheelwright
Harsant Thomas, cooper
Harsant Wm. gardener
Kemp Dd. Thomas, schoolmaster
King Harriet, schoolmistress
Morgan Rev Rowland, *Vicarage*
Pallant Thomas, landowner
Self Robert, vict. White Horse
Self Stephen, gardener

Smith Wm. farrier
Studd James, joiner
Wilkins Rev Geo. Indepdt. minister
Williams Miss Lucy, *Hill House*
FARMERS.
Barnes Alfred || Cone James
Churchman Chas. White House
Cross James || French George
Garland ——, *Grove House*
Hambling Cotton||Pallant John
Snelling Collin || Stanton Robert
SHOPKEEPERS,— Andrews Ann
Barham Eliza || Button Wm.

SAXMUNDHAM is a small but improving and well-built market town, consisting chiefly of one long street, pleasantly situated in the vale of a rivulet, which runs southward to the Alde, 7 miles N.W. of Aldeburgh, 13 miles N.E. of Woodbridge, 21 miles N.E. of Ipswich, and 90 miles N.E. of London. Its parish contains 1097 inhabitants, and nearly 1400 acres, of which only 1102 are rated, with the buildings, at the yearly value of £3370. Wm. Long, Esq., owns most of the soil, and is lord of the *manor of Hurts*, which comprises all the parish except the small manor of *Swans*, which belonged to the late Dudley Long North, Esq., and is the site of a *chantry*, founded about 1308, by Robert Swan. HURTS HALL, the seat of Wm. Long, Esq., is a large and handsome white brick mansion, situated a little south of the town, in a beautiful and well-wooded park of nearly 200 acres. The manor was held successively by the Ufford, Hare, Cutler, and Basse families, and one of the latter erected Hurts Hall, about the year 1650, but it was rebuilt in the early part of the present century, by the late Charles Long, Esq., who judiciously laid out and planted the surrounding grounds, and expanded the rivulet into a fine sheet of water, which, at each extremity, is skilfully concealed by wood. The front of the mansion consists of three semicircular projections; the entrance hall is adorned with a handsome geometrical staircase; and the whole interior is fitted up with taste and elegance. Saxmundham has a large *corn market* every Thursday; a *fair* for toys, pedlery, &c., on Whit-Tuesday, and a *hiring for servants* on the Thursday-week before Old Michaelmas-day. The market and the fair, (formerly held on Ascension Day,) were granted by Edward II., in 1310, at the request of Thomas de Verley. During the years 1842-3, a company of shareholders, at the cost of £11,000, rebuilt the *Bell Inn*, and erected a commodious *Corn Exchange*, and a large *Public Room* adjoining. The two latter are divided by a moveable partition, and can be opened out into one apartment, 106 feet long, and 32 in height and breadth. Behind the inn is a bowling green and public gardens. The *Church* (St. John,) on a bold acclivity on the east side of the rivulet, has a tower and five bells, and contains some neat monuments to the Long family, one of whom, Lieut. George Long, was a distinguished naval officer, who fell in the very moment of victory, at the storming of Trincomale, in the East Indies. The benefice is a discharged *rectory*, valued in K.B. at £8. 15s. 10d., and in 1835, at £275, but the tithes have recently been commuted for a yearly modus of £283. 17s. Wm. Long, Esq., is patron, and the Rev. Lancelot Robert Brown, M.A., of Kelsale, is the incumbent, for whom the Rev. Robert Mann officiates. Here is a good rectory house, and 11A. of glebe; and at the north end of the town is a small Independent Chapel, where the Rev. G. Wilkins of Rendham, officiates. Near the church is a neat *School*, erected about eight years ago, by W. Long, Esq., who pays for the education of about 70 poor boys and girls. Since Saxmundham joined the Plomesgate Union, the parish *workhouse* has been converted into cottages, occupied by poor families. The *Town Estate*, comprising the site of a cottage granted by the lord of the manor, in 1657, and 3A. of land, is let on lease, at the yearly rent of £8. 18s. 6d., which, after payment of a quit rent of 22s., is applied in the service of the church. The following *Charity Lands* are vested in trustees, viz.:—5A. pur-

chased in 1657, with £68, left by Edmund Cutting and another donor for distributions of bread; and 8¼A., which was given in exchange for land in Carlton, left, at an early period, for the poor of Saxmundham. The rents amount to £34 a year, of which £5. 4s. is applied in a weekly distribution of 2s. worth of bread, and the remainder in supplying the poor with coals at reduced prices. In 1746, *Wm. Corbold* charged his estates here with a yearly rent-charge of £5, for distributions of bread among the poor, and with £5 a year for the education of four poor children of this parish, at Benhall school. The estates charged with these annuities belonged to Dudley North, Esq., in 1829. The poor parishioners have an annuity of 40s., left by *Stephen Eade*, in 1716, out of land at Carlton ; and the interest of £50, left by *Alice Clarke*, in 1820. Lord Rendlesham is *president*, and Messrs. Alex. Cavell and Geo. Moor, secretaries of the Saxmundham and Wickham Market *Horticultural Society*.

SAXMUNDHAM DIRECTY.

Post Office at Mr James Smy's. Letters despatched to Ipswich, London, &c., at ¼ before 9 eveng; to Halesworth, &c., ¼ bef. 6 mng ; to Aldeburgh, 25 min. past 6 mg ; and to Leiston, at 7 morning.

Aldrich Wm. gardener and seedsman

Backhouse Wm. gun mkr. & game dlr

Berrett Henry, glove maker, and glass, &c. dealer

Berrett Robert, cooper

Bright Jerome Denny, gent

Briggs Wm. cart owner

Brightly Celia, bookseller, &c

Chambers Clark, inspector of police

Coles Henry Pearson, bank agent

Cousins Wm. basket maker

Crowe Wm. currier & leather cutter

Dale Henry, dyer

Dick George, gentleman

Eastaugh Enoch, farmer

Flick Samuel, tanner

Garrod Wm. gentleman

Garrod Edward, watch maker, &c

Howard John, gentleman

Keer Geo. gent || Lawson Mrs

King James, sheriff's officer

Long Wm. Esq. *Hurts Hall*

Mabson Mrs Frances

Mann Rev Robt. curate, *Rectory*

Mills Robert, attorney's clerk

Moore George, bookkeeper

Newson Benj. farm bailiff

Newman Joseph, bricklayer

Osborne Mrs My||Rudland Eliz.

Plant Wm. farmer

Robinson Robert, coach maker

Ruffells Mr Samuel

Scarlett Mr Robert

Shimmon John, parish clerk

Smith Ann, upholstress

Smith Edward, gardener

Smith Jonth. farrier and cow leech

Smith Mrs Sarah and Eliz.

Smy James, land surveyor

Stopher Richard, auctioneer, valuer, & clerk to Commissns. of Taxes

Stopher Wm. cowkeeper

Tennant Miss Frances

Threadkell Wm. beerseller

Upson Philip, fishmonger

Wells Jas. corn miller and merchant

Woollason Mrs. Susannah

Woolterton Jerome, watch maker, bookseller, &c.

BANKERS.

Gurneys, Turner, and Brightwen, (draw on Barclay and Co ;) Wm. and John Flatt, *agents*

Suffolk Banking Co. (draw on London and Westminster Bank ;) Hy. Pearson Coles, *agent*

FIRE AND LIFE OFFICE AGENTS.

Atlas, Thomas Mayhew

Clerical and Medical, Alex. Cavell

Legal and General, Henry and James Southwell

Norwich Union, Jerome Denny Bright

Suffolk and General County, Wm. and John Flatt

INNS AND TAVERNS.

Angel, John Lincoln

Bell Hotel, (posting house and excise office,) John Thompson

Coach and Horses, Thos. Burrell

Queen's Head, Thomas Cooper

White Hart, James Woolnough

Academies.
Austin Joseph
Berrett Mary
Dick MrsG.(bdg)
Puttock Sophia
Rudland Emma
Stopher Hannah
ATTORNEYS.
Cavell Alexander
Mayhew Thos.,
  Esq.; h*Fairfield*
Southwell Henry
  and James
Bakers & Confrs.
Blake Jn. Bryant
Crane John
Day Daniel
Blacksmiths.
Lewis Henry
Welton Richard
Boot & ShoeMkrs.
Barnes Robert
Chapman Stephn.
Cousins Charles
Hurren George
Mills Sheppard
Newman George
Sampson George
Braziers & Tinrs
Howes James
Wells Wm.
Brewers.
Blanden James
Foulsham John
  (and maltster)
Butchers.
Baxter Joseph
Berrett John
Fenton Wm.
Cabinet Makers.
Bright Jerome
Denny (glass,
  &c. dealer)
Packman Robert

Sawyer Wm.
Chemists & Dgts.
Dunn George
Packard Edward
Gardeners.
Aldrich Wm.
Cattermole Danl.
Grocers & Drprs.
Crampin Jn.Chas
Flatman Rt. (and
  seed merchant)
Flatt Wm. & Jno.
  (stamp distrs)
Woods Robt.(fur-
  niture broker)
Hair Dressers.
King James
Reeve Wm. Jer-
  mey (& toy dlr)
Whiting Wm.
Ironmongers.
Garrett Rd&Sons
  (and founders)
Wells William
  (colourman,&c)
Joiners, &c.
Robinson Wm.
Woods Wm.
Milliners.
Benns Mary
Cousins Sarah
Smy Mrs James
Stannard Eliz.
Painters, Plum-
bers, & Glaziers.
Beard John
Whaley Samuel
Saddlers, &c.
Bloomfield Hy.
Woods John
Shopkeepers.
Allen Elijah
Woods Susanna

Stone Masons.
Thurlow John
Thurlow Thomas
  (sculptor)
Straw Hat Mkrs.
Alexander Har.
Garrod Ann
Rogers My. Ann
Stopher Charlotte
SURGEONS.
Freeman Henry
Lankester (and
  registrar)
Freeman Robert

Hemming Wm. B
Ling Jno. Mitford
Tailors & Drprs.
Andrews Wm.
Hilling John
Taylor John
Whitesmiths.
Backhouse Edw.
Wells Wm.
Wine and Spirit
Merchants.
Foulsham John
Packard Edward
Waller Jabez

COACHES.
From the Bell Inn.
To London, 9 evening, and 11 morn-
ing, and to Yarmouth, at 6 morn-
ing and 3 afternoon
From the Angel Inn.
To London, 9 morning, and Hales-
worth, 6 evening
From the Angel and White Hart.
Omnibuses, to meet the London steam-
ers at Ipswich, Monday, Wednes-
day, Thursday, & Friday, 5 morn
CARRIERS.
Marked 1, *put up at the Bell;* 2,
  Angel; and 3, *at the White Hart.*
1 *London*, H. J. & R. Smith, Monday
  and Thursday
3 Aldeburgh, J. Baxter, Wed. & Sat
3 Benhall, J. Rous, Tuesday & Sat
Halesworth (see Norwich)
Ipswich, 2 J. Sawyer, and 3 Wm.
  Free and J. Rous, Mon. & Fri.;
  and 1 H. J. & R. Smith, M. & Th
3 Middleton, W. Free, Tues. & Sat
Norwich, Bungay, &c. 2 J. Sawyer,
  Tuesday and Saturday; and 1 Rt.
  Hogg, Monday and Friday
1 Yarmouth, &c. H. J. & R. Smith's
  waggon, Tues. and J. Martin, Fri

SNAPE, a small village, on a pleasant acclivity, north of the river Alde, 5 miles W.N.W. of Aldeburgh, and 3 miles S. by E. of Saxmundham, has in its parish 542 souls, and 1700 acres of land, including 300A. of open common, and the hamlet of SNAPE BRIDGE, about a mile S. of the church, and a quarter of a mile south of the village or street, where there is a good bridge and a commodious wharf and warehouses, up to which the Alde is navigable for vessels of 100 tons burthen. About 17,000 quarters of *barley* are shipped here yearly for London and other markets, by Mr. Newson Garrett, who has warehouses, &c., on both sides of the bridge; but the buildings on the south side are in the hamlet of Dunningworth and parish of Tunstall. A

large *horse fair* is held at Snape Bridge on the 11th of August. At a short distance west of the bridge, is the site of SNAPE PRIORY, which was founded for Black Canons, in 1099, by Wm. Martell, Albreda his wife, and Jeffry their son, and dedicated to the Virgin Mary. They endowed it with the manor of Snape, including the benefit of wrecks of the sea from Thorp to Orford-ness; and gave it as a cell to the Abbey of Colchester. But upon complaint made by the Countess of Suffolk, that the abbot of Colchester did not maintain a sufficient number of religious in it, according to the wills of the founders, it was, by a bull of Pope Boniface IX., made conventual, and exempted from subjection to Colchester. William de la Pole, Earl of Suffolk, in the reign of Henry VI., designed to have refounded it, and for a short period, in 1509, it was a cell to Butley. It was one of the monasteries suppressed in 1524, and given to Cardinal Wolsey for the endowment of his college at Ipswich. After the Cardinal's fall, in 1530, it was granted by Henry VIII. to Thomas Duke of Norfolk, and was then of the yearly value of £99. 1s. 11½d. Nothing now remains of this priory, except some of its stones in the walls and outbuildings of the farmhouse, called the *Abbey*, which has been more than seventy years in the occupation of the Groome family, who lately dug up many of the foundations, and found some ancient coins, tiles, and skeletons. A bed of *oysters* was found, some years ago, about five yards below the surface. Colonel Thomas Howard Vyse is now owner of the Abbey, Rookery, and other farms, and also lord of the *manor*, in which the copyholds are subject to arbitrary fines. The other principal land-owners are W. W. Page, Esq., J. C. Baker, of *Snape House*, and the trustees of the late J. Wilson Sheppard, Esq., owners of the Ash estate and the wharf. The *Church* (St. John the Baptist) stands on a bold eminence, three-quarters of a mile N. of the village, and has a lofty tower, and a very ancient and highly ornamented font, on which are sculptured an assemblage of kings, prelates, and non-descript birds, standing on pedestals. The *vicarage*, valued in K.B. at £5. 5s. 7½d., is consolidated with *Friston*. (See page 162.) In 1802, the Rev. John Lambert left £200, the interest thereof to be distributed yearly at Christmas among poor housekeepers of Snape, not receiving parochial relief. This legacy is vested in £250 three per cent. consols.

Baker Js. Cooper, gent. *Snape House*
Burrows Joseph, cattle dealer
Clarke Wm. wheelwright
Crowe John, blacksmith & par. clerk
French Samuel, farrier
Garrett Newson, corn & coal mert.
  &c. Snape Bridge (and Aldbro'.)
Garrod Charles, bookkeeper
Garrod Noah, pilot
Haill Geo. Kittle, joiner & builder
Hudson Luke, vict. Crown Inn
Lamb Wm. schoolmr. near the Church
Larter Wm. glover
Neeve Jas. brickmaker ; h *Benhall*
Rackham Wm. butcher

Boot & Shoe Mkrs.
Dale Samuel
Lawrence Wm.
Smith Stephen
Wade John
Corn Millers.
Markin Wm.
  Ezekiel
Ship Mary
FARMERS.
* *are nr. Church.*
Barnes Thomas,
  Rookery
Bloomfield Alfrd.
Braham Robt.
Day Wm.

Groome Charles,
  Abbey
*Hambling Hrbt.
*Hambling John
Knights Henry
*Moulton Rt.
Taylor Thomas
Turrill Thomas
Wollidge Wm.
Grocers & Dprs.
Debney Richd.
Gotson John
Saunders Rd.
  Whiting Mfrs.
Garrett Newson
Gotson John

CARRIERS	Regular Trading Vessels
To Woodbridge, Ipswich, &c., call at the Crown Inn, Snape	To London, &c., every Wednesday. N. Garrett, wharfinger, *Snape Bridge*. (See also Tunstall.)

STERNFIELD, a small village on the Aldeburgh road, 1½ mile S. of Saxmundham, has in its parish 193 souls, and 1106A. 2R. of land, mostly in the manor of *Hurts*, of which Wm. Long, Esq., is lord and principal owner. W. A. Shuldham, Esq., Exors. of W. W. Page, Esq., and several smaller owners, have estates here. Part of the parish is in the Hon. Mrs. North's manor of *Mandeville*. The *Church* (St. Mary) has a flint tower and porch, but its chancel was rebuilt of brick, and the nave repaired with the same material in 1766. The *rectory*, valued in K.B. at £8. 14s. 4½d., has a neat residence, 87A. 2R. 37P. of glebe, and a yearly modus of £300 in lieu of tithes. W. Long, Esq., is patron, and the Rev. J. D. Money, incumbent. The Town Estate has been held from an early period for the general benefit of the parishioners, and consists of three tenements, a stable, garden, and 45A. of land, let for about £50 per annum, which is applied in repairing the church, and relieving and educating the poor.

Ashkittle Mr George
Freeman Row. shoemaker
Money Rev Jas. Drummond, *Rectory*
Page Wm. Woods, Esq. (Executors of the late)
Robinson James, gardener
Stevenson Thomas, woodman
FARMERS.
Barnes David, *Sternfield Hall*
Edwards Onisimus || Bond Robert
Edwards Wm. || Fish Susan
Haill Wm. (parish clerk, &c)

STRATFORD ST. ANDREW in the vale of the Alde, on the Woodbridge road, 3½ miles S.W. of Saxmundham, is a small parish and village, containing 201 souls, and 638A. of good loamy land, in the Hon. Mrs. North's manors of *Stratford* and *Griston;* but part of the soil belongs to W. A. Shuldham, Esq., J. Moseley, Esq., and a few smaller owners. The *Church* (St. Andrew) is a rectory, valued in K.B. at £5, and 1835 at £137. The Queen, as Duchess of Lancaster, is patroness, and the Rev. John Mitford is the incumbent, and has 10A. of glebe. *Directory :*—Jph. Dennington, parish clerk ; Thos. Plant, butcher ; Robt. Simonds, woodman ; John Tacon, corn miller ; and Robt. Durham, John Garrod, John Hunt, John Mantle, and Exors. of Jno. Tacon, *farmers.*

SUDBORNE, or *Sudbourn*, a scattered village 1 mile N. of Orford, has in its parish 623 souls, and about 5000 acres of land, extending three miles northward nearly to Aldeburgh, along the western side of the river Alde, and including most of the *Lantern Marshes* and *Orford-ness*, on the opposite side of that river, bordering upon the Ocean, as described at page 165. The manor belonged to Ely Priory, and was granted by Edward VI. to the Bishop of Norwich; but it was soon afterwards possessed by Sir Michael Stanhope, who built the hall. Sir Edmund Withipole obtained it in marriage with Sir Michael's daughter, and his daughter and heiress carried it in marriage to Leicester Devereux, Viscount Hereford, from whom it passed to his son, whose executors sold it (about 1683) to an ancestor of the present lord of the Manor, the *Most Hon. Richard Seymour Conway*, MARQUIS of HERTFORD, EARL of YARMOUTH, and *Baron Conway*, of Ragley, Warwickshire, and of Killultagh, Ireland, who resides oc-

casionally at Sudborne Hall, a plain quadrangular mansion, which
was built about sixty years ago by Wyatt, and stands in an extensive
park, about a mile N.W. of Orford. It is chiefly used as a sporting residence, the park and neighbourhood abounding in game. Mr.
Jas. Chaplin and some other proprietors have small estates in the
parish. The *Church* (All Saints) is a small ancient structure, and is
a *rectory*, with the curacy of Orford annexed to it, valued in K.B. at
£33. 6s. 3d., and in 1835 at £577, but the tithes were commuted in
1839 for about £600 per annum. The patronage is in the Crown,
and the Rev. John Maynard, M.A., is the incumbent, and has his residence at Orford. The *Church and Poor's Estate* comprises the old
workhouse and a cottage occupied rent-free by the poor; 61A. 5P. of
marsh land, let for £161 a year; and a yearly rent-charge of £6, secured and payable under the award of the commissioners for enclosing the
common lands in this parish, in 1807. The income from these sources
is applied mostly in the service of the church, and partly with the poor
rates. The *Town House*, in Orford, belongs to Sudborne, and is in
two tenements, one occupied rent-free, and the other let for £7 a year,
with a small piece of land annexed to it. A yearly sum of about
£9. 10s. from Sir M. Stanhope's charity, (see Sutton,) is distributed
among the poor of Sudborne.

Hertford Marquis of, *Sudborne Hall*
  (and Ragley, Warwickshire)
Barnes John, shoemaker
Brows Robt. vict. *Chequers*
Chaplin Mr James, jun.
Gambles Henry, shoemaker
Levett James, blacksmith
Master James, wheelwright
Moss Isaac, butcher
Sharman Mr Offley, *Well House*
Smith Henry, shoemaker

FARMERS AND GRAZIERS.
Artis John, *Church Farm*
Brinkley Robt. || Master Samuel
Chaplin James || Eastew George
Mannell John, *Colton Farm*
Moss Ann and Hannah
Steele Frederick, *Sudborne Lodge*
Webber Ann, *Ferry*
Whayman Horace, *High House*
Whayman Wm.||Whayman Henry

SWEFLING, a small scattered village, in the vale of the river Alde,
3 miles W. by N. of Saxmundham, and 4 miles E. of Framlingham,
has in its parish 308 souls, and 1120 acres of land, lying in several
copyhold manors, but chiefly in the manor of *Dernford Hall*, now a
farm house, formerly belonging to Leigh priory, in Essex, and afterwards to the Cavendish and Plumer families. W. A. Shuldham, Esq.,
John Moseley, Esq., Mr. Robert Simonds, and a few smaller owners
have estates in the parish. The *Church* (St. Mary,) is a rectory, valued in K.B. at £9. 2s. 8½d., and in 1835, at £262; but the tithes
have been commuted for upwards of £300 per annum. Thomas Williams, Esq., is patron, and the Rev. Russell Skinner, M.A., is the incumbent, and has 9½A. of glebe, and a neat residence, built in 1831 by
the Rev. W. Collett, the late rector. The *Feoffees' Estate* comprises
two houses, occupied by paupers, and 6A. of land, let for £13. 12s. a
year; and was given by *Ezra Crisp*, in 1699, for the reparation of the
church and other public uses. The rent of the land is all applied with
the church rates. In 1568, *Henry Leggett* left, for distribution among
the poor of Swefling, a yearly rent-charge of 40s. out of Limekiln
Close. The sum of £46, received as arrears of this rent-charge, was
laid out in 1784, in building a coal shed for the use of the parish.

Blake George, corn miller
Cross Isaiah, parish clerk
Cross Robert, shoemaker and vict.
White Horse
Freeman Alfd. tailor, grocer, & dpr
Hayward Wm. blacksmith
Mills Henry, corn miller
Skinner Rev Russell, M.A. rector,
Rectory

Smith Henry, veterinary surgeon
Smith Jonth. and Son, agricultural
machine makers & wheelwrights
Snell John, hurdle maker & wood dlr
Wright Wm. tailor, grocer, &c.

FARMERS.

Bendhall Arthur || Johnson Francis
Smith Charles || Simonds Robert
Smith John || Smith Wm.

TUNSTALL, a pleasant village, 7 miles N.E. of Woodbridge, and about the same distance W. by S. of Aldeburgh, and S. by W. of Saxmundham, has in its parish 658 souls and 2642 acres of land, including the hamlet of DUNNINGWORTH, on the south side of *Snape Bridge*, on the river Alde, 5 miles W. of Aldeburgh, where there is a wharf and extensive warehouses, as noticed with Snape. The southeast part of the parish is a sandy heath, where there is a *tumulus*, in which a Roman urn was found a few years ago, containing ashes, two coins, and a piece of a sword three inches long. The Hon. Mrs. North is lady of the *manor of Banyard*, in Tunstall, but the greater part of the parish belongs to Lord Rendlesham, the trustees of the late John Wilson Sheppard, and the Rev. Thos. Garrard Ferrand. The latter is patron and incumbent of the *rectory*, which is valued in K.B. at £16. 10s. 5d., but has now 45A. of glebe, and a yearly modus of £526, in lieu of tithes. The *Church* (St. Michael,) is an ancient structure, with a tower containing six bells. *Dunningworth* was formerly a separate parish, and had a church, which went to decay in the latter part of the 16th century, when its rectory was consolidated with Tunstall. *Dunningworth Hall*, a good farm house, is the residence of Mr. John Flatt, chief constable. In *Chapel field*, where Dunningworth church is supposed to have stood, several skeletons were found in 1841. There is a *Baptist Chapel* at Tunstall, built in 1808, and enlarged in 1838; and a *National School*, erected in 1830.

Marked * reside at Dunningworth, near Snape Bridge, and the rest at Tunstall.

*Abbott Abm. timber agent, & vict. Plough and Sail
Baker Wm. bricklayer
Brook Joseph, corn miller
Burch John, vict. Green Man
Churchyard J. veterinary surgeon
Cogshall John, baker
Cutting Robert, beerhouse
Flatt John, chief constable, *Dunningworth Hall*
Ferrand Rev Thos.Garrard, *Rectory*
*Garrett Newson, merchant, *Snape Bridge Wharf*
*Grimwood Thomas, timber mercht
Gooding Rev Wm. John, Bapt. min
Harvey Henry, schoolmaster
King Wm. hair dresser
Owles Robert, tailor
Sawyer James, butcher

Sawyer Mary, butcher
Sawyer Wm. plumber and glazier
Taylor Wm. blacksmith
*Waller Jabez, ale & porter mert
Wigg Rd. relieving officer & regr
Wilson Samuel, schoolmaster

Boot&ShoeMkrs.	Sawyer Lewis
Daniels James	Whitehead **Wm.**
Harvey Henry	*Joiners.*
FARMERS.	Ellis Thomas
Cockrell Wm. (& corn miller)	Reeve Wm.
Debney Richard	*Wheelwrights.*
*Flatt John	Fairhead Saml.
Hillen Jas. jun.	(parish clerk)
Miller Thos. jun.	Reeve Robert
Miller Thos. sen.	Reeve Samuel
Sawyer James	CARRIER.
Sawyer John	Charles Stephenson, to Woodbridge, &c. **M.** Wed. & Sat.
Sawyer Wm.	
Grocers & Dprs.	
Bullock Wm.	

WANTISDEN, 7 miles E.N.E. of Woodbridge, and 4¼ miles N.W. by W. of Orford, has in its parish 110 souls, a few scattered houses, and about 1300 acres of high land, including more than 350 acres of a large open heath. N. Barnardiston, Esq., is lord of the manor, impropriator, and patron of the *Church* (St. John,) which is a perpetual curacy, valued at £64, in the incumbency of the Rev. Ellis Wade, M.A. A great part of the parish belongs to Lord Rendlesham and the trustees of the late J. W. Sheppard, Esq. The manor was held by Butley Abbey, and was granted, at the dissolution, to Lionel Tollemach. The hall, built in 1550, is now occupied by a farmer, and near it there were dug up, in 1837, many sculptured stones, some of them representing the heads of prelates. The poor parishioners have £5 a year from Sir M. Stanhope's Charity. (See Sutton.) The *farmers and graziers* are, John Cockrill, Robert Pattle, *Walnut Tree Farm ;* and Jonathan Keer, *Wantisden Hall.*

LOES HUNDRED

Comprises 18 parishes, all in *Plomesgate Union* (see page 154,) except Woodbridge and Charsfield, which are in *Woodbridge Union.* (See p.119.) It is in the *Deanery of Loes*, and Archdeaconry of Suffolk, and is of a very irregular figure, varying from 6 to 2 miles in breadth, and extending about 15 miles southward, from its broadest part, around the town of Framlingham, and near Debenham, to the estuary called Butley River. The river *Deben* winds through it by a circuitous route from Cretingham southward to Ufford, where it crosses Wilford Hundred to Woodbridge, and there becomes navigable for large vessels. The flourishing town and port of *Woobridge* is detached, at the distance of three miles, from the rest of Loes Hundred, which is bounded on the east by Plomesgate Hundred; on the north, by Hoxne Hundred ; and on the west and south-west by Thredling, Carlford, and Wilford Hundreds. It is a picturesque district, of hill and valley, watered by the Deben, the Ore, and their tributary streams, and having generally a good loamy soil, highly cultivated, and well suited to the growth of *barley, wheat*, and *beans*. The following is an enumeration of its 18 parishes, shewing their territorial extent, the annual value of their land and buildings, as assessed to the property tax in 1815, and their population in 1801 and 1841.

PARISHES.	Acrs.	Rental.	Populatn. 1801.	1841.	PARISHES.	Acres.	Rental. £.	Population. 1801.	1841.
Brandeston	1196	1873	287	555	Hoo..........	1164	1700	124	211
Butley	2000	1139	250	364	Kenton*	1210	1496	243	287
Campsey Ash ..	1814	2656	327	374	Kettleburgh ..	1400	2299	272	355
Charsfield	1290	1903	411	551	Letheringham ..	1100	1626	138	164
Cretingham	1639	2637	246	411	Marlesford....	1268	2201	315	424
Earl-Soham	1945	3261	563	741	Monewden....	1063	1571	157	220
Easton	1462	2335	304	415	Rendlesham ..	2065	2151	216	325
Eyke	2800	2283	308	502	Woodbridge*..	1650	10,819	3020	4954
Hacheston .. ⎰	1727	2327	543	507					
§Glevering .. ⎱				11	Total† ..	31,321	52,973	9578	13,894
Framlingham ..	4528	8696	1854	2523					

† The number of HOUSES, in 1841, was 2948 *inhabited*, 82 *uninhabited*, and

26 *building.* The number of *males* was 6554, and *females,* 7340. Of the males, 3437, and of the females, 3985, were 20 years of age, and upwards. Of the inhabitants, 776 were not born in Suffolk.

* *Woodbridge* and *Kenton* are detached members of Loes Hundred, which also includes part of *Bredfield* and *Dallinghoo.* (See page 140.)

§ *Glevering* is a hamlet in Hacheston parish.

☞ The CHIEF CONSTABLES are Mr. B. Gall, of Woodbridge; and Mr. Goodwyn Goodwyn, of Framlingham.

** *Loes* and *Wilford Hundreds* were incorporated for the support of their poor, but were dis-incorporated in 1827. (See page 146.)

BRANDESTON, a pleasant and well-built village, on a bold acclivity on the eastern side of the river Deben, nearly 4 miles S.W. of Framlingham, and 6 miles E.S.E. of Debenham, has in its parish 555 souls, and 1195A. 1R. 26P. of fertile loamy land. In the Conqueror's time, the *manor* was held by Odo de Campania, whose successors granted it to the Burwells, from whom it passed to the Weylands, Tuddenhams, and Bedingfields. Andrew Revett purchased it in the reign of Elizabeth, and built *Brandeston Hall,* a large brick mansion, now occupied by a farmer. The late John Revett was lord of the manor, and owner of part of the soil, but since his death, his estates have been involved in an expensive chancery suit, and the manor of Brandeston has been sold to John Wood, Esq.; but as a good title has not been made out, the purchase is not yet completed. Lord Rendlesham, the Earl of Gosford, and the Borrett, Wase, Goodwyn, and Gall families, have estates in the parish, mostly copyhold, subject to arbitrary fines. The *Church* (All Saints) was appropriated to Woodbridge priory by Sir Thomas Weyland, about 1290. After the dissolution, the advowson of the vicarage and the impropriation of the great tithes, were given to the Seckford family, but were vested many years ago in certain trustees, for the support of some dissenting chapels in London. These "certain trustees" have sold the great tithes to the land owners, and have lately purchased the advowson of the perpetual curacies of Hoo and Letheringham, which have their parsonage here. The Rev. Thos. Broadhurst, M.A., enjoys the vicarage of Brandeston, valued in K.B. at £9. 16s. 8d., and in 1835 at £100. Here is a small *Independent Chapel,* erected in 1838. The poor parishioners have 1A. 2R. of land, given by an unknown donor, and about one acre given by Mary Revett, for apprenticing poor children.

Abbott Wm. butcher
Bedwell Jas. wheelwright & joiner
Boon Wm. beerhouse
Bradlaugh John, blacksmith
Broadhurst Rev. Ts. M.A.Vicarage
Broadhurst Thos. Mitchell, gent.
Burt Rev John, M.A. incumbent of Hoo and Letheringham
Chase John, Cooper
Clark Edw. grocer and draper
Collins Henry, corn miller
Cook Isaac, shoemaker
Cook James, vict. Queen's Head
Emeney John, bricklayer
Garrod Robert, saddler

Hines Rev Wm. Indpt. minister
Manning Wm. shoemaker
Pipe Jeremiah, grocer and draper
Rogers John, tailor
Rowland Rd. plumber & glazier
Sewell Thomas, bricklayer
Smith Wm. farrier

FARMERS.

Abbott James || Abbott John
Baldry David || Benham Wm.
Boon Edward, (and *brickmaker)*
Boon Elisha || Gall Benjamin
Gall Samuel || Garnham James
Pettit Mark || Scruton John
Smyth George

BUTLEY, a scattered village, at the southern extremity of Loes Hundred, on the west side of *Butley River*, 4 miles from the sea, 3 miles W. of Orford, and 7 miles E. of Woodbridge, has in its parish 364 souls, and about 2000 acres of land, including a large open *sheepwalk*, which forms part of the sandy heath extending westward nearly to Woodbridge and Sutton. BUTLEY PRIORY, dedicated to the Blessed Virgin, was founded for Black Canons of St. Augustine, in 1171, by Ranulph Glanville, a famous lawyer, afterwards chief justice of England, who endowed it with many churches and estates. Being removed from office, the founder, in a fit of discontent, joined the crusaders under Richard I., and was present at the siege of Acre. Before he set out to the Holy Land, he divided his estates among his three daughters; and to Maud, the eldest, who married William de Auberville, he gave the patronage of this priory, which, at the dissolution, was valued at £318. 17s. 2d. Its site was granted in the 32nd of Henry VIII., to Thomas Duke of Norfolk; but in the 36th of the same reign, it was given to Wm. Forthe, in whose family it long continued. It afterwards passed to the Clyats and the Wrights. In 1737, George Wright, Esq., fitted up the *Gate-house*, and by additional buildings and various alterations, converted it into a handsome mansion. Mr. Wright left it to his widow, from whom it descended to John Clyatt, a watchman in London, by whom it was sold to Mr. Strahan, printer to George III. It was afterwards the property of Lord Hamilton, by whom it was sold, with the Rendlesham estate, to Peter Isaac Thellusson, Esq., who was afterwards created Lord Rendlesham, and under whose singular will, the present Lord Rendlesham now enjoys this and other valuable estates, subject to the control of trustees, called " The Trustees of P. J. Thellusson, Esq." He is lord of the manor, owner of most of the parish, and patron of the *Church* (St. John,) and has recently repaired the mansion, formed chiefly out of the Priory Gate-house, for the residence of the incumbent. The whole front of what was the Gate-house is embellished with coats of arms finely cut in stone; and between the interstices of the freestone are placed square black flints, which, by the contrast of their colour, give it a beautiful and rich appearance. South of the house, are some remains of several buildings, particularly of an old chapel, in which, Grose was informed, a chest of money was found arched into the wall. Some vestiges of this once large and magnificent priory may also be seen in the out-buildings of what is now called the Abbey farm, where several stone coffins were dug up in 1822, and one of them still remains in the farm-yard. In the priory church, was interred the body of Michael de la Pole, Earl of Suffolk, who fell at the battle of Agincourt. The *perpetual curacy* of Butley is now enjoyed by the Rev. Samuel Hobson, LL.B., and is worth only about £88 a year. It has been augmented with Queen Anne's Bounty, and has the curacy of the churchless parish of Capel St. Andrew annexed to it.

Bridgman Edward, grocer & draper
Crosley John, blacksmith
Clark Samuel, boot and shoe maker
Hobson Rev Samuel, LL.B. incumbent, *Butley Priory*
Hunt Wm. wheelwgt. & blacksmith
Jackson Thomas, tailor
Reed Wm. joiner
Thurlow Hannah, vict. *Oyster*
Wilkinson John, wheelwright

FARMERS AND GRAZIERS.
Catlin Thomas, Abbey farm

Clark Wm. (and constable)
Garrod Sarah || Cooper Mrs
Lyon Edward, *Butley corner*
Welton Robert *(and corn miller)*

CAMPSEY-ASH, a pleasant but widely scattered village, on the east side of the vale of the river Deben, 2 miles E. of Wickham Market, and 6 miles N.N.E. of Woodbridge, has in its parish 374 souls, and 1814 acres of fertile land, lying in several manors, and belonging to Lord Rendlesham, the Hon. Mrs. North, A. Arcedeckne, Esq., J. W. C. Whitbread, Esq., the trustees of the late J. Wilson Sheppard, Esq., and a few smaller owners. Here was a NUNNERY for a prioress and nuns of the order of St. Clare, founded by the direction of Theobald de Valoines, who gave the estate to his two sisters, Joan and Agnes, for that purpose, in the reign of King John. It was dedicated to God and the Virgin Mary, and was enriched by many subsequent benefactors. Maud de Lancaster, Countess of Ulster, obtained a license from Edward III. to found a chantry of five secular priests, to pray and sing mass in the church of this nunnery for the souls of Wm. de Burgh and Ralph de Ufford and their wives, but it was afterwards removed to Bruisyard. At the dissolution, the Nunnery was valued at £182. 9s. 5d. per annum; and it was granted in the 35th of Henry VIII. to Sir Wm. Willoughby, who sold it to John Lane. It was purchased of the Lanes by Frederick Scott, who sold it Sir Henry Wood, of Loudham, near Petistree, and it now belongs, with Loudham, to J. W. C. Whitbread, Esq. The house called the *Abbey* is occupied by Mr. Walker, with the adjacent water-mill. Six stone coffins were dug up near this house in 1842, and some remains of the abbey may be seen in the barn. *Park House,* which was attached to the Nunnery, and was, perhaps, the chantry house, was a seat of Theophilus Howard, Earl of Suffolk, and afterwards of the Brahams or Brames, but is now occupied by a farmer. In one of the rooms is a beautifully carved chimney piece, executed in the reign of King John. *High House,* now the seat of J. Sheppard, Esq., was built by John Glover, sometime servant to Thomas Earl of Norfolk; but his successor removing to Frostenden, sold it to the Sheppards. The *Church* (St. John) is an ancient structure, with a tower and four bells, and contains several neat marble tablets, one of which is in memory of Lieut. Frederick Sheppard, who distinguished himself in the late wars, and died in 1812, of a wound which he received at the storming of Badajos. The *rectory,* valued in K.B. at £14. 5s., and in 1835 at £350, is in the patronage of the Trustees of P. J. Thellusson, Esq., (represented by Lord Rendlesham,) and incumbency of the Rev. J. Pratt. The tithes have recently been commuted for £432 per annum. The "*Parish Estate*" has been appropriated to the service of the church from an early period, and consists of two tenements, and a piece of land let for £10, and a piece of waste land in which there is a sand-pit. On this waste, two poor persons were allowed to build cottages some years ago.

Beeden Samuel, shopkeeper
Kerridge George, boot & shoe maker
Mawson Thomas, grocer and draper
Miller M. schoolmistress
Paternoster J. collar & harness mkr
Paternoster Samuel, blacksmith
Pratt James, vict. Buck's Head
Pratt Rev. J. *Rectory*
Reeve J. corn miller, *Lower street*
Sheppard John, Esq. *High House*
Walker John, corn miller, *Ash Abbey*
FARMERS.
Butcher Edward||Largent John
Fish Louis, *Park House*

Goodwyn John, *Low farm*
Jeffries Henry, *Ashmoor Hall*
Newson Wm. (farm bailiff)

Rackham Robert, *Ash green*
Schofield J. ‖ Self Edward

CHARSFIELD, 6½ miles N. of Woodbridge, and 5½ miles S.S.W. of Framlingham, is a scattered village, on a pleasant eminence, and has in its parish 551 souls, and 1290A. of land. Earl Howe is lord of the manor, which was held by Wm. de Weyland in the time of King John, and afterwards by the Bedingfields and Lemans. The *Church* (St. Peter) has a tower, five bells, and a handsome porch, over which are the arms of the Wingfields. It was new roofed in 1841, and was appropriated, in monastic times, to Letheringham Priory. The benefice is a perpetual curacy, worth only about £60 a year, of which £27 arises from Queen Anne's Bounty. Earl Howe is patron and impropriator, and the Rev. W. B. Bransby is the incumbent, and has an ancient residence, called the Rectory House. The rectorial tithes of the land, not belonging to the impropriator, have been commuted for £160 per annum. Here is a *Baptist Chapel*, built in 1808, at the cost of £400. In 1816, *Joseph Kersey* left £800, to be invested in the purchase of stock, and the dividends to be distributed in bread and coals among the resident industrious poor of Charsfield, Earl-Soham, Dallinghoo, and Marlesford. With this legacy, £832. 18s. 4d. new four per cent. annuities were purchased, so that each of the four parishes receives £8. 6s. 7d. yearly.

Acfield Robert, grocer and draper
Bransby Rev Wm. B. incumbent
Garnham John, boot & shoe maker
Keer John, collar and harness maker
Leech David, tailor
Leech Wm. bricklayer and beerhouse
Leggett George, wheelwright
Leggett John, bricklayer
Marjoram Fanny, vict. Horse Shoe
Motum Thomas, blacksmith
Pemberton Wm. joiner
Read Wm. shopkeeper
Runnacles Rev John, Baptist min

Stenton George Ashford, corn miller
Taylor Robert, butcher
Thredkell Thomas, corn miller
Wright John, butcher

FARMERS.

Burch John ‖ Burch Jeremiah
Burwood John ‖ Farrer Henry
Hodgson John Robert, *Hall*
Lucock Francis‖Meadows John
Leggett James ‖ Leggett John
Mayhew John ‖ Page Wm.
Randall Samuel ‖ Thredkell Wm.

CRETINGHAM, nearly 5 miles W.S.W. of Framlingham, and E.S.E. of Debenham, is a village and parish, containing 411 souls, and 1639 acres of land, lying in three manors. Thos. Chenery, Esq., is lord of the *manor of St. Peter*, and impropriator of the rectorial tithes, which were commuted, in 1841, for £321 per annum. The *manor of Tyes* has belonged to the Revetts more than 250 years, and forms part of the Brandeston estates now involved in Chancery. (See p. 179.) The *manor of Kettlebars*, in Cretingham, was anciently held by a family of its own name, and afterwards by the Mulso and Cornwallis families. The parish is partly free and partly copyhold; and the other principal proprietors are Lord Rendlesham, W. Bigsby, Esq., Thomas Walker, Esq., N. Barthropp, Esq., (who has a handsome mansion here, erected about five years ago,) and Messrs. C. Pulham, J. Peck, and H. Lockwood. The *Church* (St. Andrew) has a lofty tower and five bells, and was in the appropriation of St. Peter's Priory, in Ipswich. The *vicarage*, valued in K.B. at £9. 10s. 10d., and in 1835,

at £142, has 22A. of glebe, and a yearly modus of £173, awarded in 1841 in lieu of small tithes. The patronage is in the Crown, and the Rev. R. B. Exton is the incumbent. The *Town Lands*, &c., were principally settled or given in or about the third of Elizabeth, by Arthur Penning and Wm. Barwick, for keeping the church in good repair, and for the general benefit of the parishioners. They were conveyed to ten new trustees, in 1826, and comprise 7A. 26P. of land, let for £19. 5s. per annum; the Bell Inn, let for £13; a cottage and blacksmith's shop, let for £10; a cottage, built at the expense of the parish, about 1826, let for £6. 10s., and three cottages occupied by poor persons, at small rents. In 1819, the *Rev. Joseph Jeaffreson* left 2A. of land, in augmentation of the vicarial glebe, but subject to a yearly rent-charge of 40s. for the poor.

Barthropp Nathl. Esq. *Rookery*
Exton Rev Richd. B., Vicarage
Fox Fras. grocer and draper
Juby Wm. blacksmith
Oxborrow Edw. corn miller
Runnacles Robert, blacksmith
Skeet Samuel, grocer and draper
Smith John, boot and shoe maker
Warren John, wheelwright

Wightman George, shoemaker
Wright John, vict. Bell
   FARMERS.—* *are Owners.*
Buck Benj. || Garrod Thomas
Harsant Martin (& brick maker)
Hicks Wm. Ling || Jeaffreson Jph.
*Peck John || *Lockwood Henry
Murrell Henry, *Sparks Farm*
Pulham Saml. || Willis Eliz.

DALLINGHOO is mostly in Wilford Hundred, and is already described at page 144, to which the following account of its charities should have been added. The *Church and Poor Lands, &c.*, comprise 12A. 3R. 9P., and seven cottages, partly copyhold of the manors of Dallinghoo and Wickham-cum-Membris. Part of this property was given by *Thos. Shawe*, in 1670, for the church and poor, and some of the cottages were built with £100 received by the parish in 1827, on the dissolution of the Hundred House of Loes and Wilford. One cottage is occupied, rent-free, by the parish clerk, and the rest of the property is let to different tenants, at rents amounting to £30. 15s. a year. This income is applied, as far as necessary, in repairing the church, and the residue is distributed in bread and coals among the poor. New trustees were appointed in 1824. The poor parishioners have also £8. 6s. 7d., yearly from *Kersey's Charity* (see Charsfield,) and it is distributed in bread and coals, together with the following *yearly doles*, viz., 10s. left by one *Roe;* 20s. from *Mill's Charity* (see Framlingham;) and 10s. left by *Henry Dade*, out of premises at Earl-Soham, called the Stableyard.

EARL-SOHAM, a large and well-built village, pleasantly situated at the junction of two vales, 3½ miles W. of Framlingham, and 4 miles E. of Debenham, is distinguished for its extensive *lamb and stock fair*, held July 23rd and 24th, and has in its parish 741 inhabitants, and 1944A. 2R. 38P. of fertile, loamy land. It is called Earl Soham from its being anciently held by the Earls of Norfolk. In the 20th of Edward I., Roger Bigod had a grant for a market and a fair here, but the former has long been obsolete: J. Crabtree, Esq., solicitor, of Halesworth, has lately purchased the manor, which is partly copyhold, subject to arbitrary fines; but the principal landowners are Lord Henniker, Sir T. G. Cullum, and the Goodwin, Henchman, Harsant, Raw, Cavell, Kent, Scotchmer, and a few other families. *Soham Lodge*, the

property of Sir T. G. Cullum, and now the residence of J. Clubbe, Esq., is an old, irregular brick building, surrounded with a brick wall and large moat. It was formerly the seat of the Cornwallis family, one of whom left it to the Corderoys, from whom it passed through various proprietors to the Aytons and Cullums. The *Church* (St. Mary) is a neat but ancient fabric, and the living is a *rectory*, valued in K.B. a £10, and in 1835, at £515. The Rev. J. H. Groome, M.A., is patron and incumbent, and has a neat residence and 35A. 3R. 16P. of glebe. The tithes have recently been commuted for a yearly modus of £484. 15s. The *Wesleyans* and *Baptists* have each a chapel here. The *Charity Land*, which has been vested in trust from an early period, for the relief of the poor parishioners, is copyhold, and comprises 46A., lying in various parts of the parish, and let at rents amounting to £62. 4s. a-year. On one parcel of the estate are five tenements, let for £9. 10s. a year. The rents are applied in occasional relief, and in regular distributions of money, clothing, groceries, &c. In 1677, *Robert Wyard* left a yearly rent-charge out of his lands in Worlingworth, to be paid to this parish as follows, viz., on the 25th of February and on the 23rd of April, 10s. for a sermon, 25s. for the poor, 5s. for ringing the bell, and 10s. for a dinner for the churchwardens, &c. on each of these days. The poor have also £8. 6s. 7d. yearly from *Kersey's Charity*, (see Charsfield,) and £6. 16s. from £195 three and a half per cent. annuities, bequeathed by the *Rev. Mr. Capper*, in 1818, for a weekly distribution of bread.

Post Office, at George Pettit's. Letters despatched at ½ past 6 mg.
Bellman Rayner, gentleman
Boulton Henry, corn dealer
Butcher Wm. bricklayer & plasterer
Catchpole Wm. painter, plumber, & glazier
Clubbe Jas. Esq., *Soham Lodge*
Crisp Edward, schoolmaster
Downing Thos. gent‖Gonner Mrs
Garlett Rebecca, schoolmistress
Groome Rev J.Hindes, A.M. *Rectory*
Gross Edw. surgeon and registrar
Harsant Mrs Lucy, *Rose Cottage*
Harsant Martin, brickmaker; house *Cretingham*
Haward Mrs Mary Wilgress
Henchman Rev Wm. White
Ling Fras. maltster; house *Bedfield*
Mauldon Wm. thatcher
Palmer Walter, watchmaker
Pickering Geo. Clarke, gentleman
Robson Rev John Udney, B.A. vicar of Winston
Stearn George, saddler
Turtill Charlotte, vict. Falcon Inn
Walpole Jno. butcher‖Tye Mrs My.

Woods Chas. glover & assist. oversr
Woods Geo. whip mkr & hairdressr

Blacksmiths.
Barker Devereux
Cole Samuel

Boot & Shoe Mkrs.
Alexander Wm.
Davy Jonathan
Hill Wm.
Leggett Wm.
Rogers Clement
Wightman Rd., (& beer house)

Corn Millers.
Bolton Alfred
Smith Wm.

FARMERS.
Bailey Thomas
Bigsby Rt. *Lodg*
Brown Wm.
Bucke Wm.
Churchyard Jas.
Goodwin Wm.
Kent Wm. Mann
Nesling Robert
Nesling Wm.
Reeve Thomas

Scotchmer Geo.
Vesey George
Wincup George

Grocers & Drprs
Aldrich Robert
Downing John C.
Knight George

Joiners.
Birch Robert
Clarke Wm.
Gosling Wm.
Scrutton Edmd.
Woolnough John

Tailors & Drprs.
Knight George
Norton Chas. (& glover)

Turners (Wood.)
Pettit George
Pettit John

Wheelwrights.
Pettit George, (& machine mkr)
Pettit Robert

EASTON, a neat village on a bold acclivity on the east side of the river Deben, 3½ miles S. of Framlingham, and 7 miles N. Woodbridge,

has in its parish 415 souls, and 1462 acres of land, mostly the property of the Most Noble Alex. Hamilton Douglas, *Duke of Hamilton* and *Brandon*, who is lord of the manors of Easton and Martley Hall, and occasionally resides at EASTON PARK, but generally in Scotland, where he has three seats; and sometimes at Ashton Hall, near Lancaster. A. Arcedeckne, Esq., has an estate here, and Mrs. Hambling and Mr. S. G. Stearne, are resident landowners. Easton was formerly held by the ancient family of Charles, from whom it passed to the Wingfields. *Anthony Wingfield*, who was created *baronet* in 1627, built the hall, and made it his seat, but one of his successors sold this and other neighbouring estates to Wm. Lord, of Zuilestein, who was created by William III. Earl of Rochford. William, the fourth Earl, sold this estate about 1760 to his younger brother, the Hon. R. S. Nassau, who married Grace Duchess-dowager of Hamilton, and whose son, the last Earl of Rochford, died here in 1830, and left this and other estates to the Duke of Hamilton. Previous to his death, the late Earl thoroughly repaired the *hall*, which is a large and handsome mansion, in a beautiful *park* of 150 acres. *Martley and Bentress Halls*, now occupied by farmers, are ancient moated mansions. The *Church* (All Saints) has a tower and four bells, and is a *rectory*, valued in K.B. at £10. 18s. 6d., and in 1835 at £242. The Duke of Hamilton is patron, and the Rev. Samuel Kelderbee, D.D., incumbent, for whom the Rev. Henry Long officiates. The glebe is 18A. and the tithes have recently been commuted for a yearly modus of £321. 5s., to which the pasture lands pay at the rate of from 2d. to 4d. per acre.

Duke of Hamilton, *Easton Park,* (here only occasionally)
Arey Robert, shopkeeper
Beard Candler, cooper
Bedwell John, wheelwright
Clarke James, grocer and draper
Gray Wm. tailor
Hill Jared, blacksmith
Long Rev Henry, curate, *Rectory*
Newson David, vict. *White Horse*
Smith Dd. Esq. land agent, *Easton Park*

Smith George, shoemaker
Snell Robert, hedge carpenter
Tuthill Samuel, shoemaker
FARMERS.(—* *Are owners,)*
Borrett Alfred, Bentress Hall
Catchpole John
Crisp Samuel and Nathan
Hill James || *Hambling Deborah
Hill John, *Martley Hall*
*Stearne Samuel Geater
Carrier, Rt. Arey, to Ipswich, Sat.

EYKE, a village and parish, 3½ miles E.N.E. of Woodbridge, contains 502 souls, and about 2800 acres of sandy land, including *Staverton*, formerly a large park. Lord Rendlesham and the Marquis of Bristol own the greater part of the parish, and the latter is lord of the manor of Staverton with Bromeswell, which was held by Butley priory, and was granted in the 32nd of Henry VIII. to Thomas Duke of Norfolk. The *Rookery*, a good house and farm, is the residence of T. Walker, Esq., and here is a small manor belonging to the *rectory*, which is also endowed with a house and land at Woodbridge, and is valued in K.B. at £15, but is now worth about £500 per annum. The Earl of Stradbroke is patron, and the Rev. W. A. Norton, M.A., of Alderton, is the incumbent. The tithes have been commuted. The *Church* is a small ancient structure, dedicated to All Saints. Here was a *chantry*, called Bennet's Chantry, of the yearly value of £8. The lands belonging to it, in Eyke and Rendlesham, were granted in

the 3rd of Edward I. to Sir Michael Stanhope and John Delle. The *Town Lands*, comprising 12A. in Eyke and 7A. in Bromeswell, are let for £28 a year, which is applied in the reparation of the church, &c., and when there is any surplus, it is added to the poor rates. It is not known how the property was acquired. The *Poor's Land*, 3A. 2R., was given by James and Henry Mason, in 1620, and is let for £6. 19s. a year, which is distributed on Easter Tuesday by the Churchwardens, together with a yearly rent-charge of £10 from *Sir Michael Stanhope's Charity*. (See Sutton.)

Baker Wm. wheelwht. & blacksmith
Braham Mrs Ann
Chapman L. wheelwright
Churchyard Jas. veterinary surgeon
Fletcher John, Wm. & James, corn millers
Gentry Daniel, policeman
Hayward Robt. grocer and draper
Keeble Charles, shoemaker
Kettle Wm. farmer
Largent George, farmer
Linn Edw. vict. Elephant & Castle
Manthorp John, shoemaker
Manthorp Rd. tailor and par. clerk
Manthorp Wm. blacksmith
Minter Wm. joiner
Parker J. shoemaker
Roper Rev Arthur Wellington, curate
Row Henry, farmer
Waller Thomas, Esq. *Rookery*

FRAMLINGHAM, a small but thriving and well-built market town, distinguished for its *stately church* and the extensive remains of its *ancient castle*, is pleasantly situated 18 miles N.N.E. of Ipswich; 10 miles N. of Woodbridge ; 8 miles W. of Saxmundham; 8 miles E. of Debenham ; 13 miles S.E. of Eye ; and 87 miles N.E. of London. It is partly on the west and mostly on the east bank of the small *river Ore*, upon an acclivity, about three miles below the source of that river, which flows south-east and joins the *Alde*, near Snape, from which place it is supposed to have been anciently navigable for small craft to this town ; and it might be made so again at a small expense, compared with the great benefit that this fertile portion of Suffolk would derive from such an easy transit for its agricultural produce, which has now to be sent by land carriage for shipment, either to Snape Bridge or Woodbridge, both distant more than nine miles from Framlingham. The PARISH encreased its *population* from 1854 souls in 1801, to 2523 in 1841, and comprises 4527A. 3R. 27P. of land, mostly having rich loamy soil, and including the small hamlets of *Apsey-Green*, 1½ mile W.; *Babylon-Green*, 1 mile N. ; *Brabling-Green* 1 mile S.; *Coles-Green*, 1¼ S.W.; *Lampard Brook*, 1 mile S.W.; and a number of scattered farms. (See list of farmers.) The Master and Fellows of Pembroke Hall, Cambridge, as Trustees of Sir Robt. Hitcham's Charities, are lords of the manors of Framlingham and Saxstead, and owners of the demesne land, about 1300 acres. The other principal landowners are the Pierson, Hotham, Moseley, Field, Sherriff, Wise, Cooper, De Horsey, Turner, and Corrance families. The custom of these manors is " *Borough English*," by which the youngest son inherits when a copyholder dies intestate ; but if the latter has no issue, his copyhold passes to his elder brother or other heir-at-law. A *court baron* is held yearly in both parishes, but the *court leet* fell into disuse many years ago. There are in Framlingham about seventy burgage holders, about as many freeholders, and a third class called " coliarholders," who pay small fines and render suit and service. The market place is spacious, and had an ancient *cross*, which was taken down many

years ago.   The *market*, held every Saturday, is well supplied with corn and provisions.   Here are also two annual *fairs* for pedlery, pleasure, &c., held on Whit-Monday and Tuesday, and on Old Michaelmas-day and the day following.   The *Framlingham Division*, formed in 1830, comprises 33 parishes, for which *petty-sessions* are held at the Crown Inn every alternate Friday.   Mr. Chas. Clubbe is clerk to the magistrates.   By the Reform Act of 1832, Framlingham was made a *Polling Place* for the Eastern Division of Suffolk.

FRAMLINGHAM CASTLE, on the south side of the town, was one of the most magnificent and formidable baronial castles of the Saxon and Norman eras, and was surrounded by a thickly-wooded park of nearly 700 acres.   Though now a mere *shell*, it has, when viewed from a distance, the appearance of being entire, its outer walls being nearly all standing in their pristine proportions, except one of the thirteen towers, which fell down Sept. 1st, 1831.   Its form is an irregular curve, approaching to a circle, and the walls, which are 44 feet high and eight thick, are composed of flints and stones of all shapes and sizes, held together solely by the strength of the cement, in which they are imbedded.   The towers which flank the walls, are 14 feet higher than the ramparts, and are square, but vary much in size and architecture, and in their distance from each other.   An ancient wreathed chimney rises from eight of the towers, and three others project from the walls. These chimneys are fine specimens of early brick work, and are all cylindrical, but variously decorated.   The entire parapet is embattled, and in all parts of the walls are chinks of various shapes.   The principal gateway is on the south side, and over it are the arms of the noble families of Howard, Brotherton, Warren, Mowbray, Segrave, and Breos, quartered in one escutcheon, with lions for supporters, and above a lion passant, resting upon a helmet.   Of the western outworks and eastern postern, enough remains to enable the antiquary to discover their construction and extent.   Within the walls, which enclose an area of 1 A. 1 R. 11 P., not a room, and scarcely a vestige of one, remains.   The interior was destroyed about 1650, by the trustees of Sir Robert Hitcham, as will be seen in the account of his charities; and so complete was the demolition of all the apartments, that though many thousand loads of rubbish have been removed during the present century, not a single foundation has been discovered in a state of preservation, sufficient to ascertain the interior arrangements.   Even the cellars, the dungeons, and subterraneous passages, of which tradition has preserved the memory of several, appear to have undergone the same fate with the upper apartments, since the whole appeared upon excavation to be one uniform mass of building materials.   The mortices that received the timbers of the floors, the marks of ancient roofs, the windows and fire places still, indeed, prove the former existence of numerous apartments ; but except the situation of the chapel, which may be easily known from its east window yet remaining, all is buried in complete confusion.   The trustees just named destroyed the whole interior chiefly for the purpose of selecting the best parts of the materials for the erection of the adjacent almshouses, and a workhouse, pursuant to the will of Sir Robert Hitcham.   *Camden* observes, that " Framlingham is a very beautiful castle, fortified with a rampire, a ditch, and a wall of great thickness, with thirteen towers : within, it has

very convenient lodgings." Sampson, Loder, and some other historians
have noticed several sumptuous apartments, which appear to have been
elegantly decorated and hung with rich tapestry. This castle was
strongly fortified both by nature and art, being effectually defended on
the west side by a lake or *mere*, fed by the river Ore (formerly extensive, but now choked up,) and on the other sides by two broad and very
deep ditches. To these means of security were added various outworks, of which some remains may yet be traced, especially those of
the barbican, a strong fortification, which stood between the two ditches,
and served to flank the grand draw-bridge. This, together with a strong
machicolated and embattled gate and portcullis, the groves of which are
still to be seen, formed a sufficient defence against all the modes of
attack employed before the invention of fire arms. The *park*, which
extended more than a mile north of the castle, is now divided into fertile farms, belonging to Sir Robt. Hitcham's Charity. It was formerly
celebrated for its noble forest trees. Evelyn says Suffolk, and particularly Framlingham, was famous for producing the tallest and largest
oaks, perhaps, in the world; and Miller informs us that the oak, which
afforded the beams of the Royal Sovereign, grew at Framlingham, and
was four feet nine inches in diameter, and yielded four beams, each 44
feet long.

The origin of this castle is lost in obscurity. It is conjectured to
have been first built in the time of the heptarchy, by some of the first
Saxon kings of the East Angles, and is generally ascribed to Redwald,
who began his reign in 593, and resided generally at Rendlesham.
St. Edmund, the king and martyr, fled to this castle in 870, from the
invading Danes, and was here besieged by them. Being hard pressed,
and having no hopes of succour, he endeavoured to escape, but was
overtaken in his flight, and put to death by his enemies, who took possession of Framlingham, and the rest of East Anglia. About fifty years
afterwards, Framlingham was recovered by the Saxons, and in their
possession it remained till the total subjection of England by Canute.
After the Norman Conquest, this castle was considered of so much importance, that it was retained by the first two monarchs; but was granted by Henry I. to *Roger Bigod*, to be held of the king *in capite*. His
grandson, Hugh Bigod, was created *Earl of Norfolk* by king Stephen,
because he attested that Henry had, on his death-bed, declared his nephew Stephen his successor, in preference to his daughter Maud. By
this nobleman the castle was either rebuilt, or much repaired, but it
was partially dismantled in 1176, by order of Henry II., because the
Earl had favoured the pretensions of his rebellious sons, as noticed at
page 51. The king, nevertheless, restored his possessions on condition,
that on the failure of heirs to the family of Bigod, they should revert to the Crown; a circumstance which actually took place in the
third of Edward II., when that monarch appointed John de Botetourt,
governor of Framlingham castle, but removed him in 1312, when he
conferred all the possessions of the Bigods on his brother Thos. Plantagenet, surnamed de Brotherton, whom he created Earl of Norfolk
and Marshal of England. This nobleman repaired the castle, and
procured a license for a *fair*, and a charter of *free warren* for all his
demesne lands in Framlingham. He died in 1338, and his only son followed him to the grave in the same year. Alice, his daughter, mar-

ried Edward de Montacut; and their daughter Joan, carried Framlingham, and the other estates of her family, in marriage to Wm. de Ufford, afterwards Earl of Suffolk, who died without issue in 1382, after which Framlingham passed to the wife of John Lord Mowbray; who was the daughter of Margaret de Brotherton and Lord Segrave. Her son, Thomas Mowbray, inherited the estates, and was created by Richard II., *Earl of Nottingham*, in 1383, and *Duke of Norfolk*, in 1397, but was banished in the same year, and died at Venice in 1413. His son Thomas was beheaded at York, in 1405, when Framlingham was given to the *Prince of Wales*, but was restored in 1413, to John Mowbray, who, in 1424, was also restored to the dignity of Duke of Norfolk.

The *Howards* succeeded to the honours and a great part of the estates of the Mowbrays, in 1483, and with them the title of Duke of Norfolk still remains; but they have had many reverses of fortune, as is well known to every reader of English history. John, the first Duke of Norfolk of the Howard family, was slain in the cause of Richard the Third, at Bosworth field, in 1485, and being attainted, all his honours were forfeited; but his son Thomas was restored to the earldom of Surrey in 1489, and was created Duke of Norfolk in 1514, after gaining a signal victory over the Scots at Flodden Field. He died, full of years and honours, at his castle of Framlingham, in 1524. By the attainder of his son Thomas, a few days before the decease of Henry the Eight, this castle and manor were again forfeited to the Crown, in which they remained during the reign of Edward VI. On the death of that prince, his sister Mary, who was then at Kenninghall, in Norfolk, repaired for greater safety to Framlingham Castle, where she remained till she went to London to take possession of the Crown, after the powerful partisans of Lady Jane Grey had been put down. The Duke of Norfolk, who had so narrowly escaped the executioner's axe by the death of Henry VIII., was released from the Tower by Queen Mary, and restored to his honours and possessions. He died here in 1554. Thomas, the next duke, was beheaded in 1572, for taking part with Mary Queen of Scots; and this castle and manor once more reverted to the Crown. James I., immediately after his accession, granted them, with other demesnes, to Thomas Lord Howard, Baron of Walden, and his uncle Lord Henry Howard.

The latter soon after resigned his moiety to his nephew, who had in the meantime been created Earl of Suffolk, and whose son, Theophilus, in 1635, sold Framlingham, and all his rights in the hundred of Loes, to Sir Robert Hitcham, for £14,000. " The title to the estate was so perplexed, that had he not had a strong brain and a powerful purse, he could never have cleared it; of which he was so sensible, that in thankfulness to God for his wonderful success, he settled it for pious uses on Pembroke Hall, in Cambridge." This he did by will dated August 8th, 1636, by which he devised the castle and manor of Framlingham, together with the manor of Saxtead, (then of the yearly value of £1000,) to the master and fellows; £100 to be expended for the benefit of the said college; and the remainder to be appropriated for the foundation of *Almshouses* at Levington and Framlingham, for the foundation of a school at the latter place, for the education of the poor of Framlingham, Debenham, and Coggeshall, (in Essex,) and for other

charitable uses in these parishes and in Nacton. He farther directed all the castle of Framlingham, " saving the stone building," to be pulled down, and the materials to be employed in the erection of an almshouse for twelve poor people, a workhouse, and a school for the poor of Framlingham, Debenham, and Coggeshall. Seven days after he had executed his will, Sir Robert died, but his heir-at-law contrived to keep the college out of possession of the manor and lands till 1653, when an ordinance was published by order of Cromwell, then Lord Protector, for settling and confirming them agreeable to the intention of the testator, but directing separate schools and workhouses to be erected at Debenham and Coggeshall, which were at too great a distance to derive any benefit from those at Framlingham. The Master and Fellows of Pembroke Hall, instead of dividing the rents as directed by this ordinance, severed the estates, which have ever since been in the hands of distinct trustees for each of the towns. The *Framlingham Trust* extends over more than 800 acres of the demesne lands of the manor, and produces a yearly income of about £920. The Rector and the Reader of prayers of Framlingham, for the time being, with other neighbouring clergy, and some of the residents of the town, have the administration of the trust, subject to the control of the Master and Fellows of Pembroke Hall, who, in 1730, purchased a house for the residence of the *Reader*, who is also *Treasurer* of the Trust. The ALMSHOUSES are occupied by six poor men and six poor women, (widows and widowers,) who have each 6s. per week, a yearly supply of clothing and coals, and medical assistance when required. The *Boys' Free School* was originally kept in a room over the Market Cross, which was taken down in 1788, when a new school was built near the Almshouses, which stand at the western extremity of what was the castle mere. The *Workhouse*, which stands near the same place, has (since Framlingham was joined to Plomesgate Union) been converted into *public rooms*, in which assemblies, &c., are held. Adjoining it is a *Girls' Free School*, which the trustees established some years ago. The two schools now afford gratuitous instruction to about 113 boys and 86 girls. The schoolmaster has a residence in the Castle yard. After providing for the support of the almspeople and the schools, the reparation of the buildings, and the payment of salaries and incidental expenses, the surplus income (about £300 per annum) is distributed in weekly stipends and occasional allowances of clothing, among the poor parishioners, or in apprentice fees. The Rev. J. W. Darby, B.A., is the *reader*, and has a yearly salary of £30, with an addition of £15 for superintending the schools, and a further allowance as treasurer of the trust.

The mansion called the *Guildhall*, on the north side of the Market hill, occupies the site of a hall which belonged to the Guild of the Blessed Virgin Mary, founded here at an early period, and dissolved about 1537. In digging the foundations of houses at a place called the *Hermitage*, on the Dennington road, several human skeletons were found some years ago. Framlingham was anciently considered a *borough*, and had its own bailiff, who served all writs and processes within its own limits, to the exclusion of the sheriff's bailiff, as was shewn by a survey made in the reign of Edward VI. Antiquaries differ as to the origin of its name, some deriving it from the Saxon words *fremdling-*

ham, (the habitation of strangers ;) and others, affirming that the *Ore* was in olden time called *Fromus,* consider that it has reference to that river, which is said to have anciently been navigable, and which still expands itself into a broad sheet, a mile below the town, called *Broad-water.* An anchor, two elephants' tusks, and large masses of petrified clay and water, with vegetable substances, shells, &c., imbedded in them, have been found in the sand pits, below the present channel of the river ; and one of the latter being cut and polished, exhibits a perfect section of a *snake stone,* seven times coiled, and ten inches in diameter.

Framlingham Church (St. Michael) is a large and handsome structure, chiefly of black flint, with a tower 96 feet high, containing a clock, chimes, and eight bells. The nave and aisles are 64 feet long and 50 broad ; and the chancel and aisles, 61 feet in length and 68½ in width. The nave is 44, and the chancel 37 feet high. The interior is in the Gothic style, and is well paved and pewed, and contains a good organ, presented by the patrons in 1708. The nave is supposed to have been built by the Mowbrays ; but the chancel is of later date, being the work of the Howards, of whom here are several splendid monuments. In the north aisle of the chancel is a magnificent tomb of black and white marble, on which lie the figures of Henry Earl of Surrey, and his Countess, with the palms of their hands conjoined ; the former in his robes of state, over armour, but without his coronet, which, as he was beheaded, is placed on the tomb by his side. Their heads rest on double cushions, curiously wrought and gilt ; and at a little distance from the east and west end of the pedistal are kneeling effigies of their two sons and three daughters, the former habited as their father, and the latter in robes of state, over mourning, like their mother. This Earl was the most learned nobleman of his time, and was brought to the block by the false accusations of the minions of Henry VIII., only nine days before the death of that monarch. This monument was erected in 1614, by his second son, Henry, Earl of Northampton ; and a little to the east of it, is a small tomb of freestone, adorned with seven fluted pilasters of the Ionic order, and erected in memory of Elizabeth, daughter of Thomas, Duke of Norfolk, who died in her infancy. Still farther eastward is a spacious monument of freestone, enriched with the effigies of two of the duchesses of the last named duke, lying in their full proportions in robes of state, one resting her head on a horse couchant, and the other on a tiger collared and chained. The tomb is enriched with Corinthian columns, coats of arms, lions seyant, &c. South of it is another spacious tomb of freestone, erected for Henry Fitzroy, Duke of Richmond, the natural son of Henry VIII. It is 9 feet 2 inches long, and 5 feet 2 inches wide. The top is plain, but has four small images standing erect at the corners, each supporting a trophy of the passion. The lower part of the four sides is adorned with 16 fluted Ionic pilasters, and between them are the duke's own arms, impaled and differently quartered with those of Howard. In small pannels above, there are represented, in basso relievo, several of the most remarkable events in the Old and New Testament, with cariatides between them. On the south side of the altar is a stately tomb of freestone, 9 feet long, 6 wide, and 5 high, bearing recumbent effigies of Thomas Howard, Duke of Norfolk, who died in 1524, and one of his duchesses, in robes of state, with coronets

on their heads. The sides of the tomb are ornamented with columns of the Composite order, and figures of the apostles and evangelists, finely executed in alto-relievo. The helmet and crest are on the north side of the tomb, upon an iron fastened in the wall. On the south side of the chancel is the monument of *Sir Robert Hitcham, Kt.*, a distinguished lawyer and judge, and a munificent benefator to Framlingham and other parishes, as already noticed. It consists of a table of black marble, supported at the corners by four angels of white marble, with gilt hair and wings, each having one knee on the ground. Under a plain gray stone, in the south aisle, lies interred *Mr. Robert Hawes*, who compiled the greater part of the "History of Framlingham," published by Mr. Loder, of Woodbridge, in 1798.

The *Rectory of Framlingham* has Saxtead annexed to it, and is valued in K.B. at £43. 6s. 8d. In 1835, it was valued at £1201, but the tithes have recently been commuted for a yearly modus of £1250 in Framlingham, and £340 in Saxtead; besides which, the incumbent has about 70A. of glebe, and a good residence, in the Gothic style. The Master and Fellows of Pembroke Hall, Cambridge, are the patrons, and after the death or resignation of the Rev. George Attwood, M.A., the present incumbent, they intend to separate it into two rectories, and to present that of Saxtead to the senior fellow of their college. The *Unitarian Meeting-house* (formerly Presbyterian) was erected in 1717, by a congregation composed of Baptists and Nonconformists, the former of whom dated their origin from the preaching of Mr. Thomas Mills, who died in 1703; and the latter from the ministry of the Rev. W. Sampson, who had officiated as rector here ten years, but was ejected from the church on the restoration of Charles II. Adjoining this chapel is a house for the minister, purchased in 1756. Here are two other chapels, viz., a *Wesleyan Chapel*, built in 1808; and an *Independent Chapel*, erected in 1823. Here is also a congregation of *Primitive Methodists*, who assemble in the *Temperance Hall*, a neat white brick building, erected in 1842, by Mr. Samuel Fruer. There are in the town several *institutions* for the Promotion of Christian Knowledge, two *Book Societies*, a *Parochial Library*, an *Horticultural* and *Agricultural Societies*, established in 1834; an Association for the Prosecution of Felons, instituted in 1798; a *Lying-in Charity*, commenced in 1826; and a "*Penny Clothing Club*," established in 1833. A company of *Volunteers* was formed here for internal defence in 1798, and disbanded at the peace of 1801, but formed again in 1803, and remained embodied till 1814. Besides the ALMSHOUSES AND SCHOOLS supported by the munificent *Charity of Sir Robt. Hitcham*, as noticed at page 189, Framlingham has eight almshouses, and charities for the education and relief of the poor, founded by *Mr. Thomas Mills*. The TOWN LANDS comprise about 32 acres, in various parcels, and were vested before the time of Edward VI. for the general benefit of the parish. They are let for £61 a year, which is applied with the church-rates. In 1701, *Richard Porter* charged a house, formerly the Griffin Inn, with the weekly distribution of 18 two-penny loaves among the poor parishioners, who have also 18 two-penny loaves weekly, left by one Warren, out of Parham House.

In 1703, THOMAS MILLS bequeathed all his messuages, lands, and hereditaments in Suffolk, for the erection and endowment of an ALMS-

HOUSE at Framlingham, for six poor people; the yearly payment of 40s. each to Framlingham and Ufford, and 20s. each to Petistree, Wickham, Dallinghoo, Parham, and Dennington, for distributions of bread in those parishes; and the residue for the education of children of Framlingham, or the relief of the poor, as his executors should think meet. He also gave £300 for the erection of the *Almshouse*, which was built in Feaks Pightle, pursuant to the testator's directions, with the addition of two other sets of rooms, so that it is occupied by eight poor people, who have each a small garden, and an equal interest in the adjoining orchard, which is let for £4 a year. The following are the particulars and rental of the estates belonging to this charity, viz., two farm-houses and 166A. 2R. 39P. of land in Ufford, let for £260 per ann.; a farm of 113A. 1R. 6P. in Petistree, let for £130; a farm called Old Hall, in Dallinghoo, containing 46A. 2R. 36P., let for £54 a year; a house and 36A. 2R. 26P. of land in Parham, let for £59. 10s. a year; a house, barn, and about 70A. of land in Framlingham, let for £110 a year; and a farm of 23A. 1R. 6P., in Dennington, let for £30 a year. Thus the total income of the trust amounts to £643. 10s. per annum. The eight *almspeople* have each a weekly stipend of 5s., and about £24 worth of coals and £10 worth of clothing are distributed among them yearly. They are also supplied with medical assistance, and are permitted each of them to take a nurse to reside with them, to whom the trustees allow about 5s. per quarter. Bread is supplied for the poor of the several parishes, in the quantities mentioned in the will. Exercising the discretionary power given them by the testator, the trustees pay yearly £17. 10s. to a *schoolmaster*, for teaching poor boys; £9 towards the support of two Sunday-schools, and £5. 4s. to the poor attending the Presbyterian (now Unitarian) Meeting-house in Framlingham; and they distribute among the poor parishioners about £5. 10s. weekly, and supply them with about £20 worth of blankets yearly, besides supplying them with 80 chaldrons of coals, at reduced prices. There is a considerable annual expenditure in repairs of the farm buildings and the almshouse; and a great part of the estate being copyhold, a sum of from £300 to £400 has to be paid for fines, &c., on every renewal of the trust. *Mr. Thomas Mills*, the founder of this valuable charity was originally a tailor at Grundisburgh, and afterwards followed the occupation of a wheelwright at Framlingham, where he became a preacher among the Baptists, and married Mrs. Groome, a widow lady possessed of considerable property, who died before him, leaving him all her estates, which he devoted to charitable uses, as stated above. At his own request, he was buried in his garden, near the almshouses, under a neat *tomb-house*, now tastefully decorated with ivy, jessamine, &c. This building has small lancet-shaped windows, and on the side next the road is a tablet of black marble, with the following inscription:—" *In memory of Thomas Mills*, (who died January 13th, 1703, aged 80,) founder of the adjoining Almshouses, and donor of several estates to charitable purposes; also, of his faithful servant, *William Mayhew*." The latter was one of the founder's trustees; and at his death, in 1713, he desired his remains to be laid beside his master's.

Framlingham Savings Bank was established in 1819, and on the 26th of November, 1842, had a *surplus fund* of £214. 14s. 10d.; and *deposits* amounting to £24,527. 13s. 3d., of which £23,174 belonged to

669 *individuals*, £767. 1s. 1d. to 24 *Charitable Societies*, and £586. 11s. 7d. to three *Friendly Societies*. The Bank is open on the first Thursday of every month, from eleven till two o'clock, at the house of Mr. G. Edwards, the cashier. Mr. W. Edwards is the *secretary*, and the Hon. and Rev. F. Hotham, J. H. Groome, Esq., and others, are *trustees*.

FRAMLINGHAM.

Post Office :— Letters arrive at 8 morning, and are despatched at 6 evening

Attwood Rev George, M.A. *Rectory*
Baldry Benjamin, gent. Castle street
Baldry Benj. jun. tax collr. Castle st
Baldwin Thos. Wardley, auctioneer, valuer, & estate agent, Fairfield rd
Barker Rev Jas.(Wes.) Woodbridge rd
Barker Mr Thomas
Bloss Miss Mary Ann, Willow cotg
Blumfield Mr Stephen, Bridge street
Bridges Mr Wm. Market hill
Bridges Edwd. beer seller, Castle st
Browning Rev Samuel Alexander, (Independent,) Hermitage street
Cage Thos. bank cashier, Bridge st
Carr Robert, parish clerk, Castle st
Catchpole George, sweep, Horn hill
Chapman Wm. land surveyor and agent, Back street
Collins Wm. millwgt. Dennington rd
Cooper Miss Maria, Church street
Cottingham John, relieving officer and registrar, Hermitage place
Crisp Wm. bookkeeper, Water side
Dallenger Mrs Susan, Wellclose sq
Darby Rev John Wareyne, B.A. rector of Shottisham and reader of Framlingham, Castle street
Day Mrs Mary, Market hill
Edwards Mrs Louisa, Back street
Everett Jas. coal dlr. White Hart ln
Field Edw.Esq.The Oaks (& *London*)
Fruer Sl. architect, Temperance cotg
Fruer Mrs Sophia, Market hill
Gall Mr John, Dennington road
Goode Rev Thomas, B.A. curate of Saxtead, Mount Pleasant
Goodwyn Mr Jasper, Hermitage pl
Hunt Mrs Mary, Woodbridge road
Keer Miss Emma, Church street
Kersey Miss Maria, Castle street
Kinnell Mrs Eliz. Church street
Leek Stpn. basket mkr. Wellclose sq
Leggett Hy. letter carrier, Horn hill
Mann John, gardener, Castle houses
Marshall Jas. hosier, Double street
Neville Mr John, Saxmundham rd

Newson Mrs Elizabeth, Castle st
Nulter Rev Chas. Case (Unitarian,) Bridge street
Oakley John, rate collr. Water side
Page Mrs. Water side
Pierson John, Esq. *Guildhall*
Pierson Misses My.&Mgt. Market hill
Punchard Mr John Baldry, Double st
Rudd Rev Wm.(Prim.Meth.)Castle st
Smith Hy. fishmonger, Castle street
Stanford Mrs Matilda, Back street
Taylor Mrs Hannah, Back street
Thurlow Charlotte, upholsteress
Walker Mr Robert, Badingham rd
Welham Robt. registrar of marriages for Plomesgate Union, Church st
Warner Henry, gent.Woodbridge rd
Webb Mr Mark, Wellclose square
Wilkinson Miss Priscilla, Saxtead rd
Wyatt Misses, Market hill

ACADEMIES.

*(Marked * take Boarders.)*

*Bennington My. & Jane, Temp. ter
*Boult Rachel, Double street
Bridges Sarah, Market hill
Gostling Mary, Castle street
*Hill Wm. Double street
Hitcham's Charity, Samuel Lane and Dinah Tucker, Castle yard
*Oseland My. & Emma, Ivy Cottage
Springett Ellen & Emma, Market hill
*Welham Robert, jun., Church st

ATTORNEYS.

Clubbe Charles, (magistrates' clerk, &c.) Market hill
Edwards Wm. Church street

BAKERS AND FLOUR DEALERS.

(are Confectioners also.)*

Aldous John, Double street
*Leek Spencer, Wellclose square
*Middleton Rt. Buckingham, Mkp
Newson Charles, Hermitage place
Whayman David, Back street
*Woods Edward, Double street

BANKERS.

Gurneys and Co. Market hill (draw on Barclay and Co.) Charles Edwards and Co. *agents*
Savings' Bank. (See page 193.)

BLACKSMITHS.
Bridges John Fruer, Fairfield road
Bridges Silvanus, Double street
Heffer George, Wellclose square

BOOKSELLERS, PRINTERS, &c.
(And Circulating Libraries.)
Freeman Wm. Dove, (and stamp seller,) Double street
Green Richard, Church street

BOOT AND SHOE MAKERS.
Bridges Samuel M. Market hill
Cone Charles, Market hill
Field James, Castle street
Freeman James, Castle street
Gardener Henry, Bridge street
Garlett John, Bridge street
Gostling George, Market hill
Hammond James, Horn hill
Johnson Henry, Back street
King Wm. Back street
Lambert Edward, Temperance place
Leggett Francis, Horn hill
Mayhew George, Wellclose square
Moss Wm. Market hill
Newson Samuel, Queen's Head yd
Read Paul, Back street
Scotchmer Wm. Saxmundham road

BRAZIERS AND TINNERS.
Harding Wm. Back street
Pratt James, Double street

BREWERS.
Grant James Burton, Castle Brewery
Lankester Edward (and wine and spirit merchant,) Back street

BRICKLAYERS, &c.
Drake Anthony, Double street
Fulcher Robert, Castle street
Fulcher Robert, jun. (plasterer)
Hall Wm. Woodbridge road
Kerridge James, Back street
Mallows Stephen, Saxtead road

BROKERS (CLOTHES.)
Aldous James, Saxtead road
Exworth Wm. Market hill

BUTCHERS.
Bilney Francis, Back street
Bloss Robert Francis, Double street
Dixon Elizabeth, Double street
Dixon John, Double street
Kerridge John, Bridge street

CABINET MAKERS.
Butcher George, Mount Pleasant
Clarke James, Woodbridge road
Dale Samuel, Market hill
Leech Wm. Wright, Double street
Wightman Samuel, *(broker)*

CHEMISTS AND DRUGGISTS.
Clutten Henry, Market hill
Manning Sarah, Double street

COOPERS.
Vice Wm. Back street
Waters Charles, Castle street
Whayman David, Back street

CORN MERCHANTS.
Goodwyn Edward, Hermitage place
Wightman Jonathan, Wellclose sq
Wightman Robt. *(and coal,)* Back st

CORN MILLERS.
Kindred John, Victoria mill
Smyth John, Saxmundham road
Woods Samuel, Saxtead road

CURRIERS, &c.
Fox James, White Hart lane
Read Jonathan, Back street

DYERS.
Kerridge Francis, Back street
Wells Thomas, Double street

FARMERS.
*(Marked * are owners.)*
Abbott James, Little lodge
Adams James, Brabling green
Barnes John, Coles green
*Bennington Henry, Easton road
*Bennington Nath. Lampard brook
Butcher George, Saxtead bottom
Carr Francis Botwright, Rookery
Catt John, Rookery
Dove Edward, Pitman's grove
Girling Matthew, Brabling green
Gooch Edward, Apsey green
*Goodwyn Goodwyn, chief constable, Fairfield House
*Goodwyn John, Saxtead road
*Goodwyn Samuel, Saxmundham rd
Hart Daniel, *Countess Wells*
Holmes Nicholas, Dennington road
Kersey Robert, Great Lodge
Keer Davie, Kettleburgh road
Larratt James, Saxmundham road
Laws John, Dennington road
Middleton Josiah, Cherry tree
*Pierson John, Lampard brook
Pipe James, Dennington corner
Rivers Wm. Pitman's grove
*Stanford John, Bedingham road
Taylor Joseph, Castle brooks
True Nathaniel, Brabling green
Turner James, Saxtead road
Turner Richard, Saxtead green
Wightman Jnthn. *Wormwood Hills*

FIRE AND LIFE OFFICES.
Essex and Suffolk Equitable, **Wm.** Edwards, Church street

Norwich Equitable, Wm. D. Freeman, Double street

Norwich Union, Rd. Green, Church st

Suffolk & General, Charles Edwards, Market place

GLASS, CHINA, &C. DEALERS.

Freeman James, Castle street

Wightman Jesse, Wellclose square

GLOVERS.

Row John, Castle street

Watling Charlotte, Back street

GROCERS AND DRAPERS.

*(Marked * are Tallow Chandlers.)*

*Baxter Joseph, Back street

Edwards Charles & Co. *stamp office,* Market hill

Freeman Edward, Double street

Thompson Henry, Market hill

Wightman Jesse, Wellclose square

HAIR DRESSERS.

Driver Henry, Market hill

Gibbons George, Castle street

Lay Richard, Market hill

Moyse John, Wellclose square

INNS AND TAVERNS.

Crown, Miller James Rodwell *(posting.)* Market hill

Crown and Anchor, Samuel Bloss, *(posting,)* Market hill

Hare and Hounds, Ann Wright, Double street

Queen's Head, Shadrach Newson, Market hill

Waggon and Horses, Fras. Bilney, Back street

White Horse, James Brunning, Wellclose lane

IRONMONGERS.

Barker Joseph, Double street

Barker Samuel Keer, Market hill

Barnes Frederick, Market hill

Bridges John Fruer, Fairfield road

JOINERS, &C.

Bridges Job, Market hill

Clutten Henry, Bridge street

Dale Samuel, Market hill

Dallestone Daniel, Saxtead road

Dallestone Henry, Back street

Waller Daniel, Back street

Wightman John, Double street

LINEN AND WOOLLEN DRAPERS.

(See also Grocers and Drapers.)

Nickols Wm. (& hatter,) Double st

MALTSTERS.

Edwards George, Castle street

Lankester Edward, Back street

Wightman Jonathan, Wellclose sq

MILLINERS, &C.

Aldrich Lydia, Castle street

Allured Elizabeth, Dennington road

Barker Elizabeth, Church street

Capon Ann, Temperance place

Capon Mary, Church street

Chenery Dinah, Double street

Garlett Mary, Double street

Lambert Charlotte, Temperance pl

Ludbrook Mary Ann, Fairfield road

Newson Sarah, Castle street

Quinton Harriet, Double street

Rivers Eliza, Double street

Wright Eliza, Double street

PAINTERS, PLUMBERS, &GLAZIERS

Fisk Wm. Castle street

Woolnough Constantine, Bridge st

SADDLERS & HARNESS MAKERS.

Blumfield George, Wellclose square

Bridges Job, jun. Market hill

SHOPKEEPERS.

(See also Grocers, &c.)

Aldrich James, Castle street

Butcher George, Bridge street

Dallestone Daniel, Saxtead road

Edwards Elizabeth, Dennington rd

Engledow Sophia, Woodbridge road

Gall Mary, Dennington road

Mallows Stephen, Saxtead road

Middleton Hezekiah, Double street

Middleton Josiah, Castle street

Noble Wm. Saxmundham road

Reeve Samuel, Back street

Smith Samuel, Back street

Waters Charles, Castle street

STONE AND MARBLE MASONS.

Clutten George, Bridge street

Thurlow Henry, Temperance place

STRAW HAT MAKERS.

Bridges Emily, Market hill

Calvert Mary Ann, Bridge street

Clarke Jane, Woodbridge road

Leek Ann, Wellclose square

SURGEONS.

Jeaffreson Wm. Market hill

Willson John, Dennington road

TAILORS.

*(Marked * are Drapers and Hatters.)*

Allured George, Dennington road

Capon Jonathan, Market hill

*Clodd George, Wellclose square

Darling Charles, Castle street

*Farrow Joseph, Wellclose square

Garlett Wm. Alexander, Double st

Measures John, Double street

Newson Stephen, Market hill

Rowland Jas. Buckingham, Castle st

Smith Wm. Market hill; h Back st
Wightman Wm. Double street
Wright Samuel, Double street
VETERINARY SURGEONS.
Rush Wm. Hermitage place
Smith Joseph, Castle street
WATCH AND CLOCK MAKERS.
Barker Samuel Keer, Market hill
Barnes Frederick, Market hill
WHEELWRIGHTS.
Heffer George, Wellclose square
Leggett John, Double street
Moor John, Saxtead road
Wightman Samuel (coach builder,)
Woodbridge road
WHITESMITHS.
Barker Joseph, Double street
Lee George, White Hart lane
WINE AND SPIRIT MERCHANT.
Lankester Edward, Back street
COACHES.
From the Crown and Anchor to *Ipswich*, at ½ past 10 morning, and to Norwich, ½ past 3 afternoon

Omnibus from the Crown, to mee the London steamers at Ipswich every Monday and Thursday

CARRIERS.
Marked 1, go from the Crown; 2, Crown and Anchor ; 3, Hare and Hounds ; 4, Queen's Head ; 5, Waggon and Horses ; and 6, from the White Hart.
To *London*, 5 Noller's Van, Tuesday and Thursday
Halesworth, 2 J. Sawyer, and 4 W. Coates, Tuesday and Saturday
Ipswich, 6 A. Hart, Tues ; 4 Wm. Coates, Mon ; and 3 S. Exworth, Wednesday and Saturday
Norwich, 1 Meen, Tues. & Sat ; 2 J. Sawyer, Tues. & Sat ; 6 A. Hart, Monday ; Chas. Hawes, Tuesday ; and J. Cole, Friday
Woodbridge, 4 Wm. Coates, Mon ; and 6 A. Hart, Tuesday

HACHESTON, a scattered village on the Woodbridge road, 4 miles S. by E. of Framlingham, has in its parish 518 souls, and 1726 acres of land, including the hamlet of *Glevering*, which is distant nearly 6 miles N.N.W. of Woodbridge, and has only 11 inhabitants. *Glevering Hall*, a large and handsome mansion, in an extensive park on the north-east bank of the river Deben, is the seat of Andrew Arcedeckne, Esq., who owns a great part of the parish. *Bloomville Hall*, a neat white-brick mansion, belongs to the Duke of Hamilton, and is occupied by T. Hanbury, Esq. ; and Mr. T. Gregory has an estate and a neat house, near the church. Hacheston has a large *fair*, chiefly for pedlery, &c., held on the 13th of November, pursuant to a charter granted in the 2nd of Henry III., to the Prior and Convent of Hickling, in Norfolk, who were appropriators of this parish, except Glevering, which was given to Leiston priory. The *Church* (All Saints) is an ancient structure on a bold eminence, and near it is a small mausoleum, belonging to the Arcedecknes. The *vicarage*, valued in K.B. at £6. 1s. 11½d., is consolidated with Parham vicarage. Fredk. Corrance, Esq., is patron and impropriator, and the Rev. J. Haggitt, M.A., is the incumbent. The rectorial tithes have been commuted for £278. 12s. 6d. per annum, and the vicarial tithes for £169. 3s. 9d. The *Town Lands*, 14A., let for £25 a year, have been vested from an early period for parochial and charitable uses. The rent is carried to the account of the poor-rates, and partly distributed in coals and clothing, by way of addition to the ordinary parochial relief. A house, occupied by paupers, was built on part of the estate many years ago. The poor have the following *yearly rent-charges*, viz., £2. 14s., left by Mrs. Warner for a distribution of bread once a fortnight ; two of £1. 6s., left by Maximilian Smyth and Edmund Coleman, for weekly distributions of bread ; and one of 13s. 4d. and another of 12s. given by unknown donors, and distributed on Eas-

ter Tuesday. In 1701, *Richard Porter* left a cottage for the residence of a *Schoolmaster*, and a yearly rent-charge of £12 out of his estate here, for the education of 12 poor boys of Hacheston and Parham. The schoolhouse was rebuilt in 1825. The churchwardens and principal inhabitants appoint the master, and his annuity is paid out of an estate belonging to the Earl of Rochford. Here is also a *School*, built and chiefly supported by A. Arcedeckne, Esq., and attended by 75 children, mostly girls.

Arcedeckne Andrew, Esq. *Glevering Hall*
Barker Chas. sweep and beerhouse
Barthropp Mrs Mary
Barthropp Nathl. maltster ; house *Cretingham*
Carver Mr Thomas
Garrett John, chimney sweeper
Gregory Thomas, gentleman
Hanbury Edw. Esq. *Bloomville Hall*
Hill James, veterinary surgeon and vict. Queen's Head
Porter John, bricklayer
Titshall Wm. & Jane, Free Schools
Tricker Php. coachmaker &wheelwg.
  Blacksmiths.
Hill James | Pawsey Abm.

Boot&ShoeMkrs.
Blaxhall Fras.
Cornish Edmund
Hunt John
Smith Henry
Tye Thomas
  Corn Millers.
Brown John, *Glevering*
Titshall Rd.
  FARMERS.
Bond Robert
Clarke Jas. Williams, *Abbey*
Cooke Jonth.
Eade Wm.

Glandfield Stpn. (bailiff,) *Glevg.*
Walker Thomas
  Grocers & Dprs.
Comyn Thomas
Hamond Blomfield
Turner Thomas
  Tailors.
Felgate George
Titshall John
  Carriers& Coaches to Ipswich and Norwich, call at the *Queen's* Head.

HOO, a small scattered village on the southern side of the vale of the Deben, 4 miles S.S.W. of Framlingham, has in its parish 211 souls, and 1163 acres of fertile land, mostly the property of the Duke of Hamilton, (lord of the manor,) Andrew Arcedeckne, Esq., and the Rev. Ellis Walford. *Hoo Hall,* now a farm house, anciently belonged to the Earls of Norfolk and Suffolk ; and an estate called Goodwins, belonging to a family of that name, and was afterwards a seat of the Wingfields. Here were formerly *Guilds*, dedicated to Holy Trinity, St. Mary, St. Peter, St. Andrew, and St. John. The *Church* (St. Andrew and St. Eustachius) was appropriated to Letheringham priory in 1470, by the Duke of Norfolk. It is a perpetual curacy, valued in 1835 at £44, and is now consolidated with that of Letheringham, in the patronage of certain Trustees, who recently purchased the advowson of Mrs. Reynolds, and have provided a Parsonage for the incumbent at Brandeston. (See page 179.) The Rev. John Burt, M.A., now enjoys the benefice, which has recently been augmented by Queen Anne's Bounty. The rectorial tithes have been sold to the landowners. A neat *School House*, for the two parishes, was built by subscription in 1843 on land given by A. Arcedeckne, Esq. The FARMERS are Edward Brooke, Ellis L. Gleed, *Hoo Hall ;* John Gooderham, Jeremiah Gosling, *Goodwin Place ;* John Lewcock, James Scoulding, Richard Hill, *shopkeeper ;* and James Saunders, *parish clerk.*

KENTON, a pleasant village, nearly 3 miles N.N.E. of Debenham, has in its parish 287 souls, and 1209 acres of land, forming a detached member of Loes Hundred. It was formerly the property of the Kentons, who resided at *Kenton Hall,* a large ancient mansion, encompassed by a double moat, and now occupied by a farmer. This hall,

with the manor to which it gives name, now belongs to Wm. Mills, Esq. *Suddon Hall*, another old mansion and manor, is the property of E. Hayward, Esq. Mr. J. Freeman owns Kenton Lodge, and W. Adair, Esq., has an estate in the parish, which is partly in the manors Blood Hall and Crows Hall. (See Debenham.) The families of Willisham, Stane, and Warreyn, were formerly seated in Kenton. The *Church* (All Saints) was appropriated to Butley priory, but was granted to Fras. Framlingham in the 34th of Henry VIII. Lord Henniker is now impropriator, and also patron of the vicarage, valued in K.B. at £8, and now enjoyed by the Rev. Nicholas Wood. The tithes have recently been commuted for a yearly modus of £154. 14s. 6d. to the impropriator, and £150. 5s. to the vicar, who has also 33A. 15P. of glebe, and a good parsonage. The *Church and Parish Lands, &c.*, comprise a double cottage and half an acre, occupied rent-free by the sexton and parish clerk; and a house and 6A. of land at Bedfield, and 10A. at Monk Soham, let together for £16 a year. In 1684, *Wentworth Garneys* bequeathed a house, cottage, and 22A. of land here, to the ministers, churchwardens, and overseers of Kenton and Debenham, for the time being, in trust that they should distribute the rents yearly among the poor of those parishes. This property is let for £31. 10s. a year. *Directory :*—Lucretia Artiss, vict., *Crown ;* Lionel Moyes, *blacksmith ;* Robt. Plant, *shoemaker ;* John Shulver, *wheelwright ;* Rev. Nicholas Wood, *vicar ;* and Abel Ashford, Wm. Bennett, John Clarke, Wm. Clement, Samuel Cupper, John Freemam, Emma Garneys, *(Lodge,)* Wm. Hill, Peter Kersey, *(Hall,)* Samuel Kersey, *(Suddon Hall,)* Eliz. Page, and Wm. Shearing, *farmers*.

KETTLEBURGH, or *Kettleborough*, a small village in a pleasant vale, 2½ miles S.S.W. of Framlingham, has in its parish 355 souls, and about 1400 acres of land. The Duke of Hamilton is lord of the manor, but the principal proprietors of the soil are A. Arcedeckne, Esq., the Earl of Gosford, and the Tollemash, Worrell, and Spedding families. *Kettleburgh Hall*, an ancient mansion, is the seat of Mrs. Garrett. Henry III., in 1265, granted a market and fair here, but they were disused several centuries ago. The *Church* (St. Andrew) is a *rectory*, valued in K.B. at £16, and in 1835 at £290, but the tithes have recently been commuted for £410 per annum. The Earl of Gosford is patron, and the Rev. G. T. Turner, M.A., is the incumbent. The *Town Estate* comprises five tenements, and 4½A. of copyhold land, let for £17. 10s. 6d., and a double cottage let for £4. 2s. per annum. The rents are distributed in coals and money among the poor parishioners.

Alderton Jane, shopkeeper
Cullum Fredk. Wm. corn miller
Garrett Mrs Sarah, *Kettleburgh Hall*
Girling Abraham, shoemaker
Grant John, vict. Chequers
Groom Wm. beerhouse
Hart Samuel, herbalist and *poet*
Jackson Wm. saddler & shopkeeper
Jeaffreson Wm. surgeon, and *Framlingham*
Kent Mary Ann, beerhouse
Kent Wm. tin plate worker
Leeder George, shoemaker

Osborne Walter, blacksmith
Smyth George, tailor
Stokes John, shoemaker
Turner Rev. Geo. Ts. M.A. *Rectory*
Wright James, parish clerk

FARMERS.

Aldrich Elijah ‖ Drew John
Barker James, *Rookery*
Barthropp Edwin Manning
Edwards John ‖ Felgate Thomas
Kindred Edmund, *Hill Farm*
Page Thos. and Pettit James
Pipe Susan ‖ Wilkinson Robert
Smith Robert, *Halfway house*

LETHERINGHAM, on the river Deben, $3\frac{1}{2}$ miles S. by W. of Framlingham, is a village and parish containing 164 souls, and about 1100A. of land. The Duke of Hamilton is lord of the manor, but a great part of the soil belongs to A. Arcedeckne, Esq., and several smaller proprietors. The knightly families of *Wingfield* and *Naunton* were formerly seated here. The *Lodge*, an ancient mansion now occupied by a farmer, is still encompassed by a moat. Here was a small *priory* of Black Canons, founded by Sir John Bovile, as a cell to St. Peter's priory, in Ipswich. It was valued at the dissolution at £26. 18s. 5d., and was granted first to Sir Anthony Wingfield, and afterwards to his daughter. Mrs. Eliz. Naunton. *Sir Robt. Naunton,* secretary of state in the reign of James I., converted it into a good mansion, to which he removed from Alderton, and his successors resided here for several generations. One of them suffered much for his loyalty to Charles I., for whom he fought under Sir Thos. Glemham. (See page 163.) In 1760, their estate devolved on Wm. Leman, Esq., who, about 1770, pulled down most of the old mansion, which contained a fine collection of paintings. What remains of it is now a farm-house. *Sir Anthony Wingfield,* who lived in the reigns of Henry VIII. and Edward VI., had a seat here and at Ipswich, (see page 62,) and one of his family, of the same name, was seated at *Goodwins* in the adjoining parish of Hoo, and was created a *baronet* in 1627. The *Church* (St. Mary) is a small ancient structure, which was repaired and re-pewed in 1797, except the chancel, which had long been in ruins, though it contained several elegant monuments of the Bovile, Wingfield, and Naunton families. Of this chancel, but few traces are now extant. A fine brass effigy of Sir John Wingfield, executed about 1399, was removed from the church many years ago, but has recently been restored by the Marquis of Northampton, after being in various hands. The benefice is a perpetual curacy, which was valued in 1835 at £42. The late Mrs. Reynolds was impropriator of the tithes, and patroness of *Hoo and Letheringham curacies,* but the tithes have recently been sold to the landowners; and " *Certain Trustees"* have purchased the advowson of both livings, which they have consolidated, in the incumbency of the Rev. J. Burt, M.A., who has a parsonage house at Brandeston, and three acres of glebe; and in 1843 received an augmentation of £200 from Queen Anne's Bounty. Near the water mill in Letheringham, several skeletons were found in 1842, in the miller's garden. The FARMERS are James Catchpole, *Abbey;* Moses Crisp, *Old Hall;* Edmund Cuthbert, Thos. Cuthbert, George Drake, *corn miller* and *merchant;* Alfred Packard, George Rivers, and Wm. Toller, *Lodge.*

MARLESFORD, in the vale of the river Ore, 5 miles S.S.E. of Framlingham, and 2 miles N.E. of Wickham Market, is a pleasant village and parish, containing 424 souls, and 1267A. of fertile land, lying in several manors, and including an open common of 30 acres. *Wm. Abm. Shuldham, Esq.,* who owns a great part of the parish, is lord of the manor of Marlesford, and resides at the *Hall,* a neat mansion, in which, on the 18th of July, 1843, he honoured the hundredth anniversary of his birthday, by giving a splendid dinner to his tenantry, and a considerable number of the neighbouring gentry. The Hon. Mrs. North, A. Arcedeckne, Esq., Rev. G. Crabbe, G. Bates, Esq., and a few smaller owners, have astates in the parish. The *Church* (St.

Andrew) is a rectory, valued in K.B. at £9. 6s. 8d., and in 1835, at £285; but the tithes have recently been commuted for a yearly modus of £380. A. Arcedeckne, Esq., is patron, and the Rev. G. H. Porter, M.A., is the incumbent, and has a good residence and 30A. of glebe. *Sir Walter Devereux*, in the 8th of James I., left a yearly rent-charge of £6, for the relief of the poor, out of a house and land here, now belonging to G. Bates, Esq., and formerly called Mapes's. The poor parishioners have also £8. 6s. 7d. yearly from *Kersey's Charity*, (see Charsfield;) and a yearly rent-charge of 52s. left by *John Smith*, in 1693, for a weekly distribution of 1s. worth of bread, at the church.

Beedon Thomas, joiner
Bloss Robert, shopkeeper
Bolton Thos. gent. *Hill House*
Cornish Robert, wheelwright
Goodwin Geo. gardener & seedsman
Kindred James, butcher
Minter Rebecca, vict., *Bell*
Pawsey Isaac, blacksmith
Porter Rev. Geo. Hy. M.A., rector, Rectory
Scrivens Thomas, shoemaker

Shuldham Wm. Abraham, Esq., *Marlesford Hall*
SolomonJohnWhite, shoemkr.&shopr
Stannard Benjamin, corn miller
Wade Wm. shoemaker
Woods John, shoemaker

FARMERS.

Cordy John || Largent John
Largent Henry, *Hall Farm*
Markham Mary || Skeet James
Wilkinson Eliz. || Thurlow Wm.
Wilkinson Robert, *Common*

MONEWDEN, a village and parish, 5½ miles S.W. of Framlingham, and 6 miles S.E. of Debenham, contains 220 souls, and about 1063A. of land. Wm. Adair, Fsq., owns a great part of the soil, and is lord of the manor, which was called *Mungaden* at the Domesday survey, and was then held by Odo de Campania, and afterwards by the Hastings and Currys. The *Church* (St. Mary) has a tower and three bells. The *rectory*, valued in K.B. at £8. 13s. 4d., is in the gift of A. Arcedeckne, Esq., and incumbency of the Rev. Geo. T. Turner. The tithes have been commuted for a yearly modus of £292. The common was enclosed in 1832, and a portion of it awarded to the poor. DIRECTORY :— John D. Bishop, *corn miller and shopkeeper ;* Thos. Hunt, *shoemaker ;* Jph. Leach, *thatcher ;* Joshua Shulver, *wheelwgt. and parish clerk ;* John Ward, *blacksmith ;* and Abm. Kersey Blofield*, *Monewden Hall ;* Zach. Button, A. Catchpole, Edward Freeman, Eliz. Garnham, Samuel Gooderham, Geo. Gooderham,* William Gooderham, Eliz. Meadows, Jas. Peck*, Thos. Threadkell*, and Thos. Todd, *farmers.* (Those marked * are landowners.)

RENDLESHAM, a pleasant, scattered village, 5 miles N.E. of Woodbridge, and 3 miles S.E. of Wickham Market, has in its parish 325 souls, and about 2065A. of land, all (except 50A. of glebe,) the property of *Lord Rendlesham, M.P.*, the lord of the manor, who resides at RENDLESHAM HALL, a large and handsome mansion, of flint and stone, delightfully situated in an extensive park, and erected since Feb. 2nd, 1830, when the old hall, called *Rendlesham White House*, was burnt down by an accidental fire, which originated in one of the conservatories, and destroyed most of the furniture, books, and pictures. The old hall stood about ¼ of a mile from the site of the present mansion. The parish is supposed to have had its mame from *Rendilus*, one of the Saxon monarchs of East Anglia. Redwald, another king of the East Angles, kept his court here, and received Christianity, but being after-

wards seduced by his wife, he is said to have had in the church an altar
for the religion of Christ, and " another little altar for the sacrifice of
Devils." Sudhelm, also King of the East Angles, was afterwards bap-
tized here, by Cedda, archbishop of York. An ancient silver crown
was found here, in the beginning of last century, weighing about sixty
ounces, and supposed to have belonged to some of the East Anglian
kings; but it was sold for old silver, and melted down. Edward I.
granted Hugh Fitz-Otho the privilege of a market and fair here. Hugh
de Naunton had a grant of free warren in Rendlesham, in the second
of Edward II. Rendlesham House, which was a stately mansion, in the
Tudor style, became the property of the Spencers, in the reign of Edward VI., and continued in that family till it was vested in James, the
fifth Duke of Hamilton, by his marriage with Elizabeth, daughter and
heiress of Edward Spencer. The Duchess resided here after the death
of her husband. At her decease, the estate descended to her son, the
late Duke, who sold it Sir George Wombwell, from whom it was purchased, for £51,400, by Peter Isaac Thellusson, Esq., who was raised
to an Irish peerage in 1806, by the title of *Lord Rendlesham,* and
greatly improved and beautified his seat here, where he and his successor were visited, not only by many of the first nobility, but also by several branches of the Royal Family. *The Hon. Frederick Thellusson,*
the third and present *Lord Rendlesham,* was elected one of the parliamentary representatives of the Eastern Division of Suffolk, in 1843, in
place of the late Sir Charles Broke Vere. He succeeded to the title in
1839, was born in 1798, and is heir to the immense property still under
the control of the trustees of the late P. J. Thellusson, Esq. The *Church*
(St. Gregory) is a small ancient structure, and the living is a *rectory,*
valued in K.B. at £4. 13s. 4d., but has now 50a. of glebe, and a yearly
modus of £420. The patronage is in the Crown, and the Hon. and
Rev. Thomas Hay is the incumbent. The *Town Estate* was appropriated at an early period for the reparation of the church and the relief of the poor; but all the rent has for many years been applied with
the poor rates. On five roods of the land, four cottages, occupied by
paupers, have been built. The other land consists of 1a. 2r. 26p., in
Rendlesham, let to the rector for £2; and 11a. 1r. 33p. in Snape, let
for £12 a year. A commodious *School* was built here, by Lord Rendlesham, in 1840, and is supported by his lordship, for the education
of poor children of this and the adjoining parishes. DIRECTORY :—
Lord Rendlesham, M.P., *Rendlesham Hall ;* Hon. and Rev. Thomas
Hay, *Rectory ;* Joseph Hassell, *schoolmaster ;* Wm. Allen, *gardener ;*
George Last, *house steward ;* George Cooper, *farmer, High House ;*
A. Sheming, *farmer, Naunton Hall ;* and Geo. Thurston, *farmer,
Red House.*

WOODBRIDGE.

WOODBRIDGE, a thriving and well-built *market-town and port*, is pleasantly situated on the western bank of the Deben, about 9 miles above the mouth of that broad river, 8 miles E.N.E. of Ipswich, 11 miles W. of Orford, 13 miles S.W. of Saxmundham, 11 miles S. of Framlingham, and 77 miles N.E. of London. Its *population* amounted, in 1801, to 3020 ; in 1811, to 4332 ; in 1821, to 4060 ; in 1831, to 4768 ; and in 1841, to 4952 souls, including 35 in the small hamlet and manor of *Kingston*. Its PARISH comprises about 1650 acres of fertile land, forming a detached member of Loes Hundred, from which it is separated by Wilford Hundred. It gives name to the *Woodbridge Union and Superintendent Registrar's District*, which has its Board-room and principal officers here, but its Workhouse at Nacton, 8 miles from the town, as already described at page 119. It is a *polling place* at the election of the parliamentary representatives of the Eastern Division of Suffolk, and may be considered the capital of the *Liberty of St. Ethelred*, which comprises the neighbouring Hundreds of Loes, Colneis, Carlford, Wilford, Plomesgate, and Thredling, commonly called the *Woodbridge Division*, for which QUARTER SESSIONS are held here, in January, April, June, and October ; and *Petty Sessions* every Wednesday. Rollo Rouse, Esq., is lord of the manor of Woodbridge, but a great part of the parish is in two other manors, one of which, called *Kingston*, belongs to the Dean and Chapter of Ely. Here are many small copyholds and freeholds. In Domesday Book, this town is called *Udebryge*, of which its present name is no doubt a corruption ; though some writers have asserted that it derived its name from a *wooden bridge*, built over a hollow way between two parks, near the road to Ipswich, where, in Kirby's time, there was a house called *Dry Bridge*. On the south side of the church, formerly stood a PRIORY of Augustine canons, founded by Sir Hugh Rous, or Rufus, and endowed with the church, one of the manors of Woodbridge, and many other possessions. It stood near the house now called the *Abbey*, and within it were interred many individuals of the knightly families of Rouse, Breos or Brews, and Weyland. On its dissolution, in the 33rd of Henry VIII., it was valued at £50. 3s. 5½d. per annum, and was granted, with the advowson of the church, to *John Wingfield*, and Dorothy his wife, in special tail male ; and on his death without issue, it was granted in fee to *Thomas Seckford, Esq.*, the founder of the richly endowed almshouses here. In his family it remained till 1673, when it passed, by the will of Mrs. Dorothy Seckford, into the family of the Norths, of Laxford, from whom it passed to the Carthews. After the decease of the Rev. Thomas Carthew, in 1791, the Priory estate was divided and sold, at which time, the mansion called the *Abbey*, was purchased by Francis Brook, Esq., of Ufford, and it is now the property of C. S. Sharpe, Esq.; but the family of Carthew still has a residence here. In 1666, Woodbridge was visited by the plague, which carried off the minister, his wife and child, and upwards of 300 of the inhabitants. The parish of *Melton* forms a handsome suburb of Woodbridge, and in it is situated *Suffolk Lunatic Asylum*, already described at page 146.

The *Town* has been much improved during the last twenty years by the formation of several new streets, and the erection of many neat houses, and several handsome public buildings. The eminence on which it stands commands a pleasant view down the broad river *Deben*, which falls into the sea at the distance of nine miles, and is navigable for vessels of 120 tons burthen up to the town, where there are two commodious quays, extensive warehouses, and a ship-yard with a patent slip. The principal street, called the *Thoroughfare*, is nearly a mile in length, and the Market place is spacious, and has in its centre a Shire-Hall, built in the reign of Elizabeth, in which the Sessions are held; but the prisoners are sent to the House of Correction at Ipswich, the old *Bridewell* here being now only used as a police station, and a place of temporary confinement, though in 1835 it had many prisoners, crowded together without any classification of the sexes, and having only one day room, eleven feet by eight. The number confined here, for various periods in that year, was 140. The cross streets though some of them are narrow, contain many good houses, and are well paved; and lighted from *Gas Works*, established in 1815, at the cost of about £6000, and now belonging to six shareholders. The town is well supplied with water, and the eminence on which it stands is remarkably healthy, and surrounded by pleasant walks, commanding fine views of the Deben, on which a numerous *Yacht Club* hold sailing and rowing matches frequently; and in July there is a grand *Regatta*, terminated by fireworks and festivities in the evening. The Market, held every Wednesday, is extensively supplied with corn and cattle; and here are two annual Fairs, viz., on the first Tuesday in April, for cattle, horses, &c.; and October 2nd and 3rd, for toys and pleasure. R. N. Shawe, Esq., is chairman, and Mr. J. Wood, jun., secretary of the *Woodbridge Farmers' Club*, which has a numerous list of members. The want of a covered market place has long been felt, and the erection of one is now (August, 1843) in contemplation. *Salt* was formerly made here, and *ships of war*, of small magnitude, were built here about seventy years ago; but one of the docks, then in use below the Common Quay, has been filled up. During the late war, there were barracks for about 6000 soldiers, about a mile from the town, near the Ipswich road. Two *Ferry Boats* cross the river to Sutton, and at Melton, about a mile above the town, is a *new quay*. The commerce of Woodbridge has much increased of late years, and there are now belonging to the port about 50 *vessels*, having an aggregate burden of about 3000 tons. The number of *coasting vessels*, which arrive and sail with cargoes, is about 350 yearly, and their aggregate burden from 15,000 to 20,000 tons; and from 10 to 15 *foreign cargoes* arrive yearly. The *exports* consist chiefly of corn, flour, and malt; there being in the town extensive granaries, and several mills and malt kilns. The *imports* are chiefly coal, timber, wine, spirits, groceries, drapery, and iron wares. Here are *bonded warehouses* for timber, wood goods, wines, and spirits; and the merchants trade regularly with London, Newcastle, Hull, Liverpool, and occasionally with the continent of Europe, and the Baltic. The *Customs* collected here in 1834, amounted to £2263, and in 1840 to £4315. The Custom House is in Quay lane, and the officers are Percy Lee, Esq., *collector ;* Mr. W. Gross, *comptroller ;* and Mr. J. Woodrow, locker and tide waiter.

Lieut. J. Holbrook, R.N., is chief officer of the *coast guard*. The Excise Office is at the Crown Tavern, but the port is in the Ipswich collection. (See page 64.) Mr. J. H. Halls is the *supervisor and port surveyor*. Mr. Merry and G. Phillips are division officers and permit writers, and Mr. Wm. Law is riding officer. Fifty years ago, only one daily coach and a weekly waggon passed through the town to and from London; but more than twelve *conveyances* (coaches, omnibuses, and carriers' waggons and carts) now pass daily between the hours of six in the morning and twelve at noon; and persons may travel from Woodbridge to London in five hours, for 10s., instead of paying three times that amount, and being thirteen hours on the road, as was formerly the case.

The Parish Church *(St. Mary)* is a spacious and handsome structure of black flint and free stone, supposed to have been built in the reign of Edward III. by John, Lord Segrave, and his wife, Margaret de Brotherton, whose arms are yet to be seen over the door of the large and lofty quadrangular tower which has, in the upper part, the stone and flints beautifully intermixed in various devices. The roofs of the nave and aisles are supported by ten beautiful Gothic pillars and four demi ones. The north portico is decorated in front with the representation, in relievo, of Michael, the arch-angel, encountering the Dragon. Since 1839, *George Thomas, Esq.*, has, at his own expense, laid out nearly £1000 in repairing and beautifying this noble edifice, which he has decorated with several beautiful stained glass windows, and improved by the erection of a new porch. Here were formerly altars of St. Anne and St. Saviour, and a celebrated image of our Lady; and in the north aisle was a chapel, dedicated to St. Nicholas. Adjoining the north side of the chancel is a private chapel, erected by *Thomas Seckford, Esq.*, one of the Masters of the Court of Requests, and Surveyor of the Court of Wards and Liveries in the reign of Elizabeth, and the founder of the almshouses here. This munificent benefactor of Woodbridge was interred in this chapel, under a large altar tomb, which was stripped of its brass inscriptions, &c., in 1643, by Dowsing, the Parliamentary visitor. He was not less distinguished in the profession of the law, than in the other polite accomplishments of the age in which he lived; and to his patronage to his servant Christopher Saxton, the public was indebted for the first set of county maps, which were engraved by his encouragement, and at his expense. He built the Sessions House at Woodbridge, giving the upper part of it to the use of the county for ever. He represented Ipswich in three Parliaments, and died without issue in 1588, aged 72. The steeple and some other parts of the church were repaired about the middle of the 15th century, as appears from numerous legacies left for that purpose. Here is a mutilated inscription of *John Albrede*, a "twill-weaver," who left 20 marks towards repairing the steeple, and was at the expense of carving, gilding, and painting the rood-loft, in which were the pictures of the cross and crucifix, the Virgin Mary, and several arch-angels, saints, and martyrs, figured, as we are told, to the life, but all destroyed by Dowsing in 1643. The benefice is a *perpetual curacy*, which was certified at £45, and valued in 1835 at £439 per annum. W. C. Betham, Esq., is the patron, and the Rev. T. S. Bomford, the incumbent.

St. John's Church was erected in 1842-'3 to supply that lack of church-room which had long been felt in this improving town. It is a fine specimen of the simple, yet beautiful early English style, and cost about £3500, raised by subscription. It has about 800 sittings ; and an elegant spire, rising 138 feet, and terminated by a finial of Caen stone, forming two crosses intersecting each other diagonally, and decorated with foliage thrown out in bold relief. The foundation stone was laid, June 30th, 1842, by George Thomas, Esq., one of the principal contributors to the fabric, and the event was celebrated by a splendid procession of Free Masons. Mr. J. M. Clark, of Ipswich, was the architect, and Mr. A. Lockwood, of Woodbridge, was contractor for the building. There are in the town two *Independent Chapels*, built in 1805 and 1841, by congregations which date their origin from 1651 and 1787. Here are also an old *Friend's Meeting House*, a *Baptist Chapel*, and a *Wesleyan Chapel ;* the latter built in 1829. The Mechanics' Institution, established here in 1835, is in a flourishing condition, and has a library of about 2000 volumes. G. Moore, Esq., is president; G. Thomas, Esq., vice-president ; and Mr. Alfred Taylor. librarian. There are in the town several Religious and Charitable Societies, Sick Clubs, and Secret Orders, a *Shipwrecked Seamen's Benevolent Society*, (established in 1840 ;) a *Savings' Bank ;* richly endowed *Almshouses ;* and several *schools and charities*, for the education and relief of the poor.

Free School :—In 1662, *Robert Marryott* conveyed to certain trustees his copyhold messuage in Woodbridge, and the buildings, yards, garden, and orchard thereunto belonging, in trust for the use and residence of a schoolmaster. By the same deed, four *rent-charges* amounting to £25 per annum, were settled upon the master for teaching ten poor children—viz., £5 given by the said Robt. Marryott, out of land called Brayes, in Bredfield ; £5 given by *Fras. Burwell*, out of a messuage at Sutton ; £5 given by *Dorothy Seckford*, out of land in Great Bealings ; and £10 given by the feoffees of the town lands, out of the Lamb Farm. By a decree of the Court of Chancery in 1800, it was ordered that the schoolmaster and the ten free scholars should be elected by the perpetual curate, the churchwardens, and six of the principal parishioners ; and that the master should charge only £3 a year each for teaching other children of Woodbridge, but might make his own terms for those sent from other parishes. The free-scholars are selected from the poor families of Woodbridge. They are instructed with the other scholars in writing, arithmetic, mathematics, and mensuration, and also in the *Latin and Greek Tongues*, when required. Besides the use of the school premises and the £25 per annum noticed above, the master has 2a. 3r. 36p. of land, left by *Francis Willard* in 1679, and now let for £8 a year. The school and master's house were repaired and partly rebuilt in 1835, at the cost of about £500. The Rev. Thos. W. Hughes, B.A., is the present master. Here is also a National School, built in 1812, at the cost of about £1500, and having room for about 150 children of either sex ; and in Castle street is another large *School*, in two apartments, connected with the British and Foreign School Society, erected in 1840, at the cost about £900, and now attended by about 80 boys and 70 girls.

The Town Lands are situated in the parish of Martlesham, ad-

joining that of Woodbridge, and consist of the *Lamb Farm*, comprising three tenements, out-buildings, and 51 A. 20 P. of copyhold land, given by *John Dodd*, in the reign of Henry VII., for the maintenance of the poor and the benefit of the town; and the *Street Farm*, containing 9 A. 2 R. 39 P. of copyhold land, given by *Jeffery Pitman* in 1687, for the reparation and maintenance of the church. They are let for £56 a year, out of which £10 a year is contributed towards the support of the free school; and the remainder, after the payment of £5. 6s. 4d. for land tax and quit rents, is applied in the service of the church. In 1660, the churchwardens and principal parishioners let on lease for 999 years, at the yearly rent of 10s., the *Town Common* (about 11 A.) which had been used from time immemorial by the parishioners; and also for the same term, at the annual rent of 2s. 6d., about a rood of land, which had been left to the poor by *John Sayer*. This property now comprises a dockyard, shipyard, quay, &c., let by the present lessee for about £400 a year, out of which he pays only 10s. yearly to the churchwardens for what was formerly the town common, and 2s. 6d. yearly for the site of a house standing on the land given by John Sayer. The POOR'S HOUSES comprise a house in Pound street, given by *Wm. Bearman* in 1668, and long used as the parish workhouse; two houses and a garden belonging to the parish, and formerly used as *pest-houses;* a house in New street, formerly used as a bridewell, and purchased by the parish in 1641; two houses in Turn lane, given by *Wm. Smith* and *Jeffery Pitman*, in 1608; and two houses in the Thoroughfare, also given by Wm. Bearman. These premises are all occupied rent-free by paupers or poor persons. Two pieces of land belonging to two of the houses, are let for £2. 4s. 6d. a year, which is carried to the poor-rates, out of which the cost of repairing the houses is paid.

SECKFORD'S ALMSHOUSES.—Queen Elizabeth, in the 29th year of her reign, by letters patent, gave license to *Thomas Seckford, Esq.*, to found an almshouse of the seven tenements lately built by him at Woodbridge, for the constant residence of thirteen poor men, twelve of them to occupy six of the tenements, and one to occupy the seventh, and to be called the Principal; and her Majesty thereby ordained that the Chief Justice of the Common Pleas, and the lord of the manor of *Seckford Hall*, (see page 130,) if he should be the heir-male of the body of the late Thomas Seckford, Esq.,—if not, the Master of the Rolls of the Court of Chancery,—should be *governors of the almshouse*, and of the lands and possessions thereof; and that they should be a body corporate, and should have power to make statutes and ordinances for the government of the almspeople. In 1587, the founder ordained that the 13 almsmen should have the use of the gardens, and about three acres of land near the almshouse, and of the well or fountain in his newly enclosed park of Woodbridge, and that they should have a yearly supply of fuel and gowns, and each an annual stipend of £5, except the Principal, who should have £6. 13s. 4d. yearly. He also gave a tenement called *Copthall*, and two acres of land, for the use of three poor widows, to be *nurses* to such of the poor men as should be sick or infirm, and to have each a yearly stipend of £2. 13s. 4d. By his will in the same year, he endowed the almshouse with various houses, buildings, yards, gardens, and other pieces of land in the parish of St.

James, Clerkenwell, London, then of the yearly value of £112. 13s. 4d. This estate is now one of the most improving parts of the metropolis, and had increased, in 1768, to the yearly value of £563. In 1826, an act of Parliament was obtained to enable the governors of the alms-house to grant building and other leases, to take down many of the old buildings, to erect new premises and repair and alter old ones, and to lay out new streets on the charity estate in Clerkenwell, which now comprises Seckford street, Woodbridge street, Suffolk street, and one side of St. John street, Aylesbury street, St. James' walk, Prison walk, and Corporation row. This estate, including the buildings upon it, belonging to the almshouse, produced, in 1830, a rental of more than £3000 per annum ; but as a great part of the most valuable building sites in the new streets were then unlet, the yearly rental is now more than £4000. The Charity Commissioners, in 1830, were informed by the governors' solicitor that no alterations had been made in the allow-ances to the almspeople, or other payments, since 1768, when the rental of the estate was only £563 per annum, but that it was the intention of the governors, as soon as the building ground was let, to apply for an act of Parliament for the future regulation of the charity funds; and that the sum of £3456, three per cent. stock, and all other savings of the income, had been expended in obtaining the act of Parliament of 1826, in redeeming the land-tax,—in building new sewers, drains, and arched cellars,—in forming new roads, and in otherwise improving the Clerkenwell estate. The *yearly sums* paid out of the rents to the ob-jects of the charity, till some years after 1830, were,—£27 to the Prin-cipal ; £20 to each of the other twelve *almsmen ;* £12 to each of the three *nurses ;* £13 to an extra nurse; £10 to the minister, and £10 to the churchwardens of Woodbridge ; £12 to the receiver of the rents ; about £152 for distributions of clothing and coals among the almspeople and other poor of Woodbridge ; about £17 for medical attendance; about £30 for repairs, &c. ; and about £10 each to Woodbridge and Clerkenwell, for distribution among the poor of those parishes. In 1838, the governors commenced the erection of a NEW HOSPITAL, in lieu of and near the Old Almshouses, for the residence of 26 *men and* 6 *nurses,* and they now allow each of the latter a yearly stipend of £20, and each of the former £25 a year, except the *Principal,* who has £80 a year, and has the superintendence of the other inmates, under the direction of the minister and churchwardens of Woodbridge. They are also supplied with coals, clothing, and medical attendance. The New Hospital is an elegant building, in the Elizabethan style, comprising two wings, with a handsome chapel in the centre. It was erected at the cost of £15,000, from a design by J. Noble, Esq., the architect. It contains two rooms for each of the 32 inmates, and they have each a small garden. The *Old Almshouses* were new fronted in 1824, and are now let at low rents to poor widows. The church-wardens of Woodbridge are the administrators of this charity, under the control of the governors.

John Sayer, in 1637, left 15a. 2r. 26p. of land at Melton, in trust, that the rents thereof should be applied in a weekly dole of 15 two-penny loaves, and a yearly distribution of clothing among the poor of Woodbridge. The land is partly copyhold, and is let for about £30 a year, which is distributed by the churchwardens in bread, of which 42

threepenny loaves are given every Sunday among the aged poor attending the church. A yearly rent-charge of 40s., left by ALICE OSBORN, in 1677, out of her messuage called the Malting Office, is distributed among the poor parishioners in coals. For a distribution of bread on Candlemas-day, they have a yearly rent-charge of 20s., left by GEORGE CARLOW, in 1738, out of a house in New street. In 1781, JOHN RUDLAND charged his estate at Hasketon with the yearly payment of £3 to the pastor and deacons of the Congregational Meeting House in Woodbridge, to be laid out in three gowns for three poor widows of the parish, on the 2nd of April.

WOODBRIDGE DIRECTORY.

POST-OFFICE: Mr. Wm. Row, *postmaster*, Cumberland street. The London Mail is despatched at ½ past 10 night, and the North Mail (to Saxmundham, Yarmouth, &c.) at ½ past 4 morning. Letters are despatched to Framlingham, Wickham market, Orford, &c., at 6 morning. The *box closes* at ½ past 8 evening.

The CONTRACTIONS occasionally used are *Mkp. for Market place ; Cumbd. st. for Cumberland street ; and Thfare. for Thoroughfare*

MISCELLANY *of persons not arranged under the heads of Trades and Professions*

(See also Melton, page 147.)

Alderson Miss Sophia, Cumbd. st
Aldrich Hy. bank agent, New street
Aldous Mr Wm. Seckford street
Alexander J.B. Esq. banker, Church st
Ashford E. pawnbroker, Thoroughfare
Amos Sarah, lodgings, New street
Amos Mr James, Castle street
Bacon Miss Sarah, Seckford street
Baldry Mrs Mary, Church street
Barton Bernard *(poet,)* Thoroughfare
Betham Misses My. & Emma. Castle st
Betts Mr John, jun. Thoroughfare
Blanden Jas. bird preserver, Castle st
Blowers Robt. whiting mfr. Quay lane
Bomford Rev T. S. *Rectory*
Borrows Joshua, farmer, Brewer's ln
Brighten Clark, gardener, Seckford Almshouses
Brooke Thomas, gent. Burkett road
Cana Robert, auctioneer and commissioner for taking special bail, Thoroughfare
Causton William, professor of music, Castle street
Chappell Wm. George, parish clerk, Church street
Clarke Mrs Sarah, New street
Cole Thos. fishmonger, Theatre st
Collett Rev Woodthorpe, M.A. curate of Bromeswell, Burkett road

Cordy Mrs H. *Burkett Lodge*
Cotton Miles, relieving officer, Cumberland street
Daniels Jph. fishmonger, Church st
Devereux Jas. eating house, Thfare
Dodman John, ship agent, &c. Brook st
Doughty Fredk. gent. Cumberland st
Dowsing Mrs Lydia, Thoroughfare
Easter Mr James, Queen's head lane
Fish Thos. sheep dresser, Seckford st
Fisher Richd. farmer, Bredfield st
Fisk Wm. carrier, Theatre street
Gall Benjamin, chief constable, sub-distributor of stamps, & secretary to Savings' Bank, Thoroughfare
Gammage William B. wharfinger, Brewer's lane
George Wm. music dlr. &c. Church st
Giles Thomas, gent. Thoroughfare
Gissing James, sexton, Seckford st
Gobbett James, farmer, *Kingston*
Godbould Geo. vety. surgeon, Thfare
Goodwin Mrs Eliz. Church street
Gourham Mrs F. D. Seckford street
Green Robert, carrier, New street
Gross Jas. bank agent, osier grower, &c. Thoroughfare
Gross Mr Robert, Cumberland st
Gross Wm. comptroller, Cumbd. st
Halls Jas. Hy. supervisor and port surveyor, Sandy hill
Hayward Rev Thos. Seckford street
Head Mrs Mary, Seckford street
How Mrs Ann, Cumberland street
Keeble Mrs Sarah, Brook street
Keeble Wm. Swedish & Norwegian vice-consul, and ship and custom house agent, Common quay

Kemp Wm. sen., colr. of poor rates, & regstr. of marriages, Market pl
Lamb George, gent. Thoroughfare
Lankester John, river surveyor, Cumberland street
Lankester Rbt. bank clerk, Cumbd. st
Lark James, inspector of police, Theatre street
Law Wm. excise officer, Castle st
Lawrence Wm. farrier, Theatre st
Leek Thos. game dlr. Thoroughfare
Leggett Mr John, Thoroughfare
Lee Percy, Esq., collector of customs, Quay lane
Linsted John, gent. Castle street
Loder Edwd. superintendent, *Seckford Almshouses*
London Wm. bank clerk, Cumbd. st
Long Mrs Martha, Cumberland st
Lynn Geo. D. physician, Church st
Mallett Mrs Eliz. Seckford street
Mason Joseph, clerk, Cumberland st
Moulton Benj. union clerk, auctioneer, &c. Thoroughfare
Nanton Miss Sarah, Cumberland st
Newson Thos. carrier, New s'reet
Olding Sarah, lodgings, Market pl
Oxborrow Edw. gun mkr. Market pl
Payne Rev J. (Weslyn.) Brook st
Packard Mrs Agnes, Thoroughfare
Read Mrs Rachel, Seckford street
Rodgers Rev Thos. curate, Seckford st
Ross Rev. John (Indpt.) Castle st
Row Wm. postmaster, Cumberland st
Russell Miss Sus. Thoroughfare
Salkeld Fras. gent. Cumberland st
Scarnell Mrs Ann, Theatre street
Shaming Thos. gent. Cumberland st
Sharpe Chas. S. Esq. *Abbey House*
Sheppard Mrs L., Cumberland st
Simpson Misses M. E. & C., New st
Sizer Mrs Ann, Thoroughfare
Skinner John, green grocer, Thfare
Smith Wm. pilot, Brewer's lane
Smith Henry, John, & Robert, carriers, Thoroughfare
Spalding Mrs Eliz. Cumberland st
Stananought Alfred, engraver, Thfare
Stimpson John, sawyer, Castle st
Sutton Mrs Charlotte, Seckford st
Syred Mrs Betty, Seckford street
Taylor Rev Hy. (Indept.) Chapel ln
Taylor Mrs Eliz. Seckford street
Thomas George, Esq. Thoroughfare
Thompson Geo. Edward, bank agent & wine mert; h Thoroughfare
Thompson Philip, gent. Thoroughfr

Thurton J. registrar of births & dths
Tills Misses Hanh. & Eliz. Seckford st
Topple Sarah, fishmonger, Thfare
Turner Robert, farmer, Brewer's ln
Vertue Simon, clerk, Brewer's lane
Wainwright Mrs M. Thoroughfare
Warren Mr A. P., Seckford street
Watson Rev Cphr. George, rector of Melton ; house Church street
Weeding John, horse letter, Thfare
Whimper Mr Wm. (R.N.) Theatre st
Wilson Wm. town crier, Angel lane
Wittey Rev John Francis, curate, Seckford street
Wood John, sen., solicitor ; h *Melton*
Woodrow James, locker and tide waiter, Quay lane
Woods Mrs Eliz. Market place
Woolnough Mr James and Mrs L., Seckford street
Wright John, bird presrvr. Brook st

ACADEMIES.

*Marked * take Boarders.*

*Aldous M. E. (ladies) Seckford st
Cadman Cath. (infant) Castle st
Fenn John, Cumberland street
British School, Wm. & Sarah Gayfer, Castle street
**Grammar School*, Rev Thos. Williams Hughes, B.A.
Hayden Wm. Thoroughfare
Hitchcock George, Theatre street
*Knight Ann, Cumberland street
National School, Godfrey and Mary Gurney, Burkett road
Patrick John, Theatre lane
Pizey M. A. Thoroughfare
Porter Robert, Cumberland street
Scarnell Lucy, Seckford street
Smyth Mary Ann, New street
Welton Jane, Cumberland street
*Winter Caroline, Cumberland st

ATTORNEYS.

*Marked * are Commssrs. for taking Acknowledgmts. of Mard. Women.*

Brooke Cooper Chas. Cumberland st. (firm, Meadows and Brooke)
*Carthew Thomas, (superintendent registrar,) Thoroughfare
Churchyard Thomas, Cumberland st
Gissing Sml. Newson, Cumberland st
Meadows & Brooke, Cumberland st
Meadows Dl. Chas.; h Cumberland st
*Moor Chas. & Son, Cumberland st. (Chas. is treasurer of Woodbrdg. Div. ; & Geo. inspctr. of corn rets)
Rouse Rolla (barrister,) *Melton*

*Wood John, jun. (coroner, & clerk to magistrates & comms. of taxes,) Church st; house Thoroughfare

AUCTIONEERS.

Cana and Moulton, Thoroughfare
Elvis George, *Melton*
Pizey Henry, (& collector of taxes,) Cumberland street

BAKERS & FLOUR DLRS.

Aston James, Castle walk
Barritt James, Church street
Daniels Wm. Cumberland street
Fisher Wm. New street
Fisher Susan, Thoroughfare
Gammage Benjamin, Thoroughfare
Gammage James, Cumberland st
Gammage Wm. Cumberland street
Hayman M., New street
King James, Seckford street
Leek Anthony, Thoroughfare
Mayhew James, Market place
Palmer Henry, Seckford street
Pooley Henry, Theatre street
Richardson Thomas, Thoroughfare
Scruton Wm. Brook street
Wright John, Bredfield street

BANKERS.

Alexanders & Co. Church st. (draw on Barnett, Hoares, and Co.)
National Provincial Bank of England, New st. (on London Joint Stock Bank ;) Henry Aldrich, agt
Suffolk Banking Co. Thoroughfare, (on London&Westminster Bank ;) Gross & Thompson, agents
Savings' Bank, Thoroughfare; Benj. Gall, *secretary*

BASKET MAKERS, &c.

Gross James, Thoroughfare
Leek Timothy, Thoroughfare
Woods Isaac, New street

BLACKSMITHS.

Butcher James, Theatre street
Dowsing John, Chapel lane
Ellis Jonathan, Sun lane
Fisher Richard, Common quay

BOOKSELRS., PRINTERS, &c.

Loder John, (& news agent) Thfare
Munro John Donald, Market place
Pite Edward, Church street

BOOT & SHOE MAKERS.

Allen John, Seckford street
Barnes Ann, New street
Barnes John, New street
Barnes Robert, (sheriff's officer,) Seckford street
Bowles James, Brewer's lane

Bumstead Charles, Thoroughfare
Carr James, Thoroughfare
Duffield Thomas, New street
Gillingham Wm. Seckford street
Hunt James, Thoroughfare
Larter Jonathan, Bredfield street
Martin Wm. Seckford street
Mickleburgh Wm. Seckford street
Patrick John, Angel lane
Spore J., Angel lane
Stanton Robert, Church street
Taylor Joseph Fuller, New street
Threadkell Wm. Cumberland street
Turner Wm. Chapel lane
Webb James, sen. Thoroughfare
Welton Nathaniel, New street
Wilson John, Market place
Wright Wm. Church street

BRAZIERS & TINNERS.

Bird John, Angel lane
Neeve John, Thoroughfare
Turner George, Thoroughfare

BREWERS.

Aston James, Castle walk
Edwards Henry, Thoroughfare
Kersey Richard, Bredfield street
Lockwood Wm. (& porter merchant) Castle brewery

BRICK & TILE MAKERS.

Peak & Dorling, *Melton*

BRICKLAYERS.

Fisk John, Bredfield street
Morrell Edward, Castle street
Sparkes Isaiah R. and Co., (& plasterers,) Haymarket

BUTCHERS.

Bolton James, Market place
Button George, Cumberland street
Brinkley Wm. Church street
Churchyard Lucy, Market place
Clark Benj. Castle street
Culham Wm. (pork) New street
Gosling Aldous, Thoroughfare
Oxborrow John, Cumberland street
Pooley Sarah, New street
Turner John, (& cattle dlr) Thfare
Turner George, Thoroughfare
Turner Wm. Church street
Turner Wm. Seckford street
Whitehouse James, Angel lane

CABINET MAKERS AND UPHOLSTERERS.

Ellisdon Joseph (*upholsterer and appraiser*) Thoroughfare
Fisher John, Bredfield street
Fisher Wm. Thoroughfare
Fisk Samuel, Market place

Gennills John, New street
Goodwin Wm. Thoroughfare
Hayward Joseph (and turner) Mkp
Head Samuel, New street
King David, Theatre street
Miles Richard, Thoroughfare

CHEMISTS & DRUGGISTS.
Buckmaster Peter, Thoroughfare
Francis Geo. (& stamp seller) Mkp
Gall and Allen (and soda water ma-
nufrs. &c.) Thoroughfare
Manning Saml. Spooner, Thrghfare
Sterry Hy. Whatling, Thoroughfare

CHIMNEY SWEEPERS.
Catchpole James, Bredfield street
Goodwin Wm. New street
Holder James, Bredfield street
Smith Wm. New street

CLOTHES BROKERS.
Ashford Eliza, Thoroughfare
Bodgener Henry, New street
Brown James, Thoroughfare
Brown Susannah, Cumberland st
Hawk Mary Ann, Church street
Mathews Wm. New street
Woodroff Elizabeth, New street

COACH MAKERS, &c.
Daniels James, New street
Downing Edward, Thoroughfare

CONFECTIONERS, &c.
Barritt James, Church street
Fisher Wm. New street
Gammage Benjamin, Thoroughfare
Leek Timothy, Thoroughfare
Mayhew James, Market place
Richardson Thomas, Thoroughfare

COOPERS.
Barnes Stephen, Cumberland street
Brightwell James, Chapel lane
Ferguson Theophilus, New street

CORN MERCHANTS.
(Marked * are also Coal merchants.)
Brown John, Cumberland street
Edwards Henry, jun. (and emigra-
tion agent) Cumberland street
Hart Daniel (and seeds) Com. quay
*Jessop Alexander, Quay lane
*Loft George, Common quay
*Manby Geo. Edwards, Thorough-
fare and Quay
Rogers Wm. Thoroughfare
*Tills Wm. Thoroughfare
Ward Noah, Castle walk

CORN MILLERS.
Bendall Frederick, Mill hill
Brown John, Cumberland street
Manby George E., Water mill

Osborn S. Theatre street
Trott Pearce, Burkett road

CURRIERS & LTHR. CUTRS.
Goodwin Edmund, Church street
Smith Thomas, Thoroughfare

DYERS & SCOURERS.
Francis Harriet, New street
Kell Wm. New street
Nob'e James, Cumberland street

FIRE & LIFE OFFICES.
Alliance, (Marine) Wm. Tills, Tho-
roughfare
Argus J. Wood, jun. Thoroughfare,
Atlas, Thos. Carthew, Thoroughfare
British Fire, and Westminster Life,
Alfred Taylor, Church street
Church of England, Wm. Henry
Brook, Church street
County, J. W. Issitt, Thoroughfare
Essex and Suffolk, and Eagle, John
Loder, Thoroughfare
English and Scottish (Law Life) and
Fam. Endowment, Meadows and
Brooke, Cumberland street
Farmers', H. Edwards, jun. Thfare
Globe, Meadows and Brooke, Cum-
berland street
Guardian and Invalid, J. Wood,
jun. Thoroughfare
Norwich Equitable, Benjamin Gall
Norwich Union, Rt. Cana, Thfare
Norwich, Thos. Giles, Thoroughfare
Phœnix, H. Neal', Thoroughfare
Protector, Geo. Francis, Market pl
Royal Exch., G. E. Manby, Quay
Suffolk, J. W. Issett, Thoroughfare
Sun, Wm. Kemp, Market place
United Kingdom, Rd. Miles, Thfare
Yorkshire, Wm. Wincopp, Mkp
York and North of England, S. S.
Manning, Thoroughfare

FRUITERERS.
Gross & Thompson, Thoroughfare
Loder Charles, Church street

GARDENERS.
Abel Robert, Angel lane
Bagster James, Seckford street
Crouch Thomas, New street
Foreman John, New street
Skinner John, Thoroughfare
Woods John & Son(& nurserymen,)
Cumberland street

GLASS, CHINA, &c. DLRS.
Morley Wm. Thoroughfare
Pite Edward, Church street

GLOVER, &c.
Goodwin Robert, Market place

GROCERS, &c.

Barnard Philip, Church street
Bachelor Richard, Market place
Fenn John (tea dlr.) Cumberland st
Flaxman Charles, Thoroughfare
Gross & Thompson, Thoroughfare
Hurren Richard, Market place
Loder Charles, Church street
Mathew Frederick, Church street
Mickleburgh Robert, Market place
Morgan John, Thoroughfare
Neale Horace, Thoroughfare
Oxx Amos, Thoroughfare
Revell Wm. Cumberland street

HAIR DRESSERS, &c.

Brighten George, Cumberland st
Dunnett Philip, Market place
Green Robert, New street
Keeble Wm. Thoroughfare
Marsh Wm. Nathan, Market place
Mathews Wm. New street
Sykes Thomas, New street
Taylor Alfred, (librarian to Mechanics' Institution, and post office clerk,) Church street
Wade George, Cumberland street

HARDWARE & TOY DLRS.

Catchpole John, Thoroughfare
Issett John Webster (and rag, horse hair, &c. dealer) Thoroughfare
Mickleburgh Robert, Market place

HATTERS.

Bays Thomas (and stock whs.) Mkp
Brown James, Thoroughfare
Goldacre Robert, Thoroughfare
Towber John (and furrier) Thfare

INNS AND TAVERNS.

Anchor, Wm. Keeble, Common quay
Angel, Saml. Oxborrow, Theatre st
Boat, Elizabeth Adams, Com. quay
Bull Inn, John Salmon, Market pl
Cherry Tree, Jno. Jeffries, Cumb. st
Cock & Pie, Jas. Mallett, New st
Cross, Henry Cork, Church street
Fox, James Frud, New street
Crown Tavern (and posting,) Michl. Cundy, Thoroughfare
Half Moon & Star, Edw. Barker, Cumberland street
Horse Shoes, Stephen Barnes, Cumberland street
King's Arms, Hy. Fisk, Thoroughfr
King's Head, Alex. Cramer, Mkp
Mariners' Arms, Js. Smyth, New st
Queen's Head, Susan Sele, Seckfd. st
Red Lion, Cath. Gross, Thoroughfr

Royal Oak, Susan Lankester, Thfr
Ship, Wm. Pleasance, Com. quay
Sun, John Betts, sen. Thoroughfare
Tankard, Wm. Mathews, New st
Waggon & Horses, George Quadling, Bredfield street
Wellington, Jph. Nunn, Cumbld. st
White Horse, John Wade, Mkp
White Swan, John Syred, Market pl

BEER HOUSES.

Aston James, Castle walk
Brightwell James, Chapel lane
Cole James, Cumberland street
Easter Abraham, Castle street
Emmerson James, Seckford street
Glanfield Wm. Bredfield street
Woods Robert, Bredfield street
Worledge Mary, Theatre street
Wright James, Castle street

IRONMONGERS.

(See also Hardware dealers.)
Bendall Jas. (and founder,) Thfare
Gall George, Church street
Issitt John Webster, (hardware dlr.) Thoroughfare
Kemp Wm. jun. Market place
Silver Ths. Temple & Son, Church st
Stananought Jno. (inspr. of weights and measures,) New street
Turner George, Thoroughfare

JOINERS & BUILDERS.

Debney John, Limekiln quay
Flaxman Wm. Limekiln quay
Grayston Thomas, New street
Lockwood Alfred (architect, and cement manufacturer) Castle street
Mumford Wm. Quay lane
Peake Thomas, Cumberland street
Shribbs James, Castle street
Thompson George, Thoroughfare

LINEN & WOLN. DRAPERS.

Barnard Philip, Church street
Barnes Charles, Thoroughfare
Brown James, Thoroughfare
Clark John, Church street
Hurren Richard, Market place
Skeet John & Co. Thoronghfare
Smith Edward, New street

MALTSTERS.

Cobbold John, Brewer's lane
Edwards Henry, jun. Cumberland st
Heard Thos. (& hop mert.) Church st
Lynn Francis, Brewer's lane
Loft George, Common quay
Manby George E. Thoroughfare
Tills Wm. Brewer's lane

MASTER MARINERS.
*Those marked * are Shipowners.*

Adams Edward, Common quay
Allen Thomas, Castle street
*Amos Wm. and Jas. Castle street
Bardwell G. S. Brook street
Braham Robert, Sun street
Bridges Wm. Brook street
Brightwell John, New street
Broomby John W. Cumberland st
Dorrell Wm. Theatre street
*Dowsing James, Thorougfare
Elmore Samuel, Castle street
Fisk John, Theatre street
Garrard Charles, Quay lane
Hart Edmund, Brook street
How John, Common quay
Hunt George, Quay lane
Keeble John, Castle street
Knights Robert, Deben street
*Levett Wm. Castle street
Marsh John, Quay lane
Marsh Wm. Quay lane
*Moor John, New street
Newson David, Brewers' lane
Nunn John, Brook street
Passiful Edward, Brook street
Read Edward Bond, and Baldry, Common Quay
Revans John, Brook street
*Row George, Cumberland street
Skipper S. Angel street
Smith Thomas, Castle street
Smith Wm. Cumberland street
Woodroffe Wm. Seckford street
*Trott George, Castle street
*Trott Wm. Chapel lane
Woods Robert, Bredfield street

MILLINERS, &c.
Cullum and Ling, Thoroughfare
Fuller Louisa, Seckford street
Gibbs Harriet, Seckford street
Haswell Caroline, Thoroughfare
Kemp Susan, Market place
Nading M. A. Thoroughfare
Olding Harriet, Thoroughfare
Simpson Ann, New street
Stanford & Freeman, Thoroughfare
Waspe Mary Ann, Quay lane
Ward Susan, Thoroughfare

PAINTERS, PLUMBERS, & GLAZIERS.
Allen Loder, Church street
Cooke Wm. and Hy. Thoroughfare
Heffer John, Seckford street
Kell James and Charles, Thoroughfr
Mallett John, New street

Mallett Wm. Market place
Moore Wm. Christopher, New st

ROPE & TWINE MAKERS.
Cork Henry, Church street
Giles John, New street

SADDLERS & HARNESS MKS.
Birch Robert, New street
Durrant Isaac, Thoroughfare
Kirby Robert, Market place

SAIL MAKERS.
Horn Wm. Bell, Common quay
Nichols John, Common quay

SHIP & BOAT BUILDERS.
Garrard Wm. (boat) Brook street
Taylor Wm. Limekiln quay Shipyard & Patent Slip; h Thorofare

SHIP OWNERS.
(See Master Mariners, &c.)

SHOPKEEPERS.
Bird Robert, Castle street
Breckles Margt. Castle street
Clark Eliza, Theatre street
Coleman Husting, Seckford street
Culham Samuel, Cumberland street
Easter Abraham, Castle street
Garrard Wm. Brook street
Glanfield Wm. Bredfield street
Hartridge Wm. horse letter & omnibus owner, New street
Hawkins Joseph, Thoroughfare
Keeble Ann, Castle street
Lambert Mary, Cumberland street
Pizey Philip, New street
Roberts Thos. S. Theatre street
Sawyer Christian, Chapel lane
Smith Elizabeth, Seckford street
Stephenson Robert, Seckford street
Turner Samuel, Bredfield street
Woods Robert, Bredfield street

STAY MAKERS.
Field Sophia, Seckford street
Leverett Caroline, Cumberland st
Quinton Elizabeth, Market place

STONE & MARBLE MASON.
Smyth James, Thoroughfare

STRAW HAT MAKERS.
Broadbank Hephzibah, Thoroughfare
Cullingford Hannah, Thoroughfare
Moore Eliza, New street
Moss Hannah, Seckford street
Pite Mary Ann, Church street
Wade George, Cumberland street
Wright Elizabeth, Brook street

SURGEONS.
Gissing Samuel, Market place
Jones Richard, Church street
Lynn Geo. D. (physician) Church st

Marshall Charles, Castle street
Moore Nathl. & Son, Church street
Welton (Wm.) and Bligh (Richd.)
    Thoroughfare and Cumberland st

SURVEYORS, *(Land, &c.)*

Lankester J. *(river,)* Cumberland st
Lockwood Alfd. (architect,) Castle st
Moulton Benj. Thoroughfare
Pattisson W. (& architect,) Brook st
Thompson Geo. (county surveyor,)
    Thoroughfare

TAILORS & DRAPERS.

Brown James, Thoroughfare
Bodgener Henry, New street
Chappell Wm. Geo. Church street
Christopher Wm. Cumberland st
Freeman Charles, Thoroughfare
Gall John, Castle street
Hunt John, Church street
Lyons Robert, Theatre street
Mallett Jonathan, Market place
Moss James, Cumberland street
Simpson Wm. New street
Whistock Wm. Thoroughfare
Wright (Jeremiah) & Stock (Saml.)
    Church street

TALLOW CHANDLERS.

Gross & Thompson, Thoroughfare
Stanford Henry, Market place

TANNER.

Bond John, Brewer's ln; h *Ipswich*

TIMBER MERCHANTS.

Colchester Wm. and Co. (& slate,)
    Common quay
Grimwood Thomas, Thoroughfare

TOY DLRS. *(See Hardware.)*

UMBRELLA MKRS.

Pooley Samuel, Bredfield street
Revett Brady, (cutler,) New street

WATCH & CLOCK MAKERS.

Baker James, Brook street
Fisher John Forsdick, Market place
Gant Robert Drake, Thoroughfare
Hildyards John, Thoroughfare
Taylor John, New street

WHEELWRIGHTS.

Calver Chas. Brett & Ts. Theatre st
Quadling Geo. Bredfield street

WHITESMITHS.

Baxter Wm. Brook street
Dowsing James, Chapel lane
Fisher Richard, Common quay
Owles Charles, New street
Smyth Henry, Seckford street
Stananought John, New street

WINE & SPIRIT MERTS.

Brook Abm. & Son, Church street

Edwards Henry, (and ship owner,)
    Thoroughfare and Brook street
Gross and Thompson, Thoroughfare
Wincopp Wm. Market place

COACHES.

Mail, to London, at $\frac{1}{2}$ past 10 night,
    and to Yarmouth, at $\frac{1}{2}$ past 4
    morning, from the Post-office
Shannon, to London, $\frac{1}{4}$ past 10 mng.
    and to Halesworth, $\frac{1}{2}$ past 4 aft;
    and the *Retaliator*, to London, 20
    min. before 8 morning, from the
    Crown ; *Original Blue*, to London,
    $\frac{1}{4}$ past 12 at noon; and to Sax-
    mundham and Yarmouth, $\frac{1}{2}$ past 2
    afternoon, from the Sun
Mail Cart, to Orford, &c. 6 morng.
    from the Royal Oak

OMNIBUSES

To meet the *London Steamers* at
    Ipswich, every Mon. and Thurs.
    from the King's Arms ; and every
    Tues. and Friday, from the Cross,
    at $\frac{1}{2}$ past 6 morning : return fol-
    lowing days to Saxmundham,
    Framlingham, Wickham-Market,
    &c. Oxborrow's Omnibus, from
    the Sun to *Ipswich*, daily, during
    summer; and Smith's, from the
    Royal Oak, to *Aldeburgh*, Tues.
    Thursday and Saturday

CARRIERS.

Marked 1, stop at the Anchor ; 2,
    Boat ; 3, King's Arms ; 4, Red
    Lion ; 5, Royal Oak ; 6, Sun ;
    7, Wellington ; 8, White Horse ;
    and 9, at the Crown Inn

Places.	Carriers.

London, &c. H. R. & J. Smith, Sat.
    Tue. & Thu. from the Thghfare
5 Alderton, A. Hill, M. W. Th. & S
3 Bawdsey, P. Cutting, M. W. & F
Bedfield, Smith, (Wagn. & Horses,)
    Friday
5 Boyton, F. Ashkettle, W. S; 3 P.
    Cutting, M. W. F; and Cooper,
    Arnold, and Flory, M. Tues. W.
    Friday and Saturday
1 Brandeston, Pratt, M. W. and Fri
1 Dallinghoo, J. Sheppard, W. Sat
1 Easton and Earl Soham. C. Pratt,
    Monday, Wednesday, and Friday
5 Framlingham, S. Exworth, Mon.
    Thursday ; and *7 mail cart* daily
2 Framsden, Flick, Tuesday
5 Fressingfield, A. Hart, Wednesday

5 Halesworth, J. Sawyer, Mon. Fri
4 Hollesley, R. Clark, Wed. & Sat
Ipswich, T. Newson and Rt. Green, from New street, daily, except Wed; 5 S. Exworth, W. & S; 3 Fisk, daily; 6 Oxborrow, daily; and 9 H. R. & J. Smith, S. and Thu; and Hartridge's Omnibus, from New street, Monday & Thu
8 Kirton, Wright, Wednesday
1 Marlesford, Chas. Hall, Wed
Norwich, (see Halesworth, Yarmouth, &c)
7 Orford, Mail Cart, daily; 5 Henry Pead, M. W. Thu. S; and 3 Wm. Mann, Mon. Wed. and Saturday
3 Saxmundham, J. Rouse, Tu. Fri. S; and 5 Wm. Free, Wed. & Sat

5 Shottisham, W. Kemp, M.W. Sat
4 Stradbroke, J. How, Mon. & Tues
1 Swefling, W. Button, Wednesday
8 Trimley, Walton, and Felixstow, Edw. Chapman and J. Page, W; and Baxter, (King's Head,) Wed
3 Tunstall & Snape, T. Cooper, M. Wednesday, and Saturday
4 Wickham-Market, M. Mayhew, daily
Yarmouth, Bungay, &c. (see Saxmundham and Halesworth,) and H. R. and J. Smith's waggon, M. Th. & S. from the Thoroughfare
TRADING VESSELS
Sail weekly to Custom House Quay, London, and to other places occasionally

THREDLING HUNDRED.

This is the smallest Hundred in Suffolk, containing only the five parishes of *Debenham, Ashfield-with Thorpe, Framsden, Pettaugh,* and *Winston,* which contained 2616 inhabitants, in 1801, and 3504, in 1841; and comprise about 10,000 acres of clayey, but fertile land, which was assessed (with the buildings) to the property tax in 1815, at the yearly value of £13,519. They are in Bosmere and Claydon Union, and in the Deanery of Claydon, Archdeaconry of Suffolk, and Diocese of Norwich. The river Deben has its source in this Hundred, which is bounded by those of Loes, Carlford, Hoxne, Hartismere, and Bosmere-and-Claydon. Mr. Lionel Dove, of Debenham, is the chief constable.

ASHFIELD-with-THORPE, the former a scattered village, 3 miles E., and the latter a small hamlet, 2 miles E. by S. of Debenham, form a parish of 343 souls, and 1565A. 2R. 19P. of land, lying in several manors, and belonging to Lord Henniker, Sir Robt. Adair, W. Mills, Esq., and a few smaller owners. The *Church at Ashfield* has been in ruins more than a century, but its burial ground is still used. *Thorpe Chapel* (St. Mary) is now used as the parish church, and was rebuilt in 1739. The living is a perpetual curacy, valued at £53, in the incumnency of the Rev. Edwin Edwards. Lord Henniker is patron, and also impropriator of the great tithes, which were commuted in 1839 for £466 per annum, and were formerly in the appropriation of Butley priory. The glebe is 4A. 1R. 23P. The FARMERS are Danl. Barker, *Thorpe Hall;* Edmund Button, cattle dealer; George Cooke,* James C. Cook, John Garnham*, James Goodwin*, *Woodhouse;* Wm. Green*, *Ashfield place;* Wm. Hammond, *Grove farm;* Jas. Juby, *Hill farm;* John Lanham, Jerh. Quinton, Jas. and Edward Rogers, and Edward Warner, *Ashfield Hall.* Those marked thus * are *owners;* and the other principal parishioners are John Bennett, *blacksmith;* and Robt. Lockwood, vict., *Swan Inn,*

DEBENHAM, so called from the river Deben, which rises near it, is a small town, on a pleasant eminence, finely interspersed with trees,

8 miles W. of Framlingham, 13 miles N. of Ipswich, 7½ miles S. of Eye, and 82 miles N.E. of London. Its parish contained 1215 inhabitants, in 1801, and 1667 in 1841, and comprises about 3271 acres of land, rated with the buildings at the annual value of £5041. 18s. 6d. The town suffered severely by fire, in 1744. The *market*, formerly held on Friday, is discontinued ; but here is still a fair for cattle, &c. on the 24th of June, and a *lamb show* on the 2nd of September. The lower part of the *Market House* is now a police station, and the upper part is the Free School. One side of the Market place is shaded by a fine row of lime trees. In Saxon times, the kings of East Anglia occasionally held their courts here; and tradition says, the *Deben* was then navigable up to the town, though it is now only a small stream, which rises little more than a mile north of the town, and does not become navigable till, by a circuitous route of nearly 20 miles, it reaches Melton and Woodbridge, where it expands into a broad tide river. (See page 204.) Some years ago, an anchor was found imbedded in the sand, at a place called the *Gulls*, near Debenham. The ancient farm-houses, called *Crows Hall* and *Ulverston Hall*, were formerly moated. The former is of considerable antiquity, but only one of its wings is now remaining. Ulverston Hall Farm, (305a. 1r. 7p.) and the *manors of Ulverston and Sackvylls*, belong to Tooley's Almshouses, in Ipswich (see p. 79.) The greater part of the parish lies in several other manors. The manor of Debenham Butley, with the rectory and the advowson of the vicarage, belonged to Butley priory. They were granted in 1542, to Francis Framlingham, and devolved, about 1600, to the Gaudys, who resided at Crows Hall ; and one of them, Sir Chas. Gaudy, was created a *baronet* in 1661. They afterwards passed to the Bridges family, of Bealings, but are now the property of Lord Henniker, who is also lord of the adjacent *manors of Scotnells-with-Haugh, Blood Hall,* and *Crows Hall.* The manors of Kenton-with-Suddou Hall, and Winston-cum-Pulham, extend into Debenham parish; and the Dean and Chapter of Ely have held the former since the time of Edward the Confessor; and Wm. Mills, Esq., is lord of the latter. Copyhold courts are held yearly for all these manors, and the other principal landowners are the Chevallier, Mills, Wade, Beck, Norris, Manning, and Kersey families. Mark Wade, Esq., has a neat mansion here, called *White Hall.* The CHURCH (St. Mary) is a handsome structure, with a square tower, formerly surmounted by a spire, which is said to have been injured by lightning, and was taken down in 1667. The four old bells, which had chimes, gave place to a musical peal of eight, in 1761, when the *Rev. J. Clubbe,* author of an " Essay on Phisiognomy," &c., was incumbent here. The nave is an elegant example of pointed architecture, divided from the aisles by six lofty clustered pillars, with exquisitely sculptured capitals, representing heads of cherubims, foliage, &c. In the chancel are some ancient monuments, but the inscriptions are entirely defaced. One of them bears recumbent effigies, supposed to represent Sir Chas. Gaudy (or Gaude,) Kt., and his lady. In the south aisle is a more modern monument, on which are figures of John Simpson, Esq., and his two sons. Lord Henniker is impropriator of the rectory, and patron of the vicarage, which is valued in K.B. at £15. 2s. 6d., and is now enjoyed by the Rev. Jas. Bedingfeld, B.A. In 1838, the rectorial tithes were commuted for £651, and the vicarial for £282 per annum.

Domesday Book notices another church at Debenham, dedicated to *St. Andrew*, but its site is unknown, though there are, near Ulverston Hall, enclosures called Church field and Chapel-field.   In the town is an *Independent Chapel*, belonging to a congregation which originated in 1700.   *Sir Robert Hitcham's Charity* to Debenham, Framlingham, and other places, is noticed at pages 189 and 190, where it will be seen that the valuable charity estates have been separated, and appropriated to the several parishes interested therein.   The Debenham Trust comprises 236A. 3R. 5P. of land at Framlingham, let for about £250 per annum, which is applied partly for the support of a *Free School* for the education of 20 poor children, and partly for the relief of the poor parishioners.   The Master and Fellows of Pembroke Hall, Cambridge, being visitors or governors of Sir Robert Hitcham's Charity, the late Parliamentary Commissioners did not inquire into it.   Here is also a *National School*, erected in 1834, and now attended by about 70 boys and 70 girls.   In 1697, *John Simpson* bequeathed, out of a farm in Debenham, a yearly rent-charge of £30 for the following uses, viz., £17. 6s. 8d. for weekly distributions of bread among the poor parishioners, and £12. 13s. 4d. to provide eight coats and six gowns, marked J.S., for as many poor men and women, on Christmas Day. The poor of Debenham have £15. 15s. yearly from *Garney's Charity*, as noticed with Kenton, at page 199.   Mr. Arthur Powell is secretary of the *Debenham Association for the Prosecution of Felons*.

DEBENHAM.

Post-Office at Mr Fras. Arnold's.— Letters arrive by foot-post from Stonham Pie, at 7 morng. and are despatched at 7 evening

Bedingfeld Rev James, B.A., vicar and rural dean
Bennett Wm. gun mkr. & whitesmith
Bolton Robert, mill manager
Butcher John, farrier
Clark Robert, gentleman
Dove Miss Mary
Freeman Miss Lydia
Houghton Michael, attorney's clerk
Jackson Wm. clerk
James Rev Thomas (Independent)
Kersey Mrs Elizabeth
Kersey Samuel, steward
Knight Mrs Elizabeth
Last Wm. cooper
Mordant Geo. Esq. Gosling's Hall
Moyse Mrs Mary
Norris James, attorney
Peck Mrs Elizabeth
Pooley John, farrier
Preston Charles Abbott, attorney
Smart Mr Richard
Smith Mrs Harriet
Smith Charles, dish turner
Theobald Mrs Susan
Wade Mark, Esq. *White Hall*

Academies.
Arnold Jas. Percy (National)
Field Eliza
Kersey My. (bdg)
Palmer Jno. *Free*
Pritty Sar. (bdg)
Ruddock Eli (and surveyor)
Ruddock Ann E.

Attorneys.
Norris & Preston
Powell Arthur

Auctioneers.
Abbott Joseph
Wythe & Palmer

Bakers, &c.
Crapnell Joseph
Field Edwd. (and confectioner)
Smith James
Thurkettle Saml.
Wythe John, jun

Bankers.
Bacon and Co. of Ipswich ; Mr Sml. Dove, agt

Blacksmiths.
Bedwell Thomas
Last Samuel

Spall George
Thurkettle Wm.

Beer Houses.
Bendall Denis
Jessop Devereux
Wright Wm.

Boot&ShoeMkrs.
Arnold Deborah
Arnold Francis
Beecroft Lionel
Crapnell John
Crapnell Joseph
Gardner Thomas
Hyde Henry
Ludbrook James (& leather cutr)
Owles Samuel
Rands Isaac
Rumsey James

Bricklayers.
Blasby Samuel
Gooding John
Gooding Wm.

Butchers.
Amass Ann
Amass George
Gooding Wm.

Cabinet Makers.
Cook Edward
Fisk Wm.

Corn Millers.
Chevallier Chas.
(Rt.Bolton,agt)
Corner Wm. sen.
(and merchant)
Cracknell Syer
Curriers.
Arnold Francis
Crapnell Joseph
Druggists.
Cunnell John
Etches James
FARMERS.
* *are owners.*
Amass Wm.
*Barker Thomas
Bennett John
Cook George
Darby Wm.
Dove Lionel, *Ul-
verston Hall*
Dove Edward,
Old Hall
Noller Samuel
*Steptoe Nathl.
*Simpson Robert
Tacon James
Thurkettle Wm.
Gardeners.
Andrews John
Barritt Wm.
Barritt Wm. jun
Lanham Thos.

Glovers.
Carter Thomas
Hunt Samuel
Rands Sarah

GROCERS
(And Drapers.)
Abbott Henry
Abbott Jonathan
Andrews Robert
DoveSaml.(news
and fire office
& bank agent)
Etches Jas. (and
clothes dealer)
Hairdressers.
Bedwell Robett
Beecroft Wm.
Carter Thomas
Inns & Taverns.
Angel, John
Wythe, jun
Cherry Tree Inn,
Edm.Tydeman
Eight Bells,John
Carter
King's Head,
Wm. Cook
Iron,&c.Foundr.
Gowers Charles
Ironmonger.
Abbott Jonathan
Joiners.
Howes Charles

Kemp Isaac
Pollard Samuel
Pyett Jonathan
Pyett Joseph
Maltsters.
Corner Wm. sen
Simpson Robert
Milliners.
Beecroft Eliz.
Houghton Mary
Lanham Hannah
*Painters, Plum-
bers, & Glaziers.*
Gunn Fenn
Wythe John
Wythe John, jun
Saddlers.
Clemence Henry
Fulcher Charles
Poole Robert
Straw Hat Mkrs.
Etches My. Ann

Fisk Rebecca
Surgeons.
Cauet Fred. C.
Lock Edward
Moore Lionel
Welham
Tailors & Drprs.
Amass Samuel
Carter George
Corner Wm.
Cunnell John
Curtis George
Curtis Sarah
Harvey Samuel
Tinner&Brazier.
Fairweather Jno.
Watchmaker.
Percy John
Wheelwrights.
Bendall Ezekial
Howes Robert

CARRIERS.

Samuel Noller's Vans, to Ipswich, London, &c. every Monday and Thursday, and to Yarmouth, &c. every Wednesday and Saturday

To *Ipswich*, John Abbot and Son, J. Mark, Hannah Page, and Joseph and Robert Alexander, Tuesday, Thursday, and Saturday

To *Stowmarket*, Wm. Smith, Tuesday and Friday

FRAMSDEN, a scattered village, 3 miles S.S.E. of Debenham, and 11 miles N. by E. of Ipswich, has in its parish 829 souls, and 2837A. 1R. 38P. of land, which has been much improved of late years by under-draining, and is now rated, with the buildings, at £3436 per annum. Here is a *fair* yearly on Holy Thursday. The manor was anciently held by the *Montealio* or *Monthalt* family, who settled it on Isabel, mother of Edward III., and after her decease, it passed to John Eltham, the king's brother. John Tollemache, Esq., is now lord of the manor, and owner of a great part of the soil ; and the remainder belongs to Viscount Acheson (son of the Earl of Gosford,) and the Hyde, Barthropp, White, Norris, and other families. The *hall* has been occupied as a farm-house more than 80 years, by the Kersey family, and is still partly encompassed by a moat. The *Church* (St. Mary) is an ancient structure, with a lofty tower, containing eight bells. In the reign of Edward III., it was appropriated to the *Minoresses*, a convent of nuns in London. J. Tollemache, Esq., is now impropriator of the rectory and patron of the vicarage, valued in K.B. at £10. 0s. 2½d., and enjoyed by the Rev. Thos. Wm. Brereton, B.A., who has a good residence, and 43A. of glebe. In 1839, the rectorial tithes were commuted for £567, and the vicarial for £344 per annum .

Abel Wm. tailor
Balls Henry, corn miller
Bennett Amos, blacksmith
Brereton Rev Thos. Wm. B.A. vicar
Crapnell Wm. shoemaker
Farrer James, shoemaker and vict.
    Greyhound
Flick Alfred, shopkeeper
Mouser David, tailor
Mouser Robert, bricklayer
Oxborrow Caleb, shoemaker
Paternoster Samuel, blacksmith
Pepper Samuel, wheelwright
Pettit Peter, blacksmith
Thurkettle Charles, tailor
Tucker Rev John Kinsman, curate
Wright John, shopkeeper

FARMERS.
Balls Wm. (and
    corn miller)
Birch James
Birch Stephen
Birch Wm.
Bond John
Bond John, jun
Church Clement
Eade Widow
Farthing John
Freeman John
Kersey Caleb,
    Hall
Kersey Hy. agent
    to J. Tolle-

mache, Esq·
    Valley farm
Last Wm.
Mouser Henry
Oxborrow Joshua
Page Thomas
Sawyer Edward
Scace Joseph
Smith Daniel (&
    brick and tile
    maker)
Smith Elizabeth
Smy Joshua
Veasy Thomas
Wood Jeremiah
Wood John

PETTAUGH, a small village and parish, 10 miles N. of Ipswich, and 3 miles S. of Debenham, contains 266 souls, and 795 acres of land, belonging to various owners, the largest of whom is John Tollemache, Esq., the lord of the manor of Abbot's Hall and Pettaugh Hall, but part of the parish is in Crowfield and other manors, and is partly freehold. The *Church* (St. Catherine) is a rectory, valued in K.B. at £9. 12s. 1d., and now having 19A. 1R. 25P. of glebe, and a yearly modus of £194. 10s., awarded in 1840 in lieu of tithes. J. Tollemache, Esq., is patron, and the Rev. Edmund Bellman, *incumbent.* DIRECTORY :—Joseph Chilver, tailor ; Wm. Cooper, wheelwright ; Stephen Moyes, shoemaker ; John Peck, blacksmith ; Lionel Pepper, corn miller ; Samuel Sheppard, vict., Bull ; John Wood, grocer and seedsman ; James Mayhew, farmer ; John Mayhew, farmer, *Pettaugh Hall ;* John Moor, farmer ; and Wm. Page, farmer, *Abbot's Hall.*

WINSTON, a pleasant village, 1½ mile S. by E. of Debenham, and 11 miles N. of Ipswich, has in its parish 399 souls, and 1470 acres of land, in which are two brick and tile yards. The Dean and Chapter of Ely are appropriators of the rectory, and lords of the manor of Winston, but part of the parish is in another manor, which formerly belonged to the nuns of Bruisyard. Lord Henniker, the executors of the late Capt. Blakely, Dr. Beck, and several smaller owners, have estates here; and Winston Hall, with the rectory, is held on lease by the executors of the late Mr. Thos. Pettit. The *Church* (St. Andrew) is a vicarage, valued in K.B. at £9. 3s. 9d., and in 1835, at £169. The Dean and Chapter of Ely are patrons, and the Rev. John Udney Robson, B.A., is the *incumbent,* for whom a new vicarage house was built in 1843. The *farmers* are —Anthony Alexander, William and Peter Bennett, Hy. Fairweather, *cattle dealer ;* Wm. Freeman, Wm. Groome, Wm. Hicks, Peter Kersey, *Malthouse farm ;* John Palmer, *auctioneer ;* Elizabeth Peck, Susan Pettit, *Winston Hall ;* S. Scace, Geo. Shearing, and Noah Simpson.

BOSMERE & CLAYDON HUNDRED

Is a fertile and picturesque district, varying from 8 to about 12 miles in length and breadth; comprising the small town and chapelry of Needham Market, 33 parishes, and parts of two other parishes; bounded on the south by the Borough of Ipswich and Samford Hundred; on the west, by Cosford and Stow Hundreds; on the north, by Hartismere and Thredling Hundreds; and on the east, by Carlford Hundred. It is in the *Union* to which it gives name; in the *Deaneries of Bosmere and Claydon*, in the Archdeaconry of Suffolk, and Diocese of Norwich. It has generally a clayey soil, well suited to the growth of corn, and is crossed by good turnpike roads, and the small but navigable *river Gipping*, which at Ipswich takes the name of Orwell, and assumes the character of a broad estuary. (See page 62.) Some parts of it are calcareous, and the following is an enumeration of its *parishes*, &c., shewing their territorial extent, the annual value of their lands and buildings, as assessed to the property tax in 1815, and their population in 1801 and 1841. The Hundred derives its name from the parish of Claydon, and a *mere* or lake near Needham Market.

PARISHES.	Acrs.	Rental.	Populatn. 1801.	Populatn. 1841.	PARISHES.	Acres.	Rental. £.	Population. 1801.	Population. 1841.
Akenham	1060	1052	105	117	Flowton	495	578	121	179
Ashbocking§ ..	1383	1646	186	321	Gosbeck†	1530	1991	284	316
Badley	1050	1186	82	83	Helmingham†	2438	2920	235	284
Barham*	1800	2251	352	576	Hemingstone	1444	1789	253	381
Barking par. } Needhm.Mkt }	3164	2709 2134	470 1348	465 1353	Henley	1233	1286	250	329
					Mickfield	1300	1796	173	263
Battisford	1542	1680	290	520	Nettlestead ..	1029	1049	87	98
Baylham	1332	1983	232	275	Offton-with- } Lit. Bricett }	1530	1560	264	417
Blakenham Gt.	842	1011	120	180					
Blakenham Lit.	1046	1302	115	119	Ringshall	2116	2458	257	356
Bramford	3247	4096	762	833	Somersham ..	1027	1252	298	485
Bricett Great	916	878	224	214	Stonham Aspal	2399	3229	578	772
Claydon	951	1653	305	418	Stonham Earl	2521	3572	575	878
Coddenham ..	2719	2747	653	924	Stonham Parva	1173	1564	257	368
CreetingAll Sts	1286	1927	279	286	Swilland......	951	1192	184	270
Creeting St My.	1441	2010	122	196	Westerfield‡ ..	..	..	59	55
Creeting StOlv.	388	472	36	30	Whitton‡	..	..	..	112
Crowfield	1700	1350	250	385	Willisham	1030	1049	154	217
Darmsden	790	548	82	61	Total	48,773	59,920	10,042	13,136

‡ *Westerfield* and *Whitton parishes* are partly in this Hundred, but mostly in the borough of Ipswich, with which their areas, rental, and population, are included, at page 50. See also pages 85 and 86.

* *Barham* includes the *Union Workhouse*, which had 429 inmates in 1831, and 183 in 1841.

§ Ashbocking includes five *extra-parochial houses*.

† Gosbeck includes 18 and Helmingham 27 *strangers*.

The *Chief Constables* are, Mr. Benj. Morgan and Mr. Wm. Hayward, of Little Blakenham, and Mr. George Morgan, of Bramford. PETTY SESSIONS are held once a fortnight, at Needham Market and Coddenham alternately.

BOSMERE and CLAYDON UNION comprises all the parishes in the foregoing table, except Whitton and Westerfield; and also includes the five parishes of Thredling Hundred, as noticed at page

216. The thirty-nine parishes of this Union have a population of 16,521 souls, and extend over an area of 91 square miles. Each parish returns one guardian, except Debenham, which has two. The average annual expenditure on the poor of this district, during 1832, '3, and '4, was £14,306; but in 1838, it was only £6983. The 34 parishes of Bosmere and Claydon Hundred were incorporated for the support of their poor, under Gilbert's Act, in 1765; and the Work-house, which is situated at Barham, was erected in the following year at the cost of about £10,000. It was made an union-house under the new poor law, in 1835, and about £200 was expended in alterations. It has room for about 500 inmates, and had 198, in 1811; 489, in 1821; 429, in 1831; and 183, in 1841. It is a spacious brick building, divided into six wards. Mr. Crisp Howard is the *master;* and Mrs. Howard, *matron.* Mr. Jacob Peele Bray, of Ipswich, is *Clerk to the Board of Guardians;* Fredk. Hayward, Esq., of Needham Market, is *Superintendent Registrar;* and the relieving officers and registrars of births and deaths are, Mr. John Simpson, for *Coddenham District;* and Mr. George Kerridge, of Barking, for *Needham Market District.* The latter is also registrar of marriages for the whole union.

AKENHAM parish, 3 miles N. by W. of Ipswich, contains 1060 acres of land, 117 inhabitants, five scattered houses, and a few cottages. It was anciently the lordship of the Rous family. Robert Baker Orford, Esq., is now lord of the manor, and resides at *Akenham Hall;* but *Rice Hall* is the seat of Robert Woodward, Esq.; and Mr. S. Rowland, W. H. Quayle, and the Ipswich Charity Trustees, own part of the parish. The *Church* (St. Mary) is a small tiled edifice, and the living is a discharged rectory, valued in K.B. at £9. 11s. 5½d., and consolidated with that of Claydon, in the patronage of Mrs. Tyley, and incumbency of the Rev. Thomas Nunn, M.A., who has 50A. of glebe, and a good residence at Claydon. The tithes of both parishes have been commuted for a yearly modus of £506. *Directory:*—Jeremiah Gooding, *Bower Farm;* Stephen Hayward, *Walnut Tree Farm;* Rt. Baker Orford, Esq., *Akenham Hall;* Samuel Rowland, farmer; Thomas Savage, *Glebe Farm;* and Robt. Woodward, Esq., *Rice Hall.*

ASHBOCKING, a pleasant village and parish, about 6½ miles N. of Ipswich and S. of Debenham, contains 321 souls, and 1382A. 3R. 33P. of strong loamy land, including an extra-parochial place of five houses, and a small manor called *Ketts de Campo.* Ash Hall, now a farm-house, is an ancient building, which was formerly moated. John Tollemache, Esq., is lord of the manor and owner of most of the soil. The *Church* (All Saints) was appropriated to Christ Church Priory, in Canterbury, from 1326 till the Reformation. The vicarage, valued in K.B. at £9. 18s. 6½d., is endowed with the rectorial tithes. The patronage is in the Crown, and the Rev. Wm. Gordon Pleas is the incumbent, and has 14A. of glebe, and a yearly modus of £375, awarded in lieu of tithes, in 1839. The *Town Estate,* consisting of 26A., let for £30 a year, was left for pious and charitable uses in 1432, by *John Austin.* The rent, after payment of land tax and quit rent, is applied in repairing the church and relieving the poor.

Alexander Wm. shoemaker
Baxter Wm. vict. Lord Nelson
Burleigh John Cecil, schoolmaster
Goodwin Philip, corn miller
Harvey John, shoemaker
Pleas Rev Wm. Gordon, vicar

Edwards Wm. || Freeman Edward
Freeman John || Gladwell Thos.

Garnham William
M'Cluer David || Pollard Charles
Todd Thomas || Wilson Wm.

BADLEY parish, 1¾ mile W.N.W. of Needham Market, contains a few scattered houses, 83 inhabitants, and about 1050 acres of land, mostly the property of the Earl of Ashburnham, who is lord of the manor, impropriator, and patron of the *Church* (St. Mary,) which is a perpetual curacy, valued at £40, and now enjoyed by the Rev. —. Hill, of Buxhall. Here was a chantry, valued at £10 per annum; and the church was given to the Templars by Robert Fitz-Jefferey, and confirmed to them by Richard Clare, Earl of Hertford. The Mortimers were anciently seated here, and from them the estate passed to the Pooleys and Crowleys. The *farmers* are, Thomas Snell Cooper, Geo. Hayward, Sarah and Samuel Jay, *corn millers;* John Kirby Moore, and Wm. Mudd, *Hall.*

BARHAM, a scattered village, 5 miles N.N.W. of Ipswich, and S.E. of Needham Market, has in its parish 1800 acres of land, and 576 inhabitants, including 183 in *Bosmere and Claydon Union Workhouse,* already noticed at page 222; and SHRUBLAND PARK, the beautiful seat of Sir W. F. F. Middleton, Bart., 6 miles N.N.W. of Ipswich. Joseph Burch Smyth, Esq., is lord of the manor of Barham, formerly held by the families of Southwell, Wood, Webb, and Burch. Sir W. F. F. Middleton owns a great part of the parish, and is lord of the manor of *Shrubland Hall,* which is partly in the adjacent parish of Coddenham, and was the seat of Edward, a younger son of Sir Nicholas Bacon, lord keeper of the great seal in the reign of Elizabeth, who acquired the estate by marrying the heiress of the Litle family. One of his descendants, Nicholas Bacon, erected a new mansion, which was taken down by Sir William Middleton, who was created a *Baronet* in 1804, and erected the present elegant mansion, to which he removed from Crowfield Hall. His son, the present baronet, succeeded in 1829, and has greatly enlarged and improved the mansion, which stands on a delightful eminence, overlooking the vale of the Gipping, in a well-wooded park of nearly 300 acres, stocked with deer, and noted for the finest Spanish chesnut trees in the county. The *Church* (St. Mary) is an ancient fabric, with a tower at the west end. In the chancel is a monument of one of the Southwells, and an inscription to Helena, wife of Edward Bacon, Esq., recording a remarkable instance of fecundity. This parish was appropriated to Ely priory, but, in the 37th of Henry VIII., the rectory, and a wood called Bergham coppice, were granted to John Southwell, Esq. The *rectory,* valued in K.B. at £12. 10s. 5d., and in 1835 at £342, is now in the patronage of J. Longe, Esq., and incumbency of the Rev. Wm. Kirby, M.A.

Sir Wm. Fowle Fowle-Middleton, Bart. *Shrubland Park*
Beaton Donald, gardener
Brown John, maltster
Care James, butler
Chandler Chas. baker, Workhouse
Cope John, vict. Sorrel Horse
Cross Charles, wheelwright

Fulcher Seth, shoemaker
Howard Crisp, master, and Mary, matron, *Bosmere & Claydon Union Workhouse*
Kirby Rev Wm. M.A. *Rectory*
Nichols Wm. schoolmaster, & Miller Eliza, schoolmistress, *Workhouse*
Palmer James, shoemaker

Smith Mr. John

FARMERS.

Barfield Sarah || Barrett John
Borley Geo. || Brook Robert

Brook Joseph, *Barham Hall*
Brook Wm.||Keen Chas. (bailiff)
Skipper Wm. || Wood Sarah

BARKING, a pleasant village and township, one mile S.W. of Needham Market, has 465 inhabitants. Its parish, which contains also the township of Needham Market, comprises 3164A. of land, including about 300A. of woodland, and a common of 50A. It is all in the manor of Barking, of which the Earl of Ashburnham is lord and principal owner. Sir Wm. F. F. Middleton, Shafto Adair, Esq., the Alexander family, King's College, Cambridge; and several smaller proprietors, have estates here. The land is mostly copyhold, subject to arbitrary fines. *Barking Hall*, a large ancient mansion, has been divided into tenements, and occupied by poor families since 1836. The manor and the advowson of the rectory belonged to the church of Ely, from the time of Edward the Confessor till the 4th of Elizabeth, when they were alienated, and retained by the Crown, until James I. sold them to Sir Francis Needham, whose son sold them to Francis Theobald, Esq. The son of the latter was highly distinguished for his skill in the Oriental languages. The *Church* (St. Mary) is a large Gothic structure, containing several monuments of the Crowley, Theobald, and other families, and having a tower at the west end, on which is this *inscription* :—" 10 Henry III. The Bishop of Ely has a grant of a *fair* at Barking, till the king is of age, to last four days, viz., on the eve and day of St. John the Baptist, and two following days." The *rectory* has that of Darmsden consolidated with it, and is valued in K.B. at £27. 10s. 7½d. The tithes of both parishes were commuted, in 1842, for a yearly modus of £800. The Earl of Ashburnham is patron, and the Rev. Francis Steward, M.A., is the incumbent. The Rectory House is a large and handsome mansion, which was built in 1819, by the Rev. C. Davy, the late rector, at the cost of £4000. In its garden are three fine cedar trees, planted in 1712. The *Charities of Barking Parish* are noticed with Needham Market.

BARKING.

Blogg Wm. shopkeeper
Codd Wm. vict. Lion
Cooke Samuel, blacksmith
Emsden Thomas, joiner
Gibson Thomas, corn miller
Hayward Edward, corn miller
Kerridge Geo. relieving officer, and regr. of births, deaths, & margs.
Last Ephraim, shoemaker
Last John, joiner
Reynolds Simon, wheelwright
Reynolds Isaac, wheelwright

Sheldrake Robert, schoolmaster
Steward Rev Fras. M.A. *Rectory*
Sykes Samuel, vict. Fox
Woollard Thomas, balcksmith
Woollard Luke, blacksmith

FARMERS.

Elliott Jph. || Gooding Martha
Gooderham Chas. || Lambert Roger
Lambert Wm. || Mullett Samuel
Noble Alfred || Preston George
Pryke Wm. || Smith Joseph
Snell Samuel || Waspe John

NEEDHAM MARKET, *in the manor and parish of Barking*, is a small town, township, and chapelry, sometimes called a hamlet, pleasantly situated on the western side of the small but navigable river Gipping, 9 miles N.W. by N. of Ipswich, 3 miles S.E. of Stowmarket, and 78 miles N.E. of London. It contains 1353 inhabitants, and about 1000 acres of land. Here is a deep lake of nearly 40 acres,

called *Bosmere*, from which this Hundred has part of its name. In 1801, the town had 247 houses; but in 1841, it had 321, of which 22 were unoccupied, and two were building, when the census was taken. It is tolerably well built, and formerly had a considerable woollen manufacture, and a weekly *market* on Wednesday; but both dwindled into insignificance after the town was visited by the plague in 1685, and soon afterwards ceased to exist. An unsuccessful effort was made, in 1838, to establish a Saturday market here. The town has still a yearly *fair* for cattle, &c., held on the 12th and 13th of October; and has enjoyed some share in the corn, malt, and flour trade, since the Gipping was made navigable from Ipswich to Stowmarket, in 1793. (See page 62.) The *Church* (St. John the Baptist) is a small plain building, with a wooden belfry, and was re-pewed in 1829. It is a perpetual curacy, valued at £91, in the patronage of the Rector of Barking, and incumbency of the Rev. Geo. Alex. Paske, M.A. Here is a neat *Independent Chapel*, built in 1837-8, at the cost of £1352, on the site of a smaller chapel, which had been rebuilt in 1717, and was founded by the congregation of the Rev. John Fairfax, M.A., who was ejected from the rectory of Barking in 1662, for non-conformity. Here is also a *Friends' Meeting House*, to which a girls' school is attached. In 1632, Francis Theobald, Esq., bequeathed a messuage called the *Guildhall*, to be taken down, and the materials to be used in erecting a *Schoolhouse* at Needham Market; and after endowing it with a yearly rent-charge of £20, he appointed certain feoffees to be governors of the school, according to the statutes made by him. These statutes direct that the trustees should appoint a graduate of the University of Cambridge, to be master of the school, and that he should teach the youth of Barking, Needham Market, and Darmsden, the first principles of *grammar*, and perfect them in reading and writing (to qualify them for apprentices) without fee or reward, except such of them whose parents the trustees should judge able to pay. Many years ago, the property on which the annuity of £20 was charged, was given up to the charity, in satisfaction of a large amount of arrears. The school estate, which comprises the Swan Inn, and about 11 acres of land called Marsh Meadows, in Needham Market, and an acre of meadow land in Barking, is now let for about £60 a year, out of which the master receives a salary of £50. He has also a dwelling-house, but is not a graduate of the University, the endowment being insufficient for the support of a regular grammar school. He teaches 17 poor children, as free-scholars, in reading, writing, and arithmetic. The ALMSHOUSES, in Needham Market, of which the origin is unknown, were repaired in 1836, and comprise two cottages, each having an upper and lower room. They are endowed with 9 acres of land at Creeting All Saints and St. Mary, let for £18 a year, out of which four poor women, occupying the lower rooms, have each 1s. 6d. a week, and a yearly supply of coals. About 20 years ago, four other poor women were placed by the trustees in the upper rooms, to live rent free, and towards their support the late James Alexander, Esq., gave the dividends of £500 three-and-a-half per cent. annuities, so that they have the same allowances as those in the lower rooms. The *Town Lands*, about 22A., let for about £40 a year, are vested in trustees, who distribute the rents in or about January, among the working poor of Barking and Needham Market, but the origin of the charity is unknown.

NEEDHAM MARKET.

Post-Office, at Jonathan Tydeman's: Letters are despatched to the south at half-past 7, and to the north at 6 evening.

Abbott Freeman and Jonth. auctioneers and land agents
Abbott Jonth. ironmonger and crown glue manufacturer
Abbott Mrs Mary
Abbott Miss Theodosia
Bedingfeld Misses Harriet & Sus.
Cane Wm. gentleman
Catchpole Mrs Susanna
Clabon Wm. wheelwright
Clarke Wm. gentleman
Elsden Edward, tea dealer
Goldsmith Ts. dressing machine mkr.
Goodchild Amos, glover, &c
Haggar Jph. rake & hurdle maker
Lingwood Edward, gentleman
Marriott Mrs Ann
Martin John Whymper, farmer
Moore John Carter, solicitor's clerk
Maw Samuel Alexander, farmer and owner
Maw Thos. bank agent and agent to the Suffolk and General Country Fire Office
Mount Wm. mousetrap maker
Paske Rev Geo. Alex. M.A. incbt.
Potter Thomas, basket maker

Rawlins Rev. Chas. B.A. curate of Creeting All Saints
Richards George, gentleman
Scopes Edward, bricklayer
Sheming Wm. tinner and brazier
Simpson James, cooper
Squire Mrs Rachel
Snell Henry, farmer
Studd George, hair dresser
Vincent Jonth. veterinary surgeon
Ward George, farmer
Ward Mrs Sarah & Mrs Sophia
Ward Sl. brickmaker & lime burner
Wells Mr John
Woodward John, farmer

ATTORNEYS.

Fox Wm. Leedes, (and *Stowmarket, Thursday)*
Hayward Fred. (Sup. Registrar and clerk to Magistrates)

BANKERS.

Alexanders & Co. (Ipswich & Needham Bank,) draw on Barnett, Hoares, & Co.: Thos. Maw, agt.

INNS & TAVERNS.

Bull, Robert Mudd
George Inn, Webster Adams
King's Head, Elizabeth Knight
Queen's Head, Richard Sage
Rampant Horse, John Mount
Swan Inn, Saml. Haggar, (posting)
Three Tuns, Wm. Tydeman

ACADEMIES.
(* *are Boarding.*)
*Diggens Misses Mary & Emily
Flatt Mary
*Grey Walter (Free Gram. School)
Payne Elizabeth
*Taylor Ann

Bakers.
Bowell Robert
Colchester Thos.
Lockwood Luke
Lucas Thomas
Overton Benj.
Race Martin

Beerhouses.
Reed Robert
Reeve Richard

Blacksmiths, &c.
Brown Edward
Claxon Edward
Tydeman Geo.
Tydeman Jonth.

Boot & Shoe Mkrs.
Baskett Robert
Brooke Robert
Deacon Walter
Farthing Moses
Groom Robert
Hearn John
Lucas Thomas
Mulley Edward
Page John, sen.
Page John, jun.
Read Robert
Read Thomas
Read Wm.

Butchers.
(* *are Pork.*)
Bennett Thomas
Hayward Geo.
*Lockwood Luke
*Mee Henry
Moore John
Smith Ezekiel

Cabinet Makers.
Godfrey Henry
Hooper Richard

Chemists & Drugt
Beales Samuel
Quinton John (& bookseller)
West Alban

Confectioners.
Dickerson Sophia
Race Martin

Corn Millers, &c.
Colchester Thos.
Hayward Edmd.
Southgate Abm.

Gardeners.
Carver J.
Lucas James
Overton Benj.

Grocers & Dprs.
Bagley James
Garrod John
Lambert Eliazar
Woodward John

Joiners, &c.
Chapman Robt.
Reeve Wm. and Son

Maltsters & Corn Merchants.
Mount John (and lime burner)
Steward George

Milliners, &c.
Booth Eliza
Deacon Mary
Moore Sar. Eliza

Painters, Plumbers, & Glaziers.
Blomfield Thos.
Coates Wm.
Cooper Samuel
Holden Ts. Jsa.
Lovick George

Saddlers.
Dearing James
Dearing Thomas

Shopkeepers.
Baskett Robert
Beales John
Garnham Stephn.
Taylor Wm.

Straw Hat Mkrs.	*Taylors.*
Chapman Sus.	Flatt Wm.
Read Mary	Green John
Surgeons.	Lambert Eleazar
Beck Henry	Mayhew Robt.
Beck Thomas	Studd John
Pennington Jas.	*Watchmakers.*
(agt. to Crown	Beard Philip
Life Office)	Davey John

COACHES

From the Swan Inn to Bury, Cambridge, &c., at half-past 11 morng.,

and 5 afternoon, and to Ipswich at 11 morning and 4 afternoon. Also, an *Omnibus* from Stowmarket to Ipswich every Monday & Thursday at 7 morning, to meet the London steamers.

CARRIERS.

Rt. Kerridge, and the *Mail Cart* to Ipswich and Stowmarket daily; and T. Theobald, Tues. and Sat. Garrod's waggons to Bury and Ipswich, M., Tu., Thu. and Fri.

BATTISFORD, a village and parish, $2\frac{1}{2}$ miles W. by S. of Needham Market, and 3 miles S. of Stowmarket, contains 520 souls, and 1542A. 3R. of land, skirted by a rivulet which runs eastward to the Gipping. It is in two *manors* called St. John's and Battisford Hall. Wm. Raikes, Esq. is lord of the former, and Mrs. Reynolds is lady of the latter; but W. Adair, Esq. and several small owners have estates in the parish. The sub-soil is a strong clay, and the *common* (about 200A.) was enclosed in 1812. The old hall, which was a seat of the Bacons, was taken down about 80 years ago. About 135 acres of land in *St. John's manor*, is tithe free, being the site of a *Hospital* of Knights of St. John of Jerusalem, which, at the dissolution was valued at £53. 10s., and granted to Sir Richard Gresham, who, with Richard Billingford, had a grant in 1545, of the manor of Battisford Hall, which had been held by the Bishop of Norwich. *Sir Thomas Gresham*, the son of Sir Richard, founded the Royal Exchange, in London, and had the frame of that edifice constructed here upon the common; and most of the timber used in the work was the growth of this neighbourhood. The *Church* (St. Mary) was repaired in 1841, and has a lead roof and small belfry. The *vicarage*, valued in K.B. at £8. 0s. $7\frac{1}{2}$d., is endowed with all the tithes, which were commuted in 1842, for a yearly modus of £400. 5s. The Rev. Edward Paske is patron and incumbent. The poor have an annuity of 20s., left by *Walter Rust*, in 1685, for a distribution of bread on the 22nd of July. Here is a small *school*, erected by subscription in 1843. *Directory :—* Robert Andrews, shopr.; Wm. L. Baker, farmer; Obdh. Brook and Daniel Brunning, *blacksmiths;* Mrs. Fayers, Thos. Studd Harwood, farmer, *Battisford Hall;* Edward Lingwood, farmer, *Manor House;* Isaac Lucky, farmer; Henry Sparrow, bricklayer; Edward Spink, wheelwright; and Samuel Wright, parish clerk.

BAYLHAM, or *Bailham*, a village and parish, 3 miles S.S.E. of Needham Market, and 6 miles N.W. by N. of Ipswich, contains 277 souls, and 1332 acres of land. In the 14th century, it was the lordship of the Burnavilles, and afterwards passed to the Andrews, Windsors, and Actons. Sir W. F. F. Middleton is now lord of the manor and owner of a great part of the soil, and the remainder belongs to Thomas Robinson, Esq., and a few smaller owners. The *Church* (St. Peter) is a rectory, valued in K.B. at £12. 4s. 9d., and now having 40A. of glebe, and a yearly modus of £300, awarded in lieu of tithes, in 1842. John Barthorp, Esq., is patron, and the Rev. William Colville, M.A., incumbent. The other principal inhabitants are Edward

Gooding, *shoemaker;* Misses Mary and Frances Rodwell; Rt. Rogers Smith, *corn miller;* Samuel Smith, *blacksmith;* and Samuel Cross, Henry Edwards, James Gladwell, John Howard, James Howes *(Hall,)* and Thomas Mount, *farmers.*

BLAKENHAM (GREAT) is a small village and parish, on the Stowmarket road, 5 miles N.W. by N. of Ipswich, comprising 180 souls, 842 acres of land, a large water-mill on the Gipping, and two good inns on the turnpike. The *manor and advowson* were given by Walter Gifford, Earl of Buckingham, to *Bece Abbey,* in Normandy; and were afterwards conferred by Henry VI. on the Provost and Fellows of Eton College, to whom they still belong; but part of the parish belongs to John Peecock, Esq., J. B. Smyth, Esq., and a few smaller owners. The *Church* (St. Mary) is a plain tiled fabric, and the rectory, valued in K.B. at £6. 16s. 0½d., is enjoyed by the Rev. Charles Robert Ashfield. The glebe is 7A. 2R. 29P., and the tithes were commuted in 1840, for a yearly modus of £195. *Directory :—* Denney Cresswell, *shoemaker;* John Deering, *shopr.;* Wm. Fuller, vict., *Chequers;* Mary Pyman, vict., *Bell;* Ann Riches, *blacksmith;* Robert Wood, *miller, maltster,* and *corn and coal merchant;* John Peecock, Esq. (and Ipswich;) John Hayward Buckingham, Charles Cooper *(Hall;)* Edward Edwards (and maltster;) Edgar Marsh and Sarah Marsh, *farmers.*

BLAKENHAM, (LITTLE,) 4½ miles N.W. of Ipswich, is a small village and parish, containing 119 souls, and 1046A. 1R. 9P. of land. Sir T. G. Cullum is lord of the manor, but part of the soil belongs to Mrs. Meynell, Mr. J. Elliston, and Mr. B. Morgan. Great quantities of *limestone* are got and burnt here for agricultural and building purposes. The *Church* (St. Mary) is a neat structure, with a tower at the west end. The *rectory,* valued in K.B. at £10. 3s. 4d., is in the patronage of Postle Jackson, Esq., and incumbency of the Rev. George Capper, M.A., who has 35A. 20P. of glebe, and a yearly modus of £253, awarded in lieu of tithes in 1839. *Directory :—* Wm. Cockerell, Louisa Cobbold, Benj. Green, Wm. Hayward, *(Hall,)* and Benj. Morgan, *farmers;* Fredk. Hayward, *lime burner;* Rev. John Jackson, *curate;* and Joseph Lewis, *hurdle maker.*

BRAMFORD, a large village on the navigable river Gipping, 2½ miles N.W. by W. of Ipswich, has in its parish 3246A. 3R. 33P., of fertile land, and increased its population from 552 souls, in 1801, to 833, in 1841. The gross annual value of its land and buildings is £5383. Here is a "common and tye" of nearly 10 acres; and 10A. 1R. 10P. is in cottage gardens. In the reign of Edward I., Bramford was the lordship of Robert de Tibetot; but for many years, the Acton family had their seat here. Sir Philip Broke is lord of the manor of Bramford; and George Thomas, Esq., is lord of Lovetofts manor, in which is *Lovetofts Hall,* a farm-house, on or near the site of the ancient seat of the Tibetots. The *Church,* with the Berewicks of Burstall and Albrighteston belonging to it, was given to Battle Abbey by William Rufus; and that Abbey had the rectory, and were patrons of the vicarage, till the 33rd of Henry VIII., when it was granted to Christ Church, Canterbury, in exchange. The Dean and Chapter of Canterbury are now the patrons, and also appropriators of the great tithes of Bramford and Burstall, which are held on lease by Sir P. Broke. They have also

a rectorial manor, in which their tenants hold by leases of 21 years, renewable every seven years, on the payment of certain fines. The *vicarage*, with the curacy of Burstall annexed to it, is valued in K.B. at £13. 3s. 4d., though it is now worth only about £80 per annum. The Rev. George Naylor, B.A., is the incumbent. Here is a Wesleyan Chapel, erected in 1842. BRAMFORD HALL, which was the seat of the Acton family, belongs to Sir P. Broke, and is now occupied by the Dowager Lady Middleton. It is a neat brick mansion, commanding a delightful view, and distant 3½ miles N.W. of Ipswich. In 1703, *Wm. Acton* gave to the poor of Bramford £200, to be laid out in land, for a quarterly distribution of bread, meat, &c. It was laid out in the purchase of a cottage and 14 acres of land, at Stow Upland, now let for about £20 a-year. The land was exonerated from tithes by Nathaniel Lee Acton, Esq., in 1796. The poor parishioners have also a yearly rent-charge of £5, left by *Francis Brooke*, out of a farm here. The *Poor's Houses* are three tenements, occupied by six widows, and repaired at the parish expense.

Bagley John, blacksmith
Basket Caleb, cattle dealer
Bowman Jas. baker & flour dealer
Burch John, saddler, &c
Chamberlain James, schoolmaster
Charlesworth Rev John, incumbent of Flowton
Clark Wm. Chapman, gent. *Lodge*
Collins Mrs Elizabeth
Doe William, bricklayer
Edwards Edward, corn miller
Harrison Francis, joiner, &c
Hewes Thomas, joiner, &c
Lovely Wm. vict. Crown
Markham Thos. vict. Angel Inn
Middleton Dowager Lady Harriet, *Bramford Hall*
Miller Thomas, tailor
Naylor Rev Geo. B.A., vicar
Pallant Thomas, butcher
Pratt John, saddler
Pyman Brice, maltster
Rogers Thomas, wheelwright

Simpson George, cooper
Smith Matilda, schoolmistress
Steward Rev Ambrose, *White House*
Stokes Robert, gent. *Lodge*
Talmash Wm. tailor
Wiggen Rebecca, vict., Cock

SHOEMAKERS.
Giles Isaac || Heiffor James
Mayes Thomas || Upton John

SHOPKEEPERS.
Brook Isaac (and draper)
Hardwick John || Parker James

FARMERS.
Button Mary || Cullum Thomas
Cullum Thos. Cutting|| Daines John
Edwards Wm. || Goss Richard
Markham Thomas||Lewes Joseph
Morgan Geo. (& chief constable)
Morgan Geo. James||Morgan John
Mumford Robert Wm. *Grove*
Wood Richard Rudland (and brick maker) *Lovetofts Hall*

BRICETT (GREAT) is a village and parish, 4 miles E. by N. of Bildeston, and 5 miles S.W. of Needham Market, containing 214 inhabitants, and 915A. 2R. 29P. of land. Here was a *Priory*, founded about 1096, by Radulfus Fitzbrian, and Emma his wife, and dedicated to St. Leonard. They endowed it with the manor and tithes of Bricett, the tithes of Smithfield in London, and other property. Americ Peche, a descendant of the founder, confirmed all the gifts of his ancestor, and founded a chantry in the chapel. This priory having been made a cell to Nobiliac, in France, was suppressed in the 5th of Henry VI., and its revenues granted to the Provost and Fellows of King's College, Cambridge, who are still lords of the manor, appropriators of the rectory, and patrons of the *Church* (St. Mary and St. Lawrence,) which is a perpetual curacy, valued at £100, and now enjoyed by the

Rev. Arthur Young. In the east window is a profusion of stained glass, representing Edward the Confessor, and other figures and devices. In the chancel is a marble monument, in memory of John Bright and his wife, of Tolmach Hall, who died in 1670 and 1679.   Geo. Mumford, Esq., of *Bricett Hall;* Wm. Adair, Esq., Gen. Grosvenor, Rev. R. Jackson, J. Shreiber, Esq., and several smaller owners, have estates in the parish.   *Directory :* James Bloomfield, parish clerk ; Chas. Clark, corn miller ; Henry Moore, farmer ; George Mumford, Esq. ; Howard Procter, blacksmith ; John Reynolds, wheelwright ; John Scopes, shop-keeper ; and Thomas Tampion, blacksmith.

   CLAYDON, a well-built village, 4 miles N.N.W. of Ipswich, is a great thoroughfare, being at the junction of the turnpikes from Bury St. Edmund's and Norwich.   It is on the east side of the navigable river Gipping, where there are *lime-kilns* and a *whiting manufactory.*   Its parish contains 418 souls, and 951A. 37P. of land.   Sir W. F. F. Middleton is lord of the manor, but a great part of the soil belongs to Tooley's Almshouses, in Ipswich, (see page 79,) Mr. W. Cockerell, and W. Corder, Esq.   The manor was formerly held by the Southwell and Acton families.   Half a mile S. of the village, is *Mockbeggars' Hall,* an ancient house occupied by a farmer.   The *Church* (St. Peter) is a rectory, with that of Akenham annexed to it, valued in K.B. at £10, and now having 50 acres of glebe, and a yearly modus of £506, awarded in lieu of the tithes of both parishes.   Mrs. Tyley is the patroness ; and the Rev. Thomas Nunn, M.A., is the incumbent.

AlexanderN1. glover & breeches mkr
Alexander Wm. hair dresser
Baker Rev. Hy. curate of Barham
Barfield Maria, postmistress (letters received and desp. at 7 morning and 8 evening)
Beer John, tollbar lessee
Bradstreet Aaron, carpenter
Calver John, cooper
Cooper Thomas, *whiting manfr*
Forsdike Isaac, carpenter
Hayward Jeremiah, gardener
Heslop Thomas, tailor
Keddington Mrs Martha & Cath.
Lord Reuben, baker
Lovely Benj. vict. *Crown*
Morgan Wm. blacksmith (*aged* 93)
Miller John, tailor
Moye Jeremiah, schoolmaster
Offord Chas. vict. *Greyhound*
Offord and Morphew, cattle dealers

Phillips Charles, Esq. R.N.
Rudland MaryAnn&Sarah, schoolms
Sawer Charles, surgeon
Waller Henry, corn miller
Webb Mr Wm.||Raffe Mr Craig

Butchers.
Groom Geo. and Samuel
Moore Elijah

FARMERS.
* *are Owners.*
Burgess Wm.(& lime burner)
Cockerell Robt.
*Cockerell Wm.
Kersey Edward, (*Mockbeggars' Hall*)
Rodwell Robert
Seaman Jonthn. (*Claydon Hall*)

*Watkins Edw.

Saddlers.
Field Wm.
Ring Richard

Shoemakers.
Bickers Jonthn.
Bridges John
Morgan Daniel
Mills George

Shopkeepers.
Ashford James
Last John (and builder)
Moore John

   CODDENHAM is a large and well-built village, with several hand-some houses, picturesquely situated near a rivulet, 3 miles E.S.E. of Needham Market, and 7 miles N. by W. of Ipswich.   It formerly had a fair on October 2nd, and has now *Petty Sessions* once a month.   Its parish contains 924 inhabitants, and 2719A. of fertile and well-wooded land, including part of *Shrubland Park,* (see page 223,) the beautiful seat of Sir W. F. F. Middleton, Bart., lord of the *manors* of Dennies-with-Sackvilles, and Shrubland Hall, which comprise the chief part of

the parish; but here is a small manor belonging to the vicarage; and Lieut. Col. Leak, and a few smaller proprietors, have estates here. The *limestone* got and burnt here is well suited both for agricultural and building purposes. The *Church* (St. Mary) is a large and handsome Gothic fabric, with a tower at the north-west corner, containing eight bells. The east window is of beautiful stained glass. In the chancel are several handsome monuments of the Bacon, Longe, and other families. Above one of them, hangs an inscription, written on parchment, in memory of Capt. Philip Bacon, second son of Richd. Bacon, Esq., of Shrubland Hall, a distinguished naval commander, who was killed in an engagement with the Dutch, on the 1st of June, 1666. This church was given to Royston Priory by Eustachius de Mere, about the year 1220. The impropriation was granted in the 36th of Henry VIII. to J. Atkyns, and afterwards passed to the *Rev. Baltazar Gardemau*, a French missionary, who was vicar here in 1736, and settled the rectory in trust for the use of the succeeding vicars for ever, but subject to a yearly rent-charge of £5 for the poor. The Rev. Robert Longe is patron and incumbent of the *vicarage*, which has that of Crowfield annexed to it, and is valued in K.B. at £12. 0s. 5d., but is now worth about £1000 per annum, having 28A. 1R. 35P. of glebe, and being endowed with a small manor and all the tithes of Coddenham, for which a yearly modus of £644 has been paid since 1841. The vicarage-house is a commodious mansion, which was partly rebuilt in 1770, when a curious representation of the crucifixion was found and deposited in the vestry. In 1753, *Lady Cathn. Gardemau*, relict of the above-named Rev. Baltazar Gardemau, gave the FREE SCHOOL which she had erected, with a garden and playground of about half an acre, and conveyed to trustees a farm of 52A. 1R., in the parishes of Mendlesham and Earl Stonham, for teaching 15 poor boys and 15 poor girls, of Coddenham, to read, write, and cast accounts, and the girls knitting and sewing also. The farm is now let for about £75 a year, of which £45 is paid to the schoolmaster, and the remainder is expended in books, stationery, and clothing, for the children, after paying for repairs, &c. The school is conducted on the national system, and the number of free scholars was increased to 50, in 1810. Children of Crowfield are admitted when Coddenham cannot supply the whole number. The Vicar is the acting trustee; and the annuity of £5, paid by him out of the rectory, as noticed above, is distributed in clothing among the poor parishioners. Here is a *Savings Bank*, which was established in 1818, and in Nov. 1842 had deposits amounting to £26,753, belonging to 894 depositors. It has a branch bank at Stowmarket; and Mr. Charles Pritty is the actuary. One of the neat *Italian Lodges*, at the principal entrances to Shrubland Park, is in this parish, and the other in Barham. (See page 223.)

Acfield John, plumber, glazier, and painter
Bird James, master of Free School
Blomfield Benj. baker
Blomfield Barrington, surgeon
Brown Sarah, blacksmith
Brown Wm. joiner
Chapman Manning, land agent to Sir W. F. F. Middleton, Baronet
Chapman Thomas, spirit merchant
Corner Wm. thatcher
Cross Charles, wheelwright
Crowe Charles, Esquire
English Richard, bricklayer
Forsdike Thomas, beerhouse
Fox John, land agent and valuer
Goodwin Geo. gent||Freeman Mrs
Gowers Mr John & Mrs Hannah

Hayward Robert, wheelwright
Hill Benjamin, parish clerk
Kirby Mrs Mary Ann
Kittoe Captain Markham
Longe Rev Rt. M.A., *Vicarage*
Moore John, butcher
Offord John, well sinker
Offord Wm. blacksmith
Page Hannah, schoolmistress
Podd Patience & Esther, milliners
Pritty Charles, Savings' Bank acty
Scoggin James, cooper
Scoggin Samuel, butcher
Smith Moses, saddler, &c
Spurling Wm. glover
Taylor Wm. bricklayer
Thorpe Wm. vict. Crown Inn (and joiner and builder)

Farmers.
Brook Fenning
Brook Robert
Diggens Thomas

Field George
Fox John (and corn miller)
Hicks Wm.
Jacobs Isaac
Lewis Richard
Morley Daniel
Pritty Charles
Rushbrooke Jno. (& lime burnr)
Salmon Thomas
Sparrow Charles
Stimson Robert
Wright Jonathan

Grocers.
Gibbons George
Mayhew Orford
Pritty Charles(& draper)
Trapnell Wm.(& baker)
Shoemakers.
Brunning Saml.
Clark Wm.
Lovett Henry
Mayhew Orford
Tailors.
Blowers Fredk.
Miller Henry
Miller Lionel

CARRIERS TO IPSWICH.
George Chaplin, daily, except Friday ; and Wm. Wells, Monday, Wednesday, and Saturday

CREETING ALL SAINTS, ST. MARY'S, and ST. OLAVE'S, are three parishes, in which the houses are intermixed, and form a straggling village, extending from 1½ to 2½ miles N.E. of Needham Market, and containing 512 inhabitants, of whom 286 are in All Saints', 196 in St. Mary's, and 30 in St. Olave's. The three parishes contain 3115A. of land, of which 1286A. are in All Saints', 1441A. in St. Mary's, and 388A. in St. Olave's. They are ecclesiastically united, and have now but one church. The Provost and Fellows of Eton College are lords of the *manor of Creeting St. Mary,* which was anciently called the Priory of Creeting, and was a cell to the abbey of Bernay, in Normandy, with which it remained till the suppression of the alien houses, when it was given to Eton College. Wm. Adair, Esq., is lord of the manor of Creeting St. Olave, which was given by Robert de Moreton, Earl of Cornwall, about 1070, to the abbot and monks of Grestein, in Normandy, who afterwards erected a priory here, which they sold in 1347 to Sir Edmund de la Pole. The manors and advowson of St. Olave's and All Saints' were held for a long period by the Bridgman family, who sold them in 1753 to P. C. Crespigny, Esq. R. Keeble, Esq. now owns a great part of All Saints', and the other principal owners of land in the three parishes are, W. Adair, Esq., the Earl of Ashburnham, Eton College, and Mr. Thomas Crane, but here are a number of smaller proprietors. BOSMERE HALL, 1 mile S.E. of Needham Market, is a neat mansion, with pleasant grounds, bounded by the river Gipping and the small lake called Bosmere. It is the property of Sir W. F. F. Middleton, and is occupied by Major General Chas. Turner. The *Church of St. Olave* was standing in 1532, when John Pinkney was buried in the chancel, but it went to decay in the 17th century, and no traces of it now remain. *All Saints' Church* stood near St. Mary's, but being very much decayed, it was taken down in the early part of the present century, and was found to have no foundations, the ground having merely been levelled and then built upon. *St. Mary's Church,* which now serves the three parishes, is an ancient structure, in good repair, standing upon a commanding eminence. The *three rectories*

are now consolidated, and are valued in K.B. as follows :—All Saints', at £10. 0s. 5d. ; St. Mary's, at £7. 14s. 2d. ; and St. Olave's, at £4· 17s. 8¼d. They are in the patronage of Eton College, and incumbency of the Rev. John George Dupuis, M.A., who has about 50 acres of glebe, and a yearly modus of £766, awarded in 1839, in lieu of tithes. *Dunche's Charity Estate*, the original acquisition of which is unknown, is vested in trustees, and appropriated to the use of the poor of Creeting All Saints, except two yearly payments of 6s. 8d. each, to the poor of St. Mary and St. Olave. It comprises about 41A., let for about £40 a year, and five tenements, occupied rent-free by poor people. In 1813, *Margaret Uvedale* left £300 to the rector and churchwardens, in trust, to distribute the interest thereof among poor parishioners of All Saints' of the age of 60, or upwards. This legacy was invested in £300 Navy five per cents. ; and the new four per cent. stock, substituted for the same, was sold by the trustees for £315, now at interest. A cottage in the churchyard is let by the churchwardens for 30s. a year, which is applied with the church rate. In 1619, *John Campe* left a yearly rent-charge of 30s., to be applied as follows in St. Mary's parish, viz., 6s. 8d. for repairing the church spire, 3s. 4d. for the repair of the chancel, and the remainder for the poor, on St. Thomas' day. *Creeting St. Peter* lies west of these three parishes, in Stow Hundred, and is described at a subsequent page.

*Marked * are in Creeting All Saints ; † in St. Olave's ; and the rest in St. Mary's.*

Beck Edward, gentleman
†Bixby Robert, corn miller
*Dupuis Rev John George, Rectory
*Fayers Eliz. corn miller, *Bosmere*
Hicks Wm. cattle dealer and vict. King's Head
Scopes George, bricklayer
Sheldrake Wm. corn miller, *Hawkesmill*
Turner Major-General Charles, *Bosmere Hall*

Blacksmiths.
*Offord George
*Stedman Thos.
*Webber Lydia

FARMERS.
Beard Wm.
†Blogg Samuel
Clover James
Elsden Edw.
*Keeble Richd.
*Kettle Sarah
Lambert Henry
Martin John

Moore Henry, *College farm*
*Mudd John
*Turner Charles
*Tydeman Edmd.

Joiners, &c.
Lockwood Benj.
Lockwood Wm.

Wheelwrights.
Page Wm.
*Roshier John

CROWFIELD, a village, township, and parochial chapelry, annexed ecclesiastically to Coddenham parish, is pleasantly situated about 4½ miles E.N.E. of Needham Market, and S.S.W. of Debenham. It has 385 souls, and about 1700 acres of fertile land, mostly a strong clay and loam. *Sir W. F. F. Middleton, Bart.*, is impropriator of the rectorial tithes and lord of the *manor;* and his family were seated here till the early part of the present century, when they removed to Shrubland Park. (See page 223.) The hall is now occupied by a farmer. Thomas Maw, Esq., Rev. H. Syer, and a few small proprietors have estates here. The *Church* is a humble fabric, with a small belfry, and is a curacy, consolidated with the vicarage of Coddenham. The *Baptists* have a small chapel here.

Cator Jeremiah, shopkeeper
Fenning Fenn, shoemaker
Gibbons John, carpenter
Graister John, blacksmith
Hayward Samuel, shopkeeper

Lockwood Robt. maltster and beerhouse; Rt. Richardson, manager
Mayhew Wm. corn miller
Rous Wm. tailor
Summers Wm. vict. *Rose*

Vincent Abraham, farrier

FARMERS.

Baskett Nathl. || Beard Charles
Calver Chas. || Coates Mary
Double Thomas || Field John

Ford Henry || Gosling Jeremiah
Greenwood Robt. || Hall John
Ling Wm. || Mayhew George
Mills Samuel || Read Robert
Mudd Timothy

DARMSDEN, a small parochial chapelry, consolidated with Barking rectory, has only 61 souls, and about 790 acres of land, 1 mile S. by E. of Needham Market. It is the property of the Earl of Ashburnham and Sir W. F. F. Middleton, Bart, and is partly in the manor of *Taston Hall,* now a farm-house. The *Church* is a small ancient fabric, and the rectory has been united with that of Barking from an early period, under the name of *Barking-cum-Darmsden.* (See page 224.) The *farmers* are, Wm. Knock, James Meadows Moore, John Mudd, and Thomas Snell.

FLOWTON, a small parish and village, 6 miles W. by N. of Ipswich, and N.E. of Hadleigh, contains only 179 souls, and 495 acres of freehold land, belonging J. Hunt, Esq., General Rebow, and a few smaller owners. The *Church* (St. Mary) is a plain tiled fabric, with a tower at the west end. The rectory, valued in K.B. at £3. 9s. 9½d., and now having a yearly modus of £140 in lieu of tithes (warded in 1839,) is in the patronage of H. S. Thornton, Esq., and incumbency of the Rev. John Charlesworth, B.D. The *Poor's Land,* 5A. 3R., was purchased with £26, given by Robert Derehaugh and Wm. Vesey, and was conveyed to trustees in 1674, for the relief of the poor parishioners. *Directory :*—John Dedman, bricklayer ; John Lewis, corn miller ; Mr. Daniel Mills ; and John Hardwick, John Holland, Samuel Moor, *(Hall;)* James Morfey, Davy Veasey and Robert Wilson, *farmers.*

GOSBECK, on the Debenham road, 7½ miles N. of Ipswich, and 5 miles E. of Needham Market, is a scattered village and parish, containing 316 souls, and 1466A. 2R. 16P. of strong clayey land. Sir W. F. F. Middleton is lord of the manor of Gosbeck-with-Newton, and J. Tollemache, Esq. is lord of a small manor here, called *Ketsalfield.* Part of the parish is in two other manors, of which R. B. Orford and J. B. Smith, Esqrs. are lords. E. B. Venn, Rt. Welham, B. Blomfield, Robert Stimson, Rev. J. Ward, Mrs. Pizzey, and several smaller owners have estates here. The soil is partly free and partly copyhold. The *Church* (St. Mary) is a neat structure, with a tower at the south west corner, and was repaired in 1842, at the cost of £60. The rectory, valued in K.B. at £8. 5s. 5d., and in 1835, at £316, is in the incumbency of the Rev. George Capper, M.A., of Wherstead, for whom the Rev. Thomas Brown officiates. — Porter, Esq., was patron in 1835. The tithes were commuted for a yearly rent-charge, in 1843.

Braham Lucy, shopkeeper
Fenning, Richard, parish clerk
Garrard Wm. shoemaker
Jay Edward, corn miller
Pizzey Mrs Mary
Smye Robert, vict. Greyhound
Taylor John, bricklayer
Ward James, blacksmith

FARMERS.

Battrum Robert
Catt Joseph, *Manor house*
Chapman James Cook
Churchyard William
Gibbons James || Mayhew Wm.
Mulner Oliver || Stimson Robert
Pizzey John Meadows
Thurmott Edward || Walne John

HELMINGHAM is a scattered village, and a well-wooded and picturesque parish, 4 miles S. of Debenham, at the junction of the turnpikes from Ipswich and Woodbridge, and about 9 miles from each of those towns. It contains 284 inhabitants, and 2438 acres of land, all (except the glebe) the property of John Tollemache, Esq., of HEL-MINGHAM HALL, a large and handsome quadrangular mansion, with a court yard in the centre, built in or about the time of Henry VIII., of red brick, which was cemented some years ago in imitation of stone. It contains a fine collection of paintings, a good library, and a considerable collection of ancient armour, and is completely surrounded by a moat, filled with water, and crossed by two draw-bridges. The moat, and the basin which feeds it, are frequented by great numbers of wildfowl of various species. The *Park* comprises 375 acres, sheltered on the north by boldly rising grounds, and stocked with numerous herds of deer, among which are a few stags, or red deer, which are remarkably large. It is finely clothed with wood, and contains some of the finest oaks in this part of the kingdom. The ancient *Family of Tollemache* has been seated here from an early period, but was settled at Bentley for some time after the Norman Conquest. Hugh de Tollemache, or Talmache, of Bentley, was summoned among the barons to attend Edward I. in his expedition to Scotland. Lionel Tollemache, having married the heiress of the Helminghams, of Helmingham, acquired this estate, and made it his residence. His grandson, Lionel, was high sheriff of Norfolk and Suffolk, in the 4th of Henry VIII.; and the grandson of the latter, of the same name, was high sheriff of Suffolk in the 34th of Elizabeth, who conferred on him the honour of knighthood. His son, Lionel, was created a *baronet* on the first institution of that dignity, in 1611. Sir Lionel, great-grandson of the first baronet, on the death of his mother, the daughter and heiress of the *Earl of Dysart*, succeeded, by the law of Scotland, to that earldom. He for many years represented Suffolk in Parliament, and was also lord-lieutenant, custos-rotulorum, and vice-admiral of the county. The fourth in succession from him was Wilbraham Tollemache, who succeeded his brother in 1799, and died without issue, when the titles and honours of the house of Dysart passed to the late Countess of Dysart, who died in 1840, and was succeeded by Sir Lionel Wm. John Tollemache, the present *Earl of Dysart and Lord Huntingtower,* whose English seats are Ham House, Surrey, and Buckminster, in Leicestershire; but the Helmingham and many other estates passed to John Tollemache, Esq., who has greatly improved Helmingham Hall, since he came into possession. The *Church,* (St. Mary,) embosomed in wood, stands by the side of the park, and with a cottage, inhabited by a person who takes care of the vault and splendid monuments of the Tollemache family, forms a beautiful and picturesque object. Here, among other gallant warriors, is interred the heir of the family, who fell before Valenciennes, in 1793. Upon the monuments are many well-executed figures, in marble, by Nollekens and other eminent sculptors. The *rectory,* valued in K.B. at £18, has 37A. 33P. of glebe, and a yearly modus of £540, awarded in 1839, in lieu of tithes. The patronage is in the crown, and the Rev. Edmund Bellman, M.A., is the incumbent. The *poor* receive from J. Tollemache, Esq., the interest of £10, left by James Gosling, in 1748, and a yearly rent-charge of 10s. out of Bottom Farm, left by an unknown donor.

Tollemache John, Esq. *Helming-*
  ham Hall
Bellman Rev Edmd., M.A. *Rectory*
Brunning Richard, shoemaker
Groom Thomas, carpenter
Jessop John, wheelwright
Lee J. gamekeeper
Oxborrow Robert, blacksmith

FARMERS.

Alexander Jph. || Colthorp Charles
Ashwell Benjamin, *Valley Farm*
Bellman John Harvey || Dove Rd.
Feaveryear James || Fulcher Saml.
Garnham James || Mahew Sarah
Kersey Joseph Hy. *Bocking Hall*
Kersey Samuel, *Old Hall*
Pasford Joseph

HEMINGSTONE, a village and parish, $5\frac{1}{2}$ miles N. of Ipswich, contains 381 souls, and 1444A. 1R. 6P. of land, mostly freehold, and belonging to Richard B. Martin, Esq., Rev. M. G. Edgar, Sir W. F. F. Middleton, Mr. L. Leedes, and a few smaller owners. Camden says that Baldwin le Petteur held lands here by the ridiculous serjeantcy of jumping, belching, and f—t—g before the king; such was the plain, jolly mirth of ancient times. A similar tenure existed at Wattisham, in Cosford Hundred. *Hemingstone Hall*, the seat of R. B. Martin, Esq., is a brick mansion, in the Elizabethan style, situated in a pleasant vale, 6 miles N. of Ipswich. It was built by Wm. Style, Esq., who died in 1655. The Shawe, Church, and Thorne families had formerly mansions here. The *Church* (St. Gregory) is a neat structure in the decorated style. On the north side it has apparently two porches; but one, called *Ralph's Hole*, is said to have been built by Ralph Cantrell, who, being a Roman Catholic, saved his property, and satisfied his conscience respecting a vow he had made, of never entering a Protestant place of worship, by erecting this oratory, in which, by means of a small aperture, he could hear divine service without entering the church. The *rectory*, valued in K.B. at £8. 11s. $5\frac{1}{2}$d., has 70A. 2R. 20P. of glebe, and a yearly modus of £369. 5s. 5d., awarded, in 1837, in lieu of tithes. Sir W. F. F. Middleton, Bart., is patron, and the Rev. Thomas Brown, B.A., incumbent.

Barker Wm. shoemaker & shopkpr
Brown Rev. Thos., B.A. *Rectory*
Chapman Wm. shoemaker
Fenning Robert, parish clerk
Fenn Simon, tailor
Fulcher James, blacksmith
Martin Richard B. Esq. *Hall*

May Henry, wheelwright

FARMERS.

Brook Benjamin || Copping Wm.
Chapman Saml. || Chapman Susan
Leedes Luke || Fenn Richard
Peacock Joseph || Page Daniel
Potter John || Walno John

HENLEY, a scattered village and parish, on the Debenham road, $4\frac{1}{2}$ miles N. of Ipswich, contains 329 inhabitants, and 1232A. 3R. 26P. of land, mostly having a strong clayey soil. A large portion of it belonged to the late Sir Charles Broke Vere, who died in 1843. (See page 125.) The Vere family had a seat here more than two centuries. The Rev. J. M. Theobald is lord of the manor, owner of part of the parish, and lessee of the rectorial tithes under the Dean and Chapter of Norwich, who are patrons of the *vicarage*, which is valued in K.B. at £10. 0s. 10d., and is now enjoyed by the Rev. Miles B. Beevor. The *Church* (St. Peter) has a tower and five bells. In 1841, the rectorial tithes were commuted for a yearly modus of £256, and the vicarial tithes for £118 per annum. The *Baptists* have a small chapel here. In 1766, *Thomas Vere, Esq.*, left £200 to be invested in the funds, and the dividends to be applied yearly as follows:—£3 to be

distributed among the poor parishioners; 10s. to be paid to the clerk; and the remainder to the vicar for a sermon on Good Friday. This legacy is vested in £215. 17s. 9d. three per cent. Reduced Annuities.

Chambers Harriet, schoolmistress
Drury Rev George, B.A. curate
Girling Mary, blacksmith
Ibbitson Miss Harriet, *Henley Hall*
MorganGeo. corn miller; h Bramford
Parker Jas. carpenter & beerhouse
Silbons — shoemaker

Warren Charles, wheelwright and parish clerk
FARMERS.
Brook Isaac || Barker Joseph
Fenn Simon || Garnham John
Mills John || Paxman Richard
Seaman John || Street James

MICKFIELD, a scattered village, 3 miles W.S.W. of Debenham, has in its parish 263 souls, and about 1300a. of land, belonging to Mrs. Huntington, R. Dalton, Esq., Rev. — Skinner, Mrs. Durham, and several smaller owners. Two *manors* are mentioned here—viz., Wolney Hall and Flede Hall. The first appears to have belonged to the alien priory of Grestein in Normandy, and to have been sold by that convent to Tydemanus de Lymbergh, about the year 1347. The *Church* (St. Andrew) is a neat building, with a tower at the south west angle. The *rectory*, valued in K.B. at £9. 11s. 0¼d., has 26a. of glebe, and a yearly modus of £390 awarded in lieu of tithes in 1838. The Rev. M. Simpson is patron and incumbent. In 1612, the *Rev. John Metcalf* left a messuage in Bread street, Woodbridge, to the churchwardens of Mickfield, in trust to pay the Easter offerings, and other common expenses of the parishioners. It is now let for £20, which, after paying 13s. 4d. for Easter offerings, is applied with the church rates, as also is £5 the rent of a cottage, adjoining another cottage appropriated to the use of the parish clerk.

Beecroft Henry, shoemaker
Berry James, blacksmith
Quinton John, shopkeeper
Shulver Wm. wheelwright
Simpson Rev Maltyward, B.A.
   Rectory

Sparrow Edgar, parish clerk
FARMERS.
Catchpool Garnies || Dove Edward
Catchpool Geo. || Gowing David
Durham Amelia || Field Wm.
Pettit Wm. || Hammond Jas.

NETTLESTEAD, a picturesque parish, 4 miles S. of Needham Market, and 6 miles N.E. of Ipswich, has only 98 inhabitants, and 1028a. 3r. 26p. of land, rising in bold undulations, divided into four farms, and belonging to W. M. Carthew, Esq., G. Tomlin, Esq., Sir W. F. F. Middleton, Mrs. Meynell, and several smaller freeholders. Jas. Cudden, Esq., is lord of the manor, but *Nettlestead Hall* is the residence and property of Mr. Edward Snell. This ancient mansion is the subject of one of Mrs. Cobbold's beautiful poems, and was a seat of the noble family of Wentworth from 1450 till the reign of Charles I., when Thomas Wentworth, Earl of Cleveland, and Baron Wentworth, of Nettlestead, sold it to William Lodge, of London. The Earls of Richmond and Brittany held the lordship of Nettlestead from the Norman Conquest, till the 17th of Henry II. Peter de Savory had a grant of it in the 25th of Henry III., and the Tibetots held it from the reign of Edward I. to that of Edward III., after which it was held for some time by the Despensers. The *Church* (St. Mary) is a neat building with a tower at the west end. The living is a discharged *rectory*, valued in K.B. at £8. 11s. 10½d., and now having 4a. of glebe and a yearly modus of £196 awarded in 1840 in lieu of

tithes.   Postle Jackson, Esq., is patron, and the Rev. John Jackson
incumbent.   The *farmers* are Samuel Cook, *Rookery ;* John Dynes,
Watering Farm ; and Edward Snell, *Nettlestead Hall* and *High Hall.*

OFFTON parish has a number of scattered houses, and a small village, 4½ miles S. by W. of Needham Market, and 7½ miles N.W. by
W. of Ipswich.   It contains 417 souls and 1530 acres of land, including the small hamlet of LITTLE BRICETT, which has only 25 inhabitants, and the farm of *Tolmage* or *Tolmach Hall,* distant more tha
a mile W. of Offton church, and now the property and manor of Wm.
Adair, Esq.   Little Bricett has been annexed to Offton since 1503,
previous to which it was a separate parish, and had a church which was
appropriated to Thetford Priory by Robert de Reims.   The hall,
now a farm house, had its name from the ancient family of Tollemache,
and was a seat of the Kemps and D'Autreys.   James Cudden, Esq.,
is lord of the manor of *Offton,* but a great part of the soil belongs to
Wm. Adair, Esq., H. W. Sparrow, Esq., C. Kersey, Esq., and several
smaller owners.   Upon a chalk hill here, once stood an ancient *castle,*
which tradition ascribes to Offa, king of Mercia, after he had slain
Ethelred, king of the East Angles, and seized his dominions.   From
the same monarch, the village also is said to have derived its name.
No vestiges of the castle are extant.   The *Church* (St. Mary) was
in the appropriation of Thetford priory, but in the 32nd of Henry
VIII., the rectory and advowson were granted to Thomas, Duke of
Norfolk.   H. W. Sparrow, Esq., is impropriator of Offton and patron
of the *vicarage,* which has the rectorial tithes of Little Bricett, and
is valued in K.B. at £7. 16s. 0½d.   The Rev. N. J. Stubbin is the
incumbent, and has a yearly modus of £189, awarded in 1839, when
£218. 10s. was awarded to the lay impropriator in lieu of the rectorial
tithes of Offton.

Ackfield Joshua, grocer and draper
Archer George, wheelwright
Archer Daniel, wheelwright
Chaplin John, cattle dealer
Church Thomas, jun. shoemaker
Cousins Thomas, blacksmith
Green Wm. carpenter
Mullett Mary, maltster
Nichols Edward, wheelwright
Shepherd Wm. thatcher
Simpson John, parish clerk
Steward John, shoemaker

Stubbin Rev Newman John, vicar of
    Offton and rector of Somersham
Tomkins Robt. vict. Greyhound
Vincent Abraham, farrier
        FARMERS.
Barber Geo. Lee || Church Thos.
Kistruck Jas. || Cranfield Saml.
Kistruck Elizabeth, *Tolmage Hall*
Menns Robt. || Raynham Dinah
Wyard My. Ann || Rush Edward
Wyard John, *Castle Farm*

RINGSHALL, a scattered village and parish, 4 miles W.S.W. of
Needham Market, and 4½ miles S. of Stowmarket, contains 356 inhabitants, and 2116 acres of strong clayey land, chiefly arable.   Wm.
Adair, Esq., is lord of the manor, which was formerly in four manors,
called Ringshall, Charles-Hall, Rokels, and Rawlins.   A large portion of the parish belongs to Sir J. R. Rowley, the Rev. R. Johnson,
and the Jenny, Hitchcock, Squirrell, and a few other families.   The
hall and manors were formerly held by the Barkers, Watsons, and
Greshams.   The *Church* (St. Katherine) is a neat fabric, exhibiting
some remains of Norman architecture; but the east window is decorated, and three in the chancel are in the perpendicular style.   The

rectory, valued in K.B. at £11. 18s. 1½d., is in the patronage of the Master and Fellows of Pembroke College, Oxford, and incumbency of the Rev. Charles Fredk. Parker, M.A. The tithes were commuted, in 1839, for a yearly modus of £562. Here was formerly a Free-Chapel, belonging to Norwich priory, and endowed with 30A. of land.

Dickinson Daniel, shoemaker
Goodchild James, shoemaker
ParkerRevChas.Fred.,M.A.*Rectory*

FARMERS.

Beaumont Isaac ‖ Gibbons Thomas
Cooper James, *Charles Hall*

Hayward Thos. *Ringshall Hall*
Hitchcock John ‖ Luffin James
Makens Robert ‖ Nicholls —
Squirrell John ‖ Squirrell Robert
Steadman John

SOMERSHAM, 5½ miles N.W. of Ipswich, and 6½ miles N.E. of Hadleigh, is a pleasant village and parish, containing 484 souls, and 1027A. of land, belonging to Mrs. Eliz. Norman, C. Kersey, Esq., the Rev. N. J. Stubbin (in right of Mrs. Stubbin, lady of the manor,) and several smaller owners, who have estates here. The Bohuns, Earls of Northampton, were many years lords of the manor, which, in 1483, was given by Richard III. to the Duke of Buckingham. It has since passed to various families. The *Church* (St. Mary) is a neat structure, with a tower at the west end, and is a *rectory*, valued in K.B. at £8, and now having 32A. 31P. of glebe, and a yearly modus of £280, awarded, in 1839, in lieu of tithes. The Rev. N. J. Stubbin, of Offton, is patron and incumbent. The *Independents* and *Baptists* have chapels here. The *Town Land*, 1A. 3R., is let for £4. 15s. a year, which is distributed among the poor at Christmas. A great part of the land is farmed by persons residing in the adjoining parishes. The following are the principal inhabitants:—

Andrews George, shopkeeper
Andrews Samuel, plumber & glazier
Bradley John, corn miller
Clover John Wm. beerhouse
Dedman Wm. beerhouse
Fenn Thomas, parish clerk
Gardiner Edward, shoemaker
Haward Henry, farmer
Haxwell Robert, blacksmith

Lait Wm. wheelwright
Moore George, butcher
Norman Peter, blacksmith & shopr
Oxborrow John, tailor and shopr
Phillips Joseph, schoolmaster
Raynham Rt. vict. *Duke of Marlbro'*
Scott Thomas, carpenter
Wellham Robert, bricklayer
Wyard Mary, farmer

STONHAM ASPALL, a large, pleasant, and well-built village, 5 miles N.E. of Needham Market, 6 miles E. of Stowmarket, and 11 miles N. by W. of Ipswich, has in its parish 772 inhabitants, and 2399A. 2R. 25P. of land. Sir W. F. F. Middleton is lord of the manor, but a great part of the soil belongs to the Turner, Taylor, Dalton, Lock, Venn, and other families. The *Aspall* or *Haspele* family were many years lords and patrons here, and their name was added to that of the parish, to distinguish it from the two neighbouring parishes of Stonham Earl and Stonham Parva. *Broughton Hall*, now a farm-house, was the seat of a branch of the ancient family of *Wingfield*, the last of whom died here in 1762. In the churchyard is a monument in memory of Anthony Wingfield, Esq., whose effigy in alabaster, much injured by time, is represented in a recumbent posture, grasping a serpent. The *Church* (St. Lambert) is a beautiful specimen of the decorated style, with a tower, containing a fine peal of ten bells, presented, during last century, by Mr. Eccleston, of Crowfield. The interior was

repaired in 1843, and in the preceding year, a new fine-toned organ was erected. The east window has a rich display of flowing tracery. The *rectory*, valued in K.B. at £19. 10s. 2½d., is in the patronage of Sir W. F. F. Middleton, and incumbency of the Rev. Charles Shorting, M.A. The glebe is about 50A.; and in 1837, the tithes were commuted for a yearly rent-charge of £666. 10s.

In 1612, the Rev. JOHN METCALF, rector of this parish, bequeathed his lands in Stonham, Pettaugh, and Winston, to be conveyed to 16 inhabitants of Stonham Aspall, for the following public uses and charitable purposes in this parish, viz.,—a tenement called *Pitts* (two cottages and gardens,) for keeping the church path from Broad green in repair ; 43A. of land, for repairing the church, paying the lord's rents, and discharging common expenses of the parishioners ; a tenement called *Smith's*, comprising a house, double cottage, stable, and 46A. of land, for a schoolmaster, to teach freely the youth of Stonham and Pettaugh, and to pay 40s. out of the rents yearly to the *usher;* a tenement called *Curtaines*, comprising a house and 7A. 2R. of land for the *usher*, conditionally that he should also do the duty of sexton or parish clerk ; a barn and 13A. of land, adjoining the glebe, and a house and 5A. 2R. 24P., for the maintenance of *four poor parishioners*, under the name of *almspeople;* and a tenement called Mouses, with Spittle-house croft, and land called Cockroyd, Abbot's close, Long Sponge, &c. ; that the churchwardens should dispose of the rents thereof, in supplying the defect of alms to the four almspeople, in paying the yearly offerings of the parishioners communicating at Easter, and the fines that may be levied on the testator's customary lands ; and that they should bestow the surplus, if any, in the common expenses of the parishioners; but that they should allow the rector to occupy the *Town Close* (8A. 2R.,) at the fixed annual rent of £5. The property given for maintaining four almspeople is let for £27. 2s. 6d. a year. The property given for repairs of the church, payment of lord's rents, and of common expenses of the parishioners, and that given for supplying the defect of alms, the payment of Easter offerings, &c., comprise together a farm of 52A. 9P., let for £53. 10s. a year, and the Town Close, let for £5. These rents, after paying £2. 10s. yearly to each of the four almspeople, and various sums for quit-rents, &c., are applied with other funds towards the reparation of the church, and the causeway mentioned in the will. The schoolmaster's house and land are worth £65 a year, but are occupied by himself. The usher occupies the house and land left for him, and they are worth £16 a year. The *School* is free to all the boys of this parish and Pettaugh for instruction in reading, writing, and arithmetic ; but the master (the Rev. Rt. Leggett, B.A.,) is allowed to take other scholars, who pay for their education. Here is also a *Girls, Free School*, supported by the rector and other subscribers; and in the village is a Ladies' Boarding School.

STONHAM ASPALL.

Allard Elijah, tailor
Ashford Rt. & Chas. grocers, drapers, ironmongers, and druggists
Berry Wm. bricklayer & whiting mfr
Blowers Thomas, cabinet maker
Blowers Wm. shoemaker
Bobbit Wm. S. bookkeeper
Catchpole Mrs Elizabeth
Cook John, corn miller
Cuthbert John, traveller
Dallaston Robert, joiner
Denny Mary Ann, ladies' boarding and day school
Higgins John, *carrier* to Ipswich
Houghton Edmd. grocer & draper
Kemp Henry, bricklayer
Leggett Rev Rt., B.A. free schoolmr
Offord Geo. blacksmith, & *Creeting*
Oxborow Kezia, schoolmistress
Oxborow Samuel, shoemaker
Pepper John, wheelwright and vict.
  Ten Bells
Reeve Benjamin, tailor

Shorting Rev Charles, M.A. *Rectory*

FARMERS.

Aldridge George || Cracknell Ann
Creasy Sarah || Freeman Edward
Fulcher Nathaniel || Higgins John
Garnham James, *Upson Hall*

Grimwade Wm. *Broughton Hall*
Martin Stephen || Mulliner John
Rolfe John || Simpson Edgar
Simpson Henry, butcher & cattle dlr
Taylor Hy. *Red House*||Taylor Wm.
Turner John || Webb James

STONHAM (EARL,) a parish and considerable village, 5 miles E.
of Stowmarket, and 1 mile S.W. of the Post-office at Stonham Pie,
contains 878 inhabitants, and 2520A. 3R. 31P. of strong clayey land.
Messrs. Holmes, Jackson, and Sparke, of Bury St. Edmund's, are lords
of the manor, which is mostly freehold, and belongs chiefly to the executors of N. H. Smith, Esq., J. Welham, J. Garnham, Fdk. Matthew,
J. H. Cuthbert, and a few smaller owners. It anciently belonged to
the Earls of Norfolk, and from them was called Earl Stonham, to distinguish it from the two neighbouring Stonhams. The Duke of Norfolk had a grant of a market and fair here in the first of Edward III.,
but they have been obsolete several centuries. *Deerbolts Hall*, now
a farm-house, was the seat of the Driver family, whose heiress married
the late Richard Moore, Esq. The *Church* (St. Mary) is a neat cruciform structure, with a tower at the west end, and has a beautiful
ceiling. The *rectory*, valued in K.B. at £17. 2s. 6d., is in the patronage of Pembroke Hall, Cambridge, and incumbency of the Rev. John
Phear, who has 33A. of glebe, and a yearly modus of £659, awarded,
in 1839, in lieu of tithes. The *Plymouth Brethren* have a small chapel here.

A close called Blunt's (3A. 1R. 2P.,) and Acre Meadow, in the manor of
Filiol, in Earl Stonham, were settled in the 19th of Edward 4th, in trust
for the common benefit of the parishioners. GEORGE REEVE, in the 42nd
of Elizabeth, settled in trustees 20A. of land, at Stowmarket and Stow-
Upland, for maintaining a *schoolmaster* to teach poor children of Earl Stonham. At the same time, the *Hall field* (7A.) was settled for apprenticing
and buying books for the poor scholars, and the *Mill field* (6A.,) for the use
of the poor. A messuage and 3A. of land called *Dunham's,* were settled, in
the 15th of Henry 8th, for the benefit of the parishioners. For the same
purpose, the Guildhall (now the *schoolhouse,*) and a barn and 20A. called
Thradstones, near Stowmarket, were settled in the 15th of Edward 4th.
Burnt House land (8A.) was purchased, in 1681, for the use of the parish,
with sundry benefactions and money arising from the sale of wood. These
CHARITY ESTATES, with some other land, purchased for and appropriated
to the general use of the parishioners, are partly freehold and partly copyhold, and are under the direction of certain feoffees, and the churchwardens
for the time being. They comprise altogether about 64 acres, let for about
£90 a year. The rents are carried to the same general account, and applied partly in paying a salary of £9 to the *schoolmaster*, who teaches eight
free scholars; in providing about £9 worth of clothes for the free scholars;
in buying gowns for two poor women; and in distributing about £14 among
poor parishioners; and the rest of the income, after paying quit-rents and
various contingent expenses, is applied towards the expenses of the churchwarden, constable, &c.

STONHAM (EARL.)

Buck Robert, farrier & vict. Angel
Buxton Hayward, bricklayer
Doe Lemon, beerhouse and baker
Dunnington Richard, corn miller

Hayles Wm. joiner
Phear Rev John, *Rectory* .
Polard Daniel, schoolmaster

Blacksmiths.
Bendall Thomas

Clark Jesse (and
machine mkr)

Runnacles Mchl.	Martin John	Roper Hannah	Thurston George
Taylor Isaac	Matthew Fredk.	Tydeman Scapy	(and butcher)
FARMERS.	Mayhew George	Welham John	
Baker Robert	Moore Samuel		*Shoemakers.*
Brown Abraham	Nunn Cornelius	*Grocers & Drprs.*	Frost Edward
Cracknell James	Plowman Saml.	Ager Jonathan	Mills Samuel
Garnham John	Plowman S. jun	Ford John	Peirpoint John
Harwood Joseph,	Robinson Edmd.	Gall James	Runnacles Mich.
Deerbolts Hall	Robinson Wm.		

STONHAM (LITTLE,) or *Stonham Parva*, a scattered village and parish, 11 miles N. by W. of Ipswich, and 5 miles E.N.E. of Stowmarket and W.S.W. of Debenham, contains 368 souls, and about 1190 acres of land. On the Ipswich and Norwich turnpike it has two good inns, one of which (the *Magpie*) is a regular *post-office*, commonly called *Stonham Pie*. At the point where the Debenham and Stowmarket road crosses the turnpike, is a large brewery and malting establishment. The parish is sometimes called *Stonham Jerningham*, from the ancient family, who were lords here for many years. It is in two *manors*, viz., Stonham Hall, of which Sir W. F. F. Middleton is lord, and Fleet Hall with Waltham Hall, of which Wm. Parry, Esq., is lord. The copyholds are subject to arbitrary fines, but a great part of the parish is freehold. The Blomfield, Hunt, Cuthbert, and other families have estates here. The *Church* (St. Mary) is a neat structure, with a fine tower. The *rectory*, valued in K.B. at £9. 17s. 8½d., is in the patronage of Wm. Haydon, Esq., and incumbency of the Rev. W. C. Leach, who has 32A. of glebe, and a yearly modus of £330, awarded in lieu of tithes, in 1842. The *Baptists* have a chapel here.

In 1481, the Rev. JOHN BEALE bequeathed his tenement called the Pie, with a piece of ground called Caxtrelis, or Catissett, and a yard called Ide's yard, to feoffees, in trust, that out of the rents thereof, they should keep the premises in repair, and lay out the remainder in repairing the highways of Little Stonham. The property thus vested in trust comprises the large ancient inn and posting-house called the *Magpie*, and about three roods of land ; and was let by the trustees, in 1696, on lease for 160 years, at the small annual rent of £3, to Jonathan Reeve, who laid out about £220 in improving the inn, and covenanted, for himself and the succeeding owners of the lease, to keep it in good repair. The inn and the land are let by the present lessee for about £70 a year. Several unsuccessful attempts have been made to set aside the lease, so that the parish might enjoy the full annual value of the estate. In 1523, MARGARET GOWLE left about 15 acres of land in Chilton, for charitable uses in Little Stonham ; and it is now let for £20 a year, which is distributed, during winter, in coals, by the churchwardens, among the poor parishioners. The TOWN FARM, 37A. 1R. 6P., let for £56 a year, was derived chiefly from the bequest of *Thos. Crowe*, in 1483, and partly from the bequests of *Barnaby Gibson*, in 1597, and *Wm. Blomfield*, in 1685. The rent is applied as a stock for the common weal of the parishioners, mostly for the reparation of the church and roads, and partly in distributions of bread among the poor; together with £5. 10s. a year, as the rent of a double cottage and garden, purchased with £20 given by Barnaby Gibson, and £10 given by the parishioners. The interest of £20, left by *Gilbert Mouse* for distributions of bread, is paid out of the rent of the Town Farm. The parish *constable* has, by ancient usage or otherwise, 3R. 38P. of land, now let for 26s. a year. In 1685, *Robert Devereaux* left £10 for the aged poor, and it was laid out in the purchase of half an acre of land, which now lets for 12s. a year, and forms part of a pightle of

1A. 18P., of which the remainder is glebe. The *Parish School* is supported by subscription.

STONHAM (LITTLE.)

Post Office, at Mr Jas. Gurr's, *Magpie Inn.* Letters are desptchd. to Ipswich, Colchester, London, &c. at 10 night; and to Norwich, &c. at 5 morning.

Buttrum Martha, schoolmistress
Cooper Valentine, shopkeeper
Crooks Robert, blacksmith
Cuthbert John Hunt, brewer, maltster, corn mert. & brick & tile mkr
Gurr Jas. vict. Magpie Inn (posting house and post office)

Jukes —, superintendent of police
Leach Rev Wm. Crowley, *Rectory*
Noy Isaac, vict. Brewers' Arms
Page Samuel, wheelwright
Pooley Wm. Thomas, brewer (j.)
Thurlow Henry, parish clerk
Tydeman Jesse, carpenter

FARMERS.

Bevans James || Blomfield John
Edwards John, *Waltham Hall*
Edwards Thomas||Whissell Robert
Williams John, *Stonham Hall*

SWILLAND, a small village and parish, 6 miles N.N.E. of Ipswich, and N. W. of Woodbridge, has 270 inhabitants, and 951A. of land. Nathl. Byles, Esq., is lord of the manor, which was formerly held by the ancient families of Berghersh and Despencer. Mrs. A. C. Barker, T. M. Gibson, Esq., W. C. Fonnerau, Esq., and a few smaller owners, have estates here. The *Church* (St. Mary) was appropriated to Wykes Nunnery, in Essex; but the rectory was granted in 1528, to Cardinal Wolsey, towards the endowment of his college at Ipswich. The *Vicarage*, valued in K. B. at £7. 9s. 4d., is now endowed with the rectorial tithes, and is in the patronage of the Crown, and incumbency of the Rev. H. C. Morrell. The tithes were commuted in 1840, for a yearly modus of £252. The *Poor's Land*, about three roods, is let to the vicar, for £2 a year, which is distributed at Christmas. *Newton Hall*, a farm-house in this parish, is occupied by a hind. *Directory :* Fredk. Buttrum, *corn miller ;* John Knight, *blacksmith ;* James Lambert, *shoemaker ;* Wm. Leach, parish clerk ; Rev. H. C. Morrell, *Vicarage ;* Robt. Stagg, cattle dealer and vict., *Half Moon ;* and Wm. Catt, Alfred Cutting, Wm. Marshall, Matthew Peacock, *(Hall,)* James Palmer, and John Parsey, *farmers.*

WILLISHAM, nearly 4 miles S. by W. of Needham Market, and 7½ miles N.W. of Ipswich, is a village and parish, containing 217 souls, and about 1000 acres of strong, clayey land, mostly the property of the Rev. E. B. Sparke, the lord of the manor, impropriator of the tithes, (commuted in 1839, for £142. 10s. per annum,) and patron of the *Church*, (St. Mary,) which is a perpetual curacy, in the incumbency of the Rev. Geo. Alex. Paske, who has £13 a year from the impropriator, and 25A. of land, purchased with Queen Anne's Bounty. It was appropriated to Trinity Priory, in Ipswich, and at the dissolution was granted to Lord Windsor, from whose family it passed to the Brownriggs. In or about 1610, *Geo. Kirk* left for two poor families, 1A. 3R. of land, to which 17P. of waste land was added about 1825. The whole is let for £4. 10s. a year, which is divided by the churchwardens, at Christmas, among poor parishioners, together with 12s. a year paid out of Willisham Hall estate, in satisfaction of a donation of £10, left by John Brownrigg, in 1661. *Directory :* Wm. Blythe, Wm. Boby, *(Hall,)* and John Harper, *farmers ;* Robert Fisk, *lime burner ;* (h. Ipswich ;) John Grimwood, *bricklayer ;* Jph. Hardwick, *shopkeeper ;* John Hood, *beerhouse ;* and Robt. Mullett, vict., *Shoulder of Mutton.*

SAMFORD HUNDRED

Forms a Superintendent Registrar's District, and its 28 parishes were *incorporated* for the maintenance of their poor, under Gilbert's Act, in 1764. It is in the *Deanery* to which it gives name, in the Archdeaconry of Suffolk, and Diocese of Norwich. It has generally a rich and loamy soil, and is a picturesque and well-cultivated district, the south-eastern portion of which forms a fertile peninsula, between the estuaries of the Orwell and Stour, terminating at the confluence of those broad arms of the sea, opposite Harwich. It is of an angular figure, and its western side is about nine, and each of its other sides fourteen miles in length. It is bounded on the south by the Stour, which separates it from Essex; on the west, by Babergh and Hartismere Hundreds; on the north, by Bosmere and Claydon Hundred, and the borough of Ipswich; and on the east, by the Orwell. It is watered by several rivulets, crossed by the Ipswich and London road, and will be intersected by the Eastern Counties *Railway*. It has no market town, but those of Ipswich, Manningtree, (in Essex,) Nayland, and Hadleigh, are near its borders. The following enumeration of its *parishes* shews their territorial extent, the annual value of their lands and buildings, as assessed to the property tax in 1815, and their population in 1801 and 1841.

PARISHES.	Acrs.	Rental.	Populatn. 1801.	1841.	PARISHES.	Acres.	Rental. £.	Population. 1801.	1841.
Belstead*	1012	1198	212	261	Holton St. My.	810	1147	190	187
Bentley	2801	3320	337	419	Raydon	2335	2916	367	592
Bergholt East	3064	5846	970	1461	Shelley	928	1147	137	139
Brantham	1922	2368	300	404	Shotley	2051	2866	284	464
Burstall	766	1074	151	223	Sproughton* ..	2380	3555	353	585
Capel St. Mary	1910	2896	401	608	Stratford StMy†	1432	2650	502	647
Chattisham ..	714	917	161	215	Stutton	2138	2479	406	492
Chelmondiston	1293	1639	320	564	Tattingstone§	1637	2279	620	628
Copdock	932	1759	225	299	Washbrook ..	1414	2309	278	506
Erwarton	1318	1450	195	199	Wenham Great	1108	1294	170	198
Freston	1414	1763	142	224	Wenham Little	970	1507	69	87
Harkstead	1727	1909	220	338	Wherstead....	2019	2759	237	238
Higham	863	1407	202	259	Woolverstone	951	1146	241	246
Hintlesham ..	2828	3569	419	583					
Holbrook	2203	2438	447	747	Total	44,940	61,607	8556	11,813

* Small portions of *Belstead* and *Sproughton* are in the borough of Ipswich.

† Stratford St. Mary had 17 visitors, in 1841.

§ Tattingstone, in 1841, included 191 persons in the *Hundred House of Industry*.

☞ The CHIEF CONSTABLES are Mr. John Brooke, of Little Whenham; and Mr. Daniel Packard, of Stutton.

The *Superintendent Registrar* of Samford Hundred is Eleazar Lawrance, Esq., of Ipswich; and the *Registrars of Births and Deaths* are Mr. Geo. Bickmore, of Capel St. Mary, for *Capel District*; and Mr. Daniel Kerridge, of Washbrook, for *Holbrook District*. The latter is *Relieving Officer* for the whole Hundred.

SAMFORD HUNDRED INCORPORATED HOUSE OF INDUSTRY is at Tattingstone, 5½ miles S.S.W. of Ipswich, nearly in the centre of the 28 parishes, which, as already noticed, were incorporated under Gilbert's Act, for the support of their poor, in 1764. The corporation of guardians, or

overseers, still exist in their original form, though they act in conformity with most of the provisions of the *new poor law*. The sum originally borrowed for the erection of the House of Industry was £8250, and the building was finished in 1766, for the accommodation of 500 paupers, many of whom were employed in spinning worsted yarn, for the Norwich manufacturers, till hand spinning was superseded by machinery. Some alterations were made in the house in 1819 and '37, for the better classification of the inmates, of whom the average number is about 220. The number in the house, when the census was taken, in 1821, was 319; in 1831, 310; and in 1841, 191. They are well lodged, clothed, and fed, under the superintendence of Mr. William and Mrs. Catchpole, the master and matron. The former is also *clerk to the corporation.*

THE HUNDRED OF SAMFORD BENEFIT SOCIETY, established in 1840, had 350 insuring, and 18 honorary members, and a stock of £700, in June 1843. Mr. Wm. Catchpole, of Tattingstone, is the honorary secretary.

THE SAMFORD ASSOCIATION FOR THE PROSECUTION OF FELONS was established in 1823. J. Gosnall, Esq., of Bentley Hall, is treasurer; and E. Lawrance, Esq., of Ipswich, solicitor.

BESTEAD, a small village, 4 miles S.W. of Ipswich, has in its parish 261 souls, and 1012 acres of land. Sir Robert Harland is lord of the manor and owner of a great part of the soil, and the remainder belongs to F. W. Campbell, Esq., Misses Innes, and a few smaller owners. The Goldinghams sold the manor, in 1560, to Mr. Blosse, a rich clothier of Ipswich; and the heiress of his family sold it, in the early part of last century, to the Harlands. The *Church* (St. Mary) is a neat structure, with one side-aisle, and a tower on the south side. It contains a handsome monument in memory of the Blosse family. The *rectory*, valued in K.B. at £7. 6s. 0½d., and in 1835 at £295, has 54A. of glebe. The Rev. John Freeman, M.A., is patron, and the Rev. Joseph Lane, M.A., incumbent. In 1794, *Charles Bedingfield* left £80 for the poor of this parish, and it was laid out in 1754, with £15 given by Mary King, in the purchase of a double cottage and 4½A. of land, now let for £15. 18s. per annum, which is distributed among the poor at Christmas. In 1765, *Mary King* left the residue of her personal estate to the successive rectors of Belstead, for the relief of poor parishioners. The sum of £200 was derived from this bequest, but £50 was lost by the insolvency of a bank at Ipswich; and the remaining £150 is vested at 3½ per cent. interest.

Britton Fredk. wheelwright	Harris Eliz. and John, farmers
Burch George, blacksmith	Harwood Thomas, farmer, *Hall*
Clark Wm. parish clerk	Josselyn John, shoemaker
Codd Wm. Frost, corn miller	Shepherd Mrs. farmer
Collett Rev Wm. B.A. curate	Warden Jph. hurdle maker & vict.
Garnham Nathl. wheelwright	Buck's Horns
Garnham Robt. blacksmith	

BENTLEY parish, 6 miles S.W. of Ipswich, and 5 miles N. by E. of Manningtree, has a small village, many scattered houses, 419 inhabitants, and 2801A. 38P. of sandy but fertile land, mostly the property of A. W. J. Deane and J. Gosnall, Esqrs. The former is lord of the manor and owner of the hall, which was a seat of the ancient family of Tollemache, who removed from hence to Helmingham. On the banks of a rivulet 2 miles S.W. of the village, is the site of *Dodnash Priory*, which was a small house of Black Canons, founded at an

early period by one of the Earls of Norfolk, and dedicated to St. Mary. It was suppressed, and given to Cardinal Wolsey, towards the endowment of his college at Ipswich, in 1524, when it was valued at £42. 18s. 8½d.   The manor of Bentley, the rectory, the advowson, and two woods called Portland Grove and New Grove, were held by Trinity Priory, in Ipswich, and were granted at the dissolution to Lionel Tollemache, Esq.   The *Church* (St. Mary) is a discharged vicarage, valued in K.B. at £6. 2s. 11d., and now having 20A. of glebe, and a yearly modus of £190. 15s. in lieu of tithes.   The old vicarage house was exchanged in 1843 for a mansion situated near the church.   The Rev. C. E. R. Keene is patron, and the Rev. Wm. Brooke, M.A., incumbent.   The tithes were commuted in 1838, when the following yearly moduses were awarded to the lay impropriators, viz., £361. 5s. to Mr. Keene, and £85 to Mrs. Deane.   In 1716, *Tolmach Duke* charged the Church House Estate with the yearly payment of £2 for a distribution of bread among the poor parishioners.

Alexander George, shopkeeper
Booth Wm. corn miller
Brooke Rev Wm. M.A. vicar
Button Joseph, corn miller
Burch Philip, vict. "The case is altered."
Gosnall John, Esq. *Bentley Hall*

Long Charles, shopkeeper
FARMERS.
Hart Wm. (& maltsr.)||Hart Chas.
Lay James || Holland John
Page Gosnall, *Lodge* || Woods Wm.
Richardson Wm. Scrivener

BERGHOLT, (EAST) a large and well-built village, with several handsome mansions and well stocked shops, is pleasantly situated near the north bank of the river Stour, 6 miles S.E. of Hadleigh, 9½ miles S.W. of Ipswich, and nearly 3 miles W.N.W. of Mannigtree, where the Stour begins to expand into a broad estuary.   It formerly had a market and a considerable manufacture of flannel, baize, &c., but they went to decay more than a century ago.   It has a *fair* for toys, &c., on the first Wednesday in July.   Its parish increased its population from 970 souls in 1801, to 1461 in 1841; and contains 3063A. 2R. 34P. of land.   Sir Rd. Hughes, Bart., C. T. Oakes, Esq., the Dowager-Countess of Morton, C. Rowley, Esq., the Rev. J. Rowley, and W. H. Travis, Esq., have estates and *handsome residences* here; and the rest of the parish belongs to the Exors. of Sir Gilbert East, J. King, W. Lott, J. Pearson, J. Green, E. Busk, J. Gosnall, E. Cook, J. Ansell, and a few smaller proprietors.   The Dowager-Countess of Morton is lady of the *four manors* called Old Hall, Illarys, Spencer's, and St. John's, in the first of which the custom of Borough English prevails.   These manors were formerly held by the Hankeys, and lately by the Godfreys.   St. John's was given by Henry II. to the Templar Knights of St. John of Jerusalem, but was granted to the Earl of Oxford in the 36th of Henry VIII.   In 1562, here were three water mills, but only one of them is now standing.   The late *Sir Richard Hughes*, of East Bergholt, was created a *baronet* in 1773.   The *Church* (St. Mary) is a neat structure, in the decorated Gothic style, but its tower is only finished to the height of fourteen feet; the sums given towards rebuilding it, about the year 1522, being insufficient for its completion.   The five bells hang in a sort of cage in the churchyard.   The *rectory*, with that of *Brantham* annexed to it, is valued in K.B. at £25. 10s., and is in the patronage and incumbency of the Rev. Joshua Rowley, M.A.,

who has about 45A. of *glebe* in the two parishes, and two yearly *moduses*, viz., £820 from East Bergholt, and £500 from Brantham, awarded in 1837, in lieu of tithes. Here is an *Independent Chapel*, belonging to a congregation which had its origin in 1689.

East Bergholt *Town Lands*, &c., were purchased in 1695, with part of a fund which had arisen from benefactions in and before the reign of Elizabeth, for providing victuals to be sold at a cheap rate, and for other charitable purposes. They were conveyed to new trustees in 1816, and comprise six cottages at Burnt Oaks, let for £17 a year; a close of 5A. 2R. 1P., let for £9 a year; and 8A. 3R. of land called Cow-Pasture, let for £30 a year. The trustees have also £80 three per cent. annuities. The yearly income (about £58) is laid out in linen, which is distributed among poor parishioners on New Year's-day. In 1720, *Edward Clarke* left three cottages for the residence of three poor widows, and endowed them with a rent-charge of £12 a year out of his farm in Tattingstone. In 1725, *Joseph Chaplin* left an estate, now consisting of a cottage, barn, and 16A. of land, to Henry Hankey Esq., and his heirs, in trust, to apply the rents thereof in providing coats and shoes for five poor men, and gowns, petticoats, and shoes for five poor women; such as receive no alms. This charity estate is let for £17 a year; and the number of objects has been increased beyond that specified by the donor. In 1758, *Elizabeth Mitchell*, in furtherance of the desire of her late brother, conveyed to trustees 4A. 1R. 19P. of land, called Annett's, upon trust, to pay the rent thereof yearly to the churchwardens, that they might lay it out and distribute it in bread. This land, with an allotment of 2A. awarded at the enclosure, is let for £10 a year, which is distributed in bread on Easter, Whit, and Advent Sundays, Christmas day, and the first Sunday in Lent. The poor of East Bergholt have also £2. 8s. 2d. yearly from *White's Charity*, as noticed with Holton. In 1589, *Edward Lamb* conveyed to trustees a *Schoolhouse* and a rood of land in East Bergholt, for a schoolmaster, to be appointed by the lord of the manor of Illary's, the rector, churchwardens, and four of the chief parishioners. In 1589, *Lettice Dykes*, to provide for the education of poor children of this parish, and four of Stratford and Langham, conveyed to trustees various lands and tenements, some of which were sold or exchanged. The property now belonging to this trust consists of a house, barn, and about 53A. of land at Langham and Dedham, let for £66. 10s. per annum, and £102. 4s. 9d. three per cent. consols, supposed to have been derived from the sale of a house, the site of which is included in the grounds of the Old Hall. Out of the income of the school property, the trustees pay £40 a year to the schoolmaster for teaching 30 boys of East Bergholt as free-scholars in reading, writing, and arithmetic; £2 each to Stratford and Langham parishes, for schooling four poor boys; and after providing for repairs, they apply the surplus to the support of a Sunday-school, and a School of Industry, for poor girls of this parish. They rebuilt the *Free School*, in 1831, at the cost of £300.

EAST BERGHOLT.

Allen John, gentleman
Askew Samuel, furniture broker
Baker Wm. gentleman
Batley Hy. linen & woollen draper, mercer, &c
Bird Eliz. plumber and glazier　-
Bowen John, Esq. & Misses D. & E.
Clarke Rev Thomas, M.A. curate
Constable Abm. corn miller and coal and corn mert. *Flatford Mill*
Constable Miss Ann, *Wheelers*
Constable S. vessel owner
Cuthbert Richard, worsted mfr.
Deynes Wm. O. gent.||Cocker Miss
Dunthorne John, plumber & glazier
Everard Robert, hair dresser
Fairfax Rev John Collins, (Indpt.)
Green Wm. gentleman
Green Abm. timber bender
Grimsey Jph. Dagnett, land surveyor
Grimsey Joseph, baker

Harvey Martha, straw hat maker
Hayward James, cooper
Hughes Sir Rd. Bart. and Dowager
  Lady Sarah, *East Bergholt Lodge*
Jackson Mr ‖ Impey Miss Mary
Jarman John Palmer, gentleman
King Joseph, sen. gentleman
Morton Dowager Countess, *Old Hall*
Nichols John, cattle dealer
Nunn John, gentleman
Oakes Chas. Tyrell, Esq. *Highlands*
Orvis Samuel, harness maker
Peck John, cooper
Ralph Henry, baker
Reynolds James, road surveyor
Rowley Chas. Esq. *West Lodge*
Rowley Rev. Joshua, M.A. *Rectory*
Spurling Jeremiah, gentleman
Travis and Drake, surgeons
Travis Wm. Hardy ; h *Hill House*
Tuffnail Rev. Wm.
Whimper Nathaniel, gentleman
Venns Selina, milliner
Woods Thomas, gentleman

INNS AND TAVERNS.
Hare and Hounds, Mary Nichols
King's Head, Thomas Heckford
Red Lion, Thomas Ralph
White Horse, Jacob Reynolds

Aacdemies.
(*take Boarders)*
Clark Mary
*Green Charles
*Hollick Hanh.
  and Susannah

Woods Thomas
Blacksmiths.
Heckford Wm.
King John
Lemon Wm.
Neville Thomas

Bricklayers.
Boore Thomas
Pearl Robert
Rudland George
Butchers.
King Wm.
Sizer Wm.
Taylor Thos. J.
Draper.
Batley Henry
Grocers, &c.
Carman Geo. (&
  Hadleigh)
Folkard Rt. (&
  beerhouse)
Grimsey Jph. D.
Harvey John
Hickinbotham
  William
Mecklenburgh
  Matthew
Parker James
Richardson Eliz.
Wells Wm.
FARMERS.
Green John (and
  maltster)
  Buck's Elm
Holden George
King Jph.*Hill hs.*
CARRIERS.
Wm. Church to Ipswich, Saturday
John Peck to Ipswich, Wed. & Fri.
  and to Colchester, Tue. Thu. & Sat.

King W.*Quintins*
Lamb Wm.
Lott John, *Valley*
Lott Ts. *Park hs.*
Lott Wm.
Pyatt Charles
Reynolds Abm.
Reynolds Jacob
Rivett Wm.
Sallows Henry
Whimper Nathl.
  Henry
Joiners.
Church Wm.
Folkard Robert
Folkard Fras.
Harvey Henry
Nichols Wm. (&
  wheelwright)
Shoe Makers.
Arnold Samuel
Dunage Samuel
Heckford Jerh.
Heckford Thos.
Moore John
Parker John
Tailors.
Downing John
Ostinelli Fras.
White John

BRANTHAM, a village 9 miles S.W. of Ipswich, and 2½ miles N. by E. of Manningtree, has in its parish 404 souls, and 1922A. 2R. 20P. of land, including the hamlet of *Cattawade*, on the north-side of the Stour, where two bridges cross two channels of that river to Essex; one a brick structure of three arches, and the other a wooden fabric of seven arches. Mrs. Spooner and Mr. J. P. Jarman own most of the soil, and the rest belongs to several smaller proprietors. The *Church* (St. Michael) is a rectory, which, as already noticed, is consolidated with that of East Bergholt, in the patronage and incumbency of the Rev. Joshua Rowley, M.A., who has in the two parishes about 45A. of glebe, and £1320 per annum, in lieu of tithes. William Rufus gave Brantham, with the berewicks of Bercold, Scotlege, Meelflege, and Benetlege to Battle Abbey, and they were granted to the Earl of Oxford, in the 36th of Henry VIII. There was anciently a chapel near the bridges at Cattawade, in which hamlet is *Braham Hall*, formerly a seat of the Brahams, but now a farm house.

Baldwin George, shoemaker
Brundell John, blacksmith
Hearsum Thomas, wheelwright
May Wm. corn miller
Martin Jas. horse dlr. & vict. Crown
Pannifer Wm. wheelwright

Taylor Saml. shoemaker & vict. Bull
FARMERS.
Cooper George ‖ Gill Wm
Page Henry, *Braham Hall*
Rand John ‖ Simpson Thomas
Welham Jph. ‖ Whaley Rt. *Hall*

BURSTALL, a small village and parish, 4½ miles W. of Ipswich, has only 223 souls, and 766 acres of land, belonging to the Alexander family, J. H. L. Anstruther, Esq., Mrs. Bond, and a few smaller owners, and lying partly in the manors of Lovetofts and Bramford. The manor of Harrolds, in Burstall, was granted to Cardinal Wolsey, as part of the possessions of St. Peter's Priory, in Ipswich. The *Church* (St. Mary) has a tower and three bells, and is a curacy consolidated with Bramford. (See page 229.) The great tithes belong to the Dean and Chapter of Canterbury, but are held on lease by Sir Philip Broke. Here is an *Independent Chapel*, built in 1842-'3. *Directory :* – Eliz. Austin, Benj. Fayers, Pp. Hicks, Robt. Keene, James Lambert, *(Hall,)* and John Lott, *farmers ;* Geo. Fayers, gamekeeper ; James Hardwick, beerhouse ; Ann Kemball, schoolmistress ; Wm. Wilken, carpenter ; and Jph. Wolledge, blacksmith.

CAPEL ST. MARY, a pleasant village in the vale of a small rivulet, 7 miles S.W. of Ipswich, and 5½ miles S.E. of Hadleigh, has in its parish 608 inhabitants, and 1911 acres of fertile land, including 60A. of wood, 34A. of roads, and the hamlet of *Cross Green*, on the turnpike, nearly a mile S. of the village. It is in three manors, viz., *Churchford Hall*, of which Isaac Everett, Esq., is lord ; *Boynton Hall*, belonging to Queen's College, Cambridge ; and *Vaux-and-Jermyn's*, of which J. Ansell, Esq., is lord. The Rowley, Goodchild, Hollick, Brook, and other families, own part of the soil, which is mostly freehold. The *Church* (St. Mary) is a neat structure, with a tower containing five bells, and formerly surmounted by a spire, which was taken down in 1818. The *rectory*, valued in K.B. at £13. 8s. 4d., has had that of Little Wenham annexed to it since 1787, and was valued in 1835 at £682. The glebe is 22A., and the tithes of Capel were commuted in 1838 for a yearly modus of £528. The Rev. Joseph Tweed, M.A., is patron and incumbent.

Bennett James, wheelwright
Bickmore George, registrar
Bird Wm. shoemaker
Boore John, bricklayer
Brooke Cooper Wm. Esq. *Cross Gn.*
Collins Wm. vict. White Horse
Cox Martha, shopkeeper
Finch Henry, shoemaker
Ford Wm. gardener and seedsman
Hardy Jph. beerhouse and shopr.
Lawrence Cook, blacksmith
May Francis, parish clerk
Ostinelli Santino, tailor
Payne Sarah, shopkeeper

Salmon John, butcher
Skitter Levi, saddler
Scrivener Wm. thatcher
Tweed Rev Jph. M.A. *Rectory*
FARMERS.
Ablewhite Wm. *Capel Grove*
Ansell Jph. jun. || Aylyard Wm.
Brooke Cooper Wm. || Day Rache
Everett Isaac jun. (and corn miller,)
    Churchford Hall
Garnham Jeremiah, *Brook Farm*
Hollick Charles || Hollick Wm.
Jacobs Thomas || Lamb Samuel

CHATTISHAM, a village and parish, 5 miles E. of Hadleigh, and S.W. by W. of Ipswich, contains 215 souls, and 713A. 3R. 7P. of land. The manor and a great part of the soil formerly belonged to Wykes Priory, in Essex, and were granted first to Cardinal Wolsey, and then to Eton College, to which they still belong. The remainder belongs to J. K. Hicks, Esq., and a few smaller owners. The *Church* (All Saints) is a plain building, with several neat mural monuments. The vicarage, valued in K.B. at £4. 13s. 4d., has 22A. of glebe, and is endowed with all the tithes, except of about 200 acres, which are tithe free. In 1840, the tithes were commuted for £142. 10s. per annum. The Provost and Fellows of Eton College are patrons, and the Rev. H. S. Dickinson, M.A., is the incumbent. Here is a small *Wesleyan Chapel*, built in 1817. The *Rev. Thomas Warren*, in 1769,

left £200, after the decease of his widow, (who died in 1815,) to the vicar of Chattisham, and rectors of Hintlesham and Copdock, in trust for the education of poor children of Chattisham, at the free school in Hintlesham, where four or five free scholars are now sent from this parish. The legacy was laid out in £212. 15s. three per cent. reduced annuities.

Bickmore Askey, blacksmith
Cole James, shoemaker
Dickinson Rev Hy. Strahan, M.A.
  Vicarage
Gentry Daniel, farmer, *Hall*
Jolly Thomas Markwell, farmer

Hicks John Kettle, yeoman, *Chattisham place*
Moss John, shoemaker
Norman John Wm. corn miller
Payne Thomas, yeoman
Smith John, parish clerk

CHELMONDISTON, a village and parish, on the south-west side of the broad estuary of the Orwell, 6 miles S.S.E. of Ipswich, and 5 miles N.N.W. of Harwich, has 564 inhabitants, and about 1293 acres of land, including the fishing hamlet of *Pin-mill,* which has about 30 *boats* employed chiefly in getting *stone* on the rocks near Harwich, for the manufacture of *Roman Cement,* at the works in Ipswich and other places. The soil is generally a light sand, and is all freehold, belonging to Archdeacon Berners, Matthew Wise, Esq., Mr. Lucas, and a few smaller owners. The *Church* (St. Andrew) is an ancient structure, which was repewed and thoroughly repaired a few years ago. The *rectory,* valued in K.B. at £8. 10s., and in 1835 at £312, is in the gift of the Crown, and incumbency of the Rev. H. Chissold, M.A. The *Wesleyans* and *Baptists* have chapels here.

Bickmore Wm. blacksmith
Chissold Rev Hy. M.A. *Rectory*
Curtis James, vict. Butt & Oyster
Doubel Charles, vict. Red Lion
Doubel Rev Isaac (Baptist)
Haggar Wm. shoemaker
Hill Peter, boarding school
Howlett John, Chas., Henry, and
  Sl., *cement stone merts. & dressers*
Howlett Wm. shopr. & stone dresser
King Robert, shoemaker
King Charles, shopkeeper
Potter Wm. baker
Spencer Rev Robert Franklin, A.B.
  L.L.B. *curate*

Sulley Charles, shopkeeper
Walker James, corn miller; h *Woolverstone*
Webb Thomas, sen. wheelwright
Webb Thomas, jun. blacksmith
FARMERS.
Carrington John ‖ Dunnett Wm.
Fuller Luther ‖ Garrod Benjamin
Garrod John Smallman
Mason Philip Bacon
Rudland Thomas Marsden
Wade Susanna
  Carriers to Ipswich.
John Scarfe, Mon. Wed. & Saturday
John Wright, Tue. Thu. & Saturday

COPDOCK parish, between two small rivulets, from 3 to 4 miles S.W. by W. of Ipswich, has a pleasant village on the London road, containing a good inn and several handsome houses, adjoining Washbrook, in which parish some of the houses are situated. Copdock has 299 inhabitants, and 932A. 33P. of rich clayey land, lying in two manors, viz., Copdock, of which A. W. J. Deane, Esq., is lord, and Copdock-Hall-with-Barons, of which Lord Walsingham is lord; but part of the soil belongs to Rolla Rouse, Esq., Mrs. Syer, Mr. R. Bruce, and a few smaller owners. The *Church* (St. Peter) is a neat fabric, with a tower and five bells; and a curiously sculptured font. The *rectory,* valued in K.B. at £9. 12s. 8½d., has the vicarage of Washbrook annexed to it, and the two united livings were valued in

1835, at £483 per annum. Lord Walsingham is patron, and his younger brother, the Hon. and Rev. Fredk. De Grey, M.A., incumbent. Here is a *National School*, built by subscription in 1841, for the parishes of Copdock and Washbrook.

Aldrich John, gent. *Copdock Lodge*
Bishop James, parish clerk
Cook Robert, blacksmith
Daldry John, shoemaker
De Grey Hon. and Rev Frederick, M.A. *Rectory*
Dickens Lieut. General Sir Samuel Trevor, K.C.H. *Copdock House*
Jay William Mumford, vict. White Elm *(posting house)*
Josselyn James, Esq

King George, wheelwright
Roberts Wm. corn miller
Marver John, *carrier* to Ipswich
Shepherd George, shoemaker
Woods Wm. schoolmaster

FARMERS. *(* are Owners)*
*Bickmore Thomas || *Bruce Rd.
*Chamberlain James, *Mace Green*
*Ranson John || Cook John
Syer Mrs Mary, *New Hall*
Woodward Chs. Fryer, *Copdock Hall*

ERWARTON, or *Arwarton,* a pleasant village, on the north bank of the Stour, near the confluence of that broad estuary with the Orwell, is distant 9 miles S.E. by S. of Ipswich, and overlooks the harbour of Harwich, on the opposite side of the Stour. Its parish contains 199 souls, and 1318A. 1R. 17P. of land, generally a sandy loam, and mostly freehold, belonging to the Ven. Henry Denny Berners, L.L.B., archdeacon of Suffolk, and Wm. Deane, Esq. The former is lord of the *manor*, which was anciently the seat and property of the *Daviller* family, whose heiress carried it in marriage to *Sir Robert Bacon*, who, in 1345, obtained a grant for a market and fair here. It afterwards passed to the Calthorpes, and was purchased by Sir Philip Parker, Kt., of Sir D. Drury, about the year 1577. Philip Parker, of Erwarton, was created a baronet in 1661 ; and the last representative of his family, Sir Philip Parker Long, died in 1741, when the manor passed to his daughter, Lady Chedworth ; and after her death, it went to the Berners family, of Woolverstone. The ancient *Hall*, which was the seat of the Parkers, is now a farm house, commanding fine views of the estuaries of the Stour and Orwell, and having an entrance *gateway*, supposed to have been built in the reign of Elizabeth, and still in good preservation. The *Church* (St. Mary) stands on a bold eminence, overlooking the Stour, and is a neat structure, which has lately been thoroughly repaired, and the chancel rebuilt. At the same time, the pews were removed from the nave and aisles, and open sittings for 250 hearers substituted in their place. Here are several monuments, in good preservation, erected to the memory of the Daviller, Calthorpe, Bacon, and Parker families. The *rectory*, valued in K.B. at £10. 13s. 4d., has that of Woolverstone annexed to it, and has now a yearly rent charge of £544 in lieu of tithes, awarded in 1838, viz., £305 for the tithes of Erwarton, and £239 for those of Woolverstone. The Ven. Archdeacon Berners is the patron, and the Rev. Ralph Berners, M.A., is the incumbent, and has here 20A. 35P. of glebe, and a good parsonage house, erected a few years ago. The poor parishioners have three cottages, and 1A. 2R. of land, left by Philip Parker, Esq. Here is a *National School*, for boys and girls, supported by subscription. *Directory:*—George Ashford, farmer, *Erwarton Hall;* Rev. Ralph Berners, M.A., *Rectory ;* William Gladwell, vict., *Queen's Head;* John Howard, farmer; John Kerridge, blacksmith and wheel-

wright; Philip Clayton Smith, farmer and owner; and Joseph Sterne, farm bailiff.

FRESTON, a small village, upon a pleasant acclivity, on the western side of the broad river Orwell, 3½ miles S. of Ipswich, has in its parish 224 souls, and 1413A. 3R. 4P. of light but fertile and well-wooded land. The Ven. Archdeacon Berners, of Woolverstone, is lord of the manor of *Freston Hall*, within which is the small manor of *Bonds*, of which Sir Philip Broke is lord. The other principal owners of the soil are the trustees of the late Rev. J. T. Bond, Sir Robt. Harland, Mrs. Christie, and E. B. Venn, Esq., of *Freston Lodge*, a large and handsome mansion, erected in 1840, on a bold eminence, commanding a fine view of the Orwell. Freston Hall, with the manor and advowson, was anciently vested in a family who took their name from the parish. The *Fretsons* were seated here from the reign of Henry III. till that of Henry VIII., when the manor passed to the *Latimers*; but in 1590, it was held by the Goodings, of Ipswich, and afterwards by the Wrights, who separated the manor and advowson, and sold their possessions to the Thurston, Tarver, and other families. Of the ancient Hall, a fine antique TOWER still remains, near the bank of the Orwell. This tower is a strong quadrangular brick building, six stories high, containing as many rooms, one above another, but only about 10 feet by 12, with a polygonal turret at each angle, terminating in pinnacles; and a winding steeple staircase projecting from the eastern side, and terminating in an octagonal lantern. The best apartment appears to have been in the fifth story, which is loftier and has larger windows than the rest, and was probably hung with tapestry, as small nails left in the wood seem to indicate. There is but one fire place, which is on the ground-floor, and even that seems to be of modern construction, and to have no chimney; hence it is probable that this building was rather an ocsional pleasure retreat, or watch tower, than a place of permanent habitation. As it is not noticed in any of the descriptions of the hall in the time of the Frestons, this tower was probably erected by one of the Latimers. Except a farm-house, at a short distance, there is no trace of any buildings near it. The *Church* (St. Peter) is a neat structure, with a tower at the west end. The *rectory*, valued in K.B. at £6.7s.6d., was in the patronage and incumbency of the late Rev. John Theodore Bond, who left it in trust to the Rev. George Murray, M.A., of Ipswich, until his brother and heir, Arthur Bond, is of age, and has taken holy orders. The glebe is 23A. 5P.; and in 1841, the tithes were commuted for a yearly modus of £376. About thirty-five years ago, several Anglo-Saxon coins were found here.

Benns Edward, wheelwright
Bond Mrs Emily, *Rectory*
Burch John, vict. Boot(&blacksmith)
Venn Edw. Beaumont, Esq., *Freston Lodge*
Sage Joseph, joiner
Zincke Rev Barham, curate
FARMERS.
Alderton Wm.
Birch John
Bradbrook Thos.
Hare Geo. jun.
Sage Benjamin

HARKSTEAD, a village and parish, 7 miles S. by E. of Ipswich, has 329 souls, and 1726A. 3R. 32P. of land, stretching northward to the estuary of the Stour, and belonging to the Ven. Archdeacon Berners and the trustees of A. W. J. Deane, Esq. The former is lord of the *manor*, which was held by Odo de Campania, at the Domesday survey.

The *Church* (St. Mary) has a tower and five bells. The *rectory*, valued in K.B. at £11. 3s. 9d., is in the patronage and incumbency of the Rev. Ralph Berners, M.A., of Erwarton, who has 55A. 1R. 26P. of glebe, and a yearly modus of £479, awarded in lieu of tithes, in 1839. Here was formerly a *chapel*, dedicated to St. Clement, and its site is still known, at the corner of a field called Chapely down, though it has long been cultivated.

Bickmore R. blacksmith
Goose Robert, shoemaker
Hart Jacob, vict. Rose
Jordan Joseph, wheelwright
Linley Thos. shoemkr. & shopkpr
Pooley Abdil, joiner
Rivers Wm. shopkeeper

Roper Robert, gentleman
Wells Wm. shoemaker

FARMERS.

Allen Samuel || Carrington Mattw.
Cross Pearl, *Nether Hall*
Garrod Joseph || Rush Robert
Rudland William

HIGHAM is a handsome village, with several large mansions, pleasantly situated on a gentle acclivity near the confluence of the rivers Brett and Stour, on the southern confines of Suffolk, 5 miles E. of Nayland, 5 miles S. of Hadleigh, and 10½ miles S.E. of Ipswich. Its parish contains 259 souls, and 863A. 17P. of fertile and well-wooded land. P. P. Mannock, Esq., is lord of the manor, but a great part of the soil belongs to Mrs. Stutter, Mrs. Dawson, and A. C. Reeve, Esq., who have neat houses here, finely shaded with trees. The *Church* (St. Mary) has a tower and six bells, and is a perpetual curacy, valued in K.B. at £5. 6s. 8d., and in 1835, at £238. It was appropriated to Trinity Priory, Ipswich, by Maude de Munchensi; but the rectorial tithes were purchased by a Mr. Gibbs or Mr. Smith, and given to the minister. Certain trustees are patrons, and the Rev. A. C. Reeve is the incumbent. The glebe is about 50A., and in 1840 the tithes were commuted for a yearly modus of £220. In the reign of Charles I., Thomas Bedfield charged his house and land here with the yearly payment of 10s. to the minister. In 1725, *Thomas Glanville* left a cottage here, for the relief of poor widows of Higham, Holton, and Raydon. *Sir Charles Witham*, of Higham Cottage, was knighted by the Lord-Lieutenant of Ireland, in 1830.

Allen George, maltster
Baker Wm. brickmkr ; h Dedham
Dawson Mrs Mary, *Higham Lodge*
Dickson George Smith, grocer
Harris Stephen and William, *seed crushers and oil millers*
Johnson Samuel, butcher
Martin Samuel, solicitor
Nairn John Charles, M.D.
Potter Joseph, vict. King's Head
Reeve Abraham Charles, Esq.

Reeve Rev Abm. Chas. incumbent
Sheen Mrs Mary
Stutter Mrs Eliz. *Higham Hall*
Smith George, blacksmith
Smith Joseph, joiner
Welham Robert, shopkeeper
Witham Sir Chas. Kt. *Higham Cotg*

FARMERS.

Blomfield John || Bush Isaac
Daldry Joseph, *Deerlands*
Lewis Wm. Partridge

HINTLESHAM, a large and well-built village, 4½ miles E. by N. of Hadleigh, and 5½ miles W. of Ipswich, is pleasantly situated on the road between those towns, and has in its parish 583 inhabitants, and 2828A. 3R. 24P. of land, mostly the property of James Hamilton Lloyd Anstruther, Esq., the lord of the manor, who resides at the *Hall*, a fine Elizabethan mansion, in the form of the letter H, standing in a beautiful *Park* of 150 acres, and containing many spacious apartments, and a

fine collection of paintings by Vandyke, Gainsborough, and other distinguished masters. The manor was anciently held by the Talbots, and for many years by the Timperlys, who sold it, about 1740, to Richard Powis, Esq., of whom it was purchased by Sir Richd. Lloyd, Knight, one of the Barons of the Exchequer. It was bequeathed to its present owner by the late Miss Harriet Lloyd, in 1837. The Cooke and some other families have small estates in the parish. The *Church* (St. Nicholas) is a handsome structure, with a tower and five bells. The nave and aisles are leaded, but the chancel is covered with tiles. In the latter are several monuments of the Timperly family, one of which is a tomb of blue marble, bearing the portraits in brass of John Timperly, Esq., and Margaret, his wife. The former died in 1400. Here is also a neat monument to the late Misses Lloyd. The *rectory*, valued in K.B. at £33. 9s. 6d., is in the patronage and incumbency of the Rev. Wm. Henry Deane, who has 44a. of glebe, and a yearly modus of £450, awarded in lieu of tithes in 1838. The *Free School* and playground of 2R. 12P. were built and given respectively by the late Misses Lloyd, in exchange for the old playground. The school estate, which was purchased by the parishioners many years ago, with the assistance of Francis Colman, is copyhold, and consists of a cottage, small barn, and about 6A. of land at Aldham, now let for £10 per annum, for which the master teaches seven free-scholars reading, writing, and arithmetic. He has also £6. 6s. a year for teaching four or five poor children of Chattisham, as noticed with that parish, and has the use of a house built by Misses Lloyd, the last of whom (Miss Harriet) died in 1837, and left £10 a year for the education of five poor children, and £10 a year to provide coals for poor parishioners. Here is also a school, instituted by Mr. John Allen, for the education of about 40 poor children, who pay weekly 1d. each for reading, and 2d. for writing. The Hundred of Samford *Benefit Society* (see page 245) holds its meetings at the *George Inn*.

Anstruther James Hamilton Lloyd, Esq. *Hintlesham Hall*
Abbott James, carpenter
Abbott My. Ann, schoolmistress
Deane Rev Wm. Henry, *Rectory*
Deekes Mary Ann, corn miller
Game Henry, shopkeeper
Kingsbury John, bricklayer
Lott Wm. Shulver, vict. *George Inn*
Meadows Amos, shoemaker
Meadows Thomas, wheelwright
Meadows Wm. shopkeeper
Norfolk James, butcher
Norfolk Wm. blacksmith

Steward Wm. shoemaker
Woods John, sen. schoolmaster and parish clerk
Woods John, jun. bricklayer

FARMERS.

Allen John
Borham Robt.
Cook Thomas
Game Thomas
Garrod James
Hardwick Sarah
Hayward Chas.
Keeble John
Lot Wm. Shulver

Makins Robt.
Mumford Wm. *Priory*
Nock John
Norman Wm. & John
Ranson Wm.
Sturgeon Geo.
Trent John

HOLBROOK is a large and pleasant village, with several handsome houses, 6 miles S. of Ipswich, near a brook or rivulet from which it has its name, and which falls into the river Stour at *Holbrook Bay*, about a mile S. of the village. Its parish contains 747 inhabitants, and 2203A. 2P. of land, including about 370 acres of woods and plantations. The Ven. Archdeacon Berners, of Woolverstone, is lord of the manor, but the greater part of the soil belongs to the Harland, Reade, Ver-

non, Deane, Rodwell, Wilkinson, Gosnall, Cornell, Cross, and a few other families. The lordship was successively held by the families of Holbrook, Daundy, Clench, Thurston, and Staunton. *Judge Clench*, who died in 1607, lies buried in the church. The late *John Reade, Esq.*, of Holbrook House, who died in 1843, had been a chief judge in India, and was sheriff of Suffolk in 1830. The *Church* (All Saints) is a large ancient fabric, with a tower, supported by massive buttresses. It was re-pewed in 1824, and has 550 sittings, one-third of which are free. The rectory, valued in K.B. at £11. 11s. 3d., is in the patronage and incumbency of the Rev. J. B. Wilkinson, M.A., who has 6A. of glebe, and a yearly modus of £490. 10s., awarded in 1838 in lieu of tithes. The *Rectory House* is a commodious mansion, erected in 1822 by the Rev. Thomas Holmes, the late incumbent. The Wesleyans have a small chapel here. The interest of £30 (arising from £10 given by two benefactors, and £20 received in 1802, on the sale of the workhouse,) is applied in the distribution of coals at a cheap rate to the poor. Two *National Schools*, for boys and girls, are supported by the rector and other subscribers; and there are in the village two respectable *boarding schools*.

Ablitt and Brown, ladies' boarding and day school
Allen James, gardener
Baker Grove, beerhouse
Berners John Esq. *Reed Hall*
Clark Joseph, tailor
Cornell Wm. corn miller & maltster
Doyley David, fishmonger
Dunnett Ellen, straw hat maker
Dunnett John, bricklayer
Flory Thomas, pork dealer
Goodwin Robert, cooper
Hare George, sen. butcher & grazr
Herbert Wm. butcher
Herbert Sarah, vict. *Compasses*
Holden Michael, *carrier to Ipswich, Tue. Thu. and Saturday*
Kenney Thomas, schoolmaster
Laker Wm. E. boarding & dayschool
Mayhew Joshua, blacksmith
Nunn Miss Harriet
Pulford John, plumber & glazier

Pytches Miss Charlotte
Reade Mrs. *Holbrook House*
Steggold Maria, blacksmith
Topple John, tailor & parish clerk
Vincent Abm. and Wm. farriers
Wilkinson Rev John Brewster, M.A. *Rectory*

FARMERS.
Abbott Edward
Baker Wm.
Clarke Thomas
Cooper, *Brook Farm*
Dale Wm.
Keeble Robert
Robinson Ismael

Joiners.
Hick Anthony
Spink Wm.

Shoemakers.
Hawes Samuel

Hines John
Levell George
Shopkeepers.
Scrivener James
Shepherd James, (and tailor)
Stollery John
Taylor John
Surgeons.
Cutting Wm.
Martin Robert
Wheelwrights.
Dunnett Thos.
Pooley James

HOLTON ST. MARY, a small parish and village, 4½ miles S.S.E. of Hadleigh, and 9 miles S.W. of Ipswich, contains 187 souls, and 810 acres of land, nearly all freehold, and mostly belonging to Corpus Christi College, Cambridge, and partly to Robert Lawrance, Esq., and a few smaller owners. The manor anciently belonged to the *Fastolfs*, afterwards to the Mannocks, and then to Sir John Williams, from whose family it passed to Sir William Rowley, Kt. The *Church* (St. Mary) is a *Rectory*, valued in K.B. at £7. 14s. 7d., and in 1835 at £257, but now having 33 acres of glebe, and a yearly modus of £220, awarded in lieu of tithes, in 1837. Sir J. R. Rowley, Bart., is patron, and the Rev. Jsha. Rowley, M.A., incumbent. The principal inhabitants

are, Rev. John Gale Dobree, M.A., *curate* of Holton, and *rector* of Newbourn; Robert Cook, *farmer, Holton Hall;* James Hammond, *farmer;* Edward Hill, *shoemaker;* James Rumsey, *farmer;* and Jas. Waller, *butcher and farmer;* house, Hadleigh.

The *Charity School at Holton St. Mary* was established and endowed by the exertions and through the pecuniary aid of the Rev. Stephen White, a late rector, and for some time it was supported chiefly by annual contributions, but the only subscription now regularly paid to it is £3. 3s. a year from Corpus Christi College, Cambridge, which is possessed of a large estate here.   The property of the school is as follows:—A school-house was erected on the waste, which, with a garden of 10 perches, was conveyed by Sir Francis Mannock, lord of the manor, to trustees, in 1749.   The *Town Pightle*, 6 acres, was demised in 1755, by the churchwardens and overseers to the rector and his successors for 99 years, for the use of the school, at the yearly rent of 18s., to be distributed among the poor at Easter.   The *Dock Meadow*, 3A., in Stratford, let for £6 a year, was given by the Rev. Stephen White, in trust, that the rents should be applied in raising premiums, to be given in October, to the children in the school, or those who have been taught there, and could bring certificates of good behaviour. Two cottages, let for £3 each, were built by the trustees, on the site of one granted by the lord of the manor, on lease, at the yearly rent of one penny. The sum of £260, contributed by the Rev. Stephen White and others, is in the hands of the rector, at five per cent. interest.   The trustees have also £100. 13s. 4d. three per cent. reduced annuities, purchased by the last named donor; and £129. 6s. 3½d., three-and-a-half per cent. reduced annuities, purchased in 1787 with surplus income.   The yearly income from these sources, is £35. 5s. 10d.   The master has £12. 12s. a year, and the use of the school premises, for which he instructs, as free-scholars, 16 boys and 9 girls in reading, writing, and arithmetic.   The remainder of the income is applied in furnishing books and rewards for the children, and a suit of clothes for each on leaving school.   The *Town Pightle*, noticed above, will revert to the poor in 1855.   A cottage belonging to the poor was sold in 1803, for £20, which was applied towards making the *Town Well*, towards repairing which a yearly rent-charge is paid out of a piece of land adjoining the churchyard.   The sum of £30, left to the poor by one Partridge and other donors, is lent on interest.   The poor parishioners have 20s. yearly from *Glanville's Charity*, as noticed with Higham.   In 1773, the REV. STEPHEN WHITE left £500 in trust, to pay one-half of the interest thereof to the rector of Holton, (provided he resides in the parish or neighbourhood ; if not, to the curate,) for his own use ; and to apply the other moiety, in four equal shares, for the parishes of Holton, Stratford, Nayland, and Brantham, for distribution among the poor.   This charity now consists of two sums of £321. 7s., one belonging to the rector, and the other to the poor of the four parishes.

RAYDON, 3¼ miles S.S.E. of Hadleigh, is a parish containing two small villages, called *Upper and Lower streets ;* 492 inhabitants, and 2335A. 1R. 3P. of land, extending to *Masons Bridge,* on the river Brett, 2 miles S. by E. of Hadleigh, and including 418A. of woodland. Mrs. C. Cripps is lady of the manor, and owner of a great part of the soil, and the rest belongs to Mrs. C. L. Leach, Mr. J. Ansell, Mr. J. Blomfield, and a few smaller owners.   Robert de Raydon had a grant of a market and a fair here, in 1310.   The manor was afterwards held by the Hastings, from whom it passed to the owners of the neighbouring manor of Shelly.   The *Church* (St. Mary) is a plain tiled building, without a tower.   The *rectory,* valued in K.B. at £14, has 48A.

2R. 6P. of glebe, and a yearly modus of £511, awarded in lieu of tithes, in 1841. The Rev. Thomas Reeve is patron and incumbent. In 1663, the Rev. John Mayler, D.D., left out of his lands here, two yearly rent-charges, viz., 10s. for the minister, and 40s. for a distribution of bread among the poor. Five poor widows of Raydon have 20s. a year from Glanville's charity, as noticed with Higham.

Archer Joseph, blacksmith
Bennett Abielene, shopkeeper
Borham Wm. tailor
Grimwade John Girling, corn miller, *Raydon mill*
Hopes Francis, gamekeeper
Kedge Wm. vict. Fox (& carpenter)
King John, wheelwgt. & par. clerk
List Christopher, vict. Chequers
Reeve Rev Thomas, *Rectory*

Smith John, blacksmith

FARMERS.

Barfield John || Brand Joseph
Cook Thomas || Hicks Edward
Hill Wm. || Hill Thos. || North Jno.
Partidge Robert, (and valuer,) *Masons Bridge*
Roper Charles || Stubbin Robert
Stubbin Francis, *Raydon Hall*

SHELLY, a small village, pleasantly situated in the vale of the river Brett, 3 miles S. by E. of Hadleigh, has in its parish 139 souls, and 849A. 2R. 26P. of freehold land, including 62 acres of woodland. Mrs. Charlotte Cripps owns 650 acres, and the rest belongs to P. P. Mannock, Esq., Mr. W. Bouttell, and the Rev. J. Halward. She is also lady of the manor, impropriator, and patron of the *Church*, (All Saints,) which has a tower and five bells, and is a perpetual curacy, valued in 1835, at £72, and now enjoyed by the Rev. William Powell, M.A. Shelly was appropriated to Battle Abbey, and was afterwards the seat and manor of the Applebys and Tilneys. It was purchased of the Kerridge family by S. Rush, Esq., and was the property of the late Sir W. B. Rush, Kt., from whom it passed to Mrs. Cripps :—*Directory* :—John Benniworth, parish clerk ; George Branch and Wm. James, *shoemakers ;* and Thomas Heath, Richard Postens, (and land surveyor,) *Priory ;* Robert Partridge, *Shelly Hall ;* and Henry Partridge, *farmers.*

SHOTLEY is a pleasant village and fertile parish, at the termination of the peninsula, formed by the confluence of the estuaries of the Orwell and Stour, opposite Harwich, and from 9 to 10 miles S.E. by S. of Ipswich. It contains 464 inhabitants, and 2051A. 3R. 17P. of land. The village is on the bank of the Orwell ; and at *Shotley-Gate,* about a mile further south, is the Bristol Arms Inn, whence a *ferry boat* plies across the broad estuary to Harwich. Several boats are employed here in collecting stone for the manufacture of Roman cement. The parish is in two *manors,* viz., Over-Hall-with-Netherhall, of which the Marquis of Bristol is lord ; and Shotley Hall, or Kirkton, of which the heirs of Wm. Lucas, Esq., are lords ; but part of the soil belongs to Frederick Schreiber, Esq., E. C. East, Esq., Archdeacon Berners, and a few smaller owners. In the 31st of Edward I., Wm. Visdelieu had a grant for a market and fair here. Mr. John Spurling has recently introduced here some fine specimens of the Durham breed of short-horned cattle. The *Church* (St. Mary) is an ancient structure, without a tower, situated on an eminence, which commands a fine view of the Orwell. The *rectory,* valued in K.B. at £20, has 54A. 3R. 14P. of glebe, and a yearly modus of £585, awarded in lieu of tithes, in 1839. The Marquis of Bristol is patron, and the Rev. Samuel Fors-

ter, D.D., incumbent. In 1591, *Andrew Barfoot*, left for the poor of Shotley, two orchards and about 5A. of land, now let for £6. 6s. a year. The churchwardens have £10, which was given to employ the interest in providing bread and wine for the sacrament.

Cooper Thomas, shopkeeper
Forster Rev Samuel, D.D. *Rectory*
Gill George, wheelwright
Grimwood Samuel, shopkeeper
Schreiber Rev John Edw.B.A.curate
Spurling John, auctioneer, valuer, and estate agent
Stevens John, vict. Bristol Arms, *(ferry boat to Harwich.)*
Wright John, shoemaker

FARMERS.
Alderton Fisher (and maltster)
Croxson Wm.|| Gardiner Samuel
King & Spurling *(and graziers)*
Markham Chas. || Rivers John
Ruffles Robert || Sturgeon Wm.

Carriers to Ipswich.
Wm. Grimwood's cart, Mon., Wed., and Sat. ; also, an *omnibus*, Tuesday and Saturday mornings
Wm. Jackaman, Tuesday and Sat.

SPROUGHTON, a pleasant village, with several neat houses on the west bank of the river Gipping, 2½ miles W. by N. of Ipswich, has in its parish 585 souls, and 2380 acres of light but fertile land, of which two farms and 16 souls are in the Borough of Ipswich. The manor and advowson were held by the Feltons, and passed with Shotley to the family of the Marquis of Bristol ; but the soil belongs to Charles Lillingston, J. B. Smyth, Mattw. Wood, J. Josselyn, J. Rawson, and R. Woodward, Esqrs. ; the Rev. G. Capper, Mrs. Wyse, and a few smaller owners. The CHAUNTRY, nearly 2 miles W. of Ipswich, is the beautiful seat of *Charles Lillingston, Esq.*, and had its name from the estate being part of the property given by Edmund Daundy, for the endowment of a chantry in St. Lawrence's Church, Ipswich. The house was erected in the early part of last century, by Edward Ventriss, Esq., of whose heirs it was purchased by Sir J. Barker, whose son, the late Sir John Fytch Barker, Baronet, resided here. It passed in 1836 to the present worthy proprietor, who has greatly improved the mansion, and the extensive and beautiful grounds by which it is surrounded. The house stands on an eminence, commanding fine views of Ipswich, the vale of the Gipping, and the surrounding country, and encompassed by green slopes, pleasure grounds, luxuriant shrubberies, and flower gardens, all tastefully laid out. In the vicinity is a large and elegant conservatory, abounding in the choicest exotics, and teeming with the richest offerings of Flora. In another part of these enchanting grounds is a fine lake, called *Beech Water*, formed a few years ago, and covering several acres. This lake is studded with little islands covered with shrubberies, and is skirted on all sides by fine beech and other trees, with a broad walk round the margin, commanding delightful prospects. In the spring of 1843, C. Lillingston, Esq. gave a grand *rural fete* here, in honour of the birth-days of two of his children, and the grounds were thronged by upwards of 1500 visitors. *Sproughton Church* (All Saints) is an ancient structure, with several interesting monuments. The *rectory*, valued in K.B. at £20. 18s. 9d., and in 1835 at £519, is in the patronage of the Marquis of Bristol, and incumbency of the Rev. Edward Gould, M.A. In 1836, the tithes were commuted for a yearly modus of £510, free from poor rates. In 1618, *Elizabeth Bull* left a double cottage here for the residence of two poor widows. For a distribution of bread, the poor of

Sproughton have a yearly rent charge of 26s. out of a field at Whitton, left by an unknown donor.

Daldry Thomas, bricklayer and vict.
  Wild Man
Gould Rev Edward, M.A. *Rectory*
Gunnell George James, Esq.
Josselyn John, Esq.
Knights Elizabeth, schoolmistress
Lillingston Charles, Esq. *Chauntry*
Marshall John, blacksmith
Neeve Henry, corn miller
Plumb Henry, carpenter
Robinson Samuel, cattle dealer
Smith Wm. and John, wheelwrights
  and blacksmiths

White Thomas, carpenter
Woodward Rev John
                FARMERS.
(* are owners, & † in Ipswich Boro'.)
† Ashford Robert
† Howard Thos. *Sproughton Villa*
*Kersey Clement || Woodgate **Wm.**
*Ranson John, *Poplar House*
Ward John Thos. *Sproughton Grove*
              SHOEMAKERS.
Green James || Phillips Obadiah
Whinney Jonathan || White George

STRATFORD ST. MARY is a pleasant and well-built village on the north bank of the river Stour, and on the Norwich and London road, 10 miles S.W. of Ipswich, 6 miles S. by E. of Hadleigh, and 5 miles W. by N. of Manningtree. Its parish has 647 souls; 1432A. 1R. 26P. of fertile and well-wooded land; several handsome houses, and good inns and shops; and a large corn mill, on the Stour, worked partly by steam. It is a great thoroughfare, and is separated from Essex by the Stour. Wm. de la Pole, in the 7th of Richard II., obtained a special charter for a court leet here, and also for a market every Thursday, and a *Fair* on the eve, day, and morrow of the Translation of St. Thomas the Martyr. The market has long been obsolete, but a pleasure fair is still held here on the 22nd of June. On an acclivity quarter of a mile S.W. of the village, overlooking the river Stour, are traces of an encampment, supposed by some antiquarians to be the Roman Station *Ad Ansam*, which Mr. Talbot places at Cattawade Bridges, four miles below, where the river makes a small island. The parish is in two manors, viz., *Vesseys*, of which Sir J. R. Rowley is lord, and *Spanbies-Sulyard*, of which the trustees of A. W. J. Deane, Esq. are lords; but the soil is mostly freehold, and the principal proprietors are Corpus Christi College, Cambridge; Sir Richard Hughes, H. Firman, Esq., Rev. T. Reeve, and the Bach, Partridge, and a few other families. The *Church* (St. Mary) is a handsome structure in the decorated style, with a tower containing five bells. The north aisle appears to have been built about 1500, and the porch about 1526. In the windows are some fragments of ancient stained glass; and on the water table, now partly overgrown with moss, are inscribed the names of Edward and Thomas Mors, and their wives, who were benefactors to the edifice in the 15th century. The *rectory*, valued in K.B. at £13, has 19A. 2R. 19P. of glebe; and a yearly modus of £325, awarded in 1839, in lieu of tithes. The Queen, as Duchess of Lancaster, is patroness, and the Rev. Charles Golding, M.A., incumbent. The Church Estate comprises two tenements and an acre of land, let for £7. 10s. a year. The *Poor's Land*, given by unknown donors, comprises two acres in Stour and Mill Meadows, let for £4. 13s. a year, which is divided among the poor, to assist them in buying coals. In 1735, £114, benefaction money, was laid out in the purchase of a house, yard, garden, and 2A. of land, which, were conveyed to the churchwardens

and overseers, for finding linen cloth for the poor. These premises were let in 1777, on a lease, for 99 years, at the annual rent of £5. 15s. 6d. The poor parishioners have also £2. 4s. yearly from *White's charity*, noticed with East Bergholt. A customary payment of 5s. a year, out of a close belonging to Mr. Partridge, is carried to the overseers' accounts. In 1731, *Robert Clarke* left a yearly rent charge of £5 out of his lands here, for the education of six poor children. Three others are taught reading and writing, under the charities of Lettice Dykes, (see East Bergholt,) and Wm. Littlebury, one of the benefactors of Dedham school, in Essex, on the opposite bank of the Stour.

Atkinson Robert, butcher
Back Alfred, maltster
Back Wm. corn miller & merchant, *Steam and Water mill*
Baines Wm. beer seller
Barnard Peter Ceal, clerk
Blyth Mr Daniel
Blyth Mrs Ann || Barnard Mrs
Bore Charles, bricklayer
Chisnall Henry, shoemaker
Cole James, shopkeeper
Cooper Samuel, carpenter
Godfrey Thomas, post horse letter
Golding Rev Charles, M.A. *Rectory*
Grimwade Samuel, baker
Groom Thomas, plumber & glazier
Hardy Caroline, schoolmistress
Harmer Joseph, tailor
Harris Wm. seed crusher
Herbert Jacob, hay trusser
King George, harness maker
Laundry James, gardener, &c
Lee Samuel, coach builder
Manistre Wm. gentleman
Mann Elizabeth, schoolmistress
Mash James, grocer and draper
Mixer John, baker
Pettit Daniel, blacksmith

Phillips Wm. gentleman
Proby Miss Mary
Purkiss Ann, postmistress
Sallows Wm. gent. || Rowell Mr W.
Spurgeon Charles, surgeon
Stopper Samuel, gardener
Stopper John, gardener
Stow Thomas, butcher
Thompson George, Esq.
Wainforth Wm. shoemaker
Waller Samuel, grocer & draper
Webb Newman, gentleman
White Frederick, tailor
Woods Thomas, shoemaker

INNS AND TAVERNS.
Anchor, Henry Smith
Black Horse, Anthony Shales
King's Arms, Matthew Smith
Swan, Richard Kerridge (& posting)

FARMERS.
Cook Edward, *(estate agent and auctioneer,)* Churchgate house
Hicks Henry, *Stratford Hall*
Hunt Francis || Reynolds James
Partridge John, *Woodhouse*
Strutt Wm. *(& birch broom mkr.)*
Syer E. M. *Four Sisters*
Waller John

STUTTON is a picturesque village and parish, on the north-side of the broad estuary of the Stour, 7½ miles S. of Ipswich, and W. by N. of Harwich, and 4 miles E. by N. of Manningtree. It contains 492 souls, and 2138A. 3R. 32P. of freehold land, belonging to John Tollemache, Esq., John Page Reade, Esq., Wm. Deane, Esq., Mrs. O'Malley, Rev. T. Mills, Mrs. Mills, and the Sackett, Western, Baker, Hall, Whitbread, and some other families. *Stutton Hall*, now a farm house belonging to J. Tollemache, Esq., is in the Elizabethan style, and is said to have been built by Sir Edmund Jermy. *Crow Hall*, a large mansion with pleasant grounds, is the seat of J. P. Reade, Esq., and was built by one of the Latimers in 1605, but has since undergone many alterations and improvements. It is in the Tudor style, and has a large drawing-room finished in the florid style of Henry Seventh's chapel, in Westminster Abbey. It overlooks the Stour, and commands a view of Harwich harbour and the ocean. *Crepping Hall*, now occupied by

a farmer, was a seat of the Wingfields, and previously belonged to Colne priory, in Essex. *Alton Hall*, another mansion in this parish, is the seat of William Deane, Esq., and stands on a pleasant acclivity about a mile north of the Stour, near the Holbrook rivulet, upon which are two corn mills. The *Church* (St. Peter) is a neat structure, with a tower and five bells, and has several handsome monuments, two of which, belonging to the Jermy family, have kneeling effigies. The *rectory*, valued in K.B. at £12. 7s. 6d., and in 1835 at £550, is in the patronage and incumbency of the Rev. Thos. Mills, M.A., who erected a *Free School* here in 1838, and has a pleasant residence near the church. The Wesleyans have a chapel here, built in 1840. The poor parishioners have an acre of land, let for £4. 4s., and the dividends of £100 three per cent. reduced annuities, for distributions of bread and coals.

Aldred James, shoemaker
Allsop Thomas, butcher
Askew John, *carrier to Ipswich*, Tuesday and Saturday
Baker Rev George, curate
Bunnett Francis, carpenter
Chisnall Charles, wheelwright
Clarke Gideon, shoemaker
Cowles Robert, gardener
Dale Nathl. vict. King's Head, (and parish clerk, overseer, &c.)
Deane Wm. Esq. *Alton Hall*
Gladwell John, thatcher
Haste Joesph, blacksmith
Hines Owen, shoemaker
Hunt John, carpenter
Mayhew John, shopkeeper
McFarlan Captain James, R.N. *Stutton Lodge*

Mills Rev Thos. M.A. *Rectory*
Ranson — corn miller
Reade John Page, Esq. *Crow Hall*
Rumsey James, beerhouse
Stannard and Death, corn millers, New mills
Stedman Wm. grocer, draper, and ironmonger

FARMERS.

Aylward John, sen. and jun.
Budd John Peyto || Aldham Saml.
Button James, (and butcher)
Long John, *Queech Farm*
Orman Wm. *Stutton Cottage*
Packard Danl. (and chief constable,) *Crepping Hall*
Stanford George, *Stutton Hall*

TATTINGSTONE, a village and parish on the banks of a rivulet, 5½ miles S.S.W. of Ipswich, and 5 miles N.N.E. of Manningtree, contains 1637A. 3R. 1P. of land, and had 437 inhabitants in 1841, besides 191 in *Samford Hundred House of Industry*, which is already noticed at page 244. Thos. Burch Western, Esq., is lord of the manor, and owner of most of the soil. His seat, called *Tattingstone Place*, is a large neat mansion, with a well-wooded park and extensive fish ponds. It was anciently a seat of the Beaumonts, but was purchased about the middle of the last century by Thomas White, Esq., who rebuilt it, and erected near it an ornamental building in the form of a church. Here is a *Free School*, built in 1841 at the cost of £205, part of which was given by the Diocesan Society, and the remainder by the rector and T. B. Western, Esq. It is supported by subscription. A house of four tenements is appropriated to the use of four poor families; a cottage and an acre of land to the use of the parish clerk; and an adjoining cottage to the use of the sexton, but the donors are unknown. The *Church* (St. Mary) is a neat structure, with a tower and five bells. The *rectory*, valued in K.B. at £6. 13s. 4d., is in the gift of Charles Elliott, Esq., and incumbency of the Rev. C. B. Elliott, M.A., who has a good residence, 39A. 14P. of glebe, and a yearly modus of £402

awarded in 1837, in lieu of tithes. The *Wesleyans* have a chapel here, erected in 1800, and rebuilt in 1842. In the 10th of Edward IV., here was a *free chapel* belonging to the Earl of Oxford.

Allcock Edward, tailor
Aldrich Timothy, shoemaker
Balls Chas. joiner and builder
Catchpole Wm. governor and clerk of Samford Hundred *House of Industry*. (See page 244)
Elliott Rev Charles Boileau, M.A. F.R.S. *Rectory*
Fulcher James, bricklayer
Hawes Joseph, shoemaker
Johnson Wm. blacksmith
Marsden Mary, vict. White Horse
Moutell Joseph, shopkeeper
Neale Rev Edward, M.A. curate
Payne Wm. parish clerk
Pratt Jonathan, joiner
Price Sarah, shopkeeper
Ramsey Abraham, shopkeeper
Tyrell Samuel, shoemaker
Western Thos. Burch, Esq. *Tattingstone Place*

FARMERS.
Cooper John, *Hall*
Norman Joseph || Norman John
Rist Isaac || Waller Frederick

WASHBROOK, a village and parish, $3\frac{1}{2}$ miles W. by S. of Ipswich, lies in the vale of a rivulet, from which it has its name, on and near the London road. Some of its houses adjoin and form part of Copdock village. (See page 250.) It contains 506 inhabitants, and 1414A. 1R. 1P. of land, of which 229 acres are copyhold. Lord Walsingham owns about 450 acres, and is lord of the manor, and the rest belongs to J. Josselyn, Esq., Mrs. Syer, Mrs. Spooner, and a few smaller owners. *Amor House*, now occupied by a farmer, with a smaller manor attached to it, was appropriated to the abbey of Albemarle in Normandy, and afterwards to Dartford nunnery in Kent; but was granted at the dissolution to Sir Perceval Hart, Kt. On the same estate was a church called *Felchurch* or *Velechurch*, of which no traces now remain. The parish *Church* (St. Mary) is a neat structure, in a secluded part of the valley, and is a *vicarage* valued in K.B. at £8. 6s. 8d., and endowed with all the tithes, except the great tithes of the copyhold land, for which a yearly modus of £52 is paid to Lord Walsingham, the patron of the vicarage, which is consolidated with the rectory of Copdock. The tithes of Washbrook have been commuted for a yearly modus of £224. 10s.

Garwood Thomas, shopkeeper
Hearn Rt. maltster and vict. *Swan*
Kerridge Danl. registrar & relieving officer
Raw John, gent. *Washbrook Grove*
Taylor Robert, bricklayer
Watcham John, painter and glazier
Wright Frederick, joiner, &c
FARMERS.
Cotton Herbert, *Amor House*
Daking John || Trent Wm.
Game John & Isaac, *Birch House*
Gentry James, *Washbrook Green*
Lott John, *Rookery*

WENHAM (GREAT) is a parish of scattered houses, from 4 to 5 miles S.E. of Hadleigh, and 8 miles S.W. of Ipswich. It has 198 souls, and 1107A. 3R. 35P. of land, mostly a strong clay. Kirby calls it Wenham Magna, or *Burnt Wenham*. The manor and advowson were anciently held by the Vaux family, and were appropriated to Leigh priory in Essex, but granted in the 28th of Henry VIII. to R. Cavendish. The parish now belongs to Mrs. J. C. Leach, Mrs. Mary Syer, and the Turner, Ansell, Talbot, and a few other families. The Rev. D. C. Whalley is patron and incumbent of the *rectory*, which is valued in K.B. at £8. 13s. 4d., and has 16A. of glebe (mostly in other parishes,) and a yearly modus of £275, awarded in 1843 in lieu of tithes.

The *Church* (St. John) is a neat structure of early English architecture, with a tower now containing three, but formerly having four bells. It is supposed to have been built in the 13th century, and was repaired and improved in 1842, when a new porch and vestry were built, and three windows in the church were re-opened. In the north aisle are some remains of a rood stair-case, and the lower part of a screen, and in the wall is a niche, supposed to have been a chrismatory. The piscina and drain are in good preservation, and in the north wall is a singular opening, supposed to have been used for viewing the burning of the lights at the altar during Easter. A sword, helmet, and banners, formerly belonging to the East family, hang in the church; and on the floor is a slab in memory of Gilbert East, dated 1768. The present rector purchased the patronage and incumbency of the Rev. J. Ashley, in 1836, and intends making further improvements in the church. *Directory :—*Rev. Daniel Constable Whalley, *Rectory;* Wm. Moutell, *carrier* to Ipswich ; John Marven Syer, gent., *Wenham Cottage ;* Wm. Pottingale, *shopkeeper ;* and Joseph Ansell, *(maltster,)* David Beaumont, Wm. Goddard, Wm. Golding, Robt. Rist, *(Hall,)* and Thos. Vince, *farmers.*

WENHAM (LITTLE), a small parish, lies east of Great Wenham, 6¼ miles S.W. by W. of Ipswich, and contains only a few scattered houses, 87 inhabitants, and about 970 acres of land, belonging to the executors of F. Josselyn, Esq., (lords of the manor,) P. Havens, Esq., and Mr. Jas. Turner. *Wenham Hall* was anciently the seat of the Brews, and afterwards of the Thurstons, but is now a farm house. Near it is a building with massive walls, dated 1569, and supposed to have been used as a chapel. The *Church* is a neat building, with a tower at the west end ; and among its monuments is one to Joseph Thurston, Esq., who died in 1732, and is supposed to have been the last of his family who occupied the hall. The rectory, valued in K.B. at £5. 8s. 11½d., has been consolidated with that of Capel St. Mary, since 1787, as noticed at page 249. The manor, with the annual quit and free-rents and fines, and the Grove estate, (61A. 2R. 2P.,) which belonged to the late F. Josselyn, Esq., were advertised for sale, June 27th, 1843. *Directory :—*James Abbott, shoemaker ; Wm. Ablewhite, farmer, *Grove ;* John Brooke, farmer and chief constable, *Hall;* Snell Cooper, farmer, *Lodge ;* Wm. Hammond, blacksmith ; and Jas. Turner, *yeoman.*

WHERSTEAD, a village and parish on the western side of the vale of the Orwell, 2½ miles S. of Ipswich, has 238 inhabitants, and 2019A. 2R. 28P. of fertile land, belonging to Sir Robt. Harland, Bart., Jas. and John Josselyn, Esqrs., and a few smaller owners. Sir Robert is lord of the manor, impropriator of the rectory, and owner of *Wherstead Lodge*, where he resided till he succeeded to the more splendid seat of Orwell Park. (See page 126.) Wm. Scrope, Esq., now resides here occasionally. Gilbert de Reymes had this lordship in King John's time ; and in the 1st of Edward IV., it was granted to Sir Jno. Howard, as part of the forfeited estates of John, Earl of Wiltshire. It afterwards passed to the famous *Lord Chief Justice Coke*, who often resided here. The *Church* (St. Mary) has a tower and three bells, and stands on an eminence, sheltered with trees, and commanding a fine view of

the river Orwell. The *vicarage*, valued in K.B. at £5. 6s. 8d., is in the gift of the Crown and incumbency of the Rev. Geo. Capper, M.A., who has a good residence, (which was enlarged and improved in 1816,) 18A. 37P. of glebe, and a yearly modus of £158. 12s. 6d., awarded in lieu of small tithes, in 1840, when £405. 8s. per annum was awarded to the impropriator in lieu of the great tithes.

Addison Daniel, parish clerk
Capper Rev George, M.A. vicar of Wherstead and rector of Gosbeck
Newton Robert, vict. *Ostrich*
Quadling Benj. wheelgt. & wood dlr
Scrope Wm. Esq. *Wherstead Lodge*
Wilsmoer Joseph, blacksmith

FARMERS.

Frost Charles, Pannington Hall
Lee Joseph || Beart Samuel, *bailiff*
Sexton George, *Thorrington Hall*
Sexton Elizabeth, *Wherstead Hall*
Sexton Robert, *Bourn Hall*

WOOLVERSTONE, on the south-western bank of the river Orwell, 4 miles S. by E. of Ipswich, is a pleasant village and fertile parish, containing 246 souls, and 951A. 2R. 39P. of land. The Ven. Henry Denny Berners, LL.B., archdeacon of Suffolk, is lord of the manor, owner of nearly all the soil, and resides at *Woolverstone Hall*, a large and elegant mansion, in a beautiful *Park* of more than 400 acres, well clothed with wood, and stocked with spotted deer; and descending to the margin of the broad river Orwell, opposite another beautiful seat, called Orwell Park. The present hall was erected, in 1776, by the late Wm. Berners, Esq., proprietor of the stately street in London called after his name. It is built of Woolpit brick, with stone dressings, &c., and a pediment in the centre of the principal front, supported by four Ionic columns. The wings are connected with the centre by colonnades. The bow front next the river commands the most pleasing views of the water and the opposite shore of Nacton, through the trees which embellish the park. The apartments are fitted up with great taste, and contain a fine collection of pictures. The stables form an ornamental building on the site of the old hall. At some distance from the house, in the park, stands a square obelisk of freestone, 96 feet high, with an ascent in the interior to the top, which is surmounted by a globe, encircled with rays. As the inscription upon it records, this pleasing object was erected, in 1793, by the late Chas. Berners, Esq., in memory of his father, Wm. Berners, Esq., who died in 1783. This estate, early in the last century, belonged to Mr. Tyson, who became a bankrupt in 1720, when John Ward, Esq., of Hackney, claimed it in right of a mortgage. The matter was brought before the Court of Chancery, and for upwards of half a century, the cause remained undecided. At length, about 1773, the property was ordered to be sold, and was purchased by the grandfather of the present proprietor for £14,000. The *Church* (St. Michael) is a neat structure, in the park, and has a north aisle, which was added to it in 1832. The *rectory*, valued in K.B. at £5. 8s. 7d., is consolidated with that of Erwarton, in the patronage of Archdeacon Berners, and incumbency of the Rev. Ralph Berners, M.A., as already noticed at page 251. The Archdeacon supports a *National School* here, which he erected in 1832.

Berners Ven. Henry Denny, LL.B. archdeacon of Suffolk, *Woolverstone Hall*
Bramwell Rev Hy. Rowland, M.A. *curate*

Dale Samuel, farm bailiff
Gibbs Robert, shopkeeper
Walker James, farmer and corn miller, *Ralph's Farm*

STOW HUNDRED

Is a fertile and picturesque district, nearly in the centre of Suffolk, averaging about seven miles in length and breadth, and bounded by Cosford, Bosmere-and-Claydon, Thedwestry, Blackbourn, and Hartismere Hundreds. It is in the *Deanery* to which it gives name, and was in the Archdeaconry of Sudbury till 1837, when it was added to the *Archdeaconry of Suffolk*, so that it is still in the *Diocese of Norwich*. It is in *Stow Union*, and is watered by the river *Gipping*, which is navigable, for small craft, from Ipswich to Stowmarket, and receives here several tributary streams. The following is an enumeration of its fourteen *parishes*, shewing their territorial extent, the annual value of their lands and buildings, as assessed to the property tax in 1815, and their population in 1801 and 1841.

PARISHES.	Acrs.	Rental.	Populatn		PARISHES.	Acres.	Rental. £.	Population.	
			1801.	1841.				1801.	1841.
Buxhall	2524	2905	385	533	Old Newton ⎰	2349	3242	451	543
Combs	3000	3653	662	1064	Dagwrth ham ⎱				169
Creeting St. Ptr.	1336	1655	123	213	Onehouse*	866	1086	180	303
Finborough Gt.	1632	1721	325	467	Shelland	509	572	90	109
Finborough Ltl.	360	453	68	64	Stowmarket† ..	1240	6043	1761	3043
Gipping	900	915	120	93	Stowupland ..	2890	3775	709	903
Harleston	620	763	87	90	Wetherden ..	1784	2304	346	515
Haughley	2700	2985	592	916					
					Total	22,710	32,072	5899	9025

☞ CHIEF CONSTABLES.—Mr. Thos. Gross, of Stowmarket; and Mr. James Ward, of Haughley.

* Onehouse includes *Stow Union Workhouse.*

† Stowmarket includes the small hamlet of *Chilton.*

STOW UNION comprises an area of 89 square miles, or 54,978 acres divided into 34 parishes, of which 14 are in Stow Hundred, 11 in Blackbourn Hundred, and 9 in Thedwestry Hundred, which see. In 1841, it had 19,675 *inhabitants*, of whom 9759 were *males*, and 9916 *females;* and 4072 *houses*, of which 113 were empty, and 29 building, when the census was taken. Its *expenditure* for the support of the poor, in 1838, was £7768, and in 1840, £7754. 9s. The average annual expenditure of the 34 parishes, during the three years preceding the formation of the Union, was £14,919. The *Union Workhouse*, standing on an eminence in the parish of Onehouse, more than 1½ mile W. of Stowmarket, was erected in 1781, as a House of Industry for the 14 parishes of Stow Hundred, which were incorporated under Gilbert's Act. It cost more than £12,000, and was described in 1810 as having more the appearance of a gentleman's seat than a receptacle for paupers. Its internal arrangement has been considerably altered since the formation of the present Union, in 1835, to afford a better classification of the inmates, of whom it had 235, in 1821 ; 189, in 1831 ; but only 91 in 1841, so that it appears to have fewer paupers from 34, than it had formerly from 14 parishes. They are maintained at the average weekly cost of 2s. 4d. per head. Each parish in the Union returns one guardian, except Stowmarket, which returns two. Mr. Edw. and Mrs. Ablitt are *master* and *matron* of the Workhouse ; Mr. E. R. Buchanan, of Stowmarket, is *Clerk to the Board of Guardians*, and also *Superintendent Registrar.* Mr. Wm. Feltham is *Registrar of Marriages* for the whole Union, which is divided into three Relieving and Registration *Districts.* The *Registrars*

of Births and Deaths are Spencer Freeman, for *Stowmarket District;* Edw. Knevett, for *Rattlesden District;* and C. M. Burcham, for *Walsham-le-Willows District.* The latter is also Registrar of Marriages for the latter district; and Mr. Wm. Feltham is Registar of marriages for the other two districts. The *Relieving Officers* are, E. Knevett, C. B. Law, and C. M. Burcham. On the 11th of August, 1843, several splendid pieces of plate, which cost £300, raised by subscription, were presented by the Guardians and other principal inhabitants of this union, to *John Henry Heigham, Esq.*, as a mark of esteem for the valuable services he has rendered as Chairman of the Board.

BUXHALL, a pleasant village, 3½ miles W. by S. of Stowmarket, has in its parish 533 souls, and 2523A. 1R. 25P. of land, now rated, with the buildings, at the yearly value of £3465. 10s. It is mostly freehold, and lies in four *manors,* viz., *Buxhall,* belonging to the Rev. Coppinger Hill, of BUXHALL LODGE; *Cockerells Hall,* belonging to the Hon. and Rev. Sir Henry Leslie, Bart., of Box Hill, Surrey; *Fen Hall,* belonging to Sir J. R. Rowley, Bart.; and *Liffeys Hall,* belonging to Mr. John Fuller. The other principal owners of the soil are Lord Ashburnham, Lieut. Garnham, of *Buxhall Vale;* R. Hillhouse, Esq., Capt. Parker, and Messrs. R. Osborn, T. Stearn, and J. Hopson. The manor of Buxhall was the property of *Sir Wm. Coppinger,* Lord Mayor of London, in 1512, who was born here, and at his death left half his property to charitable uses, and the other half to his relations, who long flourished here, and became so famous for hospitality that " *to live like the Coppingers*" was long a proverbial expression in this neighbourhood. The *Church* (St. Mary) is an ancient structure, and the living is a *rectory,* valued in K.B. at £20. 0s. 5d., and now having a yearly modus of £680, in lieu of tithes, and a neat residence. The Rev. C. Hill, M.A., is patron; and the Rev. Charles Green, B.A., incumbent. The *Rev. Henry Hill,* a late rector, patron, and lord of the manor of Buxhall, successfully practised here the drilling of wheat in rows, at the distance of 18 inches. In 1615, *Mark Salter* left a yearly rent-charge of 20s. for the poor parishioners, who have also £4. 8s. 10d. yearly from £148 three per cent. consols, left by the late Mrs. Eliz. S. Garnham.

Clover Isaac, corn miller
Fuller Robt. Osborn, Esq., *Whalebone Cottage*
Garnham Lieut. Jno. *Buxhall Vale*
Green Rev. Charles, B.A., rector of Buxhall and Harleston
Hill Rev Coppinger, M.A., *Buxhall Lodge*
Langham Robert, butcher
Richer Thomas, wheelwright
Spurr James, blacksmith
Thurlow Frederick, carpenter

FARMERS.
* are Owners.

*Barnes John
Bradbrook Jas.
Cracknall Saml.
Cropley Jermh., *Liffeys Hall*
Dykes Thomas
Goram James
Hattan Nelson
*Hunt Sarah
Kemball Wm.

Kemball Wm., junior
Melton Frederick
Rands, *Farsborn Hall*
Pike Ann
Pilgrim Thos.
Ruffell John, *Cockerells Hall*
Spink John
* Spink Wm., *Fen Hall*

COMBS, a large straggling village, 1 mile S. of Stowmarket, has in its parish 1064 souls, many scattered farm-houses, and about 3000 acres of land, rising in bold undulations, extending southward to the vicinity of Battisford, and bounded on the north by the river Gipping, which is here crossed by a brick *bridge*, which was widened and repaired

in 1842. In the 43rd of Edward III., it was the lordship of Robert de Ufford, and it afterwards passed to the Willoughby de Eresby family, and from them to Charles Brandon, Duke of Suffolk. It was afterwards possessed by the Daundys, and was for some time the seat of the Bridgmans, one of whom rebuilt the *Hall*, which was sold by his heirs to Mr. Crowley, and was pulled down about 1730. Part of the parish was granted to Dartford nunnery, and given at the dissolution to Richd. Gresham, Kt. The Earl of Ashburnham is now lord of the *manor*, but the greater part of the soil belongs to Lady Pocklington, Lady Hotham, T. R. Daniel, Esq., (who has a pleasant seat here called *Edgar House;* C. Cure, Esq., F. W. Everett, Esq., and the Crosse, Freeman, Webb, Wolton, White, and other families. The *Church* (St. Mary) is an ancient fabric, and the living is a *rectory*, valued in K.B. at £25. 17s. 8½d., but now worth £880 per annum, and having a neat residence, about a mile from the church. The Earl of Ashburnham is patron, and the Rev. Richard Daniel, M.A., F.S.A., incumbent. The *Church Land* lets for about £3 per annum.

Adams Robert, baker
Andrews Samuel, carpenter
Baker Wm. boot and shoe maker
Bone John, blacksmith
Cooper James, corn miller
Daniel Rev Richd. M.A. Rectory
Daniel Thos. Reeve, Esq. *EdgarHs*
Ellis Robert, vict. Magpie
Freser James, bookkeeper
Green Joseph, wheelwright
Grimwood Joseph, farrier
Mayhew Thomas, beerhouse & shop-
keeper, and baker
Meakens Jno. vict. Punch Bowl
Miller Wm. *carrier* to Ipswich daily
Mumford Robt, gent. *Rose Cottage*
Pilbrow Wm. gardener
Pryor Thos. boot and shoe maker
Roper John, shopkeeper
Southgate Hiram, corn miller

Southgate Samuel, shopkeeper
Southgate Thos. sen. parish clerk
Webb Bayly, maltster, and corn and
coal merchant
Webb Jph. A. & Son, tanners, fell-
mongers, and woolstaplers

FARMERS.
* are Owners.
*Baker Wm.
Battle Francis
Cobbold John,
Edgar House
Cobbold Jno.jun.
Denny Samuel
*Durrant John,
Moat Farm
Godbold Thomas
Goymour Samuel
* Green John,
Jack's lane

Mumford Geo.,
Rose Cottage
Robinson Benj.
*Robinson Jacob
Rush James
Spink William,
White House
Southgate John
*Taylor Wm.
Theobald Thos.
* Ward Ed.Beth-
el, *KemberleyHl*
Willden Samuel
Wood Ts.Fowler

CREETING ST. PETER, a village and parish, 2½ miles E.S.E. of Stowmarket, has several scattered houses, 213 inhabitants, and 1335a. 3r. 31p. of land, and lies west of three other Creetings, noticed at page 232, from which it is sometimes called *West Creeting*. It is mostly freehold. Sir W. B. Proctor, Bart., is lord of the *manor*, but Sir W. F. F. Middleton, Bart., Mdk. Lonsdale, Esq., Lady Nightingale, J. H. Hart, Esq., Sir R. Pocklington, R. and E. Willoughby, Esqs., and several smaller owners, have estates here. The farms of *Raydon* and *Braziers Halls*, two ancient houses, are the property of Mr. W. Worledge. The *Church* (St. Peter) is an ancient fabric, and the living is a *rectory*, valued in K.B. at £10. 2s. 6d., but now having a yearly modus of £401. 10s., awarded in lieu of tithes, in 1839. The Rev. Edw. Paske, M.A., is patron and incumbent, and has a handsome residence, with pleasant grounds. The other principal inhabitants are Wm. Worledge, yeoman, *Braziers Hall;* and the following *farmers:* Mrs. Burman, (and owner,) Wm. Edwards, *Creeting Hill;* Gosling

and Dorling, *Howe Farm ;* Thos. Mudd, *Creeting Grove ;* and Mrs.
Eliz. Wolton, *Creeting Hall.*

FINBOROUGH, (GREAT) a pleasant village, near one of the
sources of the river Gipping, and 3 miles W. by S. of Stowmarket, has
in its picturesque parish, several scattered farm houses, 467 inhabitants,
and 1631A. 15P. of fertile land, partly copyhold.　The *manor and hall,*
with about half of the parish, belong to Lady Hotham, but at her decease they will devolve to R. J. Bussell, Esq., nephew of R. Pettiward, Esq., her late husband. The rest of the parish belongs to the Hattan, Crosse, Webb, Eade, Hunt, Mudd, and other families.　The descendants of Ranulf Glanville gave possessions here to Butley priory,
which had the rectory and advowson of the vicarage till the dissolution ;
but in 1559, they were granted to the Bishop of Ely, in exchange.
Ralph Lord Pipard held the manor in the reign of Edward II.　FIN-
BOROUGH HALL, a large and handsome mansion, in a beautiful
park, is occupied by Capt. Robert and Robert John Bussell, Esqrs.,
and will become the property of the latter on the death of his aunt,
Lady Hotham.　It was built by Roger Pettiward, Esq., the late proprietor, in 1795, under the direction of Mr. F. Sandys. It is of Woolpit
brick, and in the centre of the front is a projecting bow, adorned with
a pediment, supported by four columns likewise of brick, formed in
moulds made expressly for this purpose.　The park comprises about
200 acres, and gently slopes from the mansion, into a valley, which
nearly forms a circle from west to south, and is watered by a rivulet,
which, after a winding course, joins the Gipping below Stowmarket.
Beyond the rivulet, the park again rises to the north, and is skirted
by a wood.　It is diversified by clumps of large trees ; and behind the
hall is an embowered walk winding to the church.　In the parish is a
large oak plantation, called *America,* from the circumstance of its
having been planted by some disbanded soldiers who had returned from
the wars in North America.　The *Church* (St. Andrew) is a small
antique fabric, containing several handsome monuments of the Wol-
lastons and Pettiwards.　One is in memory of the *Rev. Wm. Wollaston,* a late lord of the manor, and author of the " *Religion of Nature Delineated,"* of which upwards of 10,000 copies were sold within
a few years after its publication ; though it exposed him to the cen-
sure of many zealous Christians, some of whom considered him as belonging to Dr. Clarke's fourth class of Deists.　He was born at Co-
ton Clanford, in Staffordshire, and died at London in 1724, after publishing a variety of other works, distinguished by the display of powerful abilities, and great erudition.　The Bishop of Ely is appropriator
of the *rectory,* (held on lease by Lady Hotham,) and patron of the
vicarage, which is valued in K.B. at £5. 1s. 3d., and has now 7¼A. of
glebe, and a yearly modus of £146. 2s. 9d., awarded in 1841, when
the rectorial tithes were commuted for £284. 14s. per annum.　The
Rev. Frederick Herbert Maberly, M.A. (of Stowmarket,) is the
present vicar.　The *Town Estate,* which has from time immemorial
been vested in feoffees, in trust for the benefit of the parishioners, consists of two cottages, a farm house, and about 60A. of land, let for
£52. 10s. a year, which, after paying for repairs, is distributed among
the poor parishioners.　*Roger Pettiward, Esq.,* the late lord of the
manor, who died in 1833, bequeathed £666. 13s. 4d. three per cent.

Consolidated Annuities, in trust to apply the dividends thereof, in the purchase of six brown great-coats for six poor widowers, and six good red cloaks for six poor widows of this parish ; and the surplus, if any, to be distributed in coals among the said poor people on New Year's Day.

FINBOROUGH (GREAT.)

Bussell Capt. Robert & Robt. John, Esqrs. *Great Finborough Hall*
Abbott Thos. gardener, at the Hall
Aldrich Robert, auctioneer & valuer
Andrews George, vict. White Horse
Archer Felgate, shoemaker
Bradley, John, shopkeeper
Brook Wm. corn miller
Chaplin Wm. joiner
Edgar Mrs Elizabeth
Halls John, wheelwright
Halls Mr Joshua

Mudd Elizabeth and Emma, boarding and day school
Purr Wm. blacksmith
Thurlow, Jeremiah, joiner & builder

FARMERS.
(* *are Owners.*)
Boby Charles
Chaplin M.
Cooper Joseph
Crosse Henry, *Boyton*
Davis Henry, *Valley farm*
Goymour Wm.

*Hattan Charles, *Boarded barn*
*Hattan George
*Hunt John
Lawson Thomas, *Dairy farm*
Lusher Denis
*Mudd Thomas, *Mill hill*

FINBOROUGH (LITTLE,) a small parish, 3½ miles S.W. of Stowmarket, has only 64 souls, and 360 acres of land, belonging to Messrs. W. and H. Crosse, Mrs. Turner, Mr. J. Durrant, and a few smaller owners, and mostly occupied by Mr. Robert Turner, of the *Hall farm ;* and Mr. Jas. Durrant, of *Hill farm.* It is in the manor of Bricett, (see p. 229,) and was appropriated to Bricett priory, which was given at the dissolution to King's College, Cambridge, to which the manor, the rectory, and the patronage of the *perpetual curacy,* (valued at only £11,) still belong. The Rev. Chas. Frederick Parker, M.A., of Ringshall, is the incumbent. The *Church* (St. Mary) is a small thatched building, without either a steeple or belfry. The tithes, belonging to King's College, have been commuted for a yearly modus of £96. In 1671, *Wm. Fower* left for the benefit of poor parishioners, a house called Bennett's, and about 6A. of land in Ringshall, let for £12 ; and the site of a house in this parish, let for 2s. a year. The latter is held on a 60 years' lease, dated 1786.

GIPPING, a well-wooded and picturesque parish, 4 miles N.N.E. of Stowmarket, is so called from its being near one of the three springs which give rise to the *River Gipping.* (See page 62.) It is sometimes called a hamlet to Old Newton, or Stowmarket, and contains 93 souls, and about 900 acres of land, in six farms, which have commodious houses. Chas. Tyrell, Esq., of Polstead, owns most of the soil, and is lord of the manor, impropriator, and owner of *Gipping Hall,* a large ancient brick mansion in a park of 60 acres, which was long the seat of his family, but is now only occupied occasionally as a sporting seat. The Tyrells are descended from Sir Walter Tyrell, Kt., who was lord of Langham, in Essex, at the Domesday survey. Wm. Tyrell, Kt., of Gipping, was father to James Tyrell, who was captain of Guisnes, in France, in the reign of Henry VII. The *Church*, or Chapel, stands near the hall, and was built by the Tyrell family. It is an ancient Gothic structure, and its north wall is finely mantled with ivy. The living is a *donative*, exempt from episcopal jurisdiction, in the patronage of Chas. Tyrell, Esq., and incumbency of the Rev. —— Oakes,

for whom the Rev. J. Phear, of Earl Stonham, officiates. The Rev. W. H. Crawford and Dr. Beck have each a manorial right over a small part of the parish; and General Rebow, G. Falkner, and Mr. Fisher have small estates here. In the 9th of James 1st, *Margaret English* conveyed to trustees a cottage, barn, and 11A. of land, in trust to pay yearly 20s. for the poor of Old Newton, and 30s. to the poor of Stowmarket, and to distribute the residue of the rents among the poor of Gipping. The estate is let for £14 a year, so that the poor of Gipping derive from it about £9. 10s. per annum, which is distributed in coals, blankets, &c., together with a yearly rent-charge of £3. 6s. 8d., left by the same donor, out of an estate belonging to C. Tyrell, Esq. *Directory:*—James Miller, *carpenter;* and Robert Groom, Charles Halls, *Rookery;* Wm. Hunt, Richard Scotchmer, Robert Steggall, and Wm. Turner, *farmers.*

HARLESTON, 3 miles N.W. of Stowmarket, is a small parish containing only 90 souls, and 620 acres of land, partly copyhold, and partly in the manors of Haughley and Dagworth, but mostly in the manor of Harleston Hall, which belongs to Lady Hotham, who rebuilt the *Hall* in the Elizabethan style, a few years ago; but it is occupied by a farmer. Charles Tyrell, Esq., has an estate here. The *Church* is a discharged rectory, valued in K.B. at £7, and in 1835 at £175. It has 11A. of glebe in Shelland parish, and is in the gift of Lady Hotham, and incumbency of the Rev. Charles Green, B.A., of Buxhall. The *farmers* are Jacob Bradley Cooper, *(Hall;)* James Davis, Wm. Peddar, *(Moor;)* and Robert Moyes.

HAUGHLEY, an ancient village, was formerly a market town, and is picturesquely situated on a declivity nearly 3 miles N.N.W. of Stowmarket. Its parish has 916 souls, and about 2700A. of land, including an open *common* of 120A., and the small hamlets of *New Street* and *Haughley Green.* The Rev. Wm. Henry Crawford, of HAUGHLEY PARK, is lord of the manor, but a great part of the soil belongs to Charles Tyrell, Esq., (owner of the seat called *Plashwood,* now occupied by the Rev. Sir A. B. Henniker,) the trustees of the late R. Pettiward, Esq., the Rev. E. Ward and James Ward, Esq., of *Tot Hill;* the Rev. John Ward; and several smaller owners. *Haughley Park* was held by Charles Brandon, Duke of Suffolk, and passed to the Crown by purchase or exchange. It was afterwards granted to Sir John Sulyard, by Queen Mary. In the early part of the present century, it was the seat of the eldest son of Sir W. Jerningham, who married the daughter and co-heiress of the late S. Sulyard, Esq. The estate was sold for £27,840, in 1811, and the advertisements of the sale described it as "The manor of Haughley Park, extending over 2442 acres, 22 dwelling-houses, and 28 messuages, with the spacious mansion-house and offices, and a park and land containing about 396 acres." The lord of this manor formerly possessed a jurisdiction of *Oyer and Terminer,* trying all causes in his own court, of which instances are on record so late as the 11th of Elizabeth. At a court held in the 15th of Edward IV., it was ordered that the abbot of Hales, in Gloucestershire, to whom the parish was appropriated, should erect a new *gallows* in Luberlow field; and at the same time, William Baxteyn held lands here by the service of finding a ladder for the lord's gallows. The *copyholds* are subject to arbitrary fines. Some

small portions of the parish are in the manors of Dagworth, Pulham, and Bacton. The *market* anciently held here, was of a more early origin than that at Stowmarket, but it was disused some centuries ago. A *fair* for toys, pleasure, &c., is held here on the 25th of August. Near the church are the remains of a very strong CASTLE, supposed to have been a Saxon structure, and to have been the fortress called *Hageneth Castle*, which was in the custody of Ralph de Broe, and was stormed and demolished in 1173, by the army of Flemings, under the Earl of Leicester. (See pages 51 and 622.) It afterwards belonged to the Uffords, and De la Poles, Earls of Suffolk. The site of this castle is considered by some antiquarians to have been the Roman camp *Sitomagus*, which others place at Woolpit. Its form may still be distinctly traced, and approaches to a square, fortified with a deep ditch or moat. Towards the north, upon a high artificial hill, of steep ascent, and also surrounded by a deep moat, stood the *keep*, or strong tower, the foundation of which now remaining is very thick, and apparently circular. On the west side of it is a large oblong square, that seems to have been an outwork of the castle, bounded by a smaller moat, except on the east, where it abuts on the castle moat. The ground occupied or enclosed by all these works, exceeds seven acres. The CHURCH (St. Mary) is a large ancient structure, of early English architecture, consisting of a nave, chancel, and south aisle, with a tower at the west end of the latter, which has in its east window the arms of Hales Abbey, in stained glass. It is about 110 feet long, and 50 broad, and contains some neat monuments of the Crawford, Smyth, and other families. The Dean and Chapter of Westminster, as trustees of Dr. Triplett's Charity, are impropriators of the rectory, but the patronage of the *vicarage*, valued in K.B. at £7. 19s. 2d., is in dispute. The Rev. Edward Ward, M.A., is the present vicar. In 1842, the rectorial tithes were commuted for £420, and the vicarial for £350 per annum. The *Town Lands*, under the management of the churchwardens, overseers, and feoffees, consist of a garden and four tenements, formerly called the *Guildhall*, and now the *Town House*, let for £7. 7s. a year; two meadows, containing 4A. 2R.; and Broom Hall Field, 3A. 3R., in the Manor of Dagworth-with-Sorrel, let at rents amounting to £10 a year; and about a rood of land, formerly the site of a house, let for 16s. a year. The poor have also 15s. a year, left by *Thos. Ballard*, in 1599, out of land called *Shackery's*.

HAUGHLEY.

Marked 1, live at Haughley New Street ; and 2, Haughley Green.

Andrews Wm. joiner and builder
Baker Francis, corn mill
Barnes Wm. schoolmaster and baker
Barritt Alfred, tailor
Clark Thomas, joiner and builder
Cleveland Wm. grocer and tailor
Crawford Rev Wm. Henry, M.A. Fellow of St. Peter's College, Cambridge, *Haughley Park*
Denny John, vict. shoemkr. &c. *Cock*
Ebden Miss Elizabeth
Ebden Wm. surgeon
Elmer John, harness maker
Faiers Simon, vict. and shoema King's Arms
Freeman Rev Frederick Wm. M.A. curate, *Vicarage*
Frost John, bricklayer & beerhouse
Funnell George, boarding school
Funnell John, gent
Green Robert, shoemaker
Grimwood Geo. maltster, *Dagworth*
Henniker Rev Sir Augustus Brydges, Bart., *Plashwood*, (and *Newton Hall, Essex*)
Jacobs Mrs. *Dagworth*
James Samuel, baker and joiner

1 Lummis Wm. carpenter, black-smith and vict. *White Horse*
2 Plummer Amos, tailor
Pritty Jasper and Sisters, grocers, drapers, glovers, &c.
Pritty John, sash-cord manufactr
Pryke George, cooper
Pryke George, jun. shopkeeper
Ruffell Edward, butcher
2 Ruffell Wm. blacksmith
Sheppeard Samuel, harness maker
2 Simpson James, corn miller
Ward Rev Edw. M.A. vicar, *Tot Hill*
Ward James, Esq., chief constable, *Tot Hill*

Winwood James, wheelwright
FARMERS.
(* *are Owners.*)
Baker Charles, *Castle*
Barnes John, (& land surveyor)
*Clark Caudle
*Francis Wm.
2*Kerry J.
Morley Mrs
2 Munnings Jas. (and cattle dlr)
2 Munnings Jno.

Pawsey Joseph, *Haughley Bells*
1 Pawsey J. jun.
Pritty George
Steggall Wm.
Welham James
Welham James, jun. *Bushes*
CARRIER.
Firman Jno., to Stowmarket and Bury

OLD NEWTON, a straggling village, picturesquely situated on the boldly rising banks of one of the sources of the river Gipping, 3 miles N. by E. of Stowmarket, has in its parish 712 souls, and 2348A. 1R. 32P. of land, including DAGWORTH hamlet, which had 169 inhabitants in 1841, and was anciently a chapelry, and the foundations of its chapel may still be traced. *Hops* are grown at Dagworth, and a few of its houses are in Haughley parish. G. Tomline, Esq., is lord of the *manor of Newton;* Sir John Shelley is lord of *Nether Hall manor;* and the manor of *Dagworth-with-Sorrel* is held by the Rev. J. G. Haggitt, as lessee of the Bishop of Norwich. Part of the parish lies in other manors. A great portion of the soil is freehold, and the copyholds are subject to arbitrary fines. *Newton Hall* belongs to General Rebow, and the other principal landowners are C. Tyrell, Esq., T. Bond, Esq., Mrs. Rust, Mr. Kerrey, and the trustees of S. Ringe, Esq. Newton was one of the estates belonging to Margaret, Countess of Salisbury, whom Henry VIII. iniquitously, and without trial, condemned to the block, in the 70th year of her age. For sometime after the Norman conquest, it was held by the Boytons. The *Church* (St. Mary) is an ancient structure, and was appropriated by Henry II. to the abbey of St. Osythe, in Essex. The living is a vicarage, valued in K.B. at £7. 15s. 5d., in the patronage of the Rev. Wm. Burgess, and incumbency of the Rev. Charles Bridges, who has a neat residence and 12A. 2R. 31P. of glebe. The *tithes* were commuted in 1840, the vicarial for £168. 14s., and the rectorial for about £414 per annum. Of the latter, £45 belongs to the Rev. J. G. Haggitt; £18 to Mrs. Rust; and the remainder to Sir J. Shelley, as lessee of the Bishop of Norwich. The poor have 20s. a year from English's charity, as noticed with Gipping.

NEWTON (OLD.)

Marked 1, live in Dagworth; 2, Ward Green; 3, Brown Street; and the rest in Old Newton, or where specified.

3 Adams Edward, gentleman
1 Armstrong Wm. *hop grower*
Baxter Jas. blacksmith & shopkpr.
Bridges Rev Charles, *Vicarage*
Bridges Reuben, steward
Carr James, blacksmith

Clabon John, blacksmith
Clamp John, shopkeeper
Clark Francis, shopkeeper
Diaper Jonathan, shoemaker
Faiers George, shoemaker
Francis Robert, bricklayer
3 Gardiner Mrs Elizabeth
1 Grimwood George, maltster
Hayward Wm. wheelwright
Horrex Zechariah, carpenter
Nichols Francis, wheelwright

Pyman Samuel, corn miller
2 Taylor George, corn miller
Thing Ts. vict. Shoulder of Mutton
Wicks Edmund, chairmaker

FARMERS.
(* are yeomen.)
2 Aston Abrm.
3 Baker John
*Bircham Chas.

Coleby Joseph
1 Gladwell Ann
*Groom Roger
*Harvey James
Hawse Jesse

1 Jennings Jas.
   (& hop grower)
*Kersey Joseph
   Rookyard
*Lankester Wm.
   Bridge Farm
*Mayhew Geo.
*Nottidge Ralph,
   White Hall
*Nunn Thomas

1 Peck John, Red
   House
Turner Mrs My.
   Newton Hall
*Turner Philip
TurnerWm. Nether Hall
WhistlecraftJas.
   Ivy House
2 Woods Thos.

ONEHOUSE, 2 miles W. by N. of Stowmarket, is a small parish of scattered houses, containing 865A. 1R. 17P. of well-wooded land, and 303 inhabitants, including 91 in *Stow Union Workhouse*, which is situated here, and is already described at page 285. In the reign of Edward the Third, it was the seat and estate of Bartholomew de Burghersh, who was one of the twelve barons to whose care the Prince of Wales was committed at the battle of Cressy. He died here in 1369, without male issue, and his sole daughter and heiress married Edward, Baron Despenser. On the site of the old hall, encompassed by a moat, a commodious farm-house was built many years ago. The grandeur and solitary situation of the ancient mansion probably gave name to the parish, which, little more than two centuries ago, was covered with wood, except a narrow strip, which ascended from the valley to the hall. Queen Elizabeth, in one of her "progresses" through this county, breakfasted at Onehouse. The parish still abounds in fine timber trees, and on the glebe adjoining the secluded Rectory House is a wood of ten or twelve acres. Lady Hotham is lady of the *manor,* and owner of the greater part of the soil, and the remainder belongs to J. Garnham, Esq., and a few smaller owners. It is mostly freehold. The *Church* (St. John) is a small ancient fabric, with some remains of Saxon architecture. The tower is circular, and the font is of unhewn stone. The *rectory,* valued in K.B. at £7. 2s. 6d., and in 1835, at £200, has 34½ acres of glebe. Lady Hotham is patroness, and the Rev. Thomas Scott, B.A., incumbent. *Directory :*—Edward Ablitt, master of the *Union Workhouse ;* Wm. Crosse, Esq., *Onehouse Hall ;* Rev. Henry S. Marriott, M.A., curate, *Rectory ;* Mrs. Susan Page Rout, *Onehouse Lodge ;* John Green, sen. and jun., *farmers ;* Jeremiah Oxer, *farmer ;* and James Riley, maltster and vict., *Shepherd and Dog.*

SHELLAND, a small secluded village and parish, near one of the sources of the river Gipping, 4 miles W.N.W. of Stowmarket, has 109 inhabitants, and 509 acres of well-wooded land, rising in bold undulations, and all belonging to Charles Tyrell, Esq., except 20A. belonging to J. Garnham, Esq., and about two acres belonging to the glebe of Harleston and Onehouse. C. Tyrell, Esq., is lord of the manor, impropriator of the tithes, (commuted for £125 per annum,) and patron of the *Church,* which is a *donative,* valued at £40, and enjoyed by the Rev. Henry Ray. Shelland was held by the Bouchier and Devereux families, and was sold in 1591, by that great but unhappy favourite of Queen Elizabeth, Robert Devereux, Earl of Essex. *Rockylls,* now a farm, was held by the Drury family, and afterwards by the Rays. The poor have a yearly rent-charge of 20s., left by Wm. Kent, in 1712, out

of a house and orchard, on Shelland Green. The principal inhabitants are, Wm. Brett, *blacksmith;* Thos. Sparrow, *bricklayer;* Eliz. Oxer, *New Farm;* and Wm. Peddar, farmer, *Rockylls Hall.*

STOWMARKET, a small, but thriving *market town,* is pleasantly situated betwixt, and at the confluence of two branches of the river Gipping; on the road from Ipswich to Bury St. Edmund's; 12 miles N.N.W. of the former; 14 miles E.S.E. of the latter; 3 miles N.W. of Needham Market; 13 miles N. by E. of Hadleigh; and 81 miles N.E. of London. Including the small hamlet of CHILTON, half a mile W. of the town, its parish contains about 1240 *acres of land,* mostly freehold, and belonging to Mrs. M. D. Marriott, Mrs. Rust, of *Abbott's Hall,* Henry Jas. Oakes, Esq., and several smaller proprietors. It had 1761 inhabitants in the year 1801; 2006, in 1811; 2252, in 1821; 2672, in 1831; and 3043, in 1841, when its number of *males* was 1420, and *females* 1623, and its number of *houses* 632, of which 20 were empty when the census was taken. It was in a declining condition during last century, till the GIPPING was made *navigable* to it from Ipswich in 1793, since which it has doubled its buildings and *population,* and has enjoyed a considerable traffic in corn, malt, coal, &c., being nearly in the centre of the county, and there being no other navigation within the distance of many miles. As already noticed at page 62, the Gipping rises from three rivulets which unite at Stowmarket, whence it flows to Ipswich by a winding course of 16 miles, in which it has fifteen *locks,* each 60 feet long and 14 broad; three built with timber, and twelve with brick and stone. The construction of this canal cost about £27,000, and its completion reduced the price of land-carriage from hence to Ipswich more than one-half. Independently of its utility, it is a great ornament to the town, there being an agreeble walk from the basin along the towing path, nearly a mile in length, winding through fertile meadows, hop plantations, &c. The *town* has many good inns, well-stocked shops, and neat and commodious houses, especially about the *Market place,* which is spacious, and has a handsome *Corn Exchange* and *Assembly Room,* built about nine years ago at the cost of £3000, raised in £25 shares. The *Gas-works,* by which the town is now brilliantly lighted, were constructed in 1835-'6 by a speculator, who afterwards sold them to a company of shareholders, to whom Mr. G. Stevens is superintendent. The *Market,* held every Thursday, is extensively supplied with corn, and numerously attended by farmers from a considerable distance; and being well situated for the barley trade, there are in the town a number of large malting houses. Two *Fairs* are held here annually—viz., on June 10th for toys, pleasure, &c., and on August 12th for sheep and lambs, of which as many as 13,000 are sometimes shown. Each fair continues two days, and when the latter date falls on Saturday, the fair is held on the preceding Thursday. The town had formerly a small manufacture of worsted stuffs, and still gives employment to a number of persons in the manufacture of linen or "*Suffolk hempen cloth,*" and in making *sacking,* rope, twine, &c. There are in the parish several extensive *nurseries* and market *gardens;* but the *hop-grounds,* which formerly extended over about 150 acres, have been reduced to about 32 acres. *White bricks* of excellent quality are made here.

Stowmarket, from its central situation, has been the place from time

immemorial where all the county meetings, connected with the politics of the kingdom, have been held ; and until Suffolk was separated into two Divisions by the Parliamentary Reform Act, all nominations of members for the county were made here. The town was anciently a borough, and possessed a chartered incorporation. It is now a *polling place* for the Western Division of the county, and has *petty sessions* every alternate Monday. The *church-chest,* which is large and very antique, has three locks, the keys of which had been in the hands of the patron, incumbent, and churchwardens for immemorial years, until a short time ago, when the chest was opened by the *Rev. A. G. H. Hollingsworth, M.A.,* the present vicar and rural dean, and found to contain a great mass of papers, the substance of which will be found in his History and Antiquities of Stowmarket and the Hundred of Stow, now (Sept., 1843) about to be published. The old mansion-house, called *Abbott's Hall,* (now the seat of Mrs. Rust,) and the manor of Stowmarket, with the rectory and advowson of the vicarage, were given by Henry II. to the abbey of St. Osythe, in Essex, together with several neighbouring manors and churches ; and at the dissolution, they were granted to Thomas Darcie. *Richard de Amourdevil* obtained a grant for a market and fair here in the 12th of Edward III. Mrs. M. D. Marriott is now lady of the manor of Stowmarket, or Abbott's Hall, which, in 1764, was held by Wm. Lynch, Esq. The CHURCH *(St. Peter and St. Mary)* is a spacious and beautiful structure, with a square tower containing height bells, and surmounted by an elegant wooden spire, rising to the eight of 120 feet. It was repewed and beautified in 1840, at the cost of £1000, and contains several neat monuments of the Tyrell and other families, and one to *Dr. Young,* who was vicar here from 1628 to 1656, and was the tutor of *Milton,* who visited him at the ancient Vicarage, where a mulberry tree of great size bears the honour of being planted by the immortal poet. Dr. Young was one of the leaders in that war against episcopacy, which raged in the time of Oliver Cromwell and the Puritans ; but the town does not appear to have been the scene of any military conflict during the civil wars of the 17th century, though it suffered severely, like most other places in the county, from the Parliamentary taxation of those unhappy times. The *vicarage* of Stowmarket, with that of Stow-upland annexed to it, is valued in K.B. at £16. 15s., and is now worth upwards of £300 per annum. The Rev. A. G. H. Hollingsworth, M.A., is patron and incumbent, and also impropriator of part of the rectorial tithes in both parishes, but the greater part of them belongs to the landowners. His portion of them has been commuted for £33 per annum in Stowmarket, and £257 per annum in Stow-upland. The vicarial tithes have been commuted for a yearly modus of £186. Stow-upland, which had been churchless, has now a handsome church, which was finished in 1843. There are in the town five chapels belonging to the Independents, Baptists, Wesleyans, Primitive Methodists, and Plymouth Brethren. The Independent congregation here was formed in 1720, and the Baptists' in 1797. E. P. Archer, Esq., is secretary to the *Central Suffolk Agricultural Society,* which holds its annual meetings here.

The following CHARITY ESTATES AND RENT-CHARGES are under the management of feoffees for the benefit of the town, the church, and the

poor.   By a decree of the Court of Chancery in 1623, and another in 1653, it was decreed that the following estates, which had been devised with others by *Margaret Gowle*, in 1523, for superstitious uses, should be settled for the following uses—viz. the *Chilton Hall Meadow*, &c., (10A. 1R. 32P., and a cottage, let for £62. 10s. a year,) for the reparation of the church, subject to a yearly payment of 40s. for the relief of the poor; and the property called Wyles, Cross Pightles, and Perry-Field, solely for the relief of the poor.   The three latter comprise 5A. 8P. of land, and a double cottage, let for £33 a year.   The "*Common Weal Land*," comprising about 11A. called *Spoonman's*, in Stow-upland, was purchased by the inhabitants with £105, in 1716, subject to a mortgage of £40, which was paid off by borrowing that amount from Richd. Shute's charity.   This land adjoins about 10A. of land and a barn, left for the relief of the poor by James Revett, in 1586, and they are let together for £40 a year, about half of which is distributed among the poor, and the remainder is laid out in repairing the church.   The *Old White Lion Estate* was settled at some unknown period, for providing gowns for poor men and women, with the letters M. F. upon them, in remembrance of *Michael Flegg*, the donor.   It consists of a house, shop, and large yard, near the Market place, let for £22; and four houses, a warehouse, workshop, and other buildings, with gardens, &c., on the ground formerly called the George yard, let, in 1811 and 1812, to various tenants at rents amounting to £22, on lease for 44 years; the lessees covenanting to lay out certain sums in improving the premises.   The Old White Lion Inn is supposed to have stood in the George yard.   In 1686, RICHARD SHUTE left £100 to purchase land for the poor, and £40 of it was paid for discharging the mortgage on Spoonman's land, as already noticed. The remaining £60 was laid out in the purchase of 3A. 0R. 33P. in Perryfield, let for £14 per annum.   In 1712, WM. KENT left his messuages in Ipswich street, to the minister, churchwardens, and overseers of Stowmarket, to provide coats for poor men, with the letters W. K. upon them. These premises were let in 1811 on lease for 44 years, at the annual rent of £10, the lessee covenanting to lay out £240 in improving the buildings. The yearly RENT-CHARGES, held by the same feoffees for the benefit of the poor, are as follows:—£2 out of Chilton Hall Meadow, as already noticed; £4 out of Chilton Hayward, in Onehouse parish, left by *John Wage*, in the reign of Philip and Mary; £2 given by the same donor out of the same estate for schooling two poor boys; £4 given by *John How*, in 1586, out of a tenement called Bills, or Bess Garnham's; £4. 13s. 4d. left by *James Rivett*, in 1586, out of land at Stow-upland; 25s. left by *Wm. Kent*, in 1712, out of a shop formerly the George Inn; £2 left by *Charles Booth*, in 1710, out of premises in Tavern street; £3. 6s. 8d. given by *Margaret English*, out of lands at Gipping; 30s. out of other lands in Gipping, given by the said Margaret English; 30s. left by *Jacob Johnson*, in 1708, out of a house here, belonging to Mr. Smith; and £2. 12s. for bread, and 20s. for schooling poor children, given by *Thomas Blackerby*, out of the manor of Stowmarket, or Abbott's Hall, which was purchased by the late Mr. Marriott, in 1819.   The *yearly income*, derived from these estates and rent-charges, amounts to about £230, out of which the feoffees provide 2s. worth of bread every Sunday, for the poor, and distribute yearly about £18 in coats, and £26 in small sums among the poor.   The residue is applied in payment of the expenses attending the office of the churchwardens, no part having been applied for education since the establishment of the NATIONAL SCHOOLS for boys and girls, in the church-yard.   The above-named *Thos. Blackerby* charged the great tithes of Stowmarket, (lately the property of Mr. Boby,) with the following rent-charges—viz., £4 once in four years for gowns for two poor men of Stowmarket, and one of Stow-upland; 20s. yearly to the minister; and £2s. 12s. yearly to the lecturer for sermons on Thursdays.

STOWMARKET DIRECTORY.

Post-Office, Market place; Mr. John George Hart, *postmaster*. Letters are received and despatched at 7 morning and 7 evening, by Mail cart, which meets the mails at Ipswich and Bury St. Edmund's.

MISCELLANY.

Adams Thos. pipe maker, Ipswich st
Barnard Henry, dyer, Church st
Boothroyd Joseph, excise, Regent st
Bridges Mrs Sarah, Ipswich street
Buchanan Edgar Rout, superintendent registrar & Union clerk, Ipswich rd
Burch Mrs Esther, Tavern street
Burton James Wm. (excise) Regent st
Caley Samuel, fishmonger, Bury st
Colson John, gun maker, Ipswich st
Daniel Rev G. W. B., curate, Tavern st
Dorman Wm. Hy. preacher to the Plymouth Brethren, Violet hill
Earthy Richard, sexton, Church yd
Earthy Thomas, farrier, Ipswich st
Esling Mrs Sarah, Church yard
Francis Jas. umbrella maker, Bury st
Francis Jsha. hatter & dyer, Bury st
Freeman Spencer, registrar of births and deaths
Fulcher Mrs Charlotte, Ipswich st
Grimsby Mrs Mary, Ipswich street
Grimwood Robt. clothes dlr. Stwd. st
✻Hart John Geo. bank manager, Mkp
Harley Dan, musical instrument mkr. Ipswich street
Hewitt Wm. merchant, Tavern st
Hollingsworth Rev Arthur George Harper, M.A. vicar & rural dean, *Vicarage*
Hunt Jas. gent. Stowupland street
King Benj. jun. mercht. Ipswich rd
King Benj. merchant, Violet hill
Kerridge James, dyer, Church yard
Langham Chas. clothes dlr. Bury st
Larkham Mrs Lucy, Ipswich street
Lawrence Mrs Susannah, Bury st
Lingley Rev Isaac (Bap.) Bury st
Lockwood Mrs Eliz. Ipswich street
M'Lachlin Jno. surveyor, Bury street
Maberly Rev Fdk. Herbert, M.A. vicar of Great Finborough, Violet hill
Mays Edw. millwright, Bury street
Miller Mrs Sarah, Ipswich street
Mills Mrs Eliz. & Miss F. Tavern st
Offord James, cutler, Ipswich street
Offord Thomas, copperplate printer, Bury street
Paul Miss Susan, Bury street
Payne Henry, clerk, Bury street

Pettit Miss Mary, Church yard
Prentice Thos. merchant, Violet hill
Prentice Wm. mercht. Stowupland st
Pulford John, supervisor, Regent st
Purr Mrs Ann, Bury street
Rawlings Miss Ann, Ipswich street
Rout Mrs J. P. *Limetree House*
Rust Mrs Ann Sarah, *Abbott's Hall*
Sheldrake Jerh. traveller, Ipswich st
Sheldrake Thos. wine mert. Ipswich st
Stevens Geo. & Wells John, brewers, Stowupland street
Suttle James, hay dealer, Crow st
Symonds Mrs Elizabeth, Regent st
Turner Mrs Mary, Union street
Ward Rev Wm. (Indt.) Ipswich st
Williams Charles, clerk, Bury street
Webb Holman, gent. Ipswich street
Whayman Owen, veterinary surgeon, Butter market
Winwood Keziah, turner, Ipswich st
Youngman Thos. fruitr. Ipswich st

ACADEMIES.
*Marked * take Boarders.*

*Carr Geo. (Grammar,) *Chilton House*
Carter Sarah, Ipswich street
*Curtis Mary Ann, Bury street
Garrard Ann, Ipswich street
Isaac James, Tavern street
Martin Phœbe, Bury street
National School, Church yard, Wm. Cooper and Mary Frewer
Newton J. (Infants',) Violet hill
Orams Mary Anne, Ipswich street
*Paul Susan, Bury street
*Peek Harriet, Ipswich street
*Tydeman George, Stowupland st

ATTORNEYS.
Archer Edwd. Peter, top of Tavern st
Gudgeon James, Bury street
Marriott John (clerk to magistrates and commissioners of taxes,) *Camping land*
Ransom John Bayley, Bury street

AUCTIONEERS, &c.
Cole Thomas, Crow street
Downing Hy. Shuckforth, Market pl
Payne James, Butter market

BAKERS & FLOUR DEALERS.
Ayliffe Richard, Bury street
Barnard Edward, Stowupland street

Blomfield Thomas, Bury street
Blomfield Thomas Wm. Bury street
Greengrass George, Bury street
Lockwood John, Ipswich street
Pooley Thos. (clothes broker,) S. st
Tricker John, Regent street
Tricker Robert, Ipswich street
Wilkinson Thos. Eugene, Ipswich st

BANKERS.
Oakes, Bevan, Prentice, Moor, and Co. Market place (on Barclay and Co ;) J. G. Hart, *manager*
Suffolk Banking Co. Market place (on London & Westminster Bank ;) J. A. Lankester, *manager*
Savings' Bank, Market place (open Sat. from 1 to 5 ;) J. G. Hart, *agent*

BASKET MAKERS.
Collins Robert, Stowupland street
Collins Wm. Tavern street
Stevens Wm. Stowupland street

BLACKSMITHS.
Cracknell Samuel, Bury street
Gladwell Jas. (drill maker) Regent st
Harding Amos, Stowupland street
Smith Wm. Ipswich street

BOOKSELLER, &c.
Woolby Thos. (printer, news agent, stamp vendor, &c.) Ipswich street

BOOT & SHOE MAKERS.
Andrews Wm. Bury street
Chittock George, Bury street
Codd Wm. Ipswich street
Colson John, Bury street
Colson Wm. Stowupland street
Cuthbert Robert, Regent street
Diaper George, Bury street
Flack Joshua, Regent street
Gladwell Thomas, Stowupland street
Howes Benjamin, Union street
Lait Robert, Bury street
Lawrence Henry, Butter market
Ormes Samuel, Crow street
Pulmer Robert, Stowupland street
Pollard Edmund, Ipswich street
Race James, Stowupland street
Raffe James, Bury street
Reddish Edward, Market place
Roper Benjamin, Bury street
Roper David, Church lane
Runeckles Robert, Bury street
Rushbrook Francis, Violet hill
Stimpson Brice, Church lane

BRAZIERS & TINNERS.
Quinton James, Stowupland street
Salmon Edward, Bury street
Southgate Wm. Bury street

BRICK & TILE MAKER.
Fison Joseph, Onehouse road

BRICKLAYERS.
Andrews Joseph, Tavern street
Barker George, Church yard
Revett Daniel, Bury street
Webb Mary Ann, Bury street
Webb Robert, Violet hill

BUTCHERS.
Abbott Fred. Ablitt, Ipswich street
Cuthbert Thomas, Bury street
Hayward George, Bury street
Howes Benjamin (pork,) Union st
Quilter Philip (pork,) Ipswich street
Simpson Susannah (pork,) Ipswich st
Suttle Wm. (pork,) Ipswich street
Turner Wm. (pork,) Bury street

CABINET MAKERS, &c.
Bailey Wm. Bury street
Betts Francis, Bury street
Briggs John, Market place
King Wm. Ipswich street
Purr Robert (and builder,) Bur

CHEMISTS & DRUGGIST
Cutting James Bray, Market place
Simpson Thomas, Bury street

COACH MAKER.
Hewitt Wm. Tavern street

CONFECTIONERS
Fenton Eliza, Ipswich street
Greengrass George, Bury street
Pooley Thomas, Stowupland street
Steverson James (game dlr.) Mkp
Tricker Robert, Ipswich street
Wilkinson Thomas E. Ipswich st

COOPERS.
Lockwood John, Ipswich street
Tricker Wm. Bury street

CORN MILLERS.
(For Dealers, see Merchants.)
Boulter Wm. *Ford mills*
Fison Joseph, Onehouse road
Palmer Wm. (seed,) Bury street
Whitehead Cornelius, Bury street

CURRIERS & LTHR. CUTRS.
Drake Charles (leather cutter only,) Ipswich street
Lawrence Henry, Butter market

FARMERS.
Bridges Wm. Bury street
Canler Ambrose, *Chilton Hill*
Cuthbert Thos. (& cattle dlr.) Bury st
Flowerdew Thomas, Bury street
Green John, jun. *Chilton*
Hearn James, Union street
Locke John (owner,) Woodside
Matthew John (owner,) *Chilton*

Smith Wm. Bury street

FIRE & LIFE OFFICES.

Alliance, J. Green, Market place
Atlas, J. B. Cutting, Market place
County (Fire) and Provident (Life,) Richard Keen, Market place
Farmers' & General, E. P. Archer
Norwich Equitable, Jas. Gudgeon, Bury street
Phœnix and Norwich Union, Thos. Sheldrake, Ipswich street
Suffolk Amicable, T. Gross, Mkp

FURNITURE BROKERS.

Betts Fras. (appraiser,) Bury street
King Wm. Ipswich street
Payne James, Butter market

GARDNRS. & NURSERYMEN.

Barnard Valentine, Bury street
Barnard Wm. Bury street
Felgate John, Bury street
Fisher Abraham, Nursery
Girling Samuel (and florist,) *Dane croft Nursery*

GLASS, CHINA, &c. DEALRS.

Parmenter Isaac, Butter market
Reeve John, Market place

GLOVERS.

Bird Eliza, Bury street
Raffe Wm. Ipswich street

GROCERS AND DRAPERS.

Keen Richard, Market place
Lankester Jph. Antrim, Market pl
Sheldrake Thomas, Ipswich street
Whitmore Wm. (draper only,) Tav. st
Williams Robert, Stowupland street

HAIR DRESSERS.

Downing George, Market place
Langham Charles, Bury street
Parmenter Isaac, Butter market
Suttle Wm. Church yard

HATTERS.

Gooding Wm. (& clothier,) Butter mkt
Keen Richard, Market place
Lankester Joseph A. Market place
Sheldrake Thomas, Ipswich street
Whitmore Wm. Tavern street
Williams Robert, Stowupland street

HORSE & GIG LETTERS.

Bailey Thomas, Ipswich street
Cross Henry, Ipswich street
Lockwood John, Ipswich street

INNS AND TAVERNS.

Barge, John Bird, Stowupland st
Duke's Head, Jno. Hagger, Ipswich st
Fox Hotel, (posting house,) John Lockwood, Ipswich street

Fox and Hounds, Robert Aldous Bowell, Bury street
Greyhound, John Taylor, Market pl
King's Arms, Hy. Cross, Ipswich st
King's Head, Jas. Reach *(posting,)* Ipswich street
Pickerel, Samuel Pulham, Nav. bdg
Queen's Head, Edwd. Barritt, Stowupland street
Rose, Owen Whayman, Butter mkt
Tyrells' Arms, Wm. Smith, Bury st
Waggon and Horses, George Codd, Navigation wharf
White Hart, Robert Smith, Crow st
White Horse, Thos. Coleman, Stowupland street
White Lion, James Williams, Stowupland street

BEER HOUSES.

Ayliffe Richard, Bury street
Colson Wm. Stowupland street
Godbold Jas. Earthy, Stowupland st
Godbold Jonathan, Bury street
Smith Wm. Cats lane
Turner Wm. Bury street

IRONFOUNDERS, &c.

Bewley Thos. (and machine maker,) Crow street
Woods James (and agricultural implement maker,) Bury street

IRONMONGERS & BRAZRS.

Gross Thomas (and chief constable, news agent, &c.) Market place
Prentice & Hewitt, Stowupland st
Purr Wm. Watts, Ipswich street
Rust Isaac Arnold (and oil & colour man,) Bury street

JOINERS & BUILDERS.

Betts Francis, Bury street
Blomfield Wm. Bury street
Dennis Charles Elisha, Bury street
Grimwood Robert, Stowupland st
Lyas Ambrose, Church yard
Lyas Wm. Ipswich street
Payne James, Bury street
Rednall Ephraim, Regent street
Revett Daniel, Bury street
Turner Richard, Bury street
Webb Richard, Bury street

LINEN & WLLN. DRAPER.
(See also Grocers and Drapers.)
Whitmore Wm. Tavern street

LINEN MANUFACTURERS.
(See also Rope and Sacking.)
Bond Robert, Union street
Crabb Habakkuk, Ipswich street

MALTSTERS.
Byles and King, Ipswich street
Byles Jeremiah & Co. Stowupld. st
Cobbold John, Navigation wharf
Cornell Wm. Greengrass, Stowupld.st
Cowell Abm. K. Navigation wharf
Prentice Thos. & Co. Navigation whf
Webb Bayly, Ipswich street

MERCHANTS.
(Marked * are Corn & Coal Merchts.)
*Byles and King, Ipswich street
*Byles Jeremiah and Co. (and timber
  and slate,) Stowupland street
*Cobbold John, Navigation wharf
Cornell Wm. G. Stowupland street;
  house, *Ford cottage*
*Cowell Abm. K. Navigation wharf
Fison Joseph (corn, wool, and seed,)
  Onehouse road
Lockwood John, Ipswich street
Prentice & Hewitt (timber, slate, and
  bar iron,) *Patent Saw Mills*
*Prentice Thos.& Co. Navigation whf
Squirrell Rt. (corn,) *Thorney Hall*
Webb Bayly, Ipswich street

MILLINERS, &c.
Dennis Elizabeth, Bury street
Dennis Hannah, Bury street
Diaper Elizabeth, Stowupland street
Fenton Eliza, Ipswich street
Garwood Maria, Stowupland street
Halls Mary, Market place
Keene Mrs. Market place
Lee Ann, Bury street
Tillott Mary Ann, Ipswich street
Webb Sarah H. Ipswich street

PAINTERS, PLUMBERS, AND GLAZIERS.
Collin George, Ipswich street
Pearsons John, Ipswich street
Rout James, Market place
Wilson George, Stowupland street

ROPE AND TWINE MAKERS.
(Marked * are also Sacking mfrs.)
Andrews Daniel, Bury street
Andrews Wm. Bury street
*Bond Robert, Union street
*Crabb Habakkuk, Ipswich street
*Garrard Edward, Ipswich street

SADDLERS, &c.
Bethell John Ward, Ipswich street
Collins Robert, Stowupland street
Frewer Leonard, Market place
Wright Samuel, Tavern street

SHOPKEEPERS.
Blomfield Rebecca, Bury street

Felgate Isaac, Bury street
Felgate Wm. Bury street
Howes Benjamin, Union street
Leather Jonathan, Regent street
Palmer Godfrey M. Church yard
Race James, Stowupland street
Raffe John, Stowupland street
Reason Sheppard, Stowupland st
Simpson Susan, Ipswich street
Tricker Wm. Bury street

STONE & MARBLE MASONS.
Simpson and Hopson, Ipswich street
Webb Richard, Bury street

STRAW HAT MAKERS.
Collin Emily, Ipswich street
Dennis Hannah, Bury street
Halls Mary, Market place
Lambert Harriet, Ipswich street
Scoulding Shadrach, Church yard
Smith Louisa, Union street
Todd Amelia, Bury street

SURGEONS.
Bedingfield Jas. *M.D.* Stowupld. st
Bree Charles Robert, Backs Hall
Freeman Spencer, Market place
Ward Samuel, Ipswich street

TAILORS.
(Marked * are Drapers also.)
Balls George, Tavern street
*Bewley Hunter, Crow street
Brown John, Ipswich street
Drake Charles, Stowupland street
Gorrard John, Ipswich street
Garwood Joseph W. Stowupland st
*Girdlestone James, Crow street
Langham Henry, Tavern street
Raffe Henry, Tavern street
*Rust Frederick Wm. Bury street
*Salmon Thomas, Bury street

TALLOW CHANDLERS.
Bond Robert, Cats lane
Lankester Joseph Antrim, Mkp

TANNER.
Webb Joseph Antrim, Ipswich st

WATCHMAKERS, &c.
(* are Jewellers also.)
*Feltham Wm. (registrar of mar-
  riages,) Tavern street
Kersey Thomas, Market place
*Scrivener Philip, Market place

WHEELWRIGHT.
Gladwell James, Regent street

WHITESMITHS.
Cracknell Samuel, Bury street
Orams Thomas, Ipswich street
Smyth Francis, Tavern street

WINE & SPIRIT MERCHTS.

Diaper James (and porter,) Stow-
upland street
Lankester Joseph A. Market place
Sheldrake, Mumford, & Co. Ipswich st
Stevens and Co. (and brewers,) Stow-
upland street

COACHES.

From the Fox Hotel.

The *Criterion*, to meet the London
Railway trains at Colchester, on
Monday at ½ past 5 morning, and
every other morning at ½ past 7
The *Regulator*, daily, except Sunday, to Ipswich, at 11 morn. and
to Bury St. Edmund's, at ½ past
5 afternoon
Omnibuses, to meet the London
steamers at Ipswich, every Monday and Thursday

CARRIERS.

Marked 1, *stop at the Barge*; 2, *Fox
and Hounds*; 3, *Greyhound*; 4,
King's Arms; 5, *Pickerel*; 6,

Queen's Head; *and* 7, *at the
White Hart*

To London, J. Broom, Union street,
Mon. and Thurs. (*via* Hadleigh)
Bury, 4 J. Garrard, Tuesday and
Friday; Isaac Turner, Wed. and
Sat; and 6 *Mail Cart* daily
Cotton, 2 J. Baker, Tues. & Friday
Debenham, 1 C. Smith, Tues. & Fri
Haughley, 6 J. Firman, Monday,
Thursday, and Saturday
Ipswich, I. Turner, Bury st. Mon.
Tues. Fri. and Sat; Miller, from
Combs. daily; 4 Garrod, Mon. and
Thursday; 6 Firman, Friday;
and 5 Minter, Tuesday
Norwich, 6 Rt. Barham, Tues. Wed.
Fri. & Sat; 5 Minter, Sat.; and
6 *Mail Cart* daily
Rattlesden, 7 Moore, Thursday
Sudbury, 3 W. Gage, Tues. & Thurs
Thetford, 6 J. Rowley, Tues. & Fri
Walsham, 6 Firman, Thursday and
Friday, and 5 Minter, Saturday

STOWUPLAND is a township or parish of scattered houses on
the eastern acclivity of the Gipping, opposite Stowmarket, to which it
is considered a hamlet, having been ecclesiastically connected with that
parish from time immemorial. It forms a pleasant suburb to Stowmarket, extending two miles eastward from the town, and containing
903 inhabitants, and about 2890 acres of land, rising boldly from the
Gipping and two of its tributary streams, and including the hamlet of
Thorney, and an ancient farm-house called *Columbyne Hall,* which is
still encompassed by a deep moat. It lies in six *manors,* of which the
following are the names and lords :— *Thorney Hall,* Charles Tyrell,
Esq.; *Thorney-Lezens and Thorney-Mumpliers-with-Braziers,* Edw.
Bigsby Beck, Esq.; *Columbyne Hall,* Earl of Ashburnham; and
Thorney-Keebles and Thorney-Campsey, Charles Rayner Freeman,
Esq.; but part of the soil belongs to Lady Pocklington, Mrs. Marriott, (formerly of *Thorney Hall;*) Mrs. Rust, and the Boby, Holland, Jermyn, Turner, Cooper, Falkner, Dalton, and other families.
The manor of Thorney was held by the nuns of Campsey, and was
granted in the 37th of Henry VIII. to Thomas, Duke of Norfolk.
The parish is partly copyhold. The *vicarage* is consolidated with that
of Stowmarket, and the present incumbent and patron is impropriator
of those portions of the rectorial tithes, which do not belong to the
landowners, and were commuted in 1841 for £257 per annum. Stowupland was without a *Church* till 1843, when its present church or
chapel of ease, dedicated to the Holy Trinity, was erected by subscription, at the cost of £1360, of which £150 was granted by the Church
Building Society. The Marquis of Bristol and the Vicar contributed
largely towards the building, and the site, comprising half an acre,
nearly two miles E. of Stowmarket, was given by C. R. Freeman, Esq.
It is a handsome edifice, with a slender spire, and was consecrated by

the Bishop of Norwich, August 30th, 1843. The *Poor's Estate*, the acquisition of which is unknown, is under the direction of the church-wardens and overseers, and consists of a farm of 22A., let for £35 a-year, and a cottage and 23A. of land, let for £30 a-year. The rents are distributed in money and coals among the poor parishioners. A poor man of this parish has a coat once in four years from Blackerby's charity, noticed with Stowmarket.

Bauley Thomas, corn miller
Burch Robert, vict. Crown
Cross Miss, Mill house
Felgate Fuller, corn miller
Hart John, blacksmith
Pyman John, shopkeeper
Quinton John, carpenter
Taylor Wm. wheelgt. & blacksmith
Wood Thomas, corn miller
     FARMERS.—(* *are Owners.*)
Beard Rd. and Wm. *Dagar house*

*Boby John || Boby John, jun.
Boby Robert, *Columbyne Hall*
*Cooper Elizabeth || Packard Wm.
*Freeman Charles Rayner, Esq
Law Chas. Blomfield (relvg. officer)
Preston George || Pyman Edwin
Squirrell R. merchant, *Thorney Hall*
Stearn Thomas, *Sheepcote Hall*
Stedman John || Turner John
Warren James || Willden Martha
Whistlecraft William

WETHERDEN, 4 miles N.W. of Stowmarket, is a village and parish containing 515 souls and 1784 acres of land. *Wetherden Hall*, some remains of which may be seen in the farm-house bearing that name, was the seat of the ancient and respectable family of Sulyard, one of whom, *Sir John Sulyard*, was among the first to take up arms and levy men in the service of Queen Mary, against the supporters of Lady Jane Grey. For his loyalty, Mary, as soon as she was safely seated on the throne, made him a present of the manor and park of Haughley, where he erected a mansion. His son Edward adhering to the religion of his ancestors, suffered much during the next reign for recusancy, notwithstanding the unimpeached loyalty of his sentiments and conduct. The fidelity of Sir Edward, the grandson of the latter, to the cause of Charles I., brought on him imprisonment, and the sequestration of two-thirds of his estate, during Cromwell's usurpation; but when Charles II. recovered his throne, he was restored to his possessions and liberty. His descendants continued here for several succeeding generations. Lord Thurlow is now lord of the *manor*, but a great part of the soil belongs to the Heigham, Tyrell, Tanner, Prater, and other families. The copyholds are subject to arbitrary fines, but a part of the parish is freehold. The *Church* (St. Mary) is a neat but ancient structure, containing several monuments of the Sulyards. The aisle and porch were built by Sir John Sulyard, who was lord chief justice of England, and obtained a grant of free warren here in the 1st of Richard III. His arms and quarterings are finely carved round the porch and along the chancel. The *rectory*, valued in K.B. at £6. 13s. 4d., and in 1835 at £371, is in the patronage of the Crown, and incumbency of the Hon. and Rev. Sir Henry Leslie, Bart., of Box-Hill, Surrey. Here is a *Baptist Chapel*, built in 1837, at the cost of about £230. The *Town Lands* comprise 11A. 3R. 34P., let for £20. 15s. a-year, and have been conveyed from time to time to trustees, to permit the churchwardens and overseers to apply the rents and profits for the benefit of the poor. The sum of £5. 5s. a-year is applied towards the support of a Sunday-school, and the residue of the rent is laid out in the purchase of coals, which are sold to the poor parishioners

at a cheap rate. The poor have also a yearly rent-charge of 20s. out of lands in Haughley, left by *Margaret Chinery*, in 1730.

Bird John, plumber and painter
Brampton Rev John Black, curate, *Rectory*
Clark Henry, farm steward
Clark Sarah, National school
Collen John, corn miller
Dodson Thomas, shoemaker
Easlea James, corn miller
Grimwood John, maltster & beerhs
Hayward Elizah, blacksmith
Knevett Edward, relieving officer *for Rattlesden District*

Palmer Geo. wheelwgt. & blacksmith
Watchman Wm. vict. May Pole
Williams James, grocer
Wright My. boarding & day school
    FARMERS.—(** are Owners.*)
Balls Wm. || Bull James
Clark John || Edwards Robert
Hammond James, *Wetherden Hall*
Harrison John || Kerry Thomas
Hunt Sellsby Wardle *(auctioneer)*
*Martin Stephen || Munnings James
*Tanner Samuel || Ruffell Wm.

COSFORD HUNDRED

Includes the thriving market town of *Hadleigh*, and seventeen other parishes, forming a fertile and picturesquely undulated district, watered by the river Brett and its tributary streams. It is about twelve miles in length from north to south, and from four to seven in breadth, and is bounded by the Hundreds of Samford, Babergh, Thedwestry, Stow, and Bosmere and Claydon. It is in *Cosford Union*, in the *Liberty of St. Edmund*, and in the *Deanery and Archdeaconry of Sudbury*, which were taken a few years ago from the diocese of Norwich, and added to the *See of Ely ;* except the parish of *Hadleigh*, which is a *peculiar* of the Archbishop of Canterbury. It has generally a *clayey* soil, and the following is an enumeration of its 18 parishes, shewing their territorial extent; the annual value of their lands and buildings as assessed to the property tax in 1815; and their population in 1801 and 1841 :—

PARISHES.	Acrs.	Rental.	Populatn. 1801.	1841.	PARISHES.	Acres.	Rental. £.	Population. 1801.	1841.
Aldham	1715	1953	197	293	Layham	2489	3722	471	549
Bildeston	1240	1840	744	857	Lindsey	1246	1333	170	290
Brettenham	1550	1666	228	367	Naughton	854	854	120	137
Chellesworth	860	1319	234	284	Nedging	810	867	143	195
Elmsett	1974	2489	324	446	Semer†	1206	1718	203	370
Hadleigh *parish*	4288	7605	2332	3679	Thorpe Mo- rieux .... }	2428	2176	271	418
Hadleigh *hamlet**	610	446	154	232					
Hitcham	4056	4126	746	1065	Whattisham ..	1299	1381	154	240
Kersey	1510	2339	513	787	Whatfield	1571	1932	235	394
Kettlebaston	1006	1144	145	203	Total ..	30,712	38,910	7384	10,806

☞ The CHIEF CONSTABLES are Mr. Wm. Strutt, of Hadleigh, and Mr. Wm. Chaplin, of Nedging. PETTY SESSIONS are held at Hadleigh every fourth Thursday.

  * *Hadleigh Hamlet* is properly a township, in Boxford parish. *(See Babergh Hundred.)*

  † *Semer* includes COSFORD UNION WORKHOUSE, which had 165 inmates in 1811, 169 in 1821, 164 in 1831, 108 in 1841, and 150 in 1843. It was erected in 1780, as a House of Industry for the 18 parishes of Cosford Hundred, which were incorporated under Gilbert's Act, in 1779. It

cost about £8000, and is large enough for 500 inmates. It consists of a centre and two wings, and the interior has undergone considerable alterations, so as to admit of that classification of the sexes, and of the young and aged, required by the New Poor Law. The present *Union* was formed in 1835, and comprises the 18 parishes of Cosford Hundred, and 10 parishes in Babergh Hundred (which see.) These 28 parishes comprise an area of 80 square miles, and a population of 18,238 inhabitants. The average annual expenditure of this district, for the support of the poor, during the three years preceding the formation of the union, was £19,223; but in 1838, it only amounted to £7122. In 1810, when the workhouse was confined to Cosford Hundred, it was said the poor rates of that Hundred had been reduced to three-eighths of what they had been previous to 1780. Before hand-spinning was superseded by machinery, the paupers here were employed chiefly in spinning yarn for Norwich. Mr. Robert and Mrs. Jane Patterson are *master and matron* of the Workhouse, and Isaac Last, Esq., is *Union Clerk and Superintendent Registrar.* The District Registrars and Relieving Officers are Mr. Joseph Glandford Stow, of Hadleigh Hamlet, for *Hadleigh District;* and Mr. George Scott, of Cockfield, for *Lavenham District.*

ALDHAM, 1½ mile N.E. of Hadleigh, is a pleasant village and parish, containing 293 souls, and 1715 acres of land, including about 100 acres of woodland. It was the lordship of the Vere family, Earls of Oxford, till it was forfeited by the attainder of John, the 12th Earl, in 1461; after which it was given by Edward IV. to Sir John Howard. T. B. Leonard, Esq., is now lord of the manor, in which the copyholds are subject to arbitrary fines. The other principal landowners are the Rev. James Cook, J. H. L. Anstruther, Esq., and the Matthew, Gray, and Blofield families. The *Church* (St. Mary) is an ancient fabric, with a round tower, and stands upon a mound, which has a trench on two sides of it. The old oak pews are still preserved, and one of them bears the date 1537. The font is a curious relic of antiquity. The *rectory*, valued in K.B. at £10. 13s. 4d., and in 1835 at £290, is in the gift of T. B. Leonard, Esq., and incumbency of the Rev. Henry Uhthoff, who has 45A. 2R. 18P. of glebe. A great part of the Hall farm is tithe free. The poor parishioners have 20 a-year out of an estate at Raydon, given by John Goodale, in 1627. *Directory:*—John Gooch, *maltster;* Andrew Hales, carpenter; John Howlett, vict., *Sportsman;* Henry Payne, blacksmith; and Wm. Baldry, Cornelius Bull, Wm. Cone, Josiah Matthew, (and owner;) Thomas Partridge, *(Hall;)* Sl. Strand, (and owner;) and Jas. Vince, *farmers.*

BILDESTON, or BILSTON, a small town and parish, in a picturesque valley, on the banks of a rivulet, 5 miles N. by W. of Hadleigh, formerly had a weekly *market* on Wednesday, which was disused about the middle of last century, after the decay of the manufacture of *blue cloth* and *blankets,* for which the town was once famous. It has still two annual *fairs* for toys, wearing apparel, &c, on Ash-Wednesday and Holy Thursday, and contains 857 inhabitants, and 1240 acres of fertile land, mostly a strong clay. Miss M. A. Tyrell is lady of the manor, in which the copyholds are subject to arbitrary fines. The largest proprietors of the soil are T. B. White, B. Haynes, and Rt. Chinery, Esqrs. The manor was anciently held by the noble family of Bouchier, whose heiress carried it in marriage to Lord Parr. It afterwards passed to the Beals, Brands, and Alstons. The late Rd.

Wilson, Esq., built a neat cottage residence here, and owned a great part of the parish. The *Church* (St. Mary) is a large and handsome structure, on an acclivity on the west side of the town. It is in the perpendicular style, and has a tower containing six bells. The east window is large and beautiful, and in some of the other windows are fragments of ancient stained glass. The *rectory*, valued in K.B. at £12. 6s. 10½d., has a good residence, 51 acres of glebe, and a yearly modus of £435, awarded in 1840 in lieu of tithes. The Rev. Charles Johnson is patron and incumbent. Here was formerly a chapel, dedicated to *St. Leonard*, in which was Erdington's Chantry. The *Baptists* have a small chapel here, built in 1731, and a house for the minister, purchased in 1814. The town is said to have formerly extended to the church, which is now distant quarter of a mile. The *Church Land*, 20 acres, is let for £30 a year. Two cottages are occupied rent-free by poor persons, but the donor is unknown. The rent of Smock Meadow, in Chellesworth, (£5 a year,) is distributed in linen among poor widows ; and the interest of £27, in the hands of the church-wardens, is distributed among poor parishioners, in coals, but the origin of these charities is unknown.

POST OFFICE at Mrs Sarah Colman's. Letters despatched, *via* Hadleigh, at 7 evening

Abbot Charles, watchmaker
Brooks Danl. gent||Baldwin Mr Wm.
Campbell Rev John, (Baptist)
Clark Mary Ann, toy dealer
Cleghorn Ts. currier & leather cutter
Cleghorn Ralph Willoughby, wine, &c. agent, *Bildeston House*
Cooper Mr Wm.|| Death Wm. gent.
Esmand Mrs Louisa, (lodgings)
Farrow Mr Thomas
Folkard Samuel, parish clerk
French Rev Thomas, curate
Godfrey Thomas, excise officer
Goodwin Miss Elizabeth
Growse Robert, surgeon
Haynes Berry, Esq.
Johnson Rev Charles, *Rectory*
Johnson Richard, basket maker
Lucky Ann, straw hat maker
Nunn John, cattle dealer
Peacock Wm. hair dresser
Squirrell Wm. wine, spirit, porter, and hop merchant
Tydeman James, watchmaker
Ward John, letter carrier
Young Rev Walter, M.A. curate of Wattisham and Bricett

INNS AND TAVERNS.
Bull Inn, Sarah Colman
Crown, John Edwards
King's Head, Mary Simpson

Academies.
Hobart Eliz.
Hobart Henry
Lilley Sarah
Bakers.
Bull Wm.
Haste John
Lucky John
Blacksmiths.
Stow George
Woollard Edw.
Boot & Shoe Mkrs
Bull Richd. (& leather cutter)
Gill Robert
Scarfe Joseph
Scarfe Robert
Ward Ebenezer
Ward Isaac, (& porter dlr. and horse and gig letter)
Bricklayers.
Johnson W. sen.
Ward Thos. (& beerhouse)
Webb Thos.
Butchers.
Nunn Thomas
Seaman Robert Hicks
Syer Baumstead
White Wm.
Coopers.
Studd George

Syrett John
Corn Millers.
Harris Wm.
Ratcliffe Saml.
FARMERS.
Barton Joseph
Bugg Meshach
Cousens Wm.
Green John
Knapp Sergeant
Mumford Fredk.
Copthall
Squirrell Wm.
Syer Wm.
Vince Wm.
Glovers.
Bull Isaac
Vince John
Grocers & Drprs.
Gibbs Joseph
Johnson Marianne & Son, (& agents for Suffolk Fire office, & Alexander's bar iron, &c.)
Makin Eliz. (dpr.)
Osborn James
Joiners & Cabinet Makers.
Bull Wm.
Fayers Robert
Grimwade Pilbrough
Johnson Wm.

Maltsters.	Hearn Robert	COACH to Colchester, to meet the
Chinery John	Tricker James	London railway trains, at 8 in the
Emerson Henry	*Tailors.*	morning, (except Sunday)
Plumbers, Paint-	Cooper George	CARRIERS *to Ipswich :* Hy. Emer-
ers, & Glaziers.	Notcutt Godard	son, Sat ; Jerh. Gosling, Monday,
Moss John	Osborn James	Wed. and Fri ; John Webb, Tue.
Osborn Orris	Vince John	Thu. and Sat : and Saml. Wright,
Saddlers.	*Wheelwright.*	Tue. and Fri. and to *Lavenham*,
Drew Robert	Coates Edward	Wednesday and Saturday

BRETTENHAM, near the source of the small river Brett, 4 miles N.N.W. of Bildeston, and 7 miles W.S.W. of Stowmarket, is a pleasant village and parish, containing 367 souls, and about 1550 acres of land. From the signification of its name, some antiquaries suppose it to be the *Combretonium* of Antoninus ; and the vestiges of a camp, quarter of a mile S.W. of the village, seem to confirm the conjecture. Others, however, place this station at Icklingham, near Mildenhall. *Brettenham Hall,* a neat mansion in a park of 133 acres, was more than two centuries the seat of the *Wenyeve* family, but is now only occupied by a servant; the estate and the manor, vested with the trustees of the late John Camac, Esq., being now in chancery. Part of the parish belongs to Fisk Harrison, W. Brewster, and —. Foster, Esqrs. The *Church* (St. Mary) has a tower and three bells, and is a neat fabric, with a leaded nave and a tiled chancel. The *rectory*, valued in K.B. at £11. 3s. 10d., and in 1835 at £377, is in the gift of the Crown, and incumbency of the Rev. Samuel Cole. The tithes were commuted in 1843 for a yearly rent-charge. The *Church land* is 2¼A. The *poor* have an annuity of 20s. out of Church-field, left by James Durrant, in 1644.

Barrell Isaac, beerhouse
Clover Samuel, corn miller
Cole Rev Samuel, rector
Green Wm. shopkeeper
Green Wm. beerhouse
Kinzey Wm. shopkeeper
Marriott Michael, shopkeeper
Mumford John, shoemaker
Sawyer Robert, wheelwright

Seaman Robert, blacksmith
FARMERS.
Andrews Robert || Bigsby Joseph
Cooper George || Downing Daniel
Garner Robert || Jackson Isaac
Mills James || Scott John
Raker John || Roper Henry
Taylor Robert || Ward George

CHELLESWORTH, or CHELSWORTH, a small village and parish in the picturesque and well-wooded valley of the river Brett, 5 miles N.N.W. of Hadleigh, contains 284 souls, and 860 acres of fertile land. The Brett receives here two tributary streams, and skirts the rising grounds called Park-fields, where traces of an ancient mansion were to be seen some years ago, supposed to have been a seat of the Howards, who anciently held the manor, which afterwards passed to the Veres, Earls of Oxford. In 1737, the manor was purchased by Robt. Pocklington, Esq., who erected CHELLESWORTH HOUSE, now the pleasant seat of *Sir Henry Edmund Austin, Kt.*, the present lord of the manor, who was knighted in 1832, and derived the estate from the late Sir Roger Pocklington, Bart. Messrs. T. B. White and W. Ennals have small estates in the parish. The Church (All Saiuts) is a neat edifice, with a tower and one bell, and is a *rectory*, valued in K.B. at £8. 8s. 9d., and now having 30 acres of glebe, and a yearly modus

of £270, awarded in 1840 in lieu of tithes. The patronage is in the Crown, and the Rev. Fredk. Calvert, M.A., is the incumbent. Here is a small *National School.* In 1580, *Robert Nightingale* bequeathed for the use of the poor, a copyhold estate in this parish, comprising 21 acres, let for about £30 a year, which is distributed in coals and clothing. The poor parishioners have also, for a distribution of bread, a yearly rent-charge of 30s., left by *Eliz. Thurloe,* out of an estate here belonging to the lord of the manor.

Austin Sir Henry Edmund, Knight, *Chellesworth House*
Browne Rev Alex. curate
Cullum Mrs Ann, *Rose Cottage*
Disney Edward, parish clerk
Edwards Zach. farmer
Elliston Fredk. shopkeeper
Ennals Wm. yeoman
Gage Hy. Martin, butcher & farmer
Gage Peter, joiner, &c.
Gage Smith, pork butcher
Gage Wm. cattle dealer
Osborn Thomas, shopkeeper
Pocklington Robert Martin, Esq. *Chellesworth House*
Radford Captain, R.N.
Raynham Wm. farmer
Smith Mrs Rebecca
Tampion Thomas, blacksmith
Whiteman Wm. shoemaker

ELMSETT, a scattered village and picturesque parish, 4 miles N.N.E. of Hadleigh, and 8 miles W. by N. of Ipswich, has 446 inhabitants, and 1974 acres of land, including 79 acres of wood. James Cudden, Esq., is lord of the manor, but the soil belongs mostly to Bishop Andrews' Charity, the Rev. J. Y. Cook, Miss Cook, and the Sparrowe, Lott, Canham, and a few other families. The ancient Rectory House, which has recently been much improved, is nearly encompassed by a moat; and near the church is the old *Hall,* which was formerly moated, and is now a farm-house. On the descent of the opposite hill is a *Dropping Well,* which is sulphureous, and is said to possess similar medicinal properties to the Cheltenham waters. A *fair* for toys, &c., is held here on Whit-Tuesday. The REV. JOHN BOYSE, an eminent scholar and divine, was born here in 1560, at the Rectory House, and is said to have manifested such a precocity of talents, that by the time he had attained his fifth year, he could read the Hebrew Bible. He was educated at Cambridge, where he was chosen Greek lecturer. On the death of his father, he became rector of this parish. He was one of the translators and revisors of the new version of the Bible, made by order of James I., and assisted Sir Henry Savile in translating the works of Chrysostom. He died in 1643, and, notwithstanding his great learning and industry, the highest preferment he obtained was a prebend in Ely cathedral, given him by Bishop Andrews. The *Church* (St. Peter) is an ancient structure, built of flints, and covered with slate. In the chancel is a mural monument, bearing an inscription and kneeling effigy in memory of Edward Sherland, Esq., who died in 1609. The *rectory,* valued in K.B. at £13. 7s. 1d., has 50A. 3R. of glebe, and a yearly modus of £630, awarded in 1842 in lieu of tithes. The patronage is in Clare Hall, Cambridge, and the Rev. Jas. Speare, M.A., is the incumbent. The poor have 3s. a year, out of part of the glebe, called the Grove, pursuant to the bequest of the Rev. Richard Glanvill. In 1726, the Rev. Moses Coe left £15 for the poor parishioners attending the church. This legacy, with some arrears of interest, now amounts to £30, vested in Hadleigh Savings' Bank.

Archer John, wheelwright
Clarke Golding, maltster
Clarke James, vict. *Chequers*
Cole Samuel, shoemaker
Cook Wm. blacksmith
Canham Mr Thos. *Laurel Cottage*
Fenning Thomas, thatcher
Podd Wm. *carrier to Ipswich*
Speare Rev James M.A. rector, *Rectory*

FARMERS.

Archer — || Bull John
Cousens Samuel || Ford Samuel
Gardiner Rd. || Hobart John
Jacobs Susanna
Juby Henry || Ship Anthony
Stearn John, Patrick, & Wm. *Elmsett Hall*
Syer Wm. || Turner Wm.

HADLEIGH, formerly noted for the manufacture of *woollens*, and now having a large *silk-mill*, and a number of maltsters and corn merchants, is a well-built and thriving *market town*, pleasantly situated on the eastern side of the small river Brett, 10 miles W. by S. of Ipswich; 20 miles S.S.E. of Bury St. Edmund's; 7 miles N.N.E. of Nayland; 11 miles E. of Sudbury; and 64 miles N.E. of London. Its parish comprises 4288 acres of land, and its *population* amounted, in 1801, to 2332; in 1811, to 2592; in 1821, to 2929; in 1831, 3425; and in 1841, to 3679. It is a *polling place* for the Western Division of the county, and *Petty Sessions* are held at the White Lion Inn every fourth Thursday. The *town* has been much improved during the last thirty years, and its principal street (*High street*) has many good houses, shops, and inns, and is nearly three quarters of a mile in length, extending from north to south, parallel with the river, which, at each end of the town, is crossed by a good bridge. That at the north end was rebuilt in 1843, at the cost of £1150, and consists of six iron arches resting on brick pillars. The *Corn Exchange* is a commodious building, erected by subscription in 1813, and the *Town Hall* is a large room, which was originally one of the wards of the old workhouse. An inspector and two policemen, belonging to the Suffolk constabulary force, are stationed here. The town was first lighted with gas from the works of Messrs. Brown and Moy, *silk throwsters*, who erected their silk mill here in 1834, and employ about 350 boys and girls. The *market*, held every Monday, is an extensive mart for corn, sold by sample; and here are three annual *fairs*, held on Whit-Monday and Old Michaelmas day for toys, &c., and on Sept. 20th for lambs, sheep, and cattle. A *Farmers' Club* meets monthly at the White Horse and White Lion Inns, alternately. Messrs. Offord and Robinson are solicitors to the *Hadleigh Association* for the prosecution of felons, which was established in 1843. The town formerly had a *corporation*, consisting of a mayor, aldermen, and common council; but a *quo warranto* being brought against them, they surrendered their charter during the reign of James II., and no other has since been granted. It is remarkable as the burial place of *Guthrum*, the Danish chieftain, who, being defeated by Alfred the Great, consented to embrace Christianity, and had the government of East Anglia assigned to him. Here he reigned twelve years, and dying in 889, was interred in Hadleigh church, where the tomb, shewn for his, does not bear marks of such antiquity. *Dr. Rowland Taylor*, who was rector of Hadleigh, suffered at the stake in the sanguinary reign of Queen Mary, for his adherence to the doctrines of the Reformation. He was burnt on *Aldham Common*, nearly a mile east of the town, upon the spot still marked by

a stone, bearing the following mis-spelt inscription :—" Anno, 1555.— Dr. Taylor for defending what was god, on this place shed his blod." This common (77A.) was enclosed in 1729, and *Hadleigh Heath* (20A.) about thirteen years ago. On the 15th of August, 1843, Hadleigh, like many other places in the county, was visited by an *awful storm*, which commenced about two o'clock in the afternoon, and continued 45 minutes, during which vivid flashes of lightning and loud crashes of thunder followed in quick succession, accompanied by deluging torrents of rain, large hail stones, and pieces of ice, which destroyed the glass in many of the windows, and flooded the lower parts of the town. In some parts of High street, the water was 18 inches deep, and a punt was seen rowing about in it for some time after the storm had abated.

The parish is in five MANORS, of which the following are the names and lords :—*Hadleigh Hall*, Rev. E. Jermyn, (as *lessee* under the Archbishop of Canterbury;) *Hadleigh*, J. H. L. Anstruther, Esq.; and *Toppesfield Hall, Cosford Hall*, and *Pond Hall*, of which J. Tollemache, Esq., is lord; but a great part of the soil belongs to other proprietors, the largest of whom are Sir W. B. Rush, the Drapers' Company, London; Sir J. R. Rowley, Bart., the Dowager Lady Rowley, and Rt. Kersey, Wm. Strutt, and J. C. Archer, Esqrs. POND HALL, 1½ mile E. of the town, was formerly a seat of the *D'Oyly* or *Doyley* family, one of whom was created a baronet in 1663, but they left here more than two centuries ago, and the hall is now a farm house. *Peyton Hall*, a farm house, 1 mile N. of the town, is supposed to have been a seat of the Peyton family; and on the south side of the parish, at the distance of from 1 to 2 miles, are the farms of *Benton-end, Kateshill*, &c., near *Mason's Bridge*. The CHURCH *(St. Mary)* is a large and handsome structure, nearly in the centre of the town, and has a fine tower containing eight bells, and surmounted by a tall wooden spire covered with lead. It is 143 feet long by 63 broad, and has in its windows some fragments of ancient stained glass. It has several neat monuments, and the remains of a tomb, said to have been raised in memory of Guthrum, the Danish chieftain, already noticed. The organ is a handsome and fine-toned instrument, and the pulpit and font are antique and richly carved. The altar-piece, which is of beautiful carved work, was put up by Dr. Wilkins, a late rector, whose successor much improved the *Rectory House*, which was rebuilt in 1836, but has still in front an ancient brick gate, with two hexangular towers, built with the old house about 1490, by Wm. Pykenham, dean of Stoke College, and incumbent of Hadleigh. The *Rectory*, valued in K.B. at £45. 12s. 1d., is in the *patronage* and *peculiar jurisdiction* of the Archbishop of Canterbury, and incumbency of the Very Rev. Henry Barry Knox, A.M., rural dean. The *tithes* were commuted, in 1838, for a yearly modus of £1325. There are in the town four other places of worship—viz., the *Chapel at the Almshouses;* an *Independent Chapel*, erected in the early part of last century, and rebuilt on a larger scale in 1825, at the cost of about £3000; a *Baptist Chapel*, built in 1830; and a small one belonging to the *Primitive Methodists*. Here is a SAVINGS' BANK for Cosford Hundred, founded in 1818, and open every Saturday from 2 till 4 o'clock, at Mills and Co.'s, in Queen street. In Nov., 1842, it had deposits amounting to £15,944, belonging to 577

depositors, 11 Charitable Societies, and 13 Friendly Societies. There are in the town two Friendly Societies, a Lodge of Freemasons, and another of Druids. The *Charities of Hadleigh* produce a yearly income of about £900, and comprise Almshouses for 36 poor people, and a Free School for 24 poor children. Here are also *National Schools* for boys and girls, attended by 140 children; and a large *British School*, built in 1841, by J.Ansell, Esq., and divided into three apartments for boys, girls, and infants, of whom about 160 are generally in attendance, but the rooms will accommodate 300.

THE MARKET-RENTS TRUST.—By indenture, in the 17th of Henry 6th, Wm. Clopton, Esq., granted to 15 trustees, land called Church croft, belonging to the manor of Toppesfield Hall, with a building thereon used as the market-house, and all the liberties, rights, and customs belonging to the market and fairs, except the assize of bread and ale, waifs, strays, forfeitures, &c., to be held by them and their heirs at the yearly rent of 6s. 8d. The property and privileges comprised in this grant have been transferred from time to time to new trustees, upon trust, that the rents and profits should be employed for the relief of the poor, the reparation of the church, and other public uses. The trust property comprises various buildings in and near the Market place, let for about £90 a year, two large rooms in the Guildhall, occupied for public meetings, &c., and a cottage, occupied rent-free by the town crier. The trustees also derive from £12 to £15 from stallage, &c.

THE GRAND FEOFFMENT.—The estates and property derived from sundry charitable donations for the poor of Hadleigh, which have for a long period been combined, are vested in trustees, called the *Grand Feoffees*, and have been conveyed from time to time upon trust, that the rents and profits thereof should be employed for the use of the poor parishioners, and such other uses as are appointed by the several donors, with a provision that when the feoffees are reduced to six, they should elect others, to make twenty at least. The charities and properties thus combined are as follows:— *Wm. Pykenham, D.D.*, rector of Hadleigh, erected 12 *Almshouses and a Chapel* in Magdalen street (now called George street,) for 24 poor people; and by his will, in the 12th of Henry 7th, he endowed them with various lands and tenements in Whatfield, Hadleigh, Aldham, Naughton, Elmsett, and Semer, now worth about £400 per annum. *Dr. Good* erected two other almshouses for four inmates, adjoining those of Dr. Pykenham; and in 1540, *John Raven* erected four *almshouses at Benton-end*, for eight poor people, and endowed them with lands at Raydon and Holton. The 36 *almspeople* in Pykenham's, Good's, and Raven's almshouses, receive 4s. 6d. each per week from the rental of the Grand Feoffment, and the eight in Raven's houses, have also divided among them £7. 18s. per ann. from land purchased with £50, left for that purpose by John Raven, M.D., in 1636. *John Glanvel*, in 1616, gave lands for the poor in the almshouses. The other *benefactions* left for the relief of the poor, and vested with the Grand Feoffees, were £20, left by Wm. Berryffe, in 1614; £30, by Wm. Smith, in 1624; two tenements, given by Alice Parkins; £10, by Alice Humfrey, in 1632; two tenements, by Richard Glanfield, in 1636; three tenements, by John Alabaster, in 1667; £52, by John Calton, in 1614; 20 marks, by Thomas Spencer, D.D.; £10, by John Beaumont; a tenement, by Thos. Orson; £10, by Oliver Aylward; £50, by Edward Gaell; two tenements, by Wm. Gaell, in 1606; £100, by Sir Nicholas Strutt; £50, by Ann Strutt, and £40, given by Thos. Cook, D.D., in 1679. The money derived from these legacies was laid out in the purchase of land. The Grand Feoffees are also trustees of the FREE SCHOOL, to which

Elias Jordayn gave £100, in 1655, to be laid out in land; and *John Alabaster* gave 1A. 3R. of land, now forming part of the paddock of Holbecks house. The property of the Grand Feoffment, derived from these various bequests, consists of houses, cottages, and other buildings, and about 726A. of land in Hadleigh, Offton, Whatfield, Polstead. &c., and produces *a clear yearly income* of about £700, out of which about £430 is divided among the 36 almspeople; about £140 among poor parishioners, in coals, wood, cloth, &c.; and £22. 5s. is paid yearly to the *schoolmaster,* who has also £7 a year from Ann Beaumont's charity, and a yearly rent-charge of £5, out of Place Farm, left by Edward Clarke, in 1582. For these allowances and the use of the school-house, he teaches 24 *free scholars* reading and arithmetic.

Ann Beaumont, in 1701, bequeathed a messuage and lands near Hadleigh bridge, to the rectors of Hadleigh, Hintlesham, and Layham, and other trustees, upon trust, to pay £10 a year to Christ's Hospital, in London; £5 a year to the master of the Free School at Hadleigh, for instructing six poor children; and to apply the remainder of the rents in apprenticing the said free scholars, and in other charitable uses, in Hadleigh. The master and governors of Christ's Hospital refused to accept the annuity of £10, and by a decree in Chancery, in 1769, the whole benefit of the estate was vested for the use of Hadleigh parish. It comprises a cottage, a barn, and 18A. 2R. 17P. of land, let for £42 a year, out of which the following fixed payments are made, viz., £7 to the master of the Free School; £4. 18s. for providing coats and caps for the six boys taught in consideration of this charity; and £2 for providing linen, &c., for poor parishioners; and the residue, after payment of incidental expences, is applied in apprentice fees of about £12 each. In 1615, *Jno. Fiske* charged his estate at Wetheringsett with the payment of £5 per annum, to be laid out in shifting cloth for poor widows of George street; and £5 per annum, for providing bread for the poor widows of the parish. In 1643, *John Whiting* left 40s. a year, out of a house in High street, to be distributed in bread among the poor of Hadleigh. In 1743, MARY CLARK left 22A. 2R. 35P. of land at Foxearth, in Essex, to provide coats for the men and petticoats for the women in the *almshouses* at Hadleigh. The land is let for £33 a year, of which about £21 is laid out in clothing for the almspeople, and the remainder is distributed among them in money.

HADLEIGH DIRECTORY.

POST OFFICE at Mr. John Patmore Ellisdon's, High street. Letters from all parts arrive at 7 morning, and are despatched at 8 evening.

☞ *Marked 1, are in Queen street ; 2, Church street ; 3, Market place ; 4, Bridge street ; 5, Angel street ; 6, Duke street ; 7, George street ; 8, Benton street ; and the rest in High street, or where specified.*

Adam Wm. Jackson, supervisor
Ansell John, Esq. High street
Ansell Rt. draper, &c; h High st
Baker Edward, gent. Queen street
Baker Mrs Eliz. Church street
8 Batley Samuel, rake, &c. maker
Battell Edward, horse letter
Beeton Mrs Lucy, High street
Berry Mrs Ann, Market place
6 Brown and Moy, silk throwsters
Bryer Wm. gent. Church lane
2 Chapman Rev Chas. M.A. incumbent of Kersey and Lindsey
Clarey John, coachman, High st
Clarke George, fruiterer, High st

Cook John, draper; h High street
Cocksedge Hy. gunsmith, High st
Cooke Miss Hannah, Queen street
Cook Miss Maria, Church lane
Corder John, joiner, High street
Cornell Mrs Mary, Benton street
Drake Mrs Ursula, High street
Derrick, Wm. ironfounder, High st
Downs Edward Samuel, stone and marble mason, statuary, &c.
Dunthorne Thomas, gent. Queen st
Ellisdon John Patmore, postmaster and news agent
Elsden Isaac, gent. High street
Fenn George, banker's clerk

Frost Mr Edward, High street
5 Frost Shadrach, brewer
Golding Wm. tanner and fellmonger
GrimwadeWm.Esq.banker,Queen st
Grimwade Wm. jun. wine and spirit merchant, High street
Harstow Mr. Church street
Keymer Mrs Dinah, High street
Knox Very Rev Hy. Barry, A.M. rector and rural dean, *Rectory*
2 Last Charles Henry, solicitor
2 Last Isaac, Esq. solicitor, Union Clerk, and supt. registrar
1 Lee Rev Edw. Hy. B.A. curate
Maskall Mr Edward, High street
Offord Henry, Esq. solicitor; house *Hadleigh Hall*
Offord Robert, cutler, High street
Piper John Dixon, bookseller
7 Powell Rev Wm. M.A. incumbent of Shelley
Pritty Mrs Eliz. High street
Pritty Mr Thomas, High street
Rainbird Mrs Susan, High street
Rand Mrs Sarah, Duke street
Robinson John Fredk. solicitor
Robinson John Smith, auctioneer
Seeley Mr J. Market place
Sheldrake Mrs Ann, Market place
Sheldrake Mrs Cath. *Cottage*
8 Skinner Rev Richd. (Indept.)
Spraggon Walter, cattle dealer, *Cosford Bridge*
Steptoe Thos. tea dealer, High st
Strutt Miss Ann, Benton street
Taylor Wm. bank clerk, High st
Wade Mrs Susanna, High street
2 Wallace Chas. Lucas, solicitor
Whishaw Mrs Eliz. High street
Whittle Wm. fruiterer
Wilkinson Henry, gent. George st

ACADEMIES.
*(Marked * take Boarders.)*
1 Aldrich Amy M. & Catherine E.
*Golding Mary, High street
4 Grimwade John, *Free School*
6 *British Schools*, James Ashdown, My. Ann Oxborrow & My.Fidgett
3 *National*, Hy. Norford and Eliz. Palmer
8*Jaynes John Hadleigh
Pickes Esther, High street
*Tovell Edward, High street

ATTORNEYS.
Baines John Geo. Fuller, Queen st
Bunn Edward, High street

Last, Wallace, and Last, (clerks to the magistrates, and commissrs. of taxes,) Church street
Newman Richard, High street
Offord and Robinson, *Hadleigh Hall*

BANKERS.
Alexanders and Co. High street, (on Barnett, Hoares, and Co.)
Mills, Bawtree, Errington, Bawtree, and Grimwade, Queen street, (on Hankey and Co.)

FARMERS. *(* are Owners.)*
Baker Henry, Toppesfield
Beeston Robert, Coram street
*Clarke Joseph, in the fields
5 Corder John || Fenn Geo. Stone st
Frost John, Friar's farm
4 Gray Thos. |† Grimwade Wm. jun.
Hicks Philip, *Pond Hall*
Hoddy Robert, Coram street
*Kersey Caleb
*Kersey Robert, Crosshouse
4 Rand Joseph
Rand Robert, *Peyton Hall*
Sallows Robert, Kates hill
*Strutt Isaac, *Toppesfield Hall*
*Strutt Wm. *Benton end*
5 White Thomas

FIRE AND LIFE OFFICES.
Clerical, Medical, and Genl. Life, Wm. Grimwade, jun.
English and Scottish, and Law Life, Last, Wallace, and Last,Church st
Farmers', Wm. Grimwade, jun.
Freemasons' and General Life, H. Offord
Suffolk and General Country Amicable Fire, Offord and Robinson, Hadleigh Hall

INNS AND TAVERNS.
8 Barley Mow, Eliz. Scrivener
Cock, Eliz. Parker, George street
George and Commercial Inn, Thos. Chisnall, (posting,) High street
King's Head, Robt. Long, High st
Ram, Wm. Hurrell, Market place
Shoulder of Mutton, John Warren
Swan, Jph. Dynes, Benton street
Wheat Sheaf, David Pratt
White Hart, Wm. Kitson, Bridge st
White Horse and Coml. Inn, Mark Leppingwell Munson, (posting,) High street
White Lion Inn, Joseph Stevens, (posting,) High street

Bakers & Flour Dealers.
5 Chaplin Richd.
8 Death Jph.
5 Dunningham Isaac
4 Gardiner Tillett
8 Green Wm.
2 Norfolk Gregy.
5 Smith Susan
7 Spooner Wm.
Taylor John
Wells Godfrey
Basket Makers.
5 Branch Henry
7 Woollard Robt.
Beerhouses.
5 Chaplin Rd.
7 Cooper Edward
5 Frost Shadrach
8 Smith John
Whittle John, Stone street
Blacksmiths.
Beaumont John
Cook Joshua
7 Dunningham Joseph
8 Lines John
8 Lingley John
Lingley William, Heath
Payne John, Cock's corner
Booksellers, Printers, &c.
4 Grimwade Jno.
Hardacre Henry, (stamp seller, corn inspector, & organist)
Piper & Baker
Boot & Shoe Mkrs.
7 Chisnall Ann
Cook Thos.
Death Matthew
Death W. Aldam
7 Elliott John
Ellisdon John P.
Hart Wm.
May Charles
May James
5 Pettit Levi
Salmon Henry, Ipswich road
Spooner John
5 Spooner Hicks

7 Steele Thos.
Stow Edward
Braziers & Tinrs
Clayden Henry
Deeks Wm.
Simpson Henry
Simpson Thos.
Bricklayers.
Brook Robert
Cook John
Wilkinson Hy.
7 Wilkinson Rt.
Brickmakers.
Clark Mary Ann
Wilkinson Hy.
7 Wilkinson Rt.
Butchers.
Brown Wm.
7 Brown Thos.
8 Day George
Day John
Dunningham Isc.
7 Frost Henry
Hasell Benj.
4 Mott Wm.
7 Sibbons Woods
Waller James, (& Holton)
Welham Ransome
Cabinet Makers.
Bateman George
8 Clarke Joseph
1 Gardiner John
Lamb Wm. Hy.
Reeve Sarah
Smith George, Cock's corner
Woolmer Edw.
Chemists & Drugs
Story Henry
Wick James
Coach Builders.
Green Jacob
Jolly Robert
Coopers.
Faiers Robert
Faiers James Bransby
Gyton Wm.
Warren James
Corn Merchants.
Chisnall Thos.
Corder John
Fenn Josiah, sen.
Frost H. (& hop)
8 Groom Henry

Kersey Robert, Cross house
4 Rand Joseph
Syer Abm. Hy. (and porter,) Bridge cottage
Syer John Spencer, Duke st
Whittle James
Corn Millers.
Baker Hy. Toppesfield mill
Deeks Robt. Hadleigh mill
4 Syer Abm. Hy.
Curriers, &c.
* *are Leather Cutters only.*
*Death Matthew
*Hart Wm.
Scrivener Chas.
Drapers, Mercers, & Hatters.
Braham John & James
Carman George
Cook & Hansell
Garnham George Frederick
Gilbert Charles
Howchin Wm.
Piper Henry
Farriers.
8 Grimwade Jno.
Long Robert
Furniture Bkrs.
7 Allen John
Death Matthew
Lamb Wm. Hy.
5 Spooner Thps.
5 Spooner Wm.
Gardeners.
7 Deeks Wm.
7 Flack John
Syer George, Nursery
5 Whelham John
5 Wythe Stephn.
Glass, China, &c. Dealers.
Clark Emma
Clayden Henry
Death W. Aldam

Glovers.
Oxford Thomas
5 Prigg Wm.

Grocers.
(*See also Shopkeepers.*)
Botten Jas. (and clothes dealer)
Braham Jno. and James
Cook & Ansell
Gilbert Charles
Ironmongers.
Clayden Henry
Simpson Thomas, (& gas agent)
Joiners.
8 Bantock John
2 Clarke Wm.
Corder Joseph
2 Driver Thomas
Parsons Clark
Maltsters.
Chisnall Thos.
5 Corder John
Fenn Josiah, sen.
4 Fenn Charles
8 Groom Henry
5 Grimsey Wm.
4 Rand Joseph
4 Syer Abraham
7 Vince John
5 White Thos.
5 Wilson Thos.
Millwrights and Machine Mkrs.
6 Nunn Samuel
5 Wilkin Henry
Milliners, &c.
2 Brown My. Ann
7 Burch Harriet
7 Falkner Susan
1 Fenn Sarah
3 Terry M. A. & E.
Wells Sarah
Painters, Plumbers, & Glaziers.
Gardiner Benj.
Hawkins & Reeve
Lloyd Purches
Stow Thomas
Perfumers and Hair Dressers.
Bare Benj.
7 Deeks James
Ray John
Verlander Saml.
Saddlers, &c.
Goodrich Jph.
Kersey Robert

2 Sexton Thomas,
(parish clerk)
Wells John
Shopkeepers.
5 Cooper John
7 Dunningham
Joseph
4 Gardiner Tillett
5 Pettit Levi
7 Spooner Wm.
8 Staines John
8 Turner John
Straw Hat Mkrs.
8 Bantock Sarah
Braham J. & J.
Garnham Eliz.
Gyton Jane
Lloyd Purches
8 Palmer Sarah
Venn Selina
Surgeons.
Growse John
Mudd William

Tailors.
Howard John &
Samuel
Howard John
8 Howard Wm.
5 Reichter Fras.
Sage Edward
Sexton John
8 Staines John
5 Webb John
Webb John
*Tanner and Fell-
monger.*
Golding Wm.
Watch Makers.
Gurdon George
Payne Ann
Simpson Caleb
Wheelwrights.
4 Gardiner Thos.
Herbert Peter
Towns George,
turner

COACHES

From the White Lion and White Horse, every morning, except Sunday, at 8, to *Colchester,* to meet the *London Trains*

Omnibus to Ipswich, from the Shoulder of Mutton, at 9 morng. except Sunday

CARRIERS.

Those marked 1, *stop at the King's Head; and* 2, *at the White Horse*

2 John Broom, to *Colchester,* Tue. and Fri. and to Stowmarket, W. & S

2 Thos. Howard, to *Sudbury,* W. & S

2 Wm. Ruggall, to *Ipswich,* Mon. and to *Sudbury,* Tuesday

1 John Springett, to *Lavenham,* Tuesday and Friday

John Warren, from High street, to *Ipswich, Colchester,* and *London,* Tues. Friday, and Sat. mornings

HADLEIGH HAMLET is a small township of scattered houses, about 4 miles W. of Hadleigh, in the *parish of Boxford,* but in Cosford Hundred, and manor of Hadleigh Hall. It contains 232 inhabitants, and about 610 acres of land, belonging to Sir B. C. Brodie, Bart., the Executors of F. H. Child, Mrs. Mary Sheen, Miss Ann Hoy, and a few smaller proprietors. Some of its houses form part of the village of Boxford, which see. *Directory:*—Daniel Death and Richard Munson, *shoemakers;* John Watson, *carpenter and brickmaker;* and Frederick Benyon, John Clifford, Mary and John Curtis, Wm. Parmiter, Joseph Glandfield Stow (registrar,) and Daniel Tiffen, *farmers.*

HITCHAM is a large scattered village and extensive parish, 1½ mile N. of Bildeston, 7 miles N.N.W. of Hadleigh, and 7 miles S.W. by S. of Stowmarket. It has 1065 inhabitants, and comprises 4056A. of fertile, but strong clayey land, extending five miles in length, and four in breadth, and including a luxuriant *Wood* of 102A. 1R. 16P. Robert Mapletoft, Esq., is lord of the *manor,* in which the arbitrary fines paid by the copyholders average about £160 a year, and the quit-rents about £49 a year, subject to a fee-farm rent to the Marquis of Camden. He is also owner of *Hitcham Hall,* a large, handsome, commodious farm-house, which, with the manor, the wood, and Plains Farm, is now (Sept. 1843,) advertised for sale. The other principal landowners are the trustees of the late John Camac, Esq., Sir B. C. Brodie, Rev. J. Y. Cooke, and Messrs. J. Harper, R. Ennals, R. Luckey, and J. Grimwood. The manor and advowson belonged to the Bishop of Ely till the 4th of Elizabeth. The ancestors of *Sir Robert Hitcham* (see page 192,) were no doubt seated here. *Wetherden Hall,* an ancient farm-house, 2½ miles N.W. of Bildeston, is still encompassed by a moat, and was long the seat of the knightly family of Waldegrave. The *Church* (All Saints) stands near Hitcham Hall,

and is a large and handsome structure, with a tower and six bells, and a fine south porch. The interior is lofty, and the roof is beautifully carved. The *Rectory*, valued in K.B. at £26. 13s. 4d., has a good residence, 26A. 39P. of glebe, and a yearly modus of £1159, awarded, in 1840, in lieu of tithes. The patronage is in the Crown, and the *Rev. J. S. Henslow, M.A., F.L.S.*, is the incumbent, and also Professor of Botany at Cambridge University; and to him the farmers of Suffolk are greatly indebted for many valuable essays and experiments for the improvement of agricultural science. The Baptists and Primitive Methodists have chapels here. The *Feoffment Estate*, vested in trustees for the poor of this parish, comprises three tenements, usually occupied rent-free by poor persons, and 28A. 3R. of land, let for about £50 a year. The rents, after deducting incidental expenses, are distributed about Christmas among poor parishioners. The trustees are also, by custom, admitted tenants of a piece of land called *Thieves Acre*, which is held by the rector, at the yearly rent of a noble and a mark, which sum, with a voluntary addition by the rector, making in the whole £5, is distributed in bread. In 1663, *Sir George Waldegrave* gave two tenements for the residence of poor people, and they were rebuilt, about 1818, by the lord of the manor. In 1714, *Benj. Sparrow* left a yearly rent-charge of 18s. out of lands now belonging to Mr. Dakin, for schooling two poor children.

Gooch Robert, gamekeeper
Green John, vict. White Horse
Henslow Rev John Stevens, M.A., F.L.S. rector of Hitcham, and Professor of Botany at Cambridge University
Nunn John, butcher
Reynolds Wm. parish clerk
Sewell Edward, thatcher
Squirrell Jonathan, beerhouse
Stow Jane, schoolmistress

Blacksmiths.
Cobbold Thomas
Rush Joseph
Warren Zach.

Bricklayers.
Lister Thomas
Smith Wm.

Corn Millers
Barnes Robert

Clover Isaac
FARMERS.
Baker John
Baker Peter
Barton Edward
Barton Joseph
Bennett John
Cooper Esther
Cooper Syer

Death Saml. (& *cattle dealer)*
Downing Edw.
Ennals Robert
Fayers George
Grimwood Jas.
Grimwood Wm.
Harper John, Esq *Hitcham Hall*
Hitchcock Ralph *Wetherden Hall*
Hitchcock John
Jackson Thomas
Lucky Robert
Melton Robert
Pettit John
Pilgrim John, *Chapel Farm*
Poisey Wm.
Preston Joseph
Ranson Samuel

Plains Farm
Stearn John
Woollard John
Joiners, &c.
Baker Wm.
Death Wm.
Eley Jsa. (wgt.) .
Shoemakers.
Dickinson Dod. (and beerhs)
Grimwood Isaac
Lambert Elisha
Pearl John
Shopkeepers.
Bird Ebenezer
RaffeHanh.&Sar
Ward Ephraim
Taylors.
Hoddy John
Ward Wm.
Wordly John

KERSEY, a neat village, in a picturesque valley on one of the tributary streams of the river Brett, 2¼ miles N.W. of Hadleigh, has in its parish 787 souls, and 1510 acres of fertile land. It has a pleasure *fair* on Easter Monday, and is noted for the ivy mantled ruins of a PRIORY of Augustine Canons, which was first founded as a *hospital*, or *free-chapel*, about the year 1218, by Thomas de Burgh; but a few years afterwards, it was converted into a priory by his widow, Nesta de Cokefield, who endowed it with the tithes and advowson of Kersey and Lindsey. It was dedicated to St. Mary and St. Anthony, but was dissolved at an early period; and in the 26th of Henry 6th, Lord Po-

wis gave it, with all its revenues, to King's College, Cambridge, to which the site, the *Priory Manor,* &c., still belong. A great part of the parish is in two other manors—viz., *Kersey,* of which the Rev. Thomas Reeve is lord, and *Sampson's Hall,* of which the Rev. Thos. Jones is lord. The mansion called the *Priory,* near the venerable remains of the monastery, is the seat of Richard Newman, Esq., lessee of the estate and tithes belonging to King's College. The other principal landowners are Henry Offord, Jas. Bentley, and J. C. Archer, Esqrs. ; and Mr. B. Mann and several smaller owners have estates in the parish. The *Church* (St. Mary) is a neat structure of perpendicular architecture, with a lofty tower, containing six bells. It is a perpetual curacy, united with Lindsey, and valued, in 1835, at £112. The Rev. C. Chapman, M.A., is the incumbent, and the Provost and Fellows of King's College, Cambridge, are patrons and appropriators. The tithes of Kersey were commuted in 1840 for a yearly modus of £420. In 1580, *Robt. Nightingale* left in trust with the churchwardens and six of the chief parishioners, a cottage for four persons to dwell in, and 2A. 3R. of copyhold land, for the relief of the aged poor of the parish. The cottage was rebuilt at the expense of the parish, and is occupied by three families. The land is let for £5 a year.

Bull Henry, saddler
Cuthbert Joshua, baker
East George, schoolmaster
Green John, wheelwright
Grimwade Wm. farrier & vict. Bell
Newman Richd. Esq. *Kersey Priory*
Raynham Robert, bricklayer
Ruffell Ambrose, maltster and land surveyor
Vince Robert, bricklayer
Vince John, sexton
Whymark John, vict. White Horse

Blacksmiths.
Cobbold Richard
Smith Elizabeth

Corn Millers.
Hicks Rt. Jacob

Carter Christiana
Clarke John
Durrant John
Mason Benj. jun.
Ruffell Ambrose
Rush Richard
Sparrow Robert
Stow John, *Hall*
Stutter John, *Sampson's Hall*
Syer Wm.
Warren James
Welham Samuel
Mason Benj. jun.

FARMERS.
Betts John
Bouttell Thomas

Grocers & Dprs.
Rush John

Sexton, Fred. (& land surveyor)
Joiners, &c.
Pittock Saml. (& parish clerk)
Smith Edward
Woods Wm. (and beerhouse)
Shoemakers.
Kemble Thomas
Pryke John
Pryke Thomas

Tailors.
Kittle Robert
Scarf Henry

KETTLEBASTON, a small village, on an eminence, two miles N.W. of Bildeston, and 7 miles N.N.W. of Hadleigh, has in its parish 203 souls, and 1006 acres of land. Mrs. Beachcroft is lady of manor, but a great part of the soil belongs to Sir B. C. Brodie, the trustees of the late J. Camac, Esq., W. Makin, G. Richards, T. Lay, and a few smaller owners. In the 23rd of Henry VI., this manor was granted, with that of Nedging, to Wm. de la Pole, Marquis of Suffolk, to hold by the service of carrying a golden sceptre with a dove on the top, at the coronation of the king ; and a sceptre of ivory, with a golden dove upon it, at the coronation of the queen. The manor descended from the Waldegraves to the Lemans, and from them to the Beachcrofts. The *Church* (St. Mary) is a neat fabric, with a tower and three bells. The *rectory,* valued in K.B. at £13. 6s., has 15 acres of glebe, and a yearly modus of £300, awarded in 1841, in lieu of tithes. The Rev. John Robert Fiske is patron and incumbent. Here is a *National School,* built in 1838, and having about 30 scho-

lars. The *Charity Land*, one acre, is let in two lots for £6 a year, which is distributed in coals and clothing. *Directory :*—Elizabeth Beeton, schoolmistress ; Rev. J. R. Fiske, *Rectory ;* Jonathan Head, parish clerk ; and John Barton, *(Hall;)* Wm. Cole, George Cooper, James King, and Robert Makin, *farmers.*

LAYHAM, a pleasant village on both sides of the river Brett, 1¼ mile S. of Hadleigh, has in its picturesque parish 549 souls, and 2488A. 2R. 29P. of land, having a good mixed soil, and abounding in *cherry trees ;* and extending southward to *Masons Bridge*, and northward to HOLBECKS, (half a mile S. of Hadleigh,) the pleasant seat of the Dowager Lady Rowley. The parish is in two *manors*, called Overbury and Netherbury Halls. Henry Offord, Esq., is lord of both, but a great part of the soil belongs to Sir J. R. Rowley, the Dowager Lady Rowley, Chas. Rowley, Esq., Mrs. Norman, Misses E. and M. Armstrong, and the Brown, Berry, Partridge, Strutt, Thomas, and a few other families. The manors were anciently held by the *de Leyhams*, Woodstocks, and Hollands ; and passed from the latter to the Mortimers, and from them to the Greys and Howards. During the greater part of last century, they were held by the D'Oley family. The *Church* (St. Andrew) has a tower at the west end, and was repewed in 1837, when a new gallery was erected. The *rectory*, valued in K.B. at £16. 0s. 7½d., has 71A. 1R. 29P. of glebe, and a yearly modus of £800, awarded in 1840 in lieu of tithes. The patronage is in St. John's College, Cambridge, and the Rev. Henry Hunter Hughes, B.D., is the incumbent. Near the church is a *National School*, built in 1840, at the cost of about £160, and supported by the rector and principal parishioners. In 1727, the Rev. Wm. Baker left £30 for a yearly distribution of bread among the poor attending the church, and it was laid out in the purchase of an acre of land, now let for £3. 15s. a year.

Ablewhite Thomas, butcher
Berry Charles, corn miller
Berry Mrs Mary
Church Wm. carpenter and shopr
Clarke Robert, shopkeeper
Cook Robert, boot and shoemaker
Cook Edward, bricklayer
Ede Stephen, vict., *Queen's Head*
Hasell Susanna, vict. *Cherry Tree*
Hughes Rev Henry Hunter, B.D. *Rectory*
Hughes Rev George, M.A. curate
Lappage Mrs Maria
Norman Mrs Eliz. *Netherbury Hall*
Norman Jonathan, shopkeeper
Rowley Lady Susan Edith, *Holbecks*

Secker Miss Elizabeth
Smith Solomon, wheelwright
Rand Wm. butcher, & vict. *Marquis of Cornwallis*

Blacksmiths.
Cooper Wm.
Gosling Thomas Leech

FARMERS.
Berry Charles
Berry Jas. jun. Pope's green
Brown Charles, Moated farm
Fidget Richard

Norman James, *Netherbury hl*
Pratt Thomas
Richardson Thos.
Spencer Hannah
Strutt Wm. *Overbury Hall*
Strutt John
Vince Lionel
Vince Wm.
Vince Molly

LINDSEY, from 4 to 5 miles N.W. of Hadleigh, is a parish of scattered houses, containing 290 souls, and 1246A. 1R. 9P. of fertile land, in two *manors*, viz., *Beaumonts*, of which Messrs. Sparke, Holmes, and Jackson, of Bury St. Edmund's, are lords ; and *Lindsey*, of which J. Cudden, Esq., is lord. The copyholders are subject to arbitrary fines, but about two-thirds of the parish are freehold. The principal landowners are Sir H. E. Austin, the Provost and Fellows of King's

College, Cambridge; Sir J. R. Rowley, and the Mumford, Gage, Arthy, and Matthew families. The *Church* (St. Peter) is an ancient fabric, with a small belfry. The tower being much decayed, was taken down about ten years ago. The benefice is a perpetual curacy, with Kersey annexed to it, and valued in 1835 at £112. The church was appropriated to Kersey priory, and is now in the appropriation and patronage of King's College, Cambridge, and incumbency of the Rev. Charles Chapman, M.A. The tithes were commuted in 1838, for £320 per annum, of which £262 belongs to King's College, £12 to Mr. John Arthey, and £46 to Richard Newman, Esq. The latter is also lessee of the college tithes and lands; and the two small rent-charges are in right of land here, which belonged to a free chapel or some religious house, the remains of which are now a stable. Here is a small *Baptist Chapel.* A yearly rent-charge of 15s. for thirty poor widows, is paid out of a piece of land belonging to Mr. Arthy, pursuant to the bequest of one Grimsey. *Directory :*—Robert Bouttell, vict., *White Rose ;* Isaac Farthing, poulterer; William Stribbling, blacksmiths; Robert Willis, tailor; and John Arthy*, Joseph Arthy*, Joshua Clifford, Thos. Cousens, Samuel Matthew*, (and brick maker, *Raven's Hall ;)* Robert Raynham, Edward Rush, and Benj. Worters, *farmers.* Those marked * are *owners.*

NAUGHTON, a small village and parish, 2½ miles E. of Bildeston, and 5 miles N. of Hadleigh, has 137 souls, and 854A. 1R. 27P. of land, about half of which is copyhold, subject to arbitrary fines. Alexander Adair, Esq., is lord of the manor, but the soil belongs mostly to G. Cooke, C. Tyrell, and R. Kersey, Esqrs. The *Church* (St. Mary) is a small ancient structure, with a tower at the west end, and was re-pewed in 1833. The *rectory*, valued in K.B. at £10. 15s., has 57A. 1R. 6P. of glebe, and a yearly modus of £190, awarded in 1842, in lieu of tithes. The patronage belonged to the late Sir F. Ommaney, but is now in dispute. The Rev. Wm. Edge is the incumbent. The poor parishioners have the interest of £20, left by the Rev. Hy. Jones, in 1723, and 3s. 4d. yearly, out of *Gazeley's field*, left by Robt. Nightingale, in 1583. *Directory :*—Wm. Cuthbert, *shoemaker ;* George Dade, parish clerk; Robt. Piper and Thomas Tampion, *blacksmiths ;* Wm. Roberts, *wheelwright ;* Rev. Walter Melville Wright, *curate ;* and Wm. Baldry, Saml. Cooper, James Crich, Thos. Fidget, George Green, and Joseph Grimwade, (Brick House,) *farmers.*

NEDGING, a small parish of scattered houses, 1 mile S. of Bildeston, and 4 miles N. of Hadleigh, comprises 195 souls, and 810 acres of strong, loamy land. The Rev. Wm. Edge is lord of the manor, which was anciently held with that of Kettlebaston, by the coronation service noticed with that parish. A great part of the soil belongs to the Rev. J. Y. Cooke, and Messrs. J. Stutter, R. Chinery, and I. Clover. The *Church* (St. Mary) is a small structure, with a tower and two bells, and is a *rectory*, valued in K.B. at £8. 12s. 11d., and now having 30 acres of glebe, and a yearly modus of £191, awarded in 1841, in lieu of tithes. The Rev. Wm. Edge is patron and incumbent, and has a neat residence here. The other principal inhabitants are, Robert Chinery, *yeoman ;* Isaac Clover, yeoman and *corn miller ;* and Wm. Chaplin, farmer and *chief constable.*

SEMER, 2 miles S. of Bildeston, and 3 miles N. by W. of Hadleigh, is a village and parish, on the river Brett, containing 1205A. 2R. 12P. of land. It had 370 inhabitants, in 1841, including 108 in *Cosford Union Workhouse*, which is situated here, and is already noticed at page 283. This lordship was appropriated to the use of the cellarer of the abbey of Bury St. Edmund's. Mrs. Mary Ann Tyrell is now lady of the manor, in which the copyholds are subject to arbitrary fines. The other principal owners of the soil are J. C. Archer, Esq., and the Rev. J. Y. Cooke. The latter is also patron and incumbent of the *rectory*, valued in K.B. at £11. 7s. 1d., and now having a yearly rent-charge of £370, awarded, in 1842, in lieu of tithes ; and a commodious residence, with pleasant grounds overlooking the river Brett. The *Church* (All Saints) is an ancient structure, which was repewed and thoroughly repaired in 1843. Near it is a small lake or *mere*, from which the parish is supposed to have derived its name. The poor parishioners have 20s. yearly out of land at Raydon, left by John Goodall, in 1607 ; and 20s. a-year out of the poor-rates, as interest of £20 benefaction money.

Archer Joseph Clarke, Esq., *Semer Lodge*
Cooke RevJas.Young, M.A.Rectory
Cutten Wm. corn miller
Green Saml. wheelwgt. & carpenter
Patterson Rt., governor of Cosford Union Workhouse

Vince John, jun., blacksmith
FARMERS.
Green Thomas, *Semer Hall*
Green Wm. Partridge, *Semer Gate*
Marshall, Stephen
Sallows Henry, *Semer Dairy*
Smith Richd. || Watson Thomas

THORP-MORIEUX, a scattered village and parish, 3½ miles N. by E. of Lavenham, and 9 miles S.E. by S. of Bury St. Edmund's, has 418 inhabitants, and 2428 acres of land, near the source of the river Brett. It was anciently the lordship and seat of the Morieux family, and afterwards of the Risbys. Henry Sparrow, Esq., is now lord of the manor, which is mostly freehold. The other principal landowners are, F. G. H. Harrison, Esq., Thos. Poinder, Esq., and Mr. John Stearn. The *Church* (St. Mary) has a tower and three bells. The *rectory*, valued in K.B. at £18. 14. 6½d., has a good residence, 25A. of glebe, and a yearly modus of £620, awarded in 1843, in lieu of tithes. The Rev. T. T. Harrison is patron and incumbent. The poor have the interest of £10, left by Wm. Bowl.

Aves John, shoemaker
Goold Bixby, parish clerk
Harrison RevThos.Thomas,*Rectory*
North Wm. wheelwright
Rush Samuel, blacksmith
Tracey Robert, shoemaker

FARMERS.
Andrews John || Payne Robert
Edgar John || Scott Charles
Last John || Scott John
Mannington John || Scott John
Mudd Eliz. || Stearn John
Mumford Robert, *Thorpe Hall*

WATTISHAM, a small village, 2 miles N.E. of Bildeston, and 6 miles S.W. of Needham Market, has in its parish 240 souls, and 1298A. 3R. 6P. of land. In the reigns of Edward I., II., and III., the manor was held by the Wachesham family, by the same indecent service as that of Hemingstone. (See page 236.) Messrs. Last, Wallace, and Last, solicitors, of Hadleigh, now hold the manor, but the soil belongs chiefly to Mrs. Maria Mumford, the Rev. Richard Johnson,

G. T. Nichols, Esq., and S. G. Hart, Esq. The copyholds are subject to small arbitrary fines. The *Hall*, occupied by a farmer, is still moated. The *Church* (St. Nicholas) is a plain fabric, with a tower at the west end, and contains a mural tablet, recording a singular calamity which happened in the parish in 1762, when " six persons of one family lost their feet by mortification." It was appropriated to Bricett priory; and the Provost and Fellows of King's College, Cambridge, are now appropriators of the rectory, and patrons of the *perpetual curacy*, which is valued at £100, and enjoyed by the Rev. Arthur Young, together with that of Great Bricett. The tithes were commuted, in 1841, for a yearly modus of £389. 5s. 6d., and are held on lease by G. Mumford, Esq. Here is a neat *Baptist Chapel*, which was erected in 1763, and rebuilt in 1825. *Directory :*—Wm. Beaumont, parish clerk ; John Clabon, *blacksmith ;* Rev. John Cooper, Baptist minister ; John Keeble, beer hs. & shopkeeper ; Joshua Ward, shoemaker ; and Thos. Carter, *(Loose Hall,)* Wm. Harvey, *(Wattisham Hall,)* Priscilla Pilgrim, *(Judgment Farm,)* John King, Daniel Pead, and Thos. Vince, *farmers.*

WHATFIELD, or *Wheatfield,* a small village, mostly of thatched cottages, 3 miles N. by E. of Hadleigh, has in its parish 394 souls, 1571 acres of land, and nine scattered farm houses. The parish is bounded on the west by the river Brett, and has generally a strong, clayey soil, well suited to the growth of wheat, and mostly copyhold, subject to arbitrary fines. It is in three *manors,* viz., Whatfield Hall belonging to Mrs. Mary Ann Tyrell ; Barrards Hall, belonging to the Bowers Family ; and Whatfield-Furnese, belonging to Lady Austin ; but a great part of the soil is the property of G. Cook, Esq., J. C. Archer, Esq., and a few smaller owners. Kirby mentions two manors here, called Cosford and Hornham. The *Church* (St. Margaret) is a small plain structure, containing several monuments, one of which is in memory of Wm. Vessey, gentleman, who was seated at *Whatfield Hall,* now a farm-house. The *rectory,* valued in K.B. at £15. 0s. 5d., and in 1835, at £393, is in the patronage of Jesus College, Cambridge, and incumbency of the Rev. Fredk. Calvert, M.A. The tithes were commuted for a rent-charge, in 1843. The *Rev. Thomas Harmer,* a dissenting minister, eminent for his attainments in Oriental literature, and his unaffected piety, died here in 1788, and was born at Norwich in 1715.

Calvert Rev. Fred. M.A. Rectory
Garrard Edward, shoemaker
Vince John, sen. blacksmith & vict.
　Horse Shoes
Wright John, parish clerk

FARMERS.

Andrews George || Cone James
Daking Robert || Frost Edward
Nunn John, *Barrards Hall*
Richardson Grimsey || Rush Robert
Richardson Edward || Vince John

THEDWESTRY HUNDRED

Is about twelve miles in length, and six in breadth, and is bounded on the west by the borough of Bury St. Edmund's, and Thingoe Hundred; on the north, by Blackbourn Hundred; on the east, by the latter and Stow Hundred; and on the south, by Cosford and Babergh Hundreds. It is a fertile district, rising in bold undulations, and watered by many rivulets, which rise within its limits, and form or swell the sources of the small rivers Thet, Gipping, Lark, and Brett. It is in the *Deanery of Thedwestry, Archdeaconry of Sudbury, Diocese of Ely*, and Liberty of *St. Edmund*. It has no market town; but those of Bury and Ixworth are on its borders. The following is an enumeration of its 24 parishes, shewing their territorial extent; the annual value of their lands and buildings, as assessed to the property tax in 1815; and their population in 1801 and 1841:—

PARISHES.	Acrs.	Rental.	Populatn. 1801.	Populatn. 1841	PARISHES.	Acres.	Rental. £.	Population. 1801.	Population. 1841.
Ampton	870	845	75	147	*Rattlesden ..	3200	4607	814	1141
Barton Great ..	3500	3128	523	774	Rougham	3846	3933	607	969
*Beyton	626	940	231	384	Rushbrooke ..	1066	1618	122	175
BradfieldCombust	800	1106	125	192	Stanningfield..	1431	1788	248	327
Bradfield St Clare	1428	1406	131	249	*Thurston	2400	2149	354	599
Bradfield St. Geo.	2000	2110	354	479	Timworth	1220	1056	149	212
*Drinkstone	2170	2673	369	505	*Tostock	975	1390	220	367
*Felsham	1605	1930	301	398	Welnetham ⎱				288
Fornham St. Gnv.	700	731	116	70	Great ....⎰	1409	1851	222	
Fornham St. Mtn.	1200	1668	166	294	§Sicklesmere⎰				273
*Gedding	502	570	108	173	Welnetham Ltl	570	869	142	159
*Hessett	1568	1642	323	417	*Woolpit	2000	2667	625	942
Livermere Mgn..	1580	1312	259	320					
Pakenham	3696	3113	681	1102	Total ..	40,362	45,102	7259	10,947

☞ CHIEF CONSTABLES.—John Fenton, of Great Welnetham; and John Boldero, of Rattlesden.
  * The nine parishes marked thus * are in STOW UNION (see page 265;) and the other fifteen parishes are in THINGOE UNION. (See page 601.)
  § *Sicklesmere Hamlet* is partly in *Little*, and mostly in *Great Welnetham*, 226 of its inhabitants being in the latter, and 47 in the former parish.

AMPTON, a small neat village, pleasantly situated 5 miles N. of Bury St. Edmund's, has in its parish 147 souls, and 870 acres of land, all the property and manor of Lord Calthorpe, who resides here occasionally at AMPTON HALL, a large handsome mansion, in an extensive and beautiful park, which adjoins the more extensive park of Livermere. The two parks comprise about 700 acres, and the late owners, with a harmony very unusual, made a noble serpentine river through both, and built a large and handsome bridge over it, at their joint expense, by which means they ornamented their grounds to a degree otherwise impossible. In Ampton Park, the water forms a bend against the slope of a wood, which has a very noble effect. In one part, the water winds through a thick planted wood, with a very bold shore,—in some places wide, and in others so narrow, that the overhanging trees join their branches, and even darken the scene. The banks are everywhere uneven—first, wild and rough, and covered with bushes and shrubs; then, fine green lawns, in gentle swells, with scat-

tered trees and shrubs, extending to the mansions.   At the termination of the water, the abruptness and ill effect of that circumstance is taken off, by finishing with a dry scoop, which is very beautiful, the bed of the river being continued for some distance, along a sloping lawn, with banks on each side, planted and managed with great taste.   *Ampton Hall,* now only visited by its noble owner as a sporting seat, was long the residence of the Calthorpe family, which became extinct in the person of *Sir Henry Calthorpe, K.B.,* who, dying in 1788, devised all his estates to the male heir of his sister Barbara, wife of Sir Henry Gough, of Edgbaston, near Birmingham, on condition that his nephew should assume the surname of Calthorpe, which was accordingly complied with ; and in 1796, Sir Henry Gough Calthorpe, Bart., was created *Baron Calthorpe, of Calthorpe, in Norfolk.*   His second son, George Gough Calthorpe, who succeeded his elder brother in 1807, is the present Lord Calthorpe, and his principal seats are *Edgbaston House,* Warwickshire, and *Elvatham,* Hampshire.   Ampton was anciently the lordship of the abbot of Bury St. Edmund's.   The *Church* (St. Peter) is a small neat structure, and the benefice is a *discharged rectory,* valued in K.B. at £8. 2s. 1d., and in 1835, at £172.   Lord Calthorpe is patron, and the *Rev. Jas. H. Stewart, M.A.,* is the incumbent, and has a good residence here.   The tithes were commuted, in 1841, for a yearly rent charge of £155.   In 1692, *Mrs. Dorothy Calthorpe* left £100 to build an ALMSHOUSE, on Ampton green, for six poor women, of the age of 60 years or upwards, to be chosen, half out of Suffolk and half out of Norfolk.   For its endowment she left £1000, but there appears to have been a deficiency of assets to answer the testator's bequest, for the almshouse contains only *four* apartments, and the fund appropriated to its support, under her gift, consists only of £700 old south sea annuities ; but the endowment was afterwards augmented with £100, given by *John Edwards,* and now vested in a yearly rent-charge of £4.   The *four almswomen* are appointed by Lord Calthorpe, who supplies them with fuel, clothing, &c., and repairs the almshouse. Each inmate has £6 a year.   In 1692, JAMES CALTHORPE, Esq., conveyed unto Sir John Poley, Knt., and four other trustees, and their heirs, the farm of Aldeby Hall, and the manor of Aldeby, in Norfolk, and a messuage and orchard in Ampton, in trust, that the messuage and orchard should be used as a CHARITY SCHOOL, for the use and residence of a master and six poor boys, of Ampton, Great and Little Livermere, Ingham, and Timworth ; and that the rents of the manor and premises in Aldeby should be applied for the schooling, clothing, feeding, and maintaining the six poor boys, and the payment of a suitable salary to the schoolmaster ; £20 a year to the minister of Ampton, and £5 a year to the parish clerk.   The donor directed that, in cases of equal circumstances, the children of Ampton should be preferred ; that none of them, at the time of admission to the school, should be more than seven years old, nor partake of the charity longer than till the age of fourteen years ; and that they should wear blue caps and blue coats, with the letters " J. C." affixed on the breast part of the coats.   In 1715, *Henry Edwards* bequeathed £100 to the trustees of this scoool, and directed that the interest thereof should be paid to the master for teaching five other boys, one from each of the above-named parishes.   In 1733, the trustees laid out £530, saved from the school

income, in the purchase of a farm of more than 50 acres, at Stanton, now let for £78 a year. Aldeby Hall farm comprises 380A., and is let for £280 per annum ; and the profits of the manor of Aldeby average about £10 per annum. Edward's legacy, with money arising from the savings of income, was laid out in the purchase of £1017. 11s. 3d. three per cent. consols, the dividends of which swell the income of the charity to about £399 per annum, which is amply sufficient for extending the charity to the education and maintenance of two boys in addition to the six named by the founder, and also for a considerable increase of the number of boys taught without charge, but maintained by their parents. The school is conducted on the national system. The master has £140 a year, for the maintenance and teaching of six poor boys, and an addition of £5 a year is paid him as the interest of Edward's legacy for teaching five boys. He is allowed to take other scholars from the five parishes named in the foundation deed, and charges 3d. per week each for their instruction. The trustees provide the six boys with clothing, books, and other necessaries, to the amount of about £50 a-year. They also pay £20 a-year to the minister of Ampton, and £5 to the parish clerk, as directed by the founder. The Rev. H. Hasted and others are trustees. Augustine Page is the *schoolmaster ;* and the only *farmer* in Ampton is Charles Stedman.

BARTON (GREAT), a scattered village and parish, with several large houses and extensive farms, from 2 to 3 miles N.E. of Bury St. Edmund's, comprises 774 inhabitants, and about 3500 acres of fertile land, anciently the lordship of the Abbot of Bury. *Sir Henry Edward Bunbury, Bart.,* K.C.B., of BARTON HALL, is lord of the manor, and owner of the greater part of the soil, and the remainder belongs to R. P. Lankester, Esq., Capt. Bennet, John Phillips, Esq., and a few smaller owners. After the dissolution, it was the estate of the Kitsons and Cottons, and the manor was purchased of the latter by Thomas Folkes, Esq., who built the present *Hall,* and whose heiress carried it in marriage to Sir Thos. Hanmer. About the middle of last century, it descended to the Rev. Sir Wm. Bunbury, who greatly improved the mansion and grounds, and whose *baronetcy* was created in 1681. His son, the late baronet, represented Suffolk in nine Parliaments, and built the fine large room which forms part of the mansion. The *Church* (Holy Innocents) is a neat structure, with a tower and six bells, and the living is a discharged *vicarage,* valued in K.B. at £10. 15s. 7½d., and now worth about £500 per annum. The Rev. Wm. Blake, M.A., is the incumbent, and Sir H. E. Bunbury is the patron, and also impropriator of the rectory. The tithes were all commuted, in 1802, for yearly rent-charges. In 1492, *Wm. Howardly* left 40 marks, and the residue of his personal estate, to be laid out in land, the profits thereof to be applied in repairing the church, and relieving the poor of Great Barton. The charity estate now consists of three old cottages, occupied rent free ; and a farm of 48A. 2R. 30P., let for £50 a year, and allotted at the enclosure, in 1805, in lieu of the old charity lands. After paying the land tax and other incidental expenses, the remainder of the rent is carried to the general account of the churchwardens, who distribute thereout £10 a year among the poor, in bread and fuel. An *Allotment* of 50A. was awarded at the enclosure to trustees, the rents thereof to be applied in the purchase of fuel for the poor

parishioners. It is let for £46 a year, and the rent is laid out in coals, which are sold to the poor at a reduced price. The late Lady Bunbury left four almshouses, and a small endowment for poor widows of this parish.

Adams Wm. land agent
Blake Rev Wm. & Sir. Hen. Chas. Bart. *Vicarage*
Bunbury Sir Henry Edward, Bart. K.C.B. *Barton Hall*
Chilver Robert, blacksmith & edge-tool maker
Last Wm. shopkeeper
Long Wm. shopkeeper
Parsons John, parish clerk
Pollington Robert, shoemaker
Rouse Wm. wheelwright

Sharman Pearson, corn miller
FARMERS AND GRAZIERS.
Cooper Jonathan, *Manor Farm*
Denton Henry, *Cats-hall*
Hill John, (bailiff) || Foulger Geo.
Lofts Jacob || Holden John
Lankester Robert Preston, Esq. *East Barton*
Nice Richard || Manning James
Paine Frederick, *Elms Farm*
Phillips John, Esq. || Sharman P.
Carrier to Bury, Wm. Bishop

BEYTON, *Bayton*, or *Beighton*, a pleasant and well-built village, 5½ miles E. by S. of Bury St. Edmund's, has in its parish 384 souls, and 626 acres. The manor belongs to the Crown, and the soil is held by Philip Bennett, sen. and jun., Esqrs., Wm. Walpole, Esq., Mrs. Clayton, Mr. J. Nunn, and a few smaller proprietors. The *Church* (All Saints) is a small structure with a tower, which formerly contained five bells, but four of them were sold about seventy years ago, and the money expended in repairing the church. The living is a discharged rectory, valued in K.B. at £4. 3s. 9d., and in 1835 at £175. The patronage is in the Crown, and the Rev. T. L. Clarkson is the incumbent. The *Hall*, a neat mansion occupied by H. Cocksedge, Esq., is the property of W. Walpole, Esq.

Abbott Joseph, vict. *White Horse*
Aldridge John, shoemaker
Aldridge Wm. cooper
Allington Samuel, vict. *Bear*
Bishop George, butcher
Clarkson Rev T. L. *Rectory*
Cocksedge, Hy. Esq. *Beyton Hall*
Cornish John, thatcher
Hazelwood Wm. blacksmith
Howe Robert, bricklayer
Howlett Edward, woodman
Hunt John, grocer and draper
Mulley John, baker
Ransom Wm. butcher
Ray Walter, Esq. *Vincent Cottage*

Spink Henry, wheelwright
Spink John, watchmaker
Walpole Wm. Esq. *Beyton Lodge*
Webb Miss Mary, boarding school
Wiard John, shoemaker
Wiard John, lath render
Wright James, butcher
Wright Mrs Mary
FARMERS.
Bennet Ralph, *Quaker's Farm*
Cornish Wm. || Gall Abraham
Cullum George, (bailiff)
Jennings Robert || Winter John
Sturgeon Joseph, *Brook Farm*

BRADFIELD COMBUST is a small village and parish, on the London road, 5 miles S. by E. of Bury St. Edmund's, containing 192 souls, and about 800 acres of fertile land. The ancient Hall of Bradfield belonged, with the lordship, to Bury Abbey, and was burnt to the ground in 1327, during the violent attacks made on the convent and its possessions by the townsmen. (Vide page 613.) After this conflagration, the parish was called *Combust*, or *Burnt-Bradfield*. The present *Hall* was built long after this event. It is the seat of Miss Mary Young, and was the birth-place and residence of the late *Arthur Young, Esq.*, whose indefatigable exertions for the promotion of agriculture, the chief source of the prosperity of a state, entitle his name

to the veneration of all philanthropists of this and succeeding generations. For the Board of Agriculture, of which he was secretary, he surveyed this and many other counties, and published a description of their soils, produce, modes of culture, &c.; and suggested various improvements, many of which have been successfuly carried into effect. One of his ancestors purchased the hall estate, and the manor of Bradfield, in 1620, of Sir Thomas Jermyn. Part of the parish belongs to Messrs. J. and W. Steward, T. Walton, and G. Sharpe; the Rev. H. J. Hasted, and the Guildhall Feoffment, of Bury St. Edmund's. The *Hall* stands upon a range of high land, which runs through the whole county. Two small brooks, which rise here, take contrary directions, and even the highest grounds are beautifully wooded. The late Mr. Young planted on his estate above 40,000 larch and other trees, as nurses to oaks, sown twenty years before; and his father, (Dr. Young,) formed an avenue of limes, which are now remarkably beautiful. Reduced to blindness after a life of uncommon activity, Arthur Young, "the father of improved British agriculture," devoted his time, with the aid of an amanuensis, to the illustration of his favourite pursuit, nearly to the period of his death, in 1820. His estate, when in his own cultivation, presented a variety of experiments, the result of which were laid before the public in his *Annals of Agriculture*, and in a work on which he was occupied many years. The *Church* (All Saints) is a neat fabric, with a tower and three bells. The benefice is a discharged *rectory*, valued in K.B. at £4. 19s. 7d., and now having a yearly modus of £230, awarded in 1843 in lieu of tithes. The Rev. H. J. Hasted, M.A., is patron and incumbent.

Alderton John, blacksmith
Burroughs James, wheelwright
Cooke Henry, schoolmaster
Fisher John, brick and tile maker
Gould Rev Fredk. curate of Bradfield St Clare
Hasted Rev Hy. John, M.A. *rector*
Hynard Isaac, vict. *Manger*

Mower Wm. shopkeeper
Ottley George, shoemaker
Walton Wm. Thomas, maltster
Young Miss Mary, *Bradfield Hall*
FARMERS.
Sharpe George || Ince Elizabeth
Steward James, *Block Farm*
Steward Wm. *Loft Farm*

BRADFIELD ST. CLARE, a scattered village and parish, 5 miles S.S.E. of Bury St. Edmund's, has 240 souls, and 1428 acres of fertile land, formerly the lordship of the Wenyeves. T. Walton, Esq., of the *Lodge*, and a few smaller owners, have estates here; but a great part of the parish, with the manor, belongs to the Rev. Robt. Davers, A.B., who is also patron of the *Church* (St. Clare) which has a tower and three bells, and is a *rectory*, valued in K.B. at £7. 4s. 7d., and now having a yearly modus of £280, awarded, in 1843, in lieu of tithes. The Rev. S. Isaacson is the incumbent. The *Hall*, occupied by a farmer, is an ancient moated house, formerly a retreat of the monks of Bury, and near it is a wood of 300 acres, partly in the adjoining parish of Bradfield St. George.

English Wm. shoemaker
Fisher Saml. brick and tile maker
Walton Wm. Thos. maltster, & agent to the Farmers' Fire & Life Office
Walton Thos. Esq. *Bradfield Lodge*
FARMERS.
Bruce Simon

Bullock John, *Petches Green*
Cornell George, *Petches Green*
Offord George, Elm green
Offord Henry, Bradfield Hall
Scott Wm. *Parsonage*
Stukeley Ann, *Elm Green*

BRADFIELD ST. GEORGE, or *Monks Bradfield,* lies north of the two preceding Bradfields, 4½ miles S.E. by S. of Bury St. Edmund's, and is a scattered village and parish, containing 479 inhabitats, and about 2000 acres of fertile and well-wooded land. It was given by Bishop Alfric and Earl Ulfketel to the monks of Bury, and was granted in the 31st of Henry VIII. to Sir Thomas Jermyn, Kt. The Rev. Robert Davers, A.B., is lord of the manor, but a great deal of the soil belongs to Lieutenant-Colonel Rushbrooke, M.P.; R. Maulkin, Esq., and several smaller free and copyholders. The *Church* (St. George) stands on so elevated a situation, that from the steeple, though only 66 feet high, may be seen sixty churches in this and the three adjoining counties. It is a neat structure, with five bells. The *rectory,* valued in K.B. at £11. 7s. 3½d., and in 1835 at £550, is in the patronage of the Marquis of Bristol, and incumbency of the Rev. Robert Davers, A.B. The titles were commuted in 1843. Here is a small *Baptist Chapel,* built in 1835. An annuity of £2 is paid to this parish for schooling four poor children, pursuant to the bequest of Thomas Sparke. (See Rougham.)

Davers Rev Robert, A.B. *Rectory*
Elmer Thos. butcher, *Broomley lane*
Francis James, shopkeeper
Lait Robt. shoemkr. *Cross green*
Last Abi, shopkeeper, *Free wood*
Last John, woodman, *Free wood*
Last Simon, wheelwright and woodman, *Linkwood*
Levett John, blacksmith, *Maypole*
Pattison Rev Edward, B.A. rector of Gedding, *Maypole green*
Rouse Robt. tailor, *Great green*
Sturgeon Humphry, woodman

Wade Wm. blacksmith, *Great green*
FARMERS. (* *are Owners.*)
*Beddell Geo. (*auctioneer and land agent,*) *West Farm.*
Bland Charles, *Maypole green*
Chickall Walter, *Bradfield Hall*
Eversham Joseph, *Maypole green*
*Hearn Roger, (maltster, corn miller, and mert.) *Bradfield Mills*
*Johnson James, Felsham road
*Maidwell Eliz. *Smallwood green*
Mallows James, *White Hall*

DRINKSTONE, a neat and pleasant village, built round a large green, 8 miles E. by S. of Bury St. Edmunds, has in its parish 505 souls, and 2,170 acres of land, well-wooded, and having a rich loamy soil and a thick bed of gravel. It was anciently the lordship of the noble family of Bouchier. John Moseley, Esq., is lord of the manor of *Drinkstone Lovaine,* and the Rev. Dr. Kilderbee is lord of the manor of *Drinkstone Timperley;* but a great part of the land belongs to the Grigby, Franklyn, Powell, Hart, Boldero, Steggall, and other families. *Drinkstone Park,* the seat of Mrs. Grigby, is well-wooded, and comprises 230 acres, of which 129 acres are in Hessett parish. The mansion is a large and handsome fabric, which was erected about 1760, by the late Joshua Grigby, who surrounded it with extensive plantations. About the same time, the Rev. Richard Moseley, the late rector, and lord of the first-named manor, built here a large and handsome house for his residence; but though called the *Rectory House,* it does not belong to the living, and is now the seat of Henry Franklyn, Esq. The *Church* (All Saints) is a neat structure, with a tower and six bells. The *Rectory,* vatued in K.B. at £16. 17s. 1d., has a yearly modus of £546, awarded in 1840 in lieu of tithes, and is in the patronage and incumbency of the Rev. Edgar Rust, M.A. In 1564, *John Wrenn* gave 15 acres of land, to be ploughed, tilled, and

sown by poor householders of Drinkstone, for their own profit; but it
is let for £17. 10s. per annum, which is distributed in bread-corn by
the rector and churchwardens. In 1692, *Thos. Camborne* bequeathed
the residue of his real estate, to be disposed of for setting and keeping to work the poor parishioners. The property belonging to this
charity is partly copyhold. and consists of a house and about 29A. of
land, let for £46 a year, which is mostly dispensed by the trustees in
apprenticeing poor children. A cottage, garden, and piece of waste
ground, are appropriated by ancient usage to the relief of *poor widows*,
and let for about £4 a year. The *Church Land*, 5 acres, is let for
£6. 6s. a year, which, with a rent-charge of 18s. 6d. per annum, is
applied to the repairs of the church. In 1804, the *Rev. Richard
Moseley* left £700 to be invested in the funds, for the support of *Day
and Sunday Schools*, for teaching poor children of Drinkstone and Rattlesden to read and write. This legacy was laid out in the purchase of
£1091. 3s. 6d. three per cent. consols. The dividends are employed in
supporting schools here and at Rattlesden.

Barrell Robert, butcher
Clover John, corn miller
Cocksedge William, land steward, *Drinkstone place*
Cottingham Lionel, surgeon
Franklyn Henry, Esq. *Rectory*
Grigby Mrs Anna, *Drinkstone Park*
Hawkins James, wheelwright
Jewers John, maltster
Manfield Jph. shopkr. and *carrier*
Manfield Martha, schoolmistress
Mortlock Wm. shopkeeper
Nunn John S. maltster, *Tyshurst*
Nunn Wm. blacksmith

Rust Rev Edgar, M.A. rector
Steggall Rev John, incumbent of Great Ashfield
Whiten Hannah, beerhouse
FARMERS. (* *are Owners.*)
*Cottingham Lionel || Boldero Wm.
Cooper Wm. *Whitefield House*
ᶜCraske John, sen.||Craske Mrs M.
Craske John, jun. *Timperleys*
*Jewers John || Death George
*Nunn James || Nunn J. S.
Raynham John, *Drinkstone Hall*
Whiten Samuel || Winter Mrs

FELSHAM, a well-built village, pleasantly situated 8 miles S.E.
of Bury, has in its parish 398 souls, and 1605 acres of land, rising to as
great an altitude as any in Suffolk. Fisk Harrison, Esq., is lord of the
manor, which was formerly held by Bury Abbey; but a great part of
the soil belongs to the Holmes, Garnham, Brooke, Davers, Cooke,
Hotham, Goodwin, Sturgeon, and a few other families. The mansion,
called the *Castle*, now divided into four tenements, stands on a lofty
eminence, and was the seat of the Reynolds, and afterwards of the late
Dr. Scott. It is now the property of Dr. Blitsoe. A *fair* for
lambs, &c., is held at Felsham on the 16th of August. The *Church*
(St. Peter) has a tower and six bells; and the living is a rectory, valued in K.B. at £8. 4s. 7d., and now having a yearly modus of £367,
awarded in 1841 in lieu of tithes. The Rev. Thomas Anderson is
patron and incumbent. The *Town and Poor's Estate* consists of the
Church House, occupied by paupers; 8½ acres of land, let for £25 a
year; a barn and 20 acres of land, let for £25 a year; half an acre at
Drinkstone, formerly a stone quarry; and a baker's shop and garden,
in Brackland, Bury St. Edmunds, now let for £10 a year, but the rent
will be considerably increased after the expiration of the lease. From
ancient time, the above-mentioned premises have been held in trust, as
to the property in Bury St. Edmund's, to distribute the rent in bread

among the poor; and as to the rest of the estate, to apply the rents and
profits for the repairs of the church, and the surplus to be disposed of
for the benefit and advantage of the parishioners.

Anderson Rev Thomas, *Rectory*
Barnes Wm. corn miller
Bigsby Jeremiah, baker
Brewer Henry, wheelwright
Brewer Thos. bricklayer & beerhs
Davers Charles, gent
Frost James, schoolmaster
Frost George, grocer and draper
Gladwell John, thatcher
Hall Mr John, *Felsham Castle*
Howe Francis, blacksmith
Kinsey Edmund, farm steward
Kinsey Wm. vict. Six Bells
Lankester Joseph & Co. grocers &
    drapers
Marshall Wm. farm steward

Morgan Mr Robert
Raffe James, shopman
Sturgeon Isaac, gent
    BOOT AND SHOE MAKERS.
Gill Wm. || Green John
Gladwell Joseph
            FARMERS.
Garnham Eliz. *Felsham Hall*
Gould John || Bogges George
Gosling Wm. || Kerridge George
King James, *Maiden Hall*
Melton Samuel, *Brook Hall*
Nunn Thomas || Roper Elijah
Sturgeon Chas. || Smith Thos.
Watkinson William

FORNHAM ST. GENEVIEVE is a fertile and picturesque parish, on the eastern side of the small but navigable river Lark, 2½
miles N.E. by N. of Bury St. Edmund's, containing only 700 acres of
land, and 70 inhabitants. It formerly belonged to Bury Abbey, and
was granted in the 31st of Henry VIII. to Sir Thomas Kitson. It
afterwards passed to Sir Wm, Gage, and in the early part of the present century, it was the seat and property of Samuel Kent, Esq. It
was purchased, with a large estate in the adjoining parish of Fornham
St. Martin, by Charles, the predecessor of the late Duke of Norfolk,
who occasionally resided at the beautiful seat called FORNHAM PARK,
which is extensive and well-wooded, and contains a handsome mansion,
and some remains of the parish *Church*, which was consumed by fire on
the 24th June, 1782, owing to the carelessness of a man who was
shooting at jackdaws. In July, 1843, the Duke of Norkfolk sold
the Fornham Estate, (comprising about 1600A,) to *Lord John Manners*, (a son of the Duke of Rutland,) for £75,550, so that his lordship
is now owner of this and most of the adjoining parish of St. Martin.
The *Rectory* of Fornham St. Genevieve is valued in K.B. at £7. 1s.
½d., and since the destruction of the church, it has been united with
Risby, which see. The tithes of this parish have been commuted
for £140 per annum. In 1173, a splendid victory was gained here by
Robert de Lucy, chief justice of England, at the head of the army of
Henry II., over the Earl of Leicester, the general of the foreign troops
employed by the king's rebellious sons, as noticed at page 622. The
numerous barrows called *Seven Hills*, under which many of the slain
in this battle are said to have been interred, are near the Thetford road,
7 miles N. of Bury. The poor parishioners have a yearly rent-charge
of 20s. out of the manor of Lackford, left by Lady Kitson; and two
others left by unknown donors, viz., £3. 8s. out of land at Culford, and
10s. out of land at Fornham. *Directory :*—Lord John Manners, M.P.,
Farnham Park ; John Muskett, Esq., land agent; Benj. Ennals,
gamekeeper; Joseph Green, clerk; James Petch, shepherd; and
Martin Spencley and John Warnes, farm bailiffs.

FORNHAM ST. MARTIN, a neat and pleasant village on the Thetford road, and near the termination of the *Lark Navigation,* (see page 603,) 2 miles N. of Bury St. Edmund's, has in its parish 294 souls, and about 1200 acres of land. *Fornham House,* a large and handsome mansion, is the seat of John Thomas Ord, Esq., who owns about 200 acres; and the rest of the parish, with the manor and advowson, was sold in 1843, by the Duke of Norfolk, to Lord John Manners, M.P., as noticed with the preceding parish. The *Church* (St. Martin) has a tower and three bells, and the living is a *rectory,* valued in K.B. at £7. 11s. 3d., and now having a yearly modus of £350. Lord John Manners is patron, and the Rev. Edward Hogg incumbent. Part of the small tithes belong to the rector of Fornham All Saints. The *Free School,* built by the Duke of Norfolk, in 1836, is supported by subscription. The poor have four rent-charges amounting to £2. 10s. per annum, left by unknown donors, and another of £2 left by Lady Kitson, out of the manor of Lackford. The *Town Land* was exchanged at the enclosure for an allotment of 2R. 14P., now let for 20s. a-year. A cottage has been held from time immemorial by the churchwardens, and the rent applied in repairing the church.

Alderton Joseph, carpenter
Baker John, corn miller, *Wind and Water Mills*
Cocksedge Misses, E. E. F. & M. *New Cottage*
Croft Saml. gent. Fornham cottage
Cutting Henry, vict. Swan
Cutting Robert, blacksmith
Fenner Charles, shopkeeper
Gardener Wm. gentleman
Gooderham Ellen, *Free School*
Hogg Rev Edward, *Rectory*
Liddle Thomas, vict. Woolpack
Ord John Thos. Esq. *Fornham hs*
Smith Thomas, shopkeeper
Smith Joseph, shoemaker

GEDDING, a small village and parish, 8 miles S.E. of Bury St. Edmund's and W. of Stowmarket, contains 173 souls and 501A. 3R. 21P. of fertile land. The *Hall,* an ancient moated mansion, formerly the seat of the Bokenhams, is now occupied by a farmer, and belongs, with the manor, to T. L. Ewen, Esq., but a great part of the soil belongs to Mrs. Elizabeth Mudd, the executors of the late Isaac Haselwood, Esq., and the executors of the late S. Hustler, Esq. The *Church* is a small fabric, with a tower and two bells, and the benefice is a discharged *rectory,* valued in K.B. at £4. 13s. 4d., and now having a yearly modus of £150, awarded in 1842 in lieu of tithes. The Rev. Edward Pattison, B.A., is incumbent, and the Corporation of Bury are patrons; the advowson being given to them many years ago by the will of Jeremiah Catling. *Directory :*—John Golding, *corn miller;* Wm. Middleton White, *surgeon;* and John Ennals, Thomas Maidwell, *(Hall,)* Eliz. Mudd, and Wm. Wade, *farmers.*

HESSETT, 5½ miles E. by S. of Bury St. Edmund's, is a pleasant village and parish, containing 417 souls, and 1568 acres of land, formerly belonging to the Abbot of Bury, by gift of Earl Ulfketel. It was granted in the 32nd of Henry VIII. to Thomas Bacon, and was afterwards the seat and manor of the *Le Heup* family. J. H. Powell, Esq., has an estate here, but the manor and the greater part of the soil belong to Chas. Tinglin and M. E. Rogers, Esqrs., who are also patrons of the *rectory,* valued in K.B. at £12. 17s. 11d., and in 1835, at £255, and now in the incumbency of the Rev. Thos. Ellis Rogers, M.A. The tithes were commuted in 1840. The *Church* (St. Ethel-

bert) is a handsome structure, with a tower and five bells, and was built by the *Bacons*, who resided here from the reign of Henry II. to that of Charles I. The *Poor and Town Estate*, held under deeds of very ancient date, in trust partly for the use of the poor, and partly for the common benefit of the parish, consists of the Guildhall, and four cottages occupied rent-free by poor families, and 12A. 1R. of land, let for £16. 16s. 6d. a year, of which £1 is paid to the parish clerk, and £4. 19s. is distributed among the poor; and the remainder is applied in the service of the church. The poor parishioners have also the dividends of £200 old South Sea Annuities, purchased in 1726, with money left by *Sir Jeffery Burwell*, in the 23rd of Charles II.

Aldridge Robert, cooper
Groom Mr James || John, par. clerk
Lawrence James, vict. *Five Bells*
Presland Robert, carpenter and shopkeeper
Raker Joel, bricklayer
Steggall Rev Wm., M.A. curate
Steggall Robert, blacksmith
Sturgeon James, carpenter
Tiffen Joseph, maltster

FARMERS.
Alderton Robert, *Elms Farm*
Bauly James || Canham Wm.
Groom Henry || Raker Joel
Robinson Samuel, *Free croft*
Taylor Ephraim, *Woad Hall*

SHOEMAKERS.
Austin Robert || Eaves Abraham
Manning John || Wilkins Wm.
Carrier to Bury, George Hubbard, Wednesday and Saturday

LIVERMERE MAGNA, or *Great Livermere*, a pleasant village, 5 miles N.N.E. of Bury St. Edmund's, has in its parish 320 souls, and 1580 acres of land, anciently belonging to the Bokenhams, and partly to Warden Abbey, in Bedfordshire. LIVERMERE PARK, now only visited as a sporting seat, comprises about 550 acres, well watered and wooded, and adjoining Ampton Park, from which it is separated by a serpentine lake, as already noticed at page 301. It contains about 300 head of deer. The hall, which is a large handsome mansion, was much improved, as well as the grounds, by the late Nathaniel Lee Acton, Esq., whose heiress married the late Sir Wm. Middleton. (See page 223.) Sir Wm. Fowle Fowle Middleton is now lord of the manor, and owner of nearly all the parish; but his mother, the Dowager Lady Middleton, has the patronage of the *rectory*, which is valued in K.B. at £15. 8s. 11½d., and, with that of Little Livermere annexed to it, is now worth about £440 per annum. The Rev. A. A. Colville, M.A., is the incumbent. The *Church* (St. Peter) is a small thatched structure, with a tower and five bells. Here is a *National School*, built in 1836, and now having about 60 scholars. The *Town Estate*, for the general benefit of the parishioners, consists of four tenements, with a croft of 1A. 2R., occupied rent-free by poor widows; three tenements with gardens let for £9 a year; and 26A. 3R. of land, let for £30 a year. The rents are distributed in coals, clothing, &c. among the poor. The four tenements occupied by poor widows, were rebuilt at the expense of the late N. Lee Acton, Esq., in 1792. This parish also participates in the benefits of the Charity School, at Ampton. (See page 302.)

Cockrill George, gentleman
Colville Rev Asgill A., M.A. *Rectory*
Crack Jonathan, shopkeeper

Cranis Mrs Elizabeth
Downing John, thatcher
Downs John, blacksmith
Hilder John, carpenter

Mothersole Philip, bricklayer
Mothersole Robert, shoemaker
Mothersole Wm. bricklayer
Methersole Wm. woodman
Seator Sarah Walker, schoolmistress
Tradget Zachariah, gamekeeper

Wolsey George, gardener
FARMERS.
Cooke James (and butcher)
Cutting John (and *Park keeper*)
Self Samuel ‖ Halls Charles

PAKENHAM, a large and well-built village, pleasantly situated on the banks of a small rivulet, 2 miles S. of Ixworth, and 5 miles N.E. by E. of Bury St. Edmund's, has in its parish many scattered houses, 1105 inhabitants, and 3696 acres of fertile land, including a *wood* of 124 acres, and a small enclosed *fen*. It is in four *manors*, viz., *Pakenham Hall*, belonging to Lord Calthorpe; *Maulkin's Hall*, the property of Joseph Wilson, Esq.; *Nether Hall* (a neat and commodious mansion,) the seat and property of Wm. Chinery Bassett, Esq.; and *New House* (a large ancient mansion,) the seat and estate of the Rev. W. J. Spring Casborne, who is also owner of the wood, and impropriator of the *Rectory*. But part of the parish belongs to the Quayle, Rogers, Tinglin, Thornhill, and a few other families. The rectory was appropriated by Edward I. to the abbey of Bury, and was granted, at the dissolution, to the family of the *Springs*, one of whom, Thomas Spring, a rich clothier, of Lavenham, died in 1510. From him descended *Wm. Spring*, of the "New House," Pakenham, who was created a *Baronet* in 1641; but the family ended in female issue about the middle of last century, and their estate and tithes here have descended to the Rev. W. J. Spring Casborne. *Sir John Ashfield*, of Nether Hall, was created a baronet in 1626, but his family has been long extinct. The ancient family of L'Estrange had also a seat here, which was sold to the Curwens, and passed from them to the Hollingsworths. *Barton Mere House*, at the source of the rivulet, 3 miles N.E. of Bury, is the seat of T. and W. Quayle, Esqs.; and *Pakenham Lodge* is the seat of Thomas Thornhill, Esq. The *Church* (St. Mary) is a neat structure, with a tower rising from its centre, and containing five bells. The *vicarage*, valued in K.B. at £10. 3s. 9d., and in 1835, at £281, is in the patronage of Lord Calthorpe, and incumbency of the Rev. Wm. Carpenter Ray, M.A. The tithes were commuted, in 1841, for a yearly modus of £908. 2s., about two-thirds of which belong to the impropriate rectory. Here is a *National School*, with a house for the master, built in 1842, and now attended by about 110 children. The TOWN ESTATE comprises about 54A. of land, in Pakenham, Thurston, Elmswell, Hepworth, and Walsham-le-Willows, let for about £58 per annum. Part of it was given by *Robert Stoke*, in 1525, that his *obit* might be kept yearly, and the surplus profit might be used for the benefit of the church. The rest of the estate was purchased with £66, bequeathed to the poor by *Robt. Gardiner, Nicholas Palfrey*, and other donors, except about 20 acres, which were awarded to the trustees, under an act of the 42nd of George III., for *enclosing* the open fields, &c., of Pakenham; and some other allotments awarded at the enclosure of Hepworth. For many years, the trustees applied the whole of the rents in the service of the church; but in 1824, a scheme was issued by the Court of Chancery for the future application of the charity, by which it is directed that only the rent of the land supposed to have been left by Robert Stoke, should be applied in the

repairs of the church, and that the remainder of the income should be distributed among the poor not receiving parochial relief. The portion belonging to the church is about £6. 14s. a year, so that there is upwards of £50 per annum for distribution among the poor parishioners. In 1651, *John Cooke* left £100, to be laid out in lands, the rents thereof to be divided among 20 poor people of Ixworth and Pakenham. It was laid out in the purchase of 10A. in Horningsheath, now let for £15 a year. In 1713, *Thomas Bright* left £100 to provide clothing for the poor of Thurston and Pakenham. In satisfaction of this charity, £5 a year is paid out of Nether Hall estate.

Bassett Wm. Chenery, Esq. *Nether Hall*
Bloomfield Wm. collar & harness mkr
Bridges Susan, vict. *Bell Inn*
Bridges Wm. cattle dealer
Brooks John, gamekeeper
Brooks Henry, plumber and glazier
Casborne Rev Walter John Spring, M.A. *New House*
Cox James, schoolmaster
Clemence Henry, vict. *Woolpack*
Farrow Frederick, cattle dealer
Jannings Misses J. E. E. and S.
Jones Rev Charles, M.A. curate, *Vicarage*
Langham Wm. gent. *Ixworth Bridge*
Potter Amos, butcher
Quayle Thomas and William, Esqs. *Barton Mere House*
Sheppeard George, gardener
Stedman Miss Frances
Thornhill Thos. jun. Esq. *Lodge*
FARMERS.
Cockrill John, *Beaumond's Hall*
Eaton Wm. Muskett, *Brusters*
Hilder Henry, *New House Farm*
Jacob Robert, *Red Castle*

Jacob Thomas, *Barton Merc*
Matthew George W. *Maulkin's Hall*
Mothersole Charlotte
Norbrooke Wm. *Fen*
Outlaw Thomas, *Red Castle cottage*
Potter Charles, *Fen*
Robinson Henry, *Bridge Farm*
Sparke Seth, *Nether Hall Farm*
Stedman Robert, *Manor House*

Bakers.
Chandler —
Mothersole Simn
Blacksmiths.
Calver James
Melton Sophia
Boot&ShoeMkrs.
Foreman Stn. *Fen*
Harrold James
Peck James
Bricklayers.
Millican Wm. *bhs*
Simper James
Carpenters, &c.
Cooper Edmund
Edwards Joseph, *Fen*

Elsden John
Melton George
Corn Millers.
Goodrich Clemnt.
Lowe Elizabeth
Grocers & Drprs.
Batterbee Brnbs.
Goodwin Thos.
Grimston end
Steggall John
Tailors.
Palmer Edward
Potter Js. (draper and hatter)
Carrier to Bury.
Wm. Leeder, W. and Saturday

RATTLESDEN, a large and well-built village, in a picturesque valley, on one of the sources of the river Gipping, 5 miles W. of Stowmarket, and 9 miles E.S.E. of Bury St. Edmund's, has in its parish 1142 souls, and about 3200 acres of land, generally having a fertile clayey soil, and including a small enclosed *fen*, several open greens, or commons, and the hamlets of *Poy street Green* and *Hightown Green*, from 1 to 2 miles S., and *Clopton Green*, 1 mile N. of the village. The greater part of the open fields, &c., were enclosed about ten years ago, and the fen about 70 years ago. *Clopton Hall*, with the estate attached to it, is the seat and manor of Captain Windsor Parker, and was long the residence of the Clopton family. John Moseley, Esq., is lord of the manor of Rattlesden, which was held by the Bishop of Ely till the fourth of Elizabeth, and was granted, in the second of James I., to Philip Tyse and Wm. Blake. It passed to the Moseleys in the early part of last century, together with the advowson of the rectory. The Cocksedge, Boldero, Mudd, Winson, Canham, Eaton, Firman, Pettit,

and some other families, have estates in the parish, and the soil is mostly freehold. The *Church* (St. Nicholas) is a neat edifice, with a tower, containing five bells, and surmounted by a spire. The *rectory,* valued in K.B. at £20. 0s. 2½d., has about 50 acres of glebe, and a yearly modus of £775, awarded, in 1840, in lieu of tithes. The Rev. James Oakes is the incumbent, and John Barney, Esq., has the next presentation. The *Baptists* have a chapel here, built in 1808, and rebuilt in 1823. The *National School,* attended by about 160 daily, and 240 Sunday scholars, has about £16 yearly from Moseley's Charity, as noticed with Drinkstone. The *Poor's Land,* 7A., was partly given by *Wm. Clopton,* in 1711, and is let for £10 a year. A tenement belonging to the church is let to the clerk for £3 a year. Here is a *Friendly Society,* and also a lodge of Odd Fellows.

Marked 1, *are at Clopton green ; 2, Fen ; 3, High-town green; 4, Poy-street green; 5, Potash ; and the rest in Rattlesden, or where specified.*

Chandler Wm. Wilson & Mrs. *National School*
Cousins Rev Jph. M.A. *curate*
Cross Pearl, wheelwright
Death Charles, butcher
Ennals Mrs Mary Ann
3 Gowers James, beerhouse keeper
Parker Capt. Windsor, *Clopton Hall*
Poole Wm. collar and harness mkr.
Punchard Jeremiah, parish clerk
Salmon Abraham, tailor and draper
Smith George, vict. *Five Bells*
Winson Robert, corn miller
Salmon Wm. vict. *Half Moon*

Bakers.
Roper Hy. Clement
Salmon Wm.

Blacksmiths.
Chaplin Samuel
Holden Michael
3 Poole John

Boot&ShoeMkrs.
Abbott Wm.
Beeton Samuel
Fayers Benj.

3 Gowers Benj.

Bricklayers.
Firman Anderson
Firman George
Smith James
Smith George

Joiners, &c.
3 Chaplin Robt.
Plume John and Son
5 Ranson James

FARMERS.
(* are owners.)
Bird Canler, *Shelland Hall*
*Boldero John, *Whitehouse*
Bye W. *(steward) Dew's farm*
3 Chaplin Shadh.
Cobbold James
Cooper Ann
4 Edgar Ann
3 Ellis James
4*Firman Geo.
3 Friston Saml.
3 Green Benj.
Groom Charles, *Wood hall*
4 Jackson Eliz.
Jewers John
Kent, Robt. *Hall*
3 Langham Wm.
*Manfield Wm. *Holly Bush*
3*Merrington Rt.
3*Merrington W.
5 Moore Wm.
* Osborne Ann
2 Pettit Peter
Plume John
4 Reeve John
1 Salmon James

3 Sawyer Edwd *Burnt House*
Scott Jas. *Woodhouse*
4 Snell John
Sparke Robert
2 Taylor John
3*Taylor Wm.
*Winson Robt.
Maltsters.
3 Green Benj.
Jewers John
Salmon Wm.
Painters, Plumbers, & Glaziers.
Beeton Wm. and Son
Chandler Henry
Shopkeepers.
Archer Robert
Chandler Wm.
Wilson
3 Moore John
Roper Hy. Clemt.
Scolding James
3 Snelon Richd.
4 Youngman Js.
Carriers to Bury Wed. and Sat.
Moore Robert
Ramsbottom Ab.
4 Youngman Jas

ROUGHAM, a scattered village, from 3 to 4 miles E. by S. of Bury St. Edmund's, has in its parish several neat mansions and commodioue farmhouses, 969 inhabitants, and about 3846 acres of fertile land. Th, manor and most of the soil are the property of Philip Bennet, sen., Esq., of *Rougham Hall,* a neat mansion with extensive pleasure gro unds near *New Hall,* the seat of Capt. Philip Bennet, jun. ; and the remainder belongs to the Rev. N. Colvile, D.D., and a few smaller owners. The manor formerly belonged to Bury abbey, and *Eldo,* or *Old-*

haugh, an ancient house now occupied by Col. Ray, was a grange of the abbot, but was granted by Henry VIII., with other large possessions, to the Jermyns, from whom it passed through various families to the Cocksedges. Rougham Hall was long the property of the Drurys, and, in 1810, belonged to Roger Kerington, Esq. *Rookery Hall* is the seat of Robt. Bevan, Esq. " By indenture, dated 10 Henry VIII., Sir Wm. Waldegrave, kt., *sold* to Margaret Drury, of Rougham, widow, the wardship of Edmund Wrest, *to be married* to Dorothy Drury, her daughter." The same lady, by another indenture, *bought* of Robt. Radcliffe, Lord Fitzwalter and Egremont, the wardship of Elizabeth Day, a rich heiress, whom she married to her second son Francis!!! The *Church* (St. Mary) is a large and handsome structure, with a tower and five bells, and contains an ancient monument of Sir Roger Drury and his lady, who died in 1400 and 1405, and are interred beneath a flat stone, about four feet high, adorned with their figures in brass. The preservation of this antique tomb is no doubt owing to a pew, built over it, having concealed it from the view of the church spoliators of the 17th century. The *rectory*, valued in K.B. at £23. 18s. 6½d., has now a yearly modus of £940, awarded in 1815 in lieu of tithes. Philip Bennet, Esq., is *patron*, and the Rev. Robt. Davers, A.B., of Bradfield St. George, is *incumbent*.

The *Poor's Estate* consists of an *almshouse* for aged poor ; and 2½A. of land allotted at the *enclosure*, in 1813, in lieu of land purchased with the benefactions of *John Sparke and Wm. Ling.* This land is let for £6 a year. The *Poor's Allotment* consists of 9A. 2R. 30P., awarded to the poor parishioners at the enclosure, in compensation of their right of cutting furze on the commons. It is rented by the parish to employ the poor when out of work, at the yearly rent of £13. 10s. which is distributed in coals, in winter. An allotment of 3A. 25P. was awarded at the enclosure, in lieu of open field land, which had been appropriated from ancient time to the repairs of the church. In the 23rd of Charles II., *Sir Jeffery Burwell, kt.*, settled a messuage and 4A. 1R. 22P. of land at Rougham, in trust to distribute the rents in clothing poor women of the parish. There are now four cottages on the land, and the whole is let for £25 a year. Two of the cottages were built about 30 years ago at the cost of £207, which has been paid out of the rents. The sum of £80, left by *Sir Jeffery Burwell* to purchase £4 a year for apprenticing poor children of Rougham, and for paying 20s. a year to the parish clerk for keeping the donor's monument in repair, was laid out, in 1726, in the purchase of £135. 10s. 10d. Old South Sea Annuities. In 1702, *Roger Kerington* left £200 to be laid out in land, and the rents thereof to be applied in apprenticing poor boys of Rougham and the parish of St. Mary, in Bury St. Edmund's, alternately. This legacy was laid out in the purchase of 21A. 3R. 19P. of land at Barningham, now let for £35 a year. P. Bennet, Esq., is the trustee. In 1720, *Edmund Sparke* bequeathed his estates here and at Thurston for the foundation of a FREE SCHOOL at Rougham, and willed that four of the free scholars should be selected from Thurston, by the minister of that parish. The school estate comprises a house for the master, a school-room, an orchard, and 7A. 27P. of land, in Rougham ; and a farmhouse and 14A. of land at Thurston. The master occupies the school house and 3A. 35P. of land, and the remainder is let for £47 a year. He is appointed by the rector, and instructs 16 free scholars. In 1721, *Thomas Sparke* left out of 50A. of land, (now belonging to J. Case, Esq.,) a yearly rent-charge of £7. 16s. for a weekly distribution of 30s. worth of bread among the poor of Rougham ; and £4 a year for schooling eight small children of Rougham and Bradfield St. George.

Marked 1, *live at Battley's* ; 2, *Black-thorpe* ; 3, *High-Rougham* ; 4, *Howe-Corner* ; 5, *Kingshall street;* 6, *Nether street; and* 7, *at Roug-ham green.*

2 Bauly Edward, wheelwright

Bennet Capt. Philip, *New Hall*

Bennet Philip, Esq. *Rougham Hall*

5 Bennet Wm. shoemaker

Bevan Robt. Esq. *Rookery Hall*

7 Buckley Wm. shoemaker & shopr.

3 Chapman George, blacksmith

6 Crofts John, parish clerk

3 Drake John, butcher

6 Green John, schoolmaster

5 Hammond Elizabeth, shopkeeper

2 Levett John, blacksmith

7 Levett John, jun. schoolmaster

7 Oakes Rev H. A. curate of Nowton

5 Olle Francis, beer seller

5 Parish Thomas, blacksmith

7 Quayle Rev Thos. M.A. curate

2 Race John, gardener

1 Ray Colonel Philip, *Eldo House*

1 Scotman Rev Thomas

7 Stiff Charles, shopkeeper

FARMERS.

4 AbrahamRobt.

5 Cornish Geo.

5 Cornish Wm.

3 Edgar Richard

Edwards Margt.

4 Everard Thos.

2 Garnham Geo.

7 Golding Wm.

Gurling John (& miller,) *Heath*

1 Halton Daniel

Hayward Chas.

Moat Farm

7 Johnson Mrs

7 Levett George

7 Melton Chltte.

5 Olle Wm.

Roper Robert, *Rougham pl.*

7 Stiff Charles

7 Stiff Robert

RUSHBROOKE, a pleasant village and parish, on the east side of the small river Lark, 3 miles S.E. of Bury St. Edmund's, has 175 inhabitants, and 1066 acres of land, all the property and manor of Lieut. Colonel Rushbrooke, M.P., of *Rushbrooke Hall*, a large moated mansion, forming three sides of a square, and standing in an extensive and well-wooded park, skirted on the west by the river which supplies the moat, and a lake of 7 acres. It was held by the Abbey of Bury, and was granted by Henry VIII. to the *Jermyns*, who resided here, and rose to considerable eminence. Sir Thomas Jermyn was privy councillor and comptroller of the household to Charles I. His second son, Henry, was created *Lord Jermyn* of St. Edmund's Bury, in 1644, and *Earl of St. Albans*, in 1660. He died in 1683, when the earldom became extinct, but the barony devolved on his nephew, Thomas Jermyn, who died in 1703, without male issue. Henry, the younger brother of the latter, was created Baron Jermyn, of Dover, but died without issue in 1708. The heiress of the Jermyns carried their estates, in marriage, to Robt. Davers, Esq., only son of *Sir Robert Davers*, of Rougham, who was created a baronet in 1682. On the death of Sir Charles Davers, Bart., without issue male, in 1806, the Rushbrooke estate devolved to Robert Rushbrooke, Esq., whose family had anciently held, and took their name from it. The hall witnessed some of the festivities occasioned by Queen Elizabeth's progress through the county, in 1578, when " Sir Robert Jermyn, of Roesbroke, feasted the French embassadors two several times, with which charges and courtesie they stood marvellously contented." The *Church* (St. Nicholas) is a small neat structure, with a tower and three bells, and contains several monuments of the Jermyns. The rectory, valued in K.B. at £8. 1s. 5¼d., is consolidated with that of Bradfield St. George, (see page 306,) in the gift of the Marquis of Bristol, and incumbency of the Rev. Robert Davers, A.B.. The tithes were commuted in 1841. The *Almshouse* here, for three poor women and one poor man, was rebuilt by Thomas, Lord Jermyn, who endowed it, in 1700, with a yearly rent-charge of £15. 8s. 4d., out of a house in St. James's square, London, now belonging to the Marquis of Clanricarde. In 1640, William and

Henry Jermyn, Esqrs., granted to the almspeople a yearly rent-charge of £5, out of a moiety of the manor of Thorpe Hall, in West Wretham, in Norfolk.   There is also belonging to the almshouse 10A. 2R. 13P. of land, in St. Mary's parish, Bury St. Edmund's, let for £8 a year, and allotted at an enclosure, in lieu of other land given by an unknown donor.   The sum of £125 three per cent. consols, was purchased with money received some years ago for wood standing upon the land which was exchanged at the enclosure.   The almspeople have each 2s. per week, and a supply of coals and clothing yearly. Here is another almshouse of four tenements, erected by *Sir Jermyn Davers*, about 1724, but it is not endowed.   It is repaired by the owner of the Rushbrooke estate, and is occupied, rent free, by poor families.

Rushbrooke Lieut. Col. Robt. M.P. for the Western Division of Suffolk, *Rushbrooke Hall*
Denton John Fredk. farmer, *Green*
Denton Wm. farmer, *Bridge farm*
Eyres Col. Geo. Wm., *Hall*

Hammond John, shepherd
Lock Jonathan, parish clerk
Ranson Wm. shoemaker
Sturgeon George, farmer, *Hall farm*
Tooley George, gamekeeper
Wigg Joseph, gardener

STANNINGFIELD, 5 miles S. by E. of Bury St. Edmund's, is a village and parish containing 327 souls, and 1431 acres of land, including the estate and mansion called *Coldham Hall*, belonging to Sir Thomas Gage, lord of the manor, (formerly belonging to the Rokewodes,) owner of most of the parish, and patron of the *rectory,* valued in K.B. at £8. 0s. 2½d., and now having a yearly rent-charge of £350, awarded in lieu of tithes in 1840.   The Rev. Thomas Image, M.A., is the incumbent.   The *Church* (St. Nicholas) is a small ancient structure.   The parish enjoys a share of Corder's charity, as noticed with Glemsford, and some of its inhabitants are partly employed in making *Tuscan straw plat.*

Atkinson John, shopkeeper
Brett George, shoemaker
Cornish Edw. thatcher & beerhouse
Gooch John, gamekeeper
Musk John, shoemaker
Reeman James, blacksmith
Smith Joseph, surgeon
Taylor Robt. C. Esq. *Coldham Hall*

FARMERS.   (* are Owners.)
Borley Joseph || Webb Edw. *hind*
Clarke Benj. (and maltster)
Makin Abraham || Mayston E.
*Rollinson Geo. *Little Rokewode*
Sargent Thos. || Smith James
*Talbot James, *Stanningfield Hall*

THURSTON, a scattered village and parish, pleasantly situated 5 miles E. by N. of Bury St. Edmund's, has 599 inhabitants, and about 2400 acres of fertile land, belonging to W. C. Bassett, Esq. (lord of the manor of Nether Hall,) P. Bennett, Esq., James Bunbury Blake, Esq., (of *Thurston House*,) and the Stedman, Bacon, Jannings, Smith, Oakes, Armstrong, and a few other families.   *Thedwestry Hill*, in this parish, is the only place that bears the name of the Hundred.   The *Church* (St. Peter) has a tower and five bells, and was appropriated to Bury Abbey; but the rectory, and the advowson of the vicarage, were granted in the 5th of James I. to William Blake and George Tyte.   Chas. Tyrell, Esq., is now patron of the *vicarage,* valued in K.B. at £6. 13s. 4d., and in 1835 at £250, and now enjoyed by the Rev. Jas. Oakes, M.A.   The *Church Estate* consists of a double cottage and garden, and 8A. 1R. 35P. of land, in Thurston, and 3A.

17P. in Barton, let at rents amounting to £21. 11s. per annum. About 5 acres of the land was given by Thomas Rose, in 1492, but it is not known how the other part of the estate was acquired. The *Town Lands,* let for £20 a year, consist of 7A. 3R. 24P. in Stanton, and 5A. 1R. 18P. in Badwell-Ash. The land at Stanton was purchased with £53 given by Sir Robert Gardener and others. The rents are distributed among the poor parishioners, about Christmas. The *Poor's Allotment,* 10A. 3R. 14P., was awarded at the enclosure in the 43rd of George III., in trust for the poor, in lieu of their right of cutting fuel. The rent, £9 a year, is distributed in coals. The poor parishioners have £2. 10s. yearly, in clothing, from *Bright's Charity,* (see Pakenham,) and the interest of £20, left by Charles Warren, in 1662.

Bennet James, shopkeeper
Bennet Thomas beerhouse
Blake Jas. Bunbury Esq. *Thurston House*
Boreham James, carpenter
Cock Richard, plumber & glazier
Hall Jno. baker and parish clerk
Pearl Edmund, corn miller
Pridgeon Wm. vict. *Victoria*
Ranson Wm. bricklayer
Smith Mrs Alice

Blacksmiths.
Bradley Robert
Church Harriet

Marriott Mathias

Boot&ShoeMkrs.
Bennet Samuel

Drake Daniel
Simpson John
FARMERS.
(* are Owners.)
Baker Edmund, *Vicarage*
Boreham Eliz.
*Catchpole John
Cook Thomas
Jannings John, sen. & junior, *Grove*
Knights John

Last Jno. *Thedwestry Hill*
Ranson Robt.
Smith George, *Barton Mere*
Smith Wm. (and maltster)
Tailors.
Ayliffe Wm.
Baker Robert
Wheelwrights.
Bush Peter
Hawkes
Presland Thos.

TIMWORTH, 3½ miles N. of Bury St. Edmunds, is a small village and parish, containing 212 souls, and 1220 acres of land, all the property and manor of the Rev. Edward Richard Benyon, of Culford Hall, who is also patron and incumbent of the *rectory,* which is valued in K.B. at £9. 17s. 11d., and is consolidated with Ingham. The *Church* (St. Andrew) is a small neat structure, with a tower and four bells. The *Poor's Land,* (about 3A.) is let for £3. 10s., and was partly purchased with £40. 5s., arising from two benefactions. The rent is distributed among the poor parishioners about Christmas. *Directory:—* Joseph Clark, gardener; John Davey, shoemaker; Abraham Hawke, shoemaker and shopkeeper; Wm. Harrison, farmer, *Timworth Hall;* and Wm. Walton, farmer, *Timworth Cottage.*

TOSTOCK, a neat village, 7 miles E. of Bury St. Edmund's, has in its parish 367 inhabitants, and 975 acres of land. The manor belonged to Brithulf, son of Leoman, the Saxon; but Baldwin, Abbot of Bury, begged it, with other estates, of William the Conqueror. It afterwards passed to the family of the Lords North and Grey, who had their seat at Tostock Place; but the Hall was the seat of Wm. Berdewell, in 1445. The parish is now in two manors, viz., New Hall, of which Dr. Browne is lord, and Little Hall, of which Mr. Braddock is lord; but part of the soil belongs to W. and P. Ray, Esqrs., and several smaller owners. *Tostock Hall,* a neat mansion, with pleasant grounds on one of the tributary streams of the river Thet, is now unoccupied. The *Church* (St. Andrew) has a tower and five bells, and is a discharged *rectory,* valued in K.B. at £6. 8s. 6d., and now having a yearly modus of £307, awarded in 1843 in lieu of tithes. The Rev.

Wm. Tuck is patron, and the Rev. James Oakes, M.A., incumbent.
The *Poor's Estate* comprises 2A. 1R. 8P., in this parish, and 3A. in
Bayton, and was vested in trust pursuant to the directions of the Court
of Chancery, in 1817, that the acting overseer should distribute the
rents in bread and clothing among the most needy poor of the parish.
The rents amount to £10 per annum.

Flatt Thomas, vict. *Royal William*
Goold George, wheelwright
Marriott Matthias, blacksmith
Matthews Luke, vict. *Gardeners' Arms*
Oakes Rev James, M.A. *Rectory*
Pollard Jas. bricklayer and *carrier*

Boot&ShoeMkrs.
Bennington Jno.
(and shopkpr)
Crofts John
Everett John
Frost Wm.

FARMERS.
(* are Owners.)

*Bacon John
Bowen Mary
Howel Samuel
Jennings John
MarriottMathew
*Ray Walter
*Willis Harrgtn.

WELNETHAM, (GREAT) a scattered village on the east side of
the river Lark, four miles S.S.E. of Bury St. Edmund's, has in its parish 1409A. 1R. 26P. of fertile land, and 514 inhabitants, of whom 288
are in SICKLESMERE, a neat *hamlet*, which has also 47 inhabitants
in the parish of Little Welnetham. Here was a small house of *Crouched*
or *Crossed Friars*, which was dedicated to St. Thomas-a-Becket, and
was granted by Henry VIII. to Anthony Rous. Camden says great
quantities of potsherds, and platters of Roman manufacture, also ashes,
bones of sheep and oxen, many horns, a sacrificing knife, urns, and
other relics, have been found here. Sir Richard Gipps, who died at
the Manor House in 1708, found in the parish the head of a Roman
spear, a sacrificing knife, vessels, coins, bricks, and pateras, one of which
was inscribed ANISIM. The manor passed from the Jermyns to the
Symonds, and is now held by the Rev. Jas. Wm. Wenn, but the greater
part of the parish belongs to the Marquis of Bristol, the Rev. Fredk.
Le Grice, Henry Le Grice, Sir W. F. F. Middleton, and H. J. Oakes,
Esq. The *Church* is a small neat fabric, and the benefice is a Rectory, valued in K.B. at £9. 15s. 7½d., and now having a yearly modus of
£405, awarded in 1843, in lieu of tithes. Frederick Wing, Esq., is
patron, and the Rev. Henry G. Phillips, M.A., is the incumbent. In
1814, *Mrs. Mary Green* left £200 to provide for a yearly distribution
of coals among the poor parishioners, and it is now vested in £289.
12s. 6d. three per cent consols.

GREAT WELNETHAM.
Borley Wm. baker and beerhouse
Brooks Zachariah, corn miller, Cha-
  pel hill
Crick John, cattle dealer
Deakin Roger W. bricklayer
Fenton John, auctioneer, maltster,
  and land agent, *Welnetham Hall*
Fenton Samuel, jun. land agent
Hibble John, corn miller
Phillips Rev Hy. G., M.A. *Rectory*
FARMERS.
  John ‖ Fenton Frederick
Cooke John, *Water lane*
Fenton Jeremiah & Son, *Copy farm*
Fenton Samuel, *Manor farm*

Lee John, *Brundish farm*
Reeman Wm. *Skippers*
Warren Robert, *Cock's green*

SICKLESMERE.
Marked are in Little, and the others
  in Great Welnetham Parish.
*Alderton Robert, blacksmith
Bennett James, gentleman
Brundish Wm. blacksmith
Frost Mr Edward
Farrow Isaac, butcher
Gurton Mrs. cowkeeper
Holt Wm. grocer and dep. registrar
Hubbard Wm. butcher

*Hasted Rev Henry John, rector of Little Welnetham and Bradfield-Combust
*Major Wm. Dench, wheelwright and vict. *Rushbrooke Arms*
Major Lucy, schoolmistress
Pryke Wm. wheelwright
*Tooley Wm. farm bailiff

Ungless John, grocer, glover, and breeches maker
Warren Reuben, bricklayer
Wright Thomas, drawing master
Shoemakers.
Avis Thomas || Grimwood John
Osborne Joseph || *Ranson George

WELNETHAM, (LITTLE) a village and parish, 3 miles S.S.E. of Bury St. Edmund's, contains only 570 acres of land, and 206 inhabitants, of whom 47 are in the hamlet of *Sicklesmere,* which is mostly in the parish of Great Welnetham. The manor was successively held by the Weylands, Burghershes, Despensers, Langleys, and Davers, and is now held by Henry James Oakes, Esq., but part of the soil belongs to R. Rushbrooke, Esq., and a few smaller owners. The farm house at *Chapel Hill* is a very ancient structure, supposed to have belonged to the Crouched Friars, noticed above. The *Church* (St. Mary) is a small structure, with a tower and three bells. The living is a discharged *rectory*, valued in K.B. at £4. 13s. 4d., and now having a yearly modus of £155, awarded in 1843, in lieu of tithes. The Marquis of Bristol is patron, and the Rev. Henry John Hasted, M.A., is the incumbent. The other principal inhabitants, exclusive of Sicklesmere, are James Alderton, *blacksmith;* Robert Martin Carse, farmer, *Hall;* and James Ayres, farmer, *Chapel hill.*

WOOLPIT, a large and well-built village, with several neat mansions, 8 miles E. by S. of Bury St. Edmund's, and 6 miles N.W. by W. of Stowmarket, has in its parish 942 inhabitants, and about 2000 acres of land. It has a large annual *fair,* commencing on Sept. 16th, for horses, and on Sept. 19th, for cattle and toys. Dr. Gale and some other antiquaries place the Roman station *Sitomagus* here, rather than at Thetford or Haughley. (See page 271.) Woolpit is certainly an ancient place; Roman coins, &c., have often been discovered in the parish; and in a meadow near the church is a large moated area, having in its centre a fine spring, called *Lady's Well,* said to possess medicinal virtues for the cure of sore eyes. A very white and durable kind of brick, equal in beauty to stone, is made here, and is well known under the denomination of *Woolpit brick.* Many mansions in various parts of the county have been built of it. The manor and advowson belonged to Bury Abbey, and were granted by James I. to Sir Robert Gardiner. J. H. Powell, Esq., is now lord of the manor, but a great part of the soil belongs to Capt. W. Parker, George Jackson, Esq., Charles Tyrell, Esq., Rev. Sir G. W. Crauford, W. Caldecott, Esq., and a few smaller owners. The *Church* (St. Mary) is a fine Gothic structure, with a tower containing five bells, and surmounted by a spire. If was thoroughly repaired in 1843. The north porch is highly decorated, and has a room above it. Over the entrance are five niches, with ornamental finials. There is also a niche in each of the two buttresses at the corner of the chancel. Tradition reports that there was in the church a shrine to the Virgin Mary, to which pilgrims resorted, and that there was a chapel near the spring called Lady's Well, which is quadrangular and bricked, and supplies the moat already noticed. The *rectory,* valued in K.B. at £6. 18s. 9d., and in 1835 at £350, is in the

patronage of Mrs. Page, and incumbency of her husband, the Rev. L. F. Page. The Primitive Methodists have a small chapel here. The *National School* was built in 1836, at the cost of £360, and here is also an Infant School, established in 1837. The POOR'S LANDS, given for the relief of poor parishioners by *Sir R. Gardiner*, and persons named *Bitton, Kent, Webb*, and *Clarke*, comprise 15A. 2R. 5P. in Woolpit, let for £38 per annum, and 5A. 2R. 34P. in Rattlesden, let for £10 a year. Of these rents £3 is distributed in bread, and the remainder in small sums, about Christmas. In 1728, *Fras. Beales* left two tenements to provide for a quarterly distribution of bread among 52 poor parishioners, and they are now let for £5. 10s. a year. The *Church Lands*, 6A. 2R. 37P. in Woolpit and Hunston, are let for £14 a year. Three poor women are sent from this parish to *Gardiner's Almshouse.* (See Elmswell.)

POST OFFICE, at Mr G. B. Jackson's. Letters despatched to Ipswich, &c., at ½ p. 6 morning, and to Bury, &c. at 7 evening

Archer Thomas Coates, solicitor
Baker Philip, land surveyor, *Lawn Farm*
Caldecott Wm. Esq. *Kiln Farm*
Clayton Rev Edw. M.A. curate
Crabb Denny, land agt. *Kiln Farm*
Fiske Mr Thomas
Folkard Samuel, hair dresser
Garrard James, watchmaker
Howlett John, parish clerk
Hunt John, grocer and draper, and agent to the Norwich Union Fire Office
Hunt Sellsby, gentleman
Hustler Orbell, gentleman
Jackson Geo. Bridges, postmaster
Jackson Samuel, gentleman
Keeble Robert, cabinet maker
Page Rev Luke F., M.A., *Rectory*
Page Mrs. *Woolpit Cottage*
Rednall Mr John
Slater John, surgeon
Tricker Philip, saddler
Wiffan Wm. farrier
Woodgate Wm. cooper

INNS AND TAVERNS.
Crown, Richard Sage
Plough, John Avey
Swan, John Hunt Cuthbert
Beer House, Wm. Coe

Academies.
Folkard Jem
Sidney Michael
Sidney Mary
Woodgate Susan

Bakers.
Lucas Wm.
Nunn John
Potter Nathl.

Blacksmiths.
Howlett James
Moyse James

Boot & Shoe Mkrs.
Burt Robert
Green Thomas
Howe Wm.
Lummas Wm.
Pollard Robert
Rice John

Bricklayers.
Abbott Wm.
Morley Abm.

Brick & Tile Mkrs
Caldecott W. Esq
Pilbrow & Fisher
Wright Reuben
Wright Robert; h *Elmswell*

Butchers.
Graham Robert
Joyslan Robert
Morley David

Carpenters, &c.
Moore Maurice
Rednall John
Snell Edward

Corn Millers.
Bauly George
Robinson Geo.

FARMERS.
Baker Philip
Beckett Joseph
Biddell George
Blundell John
Caldecott Wm.
Hall Joshua
Palmer George
Roper Wm.
Stiff Thomas

Painters, Plumbers, & Glaziers.
Broom John
Cock John
Cock Thomas

Tailors.
Cooper George
Girdlestone Owen
Sidney John Barrett

Wheelwrights.
Blundell John & Son, *Heath*
Richer Stephen

CARRIER.
Wilden Abm. to Bury, Wed & Sat; and Ipswich, Monday & Thursday

HARTISMERE HUNDRED

Forms an *Union* under the New Poor Law, and a *Deanery*, which was formerly in the Archdeaconry of Sudbury, but was added to the *Archdeaconry of Suffolk*, in 1837, and is still in the *Diocese of Norwich*. It is one of the Geldable Hundreds of Suffolk, and the *fee* of it was granted in tail male by Edward III. to Robert de Ufford, Earl of Suffolk. J. Heigham, Esq., of Hunston Hall, is now *lord* of this fee. It is a fertile district, averaging about ten miles in length and breadth, and bounded on the north by the river Waveney, which separates it from Norfolk; on the west, by Blackbourn Hundred; on the south, by Stow, Bosmere-and-Claydon, and Thredling Hundreds; and on the east, by Hoxne Hundred. It is watered by several rivulets, running northward to the Waveney; and is a well-wooded and fertile district, rising in picturesque undulations, but subsiding in a champaign tract near the Waveney. It has generally a strong loamy soil, and has a substratum of impervious *blue clay*, lying at the depth of from one to two feet. It includes the *Borough of Eye*, and the small *towns* of Botesdale and Mendlesham; and is divided into 32 *parishes*, of which the following is an enumeration, shewing their territorial extent, the annual value of their lands and buildings, as assessed to the property tax in 1815, and their population in 1801 and 1841.

PARISHES.	Acrs.	Rental.	Populatn. 1801.	1841.	PARISHES.	Acres.	Rental. £.	Population. 1801.	1841.
Aspall........	827	997	87	132	Rishangles....	719	582	192	261
Bacton	2231	2750	585	800	Stoke Ash	1173	1471	275	423
‡Botesdale twp.	1260	1565	565	633	Stuston	798	872	180	252
*Braiseworth..	722	872	105	151	*Thorndon	2680	2768	526	732
*Brome	893	1743	278	328	Thornham Mag	1327	2287	295	374
Burgate	2034	2524	296	369	Thornham Pva.	670	875	123	203
Cotton	1922	2425	441	545	*Thrandeston	1379	1505	305	373
*Eye *Old Boro*†	4174	6475	1734	2493	Thwaite	832	1243	129	176
Finningham ..	1235	1918	373	480	Westhorpe ..	1322	1706	199	264
Gislingham ..	2251	3091	473	669	Wethering- ⎫				788
Mellis........	1344	1442	371	530	sett-cum- ⎬	3777	4696	851	
Mendlesham ..	3880	5747	1051	1340	Brockford ⎭				277
*Oakley	1280	1428	298	355	Wickhm Skeith	1770	2293	442	574
*Occold	1480	2093	397	578	†Wortham	2727	3874	784	1116
Palgrave	1475	1995	580	730	Wyverstone ..	1523	1749	243	348
‡Redgrave	2059	2740	530	719	*Yaxley	1239	1617	382	507
*Redlingfield ..	1075	1020	212	240					
Rickinghall Spr	1401	1890	565	768	Total	53,479	70,433	13,897	18,530

* The eight parishes marked thus * were added to the *Parliamentary Borough of Eye*, by the Reform Act of 1832, as also were Denham and Hoxne, in Hoxne Hundred.

‡ *Botesdale* is a town and township, in Redgrave parish.

☞ CHIEF CONSTABLES.—Mr. John Hayward, of Thorndon; and Mr. John Seaman, of Brockford.

PETTY SESSIONS, for the Municipal Borough of Eye, are held there every Saturday; and for the Hundred, they are held at *Botesdale, Stoke Ash*, and *Thwaite*, alternately, viz., 22 times a-year at the first, 11 times a-year at the second; and 12 times a-year at the last named place.

† HARTISMERE UNION has its *Workhouses at Eye and Wortham*. That at the former place had 56, and that at the latter place had 97 inmates.

in July, 1841. The former is chiefly for the reception of able-bodied poor and infants; and the latter chiefly for boys and girls, who are employed in making shoes, clothing, &c. These houses were built in the latter part of last century, by the parishes in which they are situated, but have been considerably altered and enlarged since the Hundred was constituted an Union, under the new poor law, in 1835. In 1779, Hartismere, Hoxne, and Thredling Hundreds, were incorporated for the support of the poor; but as they never raised the sum of £16,000, required for the erection of a House of Industry, the incorporation was never carried into effect; several parishes considering it more benefical to erect workhouses of their own. The 32 parishes of Hartismere Hundred and Union comprise an area of 53,479 acres, and 18,530 souls, as has been seen in the foregoing table. The average annual expenditure on the poor of these parishes, during the three years preceding the formation of the Union, was £19,212. Their expenditure in 1838 was £9258; in 1839, £8617. 11s.; and in 1842, £7891. The Guardians meet every Monday, at the Board-room, in Eye. Sir Edw. Kerrison, Bart., is *Chairman of the Board;* and the Rev. Dr. Day and Mr. J. Kirby are the *Vice-Chairmen.* Mr. Chas. Fisher Costerton, of Eye, is *Union Clerk & Superintendent Registrar;* and Mr. Geore Mudd, of Eye, is *Registrar of Marriages* for the whole Union. The REGISTRARS OF BIRTHS AND DEATHS are, Mr. R. H. Harris, for *Botesdale Division;* Mr. Philip Hart, of Brome, for *Eye Division;* and Mr. Wm. Cuthbert, for *Mendlesham Division.* The RELIEVING OFFICERS are, Mr. Charles White, for the first; Mr. P. Hart, for the second; and Mr. Anty. Gissing, for the third-named division. The Rev. Charles Notly, B.D., is *chaplain;* and the *masters and matrons of the Workhouses* are, Mr. John and Mrs. E. Thornton, at *Eye;* and Mr. D. and Mrs. S. Helsdon, at *Wortham.*

ASPALL, a parish of scattered houses, from 5 to 6 miles S. of Eye, and 2 miles N. of Debenham, has 132 souls, and 826A. 1R. 6P. of land, in which the river Deben has its source. It was formerly the seat and property of the Brookes, Lords Cobham. The manor has long been held by the family of the Rev. John Chevallier, M.D., and Charles Chevallier, Esq., of *Aspall House,* its present lords; but part of the soil belongs to J. Freeman, Esq., and several smaller free and copyholders. The latter are subject to arbitrary fines. Aspall House is a large and handsome mansion, finely embowered in wood, and was licensed, in 1833, for the reception of six *insane persons,* under the care of the owner, the Rev. J. Chevallier, M.D., who is also patron and incumbent of the *Church,* which is a perpetual curacy, not in charge, and valued in 1843 at £149. Sir Charles Gaudy settled upon the minister, for the time being, the impropriate rectory, which had belonged first to the Priory of Castleacre, and afterwards to that of Butley. The glebe is 26A. 3R.; and in 1843, the tithes were commuted for a yearly modus of £251. 13s. *Directory :*—Rev. John Chevallier, M.D., and Charles Chevallier, Esq., *Aspall House;* Mr. Joseph Blomfield; and Samuel Darby, John Freeman, (owner,) Wm. Freeman, and Thomas Page, *farmers.*

BACTON, a considerable and well built village, 6 miles N. of Stowmarket, and 8 miles from Eye and Debenham, has in its parish 800 inhabitants, and 2230A. 3R. 23P. of land. It was the lordship and demesne of the Bishop of Norwich till about 1535, when it was given to the Duke of Norfolk, who conveyed it, in exchange, in 1558, to Sir John Tyrell. George Tomline, Esq., of Riby Grove, Lincolnshire, is now lord of the *manor,* but part of the soil belongs to W. Steele, Esq.,

Mr. C. Jannings, and several smaller owners; and *Bacton Hall* has been purchased, and is now the residence of Mr. Wm. Whistlecraft. The wife of Henry Howard (who died here in 1739, aged 95,) bare him a daughter in her 58th year. The *Church* (St. Mary) is a handsome structure, with a tower, which has a peal of five bells, and is surmounted by a wooden spire. It was repaired, in 1841, at the cost of £360. The *rectory*, valued in K.B. at £19. 13s. 3½d., has a good residence about a mile S. of the church, and a yearly modus of £750, awarded, in 1841, in lieu of tithes. H. D. Hemsworth, Esq., is patron, and the Rev. E. B. Barker incumbent. At the Bull Inn is a lodge of Odd Fellows. The *Town Lands*, under the management of the overseers, churchwardens, and principal parishioners, comprise 20A. at Finning-ham, 11½A. at Old Newton, and 18A. in Bacton, let at rents amounting to about £80 per annum. The land at Finningham was vested, at an early period, for the use of Bacton; that at Old Newton was purchased in the reign of James 1., with £100; and that at Bacton, which is copyhold, was anciently held by trustees, for exoneration from taxes. A great part of the rents is applied with the church-rates, and the remainder with the poor-rates. The poor have two yearly rent-charges, viz., 13s. 4d., called *Daine's Gift*, out of the estate of the Right Hon. John Hookham Frere, and 8s., called *Warren's Dole*, out of an estate belonging to G. Tomline, Esq.

Banks Jonathan, shoemaker
Barker Rev Edw. Burton, *Rectory*
Cattermole Esther, boarding and day school
Cutting John Flowerdew, butcher
Cutting Wm. maltster & corn mert
Cutting Wm. Thomas, butcher
Finbow Wm. tailor
Flowerdew Richard, steward
Ford Wm. blacksmith
Garrard Thomas, shoemaker
Gissing Samuel, gentleman
Jannings Chas. wine & spirit mert
Jannings Charles, gentleman
Hammond Joseph, boot & shoe mkr
Hunt Wm. corn miller
Labon George, bricklayer
Leggett Henry, tailor
Osbourn Ann Maria, plumber and painter

Pizzy Wm. farrier
Potter Richard C. grocer and draper
Rose Robert, beer house
Scotchmer Thomas, wheelwright
Woods Samuel, vict. and carpenter, *Bull Inn*

FARMERS.—(* *are owners.*)
*Brand Edward || Borrett Anthony
*Cooper Edward, *Reed House*
Cooper Freeman || Canler Wm.
Cutting John || Cutting Wm.
Easlea Wm. || Finbow John
*Flowerdew Thomas
Flowerdew Robert || Ford Job
Frost Charles || Hammond Joseph
Jannings Robert || Kerry John
Lines John || Polly Joseph
*Thrower Mrs || Woods Charles
*Whistlecraft Wm. *Bacton Hall*

BOTESDALE, a small but ancient market town, with part of the adjoining villages of Rickinghall Superior and Inferior, forms a good street, three-quarters of a mile in length, upon a pleasant eminence, on the Bury and Norwich road, 7 miles W. by N. of Eye, 6 miles W.S.W. of Diss, 9½ miles N.E. by E. of Ixworth, and 87 miles N.E. of London. Though called a hamlet, it is a *township, in the parish of Red-grave*, and contains 633 inhabitants, and 1260 acres of land, including an *extra-parochial* spot, on which stands the *Grammar School and St. Botolph's Chapel*, under the same roof with the master's house. This small chapel was founded as a *chantry*, by John Sheriff, who endowed it for the support of a priest to pray for his and his wife's souls.

It overlooks the valley of a small rivulet, and from it the township was called *Botolph's dale*, now corrupted to Botesdale. The town is a great thoroughfare, eight coaches and several carriers' waggons, &c., passing daily to London, Norwich, &c. The *market*, held every Thursday, has been long disused, but an attempt is now making to revive it. A *fair* is held yearly on Holy Thursday, and a hiring for servants on the Thursday before Michaelmas. Henry III. granted a charter for a fair to be held here in the eve and day of St. Botolph, (May 17 and 18,) but it has long been obsolete. George St. Vincent Wilson, Esq., is lord of the *manor*, and owner of a great part of the soil, and the remainder belongs to Jas. Amys, Esq., of *Botesdale Lodge* (a neat residence,) and a few smaller owners. The GRAMMAR SCHOOL for Redgrave and Botesdale was founded under letters patent of the 3rd of Elizabeth, granting license to Sir Nicholas Bacon to erect a grammar school at Botesdale, on the site of the above-named chantry, or free chapel, for the instruction of boys living there and in the neighbourhood; and it was ordained that there should be two governors of the school revenues, who were thereby incorporated; and that Sir Nicholas and his heirs should appoint the master, and make ordinances for the government of the school. In the 19th of Elizabeth, Sir N. Bacon charged his manors of Skeddy and Burningham with the yearly payment of £20 to the master, £8 to the usher, and £2 for repairing the school premises. These rent-charges, subject to a deduction of £5. 12s. for land-tax, are paid to the master, the Rev. Wm. Hepworth, M.A., rector of Finningham, who lets the school to the Rev. J. Haddock, and pays him for the education of six free scholars, besides whom he has a number of boarders and day scholars. Near the school is a cottage, let by the master for £3. 3s. a year. For £21 a year, subscribed by the inhabitants, the Rev. J. Haddock performs divine service every Sunday evening in the *chapel* adjoining the school, which, after being many years disused, was substantially repaired, and neatly fitted up, by subscription, in the early part of the present century. The Dowager Lady Suffield has the appointment of the master. The founder bequeathed £20 a year to Benet College, Cambridge, towards the support of six scholars from this school; and Archbishop Tennison left an annuity of £6 for the same purpose. The *Wesleyans* and *Baptists* have each a neat chapel here, and the latter is used occasionally by the *Independents*. In the town is also a FREE SCHOOL for all the poor children of Botesdale and the neighbourhood, established in 1825, by *Mr. John Dyer*, and endowed by him with 16A. of land, worth more than £30 a year. *Petty Sessions* are held here 22 times a year, and in the town is a small *Bridewell*, or lock-up, built about 1809. The POST-OFFICE is at Mr. Benj. Taylor's. Letters are received and despatched at 7 morning and 7 evening. A *steeple chase* is held here yearly, in April. An *Allotment* of 2 acres, called the Back Hills, was awarded, at the enclosure in 1815, to the lord of the manor of Botesdale, the rector, and the churchwardens and overseers, upon trust to permit the *annual fair* to be kept upon it, and to allow the parishioners to get gravel, &c. in it for the reparation of the roads; but to let the herbage, and distribute the yearly rent (now £3. 5s.) among the poor.

BOTESDALE.

Amys James, Esq. *Botesdale Lodge*
Blowers Wm. wheelwright
Boston Noah, tailor
Boston Robert, tailor
Boyle Mary, dressmaker
Candler John, blacksmith
Claydon John, saddler
Collins Thomas, watchmaker
Cornish Robert, bricklayer
Cracknell Henry, hair dresser
Cracknell Wm. solicitor
Dawson Samuel Taylor, Esq
Doughton Verdon, baker
Dyer John, gent. *Botesdale cottage*
Flowerdew Mrs Ann
Fulcher Wm. cabinet maker
Goddard John, baker
Haddock John, chemist and druggist
Haddock Rev Joseph, incumbent of Ixworth Thorpe
Harris Robt. surgeon and registrar
Hunt Gilford, plumber and glazier
Mills Mrs Martha
Pretty John, tailor
Sparke Rev Joseph F. (Baptist)
Sword Robert, gentleman
Taylor Benj. bookseller, stationer, bank agent, stamp seller, & agent to Norwich Union Fire Office
Tricker Leonard, saddler

Vine Hy. stone and marble mason
Wiseman Richard, butcher

ACADEMIES.

Haddock Rev Jph. *Grammar School*
Larter Alfred
Whitehead Reuben, *Free School*

BOOT AND SHOE MAKERS.

Baldry Wm. || Bennet George

CORN MILLERS.

*Robinson Samuel (and maltster) .
*Robinson Wm. (and maltster)
Youngman Benjamin (and baker)

FARMERS.

Blomfield John || Nunn Joseph
Symonds George, *Abbot's Hall*
Whitehead Reuben (& leather cutter)

GROCERS AND DRAPERS.

Collins Richard || Turner Philip

INNS AND TAVERNS.

Cherry Tree, John Burcham
Cock, Wm. Howard
Crown, Wm. Cullum
Greyhound, Stephen Tillett
Queen's Head, George Chapman

COACHES pass eight times a day to Norwich, Bury, London, &c. A *Market Coach* from the Greyhound, every Wednesday morning, at 9, to Bury St. Edmund's

CARRIERS pass daily to all parts.

BRAISEWORTH, a small village and parish, 2 miles S.S.W. of Eye, contains 151 souls, and 722 acres. Lieut. General Sir E. Kerrison, Bart., is lord of the manors of Braiseworth Old Hall and New Hall with Brome, formerly held by the Earl Cornwallis, and anciently by the Sackvills; but a great part of the soil belongs to Lord Henniker, the Rev. Geo. Walker, the Rev. H. Hasted, Mr. Richard Berry, Mr. S. Hunt, and a few smaller owners. The *Church* is an ancient structure, with a modern steeple of white brick, erected, at the cost of £70, about ten years ago, when the old one was taken down. The living is a discharged *rectory*, valued in K.B. at £4. 8s. 1½d., and now having a yearly modus of £200, awarded, in 1840, in lieu of tithes. Sir E. Kerrison is patron; the Rev. H. Hasted, of Bury, incumbent; and the Rev. W. Chenery, of Stuston, curate. The FARMERS are, Noah Allen, John Cooper, Mary Dykes, *Church House;* Mary Green, Jno. Hart (owner,) Robert Jacob, *Braiseworth Hall;* John Jeffries, and Wm. Roundacre.

BROME, a pleasant village, 2 miles N. of Eye, and 4 miles S.E. of Diss, has in its picturesque parish 892A. 1R. 34P. of fertile and well-wooded land, nearly all the property of Lieut. General Sir E. Kerrison, Bart., of Oakley Park, in the adjoining parish of Hoxne, who is also lord of the manors of *Brome Hall, Davillers,* and *Ling-Hall-in-Brome.* The Brome and Oakley estates were purchased by the late M. Kerrison, Esq., of the last *Marquis Cornwallis,* who died in 1823, and whose

family had been long seated at BROME HALL, a fine old brick mansion, with curiously ornamented chimneys, said to have been built by
Sir Thomas Cornwallis, who died in 1590.   This mansion was formerly very extensive, and contained a fine collection of paintings, but it
has been considerably reduced in size, and is now unoccupied.   It is
finely embosomed in woods and plantations, and approached by a noble
avenue of full grown oaks.   The great hall, or dining room, exhibits
a perfect specimen of old English grandeur ; wainscoted with oak to
the height of ten feet, and having no ceiling, the timbers of the roof
being finished like those of churches.   The chapel, which has not been
used since about 1760, has a large bay window looking upon the lawn,
and a finely carved Gothic screen, hung with tapestry, representing
various scenes in the life of our Saviour.   *Thomas Cornwallis*, the
founder of the illustrious noble family so long seated here, was sheriff
of London in 1378.   In the reign of Henry VIII., John Cornwallis
was *knighted* for his valour at the siege of Morlaix, in Britanny, and
appointed steward of the household of Prince Edward, afterwards
Edward VI.   His son, Sir Thomas, being high sheriff of Norfolk and
Suffolk in the last year of that king's reign, raised a considerable force
in behalf of his sister Mary, who, in gratitude for his assistance in
placing her upon the throne, nominated him a member of her privy
council, treasurer of Calais, and comptroller of her household.   His
grandson Frederic was created a *baronet* in 1627.   He distinguished
himself by his adherence to the royal cause, attended King Charles in
all his military operations, and at the battle of Copredy bridge, in particular, he rescued Lord Wilmot, who had fallen into the hands of the
enemy under Sir Wm. Waller.   He accompanied Charles II. in his
exile, and that king, after his restoration, in reward of his services, not
only appointed him treasurer of his household, comptroller, and privy
counsellor, but created him, in 1661, a peer of the realm, by the title of
Lord Cornwallis, of Eye.   His grandson Charles, third Lord Cornwallis, was first lord of the admiralty, and Lord Lieutenant of Suffolk,
under William III.   To him succeeded his son Charles, the fourth
lord, joint post-master general, and pay-master general of the army, in
the reign of George I.   He had a numerous family, among whom were
Charles, the fifth lord ; Edward, who embraced the military profession,
and was, in 1762, appointed governor of Gibraltar ; and Frederic, constituted, in 1750, bishop of Litchfield and Coventry, and translated, in
1768, to the archiepiscopal see of Canterbury.   Charles, the fifth lord,
having been previously appointed constable of the Tower of London,
lord lieutenant, and custos rotulorum of the Tower Hamlets, was, in
1753, created *Viscount Brome and Earl Cornwallis*, in addition to his
former title.   Of the issue of this nobleman were Charles, the second
earl ; James, late bishop of Litchfield and Coventry ; and William, an
admiral, and distinguished ornament of the British navy.   Charles,
the second earl, was, in consideration of his splendid services as a soldier and a statesman, advanced, in 1792, to the dignity of *Marquis
Cornwallis*.   His eminent talents caused him to be selected for various
appointments of great difficulty, and the highest importance.   He
crushed the rebellion in Ireland, negotiated the peace of Amiens, and
having been a second time invested with the office of governor-general
of the British possessions in the East Indies, he died in 1805, at

Gauzepoor, in the province of Benares, and was succeeded by his only son Charles, who was colonel of the East Suffolk Militia, and died without male issue in 1823, when the Marquisate became *extinct;* but the Earldom and Barony of Cornwallis, and the Viscountcy of Brome, devolved on his uncle and heir. The present Earl Cornwallis, &c., succeeded to the titles in 1824, and resides at Linton Place, Kent. Brome *Church* (St. Mary) is an ancient structure, with a round tower, containing five bells. In the chancel are several handsome *monuments* for various members of the Cornwallis family. Sir John, who died at Ashridge, in 1544, is interred beneath a marble tomb, four feet high, upon which lies his figure in armour, with a white staff in his hand, and a greyhound at his feet. Beside him is the effigy of Mary, his wife, with a hound at her feet also. Near this monument is another, on the north side of the chancel, for Sir Thomas Cornwallis, Knight, and Anne, his wife, with their effigies. In the aisle adjoining is a third, for Henry Cornwallis, Esq., who is represented in armour, kneeling. The *rectory,* valued in K.B. at £10. 0s. 2½d., has that of Oakley annexed to it, and the joint benefices were valued, in 1835, at £561. Sir E. Kerrison is patron, and the Right Hon. and Rev. Henry William Powlett, *Lord Bayning,* is the *incumbent,* and the Rev. Wm. Ward, *curate.* In 1683, John Goldsmith left for the poor of Brome a yearly rent-charge of £3, out of his estate at Tivetshall, in Norfolk, now belonging to the Earl of Oxford. Under an enclosure act of 1808, the yearly payment of £15 was charged on an allotment in Brome (now belonging to Sir E. Kerrison,) for providing fuel for the poor, in lieu of the right they had of cutting firing on the commons.

Bailey Mark, tailor and draper
Butcher Nathaniel, blacksmith
Cooke Miss Maria
Copping Richard, *corn miller*
Curtis John, vict. Swan Inn
Gooderham John, carpenter
Hart Pp. relieving officer & registrar
Haves John, blacksmith
Lingwood Joseph, gentleman
Macey Thomas, schoolmaster

Shepherd James, *carrier* to Ipswich
Thompson Henry, boot & shoe mkr
Utton Thomas, Esq. agent to Sir E.
   Kerrison and Lord Henniker
Ward Rev Wm., M.A. *curate*

FARMERS.
Gedney Benjamin ‖ Parke Mary
Taylor Thomas, *Warren Hill*
Thompson Joseph (and grocer)

BURGATE, a village and parish, 2 miles E. of Botesdale, and 5 miles W.N.W. of Eye, contains 369 souls, and 2034A. of land, including about 100 acres of woods and plantations. It was formerly the seat and property of a family of its own name. Geo. St. Vincent Wilson, Esq., is now lord of the manor and owner of most of the soil, and the remainder belongs to Shafto Adair, Esq., the Rev. E. Jermyn, Lord Henniker, Miss Harrison, and a few smaller proprietors. The *Church* (St. Mary) is an ancient structure, with a tower and five bells. In the chancel is an old tomb, in memory of Sir William de Burgate. The rectory, valued in K.B. at £13. 10s. 10d., has about 70 acres of glebe, and a yearly modus of £550, in lieu of tithes. The Bishop of Ely is patron, and the Rev. Chas. Robt. Ashfield, B.A., is the incumbent, and has a neat modern residence near the church. The other principal inhabitants are, Wm. Betts, *blacksmith;* Wm. Hines, vict., *King's Head;* and Robt. Algar, Wm. Buck, John Chapman, Henry

Gibson, Thos. Green, Jph. Harwood, *Burgate Hall;* David Simpson, John Smith, Wm. Thirkettle, and Elizabeth Wiseman, *farmers.*

COTTON, 6½ miles N. by W. of Stowmarket, and 3 miles W. of Mendlesham, is a village and parish, containing 545 souls, and 1921A. 2R. 27P. of land, belonging to various proprietors, the largest of whom are, E. B. Venn, Charles Tyrell, W. Adair, B. Frere, and G. T. Heigham, Esqs.; the Right Hon. J. H. Frere, and Capt. Heigham. The manors of Bacton and Mendlesham extend into this parish. *Cotton Hall,* now a farm house, belongs to C. Tyrell, Esq., (lord of the manor,) and is an ancient mansion, encompassed by a broad and deep moat, which appears to have been walled on both sides. William de la Pole died seised of Cotton manor, in the 28th of Henry VIII. It afterwards passed to the Duke of Norfolk, who, in 1558, assigned it to Sir John Tyrell. The *Church* (St. Andrew) has a tower and five bells. In its windows are some fragments of ancient stained glass, and its porch has highly enriched mouldings. The *rectory*, valued in K.B. at £15. 10s. 2½d., has a good residence, which was erected in 1811, of white brick, and has extensive gardens and pleasure grounds. The glebe is 19A. 30P., and the tithes were commuted, in 1839, for £485 per annum. The Rev. Peter Eade, B.A., is patron and incumbent. The *Wesleyans* have a small chapel here. The *Town Estate,* consisting of a house occupied by paupers, a cottage occupied rent free by poor persons, and 8A. of land, let to the rector for about £10 a year, has been conveyed from time to time to feoffees, without any declaration of trust. The rent is applied to the repairs of the church and general parochial purposes, agreeably to long usage.

Eade Rev Peter B.A. *Rectory*
Finbow William, butcher and vict., *Cock and Bottle*
Leggett Geo. wheelwright
Leggett Wm. corn miller
Mullenger Joseph, bricklayer
Selby Allen, bricklayer and beerhs

FARMERS.
Berry Nathl. || Bird Canler
Canler George, (*owner*)

Cater and Foulger
Clarke My. *Hempnall Hall*
Finbow Jno. || Goodrich Wm.
Hart Jno. Cotton Lodge
Mayhew Nathl. Hill Farm
Seaman Wm. (and blacksmith)
Sheppard Samuel
Waters George, (*owner*)
Worlledge Robt. & Wm. *Cotton Hall*

EYE, an ancient *borough* and irregularly built *market town,* occupies a low situation at the confluence of two rivulets, 8 miles N. of Debenham, 21 miles N. of Ipswich, 5½ miles S.S.E. of Diss, 8 miles E. by S. of Botesdale, and 90 miles N.E. of London. Its parish had 1734 inhabitants in 1801; 1893 in 1811; 1882 in 1821; 2313 in 1831; and 2493 in 1841, when its number of *males* was 1192, and females 1301; and its number of *houses* 483, of which 16 were empty when the census was taken. The return in 1841, included 56 persons in the *Union Workhouse,* already noted at page 321. The parish comprises 4174A. 1R. 21½P. of fertile land, including CRANLEY hamlet, from 1 to 2 miles S.S.E. of the town, and a number of scattered farms. Sir Edward Kerrison, Bart., is lord of the *manors of Eye Hall,* otherwise *Priory;* *Eye Stokemere,* and *Cranley Hall in Eye;* and also of Eye Thelnetham. Thos. French, Esq., is steward of these manors, for which general courts-baron are held yearly. A great part of the parish is freehold, belonging to the Rev. Nathaniel D'Eye, Edgar Chenery, Esq., T.

Blythe, Esq., (owner of Eye Park,) and several other proprietors; and part of it is in the Earl of Stradbroke's manor of *Netherhall.* Abbo Floriacencis, who wrote in the latter part of the 10th century, describes the town as situated in his time in the midst of a marsh, and says the rivulet had been navigable to it from the Waveney. In corroboration of this, small rudders, iron rings, &c., are said to have been found in the neighbouring fields. The rivulet receives here a small tributary stream, and consequently the town is encompassed on three sides by water. The *Borough* received a charter from King John, but had long had a corporation by prescription.* The charter of the 9th of William III. was the governing charter, (though the corporation have eight other charters) till the passing of the Municipal Act of 1835; previous to which the borough was governed by two bailiffs, 10 principal burgesses, 24 commoncouncilmen, a recorder, town clerk, and inferior officers. The *freedom* was acquired by birth, apprenticeship, or election; and the number of freemen was about 130, of whom only about 60 were resident. Under the Municipal Act the borough is now governed by a *mayor, four aldermen,* and 12 *councillors;* and it has had a *commission of the peace* granted on petition. The mayor is judge of the *court of record* held every Saturday, for the recovery of debts to any amount. *Petty Sessions* are held on the same day by the mayor and the borough magistrates, at the *Town Hall,* a handsome building in Broad street, part of which was formerly a gaol, but a small new *prison* was erected in 1817, adjoining the Workhouse, at the cost of about £300, of which £50 was paid by the corporation and the remainder by the parish. But prisoners committed to the House of Correction or for trial at the Quarter Sessions, are sent to Ipswich. The *income* of the borough in 1839 was £383. 5s. 7½d., of which £36. 7s. 3d. was expended in lighting and cleansing; £42. 18s. 8½d. on public works, repairs, &c.; £94. 12s. 3d. in law expenses; and £62. 11s. 6d. on police and constables.

The *Municipal Borough* comprises only the parish of Eye; but the *Parliamentary Borough* has been extended by the Reform and Boundary Acts, to the *ten surrounding parishes* of Hoxne, Denham, Redlingfield, Occold, Thorndon, Braiseworth, Yaxley, Thrandeston, Brome and Oakley; so that it has now a population of 7403 souls, and is of an irregular figure, averaging about 7 miles in length and breadth, and lying partly in the adjoining Hundred of Hoxne. Eye regularly sent two *members to parliament* from the 13th of Elizabeth, till it was deprived of one by the Reform Act of 1832; before which, the greatest number of electors ever polled at a contested election was 129. The number of *voters* registered in 1837 was 328, of whom only 50 exercised the franchise in right of their freedom of the borough. The number of freemen now entitled to vote is only about 40. Lieut. Gen. Sir Edward Kerrison, Bart., K.C.B., of Oakley Park, has represented the borough in nine parliaments, and is also lord of the *honor of Eye.* The TOWN-COUNCIL *and Officers,* (in 1843,) are Samuel Peck, Esq., *mayor;*

---

* *Domesday Book,* states that *Edric* held Eye; that there were in it 12 plough lands in the Confessor's time. " Now, (1068,) Robert Malet holds it in demesne. There is a Park for deer, and a market to which belong 25 *Burgesses.* To the manor belongs 48 *Socmen,* (i.e. tenants in ancient demesne,) who had 121 acres; of whom 37 were the lord's vassals." It was anciently called *Aye* or *Eay,* (i.e. the Island,) because it was surrounded with water and fenny grounds.

Messrs. Robert Bishop, Hy. Gooch, S. Peck, and Thos. French, *aldermen ;* Messrs. R. Reeve, J. Parke, J. Aldred, G. Sewell, H. Sewell, G. T. Knott, C. Beales, W. Craske, J. S. Flowerdew, R. Mendham, D. Penning, and W. Harper, *councillors ;* G. W. Lawton, *town clerk ;* Mr. Richard Nurse, *treasurer ;* Messrs. R. Bishop, Hy. Gooch, R. Todand, G. Mudd, *charity trustees ;* William Thurlow and Daniel Todd, *serjeants-at-mace ;* Richard Murdock and Thomas Stannard, *chamberlains,* and Richard Remington, *crier.* P. Baylis, (of Ipswich,) J. Moore, R. Wallis, B. Cotton and T. French, Esqrs., are the *Borough Magistrates ;* and Edgar Chenery, Esq., is their *clerk.* The poor freemen of the borough, who do not occupy 10A. of land, have each the privilege of pasturing two head of cattle on the Moor, which comprises about 30A. of fertile land, about ten acres of which are mown yearly, and the grass sold to them at the rate of from 3s. to 5s. per acre. A freeman's widow is entitled to the same privilege.

The Borough was long under the political influence of the Cornwallis family, (see page 326,) but the last *Marquis Cornwallis,* who died in 1824, sold his estates and manors here, and in the neighbouring parishes, to the late Matthias Kerrison, Esq., father of their present owner, Sir E. Kerrison, Bart. *William Malet,* who came to England with William the Conqueror, had the lordship of Eye with all its appendages, conferred on him by that monarch. His son, *Robt. Malet,* built a *Castle* here, near the west end of the church, and some of its ruined walls were to be seen in Kirby's time; and on the east side of the town he founded a *Benedictine Priory,* which was afterwards enriched by various benefactors, and was subordinate to the Abbey of Bernay in Normanday, till Richard II. released it from foreign dependance. At the dissolution, it was valued at £161. 2s. 3½d., and its possessions were granted to Charles Brandon, Duke of Suffolk. The *Honor of Eye* is said to have formerly comprised 120 manors, or the greater part of them. Its second Norman lord, Robert de Malet, held the office of great chamberlain of England under Henry I., but being an abettor of Robert, that king's elder brother, in his attempt upon the crown, his estates were confiscated, and himself banished the realm. This honor was then conferred on Stephen, Earl of Boulogne, who afterwards ascended the English throne. It was given by Richard I. to Henry Earl of Brabant and Lorraine, but was again in the king's hands, 9 Edward I., and so continued till 4 Edward III., who granted it to his brother John, Earl of Cornwall ; and on his death without issue, it was given, by the same king, to Robert de Ufford, whom he had created Earl of Suffolk. With the death of his son William, the family became extinct, and this honor once more returned to the crown ; after which it was conferred on the De la Poles, Earls of Suffolk, and for a long period it was held by its late possessors, the illustrious family of *Cornwallis.* (See page 326.) In 1781, some labourers, digging in a field near Eye, discovered a leaden box, containing several hundred Roman coins and medals, all of the purest gold, well executed, and in high preservation, chiefly of the Emperors Arcadius and Honorius. They were worth about eleven shillings each, and near them was found a quantity of human bones.

Though the town has been much improved during the last forty years, it still retains many of its old thatched houses, with whitewashed

fronts. The streets are irregularly built, and generally narrow, and were neither paved, lighted, nor watched at the time of the municipal enquiry, about ten years ago; but since then, provision has been made for these necessary purposes. The *market*, formerly on Saturday, is now held on Monday; and the lower part of the Town Hall has been fitted up as a *Corn Exchange*. A fair for cattle, toys, &c., is held yearly on Whit-Monday. During this fair, and those at Finningham and Thrandeston, (over which he has control,) the Mayor of Eye holds a *court of pie poudre*. RACES are held yearly on Cranley green, in July. They were revived in 1839, and continue two days. Gurneys and Co, and the East of England Bank have branches here. There is also in the town a *Savings' Bank* for the Hundred of Hartismere, and connected with it is a " *Government Annuity Institution*," established in 1842, under an act of the 3rd of William IV. The CHURCH (St. Peter and St. Paul) is a large handsome structure, which was appropriated to the Benedictine Priory here, of which there are still some vestiges.* Sir E. Kerrison Bart., is impropriator of the *rectory*, and also patron of the *vicarage*, which is valued in K.B. at £11. 4s. 7d., and is now enjoyed by the Rev. Jas. Wm. Campbell, for whom the Rev. Jas. Whiting officiates. The net yearly value of the living is now £338, 7s. 6d. The tithes were commuted in 1842—the vicarial for £451. 5s., and the rectorial for £783. 15s. per annum. The *Wesleyans* and *Baptists* have chapels in the town. Here are *two News Rooms ;* a small *Theatre ;* several *Boarding Schools ;* a large *National School*, for both sexes, built about six years ago by Sir E. Kerrison, and chiefly supported by him ; and an endowed *Grammar School*, and several valuable *Charities*, of which the following account is derived chiefly from the Report of the Parliamentary Commissioners.

The TOWN LANDS comprise several valuable estates, and are vested in trustees appointed by the Corporation, and the rents are received and applied by an officer called the town treasurer, under the direction of the Corporation. Some of the estates are held under conveyances of very ancient date, containing no specification of trust or appropriation; others appear to have been purchased with funds belonging to the Corporation ; and the remainder have been given or settled by different benefactors, for specific charitable objects. They were conveyed to new trustees in 1822, and comprise a house and 26 acres of land in Bedfield and Worlingworth, given by *Francis Kent*, for supporting an *usher* at the Grammar School ; 14 acres at Osmondestone ; 42 acres at Newton ; 2 acres 2 roods at Hoxne ; a house and 13 acres at Gissing ; a house, 162 acres, and eight commonages in Cranley hamlet; and the *Guildhall, Town Hall*, two cottages, and about 30 acres in Eye, called the *Moor*. Such of the estates as are not noticed as belonging to the following charities, are considered to belong to the Corporation, or to be held only for general public purposes under their direction. The rental derived from the Town Lands amounts to £400 per annum, out of which are paid the expenses of the Corporation, and the salaries of the organist and parish clerk; and from £150 to £200 is distributed yearly among the poor of the parish, in coals, clothing, and money.

* One of the possessions of the Monks of Eye, was the site of the episcopal see at Dunwich, till swallowed up by the ocean. They brought from that place *St. Felix's Book of the Gospels*, which Leland saw, written in great Lombard letters of high antiquity, and by which, under the name of the *Red Book of Eye*, the common people were accustomed to swear.

The GRAMMAR SCHOOL is kept in a large room in the Guildhall; and the other rooms in that building are in the master's use, as also is the adjoining garden. In 1566, the Corporation decreed that such of the town lands as had theretofore been given and purchased to the use of a schoolmaster, should thenceforth be employed to the maintenance of a learned man, to teach a Grammar School in Eye, to be nominated from time to time, with the consent of the greater part of the feoffees of the town lands, and of the most substantial inhabitants of Eye; and that he should have £10 a year for teaching the youth of Eye in grammar and the Latin tongue. In 1593, *Francis Kent*, as noticed above, left a house and 26 acres of land, for the maintenance of an usher to teach writing and grammar in this school freely to the children of Eye, Horsham, Allington, and Bedfield. This property is now let for £40 a year. Since 1740, the offices of master and usher have been consolidated in the person of the master, who teaches 20 boys, as free scholars, in reading, writing, and arithmetic, and also in Latin, when required. In the 12th of James I., EDWARD MALLOWS left £200 to be laid out in the purchase of land, to be settled in feoffees, in trust that the rents and profits thereof should go for the maintenance of two or three scholars in the University of Cambridge, who should have been born at Eye, those of his own kindred to be preferred; and when there should be no such scholars at the University, he directed that the income should be applied for the better maintenance of the grammar school, or for the relief of the poor of Eye. The property purchased with this bequest, consists of the 13 acres of land at Gissing, noticed with the Town Lands, and is let for £30 per annum. In 1830, the rent of this land had, for a long period, been improperly carried to the general account of the Corporation.

Charities Connected with the Town Lands: – The sum of £20 left by *Matthew Hinton*, in 1640, was laid out in 1651, with money belonging to the corporation, in the purchase of the Town Lands at Cranley, which, in respect of this benefaction, were charged with the yearly payment of £1. 12s. to the churchwardens, for distribution among the poor. In 1692, £100, given by *Thomas Herring, Esq.*, was laid out in the purchase of about 12A. of the town land at Newton, now comprising 42A. 3R. let for about £62 a year, which is distributed chiefly in coals. The *Town Houses* are two cottages, occupied rent-free by poor families. They were given by Edward Golding, in the 18th of Elizabeth, in lieu of an annual rent-charge, intended to have been given by *John Hayward*.

Harwin's Charity (of unknown date) is a yearly rent-charge of £2. 10s., paid out of a house in Castle-street, for distribution among the poor. In 1654, *Wm. Small* bequeathed, out of his estate called Eye Park, a yearly rent-charge of £21, to be applied as follows, viz. : £10 to Swanton Mawley; £1 to Norwich, and £10 to Eye, for educating and apprenticing poor children. The portion belonging to Eye is all applied for the last-named purpose. In 1572, *Edward Golding*, for the purpose of carrying out the intention of *Wm. Woodman*, granted an annuity of £3. 6s. 8d. out of lands called Barhams, in Cranley, upon trust, towards finding two parish-clerks to serve in the parish church. In the 16th of Charles I., *Ann Lomax* gave a yearly rent-charge of 20s. out of a house, now called the Bull, to be distributed, on Good Friday, amongst the aged poor of Eye.

BEDINGFIELD'S ALMSHOUSES:—Nicholas Bedingfield erected tenements in Lambseth-street, for the free habitation of four poor widows or old maids, natives of Eye; and by his will, in 1636, he endowed them with a house, two cottages, gardens, and 3A. 1R. 14P. of land, (now let for £26 a year,) in trust that each of the almswomen should have 2s. monthly, a new gown of grey cloth every two or three years, and a cart load of fire-wood every year; and that the surplus rents should be divided among them, after

paying for the necessary repairs of the almshouses, which contain four low rooms and four chambers, and are occupied by eight poor women belonging to the parish. About 1780, nearly £200 was laid out in rebuilding or repairing these almshouses.

EYE DIRECTORY.

POST OFFICE, at Mr. Richard Nurse's. Letters from all parts arrive (*via* Scole) at half-past 6 morn., and are dispatched at 9 evening.
Those marked 1, *are in Broad-street;* 2, *Castle-st.;* 3, *Lambseth-st.;* 4, *Church-st;* 5, *Cross-st.;* 6, *Magdalen-st.;* & 7, *in Lowgate-st.*

1 Allison Fras. B. excise officer
1 Barber Wm. bank agent
Barker John, gent. *Richmond hill*
1 Bishop Hy. sec. to Savings' Bank
Chenery Mrs Ann, Lambseth st
2 Chenery Edgar, Esq. solicitor & clerk to magistrates
Chenery Mrs Sarah, Castle street
1 Church John, broker, and glass & china dealer
Costerton Chas. Fisher, superintendent registrar and union clerk
Cream Chas. solr. Lambseth street
Cotton Benj. Esq. Lambseth street
Denny Mrs Harriet, Lambseth st
Dykes, Robt. cooper, Church street
Eade The Misses, Castle street
2 Edwards Mrs || 3 Faires Mrs
2 Flanders Rev Mark Wm. (Bapt.)
2 French Thomas Esq. solicitor and commissioner of taxes
4 Gill John, clerk to the commissrs. of the income tax
4 Fisher John, managing clerk
Gooch Henry, gent. *Langton green*
Hayward Lionel, gentleman
2 Herbert George, parish clerk
Holmes John, dyer, Lowgate street
4 Jessop John, cattle dealer
Jones Miss Eliza, Lambseth street
2 Lawton George Warner, Esq. solr. and town clerk
4 Mahew Rev T. curate of Occold
4 Mendham Robt. artist & var. mfr.
Moore James, Esq Magdalen st
4 Moore John, assistant overseer
1 Mudd George, auctioneer, &c
4 Notly Rev Chas. B.D. incumbent of Redlingfield
1 Nurse Richard, postmaster
3 Pashley Charles, music master
Peck Samuel, gent. Langton green
3 Pretyman Robert, gent. Church st

Rands William, basket maker
Riches Richard, gent. Castle street
Ruffell Wm. postman, Church lane
2 Rush John, veterinary surgeon
2 Sadd Lancelot, temp. coffee house
4 Short George Groom, maltster
Syer Edw. solr. house Lambseth st
3 Tacon Richard & Chas. brewers
Thornton John and Mrs E. master and matron of the *workhouse*
Thrower Mrs Hannah L. Church st
2 Todd Daniel, sergeant at mace
Todd Mrs Sarah, Castle street
Turner Mrs Ann, Church street
5 Thurlow William, sergt. at mace
4 Ungless Wm. Hy. bank cashier
Wallis Reuben, gent. Prospect cotg
Watling John, inspector of police, Langton green
Welton Ann, circulat. liby. Butchery
2 Whayman George, corn chandler
4 Whayman Isaac, veterinary surg.
Wythe Mrs J. *Chandos lodge*

BANKERS.

2 East of England Bank, (on London and Westminster Bank;) Thomas French, Esq. agent
1 Gurneys & Co's. Branch of the Halesworth Bank, (on Barclay and Co.) William Barber, agent
1 Savings' Bank and Annuity Institution; open on Mon. from 11 to 12 o'clock; Henry Bishop, actuary

BOOKSELLERS, STATIONERS, PRINTERS & BINDERS.

Bishop Robert, Broad street
Nurse Richd. (and stamp vender) Broad street

FIRE AND LIFE OFFICES.

1 Alliance & Northern Union, Hy. Bishop
1 Church of England, Wm. Marshall
1 Norwich Equit. (Fire) Rd. Nurse
1 Norwich Union, William Barber
5 Royal Exchange, Wm. Thurlow
2 Suffolk & Gen. Country Amicable, Thos. French

INNS AND TAVERNS.

Black Swan, Wm. Lake, Cross st
Bull, James Robinson, Lambseth st
Cherry Tree, Jph. Martin, *Gretney*
Crown, William Moss, Magdalen st

Grapes, Jesse Sheppard, Church st
King's Arms, Hy. Collins, Castle st
King's Head, Fras. Smith, Church st
Queen's Head, Mk. Tye, Lambseth st
Red Lion, Hy. Cracknell, Church st
Star, William Button, Castle street
2 Three Horse Shoes, Lydia Ward
Victoria Arms, David Prentice,
    Butchery
White Lion Inn & Commercial Hotel,
    Henry Charles Rowling, Broad st

ACADEMIES.
(*take Boarders.)
*2 Garneys Sarh.
King Jas. *Natl.*
*4 Notly Rev Cs.
    B.A. *(Gram.)*
7 Pittick Har.
* Pretty Eliz.
    Hill House
*3 Sewell Henry
2 Todd Jane

ATTORNEYS.
2 Chenery Edgar
2 French and
    Lawton
3 Syer & Cream

BAKERS.
Cooper John,
    Church street
2 Leathers Thos.
    Fred.J.(& con-
    fectioner)
1 Mudd George,
    & confectioner)
4 Oriel Henry
5 Ramplinge
    Jesse

Beerhouses.
4 Frost Charles
4 Herbert Danl.
1 Lawrence Rt.
    (&porter mert)
Marriott James,
    Langton gn
2 Offord Edmund
2 Stannard Thos.
4 Strutt Joseph

Blacksmiths.
2 Collins Henry,
    &drill,&c.mkr.
4 Smith Joseph
5 Thurlow Wm.
2 Waterman Jno.

Boot&ShoeMkrs.
4 Borrett Geo.
4 Fearman John

Hursham Edw.
    Back lane
2 Oaks Abraham
2 Page Edward
4 Roper Mary

Brewers.
4 Flowerdew and
    Gowing
3 Tacon Richd.
    and Co.

Bricklayers.
4 Lawrence Wm.
6 Marriott Hy.
4 Murdock Rd.
3 Tye Mark

Butchers.
1 Chase Robert
4 Gissing Jno. S.
6 Self Wm.
2 Sturgeon Saml.

Chemists& Drgts.
1 Bishop Robert
2 Bush John

Coach Maker.
4 Lait Robert

Corn Millers.
Aldred Hy., Back
    lane
Chambers Jonth.
2 Offord Edmund

FARMERS.
Bate Ed. (owner)
Beales Charles,
    Moor Hall
Bolton Wm.
Carter Wm.
Case and Brock
Chambers Robt.
Craske Walter,
    Priory Farm
Edwards Thos.
    Rook Hall
Edwards Wm.
Freston Samuel,

Kiln Farm
Gooderham, Jas.
    sen. *Low Farm*
Gooderham Jas.
Gowing Edward
Gowing Eliz.
Gowing Ellis Sy-
    monds, *Cran-
    ley Hall*
Harper Wm.
Harris George,
    Cranley Green
Johnson John
Knott Garrett
    Taylor, *Eye
    Park*
Mallows Wm.
Parke James
Peck Sl. *Lang-
    ton Green*
Perry Joseph
Salter Daniel
Sewell Ann
3 Tillott James
Todd Robert
Whayman Mary

Grocers, &c.
1 Bishop Mary
3 Catt Jno.&dpr.
4 Collins Jno. (&
    tal. chandler)
4 Dove James
3 Sewell George,
    and *draper*

Hairdressers.
2 Burrows Wm.
6 Gooderham Dl.

Ironmongers.
1 Barber Wm.
7 Garrood&Sons,
    (& founders)
1 Marshall Wm.

Joiners, &c.
4 Day Daniel
7 Hindes James
3 Penning Danl.
    & bell & paper
    hanger
5 Rampling Edw.
4 Short George
2 Stannard and
    Brook

L.& W.Drapers.
4 Catt John
1 Cason Wm.
1 Nayler & Gis-
    sing

3 Sewell George
    Milliners.
1 Allinson Mary
2 Banister Har.
4 Penning Mrtha.
5 Welton Susan
*Painters, Plum-
bers, & Glaziers.*
2 Neale James
2 Sturgeon Danl.
    Saddlers, &c.
2 Marsh John,
3 Remington Rd.
7 Tricker Wm.
    Shopkeepers.
6 Dade Robert
7 Harvey Jph.
4 Strutt Joseph
Straw Hat Mkrs.
7 Borrett Mary
2 Marsh Sarah
    Stone Mason.
2 Sturgeon Danl.
    Surgeons.
2 Ashford Seaman
2 Clough Wm.
2 Miller Walter
    Wm.
6 More James
4 Strowger Saml.
    Badeley
    Tailors.
4 Bond Joseph
7 Borrett John
4 Gissing Geo.
2 Pretty Robt.
1 Read Wm.
2 Sadd Jane

Tinners & Brazs.
1 Barber Wm.
1 Marshall Wm.
Watch Mkrs.&c.
7 Batchelor Hy.
1 Calver Susan
2 Skinner Mark
    and George
    Wheelwrights.
Day Jph. Back ln
2 Girling Danl.

*Wine and Spirit
    Merchants.*
4 Flowerdew and
    Gowing(&hop,
    corn, coal, &c)
Tacon Rd.& Co.

COACHES,

To Norwich and Ipswich, pass daily through *Yaxley*, 2 mile W. of Eye

CARRIERS.

Noller's Vans from the White Lion every Mon. Thurs. & Sat. to *London, Norwich, &c.* Also, *Smith's*

Waggons same days from the King's Head

To Ipswich, Rt. Dade, from Magdalen street, Tue. and Sat.

To Norwich, Fras. Smith, from the King's Head, Friday

FINNINGHAM, a scattered village, $7\frac{1}{2}$ miles N. of Stowmarket, 5 miles S. of Botesdale, and 7 miles S.W. of Eye, has in its parish 480 souls, and 1234A. 1R. 3P. of fertile land, nearly all the property and manor of the Rt. Hon. John Hookham Frere, of Malta, whose family were formerly seated at the Hall, and who is also patron of the *rectory*, valued in K.B. at £10. 10s. 5d., and now having a yearly modus of £450. 12s. 6d. awarded, in 1840, in lieu of tithes. The Rev. Wm. Hepworth, M.A., is the incumbent, and has a good residence near the *Church*, (St. Bartholomew,) which is finely embowered in trees, and has a tower and three bells. A large *cattle fair* is held here on Sept. 4th. The *Church and Town Estate* consists of a house and some cottages, occupied rent-free by poor families; the Bull-yard, let for 5s.; and about 2A. of land, let for £7. 7s. a year. The rents are added to the church and poor rates. A yearly rent-charge of £6 is paid out of 19A. of land, at Mendlesham, pursuant to the bequests of *Ann Frere* and *Susan Edwards*, the former of whom left the interest of £50, to be distributed in bread and hempen shifts among the poor, and it was laid out in the purchase of half of this rent-charge; and the latter donor left £3. 10s. a year, to be applied—50s. for the education of four poor children, and 20s. to be distributed among poor communicants. In 1766, *Eleanor Frere* gave a yearly rent-charge of £12 out of her house and lands, called Sudbornes, in Wyverstone, to be applied as follows:—£4, for teaching six poor children to read and write; £5, for providing coats for four poor men, constantly attending divine service; £2. 5s., to be distributed in meat among poor parishioners; and 15s., to be distributed in bread, on the 12th of November.

Banks James. shoemaker
Banks Mrs Elizabeth
Blomfield John, vict. *White Horse*
Carr James, schoolmaster
Clayton Misses Ann and Eliza
Cox Jas. gardener & nurseryman
Fairweather John, tailor
Hammond Robt. currier and leather cutter
Hepworth Rev Wm. M.A. Rectory
Plummer John, officer of Excise
Potter John, saddler
Rednall Ephraim, carpenter
Rednall Edw. grocer and draper
Rednall George, shoemaker

Roper John, grocer and draper
Sands John, wheelwht. & blacksmith
Sands Thomas, shoemaker
Steggall Wm. corn miller
Wright Thomas, baker
Youngman Mary, butcher

FARMERS.

Andrews John || Driver John
Finbow Ambrose || Parker Philip
Martin George, (Hall)
Martin John and Walton, *Lodge*
Peck Samuel, *Mill Farm*
Simpson John || Smith Edmund
Steggall Charles, *Green*
Steggall Henry || Youngman Mary

GISLINGHAM, a pleasant village and parish, 5 miles W.S.W. of Eye, and $3\frac{1}{2}$ miles S.S.E. of Botesdale, contains 669 souls, and 2251A. of land, including the scattered farms of *Potash*, *Rush Green*, and *Swattisfield Hall*. The latter was rebuilt in the early part of last

century, by Chas. Bedingfield, Esq.   The parish is in two *manors*, (Swattisfield Hall and Rushes and Jennings,) of which Lord Henniker and Geo. St.Vincent Wilson, Esq., are lords, but a great part of the soil belongs to J. H. Heigham, Esq., J. H. Frere, Esq., Rd. Reeve, Esq., Mrs. Ion, Archdeacon Glover, the Rev. P. N. Joddrell, and a few smaller owners.   It is mostly freehold, and the fines on the copyholds are arbitrary.   The *Church* (St. Mary) is an ancient structure, with a tower and six bells.   The *rectory*, valued in K.B. at £26. 1s. 5½d., and in 1835 at £503, has a good residence, and is in the patronage and incumbency of the Rev. Thos. Collyer.   The tithes were commuted, in 1839, for a yearly modus of £624.   There was here a preceptory belonging to the knights of St. John of Jerusalem, and it was granted in the 7th of Edward VI., to John Green and Robert Hall.   The *Baptists* and *Methodists* have chapels in the parish.   The *Town Estate* comprises a house, occupied rent-free by poor persons; a house and 30A. of land, in Thorndon, let for £42 a year; and 2A. in Gislingham, let for £4 a year.   The rents are applied in repairing the church, the school, and poor's house, and in defraying other public charges of the parish.   In the 12th of Charles I., *John Darby* left 8½A. of land, called Park Close, in trust to pay yearly 20s. towards repairing the highways, and 20s. towards repairing the school; and to distribute the residue of the rent amongst the poor parishioners.   The land is now let for £12 per annum.   The estates here, belonging to J. H. Heigham, Esq., are charged with various annuities, amounting to £28. 10s. per annum, bequeathed by *John, Mary, and Edmund Darby, and the Rev. John, Mr. John, and Mrs. Alice Symonds*, between the years 1640 and 1702, for the following uses—viz., £17 a year to the master of the *free school*, for teaching ten boys of the parish; £3 to the schoolmistress for teaching seven poor girls; and £8. 10s. for a distribution of clothing, &c., among the poor parishioners.

Battrum Ts. grocer, draper, & tailor
Cobb Michael, corn miller
Collyer Rev Thomas, Rectory
Finch Ellis, corn miller
Land John, beerhouse
Leggett John, blacksmith
Leggett Thomas, wheelwright
Mothersole Wm. F. schoolmaster
Prike Wm. shoemaker
Selsby Thomas, shoemaker
Stagg Wm. vict. *Six Bells*
Stagg Wm. jun. blacksmith
Talbot Thos. grocer, and carrier to Ipswich, Tuesday and Friday
Todd James, saddler, &c.

Webb Wm. Woodham, surgeon

FARMERS.

Battrum John || Brett Robert
Brett Wm. || Brooks James
Brooks John, *Potash Farm*
Cole Wm. || Corbould John
Cracknell Chas. *Swattisfield Hall*
Hayward Wm. || Jacob Nathaniel
Joddrell Neville || Morley Corben
Munns James, (owner)
Shave Simon || Simpson Edward
Starling John || Steggall George
Steggall Thomas, *Rush Green*
Turner Jno. *owner* || Wells Thos.

MELLIS parish contains 532 souls, and 1344A. 1R. 30P. of land, and its houses are scattered on the margin of a pleasant *green*, or common, about a mile in length, and from 3 to 4 miles W. of Eye.   It is mostly in the two manors of *St. John's* and *Pountney Hall*.   Geo. St. Vincent Wilson, Esq., is lord of the former, which belonged to the knights of St. John, at Gislingham, and the Rev. Edward Jermyn is lord of the latter, in which the custom of Borough English prevails.

Mellis Hall, a small farmhouse at the west end of the green, is all that remains of the once extensive mansion of Pountney Hall, which was long the seat of the Clarkes, and had a large park. The greater part of his hall was taken down many years ago. Lord Henniker, Sir E. Kerrison, J. H. Frere, Esq., the London Missionary Society, Mr. H. Potter, and several smaller owners, have estates in the parish. The *Church* (St. Mary the Virgin) is an ancient structure, and had a tower which fell down in 1735, and has never been rebuilt, though £200 was subscribed for that purpose. It contains some memorials of the ancient families of Yaxlee and Clarke, and had two guilds dedicated to St. Peter and the Holy Trinity, and a noted image of St. Michael. The *rectory*, valued in K.B. at £9. 15s., has 9½A. of glebe, and a yearly modus of £333. 11s. 9d., awarded, in 1839, in lieu of tithes. The patronage is in the Crown, and the Rev. Henry Creed, A.B., is the incumbent. The advowson anciently belonged to the prior and convent of Eye, and afterwards to the Earls of Suffolk, till 1511, when it was seized by Henry VIII. The Wesleyans have a small chapel here.

Bryant Saml. vict. Falcon	Copping Zach. ‖ Cracknell Henry
Bullingham Wm. wheelwright	Dade Leonard ‖ Doggett John
Creed Rev Hy. A.B. *Rectory*	Eaton Wm. (and *corn miller*)
Larter Thomas, carpenter	Hammond John S.
Meadows Jabez, cooper	Jermyn Benjamin, *Mellis Hall*
FARMERS.	Jermyn Joseph ‖ Morley David
Calver Wm. ‖ Collins Thomas	Wells Robert, *Potash Farm*
Chenery Thomas, (*owner*)	Whitmore Mary, *Putney Hall*

MENDLESHAM, formerly a market town, consists of one long street of irregularly built houses, in a marshy situation, 7 miles N.E. by N. of Stowmarket; 7 miles S.S.W. of Eye; 6 miles W.N.W. of Debenham; and 88 miles N.E. of London. Its parish contains 1340 inhabitants, and 3880 acres of land, including the hamlet of *Mendlesham Green*, nearly a mile south of the town, and several scattered farmhouses. Hugh Fitz Otho procured the privilege of a market and fair here, in the reign of Edward I. The market was on Tuesday, but has long been obsolete. The *fair* for cattle, &c., is still held on Holy Thursday. Charles Tyrrell, Esq., is lord of the manor, but a great part of the soil belongs to J. G. Sheppard, Jas. Morrison, Rt. Pulford, E. Chapman, J. Matthew, J. Simpson, and J. Garnham, Esqrs.; Sir W. F. F. Middleton, Mrs. Parry, and several smaller free and copyholders. The latter pay small certain fines. In the latter part of the 17th century, an ancient *silver crown*, weighing about 60 ounces, and supposed to have belonged to one of the kings of East Anglia, was found here. A gold concave ring, with an inscription in the Runic character, was also ploughed up here in 1758. Camden supposes Mendlesham to have been the residence of Dagobert, one of the East Anglian kings. The *Church* (St. Mary) is a large and handsome structure, consisting of a nave, chancel, side aisles, and a lofty tower, in which is a peal of five bells. It was appropriated by Wm. Rufus to Battle Abbey. Messrs. Oakes, Bevan, and Co., bankers, of Bury, and Mr. Thomas Francis, are now lessees of the *Rectory*, under the Dean and Chapter of Chichester, and have a yearly modus of £512. 5s. 8d., awarded in lieu of the great tithes, in 1839, when the vicarial tithes were also commuted for £504. 7s. 10d. per annum. The *Vicarage*, valued in K.B. at £14. 9s. 2½d., is in the patronage of the Rev. Robt. Field, and in-

cumbency of the Rev. Henry Thos. Day, L.L.D., who has a neat and commodious residence, half a mile from the church. The Baptists and Primitive Methodists have small chapels in the parish. The following messuages, lands, &c., in this parish, are appropriated to charitable uses—viz., a building given by Peter Duck, and used partly for the residence of paupers, and partly as a school; 12 tenements near the church yard, occupied rent-free by poor families; a farm of 150A. 1R. 33P., left by *Robert Lake*, in 1473, for the payment of fifteenths and other subsidies, the repairs of the church, and the relief of the poor; a farm of 45A. 3R. 16P.; two closes, called *Birds*, containing 12A. 3R. 36P.; land, called *Salmons*, containing 10A. 1R. 3P.; a garden of 5 perches; and a blacksmith's shop and garden. These *Charity Estates* have, from time to time, been conveyed to new trustees, but the donors are unknown, except Robert Lake and Peter Duck. The rents produce a *yearly income* of about £350, and are applied as a general fund in the following manner—viz., £20 a-year to the *Schoolmaster*, for teaching 15 poor children in reading, writing, and arithmetic; £20 a-year towards the support of a *Sunday School,* and finding books for the children, and bonnets and frills for the girls; and the remainder, after providing for contingent expenses, is appropriated to the repairs of the church, and the relief of the poor; about £200 being devoted yearly to the latter purpose, in weekly distributions among widows and aged and infirm parishioners.

MENDLESHAM.

Abbs Henry B. dyer
Alders Wm. plumber, painter, &c
Buckenham Harriet, glover
Cuthbert Wm. surgeon & registrar
Day Rev Hy. Ts. L.L.D. *Vicarage*
Finbow Robert, gardener
Francis Thomas, gentleman
Gissing Walter, plumber, glazier, &c
Goddard John, cooper
Jacob Edmund, ironmonger
Percy Zephaniah, clock & watch mkr.
Pizzy Thomas, butcher
Rednell Elizabeth, vict. *Oak*
Reynolds George, vict. *King's Head*
Saunders James, machine maker and millwright

ACADEMIES.
Haxell Owen, agt to the Royal Exchange Fire &c. office
Matthew Hanh.

Bakers.
Brett Brist
Foster John, sen.

Beerhouses.
Arnold Benj.
Batley Wm.
Clark Alfred
Clark Mary
Cowlis Robert

Rose John

Blacksmiths.
Burch John
Fox Nathl.
Quinton Ishmael
Rose John

Boot & Shoe Mkrs.
Brundish Robt.
Brundish Wm.
Burnham Wm.
Clark Alfred
Fox David
Reynolds Edw.
Reynolds Geo.
Roper Thomas

Steggall Robert
Wix Robert

Bricklayers.
Blomfield Jsa.
Rodwell John

Corn Millers.
Cowles Robert
Foster Jno. jun.
Ling John

FARMERS.
(* are owners.
Bendall Sutton
*Brundish Wm.
Daggett Robert
Durham Geo. Frd
Eastall Samuel
Eldred Edward
Field Edward
*Foster Jno. sen.
Fox George
Fox Thomas
Francis Dnl. *Hall*
Francis Robert
Gissing Henry, *Herbert Green*
Gissing Spenser
*Grimwade John
Harwood Wm. *Lodge*
*Kersey Robert
*Lake Elizabeth
Matthew Edw.

Mayhew Robert
Mills Simon
*Robinson John
White Jerh. B. *Manor House*
Wilson Wm.
Wix John
Wright Wm.

Grocers & Dprs.
Ashford Alfrd. agt to Essex & Sufk. Fire Office
Codd Jane

Tailors.
Garrard Henry
Potter Robert

Wheelwrights.
Arbourn Charles
Arnold Benj.
Burch Robert
Childs Edward
Clark John
Crowe Peter
Watcham Wm.

CARRIERS.
Barker James, to Stowmarket, Mon. & Thu.
Wood Edmund, to Ipswich and Stowmarket, Tue. & Thu.

OAKLEY, a pleasant scattered village, 3 miles N.N.E. of Eye, has in its parish 355 inhabitants, and 1280 acres of fertile land, within the Parliamentary borough of Eye, and nearly all the property of Lieut.-Gen. Sir E. Kerrison, Bart., whose beautiful mansion in *Oakley Park*, is in the adjoining parish of Hoxne, but the greater part of the extensive park is in Oakley, on the western side of the small river Dove, which here divides the Hundreds of Hartismere and Hoxne, and falls into the Waveney a little below the park. This elegant seat is described with Hoxne. M. Kerrison, Esq., the father of the present possessor, purchased the manors of *Beauchamp and Hoo Hall*, in Oakley, and other estates in this neighbourhood, of the last Marquis Cornwallis, as noticed with Brome at page 325. *Oakley House*, a neat mansion, near the park, is occupied by Mrs. Bacon Frank. Mrs. Worth, of Norwich, owns a small farm in the parish. The *Church* (St. Nicholas) is an ancient structure, with a tower and five bells, and the benefice is a *rectory*, valued in K.B. at £9. 4s. 9d., and consolidated with that of Brome. (See page 326.) It is said that Oakley was anciently in two parishes, and that it had another church (St. Andrew's) in what was called Little Oakley. The *Town Estate*, consisting of a messuage occupied by poor persons, and 13A. of land, let at rents amounting to £22. 4s. 8d. per annum, has been held, from an early period, by the churchwardens for the use of the church, but it is not known how it was acquired.

Clark Wm. grocer, and bird & animal preserver
Day John, carpenter
Frank Mrs Bacon, *Oakley House*
Ling Mary, schoolmistress
Moule Solomon, wheelwright
Poppy Jas. blacksmith & vict. *Green Man*

Salter John, shoemaker

FARMERS.
Crisp Wm. || Holden Samuel
Gowing Samuel, *Warren Hill*
Owles Wm. || Rush Wm.
Sheldrick George

OCCOLD, a village and parish in the parliamentary borough, and 2½ miles S. of Eye, contains 578 souls, and 1479A. 3R. 10P. of land, including the hamlet of *Benningham Green*. The manor of Little Thorndon extends into Occold, and here is a small *Rectorial manor*. The rest of the parish is in the *manors of Occold Hall and Benningham Hall*. The Rev. B. Chapman, D.D., is lord of the former, and Mrs. Burroughs is lady of the latter, but a great part of the soil belongs to the Herman, Kerry, Wingfield, and several resident families. The *Church* (St. Nicholas) has a tower and five bells ; and the *rectory*, valued in K.B. at £19. 1s. 5⅓d., has 47A. of glebe, and a yearly modus of £404. 4s. 1d., awarded in 1839 in lieu of tithes. The Rev. — Todd is patron, and the Rev. John Ward, M.A., incumbent. *Chapelfield*, at Benningham, is said to be the site of an ancient chapel, of which no traces are extant. The TOWN ESTATE was mostly devised by *John Henman*, in 1449, for certain superstitious uses, the payment of tenths and fifteenths, the relief of the poor, and the reparation of the church and highways. It was conveyed to new trustees, in 1813, and consists of the townhouses, occupied by paupers ; a house and 4A. of land, let for £10 a year ; and a messuage, farm house, outbuildings, and 46½A. of land, in Occold and Redlingfield, let for about £58 per annum. The rents are applied in repairing the church, town houses, &c., and in paying a yearly

salary to a surgeon for attending the poor.   Mr. G. Sherman and others are the trustees.   In 1720, Wm. Lee left all his lands and tenements, in Occold, to the intent that 5s. worth of bread should be given weekly to the poor parishioners ; and 40s. yearly to the poor of Thorndon ; and that the residue of the rents should be applied in buying clothes for the poorest people in Occold.   This charity estate comprises 20A. 2R. of freehold land, and 6A. 34P. of copyhold, in the manor of Benningham Hall ; 2A. of copyhold in the manor of Occold Hall, and two cottages divided into several tenements.   The whole is let for £50 per annum. In 1724, Robt. Denny left a yearly rent-charge of 20s., out of a farm belonging to Mr. Chapman, for a distribution of bread on Ash Wednesday.

Blomfield Saml. beerhs. & wheelwht.
Capon Wm. brick and tile maker, and corn miller
Everson John, blacksmith
Everson John, shopkeeper
Everson Jno. & Ezra, edgetoool mkrs.
Hunt Eli, beerhouse
Rowe Thomas, vict. *Bottles*
Runnacres John, carpenter
Sherman Geo. jun. grocer & draper
    FARMERS.   (* *are Owners*)
Eldred Wm. || Hammond James

*Hunt Benj. || *Johnson George
Last Henry, *Benningham*
Moore Thomas || *Nicholls John
Orford Robt. Baker, *Occold Hall*
Pike Isaac, (and *maltster*)
*Sherman George, *Red House*
*Sherman Geo. sen. || *Tubby John
Weeding Kemble, *Benningham Hall*
Wells Hy. & land agent & surveyor, *White House*
Wingfield James

PALGRAVE, a pleasant village, on a shady green, in the vale of the river Waveney, 1½ mile S. of Diss, and nearly 5 miles N.N.W. of Eye, has in its parish 730 souls, and 1474A. 3R. 1P. of fertile land. Sir E. Kerrison, Bart., is lord of the manor ; but the soil belongs to Miss Harrison, and the Tuck, Potter, Howe, Taylor, Sheriffe, Bond, Roper, Tippel, and other families.   *St. John's*, a neat mansion, with pleasant grounds, one mile S.S.W. of the village, is the seat of Miss Mary Harrison, and has long been the residence of her family, who have a vault and several memorials in the church.   This lordship anciently belonged to Bury Abbey, and in the west part of the parish was a chapel of St. John the Baptist, subordinate to that monastery, where five secular priests resided, and said mass daily.   The *Church* (Saint Peter) is an ancient structure, with a tower and six bells.   In the porch, with others of his family, is interred *Thomas Martin, Esq.*, the celebrated antiquary, who wrote a history of Thetford, his native place, where he was born in 1696.   He was bred an attorney, and having married the widow of Peter Le Neve, Esq., norroy king at arms, became possessed of his noble collection of British antiquities, to which he made extensive additions.   His ambition was to deserve his cognomen of " *Honest Tom Martin of Palgrave*."   He died in 1774, poor in everything but antiquities, manuscripts, and books, which were sold to Mr. Worth, of Diss, for £600, but afterwards sold to various parties, for several thousand pounds.   His manuscripts, &c., relating to Suffolk, were purchased by Sir J. Cullum, of Hardwick, near Bury St. Edmund's.   The *rectory*, valued in K.B. at £19. 11s. 3d., has a good residence, 6A. of glebe, and a yearly modus of £441. 10s., awarded in 1838 in lieu of tithes.   Sir E. Kerrison, Bart., is patron ; and the Rev. James Cox, D.D., incumbent.   The *Town Estate* com-

prises a messuage called the Guildhall, occupied by paupers; about 2ᴀ. of land near the latter, belonging to the poor ; and a farm of 66ᴀ. 3ʀ., in Guestwick, Norfolk, let for £60 a year, which is applied in the service of the church ; and if any surplus remains, it is carried to the poor rates. Two yearly rent charges, viz., 20s. left by *Henry Bootie*, in 1653, out of a farm belonging to Miss Harrison ; and 10s., left by *John Stebbing*, in 1677, out of land belonging to Mr. Ives, are distributed in bread, at Christmas.

Alstone Miss Emma
Bond George, shopkeeper
Brown Henry, butcher
Bumstead Geo. baker and shopkpr
Chaplyn Edward, corn miller
Curson John, vict. *Swan Inn*
Doggett Robert, tailor
Ford Thomas, carpenter
Hammond Wm. shoemaker
Harrison Rev Hy *rector of Shimpling*
Harrison Miss Mary, Saint John's
Howell Wm. carrier to Ipswich and Norwich
Knott John, blacksmith
Lock Mr Gordon
Moore John, shoemaker
Payne John, plumber & glazier

Richards Wm. gentleman
Ship Robt. florist and vict. *Lion*
Smith Mr Thomas
Thurlow Hy. joiner & cabinet mkr
Thurlow Samuel, corn miller
Tilbrook Mrs Sarah, boarding school
Turner Mr Robert

FARMERS.

Browning John (& cattle dealer)
Calver Geo. || Chaplin Edmund
Crane Levi || Garrard John
Gooderham Wm. *Spring farm*
Hart Nathaniel || Haynes Robert
Howe Martin (owner)
Long Phillis || Martin Wm.
Pike Henry (and maltster)
Quinton Edw.||Rix Wm.||Rush Hy.

REDGRAVE, a large and handsome village, pleasantly situated near the sources of the Waveney and Little Ouse, 2 miles N. by E. of Botesdale, 5 miles W.S.W. of Diss, and 8 miles W.N.W. of Eye, has in its parish 719 souls, and 2059 acres of fertile land, exclusive of *Botesdale* township, which is already described at page 323. It was anciently the lordship of the Abbot of Bury, to whom it was given by Ulfketel, Earl of East Anglia. It was granted by Henry VIII., in the last year of his reign, to Thomas Darcy, from whom it passed to the Bacons. *Sir Nicholas Bacon*, lord keeper to Queen Elizabeth, made it his seat; and his descendant, Sir Nicholas, was created by James I. the premier baronet of England, in 1611. By one of his successors, the estate was sold, about the close of the 17th century, to Sir John Holt, lord chief justice of the King's Bench, in whose family it continued till it became by marriage the property of the late *Admiral Wilson*, from whom it passed to the present owner and lord of the manor, *Geo. St. Vincent Wilson, Esq.* But part of the parish belongs to the Butcher, Cobbold, Betts, Flowerdew, Barclay, Debenham, and other families. REDGRAVE HALL, the seat of Mr. Wilson, was built in 1770, by the late Rowland Holt, Esq.; who also embellished the *Park* at an expense of £30,000. It stands on the site of one which had been built by Sampson, abbot of Bury, in 1211, and is a spacious structure of Woolpit brick, with a projecting centre, the pediment of which is supported by four Ionic columns. " In the evidence room here," says Sir John Cullum, " are preserved many valuable manuscripts." The park is extensive, and beautifully clothed with wood, and the rivulet which flows through it is expanded into a fine serpentine lake, of more than 46ᴀ. On the north side of the parish, within the bounds of Norfolk

is *Lopham Gate*, where two copious springs rise in swampy ground, and, flowing in opposite directions, give rise to the rivers Waveney and Little Ouse, the former running eastward to Yarmouth, and the latter westward to Thetford and Lynn, and both forming the boundary of Norfolk and Suffolk. The *Church* (St. Botolph) is an ancient structure, with six bells; but in the early part of the present century, it was repewed, and ornamented with a neat steeple of white brick, chiefly at the expense of Rowland Holt, Esq. The organ, which cost £185, was erected in 1842. This church contains some monuments, which, for beauty of marble and sculpture, are exceeded by few in the kingdom. In the right aisle is a black table monument, upon which are the recumbent effigies, in white marble, of Sir Nicholas Bacon and his lady, executed by Nicholas Stone, at the cost of £200. In the chancel is interred that excellent judge, *Sir John Holt*, whose monument is said to have cost £1500. He is represented in white marble, sitting in a chair, in his judicial robes, with the figures of Justice and Mercy on either side of him. Two Corinthian columns support the alcove under which he is seated. *Thomas Wolsey*, afterwards the famous cardinal, was presented to the rectory of Redgrave, in 1506, by the abbot and convent of Bury. (See page 56.) Geo. St. Vincent Wilson, Esq., is now patron, and the Rev. Mdk. Wilkinson incumbent of the *rectory*, which is valued in K.B. at £25. 7s. 1d., but is now worth about £777 per annum, and has 45A. 3R.10P. of glebe, and a large and handsome Rectory house. The Wesleyans have a chapel here; and an Independent congregation was formed in this parish as early as 1672. The *Church Lands* comprise 2A., near the churchyard, let for £3; and 1A. 1R., in Hinderclay, let for £3 a year. The *Poor's Allotment* consists of 80 acres of waste land, and was awarded at the enclosure, in 1815, to be employed for providing fuel for the poor parishioners, or otherwise for their use, under such orders as to the lord of the manors of Redgrave and Botesdale, and the rector, churchwardens, and overseers, should seem most beneficial. *John Brundish* gave, for the relief of the poor, 1A. 2R. of land, now let for £3 a year. In 1686, *Mary Foster* left £18 for schooling poor children, and it was laid out in the purchase of 1A. of land, at Barningham, now let for £1. 10s. a year, which is paid to a schoolmistress, for teaching three children to read. In 1727, *John Hubbard* left a yearly rent-charge of £3. 5s., out of Calkpitt's Hole Closes, for a monthly distribution of bread; and he also gave a house, and directed that two of the rooms therein should be occupied, rent-free, by two poor widows, and that the other rooms should be let, and the rents employed in repairing the house, and in allowing 15s. yearly to each of the two widows. The *Grammar School* for Redgrave and Botesdale, is already noticed at page 324.

Adams Geo. wheelwright and machine maker

Baily Edward, blacksmith

Blake Edw. Parker, Esq. *Redgrave Cottage*

Browne John, corn miller

Bullock Wm. corn miller

Burrows Amos, tailor, &c

Chaplyn Herod, saddler, &c.

Clarke Wm. carpenter

Collins Edward, gardener

Crack George, shoemaker

Cracknell Wm. grocer, draper, and tailor

Cullingford Benjamin, shoemaker

Gates Robert, wine, spirit, & corn merchant

Hart Chas. vict. *Cross Keys*

Hart Jph. & Sons, organ builders
Holt Sibery, vict. *Fox*
Jolly John, butcher
Payne George, bricklayer
Pearce John, carpenter
Pemberton Wm. shoemaker
Rush Robert, veterinary surgeon
Taylor Baker, grocer and draper
Vyse Edward, butcher
Wilkinson Rev Marmaduke, *Rectory*

Wilson Geo. St Vincent, Esq. *Redgrave Hall*
Witting Daniel, tea dealer

FARMERS.

Butcher Osborn || Button Thomas
Darnell Henry || Darnell Samuel
Debenham Wm. Hy. (maltster)
Downing Thomas || Gates Robert
Reeve Saml. || Orves Joseph
Woodgate Robert || Wright Chas.

REDLINGFIELD, a village and parish, in the parliamentary borough, and 3½ miles S. by E. of Eye, contains 240 souls, and 1074A. 3R. 13P. of land, all, excepting about 100A., the property of Wm. Adair, Esq., the lord of the manor, impropriator of the tithes, and patron of the *Church*, which is a perpetual curacy, valued at £71, and now enjoyed by the Rev. Chas. Notly, B.D., of Eye. A *Benedictine Nunnery* was founded here, in 1120, by Manasses, Earl of Guisnes, and Emma his wife, who endowed it with the manor of Redlingfield. At the dissolution, this house was valued at £67. 0s. 1½d., and was granted to Edmund Bedingfield, from whose family it passed to that of Willis, and from the latter to the Adairs. Of this monastery, there are still considerable remains, part of it being converted into a farm-house, and its chapel being the parish church, which is a small fabric, without a tower. In a hollow part of the wall, at the west end, is a swarm of bees, which settled there about twenty years ago, when they are said to have followed a corpse brought here for interment. The tithes were commuted in 1839 for £208 per annum, to the impropriator. The *Town Estate*, vested for the reparation of the church and the relief of the poor, consists of 40 acres, in the parishes of Redlingfield, Denham, and Hoxne, let for £45 a year.

Bane Thomas, wheelwright
Bolton Robert, wheelwright
Cracknell George, carpenter
Howes Oliver, blacksmith
Rowe Wm. corn miller and beer house

FARMERS.

Barnes John || Bolton Robert
Cracknell Chas.(& tax colr.)*Rookery*
Cracknell George, *Hall*
Cracknell Mary Ann
Cracknell Thomas || Johnson Maria
Platford Edward (and owner)

RICKINGHALL SUPERIOR is 7½ miles W. of Eye, and 8½ miles N.E. by E. of Ixworth, and adjoins Botesdale, and many of its houses form part of that town. (See p. 323.) Its parish contains 768 inhabitants, and 1410A. 30P. of land, partly copyhold, subject to arbitrary fines, and held of the manor of *Facons Hall*, now a farm house. George St. Vincent Wilson, Esq., is lord of the manor, owner of most of the soil, and patron of the *rectory*, which is valued in K.B. at £9. 13s. 11½d., and has that of Rickinghall Inferior united with it, in the incumbency of the Rev. T. P. Slapp. The tithes were commuted in 1840, for a yearly modus of £1052, of which £472. 2s. is paid by Rickinghall Superior, and £579. 18s. by Rickinghall Inferior. The *Church* (St. Mary) is an ancient fabric, with a tower and six bells. The *Town Estate* consists of a house and two cottages, occupied rent-free by poor persons, and 27A. 2R. 27P. of land, let for £23 a year, which is applied in the service of the church. In the 10th of Eliza-

beth, *Francis Rookewode* and *Thomasine,* his wife, gave 12A. of land in Botesdale, in trust, that the rents thereof should be employed for the relief of the poor parishioners of Walsham-in-the Willows and Rickinghall Superior and Inferior. At the enclosure, about 1820, this land was exchanged for separate pieces allotted to each parish; and that belonging to this parish contains 2A. 3R. 11P., let for £8. 16s. 6d. per annum. The poor parishioners have also the interest of £10, left by *John Browne,* in 1731; and a yearly rent-charge of 16s., left by an unknown donor, out of land called Howechins.

Barham Robert, carrier to Ipswich, Tuesday and Friday
Bedwell Valentine, beerhouse
Boulter Wm. grocer, draper, and agent to the Suffolk Fire Office
Burroughs Rev Thomas, curate
Chapman Thomas, vict. *Garden Hs*
Clarke Thomas, cabinet maker
Crack James, shoemaker
Crack John, tailor
Cullingford Joseph, wheelwright
Damant Catherine, straw hat maker
Hamblin Mrs Mary
Rednall Henry, vict. White Horse

Rednall Lockwood, carpenter
Seddington Joseph, tailor
Smith Bernard, gentleman
Steggall Jonathan, bricklayer
Vincent Samuel Baker, surgeon
Warren David, blacksmith
Wiseman Richard, butcher

FARMERS.
Cook George, *Facons Hall*
Dodd John || Freeman Robert
Long Samuel || Newstead John
Porter Wm. || Smith Jas. Hamblin
Steggall Jonathan
Warren Issachar

RISHANGLES, a small village on the turnpike, 4 miles S. of Eye and N. of Debenham, has in its parish 261 souls, and 718A. 3R. 22P. of land. The *manor* belonged to the nuns of Redlingfield, and was granted in the 4th of Philip and Mary to Wm. Honing and Nicholas Cutler. It afterwards belonged to Lord Orwell, and is now held by Richard Dalton, Esq., but the soil belongs mostly to Lord Henniker, H. D. E. Hemsworth, Esq., Messrs. John Raw and James Wingfield, and several smaller free and copyholders. The latter are subject to arbitrary fines. The *Church* (St. Margaret) is an antique structure, with a tower and three bells. The *rectory,* valued in K.B. at £7. 13s. 1½d., and in 1835, at £323, is in the patronage and incumbency of the Rev. C. T. Elers, for whom the Rev. J. Chevallier, M.D., officiates. The Baptists and Methodists have chapels here, and there is a *brick and tile* manufactory in the parish.

Canham John, coach maker and blacksmith
Clarke Emanuel, shoemaker
Hammond Mr James
Leggett Rev Samuel Newsome (Independent,) schoolmaster
Ling Henry, carrier to Ipswich, Thursday and Friday

Seaman Robert, vict. Swan
Stevens Joseph, corn miller
FARMERS.
Barker Daniel || Bennett John
Capon Curtis || Lockwood Thomas
Jeffries Robert, *Woodhouse*
Whatling Wm. || Wright Thomas

STOKE-ASH, a village on the Ipswich and Norwich road, 3½ miles S.W. of Eye, has in its parish 423 souls, 1173A. 2R. 35P. of fertile land, and a large ancient *Inn,* where petty sessions are held eleven times a year. A *hiring for servants* is held here in October. The manor belonged to Eye priory, and was granted in the 28th of Henry VIII. to Edmund Bedingfield. Lord Henniker is lord of the manor of *Stoke-Hall-with-Thorpe;* and the Rev. G. Turner is lord of *Wood*

Hall manor, but part of the parish is in the manor of Thwaite, and the other principal landowners are G. Jackson, T. Utton, and A. Campbell, Esqrs., and the Rev. P. Wakeham. The soil is mostly freehold. The *Church* (All Saints) is an ancient structure, with a tower and four bells, and the living is a *rectory,* valued in K.B., at £11. 1s. 3d., and now having 16A. 1R. 17P. of glebe, and a yearly modus of £358, awarded in 1842, in lieu of tithes. The Rev. — Bull is patron, and the Rev. J. Ward is the incumbent, and has an ancient thatched residence near the church. The *Baptists* have a small chapel here.

Ablett Samuel, shoemaker
Bean Edward, wheelwright
Church James, blacksmith
Leggett Wm. shoemaker
Potter Zach. vict. White Horse Inn
Sparke Job, corn miller
Tyler Wm. carpenter

Ward Rev John, *Rectory*
FARMERS.
Banks Jph. || Berry Rd. *Stoke Hall*
Cobb Geo. || Canler Edw. *Rookery*
Colman Wm. || Day Wm. *Wood Hl*
Knights Thomas || Pettit Wm.
Potter Zachariah || Woods Wm.

STUSTON, a village and parish, 3 miles N. of Eye, has 252 souls, and 797A. 2R. 32P. of land, including an open *common* of 147A. on the south side of the vale of the Waveney. Sir E. Kerrison is lord of the manor of *Boylands and Facons,* in Stuston; and the manor of *Stuston Hall* belongs to Christ's Hospital, but part of the soil belongs to O. Clarke, Esq., (who has a neat mansion here,) Miss Manning, of Diss, and several smaller proprietors. The copyholds are subject to arbitrary fines. *Stuston Hall,* (taken down some years ago,) was long the seat of the knightly family of Castleton, and afterwards of the Marriotts, of whom it was purchased by Samuel Traverse, from whose trustees it passed to Christ's Hospital. The manor of Facons was held by the nuns of Flixton, and was granted in the 36th of Henry VIII. to John Eyre. The *Church* (All Saints) is a venerable thatched structure, with a round tower, containing four bells, and finely mantled with ivy. The benefice is a discharged *rectory,* valued in K.B. at £6. 16s. 8d., and in 1835, at £174. Sir E. Kerrison is patron, and the Rev. Walter Chenery, M.A., is the incumbent, and has 18A. of glebe, and a good residence, which was repaired and modernised about ten years ago. In 1710, *Eliz. Bosworth* gave 4A. of land for the use of the rector, but subject to a yearly rent-charge of 10s. for the poor. *Directory :*—John Atkinson, *blacksmith ;* Rev. Walter Chenery, M.A., *Rectory ;* Osmund Clarke, Esq.; Miss Susan Clarke, *Stuston Lodge ;* Henry Fulcher, *carpenter ;* John Land, *farmer ;* Richard Strange, vict., *Swan ;* Harriet Tippell, farmer, *White House ;* Osborn Tippell, *gentleman ;* and Charles Weaver, *farmer.*

THORNDON, a large scattered village, with many neat houses, in the parliamentary borough, and 3 miles S. by W. of Eye, has in its parish 732 souls, and 2680A. 33P. of land, including 51A. 3R. 36P. of commons, &c. It is in four *manors,* viz., Little Thorndon, of which N. C. Barnardiston, Esq., is lord ; Thorndon and Hestley Hall, of which Frederick Hayward, Esq., of Needham Market, is lord; and a small manor belonging to the Rectory. *Hestley Hall* and *Standwell Lodge* are the seats and property of J. and J. Hayward, Esqrs. The former is an ancient mansion, embowered in trees, 4½ miles S. of Eye, and the latter is a neat modern house, with tasteful pleasure grounds. The

other principal landowners are Richard Dalton, Esq., H. D. Hemsworth, Esq., Rev. J. Betts, Rev. B. Chapman, and Messrs. J. Hammond, Thomas Woodward, and J. Simpson. The copyholds are subject to arbitrary fines. In the reign of Edward III., *Thorndene* was
held by Robert de Ufford, Earl of Suffolk, and afterwards by the
De la Poles. The *Church* (All Saints) is a large ancient fabric,
with a tower and six bells. The *rectory*, valued in K.B. at £24.
11s. 10½d., has 77 acres of glebe, and a yearly modus of £711.
12s. 2d., awarded in 1839, in lieu of tithes. The Rev. Thos. Howes
is patron and incumbent, and has a commodious white brick residence
near the church. The *Town Estate* comprises a workhouse and yards,
and a cottage in Thorndon, and 94A. 2R. of land in Thorndon, Occold,
and Wetheringsett, let to various tenants at rents amounting to £147
per ann. It was vested in or before the reign of Elizabeth, for the reparation of the church, the relief of the poor, and any other public
uses that the major part of the parishioners should think proper. The
poor have 40s. a year from Lee's Charity, (see Occold,) and a yearly
rent-charge of 40s., left by one *Cullum*, out of an estate now belonging to N. C. Barnardiston, Esq.

Adams John, grocer and draper
Adams John, blacksmith
Brock David, wheelwright
Churchyard John, wheelwright
Churchyard Robert, beerhouse
Cobb George, carpenter
Cracknell Benj. vict. Black Horse
Emerson John, blacksmith
Gibbs Cornelius, tailor
Hammond Miss Charlotte, *Pool Hs*
Hayward John, gentleman, & chief
   constable, *Standwell Lodge*
Howes Rev Thomas, *Rectory*
Lock Nathan, miller and grocer
Peck James, beerhouse
Rodwell Thomas, bricklayer

Strange Mr Henry
Tyler George, carpenter
Wells Charles & James, shoemakers
   FARMERS. (* *are Owners.*)
Aston & Ward || Berry John
Brock Robert || Cook Elizabeth
Case Henry, *Hill House*
*Hammond Hy. || Hammond Michl.
Hammond Thos. Edgar, *Red House*
*Hayward John, *Hestley Hall*
Hayward Robert
Kerry Wm. *Rishangles Lodge*
*Locke Nathan || Moore David
Moore Robert || Strange Robert
Wells Charles || Woodward George

THORNHAM MAGNA is a pleasant village and parish, 3 miles
S.W. of Eye, containing 374 souls, and 1326A. 3R. 10P. of fertile land,
all except about 30A. belonging to Lord Henniker, M.P., of THORN-
HAM HALL, a large and handsome mansion, which was considerably
enlarged and improved about ten years ago, and occupies a delightful
situation in a beautiful park, which has recently been enlarged, and is
finely shaded with full grown trees and rising plantations. Thornham
was the lordship of the Kellegrews, and was the estate and seat of the
late *Sir John Major,* who was an elder brother of the Trinity House;
High Sheriff of Sussex in 1771, was elected one of the Parliamentary
representatives of Scarborough in 1761, and died in 1781. He was
created a *baronet,* with remainder to his son-in-law, the late John
Henniker, Esq., who was raised to an *Irish peerage* in 1800, by the
title of BARON HENNIKER, and died in 1803. *The Right Hon. John
Henniker Major, the present Lord Henniker,* is one of the Parliamentary representatives of the Eastern Division of Suffolk, for which
he has sat in three Parliaments. He married one of the daughters of

Lieut. General Sir E. Kerrison, Bart. The CHURCH (St. Mary) is a handsome structure, with a tower and five bells, and contains a good organ, given by the late Duchess of Chandos, and an elegant monument in memory of the late Lord Henniker. The benefice is a discharged rectory, valued in K.B. at £7. 11s. 3d., and in 1835 at £497, with that of Thornham Parva annexed to it. It is in the patronage of Lord Henniker, and incumbency of the *Rev. Sir Augustus Brydges Henniker, Bart.,* who resides at Newton Hall, Essex, and occasionally at Plashwood, Suffolk. (See page 270.) The Rev. Thomas Preston, M.A., is the curate. The *Town Estate,* consisting of the site of a tenement, and 4A. of land, let for £9 a year, was given by *John Bennett,* in 1434, for superstitious uses, the repairs of the church, and the payment of tithes and fifteens. The rent is all applied to the use of the church.

Henniker Right Honourable Lord, M.P. *Thornham Park*
Butcher Wm. and Son, bricklayers
Campling James, vict. *Horse Shoes*
Canler Wm. corn miller
GissingAnty.Sewell, relieving officer
Lamb Henry, blacksmith
Martin Thomas, wheelwright
Preston Rev Thomas, M.A. curate, Rectory
Pritty Mary, grocer and draper
FARMERS.
Barfoot Charles || Bull Seth
Green Edward || Mabson Wm. *hind*
Mullenger J. || Peck John
Steggall Charles || Wilson Charles

THORNHAM PARVA, a small village and parish, 2½ miles W.S.W. of Eye, has only 203 inhabitants, and 670 acres of land. Lord Henniker is lord of the *manor,* and owner of most of the soil, and the remainder belongs to Sir E. Kerrison, H. D. Hemsworth, and J. Gurdon, Esq. The *Church* is a small ancient edifice, with a round thatched steeple, containing only one bell. The living is a discharged *rectory,* valued in K.B. at £4. 14s. 4½d., and consolidated with that of Thornham Magna. The tithes of both parishes are about to be commuted. *Directory :*—Nathaniel Lamb, *blacksmith ;* Thomas Martin, carpenter ; and Thos. Aldridge, Richd. Anness, *Grange farm ;* Philip Youngman, *Chapel farm ;* and Robert Buck, *farmers.*

THRANDESTON, a pleasant village, scattered round a fine green, nearly 3 miles N.W. of Eye, and now in the parliamentary borough of Eye, has in its parish 373 inhabitants, and 1379A. 37P. of land. Sir E. Kerrison is lord of the *manors* of *Thrandeston Woodhall, Mavesons* in Thrandeston, and *Ampners,* near Thrandeston ; but the greater part of the parish belongs to the Rt. Hon. J. H. Frere, Thos. French, Esq., the Rev. N. D'Eye, the Rev. J. D. Hustler, Hy. Rix, Esq., and several smaller owners. *Goswold Hall,* an ancient moated house in the village, with a small estate attached to it, was granted by William the Conqueror to Walter D'Bowyer, and passed from his family to the Greys. From the latter it passed to the Rix family, and their heiress carried it in marriage to the Blakelys, who sold it lately to Thomas French, Esq., of Eye. A large *cattle fair* is held at Thrandeston, on July 31st and August 1st. The *Church* (St. Margaret) is a neat ancient structure, with a tower and five bells. In the chancel are two square stones, stripped of their brasses, and covering a vault said to contain the remains of Judge Reynolds. In the churchyard is a remarkably large oak tree. The *rectory,* valued in K.B. at £13. 6s. 8d., and in 1835 at £391, is in the gift of Sir E. Kerrison, Bart., and in-

cumbency of the Rev. Nathaniel D'Eye, M.A., who has a commodious residence, with pleasant grounds. The *Town Estate* comprises 9A., and a common right and a half, let for £18 a year, and three cottages and two hemplands, partly occupied, rent-free, by poor persons, and partly let for £6 per annum. The rents, according to ancient usage, are applied chiefly in the service of the church, and partly with the poor rates. The poor have a yearly rent-charge of £3 out of land at Brome, pursuant to an act for enclosing the open lands of that parish ; and they ought to have £2 a year out of Lady's field, but it has not been paid for some years.

D'Eye RevNathaniel,M.A. *Rectory*
Butcher Nathaniel, blacksmith
NunnMrGeo.|| NunnThos.beerhouse
Ruffell Richard, bricklayer
Wright Edwd. wheelwright & shopr
Wright Jemima, beerhouse

FARMERS. – (* *are owners.)*
Baker John || Branchflower Samuel
Hayward Charles || Rust Thomas
Kirby John, *Goswold Hall*
*Mickleburgh John || Rendall Henry
*Rix Thomas || Saunders Benjamin

THWAITE, a small village and parish, 5 miles S.W. by S. of Eye, contains 176 souls, and 832 acres of land. *Petty Sessions* are held here, at the Buck Inn, once a month. John George Sheppard, Esq., of Campsey Ash, owns nearly all the soil, and is lord of the manor, which was long the seat and property of the Reeves, one of whom, Sir George Wright Reeve, was created a *baronet* in 1661. The Countess Dowager of Leicester, the daughter and heiress of the last Sir Robert Reeve, carried the estate, by her second marriage, to John Sheppard, Esq., an ancestor of its present owner. Two *fairs* for cattle, &c., are held here on June 30th and Nov. 26th. The *Church* (St. George) is an ancient fabric, with a small belfry, and the living is a discharged *rectory*, valued in K.B. at £6. 3s. 1½d., and now having 21A. of glebe, a good residence, built in 1842, and a yearly modus of £234. 5s. 2d., awarded, in 1839, in lieu of tithes. J. G. Sheppard, Esq., is patron, and the Rev. George Wm. Kershaw, M.A., is the incumbent. The *Town Estate* comprises a cottage, occupied by paupers, and 2A. of land, let for £3. 10s., which is applied with the poor rates. The donor is un-known. *Directory:* Rev. G. W. Kershaw, *Rectory ;* Car. Rosier, vict., *Buck's Head*, (and post-office ;) Orlando Whistlecraft, *grocer, stationer, and publisher,* Minerva Cottage ; and Charles Camel, Deborah Canler, *Brockford Hall;* Thomas Sawyer, *Hill House;* James Rush and James Whistlecraft, *farmers.* The latter is also a *carpenter.*

WESTHORPE, 5 miles S. of Botesdale, and N.W. by W. of Mendlesham, and 8 miles N. of Stowmarket, is a pleasant village and parish, containing 264 souls, and 1322A. 1R. 19P. of land. Lady Nightingale is lady of the manor, and owner of a great part of the soil, and the remainder belongs to George Tomline, Esq., Mr. J. Kerry, and several smaller free and copyholders. The latter are subject to arbitrary fines. When Domesday survey was made, Westhorpe be-longed to Gilbert de Blund. Wm. de Ellingham, or Elmham, obtained a grant for a *market* and fair here in 1371, but they have long been obsolete. It was the manor of William de la Pole, Duke of Suffolk, when he was beheaded in 1450. It was afterwards granted to *Charles Brandon, Duke of Suffolk*, who married his third wife, *Mary Tudor, Dowager Queen of France*, and sister to Henry VIII., in 1571, (see

pages 603 and 630;) and here they resided in great splendour, at
WESTHORPE HALL, which was demolished many years ago. The
cloister, the chapel, with its painted window, and the original furniture, were kept up till about 80 years ago, when the whole was taken
down, and a farm house built on the site. Martin, who witnessed the
demolition, said it was done in a careless manner, all the fine chimneys
and ornaments being pulled down with ropes, and crushed to pieces.
The *Church* (St. Margaret) is a large ancient fabric, with a tower and
five bells, and contains several handsome monuments to the *Sheltons,*
who were long seated here. In the windows are some remains of ancient stained glass. The living is a discharged *rectory,* valued in K.B.
at £4. 18s. 1½d., and now having a yearly modus of £350, awarded, in
1839, in lieu of tithes. The Rev. Richd. Hewitt, D.D., is patron and
incumbent, and his son, the Rev. Richard Hewitt, jun., M.A., is the
curate. The *Town Estate* was formerly vested in trustees, but has
long been managed by the parish officers, and the rents applied with
the church and poor rates. It comprises a house and garden, occupied
by paupers; two roods of land, called Butt yard, let for 9s.; 2A. 2R.
in Car meadow, let for £3; and 9A. 2R. in Walsham-le-Willows, let
for £18 a year. A yearly rent-charge of 10s., left by *Richd. Brown,*
in 1641, is distributed among the poor on Easter Monday.

Hewitt Rev Richard, D.D. *Rectory*	FARMERS.—*(* are owners.)*
Hewitt Rev Richd. jun. M.A. curate	Anness Francis ‖ Cornell Joseph
Hails Joshua, carrier to *Bury,* Wed	*Berry Thomas Leabon
Hodgson Dudley Rose, land agent,	*Butler Wm. ‖ *Grimwood Wm.
Westhorpe Lodge	Largent Richard Davy
Largent Rd. D. architect & surveyor	Potter and Strange ‖ Leggett Chas.
Oliver Mary, vict. *Crown*	Rainbird Thomas, *Westhorpe Hall*
	Weavers Henry (and *cattle dealer*)

WETHERINGSETT-cum-BROCKFORD, the former a pleasant village, and the latter an adjacent hamlet, from 1 to 2 miles N.E. of Mendlesham, 6 miles S. by W. of Eye, and 4 miles N.W. of Debenham,
form a parish of 3777 acres of fertile and well-wooded land, and 1065
souls, of whom 277 with about 1000 acres, are in Brockford, and the
rest in Wetheringsett. They are near the source of the Dove rivulet,
which here crosses the Ipswich and Norwich turnpike, at the point anciently passed by a ford, called *Brook-ford.* Edmund Jenny, Esq.,
is lord of the manor of Wetheringsett, and J. G. Sheppard, Esq., is
lord of the manor of Brockford; but a great part of the parish belongs
to H. D. Hemsworth, R. Woodward, N. J. Scott, T. Revett, G. Hayward, S. Peck, J. Edwards, J. Seaman, and G. Tomline, Esqrs.; Lord
Henniker, Miss Alstone, Mrs. Huntingdon, and several smaller owners.
The copyholds pay arbitrary fines. Part of Brockford anciently belonged to Bury Abbey, and Wetheringsett to the church of Ely,
and afterwards to Lord Maynard. The *Church* (All Saints) is at
Wetheringsett, and is a large and handsome structure, with a lofty
tower, containing five bells. The north aisle is the property of the
Revett family, who have been seated here four centuries, but Tobias
Revett, Esq., is the last of the family. The *Rectory,* valued in K.B.
at £33. 9s. 2d., has 64A. 2R. 34P. of glebe, and a yearly modus of
£713. 19s. 10d., awarded in 1843 in lieu of tithes. A. Steward, Esq.,
is patron, and the Rev. Robert Moore, B.A., incumbent, for whom a

large and handsome *Rectory House* was built in 1843, at the cost of about £4000, of white brick, in the Tudor style. The Town Lands, &c., are under the management of trustees, and comprise 43A. 2R. 14P., let for £65 a year; a barn and 22 acres, let for £33 a year; 10 acres, formerly called Rooke's, let for £15 a year; and five tenements, (one called *Redding Poke Hall*, and another called *Mumford's*,) all occupied rent free by poor families. The rents of the land, after paying for repairs of the tenements and the church, are applied in distributions of fuel, blankets, and money, among poor parishioners; but the sum of 30s. is given as a dole to six poor widows, and the poor of Brockford have preference, in a dole of £3. In 1707, the *Rev. John Sheppard* left two yearly rent-charges to this parish, viz., 40s. a-year out of the Church Pightle, for a dinner on Lady day, to be given to 20 poor people; and 50s. out of an estate at Kelsale, for a distribution of 6 twopenny loaves weekly among six poor parishioners.

Marked 1, live in Brockford; and the others in Wetheringsett

1 Ablett James, grocer and draper
Chapman Thomas, shoemaker
Chapman Wm. shoemaker
1 Clark Thos. & Edw. carpenters
Clark Wm. carpenter
1 Cooper Thomas, shoemaker
1 Crowe Peter, beerhouse
Denny James, vict. *White Horse*
Edwards Rev Edwin, B.A. incumbt. of Ashfield
Gibbs Cornls. grocer and tailor
1 Gooderham Jas. vict. *Griffin*
Hayward Jerh. wheelwright
Hood Wm. blacksmith & wheelwgt
1 Jacob John, saddler
Moore Rev Robt. B.A. *Rectory*

Mortimer Geo. jun. shoemaker
1 Revett Tobias, Esq. *Brockford gn*
Robinson John, shoemaker
Rodwell Edward, beerhouse
Rodwell Edgar, bricklayer
Tye Thos. blacksmith

FARMERS. (** are owners*.)

1 Baskett Jonthn.
1 Cole Robert
Cowles Susan
1 Eastell Saml.
1 *Edwards Jno.
Grimwade Wm.
Hammond Robt.
Hayward Geo.
Bramham's hall
1 Howlett John
Lines John

*Mortimer Geo.
Peck Thomas
*Roper John
*Roper Sion
Rose Clark, *Potash*
1 *Seaman John
Sheldrake Mercy, *Hall*
Woodward Hy. *Lodge*

WICKHAM SKEITH, a village and parish, 3 miles N. of Mendlesham, and 6 miles S.W. of Eye, contains 574 souls, and 1770A. 1R. 25P. of fertile and well-wooded land, on which are some of the finest oaks in the county. The Rev. C. Garrad is lord of the *manor*, but the greater part of the soil belongs to J. G. Sheppard, Esq., Lord Henniker, the Right Hon. J. H. Frere, Charles Tyrell, Esq., E. B. Venn, Esq., Mrs. Amyott, Mr. W. L. Edwards, and a few smaller owners. Under an ancient oak on Wizard farm, many *Saxon coins*, of Harold, Edward the Confessor, &c., were found a few years ago, and are now deposited in the British Museum. The *Church* (St. Andrew) is a large ancient fabric, with a tower and six bells. The *vicarage*, valued in K.B. at £5. 8s. 1½d., is in the patronage of the Rev. C. Garrard, and incumbency of the Rev. Francis Howes, of Norwich. The tithes were communted, in 1839, for yearly moduses, viz., £422. 3s. to the nine *impropriators;* and £115. 6s. 1d. to the *vicar.* "The manor was given, in the reign of Stephen, to the Abbey of St. John, at Colchester, by a knight of great note in those days, named Robert de Salco Villa, who at last turned monk, upon condition that four monks of that house should be settled here to pray for his soul; and in the next reign, his son Jordan, consented that the religious should be withdrawn from

hence, and removed to Colchester, where the convent was to be increased with four religious above their old number." In the 34th of Henry VIII., this manor was granted to Richard Freston, and it afterwards passed to the Bacon and other families. The *Hall*, now a farmhouse, has near it some fine full grown oaks. The *Town Estate*, consists of two cottages, occupied rent-free by poor families; and a farm of 15A. 39P. in Brockford, let for £20 a year, which is carried to the church and poor rates. There are no writings concerning this property.

Battrum Wm. miller and farmer
Bendall Martha, vict. *Swan*
Eade Rev'Thos. French, curate,B.A.
Leggett William, wheelwright and blacksmith
Pollard James, shopkeeper

FARMERS.
Craske Edw. S. || Deck Edw. *Hall*
Edwards Wm. Lea, *Broad Oak*
Parker Charles || Parker Samuel
Steggall George
Tunmer Thomas, *Wizard Farm*
Ward John, *Abbey Farm*

WORTHAM, a widely scattered village, 3 miles N.E. of Botesdale, and S.W. of Diss, and 6 miles N.W. by W. of Eye, has its parish 1116 inhabitants, and 2726A. 3R. 31P. of land, separated by the Waveney from Norfolk, and including more than 250A. of open commons, called *Long Green* and the *Ling*, the latter of which has had its peaty soil skinned off by the parishioners for fuel. Upon this Ling is a small tumulus, and one of the *Workhouses* of Hartismere Union, already noticed at page 321. The parish is in two *manors*, viz., *Wortham Hall*, of which the Rev. Thomas D. Betts, is lord; and *Wortham Abbot's*, of which George St. Vincent Wilson, Esq., is lord; but a great part of the soil belongs to Miss Harrison, Mrs. Barber, J. J. Tuck, Esq., Mrs. Burgess, Messrs. T. Rust, and H. and R. Balding, and a few smaller owners. The *Manor House*, belonging to T. D. Betts, Esq., and occupied by John Johnson Tuck, Esq., is finely embowered in trees, and was for more than two centuries the seat of the Betts family. The *Church* (St. Mary) is a large ancient structure, but of its massive round tower, only the shell now remains. The *rectory* was in two medieties, valued in K.B. as follows:—Wortham Everard, at £13. 2s. 8½d.; and Wortham Jervis, at £13. 2s. 1½d. These medieties were consolidated in 1789, and are now in the patronage and incumbency of the Rev. Richard Cobbold, M.A., rural dean, who erected a large and handsome *Rectory House*, in 1828. The glebe is about 40A., and the tithes were commuted in 1839 for a yearly modus of £860. The full annual value of the parish is £5340, and the assessed rental £3936. The Rev. Wm. Thurlow, brother of Lord Chief Justice Thurlow, was rector here, and was buried in the chancel, about 1718. The present rector liberally supports a *Day and Sunday School*, for the education of the poor. In the 22d of James I., *Thomas Church* left 4A. of land, for the poor parishioners, and it is now let for £7 per annum.

Browne Charles Youngman, grocer and draper
Cobbold Rev Richard, M.A. curate and rural dean
Dover Miss

Fake John, wheelwright
Gamble Misses My., Ann, & Jane
Helsden John, governor, Workhouse
Potter Henry, gentleman
Roper Geo. Wm. gentleman

Smith John, beerhouse
Tuck John Johnson, Esq.*Manor Hs*

INNS AND TAVERNS.
Dolphin, John Nunn
Magpie, Mary Ann Bruce
Queen's Head, Samuel Allen
Tumble-down-Dick, James Hall

Academies.
Brock Eliz.
Moses John
Vine Thos.

Blacksmiths.
Pretty John
Salter Robert

Shoemakers.
Churchard Jas.
Crack George
Potter Robert

FARMERS.
Adams Henry, *Spears Hill Farm*
Adams Thomas, *Wood House*
Algar Robert
Balding Henry, *Wortham grv*
Balding Richard

Bricklayers.
Bobby Benj.
Edwards Saml.

Corn Millers.
Adams George
Rash John
Robinson James

Battrum Samuel
Bond David
Burgess Alfred
Cullingford Wm.
Drake Ephraim, *New Water*
Hart Thomas
Jolly John, (cattle dealer)
Marshall Chas.
Read Wm.
Roper John
Snelling John
Wright Chas.

WYVERSTONE, a scattered village and parish, 7 miles N. of Stowmarket, and 5½ miles S. of Botesdale, comprises 348 souls and 1522A. 2R. 21P. of land, mostly freehold and partly copyhold. In the Conqueror's time, it was the lordship of Gilbert de Bland, and afterwards of the De la Poles, Earls of Suffolk. The Ewers held it for some time, and after them the Barnardistons. John Moseley, Esq., is now lord of the manor, but the soil belongs to H. J. Oakes, Esq., J. S. Ord, Esq., G. Tomline, Esq., Mr. B. Leggett, the Rev. Fras Upjohn, and a few smaller owners. The *Church* (St. George) is a rectory, valued in K.B. at £8. 14s. 9½d., and is in the patronage of John Moseley, Esq., and incumbency of the Rev. James Ware, who has a good residence and 15A. of glebe. The tithes were commuted in 1839, for a yearly modus of £331. 17s. 2d. The *Town Estate* is vested in trustees for the benefit and advantage of the parish, and is partly free and partly copyhold. It comprises two houses, a cottage, and two gardens, occupied rent-free by poor parishioners; and a house, cottage, and about 30 acres of land, let for £43. 10s. a year, which is applied in repairing the church and the buildings on the estate, and for other general purposes of the parish.

Baker John, shoemaker
Berry Thomas, tai or
Chandler Mr John
Cutting Thomas, shoemaker
Garrard John, shoemaker
Marrington Robt. corn miller
Sauds Robert, blacksmith
Steggall Wm. Charles, gent
Townsend Wm. tinner & beerhouse

Ware Rev James, rector
Woods Wm. carpenter

FARMERS. *(* are Owners.)*
*Baldry James || Baker John
Barker George || Boby Hy. *Park*
Clark Joseph || Clements Wm.
*Cutting Wm. || Eaton Edward
*Howlett Robert||Nicholls James
*Osbourn William

YAXLEY, in the parliamentary borough, and 1½ mile W. of Eye, is a scattered village and parish, containing 507 inhabitants, and 1238A. 2R. 6P. of land, partly copyhold. Sir E. Kerrison, Bart, is lord of the manor, but the greater part of the soil belongs to Lord Henniker, J. Gurdon, Esq., Rev. James Lane, J. Cobbold, Esq., P. R. Welch, Esq., and several smaller owners. *Yaxley Hall*, a large and handsome mansion, in the Elizabethan style, with extensive plantations and pleasure grounds, was the seat of the late F. G. Y. Leeke, Esq., and is now the residence of his relict and P. R. Welch, Esq. The *Church* (St. Mary) is an ancient structure, with a beautiful porch, and a tower containing six bells. The *vicarage*, valued in K.B. at £6. 6s.

5½d., is in the patronage of Robert Knipe Cobbold, Esq., and incumbency of the Rev. Robert Rolfe, M.A., who has 35 acres of glebe, and a yearly modus of £139, awarded in 1842, in lieu of tithes. The rectorial tithes have been commuted for £287. 17s. per annum, of which £26. 13s. belongs to Lord Henniker; £18. 15s. to J. Cobbold, Esq.; and the remainder to Sir Edward Kerrison, Bart. The *Town Estate* has for a long period been appropriated to the use of the church, the reparation of the houses used for the poor, and the payment of the constable's expenses ; and when any surplus remains, it is applied in clothing poor children, or binding them out apprentices. The estate comprises the Guildhall and cottages, occupied rent-free by poor parishioners ; 11 acres of *common ;* and a cottage and 22A. 3R. 9P. of land in this and the neighbouring parishes, let to various tenants, in 1829, at rents amounting to £35. 19s. 4d. per annum. The poor have a yearly rent-charge of £4, left by an unknown donor, out of Yaxley Hall estate; and two others, of 8s. each, left by *John Roe* and *John Clarke*, out of a cottage and 4 acres belonging to Mr. Welton. Yaxley Hall is also charged with the yearly payment of £1. 13s. 4d. for repairing the highways.

Leeke Mrs Ann, *Yaxley Hall*
Mullenger James, wheelwright
Murton James, wheelwright
Palmer William, cattle dealer and vict. *Bull*
Reeve Robert, vict. *Red Lion*
Rockett Charlotte, shopkeeper
Sprigge Rev Wm. M.A. curate
Stanton James, corn miller
Welch Patrick Robt. Esq. barrister, *Yaxley Hall*

Welton Ann, shopkeeper
Welton Edmund, blacksmith
Woodward John, grocer & draper
Wright Mrs Ann

FARMERS.

Bate Wm. || Allen Wm.
Blofield George, *Manor House*
Drane Thos. || Elvin Thos.
Fulcher Thomas
Murton Samuel, *Bull Hall*
Tillott Robert, *White House*

BLYTHING HUNDRED.

This is the largest Hundred in Suffolk, and lies on the east side of the county, extending nearly twenty miles along the sea coast, and having its two other sides nearly of the same length, projecting westward and forming an irregular triangle, bounded on the south › y Plomesgate Hundred; on the west, by Hoxne Hundred; on the north, by Wangford and Mutford Hundreds; and on the east, by the ocean. It is in *Blything Union*, in the *Deanery of Dunwich, Archdeaconry of Suffolk*, and *Diocese of Norwich ;* and constitutes a baronial *Liberty*, of which Lord Huntingfield is *bailiff*, and Harry White, Esq., *steward ;* and for which a *Court*, (formerly having cognizance of debts under 40s.) is held yearly at Covehithe. It is watered by the river *Blythe* (from which it has its name,) and many smaller streams, flowing eastward to the sea, and some of them forming " *broads*," or small lakes, near the coast, which rises in many places in bold precipitous cliffs. The western parts form a high district of hill and dale, and have a strong and fertile loamy soil ; but on the eastern side, near the sea, a light sand prevails, and there are still some unenclosed sheep walks. It is in all

parts picturesque, and includes the thriving market town of *Halesworth ;* the decayed borough and port of *Dunwich ;* and the rising port, borough, and town of *Southwold,* an important fishing station and fashionable bathing place. Its creeks and fishing stations were formerly more numerous than at present, some of them having been choked up or washed away by the ocean, which is slowly but constantly wasting many parts of the coast. It is divided into 46 *parishes,* and one *township,* (Henham,) of which the following is an enumeration, shewing their hamlets, their territorial extent, the annual value of their lands and buildings, as assessed to the property tax, in 1815, and their population in 1801 and 1841.

PARISHES.	Acrs.	Ren-tal.	Populatn. 1801.	1841.	PARISHES.	Acres.	Rental. £.	Population. 1801.	1841.
Aldringham ⎰	628	692	221	259	Linstead Parva	554	562	134	205
Thorpe *ham.* ⎱	1108			142	Middleton- ⎰	1420	2183	488	599
Benacre	2576	1467	178	194	with-Fordley ⎱	604			
Blythburgh‖				592	Peasenhall ..	1972	2359	532	845
Bulcamp *ham* ⎰	4111	2818	886	109	Reydon*	2675	2000	317	433
Hinton *ham.* ⎱				136	Rumburgh	1370	1661	358	435
Blythford	1373	709	163	223	Sibton	2680	3039	421	564
Bramfield	2547	3300	552	746	Sotherton	1084	966	168	222
Brampton	1967	1992	236	322	Southwold§ ..	632	1849	1054	2186
Chediston	2378	2421	368	433	Spexhall	1482	1468	140	215
Cookley	1552	1719	264	324	Stoven........	762	788	125	127
Cove (South)..	1198	814	131	194	Theberton* ..	2050	1856	430	580
Covehithe	1524	808	180	186	Thorington....	1411	1340	125	157
Cratfield......	2000	2418	551	720	Ubbeston	1207	1321	177	243
Darsham	1493	2012	421	528	Uggeshall ...	1455	1656	335	295
Dunwich	1334	522	184	237	Walberswick..	1771	1496	229	339
Easton Bavents	260	370	17	11	Walpole	1624	1927	494	615
Frostenden* ..	1292	1617	266	428	Wangford .. ⎰	829	1230	477	690
Halesworth ..	1420	3894	1676	2662	Henham twp. ⎱	1500	1947	166	128
Heveningham	1900	1838	305	417	Wenhaston ⎰	2327	2580	578	971
Henstead .. ⎰	1920	1397	227	280	Melles *ham.* ⎱				123
Hulvrstreet.† ⎱				293	Westhall	2194	2300	373	412
Holton	1132	1487	328	541	Westleton	6103	2987	661	897
Huntingfield ..	2011	2258	373	397	Wissett	2260	2551	349	470
Knodishall‡ ..	1731	1516	286	397	Wrentham	1280	3114	822	1020
Leiston .... ⎰	4966	3069	823	1111	Yoxford	2670	3616	851	1251
Sizewell *ham* ⎱				66					
LinsteadMagna	1304	1471	93	92	Total	87,631	87,405	18,010	26,062

‖ Blythburgh parish includes the *Union Workhouse at Bulcamp,* which had 523 inmates in 1801, and 215 in 1841.

* Frostenden, in 1841, included 24, and Walberswick 16, *visitors ;* and Raydon 21, and Theberton 9 persons, *in tents.*

‡ Knodishall includes Buxlow, which was anciently a parish.

§ About 200 *seamen,* belonging to *Southwold,* were absent at the census of 1841. The return included 17 persons *in barges,* and 19 *in tents.*

☞ CHIEF CONSTABLES, John Aldis, *Halesworth ;* Richard Boyce, *Southwold ;* Benj. Reeve, *Wangford ;* John Potter, *Yoxford ;* John Lay, *Peasenhall ;* and James Hingeston, Frostenden.

BLYTHING UNION comprises all the 47 parishes of Blything Hundred, and also *Carlton* and *Kelsale* parishes, which form a detached member of Hoxne Hundred. These 49 parishes contained 27,321 inhabitants in 1841, and extend over an area of about 91,300 acres, or 138 square miles. All the parishes in Blything Hundred, except Dunwich, were incorporated

by an Act of the 4th of George III, (1764,) for the maintenance of their poor, in a *House of Industry*, erected in the course of the two following years at *Bulcamp*, in Blythburgh parish, nearly in the centre of the Hundred. The sum of £12,000 was borrowed on the credit of the poor rates, for the erection of this WORKHOUSE, and was repaid by annual instalments, the last of which was paid in 1791. This house was so unpopular among the poor, that before it was completely finished, it was partly destroyed by a riotous mob, which was dispersed by the military. It was opened October 13th, 1766, on which day 56 paupers were admitted. It had 352 *inmates* in April 1767, and the average number during the following years was—214, in 1790; 281, in 1795; 331, in 1800; 335, in 1810; 533, in 1817; 558, in 1818; 551, in 1820; 445, in 1825; 401, in 1830; 345, in 1835; 192, in 1840; and 264, in 1843. The Directors and Acting Guardians dissolved the incorporation in July, 1835, and at their request the present Union was formed under the control of the New Poor Law Commissioners. In the following year, about £1000 was expended in altering the Workhouse, so as to admit of a better classification of the inmates. The male able-bodied inmates are employed in a hand corn mill, in picking oakum, &c. The average annual expenditure of the 46 parishes during the seven years preceding their incorporation in 1764, was only £3085, being only about one shilling in the pound on the assessed rental. The expenditure on the poor of the 49 parishes forming the present Union was £23,777, in 1832; £23,389, in 1833; £23,752, in 1834; £11,000, in 1839; £10,005, in 1840; and £9400, in 1841; thus, it appears, that since the formation of the Union, the poor rates have been reduced about fifty per cent; but these sums are exclusive of the county rates, to which the Union contributes about £3000 per annum, which is paid out of the poor rates. Three *Guardians* are elected for Halesworth, two each for Kelsale, Leiston, Peasenhall, Southwold, Walpole, Wenhaston, Westleton, Wrentham, and Yoxford; and one for each of the other parishes. Harry White, Esq., of Halesworth, is *clerk of the Board of Guardians*, of which the Earl of Stradbroke is *chairman*, and Sir Thomas S. Gooch, *vice-chairman.* Mr. Daniel and Mrs. Forman are *master and matron of the Workhouse;* John Beales, Esq., *house surgeon;* and the Rev. Richard Day, *chaplain.* The Union is divided into 12 *Medical Districts*, each having its own surgeon. Mr. Daniel Forman is also *Superintendent Registrar* of the Union, which is divided into three districts, of which the following are the *Relieving Officers and Registrars of Births and Deaths*, viz., Mr. Wm. Fisher, of Cratfield, for the *first;* Mr. Thos. Tuthill, of Blythburgh, for the *second;* and Mr. Charles White, jun., of Wenhaston, for the *third district.* Mr. E. B. Haxell, of Halesworth, is *Deputy-Superintendent Registrar;* Mr. Wm. Fisher, of Cratfield, *Registrar of Marriages* for the whole Union; and W. C. Hotson, Esq., of Little Massingham, Norfolk, is the *auditor.* For Blything Hundred SAVINGS' BANK, see Halesworth.

ALDRINGHAM, a small village, 2½ miles N. by W. of Aldborough, and 5 miles S.E. of Saxmundham, has in its parish 1736 acres of land, and 401 inhabitants, including THORPE, which has 1108 acres, and 142 souls, and is a hamlet and fishing station on the sea coast, 1½ mile E. of Aldringham, and had a chapel, which was in use after the Reformation, and of which some vestiges still remain. Hamo de Masey, in the 12th of Edward II., obtained a charter for a *market* and *fair* at Aldringham. The former has long been obsolete, but two small fairs are now held here on October 11th and December 11th. The soil is generally a light sand, and about 250A. form an open common. It belongs mostly to W. A. Shuldham, Esq., and P. J.

Thellusson's Trustees, the latter of whom have lately purchased a great part of Aldringham of Mr. Fras. Hayle, of *Stone Cottage*, a neat house embowered in plantations, nearly a mile E. of the village. The *Church* (St. Andrew) was appropriated to Leiston abbey by Ranulph Glanvile, the founder. It is an ancient structure, and had a tower, which fell to ruin many years ago, but its remains were not cleared away till 1843, when th·· church was repaired, and a small belfry erected, at the west end. The impropriation and advowson were granted in the 28th of Henry VIII. to the Duke of Suffolk, and are now held by Lord Huntingfield, who has now a yearly modus of £205 in lieu of tithes. The benefice is a perpetual curacy, not in charge, valued at only £59, and now in the incumbency of the Rev. Henry Turner Dowler, M.A. The Baptists have a chapel in the parish.

Aldis Rev Robert, Baptist minister
Bird Edward, farmer
Chard Joshua, fisherman, *Thorpe*
Chason Charlotte, shopkpr. *Thorpe*
Cotton James, shopkeeper
Crane James, corn miller
Gildersleeves George, farmer
Gowing Robert, farmer, *Thorpe*
Hayle Francis, gent. *Stone Cottage*
Kemp Chas. vict. Parrot & Punchbowl
Kemp Thomas, blacksmith
Nunn James, farmer, *Thorpe*
Salter Jno. vict. Cross Keys, *Thorpe*
Shuldham William Abraham, Esq. *Thorpe (and Cransford Lodge)*

BENACRE, or *Binacre*, a scattered village, 7 miles S.E. of Beccles, and S.W. of Lowestoft, and 6 miles N.N.E. of Southwold, has in its parish 194 souls, and 2575A. 3R. 13P. of sandy and marshy land, extending eastward to the sea beach, near which is *Benacre Broad*, a sheet of fresh water covering more than 50 acres, and bounding in pike and other fish. It was anciently the lordship and demesne of the Pierpoints, and afterwards passed successively to the Bowetts, Dacres, and other families. It was purchased about the middle of last century of the Carthew family by Sir Thos. Gooch, who was created a *Baronet* in 1746. It now belongs to his descendant, *Sir Thos. Sherlock Gooch, Bart.*, of BENACRE HALL, a spacious mansion of white brick, in a large and beautiful park, on the west side of the parish. In 1786, one of the workmen employed in cutting the *turnpike*, which adjoins the park, found a stone bottle, containing upwards of 900 pieces of silver coin, mostly in good preservation, and none older than the time of Vespasian. Sir T. Gooch bought about 700 of them, and the remainder were sold to a Jew, who retailed them at low prices in the neighbourhood. The *Church* (St. Michael) is a neat fabric, and the living is a *rectory*, with the rectory of Easton-Bavents and the vicarage of Covehithe united with it, and valued in K.B. at £18; and in 1835, at £440. Sir T. S. Gooch, Bart., is patron, and the Rev. Wm. Gooch, incumbent. They support a daily and Sunday school, for the instruction of the poor. The other principal parishioners are Stephen Cox, vict., *Walnut Tree ;* Christopher Smith, bailiff; and Osborne Clacke, Edmund Cottingham, and James Eccleston, *farmers.*

BLYTHBURGH is a small village, pleasantly situated on the river *Blythe*, near Henham Park, at the junction of turnpikes from Beccles and Lowestoft, 4½ miles W. of Southwold, and E. by S. of Halesworth. Its parish contains 4011 acres of land, and had 837 inhabitants in 1841, of whom 215 were in the *Union Workhouse* (already noticed at page 355;) 109 in the hamlet of *Bulcamp ;* 136 in the hamlet of

Hinton ; and 373 in Blythburgh. Though now a humble village, Blythburgh was formerly a flourishing little town and port, and had a considerable fishery, and a gaol for the division of Beccles, for which Quarter Sessions were held here. It had also a weekly market, and two annual *fairs,* and one of the latter is still held on the 5th of April. Its decline is attributed to its river becoming so choked up, as to be navigable to the town only for small barges, and to the suppression of its Priory. In 1679, many of its houses, with their goods and furniture, were burnt by an accidental fire, and the damage was estimated at £18,030. A dreadful thunder storm happened here on Sunday, August 4th, 1577, during divine service, when the lightning did great damage to the church, and struck down 20 people, of whom two were killed and others scorched. The spire and part of the steeple were thrown down, and other parts of the church were "rent and torn by the tempest, which took its course to Bungay, where it did much mischief." Several Roman coins and urns have been discovered here; and it is said that *Anna, king of the East Angles,* and Firminus, his son, who were slain fighting against Penda, king of Mercia, in *Bulcamp forest,* were buried here in 654. About forty yards east of the church, are some ivy-mantled remains of a small *Priory of Black Canons.* The revenues of the church of Blythburgh being given by Henry I. to the abbot and convent of St. Osith, in Essex, they soon afterwards founded this priory, which was endowed by Richard Beauveys, Bishop of London, and other benefactors. It was suppressed in the 26th of Henry VIII., when it contained only five canons, and its revenues were valued at £48. 8s. 10d. per annum. It was granted to Sir Arthur Hopton, then lord of the manor. Here was anciently a building called Holy Rood Chapel, of which there were some remains in 1750. *Westwood,* formerly a large park, contained the ancient mansion of the former lords of the *manor,* which is now held, with a great part of the soil in this and the neighbouring parishes, by Sir Charles Blois, Bart. ; but Col. Bence, Col. Raper, F. Barne, Esq., N. Micklethwaite, Esq., the Earl of Stradbroke, Mr. Joseph Wigg, and several smaller owners, have estates here. The ancient hall having, as is conjectured from various relics found on its site, been destroyed by fire, the present edifice, called WESTWOOD LODGE, (2 miles S. of Blythburgh,) commanding a pleasant sea view, was erected about the middle of the 17th century, by John Brooke, Esq., from whom it descended to the family of Blois. It has long been let, with a fine farm of 3000 acres, now occupied by Mr. J. G. Cooper, a celebrated breeder of sheep and cattle, who has here annually an extensive stock sale. The *river Blythe* is navigable up to Halesworth for small barges, and below it forms a large " *broad,*" extending two miles to the new quay and lime-kiln at Walberswick, whence it runs, in a straight and deepened channel, about two miles in length, to the pier south of Southwold, and forms a harbour to that sea-port for vessels of 100 tons burthen. Several hundred acres of fine marsh land, on the banks of the Blythe, have been *embanked and drained* during the last fifty years. The CHURCH (Holy Trinity) is a large ancient structure, which has been extremely beautiful, but has been much mutilated by time and injudicious repairs. The windows are numerous, and have been richly decorated with painted glass and tracery, most of which

have given place to unsightly masses of brick. Internally the fine carved work has been covered with many coats of whitewash; and the carvings on the roof, consisting of angels bearing shields, have so long been in a decayed and mouldering condition, that many of them have fallen down. The porch is still decorated with grotesque heads, and at each corner stands an angel with expanded wings. In 1442, John Greyse left 20 marks towards rebuilding the chancel. The tower, which formerly had a spire, is of inferior workmanship to the nave and chancel. There were two chapels at the east end, dedicated to the Blessed Virgin, and her mother St. Anne; and in the church were several altars, and a great number of images of saints. In the 30th of Henry VI., John Hopton, Esq., founded a *chantry* here, dedicated to St. Margaret. At the east end of the north aisle, is shewn a tomb, said to be that of Anna, king of the East Angles, and in the chancel, another, for his son Firminus; but their remains are said to have been removed to the abbey church of Bury St. Edmund's. Upon an altar monument in the chancel have been raised two clumsy columns of brick, which has occasioned the remark, that the person whom it covers, whatever he might have been in his life-time, is now a firm supporter of the church. In front of two pews near this tomb, are eighteen small figures, representing the apostles and other scripture characters; and at the west end of the middle aisle, is the figure of a man, which used to strike time on a bell, now cracked, in the same manner as those at St. Dunstan's, in London. The benefice is a *perpetual curacy*, not in charge, in the patronage of Sir Charles Blois, Bart., who is also impropriator of the tithes, out of which he allows about £45 a year to the incumbent, now the Rev. Thomas Harrison. The Primitive Methodists have a small chapel here, built in 1837. HINTON hamlet extends from 1 to 3 miles S. by W. of Blythburgh, and has several scattered farm houses; and BULCAMP lies north of the village, on the opposite side of the river, and has several scattered houses and cottages, and the large *Union Workhouse*, noticed at page 355, and situated on an eminence nearly a mile from Blythburgh. The *Church Land* is in two pieces, called Thistley Meadow and Penny Pightle, let for £19 a year. In 1701, *Thos. Neale* left, out of an estate at Bramfield, a yearly rent-charge of £3, and directed £2. 10s. thereof to be applied for teaching five poor children of Blythburgh to read, and 10s. for buying bibles and other religious books for young persons. The annuity is paid by Mr. Haward, the owner of the estate, and is applied towards the support of a Sunday school. The poor of Blythburgh and Bulcamp have a yearly rent-charge of 20s., left by an unknown donor, out of land belonging to the Earl of Stradbroke.

Marked 1, reside at Bulcamp; 2, at Hinton; and the rest at Blythburgh

Bickers Wm. millwright
Elmy Esau, parish clerk
1 Forman Daniel, superintendt. regr. and governor, *Union Workhouse*
Hatcher Benj. wheelwright & beerhs
Holmes Robert, policeman
Lay John, corn merchant, &c; house Peasenhall
Patman Mary Ann, schoolmistress
Tuthill Thomas, jun. relieving officer and registrar
Truman Dorothy, vict. White Hart
2 Wigg Joseph, gent. *Poplar House*

Blacksmiths. | Whincop George
Burton Wm.

Boot&ShoeMkrs.	1 Farrow John	Tuthill Geo. and	Puttock Robert
Aldis James	Baker	William	(and tailor)
Burton James	2 Friston Judith	2 Wigg Joseph	The *Mail Cart,*
Dodd Richard	1 Ling Wm.	Woods John (and	and *Coaches &*
FARMERS.	Lyon Wm.	miller)	*Carriers* to Ips-
2 Cole James	Osbourn Ezekial		wich, Yarmth.
Cooper Js.Green-	2 Porter George	*Grocers & Drprs.*	&c. call at the
ling, *West-*	2 Stanford Adps.	Catchpole James	WhiteHartInn,
wood Lodge	2 Tacon John	Lumkin Ann	daily

BLYTHFORD, or *Blyford*, a scattered village, on the north bank of the Blythe, 2¼ miles E. by S. of Halesworth, has in its parish 223 souls, and 1373 acres of land, rising in bold undulations from the river. The *Church* (All Saints) was appropriated to Blythburgh Priory, before the year 1200, by Ralph de Criketot. It is now a donative in the patronage, impropriation, and incumbency of the Rev. Jeremy Day, who has a yearly modus of £411. 18s., in lieu of tithes, and is lord of the manor; but a great part of the soil belongs to the Earl of Stradbroke and several smaller owners. The *Hall*, an ancient mansion, near the church, is occupied by a farmer.

Algar James, boot and shoe maker	Row Robert, shopkeeper
Croft James, vict. Queen's Head	Thrower Wm. blacksmith
Cullingford Wincop, grocer, &c.	FARMERS.
Edwards John, parish clerk	Beaumont Richard ‖ Block Wm.
Phillips James, boot and shoe maker	Cross John ‖ Tyrell Abraham
Puttock Robert, bricklayer	Garrard Seaman, *Blythford Hall*
Reeve John, bricklayer	Thompson Joseph (and owner)

BRAMFIELD, a large and well-built village on the turnpike, 2 miles S. of Halesworth, and 8 miles N. by E. of Saxmundham, has in its parish 746 souls, and 2546A. 3R. 25P. of land, exclusive of roads. The manor was given by Sir John de Norwich, in the reign of Edward III., to the college which he founded at Mettingham. At the dissolution, it was granted to Thos. Denney, from whom it passed to the Rous family. The Earl of Stradbroke is now lord of the manor of *Bramfield-cum-Brook Hall*, but a great part of the soil belongs to Colonel Bence, Capt. Page, the Rev. R. Rabett, P. Tatlock, Esq., and several smaller owners. *Brook Hall* is the pleasant seat of Capt. Page; and *Bramfield Hall*, a fine old mansion near the church, is the residence of the Rev. Reginald Rabett, whose family has long been seated here. The *Church* (St. Andrew) is an ancient structure with a round tower, detached at the distance of 12 yards, and containing five bells. In the chancel is an elegant monument to Arthur, third son of the celebrated lawyer, Sir Edward Coke. On the pavement are many black marble stones, for the two ancient families of Rabett and Nelson. The *vicarage*, valued in K.B. at £6. 7s. 6d., is in the patronage of the Crown, and incumbency of the Rev. R. Rabett, who has a yearly modus of £210, in lieu of the vicarial tithes, awarded a few years ago, when the great tithes, now in the impropriation of Mr. R. Haward, were commuted for £420 per annum. Here is a small Independent Chapel, built, in 1841, at the cost of £250. An *Almshouse*, for eight poor parishioners, was built here in 1723, pursuant to the will of *Thos. Neale*, who, in 1701, left directions for its erection, and charged his real estate with the yearly payment of £3, for one of the almspeople to teach six poor

children to read the Bible, and 10s. a-year to provide them with Bibles and religious books. The testator's widow, *Mary Fowle*, in 1708, left £100 to be laid out in land, the rent thereof to be applied for repairing the almshouse, and when not wanted for that purpose, to be distributed among poor widows of the parish. This legacy, with £80 left by *Eliz. Archer*, in 1716, for schooling poor children, and finding them Bibles, was laid out, in 1727, in the purchase of a house and 10A. 2R. of land, at Metfield, now let for £13 a-year, of which about £8 is applied in relieving the almspeople, and repairing the almshouse, and the remainder is paid to the schoolmaster, together with the above-named rentcharges of £3. and 10s., for teaching 13 poor children, and finding them with 20s. worth of books yearly. The land adjoining and belonging to the almshouse is let for £2 a-year. The *School* was built and is repaired by the parishioners. New trustees were appointed in 1812. A cottage and 2A. of copyhold land have, from a remote period, been vested in trust for the benefit of the inhabitants, and are let for £9 a-year. The rent used to be carried to the churchwardens' account, but has of late years been applied in aid of the poor rates. The Rev. R. Rabett and others are trustees.

Andrews Jno. jun. veterinary surgeon
Andrews Jno. sen. veterinary surgeon
Bailey Sophia, schoolmistress
Balls Henry, beerhouse
Batterham Margaret, draper, &c.
Brown Lucy, straw hat maker
Cottermull Benj. grocer and draper
Clowe Sarah, schoolmistress
Debney Wm. grocer and draper
Feathers Robt. plumber & glazier
Fieldbank Mr Jph. *Bramfield Lodge*
Heffer Wm. butcher
Howlett Horace, vict. *Swan*
Lock Hy. tailor, *Post-office.* Letters rec. at 7 mg. & desp. at ½ p. 7 evg.
Mason Rev Christopher, curate
Page Capt. Thomas, *Brook Hall*
Rabett Rev Reginald, *Bramfield Hl*
Tatlock Paul, Esq.
Tillett Jph. vict. Queen's Head

Blacksmiths.
Hatcher John
Wright Wm.
Boot&ShoeMkrs.
Catling Charles
Cupper Arthur
Pierson Wm.
Bricklayers.
Eastaugh Nathl.
Kemp James
FARMERS.
Andrews Robt. (and miller)
Archer John
Bloomfield Robt.
Capon Stephen, *Cottage*
Craske Wm.
Croft James, (& miller)
Cross Samuel
Cross James

Fulsham Robert
Haddingham Rt.
HaddinghamStn.
Haward Robert, *Manor House*
Higham Thomas
Higham Wm. Aldis
Raynor Jnth.
Smyth James
Whiting Wm.
Winter Wm.
Wright Henry
Joiners, &c.
Button Anthony
Clowe Robert
Wheelwrights.
Eastaugh John
Hilling Joseph
Coach & Carriers pass daily to London, &c.

BRAMPTON, on the Beccles road, 4½ miles N.E. of Halesworth, is a pleasant village and parish, containing 384 souls, and 1966A. 2R. 14P. of fertile land. The *manor* and advowson have been held by the Lemans since 1600, and now belong to the Rev. George O. Leman, of *Brampton Hall*, a handsome red-brick mansion, in a small, but wellwooded park, erected after the old hall had been destroyed by fire, in 1733. The Earl of Gosford, Mr. Henry Jex, Thos. Farr, Esq., and several smaller owners, have estates in the parish, and part of it is a small manor, called Hales Hall. The *Church* (St. Peter) is a small structure, with a tower and five bells. The rectory, valued in K.B. at £20, is in the patronage of the Rev. G. O. Leman, M.A., and incumbency of the Rev. Thos. O. Leman, B.A., who has a good residence,

11A. of glebe, and a yearly modus of £420 in lieu of tithes. The Town's Houses and about 3A. of marsh land let for £8, and a house in four tenements, let for £3 a-year, are vested with the churchwardens for the relief of the poor. About 12A. of meadow land, called the *Town Fen*, is let for £30 a-year, and the rent is applied in the service of the church. The original acquisition of the property is unknown. A *Sunday School* here has £9. 6s. 8½d. yearly from Leman's Charity. (See Cratfield.)

Cleveland John, veterinary surgeon and vict. *Dog*	Suggate Thomas, beerhouse
	Todd Robert, bricklayer
Halifax Richard, blacksmith	FARMERS.
Lay Wm. joiner	Butcher John
Leman Rev George Orgill, M.A. *Brampton Hall*	Chipperfield Jno.
	Clutton Samuel, *Old Hall*
Leman Rev Ts. Orgill, B.A. *Rectory*	Crickmer John
Quadling Edw. wheelwright & smith	Gibson J.
Sales John, blacksmith	Hamblin Wm.
Suggate Austin, parish clerk	

FARMERS continued:
Hamblin W. jun.
Jex Hy. *(owner)*
Quadling Chas.
Read John
Skoulding Sarah
Squire Wm.
Woods George

CHEDISTON, a small village on an acclivity near one of the tributary streams of the Blythe, 2 miles W. of Halesworth, has in its picturesque parish 433 souls, several scattered farmhouses, and 2378 acres of land, of which nearly two-thirds are arable, and have a rich loamy soil. The manor and a great part of the soil belong to George Parkyns, Esq., who purchased the estate of the Plumer family about nine years ago, and resides at *Chediston Park*, which he has enlarged and beautified. The Hall was built by Wm. Plumer, Esq., and is a large and elegant mansion in the Tudor siyle, standing on a bold elevation in the park, and ornamented with towers, turrets, pinnacles, and an embattled pediment. Nearly all the full grown timber in the park has recently been cut down, but new plantations have been made. The Bishop, Birket, Robinson, and some other families, have small estates in the parish. The copyholds pay arbitrary fines. In a field, called the Grove, 2 miles W. of the church, are two moated sites, in one of which, a sword and two coins of the reign of Edward II. were found a few years ago, when the mound was levelled, and the trees cut down. The *Church* (St. Mary) is an ancient fabric, and the living is a *vicarage*, valued in K.B. at £6. 7s. 6d., and united with Halesworth rectory in the patronage of Mrs. E. Badeley, and incumbency of the Rev. J. C. Badeley, L.L.B., who has here an old parsonage house and 60A. 2R. 15P. of glebe. G. Parkyns, Esq., is impropriator of the rectory, and receives a yearly modus of £230, as a commutation of tithes chargeable on those estates in the parish, which do not belong to him. The *Town Estate*, consisting of a farm of 30A., let for £26 a-year, has been vested in feoffees since the reign of Henry VII., for the repairs of the church and other charges to be imposed on the parishioners. The *Almshouses* for five poor families were given by Henry Claxton, in 1575, and rebuilt, in 1832. Attached to them is a piece of land let for 20s. The poor parishioners have an annuity of 20s. out of land, at Cookley, left by the *Rev. Thos. Sagar*, and about £17 a-year from *Henry Smith's Charity* for distributions of bread. Mr. Wm. Bray, of Great Russel street, London, is clerk and treasurer of Smith's charity, which consists of an estate at Longney, in Gloucestershire.

Balls Robert, shoemaker
Balls Robert, wheelwright
Bishop Thos. land agent & valuer
Ingate John, corn miller
Parkyns Geo. Esq. *Chediston Park*
Stead Christopher, gamekeeper
Woolnough Jonth. vict. Wellington
    FARMERS.
(* *are owners.*)
Archer Harley

*Bishop Thomas
Blaxhill Samuel
Booth Wm.
Denny John
Fish John
Fryatt Lydia
Gibson Wm.
Ingate Charles
*Bishop Jonth.
Corbyn

Ingate Chas. jun·
Read Samuel
Read Thomas
*Robinson Geo.
Seamans James
Sones John
Winter Robert
Woolnough Jas.

COOKLEY, a small village on an acclivity, 2½ miles W.S.W. of Halesworth, has in its parish 324 souls, and 1551A. 3R. of land, the gross yearly rental of which is £2152.   Lord Huntingfield owns the greater part of the soil, and is lord of the manor, but *Cookley Grange* is a small manor now belonging to Geo. Parkyns, Esq., and formerly held by Sibton Abbey.   The copyholds are subject to arbitrary fines. The *Church* (St. Michael) is a discharged *rectory*, valued in K.B. at £6. 13s. 4d., and united with Huntingfield.   The *Town Estate*, consisting of two houses, a homestall, and 4A. of land, is let for about £19 a-year, which is applied for the repairs of the church, but when not wholly wanted for that purpose, the surplus is divided among the poor. In 1701, *Thos. Neale* charged his estate here with the yearly payment of £3, for teaching six poor children to read the Bible, and 10s. to supply them with Bibles, &c.

Andrews John, farrier & beerhouse
Forster James, shopkeeper
George Rev John, Indpt. minister
Hance Samuel, blacksmith
Nunn George, shopkeeper
Phillips Wm. shopkeeper

    FARMERS.
Cutts Wm.
Denny Thomas
Garrard Samuel
Haward James
Ife John

Kent Wm.
Lincolne Zach.
Mayhew John
Notley Alfred
Smith Wm.
Wright Samuel

COVE (SOUTH), a small scattered village, 3½ miles N. of Southwold, has in its parish 194 souls, and 1197A. 2R. 26P. of land, extending eastward to the sea coast, where a rivulet forms a large "*broad*" before it falls into the ocean, south of Covehithe.   Sir T. S. Gooch owns most of the soil, and is lord of the two manors, called South Cove with North-Hales, and Polfrey, or Blueflory-Cove.   He is also patron of the *Church* (St. Lawrence) which is a discharged *rectory*, valued in K.B. at £6. 2s. 11d., and now enjoyed by the Rev. R. Gooch.   The tithes have been commuted for a yearly modus of £267. 10s., exclusive of £2. 10s. on the glebe.   The *Poor's Allotment* consists of 12A. awarded at the enclosure, and now let for £12 a-year, which is distributed in coals.   The poor parishioners have also a yearly rent-charge of 3s. 4d. left by Simon Gisleham, out of a farm now belonging to Mr. Fellowes. *Directory :*—Edmund Smith, *parish clerk ;* Robt. Mitchell, vict. *Five Bells ;* and Stephen Candler, Robt. Hitcham, James Girling, James Jay, Robt. Keen, Barnabas Leman, Edward Sanders, and James Shepperd, *farmers.*

COVEHITHE, or NORTH HALES, a small village on an eminence near the coast, 4½ miles N.N.E. of Southwold, and 10 miles S.E. of Beccles, has in its parish 186 souls, and 1523A. 2R. 25P. of land, stretching nearly a mile eastward to *Covehithe Ness*, a small promontory on the German Ocean ; and southward to *Covehithe Broad*, a large

pool of fresh water within a short distance of the beach, now emptying itself into Easton Broad a little further to the south, and having a *hithe* or *quay* for loading and unloading vessels, in the time of Edward I., when the manor was held by John and Walter Cove, and had a grant of a *fair* on St. Andrew's day, now disused. Sir Thomas S. Gooch, Bart., is now owner of the soil, lord of the manor, impropriator of the rectory, and patron of the *vicarage*, which is valued in K.B. at £5. 6s. 8d., and consolidated with the rectories of Benacre and Easton Bavents, in the incumbency of the Rev. Wm. Gooch. The *Church* (St. Andrew) which has a tower and five bells, had a large nave and chancel, but was suffered to fall to ruin many years ago, except the south aisle which is still preserved and enclosed for divine service. The arches and pillars of the ruined parts, though so long exposed to the weather, are still tolerably entire. JOHN BALE, author of " *De Scripteribus Britannicis*," a work of great erudition, was born here in 1495, and became a Carmelite friar, at Norwich. Having embraced the doctrines of the Reformation, he was exposed to the persecution of the Catholic clergy, against whom he was protected by the Earl of Essex; but on the death of that nobleman, he was obliged to take refuge in the Netherlands, where he remained till the accession of Edward VI., by whom he was advanced to the bishopric of Ossory, in Ireland. But on the king's death, he was again obliged to flee, and resided in Switzerland during Mary's reign. Returning to England after the accession of Elizabeth, he obtained a prebend at Canterbury, and died in 1563. The *Poor's Allotment*, awarded at an enclosure, comprises about 40A. let for £24. 10s. a-year, which is distributed in coals; together with about £3 per annum, paid by Sir T. S. Gooch as the rent of 7A. of old poor's land, which is partly waste. *Directory:*—Robert Fox, vict., *Anchor*; and Charles Candler, Edmund Cottingham, John Goddard, and Robt. Porter, *farmers.*

CRATFIELD, a pleasant straggling village, 6½ miles W.S.W. of Halesworth, and 9 miles N. by E. of Framlingham, has in its parish 720 souls, and about 2000 acres, including four large greens, where there are many scattered houses, distant from 1 to 2 miles north of the church. Ralph Barnard held Cratfield at the Domesday Survey. It was afterwards held by the families of St. Liz and Abbeni, and one of the latter gave a third part of it with the church, to the monks of St. Neot. In 1635, John Lany, Esq., gave the Rectory House, with 2A. of glebe, and all the tithes, except the corn tithes, to the Vicarage; together with a yearly rent charge of 20 marks out of the rectory. It is now in two manors, of which Lord Huntingfield and Wm. Adair, Esq., are lords; but the Rev. G. O. Leman and others have estates in the parish. The *Church* (St. Mary) is a neat structure, with a tower and six bells, and the living is a discharged vicarage, valued in K.B. at £5. 7s. 11d., and in 1835 at £299, with that of Laxfield annexed to it. Lord Huntingfield is patron, and the Rev. J. L. Farrer, incumbent. The tithes of Cratfield were commuted in 1843 for yearly moduses—viz., £115 to the vicar; and £295 to S. Bignold, Esq., the *impropriator.* Here is an *Independent Chapel*, built in 1811 and enlarged in 1832, so as to admit of sittings for 1200 hearers. It is licensed under the new marriage act. The TOWN ESTATE consists of the Town House, and nearly 2A. of land adjoining; two farms containing about 116A. in this parish; the

fourth part of a manor, called *Bucenhams* ; and a house and 17A. of land in the parish of Horham. The rents produce a yearly income of about £180, exclusive of the Town House and 1½A. of garden ground, which are occupied rent-free by the parish clerk and six poor widows. The income is applied chiefly in paying the expenses incidental to the office of churchwarden, and in other common uses for the parishioners, but about £30 is distributed yearly in coals among the poor. The property at Cratfield was granted by the lord of the manor in the 9th of Elizabeth, in consideration of £70 given by the parishioners. The other property appears to have been conveyed to the trustees by Thos. Pooley, in 1710, in consideration of £181. The whole was conveyed to new trustees, in 1797. MARY LEMAN, in 1805, left £600 to be invested for the support of *Sunday Schools*, at Cratfield, Brampton, and Redisham, and it was laid out in the purchase of £933. 6s. 8d. three per cent consols, so that each parish receives about £9 per annum.

CRATFIELD.

Marked 1, *live on Bell Green ;* 2, *North Green ;* 3, *Silverlace Green; and* 4, *Swan Green.*

4 Balls James, poulterer
1 Betts Daniel, bricklayer
1 Bland John, tailor
1 Bickers Wm. shoemaker
1 Clutten Miss Catherine
Colling Wm. parish clerk
Edwards Sampson, tailor
Farrer Rev J. L. vicar
2 Fisher Wm. sen. registrar and relieving officer
Flatman Robert, shoemaker
1 Heath Jane, (day&boarding school)
1 Moore Joshua, butcher & vict. *Bell*
1 Morris Benjamin, shoemaker
4 Morris Samuel, schoolmaster
1 Price Rev Thos. D.B. curate
4 Woolnough Wm. vict. Swan

Blacksmiths.
1 Daniels Benj.
4 Felgate Aldmn.
1 Kemp Wm.
1 Smith Samuel

FARMERS,
2 Aldrich Elisha
1 Beales John
2 Birch Jeremh.
Bridges Isaac
2 Bridges Wm.
2 Bullock My.A.
2 Burgess John
4 Churchyard Sl.
4 Dunnett Jnthn.
2 Fisher Wm.sen.
2 Fisher Wm.jun.
4 Gibson Barnbs.
3 Girling Robt.
4 Green Henry
4 Jillings Wm.

4 Jillings Thgl.
4 Kent Richard
1 Moore Joshua
2 Morris Wm.
4 Morris Wm.jun.
4 Short Ezekiel
3 Sprint James
3 Smith Wm.
2 Tacon Henry
2 Tacon Wm.
1 Wright Benj.
1 Woolnough Jas.
3 Philpot James
1 Reeve James,
 (wheelwright)
1 Smith Samuel
Grocers & Dprs.
1 Haddock Robt.
1 Matten Jonth.
1 Short Wm. (&
 miller)
4 Smith John

DARSHAM, a scattered village, 5½ miles N.N.E. of Saxmundham, and 3½ miles W. of Dunwich, has in its parish 528 souls, and 1495A. of land, including the adjacent hamlet of *Bristle Green.* William, son of Roger Bigod, gave the manor and rectory to the monks of Thetford, about the year 1110, and at the dissolution, they were granted to the Duke of Norfolk. It is now in four *manors*—viz., Darsham-cum-Yoxford, Abbots, Austins, and Garrards, of which the Earl of Stradbroke, is lord ; but part of the soil belongs to the Earl of Gosford, and several smaller owners. The late Earl of Stradbroke, when only Baron Rous, resided occasionally at *Darsham Hall,* now a farmhouse, half a mile S.W. of the village. The *Church* (All Saints), is a small structure with a tower and four bells. The living is a discharged vicarage, valued in K.B. at £4. 10s. 10d., and in 1835 at £62. The Earl of Stradbroke is impropriator and patron, and the Rev. Wm. Weddell, M.A., incumbent. The *Town Estate* consists of eight cottages, and a piece of land in this parish, and a cottage and about half an acre in Theberton, let at

rents amounting to £29. 12s. a-year. It is not known how the property was acquired. The rents are applied in the service of the church, except £4 a-year towards the support of a Sunday school.

BazantWm. parish clerk
Collings Joseph, wheelwright
Day Henry, vict. *Fox*
Eastough Jeremiah, blacksmith
Purvis Chas. Esq. *Darsham House*
Smith James, blacksmith
Smyth George, corn miller
Stanford Fdk. Esq. *Darsham Cottage*
Snell Wm. hurdle maker
Thurrell George, tailor and beerhs.
Wink John, joiner

Boot&ShoeMkrs.
Ashford John
Bazant John
Page Wm.
     FARMERS.
Borrett George
Chapman Geo.
ChurchyardWm.
Gooda Joseph
Hatcher Jermh.
(owner)

Kemp Simon
Mann Ths. *Hall*
Mann Thomas
MarkhamHarley
Markham Nich.
FoulshamArcher
Trusson Philip
Westgate Wm.
Woods John
Shopkeepers.
Chrisp John
Clements L.

DUNWICH, on the sea coast, 4½ miles S.W. by S. of Southwold, and nearly eight miles N.E. of Saxmundham, and S.E. by E, of Halesworth, is a decayed and disfranchised *borough and parish*, now having only 237 inhabitants, and 1334A. 3R. 37P. of land, half of which is open heath and sea beach. It was the *capital of East Anglia*, and the *See of a Bishop*, and formerly held no inconsiderable rank among the commercial cities of the kingdom. Its *market*, which was held on Monday, is now obsolete, but it has still a pleasure *fair*, on the 25th of July. Though now only a small village, standing on a bold cliff, overlooking the German Ocean, it is said to have been a large town, with six or eight parish churches, and a great number of chapels and monastic institutions, all of which, except the ruins of All Saints Church, and some remains of the chapel of St. James' Hospital and the Maison Dieu have been washed away by the incursions of the ocean. It sent *two members to Parliament*, from the 23rd of Edward I., till disfranchised by the Reform Act of 1832. The privilege of returning the members was vested in 32 electors, most of whom were resident in distant parts of the country. The *constitution* of the borough was based on annual elections and universal suffrage among the resident freemen, in all matters of corporate interest. At the time of the municipal enquiry, the number of resident freemen was reduced to nine, and the non-resident to about 18, and they still elected yearly their own magistrates and officers, consisting of *two bailiffs*, a recorder, coroner, &c., who occasionally held an admiralty court, granted by charter of Edward VI., but the local jurisdiction was nearly obsolete; there was no borough gaol, and the corporation could suggest no reason for any longer retaining a separate jurisdiction, consequently the borough was not included in the Municipal Reform Act of 1835; but as the corporation are lords of the manor, and possess property and rents yielding an annual income of about £150, (including a *heath* of nearly 300A., on which the burgesses have the right of cutting fuel,) two bailiffs and other officers are still elected yearly; and the same persons are generally re-elected. The present *bailiffs* are Frederick Barne and John Robinson, Esqrs., and the former gentleman owns a great part of borough, and has a handsome seat here called *Shrubbery Hall*, but here are several smaller owners. On all coals landed on about six miles of sea beach, claimed by the corporation, they levied a toll of 3d. per

chaldron some years ago; and they claim small sums for wreck, fines, and fees; but about twelve years ago, they incurred a debt of £1000 in a legal dispute with the corporation of Southwold, about a puncheon of Scotch whisky, which had been removed from the Dunwich beach by the water bailiff of Southwold. The Dunwich corporation established their right to the whisky, but incurred this debt for the payment of costs. Only two houses in the borough were valued in 1835, at the rent of £10 and upwards. The sea is perpetually encroaching on the borough and parish, and during the last ten years upwards of 20 acres have been lost. In 1833, flood-gates were erected for the protection of the marshes. The town has a few boats employed in the herring and sprat fishery, and has a new parish *Church*, (St. James,) built by subscription, at the cost of £1600, in 1830, in lieu of the ancient church of *All Saints*, which has been in ruins and disused about seventy years. It is a neat structure of white brick, in the Gothic style, with a circular tower. The benefice is a *perpetual curacy*, worth only about £40 per annum, in the patronage of Frederick Barne, Esq., and incumbency of the Rev. Wm. Weddell, M.A.

Though many of the traditional accounts relating to Dunwich are probably fabulous, it is unquestionably a place of great antiquity. It is conjectured by some to have been a station of the *Romans*, from the number of their coins discovered here. So much is certain, that in the reign of Sigebert, king of the East-Angles, Felix, the Burgundian bishop, whom that monarch invited hither to promote the conversion of his subjects to Christianity, fixed his *episcopal see* at Dunwich in the year 630; and here his successors continued, as is related under the ecclesiastical history of the county, for more than two hundred years. When an estimate was taken of all the lands in the kingdom by Edward the Confessor, there were two carves of land at Dunwich, but one of these had been swallowed up by the sea before *Domesday Survey*, when it was the manor of Robert Malet, and contained eleven Bordarii, twenty-four freemen, each holding forty acres of land, 136 burgesses, 178 poor, and three churches. It became the demesne of the crown about the beginning of the reign of Henry II., at which time it had a *mint*, "and was a town of good note, abounding with much riches, and sundry kinds of merchandizes." The annual fee-farm rent then paid by it was £120. 13s. 4d., and twenty-four thousand herrings. This was probably the period of its highest prosperity. Under Richard I., Dunwich was fined 1060 marks, Orford 15, Ipswich 200, and Yarmouth 200, for unlawfully supplying the king's enemies with corn. These sums may afford some idea of the relative importance of those towns at that time. King John, in the first year of his reign, granted a *charter* to Dunwich, by which its inhabitants were empowered, among other things, to marry their sons and daughters as they pleased, and also to give, sell, or otherwise dispose of their possessions in this town as they should think fit. This charter, dated at Gold Cliff, 29th June, 1 John, cost them three hundred marks, besides ten falcons, and five ger-falcons. In the reign of Edward I., after this town had considerably declined, it had eleven ships of war, sixteen fair ships, twenty barks, or vessels, trading to the North Seas, Iceland, &c., and twenty-four small boats for the home fishery. In the 24th year of the same reign, the men of Dunwich built, at their own cost, and equipped for the defence of the realm, eleven *ships of war*, most of which carried 72 men each. Four of these vessels, with their artillery, valued at £200, were taken and destroyed by the enemy, while on service off the coast of France. In 1347, this port sent six ships, with 102 mariners, to assist in the siege

of Calais; but during the war with France, most of the ships belonging to it were lost, together with the lives of about 500 townsmen, and goods and merchandise to the value of £1000. A still greater loss, however, was sustained by the town in the removal of its port, a new one being opened within the limits of Blythburgh, not far from Walberswick Quay, near Southwold. This circumstance, while it greatly increased the trade of these places, caused that of Dunwich to decline in the same proportion; and, combined with the ravages of the ocean, gradually reduced this town to poverty; in consideration of which, the fee-farm rent paid to the crown was abated at various times, till Charles II. fixed the amount of it at one hundred shillings per annum. But the present decayed state of this once flourishing place, is owing chiefly to the repeated *encroachments of the ocean.* Seated upon a hill composed of loam and sand of a loose texture, on a coast destitute of rocks, it is not surprising that its buildings should have successively yielded to the impetuosity of the billows, breaking against, and easily undermining the foot of the precipices. The following general view of their principal ravages is abridged from Gardner's Historical Account:—
A wood called *East Wood*, or the KING'S FOREST, extended several miles south-east of the town, but it has been for many ages destroyed by the sea. The land must consequently have stretched far out, and have formed the southern boundary of the bay of Southwold, as *Easton-Ness* did the northern. In a furious irruption of the sea, in 1739, its impetuosity exposed the roots of a great number of trees, which appeared to be the extremity of some wood, which was in all probability part of this submerged forest, which also had another wood called *West Wood.* We have already seen, that out of two *carves* of land, taxed under King Edward the Confessor, one had been washed away at the time of the Conqueror's survey. The sea, agitated by violent east, or south-east winds, continued its conquests quite to the town, for whose preservation, Henry III., in the 6th year of his reign, not only required assistance of others, but himself granted £200 towards making a fence to check its inroads. Dunwich suffered considerable damage on the night of January 1st, 1286, from the violence of the winds and sea, by which several churches were overthrown and destroyed in different places. In the first year of Edward III., the old port was rendered entirely useless, and before the twenty-third of the same king, great part of the town, containing upwards of four hundred houses, which paid rent to the fee-farm, with certain shops and windmills, had fallen a prey to the waves. After this, the church of St. Leonard was overthrown, and in the course of the same century, the churches of St. Martin and St. Nicholas were also destroyed. In 1540, the church of St. John Baptist was demolished, and before 1600, the chapels of St. Anthony, St. Francis, and St. Katherine, together with the *South gate* and *Gilden gate*, were swallowed up, so that not one quarter of the town was then left standing. In the reign of Charles I., the Temple buildings yielded to the irresistible force of the surges, and the sea reached to the market place in 1677, when the townsmen sold the materials of the cross. In 1680, all the buildings north of Maison Dieu Lane were demolished; and in 1702, the sea reached St. Peter's church, which was dismantled and soon undermined. The Town Hall shared the same fate. In 1715, the jail was absorbed, and in 1729, the farthest bounds of St. Peter's church-yard were washed away. In December, 1740, the wind blowing very hard from the north-east, and continuing for several days, occasioned terrible devastations. Great part of the cliff was carried away by the violence of the waves, which destroyed the last remains of the church-yard of St. Nicholas, together with the great road formerly leading from the Quay to the town, leaving several naked wells, the tokens of ancient buildings. King's Holm, otherwise called Leonard's Marsh, then worth

£100 per annum, was laid under water, and covered with such quantities
of shingle and sand, as to be ever since of very little value. The Cock and
Hen hills, which, the preceding summer, were forty feet high, had their
heads levelled with their bases, and the ground about them was so rent and
torn, that the foundation of the chapel of St. Francis, situated between
them, was exposed to view. The remains of the dead were washed from
their repositories, and several skeletons appeared scattered upon the beach.
A stone coffin, containing human bones covered with tiles, was also seen,
but before it could be removed, the violence of the surges broke it in two
pieces. Near the chapel, were found at the same time, the pipes of an
aqueduct, some of which were of lead, and others of grey earth. The following year, in digging a trench for the purpose of draining the marshes
overflowed the preceding winter, were discovered several old coins, and
other curiosities, of which Gardner has given a representation in his History.
Dunwich had but one church in the time of Edward the Confessor, but in
the reign of the Conqueror, two more had been added. The erection of the
former is ascribed to Felix, the first bishop of Dunwich, to whom it was
dedicated. It is farther reported that this saint was buried here in 647,
but that his remains were afterwards removed to Soham, in Cambridgeshire." Afterwards, Dunwich contained six, if not *eight parish churches.*

St. John's Church, a rectory, was a large edifice, and stood near the
great market place, in the centre of the town. In a will dated 1499, there
is a legacy of ten marks for some ornaments for this church, with the
following clause:—" If it fortune the church to decay by adventure of the
sea, the ten marks to be disposed of by my attornies, (or executors,) where
they think best." About 1510, two legacies were given towards building
a pier against St. John's church. The last institution to it was in 1537.
The inhabitants, to prevent its being washed away by the sea, took it down
about the year 1540. In the chancel was a large gravestone, under which
was discovered a stone coffin, containing the corpse of a man, that fell to
dust when stirred. On his legs, we were told, " were a pair of boots,
picked like Crakows," and on his breast stood two chalices of coarse metal.
He was conjectured to have been one of the Bishops of Dunwich. *St.
Martin's,* likewise a rectory, is thought to have stood on the east side of the
town. The last institution to it was in 1335. *St. Leonard's* was an impropriation. It probably stood eastward of St. John's, and was early swallowed up by the sea; for in a will dated 1450, the testator devised his
house in the parish, *anciently* called St. Leonard's. *St. Nicholas',* a cruciform structure, was distant twenty rods south-east of the Black Friars. The
last institution to this rectory was in 1352. The utmost bounds of its cemetery were washed away in 1740. *St. Peter's,* also a rectory, stood about
sixty rods north-east of All Saints, and had a chapel on the north side of it,
called St. Nicholas's. This edifice, on account of the proximity of the sea,
which daily threatened its overthrow, was, by agreement of the parishioners
in 1702, stripped of the lead, timber, bells, and other materials. The walls
which alone were left standing, being soon afterwards undermined by the
waves, tumbled over the cliff. The churchyard was swallowed up by the
devouring element, not long before Gardner published his History, in 1754.
All Saints' is the only church of which any portion is now standing. It
is built of flint and free-stone. The square tower is still pretty entire,
but of the body of the church, nothing but the greater portion of the exterior
walls remains, and cattle graze within its area. It appears from Gardner, that about the year 1725, part of this edifice was demolished, and its
dimensions considerably reduced. In the south-aisle, which was then pulled
down, were magisterial seats, decorated with curious carved work, and the
windows were adorned with painted glass, which, through the carelessness
of the glazier, was broken in pieces. Most of the gravestones had brass

plates with inscriptions, all of which were embezzled by the persons employed in the work. We find that, in 1754, divine service was performed here once a fortnight, from Lady-day to Michaelmas, and monthly during the rest of the year ; but it was discontinued a few years afterwards. Recent inscriptions in the churchyard, shew that it is still occasionally used as a place of interment.

In the time of the Conqueror, all the churches then erected, or to be erected in Dunwich, were given by Robert Malet, to his priory at Eye, in his charter of endowment. The prior and convent accordingly presented to all instituted churches, and had tithes out of most of them, together with all the revenues of such as were impropriated, finding a secular priest to serve the cures. According to the *Register of Eye*, Dunwich had two other churches dedicated to *St. Michael and St. Bartholomew*, which are there recorded to have been swallowed up by the sea before 1331 ; when the prior and convent of Eye, petitioned the Bishop of Norwich to impropriate the church of Laxfield to them, alleging, among other reasons, that they had lost a considerable part of their revenues at Dunwich, by the irruptions of the ocean. Besides these churches, Weever mentions three chapels, dedicated to St. Anthony, St. Francis, and St. Katherine. The site of the first is unknown. The second stood between Cock and Hen Hills, and, as well as St. Katherine's, which was in St. John's parish, is supposed to have fallen to decay in the reign of Henry VIII. Here was a house belonging to the *Knights Templars*, and afterwards to the *Hospitallers*, endowed with a considerable estate in Dunwich, and the contiguous hamlets of Westleton and Dingle. To this establishment, belonged a church dedicated to the Virgin Mary and St. John the Baptist, built for the use of the tenants of the manor, whose houses were distinguished by *crosses*, the badge of the Knights. Here were also two monastic institutions, belonging to the Franciscans and Dominicans, or *Grey and Black Friars*. The first was founded by Richard Fitz-John, and Alice, his wife ; and its revenues were afterwards augmented by Henry III. The area encompassed by the walls of this house, part of which yet remains, is upwards of seven acres. They had three gates ; one of these, the eastern, is demolished ; but the arches of the other two, standing close together to the westward, continue nearly entire. They have nothing remarkable in their construction ; but, being covered with ivy, form picturesque objects. The largest of these gates served for the principal entrance to the house, and the other led to the church. A barn is the only building now standing in this enclosure. The *Black Friary* was founded by Sir Roger de Holish. In the eighth year of Richard II., the sea having washed away the shore almost up to this house, some attempts were made to remove the friars to Blythburg. They nevertheless continued here till the dissolution, when the site of this house, as well as that of the Grey Friary, was granted, among other possessions, to John Eyre. Both of these monastic establishments had handsome churches belonging to them. Two other ancient religious institutions here were the *Leprous Hospital of St. James*, and the *Maison Dieu*, noticed below, and of which there are still some remains.

St. James's Hospital and the Maison Dieu were very ancient hospitals, which went to decay many years ago, but what remains of their endowment has long been consolidated as one charity, under the government of a master, for the support of aged widows and poor persons of Dunwich, and particularly such as are afflicted by insanity, or loss of speech, or labour under any peculiar affliction. The master is appointed by the corporation and other principal inhabitants, by yearly election, but the same person is generally re-elected. He receives the rents, selects the objects, and dispenses the benefits of the charity, and exhibits his accounts at a public meeting on May-day. The charity estate, by means of various ex-

changes, was much improved some years ago, and now consists of two double cottages, a fish house, several out-buildings, and 96A. 23P. of land, at Dunwich, and 23A. 2R. 33P. at Heveningham. The rents amount to about £93 per annum, which, after paying for repairs and other incidental expenses, is dispensed in weekly stipends of from 2s. 6d. to 6s. among nine or ten pensioners, except about £5 paid for medical attendance, and a few pounds distributed in small sums among the general poor of the parish. An annuity of 30s., used formerly to be paid out of 30 acres of land at Brandeston, supposed to have anciently belonged to *St. James's Hospital*, which was founded by Walter de Riboff, in the reign of Richard I., for a master and several leprous brethren and sisters, and had extensive possessions, the greater part of which were lost many years ago, through the encroachments of the sea, and the rapacity of the successive masters, as was the case with the revenues of the MAISON DIEU, or *God's House*, which was dedicated to the Holy Trinity, and was abundantly endowed as early as the reign of Henry III., for a master, six brethren, and several sisters. There are still some small remains of the chapels or churches which were attached to these hospitals.

The land called *Pot Break* and *North and South Cliff Pieces*, is let for £21. 6s. per annum, and is described in the terrier as belonging to the parishioners, without any declaration of trust. The rents are applied in the service of the new church. In 1566, *John Page*, alias *Baxter*, bequeathed his estate at Carlton, to be sold subject to the yearly payment of £3 to the poor of Dunwich, and £2 to the poor of Laxfield. His executors, in the 11th of Elizabeth, conveyed the estate to trustees, for the poor of these parishes, and for a long period it has been under the joint management of the corporation of Dunwich and the churchwardens of Laxfield; the former receiving five-ninths, and the latter four-ninths of the annual proceeds. It consists of a farm of 43A. 2R. 37P., at Carlton Colville, let for £75 a year, subject to some deductions for land tax, &c. The five-ninths of the clear rent received by the corporation of Dunwich have been uniformly, as far as is known, applied as part of their private revenues, without any reservation for the poor, among whom they ought to distribute at least £3 a year.

DUNWICH DIRECTORY.—Frederick Barne, Esq., *Shrubbery Hall;* Joseph Dix, farmer and vict., *Ship;* Joseph Dix, jun., *farmer;* James B. Easy, *farmer and shopkeeper;* Wm. Easy, *farmer;* John Robinson, Esq., *Cliff House;* Wm. Wade, *farmer;* Robt. Woolner, *farmer;* and Charles Wood, *schoolmaster.*

EASTON BAVENTS, a decayed parish on the sea cliff, 1½ mile N.N.E. of Southwold, has now only 10 inhabitants, and about 260A. of land, having suffered, like Dunwich, from the encroachments of the ocean, which threatens at no distant period to completely engulph it. Formerly it was an extensive parish, and was returned as having 770 acres of land, as late as 1815. A large and bold promontory, called *Easton Ness*, anciently projected here more than two miles into the ocean, and formed the northern bounds of Southwold Bay, and the most eastern point of the English coast. In the 9th of Edward I., it was the lordship of *Thomas de Bavent*, one of whose descendants, in the 4th of Edward III., had a grant for a weekly market here on Wednesday, and a fair on the eve, day, and morrow, of the feast of St. Nicholas. What remains of it now is the property of Sir Thomas S. Gooch, and is in one *farm* occupied by Mr. Samuel Plant. A cottage, and about 60 acres of land, have gone down into the sea during the last five years. The *Church* (St. Nicholas) was standing in 1638, and had a

chapel dedicated to St. Margaret, but all vestiges of it are gone. The *rectory*, valued in K.B. at £12, is consolidated with Benacre.

FROSTENDEN, a scattered village, from 4 to 5 miles N. by W. of Southwold, and 8 miles E.N.E. of Halesworth, and S.S.E. of Bec--cles, has in its parish 428 souls, and 1291A. 3R. 35P. of fertile land. — The manor was formerly held by the De la Poles, afterwards by the Howards, Morses, and Glovers, and now by the Dean and Chapter of Westminster ; but a great part of the soil belongs to J. F. Vincent, Esq., the Rev. James Carlos, (of *Frostenden Grove,)* Mr. D. Riches, and several smaller owners. The *Church* (All Saints) is an ancient fabric, with a round tower ; and the living is a discharged rectory, va--lued in K.B. at £12, and now having 26A. of glebe, and a yearly modus of £372. — Thos. Barne, Esq., is patron ; and the Rev. Richd. Gooch incumbent ; but the next presentation has been sold to the Rev. Jas. Read. The *Church Land*, 11A. 1R. 24P., is let for £26. 15s. a-year, which is applied towards the repairs of the church. The *Poor's Allot--ment*, 4A. 2R., awarded at the enclosure, in 1799, is let for £7. 10s. a--year, which is applied in distributions of coals among the poor pa-rishioners.

Aldred Jeremiah, brick, tile, and earthenware manufacturer
Anguish Robert, blacksmith
Baker John, bricklayer
Carlos Rev James, *Frostenden Grove*
Eeles Mrs Eliza, *Ivy Cottage*
Gooch Rev Richard, rector
Pells Wm. wheelwright
Riches Daniel, jun. shipowner, sur--veyor, and land agent
White Miss Sophia
Wingard Wm. beerhouse

FARMERS.

Adams Robt. || Perry John
Foulsham Noah (and surveyor) —
Hingeston James (chief constable)
Riches Daniel (and owner)

HALESWORTH is a thriving *market town*, in the picturesque valley of the small but navigable river Blythe, 8 miles S. by E. of Bungay, 9 miles S. by W. of Beccles, 10 miles N. of Saxmundham, 8¼ miles W. of Southwold, 31 miles N.E. by N. of Ipswich, and 100 miles N.E. of London. Its parish contains 1420 acres of land, (exclu-sive of roads) generally a rich light loam, and rising in bold undula-tions from the river and several tributary streams. It had 1676 inha-bitants, in 1801 ; 1810, in 1811 ; 2166, in 1821 ; 2437, in 1831 ; and 2662, in 1841. It is a *polling place* for the Eastern Division of Suf-folk ; and the Magistrates hold *Petty Sessions*, at the Angel Inn, every third Wednesday. The *town* is well built, and consists of one long street and several short ones, extending in a curved line from both banks of the *River Blythe*, which is here crossed by a good bridge, and receives in the neighbourhood several tributary streams. Under an act passed in 1756, this small river has been made navigable up to the town for barges of from 20 to 30 tons burthen, of which there are about a dozen belonging to the merchants here, employed in carrying out corn, malt, &c., and in bringing in coal, timber, &c. The river flows about 9 miles eastward to the sea, near Southwold, as already noticed at page 357. Here is a large *iron foundry and agricultural implement manufactory*, and a number of *malting houses*. Mr. P. Stead has lately obtained a patent for making malt by a new process, and has erected a large *kiln*, in the form of a tower, fifty feet high, divided into five stories, and heated by steam pipes and a hot air blast. The green

malt is first placed on the top floor, and is moved a story lower every day, and the heat of each floor increasing as it descends, it is dried off and ready for the market on the fourth or fifth day. There is also a contrivance for regulating the temperature of the " steep," as well as the drying floors. The MARKET is held every Tuesday, for the sale of corn, cattle, &c. A handsome public room, 80 feet long, 34 broad, and 22 feet high, was erected in 1841, behind the Angel Inn, and is used as a *Corn Exchange, Assembly Room,* &c. FAIRS for pleasure are held on the Tuesdays in Easter and Whitsun weeks; and for the sale of Scotch cattle, &c., on the 29th and 30th of October. Here is also a *Hiring for Servants,* on the last Tuesday in September. The *Gas Works* were erected in 1838, at the cost of £1800, in £5 shares, and have one gasometer, capable of holding 60,000 cubic feet of gas. Mr. Wm. Garrod is secretary to the company, who have usually derived a yearly profit of $7\frac{1}{2}$ per cent. on the invested capital. Near the town is a *mineral spring,* which has been successfully employed in topical inflammations, especially those of the eye. Halesworth is a place of considerable antiquity, though little is known of its early history. Richard de Argentin, who was lord of the manor in the reign of Henry the Third, obtained a charter for a weekly market, (formerly held on Thursday,) and an annual fair on the feast of Saint Luke. From the Argentins, the manor descended to the Allingtons. Afterwards, the family of Betts had it, but sold it to Wm. Plumer, Esq. John Cutts, Esq., of Witham, Essex, is now lord of the manor of *Halesworth and Dame Margerys;* but here is a small manor belonging to the rectory, and the greater part of the soil belongs to Geo. Parkyns, Esq., Chas. Woolby, Esq.; the Rev. J. Day, J. Crabtree, Esq., Mr. Wm. Cole, Mr. J. Johnson, and a number of smaller free and copyholders. Most of the houses are built on the latter tenure, and are subject to arbitrary fines. *Sir Robert Bedingfield,* who was lord mayor of London, in 1707, was a native of Halesworth. Great quantities of hemp were formerly grown in the neighbourhood, and many of the inhabitants were employed in the manufacture of *Suffolk hempen cloth,* but the trade was discontinued many years ago.

The CHURCH (St. Mary) is a large and handsome Gothic structure, with a tower containing eight bells and a good clock. It has a spacious nave, chancel, and side aisles, and was enlarged on the north side many years ago. The benefice is a discharged *rectory,* valued in K.B. at £20, and in 1835 at £450, with the vicarage Chediston annexed to it. Mrs. Elizabeth Badeley is patroness, and the Rev. Joseph Charles Badeley, L.L.B., is the incumbent, and has a large ancient *Rectory House,* about 13A. of glebe, and a small manor. The *Independents, Baptists,* and *Methodists* have chapels here, and the first named have had a congregation in the town since 1794. On the Beccles road are commodious *National Schools,* attended by 112 boys and 70 girls, and in Pound street, is an *Infant School,* which has about 100 pupils. In the latter street is a small *Theatre,* belonging to Mr. Chas. Fisher, whose company of comedians visit it for a few weeks every alternate year. The *Town and Charity Estates,* belonging to Halesworth, produce a yearly revenue of nearly £400, as will be seen in the following account of the several trusts.

The TOWN ESTATE is vested in trustees for the public uses and ge-

neral benefit of the parishioners, and consists of premises formerly called the *Guildhall*, a stable, and about 58A. of freehold and copyhold land, let at rents amounting to about £211 per annum, which is applied in repairing the church, paying salaries to the *organist, parish clerk, sexton, &c.*, in providing sacramental bread and wine, in supporting the almshouses, in *lighting the town*, and occasionally in supplying the poor with coals at a cheap rate. Part of the property is of unknown acquisition, and the remainder was purchased at various periods. The ALMSHOUSES are six small houses near the Church, given by Wm. Carey, and two cottages given by an unknown donor. They are occupied by 14 poor widows, who have small allowances from the following charities and the poor rates. In 1611, ROBERT LAUNCE left £60 for the use of the most needy poor, and it was laid out in the purchase of 5A. 3R. 9P. of copyhold land, in the manor of Southelmham, now let for £9. 4s. a year. The sum of £60, given by JOHN PHILLIPS, and £30. 5s., given by RICHARD PHILLIPS, were laid out in the purchase of a cottage and 11A. 1R. 35P. of copyhold land, in the manor of Melles, in Wenhaston, now let for £25 a year. This and the preceding charity are dispensed in weekly doles of bread, together with an annuity of 20s., left by *Matthew Walter*, in 1589, out of an estate at Holton, belonging to the Rev. J. Day. In 1650, JAMES KEBLE left for the poor, the Bell's Pightle, which was exchanged in 1819, for 7A. 3R. 28P. of land, called Holton Common Piece, now let for about £12 a year, of which £6 is distributed in bread on St. Thomas's Day, and the remainder is given to poor parishioners in sickness, as occasion requires. In 1652, JOHN KEBLE bequeathed for the relief of poor widows, and the apprenticing of poor children, a house, barn, stable, and 26A. 2R. 18P. of free and copyhold lands, in Holton, now let for nearly £100 per annum, about four acres being garden ground. One-half of the rents is divided among 20 poor widows by the rector and churchwardens, and the other half is given in apprentice fees, of about £15 each. The legacies of £80, given by *Reginald Burroughs*, £20 given by *Matthew Mann*, and £100 given by *Wm. Vincent*, in 1804, were laid out in the purchase of 8A. 3R. 26P. of land, in the hamlet of Melles, now let for £14. 17s. per annum, which is divided in quarterly payments among poor widows. In 1700, the sum of £60, given by *Thos. Neale*, for the education of poor children, was laid out, with other funds, the whole amounting to £220, in the purchase of a house and land, forming part of the town estate, but the feoffees pay yearly £3 for the schooling of six poor children, who have a yearly rent-charge of 10s., left by the same donor, towards buying them books. In 1701, RICHARD PORTER left a yearly rent-charge of £17. 6s. 8d., out of a farm here, now belonging to Mr. Woolby, for a *schoolmaster* and *schoolmistress* to teach 20 poor boys and 20 poor girls to read, and the latter also to knit. In 1816, *John Hatcher* gave to the rector and churchwardens a pew in the south gallery of the church, in trust to apply the rent (25s.) towards the support of the *National School*, already noticed. The Blything Hundred SAVINGS' BANK is open on the last Tuesday in every month, at Mr. Thomas Tippell's, in the Thoroughfare. In Nov. 1842, it had deposits amounting to £16,065, belonging to 518 individuals, 11 Charitable Societies, and 17 Friendly Societies.

HALESWORTH.

POST-OFFICE.—Mr Wm. Watson, postmaster, Thoroughfare. Letters are despatched to London and the south, at half-past six evening, and to Yarmouth, Wangford, &c., at a quarter-past ten night.

Those marked 1, are in Bridge street; 2, Bungay road; 3, Chediston street; 4, Market place; 5, Mill hill street; 6; Pound street; 7, Quay street; 8, Quay terrace; 9, Wissett road; and the others are in the THOROUGHFARE, *or where specified.*

6 Alabaster Wm. cork cutter
4 Aldis John, chief constable, &c
3 Alexander Wm. thatcher
8 Allison Charles, lodgings
Atthill Rev Lomb, incumbt. of Rumburgh, Bridge street
4 Baas Rt. Beales, solr. & bank agt
Badeley Mrs Elizabeth, Chapel ter
Badeley Rev Joseph Chas., L.L.B. *Rectory*
Bailey Mrs Susan, Bridge street
9 Baker James, chimney sweeper
2 Banham Wm. excise officer
3 Barker James, organist, &c
Bates James C. bankers' clerk
Bayfield Mrs Elizabeth, Pound st
7 Benstead Robert, coal meter
Blandon William, wherryman, Beccles road
Bowler Mrs Amy, Thoroughfare
Bryant Chas. solr.'s clerk, Quay st
Bryant John, collector of navigation tolls, Quay
Buller Benj. well sinker, Pound st
Calver Rainbird, bank clerk, Parson's lane
Carnova Peter, jeweller & tea dealer
3 Chilvers Wm. musical instrument maker, and music teacher
2 Clapham Samuel, hawker
Clark Hy. excise officer, Beccles rd
Clarke Mrs Rebecca, Pound street
Clarke Mr James, Pound street
Cloake Mr Alfred, Bungay road
Coates Thomas, carrier, Pound st
Collins Mr Thomas, Chediston st
Corbyn Jonth. tailor; h London rd
4 Cracknell Thos. wine mercht. &c
Craggs David, foreman, Parson's ln
Crampin Rev Jph.(Bapt.) Beccles rd
Davy James, builder; h Pound st
Dean Jas. M. shopman, Beccles rd

Dennant Rev John, Pound street
Doggett Mrs Isabella, Bridge street
Drake Stephen, overlooker, Quay
4 Easterson Thomas, ironfounder and agricultural implement manfr
Ebbage Mrs Lydia, Thoroughfare
Felmingham Robert, gardener, Framlingham road
3 Fitzgerrald Edw. police superindt
3 Flick Sl. tanner (& Saxmundham)
9 Foreman James, trunk, &c. mkr
3 Forsdike James, policeman
6 Garrod Wm. solicitor's clerk
George Mrs Hannah, Pound street
6 Gilbert Wilkinson John, portrait and animal painter
Hatcher Mrs., Beccles road
Hatten Mrs Mary, Pound street
Haward Mrs Sarah, Pound street
5 Haxell Ebenezer Bentfield, gent. (deputy superintendent registrar)
Higham Mrs., Bungay road
Hill Wm. job gardener, Angel yard
Holmes Rev Edmund, Bungay road
5 Hugman Mr John & Mr Joseph
Hurrell John, overlooker
8 James Henry, bankers' clerk
3 Johnson Wm. chimney sweeper
4 Johnson Andrew, Esq. bank agent
3 Juby James, whiting manufactr
King Mrs Mary, Chediston street
Lane Thos. coach painter. Quay st
4 Lemon (Abm.) and Wade (Aldous) soda water manufacturers
Mayhew Rev Joseph Wm. (Indpt.) London road
Newson Mrs Susan, Pound street
3 Nichols James, rat catcher
8 Parslee Fred. Burrell, bankers' clk
Pipe Mr Samuel, Thoroughfare
Pipe Saml. jun. plant dlr. Quay ter
Pizzey Mrs Martha, Pound street
3 Pooley Wm. policeman
Reeve Jas. Robt. brewer; h *Castle*
Revans Miss Eliz. Mill hill street
Riches Joseph Alfred, bank agt. &c
Ringwood Hammond Ferrer, gent. Quay street
Robinson Mrs Mary, Bridge street
Sawyer Mrs Martha, Quay street
Seaman Mr John, Bungay road
5 Smith Rev Geo. L. (Independent)
Smith Henry, Robert, & John, carriers, Church lane
Smith Wm. bailiff, Pound street
Stanford Mr John, Quay street
Thompson Miss Leonora, Beccles rd

4 Todd Wm. green grocer
Trivett Mrs Ann, Quay terrace
Turner Rev Samuel Blois, B.A. incumbent of Linstead, Pound st
Tuthill Miss Hannah, Bungay road
Tuthill Miss Martha, Beccles road
Tyler Mrs Mary, Beccles road
3 Warn Benj. chimney sweeper
Watson Mrs Elizabeth, Thoroughfr
Whewell Jph. hawker, Bungay rd
White Harry, solicitor, and Union clerk, &c ; h Quay terrace
2 Wild Thos. bankers' clerk
8 Woods Wm. bankers' clerk
Woolard Mr., Mill hill

ATTORNEYS.
Crabtree Jno. (clerk to the Comnrs. of Taxes, Thoroughfare
Read John, Pound street
White & Baas, Market pl. (H. White is union clerk, steward of Blything Liberty, &c.)

BANKERS.
East of England Bank, (on London and Westminster Bank,) Robert B. Baas, manager
Gurneys & Co. Market place (on Barclay & Co.) Andrew Johnson, *agent*
National Provincial Bank of England, (on London Joint Stock Bank,) J. A. Riches, *agent*
Savings' Bank, at Mr Tippell's Thoroughfare, open last Tuesday in every month

FIRE AND LIFE OFFICES.
Alliance, J. London
Crown Life, Harry White
Freemasons' and General Life, Mr. Stevens
Norwich Union, Thomas Tippell
Farmers' & Hail Storm, J. A. Riches
Phœnix, John Read, Pound street
Protestant Dissenters' & Yorkshire, Wm. Lincolne
Royal Exchange, John Foreman
Suffolk and General Country Amicable, (Fire,) Miss Allcock
Sun, Charles Bryant

INNS AND TAVERNS.
Angel Inn, Wm. Almer
1 Hawk, My. Woolnough
4 King's Arms & Commercial Inn, George Taylor
7 King's Head, Ann Waters
3 Queen's Head, Isaac Mills
3 Rose and Crown, Wm. Palmer

Ship, Wm. Lyon, Bridge street
Sun, Edmund Rose, Pound street
Swan, Thomas Neeve, Pound street
4 Three Tuns, Aldous Wade
3 Wellington, Isaac Pinkney
Wherry, John Bryant, Quay
White Hart, James Bloomfield
6 White Lion, John Seaman

ACADEMIES.
Candler Letitia
Gorbell Mrs Eliz. & Miss Hanh.
* Harvey Joph. Pound street
Harvey Miss Sar. Chapel terrace
Infant, Ly. Bird, Pound street
Mannall Jno. Mill Hill street
National school, Beccles rd. Isc. Phillips, mstr. Anna Maria Dean, mistress
Povey John. (private teacher,) Mill Hill street
* Wilson Mrs Carol. Quay st.

AUCTIONEER.
6 Davy James
BAKERS &c.
(* *are confrs.*)
3 Baker Robert
3* Baker Wm.
4 Cattermole Jas.
6 Cattermole W.
2 Fish David
1* Kemp Saml.
3 Miller James
1* Page Thomas
6* Sones Zach.
* Took Robert
Basket Makers.
4 Buller Benj. (& parish clerk)
6 Buller Wm.
Clarke Thos. (& brush & turnry. dealer)
1 Hopson Sarah
7 Took Adam
Beerhouses.
3 Barber Robert
Bird J. Church ln.

Genery Mary, Broadway
3 Haward Chas.
7 Kent Thomas
7 Scarle Cathan.
3 Smith William
2 Wade Jno. (& fishmonger)
Blacksmiths.
Cornish Joshua
6 Cullingford J.
3 Jarmy John
Smith George
7 Symonds Robt.
6 Tilney Henry
Booksellers and Printers, &c.
Butler Rose, (stationer only)
7 Roper Chrltte.
Tippell Thos. (& Stamp office,) Thoroughfare

Boot & Shoe Mkrs.
3 Barber James
Bird J. Church ln.
Carliell Wm.
6 Chapman John
3 Chipperfield W.
1 Cowles Wm.
3 Croft Daniel
3 Cullingford W.
3 Cullingford T.
4 Fenn John
6 Hugman J.
1 Lyon Wm.
4 Sawing John
1 Shade Nathnl.
6 Spall David
3 Twates Wm.
7 Wilson Geo (& leather cutr.)
Braziers & Tinrs.
Burgess Nathnl.
Taylor Joseph
Wright George
Brewers.
2 Prime Edward

4 Reeve&Crack-
　nell
3 Self Samuel
5 Wade Denny
Bricklayers, &c.
Branch Thomas
3 Newson Saml.
3 Newson Stph.
6 SilvertonJohn
6 Woodyard C.
Brickmakers.
Butcher Geo. &
　Francis
Newson Stephen
Smith H., R.&J.
Butchers.
Brown Jph.Moss
3 Colleett James
1 Foreman Jas.
1 Keable Chas.
1 Kemp Samuel
Seaman George,
　Church yard
6 Seaman John
4 Seaman Saml.
3 Squires Wm.
3 Winter Saml.
Cabinet Makers.
Collett George
4 Godbold Geo.
Harvey Samuel

Chemists&Drgts.
Chilver George
Reynolds Wm.
Rudland George,
　Harrington
Coach Brokers.
Bunyan John W.
1 Clarke John
Coach Maker.
Rose J.Bridge st.
Coal Merchants.
George T. Quay
Harvey Joseph
Stead P. Quay
Tippell T. Quay
　Coopers.
7 Kent Thomas
5 Wade Denny
6 Wade Thomas
Corn & Flr.Dlrs.
6 BarberJeremh.
3 Barber Robert
5 Boyden John
Land William
1 Page Thomas

Corn Merchants.
Riches Jph. Alf.
7 Stead Patrick
Corn Millers.
5 Baker James
6 Barber Jemh.
Pedgriff Cornls.
Shrofield,Broad-
　way
Curriers, &c.
3 Gunter Thos.
5 Hugman Benj.
　Dyers.
3 Gray Amy.
3 Johnson Maria
3 Scraggs Eliz.
FARMERS.
3 Cole John
6 George Martin
George William
Hart C. *Hales-
　worth Hall*
Johnson Jas.*Hill
　Farm*
Punchard James
Punchard Thos.
WoodyardW.jun.
Cookley White
　house
FARRIERS.
6 Neeve Thomas
3 Smith Sidney
*Furniture and
　Clothes Brokers.*
3 Blanden Wm.
Croft George
3 Smith Wm.
*Glass,China,&c.
　Dealers.*
1 Balls Ebenzr.
7 Roper Chtte.
Tippell Thomas
　Glovers.
3 Goodwin Php.
Jefferson Chas.&
　fell onger
Grocers & Dprs.
4 Aldis J. & Son
4 Aldred James
3 Chilvers Amb.
1 Emery J. (dra-
　per only)
Foreman John
1 Goddard John
Jillings John
4 LincolneW. (&
　tallow chndlr.)

7 Marshall John
　Gun Makers.
Bezant Simon
4 Cullingford W.
*Hair Dressers,
　(* Perfumers.)*
3 AlexanderWm.
Croft George
* Swann Wm.
* Taylor Henry
　Hatter.
London John
Ironmongers.
Burgess Nathnl.
4 Cullingford W.
3 Jarmy John
Wright George
Joiners & Bldrs.
6 Davy J.& Son
6 Felgate Thos.
5 Keable Fras.
5 Kindred Phins.
7 Marshall Jno.
5 Newson John
6 Rose Edmnd.
3 Smith James
9 Woolnough W.
Lime Burners.
George Thomp.
2 Prime Edwd.
　Maltsters.
1 Atmer Wm.
George Thomp-
　son
2 Prime Edward,
4 Reeve &Crack-
　nell
2 Riches J. Alf.
3 Self Samuel
7 Stead Patrick
Milliners, &c.
6 Carmen Phœbe
7 Cook My. Ann
7 Dennant S. K.
5 Keable Sarah
5 Last Ey. Eliz.
4 Wincop Sarah
*Painters, Plum-
　bers, & Glaziers.*
Chappell Wm.
3 Rounce W. (&
　carver & gilder)
5 Smith George
6 Wright James
　Saddlers, &c.
Bunyan J. Wm.
Crisp W.New ct.

7 Hopson James
Hopson Wm.
1 Musk William
　Shopkeepers.
Carter John,
　Broadway
7 Cullingford Js.
7 Kent Thomas
6 Muttitt Wm.
3 Nicholson Rt.
6 Peachey J. (&
　rope&sack mfr)
6 Sones Hy. (tea)
3 Spore James
1 Taylor Wm.
Straw Hat Mkrs.
1 Clarke Eliza
Collett M.C.R.
6 Chapman R.A.
4 Fenn Phœbe
4 Johnson Sarah
6 Sones Sar. Ann
6 Spall Eliz.
3 Webb Carolne.
3 Winter Eliz.
　Surgeons.
4 Beales John
7 Haward Fdk.
PedriftW.Hench-
　man,Wissett pl.
Rudland George,
　Harrington
Tailors (are
　Dprs.& Hatters.)*
4 Bedwell John
5 Botham Benj.
3 Butler Wm.
* Corbyn Hart-
　well & Son
* Gobbett Hy.G.
3 Howard Stphn.
* JeffersonChas.
4 Johnson Jonth.
7 Marshall Wm.
4 Robinson Wm.
4* RobinsonWm.
　jun.
Sutton Robert
3 Wright John
Timber Mercht.
7 Farrow Jph.(&
　Bungay)
Toy& Fncy Whs.
6 Buller Wm.
4 Lincolne Wm.
　(Berlin wools,
　&c.)

Watch Mkrs.&c.	*Whitesmiths, &c.*
4 Dowsing Wm.	4 Cullingford W.
Johnson John	4 Jarmy John
Suggate G. (&	3 Newson Rd. (&
jeweller)	machine mkr.)
4 Taylor Samuel	*Wine and Spirit*
Wigg Wm. (and	*Merchants.*
jeweller)	Reeve & Crack-
Wheelwright.	nell, Market pl.
1 Smith Nelson	

COACHES.

The *Shannon* to London, at ½ past 7 mg., from the Angel & Three Tuns.
The *Eclipse* from the Three Tuns & King's Arms, to Norwich, every Sat. at 6, and Mon. and Wed. at 7 mg.; & to Yoxford, same evngs. at 8.

CARRIERS.

Hy., Robt. & J. Smith. from Church-lane & the White Swan, to *Ipswich, London, &c.*, every Mon. Wed. & Fri. at 4 mg., and to *Beccles, Bungay, &c.*, ev. Tues. Thurs. & Sat. mg.
To *Ipswich & Norwich*, Thos. Coates,

Mon. & Fri., & Hy. Tilney, Tues. and Fri. mg. (from Pound street.)
Beccles, &c., from the Hawk, Saml. Foreman, Wed. & Sat.; and from the King's Head, Ann Waters, Tuesday and Friday.
Harleston, Peter Tock, Chediston st., Thursday, 10 morning.
Laxfield, Val. Harman, (White Hart) Tuesday and Friday.
Lowestoft, Jas. Page, Chediston st., Wednesday, 6 morning.
Saxmundham, Mail Cart, from the White Hart, 6 evening; and Jas. Hogg, from the King's Arms, Monday and Friday morning.
Southwold, P. Tock, Chediston st., Wed. 10 mg.; and C. Bedingfield, and W. Newson, from the King's Arms, Wednesday and Saturday.
Stradbrooke, W. Copping, fiom the White Hart, Tuesday
Yarmouth, Martin, Tues, & W. Newson, from the King's Arms, Wed. and Saturday

HENSTEAD, a small village, 5½ miles S.E. of Beccles, and 7 miles S.W. by S. of Lowestoft, has in its parish 1920 acres of land, and 573 souls, including the hamlet of HULVERSTREET, which has 293 inhabitants, and about 800 acres of land, and has usually been returned with Wanford Hundred, within the eastern boundary of which it is situated, though only a mile W. of Henstead church. In the Conqueror's time, the manor of Henstead was held by Robert de Pierpoint, and it continued in his family till 1340. It afterwards passed successively to the Cloptons, Sydnors, Brooks, and Holodays. Thomas Sheriffe, jun., Esq., (now a minor,) of *Henstead Hall*, a handsome mansion with pleasant grounds, is now lord of the manor, and patron of the *Church* (St. Mary) which was thoroughly repaired in 1842, and is a *rectory*, valued in K.B. at £12, and in 1835 at £423. His father, the Rev. Thomas Sheriffe, is the incumbent. Sir Thos. S. Gooch, Fredk. Barne, Esq., and a few smaller owners, have estates in the parish. The *Wesleyans* have a small chapel in Hulverstreet. About 2 acres of land, let for £3 a year, and a yearly rent-charge of 20s., are appropriated to the repairs of the church. In 1599, *Henry Brandon* left his tenement, and 3 roods of land, and directed the rent to be divided as follows—one half to the poor of Henstead; 6s. 8d. of the other half to the poor of Rushmere, and the remainder to be applied towards the repairs of Henstead church. The tenement went to decay many years ago, and, about 1780, the land was let on lease for 99 years, at the annual rent of 17s., the lessee covenanting to erect a new cottage. On the enclosure of *Sotterley Common*, (partly in this parish,) an allotment of 14a. was awarded to the poor of Henstead, and it is now let for £20 a-year, which is distributed in coals.

Marked • *are in Hulverstreet, and* | *Mills Jas. schoolr. and bookbinder
the others in Henstead.*

•Butcher Charles, gardener
Candler Charles, blacksmith
•Clarke Rev Charles, curate
Fisk James, boot and shoe maker
•Fisk Edmund, vict. *Gate*
Gouldby James, parish clerk
•Howell Mary, shopkeeper
•Julings Elizabeth, shopkeeper
King Wm. tailor
Mendham David, boot & shoe maker

*Mills Jas. schoolr. and bookbinder
Newson Wm. wheelwright
Peak Elizabeth, beerhouse
•Pidgeon Wm. wheelwright
Sheriffe Rev Thos. rector; & Thos.
jun. Esq. *Henstead Hall*

FARMERS.

Andrews John ‖ Bates Robert
•Fisk Wm. ‖ Jepson Charles
Robinson Samuel ‖ Rouse Joseph
Sayer Wm. ‖ Smith Wm.

HEVENINGHAM, or *Haveningham*, a pleasant scattered village on an eminence, 5½ miles S.W. of Halesworth, and 7 miles N.E. by N. of Framlingham, has in its parish 417 souls, and about 1900 acres of land. The *manor* was held by Walter Fitz-Robert, who, in 1198, gave the advowson of the church to St. Neot's priory. It was afterwards the the lordship of a family of its own name, and passed from them about 1700 to that of Bence. It afterwards passed to the predecessor of *Sir Joshua Vanneck*, who, in 1796, was raised to an Irish peerage by the title of *Baron Huntingfield, of Heveningham*, and died in 1816, when he was succeeded by his son, Joshua Vanneck, the present *Lord Huntingfield*, who was born in 1778, and married a daughter of C. Arcedeckne, Esq., in 1810, and, in 1817, a daughter of Sir Charles Blois. Sir R. S. Adair and a few smaller owners have estates in the parish. HEVENINGHAM HALL, the magnificent residence of Lord Huntingfield, stands in an extensive park, which is partly in the adjoining parish of Huntingfield, and distant about 4 miles S.W. of Halesworth. The present mansion was commenced about 1778, by Sir Gerard Vanneck, elder brother of the late baron, from the designs of Sir Robert Taylor, but finished by Mr. James Wyatt. The west end, erected from the designs of the latter, is in a much more tasteful style than the other parts of the edifice. The front, about 200 feet in length, is adorned with Corinthian columns, and otherwise chastely ornamented. The whole building is covered with a composition which has the appearance of very white freestone. Seated on a rising ground, it appears to great advantage from various parts of the *park*, which comprises more than 600A., and abounds in fine plantations. The rivulet, which is one of the principal sources of the Blythe, divides the park into two nearly equal parts, and forms a noble sheet of water in front of the house. The interior of the mansion contains a fine collection of paintings of Dutch, Flemish, and other masters, and the avenue that leads to it from the porter's lodge, is of great length and uncommon beauty. The *ancient mansion*, which stood on the Huntingfield side of the park, was a romantic baronial residence, with a gallery continued the whole length of the building, and opening upon a balcony over the porch. Its great hall was built round six straight, massy oaks, which upheld the roof as they grew, and upon which the foresters and yeomen of olden times used to hang their cross-bows, hunting poles, &c. Queen Elizabeth was entertained here by Lord Hunsdon, and near its site is *Queen's Oak*, under which she is said to have shot a buck with her own hand. This venerable oak, now verging fast to decay, at the height of seven feet from the ground,

has measured nearly eleven yards in circumference; being now hollow, it has shrunk considerably, and is " bald with dry antiquity." The late Lord Huntingfield ornamented the whole country round his splendid residence with plantations of oak, beech, chesnut, and other trees. The *Church* (St. Margaret) is a small neat fabric, with a tower and five bells, and was new roofed in 1833 at the cost of £300. The benefice is a discharged *rectory*, valued in K.B. at £11. 6s. 8d., and in 1835 at £436. The patronage is in the Crown, and the Rev. Henry Owen, M.A., is the incumbent, and has a good residence and 40A. of glebe. The yearly value of the glebe and tithe-rent is now about £550. The *Town and Poor's Estate* have been vested from an early period for the reparation of the church and highways, the relief of the poor, and such other public and charitable uses, as to the trustees should seem meet. They comprise five tenements and gardens, let for £10. 5s.; a house and 4A., let for £6; and a farm of 52A. in Badingham, let for £63 a-year. The rents are applied in the service of the church; in payment of the clerk's salary; £6 towards the support of a Sunday School, and in occasional payments to the constable and the surveyors of the highways; and the surplus is divided among the poor parishioners. The trustees have also a rent-charge of 10s., and another of 3s. per annum, from building sites belonging to the trust estates.

Lord Huntingfield, *Heveningham Hall*
Baxter Artis, gamekeeper
Edwards Thos. boot & shoe maker
Fisk John, tailor
Giles John, vict. *White Lion*
Goldsmith Geo. brick & tile maker
Harrold James, schoolmaster
Howard John, boot and shoe maker
Malpass Mr James

Owen Rev Henry, M.A. *Rectory*
Prime George, grocer and draper
Threadkill Joseph, wheelwright
 Blacksmiths.
Grayson Sarah
Harden Thomas
 FARMERS.
Andrews Chas.
Fisher Garnham
Goodwin Wm.

Jewell Wm.
Ladbrook Joshua
Moore Robert
Read James
Stevenson Geo.
Walne Robert
Watts Robert

HOLTON, one mile E. of Halesworth, is a pleasant village and parish, containing 541 souls, and 1132 acres of land, mostly in the manor of Wissett le Rosse, but chieflly the property of the Rev. J. B. Wilkinson, J. Spink, Esq., the Executors of the late F. Robinson, and a few smaller owners. *Holton Hall*, a neat mansion, with pleasant grounds, is the property of the Rev. J. B. Wilkinson, and is occupied by the Rev. Richd. Day. The *Church* (St. Peter) is an ancient structure with a round tower. The living, a discharged rectory, valued in K.B. at £10. 13s. 4d., and in 1835 at £197, is in the gift of the Crown, and incumbency of the Rev. Wm. Taylor Worship, B.A., who erected a neat *Rectory House*, in the Elizabethan style, in 1838, at the cost of about £800. Here is a *National School*, built, in 1814, by the Rev. J. B. Wilkinson, and still liberally supported by him. The *Town House* and 4 rods of land, let for £4 per annum, have belonged to the church from time immemorial. The *Lord Nelson Public-house* did belong to the parish, but, in 1786, the churchwardens granted it on lease for 99 years, to a brewer, for a premium of £80, and no rent appears to have been reserved.

Alexander Robert Webb, brewer
Andrews Mrs Sarah
Butcher Daniel, vict. *Duke*
Butcher Fras.&Geo.mill grease mfrs.
  oil & colourmen, & sack tilt mkrs.
Carron Wm. nursery manager
Day Rev Richd. M.A. *Holton Hall*
Dunnett Miss Sarah
Garrard Mr Wm. || Maria, *school*
Keable James, joiner
Keable John, butcher
Mingay Wm. shopkeeper & beerhs.
Rednall E. nursery and seedsman
Simonds Samuel, blacksmith
Taylor Wm. corn miller
Tallent Jno. vict. *Cherry Tree*
Thrower My. Ann, vict. *Lord Nelson*

Upton Henry, blacksmith
Wade Wm. cooper || Emily, *school*
Worship Rev Wm. Taylor, *Rectory*
Boot&ShoeMkrs.
  Francis John
Mingay James
  FARMERS.
Baker James
Balls James
Butcher Isaac
Crikmore James
Dallistone Hy.
Fisk Joseph
Freeston Isaac
Hambling Peter
Jallings Robert

Pleasance John,
  Flat-moor
Prime Wm.
Smith Robert
  Wheelwrights.
Beckett Wm.
Beckett Henry
  CARRIERS
From the Cherry
  Tree, Jno. Mor-
  ton, to Hales-
  worth, Tues. &
  Jas. Page to
  Lowestoft Wed.

HUNTINGFIELD, a straggling village in the vale of one of the branches of the river Blythe, 5 miles S.W. by W. of Halesworth, has in its parish 397 souls and 2011 acres of land, including about half of *Heveningham Park*, the seat of *Lord Huntingfield*, who is lord of the manor, owner of most of the soil, and derives his title from this parish, though an Irish peer. (See page 378.) The manor was, for a considerable time after the Norman conquest, the estate and residence of an ancient family of its own name, one of whom founded Mendham Priory, in Stephen's reign. It afterwards descended to the de la Poles, Earls of Suffolk, and, in the time of Queen Elizabeth, was the property of Henry Lord Hunsdon. It was next the estate of that great oracle of the law, Sir Edward Coke, by whose descendant, the Earl of Leicester, it was sold to Sir Joshua Vanneck, grandfather of the present proprietor. Geo. Bates, Esq., and a few smaller owners, have estates in the parish, and here is a small rectorial manor. The *Church* (St. Mary) is an ancient structure, with a tower and five bells. The *rectory*, valued in K.B. at £13. 6s. 8d., and in 1835, at £800, with that of Cookley annexed to it, is in the patronage of Lord Huntingfield and incumbency of the Rev. Henry Uhthoff. The *Town Estate* consists of seven cottages and 17A. 2R. 18P. of land in this and the adjoining parishes of Ubbeston and Heveningham, let for about £40 a-year, and mostly purchased with benefaction money in the reign of Charles I. The rents are applied mostly in aid of the church and partly in aid of the poor rates. In 1725, *Berry Snelling* left for the education of poor children a yearly rent-charge of £4 out of a farm now belonging to Lord Huntingfield.

Abbey John, steward
Balls John, wheelwright and vic-
  tualler, Huntingfield Arms
Barrell Wm., corn miller
Mattin Jonathan, shopkeeper
Minter Robert, tailor
Mudd James, blacksmith
Owles James, boot and shoe maker

Owles Edward, plumber and glazier
Uhthoff Rev. Henry, Rectory
  FARMERS.
Balls Francis || Dunnett John
Goodwin Samuel Chapman, *Hall*
Robinson Robert || Potter Wm.
Robinson Samuel || Taylor George

KNODISHALL, a scattered village, including *Coldfair Green*, from 3½ to 4½ miles S.E. of Saxmundham, and N.N.W. of Aldbo-

rough, has in its parish 397 souls and 1731 acres of land, including the hamlet of *Buxlow*, which was anciently a separate parish, and had a church, the site of which is now a garden. The manor of Knodishall was for a long period held by the Jenney family, and was lately purchased by Thomas Mayhew, Esq., but the greater part of the soil belongs to James Newson, Esq., (owner of the Manor House, &c.,) Mrs. Whitaker, the Rev. Sir T. G. Cullum (owner of the Hall farm,) the Executors of the late Richard Fennell, Mr. R. G. Moor, and several smaller owners; and a small part of the parish is in the manor of Leiston. The *Church* (St. Lawrence) is an ancient structure, with a tower and south porch. The Rectory of Knodishall-cum-Buxlow, valued in K.B. at £11, and in 1835, at £350, is in the patronage of Mrs. Whitaker, of Scole Lodge, Norfolk, and incumbency of the Rev. George Ayton Whitaker, M.A., who built a new Rectory House about six years ago, and has 13A. of glebe.

*Marked * are at Coldfair Green.*

*Cockrell Nathaniel, victualler and butcher, Butchers' Arms
*Elenger James, parish clerk
*Oilee Nathaniel, corn miller
*Watling John, flour & corn dealer
Whitaker Rev. George Ayton, M.A. Rectory

FARMERS.

Backhouse Philomon || Oilee Joseph
Barber Thomas Geo. *Knodishall Hall*
Clayton Wm., *Marnells*
Cooper James, *Red House*
*Hunt James || Johnson Henry
Sewell John, *Manor House*

LEISTON is a large and well-built village, 2 miles from the sea, 4 miles N. by W. of Aldborough and E. by S. of Saxmundham, 5½ miles S.S.E. of Yoxford, and 93 miles N.E. of London. Its parish comprises 1177 souls and 4966 acres of land, including the hamlet of SIZEWELL, which has 66 inhabitants, and about 1000 acres, on the sea-coast, 4 miles N. of Aldborough, and had a chapel as late as the reign of Elizabeth, though no traces of it now remain. At *Sizewell Gap*, there is a fishing boat and coast-guard station, and the cliffs rise precipitously from the beach. The parish extends three miles N. of the church, and includes part of the *Minsmere Level*, as noticed with Theberton. *Leiston Works*, established in 1778, by the grandfather of the present proprietors, Richard Garrett and Son, is one of the largest manufactories of *agricultural implements* in the kingdom, and they are patentees of various improved machines. An ABBEY of Premontratension canons, dedicated to the Blessed Virgin, was founded in the parish about the year 1182, by Ranulp de Glanville, who endowed it with the manor of Leiston, conferred on him by Henry II., and also certain churches, which he had previously given to Butley Priory, and which that convent resigned in favour of this abbey, which stood originally in a marshy situation, near the sea and the Minsmere river, where there are still some small ruins, called *Leiston Chapel*, near Minsmere Haven, more than 2 miles N.N.E. of the village of Leiston. The situation of the first house being found unwholesome, Robert de Ufford, Earl of Suffolk, about the year 1363, built a new abbey, on a larger scale, upon an eminence about a mile N. of Leiston church, to which the monks removed. This edifice was destroyed by fire before 1389; but being rebuilt, it continued to flourish till the general dissolution, when it contained 15 monks, and its annual revenues were valued at £181. 17s. 1½d. Great part of the church, seve-

ral subterraneous chapels, and various offices of the monastery, are still standing, and applied to the purposes of barns, granaries, &c. The length of the abbey church was about 56 yards, and it appears to have been a handsome structure, decorated with ornaments, formed by an admixture of black squared flints and freestone. In the walls of the church, and other buildings, are many bricks, thinner and longer than those used at present. Near the west end is a small tower entirely of brick, but having various ornaments which have been formed in moulds. The outer walls of this abbey enclosed a great extent of ground, but they have all been removed for the sake of the materials. The old abbey, near the sea, appears to have been used by some of the monks till the dissolution; and in 1331, "John Grene, relinquishing his abbaice by choice, was consecrated an *anchorite* at the chapel of St. Mary, in the old monastery near the sea." In the 28th of Henry VIII., the site of the abbey, and the *manor of Leiston*, were granted to Charles Brandon, Duke of Suffolk, and afterwards passed to the Herveys. They now belong to Lord Huntingfield; and the other principal landowners in the parish are J. P. Thellusson, Esqr.'s, Trustees; Edward Fuller, Esq., Capt. Rowley, and Mr. J. Grimsey. The abbot obtained a charter for a market and fair at Leiston, in 1312, but both have long been disused. The parish *Church* (St. Margaret) is a long thatched fabric, with a lofty tower. The benefice is a *perpetual curacy*, not in charge, but valued, in 1835, at £376, and endowed with all the tithes, which were commuted, in 1810, for £435 per annum, and were formerly in the impropriation of Christ's Hospital and the Haberdashers' Company, London, who are the alternate patrons. The Rev. John Calvert Blathwayt, M.A., is the incumbent. The *Wesleyans* and the *Society of Friends* have chapels in the village. A *Parochial School* was built here in 1840, and is supported by subscription, for the education of about 100 poor children. In 1721, *Thomas Grimsby* left a farm of 38A., at Westleton, to provide clothing for poor widows and children of Leiston, and it is now let for £52. 10s. a year. Francis Hayle and others are trustees. The same donor also left £200, to be invested by the churchwardens, for a distribution of bread among the poor, every Sunday, at the church. Of this legacy, £150 is placed out on mortgage, and the residue has been laid out in the purchase of a cottage on *Cold-fair green*, which lies south of Leiston, and is mostly in Knodishall parish. This cottage lets for £3 a year.

LEISTON PARISH.
*Those marked * are in Sizewell.*
POST-OFFICE at Thos. Taylor's.—
Letters arrive from Saxmundham at
·8 mg. and are despatched at 6 evg
Blathwayt Rev John Calvert, M.A. incumbent
Crane Wm. gamekeeper
Curwen Robert Ewing, Esq. Cupola
Debney Rd. wine and seed merchant
Furrington Maria, straw hat maker
Garrett Robt. and Son, ironfounders, wholesale ironmongers, and agricultural implement manufacturers
Gibbs Joseph, baker & confectioner
Gildersleeves Geo. brewer & spirit mert
Goldsmith Chas. saddler & harness mkr
Gooch Edwd. Woodcock, vict. White Horse Inn
Merrells Patience, dressmaker
Mann Robert, farrier
Riggs Miss Rachel
Sauler Elizabeth, glove maker
Sewell John Jessup, surgeon
Taylor Jonathan, cooper
Theobald Theobald, Esq. Cupola
Tuffield Mr Robert

Academies.	*Corn Millers.*	Hillen Benjamin	Sawer Samuel
Adamson Wm.	Curtis Wm. (and	Hunt Joseph	*Joiners.*
Cotton Jas. *(bdg)*	stationer, &c.)	Johnson Thomas	Cunnell Wm.
Cunnell Chrltte.	WoodsWm. (and	Last Elizabeth	Riggs John (and
Smith Wm.	Aldbro')	*Merrells Wm.	cabinet maker)
Tavell Han.*(bdg)*	FARMERS.	Moor Rt. Jonth.	Simmons Jonas
Blacksmiths.	Backhouse Wm.	*Pead John	*Plumbers, Glzrs.*
Baldry James (&	Barker Daniel	Tuffield John	*and Painters.*
beer house)	Barley John	Whitworth Thos.	Garrod Henry
Johnson George	*Baxter Joseph,	*Gardeners, &c.*	Westrup John
Wyatt James	(beer house)	Garrod George	*Wheelwrights.*
Boot&ShoeMkrs.	Canham John	Smith Wm.	Alexander Robt.
Andrews Nathl.	Crisp Rt. *Abbey*	*Grocers &Drprs.*	Cutts Wm.
Chandler John	Debenham John	Geater Charles,	
Watling Wm.	Devsing William	(and tailor)	CARRIER.
Butchers.	Edward, *Hall*	Hartridge James	Taylor James, to
Halls Edmund	Garrod Richard	Holden Charles	Saxmundham
Morling George	Grimsey John	Neave Gundry	

LINSTEAD MAGNA is a parish of scattered houses, from 4 to 5 miles W.S.W. of Halesworth, comprising only 93 souls, and 1304A. of land, besides about 6A. of roads. Lord Huntingfield is lord of the manor, but part of the soil belongs to G. Parkyns, Esq., J. P. Scrivener, Sir Robt. S. Adair, Mr. G. Bates, and several smaller proprietors. The *Church* (St. Peter) stands in a field nearly in the centre of the parish. It was partly appropriated to Mendham priory, by Roger de Huntingfield. Lord Huntingfield is now impropriator, and also patron of the perpetual curacy, valued, in 1835, at £97, and now enjoyed by the Rev. S. B. Turner, B.A., together with Linstead Parva. His Lordship has a yearly modus of £315 in lieu of tithes, out of which he pays £82 to the incumbent. The FARMERS are—Geo. Bates, Mary Bedingfield, John Girling, John Holmes, Charles Lee, Joshua Moore, Alfred Read, Geo. Read, James Read, Wm. Read, *Linstead Hall ;* Robert Smith, and Edward Woods.

LINSTEAD PARVA, or *Lower Linstead,* is a parish, with its houses scattered near three *Greens,* from 4 to 5 miles W. of Halesworth. It has 205 inhabitants, but only 554A. 1R. 24P. of land, exclusive of roads. Its three Greens comprise 33A. 3R. 20P. The manor anciently belonged to Sibton abbey, and the church to Mendham priory. Lord Huntingfield is now lord of the manor, impropriator, and patron of the *Church* (St. Margaret,) which is a small structure, with a belfry. The living is a perpetual curacy, valued, in 1835, at £78, and now in the incumbency of the Rev. Samuel Blois Turner, B.A., together with that of Linstead Magna. L. Cunningham, Esq., Thos. Burroughs, Esq., the Rev. Jeremy Day, W. Cutts, F. Nicker, and a few smaller owners, have estates in the parish. A copyhold house, garden, and 1½ acre of land, called *Taylor's Pightle,* have been held from time immemorial for the reparation of the church, and are now let for £9 per annum.

Bryant Thomas, blacksmith
Chipperfield John, tailor
Godfrey Felix, shoemaker
Hammond Daniel, parish clerk
Hart Anthony, vict. Greyhound
Stagoll John, land surveyor & grocer

FARMERS.—(* are *Owners*)
Bryant Thomas
*Cutts Wm. || Dye Charles
*Nicker Thomas || Haward Jabez
Seaman Kirble || Nicker Samuel

MIDDLETON, a well-built village, on the south bank of the river Minsmere, 4 miles N.E. by N. of Saxmundham, has in its parish 599 inhabitants, and 2024 acres of land, of which 603 acres are in the adjoining hamlet of FORDLEY, which was formerly a separate parish. The united parishes are now commonly called *Middleton-cum-Fordley*, and in ecclesiastical matters, *Fordley-with-Middleton*, the former being a rectory, and the latter a vicarage. Part of them is in low marshes and the *Minsmere level*, (see Theberton,) and they are in three *manors*, viz., Middleton-Chickering and Fordley, of which the Rev. C. M. Doughty is lord; and Middleton-Austin, of which Daniel Packard, Esq., is lord; but part of the soil belongs to Mrs. Howlett, Mr. G. Randall, and several smaller owners. *Middleton Church* (Holy Trinity) is a small fabric, with a tower, containing five bells, and surmounted by a leaded spire. The roof is thatched with reeds. *Fordley Church*, of which no vestiges remain, stood in the same churchyard, and was a smaller edifice, which was suffered to go to decay many years ago. In 1620, complaint was made to the Bishop of Norwich, that when service did not begin and end at both churches exactly at the same time, the bells and steeple of one disturbed the congregation of the other. To remedy this inconvenience, the bishop directed that the same minister should serve both, and officiate in them alternately. Fordley is a *discharged rectory*, valued in K.B. at £5, and in 1835 at £569, with the *vicarages* of Middleton and Westleton annexed to it. The Rev. Harrison Packard, B.A., is patron and incumbent, and receives £8 per annum from the great tithes of Middleton, which belong to the Rev. Edmund Holland, and have been commuted for a yearly modus of £441. 10s. Middleton was appropriated to Leiston Abbey by Ranulph Glanville, and was granted by Henry VIII. to Charles Duke of Suffolk. The poor have eleven small *ground rents*, amounting to £3. 9s. per annum, but the donors are unknown. The *Wesleyans* have a chapel here, built in 1828.

Marked 1, *live on Middleton Moor, and* 2, *in Fordley*

Adams Wm. tailor
1 Andrews Wm. fishmonger
Barber Mrs Elizabeth
Barnes Jacob, beerhouse
Bedwell Wm. blacksmith
Bridges John, nursery & seedsman
Brown John, bricklayer
Broom Joseph, hawker
Davy John, schoolmaster
Foulsham Rt. wheelgt. & vict. *Bell*
Hunt Samuel, grocer and draper
Ludbrooke Wm. shopkeeper
Masterson Thomas, tailor
Noller Wm. butcher
1 Packard Daniel, gent. *Mill Farm*
Prior Thomas, gardener
Read John, gentleman
Richbell Henry and Augustus, maltsters, &c.
Savage Richard, gardener

White Rev Joseph, curate, *Rectory*

Boot&ShoeMkrs.
Bedwell Wm. (& shopkeeper)
Bezant Henry
Crisp Christphr.
Goodwin John
Rous Richard

Joiners.
Clark John
1 Eade Thomas

FARMERS.
(* *are Owners.*)
*Arnold John
*Barnes Jacob
2 Canham Geo.
2*Chandler John
Dix Robert
2 Dale William
Cloughton
Drew James

*Free Wm. & Pnh
Free Wm. junior
1 Gayfer Wm.
2 Darkins Richd.
*Geater Thos. (& corn miller)
*Hunt Keziah
*Marshlain Rt.
Newson Wm.
*Packard Daniel
*Randall George
*Richbell John
*Richbell Philip
Smith Robert

CARRIER.
Wm. Free, to Ipswich, Tuesday and Friday

PEASENHALL is a large and well-built village, in a pleasant valley, on the south side of the small river Minsmere, 5 miles N.N.W. of Saxmundham, 7 miles S.S.W. of Halesworth, and 3 miles W. of Yoxford. Its parish has 845 inhabitants, and 1972A. 1R. 37P. of land. Rt. Sayer, Esq., is lord of the manor, but the greater part of the soil belongs to R. Sheriffe, Esq., Alderman Manning, Esq., J. Rudkin, Esq., C. Baldry, Esq., Mr. T. White, J. F. P. Scrivener, Esq., and several smaller owners. In the reign of Edward I., the manor was held by Roger Bygod, and in that of Edward II., by Nicholas de Segrave. The *Church* (St. Michael) is a small ancient edifice, with a tower and five bells. The *perpetual curacy*, valued in 1835 at £117, was consolidated with the vicarage of Sibton till about the year 1818, when it was made a separate cure in the patronage of the vicar of Sibton. The Rev. Harrison Packard, B.A., is the incumbent. The principal landowners are impropriators of the great tithes, which were commuted in 1840, when the small tithes were also commuted for the yearly payment of £123. 2s. 6d. to the perpetual curate, and £9. 12s. 4d. to the vicar of Sibton. The Wesleyans have a chapel here, built in 1809. The CHURCH LAND comprises a garden and 1A. in Peasenhall, let for £6. 15s., and a cottage and 5A. 37P. of land, in Sibton and Peasenhall, let for £20. 14s. a-year. Except an allotment of about one acre, this land was devised to trustees by *Edmund Kempe*, in 1490, partly for superstitious uses, and partly for the reparation of Peasenhall church. The rents are wholly absorbed in liquidating the expenses of the churchwardens, though, according to the deed appointing new trustees, in 1807, part of the income should be distributed among the poor parishioners. About 14A. of copyhold land in Peasenhall parish, and manor of Bruisyard, has been held in trust from time immemorial, for the exoneratian of the parishioners from king's taxes, and for the relief of the poor. It is let for £14. 17s. 6d., and the rent, after deducting 24s. 6d. for land-tax and quit-rent, is distributed in weekly allowances to the aged poor. A cottage and garden in this parish, but in the manor of Sibton, were left by *Robt. Louffe*, in 1580, for the relief of the poor of Peasenhall and Sibton, but the rent (£5) is wholly distributed among the former, who have also a yearly rent-charge of 52s. left by *Edmund Cutting*, in 1639, for a weekly distribution of 1s. worth of bread. It is paid out of Hubbard's land, in Sibton.

Post-office, at Mr Ths. White's. Letters arrive at 9 morning, & are despatched at 5 evening
Andrews Moses, farrier
Block Wm. vict. *Angel*
Bradstreet Mr Wm. || Brown Rt. gent.
Brown Wm. schoolmaster
Dennison John, baker & confectioner
Cooper Elizabeth, straw hat maker
Forder Wm. plumber and glazier
Gibbs Charles, bricklayer
Girling Wm. and Son, auctioneers, land agents, and agent to the Norwich Union Fire Office.
Hunt Thomas, cooper
Lay Joseph J., M.D. || Lay Mr L.

Lay John, corn mercht. miller, &c
Rose Wm. saddler & collar maker
Row Francis, land agent
Rudkin John, surgeon, (*in firm*)
Rudkin and Lay, surgeons
Smith Robert, vict. *Swan*
Teags Thomas, drill, &c. mfr.
Tillett Robert, parish clerk
Smyth Jas. (late Smyth and Sons,) corn, seed, and manure *drill* mfr. (established in 1800)
Wright Jasper, tailor

Blacksmiths.	*Boot & Shoe Mkrs.*
Bloomfield Wm.	Barber Charles
Ludbrook John	Cable John
Ludbrook J. jun.	Gardner Sarah

Gilbert Wm.
Potter Wm.
Butchers.
Cockerell Saml.
Herring Edwd.
Pipe Robert
FARMERS.
Andrews Moses
Baker Robert
Chandler John
Cole John
Cross Samuel
Girling Wm.

Holmes K.
Ingate Wm.
Kemp John
Lay John
Mays Joseph
Moore Wm.
Prime Edw.&Bj.
Robinson Jonas
Shelley Benj.
Squires Jerh.
Westgate Wm.
White Ths. sen.

Joiners.
Ludbrook Edmd.
Welton Fulcher
Grocers & Dprs.
White Thos. jun.
(and *maltster*)
CARRIERS.
Samuel Noller, to Colchester & Norwich, and J. Sawyer, to Ipswich, Tu. and Fri. from the Swan ; and Thos. Coates, from the Angel to Ipswich, &c. Mon. and Fri.

White Wm.
Wheelwrights.
Easthaugh Wm.
(& shopkpr.)
Kent Haward
Robinson John

REYDON, a scattered village, 2 miles N.N.W. of Southwold, and 7 miles E. of Halesworth, has in its parish 433 souls, and 2675 acres of land. It was anciently a place of importance, and had a market and a park. The Hall in the latter was taken down in 1684. The old house, now called *Reydon Hall,* is occupied by those well-known literary ladies *Mrs. and Misses Strickland,* authors of the " Queens of England," and other popular works. On a branch of the Blythe, called *Wood's-end Creek,* are vestiges of a wharf, which probably fell to decay in the reign of Henry III., in consequence of the rising prosperity of Southwold, said to have been formerly a part of this parish. On the same rivulet is Wolsey Bridge, which was converted into a sluice for draining the low lands, by Sir John Rous, in 1747. This bridge is erroneously stated by tradition to have been built at the expense of Cardinal Wolsey. The Earl of Stradbroke is now lord of the manor of Reydon, but part of the soil belongs to Sir T. S. Gooch, J. Leman, Esq., and a few smaller owners. The *Church* (St. Margaret) is a small ancient structure, and is said to have had a chapel, which stood a mile further to the east. The benefice is a discharged vicarage, valued in K.B. at £13. 6s. 8d., and in 1835 at £220. The Earl of Stradbroke is patron, and also impropriator of the great tithes ; and the Rev. H. W. R. Birch, M.A., of Southwold, is the incumbent. The tithes have recently been commuted for yearly moduses of £410 to the impropriator, and £218 to the vicar. The *Church and Poor's Land* comprises about 9A. 24P., let for £9. 8s. per annum, which is applied in aid of the church and poor rates ; together with dividends of £731. 5s. three per cent. Bank Annuities, left by the late Earl of Stradbroke, who died in 1827. Part of the land (3A. 2R. 9P.) is called Gravel Pit Piece. At the enclosure of the parish, in 1800, an *allotment* of 22A. was awarded to the poor, and is now let for about £18 a-year, which is distributed in coals.

Haws Adam, shopr., shoemaker, parish clerk, and vict. *Bear*
Jermyn James, gentleman
Strickland Mrs and Misses Eliz. and Agnes, *Reydon Hall*
Wright Wm. blacksmith

FARMERS.
Adams Wm. || Bloom Samuel
Cottingham L. O. || Keen John
Diver Thomas Holmes
Leatherdale Wm.||Freeman Thos.
Mills John || Pashley Wm.

RUMBURGH, a scattered village and parish, 4 miles N.N.W. of Halesworth, and 6½ miles S. of Bungay, contains 435 souls, and 1370 acres of land, rising boldly between two tributary streams of the Blythe, and including about half of a *Green,* or common, of about 100

acres, which is partly in Wissett, and in which the copyholders are allowed to turn 109 head of cattle. The executors of the late Mrs. Weebing are lords of the manor, but a great part of the soil belongs to Mr. John Grimsey, Mr. J. Manby, W, Adair, Esq., Mr. G. Calver, Mr. C. Holmes, Mr. Thomas Ling, and several smaller free and copyholders. The latter pay arbitrary fines. Here was a *Benedictine Priory*, founded about 1065, by the monks of Hulme, and dedicated to St. Michael and St. Felix. Stephen, Earl of Brittany, made it a cell to St. Mary's Abbey, in York. It was suppressed and given to Cardinal Wolsey, towards the endowment of his college, in Ipswich, in 1528, when it was valued at £10. 12s. 11¾d. It was afterwards the property of the Earls of Oxford, and passed from them to the Cobbold, Jessup, and other families. Some traces of it may be seen in the Abbey farm-house which occupies its site. The *Church*, (St. Michael,) which adjoined the priory, is an ancient structure, which has undergone many reparations, and has a short tower, with a spiral roof. The benefice is a perpetual curacy, valued in 1835, at £130, with the vicarage of South Elmham St. Michael annexed to it. The Rev. Lomb Atthill, of Halesworth, is patron and incumbent. G. Durrant, Esq., is impropriator of part of the great tithes, and the remainder belong to the landowners. The *Wesleyans* have a neat chapel here, built in 1836. The *Town Estate* was conveyed to new trustees, in 1758, and again in 1826, upon trust that the rents should be yearly disposed of for such use and advantage of the parish, as the trustees should judge " necessary and convenient," except the rent of 14A., called Warpullocks, which should be disposed of towards discharging all tenths and fifteenths imposed on the parishioners, and the overplus, if any, be divided among the poor. This estate comprises a messuage, &c., called the Bears, and 18A. of land in Southelmham St. Peter ; a close of 14A., called Warpullocks ; a close of 7A., in Southelmham St. Michael ; and a close of 5A., at Spexhall. The rents produce about £45 per annum, and are dispensed partly for the reparation of the church, and the support of a Sunday-school, and partly in distributions of coals to poor parishioners. The Rev. J. B. Wilkinson, Rev. John Holmes, James Garrould, Edgar Woolward, and J. Howlett are the trustees. The churchwardens and overseers are trustees of the following property, viz., the *Buck Inn*, let for £15 per annum ; the *Town House Cottage*, let for £8. 15s. 6d. ; the *Town Pightle*, let for £2. 2s. ; the *Acre Piece*, let for 5s. ; and a yearly rent-charge of 3s. 4d. out of Daniel Sayer's Mill. The rents are applied in aid of the church and poor rates, and other general expenses of the parish. It is not known how the property was acquired.

Aldous Samuel, butcher
Alexander James, bricklayer
Baker David, shoemaker
Ball Wm. vict. Buck Inn
Blowers John, schoolmr. & par. clerk
Chipperfield Richard & Chas. tailors and shopkeepers
Chipperfield Wm. tailor
Cracknell Thomas, maltster ; house, *Halesworth*
Garrud Wm. joiner

Green Matthew, wheelwright
Green Oakley John, coach builder
Green Robert, blacksmith
Ling Mr Frederick Smith, *Abbey*
Rodwell James, beerhouse
Sadler Wm. shoemaker
Sayer Daniel, corn miller
Winter Wm. blacksmith

FARMERS.
Banks Wm.
Bowler A.

Butcher Wm.
Calver Samuel
Garwood Wm.

Fairhead Jonth.	Ling Thomas,	OldringGarrould	Reynolds Martin
Folkard Widow	*Abbey*	and Samuel	Short Wm.
Larter Edward	Prime, James	Reynolds David	Stockdale Robt.

SIBTON is a pleasant straggling village, on an acclivity south of the river Yox, or Badingham, 2 miles W. of Yoxford, 5 miles N. by W, of Saxmundham, and 7 miles S. of Halesworth. Its parish contains 564 souls, and 2680A. of fertile land, including the hamlet of Sibton Green, more than a mile N. of the village, and several neat scattered houses. Wm. de Casineto, or Cheney, founded a *Cistercian Abbey* here about the year 1150, and dedicated it to the Blessed Virgin. It was so richly endowed, that at the dissolusion its revenues were valued at £250. 15s. 7½d. per annum. It was granted by the abbot and convent themselves to Thomas Duke of Norfolk, Anthony Rous, Esq., and Nicholas Hare, in 1536. The *Abbey House*, a commodious mansion, built chiefly out of the ruins of the monastery, is occupied by J, E. E. Spink, Esq. J. F. P. Scrivener, Esq., is lord of the manor of Sibton, with its members, and Lord Huntingfield is lord of the manor of *Sibton Hall*, now a farm house, but a great part of the parish belongs to other proprietors, the largest of whom is Robert Sayer, Esq., of SIBTON PARK, whose mansion is a large and handsome structure, erected about 15 years ago, and standing on a pleasant eminence nearly in the centre of a fertile estate of about 1000 acres, (partly in Yoxford,) a large portion of which is laid out in beautifully timbered park meadows, pleasure grounds, and gardens, refreshed by a fine lake, well stored with fish. The *Church* (St. Peter) is a fine Gothic fabric, with a tower and five bells. The benefice is a discharged vicarage, valued in K.B. at £8. 8s. 4d., and in 1835 at £143. 13s. 2d. Robert Sayer, Esq., is patron, and the Rev. S. M. Westhorpe, M.A., is the incumbent, and has a good residence, rebuilt in 1821, and about 10A, of glebe. The tithes were commuted in 1843, but the great tithes belong to the landowners. The *Primitive Methodists* have a small chapel here, built in 1836. The TOWN ESTATE consists of a house called the *Town House*, let in four tenements for £12 a year, 1A. 1R. 7P., adjoining the glebe, let for £1. 15s.; 11A. 1R. 30P. in Huntingfield, let for £17; and a house and 3A. 3R. 24P. in Badingham, let for £14 a year. The latter was purchased in 1658, with £52 derived from a bequest to the poor by *Edmund Cutting*, in 1639, and £28 belonging to the parishioners. After paying £2. 12s. a year to provide bread for the poor, in consideration of Cutting's Charity, the rents are applied with the church rates. In 1719, *John and Dorothea Scrivener* settled an estate of 32A. 0R. 32P. in Sibton and Peasenhall, and directed one-half of the yearly rent thereof to be paid to the *Vicar of Sibton*, for reading prayers every Wednesday, Friday, and holy-day in the year, and the other half to be employed in teaching poor children reading, writing, and arithmetic, and putting out apprentices. The estate is let for £55 per annum, half of which is paid to a schoolmaster and mistress for teaching 12 poor boys and 12 poor girls. A new *School* was built some years ago.

*Marked * live on Sibton Green.*

*Ayton Abner, shopkeeper	Pipe Robert, vict. *White Horse*
Howard Joseph, joiner	Powells James, parish clerk
Larter James, shopkeeper	Sayer Robert, Esq. *Sibton Park*
	Spink John E. E. Esq. *Abbey House*

Turner John, corn miller	Goodwin John	Pipe George
Westhorpe Rev Sterling Mosley,	Gowing John	Rumsey John
M.A. *Vicarage*	Hilling William,	Stannard Ephm.
White Wm. joiner	*Mill Farm*	*Winder John
Wincup Wm. blacksmith	Jarman Thomas	White Charles
FARMERS.	Martin Wm.	*Webb Robert
Bendall George	Daines John	*Pinkeney Dvd.	Wright Wm.
*Catt James	Girling Thomas,	Payne Geo. *Hall*
	Hill House	

SOTHERTON, a scattered village, near one of the tributary streams of the river Blythe, 4 miles E.N.E. of Halesworth, has in its parish 222 souls, and 1084 acres of land. The Earl of Stradbroke is lord of the manor, but part of the soil belongs to the Day, Newson, Smith, and other families. The *Church* (St. Andrew) is a discharged rectory, valued in K.B. at £5. 6s. 8d., and in 1835, at £614, with that of Ugges-hall annexed to it. The Earl of Stradbroke is patron, and the Rev.W. C. Edgell, M.A., incumbent. The Sotherton tithes have been commuted for a yearly modus of £280, and the glebe is 12 acres. *Directory:* —Henry Scarle, vict., *Cross Bows;* and Wm. Baldry, James Hadding-ham, Edward Larter, Wm. Newson, Mary Suggate, John Stanford, My. Ann Sowter, and Wm. Underwood, *farmers.*

SOUTHWOLD is a small but improving *market-town, municipal borough, sea-port, bathing-place, and fishing station,* pleasantly situated on an eminence over-looking the German Ocean; 9 miles E. of Halesworth, 5 miles N.E. by N. of Dunwich,13 miles S. byW. of Lowestoft,12 miles S.S.E. of Beccles, and 105 miles N.E. of London. The town is well built, and consists of one long street, with several short ones; and many of its houses are neat and commodious, and have gardens, &c., extending to the edge of the cliff, and commanding extensive marine prospects. It is nearly encompassed by water; having the sea on the east, *Buss Creek* on the north, and *Blythe Haven,* near the south-end of the town, where two *piers* were erected at the mouth of the river in 1749, and 1752, under the powers of an act of Parliament for the improvement of the harbour, under a body of local commissioners, who lengthened and repaired the *Black Shore Quay,* at the entrance to Buss Creek, in 1805. Vessels of 120 tons burthen can be safely moored either in the Blythe, (see page 357,) or in Buss Creek; and the latter has its name from being the resort of fishing boats, here called *busses.* The *parish,* which is co-extensive with the borough, contains only about 632 acres of freehold land, belonging to various proprietors. It increased its *population* from 1054 souls, in 1801, to 1369 in 1811; 1676, in 1821; 1873, in 1831; and to 2186 in 1841, exclusive of about 200 sailors and fishermen, who were absent when the census was taken. The rateable yearly value of the borough is now £5387, and the gross rental £6343. The *Market* is held every Thursday, the two annual *fairs,* for cattle, &c., on Trinity Monday, and Sept. 4th. *Southwold Bay,* commonly called Sole Bay, is memorable for a sanguinary *naval engagement,* which took place in 1672, between the combined fleets of England and France on one side, and that of the Dutch on the other. The British fleet was commanded by the Duke of York, afterwards James II. The combatants were parted in the darkness of the night, during which, the Dutch withdrew their shattered fleet, which the British, being equally shattered, were unable to pursue. In this sanguinary contest

the Earl of Sandwich and several other distinguished naval commanders lost their lives. The Dutch lost only three ships of war; one burnt, another sunk, and a third captured. Their loss in men was great, but never published. The French sheered off in the middle of the action, and left the English and Dutch to fight it out. The former had two ships burnt, three sunk, and one taken, and about 2000 of their men were killed or wounded. Southwold, commonly called *Sudwald*, or *Southwood*, is not of such high antiquity as Dunwich, Blythburgh, and some other neighbouring places; but its inhabitants were enabled, not only to enter into competition with those towns, but in time to surpass them in navigation and traffic. Alfric, Bishop of the East Angles, who possessed this lordship, gave it, among other donations, to the abbey of Bury St. Edmund's, by which it was held as one manor for the victualling of the monks. It had half, and a quarter of the other half of the sea belonging to the manor, before the Conqueror's time paying 20,000 herrings; but after the conquest, 25,000. From the dimensions of this manor given in Domesday survey, Gardner calculates that the sea has since gained upon this coast one mile, one furlong, and nineteen perches. In the 43rd Henry III., the manor of Southwold was exchanged, by Simon, abbot of Bury, for other possessions, with Richard de Clare, Earl of Gloucester, who, in the year following, obtained permission to convert his house in this town into a *castle*. By his son's wife, Joan of Acres, daughter of Edward I., it was carried, on her second marriage, into the family of Mounthermer, which had been invested with the earldom of Gloucester and Hertford; but in 12th Edward III., some part of the manor was annexed to the priory at Wangford, and is now held by the corporation of Southwold, of the Earl of Stradbroke, to whom the priory belongs. In the tenth of Henry IV., Southwold was exempted from the payment of any customs or tolls, for their small boats passing in or out of the river, or port of Dunwich. Henry VII. in consideration of the industry and good services of the men of Southwold, made the town a *free burgh*, or *corporation*, to be governed by two bailiffs, a recorder, and other inferior officers, to whom, and the commonalty, he gave his lordship of the same, called *Queen's demesne revenues*, and also the *privilege of admiralty*, for the annual payment of £14. He moreover granted them exemption from all dues and customs payable to Dunwich, and conferred on the town the *rights of a haven*, which probably caused the denomination of the port of Dunwich to be changed to that of Southwold. Henry VIII. not only confirmed all his father's grants, but added to them many gifts, franchises, and immunities. These royal favours gave great encouragement to the trade and navigation of the town, of which the *fishery* constituted no small part; being carried on by merchants, who annually fitted out numerous vessels, tradition says upwards of fifty, for taking cod and other fish in the North Sea. The herring fishery off their own coast was also highly conducive to the prosperity of the town. Though Southwold was sensibly affected by the emancipation of the country from the papal supremacy, still it retained an extensive trade, and exceeded all the neighbouring towns in shipping and commerce. But the greatest calamity that ever befel this place, was on the 25th of April, 1659, when a fire, whose destructive fury was heightened by a violent wind, consumed, in the space of four hours, the town-hall, market-house, market-place, prison, granaries, shops, ware-

houses, and 238 dwelling houses, and other buildings. The greatest part of the moveable goods, nets, and tackling, of the inhabitants for their fishery, and all their corn, malt, barley, fish, coals, and other merchandize, were destroyed in this conflagration, the total loss by which exceeded £40,000, to the ruin of more than 300 families. By this disaster, many substantial persons were obliged to seek habitations elsewhere, so that the town never recovered its former importance either in trade or buildings. All the court-baron rolls were destroyed on this occasion, in consequence of which, all the copyholders of the corporation are become freeholders.

About the middle of the last century, the commerce of Southwold received a fresh impulse. The entrance to the haven, on the south side of the town, was subject to be choked up, till an act of parliament was obtained for repairing and improving it. Accordingly, one pier was erected on the north side of its mouth, in 1749, and another on the south, in 1752. The establishment of the Free British Fishery, in 1750, also contributed greatly to the prosperity of the town, where two docks were constructed, and various buildings erected for the making and tanning of nets, and for the depositing of stores. As the beach at Southwold partakes of the advantages enjoyed by other towns on this coast for sea-bathing, it has of late years derived considerable benefit from the strangers who resort to it during the summer season for that purpose, and for whose accommodation here are several bathing machines, and a number of commodious lodging houses. After its first incorporation in the 4th of Henry VII., the town received several royal charters. Until 1835, the *governing charter*, was that of William and Mary, under which the CORPORATION was styled "the bailiffs and commonalty of the town of Southwold," and consisted of two Bailiffs, twelve Aldermen, a High Steward, a Coroner, Town-Clerk, and other officers. The bailiffs were appointed magistrates of the town, judges of its civil court, and admirals of the port. By charter, a court of record, an admiralty court, and a court leet were appointed to be held, but the court of record was discontinued more than a century ago. The *Borough Gaol* was erected in 1819, at the cost of £570, and comprises only a small airing yard, two cells, and an upper chamber. Southwold never enjoyed the privilege of sending representatives to parliament. Under the Municipal Act of 1835, it is included in shedule B, amongst boroughs not to have a commission of the peace, unless on petition and grant; and under section II. of that schedule amongst those, the old municipal boundaries of which are to be taken till altered by parliament. The borough is appointed by this act to be governed by a *mayor, four aldermen*, and *twelve councillors*. The new corporation, elected under this reform act, determined to get rid of their large and long accumulating *debt*, by the sale of *corporate property*, which they sold to the amount of £5,670, in 1840; when they discharged debts and interest to the amount of £6,541. 3s. Their expenditure for the following items in the same year were:—Public-works, repairs, &c., £137; Salaries, &c., £107. 18s.; Rents and taxes, £84. 19s.; and Police and constables, £77. 8d. In 1837, the town *common* was enclosed.

CORPORATION AND OFFICERS (1843.)

Mayor, J. Sutherland, Esq. || *High Steward*, Jas. Jermyn, Esq
ALDERMEN—John Sutherland, Alfred Lillingstone, & Edwd. Chas.Bird,
Esquires ; and Mr. Daniel Fulcher.
COUNCILLORS—Messrs. Rd. Rufus Boniwell, John King, John Gayford,
Joseph Arthy, Peter Palmer, Robt. Wake, R. J. Debney, Daniel
Fulcher, Thos. Penny, Henry Smith, Hy. Gayfer, and Jas. Martin.
Assistant Justices—Jas. Jermyn, Thos. Wm. Thompson, Edw. Chas. Bird,
and Robt. Wake, Esqs.
Town Clerk, Jonathan Gooding, Esquire.
Clerks to the Justices, J. Gooding and J. Shrimpton, Esqrs.
Mr. Joseph Berry Edwards is *town treasurer ;* J. Boyce and Moses Stor-
key, *assessors ;* Richd. Boyce, *chief constable ;* G. E. Child and J. Maggs,
auditors ; James Sterry, *clerk of the markets ;* Samuel Strange, *crier ;*
S. Strange and Chas. Naunton, *sergeants at mace ;* and Chas. A. Everett,
fen-reeve.

Petty Sessions are held every Thursday, before the Mayor and Justices, at the Town Hall, a large building, which is partly used as a police station. The old *Guildhall,* which stood in front of the church,
was taken down in 1815, and a more commodious building erected in
its stead, at the cost of £757. 3s. 9d. The ancient *Market Cross* was
sold for £39, and taken down in 1809. The vane which surmounted it
was dated 1666. On the cliffs are two *Batteries,* one of which is a regular fortification, with a good parapet, and is still mounted by five
guns. The CUSTOM HOUSE OFFICERS are, Henry Burwood, Esq.,
collector ; B. S. Candler, Esq., *comptroller ;* and Lieut. Ellis, *harbour master.* The gross receipt of customs, in 1839, was £319. 17s.
8d., and in 1840, £258. 2s. 1d. Three *pilot boats* and a *life boat* are
stationed here. The latter was built by subscription, in 1841, and is
40 feet long, and 11 broad. There are about 37 coasting vessels belonging to the port, but they are mostly employed in the trade of other
places, or in the *herring and sprat fishery,* which is still extensively carried on here, though it has declined of late years. The town has a
salt manufactory, two *breweries,* two *malting establishments,* and
many *fish-curing houses.* It is said to be famous for fine *old ale,* in
consequence of the excellence of its *water,* of which it has many copious springs. On a hill called *Eye Cliff,* and several others situated
near it, are vestiges of an ancient encampment, supposed to have been
occupied by the Danes ; and, where the ground has not been broken
up, are tokens of circular tents, vulgarly denominated *fairy hills.* This
is said to be the principal part of the eastern coast, at which the *swal-
lows* land on their arrival in England, and at which they take their departure for warmer climes.

The first chapel in Southwold was probably built in the reign of
King John, by the prior and monks of Thetford, who, in right of their
cell at Wangford, were patrons of the church of Reydon, to which
Southwold was then a hamlet. This chapel was destroyed by fire about
200 years after its erection. The present parish CHURCH (Saint
Edmund) is supposed to have been commenced soon after the destruction of the old chapel. It was considered a parochial chapel till 1751,
when, being endowed with £400 of Queen Anne's Bounty, and a like
sum raised by subscription, it was separated from Reydon, and made a
distinct *perpetual curacy,* which was valued in 1835 at £60 ; but the

incumbent is usually also vicar of Reydon, and the two benefices are in the patronage of the Earl of Stradbroke, and are now held by the Rev. H. W. R. Birch. The church is a large and handsome fabric, 143 feet six inches long, and 56 feet 2 inches broad. Its side aisles are separated from the nave by seven arches and six pillars of elegant workmanship. The tower, which contains a peal of eight bells, is about 100 feet high, and is a fine piece of architecture, beautified with free-stone, intermixed with flints of various colours. The porch, erected about 1500, is highly ornamented, and bears the name of the patron saint, in large Gothic letters, over each of which is placed a crown. The north door has a niche on either side, with a figure in each, re-sembling an angel with prodigious wings, in a kind of pulpit. The pil-lars supporting these niches rise from grotesque heads. The mouldings between the receding arches of all the doors are ornamented with fo-liage, flowers, grotesque heads, and figures; as is also the fillet that runs round the body of the church, above the windows. The interior has been more highly ornamented than the exterior. It contained se-veral images; and the carved work of the rood-loft, and seats of the magistrates, now somewhat defaced, originally bore a great resemblance to those in Henry the Seventh's chapel, at Westminster. Every old pew in the church was likewise decorated with representations of birds, beasts, satyrs, or human figures; except a few on the north side of the north aisle, and others concealed by the folding doors opening into the chancel. The ceiling of the latter is handsomely painted, as is like-wise that over the screen in the nave. A new gallery, containing 140 sittings, was erected in 1837, so that the church now contains seats for nearly a thousand hearers, of which about 300 are free. The *organ* was given by Solomon Grout, Esq., in 1825, when a gallery was en-larged for its reception, and for providing 100 additional sittings, in consideration of a grant from the Society for Building and Enlarging Churches. A new altar-piece was erected by Mr. Palmer, in 1826. On altering one of the pews in the latter year, several pieces of coin were found, one of which was a silver penny of Edward I., coined at Dunwich. The INDEPENDENTS, who have had a congregation here since 1695, erected a large and handsome chapel in High street, in 1837, at the cost of £2100. It is of white brick, in the Gothic style, and has 700 sittings. Here is also a small *Baptist Chapel*, built in 1821; and a *Wesleyan Chapel*, erected in 1835.

The *Poor and Town Estate*, which has long been held in trust for the use of the poor, and of the bailiffs and commonalty of the borough of Southwold, in equal shares, consists of nearly 20A. of land, at Reydon, let for £18 a year, and taken in exchange from the late Sir Thos. Gooch, for about 18A. of land at Benacre, which had been purchased with £100, belonging, one-half to the poor, and the other half to the town. The sum of £200 was also paid by Sir T. Gooch, as a *bonus* on the exchange, and half of it is still vested at interest with the Corporation. One-half of the rent of the land is applied in distri-butions of bread and coals, in winter, among poor parishioners, chiefly of the sea-faring class. Besides the £100 just mentioned, there is a sum of £144. 12s. 3d., held by the Corporation for the use of the poor, at 5 per cent. interest, being the amount of moneys formerly raised by the sale of timber off the Benacre land. The interest of both sums is

distributed among the poor, with the rent of the poor's land. There is also a sum of £150 in the hands of the Corporation (at 4 per cent.,) given by *John Steel*, the interest thereof to be distributed yearly among poor widows of Southwold. In 1816, *John Sayer* left £200 four per cent. consols, towards the support of the *Burgh School* (established in the same year ;) but if such school should be discontinued, he directed the dividends to be divided among poor widows of pilots and masters of vessels, which is now done, the school being given up in 1818, for want of support. A *National School*, opened in 1821, was discontinued in 1826, but another has recently been instituted ; and at the Independent Chapel, a day-school for poor girls, on the system of the British and Foreign School Society, was opened in 1837. On Gunhill, in a picturesque situation near the cliff, is an octagonal building, called the CASSINO, erected in 1809, and occupied as a subscription *news room*, &c. The Southwold *Medical and Surgical Institution* was commenced in 1837, for the relief of lying-in women and other sick and infirm poor ; and attached to it is a *Self-supporting Dispensary*, which, for small weekly or monthly contributions, affords to the contributors such medical and surgical aid as they or their families may require. The Earl of Stradbroke is president, and the Rev. H. W. R. Birch and A. Lillingstone, Esq., are vice-presidents, of this useful institution.

SOUTHWOLD DIRECTORY.

Post Office at Mrs. Mary Bye's, Queen street.—Letters received at a quarter past 6 morning, and despatched at 7 evening.

MARKED 1, *are in Back street ; 2, Cliff ; 3, East street ; 4, Gun hill ; 5, Market place ; 6, Meetinghouse lane ; 7, Queen street ; 8, South end, or South green ; 9, Park lane ; and the others in* HIGH STREET, *or where specified.*

Abbott Wm. agent to the Suffolk Amicable Fire Office, St James' ter
Alexander Capt. Hy. Market place
Birch Rev. Hy. W. Rous, vicar of Reydon & incumbt. of Southwold
Blois Sir Charles, Bart. South end, (and *Cockfield Hall*)
Boyce M. Richard, chief constable
5 Button Jonthn. clerk of the market
Burwood Henry, collector of customs
4 Burwood Benjamin, lapidary
7 Candler Benj. S. comptr. of customs
Carver Chas. smallware, toy, &c. dlr
Child Mrs Sarah, Park lane
Cottingham Mr John, North Cliff
Critten James, boat builder, Beach
Day Thomas, sweep, South end
Edwards Jph. bank manager, High st
Ellis Lieut. Francis Wilson, R.N. harbour master, and agent to Freemasons' & General Life Office
French Mr Samuel, High street
Freeman Edward, gent. High street

Gayford John, ship owner, agent to the London Shipping Co., and brick and tile maker
Hawke Chas. watchmaker, Eastgrn
Hopkins Rev Wm. (Indpt.) East ln
1 Knight Misses Mary and Lydia
King John, ship builder, Black shore quay
Laws Mrs. Gun hill
Lillingstone Alfred, Esq. South end
Lloyd John, brewer, Church street
Money Wm. basket mkr. Church st
Naunton Charles, fruiterer
Newson James, carrier
Norman Mr John, Queen street
Norton Mrs. High street
Oshorn George, coast guard officer
Palmer Peter, tax collector, &c
Palmer Mrs Elizabeth, Back street
Parker John, police inspector
Perry Mr John, Back street
8 Priest Wm. excise officer
Rayley Captain Charles, R.N.

Sterry James, **deputy** harbour master
Sheriffe Mrs Sarah, Centre cliff
Spicer Captain Simon, High street
Smith Robt. engraver, &c. Back st
Sutton Wm. lime burner, Gravel pit
4 Thompson Thos. Wm. bank managr
Thompson Mrs Betsy, Park lane
Turner Mrs Girling, Gun hill
Turner Thos. basket mkr. Pinkney ln
Vanneck Thompson. gentleman
Wales John, gent. Gun hill
6 Welton Isaac, horse letter
Wright Robt. salt manfr. South end

BANKERS.

Harveys and Hudsons, High street
& Bungay (draw on Hankey & Co.)

INNS AND TAVERNS.

Crown Hotel and Posting House,
Henry Garrod, High street
Fishing Buss, Wm. Balls, Blackshore
quay
King's Head, John Crowford
3 Lord Nelson, Thomas Penny
Old Swan & Royal Hotel & Posting
House, Thos. Bokenham, Market pl
Pilot Boat, James Woodard, East st
Red Lion, Jas. Martin, South green

Academies.
Debney M. E.
Haylett Robert
Hotson Mary
Jeves Job, *Natl*
Lacy Emily, *Natl*
Twaddell Sophia
Wilkins Robt.

Attorneys.
Gooding Jonthn.
South green
Shrimpton J.,
Barnaby green

Auctioneers.
Fulsher Daniel
Maggs James

*Bakers, Flour
Dealers, and Con-
fectioners.*
7 Balls John
4 Chapman Rd.
5 Lincoln Wm.
Oldring Susan
1 Sones Elisha
Sones John
5 Strange Saml.

Beer Houses.
Benstead John
Chapman Wm.
Everett Chas.

Tink William,
Church street

Butchers.
Everett Chas.
5 Haward Saml.
Robert
5 Oldring James
3 Sampson Colbgs

Cabinet Mkrs. &c.
Fulsher James,
St James' ter
Wright & Sawyer

Chemists & Drugs
8 Athey Joseph
and Son

Coal Dealers.
Crisp Wm. & Son
King Daniel,
Skellman hill
3 Goldsmith Edw.

Coopers.
Crisp B. Church st
King John, (and
sail maker)

Corn Millers.
Crisp Wm. & Son

FARMERS.
6 Barber Michl.
6 Prettyman Wm.

FISH CURERS
and Fish Merts.
5 Button Jonthn.
3 Cragie Wm.
Harrington Benj.
Land Robert,
Church green
2 Jarvis Isaac
2 Palmer John
Palmer Edward
Reynolds John,
Church street
4 Rogers Robt.
3 Stern Daniel
4 Stannard Ann
Simpson Henry,
Beach
4 Taylor Wm.
Waters John,
Beach
Waters Samuel,
Beach
2 Williams Saml.
4 Winter Robt.
3 Woodard Jas.
(dealer in soles)

3 Robson Jonthn.

Blacksmiths.
Blower Joseph
Downing Wm.

Booksellers, &c.
Bye Benj. *(print-
er)*
5 Jeves Job, (cir.
library, &c.)
3 Scarfe Eliz.

Boot & Shoe Mkrs.
Ashmenall Michl.
Church street
8 Balls Samuel
Burgess John
Cornaby Samuel
Denton Maria
Fox Robert
7 Lincoln James
Naunton George
8 Peek Nathl.
1 Smith Robert,
(and engraver)
3 Wells Fras.

*Bricklayers and
Plasterers.*
Carter Charles
1 Howard Benj.
1 Sutton Wm.
3 Sutton Wm.

Gardeners, &c.
Hall John
Smith John

Grocers & Drprs.
5 Abbot Wm. (&
tal. chandler)
4 Debney Robert
John & Son, (&
cirl. library)
Denny George,
(draper only)
Gayfer Henry
5 Jellicoe Ts. Hy.
Lay Henry

Hair Dressers.
3 Andrews John
Mayhew George

Ironmonger.
Child Edmund,
(& tinner, &c.)

Joiners, &c.
Boniwell Richd.
Rufus, Eastgn
Carter Wm. (&
parish clerk)
Fulcher Daniel
3 Palmer Peter
Sawyer John,
Albert place

Lodging Houses.
9 Bardwell Mary
Betts Wm. Bar-
naby green
Bowls Isaac,
Skelman's hill
Hillary Eliz.,
Green lane
9 Lilly Mrs Sus.
2 Lowsey John
4 Rogers Phoebe
3 Sayer Henry
9 Wright Ann

Maltsters.
Crisp Wm. and
Son, (& brew-
ers,) East gn
6 Gayfer Saml.

Master Mariners.
(* are Pilots.)
Aldrich William,
North green
Barker John
6 Baxter Benj.
*Brown William,
Church street
8 Chittleborough
John

*Easey Wm.
3 Elmy Georgel
3 Forman Danie
6 Green David
Jarvis Isaac, master of the Life Boat
4 Laws John
1 Magob John
6 Magob Robert
May Jas. North green
1 Palmer John
8 Palmer Edw.
7 Sayer Edw.
3 Sayer Henry
3 Simpson John
8 Smith Henry
Sones John, Pinkney lane
Spicer Simon
9 Stannard Fras.
Twaddell Marshall
9 Twaddell Rld.
*Waters Wm.

Waters Thomas, Pinkney lane
1 Waters Henry
6 Waythe Edw.
6 Waythe Saml.
7 Waythe Wm.
3 Welsh James
*Wright Wm.

Milliners, &c.
7 Bowler Eliz.
7 Hotson Chltte.
7 Rogers Jare

Painters, Plumbers, & Glaziers.
3 Botham Peter
Boyce James
Eade James
8 Rounce Thos.

Rope & Twine Makers.
Goodwin Jasper, Church street
Oldring Hy. (& sail maker)

Saddler.
Haken Henry

Shopkeepers.
Burcham John
Greenard Mary
Oldring Benj. Green lane

Stone and Marble Mason.
Allen Rt. High st

Surgeons.
Bird Edw. Chas. High street
Sutherland John, M.D. High st

Wake Robert, M.D. Gun hill

Tailors.
1 Andrews John
8 Balls Thomas Girling
Botham Henry
7 Newson Richd.
Sigger Richard, Pinkney lane

Wheelwright.
3 Robson Jonthn.

CARRIERS.

To Halesworth, Norwich, &c. J. Newson, High st. Wed. and Sat; Wm. Goldsmith, Green lane, Tue. and Fri; Robt. Bedingfield, Green lane, Wednesday & Friday; and J. Martin, from the Red Lion, Tue

To Yarmouth, &c. Martin, every Wed. and Sat; and Newson, Mon. and Thursday

To Wangford, Beccles, &c. Daniel Garrod, North green, Monday, Thursday and Saturday

SPEXHALL, 2 miles N. by W. of Halesworth, is a scattered village and parish containing 215 souls, and 1482 acres of land, rising in bold acclivities from one of the tributary streams of the Blythe. The principal proprietors are, Mr. Jas. Garrould, (owner of the Hall and Grove farms,) Wm. Long, Esq., Sir E. Kerrison, Thos. Morse, Esq., and Mr. Garrard. The *Poor's Land*, given by an unknown donor, consists of 5 acres at Holton, let for £13. 10s. The *Church* (St. Peter) is a small ancient structure, and the benefice is a discharged rectory, valued in K.B. at £14, and now having 45 acres of glebe, and a yearly modus of £297. 15s. in lieu of tithes. The patronage is in the Crown, and the Rev. Richard Cruttwell, L.L.B., is the incumbent, and is known for his writings on the currency, "equal adjustment," &c. The other principal inhabitants are David Reynolds, vict., *Huntsman and Hounds;* Robert Woolnough, *blacksmith;* and Saml. Cady, Henry B. Coates, Wm. Covell, James Drake, James Garrould, *Grove;* Wm. Garrould, *Spexhall Hall;* Henry Girling, George Long, Eliz. More, Widow Noller, and Jonth. Palmer, *farmers.*

STOVEN, a small scattered village and parish, 5 miles N.E. by E. of Halesworth, has 127 souls, and 762A. 1R. 31P. of land, mostly freehold. Earl Stradbroke is lord of the manor, but a great part of the soil belongs to Mrs. Bevan, Mrs. Button, T. Norton, Frederick Barne, Esq., and a few smaller owners. The *Church* (St. Margaret) was appropriated to Wangford Priory, and at the dissolution, the rectory was granted to the Duke of Norfolk. The benefice is a perpetual curacy, valued in 1835 at £69. The Rev. George Orgill Leman, M.A., of Brampton Hall, is impropriator, patron, and incumbent, and has a yearly modus of £200 in lieu of tithes. A cottage, called the *Town House,* let to three tenants for £6. 6s. per annum; and about 2 acres

of land, let for £2. 5s., have been held by the churchwardens from time immemorial for the relief of the poor. *Directory:*—John Davy, joiner; Mr. Thomas Gooch; Wm. Vinyard, vict., *Cherry Tree ;* and Edward Andrews, Martin Gooch Button, William Eastaugh, Robert Gooch, John Rockhill, and Edgar Smith, *farmers.*

THEBERTON, a pleasant village, on an eminence, 6 miles N. by W. of Aldborough, and 3 miles N.E. by E. of Saxmundham, has in its parish 580 inhabitants, and 2050 acres of land, bounded on the north by the river Minsmere, which empties itself through a small haven into the sea, about 3 miles E. of Theberton. In 1810, an act of parliament was obtained for draining the low marsh lands, called the *Minsmere Level,* and lying within the parishes of Leiston, Theberton, Dunwich, Middleton-cum-Fordley, and Westleton. This level comprises 1459A., and is now well drained and cultivated. Harry White, Esq., of Halesworth, is clerk to the drainage commissioners. Theberton includes the hamlet of EAST BRIDGE, 1 mile E. of the church. The Rev. Charles Montagu Doughty, B.A., is lord of the manor of Theberton, and resides at the *Hall,* a handsome white brick mansion, in a small but well wooded park, built in 1792, by the late George Doughty, Esq., who served the office of sheriff. But a great part of the soil belongs to Lord Huntingfield, and Thos. Milner Gibson, Esq., M.P. The latter is one of the representatives of Manchester, and resides at *Theberton House,* (1 mile E. of the village,) a commodious stuccoed mansion, which was much improved in 1830, and has a beautiful lawn, pleasure grounds and gardens, comprising about 50 acres. The *Church* (St. Peter) is a small antique fabric, with a round tower, containing four bells. A gallery was erected at the west end in 1841. The benefice is a *discharged rectory,* valued in K.B. at £26. 13s. 4d., and in 1835 at £354. It is in the patronage of the Crown, and incumbency of the Rev. Henry Hardinge, B.A., who has 13A. 3P. of glebe, and a good residence. The patronage was formerly in Leiston Abbey. An *Infant School* was built here by subscription, in 1838, at the cost of £120.

Burley Sml. shoemkr. & shopkeeper
Doughty Rev Chas. Montagu, B.A., *Theberton Hall*
Eade Wm. land agent
Gibson Thomas Milner, Esq. M.P. *Theberton House*
Hardinge Rev Hy. B.A. *Rectory*
Hill Hammond, gardener
Kitt Sarah, shopkeeper
Pipe Wm. shoemkr. and parish clerk
Rouse James, beer house
Todd Edward joiner

Tongate Wm. grocer and draper
Ward Mary Ann, schoolmistress
Waller John, corn miller
Waller Thos. vict. White Lion

Blacksmiths.
Bailey Roger
Bailey Thomas

FARMERS.
Agissing Abm.
Ablett John
Barber James

Brown Robert
Candler Edmund
Geater Thomas
Johnson Joseph
Kitt Zach.
Plant Henry
Rivers George

THORINGTON, a straggling village, 4 miles S.E. of Halesworth, has in its parish 157 souls, and 1411 acres of land, exclusive of roads and a few acres of common. *Lieutenant Col. Henry Bence Bence,* of THORINGTON HALL, owns nearly all the parish, and is lord of the manor, which is called *Thorington Wimples,* and was anciently the demesne of Walter de Norwich. It afterwards passed to the Uffords and Cokes, but has been long held by the Bence family, one of whom, about a century ago, fixed his seat at the *Hall,* which was rebuilt in

1820, at the cost of about £15,000; and stands in a pleasant park of
nearly 200 acres, near the Beccles road, 6½ miles N.N.E. of Saxmundham. The *Church* (St. Peter) is an ancient edifice with a round tower,
and was repaired and repewed in 1836, at the cost of £200. The living
is a discharged rectory, valued in K.B. at £7, and now having 11A. 2R.
17P. of glebe, and a yearly modus of £283. 17s., in lieu of tithes. Lieut.
Col. Bence is patron, and the Rev. Launcelot Robert Brown, M.A., of
Kelsale, is the incumbent. The *Church Land* is let for £2 per annum.
The FARMERS are Robert Appleton, Wm. Catling, James Edmunds,
James Friend, James Lay, James Peek, and Jas. Rush. Samuel Marsh-
land is the *gamekeeper.* NO-WHERE-HOUSE, within the bounds of
Thorington, is *Extra Parochial.*

UBBESTON, near one of the sources of the river Blythe, 6½ miles
S.W. of Halesworth, and N.N.E. of Framlingham, is a village and
parish containing 243 inhabitants, and 1207A. 1R. 14P. of land. Lord
Huntingfield is lord of the manor, but part of the soil belongs to the
Rev. R. H. Frere, Mr. Clutterbuck, and several smaller owners. The
manor was held by St. Neots priory, and was granted at the dissolution
to John Pope, Esq. It was for a long period the seat and property of
the *Sones*, whose heiress carried it in marriage, in the 17th century, to
the ancient family of Kemp, who for some time occupied the *Hall*, now
a farm house. The *Church* (St. Peter) is a discharged vicarage, valued
K.B. at £6. 13s. 4d., but endowed with the rectorial tithes by Mrs.
Mary Sone, in 1685. The glebe is nearly 7A., and the tithes have
been commuted for a yearly modus of £316. 16s. The Rev. E. Holland
is patron, and the Rev. Samuel Badeley, L.L.B., of Yoxford, is the incumbent. The *Poor's Estate* consists of two cottages, a garden, and
a blacksmith's shop, let for £12. 3s. a year, which is sometimes improperly expended in the service of the church, instead of being distributed among the poor parishioners.

Collett Capt. Anthony
Oxborough Thos. beer house
Prime Thos. shopkeeper
Smyth Charles, corn miller
Smyth Simon, blacksmith

FARMERS.
Allen Ann || Canham James
Cobbold Thos. Ubbeston Hall
Crow John || Flaxman Hy.
Huson Robt. || Kemp James
Prime Robt. || Skeet Wm.

UGGESHALL, a parish and scattered village, 5¼ miles E.N.E. of
Halesworth, and N.W. by W. of Southwold, contains 295 souls, and
1455 acres of land. The Earl of Stradbroke is lord of the manor, but
a great part of the soil belongs to Mrs. Allen, Rev. J. Borton, Rev.
B. Chapman, Rev. J. Vincent, and a few smaller owners. The *Church*
(St. Mary) is a small ancient structure, but the tower went to decay
about a century ago. The *rectory*, valued in K.B. at £13. 6s. 8d., and
in 1835, at £614, with that of Sotherton annexed to it, is in the patronage of the Earl of Stradbroke, and incumbency of the Rev. W. C.
Edgell, M.A., who has here a neat residence and 42A. of glebe. The
tithes of Uggleshall have been commuted for a yearly modus of £390.
A pleasure *fair* is held here on Trinity Tuesday. The poor have a
cottage given by one of the Platers family, let for £4, and an *allotment*
of 4A. 37P. awarded at the enclosure in 1799, and now let for £10. 10s.
per annum. They have also 10s. a year, out of land called *Gander's
Hill*, given by an unknown donor.

Baxter Saml. shopkeeper
Bardwell Mr Thomas
Dunnett Richard, blacksmith
Edgell Rev Wm. Chas. M.A. incbt.
 Rectory
Kent Wm. wheelwgt. & parish clerk
Rockhill Wm. corn miller
Wright James, vict. Buck
Youngman Mrs. Ann

FARMERS.
Bardwell Charles, *Manor House*
Baxter Ann || Bence Philip
Churchman Edw. || Eade Wm.
Girling Jas. || Gray Samuel
Leman Timothy || Youngman Wm.
Carrier, Martin, from the Buck to
 Southwold & Yarmouth, Tuesday

WALBERSWICK, an ancient village, near the sea, on the south side of the river Blythe, 1½ mile S.S.W. of Southwold, and 3½ miles N.N.E. of Dunwich, has in its parish 339 souls, and 1771 acres of land, including about 130 acres of open salt marshes and heath, on which all parishioners have a right to graze cattle or geese. It is a place of great antiquity, and was once a considerable town, which carried on an extensive commerce both by land and sea, especially in fish: having, in 1451, thirteen barks trading to Iceland, Ferro, and the North Seas, and twenty-two fishing boats employed off this coast. The alteration of the port, which ruined the town of Dunwich, proved a source of increased prosperity to Walberswick, which continued to thrive till the middle of the sixteenth century, when the alteration made in the established religion proved highly detrimental to this, as well as to many other towns of the coast, whose principal support was derived from the fishery. From that time, Walberswick began gradually to decline, and repeated and destructive conflagrations hastened its ruin. Before 1583, it suffered severely by fire ; in 1633, a great part of it was burned ; in 1683, it was again visited by a similar scourge ; and in 1749, about one-third of the small remains of the town was consumed. But since the *haven* of the Blythe has been improved, by the erection of piers at its mouth, (see page 389,) Walberswick has encreased its population from less than 200 to 339 souls, and has now a *quay* for vessels of 100 tons, and a *lime-kiln* which burns the lime and makes coke under one process, built in 1839, by Mr. Samuel Gayfer, the present proprietor. Sir Charles Blois, Bart., is lord of the *manor*, which is mostly freehold, and the other principal landowners are Mr. Wm. Borrett and Charles Peckover, Esq. The *Church* (St. Andrew) was rebuilt by the parishioners, who commenced the new fabric in 1473, and finished it in 1493. It was a large and handsome structure, and contained a chapel of Our Lady, and images of the Holy Trinity, the Rood, St. Andrew, and several other saints. Though it suffered considerably from the puritanical visitors of the 17th century, it continued nearly entire till 1696, when the inhabitants, unable to support the charge of repairs, took down the greater part of it, reserving only the south-west angle for divine service : some of the outer walls of the chancel are, however, still standing. When entire, the church was 124 feet long, and 60 broad. The tower, which is 90 feet high, was partly blown down in 1839, but was repaired in the following year. The benefice is a *perpetual curacy*, valued in 1835 at £41, and enjoyed by the Rev. Richard Harrison, together with that of Blythburgh. Sir Charles Blois is patron and also impropriator of the tithes, which were commuted, in 1840, for a yearly modus of £193. Here is a small *Independent Chapel*, erected in 1831. *Lampland* Marsh, let for £5 per annum, has been held from time im-

memorial for the reparation of the church. Upon 34 acres of *enclosed marsh*, every householder has a right to turn one head of cattle. On 40 acres of *salt marsh*, all parishioners have the right to turn what stock they choose, and the poor avail themselves of the privilege by feeding upon it great quantities of geese. A *heath* of 84½ acres is an open pasture for all resident parishioners, who have also the liberty of cutting furze, turf, ling, &c. The tenant of Westwood Lodge (see page 357) has also the right of turning sheep upon this heath, adjoining which is 3½ acres of open marsh, stocked in the same manner. This marsh might be enclosed and improved at a small expense.

Banks John, shoemaker
Cleveland Martha, schoolmistress
Cleveland Wm. shopkeeper
Cullingford Robert, bricklayer
Easey Wm. vict. Blue Anchor
Gayfer Saml. corn miller & mercht. and lime and coke burner
Harrison Rev Richard, incumbent
Lawrence Sarah, vict. Bell

Osborn Wm. shopkeeper
Threadkill John, wheelwright
Whincop George, blacksmith
Wright Henry, master mariner

FARMERS.
Easey L. || Borrett Wm. *(owner)*
Leverett John || Gayfer James
Wigg Edward, *Manor House*
Wright Benj. || Wright John

WALPOLE, a considerable village, on a pleasant acclivity above the small river Blythe, 2¼ miles S.S.W. of Halesworth, has in its parish 615 souls, and 1624 acres of land, in the manor of Walpole-with-Chickering, of which Lord Huntingfield is lord, but part of the soil belongs to P. Tatlock, Esq., the Rev. J. Philpot, Mr. J. Borrett, and a few smaller owners. The *Church* (St. Mary) has been rebuilt of white brick, and has a wooden steeple. The rectory was appropriated to the nuns of Redingfield, but the whole parish is now tithe-free, except a yearly modus of £40. The Rev. Benj. Philpot is patron and incumbent of the perpetual curacy, valued in 1835 at £85. Here is an *Independent Chapel*, erected in 1647. Its walls are of timber frames, filled up with laths and plaster, and it contains three galleries. The *National School* here was built in 1823. The *Town Estate*, held from a remote period for the general benefit of the inhabitants, consists of 3A. of land let for £7 per annum; the site, yards, &c., of the old townhouse, let in 1824 on a forty years' lease, at 7s. 6d. per annum, the lessee covenanting to erect a new house; an acre of land called Clink, let in 1800 on a 99 years' lease at the yearly rent of £1; and three small ground rents amounting to 4s. 6d. a year. The rents are applied with the church-rate. In 1701, *Thomas Neale* left out of a farm at Cookley, now belonging to Mr. Saunders, the yearly rent-charges of £2. 10s. for schooling five poor children, and 10s. to buy them books.

Blaxhill Samuel, tailor
Bokenham Robert, wheelwright
Butcher John, bricklayer
Chapman John, corn miller
Copeman Arthur Stanhope, veterinary surgeon
Ingate Robert, corn miller
Kemp Rev Robert, curate
Kemp Charles, tailor
King James, basket maker
Lumiss Wm. parish clerk
Morse Daniel, saddler

Pashley Mr Daniel Thompson, *(owner)*
Rackham Wm. & Sar. Natnl. school
Ralph John, thatcher
Sampson Robt. surveyor & postman
Stanford Philip, joiner
Strowger Thomas, mole catcher
Walker John, gent. *White House*
White James, gardener & beerhs.
Woods John, butcher & vict. *Bell*

Blacksmiths.
Plant Edward

Winter John

Boot & Shoe Mkrs.	Goddard John	Stofer Wm.	Wright Samuel
Bellamy Fredk.	Goddard Samuel	Thurlow John	*Grocers & Dprs.*
Salter Wm.	Mongan George	Upson James	Aldis Edw.Chas.
Upson John	Pashley D. T.	White Wm.	Penstead Saml.
FARMERS.	Peck James	Wigg Herbert	Rackham Benj.
Borrett John, (& owner)	Philpot John	Winter John	(and baker)

WANGFORD is a large and well-built village, on the Yarmouth road, near a tributary stream of the river Blythe, 4 miles N.W. of Southwold, 5½ miles E. by N. of Halesworth, 8½ miles S. by E. of Beccles, and 12 miles N.N.E. of Saxmundham. Its parish is in *two townships*,—WANGFORD and HENHAM, the former of which has 829 acres, and 690 souls, and the latter 128 souls, and about 1500 acres of land, more than half of which is in the extensive *Park* of Henham Hall, the elegant seat of the Earl of Stradbroke, who owns most of the parish, and is lord of the manors. Wangford had formerly a PRIORY, or *Cell* of Cluniac monks, subordinate to Thetford, and dedicated to the Virgin Mary. It is said to have been founded before the year 1160, by Doudo Asini, steward of the king's household. It was often seized during the wars with France as alien, but was made denizen in the 17th of Richard II. At the general dissolution, its revenues were valued at £30. 9s. 5d. per annum, though it had then only a prior and two monks. It was granted, together with the monastery of Thetford, to Thomas Duke of Norfolk, whose son sold it in 1612, to Sir John Rous, Kt., an ancestor of the Earl of Stradbroke, its present owner. It stood on what is now called the *Abbey Lands*, but no vestiges of it are extant. *Petty Sessions* are held at the Angel Inn on the first Wednesday of every month. The *Church* (St. Peter) is a small structure, built partly of flints and partly of brick, and has a modern spire steeple rising from the north-west angle, and containing five bells. The interior is neatly fitted up, and has several handsome monuments in memory of the late Earl of Stradbroke and several of his predecessors. The organ was purchased in 1839. The Earl of Stradbroke is *impropriator* of the tithes, and those dues from land not belonging to him were commuted in 1840 for £93 per annum. He is also patron of the *perpetual curacy*, valued in 1835, at £79, and now enjoyed by the Rev. Wm. French. Here is a *Primitive Methodist chapel*, built in 1827, and an *Independent chapel*, erected in 1831. The small bridge, at the west end of the village, was built in 1843, after two unsuccessful attempts to obtain a good foundation. The *Town House*, consisting of two small tenements, occupied rent-free by poor widows, has been vested for the use of the poor from time immemorial. The poor parishioners have a yearly rent-charge of £5, left by an unknown donor, out of a farm in Wangford, belonging to the Earl of Stradbroke.

HENHAM township, generally called a hamlet, adjoins Wangford on the west, and has 128 inhabitants, and about 1500 acres of land, of which 850 acres are in *Henham Park*, which is still well-wooded, and has many large oaks, though 1100 of the latter were cut down in 1842, and sold for £8800. The roads from Blythburgh to Beccles and Lowestoft bound the park for about two miles on the east and west; and in the northern part of it, on a pleasant eminence, 4 miles E. by

N. of Halesworth, and W.N.W. of Southwold, stands HENHAM HALL, the elegant mansion of the Earl of Stradbroke, whose family has resided here more than three centuries. The present hall is of modern erection, having been built after the destruction of the old mansion by fire, in May 1773, the loss on which occasion was estimated at £30,000. Ralph Baynard had the lordships of Henham and Wangford at the Domesday survey. In the time of Edward I., they belonged to Robert Lord Kerdeston. About 1440, they passed to the De la Poles; and in the time of Henry VIII., to the ancient family of *Rous*, who removed hither from Dennington, where they had long been seated. In 1660, John Rous, Esq., of Henham, was created a *baronet*, and one of his descendants, Sir John Rous, the 6th baronet, was created *Baron Rous, of Dennington*, in 1796, and *Viscount Dunwich and Earl of Stradbroke*, in 1821. He died in 1827, and was succeeded by his eldest son, the present *Right Hon. John Edward Cornwallis Rous*, EARL OF STRADBROKE, &c., who was born in 1794, and is colonel of the East Suffolk Militia. His brother, the *Hon. Henry John Rous*, (M.P. for Westminster,) is heir presumptive of the estates and titles.

WANGFORD PARISH.
*Marked * are in Henham.*

*Earl of Stradbroke, *Henham Hall*
Allison Wm. tailor
Barber Wm. vict. *Swan*
Barfoot Wm. tailor || Brady Mrs My.
Cleveland Robt. veterinary surgeon
Croft John, vict. *Red Lion*
Fuller Robert, baker
Gray Arthur Baldry, vict. *Angel*
Herring John, plumber, glazier, and painter
Howse Edward, sen. beerhouse
Howse Edward, jun. pork butcher
Lay Henry, surgeon, *Abbey Lands*
Mitchell Samuel, bricklayer
Read Ezekiel, grocer and draper, *Post Office* (letters desp. 8 eveng.)
Reeve Robert, butcher
Rudland James Miles, surgeon
Smith John, glover
Smith Samuel, wheelwright
Snell and Bickers, timber merchants

Stimpson Samuel, beerhouse
Terry James, saddler
Terry Wm. yeoman
Turner Robert Godfrey, corn miller
Wales Charles, grocer and draper
Watling Hamlet, day & bdg. school

Blacksmiths.
Andrews Richd.
Cutts Robert
Nelson Milbourn
Boot&ShoeMkrs.
Barber Wm.
Bence Henry
Rich Francis
Waters Wm.
Welton Charles

FARMERS.
*Carpenter Hy.
*Ling John
Mayhew Geo. L.
*Reeve Richard
Reeve Benj. (& maltster)
Taylor William, *Barnaby green*

COACHES
To Yarmouth and Ipswich daily.

CARRIERS.
Goldsmith to Norwich, Tue. & Fri.; Martin to Halesworth, Tue.; and Saxmundham, Friday—from the Red Lion.

WENHASTON, a large straggling village, on a bold acclivity, overlooking the vale of the river Blythe, 3 miles S.E. by E. of Halesworth, has in its parish 2327 acres of land, and 1094 inhabitants, of whom 123 are in MELLES, or *Mells*, a hamlet of scattered farms and a few cottages, on the south bank of the Blythe, 2 miles E.S.E. of Halesworth, where there are still considerable ruins of *Melles Chapel*, which was dedicated to St. Margaret. *Wenhaston* was held by Sibton Abbey, and was granted at the dissolution to Thomas Duke of Norfolk. It afterwards passed to the Sparrow, Leman, and other families. It lies mostly in the *manors* of Wenhaston Grange and Thorington Hall, of which the Rev. Jeremy Day is lord; and partly in Col. Bence's manor of Thorington Wimpoles. The *manor of Melles* and a great

part of soil in that hamlet belongs to the trustees of the late — Collison, Esq. It was held by Mettingham college, and was granted at the dissolution to Thomas Denney. N. Micklethwaite, Esq., the Earl of Gosford, and the Youngs, Burgess, and some other families have estates in the parish. The *Church* (St. Peter) stands on an eminence, commanding a view of the sea, and is an ancient structure, with a tower and six bells. It has several monuments of the Lemans, who were formerly seated at the *Hall*, now occupied by a farmer. The living is a discharged vicarage, valued in K.B. at £6. 0s. 10d., in the patronage of the Crown, and incumbency of the Rev. Richard Day, M.A. The Earl of Gosford is impropriator of the rectorial tithes, which were commuted for a yearly modus of £378. 2s. 3d. in 1839, when the vicarial tithes were also commuted for £142 per annum. Here is a *Wesleyan chapel*, built in 1822, and enlarged in 1835. The Town Estate, let for £54 a year, which is applied with the church-rate, comprises a building in four tenements, anciently called the Guild-hall, granted by the prior of Blythburgh; 4A. of land, vested at a remote period for the use of the church and poor; and about 16A., formerly waste land, granted by the lord of the manor of Blythburgh, in 1770. *William Pepyn*, in 1562, bequeathed for the schooling of poor children, property now consisting of a dwelling, called the *School-house*, and 3A. 2R. 26P. of land, let for £16 a year. In 1563, Reginald Lessey left for the same purpose 3A. of copyhold land, near Blyth-burgh, now let for £10 a year. The school trustees have also £45, lent on mortgage, and derived from the sale of timber. The rents and interest are paid to a *schoolmaster* for instructing about 17 poor children in reading, writing, and arithmetic. In 1680, *Mary Collen* left a yearly rent-charge of £3, for repairing her monument and the relief of six poor widows. This annuity is paid out of about 45A. of land in Melles hamlet, occupied by Mr. Haward. Petty Sessions are held at Wenhaston every third Wednesday.

WENHASTON PARISH.
*Marked * are in Melles hamlet.*

Butcher Matthew, tailor
Cole George, schoolmaster
Coleman Henry, brewer
Dickinson James, hair dresser
Funnell Thomas, schoolmaster
Haward Mrs Amelia
*Higham Saml. S. corn miller
Mortimer Harriet, schoolmistress
Nunn James, millwright
Raven Robert, butcher & beerhouse
Watling Fredk. vict. Compasses
White Chas. tailor & parish clerk
White Chas. jun. relieving officer & registrar
Youngs Mr John, jun.

Blacksmiths.
Danford James
Newby Wm.

Swain Robert
Boot&ShoeMkrs.
Brunning Jacob

Brunning Robt.
Harper Samuel
Ludbrook Robert
Peck Wm.
Tuthill, John

FARMERS.
Andrews Wm.(& corn miller)
Butcher Francis
Burgess Thomas
Friend Wm.
*George Chpr.
Harper Eliz.
*Haward Chas.
Leggett James
Lines Wm. *Hall*
Nolloth Robert
Smith John
Plant Edward

*Turrell George
Wade Robert
* Watling George
*Wells James
Whittingham Frs
Youngs John
Grocers, &c.
Cole Wm.
Benstead Harriet (and saddler)
Burrows Wm.
Dunford Robert
Tuthill John
Joiners, &c.
Cole Wm.
Webb Robert
Wheelwright.
Peck Wm. (and shopkeeper)

WESTHALL, a small village, 3 miles N.E. of Halesworth, has in its parish 412 inhabitants, 2194 acres of land, and many scattered

houses, stretching more than two miles N.W. of the church to the source of a rivulet; and mostly situated on the margins of four *greens* or *commons*, which comprise 125 acres, on which all the parishioners have a right of pasturage, according to the extent of their farms. Robert de Burgh, Earl of Kent, had a grant of the *manor* in the 13th of Henry III. From the reign of Henry VIII. till the latter part of last century, it was held by the Bohun family, one of whom, Edmd. Bohun, Esq., who resided here, was a voluminous writer of the 17th century. The most noted of his works were, a *Geographical Dictionary*, and a *History of King James the Second's Desertion*. Wm. Adair, Esq., is now lord of the manor, but a great part of the soil belongs to Peter Foster, Esq., Thos. Farr, Esq., the Rev — White, and the Penrose, Tacon, Manning, Carlos, Newson, and other families. The *Church* (St. Andrew) is a small ancient structure, with a tower and five bells. The prior and convent of Norwich bought the advowson and the appropriation of Humberstone Abbey, Lincolnshire. The Dean and Chapter of Norwich are now appropriators of the rectory, and patrons of the vicarage, valued in K.B. at £10. 2s. 3½d., and in 1835 at £195, and now enjoyed by the Rev. Richard Mathews. The rectorial tithes have been commuted for £478. 10s., and the vicarial for £150 per annum. A cottage and two acres of land, let for £9, and two ground rents, amounting to 6s. per annum, have been vested for a long period for the repairs of the church. The parish has also two yearly rent-charges of £1. 6s. and £1. 12s., left by the *Rev. Gregory Clarke*, and Ann his wife, in 1717 and 1726, for schooling poor children. They are paid to a schoolmistress, for teaching five children to read.

WESTHALL.

Marked 1, *live on Bacon Common;* 2, *Cox Green;* 3, *Mill Common; and* 4, *Nethergate Green.*

Beddingfield Cornelius, tailor
3 Blaxhill Samuel, corn miller
3 Boyles Saml. vict. Greyhound
3 Boyles James, shoemaker
3 Coleby Joseph, shoemaker
3Cornish Joshua, tinner & blacksmth
Fisk Fras. brewer & vict. *RaceHorse*
Fisk John, parish clerk
2 Green Wm. wheelwright
3 Miller Edmund, wheelwright

Offord Wm. blacksmith

FARMERS.

2 Bates John (& surveyor)
3 Clerk Robert
3 Crisp Ellis
3 Cross Wm.
3 Davy John
3 Davy Emily
2 Driver Henry
3 Ellis James
2 Fuller Wm.
2 Green Wm.
3 Greenard Geo.

4 Greenwood Ann
3 Haddingham W
2 Hammond Sml.
3 Leman Robert
3 Newbery Jno.
4 Newbery Geo.
3 Newson Isaac
3 Norman Isaac
3 Pedgrift John
4 Rackham Roger
2 Sallows Thos.
Spelman Isaac, *Westhall Hall*

WESTLETON, a large and pleasant village, on the north side of the *Minsmere Level*, (see page 397,) 2½ miles W.S.W. of Dunwich, and 5½ miles N.E. by N. of Saxmundham, has in its extensive parish 897 souls, and 6103 acres of land, including a large portion of open sandy heath on the north; some fine salt marshes near the coast; *Minsmere Haven*, extending more than three miles S.E. of the village; and several fertile farms in the DINGLE, a narrow dale, watered by a small rivulet, running three miles northward from Dunwich, within half a mile of the sea coast. The Dingle had formerly a chapel. The parish is in *four manors*, of which the following are the names and lords: Westleton-with-its-Members, Sir Charles Blois; Westleton-Grange S. A. Woods, gent.; Westleton-Cleves, John Cutts, gent.; and Wes-

tleton Minsmere, Lord Huntingfield. The other principal proprietors of the soil are N. Micklethwaite, Esq., Fredk. Barne, Esq., Rev. J. Day, and Charles Purvis, Esq. The gross yearly rental of the parish is £6103. The land is mostly freehold. *Westleton Grange* anciently belonged to Sibton Abbey, and was granted at the dissolution to Thomas Duke of Norfolk. The *Church* (St. Peter) is an ancient structure, which formerly had a large tower, containing eight bells, but it fell down in 1770. A fine Norman arch divides the nave and chancel. The vicarage, valued in K.B. at £8, is consolidated with Middleton and Fordley, in the patronage and incumbency of the Rev. Harrison Packard. N. Micklethwaite, Esq., is impropriator of the rectory. The great tithes of Westleton have been commuted for £690, and the small tithes for £325 per annum. The incumbent resides at Yoxford, but has here 17 acres of glebe, and a parsonage-house, which was repaired and enlarged in 1843, at the cost of £600. Here is a *Primitive Methodist Chapel*, built in 1835, and a *National School*, erected in 1842, at the cost of £430. The *Church Land* is let for £17 a year, but the donor is unknown. In 1722, *Thomas Grimsby* left about 12A. of land, to provide clothing for poor widows and children of this parish, and it is now let for £14 a year. Fras. Robinson, Esq., of Dunwich, is the sole trustee.

Brown Jemima, schoolmistress
Brown John, beerhouse
Brown Wm. tailor
Bruce Joseph, policeman
Cooper John Rous, gent. *Red House*
Fisk Henry, vict. Crown
Gardener Rev Jas. Wm. curate
Goodwin Mary, dressmaker
Jude James, schoolmaster
King Samuel, baker
Mayhew Honora, straw hat maker
Newson Ann, straw hat maker
Tyrell Robert, parish clerk
Ward John, saddler
Woods Samuel Alexander, gent., *Vale House*

Blacksmiths.
Brown Joseph
Noller Charles
Noller John

Boot & Shoe Mkrs.
Blowfield John
Carver Wm.
Gould John

Hazel Joseph
Rous Richard
Spall Esau
Bricklayers.
Etridge Wm.
Parnall John
Corn Millers.
Balls John
Mann ell John
Pratt and Whitehead
FARMERS.
Blandard James
Briggs Benjamin, *Dingle*
Cooper John R.
Dix Geo. *Dingle*
Etridge John
Gibson Richard

Girling Richard
Kersey John
Marshlain Robt.
Moore John
Rous James, *Chatbourn*
Smith James
Joiners.
Mayhew Scarlet
Rous James
Shopkeepers.
Fryer Harriet
Mannell John
Mannell Thomas
Salter Wm.
Wheelwrights.
Fisk Samuel
Threadkill Thos.

WISSETT, a pleasant village, in a narrow valley, on one of the tributary streams of the Blythe, 2 miles N.W. of Halesworth, has in its parish 470 souls, and 2260 acres of land. In the reign of Henry III., it was the lordship of the Earl of Richmond, and it afterwards passed to the Earl of Savoy, and from him to John de Vaux, whose two daughters and co-heirs married Wm. de Nerford and Thomas Lord Roos, or Ross. W. E. Hartopp, Esq., is lord of the manor, called *Wissett le Rosse*, but the greater part of the soil belongs to the Parkyns, Tacon, Wilcox, Bence, Micklethwaite, Crabtree, Chase, Calver, Crisp, Wright, Pedgrift, Aldred, Button, Pattison, and other families, some of whom have neat houses here. The parish is mostly freehold, and its gross annual rental is now estimated at £3637. The *Church* (St.

Andrew) is a small antique fabric, with a round tower. The north entrance is under a fine Saxon arch. The east end was repaired seven
years ago, and the interior was new pewed in 1843, when a gallery was
erected at the west end. Wm. Edmund Hartopp, Esq., is impropriator
of the rectory, and patron of the perpetual curacy, valued, in 1835, at
£105, and now enjoyed by the Rev. Robt. Kemp, for whom a new
Parsonage was built in 1843, at the cost of about £700, towards which
the patron gave £200, and the Governors of Queen Anne's Bounty
£200. The tithes have been commuted for yearly moduses of £452.
10s. 2d. to the impropriator, and £90 to the incumbent. A house and
garden have been vested in trust, from an early period, for the reparation of the church, and were let, in 1774, on a lease of 99 years, at the
annual rent of £1. 5s. 4d., the lessee covenanting to lay out a large
sum in rebuilding the house. Here is a *School*, supported by subscription, for the instruction of about 30 poor children.

Aldrich Jno. bricklayer & whiting mfr
Algar George, tailor and shopkeeper
Barber Richard, joiner
Berry Jph. shoemaker & parish clerk
Davy Lucy, schoolmistress
Gooch Samuel, vict. Swan
Howlett Jonathan, auctioneer, &c. *Hill House*
Howlett and Lenny, auctioneers and estate agents
Howlett Wm. beerhouse keeper
Hufflett George, blacksmith
Keable John, corn miller
Kemp Rev Rt. incumbent, *Parsonage.*
Lenny Charles, auctioneer, &c.
Markham Wm. shoemaker

Pedgrift Wm. Henchman, surgeon, *Wissett Place*
Phillips John, gentleman
Watson Henry, blacksmith
Woods Wm. brewer and shopkeeper

FARMERS.—(* *are Owners.*)

*Aldred Robert	Goldsmith Jas.
Allen Richard, *Red House*	Mayhew Edward
	Moore Jno. Robt.
*Banks Wm.	Prime Philip
Banks Wm.	*Self Thos. (and gardener)
Bootman Eliz.	
*Button John, *Brook Hall*	Tillott Jno. *Lodge*
Chase Elizabeth	Walker John
Ecclestone Jas.	Walker John
	Winter James

WRENTHAM, a large and well-built village, partly on the Yarmouth road, 9 miles S.S.W. of Lowestoft, 5 miles N. of Southwold, and
8 miles S.E. by S. of Beccles, has in its parish 1020 souls, and 1280
acres of land. At the Domesday survey, Robert de Pierpoint held the
manor of the famous Earl Warren. It afterwards passed to the Poin-
ings. In the reign of Edward VI., it was purchased by the *Brewsters*,
who built the *Hall*, which was taken down several years ago, after the
manor had been sold to Sir T. S. Gooch, Bart., its present lord. Part
of the soil belongs to the Dean and Chapter of Westminster, and several smaller proprietors. The *Church* (St. Nicholas) is a neat structure, with a tower and five bells. It has recently been re-pewed, repaired, and furnished with 312 additional sittings, at the cost of nearly
£700, towards which the Society for Building and Enlarging Churches
gave £250, and £243 was levied by rate on the parishioners. The remainder, and the organ, were contributed by the present incumbent,
who, in 1842, erected a new Rectory House, at the cost of £1000.
The rectory, valued in K.B. at £21. 6s. 8d., has now a yearly modus
of £578. 1s. 11d., awarded, in 1839, in lieu of tithes. Sir T. S. Gooch
is patron, and the Rev. Stephen Clissold, M.A., incumbent. The
pious *Bishop Ebor* resided many years at the old Rectory House.
Here is an *Independent Chapel*, built in 1778, by a congregation which
originated in 1647 ; and also a small *Primitive Methodist Chapel*, built

in 1841. The *National School*, for children of both sexes and infants, is a neat building, in two large rooms, with a dwelling for the teachers, erected in 1834, at the cost of £745. 14s. 5d., subscribed by the lord of the manor, the rector, and other contributors, except £131 granted from her Majesty's treasury, and £80 given by the National School Society. About 100 children attend, and each pay 1d. per week. Here is also a large school connected with the *British and Foreign School Society*, erected in 1837, at the cost of £200, and attended by about 50 children. The *Town House* has been vested for the use of the poor from an early period, and is in three apartments, two occupied rent-free, and the other let for £3. The *Town Meadow*, three acres, let for £2, has also belonged to the poor from an early period; and they have £3 a year from the *Bull Fen*, given in 1632, and an *Allotment* of 25A. 1R. 18P., awarded at the enclosure, in the 37th of George III., and now let for £37 a year. They have also a yearly rent-charge of 20s., left by *Robert Edgar*, out of that part of the Frostenden estate situated in Wrentham parish, and belonging to the Dean and Chapter of Westminster. The income from these charities is applied in distributions of coals, clothing, &c.

WRENTHAM.
*Marked * reside at West end.*
Post Office at Mr Edw. Kemball's.
Letters received at 6 morning, and despatched at 8 morning
Artis James, bricklayer
Artis Alfred Joseph, bricklayer
Algar Sarah, baker
Angel Miss Mary Ann
Baldry James, watch and clock mkr
Baxter Wm. beerhouse
Bullock Edward, watch & clock mkr
Chancellor Henry, tailor & draper
Chipperfield Rd. beerhs. & butcher
Clissold Rev Stephen, M.A. *Rectory*
Cutts Francis, shopkeeper
Dade Rebecca, beerhouse
Exeter Rev John, curate
Farrer Fredk. veterinary surgeon
Fisk Samuel, beerhouse
Goff Johnson, corn miller
Harmer Alfred, surgeon
Harmer John, druggist
Hasilup Samuel, tailor and draper
Hitcham Mrs
Howard Sarah, corn miller
Johnson Henry, butcher
Kemball Eliz. day & bdg. school
Lenny John Grimsby, land agent
Lenny & Croft, land agents & surveyors; and Bury St Edmund's
Lilly Royal Wm. plumber & glazr
Mealing John, cooper & shopkeeper
Mills Joseph, wood turner
Parry, Maria, day & bdg. school
Primrose and Harmer, surgeons

Quadling Wm. ironmonger & joiner
Ritchie Rev.— Independent minster
Roberts Samuel, sawyer
Scarlett Mary Ann, vict. Eagle
Smith Sidney, farrier, &c
Stutter Miss, *British School*
*Vincent John Francis, gent
Wright Edward, saddler
Wright Stephen, stationer, &c
Wright Wm.& Miss S.*National School*
Wroot James, tailor
Wroot Misses Mary and Martha

Blacksmiths.
Burcham Thos. (ironmonger)
Lovett Wm.
Lloyd James
*Wilson Wm.

Boot & Shoe Mkrs.
Allger Alfred
Allger Charles
Fox Samuel
Wilson Thos.
Woolnough John

FARMERS.
Baxter W. Stone
*Bence Wm.
Candler Chas.
Candler James
Carter Willber
*Cottingham W.
*Crisp Baker
Denny John
*Denny Robert
Girling Thos.
Goff John

Kent John
Tacon John
*Wigg Neriah

Grocers & Drprs
Girling & Scalett
Martin John
Newson Wm.
Read John

Joiners.
Dade John
Waters John

Wheelwright.
Cox Stephen

COACHES daily to Yarmouth, Ipswich, &c
CARRIERS.
Goldsmith, to *Norwich, &c.* Tues. and Fri
Martin, to *Southwold*, Mon. W. and Saturday

YOXFORD is a large and remarkably neat and pleasant village, seated in a fertile vale, sometimes called " *The Garden of Suffolk*," on the banks of the small river Yox, or Minsmere, and on the Ipswich and Yarmouth road, 4 miles N. by E. of Saxmundham, 6½ miles S. of Halesworth, and 94 miles N.E. of London. Its parish increased its population from 851 souls, in 1801, to 1251, in 1841, and comprises about 2670 acres of land, and several large and handsome mansions. *Petty Sessions* are held every fourth Wednesday, at the Three Tuns Inn, which is a large posting-house. Besides the *manor* of Darsham-with-Yoxford, which belonged to the monks of Thetford, here is also another manor, which belonged to Sibton Abbey. The Earl of Strad-broke is lord of the former, and Sir Charles Blois of the latter ; but a great part of the parish belongs to other proprietors, the largest of whom are R. Sayer, Esq., D. E. Davy, Esq., the Misses Colmer, F. Clayton, Esq., and Mr. Robert Barker. COCKFIELD HALL, on the north side of the village, is the seat of Sir Charles Blois, Bart., and is a large and handsome mansion, in the Tudor style, on a gentle elevation, in a beautiful park, skirted on the south by the river Yox, or Mins-mere. It was formerly the seat of the Brook family, and passed from them to Sir Charles Blois, of Grundisburgh, who was created a baro-net in 1668, and soon afterwards made Cockfield Hall his chief resi-dence. GROVE HOUSE, a handsome mansion, in a small park, on the south side of the village, is the property of D. E. Davy, Esq., but has been unoccupied since the death of its late occupant, the Right Hon. Thomas Manners Sutton, the first *Baron Manners of Foston*, who died in 1842, and had been Lord Chancellor of Ireland, and was raised to the peerage in 1807. He was the sixth son of George, the third son of John, third Duke of Rutland ; and his son and successor pur-chased Fornham Park, in 1843. The ROOKERY, another neat seat near Yoxford, was much improved by its late owner, Robert Colmer, Esq., and is now the residence of his daughters. The CHURCH (Saint Peter) is a neat structure, with a tower, containing six bells, and sur-mounted by a leaded spire. It was enlarged in 1837, at the cost of £1200, a great part of which was contributed by the Society for Building and Enlarging Churches, who stipulated that about 400 of the 935 sittings should be free. The benefice is a vicarage, valued in K.B. at £5. 14s. 2d., aad in 1835 at £161. The Rev. Saml.Ths.Roberts, LL.D., is the incumbent, and the Earl of Stradbroke is patron and impropriator. The tithes were commuted in 1839 for yearly moduses of £284 to the impropriator, and £171 to the vicar, who has also 5A. of glebe, five cottages, and a small parsonage, but does not reside in the parish. Here is a small *Wesleyan Chapel*, built in 1834, and a *National School*, erected in 1837, at the cost of £400, and having two large rooms for boys and girls. The *Town Land*, about 1½A., let for £2. 1s. a year, is by ancient usage appropriated to the service of the church. In 1651, *Robert Sillett* left a yearly rent-charge of £5 out of 10A. of land, (now belonging to D. E. Davy, Esq.,) for providing cloth-ing for the most needy poor of Yoxford. A legacy of £50, left for the poor by *Anthony Bedingfield*, was laid out in 1716, in the purchase of a rent-charge of £2. 10s. a year, out of two closes in Darsham, now belonging to the Purvis family. Mr. Robert Hughman is secretary to *Yoxford Farmers' Club*.

YOXFORD DIRECTORY.
Marked 2, reside in Little street.

POST OFFICE at Mrs Emma Bird's.
Letters are received & despatched at 7 morning, & $\frac{1}{2}$ past 7 evening

Arnold John, farrier, &c
Badeley Rev Samuel, L.L.B. vicar of Ubbeston, &c. *Red House*
Barnaby, Mrs Julia, *Vine Villa*
Blois Sir Chas. Bart. *Cockfield Hall*
Borrows Robt. tinner and brazier
Cable Francis, coach builder
Clabyn Thomas, postman
Clayton Christopher, gent
Cooper Edward, coachman
Colmer Misses C. J. E. & E. *Rookery*
Cullingford Stephen, fishmonger
Frier Mrs Lucy
Goldsmith Wm. policeman
Haward Robert, corn miller
Helwig Henry, dyer
Kerrison R. A. gentleman
Lee Mr John, sen. ‖ Lay Mr John
Lyons Mr Thos.‖Mabson Mr Edw.
McCormick Rev John, *curate*
Miller Mrs Sarah
Packard Rev Harrison, M.A. incbt. of Middleton, Fordley, Westleton, and Peasenhall
Pallant Mr James
Potter John, magistrates' clerk
Weddell Rev Wm. M.A. vicar of Darsham
Whincop Wm. agent to Garrett and Son, of *Leiston*, founders and agricultural implement makers
Woolnough James, horse letter
Wright James, gamekeeper
2 Wright Wm. farrier

Academies.
Jones Sus. (bdg)
Hughman Robt. (boarding)
Rickards Ths.' (& parish clerk)
Smith Catharine
Spall Ann, *Natl.*
ATTORNEY.
Cavell Alex.
Bakers & Flour Dealers, &c.
CattermoleJohn, (Temp. Hotel)
Dennison Wm.
Fisher Robert
Basket Maker.
Ralph John

Blacksmiths.
Dalby Jeremiah
2 Dalby George
Bookseller, &c.
Bird Emma
Boot&ShoeMkrs.
Borrett John(and beer house)
Chambers Wm.
2 Cooper John
Crane John
Curtis Robert
2 Payne Thomas
Spalding Wm.
Spall Joseph
Wright George
Bricklayers.
Bloomfield John

Calver Wm. (& marble, &c. mason)
Butchers.
Foulsham Jph.
Smith Robert
Wenden Daniel
Cooper.
Clayton John
Druggist.
Bird Emma
Currier, &c.
Crow Wm.
FARMERS.
* *are Owners.*
Balls Joseph
*Barker Robert, *Wolsey Farm*
Breaton Thos.
Cunningham Rt.
Davy Thomas
Ellis Henry
Girling Fredk.
*Gobbett Wm.
GobbettWm.jun
Howlett Samuel
Paxman Chpr.
Sewell Joseph
Spall Saml. *Hill Farm*
Tallant Thomas
Grocers & Drprs.
Lee John, jun.
Nun Wm.
Revans Edw. & Son
Hair Dresser.
King Robert
Inns & Taverns.
Griffin, H.Porter
Three Tuns,Jno.
Barnes (posting house)
Ironmongers.
Dalby Wm.
Garrett Rd. and Son, (& *Leiston)*
Joiners&Buildrs.
Clayton Aldermn

Cotton Ezra
Spenling George
Sunniss Wm.
Milliners, &c.
Bailey Sophia
Clark Charlotte
Garrod & Filby
Row Mary Apn
Painters,Plumbers, & Glaziers.
Fisk Henry
Stapleton Wm.
Saddlers, &c.
Row Geo. &.John
Shopkeepers.
2 Danford John
Foulston My. A.
LastJoseph (corn & flour dealer)
Sewell Phœbe
SURGEONS.
LanchesterThos. W., M.D.
Wilson Charles
Wase Jeremiah
TAILORS.
Creighton Wm.
DaleJas.(sexton)
Daniels Richard
King Alfred (& stay maker)
Masterson Jno.
Tillett John
WATCHMAKERS
Bullock Wm. D.
Bailey Joseph
Green John (and jeweller)
Smyth Luke
Wheelwrights.
Cable Frs.(coach builder)
Elmy John (and beer house)
2 Phillips John
Short Jph. (gunsmith)

COACHES.
(From the Three Tuns Inn.)
Mail, to London, at 8 evening ; & to Yarmouth, 6 morning
Shannon, to Halesworth, at 7 evg ; and to Ipswich, $\frac{1}{2}$ p. 8 morning
Eclipse, to Norwich, every Monday & Wed. at 6, & Sat. at 5 morng

Old Blue (from the Griffin) to Ipswich, 10 mg; & to Yarmouth, ½ past 3 afternoon

Jas. Woolnough's *Omnibus*, to Ipswich, Mon. Tu. Th. & Fri; and to Halesworth, Tu. Th. Fri. & Sat

CARRIERS.

H. R. and J. Smith's Waggon, (from the Tuns,) to Ipswich,London,&c Mon. Tu. & Thu; and to Halesworth, Norwich, &c. Tues. Fri. and Saturday

WANGFORD HUNDRED

Forms a *Superintendent Registrar's District*, and an *Union* under the new poor law; and is divided into the *Deaneries* of Southelmham and Wangford, as noticed below. It is about twelve miles in length, from east to west, and about five in breadth; and is bounded on the north by the navigable river *Waveney*, which separates it from Norfolk; on the east, by Mutford Hundred; on the south, by Blything Hundred; and on the west, by Hoxne Hundred. It is a fertile district, especially in the broad vale of the Waveney, where there is an extensive tract of rich marshes, celebrated for feeding cattle. On the south side of the vale, the land rises in bold undulations to a high champaign tract of strong loam, comprising nearly all the rest of the Hundred. Bungay and the four Ilketshalls are in the *Duke of Norfolk's Liberty*, but the other parts of the Hundred are among what are called the Geldable manors of Suffolk. It comprises the two thriving market towns of *Bungay* and *Beccles*, in the vale of Waveney; the four parishes of *Ilketshall;* the seven parishes of *Southelmham;* and fourteen other *parishes*, as will be seen in the following enumeration, shewing their territorial extent, the annual value of their lands and buildings, as assessed to the property tax in 1815, and their population in 1801 and 1841 .—

PARISHES. ‖	Acrs.	Rental.	Populatn. 1801.	Populatn. 1841.	PARISHES.	Acres.	Rental. £.	Population 1801.	Population 1841.
Barsham	1871	1962	162	250	Shadingfield ..	1370	1306	157	177
Beccles*........	1994	7976	2788	4086	Shipmeadow‡..	800	865	442	265
Bungay Holy Trinity	2090	2896	903	1861	Sotterley	1594	1358	254	223
BungayStMary		4621	1446	2248	*Southelmham—* All Saints§..	1150	1548	192	224
Cove (North)....	1082	1074	178	219	St. Cross ..	1301	1331	203	258
Ellough	1074	1068	157	155	St. James ..	1302	1721	243	289
Flixton	1762	1507	219	192	St. Margaret	589	2375	186	181
Homersfield†	981	809	147	291	St.Michael..	816	924	107	145
Ilketshall—					St. Nicholas§	500	§	93	90
St. Andrew..	1696	1631	368	548	St.Peter	576	626	129	91
St. John	743	792	51	71	Weston	1551	1592	170	211
St. Lawrence	988	1329	113	221	Willingham ..	890	965	136	156
St. Margaret	2093	705	295	315	Worlingham ..	1727	1641	168	208
Mettingham	1706	2367	270	409					
Redisham	733	779	138	165	Total ..	34,679	48,226	9972	13,860
Ringsfield	1700	2458	257	311					

‖ *Hulverstreet*, a hamlet of Henstead parish, is within the bounds of Wangford Hundred. (See page 377.)

* Beccles included 32 persons in the *House of Correction*, in 1841.

† Homersfield included 18 persons in tents and the open air, in 1841; and Bungay included six persons in barges.

‡ Shipmeadow includes the *Union Workhouse,* which had more than 300 inmates, in 1801, and 133 in 1841.

§ The annual value of *St. Nicholas* is included with *All Saints,* and they are now united as one parish and township.

☞ CHIEF CONSTABLES—Mr. Wm. Dyball, of Bungay; and Messrs. James Halls and James Boydon, of Beccles.

DEANERIES.—The seven parishes of Southelmham, with those of Flixton and Homersfield, are in *Southelmham Deanery ;* and all the other 19 parishes are in *Wangford Deanery.* The whole Hundred is in the *Archdeaconry of Suffolk,* and *Diocese of Norwich.* For Southelmham Deanery, the Archdeacon's Visitations are held at Stradbroke; and for Wangford Deanery, at Beccles.

WANGFORD UNION.—The Hundred of Wangford was incorporated for the support of its poor, under Gilbert's Act, in 1764; and in the following year, the guardians and overseers of the 27 parishes (Southelmham, All Saints and St. Nicholas being united as one) erected a large *House of Industry* at Shipmeadow, about three miles from Beccles and Bungay, at the cost of about £8500. This WORKHOUSE has room for about 450 paupers, and since the incorporation was dissolved, and the Hundred formed into an union under the new poor law commissioners, its internal arrangements have been considerably altered, so as to admit of a better classification of the sexes, and the aged and young. Eight *guardians* are elected for the two parishes of Bungay, 6 for Beccles, two each for eight of the other larger parishes, and one each for the 16 smaller parishes. The total *expenditure* for the relief of the poor of the 27 parishes, during the *quarter* ending March 21st, 1843, was £1748. 2s. 1¾d., exclusive of £8. 17s. 6d., for *registration fees,* and £6. 9s. 6d. for *vaccination fees.* Rt. W. Clarke, Esq., is *Union Clerk and Superintendent Registrar.* Mr. Wm. Stanford is relieving officer and registrar of births and deaths for *Beccles District,* of which Mr. J. C. Webster is registrar of marriages; and Mr. Bloomfield Sewell is registrar of births, deaths, and marriages, for *Bungay District,* of which Mr. Robert Butcher is relieving officer. Mr. Thos. and Mrs. Balls are *master and matron of the Workhouse,* which had 261 inmates in 1811, 206 in 1821, 250 in 1831, and 133 in 1841, when the census was taken in those years.

BARSHAM, a scattered village on the south side of the vale of the Waveney, 2½ miles W. by S. of Beccles, has in its parish 250 souls, and 1871 acres of fertile land. Its gross annual value is now £2343. 4s. 8d. It was anciently the lordship and seat of the Itchinghams, whose heiress carried it in marriage to the Blennerhassetts, in the reign of Edward VI. Robert A. Suckling, Esq., is now lord of the manor, but a great part of the soil belongs to Sir E. Kerrison, N. Micklethwaite, Esq., J. Garden, Esq., and the Rede, Gower, and other families. *Ashmans,* a large mansion, on an eminence, 1 mile W. of Beccles, is the seat and property of the Rev. Rede Rede, and gives name to a manor which extends into Beccles parish. *Barsham House,* a neat mansion, on a bold acclivity, half a mile W. of the church, belongs to R. A. Suckling, Esq., and is occupied by C. R. Bewicke, Esq. The *Church* (Holy Trinity) is an ancient fabric, with a round tower, a thatched nave, and a tiled chancel; and on its floor is a brass effigy of one of the former lords of the manor. The rectory, valued in K.B. at £15. 6s. 8d., is in the patronage and incumbency of the Rev. Alfred Inigo Suckling, who has now a yearly modus of £445 in lieu of tithes, and 72 acres of glebe, besides 8A. forming the garden and grounds surrounding the *Rectory House,* a large old mansion, finely embowered

in trees. *Lawrence Eachard, A.M.,* an eminent divine and writer, was born here in 1671. After receiving his education at Cambridge, he settled in Lincolnshire. In 1699, he published the first part of his *Roman History,* which, in 1702, was followed by a *General Ecclesiastical History,* a work which has gone through numerous editions. His next work was a *History of England* down to the Revolution. In 1712, he was presented to the archdeaconry of Stow; and in 1716, he published a small volume, called " The Gazetteer's or Newsman's Interpreter," which may be considered as the model of the Gazetteers of the present day. He died in 1730. An acre of land, called *Town Land,* has belonged to the poor parishioners from time immemorial. The rent, 20s., is applied with the poor rates.

Bewicke Calverly Richard, Esq. *Barsham House*
Candler Saml. blacksmith & beerhs
Fisher Wm. shoemaker
Howlett John, joiner
Rede Rev Rede, *Ashmans*
Rix Mrs Martha, *Ashmans*

Suckling Rev Alfred Inigo, *Rectory*
West George, cattle dealer
FARMERS.
Bond Wm. ‖ Draper Sarah & Sisters
Ebbs Wm. ‖ Page John
Gower James, *Barsham Hall*
Howlett Benjamin ‖ Gower Zach.

BECCLES is a well built and improving *market town,* and *municipal borough,* seated on a dry and pleasant acclivity, on the south side of the *river Waveney,* which separates it from Norfolk, and is navigable for sea-borne vessels from the Norwich and Lowestoft Navigation, and for small craft, to Yarmouth and Bungay. It is subject to the port of Yarmouth. The town is well paved, and has several good streets, which terminate in a spacious *Market place.* It is distant 6 miles E. of Bungay, 10 miles W. by S. of Lowestoft, 40 miles N.E. by E. of Ipswich, 14 miles S.W. by S. of Yarmouth, 18 miles S.E. of Norwich, and 109 miles N.E. of London. The *parish,* which is co-extensive with the municipal borough, contains 1994 acres of land, and had 2788 inhabitants, in 1801; 2979, in 1811; 3493, in 1821; 3862, in 1831; and 4086, in 1841. It is a *polling place* for the Eastern Division of Suffolk, and gives name to a division of the county, for which here is a House of Correction, and a Hall, in which *Quarter* and *Petty Sessions* are held. An *Act of Parliament* for paving, lighting, cleansing, and otherwise improving the town, was obtained in the 36th of George III. The *Gas Works* belong to Mr. James Malam, and were erected in 1837. They have a gasometer of 10,000 cubic feet, and supply 108 street lamps, paid for by the Corporation. The *Market,* held every Saturday, is well supplied with corn and provisions; and here is a large *fair* for cattle, &c., on Whit-Monday. A fair is also held on July 11th, and a hiring for servants in October, but they are now of trifling consequence. *Horse Races* are held on the large common on the east side of the town, early in August, either the week before or after Yarmouth races, and they are numerously attended. The principal *trade* of the town is in corn, malt, and coals, which is much facilitated by the navigation of the Waveney, on which there are several commodious *wharfs.* In 1831, an Act of Parliament was obtained by the Corporation, and other Commissioners, for deepening the river Waveney from Beccles to the point at which it communicates with the Norwich and Lowestoft Navigation, finished in 1833. (See Lowestoft.) That part of the Waveney deepened by the Beccles

Navigation Commissioners, extends eastward, by a winding course of about eight miles, to the vicinity of Oulton, and in conjunction with the last-named navigation, opens a communication for sea-borne vessels to this town and the city of Norwich, without breaking bulk, or discharging their cargoes into small craft, as formerly, at Yarmouth, from whence barges and wherries are still allowed to pass along the Yare and the Waveney, without paying any dues to either of the navigation companies. The *Beccles Navigation* proved an unprofitable speculation to the original proprietors, and has been sold to a company of shareholders for £5000. The Commissioners and other principal inhabitants are now (1843) making an effort to improve the trade of the town, by applying for an Act of Parliament to materially reduce, or utterly abolish, the present heavy *port dues*, which have caused much of the traffic to be still carried on in small craft from Yarmouth, whence vessels to Beccles, Bungay, &c., have the use of the navigation, in consideration of the yearly payment of £196 by the haven and pier commissioners of that port. Mr. E. C. Sharpin is *clerk* to the Beccles Navigation Commissioners. In 1586, the town sustained great injury from a *conflagration*, which destroyed more than eighty houses, and property to the value of £20,000.

Beccles was formerly in two parishes, but that called *St. Mary Endgate*, at the south end of the town, had its church demolished by order of Queen Elizabeth, on the plea " that the parishes of *Beccles and Endgate* had been for so many years blended together, that the bounds and limits of them could not be known in 1419; when a legal agreement was made by the bishop, patron, and rectors of both parishes, that the rector of Beccles should take the whole tithes of both parishes, and pay the rector of Endgate £6. 13s. 4d. yearly, in the parish church of Endgate : so that the inhabitants of Endgate, have, time out of mind, been esteemed parishioners of Beccles." The parish comprises about 1400A. of marshes and common, which formerly belonged wholly to the inhabitants, under the name of BECCLES FEN, but about 450 acres have been sold at various periods, and a large portion of the remainder is now enclosed, and let by the corporation, who apply the rents in aid of the borough rates, or otherwise, for the general benefit of the town. The extensive *common* on which the races are held, is still open, and upon it all the inhabitants have the free right of grazing a certain number of cattle, according to the rentals at which they are respectively assessed to the parochial rates. This common is of great benefit to the poor, and is very fertile, but is so fully stocked as to be generally rather a bare pasture. The Earl-of Gosford is lord of the *manor of Beccles*, but part of the parish is in the Rev. Rede Rede's *manor of Ashmans*, which is partly in the adjoining parish of Barsham, and includes the ancient manor house of *Roos, or Ross*, now occupied by a farmer, and formerly the property of the Garneys, from whom it passed successively to the Tolbys, Sucklings, and Riches. Nathaniel Micklethwaite, Esq., and several smaller free and copyholders have estates in the parish. The manor and advowson of Beccles were granted to the Abbey of Bury Saint Edmund's, by King Edwy, about the year 960. At this period, it is supposed the tract of marshes extending from Yarmouth to some distance above Beccles, was a broad *estuary*. Some years afterwards, pro-

bably by the shifting of the sands off the coast, the mouth of the estuary began to be obstructed, and the sea to be excluded; in consequence of which, the extent of the marshes was gradually increased, and, in process of time, rendered fit for the pasturage of cattle. These *marshes*, however, were so slowly reclaimed from the water, that, at the time of the Conqueror's survey, there appears to have been no more than ten acres belonging to the Abbot's manor of Beccles. That portion called *Beccles Fen*, was, for a great number of years, of little value, and was probably given up to the inhabitants of the town by the abbot, because it was not of sufficient worth to deserve his notice. At first, perhaps, its chief value arose from the *rushes* which it supplied for covering the roofs and strewing the floors of houses, &c. A yearly rent of ten marks was paid to the abbot for the fen, and it was governed by four fen reeves, and ultimately increased by drainage to an area of about 1400 acres. In the transactions which took place after the dissolution of the monasteries relative to the procurement of a grant of the fen from the king, there seems to have been much misunderstanding and contention among the inhabitants. "These disputes continued for a number of years to be maintained with great acrimony, and on one or two occasions with bloodshed; and as they occasioned great expense in law proceedings, they were the original cause of enclosing several parts of the fen, and devising them, for terms of years, in order to defray the expenses. In 1540, Henry VIII. granted the fen to William Rede, merchant, and his heirs, in trust, for the benefit of himself and other inhabitants of the town of Beccles. The sum paid for this grant was £120. Great jealousies existed among many of the inhabitants, on account of the exclusive powers given by it to the family of Rede, of making rules, &c., for the government of the fen; and in 1543, they succeeded in procuring its revocation, on the ground of non-performance of certain conditions, and obtained a *new grant*, by virtue of which the fen was to be governed by *four fen reeves*, chosen annually from among the inhabitants. This gave satisfaction for a time to the townspeople, as it was nearly what they had been accustomed to under the abbots. But considerable expense had been incurred in law proceedings, to defray which it was resolved to resort to the former expedient of enclosing and demising; and this led the way to fresh disputes and a renewal of the quarrel with the family of Rede. For forty years, these animosities were kept up with the utmost rancour on both sides, during which time various suits at law were prosecuted, which proved very expensive, and decided nothing. The peaceable inhabitants refused to attend at the election of fen reeves, on account of the desperate affrays which usually took place on those occasions. At length the authority of the fen reeves was set at defiance, and most of their leases, account-books, and other writings were seized and destroyed. The issue of these disputes and riotous proceedings was a *surrender* of the fen to Queen Elizabeth, by an act of the inhabitants, assembled at the church, January 25th, 1584. But although this surrender was sanctioned by a majority of the inhabitants, there was still a large party in opposition to the measure. The poor were made to believe that their rights were to be done away with, and that certain individuals were about to purchase the fen to themselves and their heirs, and consequently fresh riots and disturbances arose; the pound

gates were destroyed, and the windows of the guildhall demolished. The measure, however, which met with so much opposition, was the most prudent that could possibly have been pursued. The instrument of surrender set forth, that it was made to the intent and purpose that the fen might be re-granted in a more effectual manner, to a select body of the inhabitants, to be incorporated under the name of the *Portreeve, Surveyors, and Commonalty of the Fen of Beccles.* Letters patent were accordingly granted in July, 1584, by which the Corpora-tion was constituted in the form which it retained till it was altered by the municipal act of 1835. Still many of the inhabitants were dissatis-fied, and at length a commission was issued to Sir Robert Wingfield and others to act as arbitrators. Their award was in favour of the corporation ; and on the 3rd of February, 1588, the Queen ratified and confirmed the *charter.* On the 19th of May, 1605, the charter was further confirmed by James I. The fen is held of the Crown by fealty, and a yearly *fee farm rent* of 13s. 4d.

The old *corporate body* consisted of a portreeve and 36 burgesses, dis-tinguished by the appellations of *the twelve,* and *the twenty four.* The office of portreeve, or chief magistrate,was held in rotation by the former, who were styled the 12 principal, and the latter the 24 inferior burgesses. They had a common clerk, or prothonotary, and were themselves the "surveyors," who inspected and regulated the fen, and the rights of the inhabitants to pasturage thereon. Though the original incorporation appears to have referred only to the management of the fen for the benefit of the town, the borough is included in the Municipal Reform Act of 1835, under which it is now governed by a *Mayor, four Alder-men,* and *twelve Councillors.* It has no commission of the peace, but the mayor is a magistrate ex-officio, and during the year following his mayoralty; and the county magistrates have concurrent jurisdiction in the borough,and hold *petty sessions here weekly.* The TOWN COUNCIL and OFFICERS, (1843,) are as follows : H. W. R. Davey, *mayor;* W. H. Crowfoot, Fredk. Wm. Farr, Wm. John Crowfoot, and Richd. Bohun, Esqrs, *aldermen;* Messrs. Amos Barber, Robt. Newman, Chas. Chenery, John Garrod, R. W. Clarke, James Crisp, H. W. R. Davey, John Garnham, Thos. Gilbert, W. H. Leavold, Robt. Tacon, and W. K. Barker, *councillors;* E. C. Sharpin, Esq., *town clerk;* Abraham Clarke, *treasurer;* John Nichols, *mace bearer;* and Joseph Hawkins Fiddes, *crier.* The COUNTY MAGISTRATES, who usually preside here at petty sessions are J. Garden, Esq., Rev. Hugh Owen, Rev. Charles Clarke, and E. P. Montagu, Esq. ; and Sir Thomas Sherlock Gooch, Bart., is chairman of the quarter sessions. Mr. John Reynolds is *in-spector of corn returns;* and Mr. Abm. Clarke, *distributor of stamps.* The INCOME OF THE CORPORATION for the year ending September 11, 1842, was £2385. 15s. 11½d. ; of which £1845 arose chiefly from the rents of the marshes. Their *debts* amounted to £1700, borrowed of Miss Smith, and Mrs. Lillingstone, £1125, owing on old and new tontine bonds, and £50 belonging to Girling's charity ; and their *dis-bursements,* including the interest of these sums, amounted in the same year to about £1770 ; leaving a balance of £566 in the hands of the treasurer. Among the principal items of *expenditure,* during the year, were—Labour on the fen, £205; Watchmen, police, and constable £128; coats, for ditto, £38. 6d. 6d. ; Poor rate, £169; Land Tax, £51. 12s. ;

Subscription to the poor, £50; Donation to National, British, and Infant Schools, £30; Carpenters' and Blacksmiths' work on the fen, £23. 12s. 9d.; Magistrate's Clerks, £23. 8s. 7d.; Alteration and repairs of Assembly Rooms, £138. 12s. 8d.; Mayor's Salary, £25; and Town-clerk's salary, £30.

The TOWN HALL, in which Quarter and Petty Sessions are held, is a neat and commodious building in the New-Market place. The GAOL, or HOUSE OF CORRECTION, for Beccles division of the county, is in Newgate-street, and stands apart from other buildings in an airy situation. It was much enlarged and improved about twenty years ago. A part only of the area, enclosed by the boundary wall, is occupied by the prison buildings and yards; the remainder being garden ground in the occupation of the governor. The buildings consist of a centre, two wings, and irregular projections, and comprise cells, and day rooms, for 18 males and 6 females, besides a ward for vagrants and others committed for short periods. The *tread-mill* is in two partitions, so that felons working in one, can have no communication with misdemeanants working in the other. Mr. Samuel Drewell is *governor*, and Mrs. Drewell, matron. The *Suffolk Rural Police* has an inspector and two men here, and a *Station* in Smallgate.

The Parish CHURCH (St. Michael) is a large and handsome Gothic structure, in the highest part of the town, overlooking the river Waveney, and having an octagonal tower, standing at some distance from the south east corner of the chancel, and containing a peal of ten bells. The south porch is a fine specimen of what is called the florid Gothic; and on the north side, is another porch of plainer architecture. It is supposed to have been built about the year 1369. The church-yard commands extensive prospects, but being too small for the present encreased population of the town, another burial ground was consecrated at the foot of Blyburg-gate, in 1823, and has a small ivy-mantled building in which the funeral service is read. The *rectory*, valued in K.B. at £21. 12s. 3½d., and in 1835, at £241, is in the patronage of the Earl of Gosford, and incumbency of the Rev. Hugh Owen, D. C. L. The tithes have been commuted for a yearly modus of £350. As noticed at page 413, here was another parish church, called *St. Mary Endgate*, which was a discharged vicarage, valued in K.B. at £7. 6s. 8d., but it was consolidated in the reign of Elizabeth with the rectory of St. Michael. The foundations of this church were removed some years ago, and the site is now occupied by cottages. Beccles had formerly a *Chapel of St. Peter*, near the old market; a Chapel of St. Mary Magdalen, belonging to a small hospital, on the hill near the Free School; and a *chapel, or hermitage*, near the bridge over the Waveney, where priests used to stand to collect the alms of passengers. The *Independent Chapel*, in Hungate, is a neat building, which was enlarged in 1836, at the cost of nearly £1000, and will now seat about 1000 hearers. It stands in a small burial ground; in addition to which, a small plot of ground at the south end of the town, belonging to the chapel, was enclosed, and appropriated to the purpose of a *cemetery*, in 1841. The Rev. John Flower is pastor, and his congregation date their origin from 1652. The *Wesleyans* have a Chapel in Northgate, built in 1833; and the *Baptists* have one in Newgate, opened in 1808. In Smallgate, is an old *Friends' Meeting-house*, with a small burial ground, but it is now used as an

Infant School. The various congregations in Beccles, liberally support *religious and charitable institutions* for the relief and instruction of the poor parishioners, who also derive considerable benefit from the *Fen* or *Common* already noticed, and from other *trust estates* and *benefactions.* The BECCLES MEDICAL DISPENSARY was established in 1822, and has the gratuitous services of Dr. Crowfoot, and W. E. Crowfoot, and H. W. R. Davey, surgeons. Since its institution, it has had about 5000 patients, of whom about 3500 have been cured. The Earl of Gosford is patron, and Mr. J. Crickmay, secretary.

The TOWN ESTATE has been vested in *feoffees* from an early period, for the payment of tenths, fifteenths, and subsidies chargeable on the poorer parishioners ; and for the general benefit of the inhabitants. This trust property comprises the *Guildhall,* now used as a national school ; part of the site of the White Lion, let for £6. 6s. a year ; four tenements in Puddingmoor-street, occupied rent-free by eight poor widows ; a piece of land on which the workhouse formerly stood, but occupied since 1787, by the house of correction, at the yearly rent of £5 ; various parcels of land, in the parish of Beccles, containing in the whole 97A. 2R. 2P., let for £250. 17s. per annum ; and 6A. in the adjoining parish of Gillingham, in Norfolk, let for £9 a year. Since 1827, the income arising from these sources has been applied in distributions of money and coals among poor parishioners, and in subscriptions towards the support of a national school, a clothing charity, a lying-in-charity, and the dispensary. The site of the Assembly Rooms also belongs to this trust, and was let in lease for 200 years, in 1785, to the corporation, for the yearly acknowledgment of one shilling. In consideration of £50 left by *Robert Girling,* in 1672, the corporation pay £3 a year for apprenticing a poor child of Beccles. A yearly rent-charge of £2. 12s., left by one *Ward,* is paid out of a house and 6A. of land, for a weekly distribution of 1s. worth of bread.

Hospital Lands : Charles II., in the 26th year of his reign granted to the Corporation of Beccles Fen, three acres of land, with an ancient chapel, then wasted, and a house also wasted, reputed to have been an ancient hospital for lepers ; also two cottages, 3 acres of marsh land, and a yearly rent of 25s., formerly payable to the said late hospital out of the manor of Barsham ; provided that the corporation should, from time to time, convert all the rents and profits of the premises to the maintenance of the poor of Beccles. In 1788, these lands and tenements were let on lease for 200 years to Thomas Rede, Esq., for the yearly rent of £13. 4s. 8d. The lessee expended upwards of £1200 in erecting a mansion upon the land for the residence of himself and family. The rent and an annuity of 25s. are carried to the general account of the Corporation, who expend considerable sums annually for charitable purposes.

The FREE SCHOOL was founded by *Sir John Leman, kt.,* who, in 1631, bequeathed a messuage to be used for the school and master's house in Ballygate, and the undermentioned lands, &c., to the Corporation of Beccles, in trust that the schoolhouse, with the garden and appurtenances, should be a free school for 48 children, 44 of them to be inhabitants of Beccles, 2 of Ringsfield, and two of Gillingham, and that they should be taught English reading, writing, and arithmetic, by a master and usher, appointed by the Corporation, whom he willed should be governors of the school, and should dispose of the rents and profits of the school estates as follows viz., £18 yearly to the usher, and the residue to the master. These estates comprise a house and 14A. 1R. 21P. of land, mostly in Gillingham, let for £34. 10s. per annum, and two barns and 98A. 3R. 31P. of land, in Ilketshall-St. Andrew, and Barsham, let for £149 per annum. The yearly income (£183.

10s.) after the payment of taxes and repairs, is divided into three parts, two of which are retained by the master, and the other is paid to the usher. The master's house was considerably improved in 1762.

GRAMMAR SCHOOL: – In 1712, *Dr. Henry Fauconberge* bequeathed all his real estate in Corton and Flixton, for the support of a person well-learnt and experienced in the Latin and Greek tongues, to teach school in Beccles, for the purpose of fitting youth for the Universities. The testator directed that the said schoolmaster should be appointed by the bishop of Norwich, the archdeacon of Suffolk, and the rector of Beccles, or any two of them, and that they should have power to remove him for misconduct, &c. The estate was conveyed to trustees pursuant to the testator's direction, and consists of a house, a cottage, and 132A. 3R. 30P. of land, mostly situated in Corton, and let to two tenants at rents amounting to £183. 15s. per annum. After deducting £6. 18s. a year for land-tax, and the expense of repairs, the rest of the income is paid to the Rev. Hugh Owen, D.C.L., who was appointed to the office of schoolmaster in 1815, and has since become rector of Beccles. There is no school-room belonging to this institution, but five or six boys occasionally attend Dr. Owen four hours a day for instruction in classical learning, and attend other schools to be taught writing and arithmetic. He receives 21s. a quarter from each, and it is considered that the testator's object was rather to induce a person properly qualified to reside in Beccles, and there afford the means of young men being fitted for the University, than to establish a free grammar school, for gratuitous instruction in the primary elements of grammatical learning. Scholars from Beccles participate with others in ten exhibitions at Emanuel College, Cambridge. Here are two NATIONAL SCHOOLS for 140 children of both sexes, and BRITISH SCHOOLS for about 150 boys and 150 girls. The THEATRE is a neatly fitted up building behind Queen square; and near it are the ASSEMBLY ROOMS, formerly used partly as a theatre, and now containing a handsome suit of rooms for assemblies, &c., and a *Subscription Library*, established in 1835, and now comprising upwards of 2000 volumes. Mr. J. Crickmay is the librarian, and has at his own house a *Subscription Newsroom*.

BECCLES DIRECTORY.

POST-OFFICE, Smallgate street: —Mr. John Crickmay, *postmaster*. Letters are received by Mail Cart from Wangford at 20 min. before 7 morning; and are despatched at a quarter-past 6 evening.

Aldous Mr Wm. London road
Aldridge Thomas, mail cart owner, Smallgate street
Bachelor Mrs Eliz. Blyburgate st
Bales Mrs Ann, Blyburgate street
Barber Robt. carter, Raven's meer
Barker Thos. ironmgr.; h Nmarket
Barnard Mrs R. Smallgate street
Barnby John, carter, London road
Barnby Isc. letter carrier, Falcon yd
Bardwell Richd. cashier, Old mkt
Bardwell Mrs Sarah, Old market
Barnes Mr Joseph, Hungate lane
Bobbett Chas. bookpr. Blyburgate
Bobbett Jas. parish clerk, Rock ln
Bohun Rd. solicitor ; h Ballygate
Boult Mr Benj. Sheepgate street

Boydon Miss Cath. Old market
Carlow Saml. Green, gent. Northgt
Carter Wm. coast waiter, Northgt
Chambers Wm. H. agent, *Gas works*
Chaplin Mr Edwd. Northgate street
Chaplin Mrs Harriet, Northgate st
Clarke Abm. stamp distributor and comssr. of special bail, Smallgate
Clarke Mrs Ann, New market
Clarke Rt. Welham, solr. union clerk, and supt. regr. Ballygate street
Copeman Mrs Eliz. Smallgate street
Copeman Rd. swine dlr. Blyburgate
Copland Miss Cath. Smallgate
Crabbe Miss, New market
Crisp Miss Emily, Smallgate street
Crowfoot Wm.John, M.D. Saltgate st

Cutting Thos. turnkey, Newgate st
Darby Mr Richard, Newgate street
Dashwood Chas. gent. New market
Dashwood Rev George, Saltgate st
Davey Hy.Wm.Rt. surgeon ; h New market
Day John, Esq. Hungate street
Delf Thos. draper ; h London road
Delf Wm. Esq. St. Mary's, Ballygt
Doy Money, sweep, Raven's meer
Drewell Samuel, governor, *House of Correction*
Fairweather Mrs Eliz. Hungate ln
Farr Fdk. Wm. brewer ; h Blyburgt
Farr Henry, gent. London road
Fiddes Miss Eliz. Manor house
Fiske Robt. solicitor ; h *Kessingland*
Foulger Miss Eliz. Blyburgate st
Flower Rev John, (Indpt.) Hungate
Francis Rev Rt. John, London road
Garnham Geo. police inspr. Smallgt
Gibson Mrs. Hungate street
Goldsmith Mr Robert, Ingate
Gordon John Rolfe, gent. London rd
Gostling Mrs Hanh. Newgate street
Hall Mrs. Hungate street
Harvey Henry, gent. London road
Holmes Mr John, Peddars lane
Houghton Mr James, Smallgate st
Howe John, postman, Northgate st
Howman Miss Dorothea, Ballygate
Kent Wm. draper ; h New market
Kerridge Daniel, gent. Ballygate
Kirk Thomas, excise officer, Ballygt
Last Samuel, gent. London road
Last Mr Wm. Haward, Smallgate
Lawes James, cattle dlr. Raven's mr
Lenny Misses Har. & Sus.Queen's sq
Lillingstone Mrs Eliz. New market
Martin Wm. shopman, Hungate st
Mayhew Jas. boat owner, Blyburgt
Mayhew John, boat owner, Northgt
Montagu Edw. Proudfoot, Esq. Ngt
Mouser John, carter, Northgate st
Neach Saml. cattle dlr. Raven's mr
Nusson Kezia, midwife, Northgt. st
Owen Rev Hugh, D.C.L. *Rectory*
Pollard Mr Thomas, Ingate street
Pymar Thomas, organist, Saltgate
Read Mr Wm. Peddars lane
Rede Rev Rede, *Ashmans*
Reynolds John, corn inspr. Old mkt
Rix Samuel Wilton, solr ; h Saltgt
Rogerson Mrs Mary Ann, New mkt
Sayer Mr James, New market
Sayer Mr Wm. Ballygate street
Sloper Mrs Mary Ann, Smallgate st

Shipley Edward, postman, Northgt
Smith Mrs Susanna, New market
Smith Wm. compositor, Blyburgate
Sprunt John B. bookpr. Raven's mr
Stanford Wm. relieving officer and registrar, Northgate
Stone Mrs Elizabeth, Ballygate st
Tallent Mr Edgar
Taylor Mrs Mary, New market
Thompson Miss Sophia, Blyburgate
Thurlow James, gent. Northgate st
Tiptod Wm. gent. London road
Turrell Robert, carter, Pudding lane
Woolner Mr James, Blyburgate st
Woolner Mrs Sarah, Hungate street
Wright Rev Geo. (Bapt.) London rd

ACADEMIES.
(Marked * take Boarders.)
British Schools, Peddars lane : Edw. Evans and Mary Ann Dobell
*Cowles Wm. Northgate street
*Crowe Isabella, Ballygate street
Free School, Ballygate street : Chas. James Sayer and John Hayward
Grammar School : Rev H. Owen, D.C.L.
*Fuller Jemima, New market
National Schools, Newgate street : James Wiseman & Eliz. Peachey
*Sayer & Crickmay (ladies) Northgt
*Winn Jemima, Saltgate street

ANIMAL PAINTERS, &c.
Drewell Robert, Smallgate street
Fenn George, Goosegreen lane

ATTORNEYS.
Bohun & Rix, Ballygate street
Fiske & Clarke, Ballygate street
Francis Robert Henry, Ballygate st
Sharpin Edward Colby and William Robert, Blyburgate street, (E. C. Sharpin is town clerk, &c.)
Webster John Crisp, (registrar of marriages,) Old market

AUCTIONEERS, &c.
Fenn George, Goosegreen lane
Oswald Robert, Northgate street

BAKERS & FLOUR DLRS.
(Marked * are also Confectioners.)
*Aldred James, Northgate street
*Bird John, Ballygate street
Denny James, Blyburgate street
*Ecclestone John, Saltgate street
Fairweather John, Blyburgate st
Hurren Fanny, Ingate street
Julians Ezekiel, Blyburgate street
Knights George, Northgate street
Mayhew James, New market

*Mayhew Jeremiah, Smallgate st
Rich Jeremiah, Blyburgate street
*Smith James, Northgate street
*Thrower Benjamin, New market
Winson Henry, Sheepgate street

BANKERS.
Gurneys, Turner, and Brightwen, Ballygate street (draw on Barclay and Co.) Bohun & Rix, *agents*
Lacons, Youell, & Co. Queen square, *and Yarmouth*, (on Glyn and Co.) Mr John Mayhew, *agent*

BASKET MAKERS.
Hopson Wm. New market
Long Charles, Northgate street

BLACKSMITHS.
Alecock Wm. jun. Smallgate street
Burwood Richard, Northgate street
Cutting Denny, Old market
Holland Anthony, Blyburgate street
Pleasants George, Hungate street

BOAT BUILDERS.
Jones John, near Old market
Wright Wm. Northgate street

BOOKSELLERS, &c.
Cattermole Samuel (lib.) New mkt
Gaze Edward, Sheepgate street
Grimwade Wm. (lib.) New market
Jarman Robert Barnett (&printer) Ballygate street
Loyns Simon (and printer) New mkt

BOOT & SHOE MAKERS.
Barber Benjamin, Ingate street
Benns Philip Coleman, Queen square
Crowe Matthew, New market
Dennant Jeremiah, Saltgate street
Ellis James, Smallgate street
Feltham Jas. New mkt. & *Yarmouth*
Goffin George, Smallgate street
Hayward Vice, Northgate street
Hindes Robert, Saltgate street
Jermy Philip, Ballygate street
Mendham Samuel, Blyburgate st
Mills Robert, Northgate street
Smith Richard, Ballygate street
Stimpson John, Saltgate street
Spratt Robert, Ingate street
Thrower Robert, Rook lane
Welton John, Northgate street
Woolner George, Northgate street
Wyatt Thomas, Newgate street

BRAZIERS & TINNERS.
Goldsmith Robert, Ingate street
Johnson Jonathan, New mkt. & Ngt
Kent John & Joseph, Hungate st
Taylor George, New market

BREWERS & MALTSTERS.
Atkinson Samuel Emms, Northgt. st
Farr Thomas & Son, Blyburgate st; h Pudding moor
Lenny Wm. Ballygate street
Rogers Wm., Hungate ; h Newgt. st
Tacon Rt. & Wm. Hy. Blyburgt. st

BRICK & TILE MAKERS.
Aldous John (and earthenware manufacturer,) Ingate street
Fenn George, Ingate street

BRICKLAYERS.
Barnes James, Newgate street
Goldsmith Benjamin, Blyburgate st
King Wm. Northgate street
Lockwood Wm. Blyburgate street
Meacham Edward, Northgate street
Pedgrift John, Northgate street

BUTCHERS.
Copeman Hanh. (pork) Blyburgate
Copeman Wm. New mkt ; h *Toft*
Crickmore James, Hungate street
Crickmore My. Ann, Blyburgate st
George Rebecca, New market
Holmes Thomas, Bridge street
Jordan Henry, New market and Northgate street
Jordan Robert, New mkt. & Ballygt
Lay John, Northgate street
Nicholls John, Old market
Stevens James, New mkt ; h Newgt

CABINET MAKERS, &c.
Aldous John, Rooks lane
Brooks John Bobbett (upholsterer) New market
Clarke Stephen, Smallgate street
Hayward Richard, New market
Hindes Wm. Rooks lane
Love John Alger, Saltgate street
Syder George, New market
Woolnough George, New market

CHEMISTS & DRUGGISTS.
Corbyn Joseph Bishop, New market
Steel Samuel, New market
Taylor Robert, Old market

CLOTHES BROKERS.
Barkway Edward, Smallgate street
Custance Mary, Smallgate street
Garrod Wm. Northgate street
Piper Isaac, Sheepgate street

COACH MAKERS.
Gilbert Thomas, Hungate street

COAL MERCHANTS.
Atkinson Wm. Emms, Northgate
Atkinson Wm. Milnes (and coke burner) Raven's meer
Buck Timothy & Edw. Northgt. st

Chambers Wm. Henry, Fen lane
Hursthouse Charles, Fen lane
Knights Thomas, Ballygate street
Ludbrooke John, Ingate street
Ward Frances, Pudding moor
COOPERS.
Barkway Thomas, New market
Collins Barney, New market
Hayward Robert, Bridge street
Hayward Robert, Smallgate street
Nutman Samuel, New market
Roberts James, Sheepgate street
CORN & COAL MERCHTS.
Boydon Jas. (chief constable) Ngt. st
Clarke Abraham, jun. Rook lane; h
Smallgate street
Crisp James, jun. Northgate street
Crisp John, Pudding mr; h Smallgt
Crisp John, jun. Bridge wharf; h
Blyburgate street
Dowson Edward Hutton, Northgate
street; h *Geldeston*
Leavould Wm. Hy. Corporatn. wharf
Read Robert, Ingate street
Tacon Robert & Wm. Henry, Bly-
burgate street.
CORN & FLOUR DEALERS.
Green James, New market
Money Jas. (and bacon) Hungate st
Sayer Thomas, Bridge street
Winter Henry (& seed) Northgt. st
CORN MILLERS.
Bullock George, London road
Burtsal Robert, London road, and
Ellingham
Crisp James, Ingate mill
Devereux Jph., Old mkt. & Common
Leavould Wm. Henry, Tower mill,
Ingate street
CURRIERS, &c.
Garrod John, Queen square
Smith Ellen, Northgate street
DYERS.
Marshall James, Sheepgate street
Pond Alice, Northgate street
FARMERS.
*Marked * are Cowkeepers only.*
Barber Amos, *Roos Hall*
Barber Eliel, Ballygate street
Bartram Stephen, Ingate street
Chenery Charles, Old market
Copeman Charles, Smallgate street
*Davy David, Pudding moor
Forder John, London road
*Foreman John, Ravens meer
Gibbins John, Swines green
Lark John, Ballygate street

*Nichols John, Ravens meer
*Smith Jas. (& hay dlr.) Raven's mr
*Wigg George, Raven's meer
FELLMONGERS.
Buck Timothy and Edward (& bone
merchants) Northgate street
FIRE & LIFE OFFICES.
Atlas, Robert H. Francis, Ballygate
County Fire & Provident Life, John
B. Brooks, New market
Dissenters' & General, S. W. Rix,
Ballygate street
Farmers', T. & E. Buck, Northgt
Freemasons', S. Cattermole, New
market
Family Endowment, S. Steel, New
market
Manchester, Minerva, & National
Endowment, W. W. Garnham,
Blyburgate street
Norwich Equitable, H. J. Kerrison,
New market
Norwich Union, A. Clarke, Smallgt
Phœnix, J. C. Webster, Old markt
Royal Exchange, Wm. Grimwade,
New market
Suffolk and General County, Chas.
Bobbett, Blyburgate street
Sun, E. & W. Sharpin, Blyburgt. st
Yorkshire, J. Crickmay, Smallgate
FISHMONGERS.
Chaplin Robert, Old market
Prime Joseph, Newmarket
Tillott Frederick, New market
GARDENERS.
Arnoup Israel, Newgate street
Botwright John, Smallgate street
Bradnum Wm. Pudding moor
Copeman Edward, Swines green
Copeman Isaiah, Swines green
Copeman John, Blyburgate street
Delf John, Ingate street
Elvin Benjamin, Swines green
Flowers James, Pudding moor
Grant Sarah & Charlotte, Newgt. st
Harmer Eleanor, Blyburgate street
Jermy Benjamin, Raven's meer
Mobbs Aaron, London road
Mobbs Samuel, Pudding moor
Morgan Edward, London road
Reynolds John, Old market
Rouse Wm. London road
GLASS, CHINA, &c. DLRS.
Fiddes Joseph Hawkins, New mkt
Garrett Robert, Hungate lane
Gooderham John, Northgate street
Smith & Shepherd, Old market

GLOVE MAKERS.

Buck Timothy & Edw. Northgt. st
Page Robert, Hungate street

GROCERS & TEA DEALERS.

Bird Robert, Northgate street
Bulwer Wm. John, Saltgate street
Burtsal Robert Aggas, New market
Chenery Joseph, Hungate street
Collins Elizabeth, Smallgate street
Hill James, Hungate street
Smith Shepherd, Old market
Thirtle James, New market
Ward Robert & Son, Queen square

GUNSMITHS.

Boreham John Bales, New market
Sutton Edward (and game dealer)
    Blyburgate street

HAIR DRESSERS.

Garrod John, Northgate street
Ife Edward, Sheepgate street
Layton Charles Hardingham, New
    market
Peachey David, Newgate street
Smith Wm. Smallgate street
Woodward Wm. New market

HATTERS.

Collins Chas. Jas. (mfr.) New mkt
Holdron Wm. New market

HOTELS, INNS, & TAVERNS.

Angel, Rd. Warner, Ballygate st
Bear & Bells, Han. Lawes, Old mkt
Black Boy, Wm. Read, Blyburgt. st
Chequers George Youell, Smallgt. st
Cross Keys, Rt. Warner, Hungate st
Crown, Francis Mills, Blyburgt. st
Crown & Anchor, Thomas Knights,
    Ballygate street
Dolphin, Jonth. Grey, Market row
Duke of Cumberland, Geo. Crowe,
    Ballygate street
Falcon, Ann Fiddes, New market
George and Dragon, John Press,
    Hungate lane
Hermitage, Rd. Darby, Bridge st
Horse & Groom, Hy. King, New
    market
King's Head Inn & Posting House,
    Robert Newman, New market
Marquis of Granby, Saml. Atmeare,
    Northgate street
Pickerel, Benj. Elvin, Pudding ln
Prince of Wales, Samuel Barkway,
    Saltgate street
Red Lion, Wm. Knights, Blyburgt
Ship, Wm. Darby, Bridge street
Three Pidgeons, Mary Downing,
    Pudding moor

White Horse, Jth. Nobbs, New mkt
White Lion Inn and Excise Office,
    James Harvey, Smallgate street
White Swan, Hy. Cooper, New mkt

BEER HOUSES.

Arnold Elizabeth, Ravens meer
Barker Charles, Ingate street
Chapman Jeremiah, Bridge street
Elvin Benjamin, Swines green
Garrod John, Northgate street
Grey George, Ravens meer
Groom George, Smallgate street
Hatcher John, Ravens meer
Hunt John (brewer) Ingate street
Hollen Robert (brewer) Newgate
Knights James, Pudding moor
Lawes James, Raaves meer
Peck Samuel, Smallgate street
Piper Isaac, Northgate street
Playford Daniel, Blyburgate street
Sayer Thomas, Bridge street
Smith Eddy (brewer) Newgate
Utbert Wm. Henry, Queen square
Wright Wm. Northgate street

IRONMONGERS.

Barker Wm. Keer, New market
Kent John & Joseph, Hungate st
Taylor George, New market

JOINERS & BUILDERS.

Barber Robert, Queen square
Boast George, Smallgate street
Grey George, Ravens meer
Moore John, Blyburgate street
Norman John, Hungate street
Pell Nathaniel, Pudding moor
Utton James, Pudding moor
Woodroffe Thomas (and slate dealer)
    Northgate street
Woods John, Northgate street

LIME BURNERS.

Chenery Charles, Pudding moor
Pell Nathaniel, Pudding moor

LINEN & WLLN. DRAPERS.

Bird Robert, Northgate street
Chenery Joseph, Hungate street
Collins Elizabeth, Smallgate street
Delf & Kent, New market
Garnham John & Son, Blyburgate st
Kerrison Henry James, New market
Mayhew John & Son, Queen square
Stacey George Granby, New market

MALTSTERS.

(See also Brewers, &c.)

Crisp James, jun. Northgate street
Crisp John, Pudding mr; h Smallgt
Crisp John, jun. Bridge wharf

Dowson Henry Gibson, Northgate street, and *Geldeston*

MILLINERS.

*(Marked * are Straw Hat Makers.)*

Barber Eliza, Mary Ann, and Matilda, Queen square

Cattermole Louisa, Hungate street

*Cooke Mary Ann, Smallgate street

*Garnham John & Son, Blyburgt. st

Gosling Eliza, Newgate street

*Jarman Mary, Ballygate street

Oakes Elizabeth, Smallgate street

Sayer Hepzibah, New market

Shaw Elizabeth, Blyburgate street

Titshall Mary, Ingate street

Weavers Elizabeth, Blyburgate

Wheeler Eliza, Smallgate street

Winson Georgiana, Sheepgate street

MILLWRIGHT.

Martin Robert, Ingate street

NURSERY & SEEDSMEN.

Fenn (Geo.)&Laws (Thos.)Goose grn

Gill Hubert Wm. Bridge street

PAINTERS, PLUMBERS, and GLAZIERS.

Everett Edward, Sheepgate street

Hall James (& gas fitter,) Smallgate

Lark Henry, Bridge street

Sayer Thos. Hanby, Ballygate street

Swan Lionel, New market

Thompson John, Smallgate street

PATTEN & CLOG MAKERS.

Barkway Robert, Smallgate street

Barkway Thomas, New market

PAWNBROKER.

Stubbins Wm. Rooks lane

PUMP MAKERS, &c.

Edwards Noah, Newgate street

Youell George, Smallgate street

ROPE & TWINE MAKERS.

Ingram George, Smallgate street

Piper Wm. Northgate street

SADDLERS, &c.

Allcock Robert, New market

Boon Alfred, Hungate street

Frankland Wm. Smallgate street

Grigson George, Queen square

SHOPKEEPERS.

Artis James, Ingate street

Aston Edward, Blyburgate street

Barkway Edward, Smallgate street

Brunning Charlotte, Blyburgate st

Custance Mary, Smallgate street

Goldsmith Charles, Ingate street

Gooderham John, Northgate street

Hatcher John, Ravens meer

Hunt Ann, New market

Leavould Robert, Ingate street

Moore John, Blyburgate street

Norman Joseph, Ballygate street

Rand John, Northgate street

SILVERSMITH, &c.

(See also Watchmakers, &c.)

Grimwade Wm. (& toy dlr.)New mkt

STONE & MARBLE MASONS.

Haward Samuel, Bridge street

Whitehead John Fryer, Northgate st

SURGEONS.

Crowfoot Wm. John, M.D. Saltgate

Crowfoot Wm. Henchman, Northgt

Crowfoot Wm. Edward, New mkt

Dashwood Robert, New market

Davey Henry Sallows & Son (Henry Wm. Robert,) Oldmarket

Gray John, Northgate street

TAILORS.

Aldous John (& draper,) Smallgate

Barber Robert, Northgate street

Buck Robert, Ballygate street

Buck Wm. Ballygate street

Butler John, Bridge street

Clarke Stephen, Ingate street

Cutting Henry, Newgate street

Fish Amos, Horse and Groom lane

Garnham John & Son, Blyburgate st

Holdron Wm. (& draper,) New mkt

Leavould Robert, Ingate street

Piper Isaac, Sheepgate street

Piper Isaac, jun. Hungate street

Piper James (and draper,) Northgt

Spratt Wm. Ingate street

Waud Wm. Sheepgate street

TANNER.

Garrod John King, Northgate street

TEA DEALERS.

(See Grocers, &c.)

Cattermole Samuel, New market

Grimwade Wm. New market

TIMBER MERCHANTS.

Bartram Stephen, Peddars lane

Hursthouse Charles, Corporation wf

TOBACCO PIPE MAKERS.

Copeman John, Peddars lane

Knights Wm. Blyburgate street

Woolnough Charles, Blyburgate

Woolnough John, Newgate street

TURNERS (WOOD.)

Barkway Thos. (bowl,) New market

Cudden John, Blyburgate street

Hayward Richard, New market

VETERINARY SURGEONS.

Cleveland James, Blyburgate street

Hindes Edward, Northgate street

WATCHMAKERS, &c.

Ayers Edward, Blyburgate street
Bullock Robert, Smallgate street
DurrantRt.(& jeweller,)New market
Jones Garwood, Blyburgate street

WHEELWRIGHTS.

Titshall Wm. Ingate street
Warren Wm. Smallgate street

WHITESMITHS, &c.

*Marked * are Agricultural Imple-ment Mfrs. & † Brass & Iron Fndrs.*
*Alecock Wm. Sheepgate street
†Ayres Robert, Blyburgate street
*†Harper Wm. Hungate street
Welch Wm. New market

WINE & SPIRIT MERCHTS.

Buck Timy. & Edwd. Northgate st
Farr Thomas & Son, Blyburgate st
Harvey James, Smallgate street
RogersWm.Hungate st; h Newgt.st
Tacon Rt. & Wm. Hy. Blyburgate st

WOOL MERCHANTS.

Boydon James, Northgate street
Buck Timy. & Edward, Northgate st

COACHES.

From the King's Head, *to London*,
6 evening, daily, except Sunday;
to Bury, every Tues. Thurs. and
Sat. at ½ past 9 mg ; *to Lowestoft*,
Mon.Wed.&Sat. 7 mg ; *toNorwich*,
Mon. & Wed. 8 mg. & Sat. 7 mg ;
and *to Yarmouth*, Mon. Wed. and
Friday, 6 evening

From the White Lion, *to London*,
Mon. Wed. & Friday, at ½ past 9
mg ; and *to Yarmouth*, Tues. Th.
and Sat. at ½ past 2 afternoon

CARRIERS.

Marked 1, *go from the Cross Keys ;*
2, *King's Head ; 3, Red Lion ;*
4, *White Horse ; and 5, from the*
White Swan

Places.	Carriers.

4 *London, &c.* H. R. & J. Smith's
waggons, Mon. Thurs. and Sat
4 *Bungay*, Wm. Page, Mon. Thurs.
and Sat. at 4 aftn ; and J. Neave
(Chequers,)Mon.Wed.&Sat. 7 evg
1 *Halesworth*, S. Firman, Wed. and
Sat. 2 aftn ; and Waters, from the
Bear & Bells, Tues. & Fri. 2 aftn
Lowestoft, John Elliot, Hungate,
Mon. & Thurs. 9 mg ; and John
Watson(Falcon,)Wed.& Sat.6 mg
5 *Norwich*, Edw.&Wm. Goldsmiths'
Van, Tues. and Fri. 12 noon; J.
Watson (Falcon,) Tues. and Fri.
noon ; and J. Elliot, Hungate,
Tues. noon, and Sat. 6 morning
2 *Southwold*, D. Garrod's van, every
Mon. Thurs. & Sat ; and 5 E. and
W. Goldsmith's van, Wednesday
and Saturday, 6 evening
Wangford, T. Aldridge (mail cart,)
daily, 6 evening
3 *Wrentham*, J. Golder, Mon. Th.
and Sat. at ½ past 3 afternoon
Yarmouth, Isaac Piper, Northgt ;
and James Neave, from the Che-quers, 6 morning

TRADING VESSELS.

The *London & Beccles Shipping Co.'s*
Vessels, weekly, from Corporation
wharf ; Wm. Hy. Leavould, *agent*
Wherries to *Yarmouth and Bungay*,
daily, W. H. Leavould and Wm.
Darby, *agents*
Vessels occasionally to *Norwich, &c.*

BUNGAY, a well-built and flourishing market town in two parishes, and in the Duke of Norfolk's Liberty, is pleasantly situated on an eminence, skirted on the east and west by the navigable river Wave-ney, which divides it from Norfork, and is here crossed by two good *bridges,* and by a circuitous reach in the form of a horse-shoe, encom-passes a fertile common called Outney, on the north side of the town. It is distant 40 miles N.N.E. of Ipswich, 40 miles N.E. by E. of Bury St. Edmund's, 14 miles S.S.E. of Norwich, 20 miles S.W. by W. of Yarmouth, 6 miles W. of Beccles, 16 miles W. of Lowestoft, 9 miles N. of Halesworth, and 109 miles N.E. by N. of London. The Wave-ney is navigable to it for barges from Yarmouth, and connects it with the Norwich Lowestoft navigation. It enjoys considerable traffic in corn, malt, flour, coals, &c. It was formerly noted for the manufac-ture of knitted worsted stockings and " Suffolk hempen cloth," but

these trades are now obsolete. In Ditchingham, a suburb on the Norfolk side of the river, is a large *silk mill*, erected in 1832, and employed in the manufacture of *crape*, by Messrs. Grout and Co., of Norwich. In the town is a *paper mill*, and the extensive *printing office* and stereotype foundry of Messrs. Childs and Son, established in 1795, by Mr. Charles Brightley, who was joined in business by Mr. J. R. Childs, in 1808, and for many years they were among the largest printers and publishers of periodical works in the kingdom. The present proprietors are now only printers for London and other publishers, and their stock of stereotype plates is said to weigh about 300 tons. The *market*, held every Thursday, is a considerable corn mart ; and here are two large annual *fairs* for cattle, horses, &c., on the 14th of May and 25th of September. The latter is also a "sessions" or hiring for servants. The county magistrates hold *petty sessions* here every Thursday. The *Market-place* is a spacious but irregular area, lined with good shops, inns, &c., and having an octangular *Butter Cross*, built in 1690, and covered with a leaded dome, surmounted by a fine figure of justice. Here was another market cross, called the *Corn Cross*, but it was taken down in 1810. The Market-place is considered one of the handsomest in the county. It occupies a gently rising ground, nearly in the centre of the town, and the *streets* which diverge from it to the principal roads, are spacious and well-paved, and are lighted with *gas*, from works erected by Mr. Malam in 1837. The inhabitants are amply supplied with excellent water from numerous *springs*, some of which are said to possess medicinal properties ; and the houses have generally a modern appearance, nearly all of them having been built since March 1st, 1688, when a *fire* broke out in an uninhabited dwelling, and spread with such rapidity, that the whole town, with the exception of one small street and a few detached houses, was reduced to ashes in the space of a few hours. The property destroyed by this conflagration was valued at about £30,000, and comprised 190 dwelling houses, one of the churches, the free-school, three almshouses, two ancient market crosses, and various other buildings.

The two *Parishes of Bungay Holy Trinity and St. Mary*, comprise about 2090 acres of land, and their *population* amounted to 2349 souls in 1801 ; 2828 in 1811 ; 3290 in 1821 ; 3734 in 1831 ; and 4109 in 1841 ; so that the town has nearly doubled its buildings and inhabitants during the last half century. Its number of *houses*, when the census was taken in 1841, was 965, of which 936 were occupied, 24 empty, and 5 building ; and the number of *males* was 1913, and *females* 2196. The rateable *yearly value* of the land and buildings in Holy Trinity parish, is £5028. 3s. 6d., and in St. Mary's, £5722. The former has about 1300 acres and 1861 souls, and the latter has about 800 acres and 2248 souls, and their *boundaries*, which were very intricate, have recently been clearly defined by commissioners under the tithe commutation act, as those between Mettingham and Bungay were in 1814, under an enclosure act. OUTNEY COMMON, a fine pasture of about 402 acres, is extra-parochial, and is skirted on the south by the town, and on its other sides by the river Waveney. It is under the management of *common-reeves*, appointed by the owners of the "beast-goings," or common-rights, of which it is restricted to about 150, each having pasturage for two head of cattle,

and formerly attached to the different properties in the two parishes; but, being freehold, part of them have been sold to non-residents, who, as well as the resident owners, can either let them or occupy them themselves. Six of these " goings," let for about £14 a year, are held by feoffees, as part of the Town Lands, to which trust there also belong " two goings" on STOW FEN, another extra-parochial common, on the south side of the town, comprising 88 acres, under the management of *fen-reeves*. The banks of the Waveney, which sweeps in the form of a horse-shoe round Outney common, afford delightful promenades; and on the Norfolk side of the river, is a remarkable *cold bath*, enclosed in a dilapidated building, erected in 1725, and supplied by a spring issuing from the foot of a lofty and abrupt acclivity. On the north side of the town are traces of a *Roman-dyke*, extending east and west to the two bends of the river, and affording, in former times, the means of completely insulating Outney common. About 98 acres of land, near the Roman road, called *Stone-street*, about 4 miles S. of Bungay, is a detached number of Holy Trinity parish. The Duke of Norfolk is lord of the manors of *Bungay-Burgh, Bungay Priory*, and *Bungay Soke*, but part of Holy Trinity parish is in the manor of *Ilketshall Bardolf*, of which Sir Wm. Wyndham Dalling, Bart., is lord. The soil belongs to various free and copyholders, and the latter are subject to arbitrary fines. Bungay was anciently described as *Bungay-Burgh and Boyscott*, meaning the town and hamlet, without any reference to the two parishes, and it is still so treated by the Crown in the collection of the land tax. East of the town, on the Beccles road, is Duke's Bridge, which crosses a small rivulet near *Duke's Bridge House*, the pleasant seat of Mrs. Barlee, who has an estate here. *The Grove*, a large mansion, 1 mile S. of Beccles, is the seat and property of Robert Butcher, Esq. Among the other proprietors are the Rev. George Dashwood, owner of part of the Uplands; Sir E. Kerrison, and Lord George Beresford, owners of farms, near the Beccles road; Mr. Richard Mann, owner of Wainford Mills; Mr. Wm. Denny, of *Duke's Farm;* and Mr. J. Gower, and Mrs. Fisher, who have each a farm in the *Uplands*, which occupy a bold elevation 1½ mile S. of the town. *Courts Leet and Baron*, for the Duke of Norfolk's three manors, are held generally twice a year, before J. Muskett, Esq., the steward.

In ancient times the Waveney was a much broader stream than it is now, (see page 412.) and Bungay was called *Le-Bon-Eye*, or the good island, being then nearly encompassed with water, as it still is on three sides. It was granted with 116 other manors, by William the Conqueror, to Roger Bigod, who was afterwards created Earl of Norfolk, and is supposed to have built BUNGAY CASTLE, which, from its commanding situation, on a bold eminence overlooking the river Waveney, and the great strength of its fortifications, was boasted of by Hugh, the next Earl, as being impregnable; but in 1140, it was stormed and taken by King Stephen, though the refractory Earl had said, "*Where I in my Castle of Bungay, upon the waters of Waveney, I would not set a button by the King of Cockney.*" It was, however, soon afterwards restored to the Earl, who was obliged to surrender it to Henry II., in 1155, but had it restored to him again in 1163. This Earl, as noticed at pages 51, 188, and 622, espoused the cause of the rebellious sons of Henry II., in 1173; and his castles at Ipswich, Framlingham, and Walton, being

taken by the king's forces, he purchased the royal pardon by humble submission, and a fine of one thousand marks. His Castle at Bungay, (as well as his other strong-holds,) was demolished by order of the King, and on its site was erected a mansion which, in the 22nd of Edward I., Roger Bigod, Earl of Norfolk, and Earl Marshal of England, obtained permission to embattle. In 1348, Joan, daughter of Alice de Montacute, and granddaughter of Thomas de Brotherton, Earl of Norfolk, was born here. The form of the Castle appears to have been octangular. The ruins of two round portal towers, and portions of the west and south west angles are still standing, as also are three sides of the great tower or keep, the walls of which are from 7 to 11 feet thick, and from 15 to 17 feet high. In the midst of the ruins, on what is called the terrace, is a mineral spring, now disused, and near it is a vault or dungeon of considerable depth, descended by a sort of stone chimney. Detached portions of the walls and their foundations are spread in all directions in the castle grounds, a ridge of which, about 40 yards long, forms the southern boundary of a bowling green, which commands delightful prospects. The mounds of earth, raised for the defence of the castle, still retain much of their original character, though considerably reduced in height. One of them facing the south, was partly removed in 1840, with the intention of forming a cattle market. At Earsham, on the Norfolk side of the river, nearly opposite the castle, some tumuli and traces of a Danish camp were removed about thirty years ago. Near St. Mary's Church, are the ruins of a PRIORY of Benedictine Nuns, some portions of which, facing Olland street, were taken down in 1843, and the space which they occupied was added to the churchyard, together with the site of the old parsonage house and garden. This nunnery was founded in 1160, by Roger de Glanville, and his wife, the Countess Gundreda, in honour of God, the Blessed Virgin Mary, and the Holy Cross. At the dissolution it had a prioress and eleven nuns, and was valued at £62. 2s. 1½d. Its site and possessions were granted by Henry VIII., to Thomas Duke of Norfolk. A silver seal is extant of " Marie d' Huntingfeld," who was prioress here, in the year 1200. Upon another seal of the nunnery, dated 1360, the town is called BVNGEYA. The records of the castle and nunnery are supposed to have been destroyed by the great fire already noticed. The Almshouse, in Olland street, which escaped the flames of this conflagration, is supposed to have been an Infirmary, attached to the nunnery. At the bottom of its windows, are some curious carvings, of the time of Elizabeth. In the town, is the figure of a crusader, carved in wood, supposed to have been removed from this house, and to represent Ranulph Glanville, who accompanied Richard I. to the holy wars, and was present at the siege of Acre. About 30 years ago, an earthen pot containing several hundred *Roman brass-coins*, was ploughed up, on the Norfolk side of the Waveney, opposite Outney common. Some of these are now in the possession of Mr. G. B. Baker, who has also a tournament spur, of the time of Edward III., and several other antiquities, among which is half of a chimney piece, removed from the last named house, and curiously inlaid with wood of various shades, representing a court-yard with embattled buildings, and bearing the arms of Bedingfeld, and the date 1572. A silver penny, of Offa, King of Mercia, was found here, some years ago. In 1826, Mr. T. Utting, on removing some of the walls of the castle, which had fallen into his

garden, found a rude leaden seal, inscribed "S. G. ROB. BLOKOO;" and in the following year, Mrs. Barlee found in her garden, at Duke's Bridge House, a coin of Gordianus Pius, who was killed in A.D. 224; and not far from the same spot was found, in 1840, the skeleton of a man imbedded in clay. In monastic times, there were in the town two *crosses*, one on the site of the Pound, and the other on the site of the Independent chapel. The land called *Ollands*, is described in a deed of the time of Edward III., as the "*Campo de Ilketshale.*" Less than a century ago, Bungay was the residence of several families who kept their carriages, and was so gay a place, that its balls were considered next in gentility to those of Bury, and it was designated "Little London."

The two PARISH CHURCHES of *Holy Trinity* and *St. Mary*, and another church dedicated to *St. Thomas*, and appropriated to the nunnery, are supposed to have been formerly enclosed in one extensive churchyard. The latter was in use after 1500, but no traces of it now remain. Here was also a chapel, dedicated to *St. Mary Magdalen*, which stood on the site of the house now occupied by Mr. Everson, mill-wright, on the Flixton road, and was probably attached to the *Hospital of St. John*, which stood near it, and is mentioned in several old deeds and in the Duke of Norfolk's court books, though nothing is known of its origin or dissolution. Human bones have often been found near the site of the chapel, and also in Trinity street, between the two parish churches, where there was formerly only a foot-path. HOLY TRINITY CHURCH is a small ancient edifice with a fine round tower, on the top of which are battlements, and several shields bearing the arms of Thos. de Brotherton, Earl of Norfolk, and son of Edward I., and the Montacute, Bigod, Beauchamp, and other families. It contains a brass plate in memory of Margaret Dallinger, who was prioress here; and some of the antique carved ends of its former benches still remain. Among its monuments is a handsome one in memory of the Rev. Thomas Wilson, a late learned and pious vicar, who died in 1774. This church was appropriated to Barlings Abbey, in Lincolnshire, and after the dissolution to the See of Ely. The *vicarage*, valued in K.B. at £8. 5d., and in 1835, at £256, has a good residence and a few acres of glebe. The Rev. Thomas Collyer, M.A., is the incumbent, and holds the rectorial tithes on lease from the Bishop of Ely, the patron and appropriator. ST. MARY'S CHURCH is a large and handsome structure, with a lofty tower containing 8 bells, a clock, and chimes. It is of flint and free-stone, and was mostly rebuilt between the years 1689 and 1701, after the fire of 1688, by which it was reduced to a ruinous shell, some interesting portions of which still remain at the east end; the original fabric being much larger than the present one. The old steeple was struck by lightning in 1577, and two men were killed in the belfry. The roof is supported by light and elegant pillars, and the interior was re-pewed a few years ago, when 245 additional sittings were provided, and 125 of them appropriated for the free use of the poor. The benefice is a *perpetual curacy*, valued in 1835 at £115, and having a commodious parsonage house, erected some years ago, in the precincts of the nunnery. The Duke of Norfolk is patron and impropriator, and the Rev. Henry Parker Cookesley, B.A., is the incumbent. The tithes of the two parishes were commuted in 1843. In the town are three neat CHAPELS of white brick, one belonging to the *Independents*, erected in 1776, and enlarged in

1811; one to the *Wesleyans,* erected in 1836, and the other to the *Roman Catholics,* built about 20 years ago, and having a house erected ten years ago, for the use of the priest. The *Baptists* have recently opened a place of worship here. *Religious and Charitable Institutions,* for the relief and instruction of the poor, are as numerous and as liberally supported in Bungay, as in most other places of the same magnitude; and the town enjoys the benefit of an endowed Grammar School, a number of Almshouses, and various trust estates for the poor, and the general benefit of the parishioners.

The *Town Lands and Premises* comprise several tenements, and upwards of 170 acres of land, in Bungay, Hempnall, Earsham, and other adjacent parishes, let at rents amounting to about £470 per annum, and vested with feoffees and the town-reeve, partly in trust for the common benefit of the town, and partly for the support of particular charities mentioned below. The oldest trust deed relating to these lands, which is now extant, is dated 1639; and the last conveyance in trust was by deeds of Dec. 1st and 2nd, 1809. The rents are collected by the clerk or receiver, and the accounts relating to the trust are settled annually in December, at a meeting of the *feoffees* and *town-reeve.* ALMSHOUSES, comprising 18 rooms, occupied by poor people, belong to this trust.

GRAMMAR SCHOOL.—In the 34th of Elizabeth, *Thos. Popeson, A.M.,* schoolmaster at Bungay, granted to the master, fellows, and scholars of Emanuel College, Cambridge, a yearly rent-charge of £6 towards the augmentation of the ten scholarships in that college, founded by Sir Walter Mildmay, for boys from Bungay school. At the same time, the feoffees of the town lands gave an annuity of £6 for the same purpose. By another indenture in the same year, reciting that the said Thomas Popeson and the feoffees of the town lands had made, and meant further to make, provision for the perpetuity of a free grammar school in Bungay,—the said Thomas Popeson conveyed to the feoffees his messuages, lands, and premises, for the use and support of the free grammar school, except one of the houses, which was then and was to be continued an *almshouse* for four impotent widows of St. Mary's parish, and except the yearly rent-charge of £6, given out of the same premises for augmenting the ten scholarships, as above named. Of the property settled by Popeson, some part appears to have been sold for the redemption of the land tax on the town lands; and the remainder, except the almshouse, is let for about £14 a year, which is added to the general account of the town feoffees. In 1728, *Henry Williams,* for the better support of a schoolmaster at Bungay, for instructing youth in the rudiments of good learning, granted to J. Bedingfeld, C. Garneys, and other trustees, the perpetual advowson of the vicarage of Ilketshall Saint Andrew, upon trust that they and their heirs, &c. should present the same to the schoolmaster of Bungay. In 1728, *Robert Scales* devised his estate at or near Ilketshall St. Lawrence, to trustees, upon trust that, if the schoolmaster of Bungay should be a minister of the Church of England, and should read, or cause to be read, divine service at the church of Saint Mary, every Wednesday and Friday, and also teach so many poor boys as the trustees should appoint, the clear rents and profits of the estate should be paid to him yearly. This estate was conveyed to 33 new trustees, in 1809, and consists of a farm of 33A., let for £50 a year, which is paid to the *deputy master,* (the Rev. Fredk. Barkway,) who performs the duties of the school for the Rev. John Gilbert, who was appointed master of the school by the Master and Fellows of Emanuel College, and was presented in consequence to the vicarage of Ilketshall St. Andrew, pursuant to the bequest of Henry Williams. The deputy master occupies the school premises,

which are large and old, and are repaired by the town feoffees, who also pay the parochial charges thereon. The school is free for ten boys of Bungay, for instruction in the classics, but they are each charged two guineas a-year for instruction in English, writing, and arithmetic. If the Master and Fellows of Emanuel College neglect to appoint a master, for four months after a vacancy, the nomination for that time is in the feoffees of the town lands, who have also power to remove the master for misbehaviour or neglect. The free scholars are admitted on application to the town-reeve. In consequence of the smallness of their endowment, the ten scholarships noticed above have been reduced to four. The NATIONAL SCHOOLS, adjoining the Common, form a handsome building, erected in 1834, at the cost of £367, and are attended by about 110 boys, 60 girls, and 120 infants. Here is also a large school connected with the *British & Foreign School Society*, erected in 1835, for 150 boys and 80 girls, but attended only by about 80 of the former, and 50 of the latter. A BOOK CLUB has existed here since 1770, and at Mr. Edward Sims', is a *News and Reading Room*. Here is also a neatly fitted up *Assembly Room*; and in Broad street is a *Theatre*, built in 1827, and opened for a few months every alternate winter.

THOMAS WINGFIELD, in 1593, left £170 to be laid out in lands to be vested in trust, that the rents and profits thereof might be applied mostly to the relief of the poor, and partly towards the support of two poor scholars in Cambridge, and for other uses. This £170, with £20 given by the inhabitants, was laid out in the purchase of 9A. of land in Bungay, let for £24 a-year, and 8A. 2R. 14P. at Ilketshall St. John's, let for £18. The latter has for a long period been attached as part of the Town Lands. Out of the rent of the former, about £18 is distributed yearly among the poor of the two parishes of Bungay; and 10s. is paid for a sermon, 10s. for the entertainment of the trustees, and 20s. towards the support of a Sunday School; no part of the income having for a long period being applied to the support of students at the University. In 1712, HENRY WEBSTER left an acre of land, at Ditchingham, and the sum of £20, to provide for the instruction of poor children in reading and writing. The £20 was laid out in the purchase of an acre of land, at Earsham. At the enclosure of Ditchingham and Earsham, allotments were awarded in lieu both of the charity lands and of some lands in each parish belonging to the churchwardens of St. Mary, in Bungay. These allotments are thrown together, and let for £29. 5s. a-year, of which £8. 16s. is appropriated to Webster's charity, and is paid to the funds of the National Schools. From *Henry Smith's Charity*, for the benefit of the poor of several parishes, Bungay receives about £36 yearly, which is distributed in bread during winter, among poor persons not receiving parochial relief; two-thirds in St. Mary's, and one-third in Holy Trinity parish. ST. MARY'S PARISH has church land producing about £20. 9s. a year, as noticed above, with Webster's charity. In 1730, *Thos. Bransby* left a yearly rent-charge of £5 out of his estates in Shottisham, in Norfolk, to be distributed among the poor of Bungay St. Mary, on Christmas-day. The *Church Estate*, which has been vested from time immemorial with the churchwardens of *Holy Trinity parish*, comprises 4A. of land in Mettingham Meadow, and an allotment of nearly one acre on Mettingham Green, let for £9 a year; about three roods, called Clubb's Piece, let for £3. 3s.; Trinity Meadow, let for £1. 10s.; a shop and chamber, at Harleston, let for £2. 10s. a year; and an annuity of 20s. out of Nettleholme Meadow. The rents are applied in the reparation of the church. In 1577, *Christiana Wharton* left her five ALMSHOUSES, in Holy Trinity parish, in trust, to permit five well-disposed poor persons to dwell therein, rent free. They are occupied by five poor widows, placed in them by the churchwardens. In 1786, certain land, and a tenement and shop, then producing

£3. 12s. a year, were held for the benefit of the poor of Holy Trinity parish, and stated to have been given by persons named *Duke* and *Richer*, but they have for many years been unknown, and may perhaps be included in the property appropriated to the service of the church.

Here are two *Clothing Societies*, a *Lying-in Charity*, and a *Dispensary*. The latter was established in 1828, and is liberally supported by subscription. The SAVINGS' BANK, for Bungay and the neighbourhood, was instiuted in 1818, and is open every Thursday, from ten to one o'clock. In 1842, its deposits amounted to £14,230. 9s. 5d., belonging to 463 individuals, and 20 Charitable and Friendly Societies. Mr. G. B. Baker is the secretary.

BUNGAY DIRECTORY.

Post Office, Olland street : Mr Daniel Stock, *postmaster*. Letters are received at 20 min. before 7 morning, and despatched at 7 evening, by mail cart from Scole.

(Ditchingham is a suburb, in Norfolk.)

Adkin Wm. gun maker, Earsham st
Angell Mrs Harriet, Earsham st
Ayers Mrs Charlotte, Back lane
Baker Mrs Ann, Plough street
Baker Graystone Bucke, bank agent, Market place
Baker Wm. Thompson, agent, Plough street
Baker Mrs Letitia, Broad street
Balls Mrs Elizabeth, Broad street
Barkway Rev Frederick, reader at St. Mary's, & dep. master of grammar school, Earsham street
Barlee Mrs Frances Sarah, *Duke's Bride House*
Barnes Mrs Betsy, Earnshaw street
Bewicke Mrs Sarah, Trinity street
Blackie Mrs Ann, Upper Olland st
Botwright Mrs Ann Maria, (& Ambrose, *clerk*,) Lower Olland st
Browne John, organist, Lwr. Olland st
Burstall Henry, gent. & Mrs Lucy, Grove road
Butcher Robert, Esq. *The Grove*
Butcher Mrs Mary, Trinity street
Butcher Rt. relvg. officer, New rd
Butcher Wm. mole catcher, Back ln
Butcher Wm. traveller, Plough st
Camell Mrs , *Ditchingham*
Chamberlain Thomas, compositor, Providence place
Carver Miss Ann, Plough street
Chambers Mrs Davis, Lwr. Olland st
Chaston Daniel, gent. New road
Chaston Mrs My. Ann, Almshouse st
Childs Chas. printer ; h Earsham st
Chenery Mrs Martha, Bridge street

Clarke Rev Thos. (Indpt.) Olland st
Colborne Thomas, bookpr. Olland st
Cole James, gent. Trinity street
Collett Mrs Sarah, Earsham street
Collyer Rev Thomas, M.A. Vicarage
Cook Charles, clerk, Trinity street
Cookesley Rev Henry Parker, B.A. incumbent of St. Mary's
Cornish Joshua, sweep, Broad st
Crick Wm. manager at *Ditchingham silk mills*
Dreyer Mrs Eliza, Trinity Hall
Duck-Rev Jas. (Catholic,) Olland st
Earl Mr Richard, Earsham street
Ebbage Robert, gent. Trinity street
Edwards Wm. artist, Grove road
Feltham John, gent. *Olland House*
Hancey Hy. & Sml. carters, Broad st
Halls James, manager, *Gas works*
Hartcup Wm. solr. ; h Mkt. place
Haward Miss Mary, Grove street
Hawes Mrs Jane Jemima, Plough st
Hodgson Jesse, brush dealer, Two Brewers street
Jarvis Thomas, upholsterer, Providence place
Kerridge Mrs Kph. Trinity street
King James, sweep, Lower Olland st
King Chas. excise, Upper Olland st
Larke Wm. bookpr. Broad street
Lee Mr Henry, Grove road
Leggett James, carter, Broad street
Kingsbury Mrs Elizabeth, Broad st
Mann Richard, gent. Earsham st
Margitson James Taylor, solicitor ; house *Ditchingham House*
Matthews Edward, stereotyper, Providence place

Minns Mr John, Lower Olland st
Morell Mrs Sophia, Broad street
Mullenger Wm. postman, New road
Palmer David, pump maker, Upper
    Olland street
Palmer Mrs Jamima, London road
Palmer Mr Ralph, Earsham street
Piggott Rev John, (Wesl.)Plough st
Plowman Mrs Mary, Bridge street
Plowman Mrs., Earsham street
Plumb Edward, farrier, Back lane
Pratt Mr Hy. & Mrs. Ann, Olland st
Putterill Mrs Maria, Plough street
Rackham Mrs Sarah, Common side
Raphael John, gent. *Rose Villa*
Reade Mr Wm. Broad street
Reeve Samuel, gent. Trinity street
Roberts Mr George, Almshouse st
Scott John Barber, Esq. Earsham st
Scott Samuel, Esq. Earsham street
Sewell Bloomfield, regr. Plough st
Sillett John, policeman, Olland st
Sims Edward, news room keeper,
    Earsham street
Smith Mrs Ann, Earsham street
Smith Mrs Elizabeth, Olland House
Smith Mr Joseph, Providence place
Smith Mr Samuel, Castle hills
Smith Samuel, agent, Lwr. Olland st
Smith Thomas, traveller, Grove cot
Stockdale Noah, foreman, Olland st
Taylor Jph. Helor, gent. Plough st
Utting Thomas, gent. *Ditchingham*
Webster John, gent. Upr. Olland st
West Wm. gent. Plough street
White Warren, gent. Plough street
Winter John, artist, Earsham street

ACADEMIES.
*(Marked * take Boarders.)*
*Abel Matthias, Broad street; house
    Providence place
Blake Charlotte, Earsham street
British School, Plough street, Henry
    and Elizabeth Foreman
Catchpole Elizabeth, Broad street
FreeGrammar, Rev Frederick Bark-
    way, Earsham street
*Jonas Charles Paul, Bridge street
National Schools, John Abel, Louisa
    Cocks, and Sarah Marston
*Owles Harriet, Trinity street
*Scammell Mary, Trinity street
Spilling Sarah, Earsham street
*Tovell John, Upper Olland street
Towler Denny, Lower Olland street
*Woolnough Mary, Trinity terrace

ATTORNEYS.
Bellman Henry, Earsham street
Drake Charles, Trinity street
Elswood Azariah, (clerk to magis-
    trates,) Earsham street
Freestone Edward, Broad st,(attends
    Thursday;) house *Norwich*
Margitson & Hartcup, Broad street
Smith Samuel, Earsham street

AUCTIONEERS.
Baker George, (and *land surveyor,)*
    Earsham street
Dalliston Blyth, (and land agent,)
    Olland street
Spall Heny, (& rate colr.) New rd

BAKERS & FLOUR DLRS.
Alexander Wm. Bridge street
Barnes Elisha, Earsham street
Bidwell Mark, Lower Olland street
Clarke John, Bridge street
Draper Francis, Bridge street
Ecclestone Bobert, Upper Olland st
*Fryer Jonathan, (confecr) Mkt.
*Mayhew Jerh.(confecr.)Earsham st
Redgrave Samuel, Broad street
Sayer Manning, Upper Olland st

BANKERS.
East of England, Bankg. Co., Ear-
    sham street, (on London and West-
    minster Bank,) Mr Sl. Smith, agt.
Gurneys and Co. Broad street, (on
    Barclay & Co,) Mr John Taylor
    Margitson, *agent*
Harveys & Hudsons, Market place,
    (on Hankey & Co.) Mr G. B. Ba-
    ker, *agent*
Savings' Bank, Market place, (open
    Thurs. 10 till 1,) Mr G. B. Baker,
    secretary

BASKET MAKERS.
Cudden James, Olland street
Glover Charles, Bridge street
Turner Eleanor, Upper Olland st
Waller Robert, Two Brewers street

BLACKSMITHS.
(See also Veterinary Surgeons.)
Fryett George, Upper Olland street
Gardiner Simon, Bridge street
Jay George, Broad street
Smith Wm. *Ditchingham*
Woolnough George, Upper Olland st

BOOKBINDERS.
Bollingbroke George, Broad street
Marston Thomas, Mill lane
Reeve Edward, Earsham street

BOOKSELLERS, PRINTERS, AND STATIONERS.

Ashby John Samuel, (and depository of Christian Knowledge Society,) Olland street
Childs John and Son, (*printers and stereotype founders,*) Broad street
Dyball Wm. Market place
Morris John Money, (*publisher,*) Broad street
Smith George, Olland street
Stock Daniel, Olland street

BOOT & SHOE MAKERS.

Beare Robert, Upper Olland street
Beare Wm. Upper Olland street
Cattermole James, Lower Olland st
Cattermole Jph. (& clerk of Trinity church,) Lower Olland street
Cattermole Wm. Broad street
Claxton Robert, Bridge street
Cobb John, Broad street
Codenham Wm. Lower Olland st
Codling Wm. Turnpike lane
Copeman Job, Olland street
Cornaby Edward, Market place
Cornaby Matthew, Bridge street
Cornish Frederick, Broad street
Cross Wm. Earsham street
Darby Stephen, Providence place
Ebbage Robert, Earsham street
Fenn Thomas, Turnpike lane
Fenn Wm. Bridge street
Gibbs James, Olland street
Martin George, Market place
Mayhew John, Olland street
Page Wm. Upper Olland street
Scarlett Samuel, *Ditchingham*
Tibnam Samuel, *Ditchingham*
Tilley Charles, Bridge street
Woor James, Upper Olland street

BRAZIER & TINNER.

Norman John, Market place

BREWER.

Clarke John, Bridge street

BRICKLAYERS.

Betts Robert C. Broad street
Bull Isaac, Broad street
Fenn Wm. Upper Olland street
Nunn Robert, Plough street

BUTCHERS.

Aldous Richard, Olland street
Baldry George, Upper Olland street
Beecroft Wm. Bridge street
Chase Robert, Bridge st. & Olland st
Cutting Wm. *Ditchingham*
Fisher Susanna, Market place
Girling John Wm. Earsham street

Honting Harley, Lower Olland st
Howe Stephen, Earsham street
Reeve Wm. Earsham street

CABINET MAKERS, &c.

Cuddon James, Olland street
Mayhew Edward (*and printers' joiner,*) Upper Olland street
Pulford Charles, *Ditchingham*
Rowe Robert, Upper Olland street
Taylor Nathaniel, Earsham street
Waller John, Two Brewers street

CHEMISTS & DRUGGISTS.

Churchyard Wm. Olland street
Meadows Wm. Henry, Earsham st
Parkinson Samuel, Market place

CLOTHES DEALERS.

Botwright Thos. Upper Olland st
Claxton Robert, Bridge street
Francis Wm. Lower Olland street
Sutton John, Olland street
Townsend George, Bridge street

COACH MAKERS.

Dutt Wm. *Ditchingham*
Spall Wm. Upper Olland street

COAL DLRS. (*See Corn, &c.*)

Draper Wm. Bridge street
Knights Thos. Providence street
Lodge Samuel, Bridge street

COOPERS.

Foreman Robert, *Ditchingham*
Harding Simon, Bridge street
Hinsby Wm. Lower Olland street
Newson Richard, Olland street

CORN & COAL MERCHTS.

Butcher Ed. (*& lime burner,*) Staith
Cuddon Wm. Olland st & *Ditchingham*
Mann Richard and Wm. *Wainford*
Reynolds Henry, Lower Olland st
Smith Saml. (& seed,) Upper Olland st

CORN & FLOUR DEALERS.

Chittleburgh James, Earsham street
Cocks Wm. (and seed,) Broad street
Glover Charles, Bridge street
Hill Edward and Co. Olland street
Jennings James, Bridge street

CORN MILLERS.

Burstall Robt. Wainford Mills and Grove road; house Ellingham
Money Joseph, Grove road
Moore John, Grove road
Sayer Manning, Upper Olland st
Wright Robert, Grove road

CURRIERS, &c.

Parker Samuel, Upper Olland street
Reeve John Rising, Bridge street

DYERS.

Hallows Addington, Earsham street

Kerridge Wm. *Ditchingham*

FARMERS.

Bullen Thomas, Broad street
Butcher Walter, Uplands
Denny Wm. *Duke's farm*
Gower James, *Uplands House*
Hamblin My. Ann || Hemnell Fras.
Laws Sarah, *Ditchingham*
Leggett Robert, Back lane
Malham Wm. Bridge street
Paine Charles, Duke's bridge
Pass John, Common lane
Redgreave Samuel, Back lane
Smith John, Uplands
Smith Salah, Duke's bridge
Smith Wm. Upper Olland street

FIRE & LIFE OFFICES.

Family Endowment, Wm. Church-yard, Olland street
Crown Life, C. Garneys, Trinity st
Farmers', Danl. Stock, Olland street
Globe, Hy. Bellman, Earsham st
London Assurance Co., C. P. Jonas, Bridge street
Norwich Union, Margitson & Hart-cup, Broad street
Protector Fire and Phœnix Life, J. Botwright, Upper Olland street
Suffolk and General Country, Saml. Smith, Earsham street
Sun, George Baker, Earsham street
West of England, Charles Drake, Trinity street

FISHMONGERS.

Allen James, Back lane
Ling Isaac, jun. Lower Olland st
Plumb Samuel, Back lane
Prime Elizabeth, Bridge street
Prime Wm. Bridge street
Tillett Benjamin, Broad street

FURNITURE BROKERS.

Baker John, Broad street
Knights Daniel, *Ditchingham*

GARDENERS, &c.

Cullingford Frances, Lwr. Olland st
Earl Robert, Castle hills
Smith Wm. Lower Olland street
Wigg Joseph, Olland street
Wisken Martha, Lower Olland st

GLASS, CHINA, &c. DLRS.

Chenery Phœbe, Earsham street
Gosling George, Market place
Smith Henry, Olland street

GROCERS & TEA DEALERS.

*(Marked * are Tallow Chandlers.)*
Ashby Richard D'Urban, Olland st
Cane Abel, Bridge street

Cock Gilbert, Earsham street
Durrant Fdk. Augustine, Olland st
Fisher Samuel, Market place
Haward Edwin, Earsham street
More Robert, Olland street
Owles Thomas, Trinity street
Pearce Maria (& foreign fruit dealer,) Market place
Weavers John, Olland street
White Robt. (& British wine dealer,) Market place

HAIR DRESSERS.

Atty John Wright, Lower Olland st
Blackbon Aaron (and circulating library,) Three Butchers street
Colby George, Olland street
Ife Charles, Bridge street
Taylor John, Earsham street

HATTERS.

Clarke Jeremiah, Earsham street
Lusher Randal (and glover,) Mkp
Sutton John, Olland street

INNS & TAVERNS.

Angel, Jas. Clamp, Lower Olland st
Black Horse, Eliz. Hogg, Earsham st
Butchers' Arms, Robert Read, Providence place
Chequers, Daniel Pattle, Bridge st
CherryTree, Danl. Spink, Common ln
Crown, Charles Battelle, Market pl
Falcon, Wm. Godbold, *Ditchingham*
Fleece Inn, Jas. Martin, Olland st
Green Dragon, Isaac Smith, Bridge st
Horse & Groom, Isaac Sadd, Broad st
King's Arms, Danl. Legood, Bridge st
King's Head (posting house,) Samnel Todd, Market place
Pickerel, John Rush, Market place
Plough, Wm. Watson, Plough st
Prince of Wales, Jas. Rant, Olland st
Queen's Head, Rt. Chase, Market pl
Red Lion, Edw. Betts, Upr. Olland st
Rose and Crown, George Baldry, Upper Olland street
Ship, Rt. Woodrow, Lwr. Olland st
Swan, John Stockdale, Market place
Thatched House, Robert Godbold, Grove cross roads
Three Jolly Butchers, Wm. Gibbs, Three Butchers street
Three Tuns, (posting house,) Susan Garrard Buckenham, Market pl
Two Brewers, Hannah Cullingford, Two Brewers street
Watch House, John Ellis, Wainford cross
White Horse, Wm. Chalker, Staith

White Lion, Rt.Ebbage, Earsham st
BEER HOUSES.
Brighton George, Duke's bridge
Chaney John, Earsham street
Newson Richard, Olland street
Revell Joseph, Common side
IRON FOUNDERS, &c.
(And Machine Makers.)
Cameron Daniel, Earsham street
Richmond Wm. Bridge street
IRONMONGERS.
Balls John, Market place
Booty Wm. Lower Olland street
Bushell Charles, Olland street
Cameron Daniel, Earsham street
Delf Robert (and iron merchant,) Market place
JOINERS & BUILDERS.
Botwright Jeremiah,Upper Olland st
Darby Robert, Providence place
Day George, Broad street
Ebbage Francis, Earsham street
Foulger Joseph, Upper Olland st
Smith Wm. Two Brewers street
Stockdale John, Market place

LINEN AND WOOLLEN DRAPERS.
Fisher Samuel, Market place
Grigg Thomas, Market place
Nickless Frederick, Olland street
Riches John, Earsham street
Thirtle John, Market place
Thomas Charles Johnson (wholesale and retail) Market place
MALTSTERS.
Butcher Edward, Staith
Mann Richard & Wm. *Wainford*
MILLINERS, &c.
Atmare Susanna, Upper Olland st
August Susanna, Upper Olland st
Bardwell Martha, Earsham street
Botwright Ann, Lower Olland st
Cattermole Susan, Bridge street
Clarke Sarah Ann, Earsham street
Cornaby Elizabeth, Market place
Church Mary Ann, Two Brewers st
Gould Harriet, Providence place
Newson Margaret, Olland street
Palmer Emily, Lower Olland st
Richards Harriet, Lower Olland st
Richardson Esther, Broad street
Sutton Lily, Olland street
Taylor Susanna, Lower Olland st
MILLWRIGHTS.
Everson John, Upper Olland street
Harvey Charles, New road

PAINTERS, PLUMBERS, AND GLAZIERS.
Barcham (Edw.) & Farman (Saml.) Earsham street
Brown Wm. Bridge street
Cattermole Robert, Bridge street
Cornaby John, *Ditchingham*
Gibson George, Lower Olland street
Holley Wm. Two Brewers street
Peirson Robert, Olland street .
Redgrave Samuel, Earsham street
Spooner John, Upper Olland street
Winter John (and glass stainer) Earsham street
PAPER MAKER.
Burgess Charles, Staith
SADDLERS, &c.
Archer John, Olland street
Cattermole Alfred, Upper Olland st
Reynolds James, Broad street
Smith Robert, Castle hill
Walesby Edmund, Earsham street
SHOPKEEPERS.
Alpe Wm. Upper Olland street
Banham Wm. Providence place
Borrett Wm. Bridge street
Buck Susanna, Market place
Codlen John, Almshouse street
Farrants Benjamin, Broad street
Frances Wm. Lower Olland street
Gosling George, Market place
Gowing Elizabeth, Upper Olland st
Hallows Addington, Earsham st
Knights Daniel, *Ditchingham*
Mills Ann, Lower Olland street
Tilley Elizabeth, Bridge street
Wisken Martha, Lower Olland st
SILK, CRAPE, &c. MANFRS.
Grout & Co. Ditchingham (and Norwich, Yarmouth and London) Mr Wm. Crick, manager
STONE & MARBLE MASONS.
Nursey Henry, Upper Olland st
Nursey James, Lower Olland street
STRAW HAT MAKERS.
Botwright Harriet, Lower Olland st
Clarke Louisa, Earsham street
Draper Eliza, Bridge street
Gardener John (and blocker) *Ditchingham*
Minns Sophia Anne, Bridge street
More Louisa, Olland street
Prime Harriet, Bridge street
Smith Rachel, Olland street
Spooner Emma, Upper Olland street
SURGEONS.
Currie John, Trinity street

Fisher Nathl. Briggs, Upr. Olland st
Garneys Charles, Trinity street
Webb Thomas Ernest, Broad street
TAILORS.
Barker James, Upper Olland street
Felby John, Three Butchers street
Knights Matthew, Broad street
Masterson James, Lower Olland st
Mayhew Amos, Broad street
Porter Wm. Lower Olland street
Riches John (draper) Earsham st
Sadd John, Bridge street
Smith Alfred, Market place
Sutton Saml. (& draper) Market pl
Weeding Nathl. Upper Olland st
Woolnough John, Upper Olland st
TEA DEALERS.
(See also Grocers & Shopkeepers.
Botwright George, Lower Olland st
Chenery Phœbe, Earsham street
Minns Charles, Bridge street
Smith Henry, Olland street
TIMBER MERCHANTS.
Cuddon Wm. (English) Olland st.
and *Ditchingham*
Farrow James, Lower Olland street
TOY AND FANCY WAREHS.
Cattermole Susan, Bridge street
Dyball Wm. (& silversmith) Mkp
TURNER (WOOD.)
Brighting Elijah, Mill lane
VETERINARY SURGEONS.
Archer Rt. (& forge) Upr. Olland st
Duffield Robert (& forge) Bridge st
WATCH & CLOCK MAKERS.
Bullock Robert Henry, Olland st
Carley Enoch (& pawnbkr.)Bridge st
Chenery Frederick, Olland street
Mills Edward, Bridge street
Paul Philip, Bridge street
WHEELWRIGHTS.
Gooding Samuel, *Ditchingham*
Haward Wm. New road; h *St. Lawrence's*
King Michael, *Ditchingham*
WHITESMITHS, &c.
Balls John, Market place
Booty Wm. Lower Olland street
Cameron Daniel, Earsham street
Richmond Wm. Bridge street
Waters James, Lower Olland street
WINE & SPIRIT MERCHTS.
Sexton Robert Atto, Broad street

Smith Isaac, Bridge street
COACHES.
From the King's Head, to *London*, ½ past 8 morning; to Beccles, ½ p. 5 evening; to *Norwich*, Monday, Wed. and Sat. 8 morning; to *Ipswich*, *Yoxford*, &c. Mon. Wed. & Sat. 6 evening; and to *Yarmouth*, Monday, Wed. & Fri. 5 evening.
From the Fleece Inn, to *Ipswich*, ¼ before 10 mng. and to *Norwich*, ½ p. 2 aft. daily; and Hogg's omnibus, to Norwich, Monday, Wednesday, and Saturday, 8 morning.
From the Three Tuns, to *Bury*, Mon. Wed. & Fri. ½ p. 10 mng.; and to *Yarmouth*, Tues. Thursday, and Saturday, ½ past 1 aftn.
CARRIERS.
To *London, Ipswich, &c.*; Samuel Noller (*via Eye and Diss*) from the Fleece, Wed. & Fri. 5 mng.; H. R. and J. Smith (*via Halesworth*) from the Queen's Head, Mon. Thurs. & Sat. 2 aftn.; and Jas. Sawyer (*via Framlingham, &c.*) from the Fleece, Wed. Thu. and Saturday, 8 evening.
To *Beccles*, Wm. Page, Broad st. Mon. Thurs. & Sat. 10 morning.
To *Halesworth*, Henry Tilney, from the Angel, Monday, Wednesday, and Saturday, 3 afternoon.
To *Harleston*, Wm. Beare, from the White Lion, daily.
To *Norwich*; Rt. Hogg's Van, from Bridge street, Mon. and Wed. 8 mng.; & his waggon, Tue. Thu. and Sat. 6 morning; also, Hart, from the Tuns, Tue. & Fri.; and Sawyer, from the Fleece, Tues. Wednesday, and Friday, 2 aftern.
To *Saxmundham*, Rt. Hogg, Bridge st. Monday & Friday, 4 morning.
To *Scole and Bury*, mail cart, from the Fleece, every evening, at 7.
To *Stradbroke*, Wm. Meen, from Queen's Head, Wed. & Fri. 2 aft.
To *Yarmouth*, Jas. Neave, Broad street, Mon. Wed. & Sat. 5 mng.
WHERRIES from the Staith, daily to *Yarmouth*; Edward Butcher, *wharfinger*

COVE, (NORTH) a small scattered village, 2½ miles E. by S. of Beccles, has in its parish 219 souls, and 1081A. 3R. 10P. of land, exclusive of 114 acres, called *Worlingham Peter*, or *Parva*, formerly

a separate parish, but now paying tithes to Worlingham All Saints, and poor rates to this parish, which is in the Earl of Gosford's manor of *Wade Hall*, a farm-house, 3½ miles E. of Beccles, formerly the seat of the Wasbys and Jernegans, from whom it passed to the Yallops. *North Cove Hall*, an ancient mansion, with pleasant grounds, is the seat of John Cooper, Esq., who owns a great part of the parish. The copyholds pay arbitrary fines. The *Church* (St. Botolph) is a thatched fabric, with an embattled tower. The living is a discharged rectory, valued in K.B. at £10, and in 1835 at £353, with that of Willingham annexed to it. The patronage is in the Crown, and the Rev. Richard Gooch, of Frostenden, is the incumbent. The tithes of North Cove have recently been commuted for £220, and those of Willingham for £242 per annum, besides which, the rector has a few acres of glebe, but no parsonage-house. The *Wesleyans* have a small chapel here. The *Town Land*, 1A. 2R., is let for £4. 10s. a year, which is distributed in fuel among the poor.

Cooper John, Esq. *North Cove Hall*
Andrews Benj. jun. shoemaker
Huke Charles, woodman
Huke Mr Jas. || LancasterMrWm.
Lee Martha,vict. *Three Horse Shoes*
Patrick Thos. plumber and glazier
Peirson Wm. shopkeeper

Tills Philip, parish clerk

FARMERS.

Andrews Benj. || Ayers Thomas
Bloomfield Wm. || Brock Oliver
Candler Rt. Newdigate, *Wade Hall*
Gent Robt. || Ling Wm.

ELLOUGH, in the vale of a rivulet, 3½ miles S. by E. of Beccles, is a small scattered village and parish, containing 155 souls, and 1673A. 3R. 32P. of fertile and well wooded land. The Earl of Gosford is lord of the manor, which formerly belonged to the Playters, but part of the soil belongs to Fredk. Barne, Esq., and several smaller owners. The *Church* (All Saints) is an ancient structure, with a lofty tower, and the living is a discharged rectory, valued in K.B. at £12, and in 1835 at £257. The Earl of Gosford is patron, and the Rev. Richd. Aldous Arnold incumbent. The rectory-house was enlarged about ten years ago, and the glebe is 35A. 28P., of which 16A. 3R. 28P. is in Willingham parish. The FARMERS are, Susan Artis, Chas. Debenham, Wm. Green, George Hamby, *East House ;* Samuel Holmes, *Ellough Hall ;* Thomas Paine, Samuel Pells, John Pleasants, and Samuel Weavers. Nathaniel Money is the *gamekeeper.*

FLIXTON, a small village, pleasantly situated in the vale of the Waveney, 2½ miles S.W. of Bungay, has in its parish 192 souls, and 1762A. of land. Here was a *Nunnery* of the order of St. Augustine, founded by Margery, widow of Sir Bartholomew de Creke, about the year 1258. She endowed it with the manor of Flixton. It was dissolved by the second bull of Pope Clement VII., in 1528, and intended for Cardinal Wolsey, towards the endowment of his college at Ipswich ; but he declining it, Henry VIII. granted it to John Tasburgh, who received it from Elizabeth Wright, the last prioress, in 1532, when it was valued at £23. 4s. 1d. per annum. Its site is now occupied by a farm-house, called the Abbey. *Flixton Hall* belongs, with the manor, and nearly all the parish, to Wm. Adair, Esq., but is the seat of *Sir Robert Shafto Adair,* who was born in 1763, and created a *baronet* in 1838. It was built in 1615, and was originally surrounded

by a moat, which was filled up many years ago. It is in that style of architecture which has been designated " Inigo Jones's Gothic." It has a noble entrance hall, and elegant staircase. Its apartments are spacious; and on the south side was an open colonnade, now closed up, and converted into separate rooms. The park comprises 300 acres, and is well wooded and stocked with deer. The Tasburghs were long seated here, and from them the estate descended to the Wyburns, of whom it was purchased by the late Wm. Adair, Esq. The *Church* (St. Mary) is an ancient fabric, with a tower and three bells, but its chancel is an ivy-mantled ruin. The benefice is a discharged vicarage, valued in K.B. at £6, and in 1835 at £140. Wm. Adair, Esq., is patron, and the Rev. George Sandy is the incumbent, and has a neat parsonage house, built in 1843. He is also incumbent of the rectories of Southelmham All Saints and St. Nicholas. The *Town Lands*, &c. comprise a house and 10 acres, let for £22, and two pieces of land, the precise situation and extent of which are unknown; but the yearly sums of 30s. for one, and 10s. for the other, have been paid for them as far as is known. The rents are applied in the service of the church, and other public uses. In 1782, Wm. Adair, Esq., bequeathed £300 three per cent. consols in trust, to pay the dividends yearly for the relief of the poor of Flixton, Homersfield, and Southelmham St. Cross. He also left £700, and as much money as should be found in his charity bag at the time of his death, to be invested at interest, and the yearly produce thereof to be dispensed by the successive owners of the testator's estate at Flixton, in such charitable uses as they should think proper. The £700, with £320. 13s. 7d. found in the testator's charity bag, was laid out in the purchase of £1704. 13s. 8d. new South Sea Annuities. The dividends, £51. 2s. 8d. a-year, are applied in gratuities to proper objects of charity, in the purchase of coals sold to the poor at reduced prices, and in the support of schools for the education of poor children in the three above-named parishes.

Adair Sir Robert Shafto, Baronet, *Flixton Hall*
Adair Alex. Shafto, Esq. *Hall*
Adair Hugh A. Esq. *Hall*
Beaumont John, vict. *Buck*
Ling James, blacksmith
Sandby Rev George, vicar of Flix-

ton, and rector of Southelmham All Saints

FARMERS.

Beaumont John || Beaumont Wm.
Brook Joseph || Cooper John
Howard Charles, *Abbey Farm*
Gower Sparling || Read John

HOMERSFIELD, a pleasant village, on the south bank of the river Waveney, 5 miles S.W. of Bungay, and 3½ miles E.N.E. of Harleston, has in its parish 291 souls, and 981 acres of land. Wm. Adair, Esq., is lord of the manor, owner of most of the soil, and patron of the rectory, valued in K. B. at £5. 6s. 8d., and in 1835 at £360, with that of Southelmham St. Cross annexed to it. The Rev. Courtenay Boyle Bruce is the incumbent. The tithes of Homersfield have been commuted for £143, and those of St. Cross for £220. 10s. per annum. The *Church* (St. Mary) is a small fabric, with a tower and three bells. A market and fair here were granted to the Bishop of Norwich, in the second of Henry III., but they were obsolete several centuries ago. The *Poor's Land*, 2½A., was given at an early period by Sir Nicholas Howe, and is let for £2. 10s. per annum. The small manor of *Lymborn*, in Homersfield, was held by the nuns of Bungay,

and was granted by Henry VIII. to the Duke of Norfolk, and by Edward VI. to John and Thomas Wright. Sir B. Gaudy died seized of it in 1569. DIRECTORY:—Samuel Bailey and Geo. Borrett, *shoemkrs.*; Horace Beaumont and Edward B. Marsh, *farmers;* Eliz. Church, vict., *Swan;* Joseph King, *grocer and draper;* and Thomas Smith, *parish clerk.*

ILKETSHALL ST. ANDREW, 4 miles S. E. of Bungay, and S.W. by W. of Beccles, is a parish containing 548 souls, and 1696A. of strong loamy land. Its houses are scattered round the margins of several *greens,* lying east of the other Ilketshalls, and being, like them, in the Duke of Norfolk's Liberty. The soil belongs to Wm. Adair, Esq., Lord George Beresford, Rev. J. Day, J. Garden, Esq., Rev. C. Clark, Thomas Farr, Esq., and several smaller owners. The *Church* (St. Andrew) is an ancient structure, on a commanding eminence. It is of flint and stone, and its tower is circular at the base, and octangular at the top. The benefice is a discharged vicarage, valued in K.B. at £5. 13s. 4d., and in 1835 at £139. It has 28A. of glebe, and a small parsonage, and is in the patronage of Bungay Grammar School, (see page 429,) and incumbency of the Rev. John Gilbert. The rectorial tithes belong to Mrs. Ann Scott, and several of the principal landowners. The *Wesleyans* have a small chapel here, of flint and white brick, erected in 1840. The *Town Estate* comprises a double cottage, and 2A. of land, let for £11. 10s. a year; and 7A. called Redisham Close, let for £10 a-year. One half of the rents is applied to the reparation of the church, and the remainder in defraying other public expenses of the parish.

Booker Anthony, tailor
Branch Mr John
Brighten Robert, shopkeeper
Cullum Stephen, butcher
Gardner Hannah, beerhouse keeper
Green David, corn miller
Green John, vict. Hare & Hounds
Hambling Ann, shopkeeper
Hambling Jeremiah, blacksmith & ironmonger
Haney Robert, blacksmith
High James, wheelwright
Howlett Benjamin, wheelwright
Hunting Chas. veterinary surgeon
Kemp James, shoemaker
Kemp Robert, parish clerk

Morris James, joiner
Oldring J. shoemaker
Sayer Meshach, tailor & shopkeeper
Stanard Geo. bricklayer & shopkpr
Turrell James, joiner
Wyatt Wm. beerhouse

FARMERS.
Adams George
Breese James
Burgess Thomas
Buskard Wm.
Button Ephraim
Calver James
Chaston Robert
Clarke Samuel
Cullum Wm.

Howlett Jonth.
Newby George
Nurse James
Phillips James
Sadd John
Salter John
Salter Wm.
Tooke Peter
Turner Robert

ILKETSHALL ST. JOHN, 2 miles S. by E. of Bungay, is the smallest parish among the four Ilketshalls, having only 71 souls, and 743 acres of land, five scattered farm houses, and three cottages. John Day, Esq., is lord of the manor, but part of the soil belongs to the Rev. R. Day, Mr. John Hall, and two smaller owners. The *Church* (St. John) is a small stuccoed edifice, covered with blue slate, and standing on a bold eminence. The rectory, valued in K.B. at £8. 13s. 4d., and in 1835 at £311, is in the gift of the Crown, and incumbency of the Rev. Charles James Hutton, A.B., who has a pleasant residence, and about 60A. of glebe. The tithes have been commuted for a yearly rent of £230, besides which the rector has about £50 a year from the tithes

of the other three Ilketshalls. The HALL, a neat mansion of white brick, belongs to the Rev. R. Day, but is occupied by Richard Day French, Esq. The FARMERS are John Chilvers, *Manor House ;* Geo. Dixon, and John Hall.

ILKETSHALL ST. LAWRENCE, comprises several scattered houses near the church, on the Halesworth road, 3 miles S.S.E. of Bungay, and the hamlet of *St. Lawrence Green,* 1½ mile S. of the church. Its parish contains 221 souls, and 988 acres of land. It is mostly in Sir W.W. Dalling's manor of Bardolph, (see page 426,) but the soil belongs to the Rev. J. Day, Sir E. Kerrison, Col. Bence, Lady Beresford, Wm. Adair, Esq., the Rev. R. A. Arnold, and a few smaller owners. The *Church* (St. Lawrence) is a small structure, and the benefice is a perpetual curacy, valued in 1835 at £47. The Rev. J. Day, of Hethersett, Norfolk, is patron and impropriator, and the Rev. James Culling Safford, of Mettingham, is the incumbent. It was appropriated to the nuns of Bungay. Part of a large ancient *Hall* is divided into small tenements, and the remainder was taken down many years ago.

Those marked † are on the Green.

FARMERS.
(* *are owners.*)

Bedingfield James, parish clerk	Becket Robert	*Knights James
†Day John, shoemaker	†Chandler Geo.	†Newham Wm.
†Howard Wm. wheelwright	*Dunnett Rd.	†Tye John
†Morris James, joiner	*Girling Thomas	Walne George
†Moulding Wm. corn miller & shopr.	Howard James	Warner Wm.
†Woolnough Rt. vict. & blacksmith, *Royal Oak*		*The Grove*

ILKETSHALL ST. MARGARET, 4 miles S. by E. of Bungay, is a straggling village and parish, containing 315 souls, and 2090A. 2R. 16P. of land. Wm. Adair, Esq., is lord of the manor, but a great part of the soil belongs to Lady Beresford, Mr. J. G. Chaston, and several smaller owners. The *Church* is a small structure, with a tower and three bells, and the living is a discharged vicarage, valued in K.B. at £5. 13s. 9d., and in 1835 at £131. Mrs. Patteson is patroness and impropriator, and the Rev. Patrick Bassinghall Beath incumbent. The glebe is 15 acres. The tithes have been commuted for yearly moduses of £528 to the impropriator ; £121 to the vicar ; and £15 to the rector of Ilketshall St. John. The *Town Estate,* consisting of two tenements and 24A. of land, let for £28 a year, has been vested from an early period for the reparation of the church and other public uses. The poor have about £5 yearly, left by Henry Smith, in 1626, out of an estate at Tolleshunt-Darcy, in Essex. A limited number of the tenants of the four parishes of Ilketshall, have the privilege of pasturing a certain number of cattle on *Stow Fen.* (See page 426.)

Baldry John, blacksmith	Candler Geo. jun.	Ling Rachel
Clutton Oliver, shopkeeper	Cutton Oliver	Martin Benjamin
Collings Hy. horse breaker and vict. *Greyhound*	Dodd Joseph	Meddle John
	Edwards James	Neal Thomas
Harvey Mrs Eliz. and Mrs Ann	Foyster Robert	Owles John
Martin Jph. shoemaker and shopr.	Harvey James	Pass John
Martin Thomas, shopkeeper	Holden Samuel	Rope Mark
Masterson Wm. tailor.	Holden Joseph	Spurgeon John
FARMERS. Andrews James	King Henry	Wright John
Adams James		

METTINGHAM, a pleasant village on the southern acclivity of the vale of the Waveney, 2 miles E. of Bungay, and 4 miles W. of Beccles, has in its parish 409 souls, and 1706A. 1R. 16P. of fertile land. About half a mile south of the church are the ruins of METTINGHAM CASTLE, which was of considerable extent and strength, and was built by John de Norwich, who, in the 17th of Edward III., obtained permission to convert his house here into a castle; in which he also founded a COLLEGE, to which he had the king's license to translate the priests from his college at Raveningham. This college was dedicated to God and the Blessed Virgin, and consisted of a master and thirteen chaplains or fellows, who were endowed with the castle for their residence, and with the manors of Mettingham, Bungay-Soke, and several others in Suffolk and Norfolk. They educated and maintained a number of boys at the annual charge of £28. Richard Shelton, the master, and nine fellows, subscribed to the king's supremacy in 1535, but were allowed to remain till 1542, when their revenues were valued at £202. 7s. 5½d. per annum, and their possessions were granted to Sir Anthony Denny. The founder died in 1363, and left his estates to his grandson, whose cousin, Catherine de Brews, afterwards inherited, but having assumed the veil, her estates devolved to the Ufford family. After the dissolution of the college, Mettingham was purchased by the Buxton family, who sold it about 1660 to the Bacons, of whom it was purchased by the Hunts. From the latter, it descended to the Saffords. In 1826, Samuel Safford, Esq., sold one moiety of his estates to Charles Day, Esq., of Ilketshall St. John. A great part of the parish of Mettingham belongs to various owners, and the remainder to the Rev. J. C. Safford, A.B., who is lord of the manor, impropriator of the rectory, and patron and imcumbent of the vicarage, and has a neat modern *mansion* within the area of the *castle ruins*, pleasantly seated on a well-wooded lawn. From the remains of its shattered walls, the castle appears to have been an extensive quadrangular structure, of which the gate-house is still tolerably entire. The *Church* (All Saints) is an ancient fabric with a round tower, and stands on a bold eminence overlooking the vale of the Waveney. The living is a discharged vicarage, valued in K.B. at £6. 17s. 3½d., and in 1835 at £140. The *Town Estate* is partly in Shipmeadow parish, and comprises a cottage, blacksmith's shop, 36A. of land, and two cattle-gates in Stow Fen. It is under the management of feoffees chosen by the parishioners, and has been vested from an early period for the payment of public charges of the parish, and the support of the poor. It is let for about £80 a year, of which a large portion is applied in the service of the church, and about £10 is distributed in coals among poor families.

Cock Chas. shoemkr. & parish clerk
Dains Robert, wheelwright
Parrington Joseph, Esq.
Safford Rev Jas. Culling, A.B. *Mettingham Castle*
Spalding Thomas, gentleman
Warren Sidney, blacksmith

FARMERS. | *Baley Jeremiah
(* are owners.) |

Bezant Esther
Bird John
Clutton Sarah
*Culham Thos.
Dains Widow
*Draper George
Durrant Samuel
Peck Chas. *Castle Farm*

Scarlett Francis
Strange George
Minns
Sutton John
*Tallent Ann J.
*Tallent John
Packard
*Woods Mary

REDISHAM, (GREAT) a small village, 4½ miles S. by W. of Beccles, and 6 miles S.E. of Bungay, has in its parish 165 souls, and 733A. 2R. 21P. of land, having a strong loamy soil, and rising in bold undulations. John Garden, Esq., is lord of the manor, but a great part of the soil belongs to the Earl of Gosford, and several smaller owners. The copyholds are subject to arbitrary fines. The *Church* (St. Peter) is a small fabric with a wooden belfry, and was appropriated to Butley Priory. The Earl of Gosford is now impropriator and patron, and receives a yearly modus of £100 in lieu of tithes, from the lands which do not belong to him. The perpetual curacy, valued in 1835 at £50, is now enjoyed by the Rev. Richd. Aldous Arnold. The parish has £9. 6s. 8d. yearly for the support of a Sunday school, from Leman's charity, as noticed with Cratfield. DIRECTORY:—John Buxton, *parish clerk ;* Thos. Dugdale, *shoemaker ;* Thos. Gymer, *blacksmith ;* John Maplestone, *land agent ;* John Mills, *joiner ;* Edward Westrup, vict., *Wig ;* and Robt. Gower, Michael Mahew, Stephen Sewell, Thomas Smith, (and cattle dealer,) and Robert Westrup, *farmers.*

RINGSFIELD parish has its church and a few farm-houses in a secluded valley, 2½ miles S.S.W. of Beccles, and 5 miles E. by S. of Bungay, and a larger assemblage of cottages and houses at the *Cross-roads*, about a mile further to the south, overlooking the vale of another rivulet, near the small hamlet of LITTLE REDISHAM, which was anciently a separate parish, but has long been consolidated with Ringsfield, though there are still some remains of its church, in a field, fenced round with wooden palisades. *Little Redisham Hall*, the pleasant seat of John Garden, Esq., is a neat modern mansion, on a bold acclivity, 4 miles S.S.W. of Beccles, and a quarter of a mile south of the ruins of the church. The parish of Ringsfield, including this hamlet, comprises 311 inhabitants, and about 1700 acres of land. John Garden, Esq., is lord of the manor, and purchased Little Redisham of the late Robert Sparrow, Esq. The Earl of Gosford, Richard Bohun, Esq., Col. Bence, N. Micklethwaite, Esq., Mrs. Mobbs, and a few smaller owners have estates in the parish. *Ringsfield Church* (All Saints) is an ancient thatched structure, and contains several monuments, upon one of which, inlaid with brass, are effigies of Nicholas Garneys and his wife. The benefice is a rectory, with that of Little Redisham annexed to it, valued in K.B. at £12, and in 1835 at £488. Edward Postle, Esq., is patron, and the Rev. Frederick Leathes, of Reedham, Norfolk, is the incumbent, and has a good Rectory House and 36 acres of glebe, occupied by the curate.

Marked † are at the Cross roads.

Garden John, Esq. *Little Redisham Hall*
†Battram Robert, vict. and hurdle maker, Horse Shoes
†Battram Wm. hurdle maker
†Bezant James, blacksmith
†Calver Manning, bricklayer
Colls Rev Thomas Arthur, curate, *Rectory*
†Harvey Elijah, shopkeeper
†Howlett Benjamin, wheelwright
†Mobbs Mrs Martha
†Pratt Philip, shoemaker

FARMERS.
Balls Thomas
Banyard James
Blomfield John
Chandler John
George Wm.&Rt
Holland Robert
Mathews Samuel
Skoulding Fras.
Wilson Wm.

SHADINGFIELD, a scattered village, with several neat houses, on the turnpike, 4½ miles S. of Beccles, and 6 miles N.E. by N. of

Halesworth, has in its parish 177 souls, and 1369A. 2R. 9P. of land. John Garden, Esq., is lord of the manor, which he purchased of the late Robert Sparrow, Esq.; but a great part of the soil belongs to the Scott, Peirson, Leman, Farr, Barne, Atkinson, and a few other families. *Shadingfield Hall*, a large white brick mansion, with well-wooded grounds, is the seat of Thomas Charles Scott, Esq., and was long the residence of the Cuddon family, who sold it in the latter part of last century. The *Church* (St. John) has a lofty tower, and near it is a small parsonage house, and 7½ acres of glebe. The benefice is a discharged rectory, valued in K.B. at £12, and now having a yearly modus of £303. 5s. in lieu of tithes. Lord Braybrooke is patron, and the Rev. C. T. Scott, B.A., incumbent. The latter supports a school for 30 poor children.

Bradley Benj. blacksmith
Chapman Edward, joiner
Chipperfield James, tailor
Coleby Joseph, shoemkr. (*Post Office.*
  Letters desp. ½ past 6 evening)
Cottingham Lionel, gent
Lewis John, hoop & hurdle maker
Nunn James, schoolmaster
Peirson Charles, corn miller
Peirson John Bliss, gent

Scott Rev Chas. Thos. B.A. rector; and Thomas Chas. Esq. *Shadingfield Hall*

FARMERS.

Atmare Samuel || Balls Stephen
Clarke William, Church farm
Clutten Wm. || Sadd John
Oswald Robert, jun. *White House*
Sadd Thos. *West End House*
Scarff Wm. *South House*

SHIPMEADOW, a scattered village in the vale of the river Waveney, 3 miles E. of Bungay and W. of Beccles, has in its parish about 800 acres of land, and had 265 inhabitants in 1841, including 133 inmates in the *Wangford Union Workhouse*, which is situated here, as noticed at page 411. R. A. Suckling, Esq., is lord of the manor, but part of the soil belongs to several smaller proprietors. The copyholds are subject to arbitrary fines. The *Hall*, a small neat house occupied by the curate, is the property of the Misses Draper. The *Church* (St. Bartholomew) stands on an eminence overlooking the vale, and has a thatched nave and short tower. The living is a discharged rectory, valued in K.B. at £10, and in 1835 at £214. The patronage is in certain Trustees, and the Rev. J. C. Badeley, L.L.B., of Halesworth, is the incumbent. Here are about 28 acres of glebe, but no parsonage house. The tithes were commuted in 1839 for a yearly modus of £220. The poor have a yearly rent-charge of 10s., left by Francis Wormall, in 1709.

Balls Thos. governor, Union House
Barber Jonathan, joiner
Cherry Thomas, shoemaker
Crickmer Mrs Isabella
Cullum Charles, shopkeeper
Herschell Rev Jno.Fras.curate,*Hall*

Mills Phœbe, shopkeeper
West Wm. shopkeeper
  FARMERS. (* *are Owners.*)
*Derry James || *Haughton George
Jex John || Johnson Samuel
Salter Wm.||*Tiptod Wm. *beerhouse*

SOTTERLEY parish, 4½ miles S.S.E. of Beccles, and 7 miles N.E. of Halesworth, has its houses mostly scattered round the margin of an extensive park, and contains 223 souls, and 1593A. 3R. 5P. of land. The Earl of Gosford and T. C. Scott, Esq., each own a farm here, and all the rest belongs, with the manor, to Frederick Barne, Esq., of SOTTERLEY HALL, a large and handsome mansion, in a richly wooded and finely undulated *Park*, comprising 489A. 1R. It has re-

cently been embellished with an elegant portico of the Corinthian order, and was formerly the seat of the *Players,* who held the manor as early as the reign of Edward II., and one of whom was created a baronet in 1623, but the title is now extinct. The *Church* (St. Margaret) stands in the park, near the hall, embowered in trees. It has a lofty embattled tower, and contains several ancient monuments of the Player family. The living is a discharged rectory, valued in K.B. at £10, and now having a good residence, about 34 acres of glebe, and a yearly modus of £290. 18s. 11d., awarded in 1840 in lieu of tithes. Frederick Barne, Esq., is patron, and the Rev. G. F. Barlow, M.A., incumbent. In 1616, *Thomas Jollye* left a yearly rent-charge of £6, out of the manor of Benacre, for the poor of Sotterley, who have also an *allotment* of 5A., awarded at the enclosure, and now let for £6. 10s. a year. Two tenements, called the *Town House,* are occupied rent-free by poor families. The *School* was built in 1840, at the expense of the rector.

Barne Fredk. Esq., *Sotterley Hall* and *Dunwich*
Barne Mrs Mary, *Sotterley Hall*
Bowater Major General Sir Edward G. C. H. equerry to Prince Albert, *Sotterley Hall*
Benns Wm. corn miller
Briggs Chester, blacksmith
Briggs Jonas, vict. *Board*
Doddington Wm. wheelwright

Raven Eliz. schoolmistress
Warmoll Rev Sayer Stone, B.A. curate, Rectory
Watling Robert, land agent
West James, brewer and grocer

FARMERS.
Brunning James||Chenery George
Garrod Thos. || Mann Mary
Goodwin William

SOUTHELMHAM All Saints and St. Nicholas are two united parishes, 5 miles S. by W. of Bungay, the former containing 1150A., 224 inhabitants, and a village scattered near a *green* of 52A.; and the latter having about 500 acres, 90 inhabitants, and nineteen scattered houses. Wm. Adair, Esq., is lord of the manor, but part of the soil belongs to Dr. Crowfoot, Mr. G. Durrant, and several smaller proprietors. *St. Nicholas' Church* was in ruins more than two centuries ago, but a small portion of one of its walls is still standing. *All Saints Church* is an ancient structure, with a round tower and leaded roof. They are both discharged rectories, valued in K.B., the former at £6, and the latter at £8, but they have long been consolidated, and have now about 32 acres of glebe, and a yearly modus of £274 in lieu of tithes. Wm. Adair, Esq. is patron, and the Rev. George Sandby, of Flixton, is the incumbent. The two parishes have two cottages and 1A. 2R. of land, let for £9. 11s. 6d. a year, and vested with the churchwardens for the reparation of the church. The Deanery of South-elmham comprises the seven adjoining parishes of Southelmham, and the two parishes of Flixton and Homersfield. The Trust Estates belonging jointly to these *nine parishes,* have been vested from an early period in trust, that the rents and profits should be applied for payment of the leet fee, or common fine of the leet of the *manor of Southelm-ham,* (which comprises the nine parishes,) and for repairing the highways, bridges, &c., in the seven Southelmhams. The estates consist of a farm of 27A. in Aldborough and Wortwell, Norfolk, let for £46 a year; and 18 acres of land in Flixton and Southelmham St. Margaret, let for £20 a year. Since 1814, the trustees have, out of these

rents, divided £11. 11s. yearly amongst the poor of the nine parishes. The Bishops of Norwich had anciently a *Palace* at Southelmham, as well as at Northelmham, in Norfolk, and other places. In the 12th and 13th century, they are said to have occasionally resided here in great splendour, especially Bishop Suffield, who made a valuation of all the ecclesiastical revenues in the kingdom, for Pope Innocent, and died in 1258.

Marked † are in St. Nicholas', and the others in Southelmham All Saints

Aldrich Elisha, wheelwright
Foyster David, vict. *White Lion*
Huke George, grocer and draper
†King James, blacksmith
†Smith Thomas, bricklayer
Thurston Robert, corn miller and shopkeeper
Wakeling Mrs Martha

FARMERS.

Blackburn John
Blackburn Geo.
†Button James
Chambers Edw.
Coates Jeremiah
†Danby James
Greenard James
Huke George

†Mathews Hanh.
Meers Wm.
†Newson Wm.
†Page Peter
Rackham Simon
Swallow John
Thurston Thos.
Whealey John

SOUTHELMHAM ST. CROSS, or ST. GEORGE, *alias* SAN-CROFT, is a pleasant scattered village, on an acclivity on the south side of the vale of the Waveney, 5 miles S.W. by S. of Bungay, and 4 miles E. of Harleston. Its parish contains 258 souls, and 1300A. 2R. 7P. of land. Wm. Adair, Esq., is lord of the manor, and owner of most of the soil. The manor of all the Southelmhams was formerly held by the Bishops of Norwich, and the ancient family of *Sancroft* had an estate here of their own name. The *Church* is a small ancient structure, with a tower and four bells, and was repaired and repewed in 1841, when a new gallery was erected, and 107 additional sittings provided, and appropriated to the free use of the poor. The organ was presented in the same year, by Mrs. Mary Chaston. The *rectory*, valued in K.B. at £10, is consolidated with that of Homersfield. (See page 438.) The tithes of the two parishes have been commuted for £363. 10s. per annum, and the incumbent has here 25A. of glebe, and a good *Rectory House*, built in 1834, at the cost of about £1000.

Bruce Rev. Courtenay Boyle, B.A. rector
Chenery Wm. wheelwright
Fountain Henry, blacksmith
Ling John, cow leech and vict. *Fox and Hounds*
Squires Wm. corn miller

FARMERS.

Borrett George ‖ Danby Daniel
Moore Joshua ‖ Robinson Isaac
Smith John ‖ Sadd Jacob
Shearing Wm. (and land surveyor)
Squires Noah

SOUTHELMHAM ST. JAMES, a straggling village, 6 miles N.W. by W. of Halesworth, and 7 miles S. by W. of Bungay, has in its parish 289 souls, and 1301A. 3R. 10P. of land, part of which, on the south side of the parish, is called *St. James's Park*, and was anciently a demesne of the Bishops of Norwich, who occasionally resided here in the 12th and 13th centuries, as already noticed. Wm. Adair, Esq., is lord of the manor, but part of the soil belongs to N. Mickle-thwaite, Esq., the Rev. John Lewis, and a few smaller owners. The *Church* is a small structure, with a tower and four bells, and the bene-fice is a discharged rectory, valued in K.B. at £8, and now having a yearly modus of £384. 10s., in lieu of tithes. Wm. Adair, Esq., is patron, and the Rev. Courtenay Boyle Bruce, B.A., incumbent. The

Town Estate, consisting of a house, outbuildings, and 15A. of land, let for £20 per annum, was left in 1679, by *Catherine Skaiffe,* for the repairs of the church and superstitious uses ; but after the Reformation, it was vested in trust to apply the rents so far as necessary in repairing the church, and to pay one-half of the overplus towards easing the poor rates, and apply the other half in such charitable uses as the trustees should think fit. The *Town House,* formerly the poorhouse, is let on lease for £2. 10s. a year, which is applied with the rent of the Town Estate.

Brown Joseph, tailor & shopkeeper	Butcher Henry	Lay James
Buxton John, blacksmith	Chambers James	More Richard
Burton James, vict. White Horse	Chambers Geo.	Page James
Mann Job, boot and shoe maker	Chambers Wm.	Thurston Wm.
Page Wm. wheelwright	Cunningham J.	(and farrier)
FARMERS. Buckingham Jas.	Hunting John	
Aldrich John		

SOUTHELMHAM ST. MARGARET, 5 miles S.S.W. of Bungay, is a village and parish, containing 181 souls, and 589 acres of land, now rated at the annual value of £1008. 5s. Part of it belongs to several small proprietors, and the remainder to Wm. Adair, Esq., the lord of the manor, and patron of the *Church,* which was repaired and repewed in 1838, and is a small structure, with a tower and five bells. The living is a discharged rectory, valued in K.B. at £6. 2s. 11d., and consolidated with that of Southelmham St. Peter, in the incumbency of the Rev. Adolphus Holmes, M.A. The tithes of this parish have been commuted for £136, and those of St. Peter's, for £145 per annum, exclusive of the yearly payment of £2. 2s. to the Dean and Chapter of Norwich, £1. 8s. to Wm. Adair, Esq., and 10s. 6d. to Lord Berners. The Town Estate comprises a house and about 50A. of land, let for £65 a year. It is partly freehold and partly copyhold, and has been vested in feoffees from an early period, in trust to apply the rents in discharging the fifteenths, tenths, taxes, and such other common charges of the parishioners, as the feoffees should think necessary. The income is mostly applied in the service of the church, and the remainder is added to the poor rates. A cottage, called the *Town House,* and a small piece of land adjoining, were appropriated at an early period for the reparation of the highways. They are let for 30s. a year, which is added to the rent of the Town Estate.

Chaston Mrs Mary, *Villa*	FARMERS. *(* are Owners.)*
Danby John, shoemaker	Aldrich Elijah ‖ *Danby John
Holmes Rev Adolphus, M.A. and	*Durrant George ‖ Gibborn Francis
F.L.S. *Rectory*	*Freeston George Anty. ‖ Larter —
Howe James, joiner & parish clerk	*Moore Thos. ‖ Moore John Last
Lushey George, shoemaker	Moore Robert ‖ Howlett K.
Woods Mr Stephen	

SOUTHELMHAM ST. MICHAEL, a small village and parish, 4 miles S. of Bungay, contains 145 souls, and 816A. of land. The Earl of Brittany and Richmond had lands here at the domesday survey. The *Church* is a small ancient structure, and the benefice is a vicarage, valued in K.B. at £4. 7s. 11d., and consolidated with the perpetual curacy of Rumburgh, in the patronage of the Rev. Lomb

Atthill, of Halesworth. (See page 387.) Wm. Adair, Esq., is lord of the manor, but part of the soil belongs to the Hurry, Johnson, and other families. The church and poor have had from an early period 2A. 1R. of land, now let for £3. 5s. a year.

Hammont Eliz. vict. Jolly Farmers
King Samuel, blacksmith
Mann Rachel, boot & shoe maker
Stenton Wm. corn miller
Thurston Jas. corn miller & shopr

FARMERS.
Blackburn George || Carley James
Chase Harry || Fisher Robert
Hammont Robt. || Owles Elizabeth

SOUTHELMHAM ST. PETER, a small parish, on an eminence, 3 miles S. of Bungay, contains only 91 souls, and 576A. 2R. of land, now estimated at the yearly value of £926. The *Hall* is an ancient building, occupied by a farmer. William Adair, Esq., is lord of the manor, owner of the greater part of the soil, and patron of the *Church*, a small structure with a tower and three bells. The rectory, valued in K.B. at £8, is consolidated with that of Southelmham St. Margaret, in the incumbency of the Rev. A. Holmes, A.M., who has here 25A. of glebe. The poor parishioners have about £9. 10s. yearly from Henry Smith's Charity estate at Tolleshunt-Darcy, in Essex. *Directory:*—Horace Freeston, gent.; Robert Knights, shopkeeper and vict., *Hawk;* and James Barber, Joseph Brown, Wm. Brown, Robert Cunningham, and Humphrey Durrant, *farmers.*

WESTON, a parish of scattered houses, mostly in the vale of a rivulet, 2½ miles S. of Beccles, contains 211 souls, and 1550A. 2R. 28P. of strong loamy land. *Weston Hall,* a small structure, in the Elizabethan style, belongs to Frederick Barne, Esq., and is occupied by a farmer; but *Walpole Hall* is the ancient manor-house, and belongs to Thos. Farr, Esq., the lord of the manor, which is mostly freehold. The Earl of Gosford and the Rev. — Sheriffe, have each a farm in the parish. The *Church* (St. Peter) is a small thatched fabric, and the benefice is a discharged *rectory*, valued in K.B. at £13. 6s. 8d., and in 1835, at £260. The patronage is in the Crown, and the Rev. John Mitford is the incumbent, for whom the Rev. C. T. Scott, B.A., officiates.

Farr Frederick Wm. (brewer) *Walpole Hall* and *Beccles*
Foulger Jas. vict. Duke of Marlbro'
Howlett Samuel, jun. joiner
Newson Wm. corn miller
Sarbeth John, parish clerk
FARMERS.
Andrews John, *Hill House*
Ayers Phillis, *Church Farm*

Boon Edward, *North House*
Cole Philip, *Horse-Shoe Farm*
Crisp Thos. (bailiff,) *Hungry Hall*
Foulsham Jph. Simpson, *New House*
Godbold Wm. *Kiln Farm*
King Elizabeth, *Old Farm*
Meen James, *Weston Hall*
Read Maria, *Harmony Hall*
Stammers Stephen, *Kiln Cottage*

WILLINGHAM, a small village, 4 miles S. of Beccles, has in its parish 156 souls, and 890 acres of land, fertile and well-wooded. Frederick Barne, Esq., owns the greater part, and the remainder belongs chiefly to the Earl of Gosford (lord of the manor,) and G. Kilner and T. C. Scott, Esqrs. The *Church* (St. Mary) went to ruins more than two centuries ago, and only a small part of its west wall now remains. The *rectory*, valued in K.B. at £6. 13s. 4d., is consolidated with that of North Cove, and the church there serves both parishes, though distant three miles N.N.E. of Willingham. (See page 437.) *Direc-*

tory :—Mary Grint, vict., *Fox ;* Robert Hallifax, *blacksmith ;* Nathl. Mole, *wheelwright ;* Richard Raven, *joiner ;* and Saml. Bates, Robt. Eade, Cornelius Gibson, *(Hall,)* and David Mendham, *farmers.*

WORLINGHAM, a pleasant scattered village, on the south side of the vale of the Waveney, from 1¼ to 2 miles S.E. of Beccles, has in its parish 1660 acres of land, and 208 inhabitants; exclusive of *Worlingham Parva, or St. Peter,* a decayed parish, containing neither house nor church, and having only 114A. acres of land, which pays tithe to Worlingham, and poor rates, &c. to North Cove, as already noticed at page 436, and belongs to J. Cooper, Esq. The *Right Hon. Archibald Acheson,* EARL OF GOSFORD, is lord of the manor, and owner of nearly all the parish of Worlingham. His father, of the same name, was created *Earl of Gosford and Viscount Acheson, in Ireland,* in 1806. He succeeded his father in the following year, and in 1835, was raised to a peerage of the United Kingdom by the title of BARON WORLINGHAM, of Worlingham, in the county of Suffolk; having derived this and other estates, by marrying the daughter and heiress of the late Robert Sparrow, Esq., of *Worlingham Hall,* a large and handsome mansion, in an extensive and well-wooded park, formerly the seat of the Feltons, Playters, and Robinsons, the latter of whom sold it to the Sparrows, about the middle of last century. The Earl of Gosford is Lord-Lieutenant and Custos Rotulorum of the county of Armagh, and resides generally at Cosford Castle, Ireland. His only son, VICOUNT ACHESON (born 1806,) resides at Worlingham Hall, and is one of the Parliamentary representatives of the county of Armagh, and married a daughter of the Earl of Meath. *Worlingham Church (All Saints)* is a neat structure, with a lofty embattled tower, and contains an elegant monument by Chantrey, in memory of the late General Sparrow and his son. The benefice is a rectory, with Worlinham Parva annexed to it, and is valued in K.B. at £12. It has a neat Rectory House, and 47A. of glebe ; and the tithes have recently been commuted for yearly moduses, viz., £303 for Worlingham, and £32 for Worlingham Parva, which had a church dedicated to *St. Peter,* but no vestiges of it are now extant. The patronage is in the Crown, and the Rev. Dd. Hillcoat Leighton, M.A., is the incumbent. On the farm occupied by Mr. Rackham, is a venerable *Oak,* in the hollow trunk of which a shoemaker, for several years, followed his occupation. The *Town Estate,* the original acquisition of which is unknown, consists of the Guildhall, let for £5; a house, blacksmith's shop, and 3A. 21P. of land, let for £10; 9½A. of land, let for £10. 10s. 6d.; and 2A. in Ellough, let for £3 per annum. The rents are applied in paying the leet fee of the parish, in repairing the church, in apprenticing poor children, and in other charitable and public uses.

Right Hon. EARL of GOSFORD, *Worlingham Hall,* (and Gosford Castle, *Ireland*)
Right Hon. Archibald, VISCOUNT ACHESON, M.P. *Worlingham Hl*
Hewson Wm. gamekeeper
Howes John, blacksmith
Leighton Rev David Hillcoat, M.A. *Rectory*

Mills James, wheelwright
Read Henry, Esq. land agent
Snell Walter, hoop & hurdle maker
Sutton George, jun. shoemaker
Wyatt Thomas, shopkeeper

FARMERS.

Foreman Daniel || Hanby Wm.
Read Henry, jun. || Sutton George
Rackham Thomas

HOXNE HUNDRED

Is in the Eastern Division of Suffolk, in the *Deanery of Hoxne, Arch deaconry of Suffolk*, and *Diocese of Norwich*. lt has two detached parishes (Carlton and Kelsale) in Blything Union, and its other 24 parishes form the *Hoxne Union*, and constitute a fertile district, averaging about nine miles in length and breadth; bounded, on the north, by the river *Waveney*, which separates it from Norfolk; on the east, by Wangford and Blything Hundreds; on the south, by Plomegate, Loes, and Thredling Hundreds; and on the west, by Hartismere Hundred. It is watered by several rivulets, flowing northward to the Waveney; and on its southern side are the sources of the river *Alde*, (see page 155,) and near Laxfield the chief source of the *Blythe*. (See p.371.) It has generally a strong loamy soil, well cultivated, and rising in picturesque undulations, but subsiding in a champaign tract, in the vale of the Waveney. It has only one small market town, (Stradbroke,) but those of Framlingham, Saxmundham, Eye, and Harleston, are near its borders; and it has within its limits several large villages. The following enumeration of its 26 *parishes* shews their territorial extent, the annual value of their lands and buildings, as assessed to the property tax in 1815, and their population in 1801 and 1841 :—

PARISHES.	Acrs.	Rent £.	Populatn. 1801.	1841.	PARISHES.	Acres.	Rental £.	Population. 1801.	1841.
Athelington ..	488	711	70	111	Metfield	2160	3001	600	702
Badingham ..	3200	5252	607	864	Monk Soham ..	1569	2072	329	404
Bedfield	1269	1748	295	358	Saxstead	1202	1784	391	447
Bedingfield ..	1754	2062	252	336	Southolt	799	1077	211	211
Brundish ..	2077	2593	330	525	Stradbroke ..	3634	5283	1215	1637
*Carlton	548	805	108	133	Syleham......	1603	1951	257	399
†Denham	1260	1682	219	313	Tannington ..	1600	1949	202	252
Dennington ..	3262	5185	726	979	Weybread	2476	3268	662	771
Fressingfield..	4564	5788	1044	1456	Wilby	1844	2535	443	623
Horham	1434	2037	394	442	Wingfield	2443	3791	521	668
+Hoxne	4258	6345	972	1333	Withersdale ..	880	1268	115	184
*Kelsale	3047	4994	1020	1126	Worlingworth	2447	3220	653	786
Laxfield	3630	5383	1008	1172					
Mendhm.,§part	2200	4471	541	566	Total ..	55,648	80,255	13,185	16,798

* Carlton and Kelsale are detached members of Hoxne, and are in *Blything Union*, (see page 354,) and all the other 24 parishes are in Hoxne Union.

† Denham and Hoxne parishes have been added to the *Parliamentary Borough of Eye*. (See page 329.)

§ Mendham parish is partly in *Norfolk*, where it has 257 souls, and about 800 acres.

☞ CHIEF CONSTABLES.—Messrs. Alfred Read, of Syleham, and Joseph Bloomfield, of Laxfield.

HOXNE UNION, as already noticed, comprises 24 of the 26 parishes of Hoxne Hundred, and contains 15,800 inhabitants, of whom 257 are in the Norfolk part of Mendham parish. Its area is about 80 square miles, or 50,000 acres. The Union was formed by the New Poor Law Commissioners, in 1834, and its Workhouse, at Stradbroke, was erected during that and the following year, at the cost of about £10,000, and has room for 300 inmates, but has seldom half that number, and had only 120 in 1841, when the census was taken, and 86 in October 1843. The average annual expenditure of the 24 parishes, for the support of their poor, during the three

years preceding the formation of the Union was £19,930, but during the following year it did not exceed £12,000, including the great expense of migrating many pauper families to the manufacturing districts. The Commissioners, in their report, say this reduction has not been accomplished by causing the aged and infirm to suffer privation, but by carefully investigating the cases of the applicants for relief, detecting imposition, and gradually but firmly withdrawing all out-door relief from able-bodied paupers. Previous to the formation of the Union, there were usually, in the winter months, upwards of 800 labourers without employment, receiving out-door relief in the 24 parishes. During the first quarter after the opening of the workhouse, in January 1836, only 52 able-bodied persons accepted temporary relief within its walls. The expenditure of the Union, in 1838, was £7312, and in 1839, £8279. 4s. The Workhouse is a large cruciform brick building, admirably adapted for the most approved system of classification; and within the same enclosure, a *Fever Ward* has been built, at the cost of £600. Mr. W. L. B. Freuer, of Weyhread, is *Superintendent Registrar and Clerk to the Board of Guardians ;* to whom Sir E. Kerrison is *chairman,* and the Rev. W. B. Mack, *vice-chairman.* Mr. John Sims is the *auditor ;* and the relieving officers and district registrars are Mr. Thomas Thurston, for *Stradbroke District,* and Mr. Wm. Bloss, of Brundish, for *Dennington District.* The Rev. J. Knevett, of Syleham, is *chaplain* to the Union ; and Mr. Wm. Coyte is *master,* and Mrs. Wright, *matron* of the Workhouse.

ATHELINGTON, or *Allington,* 4 miles S.E. of Eye, is a small parish of scattered houses, containing only 111 souls, and 487A. 36P. of fertile land, nearly all freehold, and belonging to Thomas Green, Esq., of Sidmouth. The *Hall* is a neat residence, occupied by a farmer. The *Church* (St. Peter) is a small ancient structure, with a tower and three bells. The benefice is a discharged rectory, valued in K.B. at £6. 14s. 2d., and now having a yearly modus of £150, and 13A. 3R. 12P. of glebe, of which 1A. is in Horham. The patronage is in the Crown, and the Rev. R. B. Exton, of Cretingham, is the incumbent. Before the Reformation, the prior and convent of Butley were patrons. The *Poor's Land,* 1A. 3R., is let for £1. 16s. a year, which is applied with the poor rates. Two boys from this parish are sent to the endowed free school at Worlingworth. The principal inhabitants are, Thomas Betts, maltster, and brick and tile maker ; David Pettit, carpenter ; and Fras. Baldry, *Grove ;* Robert Garrard, (*Athelington Hall,*) Richard Hawes, and Robert Hawes, *farmers.*

BADINGHAM, a widely scattered village, having several assemblages of houses, near the sources of the river Alde, from 3 to 4½ miles N.N.E. of Framlingham, has in its parish 864 souls, and 3200A. of fertile land, in the manors of *Badingham Hall, Colston Hall,* and *Oakenhill Hall.* Robert Sayer, Esq., is lord of the two former ; and the Rev. J. Baldry of the latter. They each hold General Courts Baron, at which the copyholders, and all owing suit and service, are summoned to attend ; but a great part of the parish is freehold. W. A. Stanford, Esq., has an estate and neat seat here, called the *White House ;* and the Horsey, Peckover, Moxon, Alderson, Scott, Webster, and several other families, have estates in the parish. *Badingham Hall,* now a farm-house, was long the seat of the Rous family ; and *Colston Hall* formerly belonged to the Holts. The *Church* (St. John) is an ancient structure, with a tower and five bells. The chancel was rebuilt of white brick, by the Rev. T. F. Chevallier, the late rector and patron, and con-

tains several monuments of the Rous family, and one bearing effigies of Wm. Cotton, his wife, and two children, erected about 1622. The font is antique, and richly carved. The *rectory*, valued in K.B. at £22. 16s. 8d., and in 1835 at £582, is in the patronage and incumbency of the Rev. Robert Gorton, who has a commodious rectory-house, with beautiful pleasure grounds, which he has much improved during the last few years. The Primitive Methodists have a small chapel in the parish. In 1715, *Elizabeth Rous* left £52 to provide for a weekly distribution of bread among the poor; and in 1735, *Dorothy Rous* left £150 for the same purpose. These legacies were laid out in the purchase of about 10A. of land, called Oldway Pieces, in Framlingham, now let for £24 a year. The churchwardens distribute 8s. 6d. worth of bread every Sunday, and the remainder of the rent is divided among the poor at Whitsuntide. A house, occupied rent-free by poor parishioners, was purchased in 1801, with £60 given for charitable and public uses.

Baker J. vict. *Bowling green*
Beales Charles, tailor
Bishop Joseph, beer house
Cook Joshua, shoemaker
Dale Michael, wheelwright
Day George, bricklayer
Etheredge Wm. carpenter
Fleming Hannah, beer house
Gissing Robert, shoemaker
Gorton Rev. Robert, *Rectory*
Ingate George, plumber, glazier, and grocer
Kell Saml. wheelwt. & machine maker
Kemp Henry, bricklayer
Kemp Henry, grocer
Newson Francis B. miller
Pooley Jph. grocer &vict. *White Horse*
Read Joseph, parish clerk *(aged 90)*
Rowe Jonathan, schoolr. and grocer
Smith John, carpenter

Stanford Wingfield Alexander, Esq. *White House*
Welton John, blacksmith
Welton Richd. grocer and blacksmith

FARMERS.
(* *are Owners.*)
Ashford Thomas
Baker John
Barham John
Barham Wm. (& cattle dealer)
Bird Wm.
Blomfield Joseph
Brown Wm.
Capon & Girling
Carley Richard
Chandler Samuel
*Doggett Jerh.
Eagle John
Everson Emanl.
Field Alfred

*Girling John (& miller,) *Colston Hall*
Goddard James
Grinling Edgar
*Lancheter Saml.
Mann Samuel
Moore Hy. *Red House*
Moore Hy. *Hall*
Pooley Joseph
Roper Osborn
Stanford John
Stofer Samuel
Symonds Joseph
Welton Robert

BEDFIELD, a straggling village, 4 miles W.N.W. of Framlingham and E.N.E. of Debenham, has in its parish 358 souls, and 1268A. 3R. 14P. of land. The *manor* and *advowson* formerly belonged to Eye Priory, and were granted, in the 36th of Henry VIII., to Sir Jno. Rous. They now belong to the Earl of Stradbroke, but the Hall estate is the property of Lord Henniker; and F. G. Doughty, W. Cupper, and W. Creasy, Esqrs., own farms here. The copyholds are subject to arbitrary fines. The *Church* (St. Nicholas) is an ancient structure, with a tower, containing five bells. The benefice is a discharged rectory, valued in K.B. at £14, and now having a yearly modus of £383, awarded, in 1842, in lieu of tithes, and including £8 on the glebe. The Rev. H. W. R. Birch, of Southwold, is the incumbent, and the Rev. A. H. Groom, jun., curate. Two houses, occupied rent-free by poor persons, and a barn and 39A. of land, let for £56 a year, are vested in trust for the relief of poor parishioners, but the original acquisition of the property is unknown. The rent is dis-

tributed by the churchwardens in coals and clothing. In the parish is an open *green* of 48 acres.

Bacon Wm. corn miller
Ellett Robert, carpenter
Freuer Rev Edward, B.A.
Jannings James, wheelwright
Nesling Robert, vict. Dog
Stannard John, blacksmith
Stannard Wm. beer house
Wright Simon, blacksmith

FARMERS.
(* *are Owners.*)
Aldous Wm. Bedfield Hall
Bolton Lewis
Creasy John, Bull's Hall
*Cupper Wm.

*Freuer Mrs Sar.
Jarvis Robert
*Ling Francis
Pepper Wm.
Runacles Wm.
Walpole Wm.
Warner Wm.

BEDINGFIELD, a scattered village, near the source of a rivulet, 4 miles S.S.E. of Eye and N. by E. of Debenham, has in its parish 336 souls, and 1753A. 1R. 7P. of fertile and well-wooded land, in the *manors* of Bedingfield and Bucks green. Sir H. R. P. Bedingfeld, Bart., is lord of the former, and H. D. Hemsworth, Esq., of the latter; but the soil belongs chiefly to John James Bedingfeld, Esq., Lord Henniker, J. Freeman, Esq., and the Shulver, Percy, and a few other families. The Bedingfelds, of Norfolk, took their name from the parish, and were formerly seated here. The manor was held by Snape Priory, and was granted first to Cardinal Wolsey, and afterwards to Thomas Duke of Norfolk, and in the 7th of Edward VI., to Thomas and George Golding. It passed soon after to the Bedingfelds, who were seated at *Flemings Hall,* an old moated house, now occupied by a farmer. *Bedingfield Hall,* the property of Lord Henniker, is another ancient farm-house, still encompassed by a large moat, which was cleansed in 1821, and had a drawbridge till a few years ago. The *Church* (St. Mary) is an ancient fabric, and the benefice is a discharged rectory, valued in K.B. at £8, and now having a yearly modus of £400. 10s., awarded in 1839; about 3A. of glebe, and a neat Rectory House, in the Elizabethan style. J. J. Bedingfeld, Esq., is patron, and the Rev. James Bedingfeld, B.A., of Debenham, incumbent. The *Town Estate* consists of 23A. 1R. 30P. of land in Debenham and Kenton, let for £35 a year; and it has been held in trust from an early period, for the general benefit of the parish, the payment of fifteens, &c. It is under the management of the churchwardens, with the consent of the trustees and parishioners. The rent is applied in paying the expenses incidental to the offices of churchwarden and constable. In 1547, *Stephen Pake* left 4½A. of land, called Dentoms, for the relief of the poor, and it is now let for £10 a year. In 1673, *Philip Bedingfeld,* in satisfaction of £50 left by his uncle Anthony, devised a yearly rent-charge of £3 for the relief of the poor, out of his estate here, still belonging to his family. This annuity is distributed at Christmas.

Attwood Rev Wm. Hamilton, B.A. curate, *Rectory*
Cracknell Syer, corn miller
Gostling James, blacksmith
Moore Wm. vict. *Lion*
Peck Joseph, wheelwright
FARMERS.
Colthorp Charles, *Church Farm*

Colthorp Mary, *Plash Farm*
Edwards James ‖ Freeman George
Edwards John, *Flemings Hall*
Johnson John, *Bedingfield Hall*
Pulham Charles
Punchard James ‖ Read John
Shulver James ‖ Shulver Mary

BRUNDISH, a widely scattered village, near the source of the river Alde, from 4 to 5 miles N. by W. of Framlingham, has in its parish 525 souls, and 2077A. 1R. 1P. of freehold land, belonging to various owners, each having the manorial rights of their own estates. Here was a famous *Chantry*, founded by Sir John Payshall, rector of Caston, and one of the executors of Robert de Ufford, Earl of Suffolk, in the 7th of Richard II., for six chaplains to pray for the soul of the said Earl. It was valued, at the dissolution, at £13. 0s. 7½d. per ann., and granted to Richard Fulmerston. On its site is a commodious mansion, occupied by Thomas Gooch, Esq., who holds the *Chantry Farm* of the Crown. *Brundish Hall*, another neat residence, embowered in lofty trees, is the seat and property of J. N. Gooch, Esq. *Brundish Lodge*, formerly the seat of the Calverts, is now the residence and property of James Chaston, Esq. The Earl of Stradbroke, Sir R. S. Adair, and the Wardley, Gwilt, Fisher, and some other families, have estates in the parish. *Sir Frederick Adair Roe*, formerly residing here, was created a baronet in 1836. The *Church* (St. Lawrence) is a neat structure, with a tower and three bells, and contains several ancient monuments. Mrs. Mary Waller, of Hollesley, is impropriator of the rectorial tithes, and the benefice is a curacy, consolidated with the vicarage of Tannington. The great tithes of Brundish have been commuted for £470, and the vicarial tithes for £105 per annum. The glebe is 9A. 19P. The parishioners have a house for the residence of poor families, and 4A. of land, let for £6 a year, which is applied with the church rates.

Bloss Wm. registrar, relieving officer, agent to the Farmers' Insnce. Office, & sec. to E. Suffolk Agrl. Protective Socty. *Brundish House*
Branch Benjamin, wheelwright
Chaston Jas. Esq. *Brundish Lodge*
Cook Nathan, carpenter and grocer
Fenn John, cooper
Gooch John N. Esq. *Brundish Hall*
Gooch Thos. Esq. *Chantry Farm*
Green Thomas, miller and grocer
Howes Henry, blacksmith
Kemp Wm. blacksmith

Spurling George, carpenter
Spurling James, vict. *Crown*
Vincent George, corn miller
FARMERS.—(* *are Owners.*)
Baker Benjamin || Bloss Wm.
Button Dorothy (St Edmund's)
Button James || Brady John
*Chandler Edmund, senior
*Chandler Edmund, junior
*Coote Edward || Coote Wm.
Garrard Robert || Girling Anthony
Lenney Simon || Martin Susan

CARLTON, a scattered village, one mile N. of Saxmundham, has in its parish 133 souls, and 548 acres of rich loamy land, forming, with Kelsale, a detached member of Hoxne Hundred. A *Chantry* was founded here, about 1330, by John Framlingham, rector of Kelsale, for three chaplains to pray for the soul of Alice, the first wife of Thos. de Brotherton, Earl of Norfolk. It was granted, in the 36th of Henry VIII., to Wm. Honing. Edward Fuller, Esq., owns most of the soil, and is lord of the manor; but his seat, *Carlton Hall*, a large handsome mansion, in an extensive and well-wooded park, is now occupied by the Hon. Charles Andrew Vanneck, eldest son of Lord Huntingfield. (See page 378.) There is another handsome seat here, called *The Rookery*, belonging to Mr. Fuller, and occupied by Robt. Knipe Cobbold, Esq. The Rev. E. Hollond, Colonel Dove, and Mr. S. Howlett, have small estates here, and part of the parish is copyhold of the

manor of Kelsale. The *Church* (St. Peter) is a small fabric of flint and stone, with a brick tower, and stands on an acclivity near the Hall, embowered in wood. The living is a rectory, valued in K.B. at £3. 11s. 0½d., and consolidated with that of Kelsale, which see. The sum of £40, left for the poor of Carlton by *Stephen Alcock*, and £5, given by Wm. Feveryare, were laid out, in 1659, in the purchase of 2½A. of land at Sweffling, vested in trust to pay 20s. yearly for a sermon, and to distribute the remainder of the rents among poor parishioners, on the 5th of November. In 1716, *Stephen Eade* charged his land here (now belonging to Mr. Fuller,) with the payment of £4 yearly, as follows :—50s. for distributions of bread, 20s. for a distribution of money among the poor, and 10s. for a sermon. The *Town Estate* has been held from a remote period for the reparation of the church and the payment of other parochial charges, and consists of a farm of 36A. 2R. 10P., let for £55 a year. About 11A. of it is freehold, and the remainder is copyhold, in the manors of Carlton, Kelsale, and Benhall.

Vanneck Hon. Charles Andrew, *Carlton Hall*
Cobbold Robt. Knipe, Esq. *Rookery*
Fuller Edward, Esq. *(abroad)*
Backhouse John, farmer
Barber James, farmer
Brady Wm. farmer, Park Farm

Chandler Edward, gardener
Clarke Elizabeth, beer house keeper
Clarke Wm. farmer
Crane Wm. gamekeeper
Kerridge George, bricklayer
Lowe George, thatcher

DENHAM, a scattered village and parish, 3 miles E. of Eye, contains 313 souls, and 1259A. 1R. 38P. of land. It has been added to the Parliamentary borough of Eye, as noticed at page 329. It is in Sir E. Kerrison's manor of Denham with Flemworth, and he owns all the soil except about 200A. belonging Messrs. Hazard and Howlett ; and is also impropriator of the rectory, and patron of the *vicarage*, which is valued in K.B. at £5. 0s. 10d., and united with Hoxne. The *Church* (St. John) is a small neat fabric, and the *Hall*, now a farm house, is an ancient moated residence.

Baylis John, beerhouse
Canler Thos. F. corn miller
Cook James, beerhouse
Stannard Robert, blacksmith
Wright George, wheelwright
FARMERS.
Canler Wm. || Clutten James

Cracknell Bj. exors. of, College farm
Dallestone Mark || Hall James
Kerry Thos. Rodwell, *Denham Hall*
Moore John || Moore Rachel
Mutimer Eliza || Precious Allen
Whatling Robert
Wilson John || Wilson Robert

DENNINGTON, a large pleasant village, in the vale and near the source of the river Alde, 2½ miles N. of Framlingham, has in its parish 979 souls, and 362A. 1R. 32P. of fertile land, rising in bold undulations, and well cultivated. It was anciently the seat and manor of the Phelip family, of which *Sir John Phelip* served with great distinction under Henry V. in France. His successor, Sir William, acquired the title of Lord Bardolph by marrying the heiress of the Bardolf or Bardolph family. In the 5th of Henry VI., he founded a *chantry* in the church here, for two priests to celebrate mass daily at the altar of St. Margaret, for the welfare of himself and wife during their lives, and for their souls after their decease. By his will, he bequeathed his body to be buried with those of his ancestors before the said altar, and directed a thou-

sands masses to be said for his soul, by the monks of Norfolk and Suffolk, as soon as possible after his death, allowing them four-pence for each mass. He also gave to the church, a certain mass-book, called a gradual, a silver censer, and a legand ; but by a codicil ordered his body to be interred in the church-yard. He left only one daughter, who carried her estates in marriage to John, Viscount Beaumont. The Hall, (now a farm house,) the manor, and a great part of the soil, belong to the *Earl of Stradbroke*, the present head of the ancient *family of Rous*, who were formerly seated here, as noticed at page 402. Leland says, " All the Rouses that be in Suffolk come, as far as I can learn, out of the house of Rous of Dennington," where " divers of them lie in the church under flat stones." Mr. Thos. Capon, Lord Huntingfield, the Earl of Gosford, Thos. Green, Esq., D. Alexander, Esq., and several smaller owners, have estates in the parish, and the copyholds are subject to arbitrary fines. Roman and other coins and antiquities have been found here at various periods. The *Church* (St. Mary) is a large antique fabric, with a tower and five bells. It formerly had two *chantries*, one at the altar of St. Margaret, noticed above, and valued at the dissolution at £26. 4s. 7d., and the other at the altar of St. Mary, valued at £9. 0s. 7½d. Both of them were granted to Richard Fulmerstone. The benefice is a *rectory*, valued in K.B. at £36. 3s. 6d., and in 1835 at £841 ; but now having a yearly modus of £1092, awarded in 1838 in lieu of tithes ; 152A. 2R. 27P. of glebe ; and a large and handsome *Rectory House*. Edward Daniel Alston, Esq., is patron ; and the *Hon. and Rev. Frederick Hotham, A.M.*, (a younger son of the late Lord Hotham, and a prebendary of Rochester,) is incumbent.

The property, called the TOWN LANDS, is under the management of the churchwardens, and is let for £55 a year, of which £14 is applied in repairing the church, and the remainder, after providing for repairs of the buildings, and other incidental expenses, is distributed in coals and money among the poor. This trust estate comprises 11A 21P. of land, called *Cannons and Cobalds*, and settled before the year 1483, for the reparation of the church, or such other public uses as the trustees should think expedient ; a house, cottage, and 14A. 2R. 2P. of land, called *Goldings and Sowgates*, conveyed to trustees by the *Rev. Edward Green*, in 1606, for the relief of the poor ; and the Queen's Head public-house, with out-buildings, yards, and gardens, purchased in 1694, with some old benefactions, and other money belonging to the poor, and vested in trust for the payment of taxes, &c., levied on the town-lands, and the relief of poor parishioners, except 20s. to be paid yearly towards the expenses of the inhabitants at their Easter meeting. *Nathan Wright, Esq.*, left £102, which was laid out in 1657, in the purchase of 7A. 11P. of land, at Kettleburgh, now let for £9. 9s. a year, and the rent is applied in apprenticing poor children. The sum of £50 given by Robert and Nathan Wright, was laid out in the purchase of 3A. 34P. of copyhold land in Framlingham, now let for £9 a year, which is applied in a supply of coals to the poor at reduced prices. In 1688, *John Paul* left one-third of the rent of his lands in Cratfield to the poor of Dennington, who now derive from this charity £7. 15s. a year, which is applied in distributing 1s. worth of bread weekly, and in a yearly distribution of coats to six poor men. A yearly rent-charge of 10s. has been paid to the churchwardens since 1764, in lieu of the rent of the *Bell Acre Land*, which is undefinably intermixed with land, called Wells' Tenement. The poor of Dennington have also 5s. worth of bread four times a year from *Mills' Charity*, (see Framlingham ;) and ten poor families not receiving

parochial relief have divided among them £5 yearly from Warner's Charity. *(See Boyton.)*

DENNINGTON.

Hotham Hon. and Rev. Frederick, A.M. *Rectory*
Barnes, Thomas, gentleman
Baldry Isaac, shoemaker
Braham Benj. grocer and draper
Capon Geo. land agt. *Dennington Hl*
Capon Thomas, corn miller
Cook Edward, vict. Queen's Head
Dunthorpe Edw. grocer and draper
Durrant Samuel, corn miller
Easter George, wheelwright
Gissing John, shoemaker
Godbold Thomas, beerhouse
Hammond Bloomfield,grocer&darper
Heffer Robert, butcher
Hayward James, blacksmith
Miller Rev Stanley, incumbent of Tannington and Brundish
Mumford Richard, tailor
Sharman John, tailor
Smith George, tailor
Storey Samuel, shoemaker
Studd Wm. carpenter
Wright Joseph, blacksmith

FARMERS. (* *are owners.*)
Capon John || Capon Mary
*Capon Thomas, *Denninton Hall*
*Cook Daniel || Cook Edward, jun.
Fenton Chltte. || Sheldrick James
Snowling John || *Tungate Wm.
*Wells Jas. || Whitmore Rt. & Wm.

FRESSINGFIELD, a large and well-built village, on a pleasant acclivity, 3½ miles N.N.E. of Stradbroke,4½ miles S. of Harleston, and 9 miles W. of Halesworth, has in its parish 1456 souls, 4564 acres of fertile land, the hamlets of *Chepenhall Green* and *Ufford Green*, from 1 to 2 miles S.E. of the village, and many scattered farm-houses, several of which are large ancient mansions, formerly the seats of the owners of the *four manors,* of which the following are the names and lords; viz., *Chepenhall,* Sir R. S. Adair; *Ufford Hall,* Lord Henniker, *Whittingham Hall,* Henry Newton Heale, Esq. ; and *Vales Hall,* Rev. Augustus Cooper. J. H. Frere, Esq., Rev. J. Arnold, G. Rant, Esq., Mrs. Scrivener, W. S. Holmes, Esq., and several smaller owners, have estates in the parish, which anciently belonged partly to the De la Pole family, and partly to Bury Abbey and Eye Priory, by gift of persons named Swartingstone and Thirketel. That excellent prelate, *Dr. Wm. Sancroft,* Archbishop of Canterbury, was born at Ufford Hall, in this parish, where he resided after he had sacrificed to conscientious scruples the high dignity which he enjoyed. He was interred in the churchyard, under a handsome monument, and perpetuated his name in his native parish, by several benefactions, as noticed below. The *Church* (St. Peter and St. Paul) is a large antique structure, with a tower and eight bells. The benefice is a vicarage, valued in K.B. at £17. 17s. 1d., and in 1835 at £597, with the rectory of Withersdale annexed to it. The Master and Fellows of Emanuel College, Cambridge, are patrons ; and the Rev. Thos. Allsopp is the incumbent, and has here a good residence. The tithes were commuted in 1840, for yearly moduses ; viz., those of Withersdale, for £330 ; the vicarial tithes of Fressingfield, for £399. 19s. ; and the rectorial tithes, for £919. 1s. H. N. Heale, Esq., of Hemel-Hempstead, in Hertfordshire, is impropriator of the latter. Here is a neat *Baptist Chapel,* erected in 1835, and having seat-room for 700 hearers. The present annual value of the parish is £7133. 15s. The FEOFFMENT ESTATE comprises three tenements, given by Edward Bohun, in the 13th of Henry VII., and occupied rent-free by poor families ; and the Guildhall, and 8A. 1R. 32P. of land, given by *Wm. Sancroft, Esq.,* in 1704, for the benefit of the parishioners. The upper room of the Guildhall is used as a school-

room, and the lower part of the building is a public-house, (the Fox and Goose,) and is let with the land for £25 per annum, which is applied in the service of the Church. In 1685, *Dr. Wm. Sancroft, Archbishop of Canterbury,* settled upon the Vicar of Fressingfield certain fee-farm rents, amounting to £52. 17s. 10½d. per annum, for increasing his maintenance, but subject to the yearly payment of £10 to the master of the school in the Guildhall, for teaching five poor boys to read, write, and cast accounts; and £6 to the parish clerk, for whose residence the same donor also gave a house, on the west side of the churchyard. In compliance with the desire of the same Archbishop, William Sancroft, Esq., in 1703, gave a yearly rent-charge of £3. 17s. out of the manor of Ufford Hall, for distribution among the poor of the parish. In 1722, the *Rev. John Shepheard* left £20, and directed the yearly interest thereof to be given in bibles and prayer-books, on Good Friday, to such boys as can give the best account of the catechism, responses, &c.

*Marked * are Land Owners; and † are at Chepenhall Green.*

Allsopp Rev Thos. and Rev George, *Vicarage*
Balls Thomas, cooper
Barkway Charles Edward, printer
Barkway Mary, dressmaker
Borrett Thomas, baker
Chandler John, gentleman
Clutten Mr Valentine
Cousins John George, saddler, &c.
Doddington Mary, straw hat maker
Dunnett John, plumber, glazier, &c.
Girdlestone Owen, whitesmith
Hart Emma, dressmaker
Rowe Lewis, hair cutter and glover
Spratt Rev George Denny (Baptist)
Thurston James, veterinary surgeon
Tibbenham John, gentleman

Academies.
Barkway Charles
Chappell Lucy Eliz. (boardg.)

Blacksmiths.
Aldous Henry
Aldous Hy. jun.
Barber James

Boot & Shoe Mkrs.
Borrett Daniel
Meen James

Bricklayers.
Borrett William
Chapman Lewis
Elliott William

Butchers.
Chase Martha
Mott Jas. (*baker*)

Corn Millers.
Chase Martha

† Sheen Samuel

FARMERS.
†Balls Charles
Barber James
Barkway Caroln.
Borrett Thomas
*Buskard Chas.
Chandler Henry, *Ufford Green*
*Chase Martha
*Clark Eliz.
†Clutten Edward
*Clutten Wm.
Cracknell Fras.
*Davy Wm.
*Dunnett John
Ebden Jas. *Whittingham Hall*
Ebden Wm. Jas. (*executors of*)

Woodlands
Fisher Jno. *Fressingfield Hall*
Goodchild ——
Green David
Green George
Green Thomas, *Ufford Hall*
Hart Roger
*Hines John
Hudson Henry
Lombard
Keable Sarah
Larter James
Larter John
Larter Thomas
Larter Thos. jun.
Leftley Saml. Js.
Lepingwell Wm.
Rix, (*Lodge*)
Meen Samuel
Mills Benjamin
Moore Wm.
Muskett Charles
†Parsley Wm.
Pearce Charles
Read Robert
Ringer Edward
Rope Hannah.
Chepen Hall
Rush Wm. (& timber mert)

*Seaman John
Websdale Henry
†*Whatling Geo.
*Wightman Jno.

Grocers & Drprs.
Bond Henry
Churchyard Rt., (& stationer)
Clutten Thomas, Selby

INNS.
Angel, Martha Chase
Fox and Goose, James Mott
Swan, Jonathan Rodwell

Beerhouses.
Chandler Martha
Etheridge James
Watson Lot

Joiners, &c.
Etheridge John, (and builder)
Vincent John

Tailors & Drprs.
Doddington John
Meen James

Wheelwrights.
Smith George
Welton Edmund

CARRIER.
Alfred Hart, to Ipswich, Mon. and Thu. ; & to Norwich, Tue. & Fri.

COACHES.
To Ipswich and Norwich, daily, from the Swan Inn

HORHAM, a scattered village, 5 miles S.E. of Eye, and 7½ miles N.N.E. of Debenham, has in its parish 442 souls, and 1433A. 2R. 11P. of land. Sir E. Kerrison, Bart., is lord of the manors called *Horham, Thorpe Hall-with-Wooten,* and *Horham Jernegans;* but a great part of the soil belongs to Thos. Green, Esq.; Alex. Denovan, Esq.; and the Crowe, Depper, Naylor, and several other families. Sir Herbert Jernegan, who died in 1239, had his seat here; but his son removed to Stonham, and the grandson of the latter to Somerleyton. The *Church* (St. Mary) is a neat ancient structure, with a large embattled tower, containing eight bells. The south porch has a handsome Norman arch, and the east window is richly decorated with stained glass, of which there are also some fragments in the other windows. The font is a much admired relic of antiquity; as also is the Parish Chest, which is entirely covered with iron plates and hoops. The *rectory,* valued in K.B. at £12. 7s. 1d., has a handsome and commodious residence, 23 acres of glebe, and a yearly modus of £452. 10s., awarded in 1838, in lieu of tithes. The Rev. Wm. Mack, of Metfield, is patron; and the Rev. Wm. B. Mack, B.A., incumbent. The *Baptists* have a small chapel here. The parish has had, from time immemorial, about 4 acres of land in Debenham, now let for £7 a year, which is applied by the overseers towards the support of the poor, and the repairs of the church. The following yearly *rent-charges* are distributed in bread among poor parishioners; viz., 10s., left by *Richmond Girling,* out of land at Strad- brook; 6s. 8d., left by the *Rev. John Clubbe,* in 1693; and 40s., left by *Lewis Hynton,* in 1706. The two latter are paid out of land in this parish, now or lately belonging to J. Goddard and U. Bolton.

Mack Rev Wm. Bumpstead, B.A., *Rectory*
Baldry Wm., vict. and wheelwright, Green Dragon
Cook Abel, shoemaker
Haward Robert, schoolmaster
Hawes Samuel, shopkeeper
Muddock John, vict., *Eight Bells*
Roe Samuel, corn miller
Rope John, carpenter and wheelwgt
Taylor George, grocer and draper
Thorndick John, blacksmith
Whatling James, shoemaker
Wretts Mr John
Wright Henry, blacksmith
FARMERS. *(Marked * are Owners.)*
* Alton Uriah || * Bolton Ziba
Creasy Lionel || Cossey Mary
Cunnell Joseph || * Greenard George
Jennings James || Jennings Wm.
*Pipe John
Plant Hy. agricultural machine mkr
Sheldrick Mary || Turner James

HOXNE is a large and well-built village, pleasantly situated on the south side of the river Waveney, near its confluence with the small river Dove, 3½ miles N.E. of Eye, 5 miles E.S.E. of Diss, and 6 miles S.W. of Harleston. Its parish has been added to the Parliamentary borough of Eye, and comprises 4257A. 2R. 11P. of fertile land, and en- creased its population from 972 souls, in 1801, to 1333, in 1841. It has a large old corn mill on the Waveney, which has recently been con- verted into a *flax mill and linen manufactory,* as also has another large mill at Syleham, about a mile and a half below. It has a *fair* for chapmen on December 1st, and had formerly a cattle fair on the same day, but it was removed to Harleston, in Norfolk, in 1780. It gives name to Hoxne Hundred and Union, but the workhouse for the latter is at Stradbroke. Hoxne, anciently denominated *Eglesdune,* is the place to which king Edmund fled, after his last unsuccessful en-

counter with the Danes, in 870, as noticed at page 607. "Tradition relates that in the hope of escaping his pursuers, he concealed himself under a bridge near the place, now called Gold Bridge, from the appearance of the gilt spurs which the king happened to wear, and which proved the means of discovering his retreat. A newly-married couple returning home in the evening, and seeing by moon light the reflection of the spurs in the water, betrayed him to the Danes. Indignant at their treachery, the king is said have pronounced a dreadful curse upon every couple who should afterwards pass over this bridge in their way to the church to be married." Such was the regard paid to this denunciation, that until the bridge was rebuilt about 15 years ago, most couples, going to the church to be married, never failed to avoid it, even if they were obliged to take a circuitous rout. Here also the remains of the unfortunate "king and martyr" were first interred. Over his grave was erected a chapel, composed of trees sawn dawn the middle, and fixed in the ground, with the interstices filled with mud or mortar, and a thatched roof. From this rude structure, the body of the reputed saint was removed, about 30 years afterwards, to its more splendid receptacle at Bury. (Vide page 605.) Some years afterwards, the chapel here was converted into a *cell* or *priory*, inhabited by seven or eight monks of the Benedictine order, governed by a prior, nominated by the prior of Norwich, and called the cell or chapel of the blessed St. Edmund king and martyr. In 1226, Thomas de Blundeville, bishop of Norwich, confirmed all revenues to God, and the chapel of St. Edmund, at Hoxne, which, at the dissolution, was valued at about £40 per ann. The Hall, manor, rectory, and advowson of the vicarage of Hoxne, belonged to the bishops of Norwich, who frequently resided here, till 1535, when they were given up by act of Parliament to Henry VIII., who granted them to Sir Robt. Southwell. They afterwards passed to the Maynard family, who erected on the site of the cell or priory, a neat mansion in the Italian style. Charles, the last Lord of Maynard who resided here, died in 1775, and the estate afterwards passed to the late Sir Thomas Maynard Hazlerigg, Bart., and from him to the late *M. Kerrison, Esq.*, who purchased the Oakley, Brome, and other estates in this neighbourhood, from the last Marquis Cornwallis, as already noticed at pages 325 and 339. His son, *Lieut.-General Sir Edward Kerrison, Bart.*, K.C.B., G.C.H., M.P., and colonel of the 14th Royal Dragoons, was born in 1774, and created a baronet in 1821. He resides at OAKLEY PARK, which comprises about 500 acres of land, more than half of which is on the western side of the small river Dove, in Oakley parish; but the mansion, formerly called *Hoxne Hall*, is on the eastern side of the valley, in Hoxne parish, and has been nearly rebuilt by the present worthy proprietor, from a design by Sidney Smirke, Esq. It is a spacious and elegant Grecian structure, and its principal apartments are of noble proportions, and finished with exquisite taste. A gallery 80 feet long is supported by eight Italian marble columns of unrivalled beauty. The Banqueting Hall is filled with fine statuary. The Saloon, Library, Dining Room, &c., contain many fine paintings, by Vandycke, Reubens, and other distinguished masters. The furniture is magnificent, and mostly in the style which prevailed in the age of Louis IV. The mansion stands on the western side of the park, nearly half a mile south of the village, overlooking the lovely valley of

the Dove, and surrounded by fine terraces and pleasure grounds, laid out in the Italian style, and ornamented by statuary of stone and marble. In 1842, a beautiful Gothic cross was erected on the park terrace, called St. Mary's Cross, to commemorate the gallant general's favourite charger, which carried him in the campaigns of Holland, the Peninsular War, and in the Battle of Waterloo.   The park is richly clothed with noble oaks, beech, and other trees, and that portion of it lying in Oakley parish was added to it by the present owner *Sir E. Kerrison, Bart.*, who represents the borough of Eye in Parliament, and is father-in-law of Lord Henniker and Viscount Mahon.   He is lord of the *manors* of Hoxne Hall and Priory, and owner of the greater part of the parish, and the remainder belongs to the Rt. Hon. J. H. Frere, of Malta; Mr. W. Richards, Mrs. Worth, Mrs. Leek, Mr. G. Seaman, and a few smaller owners.   THORPE HALL, 3 miles S.S.E. of the village, and many other scattered farm houses, are in Hoxne parish, as also is the small hamlet of HILTON, which is connected with it by a long narrow strip of the parish, and lies near Athelington, 5 miles S. of Hoxne village.   The CHURCH (St. Peter and St. Paul) is a handsome structure, consisting of a nave, chancel, north aisle, and a lofty tower, in which is a peal of five bells.   The benefice is a vicarage, with that of Denham annexed to it, valued in K.B. at £12. 3s. 6½d., and in 1835 at £450.   Sir E. Kerrison, Bart., is patron, and the Rev. John Hodgson, M.A., is the incumbent, and has a neat residence near the church. The great tithes of Hoxne parish were commuted, in 1843, for the following yearly payments—viz., £785 to Miss Doughty, of Ufford, the principal impropriator; £9. 16s. to the Rector of St. Helen's, Ipswich; and £5. 4s. to Sir E. Kerrison.   The two latter payments are from 58A. 1R. 35P., called *Pountney Land*, from its having been appropriated to the chapel of St. Edmund-a-Pountney, in Ipswich.   (See page 69.)   The *vicarial tithes* of Hoxne, were commuted at the same time for the yearly modus of £405.

Certain fee-farm rents, amounting to £5. 3s. 6d. per annum, have been paid for the use of Hoxne church from an early period, under the name of *Hallowmass Rents*.   The TOWN ESTATE is vested in trustees, and is copyhold of the manor of Hoxne Hall, but how it was acquired is unknown, except some cottages and about 4A. which were purchased by the parishioners.   It comprises about 50A. of land, five cottages, a barn, and a garden, let at rents amounting to about £82 a year, which is mostly expended in the service of the church, and partly in relieving the poor.   It is supposed to be charged with an annuity of 20s. left to the poor, in 1710, by John Hobart.   In 1734, THOMAS MAYNARD devised his real estate in Hoxne, to Charles Lord Maynard, upon trust that he should lay out £300 in erecting houses for a schoolmaster and schoolmistress to reside in, and that he should pay yearly out of the rents of the estate £40 to the master, and £10 to the mistress, for teaching freely all the boys and girls of the parish that should be sent to them, in reading, writing, and arithmetic, and the girls, also in needlework.   This devise was considered void under the statute of Mortmain, but Charles Lord Maynard erected *two dwellings and two school-rooms*, and conveyed them to trustees in 1742, together with a yearly rent-charge of £54 out of the manor of Hoxne Hall, to be paid as follows:—£40 to the schoolmaster; £10 to the mistress; and £4 for providing coals for the two schools.   About 30 boys and 20 girls are instructed as free scholars.

HOXNE DIRECTORY.

Kerrison Lieut Col. Sir Edward, Bart. K.C.B., G.C.H., and M.P. *Oakley Park*
Kerrison Edward Clarence, Esq. *Oakley Park*
Browning Edward, butcher
Barkway James, carpenter
Barkway Stephen, carpenter
Cracknell Thomas, agent to the London Assurance Company
Coleby Thomas, jun. linen manufacturer and spinner
Farron John, plumber, &c
Fisk Benjamin, bricklayer
Fisk John, beerhouse
Hodgson Rev John, M.A. *Vicarage*
Huggins Robert, bricklayer
Kent Wm. wheelwright
Moore John Lines, auctioneer and surveyor
Moore Robert, saddler
Payne John Page, surgeon
Scott Nathl. Esq *Reading green*
Sharman Henry, corn miller
Smithies Carlton, Esq. land steward to Sir E. Kerrison, *Oak farm*
Sowter Jonathan, saddler, &c
Stollery Wm. tailor
Academies.
Aldous My. *(free)* | Pearle Misses, (boarding)

Ward Herbert, *(free)*
Blacksmiths.
Freeston Isaac
Musk Lionel
Potter Hy. (beerhouse)
Wright Stephen
Boot & Shoe Mkrs.
Butcher Wm.
French James
Rayner and Warden
Smith Jonas
FARMERS.
Bayles Thomas, *Thorpe Hall*
Canler George
Clubb George
Clutten John
Wroots, *Red hs*
Colby James
Cracknell Geo *Fairstead*
Elvin George
Garrod Robert
Hall John
Harper James
Harris Richard
Huse Wm.
Lines Wm.

Marshall Robert, *Gissing farm*
Mutimer John
Palmer Robert
Pipe Benjamin, *Park farm*
Reed Alfred
Reed Hart
Rush Charles
Rush Chas. jun.
Rush John
Rush Robert
Smith Jonas
Wilson John, *Abbey farm*
GROCERS
And Drapers.
Coleby Thomas
Cracknell Phillis
Taylor John
Woods Wm. (and druggist, and agt. to Suffolk Fire office)
INNS.
Grapes, J. Pipe, & vety. surgeon
Red Lion, Alfred Kent
Swan, Wm. Huse

KELSALE, a large neat village, picturesquely situated on an acclivity in the vale of a small rivulet, 1½ mile N. of Saxmundham, encompassed by boldly rising hills, and having in its parish 1126 inhabitants, 3047 acres of fertile land, many scattered farm-houses, and the *hamlets* of East Green, North Green, Cullar Green, and part of Carlton Green, extending from 1 to 1½ mile north east and west of the church. The parish is now valued at the gross annual rental of £3726. 3s. 6d. John, Duke of Norfolk, obtained it in marriage with the heiress of the Mareschals, but being attainted for siding with the house of York against Henry Duke of Richmond, it was seized by the Crown, and given to John de Vere, Earl of Orford. In 1545, it was again in the Duke of Norfolk's family; and in the reign of James I., it was held by Sir Thomas Holland. Since the reign of Charles II., the manor has been held by the Bence family. Lieut.-Colonel Henry Bence Bence, of Thorington Hall, is now lord of the manor, but a great part of the soil belongs to many other proprietors, and a large portion is copyhold, subject to arbitrary fines. *Kelsale Lodge*, an old seat, 2¼ miles N. of Saxmundham, occupied by a farmer, is the property of Sir Charles Blois, Bart. *Kelsale House*, a neat mansion, more than a mile N. by W. of the village, is the seat and property of Stephen Capon, Esq., who owns several farms here. *Maple House*, 1 mile E. by S. of Kelsale, belongs to the Garrod family, but is occupied by John Lee Farr, Esq. S. Clouting, Esq., has a neat residence and a large

estate in the parish. The *Church* (St. Mary) is a neat structure, with a tower at its south-west angle, containing a peal of eight bells, two of which were added in 1831, when a new clock and organ were given by S. Clouting, Esq. Among the monuments is a fine altar tomb to one of the Russell family. The *rectory* of Kelsale, with that of Carlton consolidated with it, is valued in K.B. at £20. 0s. 5d., and has now 58A. 2R. 38P. of glebe, a commodious residence, and a yearly modus of £714. 10s., awarded in 1843 in lieu of tithes. Lieut. Col. Henry Bence Bence is patron, and the Rev. Lancelot Robert Brown, M.A., incumbent. The CHARITY ESTATE, belonging to Kelsale parish, comprises various free and copyhold lands, &c., which have been derived under various old grants and surrenders, the trusts and purposes of which can in few instances be distinctly ascertained. A general deed of trust, comprising all the freehold parts of the estate, was made in 1765, and the trusts thereby declared are, that the rents should be employed for the maintenance of a *Free School* for ten or more poor children to be instructed in reading, writing, accounts, and grammar learning ; for apprenticing poor children of the parish, or maintaining some of the grammar scholars at the University of Cambridge, as the trustees should think fit ; for repairing the church, and the surplus for the relief the poor and the general benefit of the parish. The copyhold parts of the estate are held of the manors of Kelsale, Middleton, and Westleton, and were given at an early period for the use of the town and the poor ; but in 1714, that part in the manor of Kelsale was surrendered upon trust to pay a yearly sum of not more than £30 to the *schoolmaster*, and to dispose of the remainder of the rents in repairing the church and the tenements on the estate, and in relieving the poor. New trustees were appointed in 1810, and the charity estate vested with them, consists of the Guildhall, (occupied by paupers,) a house, blacksmiths' shop, cottage, garden, a farm of 79A. 2R. 19P., a farm of 63A. 1R. 19P. called Palmers, 8A. of other land, and a *School*, with a house and garden for the master, all *in Kelsale ;* a house and 52A. 0R. 2P. of land, *in Middleton-with-Fordley ;* and a house and 4A. 3R. 37P. of land, *in Peasenhall.* The *yearly income* derived from these sources is about £341, which, after payment of land tax, quit rents, &c., is dispensed in repairing the church ; supporting the free school, supplying coals and clothing for the poor, paying weekly pensions to poor widows, and in apprenticing poor children. The *Schoolmaster* has a yearly salary of £50, for which, and the use of a house and garden, he teaches about 90 children (mostly boys) in reading, writing, English grammar, arithmetic, &c., and is also required to teach the scholars of a Sunday school. For weekly distributions of bread, the poor have 52s. a year out of land at Peasenhall, left by *Edmund Cutting*, in 1639, and the interest of £100, left by *Thomas Grimsby*, in 1754. They have also two annuities of 40s. each, left by Stephen Eade, (in 1716,) and *Sir Beversham Filmer*, and the rent of a house, left a few years ago by *Mr. Edmund Turner*, and now let for £6 a year. These are added to a yearly subscription of £20 or £30, and distributed in clothing and money among the most destitute parishioners. The school just noticed, is commonly called the *Grammar School.* Here is also a *Free School for poor girls*, supported by the rector, and attended by about 50 scholars.

KELSALE DIRECTORY.

Marked 1, are at East Green; 2, Carlton Green; 3, Cullar Green; 4, North Green; and the rest in Kelsale Village, or where specified.

Andrews Potter John, watch and clock maker
Bedwell James, cooper
Bedwell Wm. beerhouse keeper
Blaxtell Rachel, *Girls' Free School*
Brown Rev Lancelot Robert, M.A. rector of Kelsale, Carlton, and Saxmundham, *Rectory*
Capon Stephen, gent. *Kelsale House*
Clouting Samuel, Esq.
Cooper Geo. gent. || Blackett Mr Jn.
Dennison Wm. glove maker
Eade Maria, school || Dale Mrs Sus.
Farr John Lee, Esq. and Rev John, curate, *Maple House*
Garrard Mary Ann, dressmaker
Hurren Anty. butcher & cattle dlr
Oldring Benjamin, saddler
Rose Thomas, tailor
Sillett Lionel, vict. and butcher, *Six Bells*
Watling Henry, *Grammar schoolmr.*
3 Woolnough Wm. cattle dealer
Wright Mr Wm. || Wayling Mrs S.

Blacksmiths.
Elmey James
Fisher Joseph

Boot & Shoe Mkrs.
Briggs Thomas, (parish clerk)
Benns Philip
Dalby John
Drew Henry
Fisher James
Spalding John
Warne John

Woolnough Edw.
Woolnough Wm.
Bricklayers.
Fisk Wm.
Kerridge George
Brick Makers.
Collings John
2 Smith John
Corn Millers.
Harvey Wm.
Skoulding Thos.
FARMERS.
(* *are Owners*).
Ablett Thomas, *Slough Hall*
1 *Backhouse Bj.
Bird Samuel
Blake Andrew
Capon James
Capon Stpn. jun.
Church James
1 Cooper Edmd.
*Denny Sarah
Elworthy Sarah, *Clay Hill*
Fairs George
4 Goddard Geo.
1*Gooda Geo.
Hurren David
Hurren Davy
Jasper Marga-ret, *West End*
2 Jasper Wm.
Knight John, *Church Farm*

Lee Chas. *Fargt*
1 *Marshlain Jn.
Nichols Robert Briggs
2 *Noy Richard
1 Sewell Daniel
Skoulding Fran-cis, *Lodge*
1 *Smith David
Smith Wm.
1 Steptoe Nathl.
*Tidman Geo., sen. and jun., *Whim*
Whiting James
Wright Samuel, *Fargate*
1 Wright Wm. *East Green*
Wright Wm. *Gardeners, &c.*
Manning Thos.
2 Markham Jas.
Grocers & Dprs.
Backett Isc. jun.
3 Ife James
Sillett John
Tongate John, (and tailor)
Joiners, &c.
Bedwell Richard
Denny Thomas
3 Page John
Webb John

LAXFIELD, a large and pleasant village, near the source of the river Blythe, 6 miles N. by E. of Framlingham, and 4 miles E.S.E. of Stradbroke, has in its picturesque parish 1172 souls, and 3650 acres of land, including many scattered farm-houses, and the hamlet of *Banyards Green*. It is in three manors, one of which, with the rectory and advowson, was granted by Robert Mallet to Eye Priory, and was granted, in the 28th of Henry VIII., to Edmund Bedingfield. Another manor was granted, as part of the possessions of Leiston Abbey, to Charles Brandon, Duke of Suffolk, in the same year. John Wingfield, in Edward IV.'s reign, obtained a grant for a weekly *market* here, which was formerly much resorted to, and still the neighbouring farmers meet a number of buyers at the Royal Oak Inn, every Monday, for the purpose of selling corn by sample. Two large cattle and sheep *fairs* are held here annually, on May 12th and Oct. 25th. Lord Huntingfield is now lord of the manors of Laxfield and Laxfield Rectory, which comprise all the parish, except the small manor of *Stadhaugh*, which belongs to Smith's Charity, as afterwards noticed. A great part of the parish is copyhold, subject to arbitrary fines; and among the other principal proprietors are, the Earl of Gosford, Sir E. Kerrison,

Thos. Green, Esq., J. N. Gooch, Esq., and the Parnther, Lucas, Lewis, Butcher, Cooper, Groom, Bryant, Hiues, and a few other families. *John Noyes*, a shoemaker of Laxfield, after suffering imprisonment at Eye and Norwich, for his adherence to the reformed religion, was brought back to his native place, and burnt at the stake, on Sept. 22nd, 1557. *Wolfren Dowsing* took a conspicuous part in the affairs of the parish at the time of Noyes' martyrdom ; and from a brass inscription in the church, it appears his daughter married John Smyth, then seated at *Parkfield*, now a farm-house. The *Church* (All Saints) is a large and handsome structure, with an embattled tower, containing six bells, and crowned by four large and elegant pinnacles. Towards building the steeple, many legacies were left about the middle of the 15th century. The chancel was rebuilt of white brick about three years ago, when a new Vicarage House was erected of the same material. The benefice is a discharged vicarage, valued in K.B. at £9. 13s. 4d., and consolidated with that of Cratfield, as already noticed at page 363. Lord Huntingfield is impropriator of the rectorial tithes of Laxfield, which were commuted in 1841 for £617. 10s., and the vicarial tithes for £220 per annum. He is also patron of the vicarage, but has sold the next presentation to the Rev. E. Hollond, of Benhall Lodge. Here is about 13 acres of glebe, which, with the vicarage-house, is occupied by the curate. The Rev. J. L. Farrer, M.A., of Hackney, near London, is the incumbent. The *Baptists* have a place of worship here, and the parish has two *Free Schools*, and several valuable charities.

The PARISH AND CHARITY ESTATES are under the management of the churchwardens, and comprise the following property ; viz., the Town House and a cottage, occupied rent-free by poor parishioners ; a farm of 28A. 2R. 38P. in Wilby and Brundish, let for £39 a year, and vested for the use of the church and poor ; a house, barn, and 9A. 2R. 9P. of land in Weybread, let for £18s. 10s., and purchased by the parish, in 1629 ; four-ninths of a farm of 43A. 2R. 37P. in Carlton Colville, let for £72 a year, and bequeathed, in 1566, by John Page to this parish, and that of Dunwich, partly for the poor ; two-thirds of 14A. of land at Cratfield, let for £23. 7s. a year, and given, in 1688, by *John Paul* to this parish and Dennington, for the poor ; 3½A. of land in Laxfield, let for £6, and left by *John Smith*, in 1718, for a weekly distribution of bread ; and a yearly rent-charge of £2. 12s., given by *John Borrett*, to be distributed in bread, and now paid out of an estate here, belonging to Lord Huntingfield. The yearly income derived from the above property is about 160, and has usually been blended in one account with the church-rates ; but from £20 to £30 is distributed yearly among the poor in bread, coals, blankets, &c. In 1718, JOHN SMITH left his *manor of Stadhaugh*, in Laxfield, and all his freehold lands in this parish, to the churchwardens and overseers, in trust that they should apply the rents of the first year towards building a *School*, and afterwards pay £40 per annum to a schoolmaster, for teaching 20 poor boys of Laxfield to read, write, and cast accounts ; and £40 per annum towards putting out apprentice 8 of such 20 poor boys to some good handicraft trade, and dispose of the overplus rent in keeping the estate and premises in good condition, or, when not wanted for that purpose, in augmenting the apprentice-fees. The estate consists of a farm of 112A. 1R. 25P., let for £168 a year ; and the profits derived from the manor of Stadhaugh yield from £3 to £5 per annum. The schoolmaster teaches from 25 to 30 free scholars, and for instructing them he receives £2 per head per annum from the trustees who also pay yearly about £8 to a schoolmistress, for teaching 20 poor girls ; and £8 towards the support of a

Sunday-school. Apprentice-fees of from £15 to £20 are given with each apprentice, and the trustees also occasionally supply clothing to the boys during their apprenticeship. In 1721, ANN WARD charged her estates in Laxfield (now belonging to the Earl of Gosford) with the yearly payment of £30, in trust to pay £20 thereof to a schoolmaster for teaching ten poor boys to read and write ; and £10 to a schoolmistress for teaching 10 girls to read, knit, and sew. The latter are instructed with the girls sent to school under Smith's charity, and the former with other boys attending the *National School*, built by subscription, in 1843, at the cost of about £400, on land purchased for nearly £100. This school is in the Gothic style, and it is intended shortly to erect near it a house for the master. In 1455, *Wm. Garneys* charged his estates here with a yearly rent-charge of £2. 6s. 8d., but only 20s. a year has been paid since 1782, and distributed among the poor. This annuity (20s.) is paid out of Parkfield Farm, belonging to the Earl of Gosford.

LAXFIELD DIRECTORY.

Foot Post to Framlingham, every Tuesday, Thursday, and Saturday

Atkins George, butcher
Bultitude Mr John
Carley Robert Row, surgeon
Garrard Joseph, baker
Gibson John, bricklayer
Ives Charles, currier, &c
Lockwood Wm. bricklayer
Monkhouse Rev Henry, B.A. curate, *Vicarage*
Pepper Elias, plumber, glazier, &c
Pead Isaac, *postman*
Totman Rev James (Baptist)

Academies.
Barker Jno. (*National*)
Catchpole Righteous Wake
Goodwin John (& collector,) *Free School*
Jarman Sarah
Blacksmiths.
Aldred Peter
Felgate Henry
Boot & Shoe Mkrs.
Bickers Wm.
Cann Wm.
Copping Henry
Elnaugh Thomas
Morgan Wm.
Ransby Richard
Corn Millers.
Blomfield Robert

Newson Robert
FARMERS.
(* *are Owners.*)
Aldridge Wm.
Atkins James
*Bryant Samuel, *Banyards green*
Crouch John
Crouch Wm.
Dalliston Geo., *Rookery*
Fisher Garnham, *Manor House*
Fisk Sml. *Batleys*
Garrard Jonthn. *Boltons*
Goddard John, *Hill House*
*Gooch George, *Baldry's*
Gooderham John

*Grinling Jno. sen
Grinling Jno. jun.
Dowsing's
Grinling Wm. (& maltster)
*Hines Thomas
Huson John
Pead Joseph
Pepper James, *Banyards green*
*Phillimore John
*Randell John
Read James, sen
Read James, jun.
Parkfield Farm
Read Thomas, *Banyards green*
Read Thomas, *Stadhaugh*
Rounce John
Scace Robert
Scace Robt. jun
*Scoggings Isaac
Smith Jeptha, *Wood Farm*
Thurston Thos., *Blue House*
Webb Robert
Wells John
Wright Mary
GROCERS. (*Drapers, &c.*)
Brightley Adolphus (& printer and druggist)
Grinling William and Son

Backhouse Saml.
INNS.
General Wolfe, Robert Giles
King's Head, Thomas Hines
Royal Oak, Jas. Smith (and butcher)
White Horse, James Balls
Beer Houses.
Chaston Wm.
Lockwood Jph.
Phillimore John
Saddlers.
Read George
Wilson Edward
Tailors.
Cracknell John
Kemp Joseph
Masterson Wm.
Wheelwrights and Carpenters.
Bezent Henry
Chaston Wm.
Elmore Thomas
Flatman Henry
Hines Thomas
Pepper James, *Banyards green*

CARRIER.
Harman Valntn. to Halesworth, Tues. and Fri.

MENDHAM, a neat and pleasant village, on the south bank of the river Waveney, nearly 2 miles S.E. of Harleston, 8 miles S.W. of Bungay, and 10 miles W.N.W. of Halesworth, has in its parish 823

inhabitants, and upwards of 3000 acres of land, of which 267 souls and about 800 acres, are on the north side of the Waveney, in Earsham Hundred, Norfolk, forming a suburb to the town of Harleston, and including Dove House, several farms, and *Shotford Bridge*, which crosses the river by three arches, 1 mile S. of Harleston. Near the church, in the Suffolk part of the parish, was a *Cluniac Priory*, founded by William, son of Roger de Huntingfield, in the reign of King Stephen, dedicated to the Blessed Virgin, and subordinate to Castle-Acre Priory, in Norfolk. It was granted, at the dissolution, to Richard Freston and Ann, his wife, and some remains of it may still be traced in a farm-house standing on its site. The parish is in three manors, called *Walsham Hall* and *Mendham King's Hall and Priory*. Wm. Sancroft Holmes, Esq., of *Gaudy Hall*, on the Norfolk side of the river, is lord of the first, and Wm. Adair, Esq., of the two latter ; but a great part of the soil is copyhold, subject to arbitrary fines, and belongs to Thos. Thornhill, Esq., Geo. Rant, Esq., Lady Beresford, the trustees of Bethel Hospital, Norwich, the Chaston family, and several smaller proprietors. A large estate here, which had been forfeited by the attainder of John, Earl of Oxford, was granted to Sir Jno. Howard, in the 15th of Edward IV. An estate or manor here, called *Winchenden*, was granted to Richard and Wm. Freston, in the 1st of Edward VI., as parcel of the possessions of Holy Trinity Priory, Ipswich, which had a share of the rectory, by gift of Robert, the son of Angat. The *Church* (All Saints) is an ancient structure, with a tower and six bells ; and the benefice is a discharged vicarage, valued in K.B. at £5. 5s. 2d., and in 1835 at £122. The Rev. George Ayton Whitaker, M.A., of Knodishall, is patron an incumbent, and the Rev. S. M. Cole, of Redenhall, curate. The rectorial tithes of the greater part of the parish have been purchased by the landowners, and Wm. Adair, Esq., is impropriator of the remainder, which were commuted for a yearly modus of £270, in 1841, when the vicarial tithes were commuted for £52. 8s. per annum. Here is an Independent Chapel, belonging to a congregation formed in 1796, and also a place of worship for the Wesleyans. In 1725, Wm. Dennington charged his estate at Shimpling, in Norfolk, with the yearly payment of 12s., for a monthly distribution of 12 penny loaves among 12 poor people of Mendham ; and with 20s. a year for the sexton, for looking after his grave in the churchyard.

MENDHAM.
(See also *Harleston*.)

Buckingham Samuel, blacksmith
Bumpstead Edmund, grocer & draper
Flatman E. carpenter
Goodwin Philip, vict. *Red Lion*
Mobbs Samuel, musician, and repairer of musical instruments
Rant George, Esq.

FARMERS.—(* are *Owners.*)
(*Marked* 1, are in *Norfolk.*)

Beaumont George, *Middleton Hall*
Beaumont James || *Beaumont Mary

Brooks James || Broughton Wm.
1 Cooper Arthur || *Calver George
Denny John Harvey
Gedney Elizabeth, *Walsham Hall*
Girling Peter || Godbold Wm.
Johnson Chphr. Betts (& corn miller)
1 Kersey Edward, *Shotford Hall*
1 Mayhew Eli
Rackham Samuel || *Rant Edward
Riches Francis || Shearing Damarias
Riches Henry, *Thorp Hall*
Sadd John || 1 Sheppard Ann

METFIELD, a large village, 8 miles S.S.W. of Bungay, 5 miles E.S.E. of Harleston, and 7 miles W. by N. of Halesworth, has in its parish 702 souls, and 2160 acres of land, including a common of 41A. It is now estimated at the annual value of £3726. Capt. Chas. Rayley, R.N., of Southwold, is lord of the manor of Metfield, but part of the parish is in the manors of Mendham and Walsham Hall. Captain Rayley owns a large estate here, and *Metfield Hall*, a moated farmhouse, which was rebuilt about five years ago. The rest of the parish belongs to Wm. Adair, E. Freeston, N. Micklethwaite, and J. Burkett, Esqs. ; Lord Henniker, Lady Beresford, and several smaller proprietors. *Mrs. Susan Godbold*, who was born at Flixton, has resided here 80 years, and walked round the village on her 104th birth-day, Sept. 13th, 1843. The *Church* (St. John) is an ancient structure, with a tower and three bells, and the benefice is a *donative*, valued, in 1835, at £69. The parishioners are the patrons, and the Rev. Edwd. Thos. Alder, M.A., is the incumbent, and has about 45A. of glebe, and a neat Parsonage House, about a mile from the church; but he has only a yearly modus of £11, in lieu of small tithes. N. Micklethwaite, Esq., is impropriator of the great tithes, which were commuted, in 1843, for a yearly modus of £400. A rent-charge of 6s. 8d. per annum, left by *Thos. Maplehead*, in the 33rd of Henry VIII., for the repairs of the church, is paid out of land called Rooks. The poor have two yearly rent-charges of 20s. each, for distributions of bread, left by *Jas. Scarlet and Richd. Knapp*, in the 43rd of Elizabeth and 1762. *John Welton*, in 1556, left for the poor of this parish, about 3 acres of land in Withersdale; but it is undefinably mixed with other land now belonging to Mr. Burkett, and all that the poor derive from it is the yearly sum of 30s.

Alder Rev Edw. Thos., M.A. incbt
Aldis Richard, surgeon
Bryant Samuel, tailor and draper
Collins Robert, schoolmaster
Collins Samuel, bricklayer
Mack Rev Wm. Metfield Cottage
Poppy Charles, beer house
Poppy Edw. vict. Huntsman&Hounds
Squire Wm. beer house

Blacksmiths.
Feltham Elijah
Thain Josiah
Boot&ShoeMkrs.
Aldous Wm.
Easthaugh John
Freeston Wm.
Butchers.
Aldous Samuel
Moss John

Corn Millers.
Chase John
MeenJno.&Robt.
More Robert
Grocers & Drprs.
Catchpole Robt.
Edwards Benj.
Squire John
Wheelwrights and Carpenters.
Eastaugh John

Godbold George,
(and builder)
Self Wm.
Wiles Robert

FARMERS.
Baker Robert,
Rookery
Barrett Colin
Briton Thomas
Briton William,
(owner)
Carley John
Carley James
Chambers Edmd
Edwards Alfred
and James
Edwards Alfred,
senior

Fisher James
Gibbon
Godbold George
(and brick and
tile maker)
Godbold Samuel
Hatten Wm.
Keable John
Keable Wm.
More John, *Metfield Hall*
More Robert
More Wm.
Parsley James
Rumsey John
Squire John
Squire Nathan
Waters George

MONK-SOHAM, a village, near the source of a rivulet flowing to the Deben, 3 miles E. by N. of Debenham, and 6 miles W. by N. of Framlingham, has in its parish 404 souls, and 1569A. 2R. 33P. of land, rising in bold undulations, and now rated at the yearly value of £2243. It formerly belonged to the monks of Bury, by gift of Alfric, bishop of

East Anglia. It was granted, in the 37th of Henry VIII., to Anthony
Rous, and sold by Thos. Rous, in the 3rd of Elizabeth, to Lionel Tolmach. Anthony Deane, Esq., is now lord of the manors of *Monk-
Soham Hall*, and Blomvilles, or *Woodcroft Hall*, the latter of which
extends into the adjoining parishes. Both halls are ancient mansions,
now occupied by farmers. Most of the parish is copyhold, subject to
arbitrary fines, and a great part of it belongs to Lord Henniker, the
Earl of Gosford, and several smaller owners. The *Church* (St. Peter)
is a large, neat structure, with a tower and five bells; and the benefice
is a rectory, valued in K.B. at £19. 5s. 2½d., and now having 82A. 3R.
16P. of glebe, and a yearly modus of £445, awarded, in 1840, in lieu of
tithes. The Rev. John Hines Groome, of Earl Soham, is patron and
incumbent. The *Wesleyans* have a chapel here, in which other denominations preach occasionally. The *Town Lands* are vested in trustees for the relief and support of poor parishioners, and comprise a
messuage called the Guildhall, two cottages, and a garden, all occupied
rent-free by poor persons; 20A. 1R. 29P. of land, called *Towes*; 18A.
3R., called Fulgood; and 9A. 1R. 6P., in various parcels. The rents
amount to about £80 a year, and after paying for the repairs of the
tenements, &c., are applied in providing 2s. worth of bread for distribution every Sunday at the church, and in yearly distributions of coals
and money among the poor.

Bond John, shoemaker
Coleby Thomas, corn miller
Leggett Henry, blacksmith
Noble John, machine maker
Peck Samuel, gentleman
Pepper Mr Lionel
Rodwell Maria, schoolmistress
Symonds Mr Nathaniel

FARMERS.
(* *are Owners.*)
*Adams Joseph
Barker Charles
Blomfield Chtte.
Cook Wm.
Cracknell Thos.
*Creasy Wm.
Driver Thomas

Edwards George,
  *Monk - Soham
  Hall*
Gooderham Wm.
Grant James
*Hall John
Hammond Jas.
Hammond John,
  Woodcroft Hall
Pepper Thomas

SAXTEAD, a scattered village, 2 miles N.W. of Framlingham, has
in its parish 447 souls, and 1202 acres of land, including the hamlet of
Saxtead Green, 2 miles W. by N. of Framlingham. The soil is a
strong fertile loam, on a substratum of flint and gravel. The manor
and the greater part of the soil belong to Sir *Robert Hitcham's Charity*, of which the Master and Fellows of Pembroke Hall, Cambridge, are trustees, as already noticed at page 189. About one-
third of the parish is copyhold, subject to arbitrary fines, and the
custom of Borough English. The Mayes, Meadows, Webber, Waller,
Pallant, Holmes, and a few other families, have estates here. The
Church (All Saints) is a small ancient fabric, which had an embattled tower, but it fell down July 8th, 1805, and part of the materials
were used in building a vestry, with a small belfry over it. Thomas
de Brotherton, Earl of Norfolk, who died in 1307, is supposed to have
founded or rebuilt the church. The benefice is a rectory, consolidated
with Framlingham, as already noticed at page 192. The tithes of Saxtead have been commuted for a yearly modus of £340. In 1831, some
labourers in digging a drain behind the Volunteer Inn, found a human
skeleton, the remains of a wooden coffin, a two penny piece of Henry
Vl., and a *gold ring* weighing 2dwts. 21grs., and bearing emblems of

the Trinity, a figure of the Virgin Mary, and round the inside, the inscription, "*de bon cuer*," in Old English characters. The *Town Estate* comprises a cottage, occupied by paupers, and 15A. 2R. 5P. of copyhold land, let for £45 a year. It has been held from a remote period, in trust, for the reparation of the church, and the residue for the relief of the poor. New trustees were appointed in 1805.

Borrett Mr Joseph
Borrett Joseph, jun. blacksmith
Cattermole Wm. shoemkr & shopkpr
Cook Wm. shopkeeper
Davy Thos. wheelwright & par. clerk
Girling John, cooper
Herring John, shopkeeper
Holmes Geo. Wm. corn miller
Pipe Amelia, vict. *Volunteer Inn*
Reeve Benj. shoemaker
Thrower Jacob, shoemaker
Thrower Priscilla, beerhs. keeper
White Henry, tailor

FARMERS.
(* *are Owners*.)

Ashford Henry
*Holmes Robert
Holmes Robt jun.
James John
*Mayes George Bridges
*Meadows Wm.
*Smith Andrew
Taylor Penelope
*Webber Wm.
Webber Wm. jun.
Wightman Chas.
Wightman Clmnt
*Wightman John
Wightman Saml.

SOUTHOLT, a small village scattered round a green, 5 miles N.N.E. of Debenham, has in its parish 211 souls, and 798A. 2R. 12P. of land. Edgar Chenery, Esq., is lord of the manor, and owner of a great part of the soil; and the remainder belongs to C. Clark, Esq., Lord Henniker, Wm. Adair, Esq., Sir James Flower, and a few smaller proprietors. The *Church* (St. Margaret) is a curacy, consolidated with the rectory of Worlingworth; and the incumbent has here a yearly modus of £237. 10s., in lieu of the great and small tithes. The Rev. Edward Freuer is the officiating curate. The *Town Lands*, vested with 14 trustees, comprise a house and 28A. 3R. 37P. of land, in this parish, and 22A. 2R. 29P., in Bedfield. The rents amount to £61 per annum, and are applied towards the payment of the churchwardens' expenses, the support of a Sunday school, the purchase of clothing for the poor, and the reparation of some houses occupied by paupers. Mr. John Johnson, of Bedingfield Hall, owns a farm here, and occupies three others; and the resident *farmers* are, Lionel Creasy, Wm. Read, and Wm. Shulver; John Bloomfield, vict., *Plough;* and John Smith, *wheelwright*.

STRADBROKE, or STRADBROOK, a small market town, gives the title of Earl to the Rous family, as noticed at page 402, and is a polling-place for the Eastern Division of Suffolk, pleasantly situated near the source of a rivulet, 7 miles E.S.E. of Eye, 8½ miles N. by W. of Framlingham, and 9 miles N.E. by N. of Debenham. It consists chiefly of three streets, and its parish comprises 3654 acres of land, and had 1637 inhabitants in 1841, including 120 paupers in *Hoxne Union Workhouse*, which is situated here, as noticed at page 449. The estimated annual rental of the parish is £6963; and many of its houses and cottages are scattered round several small *greens*, which were enclosed about thirty years ago, viz., *Ashfield Green*, 1½ mile E.; *Barley Green*, half a mile S.E.; *Battlesey Green*, 1½ mile N.; *Pixey Green*, 1½ mile N.E.; and *Wootten Green*, half a mile S. of the town. Stradbrook had a *market* every *Friday*, pursuant to a charter of Henry III., but it was disused more than a century ago. Of late years, a corn market has been held here every *Tuesday*, by the neighbouring farmers and dealers, who attend on that day at the principal

inns alternately, to transact business. During spring and summer, here is a market every *Monday*, for the sale of calves. Here is also a *fair* for cattle and pedlery, on the third Monday in June, and a session or hiring for servants on the 2nd of October. *Petty Sessions* are held at the Queen's Head, every alternate Tuesday. The parish has sent about 200 pauper emigrants to America, since 1830. It is in two manors, viz., *Stradbrook-with-Stubcroft*, and *Shelton Hall-with-Wilby.* Sir E. Kerrison is lord of the former; and Thos. Geo. Corbett, Esq., of Elsham Hall, Lincolnshire, is lord of the latter. *Barley Hall* and *Hill Hall*, now farm houses, formerly gave name to two small manors, the writings of which were lost many years ago. Lord Henniker, Sir R. S. Adair, Lord Berners, and the Crabtree, Holmes, White, Jeffries, Arnold, Smith, Jolly, Greenard, Tomline, Green, Thurston, and other families, have estates in the parish. Shelton was anciently the seat of a family of its own name, and had a chapel, which was in use from 1306 till 1455. The De la Poles held Stradbrook in the 14th and 15th centuries, and it passed from them to the Howards. *Robert Copley*, or *Grossette*, the learned and pious bishop of Lincoln, who died in 1253, was born here, and was such an adversary to the unholy proceedings of Pope Innocent IV., that his holiness wished to have his body taken up and burnt. The *Church* (All Saints) is a large ancient fabric, with a tower and six bells, and was re-pewed and thoroughly repaired in 1823-4, when the late vicar, the Rev. Wm. White, who had an estate here, filled the east window with beautiful stained glass, at the cost of £100, and placed over the communion table a fine painting of Christ, taken down from the cross, which he purchased in Italy. The organ was purchased by subscription, in 1835, at the cost of £150. In the chancel are several neat monuments, and the ceiling is finely groined and carved. The benefice is a discharged vicarage, valued in K.B. at £9. 18s. 4½d., but it is endowed with the rectorial tithes, which were granted to the see of Ely in the 42nd of Elizabeth, and to the incumbent in the reign of Charles II., subject to the payment of a yearly rent of £8, and a fine of £60 every seven years to the Bishop of Ely, who is also patron of the vicarage. The Rev. J. T. Allen, M.A., is the incumbent. The tithes were commuted in 1840, for a yearly modus of £1050; and there is 6A. 1R. 2P. of glebe, and a neat vicarage house. The *Baptist Chapel* here was erected in 1814, and rebuilt in 1841; and attached to it is a school for poor girls. Here is a *Book Society*, established in 1836; an endowed school, and several other charities; and in 1843, the parishioners purchased a *fire-engine*, at the cost of £106.

The trust deeds relating to the CHARITY ESTATES of Stradbrook have been lost, and the estates and charities are now under the management of the churchwardens. The *Town House*, partly used for a *school*, and partly for the residence of the poor, was given by Michael Wentworth, Esq., the lord of the manor, in 1587. *Wm Grendling*, in 1599, left a farm of 76A. 2R. in Westhall, (now let for £90 a year,) to the feoffees of Stradbrook, in trust for the reparation of the church, the relief of the poor, the payment of five marks each per annum to the minister and schoolmaster, and five marks towards repairing the highways. In 1625, £200 *town stock* was laid out in the purchase of a house and 16A. of land at Syleham, now let for £24 a year, and vested in trust for binding poor children apprentice to trades, and for such other purposes as should be thought most fit for the

benefit of the parish. In 1667, *Giles Borrett* gave 3A. 2R. of land for the relief of the poor, and it is now let for £6. 8s. a year. The rents of the above estates are carried to one account, and the following sums are paid thereout yearly, viz. : —£3. 6s. 8d. to the vicar, £3. 6s. 8d. to the surveyor of the highways, and £5 to the schoolmaster ; and the remainder is applied mostly in defraying the expenses attending the office of churchwarden, and partly in apprentice fees, and the relief of the poor. The church was new pewed about 1823, and the expense was paid out of the rents of these charity estates. In 1698, *John Borrett* charged his lands here, called Lawrence Meadow and Wall hill, with a yearly rent charge of £5. 12s., to be applied as follows, viz. : 52s., for a weekly distribution of 1s. worth of bread among six poor parishioners ; and £3 to supply the said poor people with clothing, twenty days before Christmas. The poor parishioners have the following *yearly doles*, viz., 20s. left by Henry Austin, in 1661 ; 16s. left by Nicholas Borrett, in 1668 ; and 30s. left by Richmond Girling, in 1658. The *schoolmaster* teaches five poor children for £5 a year received from the above-named charity estates ; and 12 for the yearly sum of £15 paid to him by the *Trustees of Warner's Charity*, (see Boyton,) by whom and the parishioners he is appointed. The poor derive considerable benefit from 52A. of land, let to them in small *allotments*, at the rate of £2 per acre.

STRADBROKE.

Post-office, Queen's Head st : Henry Aldous, postmaster. Letters arrive at 9½ o'clock morning, and are despatched at a ¼ to five afternoon.

Those marked 1, *live in Chapel street*; 2, *New street*; 3, *Queen's Head street* ; 4, *Ashfield green*; 5, *Barley green*; 6, *Battlesey green* ; 7, *Pixey green* ; *and* 8, *at Wootten green.*

Allen Rev Jno. Taylor, M.A. *Vicarage*
3 Aldous Henry, postmaster
2 Bayne Rev Robert, (Baptist)
2 Berry James, post to Eye
Bradfield Charles, Esq
2 Brown John, post to Harleston
3 Burgess Henry, pork butcher
Bullard John, cryer & parish clerk
5 Catchpole James, linen weaver
4 Carpenter Mr John
1 Copping Wm. coal dealer
Coyte Wm. govnr. *Union House*
3 Gooch Jas. Wyard, surgeon
2 Holland Mr John
2 Houghton Geo. R. brazier & tinner
2 Lay Mr Robert Preston
2 Markwell John, basket maker
Mayhew George, surgeon
Mayhew Jonathan, bookbinder
Mayhew Wm. gardener
3 Meek Rev James, B.D. curate
3 Pryke George, cabinet maker
4 Pulham Mr. James
3 Roper Anthy. veterinary surgeon

5 Smith Stephen, artist
Thurston Thomas, relieving officer and registrar
2 Woodard Jonathan, seedsman
3 Worledge Isaac, cooper
Wright Mrs Mary Lorn, matron, *Union House*

FIRE AND LIFE OFFICES.
Clerical, Medical, & General (Life,) John Edward Bacon, agent
Essex & Suffolk Equitable, Anthony Gissing, agent
Norwich Union, Geo. Barnes, agt.
National Provident, John Edwd. Bacon, agent

Academies.
3 Chenery Matda.
Headdey James, Workhouse
Mayhew Henry
2 McKain Archb.
3 Millett Prcla.

Attorneys.
2 Bacon Jno. Edw.
Coyte Wm.

Bakers.
2 Burgess Hy.
3 Davy Jonth.
2 Parsons Chpr.

BANK.
East of England, Geo. Barnes, agent

Blacksmiths.
1 Beecroft Robt.
2 Borrett Robt.

1 Botwright Wm. (and gig mkr.)
1 Eastaugh Job
3 Mills John
3 Norman Robt.
4 Pendell Edw.
Boot & Shoe Mkrs.
3 Edwards Geo.
2 Holmes Saml.
1 Howes John
1 Newman Edw.
2 Mills Simon
3 Richards Chs.
2 Sillett James
1 Smith John
Bricklayers.
Betts Charles
6 Betts George
Chenery John
Butchers.
1 Rush Wm.

3 Woods Henry
Cattle Dealers.
8 Borrett Lionel
8 Chase Robert
5 Cook Elisha
8 Cook Thomas
1 Copping Jas.
2 Elvin John
Corn Millers.
1 Bayles Robert
3 Davy Jonth.
6 Farrow Robert
Druggists.
1 Robinson John
2 Smith Lot

FARMERS.
(* are Owners.)
Adams George,
Stradbroke Hall
Baldry John,
Low farm
4 Baldry Robert
3 Bayles Thos.
5 Bayles Widow
8 Bickers James
4*Blomfield Eliz.
8 Borrett John
2 Botwright John
5 Brook Wm.
4 Chandler Jas.
4 Chase Wm.
Clark Hy. North
lane

5 Cracknell John
Dale Wm.
3 Davy Jonth.
Elvin Thomas
Garrod Robert,
Hill Hall
4 Girling Abrm.
Gissing Anthy.
Gooch Jno. *Bat-
tlesey Hall*
4*Green Mattw.
4 Grinling Isaac
7 Harvey George
8 Jennings Saml.
4*Larter James
5 Laws John
4 Norman Jno. S.
6*Palmer Wm.
Pipe John, *Park
farm*
7 Pipe Philip
7 Pulham Chas.
5 Rumsey Philip
7 Rush Charles
1 Thurston John
Wharton Elijah,
Barley Hall
7*Wharton Jthn.
Wightman Chs.
Carsley Hall
8 Wilson Saml.
GROCERS
And Drapers.
3 Barnes George

2 Bryant Rt. Wby.
2 Manser Edw.
1 Robinson John
2 Smith Lot
Hair Dressers.
3 Aldous Henry
3 Beecroft Richd.
INNS.
3 Queen's Head,
Abrm. Girling
White Hart, Ja-.
Aldridge
Beerhouses.
3 Fisher Wm. (&
brewer)
3 Girling Wm. (&
linen mfr.)
2 Howes Joshua,
(& maltster)
2 Robinson Wm.
(& glover)
Joiners.
1 Brewster Edw.
2 Copping John
2 Howes Robert
Milliners.
1 Bayles Dinah
1 Bayles Hanh.
3 Girling Maria
CARRIERS.
1 Cole Joshua, to Ipswich and Norwich, Monday and Tuesday
3 Meen Wm. to Ipswich, Mon. and
Fri. and to Norwich, Tue. & Fri.

*Plumbers, Glazi-
ers, & Painters.*
3 Fisk Leonard
2 Holland Wm.
(and mason)
Saddlers.
3 Aldous Robert
3 Muttitt Wm.
1 Wilson Edw.
Surgeons.
3 Mayhew and
Gooch
Tailors.
2 Bayles Chas.
2 Lay Wm.
2 Wilson Wm.
Watchmakers.
3 Jacob Garrard
2 Percy James

*Wine, Spirit, and
Porter Mert.*
2 Thurston Frdk.
Wheelwrights.
1 Beecroft John
1 Forsdyke Caleb
4 Green Mattw.
2 Howes Robert
1 Pulham Chas.

SYLEHAM is a scattered village on the south side of the river Waveney, which separates it from Norfolk, 3½ miles N. by W. of Stradbroke, and 4 miles S.W. by S. of Harleston.   Its parish contains 399
souls, and 1603 acres of fertile and well-wooded land.   Here is a good
bridge which crosses the river to Brockdish; and also an extensive
water *corn mill*, the greater part of which was converted into a linen and
cotton manufactory, about five years ago.   The low *marshes*, near the
river, are now well-drained, but were formerly so swampy that the *ignis
fatui*, commonly called *Syleham lamps*, were frequently seen, and often
led benighted travellers astray. Thos. Dyson, Esq., is lord of the manor
of *Syleham Comitis*, which anciently belonged to the De la Poles, Earls
of Suffolk. Roger Bigod, Earl of Norfolk, had lands here, which he obtained in exchange from Bishop Herbert, and settled upon the monks
of Thetford, from whom the estate obtained the name of *Monks Hall.*
The parish is mostly leasehold, and partly free and copyhold.   The
principal proprietors are Henry Sept. Hyde Wollaston, Esq., T. Dyson, Esq., Rev. A. Cooper, Rev. W. Manning, Thos. Bridge, Esq.,
Sir E. Kerrison, and the Rt. Hon. J. H. Frere.   The *Church* (St.
Mary) is an antique fabric, with a round tower, containing three bells.
The living is a *perpetual curacy*, valued in 1835 at £88, and now in

the patronage and incumbency of the Rev. Augustus Cooper, B.A., of *Syleham Hall*, a large and handsome mansion, with well-wooded plea-sure grounds. About half the parish is tithe-free, and Miss Doughty, of Ufford, and George and Edward Press, Esqrs., of Norfolk, are im-propriators of the great tithes of the remainder, which were commuted for £245 per annum, in 1842.

Cooper Rev August.B.A. *Syleham Hl*
Crickmore James, beerhouse keeper
Dye George, corn miller
Godbold Charles, wheelwright
Knevett Rev John, incumbent of
  Needham, Norfolk
Richards Hy. vict. *White Horse*
Robinson Ray, corn miller
Rush Edward, blacksmith
Thurtell Caroline, boarding school

Warne Hy. and Sons, cotton & linen
  manufacturers, *Saleham mills*
FARMERS.
Denny George || Evans Wm.
Juby Charles || Rush James
Read Alfred, *Monks Hall*
Richards John, senior
Rush Robert, *(& cattle dealer)*
Stanford Daniel
Stannard Henry, *Red House*
Titlow John || Young Mark

TANNINGTON, a village scattered round an open *green* of nearly nine acres, 4 miles N.E. of Framlingham, 7 miles W.N.W. of Deben-ham, and 5 miles S. of Stradbroke, has in its parish 252 souls, and 1600A. 1R. 26P. of land, all freehold, belonging to the Earl of Strad-broke, (lord of the manor,) Lord Henniker, Sir Robert S. Adair, and the Meadows, Whitbread, Clutten, and a few other families. The Dades had formerley a seat and estate here. The *Church* (St. Ethel-bert) is an ancient structure, with a tower containing five bells. The living is a discharged vicarage, valued in K.B. at £12. 10s. 2½d., and in 1835 at £196, with the curacy of Brundish annexed to it. The Bishop of Rochester is patron, and the Rev. Stanley Miller, of Den-nington, is the incumbent. Mrs. Waller, of Wollesley, is impropria-tor of the great tithes, which were commuted for a yearly modus of £320. 18s. 6d. in 1841, when the vicarial tithes were commuted for £83. 10s. per annum. The glebe in Tannington is 4A. 1R. 30P. The *Town Estate* is vested in trustees for the repairs of the church, and the relief of the poor, and consists of 27A. 1R. 8P. in Tannington and Brun-dish, let for £34 a year; 18A. 3R. 26P., at Worlingworth, let for £22; and a cottage and garden given by Benj. Dunn, and let for £4 a year. Most of the rents are expended in repairing the church and support-ing the Sunday school, and the remainder is distributed in coals and clothing. Two cottages, given by one Godbold, are occupied by pau-pers. The trustees are Messrs. S. Ray, H. Sutton, R. Turner, and V. Clutten.

Butcher James, shopkeeper
Noble Syer, blacksmith
Pendell Wm. jun. carpenter
Pendell Wm. wheelwright
Whitmore John, shopkeeper & vict.
  Three Horse Shoes
    FARMERS. *(* are owners.)*
*Capon John || Carley John

Clutten Valentine || Oxborrow Jno.
Pattle Robert, Braizworth Hall
Ray Samuel || Ray William
Read John || Revett Charles
*Sutton Harsant, *Moat farm*
Turner Richard, *Long Lane farm*

WEYBREAD, a large and well-built village, pleasantly situated on the southern acclivity of the vale of the Waveney, 2½ miles S. by W. of Harleston, and 8¼ miles E.N.E. of Eye, has in its parish 771 souls,

and 2476A. 2R. 35P. of land, including roads, &c. Here are two large corn mills on the Waveney, and a little below is *Shotford Bridge,* crossing the river to Brockdish, in Norfolk. The parish is in four manors, of which the following are the names and lords :—*Weybread Hall,* Mr. Jennings Booty ; the Rectory Manor, John Cutts ; *Hoblins,* Wm. Cook, Esq. ; and *Instead,* Mr. Wm. Richards ; but the greater part of the soil belongs to other proprietors, the largest of whom are Mrs. Cotton, J. Clark, Esq., Wm. Adair, Esq., Isaac Wilcox, Esq, and Messrs. H. and T. Drane, Robert Tibbenham, T. G. Brown, J. Vipond, and Wm. Mann. *Instead Manor House,* anciently the seat of the Hobarts and Astleys, and now occupied by a farmer, has several of its apartments lined with fine old oak wainscot. The Inghams and Colemans were formerly lords of the manor of Weybread Hall, another fine old mansion, occupied by Mr. J. Booty, its present owner. Mrs. Cotton, J. Clark, Esq., and a few other owners, have neat houses here. The *Church* (St. Andrew) is an ancient structure, with a tower containing three bells. The living is a discharged vicarage, valued in K.B. at £4. 15s., and in 1835, at £102. The Rev. John Edge Daniel, M.A., is patron and incumbent, and has 9A. 1R. 11P. of glebe, and a neat white brick residence, built in 1838, at the cost of about £1000. In 1840, the *vicarial tithes* were commuted for £90. 6s., and the *rectorial tithes* for £543. 1s. per annum. The latter belong mostly to the Rev. Robert Ward, of Thetford, and the remainder to several of the principal land owners. The *Poor's Land,* 8A., is let for £12 a year, and the rent is distributed in clothing among the poor parishioners, who have also a yearly rent-charge of 25s., left by a *Mr. Harling,* in 1731, out of land called *Potter's Pits.* A large and handsome *National School,* in the Gothic style, was built here in 1842-'3, at the cost of about £500, and was publicly opened Sept. 14th, 1843, by a sermon and cold collation, attended by the principal parishioners and many of the neighbouring gentry and clergy. Towards the erection of this school, £100 was granted by Government, £65 by the National School Society, and £50 by the Diocesan Society ; and the remainder was raised by subscription.

Aldous Thomas, vict. *Heath House*
Algar Mrs Sarah
Clark John, Esq
Cotton Mrs Alice and Fredk., Esq
Crane Robert, acting overseer
Daniel Mrs Ann, *Weybread Cottage*
Daniel Rev Jno. Edge, M.A. *Vicarage*
Robertson Thomas, cattle dealer
Sims John, accountant and agent to
  H.N.Heale, Esq. *Weybread Lodge*
Ward Mr Stephen

Beer Houses.
Edwards Sampsn.
Gardner Daniel
Preston Richard
  Blacksmiths.
Barber James
Gostling George
Gostling John

Boot & Shoe Mkrs.
Gostling Jonthn.
Larter Wm.
  Corn Millers.
Bacon Robert (& merchant)
Drane Henry

FARMERS.
(* *are Owners.*)
Adams —
Bond John
Bond Robert
*Booty Jennings, *Weybread Hall*
Brown Thomas
  Goldsmith
Bryant Wm.
*Carpenter Thos.
*Drane Henry
*Drane Thos. jun
Elliott John
Feavearyear Jno.
*Fordham Thos.
Freuer Wm. Lord
  Basford, *Instead Hall*
Hart Henry

*Jeffes Leonard
  Palmer
*Matthews John
Millican Charles
Parker Ann
Pegg Wm.
Spurling Wm.,
  Green gate
Stevenson James
Vipond Jno. jun
Watling Henry
  Shopkeepers.
Gilley Wm.
Gooch Philip
Theobald Mary
  Wheelwrights.
Edwards Sampsn.
  (& beer house)
Kent Samuel

WILBY, a neat village, 1½ mile S.S.E. of Stradbroke, and 6 miles N.N.W. of Framlingham, has in its parish 623 souls, and 1846A. 1R. 20P. of land. T. G. Corbett, Esq., of Elsham Hall, Lincolnshire, is lord of the manor of *Wilby with-Shelton Hall*, but the soil belongs to various free and copyholders, the latter subject to arbitrary fines. The largest owners are the Rev. T. B. Stane (lord of a small manor called *Russells*,) Sir R. S. Adair, Lord Henniker, Sir E. Kerrison, and the Collinson, Burch, Green, Mack, Carlos, Smith, and Wilkinson families. The Nevils and Wingfields were anciently owners of most of the parish. The *Church* (St. Mary) is a handsome structure, with a tower and six bells; and in its windows are some beautiful fragments of stained glass. The south porch is highly enriched, and the architecture of the whole fabric is much admired. The benefice is a *rectory*, valued in K.B. at £26. 6s. 10½d., and now having 52A. 2R. 4P. of glebe, a neat and commodious thatched residence, and a yearly modus of £506, recently awarded in lieu of tithes. The Rev. H. Owen is patron, and the Rev. George Mingaye, M.A., incumbent. The present gross annual value of the parish is £3152. 11s. 6d. The *Town Estate*, comprising two houses and 48A. 2R. 2P. of land in Wilby, 2A. 1R. 16P. in Hoxne, and a house and 3A. 3R. 13P. in Bedfield, are let for £77. 10s. per annum, and are all freehold, except about 7½ acres. There is no account of the original settlement of these estates for charitable or public uses, except the property in Bedfield, which appears to have been given by persons named Wade and Borrett, in the reign of James I., for the relief of the poor of Wilby. The rents are received by the trustees, and paid over to the churchwardens, who expend the greater part in liquidating the charges incidental to their office, and pay the remainder to the overseers, who apply it with the poor rates. Mr. C. W. Notley, Mr. G. Seaman, and others, are the trustees.

Chase Wm. beerhouse keeper
Chenery Jonathan, shoemaker
Coleby Wm. bricklayer
Clutten Thos. Selby, grocer & draper
Cockerill Henry, blacksmith
Cook Wm. shoemaker
Copping George, carpenter
Feavearyear Edward, blacksmith
Fenton Charles, butcher
Godbold Thomas, wheelwright
Harvey Rev. Matthew (Baptist)
Newson Henry, blacksmith
Noble Alfred, wheelwright
Page William, tailor
Plant Henry, gig maker
Plant Jno. vict. & farrier, *Swan Inn*

FARMERS.
(* *are Owners.*)
Aldous James
Aldridge Jas. (& assessor)
Baldry James, *Wilby Hall*
Bayles Benjamin, *Wilby green*
Blomfield Thos.
Borrett John
Borrett Wm.
Bryant Benaiah
Cracknell Thos.
Darby Wm. *Red House*
Garrard Samuel, *Moat House*

Greenard Wm. *Church Farm*
Jeffries Robert
Lenny Robert
Notley Chas. Wilson, Russells grn
Plant Edmund
Rumsey Jemima
Scace Barnabas Gibson, *Wilby green*
*Seaman George, *Rookery*
Stearn Henry Bullock, *Foals green*
Wilson Robert

WINGFIELD, a pleasant but widely scattered village, with several neat houses, 4½ miles S. by W. of Harleston, and 7 miles E. by N. of Eye, has in its parish 668 souls, and 2442A. 3R. 38P. of fertile land, mostly free and partly copyhold, and lying in the manors of *Chickering-with-Wingfield*, of which Sir E. Kerrison is lord; and *Wingfield Castle and Hall*, of which Lord Berners is lord. The greater part of

the soil belongs to other proprietors, the largest of whom are Sir R. S. Adair, J. Wright, Esq., Rev. S. Cook, Mrs. L. Walker, Mrs. A. Cotton, Robt. Butcher, Esq., Rev. A. Cooper, Rev. J. Arnold, Mr. J. Dunnell, and Mr. S. Pallant. Early in the 14th century, *Richard de Brews* was seated at Wingfield, and he obtained a grant for a fair here in 1328. The *Wingfields*, who took their name from the parish, had a seat here from the time of the Norman Conquest till their removal to Letheringham and Easton, in the 14th century. (See pages 185 and 200.) In the reign of Henry VIII., there are said to have been eight or nine knights of the *Wingfield family*, all brothers, and two of them invested with the order of the Garter. By the marriage of Katherine, daughter and heiress of Sir John Wingfield, to Michael de la Pole, Earl of Suffolk, about the year 1370, the estates of the Wingfields, in this parish, passed to that nobleman, who obtained a license to convert the manor-house into a CASTLE, of which there are considerable remains, about half a mile north-west of the church, in rather a low situation. This castle appears to have been a large and handsome structure, without any earthworks for its defence, except the moat, which is crossed by an old draw-bridge. The south front, or principal entrance, is still tolerably entire, and the west side is now a farm-house, but was the property and residence of the late Robert Leman, D.D., who died here in 1779, and to whose family the estate descended from the *Catalynes*, who held it for several generations. At the south-east corner of the church-yard, a COLLEGE was erected about 1362, by the executors of Sir John Wingfield, for a provost or master and nine priests. It was dedicated to St. Mary, St. John the Baptist, and St. Andrew, and was valued at £50. 3s. 5½d. at the suppression, after which it was granted by Edward VI. to the Bishop of Norwich. It was a quadrangular building, and some remains of its western side may still be seen in the farm-house now standing on its site. The CHURCH (St. Andrew) which was appropriated to the College, is a large and handsome structure, with a tower and six bells. Being built of flint and stone of different colours, it exhibits a singular and beautiful appearance. The chancel is in a rich style of architecture, and contains some splendid monuments of the Wingfields and De la Poles. Upon one are recumbent effigies, in alabaster, of Michael De la Pole, Earl of Suffolk, and his countess, who died in the reign of Richard II. Upon another are figures of John, the second Duke of Suffolk, and his duchess, sister of Edward IV. The effigy of *Wm. De la Pole*, the first Duke of Suffolk, lies alone upon his altar-tomb, his duchess being buried at Ewelme, in Oxfordshire. He was created *Marquis of Suffolk*, in 1444, and *Duke of Suffolk* in 1448. Humphrey Duke of Gloucester was said to have been murdered by him at Bury, as noticed at page 625. This and other atrocities were signally avenged in his own untimely fate; his head being struck off on the gunwale of a boat, in Dover roads, and his body thrown into the sea; but being cast on shore, it was brought and buried here in 1450. The founder of the De la Pole family was a rich merchant of Ravenspurn, at the mouth of the Humber, who, after that port had been ingulphed in the ocean, in the early part of the 14th century, removed to Hull. His family rose from obscurity to the greatest splendour and the highest offices of state, but suffered many reverses of fortune. By the attainder of Ed-

mund De la Pole, Duke of Suffolk, in 1513, all his honours and estates were forfeited to the Crown, and the family became extinct in the male line by the death of his brother Richard, who fled to Italy, and was killed at the battle of Pavia, in 1525. On the north wall of the chancel is a tablet, in memory of the *Rev. John Bucker*, the late incumbent, who died in 1836, and was buried under the pavement of the *National School*, in the churchyard, which was built in 1834, at the cost of £200. The benefice is a *perpetual curacy*, valued in 1835, at £100, but lately augmented to the yearly value of £150 by the Bishop of Norwich, the patron and appropriator. The Rev. E. D. Bolton, M.A., is the incumbent. The tithes were commuted in 1840, for a yearly modus of £698. 3s. 3d., and are held on lease of the Bishop of Norwich by Lord Berners. About 200 acres of the *Castle and College farms* are tithe-free. The former belongs to Lord Berners, and the latter to Rt. Butcher, Esq. Under the summer house, in his garden, *Mr. Absalom Feavearyear*, a carpenter, of Wingfield, has constructed a vault, in which himself and son intend being buried. The Town Estate consists of a house and garden occupied by the poor, and a farm of 35A., called Trower's, let for £45 a year. It was bequeathed by *John Trower*, in 1513, and was conveyed to new trustees in 1816, upon trust that the rents should be yearly employed in the relief of poor parishioners, the reparation of the church, and in other public uses. For a distribution of bread, the poor have a yearly rent-charge of 25s., left by a *Mr. Harling*, in 1731, out of a farm now belonging to Mrs. Walker.

Barber Elijah, National schoolmr.
Bolton Rev. Edward Dykes, M.A. incumbent
Bryant John, corn miller
Burrows Maria, grocer
Crosskill Eliz. National schoolmrs.
Davis Wm. blacksmith
Feavearyear Absalom, carpenter
Feavearyear Fanny, beer house
Fisk David, tailor
Grice Christopher, wheelwright
Precious Wm. blacksmith
Robertson Jas. W. vict. King's Head
Spall John, beer house

FARMERS.
(* are Owners.)
Bolton James
Brighton Wm.
Park Farm
Bond Thomas

*Buskard Joshua
Crisp Jno. *Wingfield Hall*
Dunnell Rebecca
Farrow Bilby
Feavearyear Absalom
Filby Isaac
Gowing Hannah
Gowing Robert
Harris Samuel
Hart Jonathan jun. *Abbey*
Hill Wm.

Hart Jonathan,
Kerry Lionel, *Chickering Hl*
Masterson John
Mobbs Thomas
Page Wm.
Pretty George
Fenn, *College Farm*
Self Wm.
Sheldrake John
*Stead Wm.
Stevenson Joseph
Tacon J. *Castle*

WITHERSDALE parish comprises 184 souls, 880 acres of land, in several detached portions intermixed with other parishes ; and a pleasant village, which has a suburb in Mendham parish, and is distant 3 miles S.E. of Harleston, and 6½ miles N.E. by N. of Stradbroke. Captain Rayley is lord of the manor, but part of the soil belongs to Lord Henniker, Nathaniel Micklethwaite, Esq., Mr. Thomas Barham, George Rant, Esq., and a few smaller owners. The copyholds are subject to arbitrary fines. The *Church* (St. Mary) is a small antique fabric, with a wooden belfry, in which hang two bells. The living is a discharged rectory, valued in K.B. at £6. 16s. 8d., and consolidated with the vicarage of Fressingfield, as already noticed at page 456. The

tithes here were commuted in 1840 for a yearly modus of £330. The *Poor's Land*, 2 acres, let for £3 a year, was conveyed to new trustees in 1805, upon trust, to apply the rent for the benefit of the poor parishioners.

Aldous Samuel, butcher
Buckingham Samuel, wheelwright and blacksmith
Edwards Arthur, tailor
Feltham Elijah, blacksmith
Francis Wm. confectioner
Golding John, vict. *Cross*
Hill John, gentleman

Jackson James, shopkeeper
Poppy Thomas, tailor
Short Henry, boot and shoe maker
Wiles Samuel, wheelwright
Wilkinson John, blacksmith

FARMERS.

Barham Robert, (owner,) *Hall*
Chase Wm.||Cock Jerh.||Rush Robt.

WORLINGWORTH, a large and well-built village, pleasantly situated near the source of a rivulet, 5 miles N.W. of Framlingham, and 6½ miles N.E. by E. of Debenham, has in its parish 786 souls, and 2446A. 2R. 6P. of fertile land. The large *common* here was enclosed in 1831 '2, and from the luxuriant growth of the hedges and plantations, it can now scarcely be distinguished from the old enclosures. Lord Henniker is lord of the *manor*, and owner of about half of the soil; and the remainder belongs to Sir R. S. Adair, T. W. F. V. Wentworth, Esq., and several smaller owners. It is mostly free, and partly copyhold. *Worlingworth Hall*, now occupied by a farmer, was the seat of *Sir John Major, Bart.*, who died in 1781, and whose son-in-law, John Henniker, Esq., succeeded to his estates, and was created a peer by the title of *Lord Henniker*, as already noticed at page 346, with Thornham Magna, where the present Lord Henniker has his seat. Bishop Alfric gave the lordship of Worlingworth, and the advowson of the church, to Bury Abbey; and they were granted, in the 31st of Henry VIII., to Anthony Rous. The *Church* (St. Mary) is a neat fabric, with a tower and six bells, and contains a beautiful Gothic *font*, which once adorned the abbey church at Bury. The benefice is a *rectory*, valued in K.B. at £19. 12s. 3½d., and in 1835 at £777, with the curacy of Southolt annexed to it, but now having a yearly modus of £680, awarded in 1838, in lieu of tithes; 52A. 2R. 15P. of glebe, and a good residence. Lord Henniker is patron, and the Rev. Edward Barlee, incumbent.

The Town Lands, &c., of Worlingworth, were conveyed to new trustees in 1817, but the original acquisition of them is unknown. They comprise the Guildhall, and several cottages, occupied rent-free by poor persons; a farm of 49A. 2R. 15P., let for £65 a year; 7A., called Blakeland, let for £10 a year; a cottage and garden, let for £3; a house, barn, and 6A. 2R. of land at Tannington, let for £10; and a house, barn, and 37A. 2R. 24P. of land at Bedfield, let for £43 a year. The rents, amounting to £131 per annum, are applied in the payment of £4 to Baldry's charity; £5 to Godbold's charity; in the repairs of poor's tenements, the church, &c.; in the payment of the salaries of the parish clerk and sexton; in the payment of £7 a year for the support of a Sunday school; and in the distribution of coals among poor parishioners. In 1689, *John Baldry* bequeathed his copyhold messuage, and 20 acres of land, in Monk Soham, (now let for £28 a year,) to the feoffees of Worlingworth, in trust for the support of a *schoolmaster*, to teach poor children of this parish to read, write, and cast accounts; and his land, called *Gardiner's Pightle*, in Bedfield, he left for the relief of the poor. This pightle is let with the Town Lands, but the feoffees pay for it

£5 a year. In 1698, JOHN GODBOLD left £120 for increasing the salary of a schoolmaster to teach the youth of Worlingworth and Athelington in grammar, writing, and arithmetic; and he gave to the use of the poor of Worlingworth, two messuages and 1A. 2R. 5P. of land, (now let for £13 a year,) to the intent that the churchwardens should distribute two shillings' worth of bread every Sunday at the church, and disribute the remainder on Ash-Wednesday, except 10s. to be paid to the minister for a sermon on that day. The £120 was laid out in the purchase of 9A. 2R. 3P. of land, now let for £13 a year, which is paid to the schoolmaster, who has also, after payment of repairs, &c., the rent of the farm of 20A. at Monk Soham, noticed above. A new *School* was erected some years ago, out of the endowment, and a house for the master was built in 1825, at the expense of Mr. John Corby, of Woodbridge, on land belonging to the parish. The school is free to the children of all parishioners who occupy at rents not exceeding £10 a year, and also to two boys from Athelington.

WORLINGWORTH.

Barlee Rev Edward, *Rectory*
Blowers Charles, saddler
Cavalli Julius, vict. Swan
Clark James, grocer and draper, and wine and spirit merchant
Cornish James, blacksmith
Goymer Clarissa, schoolmistress
Ives James, boot and shoe maker
Moulton Henry, corn miller
Mullenger Thomas, *Free School*
Newson James, wheelwright
Preston Henry, auctioneer, land agt. and surveyor
Reeve Wm. blacksmith
Riches Thomas, carpenter
Southwell Elizabeth, ladies' boarding school, *Hall*

Wells Kitty, grocer and draper

FARMERS.
(* are Owners.)
*Adams Joseph, (and maltster)
Ashford Walter
Blomfield John
Clark James
Copping Joseph
Cornish Henry
*Emmerson Jas.
Freuer Alfred
Fulcher Henry
Garnham James
Moss James
Moulton Thomas
Pipe Benjamin

Plant Robert
*Plant Wm.
Preston Henry
Reeve John
*Reeve Wm.
Spurling John
Spurling William, *Hall*
Taylor Wm.
*Wardley Saml.
MAIL CART to Stradbroke, at 9 morng. and to Woodbridge 5 afternoon

---

MUTFORD & LOTHINGLAND.

Mutford and Lothingland Hundred is the north-eastern apex of Suffolk, averaging only about five miles in breadth, but extending fifteen miles from north to south, along the shore of the German Ocean, which bounds it on the east, except about three miles at the north end, where the river Yare, and the narrow peninsular strip of land on which Great Yarmouth is built, intervene between it and the sea. On the north, it is bounded by *Breydon Water*, the broad receptacle of the *Yare and Waveney;* and on the west, the latter river bounds it for about nine miles, and separates it from Norfolk. Its southern division, forming what was formerly called the *Half Hundred of Mutford*, is about five miles in length and breadth, and is bounded on the west by Wangford Hundred; on the south, by Blything Hundred; on the east, by the sea; and on the north, by *Oulton Broad* and *Lake Lothing*, through which the river Waveney anciently passed to the ocean, near Lowestoft. The northern division has another large lake, called *Fritton Decoy*, which abounds in *wild fowl*. It was called the *Half Hundred*

of Lothingland, till 1763, when it was *incorporated* with the Mutford Division, for the maintenance of the poor of their twenty-four parishes, as afterwards noticed.   LAKE LOTHING, extending nearly three miles in length, from east to west, comprises more than 200 acres, and is crossed near the centre by *Mutford Bridge;* and the western part of it is usually called *Oulton Broad.*   As noticed with Lowestoft, the *Norwich and Lowestoft Navigation,* opened in 1833, for sea-borne vessels, passes through this lake, so that Lothingland is now completely insulated, as it was in ancient times, when it was called the *Island of Lothingland,* and when the waters of the *Waveney* passed by the same route to the sea, near Lowestoft, instead of turning abruptly to the north, as they do now, above Oulton, in their route to the estuary of the Yare.   The whole Hundred is in the *Deanery of Lothingland,* and *Archdeaconry of Suffolk,* and has its *Workhouse* at Oulton, and an *Infirmary and Dispensary at Lowestoft,* its only market town and port, which is extensively engaged in the *herring fishery,* as also is *Pakefield* and many of its other villages on the coast.   It is one of the *geldable* Hundreds of Suffolk.   In judicial affairs, it forms part of the Beccles Division; and in the Parliamentary franchise, part of the Eastern Division of the county.   It was anciently a demesne of the Crown, and a great part of it was formerly held by the Fitz-Osbert and Jernegan families, but it now belongs to various owners, the largest of whom is Lord Sydney Godolphin Osborne, who is lord of most of the manors, having recently succeeded to the large possessions of the late *Rev. G. Anguish.* (Vide Somerleyton.)   The *soil* is in many places a rich strong loam, on a substratum of clay ; but a light fertile sand prevails along its eastern side, and near Lake Lothing, with an occasional mixture of clay and brick earth, in many parts wet, and full of springs. In the vale of the Waveney is a broad tract of rich *marshes.*   Most of the *farms* vary from 50 to 200 acres, but a few of them extend to 400 acres, and they are generally well cultivated.   The following is an enumeration of the 24 *parishes* of this Hundred, shewing their territorial extent, the annual value of their lands and buildings, as assessed to the property tax in 1815, and their population in 1801 and 1841 :—

PARISHES.	Acrs.	Rent £.	Populatn. 1801.	1841	PARISHES.	Acres.	Rental £.	Population. 1801.	1841.
Ashby........	1045	558	42	53	Gunton	862	1306	36	77
†Barnby*	1029	1177	188	296	Herringfleet ..	1309	1297	160	197
Belton...... ⎰	2009	1941	350	401	Hopton	1267	1669	202	251
⊦ Browston.. ⎱				64	†Kessingland*	1616	2419	475	658
Blundeston* ..	1573	2397	386	592	†Kirkley*	514	823	177	433
Bradwell*	2295	3372	199	270	Lound*	1242	2263	332	412
Burgh Castle..	1497	2264	189	327	‡Lowestoft*..	1486	7451	2332	4647
†CarltonColvle*	2780	3359	497	785	†Mutford*	1499	2382	290	415
Corton*	1180	1594	242	442	‡Oulton*......	1979	2020	522	660
Flixton	602	918	41	23	†Pakefield* ..	670	896	282	495
Fritton*	1478	1441	174	223	†Rushmere ..	780	872	127	134
†Gislehain* ..	1344	2120	198	254	Somerleyton*..	1380	2398	240	504
Gorleston ..⎰	1335	3796	1728	2351					
§South Twn.*⎱	597			1428	Total*..	33,368	50,73:	9,409	16,392

* When the census was taken, in 1841, there were 467 *fishermen* absent from the sixteen parishes marked thus *, so that the *total population* of the Hundred

was then 16,859. Of these fishermen, 190 belonged to *Lowestoft*, 86 to *Pake-field*, and the remainder to the other fourteen parishes.

§ South Town, or *Little Yarmouth*, is a suburb of Great Yarmouth, and form part of that *borough*, to which Gorleston was added by the Reform Act.

‡ In 1841, Lowestoft included 11 persons in *Mutford and Lothingland Infirmary*; and Oulton 141 in the *Hundred House of Industry*.

† The eight parishes marked thus † form the *Mutford Division*, or *Half Hundred*.

☞ CHIEF CONSTABLES.—Messrs. Charles Pearse, of Carlton Colville; Robt. Bonfellow, of Lowestoft; and Geo. Thurtell, of Flixton.

The HOUSE of INDUSTRY, *belonging to the Incorporated Hundred of Mutford and Lothingland*, is at Oulton, about 2½ miles W. of Lowestoft, and was built in 1765, at the cost of about £3000. The 24 parishes of this Hundred were incorporated for the maintenance of their poor, by an Act of Parliament, passed Nov. 15th, 1763. This Act was amended, and its powers enlarged by another Act, passed in 1833. Notwithstanding the passing of the general Poor Law Amendment Act, in the following year, this incorporated Hundred still continues under its own local management, the Board of Guardians adopting only such suggestions, made by the Poor Law Commissioners, as they think useful and necessary. In 1836, they enlarged the House of Industry, and made some alterations for the better classification of the inmates, at the cost of about £1100. When the census was taken, the number of inmates in the following years was 233 in 1821; 221 in 1831; and 141 in 1841. During the quarter ending June 24th, 1843, the number of *out-door paupers* was 1739, and *in-door*, 210; and the expenditure for the same quarter was £1039. 8s. 11¾d., exclusive of £10. 19s. 6d. for registration fees. The Poor Law Commissioners, in their first report, speak highly of the comfort and economy exhibited in this House of Industry, and also of the general management of the Incorporated Hundred, which is vested with a *Board* of 24 *Directors* and 36 Guardians, elected at annual vestry meetings. Mr. Edmund Norton, of Lowestoft, is their *clerk*, and is also magistrates' clerk and *superintendent registrar of the Hundred*, of which Mr. G. S. Crisp is *Registrar of Marriages*. Mr. Henry Harrison is *governor* of the House of Industry. Mr. E. Norton is also clerk to the Mutford and Lothingland *Association for the Prosecution of Felons*. Sir T. S. Gooch is president, and Mr. R. H. Reeve secretary to the SUFFOLK HUMANE SOCIETY, which has *life-boats* at Lowestoft and Pakefield, and various apparatus on the shore for communicating with stranded vessels.

ASHBY parish, nearly 6 miles N.W. of Lowestoft, and S.W. by S. of Yarmouth, contains only 53 souls, 1045 acres of land, one farmhouse, and a few scattered cottages. It is bounded on the north by the large *broad* called Fritton Decoy. It anciently belonged to the Inglosse and Jernegan families. A small part of it now belongs to J. F. Leathes, Esq.; and the remainder, with the manor, has long formed part of the Somerleyton estate, now the property of Lord Sydney Godolphin Osborne, who is also patron of the *Church*, (St. Mary,) a small thatched fabric, with an embattled tower, round at the base, and octangular above. It is of great antiquity, and stands alone upon a pleasant eminence. The benefice is a discharged *rectory*, valued in K.B. at £6, and in 1835 at £214. It has 11A. of glebe, and is now enjoyed by the Rev. Edward Thurlow. Mr. John Slipper, *farmer and grazier*, occupies most of the parish.

BARNBY, a pleasant scattered village, 4½ miles E. by S. of Beccles, and 6 miles W.S.W. of Lowestoft, has in its parish 296 souls, and 1029 acres of land. Lord Boston is lord of the manor, but part of

the soil belongs to the Earl of Gosford, Mrs. Reeve, and a few smaller owners. It extends northward to the Waveney, where it has about 400 acres of rich marsh land. The *Church* (St. John) is an ancient thatched fabric, and the benefice is a discharged rectory, not in charge, but rated at £130, and consolidated with the vicarage of Mutford and the rectory of Wheatacre All Saints. The latter is in Norfolk, and the value of the three joint livings in 1835 was £660. The Masters and Fellows of Gonville and Caius Colleges, Cambridge, are patrons; and the Rev. Wm. Oakes M.A., of Wheatacre, is the incumbent. On the enclosure of the common, 13A. of land was allotted to the poor parishioners, in lieu of their right of cutting furze, and it is now let for about £9 a year, which is distributed in coals during winter. The present gross annual value of the parish is £1013. 10s.

Baldry Wm. shoemaker
Bloomfield Robert, corn miller
Doddington Hy. vict. *Blind man's gate*
Everitt Wm., iron founder, &c.
Moore Joseph, victualler, *Swan*

Newby Charles, blacksmith
Wigg George, wheelwright

FARMERS.

Algar Wm. || Clark John
Patrick Parlet || Scarlett James
Woodthorpe John

BELTON, a small scattered village, in a picturesque dell, opening to the vale of the Waveney, five miles S.W. of Yarmouth, has in its parish 465 inhabitants, and 2009 acres of land, including about 300A. of marshes on the banks of the Waveney, and the hamlet of BROWSTON, which has 61 inhabitants, and is more than a mile S.E. of the church. Lord S. G. Osborne is lord of the manor of *Gapton*, in this and the neighbouring parishes, which anciently belonged to the Fastolf family. A great part of the soil belongs to Lord Boston, Magdalen College, Oxford, and the Fowler, Harper, Glasspole, and other families. *Browston Hall* is a fine old mansion, with tastefully planted grounds, in a low but agreeable situation. It was formerly a seat of the Symonds and Le Grys families, but now belongs to Mr. Harper, and is occupied by J. Baker, Esq. *Belton Hall*, half a mile south of the church, is the residence and property of Mr. G. Glasspole. The *Church* (All Saints,) an ancient structure, stands on an acclivity, and had a round tower, which went to ruin many years ago. The bell hangs in a wooden belfry over the porch. A neat screen, with folding doors, divides the nave and chancel, and they contain several neat monuments, one of which is in memory of *John Ives, Esq., F.R.S. and F.A.S.*, who was born at Yarmouth, and died here in 1776, aged 26. He was author of "Select Papers relating to English Antiquities," a M.S. "History of Lothingland," &c. At the foot of his monument is carved an oak tree, broken in the middle, from which a few acorns have fallen ;—a touching and appropriate emblem of the untimely death of this accomplished antiquary, whose father had large estates in this neighbourhood. Over the communion table is an ancient painting of the Last Supper, and in the north windows are a few fragments of stained glass. The benefice is a discharged rectory, valued in K.B. at £17. 15s., and now having a yearly modus of £440, about 12A. of glebe, and a neat modern residence. The Bishop of Norwich is patron, and the Rev. T. G. F. Howes incumbent. Here is a *National School*, built in 1835. The *Church Land* comprises 1A. 2R. 18P., occupied by the parish clerk rent-free, and 5A. 2R. 18P., let for £6. 6s. per annum. At the *enclo-*

sure of the common in 1810, an allotment of 9A. 9P. was awarded to the poor, and it is now let for £12. 12s. a year, which is distributed in coals.

Marked * are in Browston, and the others in Belton.

*Baker John, Esq. *Browston Hall,* (and solicitor, at Yarmouth)
Bedingfield Michael, blacksmith
Bracey James, vict. King's Head
Bussey Wm. blacksmith
Cutting Thos. butcher (& overseer)
Fowler Rev. Thos. C. & John C. Esq.
Goffin Thomas, joiner
Howes Rev. T. G. F. *Rectory*

Jenner James, schoolmaster
Jermy Michael, gardener
Pool Noah, joiner, and Hy. shoemkr
Skipper Daniel, shoemaker
Thompson Arthur Fisher, gent

FARMERS.

Booth Robert ‖ Goldsmith James
Glasspole George, *Belton Hall*
Hammond Chas. ‖ *Hammond Isaac
*Newark James ‖ *Sheppard James
*Stannard Edward ‖ Sheppard Robt.

BLUNDESTON, a pleasant scattered village, with several nea houses, 3 miles N.N.W. of Lowestoft, has in its parish 1573A. 1R. 37P. of land, and had 592 souls in 1841, exclusive of 11 fishermen. Lord S. G. Osborne is lord of the manor, which was anciently held by a family of its own name, and afterwards by the Yarmouths, Sydnors, Allens, and Anguishes; but a great part of the soil belongs to Charles Steward, Esq., Mr. John Owles, Mr. Thomas Morse, and Mr. William Woods. The *Church* (St. Mary) is an ancient thatched structure, without aisles, and has a round embattled tower. The nave and chancel are separated by a beautifully carved screen, and contain several neat monuments of the Bacon, Sydnor, and other families. The tower has two bells, one of which was brought from Flixton; and near the south door is a niche, formerly used to contain the sprinkling water. The living is a discharged rectory, valued in K.B. at £3 16s. 8d., and in 1835, at £617, with that of Flixton annexed to it. Lord S. G. Osborne is patron, and the Rev. Edward M. Love, of Somerleyton, is the incumbent. The glebe is 12A. 31P., and the tithes of Blundeston have been commuted for £455 per ann. Here is a small *Wesleyan Chapel,* built in 1816. The *Town Estate* comprises three cottages, and about 5A. of land, and has been held from an early period for the benefit of the poor. One cottage is occupied rent-free by a poor family, and the other two and the land are let at rents amounting to £19 a year, which is applied with the poor rates. A house, barn, and 1A. 32P. of land, left for the poor by *Anthony Bays,* are let for £8 a year. The POOR'S ALLOTMENTS, awarded at the enclosure, comprise 10A. 2R. 34P. of *marsh land,* let for £33, and 15A. 2R. 38P. on *How Heath,* let for £27 per annum. The rents are distributed in coals among poor parishioners. A yearly rent-charge of 10s. for poor widows, left by *Elizabeth Ayton,* is paid out of land called Dale Pightle. In 1726, the *Rev. Gregory Clarke* left a house and 1A. 2R. of land for the support of a school for poor children. The *school* and master's house were rebuilt in 1823, and the school land now consists of 2A. 2R. 9P. The sum of 20s. a year is paid to the master, for each of the *free scholars,* who are generally about 12 in number. The present gross *yearly value* of the parish is £3124.

Albrow Wm. painter
Blistow Barny Wm. maltster, brewer and beer house keeper

Boyce Wm. blacksmith
Candler James, blacksmith
Chapman Joseph, Esq.

Cleveland James, wheelwright
Cooper Thomas, corn miller
Cooper John, bricklayer
Cory Rev. R. W. curate
Glasspole Mrs Ann
Jackson Bj. bldr. & brick & tile mkr
King David, joiner
Line John, schoolmaster, parish clerk, and overseer

Morse Thomas, farmer and owner
Newson Wm. shopkeeper
Owles John, gentleman
Steward Charles, Esq.
Skinner John, btchr. & vict. Plough
Welton Wm. joiner and beer house
Woods Wm. gent. *Blundeston Hall*
Boot and Shoe Makers.—Geo. Gillings, John Porter, & Wm. Surrel¡

BRADWELL, a scattered village, pleasantly situated nearly three miles S.S.W. of Yarmouth, has in its parish 274 souls, and 2295A. 2R. 32P. of land, including 600A. of marshes near the mouth of the river Yare. Lord S. G. Osborne is lord of the manors here, called *Caxton Hall* and *Gapton Hall.* The former belonged to the knights of St. John of Jerusalem, and the latter to Leigh Priory, in Essex. They were both granted by Henry VIII. to — Cavendish, Esq., and afterwards passed to the Jernegans, and the successive lords of Somerleyton; but the greater part of the soil is freehold, and belongs to the Fowler, Barber, Fisher, Crow, and a few other families. On the south side of the parish is *Hobland Hall,* formerly a seat of the Jarrets, lately of J. Penrice, Esq., and now of T. Barber, Esq. It has a large garden, with extensive green-houses, graperies, &c. The *Church* (St. Nicholas) is an ancient structure, with a round tower, containing three bells. In the chancel is a curious monument of Wm. Vesy, Esq., dated 1644, and bearing a group of figures in coloured plaister, assembled round an altar. The rectory, valued in K.B. at £28, has a neat residence, built about twenty years ago; and a yearly modus of £632, recently awarded in lieu of tithes. Lord S. G. Osborne is patron, and the Rev. Wm. Trivett, M.A., is the incumbent. Here is a small *National School,* built in 1841. The present estimated yearly rental of the parish is £3934, 12s.

Barber T. gent. *Hobland Hall*
Bracey Elizabeth, vict. *Sun Inn*
Chastney Margaret, schoolmistress
Clark Wm. corn miller
Elder Mr Robert
Mallett John, blacksmith
Smith Robert, boot & shoemaker

Trivett Rev. Wm., M.A. *Rectory*
FARMERS.
Cobb Wm. ‖ Woods George
Crow Robert, (*and owner*)
Osborn James ‖ Marjorum Wm.
Sheppard Wm. *Wheatcroft Hall*

BURGH-CASTLE, a Roman remain, near the confluence of the Waveney and Yare, gives name to one of the most romantic little villages in Suffolk, mostly situated on a boldly rising acclivity, overlooking the marshes on the banks of the rivers, and a large extent of the adjacent country. It is distant nearly 4 miles W.S.W. of Yarmouth, and has in its parish 327 souls, and 1496A. 3R. 1½P. of land. Camden and many other antiquarians, insist that Burgh Castle is the remains of the *Garianonum* of the Romans; but Spelman and some others place that station at Caister, on the coast two miles N. of Yarmouth, to which the estuary of the Yare formerly extended, prior to the formation of the sand on which Yarmouth stands. No doubt this broad estuary was guarded by a station on either side, but that at Caister was probably a summer camp, dependant on the more formidable fortress of Burgh Castle, of which there are still extensive remains,

standing on an eminence near the conflux of the rivers, and forming three sides of a quadrangle, 214 yards in length, and 107 in breadth, and occupying an area of 5A. 2R. 20P., including the walls, which are about nine feet thick, and are constructed of grout-work, faced on the outside with Roman bricks, interlaced in separate courses between layers of cut flint, and supported at intervals by six round towers, or rather solid cylinders, about fourteen feet in diameter, banded likewise with bricks. These towers appear to have been built after the walls, to which they are not joined, except at the summit, where they had each a round hole, two feet deep, and two feet in diameter, designed no doubt for the sentinels, who kept watch while the troops reposed in their tents within the area, which is supposed to have had no other defence on the western side but the waters of the estuary, which formerly washed the foot of the hill. Considering their great age, some parts of the walls are still tolerably entire, particularly on the south and east sides. Their height throughout has been fourteen feet. At the south-west corner is a circular mount, supposed to have been raised by the Saxons, who occupied the fortress after the departure of the Romans. The south tower fell down many years ago. The principal entrance was on the east side, where an adjoining field is supposed to have been the burial place of the garrison, from the great number of *Roman urns* that have been found in it. These urns are not remarkable either for workmanship or materials, being made of coarse *blue clay*, brought from the neighbouring village of Bradwell, ill-formed, brittle, and porous. In 1756, a space of five square yards was opened in this field; and about two feet below the surface, a great many fragments of urns were discovered, which appeared to have been broken by the ploughs and carts passing over them. One of them, taken up in several pieces, was found to have contained a considerable quantity of bones and ashes, several coins of Constantine, and the head of a Roman spear. In pulling down part of the hill which formed the Prætorium, urns and ashes were found in great abundance, and among them was a stratum of wheat, quite black, as if it had been burnt, and a great part of it reduced to a coarse powder. At the same time was found a Roman spoon, with a long, sharp-pointed handle. Rings, buckles, fibulæ, and other instruments, are frequently found here, as also are coins of silver and copper, mostly of the Lower Empire; and many skeletons were dug up within the area of the castle in 1842. Mr. Ives, in his ample and ingenious remarks on this castle, fixes the era of its erection in the reign of the Emperor Claudius, and conjectures that it was built by Publius Ostorius Scapula, who conquered the *Iceni*, who were the aboriginal inhabitants of this and the adjacent counties. We are informed in the Notitia Imperii, that this station was garrisoned by the Stablesian horse, under the command of *Præpositus*, who was sometimes styled *Garienninensis*, from the estuary which he was appointed to guard.

A little north of the castle, are some vestiges of a *monastery*, built by Furseus, an Irish monk, who, under the patronage of Sigebert, the first Christian King of the East Angles, and Felix, the first Bishop of Dunwich, collected a company of religious persons under the monastic rule, and placed them at Burgh, then called Cnobersburg, after the name of a Saxon chief, who had formerly resided here. On the

death of Sigebert, Furseus quitted his monastery at Burgh, and retired to France, after which the establishment gradually dwindled to nothing. The authors of *Magna Britannia* observe, that, according to a tradition current here, this monastery, after its desertion by the monks, was inhabited by Jews, and add, that an old way leading to the entrance, called the Jews' way, seems to give it some colour of truth. The Domesday survey informs us, that in the time of Edward the Confessor, Stigand, Bishop of Norwich, held Burgh by soccage. Under William the Conqueror, Radulph Balistarius was lord of this manor, which was always a demesne of the Crown, being held by the tenure of serjeantry, by Roger de Burgh, Ralph, his son, and Gilbert de Weseham, at whose decease, being surrendered into the hands of Henry III., he granted it, with all its appurtenances, to the priory of Bromholm, in Norfolk, to be held by the same tenure. To this religious house the castle and manor belonged till the dissolution, when they reverted to the Crown, in which they remained till they were sold by Queen Mary to Wm. Roberts, town clerk of Yarmouth. Mrs. Lydia Baret, of Thwaite, Norfolk, is now lady of the *manor of Burgh Castle*, but part of the parish belongs to several other proprietors, a few of whom have neat houses here. The *Church* (St. Peter) is a small structure, with a round tower, containing three bells; and the benefice is a discharged rectory, valued in K.B. at £6. 13s. 4d., and in 1835 at £400. It is in the patronage of the Crown, and incumbency of the Rev. Charles Green, who has 47A. 3R. 13P. of glebe, and a yearly modus of £369. 10s., recently awarded in lieu of tithes. The *Rectory House*, rebuilt in 1832 at the cost of about £1000, is a handsome mansion, with pleasant grounds, on the summit of an eminence, from which there is a descent to the marshes through a narrow defile, overshadowed on the south with trees and underwood, almost to the margin of the river, where a winding path passes under the walls of the castle. The *Poor's Allotment*, awarded at the enclosure of the common, comprises about 15 acres, let for £27. 10s. a year, which is distributed in coals among the most destitute parishioners. The *School* was built in 1836, at the cost of about £80, raised by subscription. The main beam in its ceiling was removed from a decayed house, and has a long black letter inscription, showing that the house from which it was removed, was rebuilt by Robert Thorne, the parson, in 1548.

Burgess Thomas, parish clerk
Cory Charles, solicitor, *(& Yarmouth)*
Ferrier Rd. Esq.||Nash Mr John
Green Rev Charles, *Rectory*
Lake Rhoda, shopkeeper
Palmer Ambrose, Esq. *RoseCottage*
Ward Matthew, vict. *Burgh Castle*

FARMERS.
Brewington Jacob || Neslen Geo.
Clark Richard, *(& corn miller)*
Crow James || Carrison James
Martin James Darby
Newark James || Utton Charles

CARLTON-COLVILLE, a pleasant village, on an eminence, 3½ miles S.W. of Lowestoft, has in its parish 2780 acres of land, and 800 inhabitants, including 15 fishermen who were absent when the census was taken, in 1841. It extends two miles northward to the hamlet of *Mutford Bridge*, on the Lake Lothing. (See page 480.) Lord S. G. Osborne is lord of the manor, which anciently belonged to the Colvilles, but the greater part of the soil belongs to Samuel Tolver, Esq., Isaac Preston, Esq., Wm. Woodthorpe, Esq., the Rev. Mark Waters, and

the Pearse, Warne,Woolnough, and a few other families. The *Church* (St. Peter) is a small ancient structure with five bells, but they have not been rung in peal since the tower was damaged by lightning about thirty years ago. The living is a discharged rectory, valued in K.B. at £12. 10s. 7½d., and now having a yearly modus of £387, a good residence, and about 18A. of glebe. Lord S. G. Osborne is patron, and the Rev. Edward Jermyn, M.A., incumbent. A *National School* was built in 1843, at the cost of about £200, of which £70 was given by the late patron, the Rev. George Anguish.

Marked † are at Mutford Bridge.	*Blacksmiths.*	*Warne John
†Balls Francis, shopkeeper	Moyse John	*WoodthorpeJno.
Brewster Wm. land agent, *Hall*	Wright Wm.	*Woodthorpe W.
Chipperfield Edw. butcher and vict.	*Boot&Shoe Mkrs.*	*Woolnough Jno.
Bell	Gooch Wm.	Wright Wm.
†Gent Mrs Frances	Mitchell John	*Joiners, &c.*
†George John, grocer and draper	Ratcliffe John	Balls Charles
Harming John, vict. *Ship*	Salter Colby	Bull Wm.
Jermyn Rev Edw. M.A. *Rectory*		Wright Wm.
†Kemp Robt. saddler and vict. *Lady*	FARMERS.	*Wheelwrights.*
of the Lake	*(* are Owners.)*	Rouse Samuel
†Knight John, bricklayer	*Eastaugh Robt.	Sherman Martin
Nelgin Rev Wm. curate	Fairhead John	COACH toLowes-
Smith Samuel, surgeon & registrar	*Fulcher George	toft, Norwich,
Snelling Frdk. dep. regr.&schoolmr.	Gould Rt. Alex.	&c.Wed.&Sat.
Strowger Robert, vety. surgeon	*Johnson Benj.	and *Van* toNor-
Thorpe John, shopkeeper	*Pearse Charles,	wich Tu. &Fri.
Woodthorpe Wm. Esq. *Uplands*	(chief constable)	from the Ship
	Pye J. Benjamin	

CORTON, a village three miles N. of Lowestoft, is situated on a high cliff commanding extensive prospects of the ocean. It has several neat houses, and its parish contains 1180A. of land, and 464 inhabitants, including 22 fishermen. From the foundations of old houses, which have often been discovered, it is supposed to have been much larger formerly than it is at present. Some centuries ago, there was on the east side of Corton, a parish called Newton, of which scarcely any other vestiges remain, than a stone which supported a cross, denominated Newton Cross, and a small piece of ground, known by the name of Newton Green; every other part of it having been swallowed by the sea. The *cliff*, which rises fifty feet above the beach, is composed of a soft sandy loam, and is often undermined by the ocean. After a storm, in 1812, a layer of oak planks was found at the base of the cliff, where coins and other antiquities have occasionally been discovered; and in the neighbourhood, bones of the *mammoth* and other antediluvian remains have been dug up at various periods. Lord S. G. Osborne is lord of the *manors* of Corton and Newton with Stalhams-in-Lound. They were anciently held by the De Herlings, who had free warren here; and they afterwards passed to the Jernegan, Wentworth, and Garneys families. In 1672, they were purchased by Sir Thomas Allen, and have since descended with the manor of Somerleyton. Mrs. S. Fowler, Beccles Grammar School, and the Taylor, Woods, and other families, have estates in Corton parish. The *Church* (St. Bartholomew) stands nearly a quarter of a mile from the edge of the cliff, and has been long in ruins, except the

chancel, which is still kept in repair for divine service. It has been an extensive and elegant structure. The side walls of the nave are standing, and with the porch are finely mantled with ivy. The tower, which rises to the height of ninety feet, is still nearly entire, and is a conspicuous sea-mark, of great importance to mariners wishing to anchor in Corton Bay. The length of the fabric was 120 feet, and its breadth about 32. It was dilapidated about 150 years ago, when license was obtained from the bishop to maintain only the chancel, which was again repaired in 1776, when the lead from the nave was sold to defray the expense. It was appropriated to Leiston Abbey. After the dissolution, Henry VIII. granted the *impropriate rectory* to Charles Brandon, Duke of Suffolk ; and passing through various families, it became, in the last century, the property of the Ives family, from whom it came to the Fowlers, of Gunton, its present proprietors, one of whom, the Rev. Frederick Fowler, B.A., now enjoys the discharged *vicarage*, which is in the patronage of the Crown, and was certified in K.B. at £10, and valued in 1835 at £119. The tithes were commuted in 1839 for yearly moduses—the rectorial for £405, and the vicarial for £120. The present vicar erected a handsome parsonage house in 1841, at the cost of £1300, but it is occupied by the curate. A small school for poor children is supported by the vicar. The *Town Pightle*, about 1A., is let for £1. 11s. 6d. a year, which is paid to the parish clerk. The *Poor's Allotment*, awarded at the enclosure, contains 11A. 2R. 17P., and the rent is distributed yearly among the poor parishioners, who have also an annuity of 20s. left by *Robert Briggs*, in 1718, out of a farm belonging to Mr. Fowler.

Baker George, blacksmith
Hibbs Rev Richd. B.A. curate, (boarding academy,) *Vicarage*
Hill Elizabeth, schoolmistress
King Edward, corn miller
Read Robert, beerhouse keeper
Read Robert, blacksmith
Savage Lieutenant Wm. R.N.

Scarfe Wm. shopr. and vict. *White Horse*
Smith John, boot and shoe maker
Sone Esther, shopkeeper
FARMERS. (* are Owners.)
Roe Wm. Bradley || Harvey Jas.
Stannard Wm.
*Taylor Wm. || *Woods Thomas

FLIXTON, a small churchless parish, nearly 3 miles N.W. of Lowestoft, has only 23 inhabitants, and 602A. 1R. 38P. of land, including a *decoy* of 16 acres. Lord S. G. Osborne is lord of the manor, but part of the soil belongs to Lord Boston, and a few smaller owners. The *Church* (St. Andrew) being much decayed was reduced to a roofless ruin by the great hurricane of Nov. 27th, 1703. Only a small portion of the side walls are now standing, thickly covered with ivy. The rectory, valued in K.B. at £14, has been consolidated with that of Blundeston since the destruction of the church. The tithes have been commuted for a yearly modus of £158. 9s., though the gross annual value of the parish is only £854. 10s. 10d. The *farmers* are John Button, *Flixton Hall*, and George Thurtell, *chief constable*.

FRITTON, a small village, pleasantly situated at the west end of a large *lake* or *decoy*, one mile east of the river Waveney, on the high road, 8 miles N.E. by N. of Beccles, and 6 miles S.W. of Yarmouth, has in its parish 230 souls, and 1478 acres of land, including some rich marshes on the east bank of the river, near St. Olave's Bridge. The manor of Fritton was formerly held by the Sydnors, afterwards by the

Allens and Fullers, and now by A. G. Johnstone, Esq.; but *Caldecot Hall*, now a farm house, gives name to a manor in this parish, belonging to Magdalen College, Oxford. *Fritton Hall* is now the seat of D. Dunnell, Esq.; and Fras. Turner, Esq., the Rev. F. W. Cubitt, and a few smaller owners, have estates in the parish. *Fritton Decoy* is a fine fresh water lake, more than two miles in length from east to west, and in some places more than a quarter of a mile broad. It abounds with a great variety of fish, and is the resort of widgeons, ducks, teal, and other wild fowl, during the season, which begins in October and ends in April. Vast quantities are taken yearly, and produce a considerable revenue to the proprietors. The banks of this fine sheet of water are fringed with wood, and are highly picturesque and beautiful. Near it is a pleasant sporting cottage, which is the occasional residence of Capt. G. W. Manby, of Yarmouth, the ingenious and humane inventor of the apparatus for the preservation of lives from shipwreck. The *Church* (St. Edmund) is a venerable fabric with a low round tower, a nave, and chancel. The latter is circular at the east end, and is a perfect specimen of Saxon architecture. In the windows, are some fragments of ancient stained glass. The benefice is a discharged rectory, valued in K.B. at £6. 15s. 4d., and now having 13A. of glebe, and a yearly modus of £270 in lieu of tithes. The Rev. Fras. Wm. Cubitt is patron and incumbent, and has a neat residence here at the west end of the decoy, but it does not belong to the benefice. The *Poor's Allotment*, awarded at the *enclosure*, consists of 14A. 2R. 38P., let for £12. 12s. a year, which is distributed in coals. A small school, for the instruction of the poor, is supported by subscription.

Bee James, wheelwright
Cubitt Rev Francis Wm. rector
Dunnell David, Esq. *Fritton Hall*
Rivett Wm. cattle dlr. & beerhs. kpr.
Sayer John, baker and shopkeeper
Woolner Sarah, beerhouse keeper

FARMERS.
Bond Edward || Benns George
Gayton Robert || Pettingale J.
Larkman James, *Caldecot Hall*
Rivett Wm. || Youngman Benj.

GISLEHAM, a small scattered village, nearly 5 miles S.W. by S. of Lowestoft, and 7 miles E.S.E. of Beccles, has in its parish 260 inhabitants, and 1344 acres of land. Lord Boston is lord of the manor, which formerly belonged to the Garneys family; but Mrs. Reeve, Mr. J. Reeve, Mr. T. Woodthorpe, and a few smaller owners, have estates in the parish. The *Church* (Holy Trinity) is an ancient thatched structure, with a tower, round at the bottom, and hexagonal above, and formerly containing four, but now having only two bells. The ancient screen which divided the nave and chancel, being much decayed, was removed in the early part of the present century. On the outside of the south porch are figures of two angels in a kneeling posture. In one of the north windows is some painted glass, representing an *Ecce Agnus Dei*, with the saint broken. Under another small mutilated saint, standing with an arrow in his left hand, and his right against his breast, is inscribed, " *St. Edmund.*" There are also two small figures of a man and woman kneeling, inscribed, " Wm. Gange and Margaret;" but the heads of both are wanting. In several of the windows are crowns of painted glass, alluding probably to the royal martyr, St. Edmund. The benefice is a discharged *rectory*, valued in K.B. at £13. 6s. 8d., and now having a yearly modus of £410, and a good residence.

The patronage is in the Crown, and the Rev. Robert Collyer, M.A., is the incumbent.   Here is a small *School*, endowed by the late Rev. M· Reynolds, and vested in trust with the rector, and the Archdeacon of Suffolk.

Collyer Rev Robt. M.A. *Rectory*
Farrow John, gardener
Spenton George, blacksmith
FARMERS. (* *are Owners.)*
Andrews James || Boyce Wm.

Button Louisa Ann || Crafer Wm.
Lark Alfred || Lark Wm.
Nave Wm. *(miller)* || Weavers Wm.
*Marsham Jsa. || *Woodthorpe Thos.

GORLESTON and SOUTHTOWN. (*See Yarmouth.)*

GUNTON, a small parish, on the coast, from 1 to 2 miles N. by W. of Lowestoft, has only 77 inhabitants, and 862 acres of land.   The path on the crown of the cliffs, and the *denes* beneath, are luxuriantly covered with *hare-bells* and purple-hued heath flowers, affording at all times a verdant carpet for the pedestrian.   The manor of Gunton was anciently the property of the Lowdhams, and afterwards of the Blomville, Wroth, Holles, and Luson families.   It was purchased of the latter by Sir Chas. Saunders, Kt., a distinguished vice-admiral, who died in 1775.   His successor, Dr. Saunders, bequeathed it to his two daughters, who sold it to the late Thos. Fowler, Esq., whose relict, Mrs. S. Fowler, holds the manor and estate for her life, and occupies the *Old Hall*, near the church-yard.   In 1803, the late Mr. Fowler erected the *New Hall*, a handsome mansion on the north side of the parish, two miles from Lowestoft, surrounded with plantations of forest trees, and now occupied by two of his heirs.   Some years ago, the old hall was occupied by *J. D. Downes, Esq.*, a celebrated falconer, who kept here an excellent breed of hawks, and afforded the neighbouring gentry an opportunity of witnessing the ancient sport of *hawking*, so long the favourite amusement of our forefathers, but now nearly extinct, not only in England, but in Europe.   The *Church*, (St. Peter,) which was repaired and partly rebuilt by Charles Boyce, Esq., in 1700, is a small structure, consisting of a nave, chancel, and low round tower, and having its burial-ground shaded on every side by lofty elms.   It was repewed in 1839.   The living is a discharged rectory, valued in K.B. at £5. 6s. 8d., and now having about 9 acres of glebe, and a yearly modus of £145. 14s. 4d., awarded in 1839 in lieu of tithes.   The heirs of the late T. Fowler, Esq., are patrons, and the Rev. Fredk. Cooke Fowler is the incumbent.   In 1756, Hewling Luson, Esq., discovered a bed of fine *clay* on his estate here, and erected a small pottery for the purpose of manufacturing it into a sort of *china-ware* ; but the project did not succeed, though it was afterwards tried on a much larger scale, at Lowestoft, by Messrs. Aldred, Richman, and Brown.   The principal inhabitants of Gunton are, Mrs. S. Fowler, *Old Hall ;* Robt. Cooke Fowler, Esq., and Rev. Fredk. Cooke Fowler, *New Hall ;* Robert Allen, *parish clerk ;* and Allington Carman and Thos. Cooper, *farmers.*

HERRINGFLEET, a small scattered village, on the eastern side of the vale of the Waveney, 7½ miles S.W. by S. of Yarmouth, and 6 miles N.W. of Lowestoft, has in its parish 197 souls, and 1309 acres of land, extending northward to Fritton Decoy and *St. Olave's Bridge,* which crosses the river on the Beccles and Yarmouth road, near the remains of *Herringfleet Priory,* which was dedicated to St. Olave, the Virgin Mary, and St. Edmund, and was founded by Roger Fitz Osbert,

for Black or Augustine canons, about the year 1216. Its endowment was augmented by many subsequent benefactors, and its clear yearly value at the dissolution was £49. 11s. 7d. The remains of this monastery were mostly cleared away in 1784, and the boundary walls were afterwards used in repairing a new road. Except a low-arched vault or crypt, and some of the materials in the out-offices of an adjacent house, all traces of it are gone. Its site, with the manor of Herringfleet, and the advowson and impropriation of the church, was granted in 1546 to Henry Jerningham, Esq., and his wife. His successor sold it, in the reign of James I., to the Taverners, from whom it passed to the Bacons. About the middle of last century, it passed to *Hill Mussenden, Esq.,* who bequeathed it to his elder brother, Carteret Mussenden, Esq., who assumed the surname of *Leathes*. John Francis Leathes, Esq., is now lord of the manor, and owner of nearly all the parish. He resides at HERRINGFLEET HALL, a handsome modern mansion, in an elevated situation, having a verdant paddock in front, bordered with luxuriant plantations. In the apartments is a large and valuable collection of paintings, among which are many fine cabinet pictures of Herman Vander Myn, who died in 1741. The pleasure-grounds were designed by the late Rev. Norton Nichols, and contain a rich variety of thorns, hollies and flowering shrubs. The old *Manor House,* half castellated in its appearance, stands near the church, and was formerly surrounded by a moat, part of which still remains. *Blocker Hall,* another ancient mansion in this parish, is occupied by a farmer. It is in the Elizabethan style, and its principal entrance is approached by a lofty flight of steps. The *Church* (St. Margaret) is a neat single pile, consisting of a nave, chancel, porch, and round tower, containing five bells. It was appropriated to the priory, and was thoroughly repaired about twenty years ago. The south door within the porch has a fine Saxon arch. The windows are all new, the materials for the Gothic stone-work of which were supplied from the ruined arches of the priory. The altar-window is a fine piece of architecture, and exhibits a rich display of stained glass, mostly ancient fragments, rescued from a monastery in France, at the commencement of the Revolution. There are also some fine specimens of ancient and modern stained glass in several of the other windows. The benefice is a lay impropriation belonging to J. F. Leathes, Esq., the lord of the manor, who appoints the curate, and remunerates him as he thinks proper, the cure being considered a " donative." The *Poor's Allotment,* 6A. 35P., awarded at the enclosure, is let for £13. 15s. a year, which is distributed in coals. About twenty years ago, *Mrs. Elizabeth Merry* bequeathed £20 for the education of poor children of this parish; and, to provide for this annuity, a sufficient sum of money was laid out in the purchase of stock in the public funds. The annuity is applied as follows:—£5 for the rent of a house, school, and garden; £12 to the schoolmaster; and £3 for books and rewards for the children.

St. Olave's Bridge, which crosses the Waveney, near the site of Herringfleet priory and the Bell Inn, was rebuilt in 1770. The following account of its origin is extracted from a manuscript of the late Bishop Tanner :— " King Edward I., in the 25th year of his reign, sent out a writ to Wm. de Kerdeston, Sheriff of Norfolk and Suffolk, to inquire what detriment it would be to any person, for him to grant leave to Jeffery Pollerin, of Yar-

mouth, to build a bridge over the river at St. Olave's Priory; and a Jury being empannelled, returned that one Sireck, a fisherman, called after-wards John Atte Ferrys, began several years before to carry over passengers in his boat there, and received for his pains, bread, herrings, and such like things, to the value of 20s. per year; after his death, William, his son, did the like, and made it worth 30s. per year; and after him, Ralph, his son, performed the same service, and had of his neighbours, bread and corn, and of strangers money; and because the Prior of Toft hindered passengers from going through his marsh, the said Ralph purchased a passage through the prior's marsh, with a fleet on each side, paying 12s. per year; and of the commoners of Herringfleet, he purchased a way through their common, and was to carry them over at all times free for it, and then it became worth £10 per year. After Ralph's decease, John his brother, had it, and it was valued at £12 a year. John sold it to Roger de Ludham, who then held it, so that the building of a bridge there would be to the detriment of Roger de Ludham and the Prior of Toft, but it would be to the great benefit of the country; whereupon, leave was given and a bridge began, as it is supposed, but perhaps not finished in a durable manner, for among the patents of the 9th Henry V., is one for building a bridge over the water between Norfolk and Suffolk, at ' Seent Tholowes (St. Olave's) Ferry;' what was then done does not appear, but probably not much, for in King Henry VIII. reign, it is generally believed that Sir James Hobart built the present bridge, or put it into the present form."

HERRINGFLEET.

Leathes John Fras. Esq. *Herring-fleet Hall*
Mallett John, maltster, coal dlr. and vict. Bell Inn, *St. Olave's bridge*
Mitchell Wm. schoolmaster
Newman Wm. gardener
North Rev. Henry, curate
Sinnett Wm. boot and shoemaker

FARMERS AND GRAZIERS.

Boxfield John||Minjaye William
Hayward Francis, *Blocker Hall*
Maddison Wm. H.||Pope Wm.
Wigg Thomas, Edmund, & George

COACHES AND CARRIERS

From the Bell Inn to Yarmouth, Beccles, Ipswich, Bury, &c. daily

HOPTON, a small scattered village near the sea, 4½ miles S. of Yarmouth and N. of Lowestoft, has in its parish 251 souls and 1267 acres of fertile land, including the small hamlet of *Brotherton*, on the west side of the turnpike. A large tract of heath or *common* in this and the neighbouring parishes, was enclosed about thirty years ago, and is now in a high state of cultivation. Lord S. G. Osborne is lord of the manor of Gapton Hall with Belton, which comprises most of this parish, but the soil belongs chiefly to the executors of the late Wm. Jex Blake, Esq., Samuel Palmer, Esq., Wm. Everitt, Esq., and a few smaller owners. The estate of the late W. J. Blake, Esq., comprising 323 acres, and a neat mansion with well wooded grounds, was advertised for sale in 1843. The Dean and Chapter of Norwich are lords of the small manor of Hopton Hall, and also appropriators of the rectory, and patrons of the *Church*, (St. Margaret,) which is a perpetual curacy, valued in 1835 at £102, and now enjoyed by the Rev. Thomas Wm. Salmon, M.A. It is an ancient structure with a thatched roof, a square tower, narrow-pointed windows, and a curiously sculptured font. Fras. Barber, Esq., is lessee of the tithes, which have recently been commuted for a yearly modus. The glebe is 6A. 1R. 36P. The *old manor house*, near the church, was divided into tenements many years ago. The *Town Land*, 20A., was awarded at the enclosure, in lieu of other land, and is let for £25 a year, which is applied with the

poor rates. A rent-charge of 6s. 8d. per annum, for poor widows, is paid out of a farm belonging to T. Thornhill, Esq., but the origin of the charity is unknown. *Directory:*—Rev. Thos. W. Salmon, M.A., *incumbent*; Jeremiah Armon, vict., White Hart; Wm. Jex, Wm. Green, and Wm. Smith, *farmers.*

KESSINGLAND, a large and well-built village and fishing station, on the coast, 5 miles S.S.W. of Lowestoft, and 8 miles E.S.E. of Beccles, and N.N.E. of Southwold, has in its parish 1616 acres of land and 676 inhabitants, including 18 fishermen, who were absent when the census of 1841 was taken. It was anciently a place of considerable importance, and had a weekly market on Tuesday, and a fair on Nov. 20th. It is in four *manors*, formerly held by the Proctor family, and now by Sir T. S. Gooch; but the greater part of the soil belongs to Thomas Morse, Esq., Robert Fish, Esq., and several smaller proprietors. The impropriation of the church was given, in the reign of Edward III., to the nuns of St. Clare, or Minoresses, of London, to whom it belonged till the Dissolution. It was then vested in the crown, till granted in the 6th year of James I. to Francis Philips and Richard Moore. After having passed through several hands, the impropriation was purchased by the celebrated *William Whiston*, then vicar of this parish, and settled by him on the vicarage for ever. The *Church*, (St. Edmund,) while it belonged to the nuns, was considerably larger than the present building, as is evident from the ruins of the old structure, which still remain; but after the suppression of the religious houses, being deprived of the assistance which it was accustomed to receive from that source, it soon fell to decay. In 1686, the roof was in such a ruinous state, that the whole of it fell in, and the timber and seats were carried away and burned. Divine service was in consequence discontinued, till, in 1694, the rebuilding of it in its present contracted form was commenced by Thomas Godfrey and John Campe, with contributions collected by them for the purpose. It has a lofty square steeple, which contains five bells. The font, of very ancient workmanship, is of an octagonal form, having on each of the eight sides, the figure of a saint in a sitting posture, and underneath each of these, the figure of another saint, standing on a pedestal. On that side which faces the body of the church, is a small figure of St. Edmund, sitting with an arrow in his left hand, and holding the point of his beard with his right. Over the arch of the west door in the churchyard are two angels and a small figure of St. Edmund sitting between them, in the same manner as on the font. The old *Vicarage House*, called the *Nunnery*, was burnt down in 1833, and near its site is a flint wall, about 40 yards long, and an ancient house with buttresses, supposed to have formed part of a monastery. The benefice is a discharged vicarage, valued in K.B. at £10, but endowed with all the tithes, as noticed above, and now having 53 acres of glebe, a neat residence, built in 1831, at the cost of nearly £2000, and a yearly modus of £405. 12s., awarded in 1839. The Bishop of Norwich is patron, and the Rev. D. G. Norris, incumbent. The *Wesleyan*s have a small chapel here. On the beach is a *Coast Guard Station*, with dwellings for seven families, erected in 1823 at the cost of £1200. The guard consists of a lieutenant and nine men. In 1598, *John Buckman* left for

the maintenance of the church and the benefit of the poor, a house and 14A. 1R. 28P. of land, now let for £34 a year, which is mostly applied in repairing the church. At the enclosure, an *allotment* of 35A. of land was awarded for the purpose of providing firing for the poor. The yearly rent, £35, is distributed in coals at Christmas. In the village is a *National School*, attended by about 120 children, and supported chiefly by the vicar. The present gross yearly rental of the parish is £3185. 13s. 6d.

Post Office at Mrs Eliz. Manthorp's.
 Letters received and despatched at 6 morng. and ½ past 7 evening
Allen Mary, beerhouse
Chipperfield Daniel, butcher and vict. *Queen's Head*
Cunningham Thomas, wheelwright and vict. *King's Head*
Cunningham Mrs Esther
Elliott Robert, cattle dealer
Fisk Robert, solicitor
Green James, grocer and draper
Gross Henry, machine maker
Hammond Richard, butcher
Irby Rev Thomas William, rector of *Rushmere*
Manthorp Robt. joiner & beerhouse
Manthorp Elizabeth, shopkeeper
Newson Shadrach, parish clerk
Niker John Mower, *National Schoolmaster* & beerhouse keeper
Norris Rev Denis Geo. *Vicarage*

Nunn John, saddler
Parr Timothy, grocer and draper
Pleasance John, blacksmith
Ritches Lieut. Thos. Watson, R.N.
Robson Jeremiah, tailor
Tripp James, shoemaker
Tripp Wm. cooper
Waterson Mr Thomas
Waterson Thomas, auctioneer, &c.
Wright John, glover & hair dresser
Welsh Capt. George, R.N. *Cliff*

FARMERS.
(* *are Owners.*)
Barfoot Robert
 Borrett
*Bean James
Cooper Chas.
*Cooper Wm.
Crowfoot John, Sibel, *Manor House*
*Davie David
*Davie John
Durrant Edward
 Wilcox
Fisk James
Foster Wm.
Girling Richard
FISH CURERS.
Catchpole Jas.
Davie John
Durrant James
Durrant John
Foster William
Goldsby George

KIRKLEY parish, on the coast 1½ mile S.S.W. of Lowestoft, comprises nearly half of the large *village and fishing station*, which is commonly called *Pakefield*, the greater portion of it being in the adjoining parish of Pakefield. Kirkley has only 514 acres of land, but increased its inhabitants from 374 in 1801, to 467 in 1841, including 34 fishermen who were absent when the census was taken in the latter year. It adjoins Pakefield on the west, and extends northward to the east end of *Lake Lothing*, which formerly communicated with the sea by a small channel called *Kirkley Ham*, which, at its mouth, still forms a small creek or harbour for fishing boats. The *Church* (All Saints) was for many years anterior to 1749 in a dilapidated state, but the minister officiated in Pakefield church on one part of the Sunday, alternately with its own minister. In this manner, both parishes were for a considerable time supplied; but at length the incumbent of Kirkley not only refused to perform divine service in Pakefield church any longer, but also to allow anything to the minister of Pakefield for officiating in his stead, alledging that he could not be legally compelled. The Rev. Mr. Tanner, vicar of Lowestoft, and at that time commissary and official in the archdeaconry of Suffolk, used all the mild and persuasive arguments in his power to prevail on the incumbent of Kirkley to make an allowance, but to no purpose. He therefore left him with this threat: "If, Sir, you will not officiate in Pake-

field church, I will build you a church a Kirkley, and in that you shall officiate." Mr. Tanner was as good as his word, for, partly at his own expense, and partly with the contributions of others, he fitted up the present church in 1750, partly out of the remains of the old one. The latter was much larger than the present church; and in clearing away the rubbish from the site of the north aisle, several brass-plated stones were found, and laid under the pews of the south aisle, which forms the present fabric. The old tower, about 72 feet high, is still standing, and is a conspicuous sea-mark, but is much decayed, and has now only one bell. The benefice is a discharged rectory, valued in K.B. at £5. 16s. 10½d., and now having about twenty acres of glebe, and a yearly modus of £142. 10s. The Hon. G. J. Irby, son of Lord Boston, is patron, and the Rev. R. J. Francis, incumbent. The poor parishioners have an *allotment* of 20A. 2R. 18P. awarded at the enclosure, and now let for £15 a year, which is distributed in coals.

PAKEFIELD, on the coast 1½ mile S.S.W. of Lowestoft, forms with *Kirkley* a large *village and fishing station*, containing 1048 inhabitants, of whom 581, including 86 fishermen, are in *Pakefield Parish*, which now comprises only 670 acres of land, having suffered much from the encroachments of the ocean, which has washed away about 70 acres during the last twenty years, together with several houses on the cliff. The Kirkley part of the village is separated from the Pakefield part only by the high road. Lord Boston is lord of the manor of Pakefield, but the soil belongs to various owners. The *Hall*, an old mansion in the Elizabethan style, is occupied by Mr. J. Cattermole. A *Light House* was erected here in 1831, at the cost of about £1000; and near it, is a deep and rugged ravine in the cliff, called *Crazy Mary's Hole*, from its having been the favourite haunt of a deranged love-sick maid. Pakefield *Church* is said to be dedicated to All Saints, but the ancient silver communion cup is inscribed " *Pakefield Sante Margaret*, 1337." It consists of two aisles, built nearly uniform, and its steeple contains four bells. It was thoroughly repaired and beautified about fifty years ago by the Rev. Dr. Leman, a late incumbent, who erected a new pulpit, and placed over the curious old font a handsome model of the tower and spire of Norwich cathedral. On a brass plate in the north aisle, is the representation of a man, his wife, and eleven children, and an inscription in memory of John Bowf, who died in 1417. The benefice is a discharged *rectory*, valued in K.B. at £14, and has now a yearly modus of £205, recently awarded in lieu of tithes. The Earl of Gosford, D. Tanner, Esq., and other trustees of the late B. Sparrow, Esq., are patrons, and the Rev. Francis Cunningham, of Lowestoft, is the incumbent. Many shipwrecks having occurred on this coast, an excellent *life boat* was stationed here a few years ago, similar to the one at Lowestoft. In a *barrow* on Bloodmoor hill, near Pakefield, was found in 1768, a skeleton, round whose neck hung a gold medal, and an onyx set in gold. The legend round the medal was D. N. T. AVITVS. On the obverse, a rude head helmeted, with a cross on the shoulder; on the reverse, VICTORIA AVGGG. exergue CONOB., and a rude figure of Victory. On the onyx, was a man standing by a horse, and holding the reins, with a *hasta pura* in his right hand, and a star on his helmet. The *Town Estate* comprises the site of three tenements, let for 7s. 6d. a year;

the site of two tenements, let in 1816 on a 99 years' lease, at 20s. per annum; about 1A. 1R., let in gardens, at rents amounting to £3. 7s. per annum; and about a rood of ground on which the *parish school* was built in 1817, at the expense of the rector. The rents of the land are applied in repairing the church. The *Poor's Allotment*, 15 acres, is let for about £20 a year, and was awarded to the poor at an enclosure, in lieu of their right to cut turves. The rent is distributed in coals among poor parishioners, who have also a yearly rent-charge of 20s., left by *Mary Selling*, out of lands now belonging to Mr. J. Matchett. Ten aged parishioners have £5 distributed among them yearly, from the dividends of three per cent. reduced annuities, purchased with the bequest of *Mrs. Dodd*, who died in 1814. Besides the school above noticed, here is an Infant School, and they are each attended by about 100 children, who pay one penny each per week.

KIRKLEY AND PAKEFIELD DIRECTORY.

Allen Wm. blacksmith
Blakely Miss Sarah||Olley Mrs A.
Catchpole Wm. sawyer, *Saw Mill*
Foreman Emanuel, corn miller
Francis Rev Robert John, *rector of Kirkley*
Fuller John, vict. *Mill*
Goodwin Geo. M. keeper of *Pakefield Light House*
Leggett Thomas, gentleman
Peek James, corn miller
Peek Samuel, vict. *Ship*
Rump Rev John, curate of Pakefield
Smith Mr Jacob and Mr Wm.
Tyrrel Robert, joiner
Wyatt Wm. vict.*George and Dragon*

Academies.
Feltham Chas.
Peirson Hannah

Bakers.
Chandler Geo.
Colby Benj.
Sustins Edward

Wright Michael, (& joiner)
Beer Houses.
Hellin James, (& joiner)
Horning John
Lincoln Amos
Boot & Shoe Mkr.
Mickleburgh Jas.
Bricklayers.
Annis Edward
Annis Wm.
Brown James
Welham Emanl.
Butcher.
Branch John
FISH CURERS.
Colby Wm.
Fuller John
Fuller Wm.

Matchett John
Wyatt Wm.
FARMERS.
Bird John
*Cattermole Jas.
  Pakefield Hall
*Davie George
Frost Thomas
Gray Thomas
*Grimmer Chas.
Ling Henry
*Matchett John
Shopkeepers.
Barber Sarah
Crowe Edward
Pedgrift Thos.
Searles Abrm.
Tailor.
Sargeant Wm.

LOUND, a pleasant village, 4½ miles N.N.W. of Lowestoft, and 6½ miles S. by W. of Yarmouth, is situated on a fertile plain, watered by a small rivulet, which flows northward to the large lake called Fritton Decoy. Lord S. G. Osborne is lord of the manor, but a great part of the soil belongs to the Morse, Penrice, Thompson, and other families. Near the mill water, several pieces of ancient armour and coins were found some years ago. Nearly a mile south of the church is the handsome mansion of Thomas Morse, Esq., finely embowered in wood. This gentleman is now (1843) in his 99th year. The *Church* (St. John the Baptist) is a single building, with a thatched roof and a round tower, containing three bells. In its windows are some fragments of stained glass. The font is very ancient, and on the right of the altar is a piscina, rather elegantly arched. The benefice is a discharged rectory, valued in K.B. at £8; and in 1835, at £458, and is in the patronage of Lord S. G. Osborne, and incumbency of the Rev. Edward Thurlow, who has a neat thatched residence, built in 1819. The glebe comprises about eleven acres, and the tithes have been commuted for a yearly modus of £415. The *Poor's Allot-*

ment, 20A. 2R. 18P., awarded at the enclosure, is let for about £34 a year, which is distributed in coals among the poor parishioners, who have also a yearly rent-charge of 6s., left by John Spalding.

LOUND DIRECTORY.

Glaspoole George, grocer
Green James, corn miller
Howes Charles, shoemaker
Jenner Miss Mary Ann
Mitchell Sarah, schoolmistress
Morse Thomas, Esq. *Lound Hall*
Newson Jonathan, wheelwright
Pank Henry, blacksmith
Reynolds Charles, saddler
Rudrum John, farrier and overseer

Seely John, wheelwright
Smith Wm. shoemaker
Smith George, tailor
Thacker James, vict. *Village Maid*
Thurlow Rev. Edward, rector of Lound and Ashby
Woolner Wm. gardener

FARMERS.
Cobb John || Flatman Robert
Morse Jph. Ramsey || Newson Jph.
Thurtle George || Wigg William

LOWESTOFT ranks next Yarmouth among the most important fishing stations on the eastern coast, and is a handsome and improving *market town, bathing-place,* and *sea port;* pleasantly situated on the most easterly point of England, upon a lofty eminence, rising abruptly from the German ocean, 11 miles E. by N. of Beccles, 10 miles S. of Yarmouth, 25 miles E.S.E. of Norwich, 45 miles N.N.E. of Ipswich, and 114 miles N.E. of London. Its parish comprises 1486 *acres of land,* and the small hamlet of *Normanston,* at the east end of Lake Lothing. It increased its *population* from 2332 souls in 1801, to 3189 in 1811; 3675, in 1821; 4238, in 1831; and 4837, in 1841; including 190 fishermen, who were absent when the census in the latter year was taken. Thus, it appears to have more than doubled its inhabitants and buildings since 1801. Its number of *houses* in 1821 was only 782, but in 1841 they had increased to 1104, and its number of *males* was 2157, and *females* 2680. Lowestoft, when viewed from the sea, has the most picturesque and beautiful appearance of any town on the eastern coast. It consists chiefly of one principal street, extending about a mile in length, in a gradual descent from north to south, and intersected by several smaller streets and lanes from the west. The High street is on the summit of the cliff, so that the houses on the east side of it face the sea. The declivity, formerly barren sand, has been converted by modern improvements into beautiful *hanging gardens,* richly planted with trees and shrubs, interspersed with alcoves and summer-houses, and descending to the foot of the hill. At the bottom of these gardens a range of buildings, appropriated to the purpose of curing fish, extends along the beach, nearly the whole length of the town. From the situation of these fish-houses, the inhabitants derive the two-fold advantage of the easy conveyance of the herrings from the boats, and a total exemption from the disagreeable effluvia arising from them during the process of curing. Some invalids complain that the distance of the town from the water is an inconvenience, but the descent to the beach has been rendered easy and agreeable by several winding roads from the main street, with occasional flights of steps. The shore is peculiarly favourable for sea bathing, having a regular descent, and consisting of a hard sand, intermixed with shingle, and perfectly free from ooze, and those beds of mud which are frequently met with on other coasts. It often presents a very busy scene, and a stroll upon it may be very agreeably employed in selecting a variety of very curious peb-

bles, with amber and jet, thrown upon it by the tides. The beach is stored with several excellent *bathing machines*, and every other convenience for the numerous visitors who now resort hither in summer, and for whose accommodation there are in the town many commodious lodging-houses and several large inns, some of them commanding extensive prospects of the sea and the coast. Hot and cold baths were established here many years ago by Mr. Wells; and in 1824, a *New Bath House*, upon a more extensive plan, was erected on the south beach, by four gentlemen, who sold it in 1830, to Mr. Walter Jones, its present owner. It is an oblong pebble building, with rusticated angles, and has a spacious reading room, convenient hot and cold baths, and also a sulphureous medicated bath, upon an improved principle. The approach to it has received extensive improvements, and is a gradual descent from the town, forming an excellent carriage way and promenade.

From the dryness of the soil and the absence of all damps and noxious vapours arising from low marshes, the air of Lowestoft is highly salubrious, as is evident by the general longevity of its inhabitants. In the adjacent country are many delightful walks and drives; and at the south end of the town the NORWICH and LOWESTOFT NAVIGATION enters the ocean by a short cut from Lake Lothing, and opens a communication for sea-borne vessels to Norwich and Beccles, as noticed at pages 412 and 413. The Act of Parliament for making this navigation was obtained in 1827 by a company of shareholders, chiefly merchants and manufacturers of Norwich, desirous of making that city a port for sea-borne vessels, instead of having its merchandise conveyed in small craft to and from Yarmouth. The work was commenced in the same year, and was finished September 30th, 1833, at the cost of more than £100,000; but, having proved an unprofitable speculation, it was sold in 1842 for a comparatively small sum to new proprietors, who, by lowering the dues and making various improvements, have considerably augmented the traffic upon it, and will no doubt find ample remuneration for their invested capital. This navigation pursues the deepened channel of the river Yare from Norwich to Reedham, whence by a cut about 2½ miles in length, it is carried across the marshes to the river Waveney, along which it passes to Oulton Dyke, whence by another artificial cut of about two miles, it enters the western division of *Lake Lothing*, commonly called Oulton Broad, as noticed at page 480. This lake is about three miles in length, extending eastward to within little more than a mile of Lowestoft, and now communicating with the ocean by a deep channel cut through the sea bank, and terminating in a *lock* 400 feet long and 50 broad, crossed by a handsome swing-bridge, of cast iron. At Mutford Bridge, an embankment and another lock divide Lake Lothing into two nearly equal parts; the Oulton side containing fresh water, and the Lowestoft side salt water, and forming a spacious harbour of the average depth of from 15 to 17 feet. Upon both divisions of this beautiful lake, *regattas* or water frolics are held annually, and exhibit the usual fetes of rowing, sailing, and other attractions. The Oulton frolic takes place in July, and is succeeded by the Lowestoft frolic in August. Both are numerously attended, and enlivened by bands of music, and a gay display of highly decorated pleasure barges. The lake abounds with all the common species of the finny tribe, and fishing parties may at all times, for a

small gratuity, procure boats at Mutford Bridge, either for fresh or salt water angling. The sea having receded considerably from the north end of the town, has left a broad tract between the sands and the cliffs called the *denes*, extending northward to Corton, and forming a pleasing ride and promenade, affording many botanical specimens, and in some places good pasturage for cattle ; but those parts near the town are often covered with the nets and other tackle of the fishermen spread out for the purpose of being dried or repaired.

There are here about 80 *fishing boats* employed in the herring and mackarel fisheries, each averaging about 40 tons burthen, and employing 9 or 10 men and boys. The principal part of the commerce of Lowestoft is derived from the HERRING FISHERY. The season commences about the middle of September, and lasts till about the middle of November. The boats stand out to sea, to the distance of about thirteen leagues north-east of Lowestoft, in order to meet the shoals of herrings coming from the north. Having reached the fishing ground in the evening, the proper time for fishing, they shoot out their nets, extending about 2200 yards in length, and eight in depth ; which, by means of small casks, called bowls, fastened on one side, are made to swim in a position perpendicular to the surface of the water. If the quantity of fish caught in one night amounts to no more than a few thousands, they are salted, and the vessels, if they meet with no better success, continue on the fishing ground two or three nights longer, salting the fish as they are caught. Sometimes, when the quantity taken is very small, they will continue on the ground a week or more, but in general the fish are landed every two or three days, and sometimes oftener when they are very successful. As soon as the herrings are brought on shore, they are carried to the fish-houses, where they are salted and laid on floors in heaps about two feet deep. After having remained in this state about fifty hours, they are put into baskets, and plunged into water to wash the salt from them. After this, they are spitted and hung in tiers upon rafters, which form a chequer work up to the roofs of the drying-houses. Each rafter supports between three and four thousand herrings, and on these they hang till they are sufficiently dried and smoked by wood fires, kindled in different parts of the floor. After hanging about a fortnight, unless for foreign market, when they remain much longer, they are taken down and packed in barrels for sale, each containing about 900. For many years previous to 1780, only about 33 fishing boats were employed here, and the quantity of herrings caught averaged 21 *lasts*, (each containing 10,000 herrings,) to a boat. After that time, owing to the war with the Dutch and other powers, the number of boats engaged in the herring fishery here rather diminished ; but the bounties granted by an Act of Parliament, passed in 1786, for the encouragement of the fisheries, gave new vigour to this valuable branch of industry, so that only three years afterwards, the boats fitted out by this town amounted to 44. In 1802, the herrings caught by about 30 boats of Lowestoft, sold for £30,000 ; and in the following year, they earned in six weeks £10,000 by mackarel, exclusive of the other fish caught during that period, but these were unusually prosperous seasons. The superiority of the Lowestoft herrings is evident from their fetching a higher price in the market than those of Yarmouth or other places, and is attributed solely to the ar-

rangement of the curing houses, which secures to them the benefit of a free and unobstructed current of air. The principal advantage derived by the owners of the fishing boats here from the *Mackarel Fishery*, consists in it furnishing employment for the fishermen, and keeping them at home for the herring season. Lowestoft formerly fitted out about thirty boats annually for the North Sea and Iceland fishery, which gradually declined, and was entirely relinquished about the middle of last century. On the denes, a little north of the town, may still be seen a trench were stood the blubber coppers, in which the livers of the fish brought home from this voyage used to be boiled. Between the long range of fish-houses and the sea, the numerous boats employed here in the herring and mackarel fisheries, are arranged on the shore to a considerable extent. At different periods of the year, when preparing to go to sea, they create a general interest on the beach ; the variety of employments in which the sailors are engaged, and the picturesque appearance of the boats when rigged and ready to be launched, presenting a busy and highly interesting spectacle. Other sorts of fish are caught here by a more humble class of fishermen, who go out in their own small boats in search of whatever fish they can meet with, and by the sale of which many of them contrive to support large families.

Lowestoft is an *out-station*, under the port of Yarmouth, and belonging to the custom-house establishment of that place, here is a principal coast-officer. In consequence of extensive shoals and sands, the coast here is extremely dangerous, and sometimes presents a scene of devastation scarcely to be described. But the mariners who are so unfortunate as to become entangled with these shoals, have every prompt and effectual assistance that can be afforded by two excellent *life-boats*, stationed here and at Pakefield, and by the celebrated apparatus of Capt. Manby. These and other provisions for the assistance of persons shipwrecked on this coast, have been made by the *Suffolk Humane Society*. The two life-boats are efficiently manned, and each cost about £700. There are two *light-houses* at Lowestoft, and another at Pakefield, nearly two miles S. of the town ; and there is a *floating light* in the *Stanford Channel*. The HIGH LIGHT-HOUSE, at Lowestoft, stands on the crown of the cliff, at the north end of the town, and was erected in 1676, by the brethren of the Trinity House, Deptford, who repaired and considerably improved it in 1778, 1825, and 1840. It is a round cemented tower, about 40 feet high, surmounted by a lantern 7 feet high and 6 in diameter, glazed with plate glass, and lighted by 11 lamps with plated reflectors. Adjoining it are two neat houses for the keepers, built in 1840-1. The *Low Light-House*, on the beach, is a frame of wood-work, capable of being shifted at pleasure, to accommodate it to the changes which are frequently taking place in the situation of the sands. It was removed from the denes to the beach in 1832, and has three lamps and reflectors, and a wooden dwelling for the keeper. Vessels coming into or going out of Lowestoft roads in the night, are enabled, by keeping this beacon in a line with the High Light, to pass in safety through the Stanford Channel, which is about a quarter of a mile broad, and lies between the *Home and the Barnard Sands*. The lights are kept burning from sunset to sunrise throughout the year.

During the late war, Lowestoft was protected by *three fortifications*,

one at each of the north and south extremes, and the lower battery, near the Ness. They were all of the usual fort construction. That to the north mounted four eighteen pounders, had a breastwork with four angles, a guard-house, and other conveniences. The south fort had thirteen pieces of cannon, viz., ten thirty-two pounders, and three eighteens : while the lower battery had four thirty-two, and two nine pounders, which were then considered amply sufficient for all the purposes of defence. The cannon was removed after the general peace ; but a fort-keeper still resides at the *South-end Battery*, which is now the station of a *coast-guard*, consisting of a lieutenant and twelve men. *Petty Sessions* are held weekly at the Queen's Head and Crown Inns alternately : and in Duke's Head street is a *Police Station*, with an inspector and two men. The town has a clean and neat appearance, and is well paved and lighted. The *Gas Works* were built in 1837, at the cost of £2500, by Mr. James Malam, the present proprietor, and have a gasometer of the capacity of 8000 cubic feet. The MARKET is held every Wednesday, and is abundantly supplied with provisions. Here are also two annual *fairs* for pedlery, &c., held May 12th and October 10th. Henry IV. granted to Wm. de la Pole, Marquis of Suffolk, " one market and two fairs, *below* the village of Lowestoft." The market was removed from beneath the cliff to the area near High street, now called the Old Market ; but in 1698, when the *Corn Cross* was erected, it was removed to the present market-place, nearly in the centre of the High street. The Corn Cross, with some additions and alterations, is now the *Town Hall*, and the greater part of it was a chapel of ease till the completion of St. Peter's Chapel, in 1833, when it was purchased for the use of the town. That part intended for the sale of corn was converted into a vestry and passage to the chapel, in 1768 ; but the chamber over it was always used for the public meetings of the parishioners. Adjoining the Queen's Head Inn, on the south side of the Market-place, butter, eggs, poultry, &c., are exposed for sale under a *piazza*, over which is the *Assembly Room*, a handsome modern apartment, 42 feet long and 20 broad, with a dome ceiling. The *Theatre*, a neat building in Bell lane, was erected about 20 years ago, by Mr. Fisher, whose company of comedians visit it for a few weeks every alternate year.

Lowestoft is supposed to have been a fishing station as early as the time of the Romans ; but the *ancient town* is supposed to have been washed away at an early period by the ocean ; for there was to be seen, till the 25th of Henry VIII., the remains of a *block-house*, upon an insulated spot, left dry at low water, about four furlongs east of the present beach. The origin of its name has given rise to various conjectures, one of which supposes it to have been derived from *Lodbrog*, the Danish prince, who was murdered near the mouth of the Yare, as noticed at page 606. In a charter of Edward III., it is written *Loystoft*, and *Lowystofte*. Being an ancient demesne of the Crown, it obtained from several monarchs various privileges, which were confirmed by Elizabeth and Charles I. ; but they are now obsolete, or of little use to the inhabitants, except their exemption from serving on juries at the Assizes and Quarter Sessions. The *manor of Lowestoft* formed part of the large possessions of the Fitz Osberts, after the Norman conquest ; and it passed from them by marriage to the Jernegans, or Jerninghams. It has ever since been dependant upon, and descended with the manor of

Somerleyton, now vested with Lord Sydney Godolphin Osborne, who holds a court leet, &c. annually. The soil and buildings belong to various proprietors, one of whom is Edward Leathes, Esq., of NORMANSTON HOUSE, a handsome mansion, more than a mile west of the town, with beautiful pleasure grounds, descending southward to the expansive waters of Lake Lothing, through which the river Waveney anciently passed to the sea, through the now small creek called *Kirkley Ham*, a little south of the present lock of the Norwich and Lowestoft Navigation, (see pages 480 and 498.) The town suffered severely from that dreadful pestilence, the *plague*, in 1349, 1547, 1579, 1585, and 1603. In the latter year, 316 of its inhabitants fell victims to the contagion. It has, on several occasions, sustained heavy losses by *conflagrations*, the most destructive of which happened March 10th, 1645, when property in dwelling-houses, fish-houses, and goods to the value of £10,297, were consumed. Fires of smaller extent occurred in 1546, 1606, 1670, 1717, and 1780. In the first of these years, the Vicarage House, with many of the town records, was destroyed ; and, after being rebuilt, it shared the same fate in 1606. In the year of the threatened Spanish invasion, Lowestoft was compelled to raise upwards of £200 for the purpose of raising bulwarks, and fitting out a pinnance for the defence of the coast. During the civil wars, it distinguished itself by its attachment to the cause of Charles I. ; but the neighbouring town of Yarmouth took the side of Parliament, and the consequence was, frequent contests between armed vessels fitted out by the two places, especially in 1643-4, when the Lowestoft men were generally the victors, and succeeded in capturing a great number of the Yarmouth vessels, under the command of *Capt. Allen*, (afterwards the famous admiral,) and some other spirited inhabitants. After some show of resistance, *Oliver Cromwell* was allowed to march into the town, in 1644, at the head of 1000 cavalry, and fix his head quarters at the Swan Inn. After Oliver and his soldiers had lived for some time almost at free quarters in the town, they marched to Cambridge, taking with them Sir John Pettus, Sir Edward Barker, Capt. Allen, and several other gentlemen, as prisoners. On the 3rd of June, 1665, one of the most sanguinary naval engagements that took place during the war with the Dutch, under Charles II., was fought off Lowestoft, and continued from three in the morning till seven in the evening. The *Dutch fleet* consisted of 102 men-of-war, and 17 yachts and fire-ships ; and the *English fleet* of 114 men-of-war, and 28 fire-ships. The former was completely routed, with the loss of 18 ships captured, and 14 sunk or burnt. About 4000 of the enemy were killed, and 2000 taken prisoners. The English lost only one ship and 250 men, and their wounded did not exceed 350.

Among the celebrated *naval commanders* to whom Lowestoft has given birth are the following :—Sir Thomas Allen, who, during Cromwell's protectorate, was stedfastly attached to the royal cause, was, soon after the restoration, appointed to a command in the Royal Navy. In 1664, he was sent as commander-in-chief into the Mediterranean, where the following spring, on the commencement of the war with the Dutch, he fell in with their Smyrna fleet, consisting of forty vessels, some of which were very strong, under convoy of four ships of war. After an obstinate engagement, in which the Dutch commander fell, Sir Thomas, who had only eight ships, made prize of four of the richest of the enemy's fleet. In the obstinate engagements off Lowestoft, in 1665, and near the coast of Flanders and the

North Foreland, in 1666, Sir Thomas bore a distinguished part. On the conclusion of the first Dutch war, he was again sent into the Mediterranean to chastise the Algerines, and after his return, was, in consideration of his numerous services, created a baronet in 1669. About the same time, he purchased the estate of Somerleyton Hall, and removing thither from Lowestoft, passed the rest of his life in retirement. ANDREW LEAKE, after several progressive steps in the navy, was appointed to the command of a ship in 1696. He afterwards received the honour of knighthood, and in 1705 commanded the Grafton of 70 guns, in the attack on Gibraltar. In the engagement off Malaga in the same year, he led the van of the division under the commander-in-chief, Sir George Rooke; but received a wound, of which he expired during the action. After it had been dressed, he wrapped a table-cloth round his body, and though life was fast ebbing, he placed himself in his elbow-chair, in which he desired to be again carried upon the quarter-deck, where he undauntedly sat and partook of the glories of the day until he breathed his last. From the remarkable comeliness of his person, Sir Andrew is said to have been distinguished by the appellation of Queen Anne's handsome captain. REAR ADMIRAL RICHARD UTBAR, who took an active share in most of the hard fought engagements with the Dutch, in the early part of the reign of Charles II., died in 1669, and was buried here, as also were *Admiral Sir John Ashby* in 1693, and his nephew *Vice Admiral James Mighells* in 1733. It is worthy of remark that the five naval heroes of Lowestoft above noticed were all related either by consanguinity or marriage. THOMAS NASH, a facetious writer of considerable reputation in the latter part of the 16th century, was also a native of Lowestoft. The most witty of his productions is a satirical pamphlet in praise of *red herrings ;* intended as a joke upon the great staple of Yarmouth, and the pretensions of that place to superiority over Lowestoft. In the church are memorials of *Capt. Thomas Arnold,* who died in 1737, and several other worthies of Lowestoft, besides those just enumerated. SAMSON ARNOLD MACKAY, a natural son of Captain Arnold, died at Doughty's Hospital, in Norwich, in July, 1843, aged 78. He was born at Haddiscoe, in Norfolk, and apprenticed to a shoemaker at Walton, in Suffolk. The first subject that called his attention from his useful, but humble occupation, was the *crag deposit* of this county, and in his endeavour to account for the sinister turn of the whelks and other shells found in the different strata, he was led to contemplate those systems of cosmogony which ascribe a greater antiquity to the earth than the sacred records. He had long been known to many of the scientific persons in the kingdom, and was remarkable for the orinality of his views upon the very abtruse subject of mythological astronomy, in which he exhibited great sagacity, and maintained his opinions with extraordinary pertinacity. In 1822, he published his first part of Mythological Astronomy, and gave lectures to a select few upon the science in general ; and in 1825, his Theory of the Earth, and several pamphlets upon the antiquity of the Hindoos. His room in which he worked, took his meals, slept, and gave his lectures, was a strange exhibition of leather, shoes, wax, victuals, sketches of sphinxes, zodiacs, planispheres, geographical maps, &c. The two poor widows noticed at page 626, as being executed at Bury for *witchcraft,* were natives of Lowestoft. Their names were Rose Cullender and Amy Duny, and their chief accuser was Samuel Pacy, a fanatical dissenter, who imagined that they had bewitched his two daughters.

The PARISH CHURCH (St. Margaret) is inconveniently situated about half a mile west of the town, and is thought to have been placed at that distance to protect it from being undermined by the sea, which at the time of its erection, approached much nearer to the cliff than it does now. It is nearly 183 feet in length, 57 in breadth, and 43 in

height, and has at the west end a square tower, surmounted by a leaded spire rising to the height of 120 feet. It is a handsome structure in the later style of English architecture, and the aisles are separated from the nave and chancel by two rows of handsome pillars. A stately porch on the south side forms the principal entrance, and has on its ceiling an ancient symbol of the Trinity, and over it a room, called the Maids' Chamber, as tradition says, from two sisters who resided in it several years in religious seclusion, before the Reformation. It is also said that these sisters caused two wells to be sunk at their own expense, between the church and the town, for the use of the inhabitants. A screen formerly separated the nave and chancel, and over it was the rood loft. The chancel is remarkably neat and elegant, being repaired and beautified by the Rev. John Tanner and the Rev. John Arrow, two late vicars, who died in 1760 and 1789. The latter erected a new altar piece, enclosed the communion table with handsome iron railing, and opened out the lower part of the east window, which had been bricked up. This window is now filled with beautiful *stained glass*, which was presented about twenty years ago by *Mr. Robt. Allen*, an ingenious gentleman of Lowestoft, who executed it himself. The font is very ancient, and round it are two rows of saints, which were much injured, in 1644, by Dowsing, the parliamentary church spoliator, who tore up all the brasses from the grave stones, except a few which escaped his notice. In 1778, a gallery was erected at the west end of the middle aisle; and in 1780, a good organ was placed in it. The church contains many handsome monuments, and was rebuilt, except the tower, in the fourteenth century by the prior of St. Bartholomew, in London, to whose monastery Lowestoft was appropriated by Henry I. In the middle of the chancel is a stone with the effigy of a bishop carved upon it. This is all that remains of the monument of *Thomas Scroope*, bishop of Dronmore in Ireland, and vicar of Lowestoft, who died here in 1491, aged nearly 100 years. He was of a restless and fanatical disposition : at first a Benedictine, and afterwards a Carmelite monk ; sometimes retiring to his convent for several years, and at others wandering about the country, clothed in sackcloth, girt with an iron chain, and crying out in the streets and lanes that " the New Jerusalem, the bride of the Lamb, was shortly to come down from heaven, prepared for her spouse, and that with great joy he saw the same in spirit." On the first step leading to the communion table, is an inscription in memory of the *Rev. John Tanner*, who was vicar here 51 years, and died in 1759. He was brother to Bishop Tanner, author of the *Notitia Monastica*, of which he completed and published the second edition after his brother's death. He rebuilt part of Kirkley church, (see page 494,) and was for some time commissary and official to the archdeacon of Suffolk. He was distinguished for his activity in promoting the interests of religion, and expended a large sum in repairing and embellishing this church. In 1719, with the aid of £200 from the Governors of Queen Anne's Bounty, and the contributions of the gentlemen of the town and neighbourhood, he purchased the *impropriate rectory* of Lowestoft for £1050, and settled it upon the *vicarage* for ever ; so that the living is now worth about £350 per annum, though valued at only £10. 1s. 0½d. in King's Books, and at £43. 16s. 6d. in the reign of Queen Anne. The Bishop of Norwich is patron, and the Rev. Francis Cunningham

incumbent. In the churchyard are many neat monuments, one of which is in memory of the Rev. Robt. Potter, a late vicar, who died in 1804, and is well known in the literary world as the translator of *Æschylus, Sophocles,* and *Euripides.*

ST. PETER'S CHAPEL OF EASE was erected in 1832-3, in lieu of the old chapel, now forming part of the Town Hall. (See page 501.) It is a handsome Gothic fabric, of white brick, and was finished in 1833, at the cost of £3400, of which £600 was given by the Society for Building and Enlarging Churches, and the remainder was raised by subscription, except about £900, obtained by the sale of pews. It was repaired and beautified in 1842, with money raised by the Rev. F. M. Cunningham, the curate. The great distance of the parish church from the town, rendered it necessary, at an early period, to have a chapel of ease in a more convenient situation. Before the Reformation, there were two chapels here, viz., *Good Cross Chapel*, which stood near the south end of the town, but was destroyed by the sea many years ago ; and the *Old Chapel*, a small thatched fabric, in the centre of the town, which was taken down and rebuilt in 1698, with the corn cross and town chamber adjoining it, at the cost of about £350. As already noticed, this building was used as a chapel of ease till the completion of St. Peter's Chapel. The INDEPENDENTS had a large congregation here as early as 1689. They worshiped in a barn in Blue Anchor lane till 1695, when their present chapel in High street was erected. This building has a good organ, and will hold 550 hearers. The METHODISTS made their first appearance here in 1761, and in 1776, they erected their chapel in Friary lane, which was opened by their celebrated founder, the Rev. John Wesley, A.M. It was enlarged in 1803, and will seat 700 hearers. It has a good organ, purchased in 1839, and attached to it is a house for the minister, and a Day and Sunday school, built in 1821, and enlarged in 1828 and 1843. Here is also a small *Baptist Chapel*, built in 1812, by Mr. Richard Kemp. Lowestoft enjoys the benefit of several valuable *charities, two endowed schools,* and several other schools and *public institutions*, supported by subscription. It has also a *public library*, a subscription *news room*, an *assembly room*, a *theatre*, and other sources of amusement and instruction for the inhabitants, and the numerous visitors who resort to it during the bathing season.

The *Poor and Town Estate* comprises 104A. of land, let for about £271 per annum. It has been vested with feoffees from a very early period, in trust for the repairs of the church, and other public uses, except 28A., which were purchased with £60, given by the will of *Wm. French*, in 1592, to be laid out in land, the rents thereof to be applied in the payment of 13d. a week to 13 poor people of Lowestoft, every Sunday, and 3s. 4d. to the churchwardens, for their trouble in managing the charity. By a decree of the Commissioners of Charitable uses, in 1614, it was ordered that £20 a year (then the value of French's Charity Land,) should be distributed among the poor; that £10 a year should be employed in apprenticing poor children, or in setting poor people to work ; and that the residue of the rents and profits of the town estate should be applied to the repairs of the parish church, and to such other public uses, for the benefit of the town, as the churchwardens and principal inhabitants from time to time agree upon. The site of a house given to the poor by *Ann Girling*, in 1584, is let for 20s. a year ; and a house, garden, and half an acre of land, given to them

by *James Wild*, are let for £8 per annum. In 1772, nearly 3 acres of land was enclosed from the waste on the North Common, and appropriated for the relief of the poor. It is now let for £8 a year. The *Poor's Houses*, which were given by various donors, comprise 25 dwellings, of which 13 are in Fair lane, 8 in Bell lane, and 4 in High street. They are under the care of the churchwardens, and are occupied rent-free by poor parishioners. They are repaired out of the *General Charity Fund*, which amounts to about £121 per annum, of which £47 arises from the before-mentioned charities, and the remainder from the charities of Thomas Annott and John Wilde, afterwards noticed. This fund, after providing for the reparation of the poor's houses, and other incidental expenses, is applied yearly in paying £34. 10s. for the support of Annott's school; £6. 10s. to the master of a Sunday school; £2 for providing books, &c., for the latter; and about £52 for distributions of coals, bread, shoes, clothing, and money among the poor parishioners, who have also a yearly rent-charge of 52s., left by John Hayward, in 1716, out of two houses in High street; the dividends of £200 three per cent. stock, given by *Thomas Baker* and *Anna Arnold*; and the profits of a velvet pall, which was purchased with £30 given by the *Rev. Thomas Troughton* and the *Rev. — Tanner*, and let out to hire for the benefit of the poor. Six neat ALMSHOUSES, each having three rooms, were built by subscription, in 1838, upon the beach, for the residence of six of the oldest and poorest master fishermen of Lowestoft. They have no endowment, but the inmates participate in the charities for the relief of the poor parishioners.

ANNOTT'S SCHOOL.—In 1571, *Thomas Annott* charged his two messuages, called Garbag's and Bennett's, situated at Wheatacre, in Norfolk, with the yearly payment of 20 marks, for the support of a free-school for 40 children of Lowestoft. His heir-at-law increased this annuity to £16 a year, out of which £3. 4s. is deducted for land-tax. The property charged belongs to A. Adair, Esq., who pays £12. 16s. yearly, which is added to the General Charity Fund, out of which £23 per annum is paid to the schoolmaster for teaching 23 boys reading, writing, and arithmetic; and £11. 10s. is expended yearly in finding books and stationery for the scholars, who are appointed by the minister and churchwardens. The master is nominated by the Chancellor of Norwich. This school was enlarged, in 1843, at the cost of £220.

WILDE'S CHARITY.—In 1735, *John Wilde* bequeathed his houses, tenements, lands, &c., in Lowestoft and Worlingham, to the minister and churchwardens of Lowestoft, upon trust, to pay yearly £40 to a schoolmaster, for teaching 40 boys to read, write, and cast accounts; and 21s. to the minister, 10s. to the clerk, and 5s. to the sexton, on condition that a sermon should be preached on December 23rd, from the text, "Train up a child," &c. After paying these yearly sums, the testator directed that the remainder of the rents and profits should be applied to such charitable uses as the trustees should think proper. The estate at Worlingham was exchanged, in 1791, for *Croatfield Farm*, consisting of 118A. 1R. 22P., near Laxfield, now let for £105 a year. The other parts of the charity estate are in Lowestoft parish, and consist of two cottages and a shop, let for £12. 8s. a year; a fish-house, let for £25 a year; a meadow of 1A. 2R., let for £11 a year; and several "*Dole Lands*," which are undistinguishably mixed with the town lands already noticed. Out of the income of this charity (amounting to about £153 per annum,) are paid the following yearly sums, viz., £40 to the schoolmaster; £20 to find books and stationery for the 60 free scholars; £10 for fuel and other necessaries for the school; and £1. 16s. to the minister, clerk, and sexton. The surplus, after providing for repairs, &c., amounts to about £61 per annum, and is carried

to the General Charity Fund, already noticed. The school was built by the trustees many years ago, and the master has the use of a house belonging to the charity, and now instructs 60 boys as free scholars. A GIRLS' SCHOOL and an INFANT SCHOOL, each attended by about 100 children, are supported by subscription. A school connected with the British and Foreign School Society, was established here in 1843.

The *Mutford and Lothingland General Dispensary and Infirmary* is at Lowestoft, and was established in 1822 ; but the handsome and commodious building which it now occupies was not erected till 1839-40, after a subscription of £1018 had been raised for that purpose. The New Infirmary was opened in the spring of 1840, and comprises two spacious wards, well aired and ventilated, and each having room for eight beds. It has also a smaller ward for cases requiring quietude and extra attention. It receives from 70 to 80 patients yearly, and the number of out-patients relieved yearly by the Dispensary is upwards of 300. E. Norton, Esq., is secretary and treasurer of this useful charity, which receives the gratuitous services of several medical gentlemen, and the support of a numerous list of annual subscribers. The *Lowestoft Merchants' Friendly Insurance Association* was established in 1841, and with it nearly all the fishing boats and other craft belonging to the port, are insured from loss and damage at sea. Mr. Thomas Balls is its *secretary*. Here is a SAVINGS' BANK, established in 1818, and now having deposits amounting to upwards of £14,000, belonging to about 400 individuals, and 11 charitable and 14 friendly societies. J. F. Leathes, Esq., is president, and Mr. T. B. Bird secretary, of this provident institution.

LOWESTOFT DIRECTORY.

POST-OFFICE at Mr. Thomas Pratt's, High street.—Letters are received and despatched at 20 minutes before 7 morning, and at 7 evening.

Marked 1, *reside at Alexander place;* 2, *Beach;* 3, *Bell lane;* 4, *Chapel street;* 5, *Dove lane;* 6, *Duke's Head street;* 7, *Factory lane;* 8. *Gall's lane;* 9, *Gun lane;* 10, *Infirmary place;* 11, *London road;* 12, *Mariners' lane;* 13, *Nelson street;* 14, *Old market;* 15, *St. Peter's street;* 16, *South end;* 17, *Terrace;* 18, *West end;* and the others in HIGH STREET, *or where specified.*

11 Archer Robert John, pilot
Arnold Miss Elizabeth
Arthorn Wm. solicitor's clerk
Balls Wm. gent. || 6 Phœbe, carrier
Balsham Mr Wm. || Barnes Mr Jph.
15 Barnes Richard, land surveyor
10 Barrott John, bellman & sexton
11 Baxfield Wm. master mariner
7 Bird T. B. collector, and secretary to Savings' Bank
Bonfellow Robert, chief constable, *Normanston*
15 Brame Robert, gentleman
Brewster Mr John
Browne Robert, professor of music
14 Bugg Daniel, wood turner
1 Butcher Maria (lodgings)
10 Callow Mr Jas. || 11 Mr John
11 Carter Capt.Sl. || Capps Miss My.
3 Carver Charles, cowkeeper
11 Carver MrJs. || 11 Cavell Mrs My.
12 Carver Nelson, cartowner
Chambers Mr Samuel
5 Chapman Rev. Wm. Indpt. min
Cleveland Jas. gent. *White House*
17 Coates Christopher, gentleman
Crisp Geo. Steffe, regr. of marriages
13 Crisp My. || 11 Crowe Miss Eliza
Crowe Thomas, tallow chandler
Cunningham Rev. Francis, vicar
Cunningham Rev. Francis M. curate
11 Dann Mr Wm. || Curtis Mrs E.
11 Dann Mrs F. || Deane Rd. police
Dent Aaron, corn miller, Tower ml
17 Disney Henry Beverley, pilot
11 Eastaugh Jth. Derby, corn mert
15 Ebbs Mr Saml. || 11 Ellis Mrs M.
17 Everard James, gentleman
1 Farrer Sarah (lodgings)
15 Ferrett Cornelius, pilot

15 Freeman Edward, coach builder
Garwood Mrs Mary
3 Gover Rev. Robt. Meth. minister
Gowing Stephen, gentleman
17 Green Wm. Esq. proctor
10 Harvey Geo. veterinary surgeon
Harvey John, High light keeper
15 Hodges Henry Wm. gentleman
2 Hudgell Wm. mast & block maker
Hunt Jph. postman, Black Boy yard
11 Hursthouse Charles, timber mert
Jenner Mr Charles (lodgings)
11 Joachim Lieut. Richard, R.N.
16 Johnson Miss Ann || 13 Mrs Sus.
Johnson Charles, gent. *South Bridge*
Jones John, chimney sweeper
Jones Walter, propr. of *New Baths*
King George, *Battery keeper*
Leathes Edw. Esq. *Normanston hs*
Lincoln John, gent || Lettis Mrs Jn.
6 Loveday Wm. horse breaker
15 Markham Thomas, coachman
Masterson Mrs Sus. || 2 Thos. pilot
17 Martin John, gentleman
11 Matthews Rt. Bates, harbour mr
16 Mendham James, cowkeeper
Morris Mr Rt. || Miller Mrs Mary
15 Neeve Mr Benjamin
Newson Holbert, parish clerk
3 Olley Mrs Mary
Page George, Low Light keeper
Page Wm. glover
13 Parker Mr John
12 Peirson Benjamin, leather seller
Persival Mr Richard
11 Pratt Wm. gentleman
11 Priestley Mrs Elizabeth
Preston Thomas, gentleman
4 Pritty Samuel, chimney sweeper
Randall Rev. John Montagu, assistant curate
Reeve Mrs James
15 Roe Mr Michael Richardson
Rogers Rev. John, Indpt. minister
11 Russell Mr Wm. || 17 Scott Mrs.
Scarlett Wm. pawnbroker
Seaman Edward, bank agent, and
   sub-distributor of stamps
Sheppard Lieut. Richmond, R.N.
Shuckford Isaac, basket maker
3 Simpson Mrs Mary
Smith Elizabeth, eating house
Smith Lady P. || Spall Mrs Susan
6 Sparham Mr Jno. || Thirtle Mr Js.
15 Taylor Charlotte, chimney sweepr
5 Tilmouth Charles, solicitor's clerk
5 Tripp Mr John Neeve

16 Watson Mrs Sar. || Ward Miss M.
3 Watling Mrs Anne || White Miss
10 Wayth Mr Daniel
Wilson Mr James
Wright Wm. brick and tile maker
15 Wright Capt. William
10 Wright William, dyer
Woodgate Rev. Philip, Baptist min
Woods Wm. Jones, coal merchant
Woods Miss Mary
Youngman Hy. corn & flour factor
11 Yaxley Hercules, coast officer

ATTORNEYS.
13 Barnard Wm. Vince (conveyancer and shipping agent)
Hickling James Wigg (and notary)
Norton Edmund, superintendent registrar, clerk to magistrates, &c.
Seago Wm. Rix (and notary)

BANKERS.
Gurneys & Co. (on Barclay and Co.)
   John Brown Chaston, *agent*
National Provincial Bank (on Lon-
   don Joint Stock Bank) J. W.
   Hickling, *agent*
Lacons & Co. (on Glyn & Co.) Edw.
   Seaman, *agent*, Stamp office
Savings' Bank, Town Hall ; Mr. T.
   B. Bird, *actuary*

FIRE & LIFE OFFICE AGTS.
7 Atlas, Thomas Bates Bird
Crown Life, J. Hole
Guardian, J. B. Chaston
London Assurance, Saml. F. Abbott
Norwich Union, Wm. Rix Seago
   and J. W. Hickling
Phœnix Fire, Richard Salmon
Suffolk Amicable and Country Fire
   and Family Endowment Society,
   Thomas Crowe
Sun Fire, Edmund Norton

HOTELS, INNS, & TAVERNS.
Blue Anchor, Wm. Smith
2 Bowling Green, Thomas Jarvis
5 British Queen, Edward Banham
5 Compasses, James Jarvis
Crown Inn, (and posting house,) Su-
   sanna Balls
Crown and Anchor, Thomas Balls
Dutch Hoy, Joseph Allerton
5 Ferry Boat, James Nobbs
13 Fox & Hounds, Wm. E. Godfrey
George & Dragon, Wm. Nobbs
Globe, Edward Johnson
Herring Fishery, Robert Watson
Jolly Maltster, John Plant
12 King's Head, Robert Holbrock

12 Mariners, Edward Cox
Queen's Head Inn, (and posting-house,) Thomas Punchard
Ship, William Day
11 Suffolk Hotel, Philip Westrup
Three Herrings, Thomas Utting

Academies.
14 Cunningham J.
Drackett Mrs R.
Garwood Margt. and Jane
16 George E.
17 Greathead Jas. Thomas
Greenfield John
Gurney Eliz.
Hubart & Smith
2 Roger Walter
Salter Louisa and Susan
Tooke Sarah
Tooke William
Woodgate Philip

Auctioneers.
Balls Thomas
Catchpole Thos.
Haward Samuel

Bakers, &c.
Adams George
5 Adams James
12 Barber James
Capps John
13 Cook Wm.
Cook Samuel
Feek Joseph
6 Kersey Aldiss
3 Nevill Townsend
Redgrave John
Searle Richard
3 Smith James
12 Wicks Saml.

Beer Houses.
6 Allerton Saml.
2 Capps Francis
Cooper Jn. *(retlr.)*
Day John
2 Day Susannah
2 Dann Wm.
12 Dowson Ham.
2 Gowing Robt.
3 Gray John
7 Hott John
Holbury Wm.
4 Livock Wm. (porter)
2 Pye Walter

4 Raven Robert
Redgrave James
2 Saunders Rd.
Sharman George
2 Simmonds Rd.
3 Strowlger John
3 Tongate Mary

Blacksmiths.
7 Aldiss Robt.
3 Aldiss Robt.
14 Baines Benj.
9 Cannell James
8 Clark Robert
3 Cooper James
2 Durrant Joseph
6 Mills Francis
Neslen Robert, Beccles road

Boat Builders.
Barcham Bachelor
2 Sparham Saml.

Boat Owners.
(See Fish Curers.)

Booksellers, Printers, &c.
Crisp Geo. Steffe
Crowe Thos. (& fancy repository)
Salmon Rt. Hy.
Taylor James, *binder*

Boot & Shoe Mkrs.
11 Albrow Chas.
3 Brown John
Burgess John
Colby Saml.
Cords Mary
16 Cornaby Thos.
13 Downing Wm.
6 Durrant John
Edmonds John
12 Fucher Aaron
2 German John
6 Ling Job
15 Mickleburgh Edward
3 Outon Wm.
Porter Thomas
4 Rampling Rd.

15 Saunders Jph.
3 Thaker Chas.
5 Townsend Thos.
Winyard Robt.
6 Woods John

Braziers & Tinrs.
4 Clark Samuel
Bishop Jn. Porter
Foreman John

BREWERS and Maltsters.
Everitt Geo. and William
3 Morse Fredk.
Youngman Wm. and Son

Bricklayers.
11 Balls James
12 Newson John
12 Pearce Eliz.
12 Rix George
Searle Wm.
Simmonds James
8 Smith John
16 Swatman Ths.
15 Sustins Geo.

Butchers.
Beecroft Wm.
Branch John
Branch Samuel
Buffham James
Chipperfield Ths.
9 Martin John
4 Martin John
Rackham Wm.
4 Smith George
12 Smith John

Cabinet Makers & Upholsterers.
Brewster Robert
Gill Henry
Scarll Wm.
Titlow Wm.

Chemists & Drgs.
Edmonds Benj. Morris
Morris Robert
Snell Francis

Clothes Dealers.
Capps Wm.
12 Ceiley Robt.
Corbyn George

COOPERS.
6 Barber John
2 Capps Samuel
5 Dunham Wm.
10 Jarvis Thos.

2 King George
Redgrave John
7 Peake Wm.
2 Stannard Eliza
2 Tripp Robert

FARMERS.
10 Burton John
Coleman Edw.
Jenner John
18 Mobbs Robt.
Roe Michael R.
Pearce John
Pye Wm.

FISH CURERS and Boat Owners.
15 Allerton Geo.
Allerton Joseph
Allerton Thomas
Allerton and Barcham
Balls Wm. jun.
Balls Thomas, *(salesman)*
Baines Benj.
2 Barber John
Barcham Bachelor
2 Burgess Wm.
11 Butcher John
Carr John
2 Cleveland Wm.
Cox George
Everitt Geo. and William
6 Folkard Saml.
2 Gall John
Gowing G. Sead, (agt. to Lloyds)
6 Hammersley R.
7 Hott John
2 Jarvis James
2 King & Culley
Lincoln William, *(salesman)*
15 Lincoln Wm.
2 Livock Wm.
2 Masterson Wm.
2 Matchett John
17 Nash Samuel
11 Porter Thos.
Redgrave John
2 Roberts John
2 Richmond Wm.
6 Sharman Shadh.
2 Simmons Rd.
2 Sparham Saml.
2 Stannard Eliza

11 Sterry Jas. G.
Sterry John
3 Sterry Robert
2 Taylor Benj.
2 Taylor James
2 Thirtle & Pratt
Thirtle James
2 Tilmouth Chas.
2 Tripp Robert
6 Ward Saml. L.
2 Wilson James
Woods W. Jones

*Gardeners and
Seedsmen.*
Ashman George
Church Wm. (&
porter dealer)
15 Cowles Benj.

*Glass, Earthen-
ware, &c. Dealers*
Day James
Hill J. B.
6 Parr Wm.
Smith John

GROCERS,
Tea Dealers, &c.
Abbott Saml. F.
Blaxhill Samuel
Browne Rt. sen.
Butcher Samuel,
South bridge
Cornaby Thomas
4 Cowling John
Crisp Geo. Steffe
Curtis James
Day James
Devereaux John
Farrar John
Fisher James
Smith J. Sharman

Gun Makers.
Dale Robert
15 Morter Edw.

Ironmongers.
Farrer John
Precious Robert

Joiners, &c
14 Bemmant Jph.
7 Beckett James
Brewster Robt.
11 Brown Chas. R.
10 Callow James
12 Cullingham P.
2 Hall Robt.
3 Neslen Samuel

*Linen & Woollen
Drapers.*
Chaston John
Brown
Fuller Robert
Hunwick Fras.
Pratt Thomas
Salter Rt. & Wm.

*Marine Store
Dealers.*
16 Allerton Btw.
Balls William
2 Cullingford Ts.
2 Garwood Eliz.
10 Martin John

Milliners, &c.
6 Adams Sophia
Fuller Robt.
Jenner Matilda

*Painters, Plumb-
ers, & Glaziers.*
13 Barrett Robt.
12 Hicks Wm.
Johnson Saml.
11 Ling John
6 Rackham Geo.
15 Whincup Geo.
4 Winter Wm.

*Perfumers and
Hair Dressers.*
Emms Joseph
Chambers Saml.
Fisher Edward
4 Harris Wm.
6 Robins Wm.
Salter Robert

*Saddlers & Har-
ness Makers.*
Drewell Samuel
Martin John

Sail Makers.
Brewster Edw. &
Wm. Northend
14 Tilmouth Chs.
4 Tilmouth Btwt.

Shopkeepers.
13 Allum Eliz.
3 Broom Fras.
2 Butcher Ann
2 Dann Wm.
Day John
13 Downing Wm.
4 Goldsmith Chs.
Hill J. B.
4 Killett Robert
12 Salmons My.
2 Saunders Rd.

12 Smith John

Straw Hat Mkrs.
Jones Walter
11 Rogers Jane
Smith J. S.

SURGEONS.
Brame Samuel
Sharman
11 Hodgkin Jph.
17 Hole John, (&
registrar)
Prentice John
Worthington W.
Collins

TAILORS.
Abbott Edmund
8 Brame Thomas
Capps Wm.
5 Cooper John
Freeman Thomas
Tripp
10 Gardener Fras.
Golder Michael
Hogg Henry
2 Mitchell Wm.
Punchard Chas.
Robinson Thos.
Titlow Thomas
Ward Philip

TEA DEALERS.
*(See also Grocers
& Shopkeepers.)*
Crisp G. F.
2 Jenkinson Saml.
Taylor James

*Twine and Rope
Spinners.*
15 Bly Abel

8 Capps Robert
8 Crisp Thomas
2 Cook Cotton
15 Folkard Thos.
8 Gall John
Gardener James
Gowing George,
Denes
6 Hammersley J.
7 Holt John
2 Holt Richard
15 Jarvis James
2 Leggett James
15 Masterson W.
6 Parr Wm.
2 Saunders Wm.
15 Sterry John

*Watch and Clock
Makers.*
Crake Edmund
Dye John, (and
engraver)
2 Lederer Jacob
Naylor Thos.
Sharman Geo.

Wheelwrights.
12 Cox Edward
15 Drackett Robt.
15 Freeman Edw.
(& coach bldr)
15 Spurgeon Jcb.

*Wine and Spirit
Merchants.*
Balls Thomas
Everitt Geo. and
Wm.
2 Morse Fredk.

COACHES.

Mail and *Telegraph* to Ipswich and
London, at 7 evening ; and to Yar-
mouth, at 20 min. before 7 morn-
ing ; (from the Crown.)
Coaches from the Queen's Head to
London, ½ past 8 morning ; and to
Yarmouth, ½ past 5 aftn. daily ; to
Norwich, Monday and Wed ; and
in summer also on Tues. Thurs.
and Fri. at 7 morning

CARRIERS.

To *Beccles, Norwich, &c.* J. Watson,
Wed. & Sat ; and J. Elliott, Mon.
and Thursday ; (from the Crown
and Anchor)
To *Halesworth,* James Page, Wed ;
(from the Crown and Anchor)
To *Yarmouth,* &c. Phœbe Balls'

Van, three times a day; and **J. Burton's Van**, Tues. Thu. & Sat. at 9 morng. from the Crown and Anchor; also *Sarah Martin*, from the Blue Anchor, Monday, Wed.

and Sat; and to *London*, Monday and Thursday

TRADING VESSELS

To London, every week; & Wherries to Yarmouth, every alternate day

MUTFORD, a straggling village and parish, 5 miles E.S.E. of Beccles, and 6½ miles S.W. of Lowestoft, is situated at the south-west angle of the southern division of this hundred, to which it gives name. It has 422 inhabitants, and 1499 acres of land, forming a champaign, but fertile tract. Lord S. G. Osborne is lord of the manor, but the chief part of the soil belongs to the Rev. C. Clark, Mr. Robert Gilbert, Mr. Robinson, and a few smaller owners. The *Church* (St. Andrew) is a small antique fabric with a tower, round in its lower parts, and octangular at the top. The *vicarage*, valued in K.B. at £7. 17s. 1d., is consolidated with the rectories of Barnby and Wheatacre All Saints, as already noticed at page 482. The patronage and the great tithes of Mutford belong to Gonville and Caius College, Cambridge. The present estimated yearly rental of the parish is £2198. 15s., and the tithes have been commuted for £280 per annum. Here is a small *Wesleyan Chapel*, built in 1828; and a *National School*, erected in 1842, by the Rev. Wm. Okes, the rector, who resides at Wheatacre, in Norfolk. The *Poor's Allotment*, about 15 acres, was awarded at the enclosure of the common, about the year 1800, and is let for about £16 a year, which is distributed in coals among the poor parishioners, who have also the interest of £10, left by John King.

Candler Mrs Mary
Chamberlin P. schoolmistress
Larke Alfred, bricklayer
Lay Stephen, shopkeeper
Mapes John, farrier
Mills Wm. shoemaker
Neeve Philip, corn miller
Pleasence Thomas, blacksmith
Ratcliffe Wm. coach builder
Smith Samuel, shopkeeper

Stratford Robert, beerhouse
Suggate Wm. thatcher

FARMERS.

Buckham Joseph || Brown John
Candler Stephen || Catchpole Robt.
Chalker Elliott || Fairhead Robert
Hunt Harry || Ives Edward
Keer Wm. || Lambrass John
Smith Wm. (*owner*)
Woodthorpe Maria || Leath Widow

OULTON is a pleasant scattered village, 3 miles W. of Lowestoft. Its parish is bounded on the west by the river Waveney, and on the south by the western part of *Lake Lothing*, commonly called *Oulton Broad*, on which an annual *Regatta* is held. (See pages 480 and 498.) It comprises 1970A. 3R. 32P. of fertile land, and had 675 inhabitants in 1841, including 15 fishermen, who were absent when the census was taken, and 141 paupers in the *Mutford and Lothingland House of Industry*, which is situated here, as already noticed at page 481. R. M. Baxter, Esq., is now lord of the *manor of Oulton*, which was successively held by the Bacon, Fastolf, Hobart, Reeve, Heythuson, Allen, Graves, and Bucknell families; but Lord S. G. Osborne, as owner of Somerleyton, has a paramount jurisdiction, and a great part of the soil belongs to John Penrice, Esq., the Rev. R. A. Arnold, Mrs. Reeve, J. Chapman, Esq., H. Mileham, Esq., Mr. T. Roe, and *Mr. George Borrow*. The latter gentleman is author of "The Bible in Spain," &c., and has a handsome residence on the north side of the lake. The *Church* (St. Michael) is an ancient cruciform structure, with a tower

rising from its centre ; but the south transept went to ruin many years ago, and has never been restored. The rest of the fabric was thoroughly repaired in 1836. The tower contains five bells, and was formerly surmounted by a spire. In the south porch are many small-pointed niches, and over the inner door is a fine Saxon arch. In the windows are some fragments of ancient stained glass, and on the chancel floor is a large stone, bearing effigies in brass of John Fastolf, and Katherine his wife, with their feet resting on a greyhound. The former died in 1445, and the latter in 1478. Upon another stone is a full-length brass of a priest, probably one of the Fastolf family, who were formerly seated here, and were great benefactors to the church. The benefice is a *rectory*, valued in K.B. at £14. 3s. 4d., and in 1835 at £378, in the patronage of Lord S. G. Osborne, and incumbency of the Rev. E. P. Denniss, B.C.L., who, in 1836-7, erected a large and handsome *Rectory House*, at the cost of £1600, of which £800 was advanced under the provisions of the Gilbert Act. This mansion has extensive gardens, and is pleasantly situated nearly in the centre of the *glebe*, which comprises upwards of 49 acres. The tithes have been commuted for £462 per annum, including the quota on the glebe. The *Parochial School* is a neat building, surrounded by trees and shrubs, and situated at the entrance to the rectory grounds. It was built in 1843 by the rector, aided by subscription, and a donation of £50 by the late Rev. G. Anguish. It is supported by the rector for the education of about 30 boys and 40 girls, and he generously clothes 20 of the latter. About 40a. of marsh land is held by the rector, churchwardens, and overseers, in trust for the poor parishioners, for whose benefit the produce thereof is yearly sold by auction, and the proceeds distributed in coals, during the inclemency of winter. The present gross estimated yearly rental of the parish is £2931, and the rateable value £2597. 10s. *Oulton* is supposed to have been formerly called *Old Town*, and part of its houses are near MUTFORD BRIDGE, which crosses Lake Lothing 2 miles W. of Lowestoft, and has a suburb on the south side, in Carlton Colville parish, (see pages 487 and 498.)

Bickers George, shoemaker, *Mutford Bridge*
Beaumont Isaac, victualler, Wherry, *Mutford Bridge*
Borrow George, gentleman
Bultitude Geo. shoemaker and vict. *Boar*
Crickmay Lincoln, butcher
Denniss, Rev Edwin Proctor, B.C.L. *Rectory*
Draper Sarah, beerhouse keeper
George Henry, corn miller
Harrison Henry, govnr. *Workhouse*
Gosling John, schoolmaster
Henry John, beerhouse & shopkpr.
Kiddle James, ironfounder

Knight John, corn miller and cement manufacturer
Knight Pleasance, lime burner
Mileham Henry, Esq.
Osborn John, shoemkr. & overseer
Roe Thomas brick and tile maker
Smith Thomas, wheelwright
Woods John J. maltster and corn merchant

FARMERS.

George Johnson || Farman Robert
Goff Thomas || Goldsmith Philip
Owles Wm. *Marsh*
Page Alfred || Roe Thos. (owner)
Roll Daniel || Utting Samuel

PAKEFIELD, (see page 495.)

RUSHMERE, a scattered village and parish, on the northern acclivity of a pleasant valley, 6 miles E.S.E. of Beccles, and S.W. of Lowestoft, contains 780 acres of land, and 134 inhabitants. Lord Bos-

ton is lord of the manor, but nearly all the soil belongs to Wm. Tallent, Esq., of Rushmere Hall. The *Church* (All Saints) is a thatched fabric with a round tower and two bells. The benefice is a discharged rectory, formerly in two medieties, valued in K.B. at £7. 6s. 8d., and in 1835 at £217. Chas. Gurney, Esq., is patron, and the Rev. Thos. Wm. Irby incumbent. The tithes were commuted in 1843, and it is in contemplation to erect a parsonage-house. About 20 perches of land, on Hannah's Green, was given, many years ago, by the lord of the manor, for the use of the poor, and is let for 12s. a year. The poor parishioners have also 6s. 8d. yearly from *Branden's Charity*, (see Henstead.)

Blowers Elizabeth, vict. *Tuns*
Chittleborough John, grocer & drpr.
Cooper Wm. boot and shoe maker
Crickmore Samuel, butcher
Lydamore John, farmer
Owles Thomas, farmer
Spanton Wm. blacksmith
Tallent Wm. Esq. *Rushmere Hall*

SOMERLEYTON, a pleasant scattered village, 4½ miles N.W. of Lowestoft, and 8 miles S.S.W. of Yarmouth, has in its parish 514 inhabitants, and 1380 acres of fertile land. Lord Sydney G. Osborne, is Lord of the manor, but part of the soil belongs to several other proprietors. In the reign of the Norman Conqueror, this manor was held by William, Earl of Warren, from whom it passed to the *Fitz Osberts*, who were lord-wardens of Lothingland, and had many other manors in Suffolk. In the latter part of the 13th century, Sir Walter Jernegan, Knight, of Horham and Stoneham-Jernegan, married Isabella, daughter, and at length sole heiress, of Sir Peter Fitz Osbert. The *Jernegans*, or *Jerninghams*, were ancestors of Lord Stafford, of Costessey Hall, Norfolk, and a principal branch of them were seated here until the reign of James I., when Henry Jerningham, Esq., of Costessey, who married the daughter of Sir John Jernegan, of Somerleyton, sold his estate and manors in this neighbourhood to John Wentworth, Esq., whose nephew, John Garneys, Esq., succeeded to them in 1652, but his son Thomas sold them to *Amiral Sir Thomas Allen, Bart.*, of Lowestoft, as noticed at page 502. Sir Thomas Allen, the son of this distinguished admiral, died a bachelor, and his estates passed to his nephew, *Richard Anguish, Esq.*, on condition of his taking the name and arms of Allen, which he did, and was created a *baronet* in 1699, but the title became extinct in 1794. Thomas Anguish, Esq., dying a bachelor in 1810, the Somerleyton estate and its dependencies passed to the late Rev. George Anguish, M.A., who died about a year ago, when they passed to *Lord Sydney Godolphin Osborne*, son of the third Duke of Leeds, by his second wife, Catherine, who was sister to the late Mr. Anguish. Lord S. G. Osborne is lord of many of the manors in this Hundred, and has a paramount jurisdiction over several others. He is about to reside at SOMERLEYTON HALL, which was built by Sir John Jernegan in the reign of Elizabeth, and stands in a beautiful park finely clothed with trees and evergreens. When Fuller visited it, he exclaimed, " It well deserves the name of Summerley, because it was always summer there, the walks and gardens being planted with perpetual greens." It is a brick building, having a high roof with dormers, stone pilasters, and a cornice. The quoins and dressings of the windows are of stone. The centre is very bold and imposing, and the extremities have curved pediments, terminating in scrolls, of considerable magnitude.

The windows of the great hall are richly decorated with stained glass, and some of the other apartments are of excellent proportions, and exhibit some fine specimens of carving by the ingenious Gibbons.   In an adjoining park of 40 acres, stands the *Rectory House*, a large and handsome mansion of white brick, erected in 1773; and at a short distance is another neat mansion, which was the seat of Cammant Money, Esq., and stands near a small lake called *Wicker Well*, having its banks fringed with drooping shrubs.   The *Church* (St. Mary) is situated near the hall, and is a neat fabric, with a tower and five bells.   It contains several memorials of the Jernegans, Wentworths, Garneys, and Allens, formerly seated here.   The venerable altar-tomb of Sir Thos. Jernegan formerly bore this inscription, "*Jesus Christ, both God and Man—Save thy servant Jernegan,*" but it has lost its brasses and ornaments, except several shields of arms.   The *rectory*, valued in K.B. at £12, and in 1835 at £386, is in the patronage of Lord S. G. Osborne, and incumbency of the Rev. E. M. Love, M.A., who succeeded his father in the living.   Here is a small National School, established in 1835.   The *Poor's Allotment*, 11A. 1R. 27P. of marsh land, was awarded at the enclosure for providing fuel for the poor parishioners, and is now let for about £35 per annum.

Osborne Lord Sydney Godolphin, *Somerleyton Hall*
Love Rev Edward Missenden, M.A. *Rectory*
Balls James, vict. Duke's Head
Bowler John, wheelwright
Ellis Susan, gardener
Farrow Thos. shopr. and shoemaker
Farrow Mary, wheelwright
Flowerdew Charles, corn miller
Flowerdew Maria, shopkeeper
Green Mr James
Green John, brick and tile maker
Harding Wm. blacksmith
Havers Robert, bricklayer
Horn Wm. blacksmith
Pope Richard, beerseller
Sinnet Samuel, shoemaker

FARMERS.

Balls James || Flatman Robert
Creighton John || Green John
George Rd. || Crich Rt. Cammant
Glasspole John || Larkman Robert

GORLESTON is a large and handsome village, pleasantly situated on the crown of a hill, about two miles S. of Great Yarmouth, overlooking the river Yare, which flows in a rapid stream at the foot of the acclivity, and about a mile below, is lost in the wide expanse of the German Ocean, after being separated from it for about three miles, only by the narrow strip of land upon which Great Yarmouth is built.   The PARISH OF GORLESTON comprises also the populous hamlet of *South Town*, or *Little Yarmouth*, which was anciently a separate parish, and was added to the *Borough of Great Yarmouth* in 1681, as also was Gorleston by the Parliamentary and Municipal Reform Acts of 1832 and 1835.   It comprises 1931A. 1R. 11P. of land, and increased its population from 1728 souls in 1801, to 3779 in 1841.   Of these contents 596A. 2R. 23P. and 1428 souls are in *South Town* hamlet, and 1334A. 2R. 28P. and 2351 souls in *Gorleston*.   According to Domesday Book, the whole parish was in one manor, held by *Earl Guert* in the Confessor's time, and having five caracutes of land, 20 villeins, five bordars, two caracutes in demesne, three salt pans, 300 sheep, and 24 fishermen.   Afterwards the parish was in four manors, a paramount, a principal, and two mesne, of all of which the Jernegans were lords. It is now only in two, viz., the paramount *manor of Gorleston*, of which

Lord Sydney Godolphin Osborne is lord ; and the small *manor of Bacon's*, which is held in fee by James Barber, Esq. The former has all the royalties and the two ferries, but the soil and buildings belong to various owners, the largest of whom are the Earl of Lichfield (owner of most of the land in South Town,) Jas. Barber, Esq., J. Garnham, Esq., J. S. Bell, Esq., W. D. Palmer, Esq., Mr. and Miss Rope, Mr. G. Glasspool, and Mr. M. Goody; several of whom have handsome houses here. The greater part of South Town is let on building leases for the term of 99 years. The present estimated *gross yearly rental* of the parish is £12,533. 11s. 3d., viz., Gorleston, £5239. 13s. ; and South Town, £7293. 18s. 3d. The two divisions maintain their poor conjointly as one township, and are in the incorporated Hundred of Mutford and Lothingland, which has its workhouse at Oulton, as noticed at page 481. The *waste lands* in the parish, were enclosed under an act passed in 1812. Tradition says, that Gorleston had once a weekly market ; and the Index Monasticus informs us, that in 1372, it had a *house of lepers*, but the site is unknown. By custom, it has a small fair at Whitsuntide, for toys, &c. In 1797, the mutilated remains of a stone cross were visible, a little south of the village, but they disappeared many years ago. Almost every part of Gorleston commands a sea prospect over the river Yare and the narrow denes of Yarmouth, where the *Norfolk Naval Column*, erected in 1817, in memory of that gallant admiral, *Lord Nelson*, is a conspicuous and pleasing object. The village has many excellent houses for the accommodation of sea bathers. The *South Pier*, which projects into the sea, at the mouth of the Yare, was greatly enlarged some years ago ; and a continuation of it, in a fine curve, carried up the river, forms an extensive and excellent wharf. It is constructed chiefly of large timber trees, joined and braced together by cross beams of iron work ; and measures 340 yards in length, 30 feet in breadth, and 30 feet in depth ; of which latter, 26 feet are generally under water. This pier, and about 30 acres of marsh land, called *Cobholm Island*, belong to Yarmouth parish, though on the Gorleston side of the river. The *white cliffs*, which extend in an uninterrupted curve from Gorleston to Lowestoft, are of considerable elevation, and afford delightful views of the harbour, the town, the ocean, and the adjacent country. A little south of the village is *Battery Hill*, so named from a platform of guns placed there during the late war. The sloping edge of this eminence is occupied by a range of neat houses, all built during the present century. The *Parish Church* (St. Andrew) is a large ancient structure, on a commanding eminence a little south west of the village. Its has a thatched nave, chancel, and side aisles, and a substantial square tower, containing a peal of six bells ; the tenor of which weighs 13 cwt. It is of plain architecture, and is constructed chiefly of flint, and lighted by sixteen windows. The benefice is a *vicarage*, with the *rectories* of the decayed parishes of South Town and West Town annexed to it ; and valued in K.B. at £11, and in 1835 at £381. The Rev. Francis Upjohn, M.A., is patron and incumbent, and has the great tithes of South Town, and also the tithes of wood, hay, and clover in Gorleston, wher the corn tithes belong to the Brown family. Here is a chapel, belonging to the *Independents*, and another to the *Wesleyans*. In the village are *National Schools*, forming a neat brick building, and attended by about 110 boys, 80 girls, and 70 infants.

South Town, or Little Yarmouth, is a hamlet of Gorleston parish, and a handsome western suburb of Great Yarmouth, with which it is connected by a good bridge across the Yare, which is here lined on both sides with extensive ranges of wharfs, quays, warehouses, docks, and ship-yards, but most of the latter are on the South Town side of the river. The hamlet of South Town, as already noticed, was added to the borough of Great Yarmouth, in 1681, and comprises 596A. 2R. 26P. of land, and 1428 inhabitants, though it was a very small and inconsiderable place till about 1806, when the merchants of Great Yarmouth began to erect neat and commodious houses here. It anciently formed two small parishes, called *South Town and West Town*, the churches of which were dedicated to *St. Mary and St. Nicholas*, but went to decay before the year 1559, when the remains of the former were used in repairing the piers. In 1831, a handsome *Chapel of Ease*, dedicated to St. Mary, was erected here by subscription, at the cost of about £3000, on land given by the Earl of Lichfield. It is built of white brick and flint, and lighted by lancet-shaped windows. It has seats for 1000 hearers, and its present minister is the Rev. J. E. Cox, M.A. Near the road, a little west of the Greyhound public-house, are some vestiges of a religious house, supposed to have been an *Augustine Friary*, founded by Wm. Woodrove, and Margaret, his wife. Fragments of the chapel, and the dormitories of the Friars, are still visible; but a large portion of the ruined walls were many years ago converted into a barn, which has since been transformed into cottages. The *Church of St. Nicholas*, the parish church of West Town, was attached to this friary, and stood on the west side of the High street in Gorleston. The eastern face of its lofty tower was standing till 1813, when it fell down during a high wind, and its materials were used in erecting a lofty wall round what was formerly part of the churchyard. The adjacent grounds exhibit marks of having been used for interment. In a garden adjoining the site of the tower, a brick vault was opened about twenty years ago, and in it was found an entire skeleton. The friary was endowed by several benefactors, and was granted, in 1544, to John Eyre. There was anciently a *Hermitage* here, but its site is unknown, as also is the site of a prison, noticed in the church books of Yarmouth as having been broken open by Simon Blaking, in 1297. Near the bridge, in South Town, is "*Yarmouth Proprietary Grammar School,*" a neat cruciform building of white brick, erected in 1833, by a company of proprietors, in 100 shares of £15 each. The *Royal Armory* here was built in 1806, by government, at the cost of £15,000; and during the war, about 10,000 stand of arms were arranged in it, but it has been unoccupied since the general peace. *Captain Manby*, the inventor of the machine for conveying ropes to stranded vessels, has a neat residence in South Town, and near it he has erected a handsome pedestal, in commemoration of the 12th of Feb., 1808, when his machine was first successfully used. He has now the pleasing satisfaction of knowing that more than a thousand lives have been saved by his invention.

GREAT YARMOUTH, on the eastern side of the river Yare, opposite South Town and Gorleston, is the principal *sea port*, and second town of magnitude in Norfolk, and stands pre-eminent for its prolific *herring and mackarel fisheries*. It also enjoys an extensive

traffic in coal, corn, &c., and is in great celebrity as a bathing-place, being pleasantly situated on that narrow peninsular strip of land, which is less than a mile in breadth, and stretches about five miles in length from north to south, between the German Ocean and the river Yare; 123 miles N.E. of London; 19 miles E. by S. of Norwich, and nearly 10 miles N. of Lowestoft. Its parish comprises 1270 acres, and its population increased from 14,845 in 1801, to 24,262 souls in 1841. It is in the East Flegg Hundred of Norfolk, and is an ancient *borough*, to which the suburbs of South Town and Gorleston have been added, as already noticed. The *town*, from the shape of the peninsula on which it stands, is built in the form of a long and irregular parallelogram, comprising about 133 acres, extending more than a mile southward, along the banks of the river, and about half a mile eastward, towards the sea beach. On the east, north, and south, it is encompassed by extensive remains of an embattled *wall*, 2238 yards in length, and formerly having ten *gates* and sixteen *towers*, mostly of flint; but all the former, except Pudding-gate, have been removed since 1790, for the improvement of the entrances to the town, and, though many of the towers remain, they have been variously disfigured and altered. The principal streets except two, are uniformly in the direction of north and south, and are connected by more than 150 narrow lanes or alleys, called *Rows*, and distinguished only by numbers. The *markets*, held every Wednesday and Saturday, are well supplied with corn and provisions. A *fair* for all kinds of merchandise, except cattle, is held on the Friday and Saturday after Easter; and a pleasure fair on Shrove Monday and Tuesday. *Races* are held on the denes in the latter part of August. As a *bathing place*, few towns possess more attractions than Yarmouth; for, besides excellent inns and hotels, here are a considerable number of comfortable boarding and lodging houses; baths and bathing machines of the best description, and several beautiful public gardens and bowling greens. Pleasure and exercise may be at all times enjoyed in a variety of forms. To such as delight in the bustle of mercantile pursuits, the unrivalled Commercial Quay, and the wharfs, docks, ship yards, &c., extended on both sides of the Yare, offer an enlivening treat; whilst the admirers of nature, in her quiet and rustic garb, may solace themselves in the more remote parts of the beach and the denes, where the lover of scenery may enjoy extensive marine views, and the botanist amuse himself by examining a variety of rare plants. The town has *three churches*, about *twelve chapels*, several charity schools and hospitals, and a variety of public institutions for the solace of age and poverty, and for amusement and instruction. Its *History* is long and interesting, and will be found in our *Norfolk Work;* but as its trade and commerce are closely connected with the county of Suffolk, we subjoin the following *Directory* of its principal inhabitants, together with those of *Gorleston* and *South Town*, on the west side of the haven.

YARMOUTH DIRECTORY,

Including SOUTH TOWN AND GORLESTON.

POST-OFFICE, Short Quay; Mr. David Hogarth, jun., postmaster. Letters *despatched* to London and the south, at 6 evening; to Birmingham, Lynn, and all parts of the north and west, at half-past 4 afternoon; and to Norwich, &c.. at a quarter before 2 afternoon.

The CONTRACTIONS occasionally used for the names of streets, &c., are Bpl., for Belgrave place; Cht., Charlotte street; Chq., Church square; Csq., Chapel square; Cpl., Clarence place; Fgt., Factorygate; Fqy., Fishers' quay; Glt., Goal st.; Gst., George st.; Gtn., *Gorleston;* Hst., Howard st.; Jrd., Jetty road; Kst., King st.; Mgt., Marketgate; Mkp., Market place; Mrw., Market row; Nbh., North beach; Nqy., North quay; Ntc., North entrance; Qsq., Queen square; R., Row; Rst., Regent street; Sqy., Short quay; Psq., St. Peter's square; Sbh., South beach; Sgt., St. George's gate; Sdn., South denes; Stn., *South Town;* Tpn., Theatre plain, or gate; Upl., Union place; Wpl., Wellington place; and Wqy., for West quay.

MISCELLANY *of Gentry, Clergy, Partners in Firms, and others not arranged in the succeeding Classification of Trades and Professions.*

Absolon Mrs My. Kst
Adams Thos. landing, surveyor; h Stn
Ainsley Capt. C. Kent pl
Aiken Mrs Eliz. 51 Mkp
Aldis John, clerk, Ntc
Aldis Thos. clerk, Kst
Algar John, clerk, Gtn
Allen Jas. clerk, Stn
Amis Edw. gent. East st
Andrews Mr Robt. Bpl
Armstrong, Mrs M. A. King street
Artis Mrs Eliz. Gaol st
Ashley Lieut. Benj. Stn
Atkinson Mrs Cht. Chq
Atthill Edw. gent. Kst
Auckland Wm. landing waiter; h South Town
Bacon Mrs S. Bath pl
Baker Mrs Ann, King st
Baker John, solr; house *Browston Hall*
Bales Jno. Barnet, serjt. at mace, Charlotte st
Banks Isaac, master of . floating light, 139 Gaol street
Banyer Mr Wm. King st
Barber Jas. Esq. Gtn
Barber Rt. Dvd. clerk to comssrs. of taxes, Hst
Barcham Mrs. Nquay
Barnaby Rt. Andrews, sheriff's officer, Kst
Barnes Rt. mert. Rst
Barrett Mrs Ptnc. Stn

Bartley Mrs M. A. Stn
Barton Mr Samuel, Stn
Batcheler Ths. Horace, gent. King street
Bateman Geo. surgeon, Market place
Baxfield Jph. organist, Charlotte street
Baynes Capt. Wm. H. E.C. North quay
Beart C. J. gent. Kst
Beckett Mrs. Wesley st
Beckett Wm. colr. Nqy
Belden J.H. teacher, Stn
Bell Mr Carsey, Stn
Bell John, Penrice, solr; house Gorleston
Bell Rd. Esq. collector of customs; h Gtn
Bell Wm. P. gent. 36 Cht
Beloe Hy. gent. Stn
Beloe Mrs M. Fuller's hl
Bell Rev G. R. Gtn
Berners Lord, N. beach
Betts Rev Hy. (Bapt.) North quay
Bickerton Geo. gent. Hst
Bircham Wm. gent. Sbh
Bird Mr Jas. quay, Stn
Blackburn Mrs Maria, South Town
Blake Mr Thos. Seymour place
Bly Isc. customs, Gtn
Bly John, gent. Bath hs
Boast John, clerk, Mgt
Bond Mrs Amy, Bath pl

Bond Mr. South Town
Borrett Mr Geo. Bath pl
Borrett Mr Simon, Mg
Bossley Wm. gent. Stn
Bowen Mrs Louisa, Jrd
Bowers Mrs Hanh. Ntc
Bowgin John, gent. Stn
Brady Mrs Sarah, Ntc
Branch John, 14 Rst
Brand Mr Wm. Ntc
Breeze Mrs Martha, 45 George street
Brewer Mrs Sus. Hst
Brightwen John, Esq. banker; h Short quay
Brightwen Thos. Esq. banker; h King st
Bristow Mrs Cath. Gtn
Brock Miss Sarah, Stn
Brock Misses, Stn
Brown Miss Ann, Gst
Brown John, silk mfr; h Bauleah cottage
Brown Mrs M. May pl
Brown Wm. jun. mert. Gaol street
Browne Rt. gent. Bath hl
Browne Wm. Hutton, Esq. barrister, Barrcks
Buck Chas. register office, Row 61
Budds W. customs, Sqy
Bullen Saml. police, Gtn
Burman James, parish clerk, Church trees
Burrows Rev Hy. N.,

M.A. propy. gram. school, South Town

BurtonT. gent.Union pl

Cable Wm. coachman, Theatre plain

Candler Mrs Eliz. Hst

Candler Mr Thos. Ntc

Capon Mrs J.Wesley st

Carrington Mrs Eliz. Exmouth place

Cartman John, B.A. Propy. gram. school

Carver Jas. pilot, Gtn

ChambersMrs, S. quay

Chandler Thos clerk, South Town

Chevallier Mrs S. Stn

ChristmasMrsAnn,Ntc

Clarke Mrs Ann, Ntc

Clarke Mrs Ann, Stn

Clarke Mr John, Ntc

Clarke Mrs M.Royal pl

Clarke Rd. French polisher, 45 George st

Clarke Misses S. & A. Union place

Clarke Rev Wm. Hy. M.A. incbt. of St Peter's, South quay

Clowes G. W. ironmonger, Howard street

Clowes John, solr; h Ormesby St Margt.

Coaks John, Rd. gent. South Town

Cobb Capt. Benjamin, Barracks

Cobb Mrs H. M. Stn

Coble Peter G. clerk in customs, Pudding gt

Cohen Morris, Jewish Rabbi, 85 King st

Coleby Rev Wm. Gtn

ColemanG. police, Row 121

CollierEdw. excise,Gtn

CollinsMattw.gent.Ntc

Collins Rt. porter, Sqy

Convers Mrs Eliz. Kst

Cook John, clerk, R. 60

Coote Hy. gent. Gtn

Costerton Geo. colr. of pier dues, South quay

Costerton Lieut. Saml. R.N. Jetty road

Cox Rev John Edmd. M.A. incumbent, Stn

Crane Mr John, Gtn

Coy JeffryS.excise,Gtn

Creak Alex. gent. Gst

Cretton J. turnkey, Glt

Crockett Mrs S. Wesley street

Cross Miss Jane, Gtn

CrossMrWm.North ter

Crow Mr John, Row 53

Crow Lieut. Wm. Hst

Crowe Saml. gent. Stn

Cudden Mr Wm. Tpn

Cummins Wm. excise, George street

Dalby D. tide waiter, Row 93

Davey Danl. gent. Mgt

Davie Mrs Ann, R. 57

Davie Wm. Trinity House agt. South st

Dawson Mrs Jane, Kst

Dawson Lieut. John, R.N. Church trees

Day Chas. gent. Kst

Dean Jas. Gas works

Deeks Fras. gent. Upl

Devereux Edw. pilot, 5 Smiter's buildings

Digby Lieut.Edw.R.N. Royal barracks

Diggins Mrs. Stn

Dimond Mr Wm. Archer's place

Diver Rd. gent. King st

DixonRev Isaac,Indpt. min. Garden lane

Dixon Mrs Bath place

Doughty Mrs Maria, Union place

Douglas Jas. silk manager, Market place

Douglas T. gent.East st

DouglassRt.chief mate, revenue cutter, Jetty road

Downing Mrs Esther, Row 73

Dowson Sept. mercht; house South Town

Drake Mrs Amelia, Stn

Durant Mrs Prospt. pl

Dye Jno. ironmgr. Nqy

Dye Mrs Matilda, Kst

Easter Mrs Phœbe, Kst

Eller Mr Jph. R. 120

EllettW. locker, R. 100

Ellis John, R.N. Stn

Emes Mrs E.Fuller's hl

EmesRd.clerk,Ch trees

Fabb Miss R. Stn

Farrow John,clerk, Stn

Farrow Mrs S. King st

Fear John, gent. Sqy

Fiddis John, gent. Chq

Field Mrs M. Crown pl

Fill Mr Jas. Gaol st

Fill Mr Jph. Theatr. gt

Fill Saml. John, ship chandler; h Albert pl

Fish Mr Samuel, Stn

Fisher JohnGoote, solr; house South quay

Fitt Geo. baker's clerk, 6 St James' terrace

Flowerdew Wm. ship breaker, South Town

Foreman Mrs E. Exmouth place

Foster Mrs Gaol street

Fowler Rev Wm. Stn

Fox Miss Deborah, Stn

Fox Geo. pilot, Gtn

Fransham Mr Rt. Ntc

Frere Rev Edw. Kst

Fulcher MrJph.Gaol st

Fulcher MrW. King st

Fuller John, gent. Stn

GallantMrs M.A.,R.50

Garneys Lieut. Thos. R.N. South Town

GardinerWm. gent. Stn

Garnham John, Esq. Hill house, Stn ; (& Buxhall Vale)

Garred Mrs My. R.140

Gedney Jas. gent. Stn

Gibbs Mrs E. Brunswick place

Gibbs Hy. Harris,gent. South Town

Gibson Mr Robt. Stn

Giles Mrs Queen's pl

Giles Mrs Sarah, Ntc

Gilham Mrs Mary, Stn

Gill Lieut. Wm. R.N. 5 St James' terrace

Glasscock Kickweed, coach guard,Pavd rw

Gooderham Mrs E. Sqy

Goodwin John, gent. 10 Prospect place

GoodyMattw. gent.Gtn

Goss Rev Wm. Bapt. min.Row85, King st

Gotts W. excise, Conge
Gourlay Mrs Susan,Tgt
Gowen Serjt. J. Nelson place
Gowing Mrs Ann, St Peter's walls
Greathead Fras. excise officer, Conge
Green Mr James, Stn
Green Thos. gent. Stn
Greenwood Edw. Thos. mason ; h Market gt
Giscard Mr John, Mgt
Gunton Misses Ann & Susan, Priory place
Guthrie Capt. Jas. Upl
Guy Mr James, Stn
Halfnight Jas.pilot,Gtn
Hallmarke Mrs E. Kst
Hammond Ths. ballast master, South quay
Hammond Wm. Esq. North quay
Handley Mrs Ann, Stn
Hanks Wm. gent. Sqy
Hardy Mrs Eliz. Jrd
Harley Mr C. G. Chq
Harley Mr George,Gtn
Harman Mr Jas.Bath pl
Harmer Capt. Sl. Fielding, R.N. 3 Bath pl
Harney Mrs Jemima, North entrance
Harrison Miss Mary, 1 Cambridge place
Hawkins Lieut. George Drew, R.N. Stn
Hickleton Mr Wm. Stn
Hitcham Hy. town missionary, Belgrave pl
Holland MrsMargt.Stn
Hook Mrs Hanh. Kst
Houghton Mrs Sus. Kst
Howes John, pilot, Gtn
Howlett Mrs S. row 141
Huke Mr Wm. row 121
Humphries John, clerk, Gorleston
Hunt Hy. watch maker, Clarence place
Ionn Wm. clerk, Mgt
Jackson Jas. traveller, Trafalgar place
James Mrs Jane Eliz. South Town
Jay Mr Hy.D.,Ch.trees
Jay Wm. wharfgr. Kst

Jeffery J. G. gent. Stn
Jeffery Mrs Sar. Chq
Jeffries Capt. Jas. Stn
Jermy Isaac Esq. Sbh
Jex Jas. gent. Jetty rd
Johnson Isc. pilot, Gtn
Johnson J.crier,Row 36
Kemp Rt. Palmer,Esq. South Town
Kerrison Jno. gent. Ntc
King Chas. pilot, Gtn
King John, pilot, Cliff Gorleston
King Miss M.Churchpln
Lacon Sir Edmd. Hy. Knowles, Bart. ̓bank-er ; house *Somerton*
Lacon John Edw. Esq. banker ; h *Ormesby*
Lacon John Mortlock, Esq. Short quay
Lamb Mrs Mary, Stn
Lamb Rd. clerk of St Peter's, Row 92
Larke Mrs Margt. R.87
Larlham Chs. Hy. tide waiter, Row 129
Larter Mrs Sus. Gaol st
Last Mr Wm. Row 92
Laws Miss E. Gaol st
Lawton Miss E.L. Nqy
Layton Hy. gent. Stn
Layton Mrs M. Nqy
Leggett Chas., Henry, Isaiah,& Edw. pilots, Gorleston
Leman Hy.clerk,Easthl
Lemmon Jno. gent. Stn
Lermitte Miss Matilda, Gorleston
Lettis Mrs Eliz. Hst
Libbis John, gent. Stn
Loddy Geo. gent. Stn
Long James, R.N. Gtn
Lonsdale Rd.Sibbs,Esq. bank agent, S. quay
Lonsdale Miss Sus. 4 St James' terrace
Lopez Rev Claudia, Catholic Priest, Gst
Louttid Edwin Duncan, Town Hall keeper,&c
Love Capt. Benj. L. supt. of police, Town Hall
Lovewell Mrs Eliz. Stn

Lowen Mrs My. Ann, Gorleston
Lowne MissE.Prospt.pl
Lucas Geo. solr; h *Filby*
Macavey Jph. pilot,Gtn
Mackrell S. pilot, Gtn
Manby Capt. Geo.Wm. R.N. South Town
Mann Serjt. John, Qpl
Marsh Saml Chas. wine mert. and Mrs A. Sqy
Marshall MrJermh.Ntc
Marston Mr G.Prospt pl
Marston Mrs Htte. Stn
Martin Mrs Mary, Crown place
May Charles, soap mfr. North quay
May John, clerk, Stn
Meffin Rev.John (Huntington min.) Mgt
Metcalfe Wm. Leopold, soap mfr; h Mkp
Miles Mrs Sar. Row 112
Miller J.T. collr. of port dues, South quay
Miller Richard, harbour master, South Town
Miller Stphn. gent. Gtn
Mills Mr Thomas, Gtn
Moon Mrs Prudence, North entrance
Moore Mrs Mary Ann, Town Hall row
Morland MrDl. Row 92
Morley Jacob, clerk, Row 36
Moss Philip, pilot, Gtn
Moss Wm. shopman,Gst
Mountjoy Wm. shopmn. Charlotte street
Moxon Miss E. King st
Moyse Mrs J. South qy
Nash Mrs Susanna, Stn
Naulton Mr Wm. Stn
Neale Mr Php. Row 36
Nesbitt Mrs M., Nqy
Newson Php. pilot, Gtn
Nichols Mr Ths. Conge
Nightingale MrJno.Gtn
Nightingale Samuel, brewer, Nth. entrance
Nightingale Wm. Ntc
Norton Mrs J. Bath hill
Nunn Mr Joseph, Stn
Oakes Mrs Sar. Paved row

Oliver Thos. Hutchinson, gent. South Town

Page Mrs Anna, Stn

Page Mr Rd., North qy

Page Robt. police, Tpn

Paget Charles John, brewer; h South quay

Paine Thomas, R.N. King street

Palk Capt. Rt.R.N., Jrd

Palmer Chas. John, Esq. solr; h South quay

Palmer Mrs Eleanor, Stn

Palmer Fdk. surgeon; h 9 Regent street

Palmer Robt. postman, Gorleston

Palmer Wm. Danby, Esq. South Town

Parker Admiral Sir Geo. K.C.B. South Town

Parmeter Mr John, Stn

Parsons Mrs Rbca. Stn

Pattenson G. gent. Stn

Paul Rd. crier, Row 55

Pearse S. Barrack kpr

Pearson Captain James, R.N., South quay

Pellew Hon & Rev Edw. incumbent of St Nicholas, Church trees

Pells Mrs Mgt. Gtn

Pells Mr Thomas, Gtn

Pells Mr Wm. North ter

Penrice John, Esq. Kst

Pestell Mr Wm., Gtn

Pettel Mrs Mary, Gtn

Pickard Hy. relieving officer, Market gate

Pike Capt. John, S. quay

Pike Joseph, town missionary, Belgrave st

Pitt Wm., R.N., Stn

Playford Mr D. Prospect place

Plummer Mr J. Row 56

Poole Joseph, landing waiter, South Town

Pope Thos. ferry, Stn

Porter Jas. coach proprietor, South Town

Porter Mr Rt. Row 135

Postle Mrs Martha, Stn

Powell Mrs A. East st

Pratt Mrs Han. Row 61

Preston Danl. collector's clerk, North quay

Preston Edw. Harbord Lushington, Esquire, North quay

Preston Isaac, junior, solicitor; h Crown pl

Preston John, Esq. comptroller, S. quay

Pullyn Miss C. Prospect place

Pullyn Capt Jas. coast guard, St Peter's

Pullyn Philip, gent. 8 Harrison's buildings

Purdy Wm. meter, Glt

Randall Wm. E. gent. South Town

Randall Mr William, Row 129

Ranney John Freame, solicitor, Priory pl

Ransome Mrs Ann, Ntc

Raven James, gent. Gtn

Redgrave Mrs Sus., Sgt

Reed Mrs Ann, Sgt

Reid Walter, gent. Tgt

Reynolds Fras. Riddell, solicitor; h King st

Ringwood Mr Saml. Ntc

Rising T. pilot, Row 130

Rivett James, gent. Stn

Rix John, mert. South qy

Roberts Mrs M. Royal pl

Roberts Mrs Sus., Stn

Roberts Wm. Geo., Stn

Roche James, landing waiter, 3 St Jas. ter

Rope Rt. M. gent. Gtn

Rowell Jno. coach proprietor, Nth. entrance

Rundle Hy. pilot, Gtn

Sacret Mr Thomas, Stn

Salmon Rd. pilot, Gtn

Sampson Mr Moses, Hst

Savory Mr Wm. Mgt

Sawyer Mrs Chtte. Jrd

Say Rev Hy. Gorleston, and *Swaffham*

St Quintin Lieut. Jas. R.N., Gorleston

Scott J. gent. Queen's pl

Scott John, gent. Stn

Screeton Mr J., Ch plain

Seely Mrs Sar. 27 Rst

Sharman Mrs Eliz. Ntc

Shaul Edw. pilot, Gtn

Shearing Mr Wm. Mgt

Shepherd Mrs Sarah, Sgt

Short Mr John, Tpn

Shuckford Wm. governr. Borough Gaol

Silvers Brighten, tide surveyor, Gorleston

Simmons Geo. excise, 9 Prospect place

Simonds Jas. gent. Stn

Simpson Mrs C., S. quay

Simpson Mrs My. Ann, North beach

Simpson Mrs. Church sq

Sims Wm. relieving officer, Jetty road

Sizland Geo. coachman, 5 Albert place

Skinner Mr Thomas, Sgt

Slapp Mr Thos. Row 36

Smith John, librn. Gst

Smith Michael, bathing machine owner, Gst

Smith Wm. gent. Qsq

Smyth Capt. Spencer, R.N., pier mr. Pier

Soanes Mrs A. North ter

Southam Mrs Mary, Fuller's hill

Spence Mrs Frances, Stn

Squire Rev Hy. South qy

Stagg Benjamin, clerk in customs, Broad lane

Stagg Jas. clerk, Mgt

Stanford Mrs Eliz. Nqy

Stanford Mrs Sar. Stn

Steele Lieut. Edw., Glt

Steward Mrs Eliz. Nqy

Steward Thos. Fowler, Esq., solr. and bank agent, 19 Regent st

Stringer Mr Thos. Tgt

Suggate Mr Wm. Kst

Sussards Mrs E., Row 60

Swann Mr James, Ntc

Symonds John, gent. Kst

Symonds Richd. bookkeeper, East hill

Tagg Mr Thos. Market gt

Tanqueray Mrs E. Gtn

Tallent Wm. clerk, Stn

Teasdell Jas. agent, Glt

Teasdel Wm. engineer, Gorleston

Taylor Mrs M. Gorleston

Temple Mrs Christiana, 7 Seymour place

Thackrah Rt. gent. Stn

Thomas Mrs Mary, Chq

Thompson Geo. Edwd. Esq., Denes House

Thompson Thos. met-farm officer, Gaol st

Thorndick Mrs R., Glt

Thorndick Mr Wm., Glt

Thornton Thos. reliev-ing officer, Ntc

Thrower Aaron, gent. South Town

Thurtell W.gent.S.quay

Todman Mrs H.Row 105

Tolver Samuel, solr. and town clerk, Town Hall row

Tomkines Wm. gent. 2 St James' terrace

Tomlinson Rd. gent.Tpn

Tooley Wm. serjeant at mace, Gaol paved row

Travis Sir Eaton, Bart. S.quay & *Ditchingham*

Tuubridge Thos. gent. Gorleston

Turner Dawson, Esq. banker ; h Short quay

Turnor Chas. gent. Stn

Tuthill Mr Wm. Upl

Tydeman Miss Ann, Town Hall row

Upjohn Rev Fras., M.A. vicar, Gorleston

Vale John, gent. Stn

Waits Mr Wm. King st

Walpole Wm. gent. Stn

Walton Mr Edward, Ntc

Ward Wm. contractor, 3 Cambridge place

Warner Mrs Mary, Stn

Warren Mr Jas., Row 96

Waters Jas.Denew,solr. and clerk to magis-trates ; h Priory pl

Waters John, gent. Stn

Waters Rev Mark, B.A. incbt. of St George's

Waters Mrs M. M., Stn

Watling Mrs M.A. 92 R

Watson Wm. gent. Stn

Watts George, gent. Stn

Wheeler Saml. gent.Stn

Wheeler Thos. gent. Stn

Whiley John, pilot, Gtn

Whiteside Mrs A.,Pudgt

Wicks Mrs Mary, Stn

Williams Thos. gent.Stn

Williams Rev William (Wes. min.) Gaol st

Womack Mrs Margaret, Brunswick place

Woods Chas. pilot. Gtn

Woodthorpe John, R.N. Gorleston

Woodward S. gent. Tgt

Woolsey Mrs My. Ann, Southgate

Woolston G.N.clerk, Stn

Woor Thos. Williams, gent. Theatre plain

Worship Harry Verelst, Esq. King street

Yallop Mr Wm. Ntc

Youell Edw Esq.bankr. house Short quay

Youell Jno.gent.White-horse plain

Youngs Mr John,Row 97

ACADEMIES.

(* take Boarders.)

Bammant Harr.,N.quay

Barker Susanna,Gaol st

*Barnes Amelia, Gtn

*Barrett Benj., N. quay

*Bassingthwaighte Re-becca Matilda, Kst

*Casborne Frances, Gst

Charity School,G. & A. Davie, Theatre plain

*Church Edw. Forster, Theatre plain

Clark John, Row 24

Collett Thomas, Row 63

Cooper Wm. Gorleston

Crow Mary, George st

Farman J. B., Sgt

Fill Eliz. Gaol street

Grammar School (Pro-prietary,) Rev Hy.N. Burrows, M.A. ; J. Cartman, B.A. ; & J. H.Belden,South Twn

Greaves Sar., George st

Hales Isabella, Hst

Hastings Lavinia, Glt

Holland Jas., Gaol st

*Hospital School,*Market place, J. W. Hewke and Mary Crowther

Infant Schools, Eliza-beth Brindy & Livey Rumsey

Jackson Joseph, King st

Jarmeny M. A., Mktgt

*King & Hewett, Kst

Laws Mary, Gaol st

Lincoln Sarah, N. quay

Marston Margaret, Stn

Massey Mr., Gorleston

Meall Sophia, Queen st

Mills Phillis, Gorleston

National Schools, Gtn. ; Thomas Burch, Ann, James, and Elizabeth C. Barrett

Peterson My. Ann, Kst

*Plummer Jph. G., Kst

Read Ann, Gaol street

Reeve Cath., George st

Rofe Sar. Ann, Gaol st

School of Industry, Sar. Brecknell, King st

*Silvers Ann, King st

Skakel John, Hst

Smith Sarah, Gaol st

Steward Eliz., N. quay

Tuck Thurza, Conge

* Walpole Charlotte,Gst

Webb Eliz.,North quay

Wilson Sar. & My., Gtn

* Woolsey Sarah, N.quay

*Yallop G., George st

AGENTS. *(Ship, &c.)*

Agnew James, Row 104

Barber Robt. Dvd. Hst

Barber Saml.Smith,Sqy

Bird Wm. South Town

Bunn Thos. South Town

Butcher Matthew and Sons, Jetty road

Cherry Jas. Short quay

Crowe Frdk. Howard st

Day Starling, Stn

Feek John Townley, jun. Queen street

Garson Geo. (to Lloyds,) Gaol street

Jermyn D. Custom hs.qy

Laws James E. Gaol paved row ; h Stn

Linder Saml. H. Gtn

Palmer James Hurry & Co. Regent street

Rivett John Grimes,Gtn

Saunders Wm. S. quay

Shelly John & Co. S.quay

Teasdell Robt. and Son, Quay

Woolston Jno. Gaol st

ANCHORSMITHS.

Minister John, Gaol st

Moore Saml. South quay
ARCHITECTS, &c.
Hulley Thos. Spencer,
North entrance
Norfor Wm. St Geo. gt
Tillett Abel T. (town
surveyor,) King st
ARTISTS.
Haw Misses, Regent st
Slann Rd. South Town
Winter Cornls. J. Kst
ATTORNEYS.
(* are Notaries)
*Baker & Bell, Qst
Barber Hy. Regent st
*Barth Samuel Jeffries,
Town Hall row
*Bell Charles, King st
Catchpole Wm. Smith.
Market place
* Clarke Wm. Thomas,
South quay
Clowes Thos. & Son,
Rst ; h Caister
*Cobb Jas. 2 Regent st
*Cory Chas. Gaol st
Cory Saml. Barnett, 7
Regent street
Costerton Fredk. Saml.
Regent street
*Crickmay Thos. Rst;
h South Town
Cufaude John Lomas, 5
Regent street
*Everitt EdwinChurch,
Queen street
*Fisher, Lucas, and
Steward, Gaolpvd. rw
Hodskinson Fredk. Sqy
*Holt Geo. Wells, (ma-
gistrates' clerk,) Glt
*Palmer Edmd. Reeve,
29 Regent street
Palmer Nathl. Rst
*Palmer Saml. 61 Hst
*Preston Edmund, Nqy
Ranney and Waters,
Priory place
*Reynolds and Palmer,
28 Regent street
Sayer Chpr. Queen st
Sherrington Saml. Benj.
25 Regent st ; h Acle
*Tolver & Preston, Sqy
Woods Alex. King st
*Worship Wm., Short
quay & 18 Regent st

AUCTIONEERS.
Clark John Shelly, Sgt
Cory Edw. Wesley st
Davey Jph. Regent st
Forder Thomas, Cht
Pettingill Walter Dou-
glass, 22 Regent st
Rix Benj.Town Hall rw
BAKERS & FLOUR
DEALERS.
(See also Confectioners.)
Allgar Wm. South quay
Ames Hy. Forder st
Bales Wm. Ellis, Cht
Barham Rt. Gorleston
Barber George, Sgt
Barnaby Thos. Ntc
Bayfield Ts. Fuller's hl
Boulter John, Hst
Bristow Samuel,Gaol st
Chasteney E. Crown pl
Church John, Gst
Claxton Jas. Row 34
Craske John H. Wpl
Day T. St Peter's walls
Ellis Wm. Gaol street
Farman My. North qy
Feek J. Town Hall rw
Fenner John, Gaol st
Fransham John, Ntc
Garwood Wm. Row 66
Gillings John, Gtn
Hacon Jas. George st
Hawkins John, Nqy
Hewett S. Victoria pl
Houchen G. Howard st
Howard John, Cht
Jackson John, Ntc
Jay Fras. King street
Julier Mathw. South st
Kemp Wm. Gaol st
Kent Wm. East street
Larke Wm. Row 30
Laws Joseph, South qy
Layton Hy. Howard st
Matthews Benj. Glt
Matthews Jasper, Gtn
Mayers Samuel, Mgt
Mobbs Saml. Market gt
Punchen Charles, Gst
Powley Rd. Jetty road
Sayer Henry, Ngt
Sayer Saml. South st
Sayer Thos. B. Glt
Stevenson Saml. Gtn
White Henry, Row 141
Woodrow Edmund, Kst

Woolston Benj. Glt
BANKS.
East of England Bank,
Regent st. (on Lon-
don and Westminster
Bank ;) Thos. Fowler
Steward, Esq. mangr
Gurneys, Turner, and
Brightwen, Short qy.
(on Barclay & Co,)
Lacons, Youell, & Co.
Short quay, (on Glyn
and Co.)
NationalProvincial Bk.
South quay, (on Lon-
donJointStockBank ;)
Rd. Sibbs Lonsdale,
Esq. manager
Savings' Bank, Howard
st. (open Wed. from
11 to 1 o'clock ;) R.
D. Barber, secretary
BASKET MAKERS.
Blake George, Row 19
Blake Joseph, Row 3
Haines Wm. C. Nqy
Lamb James, Row 15
Miller John, King st
Moore Wm. Jas. Nqy
Page Wm. South quay
Shuckford B.&Son,Mkp
Shuckford Wm. Gst
BATH KEEPERS.
Bly Saml. Walker, Nbh
Larke James, Denes
Bird, &c. Preservers.
Colby Wm. Jetty road
Harvey Alfred, Row12
Hubbard Chas. Hst
BLACKSMITHS.
Brooks John, Row 141
Crane Jno. Wm. Tpn
Fulcher I. Church pln
GoodaWm. South Town
Harbord John, Nqy
Ingram John, Row 1
Jex Hy. Gorleston
Lovick Thomas, Ntc
Lubbock Thos. Ntc
Manning W.Puddidg gt
Masterson Wm. Gtn
Newman Charles, Ntc
Read John, Gorleston
Read Saml. Gorleston
Smith John, North end
Smith Samuel, Sgt
Springall G. Row 63

Wavers John, Gtn
BOAT BUILDERS.
(See also Ship Buildrs.)
Burwood Hy. South qy
Foreman George, Stn
Forsdick Thos. Row 45
Hastings Henry, Jph.
& Geo. South quay
Houghton Philip, Nqy
Jermyn & Mack, Stn
Pigg Joseph, South Tn
Westgate Rt. South qy
BOOK BINDERS.
Kile Fredk. Row 110
Maryson Fras. Row 101
Palmer Wm. St Peter's
walls
Paul Thos. (& periodical
pdblisher,) Gaol st
Smith Wm. Row 55
**BOOKSELLERS,
PRINTERS, &c.**
Alexander Wm. Kst
Barber Chas. Short qy
Denew Jas. M. Row 52
Duncan Alex. 4 Mrw
Foreman John, Tpln
Foster Saml. 15 Mrw
Gooch Borrett, Mkp
Purdy Jph. Hy. Row 66
Sloman Chas. King st
**BOOT AND SHOE
MAKERS.**
Ames Ths. Charlotte st
Baldwin Chas. Ntc
Barrell John, Row 57
Bartram J. Jetty road
Beavers Ths. Elm walk
Beckett G.W. Broad rw
Bee James, Gaol street
Bee Robert, Morket pl
Blyth John, Market pl
Blyth Thos. East street
Browne Benj. Row 51
Bull Wm. Row 61
Bulley Jph. Row 122
Bullimore Robt. Tpn
Bunn James, Broad rw
Buston J. T. Paved row
Butler Rt. Market gt
Cassidy Thos. Gtn
Clarke Wm. Market rw
Crane Clmt. Gaol st
Deeks Jas. Pudding gt
Dawson Ann E. Cht
Diboll Jph. George st
Dillistone Wm. Kst

Dunnell & Yarham, Glt
Dunt Wm. Howard st
Durrell S. Gorleston
Eastick Wm. Goal st
Farey Thos. Cht
Feltham Geo. Mkp
Fisher Hester, Gst
Fisk Robt. Howard st
Flowerday Job, Gst
Fountain Rt. Prov. hill
French Wm. George st
Fromow Thos. Gaol st
Gibbs Saml. Ntc
Hannant Jph. Belgv. pl
Harrison John, Gst
Hawkins B. Broad row
High Wm. Gaol street
Jellings Bj. Gaol st
Kemp Wm. Market rw
Lake Thos. Row 78
Lane Benj. Row 95
Langley S. Gorleston
Laxon Hy. North quay
Leggett James, Gtn
Lockart Adam, Kst
Magness James, Ntc
Magness Jas. Gaol st
Martin Saml. Gaol st
Miller Wm. South quay
Newrick Wm. Stn
Newton Wm. Stn
Nichols Edward, Mgt
Nolloth Wm. Gaol st
Panks Hy. Wesley st
Pitcher Wm. North qy
Rainer Fras. King st
Read Wm. Market gt
Remlance W. South st
Rushmer S. Broad row
Sacret Rt. Howard st
Scarle John, Church sq
Simpson Wm. J. Mrw
Smith Benj. George st
Smith Thos. Gaol st
Smith Wm. Gaol st
Spratt George, Gaol st
Swanston Wm. Row 57
Theobald Benj. Glt
Thompson Jas. Tgt
Tripp Wm. Row 85
Vince Isc. Church sq
Vincent Jas. South st
Walker Wm. South st
Watson George, Ntc
White P. Church pln
Woodcock J. North end
Wright James, King st

Wright James, Row 60
Wright Richd. King st
Wright W. H. Row 85
Wyatt Hy. Gaol st
Yarham Benj. Goal st
BRAZIERS & TNRS.
Barber Saml. Row 32
Child Rt. & John, Sqy
Crisp Saml. B. Row 41
Grice Wm. Row 12
Hammantt Robt. Gst
Hammantt Robt. Gtn
Hatch Robt. Pudngate
Smith Richd. Row 130
Webb Wm. George st
**BREWERS AND
MALTSTERS.**
Bell John Sayers, Gtn
Chasteney Everson,
Crown place
Cullingford Wm. May pl
Ferrier Richd. Gaol st;
h *Borough Castle*
Howes Benjamin, Ntc.
Lacon Sir E.H.K. Bart.
and Sons, Church sqr
Lubbock Chas. Conge
Minter John, St Peter's
Paget Sl. & Son, Nqy
Palmer J. H. jun. Kst
Scarce J. Gorleston
Tomlinson Joseph, Hst
Brick, Tile,& Lime Dls.
Nuthall Philip, Garri-
son walk
Quinton, Henry, Stn
BRICKLAYERS.
Arbon Daniel, Sgt
Arbon Geo. South open
Benslyn Noah, Gtn
Bracey Wm. Nqy
Bull George, Gorleston
Burrage John, Gst
Burwood Wm. King st
Deekins James, Mkgt
Dyboll Thomas, Nqy
Hockley Chas. Puddgt
Johnson Robt. Townhall
row
Key John, North quay
Maddeys T. & J. Hst
Mitchell Thos. King st
Nickerson Robt. Gst
Page James, Row 119
Pratt Jas. North quay
Pratt Robert, Row 100
Pyle John, Bellgrv. pl

Sadler T. Gorleston
Sadler Wm. Gaol street
Thompson James, Mgt
Tooley Edm. Forder st
Worlidge Walter, Nqy
BRUSH MAKER.
Ellis Chpr. Market pl
BUTCHERS.
Balls Fras. Market pl
Barnes Jermh. Mkp
Bayes Benj. Gaol st
Bellamy Robert, Kst
Bellamy Wm. King st
Burman Edward, Cht
Carsey Wm. Market gt
Draper John, Mkp
Draper Joseph, Mkp
Fields Michl. jun. Gst
Gunton Simon, Mkp
Hacon Henry, George st
Hallifax Samuel, Gtn
Hammond Edgar, Mkp
Hering C. G. King st
Howard John, Mgt
Jex Jacob, Gorleston
Keable John, Market pl
Lamb Tennason, Glt
Lane Robert, Row 44
Marsh Wm. George st
Newman S. Gorleston
Powley Wm. George st
Presant G. South quay
Presant Wm. Jno. Glt
Savory Wm. Market gt
Shipston Samuel, Cht
Smith Rt. Gorleston
Swann Wm. Market pl
Waters Saml. Gorleston
Winter Hy. Market pl
Wright Edw. King st
CABINET MKRS.
(* are Upholsterers.)
Atkins Robert, Tgt
*Blowers Mark, Cht
Clayton John, Sgt
Crane Hy. Pratt, Gst
Ding John, North entc
Feltham and Goodrick,
    Market place
Fish John, Howard st
Goffin Rt. North quay
Gyton George, Gaol st
*Hart Wm. George st
Lake Thos. C. Row 54
*Moon Philip, Cht
Moon Wm. South Town
*Norman Simon, Cht

Reddish James, Geo. st
Richmond John, Hst
Soanes Wm. George st
*Utting Robt. Le Neve,
    Gaol street
Yallop Ephraim, Gst
CARPET DLRS.
Blowers Mark, Cht
Hart Wm. George st
Johnson Wm. & Son, Cht
Moon Philip, Cht
CARVERS AND
    GILDERS.
Errington Thos. Kst
Foslin Chas. Jetty road
Townshend Ts. Row 30
Winter C. J. W. Kst
Woolby G. Townhall rw
Wormald James, Stn
Cheese, Bacon, & Butter
    Factors.
Lucia Wm. King street
Porter John & Co. Nqy
Pulford Geo. 31 Mkp
CHEMISTS AND
    DRUGGISTS.
Bond John, King street
Davie Cufaude, Sqy
Davie Fredk. Mrw
Goddard H. E. Chu. pln
Hedges Edward, Cht
Hitchman T. H. Broad
    row
Jay Edw. Ward, Kst
King Fdk. Rt. M. Gtn
Mabson Wm. Market pl
Markland Edwin, Mkp
Owles John, George st
Priest John Paul, Mkp
Shingles Geo. Gaol st
Steward C. S. D. Mkp
Walpole Wm. W. Jet-
    ty road
CLOTHES DLRS.
Duffell Robt. George st
Felstead John, Gaol st
Hart L. J. Broad row
Huby Eliz. George st
Isaacs Isaac, Cht
Isaacs Philip, Cht
Laycock Isaac, Gst
Newman John, Gst
Smith Wm. George st
White Anthony, Cht
COACH BLDRS.
Borrett Henry, Ntc
Colman James, Stn

Crisp Edm. Belgrave pl
Gilbert Thos. jun. Stn
Gill Wm. Fuller's hill
West Wm. Daniel, Mgt
COAL MERCHTS.
Blake Garson, Stn
Briggs Wm. S. quay
Clark Jas. South quay
Costerton Geo. B. Rst
Foreman Thomas, Kst
Jay Benj. Short Quay
Morley Thomas, Gtn
Nudds Samuel, Stn
West & Richmond, Stn
CONFECTIONERS.
Ames James, George st
Archer Thomas, Jetty rd
Beecroft Peter, Cht
Beevor Wm. Gaol st
Boulter Hy. & Son, Ntc
Cocks Moses, Gtn
Ellerd R. W. Broad rw
Emms James, King st
Foreman Thos. King st
Franklin John, Stn
Gooda Chas. King st
Harbourd John, Gst
Laws Ann, George st
Layton H. M. Stn
Leeder Archd. Mkp
Naunton Geo. 34 Mrw
Naunton L. Gaol st
Reynolds George, Gtn
Rivett Richd. King st
Robinson Francis, Cht
Sharman John, King st
Tuffs Robert, Gaol st
CONSULS (VICE).
America, John Shelly
    and Co., South quay
Denmark, France, Ne-
    therlands, &c., Isaac
    Preston, South quay
Spain, Samuel Paget,
    South quay
COOPERS.
Barrett Hy. South quay
*Bennett J. B. Gaol st
Brunning James, Gtn
*Callow John, Row 63
Earl Rt. Oldtower rd
Forman Wm. George st
Fox Samuel, Market gt
Francis John, Row 135
Gillings Wm. Psq
Godbolt Chpr. Gtn
Godbolt J. Oldtower rd

Godbolt Jph. jun. Stn
Gyton Wm. Row 45
Palmer J. Belgrave pl
*Silver Wm. Fuller's hl
*Smith Elizabeth, Cht
Valient Chas. Row 139
Wolverton My.Row 130

CORK CUTTERS.
Burman Js. Church pln
Hallett Wm. Chq

CORN & FLOUR DEALERS.
Alcock Rt. Howard st
Baverley S. Church pln
Bullent Robert, Tpn
Child Charlotte, Ntc
Collins Rt. Howard st
Crow J. Fuller's hill
Ellerd J. Row 50
Foreman B. Short quay
Gallant David, Row 54
Hall W. M. Prov. hill
Hood John, Ntc
Last Jas. Church plain
Suffling Juo. Church sqr
Tooley Rt. Church sqr

CORN MERCHTS.
Allan Jno. and Co. Stn
Bird Wm. South Town
Brown Chas. 30 Rst
Bunn Ts. South Town
Dowson B. Short quay
Dowson B. U. & Sons, South town
Eller John, Row 36
Kidman Wm. Ntc; h South quay
Orfeur J. South quay
Watling Robert, Stn
Wigg Saml. Church pln

CORN MILLERS.
Branford Richd. Stn
Cole A. South mill
Cooper Thomas, Stn
Foreman B. Short quay
Freeman Edm. East hl
Green Rt. Gorleston
Hammond W. Gorleston
Last James, East hill
Mayers John, Gaol st
Perry Wm. Gaol st
Pinch A. East hill
Ransom J. B. North ml
Skinner Wm. Marketgt
Tooley Rt. Pudding gt
Waters Rt. South Town
Wilson & Reynolds, Stn

COWKEEPERS, &c.
(* are only Cart Owners; and † Farmers.)
†Annis James, Gtn
†Barber Alfred, Gtn
†Barber James, Gtn
Balls Benj. Market gt
Bartle Juo. Northquay
†Bateley Stephen, Stn
Beales Daniel, Psq
Beevor Charles, Gaol st
Bentley Henry, Stn
Bland Arthur, Row 129
Bowman Jas. Bath hill
Buckle John, Nqy
Buckle Wm. Tower p
†Bunn Jas. Gorleston
Burgess John, Stn
*Burrell Robert, Hst
Chapman Wm. Row 141
Cox Arthur, East hill
Crisp John, Row 105
†Crow James, Gtn
*Durant Edw. Mktgt
*English Chas. Mktgt
Finch John, Row 79
Fisk Henry, Tower pl
†Fowler George, Nqy
Fox John, Row 54
Glanfield Jas. Row 41
Godbolt J., Old tower rd
†Gowen Henry, Stn
†Hammond James, Gtn
†Hammond John, Gtn
Harbourd Jas. Row 118
*Harris John, Gorleston
Haynes John, N. quay
*Hepper John, Ntc
*Johnson Isaac, Psq
Julier Saml. Row 17
†Layton J. Cobholm
London Rt. Forder st
*Nockolds & Holloday, St Peter's walls
Page John, North quay
Patterson Edw. Row 73
Sampson Benj. Ntc
Starling James, Row 3
†Thrower Wm. Gtn
Todd George, Row 28
Wade Elizabeth, Nqy
Watlow Wm. Nqy
Wiseman Peter, Maypl
Withers Joseph, Sgt
*Wooden Jacob, Row 41

CRAPE & SHAWL MANFRS.
Grout & Co.,Silk Mills, (& Norwich)

CURRIERS, &c.
Cobb Benj. George st
Cobb Simon, Cht
Godfrey Samuel, Row 63
Harvey Joseph, Cht
Nash Dd. Broad row
Nash John, King st

CUTLERS, &c.
Artis James, Row 54
Lawrence John, Mkp
Offord Duffield, Kst
Platts Geo. Market row
Sumner Wm. Paved row
Whittleton Edm. Gtn

DYERS.
Borking Jas. George st
Gibbins John, Row 60
Hubbard John, Hst
Palmer Jonathan, Chq
Royall Paul, Row 40
Wright Thos. King st

EATING HOUSES.
Beckett Jas. Paved row
Howard Jas. Gaol st
Juliers Matthew, Mkp
Mapes Wm.Charlotte st
Platford James, Hst
Smith Rt. Church sq
Yaxley Fras. South qy

ENGRAVERS.
Christmas James, Gst
Freeman Wm. Gaol st

ESTATE AGENTS.
Bateley Stphn. G. Stn
Cory Edw. Wesley st
Glenister N., Kent pl
Pettingill W.D., Rst
Rix Benj. Townhall rw
Fancy & Toy Warehs.
Aldred S.H. & Son, Gst
Andrews G. Broad row
Gourlay D. A. 29 Mrw
Louttid Wm. 33 Mrw
Mordecai & Mayers, 11 Market row
Seaman F.D.& M., Kst
Starling John, Mkp

FARMERS.
(See Cowkeepers.)

FIRE & LIFE OFCS.
Alliance, A. T. Tillett, King street
Argus, B. Gooch, Mkp

Atlas, T.Crickmay,Rst
Clerical & Medical, E.
Markland & F.'S. Cos-
terton
Dissenters' & General,
G.Blake, SouthTown
Eagle,R.D.Barber,Hst
Essex & Suffolk, Wm.
Turner, Paved row
Family Endowment, E.
Everitt, Queen sq
Guardn.WMabsonMkp
Imperial & Palladium,
Reynold&Palmer,Rst
London, J.Harvey, Cht
National Mercantile,C.
S. D. Steward, Mkp
Norwich Equitable, J.
D.Waters& J.Greeves
Norwich Union, Thos.
Clowes & Son, 3 Rst
Œconomic,CDavie,Sqy
Phœnix & Pelican,Jph.
Davey&W.Alexander
Royal Exchange, Jas.
D.Waters, Priory pl
Suffolk Amicable, E.R.
Palmer, 29 Rst
Sun, Walter Douglas
Pettingill,22Regent st
Victoria,F.Crowe, Hst
West of England, D.B.
Palmer, 20 Regent st
Western,H Barber,Rst
Yorkshr. F.Crowe, Hst
FISH CURERS.
Amiss Samuel, Row 44
AtmoreW., St.Ptr's ter
Balls John, Row 18
BarnbyW.H.&Son,Cht
Barwood S., South st
BaylyJas.M., Welling-
ton place, &Norwich
Bennett John B., Glt
BishopT., St.Ptr'swalls
Blake Jas. Gaol st
Blake Robt. Pudding gt
Burling Wm. Gaol st
Burwell James, Row95
ButcherMtw&Sons,Jrd
CampbellAnn,Tower pl
Cannell Jas. G. Jrd
Combes Mns. Gaol st
Darnell Jas. Row 78
Darnell Wm. Thos. Stn
Denny & Brock, Sbh
Dye Robt. South Town

Earl Rt. Old tower rd
Eastick S. S., Jetty rd
Fenn Benj. Theatre gt
GardnerWm. North ter
Gayfer J. North quay
George Saml. South st
Giles Geo. Theatre gt
Giles Wm. Fredk. Mgt
Gilling Wm. St Ptr's st
Good Edw. South quay
Gosling Wm. Jetty rd
Green Wm. St Peter's
Hammond T., South qy
HarrisonW.&Sons, Glt
Hubbard Danl. Row 23
IngramWm.North entc
Kemp Rd.& Robt. Sgt
King and Carver, Gtn
King Edw. Gorleston
LaceyBenj.Charlotte st
Lacey M. North quay
Larn Jas. North quay
Lettis Thos. & Son, Sgt
Lincoln Jas. Market gt
Lonsdale Rd.Sibbs, Jrd
Mann Robert, Row 54
Mann Wm. George st
Minter John, St Peter's
Norman Rd. B. Hst
Palmer G. D. South qy
PalmerJas.Hurry& Co.
Regent street
RivettJno.G. Gorleston
Rook W. Rainbow cnr
Rundle Wm. jun. Gtn
Runniff John, King st
Rust James, Row 35
Salter Wm. Market gt
Scarf James, Jetty rd
Sewell Joseph, South st
Sharman Robert, Nbh
Shuckford B. & Sons,
Market place
Soanes My. A. Row 71
Stevenson J. King st
Swan Wm. & Co. Mgt
Thirkettle John, Ntc
Thompson Jas. High st
Turrell T., South quay
Woods Simon, Row 41
Worts Robt. Gaol st
Yaxley Jas. Market gt
YaxleyJohn,Market gt
YaxleyRobt.Market gt
Fishing Tackle Mkrs.
Barnes Chas. Gorleston
Colby Wm. Jetty road

Gold J., South quay
Symonds Sar. High st
FISHMONGERS.
Amiss Saml. Row 44
BanksAnn,Churchtrees
Dixon Jno. Charlotte st
Glasscock W. Row 127
Miller Isaac, Row 47
Minikin John, Cht
Neale Stph. 26 Mrw
Runniff Jas. Row 14
Runniff John, King st
Smith Dl. Market gate
SpillingJohn,Gorleston
Steffe Wm. Market gt
Yaxley C. Orford sq
FRUITERERS.
Bales Jas.Market place
CohenDd.Leyser, Mrw
FURNITURE BKRS.
Bezance John, Cht
Cox Arthur, Cht
ForderThos. Charltte.st
Howlett John, Gaol st
MallettWm.Charltte.st
NewarkJno. Charlttest
PattrickWmCharltte.st
Poppy Jonthn. Gaol st
TurnerJph. Charltte. st
FURRIERS.
Cohen D. L.Market rw
Isaacs Philip, Cht
Samuel Jph., Row 58
GAME DEALRRS
Harvey Mary, Row 42
Hubbard Chas.High st
GARDENERS, &c.
* are only Green Grcrs.
Aldrich Elijah, Gtn
*Balls Wm. Gaol st
*Bond John H. Gaol st
*Bowles Edw. Jetty rd
Bush Edw. Charlotte st
Cook T. Apollo walk
Dye Robt. South Town
Farrow John, Gaol st
Goose John, North entc
JenningsJ. Apollo walk
*King Alfred, High st
Margetson Hy. Mkt gt
*Neeve M. Apollo walk
*Page Fras. George st
Youell & Co. (nursery-
men and florists to
her Majesty) Mkt pl

GINGER BEER MANFRS.

BarchamWm. N. quay
Ives Saml. Howard st
Moore Eliz. Row 66
Rogers J. R., Row 63

GLASS, CHINA, & EARTHNWR.DLRS

Cunningham Hambleton, Market place
DybollAnn,Market row
Field Michael, 14 Mrw
Hickling Robt. King st
Howes Wm. Gorleston

GLOVERS & LEATHER SELLERS.

Farrow Wm. North ter
Pratt Mark, Church sq
Townshend John, Fuller's hill

GROCERS.

* are Tallow Chndlers.

Alcock Hy. Chas., Cht
BlaggThos. 30 Mkt rw
Bradnack Isc. R., Kst
Browne Thos. T., Kst
BumpsteadGeo. Mkt pl
Clowes John, Short qy
Crawford Kennedy,Cht
*Fenn John, Market pl
*Fulcher Wm. Mkt pl
Girling Richd. King st
Good John, King st
Greeves John, Gtn
Gunn Rt. Church pln
*HammondRd. Ch. pln
Harrison Wm. Gaol st
*Laws Wm. George st
Little David, 17 Mrw
Lorimer John, 32 Mrw
Norton A. C. 11 Mrw
Orford Wm. Broad row
Page James, Gorleston
Pickard W., Fuller's hl
Pleasants Wm., S.quay
*Pizey Rt. Market pl
Ranney Wm. Gaol st
Rising Wm. Jetty rd
*SewellEdw. Market pl
Skinner Owen,Gorlestn
Taylor Bnj. South quay
Tuttle Wm. King st
Woodrow N. F. Gaol st

GUN MAKERS.

Breeze Rt. Market pl
Mayor J., Fuller's hill
Sawyer John, George st

HABERDASHERS.

Annison Ann, King st
Barker Mary, 22 Mrw
Cox Eliz. Broad row
Gourlay D. A. 29 Mrw
Lane Eliz. King st
Loutted Wm. 33 Mrw
Ranney Wm. Gaol st
Seaman F.D. &M. Kst
SimpsonWm. J.21Mrw
Simpson Wm. Broad rw
Starling John, Mkt pl
Todd John, Gaol st

HAIR DRESSERS.

Andrews G. Broad row
Arkwright G. Prov.hill
BarnesChas. George st
Breeze F., Archer's pl
Chapman J., Gaol st
Colby Wm. Jetty road
*Crowe Thos. 18 Mrw
Dillistone J. Gaol st
Fisk Geo. Charlotte st
Forder Edw. H. Mrw
Fulcher Edw. Mkt pl
Gold John, South quay
Holliday Daniel, Kst
Houston Wm.Gorleston
Hay John, Charlotte st
HubbardIsaac,South st
Joslyn Chas. Jetty rd
LaytonWm.Theatre pn
Morse Wm. North entc
PagePhilip, Howard st
Pratt Alfred, Gaol st
Quinton John, King st
Rainbird Jonathan,Hst
Smith James,George st
Watson Geo 28 Mrw

HATTERS.

Bacon Rt. Pudding gt
Moon Mary, 5 Mkt row
Starling J. & Son, Mrw

Horse, Chaise. & Gig Proprietors.

* Stables only.

Botwright Wm. Hst
Bullent Hy. Market gt
*Burward Robert, St. Peter's walls
Catchpole Robert, Mgt
Clifton John Thos. Ntc
Coman William, Sgt
Crisp Ann, Row 104
*Edmunds Wm. Pudgt
Hall Henry, Priory pl
*HichamS.Oldtower rd

Larlham Wm. Gaol st
Martin F. 4 Seymour pl
Mihill J. South Town
*Newman Thomas, Sgt
Rivett Hy. Priory pln
Thorndick H. J., Psq

INNS & TAVERNS.

Albert,John Smith,Sqy
Archor & Hope, Abel King, Pier
AngelInn,Jno.Browne, Market place
Angel, Hy. Farman, South Quay
Angel, S. Thrower, Stn
Anson's Arms, Eliz. Harcourt,SouthTown
Apollo Gardens, Chtte.
Atkinson, N. entrnc
Ballast Keel, Wm.Paston, South Quay
Barge,R. Mitchell,Sqy
Barking Smack, John Benj. Day, Jetty rd
Bath Hotel, Samuel Walker Bly, N. beach
Bear Hotel, Robert Puncher, Sth.Town
Black-a-Moor's Head, Geo. Alexander, Glt
BlueAnchor, Wm.Parmenter, Market pl
Bowling Green, Wm. Parmenter, N. quay
Britannia, Richd. Holland, South quay
BritishLion,JohnKing Market place
Buck, Sus. Kerrison, Short quay
Bull, Rd.Watson, Mkp
Bush, John Freeman, South quay
Carpenter'sArms,Thos. Purdy, Howard st
Cock, D.Chapman, Glt
Commercial,Willm. C. Haines, Short quay
Commodore, H. Robt. Stringer, Church rd
Cross Keys, Mary Ann Doughty, Gaol st
Crown & AnchorHotel. Wm. Reeve, S. quay
Dog & Duck,James N.
Brereton, South quay
Dolphin,Jas.Larn,Nqy

Duke of Sussex, Robt. Bullimore, Mkt pl

Duke's Head Inn, Stn. Kemp, Short quay

Duke's Head, William Morfee, Gorleston

Earl Grey, S. Tooke, Gtn

Earl St. Vincent, Thos. Mitchell, King st

East and West Flegg House, Maria Manship, N. entrance

Elephant & Castle, Ths. Green, Market place

Emperor Steam Packet, W. C. Haines, Nqy

Feathers Inn, Jas. Lincoln, Market gate

Feathers, A. Woods, Gtn

Ferry Boat, Chas. Hurrell, South Town

First and Last. Sarah Newton, South quay

Fish Hill House, Robt. Whiley, Market pl

Fishing Boat, Rt. Rainbird, Gaol street

Fishing Boat, Edward Green, North beach

Founders' Arms, Thos. W. Downing, Gaol st

Fourteen Stars, Wm. Nichols, Gaol street

Gallon Can, Fras. B. Wooden, Gaol st

Gallon Can, R. E. Carter, South quay

Gallon Can, Chas. Hill, Fuller's hill

George & Dragon, Wm. Flaxman, King st

George & Dragon, Wm. Hallett, Church sq

George & Dragon, Sml. Gunn, Gorleston

Globe, Jno. Hogget, Gtn

Golden Anchor, Robert Fisk, Queen street

Golden Ball, Hy. Audley, George street

Golden Can, Geo. Swan, Howard street

Golden Lion, Joseph Youngs, George st

Grapes, J. Holl, Geo. st

Green Man, Rd. Miles, Charlotte street

Greyhound, W. Allen, South Town

Half Moon, Rt. Plane, Market place

Happy Jack, Hy. Scott, St Peter's street

Holkham Hotel, Jas. Berry, North beach

Hope and Anchor, J. S. Ward, Church sq

Humber Keel, Ann Sims, King street

Huntsman and Horn, Jas. Last, N. entrnc

Jolly Farmers, Thomas Lewis, N. entrance

Jolly Maltsters, Thos. Barber, Howard st

Jolly Tar, John Scott, Belgrave place

Jolly Watermen, Robt. Maysten, Fuller's hill

King's Arms, Thomas Wigg, N. entrance

King's Hd. Inn (empty)

King's Head, William Naunton, King st

Lion and Lamb, Saml. Wright, King street

Lichfield Tavern, Wm. Bowles, Charlotte st

London Tavern, Chas. Botwright, Gaol st

Lord Collingwood, Jno. Bessey, North quay

Lord Nelson, Jno. Rackham, King street

Lord Nelson, John Gillings, King street

Lord Nelson, Richard Parmenter, N. quay

Marine Hotel, Henry Roper, South beach

Mariners, W Capon, Hst

Mariner's Compass, Ntl Engate Page, Sqy

Neptune, Hy. Rivett, Priory place

Newcastle Tavern, Rt. Townshend, Sth. quay

New Fountain, Samuel Wells, Gaol street

New White Lion, Jas. Suffling, King street

Norfolk Hero, William King, Gaol street

Norfolk Tavern, John Annabell, Charltte. st

Norfolk Tavern, James Paston Dublack, Glt

Norwich Arms, Benj. Howes, North quay

Odd Fellows' Tavern, Edw. Daniells, Glt

Old White Lion, Wm. Howes, King street

Pleasure Boat, John Besford, North quay

Pot - in - Hand, Wm. Hawkins, King st

Prince Albert, John Haines, Howard st

Prince of Wales, Danl. Maryson, Charltte. st

Princess Charlotte, Sar. Gold, George st

Quay Mill, H Balls, Nqy

Queen's Arms, J. Mihill, South Town

Queen's Head, Charles Bullen, Charlotte st

Railway, Sl. Gibbs, N tc

Rainbow, Matilda Manship, Rainbow corner

Red Lion, Wm. Marshall, Gaol street

Red Lion, Edwd. West Woods, Gorleston

Rising Sun, Robert Wright, South Town

Rose, Thomas Hudson, King street

Rose and Crown, Sarah Breeze, Charlotte st

Rose and Thistle, Danl. B. Holl, Gaol street

Royal Exchange, Wm. Wolton, South quay

Royal Hotel, Wm. Bird, South beach

Royal Oak, Hy. Hunn, Town Hall row

Rumbold Arms, James Chapman, South Town

St. Andrew's Hall, Jno. Land, South Town

St. John's Head, Thos. Purkis, North quay

Saracen's Head, Noah Agus, Church square

Sawyers' Arms, Thos. Scrivener, Fuller's hl

Shakespeare,Rt.Cruck-
nell, King street
Ship, Chas. Todd, Gtn
Silk Mills, Mattw.Cop-
land, Pudding gate
Sir Samuel Hood, Luke
Stanford,Charlotte st
Sons of Commerce,Wm.
Mann, South quay
Sovereign Steam Pack-
et,W.C.Haines, Nqy
Spotted Cow, Elijah
Seely, South Town
Spread Eagle, William
Beales, King street
Star Hotel, Mary Pes-
tell, Short quay
Star and Garter, Wm.
Riches, Short quay
Swan-with-two-Necks,
Robt. Ellis, Mkt pl
Tanners' Arms, Isaac
Forder, Forder st
Theatre Tavern,Nathl.
Sterry, Theatre pln
Three Herrings, Robt.
Wigg, South quay
Three Tuns,Dd.Denton,
South Town
Two Brewers, Thomas
Faulke, George st
Trinity House, Benj.
Howard, South quay
Turk's Head, Wm.Hy.
Draper, Gaol street
Unicorn,Thos.Wooden,
South quay
Vauxhall Gardens,Jno.
Symonds,Susp.bridge
Victoria Hotel, James
Balls, South beach
Victoria Tavern, Eliz.
Nixon, Charlotte st
Victoria,Sml.Aldridge,
North entrance
Waggon & Horses,Wm.
Emms, Ntc
Waterman's Arms, Bnj.
Burton, North quay
Weaver's Arms, Geo.
Townshend, Mkp
Wheel of Fortune, Rt.
Spinks, Gaol street
White Hart, Frances
Betts, Church square
White Horse, Mark
Carrick, Church pln

White Horse, Mattw.
Joseph, King street
White Horse, James
Howard, Gaol street
White Horse, Thomas
Cuddon, Gorleston
White Lion, Jno. Gar-
wood, Gorleston
White Swan, Wm. La-
key Tuck, South qy
White Swan, Bnj.Mun-
ford, North quay
William IV. Maria
Eliz. Garwood, Stn.
William IV.Godfry Sy-
monds, George st
Wiltshire Arms, Chas.
Thornton, Ntc
Wine Coopers' Arms,
Jn. Warnes, Pud. gt
Wrestlers,Chs.Weston,
Church square
Yarmouth Arms, My.
Lacey, Townhall row
York Hotel, Ths. Stan-
ford, North beach
BEER HOUSES.
Barber Charles, Mgt
Bonney Wm. Gorleston
Brown Fdk. Jetty road
Burwood Ic. South qy
Bush Edward, Cht
Denny Joseph, Sbh
Dye Hy. Charlotte st
Hawkins Wm.John,Sgt
Limmer Samuel, *Fort*
Mills Wm. Gorleston
Nuthall Wm. Gaol st
Plummer Hy.George st
Stannard Erasmus, Gtn
Wright Edm. East hill
IRON AND BRASS
FOUNDERS.
Rogers Jas. M. Nqy
Yetts Wm. (and patent
windlass mfr.) Kst
IRON MERCHTS.
Brown Wm. & Son, Stn
Sherrington Jas. Nor-
ton, Fuller's hill
Thompson Rt. Gaol st,
(and Norwich)
IRONMONGERS.
(* are *Braziers, &c.*)
Bradnack Isaac,R. Kst
*Breeze Robert, Mkp
*Clowes and Dye, Hst

*Gray Thos. Edw. Kst
Morton Thomas, Cht
Pleasants W. South qy
Sherrington J. N. Chq
*Stagg John, Broad rw
*Thompson Simon,(and
optician,) Broad row
*Youell John Fuller,
Broad row
JOINERS.
Barrow George, Ntc
Beets John, Crown pl
Brock Rd. North quay
Burgess Jas. Gorleston
Clare John, George st
Cooper Thomas, Mgt
Dyball John, Row 51
Dye Rt. Barrell, Gtn
Frances Js. Fuller's pl
Gaze Benj. St Peter's
Greenacre Thos. Ntc
Greenwood Edw. Mgt
Johnson Job, Thatr.pln
Larke Jas. Row 118
Newson B. South quay
Newson Freeman, Stn
Norfor Hy. Jas. Sgt
Panchen John, East st
Plummer John,Row 56
Prentice Wm. Gtn
Proudfoot Edm. Row 73
Read James, North ter
Savage John, Stn
Sherwood Rt.Belgve.pl
Spilling Joseph,Row 50
Spilling Wm. Stn
Steward Rd. Row 46
Storey J. South Town
Swirles David, Mgt
Taylor D.& Son, Conge
Taylor Jas. Row 118
Turrell and Farrants,
Wellington place
Ward Geo. Green, Stn
Westgate Saml. Camb-
den Town
Wragg John, Row 128
Wright Saml. King st
Wright Wm. Ntc
LACE, &c. DLRS.
Swingston Wm. 1 Kst
Simpson W. J. 21 Mrw
LAST MAKER.
Freeman John, Mrw
LIBRARIES.
Alexander Wm. Kst
Bales James, Mkp

Foreman John, Tpn
Lincoln Hy. North qy
Sloman Chas. King st
Subscription, South qy.
John Smith, *lib.*
Thompson Eliza, Gst

LINEN AND WLN. DRAPERS.

Burton Wm. Algar, Mkp
Chalmers and Smith, (travelling,) Row 63
Chapman Jas. King st
Denby Fdk. King st
Ecclestone Rich. Broad row
Fyson Joseph, Mkp
Greeves John, Gtn
Hunt Wm. Market pl
Hunter Henry Levick, Fuller's hill
Jay Edw. 1 Market rw
Johnson Wm. and Son, Market row
Lake John, Market pl
Miller Charles, Mkp
Miller C. jun. Broad rw
Moore Charles, Mkp
Palmer Garwood Burton, Market place
Rackham Chs. Truman, Church plain
Whittleton Thos. Mkp
*Wilkinson Jas. Gst

LODGING HS.

Andrews Hy. Devonshire place
Ansell Ann, North bh
Bacon Hy. St Jno's. bds
Bailey Mrs My. A. Jrd
Bailey Rt. Wiltshire pl
Baker Mrs Eleanor, Sgt
Ball S. A. Harrison's buildings
Barber Sar. Beach cotg
Barber T. T. Seymour pl
Barker Mattw. Bath pl
Barnes John, King st
Bartram John, 12 Jrd
Bennett Abraham, Sgt
Bensley G., Beach
Boult James, Mill rd
Brown Rt. Kent place
Browne Wm. St Peter's walls
Burbridge P. R. East hl
Burgess Rd. St Peter's
Butcher Mrs Archer's pl

Butcher Miss My. Ann, 6 Cambridge place
Carr O. 1 Wiltshire pl
Carter Mrs Maria, Mgt
Chailey Sus. 1 St John's buildings
Chapman Rt. Gaol st
Chaston Geo. Jetty road
Church Mrs. St John's buildings
Clarke Wm. Howard st
Collett James, Kent pl
Cook Mrs Margt. 1 St James' terrace
Cutting My. A. R., Jrd
Ding Daniel, Bath pl
Dye George, Gorleston
Eastland Martha, Gtn
Ebden My. Ann, Row 71
Emms Mrs My. Jetty rd
Enders John, Sgt
Ettridge John, Jrd
Feek John T., Tgt
Forder Mrs My., Psq
French Aldred, Upl
Garwood Thos., F. Sbh
Gaze Miss Mary, Mgt
Gaze Benj. Union pl
Gaze Mrs Hanh. Jrd
Giles Geo. 4 Bath pl
Giles Jp. Harrison's bds
Goodens My. Row 20
Goulding J. 4 Camb. pl
Greenwood Thos. Jrd
Guild Mrs Sarah, Jrd
Gunton Jane, Harrison's buildings
Hall Wm. Victoria pl
Harvey John, East hl
Harwood Ann, St John's buildings
Hewitt Daniel, Mgt
Holmes Eliz. Crown pl
Hurst Thos. Jetty road
Isaac Edw. Union pl
Jackson T. Prov. hill
Joy James, Archer's pl
Kendall Miss, Crown pl
Kent Sus. Seymour pl
Larke James, Denes
Lee Mrs Ellen, Denes
Leader Miss Harriet, Denes
Leggett John, Gtn
List Eliz. Mill road
Lutson Mrs Jane, Denes

Mann James, Tpn
Martyn Mrs N. Jetty rd
Mason Mrs Sar. Denes
Masterson Hy. B., Denes
Mayhew Mary, Ann Denes
Money Mrs Maria, Sgt
Morley Edm. N., Rst
Morley Mary, Denes
Moss Thos. Jetty road
Moss Wm., Denes
Nash Mrs My. Ann, Jrd
Neech Mrs F. Denes
Nightgale C. Denes
Nuthall Robt. Denes
Orfeur Abdial, Denes
Page Saml. D. Nbh
Page Wm. Denes
Palmer Chas. Jetty rd
Palmer John, Denes
Parker Sarah. Row 66
Pate Mrs My. Denes
Patts John, Bath place
Pestell Mrs Ann, Sgt
Pestell Edm. Crown pl
Pickers Emma, Denes
Porter Wm. Crown pl
Quintou My. A. Denes
Rainer Wm. Denes
Read Lydia, Row 93
Rushmer Hanh., Denes
Salmon Joseph, Gtn
Seaman Maria, Jrd
Short Mary Ann, Kst
Simmons Ann, Jetty rd
Smith Mrs Eliz. Sbh
Smith Mrs Lucy, Sbh
Smith Mrs Mary, Jrd
Smith My. Eliz. Denes
Start John, Denes
Tedford Mary, Jetty rd
Tilson Louisa, Row 78
Turrell Mary, Denes
Tuttle Eliz., Row 99
Walker Maria, Denes
Warby John, Gorleston
Warters Ann, Row 74
Warren Thos. Kent pl
Webb Rd. Bell, Denes
Wells W. St Peter's st
Willby Rd. Howard st
Wilkinson Richd. Stn
Woods John, Bath pl
Woods Mary, Denes
Wright Chltte. Denes
Wright Robert, Denes

MALTSTERS.
(See also Brewers.)
Branford Richard, Ntc
Brown Chas. Regent st
Combe Harvey, Stn
Dowson Benjamin, Sqy
Dowson B. U. & Son,
  South Town
Gedge Adam, Row 78
Last James, Row 52
Martineau Richd., Stn
Nightingale Sml., Ngts
Reed Chas. North quay

MARINE STORE
DEALERS.
Burton & Flowerdew,
  South Town
Carter Wm. South st
Clarke Thos. South end
Clipton John, Ths. Ntc
Crane P. Fuller's hill
Cullingford Saml. Row
  139, and South quay
Goffin A. Fuller's hill
Houston Wm. Gorlestn
King Abel, Pier
Mallett Saml. Gaol st
Norman Rd. B. Hst
Prior Charles, South st
Thompson Henry, Glt
Wavers John, Gtn
Welton W. South quay

MAST, BLOCK, &
PUMP MAKERS.
Budds Alfred, Southgt
Colman and Felgrave,
  South quay
Eabbage Wm. Boult,
  Cambden Town
Ellett James, South qy
Knowles Henry, Nqy
Lubbock Wm. Nqy
Townshend Rt. Sqy
Veale Robert, South qy
Wooden Thos. South qy

MASTER MARNRS.
Appleton Jas., Row 116
Axup Jas. Jetty road
Ballard Joseph, Gtn
Barker Wm. North qy
Bateman Robt., Conge
Bateman Wm. South qy
Bayley James, King st
Blyth John, Row 74
Boult John, Row 75
Boyce J. Victoria pl
Bristow Nathl. Denes

Bristow Wm. Row 74
Buxton Wm. Miller,
  Row 142
Byfield T. St Peter's rw
Candler James, King st
Carter Wm. Denes
Clare Matthw. King st
Clarke George, Denes
Cordren Wm. Row 61
Crisp Joph. South Twn
Dabnaham J. Row 121
Darnell Thos. Denes
Dawson Rt. South qy
Dorking Robt. East hl
Doughty John, Sgt
Durrant Robt. Row 97
Eastoe Wm. Row 96
Eaton J. St Peter's st
Ellen J. Albert place
Emerson Jno. Row 129
England James, Stn
Fill Thomas, Row 121
Fish Simon, South Twn
Fish Sowdan, Row 139
Fuller Samuel, Denes
Gardiner J. Row 106
George Thos. Row 93
Gowing Henry, Jrd
Gowing John, Row 119
Green John, Row 31
Grimmer E. Row 142
Gunton Saml. King st
Hanson Wm. Row 99
Harling Wm. Kst
Harlock J. Row 138
Harrison Hy. East hill
Hawkins Jph. Row 118
Holmes Jthn. Row 54
Holmes Robt. Row 60
Howes Jonas, Stn
Howlett John, Hst
Julier John (pilot cutr.)
  3 St John's buildings
Kenney Edmd., Denes
King B. Gaol street
King Edw., Gorleston
Mansfield J. Row 101
Maryson John, Gst
Newark Isaac, Row 31
Newson John, King st
Norton Robt. Row 92
Norton Thos. Rd. Stn
Olley Thos. North quay
Orfeur John, Jetty rd
Orfeur Thomas, Denes
Palmer John, Row 121
Pile John, Row 118

Powdicks Wm. Row 109
Punchard Isaac, Kst
Rees Geo. Row 92
Rhoades Edw. 106
Rice Edmd. Paved row
Rice Geo. Gaol street
Rogers Jph. Boyle Sgt
Rogers W. Veales bldgs
Rounce John, Row 109
Rushmore, S. Row 104
Scott Wm. Row 60
Sewell W. F. Veales' bds
Shepherd S. Row 130
Smith Chas. Row 119
Spurgeon Thos. Row 45
Taylor Edw. Row 93
Teasdell Saml. Row 142
Thompson B. Row 60
Thurtell John B. Upl
Waller Thos. Sgt
Watson Geo. Gaol st
Welch Henry, Stn
Whincopp Philip, Sgt
Wilkinson Thos. Gtn
Winter John, Denes
Winter Saml. Row 56
Womack Geo. Denes
Woolverton Jas Jrd
Wright Geo. Victr. pl
Wright M. J. Gaol st

MERCHANTS.
(and Ship Owners.)
Barber Sl. Smith, Sqy
Brown Chas. 30 Rst
Cherry Jas. Short quay
Costerton John Fisher,
  South quay
Culley Saml. Regent st
  (and *Norwich*)
Laws James Eastmure,
  Gaol paved row; h
  Gorleston
Lettis Thos. & Son, Sgt
Palmer Edmund Ste-
  phen & Co. Queen st
Palmer Jas. Hurry, Rst
Preston Isaac & Son,
  South Town quay
Saunders Wm. South qy
Shelly John & Co. Sqy
Watling Robert, Stn
White Hy. L. King st
Yetts Wm. King street

MILLINERS, &c.
Aiken Sarah, Geo. st
Allcock Sarah, 7 Mrw
Clarke Sarah, 13 Mrw

Ding Eliz. Market pl
Ellerd E. & M. A. Sgt
Fookes E. Broad row
Forder Sar. Paved row
Garson Maria, 22 Mrw
Glanfield Augusta, Kst
Green M. A. South qy
Harling E. Paved row
Hastings S. Broad row
Howlett Susan, Hst
Howes E. Archer's pl
Keymer Ann, Broad rw
Maddys Eliza, Hst
Mann H. King street
Newman M. George st
Page Jane, Cht
Page My. Ann & Car.
  Howard street
Ward E. & M. Row 135
Watts Hanh. Row 73
Wilshack M. Conge

MILLWRIGHTS.
Stolworthy Jas. & Robt.
  North entrance

MUSIC DEALERS
and Preceptors.
Hawe Jane, Regent st
Meyrick Wm. King st
Street Saml. (and organ
  builder,) King st

NEWS AGENTS.
Alexander Wm. Kst
Barber C. South quay
Hoy John, Cht
Purdy J. H. Row 66

OPTICIANS, &c.
Fisher Thornton & Son,
  South quay
Thompson Simon, Broad
  row

PAINTERS,
PLUMBRS. & GZRS.
Arbon Noah, King st
Barrow Henry, Geo. st
Burgess Benj. Ntc
Burton Wm. & Son, Glt
Cooper Clarke, Gst
Cubitt Rt. Town Hall rw
Doughty Thos. W. Glt
Goffin John, King st
Goffin John, jun. Stn
Hatch Wm. Howard st
Horn Jno. Simpson, Gtn
Howes Wm. Gorleston
Hunt Chas. Benj. Gst
Lawrence Wm. 8 Rst

Norman John and Son,
  Theatre plain
Plummer Jph. A. Glt
Sandall John Nightin-
  gale, North quay
Sowells Thos. & Js. Glt
Sumner Geo. Paved row
Sumner Wm. King st
Teasdell Samuel, Stn
Thompson Rd. Glt
Tuck & Fish, Ch. plain
Woodhouse Chas. Jas.
  Queen street
Woodhouse Jas. Tpn
Woolverton Chas. Sqy
Wright James, Gtn

PAWNBROKERS.
Howlett Samuel, Hst
Maryson Fras. Hst
Mouse John, George st
Playford Hannah, Cht
Playford John, King st
Popay Susan and Ann,
  Fullers hill

PHYSICIANS.
Borrett James, King st
Impey Alfred Johnes,
  Fullers hill
Penrice Geo. King st
Smith Jas. Market pl

PLASTERERS.
Lambert Stenton, Gst
Popay Geo. S. Gtn
Wright Wm. Henry,
  Row 87

PFRS. of DANCING.
Bassingthwaight Re-
  becca M. King st
Noverre Frank, Wes-
  ley st (& *Norwich*)
Seely Louisa, 22 Rst

ROPE & TWINE
MAKERS.
(* *Make Twine only.*)
Aldridge Samuel, Ntc
Barber Robert Jrd
*Blowers Wm. Nqy
Bracey Jno. Jetty rd
Butcher M. & Sons, Jrd
*Clarke Robert, Jrd
Everit John, King st
*Gardner W. North ter
*Giles Geo. jun. Tgt
Gosling Wm. Jetty rd
Green Wm. St Peter's
Holmes Edward, Ntc
Ingram Wm. North end

Jenkinson W. Belg. pl
Keeler James, Denes
Lettis Thos. & Son, Sgt
Norman Rd. B. Hst
Rackham John, Kst
*Smowton J. South st
*Stevenson J. Kst
*Teasdell John, Csq
Welch Benj. Denes
*Wells Thomas, Ntc
*Woodhouse Rt. Row 22

SADDLERS, &c.
Allcock Wm. Cht
Beazer Martin, Cht
Burrell Chas. Gtn
Stowe Wm. Isaac, Mkp

SAIL MAKERS.
Barber Alfred, Paved rw
Bradbeen S., Row 100
Chambers W. & Son, Glt
Ingram Chas. Nqy
Lott John Hy. Kst
Miller Benj. Row 104
Pike Rt. South Town
Swanbrown J. Row 124
Swanton John, Row 57

SALT MERCHTS.
Brown Wm. & Son, Stn
Culley Saml. Rst
Lettis & Son, Cobholm
Palmer Edmd. S. & Co.
  South Town
Preston Edm. Cobholm

SEED AND CAKE
MERCHANTS.
Bunn Thos. South Tn
Culley Saml. South qy
Jenner Jas. South Tn
Palmer E. S. & Co. Stn

SHIP BROKERS, &c
Barber S. S. & Son, Sqy
Blake Garson, Stn
Bunn Thomas, Stn
Costerton Geo. B. Rst
Jermyn Danl. Custom
  House Quay
Lewis Jas. E. Paved rw
Palmer Jas. Hurry and
  Co. Regent street
Shelly Jno. & Co. (*agts.*
  to Lloyds) South qy

SHIP BUILDERS.
Barber Ts. South quay
Beeching J. South qy
Branford Ts. Womack,
  South Town
Chapman James, Stn

Fellows Hy. South Tn
Holmes Fras. & James, South Town
King Danl. South quay
Lubbock Ts. South qy
Palmer Ambrose, Stn
Palmer A. R. South qy
Preston Fredk. Stn

SHIP CHANDLRS.
Clarke & Fill, S.qy
Greeves John, Gtn
Lott John Hy. King st
Teasdell Henry, Stn

SHIP OWNERS.
(See Merchants also.)
Amess Thos. Gaol st
Barber S. S. South qy
Barker John, Queen st
Barnby Wm. Hy. Cht
Bessey Wm. North qy
Betts John, South Tn
Bracey J. St Geo. ter
Butcher Matthew, Kst
Carter Rt. South Town
Christmas Wm. Glt
Clark J. South quay
Crickmay Thomas, Rst
Crisp Wm. Row 119
Draper Wm. Hy. Glt
Foreman T. S. East hl
Garson Geo. Gaol st
Gourlay Dd. A. Mrw
Hammond Richd. Nqy
Hammond Wm. Nqy
Ivey Wm. Peter, Glt
Jay George, South Tn
Jay Hy. Albert place
Johnson James, Stn
Johnshn Jas. W. Stn
Kenney Edm. Gaol st
Lowne Jph. South Tn
Martin Hezekiah, Stn
Nave Jas. St Geo ter
Orsborn Wm. Row 45
Palmer Geo. D. Squay
Palmer W. H. Stn
Plane Thos. North ent.
Purdy Robins, King st
Scott James, Albert pl
Sewell Wm. Gaol st
Smiter William, St Peter's terrace
Steward Arthur, Stn
Steward Hy. South qq
Steward Sames, Hst
Stone Wm. Howard st
Ward Samuel, Conge

SHOPKEEPERS.
Alpe Susan, Forder st
Annison Ann, Kst
Ayers Sus. Row 129
Baldwin Ann, Cht
Barrow Ann, Cht
Beckett C. T. Puddingt
Bell George, Geo. st
Belson Wm. Gaol st
Bentley Thos. Gaol st
Blake Eliz. George st
Briggs Samuel, Cht
Bullent John, Gst
Burgess My. North end
Burling Wm. Gaol st
Burward John, Glt
Burrage Marena, Gtn
Rush Edward, Cht
Buston John T., Ntc
Butler Sarah, Gtn
Candler Harriet, Hst
Chase John, Gaol st
Claxton Eliz., Nqy
Collins Wm. Gaol st
Crane Jno., Gaol street
Downing P. South st
Dyboll Joseph, Gst
Edwards Robert, Gst
Everitt John, King st
Farman Harriet, Stn
Field Susanna, Gaol st
Frosdick C. W., Tgt
Godbolt Joseph, Stn
Guy Mary Ann, Stn
Halfnight James, Gtn
Hammond Wm., Stn
Harnton Ann, Ntc
Harrison Debh. E. and Eliz., Victoria place
Hicks Mary B., Cht
Holmes Joseph, Gst
Ives Saml. Howard st
Johnson Eleanor, Stn
Johnson Joshua, Row 99
Lacey Benjamin, Cht
Lockett Wm. (oyster pits,) South Town
Lumber Charles, Gst
Mann Wm. George st
Mills Wm. Gorleston
Money Rt. North quay
Moore James Burwood, Leicester terrace
Olley Sarah, Row 138
Page Wm. South quay
Palmer W. St Ptr.'s wls
Pedro Wm. Gorleston

Pitcher Wm. North qy
Pike Maria, Hst
Pitt James, Cht
Pratt Richard, Row100
Pye Mary Ann, Glt
Randall Jas., Mkt gate
Ray Samuel, George st
Read Ann, Gaol street
Remmonds James, Gst
Ridley Judith, Nqy
Roberts Samuel, Gtn
Runacre James, Gaol st
Sago Samuel, King st
Shaul John, Gorleston
Simpson Elizabeth, Gtn
Smith Jane, Sgt
Smith Wm. Gaol st
Spurgeon Elizbth. Hst
Starling Jonth., Hst
Taylor My. A., Forder st
Warren Samuel, Gtn
Whisken George, Gtn
Worledge Walter, Nqy
Wright Ann, George st
Wright D. Fuller's hill
Wright Sml. Crown pl

SILVERSMTHS. &c.
(See Watchmakers.)
Durrant George, Mrw
Mason Wm. (working,) Howard street

SLATER.
Quinton Henry, Stn

SOAP MANFRS.
May & Metcalfe, Nqy

STAMP OFFICE.
Palmer Jas. Hurry, Esq. Regent street

STONE MASONS.
Burgess John, Nqy
Larke & Bartram, Nqy
Lydamore and Greenwood, Nth. entrance

STRW. HAT MKRS.
(* are Blockers.)
Ayers Martha, Hst
*Bond Val., Row 54
Cain Eliz. George st
*Edwards W., Gaol st
Godbolt Sarah, Stn
*Popay T. Paved row
Rackham Hannah, Glt
*Read Wm. Howard st
Rising Susanna, Hst
Self Hannah, Gaol st
*Swanston Samuel, Glt
Woolsey Mary, King st

SURGEONS.
Aldred Chas. 12 Rst
Bateman and Palmer, Market place
Bayly Joseph, King st
Bellin Benj. South quay
Burgess Wm. Jetty rd
Costerton Charles, Sqy
Dashwood Chas.B.,Kst
Ferrier Wm. King st
Jay Simon, Regent st
Jeffery Edw.& Son,Chq
Larter John, Gaol st
Norman Rd.Rt. B., Sgt
Palmer Fdk. Nath.,Rst
Pritchard John, 2 Kst
Sabine John, M.D., Rst
Smith Jno. Caporn, Kst
Smith Jno. (regr.) Gtn
Smyth S. T., Gorleston
Taylor Charles, Mkp
Woolnough Jph., Stn
Worship Harry (regr.) Regent street

TAILORS.
Baker John, Cht
Barber Jas. Forder st
Barber Wm. Short qy
Barwood S., South st
Brand Wm. Broad row
Brianton J., Row 71
Bristow Wm.,Gorleston
Brock G. W., Forder st
Brock John, Row 40
Burgess Thos.,Row129
Burkitt Wm., Row 32
Cassidy Thos., Geo. st
Child Wm., Queen st
Cocks John, King st
Corbyn H. Paved row
Crickmay Edward, Gtn
Crickmay Samuel, Gst
Culham J., South st
Edwards E.R.,Row104
Edwards Thomas, Gst
Flower Joseph, Hst
Forder John, Paved rw
Gilham James, Row 14
Hogarth David, Mkp
Isaacs Hy., Broad row
Lark Robert, Gaol st
Lawn Jas., Broad row
Lincoln Hy., North qy
Mingay Jonth., Nqy
Mack Wm. South Twn
Mitchell Michael, Cht
Moore Wm., Ch. trees

Nolloth John (& woollen draper,) Hst
Olley Henry, 16 Mrw
Page Wm. Php., Hst
Peak Samuel, Row 129
PickersThos.R.,Row60
Portwood Wm., Row 32
Rackham Samuel, Mrw
Pratt Leonard, Gaol st
Rainer G. Paved row
Scott Jas. A. East hill
Shreeve Hy. S. Row 38
Steward C. Broad row
Stewart Charles, Hst
Tricker John, King st
Walker James, Gtn
Webster &Lummis,Qst

TALLOW CHDLRS.
(See Grocers.)
Tunbridge Rd. Row 54

TANNERS.
Cobb Benjamin, Stn
Harvey Joseph, Cht

TEA & COFFEE DEALERS.
Alexander Wm., Kst
Bales James, Mkp
Dowsing Isaac, Nqy
Springall Robert, Gst

TIMBER MERTS.
Coaks Richard, South Town (& Norwich)
Craske Job, Ntc
Culley Samuel, South entrance (and Norwich,) J. H. Palmer and Co., *agents*
Fellows, Barth, and Palmer, South Town
Nuthall P.Garrison wk
Preston I. & Son, Stn
Steward Rt. & Co., Stn
WrightWm.North ente

TOBACCONISTS.
Addison Lydia,Brd. row
Cohen David L., Mrw
Joseph Matthew, Kst
Springall Robert, Gst
Tobacco Pipe Makers.
Page Thos. G., Row 47
Taylor James, Row 51

TRUNK MAKERS.
Alexander J., Row 23
Chapman J., Row 4

TURNERS(WOOD.)
Pattman Charles, Nqy
Puttuck Edw., Row 37

Simmons P., Priory pl
Woodrow J., Conge

UMBRELLA MRS.
Spilman My., Row 26
Turner Mary, 12 Mrw

VETRNY. SURGNS
Harvey George, Stn
Hindes Rd., North qy
Smith Wm. Mkp

WATCHMAKERS.
Aldred S. H. & Son,Gst
Archbold Henry, Gtn
Ayers Thos. Howard st
Christmas James, Gst
Cotton Wm. Paved row
Davy Elijah, sen., Sqy
Davy Elijah, jun., Ntc
Davy Robert, Cht
Durrant Geo. 35 Mrw
HuntAbm.&Son,Bd. rw
Lamb Thos. Paved row
Munford Edward, Mkp
Odell Thos. Archer's pl
Shorto James, Gtn
Simpson W., Broad rw
Solomon Abm., Kst
Symonds Thomas, Hst
Woolston Wm. W., Hst

WHEELWRIGHTS.
Cox Arthur, George st
Drake James, Jetty rd
Frayer Thomas, Ferry boat row
Gooda Wm. South town
Hoggett James, Gtn
Howes Samuel, Gtn
Page Wm. Woods, Gtn

WHITESMITHS.
(* are StoveGrateMfrs.)
Brooks John, Row 142
Buckingham T.Row128
*Bullen Wm. Cht
Cobb Wm. North quay
Cubitt Robert, Row 91
Dickie Geo. May place
Elwin Robt. South quay
Elwin Wm. Row 118
Flaxman Rt. North qy
Harbord J. North quay
Minter John, Row 136
Moore John C. Row 72
Moore Saml.Velzie,Sqy
*Morter Thomas, Cht
Newark Wm.Broad row
Newman Saml. Row 20
*Nutman Sl. Fuller's hl
Plant Jno. South quay

Platford Geo.Fuller's hl
*Sherrington J. N. Chq
Springall Rt. Row 63½
Veal Henry, Row 123
WINE, SPIRIT, &
PORTER MERTS.
Barnby Wm. Henry &
Son, Charlotte street
Beart Rt.Hayward,Kst
Bell John Sayers, Gtn
Burroughs W. N. Mkp
Christmas C. H. & Co.
King street
Diver Wm.Holmes, Kst
Ferrier Richard, Glt
Lacon Sir E.H.K.Bart.
and Sons, Chq
Marsh and Barnes, Kst
Paget S. & Son, Nqy
Pratt James, High st
Preston Jacob, Qst
Tomlinson Joseph, Hst

COACHES.
From Crown & Anchor.
To *London*, 6 evng. &
½ past 7 mg.; to *Bir-
mingham*, ½ p. 4 aft.; &
to *Cambridge*, Tues. Thu.
& Sat. at 8 morning
From the Angel Inn.
To *Norwich*, ¼ bef. 2
aftn., and at 8 mg.; and
to *London*, ½ p. 7 morng.
*From the Royal Hotel &
Duke's Head.*
To *Norwich*, at 7 evg.;
and to Bury, Mon. Wed.
and Fri. at 8 morning
STEAM PACKETS.
To LONDON, the *Ra-
mona*, every Wed., Jas.
Cherry, agent; and the
Aisla-Craig, Friday, R.
Teasdell & Son, *agents*
To HULL, &c., the *Al-*

batros, every Tuesday, R.
Teasdell & Son, agents;
and the *Iris*, every Sat.,
Wm. Saunders, agent
To NORWICH, &c., the
British Queen, daily, at
4 aftn.; the *Sovereign*,
every M. W. and Fri., at
9 mg.; and the *Emperor*
and *Dahlia*, every Tues.
Thu. and Sat. 9 morng.
They also leave on Sun-
days, at 7 mg. and ½ p. 3
aft. The *fare to Norwich
and back* is 1s. 6d.
☞ Henry Brown &
Co., and Denny & Brock,
convey passengers in
their boats to and from
the *Leith, London, and
other Steamers*, passing
Yarmouth Roads.
SAILING VESSELS.
To *London*, several regu-
lar trading vessels, weekly, from the Quay; R.
Teasdell & Son, S. S.
Barber and J. E. Laws,
agents.
To *Hull, Goole, Selby,*
&c., two vessels weekly,
R. Teasdell & Son, and
W. Saunders, *agents.*
To *Newcastle-on-Tyne,*
weekly; R.Teasdell and
Son, and S. S. Barber,
agents.
To Norwich, Beccles,
and Bungay, wherries
from the Quay, daily
*CARRIERS BY
LAND.*
*Sarah Martin's Wag-
gons*, from Marketgates
to Lowestoft, Yoxford,
Woodbridge, Ipswich,
London, &c., every Mon.
and Thurs., at 1 aftn.

FROM THE INNS.
Marked 1, *stop at the
Black Swan;* 2, *Buck;*
3, *Duke's Head;* 4,
Feathers; 5, *Hunts-
man and Horn;* 6,
George and Dragon;
7, *Jolly Farmers;* 8,
Swan-with-two-Necks;
and 9, *White Horse.*
Places.   Carriers.
1 Beccles, I. Piper,Wed-
nesday and Saturday
3 Bungay, Jas. Neave's
Van, M. W. and Sat.,
4 afternoon
6 Catfield, J. Henson, S.
Cromer, (King's Head,)
Wm. Foulger; and 4,
J. Wiseman, Sat. noon
9 East Ruston, J.Bowen,
Saturday
1 Halesworth, J.Newson,
Tuesday and Friday
Happisburgh, (Wag. &
Horses,) E. Prest, S.
8 Hickling,J Forman, S.
3 Loddon,Leggett's Van,
Wed.; 2, C. Fairhead;
and W Middleton,from
the Bear, Wed. & Sat.
2 Lowestoft, P. Balls, 3
times a day; and 3, J.
Burton, Tu. Thu. &
Sat., 6 evening
7 Ludham, John Hall, S.
Martham, (Wag. & Hor-
ses,) J. Gedge,W.&S.
9 North Walsham, R.
Coe, Wed. and Sat.
7 Palling, S. Pestell, S.
6 Repps, M. Yallop, Sat.
6 Somerton, W. Child, S.
Southwold, (see Hales-
worth and Lowestoft)
Sutton, (King's Head,)
— Lake, Saturday
5 Winterton, J. Kittle &
R. Brown, Wed.& Sat.

BABERGH HUNDRED.

Babergh Hundred, in the south-western part of Suffolk, and Liberty of St. Edmund, is a fertile and picturesque district, having many large and well-built villages, and several *silk and worsted manu- factories.* It extends 16 miles in length, from north to south, and averages about eight miles in breadth. The navigable *river Stour*, in a winding course of more than twenty miles, bounds it on the west and south, and separates it from Essex; and its other boundaries are Ris- bridge and Thingoe Hundreds, on the north-west; Thedwestry Hun- dred, on the north; and Cosford and Samford Hundreds, on the east.

It is watered by many rivulets, flowing southward to the Stour, and is in *Sudbury and Cosford Unions*, in the *Diocese of Ely*, and in the *Archdeaconry and Deanery of Sudbury*, except *Monks Eleigh*, which is a *Peculiar* of the Archbishop of Canterbury. Its ancient markets of *Nayland* and *Lavenham* are obsolete ; but it has *fairs* at those places and at eight other villages ; and the market town and borough of *Sudbury* lies within its limits, though a separate jurisdiction. It comprises 32 *parishes*, of which the following is an enumeration, together with Sudbury, shewing their territorial extent, the annual value of their lands and buildings, as assessed to the property tax in 1815, and their population in 1801 and 1841 :—

PARISHES.	Acrs.	Rent £.	Populatn. 1801.	1841.	PARISHES.	Acres.	Rental. £.	Population. 1801.	1841
Acton	2729	3035	461	555	MelfordLong..	5186	7724	2204	2597
Alpheton	1212	1324	204	321	*Milden	1332	1473	130	186
Assington	2974	3829	471	778	*Monks Eleigh	2099	2520	542	732
*Boxford§	1802	3102	636	889	Nayland	942	2134	881	1114
Boxted	1367	1460	171	200	Newton-near } Sudbury .. }	2198	2737	354	443
*Brent Eleigh	1625	2200	243	289					
Bures St. Mary‡	2542	3339	702	984	*Polstead	3402	3936	655	989
Cavendish	3393	4406	1042	1353	*Preston......	1970	2111	309	406
Chilton	868	1118	79	98	Shimpling	2699	3050	441	517
*Cockfield	3626	4086	739	951	Somerton	1040	1149	117	143
Cornard Great	1550	2191	535	938	Stanstead	1162	1453	258	387
Cornard Little	1600	1811	279	396	Stoke by Nayld	4600	6744	1041	1362
*Edwardstone	1872	2104	362	495	WaldingfieldGt	2424	3328	564	676
Glemsford	2293	3675	1215	1366	WaldingfieldLt	1700	2104	338	420
*Groton	1572	1719	516	624	Wiston	1170	1889	220	252
Hartest	1964	2905	646	812	*Sudbury Boro'†*	1250	3471	3283	5085
*Lavenham ..	2812	3755	1776	1871					
Lawshall	2907	3428	554	925	Total..	71,882	95,310	21,968	29,154

* The ten parishes marked thus are in COSFORD UNION, (see page 283,) and all the others are in SUDBURY UNION.

§ *Boxford* parish includes *Hadleigh Hamlet*. (See page 294.)

‡ The parish of *Bures St. Mary* is partly in Hinckford Hundred, *Essex*, and comprises altogether 4131 acres, and 1596 souls.

† The BOROUGH OF SUDBURY is in three parishes, viz., *All Saints*, which had 1262, *St. Gregory*, which had 1893, and *St. Peter*, which had 1926 inhabitants in 1841. It also comprises 4 persons in the extra-parochial house called *Saint Bartholomew*. The return of the parish of St. Gregory, in 1841, included 196 paupers in the *Union Workhouse*.

☞ CHIEF CONSTABLE, Mr. Samuel Ruffell, of Shimpling.

SUDBURY UNION comprises the Borough of Sudbury, and 41 other parishes and townships, of which 22 are in Babergh Hundred, as just noticed, one (Hawkeden) in Risbridge Hundred, and 18 in *Hinckford Hundred, Essex*. The latter are, Alphamstone, Ballingdon, Belchamp-Otten, Belchamp St. Paul, Belchamp-Walter, Borley, Bulmer, Bures-Hamlet, Foxearth, Gestingthorpe, Henny Great, Henny Little, Lamarsh, Liston Middleton, Pentloe, Twinstead, and Wickham St. Paul. The whole Union forms a *Superintendent Registrar's District*, and had 30,148 inhabitants, in 1841. It embraces an area of 119 square miles, and its average annual expenditure for the relief of its poor, during the three years preceding the formation of the Union, in 1835, was £26,449 ; though in 1838 it was only £17,526, and in 1840, £15,745. The WORKHOUSE is at Sudbury, and is a large brick building, erected in 1836-7, on the site of a smaller one, which belonged to the three united parishes of Sudbury. It has room for 350 inmates, but has seldom more than 250, and in summer only about 200. Rt. Mapletoft, Esq., is chairman, and N. C. Barnardiston, Esq., vice-chairman,

of the *Board of Guardians.* Mr. Wm. Harvey is *governor* of the Workhouse ;
Edmund Stedman, Esq., *union clerk and superintendent registrar ;* and Mr. J.
Durrell *registrar of marriages.* The RELIEVING OFFICERS are, Mr. F. W.
Ellis, for Melford District ; Mr. S. Ramscar, for Bulmer District ; Mr. R. Pratt,
for Bures District ; and Mr. W. Steggles, for Sudbury District. The Union is
divided into five REGISTRATION DISTRICTS, of which the following are the
names, and the *Registrars of Births and Deaths,* viz.,—*Sudbury,* Mr. Wm.
Steggles ; *Hartest,* Mr. F. W. Ellis ; *Melford,* Mr. G. Green ; *Bulmer,* Mr. S.
Ramscar ; and *Bures,* Mr. R. Pratt.   Robt. Mapletoft, Esq., of Stanstead, is secretary to the Hundred of Babergh *Association for the Prosecution of Felons.*

ACTON, a pleasant village, 3 miles N. by E. of Sudbury, has in its
parish 555 souls, and 2729A. of fertile land, nearly all the property of
Earl Howe and Sir Hyde Parker, Bart.   The former is lord of the
manor, which was formerly called *Aketon,* and was held by Robert de
Buers, in the reign of Edward I., but was given by Edward IV. to
Henry, Lord Bouchier, for his faithful services to the house of York.
It afterwards passed to the Bacons.   ACTON PLACE, about half a
mile west of the village, was a seat of the Daniels, who sold it in the
early part of the 18th century, to Robert Jennens, Esq., who began
the erection of an extensive and splendid mansion, which was finished
by his son, Wm. Jennens, Esq., who died in 1791, aged nearly 100,
with the reputation of being the richest subject in the kingdom.   On
his decease, the fine tapestry was torn from the walls, and sold, with
the furniture and other moveables.   This noble mansion remained un-
tenanted, except by an old man and old woman, till about 18 years ago,
when it was taken down, except the servants' wing and a few out-
offices. The extensive park and gardens by which it was encompassed,
are now cultivated fields.   The *Church* (All Saints) is a neat structure, with a tower and five bells, and had anciently a chantry, of the
annual value of £67. 2s. 8d.   Earl Howe is impropriator of the great
tithes, and patron of the *vicarage,* valued in K.B. at £9. 6s. 8d., and
now enjoyed by the Rev. Lawrence Ottley, M.A., who has a neat parsonage.   The tithes were commuted in 1838, for a yearly modus of
£750, half of which belongs to the Vicar.   Here is a *National School,*
built by Earl Howe, in 1839.   *Ambrose Kerrington,* in 1691, charged
three closes, called the Coppice, in Great Waldingfield, with the distribution of twopenny-worth of bread every Sunday, and one pair of
shoes each, to six poor widows of Acton, on the 24th December.

Broom Thos. maltster & vict. Crown
Green Mrs Susanna
Hogger John, wheelwright
Meggs John, blacksmith
Mills Henry, shoemaker
Mills James, carpenter
Mills Jas. jun. shopkpr. & carpenter
Nice James, shoemaker
Ottley Rev. Lawrence, M.A., *Vi-
carage*

Poole George, bricklayer

FARMERS.
Branwhite John || Bear Wm.
Cadge Robert, *Barsons Hall*
Coe Wm. || Cook Henry
Green John, *Green Farm*
Tiffen Amos
Tiffen Samuel, *Babergh Heath*
Underwood Ann, *Acton Hall*

ALPHETON, a scattered village and parish, on the eastern side of a
rivulet, 6 miles N. of Sudbury, contains 321 souls, and 1202 acres of
land, anciently the lordship of the Welnethams, and afterwards of the
Raynsforths and Littles.   N. C. Barnardiston, Esq., is now lord of
the manor, but part of the soil belongs to Messrs. Wm. Gardener, S.

Death, and J. Gosling. About 200 acres are copyhold, subject to arbitrary fines. The *Church* (St. Peter and St. Paul) is an ancient tiled fabric, with a tower and two bells. The *rectory*, valued in K.B. at £10. 1s. 8d., is in the patronage and incumbency of the Rev. T. G. Dickinson, and has a yearly modus of £275, awarded in 1843 in lieu of tithes. The poor parishioners have the interest of £10, left by Geo. Clopton, and also 27s. yearly from Corder's charity, as noticed with Lavenham.

Baldwin John, wheelwright	Gardener Wm. maltster & corn miller
Crossman James, vict. *Red Lion*	Gardener Christian, farmer
Death Samuel, farmer, Hall	Goshark John, carpenter
Dickinson Rev Thomas Gustavus, *Rectory*	Melton James, farmer
	Underwood George, blacksmith

ASSINGTON, a pleasant and scattered village, 4½ miles N.W. of Nayland, and E.S.E. of Sudbury, has in its picturesque parish 778 souls, and 2974 acres of fertile and well-wooded land, nearly all the property of John Gurdon, Esq., the lord of the manor and impropriator, whose family has been long seated at *Assington Hall*, an ancient brick mansion in a fine park of 60 acres, adjoining an old wood of 50 acres. The Corbets were seated here from the reign of Edward I., till the time of Henry VIII., when Sir Richd. Corbet sold the estate to Robert Gurdon, Esq.. The ancient family of Gurdon are descended from a Welchman, who was driven by the Saxon occupation of his property into Bretagne, in the fifth century, carrying with him the name of *Gurdon* or *Greenhill*, as a memorial of his ancient pastoral estate. His descendants were among the Norman followers in the eleventh century, and obtaining a share of the Conqueror's favours, remained in this part of the kingdom. Since their settlement at Assington, the Gurdons have at various periods represented Suffolk, Ipswich, and Sudbury, in Parliament, and have several times been sheriffs of the county. For taking part against the Royalists, much of their property has been confiscated, and there are now hanging in the hall four general pardons for high treason. The *Church* (St. Edmund) is a neat structure, with a tower and four bells, and was built by Canute the Great, on the site of the last battle fought between the Saxons and the Danes, in which the latter were the victors. The hall, which stands near it, was raised originally as a religious house, in which priests prayed for the souls of the slain. The benefice is a discharged *vicarage*, valued in K.B. at £10, and now in the patronage of John Gurdon, Esq., and incumbency of the Rev. John Hallward, M.A., who has 15A. of glebe. The tithes were commuted in 1837 for the yearly moduses of £447. 17s. 10d. to the vicar, and £361. 15s. 3d. to the impropriator. In the *crag deposit* in this parish are found many curious shells and other relics of the antidiluvian world. A large petrified vegetable pod, found here some years ago, is now preserved in the British Museum. In 1598, *John Winterflood* gave the poor of Assington, four bushels of wheat at Christmas and four bushels at Easter, payable out of the farm at *Avely Hall*, and the rectorial tithes. In 1665, £16, given by the Gurdon family for supplying linen for shirts and shifts for the poor, was laid out in the purchase of 2½ acres of land, in *Aldfleet Meadow*, now let for £3 a year. The poor parishioners have also a yearly rent-charge of 26s. left by *Thos. Alston*,

in 1690, for the weekly distribution of six penny loaves ; and another of £2. 15s. left by John Gurdon, Esq., in 1752. Both these annuities are paid by the present Mr. Gurdon. The parish has a National School, and sends two boys to the Grammar school at Boxford, in consideration of £100 bequeathed for that purpose by John Gurdon, Esq., in 1777.

Gurdon John, Esq., & Coulson T.L., Esq., *Assington Hall*
Butcher Charlotte, schoolmistress
Butcher George, broom maker
Butcher Thomas, beer house
Bibby Robert, grocer and draper
Carter Henry, beerhouse
Fearon Rev. Daniel Rose, curate
Gilby Robert, grocer & draper
Gladwin Henry, tailor
Godden Charles, butcher and vict. Shoulder of Mutton
Green Elizabeth, wheelwright
Hawkins Thos. corn miller, *Moor*
Warren Mr Daniel

Blacksmiths.
Carter Thomas
Halls Alfred
Warren Thomas
Boot&ShoeMkrs.
Gentry Wm.
Good James
Griggs Jonathan
Jackaman Wm.
Plampin Edw.
Carpenters.
Aldam Jonathan
Griggs Smith
FARMERS.
Crisell John

Coe Jane
Dyer John
Godfrey John
Hawkins Thos.
Hudson Nathl.(& land agent)
Norden George
Parson Charles
Sandle James, *Darking Tye*
Thurban Wm., *Honey Tye*
Underwood Danl. *Avely Hall*
Underwood Thos

BOXFORD is a large and well-built village in a fertile valley, 5 miles N.W. of Nayland, and W.S.W. of Hadleigh. Some of its houses are in Groton and Edwardstone parishes. Its own parish comprises about 1800 acres of land, and 889 inhabitants, exclusive of *Hadleigh Hamlet*, which lies nearly two miles east of the church, in Cosford Hundred, as already noticed at page 294. Boxford has several well-stocked shops, good inns, and a number of malt kilns. It has a pleasure *fair* on Easter Monday, and on the small river which runs past the village, are several corn mills. The soil belongs to Wm. Green, Esq., Sir Hy. Peyton, Chas. Tyler, Esq., Sir J. R. Rowley, H. Green, Esq., and a few smaller owners. W. Green, Esq., resides at and is lord of the manor of *Codenham Hall*, an ancient mansion, which was formerly the seat of the Brands and the Bennets. *Peyton Hall*, a farm house, on the south side of the parish, was anciently a seat of the Peyton family, to whom it still belongs, with the manor to which it gives name, though it was for some time held by the Dashwoods. On the west side of the rivulet opposite Boxford, is the hamlet of *Stone Street*. The CHURCH (St. Mary) is a large handsome structure, with a tower 74 feet high, containing eight bells, and surmounted by a small wooden spire. The porch is on the south side, and over the entrance are seven niches, with a number of inscriptions, now nearly obliterated. The benefice is a *rectory*, valued in K.B. at £20, and now having a good residence, about 33 acres of glebe, and a yearly modus £658. 10s. awarded in 1843, in lieu of tithes. The patronage is in the Crown, and the Hon. and Rev. F. A. Phipps is the incumbent. In the village, but in Edwardstone parish, is an *Independent Chapel*, with a school and a house for the minister, erected in 1823 by J. and R. Ansell, Esqrs., at the cost of nearly £2000, including the purchase of a small endowment. Boxford has an Infant School, a *National School*, built in 1839, an endowed Grammar School, and several charities.

Boxford Grammar School was established by a charter of Queen Elizabeth, in the 38th year of her reign, which, after reciting that John Snelling and Philip

Gostlinge, in order to promote learning, and the instruction of the youth of *Box-ford*, *Groton*, and *Edwardstone*, had granted to John Gurdon and others a messuage, garden, and orchard, in Boxford, ordained that there should be a Free Grammar School there, to consist of a master and usher, and that 37 persons therein named should be governors, and be incorporated.   The *school property* now consists of a house and garden, occupied by the master; 10A. 19P. of land, at Edwardstone, let for £20 a year, and £442. 3s. 3d. three per cent. stock, of which £100 was left by John Gurdon, Esq., in 1777, for the instruction of two poor boys of *Assington*. Owing to the smallness of the endowment, and the absence of any demand for the dead languages, the master is only required to teach reading, writing, and arithmetic, to eight free scholars,—two from each of the four parishes. The TOWN LANDS, about 15A., (including a moiety of Moore's Charity, noticed with Groton,) are let for about £36 a year, and the rents are applied with the poor rates. Two cottages are used as *almshouses* for poor people, placed therein by the churchwardens, but the donor is unknown.   *Bennet's Charity Estate* consists of about 9A., at Polstead, let for £9 per annum, which is applied in teaching poor children to read. Respecting this charity no writings can be found. A yearly rent-charge of 40s., out of land at Polstead, was left by *Robert White*, in 1713, and is paid to a mistress for teaching four poor children to read. The poor parishioners have £16 per annum for *quarterly distributions of bread;* viz., £9, from 4A. 1R. 34P. of land, called Lynn's Croft, left by *John Plumb*, in 1623; and £7 from 5A. 2R. 9P., near Slade Green, in Edwardstone, called Doggett's Charity, but no writings exist concerning it.   The poor parishioners have also £3 a year from Brand's Charity. (See Edwardstone.)

BOXFORD DIRECTORY.
Marked 2, are in Groton parish.

Bouttell Mr Jonth.||Ayres Mr G. N.
Butler James, currier
Cooper Samuel, saddler
Faires John, parish clerk
Foster Rev. Cavendish, curate
Gardiner Wm. currier
Green Wm. Esq. *Codenham Hall*
Gurdon Theophilus Goate, surgeon
Hawkins Wm. clothes dealer
Hazell Hannah Maria, schoolmrs
Kiddell Sherlock Whitby, plumber & glazier
Last, Wallace, and Last, solicitors, *Hadleigh* (attend Wed. & Friday)
Lewis John, gentleman
Mann Charles Parker, surgeon
Moore Rev. Benj. (Independent)
Phipps Hon. & Rev. Fred.Augustus, *Rectory*
PlumeRev.Wm.M.A., master of the Grammar School
Salter Miss Jane
Stevens Enoch, National schoolmr
Swan Rt. Fras. *postmaster*, & agent to the Yorkshire Fire & Life Office. Letters despatched at 6 evg
Tucker Elizabeth, schoolmistress
Vine Eliz. Ann, schoolmistress
Warren John, beerhouse
Watkins John, excise officer

INNS AND TAVERNS.
Chequers, John King Cook
Fleece, John Peggs, (& hair dresr)
Swan, Samuel Prentice

White Hart, John Moye (& brewer)

Bakers.
Bare George
Marsh Jph. (& basket maker)
Sharman John

Blacksmiths.
Cook John King
Stribling Chas.

Bricklayers.
Howe Wm.
Kingsbury Fdk.
Kingsbury Rt.B.
2Kingsbury Wm. (brick maker)

Butchers.
Coates James
Herbert John

Corn Millers.
Gosling Edith
Newman Thos.
Smith T.
Sowman Thomas
2 Tiffen Thomas

FARMERS.
Alderton Chas.
Bouttell Joseph
Bouttell Robert
Bouttell Samuel
Cardy Daniel
Daking Abm.
Green Hugh, sen.
Lungley Brook
M. *Peyton Hall*
Parson Edward
Scowen Chpr.

Grocers & Dprs.
Lambard Samuel
Phillips James
2 Sadler John
Smith Thomas
Sowman John

Joiners.
Balaam Wm.
Phillips George
Phillips & Kemble

Maltsters.
Atterton Wm.
Atterton Thomas
Cardy Daniel
Hitchcock Simon (& porter mert)
Lambard Saml.
Scowen Chpr.
2 Tiffen Benj.

Shoemakers.
Bragg Mary Ann
Bull Wm.
Elmer Edward
Scoffield Wm.
Street John, sen. and junior
Watson Joseph

Tailors.
Hart Thornton
Stribling Chas.

CARRIER.
John Sowman, to Colchester, Wed and Saturday

BOXTED, a pleasant village, in a picturesque valley, 6 miles N.E. by E. of Clare, and 7½ miles N.N.W. of Sudbury, has in its parish 200 souls, and 1367 acres of land. Geo. Weller Poley, Esq., is lord of the manor, and resides at the Hall, an ancient brick mansion, in a small park, crossed by the rivulet which supplies the moat by which the mansion is still encompassed. Part of the parish belongs to the Marquis of Downshire and Mrs. Gee. The manor was anciently held by Bury Abbey, and afterwards by Robert Harleston, after whose attainder, in the reign of Edward IV., it was given to the Duke of Gloucester. It afterwards passed to the Poleys, many of whom were distinguished knights, and were seated here, and at Columbine Hall and Badley. About the middle of last century, Boxted Hall and manor passed to the *Wellers*, who assumed the name of Poley. The *Church* is a neat structure, with a tower and two bells, and contains several handsome monuments. The living is a *rectory*, consolidated with that of Hartest. The tithes here were commuted, in 1839, for a yearly modus of £375. 10s. In 1572, JOHN POLEY, Esq., bequeathed his lands and tenements at Burwell, Exning, and Fornham All Saints, in trust for equal division among the poor of *Boxsted, Hartest, Stanstead, Glemsford*, and *Somerton*. He directed that two or three persons of each of these parishes should be trustees. The estate belonging to this *charity* now consists of 24A. 2R. 16P. of land at Burwell, allotted at an enclosure in 1828, in lieu of the old charity land at Burwell and Exning, and now let for £42 a year; and 15A. 3R. of land in Fornham, let on a lease for 99 years, in 1794, at the yearly rent of £13, and now forming part of the park of Hengrave Hall. After deducting the payments for land-tax, drainage, &c., the clear income of the charity is divined among the poor, for which purpose each of the five parishes receives about £8 yearly.

Poley Geo. Weller, Esq. *Boxted Hl*
Josling Joseph, blacksmith
Westrup MrsMaryAnn, *MoorHouse*
FARMERS.
Cross Henry, *Truckett's Hall*

Golding Edward, *Boxted Lodge*
Hale Jph. (& maltster)|| Smith John
Harvey Thomas, *Park Farm*
Westrup John Spencer, *Moor House*

BRENT-ELEIGH, a small scattered village on the acclivities of a picturesque valley, 2 miles E.S.E. of Lavenham, and 4 miles W. by S. of Bildeston, has in its parish 289 souls, and 1625 acres of land. Thos. Brown, Esq., M.D., of London, is lord of the manor, and owner of most of the soil, and the remainder belongs to Wm. Adair, Esq., and a few smaller owners. The manor was formerly held by the Sheltons, who procured the grant of a market, which has long been obsolete. It afterwards passed to the Colmans, and from them to the Goates. The *Hall*, a handsome mansion with pleasant grounds, is now unoccupied. The *Church* (St. Mary) is an ancient structure, with a tower and three bells, and stands on an eminence, embowered in thriving plantations. At the end of the chancel is a *Parochial Library*, which was built and furnished with books by *Dr. Colman*, of Trinity College, Cambridge, about the year 1700. The *rectory*, valued in K.B. at £8, has a good residence, 9A. of glebe, and a yearly modus of £393. 15s., awarded in 1838, in lieu of tithes. Dr. Brown is patron, and the Rev. Richd. Snape, A.B., incumbent. Here is an ALMSHOUSE in six tenements for the residence of poor men and women, erected by *Edward*

Colman, Esq., who, in 1736, endowed it with a farm of 77a. at Pres-ton, now let for about £80 a year. The rent is applied, after paying for the repairs of the almshouse and other necessary expenses, in dis-tributions of clothing, fuel, and money among the almspeople, and in providing them with medical attendance. They are generally widows and widowers, chosen by the trustees, on the recommendation of the rec-tor. The trustees, in 1828, were Sir Wm. Rowley, Bart., Rev. Joshua Rowley, H. Scourfield, and W. Goate, Esqrs. The rent of five tene-ments, called *Poor's Houses*, is divided among poor parishioners, as also is the rent of half an acre of land at Monks-Eleigh, let for 18s. a year. In 1698, *Edward Colman* left £200 to be laid out in land, the rents thereof to be employed in binding poor boys of this parish appren-tice to substantial tradesmen or farmers. This legacy was laid out in the purchase of 3¼a. of land at Lavenham, now let for £10 a year. The rector and churchwardens are trustees.

Bowers Thomas, carpenter
Everett Francis, beerhouse
Hogger Peter, wheelwright
Pryke Isaac, corn miller
Ruffell Wm. shoemaker
Snape Rev Richd. A.B. *Rectory*
Underwood Thomas, blacksmith

FARMERS.
Ayers Wm. || King John
Cooper Joseph, *Bridge Farm*
Cooper and Hitchcock
Fayers Charles, *Marles Hall*
Watkinson John, *Wells Hall*
Woodgate John || Woodgate Wm.

BURES ST. MARY is a large and well-built village, on both sides of the navigable river Stour, 5½ miles S.S.E. of Sudbury, and nearly 5 miles W. of Nayland. It contains about 1500 inhabitants, and has a large tan yard, several extensive malting establishments, good inns, and well-stocked shops. It has a *fair* on Holy Thursday, and its parish is divided into two *townships*—viz., *Bures* and *Bures Hamlet.* The former contains 984 souls, and 2542a. 1r. 12p., and the latter is on the south side of the river in Hinckford Hundred, Essex, and has 612 inhabitants, and 1588a. 3r. 17p. of land. Osgood Hanbury, Esq., is lord of the *manor*, and owner of a great part of the soil in both town-ships, which are connected by a good bridge. The other principal landowners are Sir J. R. Rowley and Mrs. Holmes, in Bures, and Col. J. Rolt and Major Brock, in Bures Hamlet. Galfridus de Fontibus says, St. Edmond was crowned king of the East Angles at Bures, but most other writers are agreed that that ceremony took place at Bury. In the reign of Edward I., Hugh Lord Bardolf held the manor of Bures. Edward IV. granted the estates or manors of *Overhall* and *Netherall*, otherwise *Sylvester Hall*, in this parish, to Ann, wife of Lord Boucher. *Smallbridge*, now a farm house, was long the seat of the ancient family of Waldegrave. The *Church* (St. Mary) is a neat structure, with a tower containing six bells, and formerly surmounted by a handsome spire, which was set on fire by lightning, in 1733, and burnt down, together with all the wood work in the tower, where the heat was so great that the bells were melted. In the chancel are seve-ral monuments of the *Bures* or *Buers*, who took their name from the parish, and of the knightly family of Waldegrave. Upon a tomb on the north side, lies the cross-legged figure of a knight, supposed to re-present one Cornard, who is said to have sold the farm, called *Corn Hall*, for fourpence, in the time of Henry III. The benefice is a *vicarage*, valued in K.B. at £12. 6s. 6d., and in 1835 at £273, but now hav-

ing a yearly modus of £327, awarded in 1840, when the great tithes of the parish were commuted for £844. 10s. per annum, payable to O. Hanbury, Esq., and other impropriators. Mr. Hanbury is patron, and the Rev. Arthur Hanbury, M.A., incumbent. The late *Wm. Martin, Esq.*, of Lincoln's Inn, London, left £2000, in trust among other things, to pay £40 a year to the vicar of Bures. Here is a small *Baptist Chapel*, built in 1834, and a large *National School*, erected in 1840. *Mrs. Dorcas Bridges*, in 1803, left £353. 17s. 7d. three per cent. stock, the dividends thereof to be distributed yearly on Christmas-day, by the minister and churchwardens, among the poor widows of the parish, not receiving parochial relief. In 1825, *John Dupont* left 20s. a year out of a house in Bures hamlet, for poor widows of that hamlet.

BURES ST. MARY.

*Marked * are in Bures Hamlet, Essex.*

Anderson Rev Alex. (Baptist)
Boggis Mrs Elizabeth
Chaplin Wm. Elijah, farrier
Death Isaac, parish clerk
*Dupont Joseph, carpenter
Faires Wm. cooper
Garrad John & Son, tanners, brick makers, &c.
Garrad Rt. gent. and Mrs Mary
Gilby John, saddler
Hanbury Rev Arthur, M.A. incbt.
Hardy Abm. agent to Norwich Fire office
Howard Wm. National schoolmr.
*Kemp Mrs Eliz. White House
Lewis Hy. boarding and day school
Pilgrim Robert, carpenter
Pratt Rd. relieving officer & registrar
Salmon Henry, gentleman
Scowen Thomas, beer house
Siggers Willoughby, glover
Simmonds Benj. Francis, surgeon
Stannard Robert, corn miller
Steed Eliz. plumber and glazier
Stow John, hair dresser
Wyatt John, hair dresser

INNS AND TAVERNS.
Angel, Charles Humpherys
*Eight Bells, Charles Burch
Queen's Head, Lydia Hurrell
*Swan, Elizabeth Turner

Bakers.
*Burch Thomas, Smith
Cant Samuel
Layzell John
*Mole Nathl.
Blacksmiths.
*Dansie Wm.
Death Isaac
Death Saml.(and beerhouse)
Bricklayers.
Deeks Wm.
Mussett Wm.
Pilgrim James
Butchers.
Humpherys Chs.
*Miles Wm.
FARMERS.
Boggis Golding, Fish House
Boggis John, Gt. Bevell
Boggis Sarah
Bush My. *Overhall*
Dalton Henry
Davey George
*Garrad John
Good Sarah, *Small bridge*
*Goldsmith Wm.
Grimwood Saml. (& brickmkr.)
Hurrell Ralph, *Gazeley-gate*
Layzell John

Lungley Thos. *Corn Hall*
*Nott John
*Pettit Hugh
*Pettit Zach.
Phillips Samuel
*Rayner Joseph
Seaman Simon
*Townsend Chs.
*Wass John
Wood Grimmard
Grocers & Dprs.
*Dupont Maria
Ffitch George
Good Elizabeth
Maltsters and Corn Merchts.
Boggis George
Boggis Joseph Davey
Dalton James
Garrad John and Son
Shoemakers.
Goody Robert
Mole Nathaniel
Mole Wm.
Scowen Wm.
Warren Thomas
Tailors.
Cardy Henry
Good Edward
Steed Joshua
Wheelwrights.
Hawkins Wm.
*Hayward Jph.

CAVENDISH, a large village, on the north bank of the river Stour, nearly 3 miles E. by N. of Clare, and 6 miles N.W. of Sudbury, has in its parish 1353 inhabitants, and 3392A. 3R. 3P. of fertile land. It has a *fair* for cattle, &c. on June 11th, and for pleasure on the two following days; and is remarkable for giving name to one of

the most illustrious families in Great Britain. A younger branch of the *Gernons*, (who were of considerable note in Norfolk and Essex,) being seated here, assumed the sirname of *Cavendish*, and produced several individuals of great eminence. One of these, *Sir John Cavendish*, was born here in the 46th of Edward III., and became chief justice of the court of King's Bench, which office he filled with great reputation till the 5th of Richard II., when the people of Suffolk, instigated by the example of Wat Tyler and Jack Straw, rose in rebellion, under John Raw, a priest, and Robert Westbroom. The chief justice falling into the hands of the rabble, who were exasperated at the intelligence of the death of Wat Tyler, by the hand of his son, was dragged to Bury, and there his head was struck off, and set upon the pillory at the market-cross. His remains were interred at Cavendish. He left two sons and two daughters. It was his youngest son, John, one of the esquires of the body of Richard II., that dispatched Wat Tyler, in Smithfield, for which service he was knighted on the spot by the king, who also settled a pension of £40 on him and his heirs for ever. *Sir William Cavendish*, having in the reigns of Edward VI. and Mary, held various important offices at court, obtained a considerable portion of the possessions of the dissolved monasteries, and thus laid the foundation of the subsequent splendid fortune of his house. His son William was created, by James I., *Baron Cavendish, of Hardwicke*, and *Earl of Devonshire;* and the great-grandson of the latter was created *Duke of Devonshire* in 1694. These titles, with others subsequently conferred, are now held by the Most Noble William Spencer Cavendish, Duke of Devonshire, &c., whose chief seat is Chatsworth, in Derbyshire, popularly called, from its extent and magnificence, the Palace of the Peak. From another branch of the same family, descended the Cavendishes, Dukes of Newcastle, who became extinct in 1711. The present *Earl of Burlington*, whose father was raised to that dignity in 1831, is cousin and heir to the Duke of Devonshire. J. R. Brice, Esq. is now lord of the *manor* of Cavendish, but a great part of the soil belongs to Earl Howe, C. Heigham, Esq., and several smaller proprietors. The *Church* (St. Mary) is a handsome structure, with a square tower, containing six bells, and said to have been built by one of the abbots of Bury. The *rectory*, valued in K.B. at £26, and in 1835 at £547, is in the patronage of Jesus College, Cambridge, and incumbency of the Rev. Thomas Castley, M.A., who has a good residence, and 61A. 31P. of glebe. The *Independents* have a small chapel here. CAVENDISH HALL, an elegant modern mansion, in a park of 50 acres, was built by the late Thomas Hallifax, Esq., banker, of London, and is situated on the north side of the Stour, about a mile west of the village. It is the property of the Ogden family, but is occupied by Mrs. Sarah Yelloly, relict of the late Dr. Yelloly, who was physician to George the Fourth. *Houghton Hall*, another neat mansion in the parish, belongs to C. Heigham, Esq., but is now unoccupied. *Blackland's Hall*, an ancient mansion, is now a farm-house, as also are *Duck's Hall* and *Nether Hall*.

CAVENDISH FREE SCHOOL was founded in 1696, by the *Rev. Thomas Grey*, who endowed it with a farm at Pentlowe, in Essex, then of the yearly value of £25, of which he directed that £15 should be paid yearly to the master, for teaching 15 poor children of this parish in the English, Latin, and Greek tongues; that £2 should be laid out in providing books and stationery for the said free-scholars; and that the remaining £8 per annum should be employed either in

apprenticeing some of the free-scholars, or in preparing one or two of them for the University of Cambridge, and in assisting to maintain them till they took the degree of bachelor of arts. The school farm comprises 79A. 0R. 19P., and is let for £100 per annum. By an order of the Court of Chancery, in 1816, the powers of the trustees were extended, and there are now 20 free-scholars, for whose instruction the master receives £30 a year, and a further sum of £10 to find them books, &c. The direction as to fitting out children for the University does not appear to have been ever acted upon; but apprentice fees of from £8 to £20 each are given with two or three of the boys every year. In 1828, the trustees had in the bank a balance of £207; and they afterwards suffered the savings of the income to accumulate, for the purpose of providing a fund for repairing the school premises, and re-establishing the charity on its former footing of a classical school; the late master, who held the office a great many years, having, through age and infirmities, confined his attention, for some years before his death, solely to the free-scholars, none of whom required instruction in Latin or Greek. The rector has the nomination of the free-schoolars, and, with the consent of two or more of the trustees, appoints the master.

Ambrose Rd. & Thos. butchers
Baker Mr John
Baker Peter, bricklayer
Bolton Wm. beerhouse
Brockwell June, parish clerk
Byford Jph. carrier to London, *via* Clare, Monday & Thursday
Carter Geo. watch & clock maker
Castley Rev Thos. M.A. *Rectory*
Clark Henry, cabinet maker
Evens Thos. baker, *Post Office*
Hardy John, ironmonger
Mason Robt. watch cleaner
Page Robt. cabinet maker
Pledger Jas. glover & breeches mkr
Rice Jacob, plumber and glazier
Rose Wm. butcher
Thompson Wm. collar & harness mkr
Turpin George, baker
Waring Thos. Walter, surgeon
Yelloly Mrs Sarah, *Cavendish Hall*

INNS AND TAVERNS.
Bull, Edward Deeks
Five Bells, John Ely
George, John Offord
White Horse, Ann Churchyard

Academies.
Ambrose Mary
Everett Simon
Jay Sasanna
Simpson Robert, *Gram. School*

Blacksmiths.
Deeks Isaac
Durrant James
Hammond Edw.
Mott Chas.

Grocers & Drprs.
Bocock George
Brockwell Stpn.
Hale John
Spice Wm.

FARMERS.
(* *are Owners.*)
Ambrose Ann
*Coldham Wm., *Duck's Hall*
Hickford James, *Blacklands Hl*
*Murrills Wm., *Kimsing*

Norton Albion Julius Cæsar, *Robbs Farm*
Raymond Timy.
Smith Ambrose *Nether Hall*

Joiners, &c.
Stammers Henry
Woods Wm.

Maltsters & Corn Millers.
Garrett Joseph
Stammers
Offord Dl. & Geo.

Shoemakers.
Golding Fredk.
Howe George
Underwood Geo.
Woods Thos.

Tailors.
Everett Robt.
Braybrook Wm. and Sons

Wheelwrights.
Hardy Edward
Spencer Robt.

CHILTON parish, one mile N.E. of Sudbury, has only a few scattered houses, 98 inhabitants, and 968A. 3R. 35P. of land, under which is a stratum of lime, which is burnt here for agricultural and other purposes. The Rev. L. Newman has a small estate in the parish, and nearly all the rest belongs to Wm. Howe Windham, Esq., the lord of the manor, and patron of the *Church*, which is a discharged rectory, valued in K. B. at £5. 6s. 5½d., and now enjoyed by the Rev. William Coyte Freeland, B.A., who has a good residence, and 25A. 3R. 31P. of glebe. The tithes were commuted, in 1839, for the yearly payment of £208 to the rector of Chilton, and £80 to the rector of Great Waldingfield. *Chilton Hall*, now a moated farm-house, was formerly very extensive, and was long the seat of the knightly family of *Crane*, of whom there are several monuments in the church. One of them was

created a baronet in 1627, but the family became extinct many years ago, when the manor passed to the Woodhouses, who sold it to the Goldings. The *common* was enclosed in 1813. *Directory :* Thomas Fenn Addison, Esq., *Chilton Lodge ;* Henry Baldwin, *lime burner ;* Rev. W. C. Freeland, *Rectory ;* Robert Horner, farmer ; and Henry Meeking, farmer, *Chilton Hall.*

COCKFIELD, or *Cokefield,* is a widely spread village, scattered round several greens, near the source of a rivulet, from 6 to 7 miles S.S.E. of Bury St. Edmund's, and 4½ miles N. by W. of Lavenham. Its parish contains 951 souls, and 3626a. 1r. 25p. of land, in the manors of *Cockfield Hall* and *Earl's Hall,* now farm-houses, the former belonging to Samuel Buck, Esq., and the latter to R. M. Carss, Esq.; but Sir H. Bunbury, C. F. Barnwell, Esq., C. A. Brooke, Esq., and a few smaller owners, have estates in the parish. James Cuddon, Esq., of Norwich, is steward of the manors, for which he holds courts yearly. The copyholds are subject to arbitrary fines, but a great part of the parish is freehold. Cockfield Hall formerly belonged to Bury Abbey, and afterwards to the knightly family of Spring. Earl's Hall was so named from its ancient proprietors, the Veres, Earls of Oxford, who held it till the death of the last earl of that family, in 1702, after which it passed to the Moores, of Melford. On the west side of the parish are traces of an *encampment,* supposed to have been occupied by the Romans and Saxons. The *Church* (St. Peter) is an ancient structure, with a tower and six bells. The *rectory,* valued in K.B. at £30, and in 1835 at £635, is in the patronage of St. John's College, Cambridge, and incumbency of the Rev. Richd. Jeffreys, who has a good residence, and a yearly modus of £1050, awarded in 1843 in lieu of tithes. Here is an *Independent Chapel,* built in 1841 ; but the Presbyterians are said to have had a meeting-house in the parish as early as the reign of Elizabeth. In 1720, the *Rev. Fras. Robins* left £3 a year for the poor of Cockfield, and it is now paid out of the estate of Sir J. Filmer, Bart., of East Sutton Park, in Kent. The poor parishioners have also the following yearly doles ; viz., 20s. from *Corder's Charity,* noticed with Glemsford ; £3. 10s. from a house occupied by paupers, and formerly called the *Town House ;* and a rent-charge of 24s. out of Church Close, in Bradfield St. Clare, left by Edward Nice, in 1671.

Duffell Robert, corn miller
Fenton Saml. corn mert., maltster, auctioneer, land agent, and valuer
Gooch Robert, vict. *King's Head*
Hammond Wm. blacksmith & beerhs
Harper Wm. cattle dealer
Howe John, schoolmaster
Howe Mary, schoolmistress
Hudgell J. saddler
Hunt Wm. vict. *Greyhound*
Jeffreys Rev Richard, *Rectory*
Josling Wm. blacksmith
Little Robert, vict. *Punch Bowl*
Lucas James Owen, surgeon
Malton Robert, beerhouse
Moreham George, corn miller
Morley Ephraim, wheelwright

Sheppard Mr John
Talbott Benjamin, wheelwright
FARMERS.
Andrews John
Baldwin Wm.
 Pepper's Hall
Bligh Mary, (owner)
Borley Wm.
Bowle James
Edwards Benj.
Gosling Chltte.
Head Fredk.
Hilder Edward
Hilder Richard
Kennington Wm.
Kerridge Saml.

King Samuel (& butcher)
Langham John
Mumford George, *Earl's Hall*
Payne Robert
Russell Eliz.
Sansum Samuel
Sergeant John
Scott Geo. (regr.)
 Hill farm
Talbott Hy. Jno. *Cockfield Hall*
Grocers, &c.
Chaplin Thomas

Hilder & Co.	*Shoemakers.*	Steel Wm.	Bury, W. & S.,
Lambert Joshua	Fayers Henry	CARRIER.	and to Ipswich,
Thornton Eliz.	Pearson John	Osborn Isaac, to	M. and Thu.

CORNARD, (GREAT) a well-built village on the north bank of the navigable river Stour, one mile S.E. of Sudbury, has in its parish 938 souls, and 1550 acres of land, under which is a fine bed of limestone. The executors of the late J. G. Sparrow, Esq., are lords of the manors, impropriators of the rectory, and patrons of the *Church*, (St. Andrew,) which is a neat fabric with a tower, containing five bells, and surmounted by a wooden spire. The *vicarage*, valued in K.B. at £9, and in 1835 at £155, is enjoyed by the Rev. Charles Edward Holden, M.A. The tithes were commuted, in 1839, for the yearly payment of £360 to the impropriators, and £145. 15s. 6d. to the vicar, who has also about 10 acres of glebe. The common was enclosed in 1813. The parish belongs to various owners, many of whom are residents. *Grey's Hall*, a commodious mansion, now the property and residence of Mr. Thos. Fitch, has its name from the *De Greys,* who were anciently lords of the manor of Greys, in Great Cornard and Newton. The *Town Land*, about three acres, is let for 40s. a year, which is distributed among the poor parishioners, who have also 10s. as the rent of a small garden, given by an unknown donor.

Baldwin James, working jeweller
Bell Mrs Ruth || Canham Mr Robt.
Carrington Henry, shopkeeper
Clark Mr John || Dyer Mrs
Emmerson Thomas, cattle dealer
Ginn Thomas, brickmaker
Goddard Thomas, shoemaker
Hunt Hanh. brickmaker and coarse earthenware manufacturer
King Wm. gentleman
Lee Robert, corn miller and mert
Leggett Cornelius, schoolmaster
Newman George, shoemaker
Poley John, vict. *Five Bells*
Rayner Abraham, blacksmith
Siggers John, beerhouse
Smith Wm. carpenter
Studd Jonth. Abbott, gentleman
Tiffen John Lazell, gentleman
Turketine Edward, blacksmith
Wakelin Jonathan, wheelwright and victualler, King's Head
Wilkinson Rev Watts, M.A. curate, *Vicarage*

FARMERS. (* are *Owners.*)
*Brand Oliver (and maltster)
*Brand Thomas || Dyer Thomas
*Fitch Thomas, *Grey's Hall*
*Mumford Wm. || Howlett James
*Taylor Wm. || * Poley John

CORNARD, (LITTLE) a small scattered village, in the vale of the Stour, 2½ miles S.S.E. of Sudbury, has in its parish 396 souls, and about 1600 acres of land, mostly in the manor of *Caustons*, anciently belonging to the De Greys, but now to J. N. Sparrow, Esq. A great part of the soil belongs to Lord Walsingham, H. T. Jones, Esq., and several small owners. The *Church* (All Saints) is a small neat fabric, and the benefice is a rectory, valued in K.B. at £8. 2s. 8½d., and now having about 50 acres of glebe, and a yearly modus of £500, awarded in 1842. The Rev. Wm. Pochin is patron and incumbent. In 1628, *Thos. Stephens* left two yearly rent-charges out of land called Bones ; viz., 20s. for five poor parishioners, and 6s. 8d. for the minister. The interest of £100, left by *Henry Crossman*, in 1790, is applied towards the support of a Sunday-school.

Pochin Rev Wm., Rectory
Rayner Wm. blacksmith
Tricker Edmund, brickmaker
FARMERS.
King George Church, *Peacock Hall*
Mumford George, *Caustons Hall*
Sandle Wm. || Bell John
Segers Henry || Taylor Ann

EDWARDSTONE, a scattered village, in the vale of a small river, 5 miles E. of Sudbury, has in its parish 495 souls, and 1872 acres of land, mostly arable, but including 105A. of wood. The distinguished family of *De Monte Canisio*, or Montechensy, were anciently seated here, and their heiress carried the *manor* in marriage to the Waldegraves, who sold it, about the year 1598, to John Brand, clothier, of Boxford. The Kemps obtained it by marrying the heiress of J. Brand, Esq., and in 1714 sold it to Wm. French, draper, of London. Charles Dawson, Esq., is now lord of the manor, and owner of nearly all the soil. He resides at the *Hall*, an ancient mansion with pleasant grounds, and is patron of the *Church*, (St. Mary,) and lessee of the great tithes, which belong to the Bishop of Ely. The *vicarage*, valued in K.B. at £4. 13s. 4d., is enjoyed by the Rev. G. A. Dawson, M.A., of Groton, who has a yearly modus of £263, awarded in 1840, when the rectorial tithes were commuted for £373 per annum. Here was formerly a *cell* to the monastery of Abingdon, near Oxford; but the monks were removed to Colne Priory, in Essex, which obtained the appropriation of the rectory, afterwards annexed to the See of Ely by Queen Elizabeth, in exchange for some valuable manors. Here is a *National School*, built in 1843, at the cost of £250, subscribed by C. Dawson, Esq., and other contributors.

In 1709, ISAAC BRAND left £100 to be laid out in land, the rent thereof to be distributed among the most aged and industrious poor of Edwardstone, on Easter Sunday. This legacy was laid out in the purchase of a cottage and croft, which were sold in 1804 for £205, which was laid out in 1823 in the purchase of £249. 17s. three per cent. reduced annuities. The dividends, £7. 8s. a year, are distributed in linen cloth by the churchwardens. In 1722, JOHN BRAND left two yearly rent-charges of 20s. each, to be laid out in bread for the poor of Edwardstone and Boxford, but these payments having become void, *Joseph Brand*, in 1722, in order to revive the charities, conveyed to nine trustees two tenements in Sherborne street, with half an acre of land adjoining, in trust to distribute the clear yearly rents thereof, in bread, among the poor of Edwardstone and Boxford, on the 5th of November. The two tenements were burnt down about 43 years ago, and a new cottage was built on the site, at the expense of *Boxford parish*, which receives the whole of the rent—£3 per annum. In 1725, JOSEPH CHAPLIN left £250, to be laid out in land, for providing coats and shoes for five poor men, and gowns, petticoats, and shoes for five poor women of the parish of Edwardstone. This legacy, and £53 left by *Sir Joseph Alston*, were laid out in 1809, in the purchase of a barn and 22A. 2R. of land at Polstead, now let for £26 a year, with an allotment of 1A. awarded to it in 1817. The vicar is one of the trustees, and distributes the rent in coats and gowns. The TOWN LANDS are in three small plots, let for £8 a year, of which £5. 10s. is paid to the master of the Sunday school, and the remainder is distributed in clothing. It is unknown how the parishioners acquired this land, and there stands upon it a building, long used as a workhouse. The parish sends two free scholars to *Boxford School*, and the poor have a yearly rent-charge of £2 out of Edwardstone Hall, supposed to have been left by *Wm. French*. In 1758, EDWARD APPLETON left three yearly rent-charges out of a farm here called Hockets, viz., 40s. each to Great and Little Waldingfield, and 20s. to Edwardstone, for the poor of those parishes. These annuities have not been paid during the last twenty years, but the land charged is supposed to belong to the Dawson family.

EDWARDSTONE.

Broadhurst Wm. gentleman
Cooper Mr Edward
Dansie Wm. blacksmith
Dawson Charles, Esq. *Hall*
Emerson Elizabeth, schoolmistress
Goat John, beerhouse keeper
Hallifax Rev John, M.A. rector of *Groton*
Smith Saml. miller & beerhouse kpr
FARMERS.
Cooper Edw. jun. || Crossby —
Emerson Henry || Game James
Hart Wm. || Hurrell Charles

Hills Samuel, *Priory*
Lord James ‖ Keeble Francis

Cook William ‖ Hart William
Hurrell Charles ‖ Kensey John

GLEMFORD, a large straggling village, on an eminence, 4½ miles E.N.E. of Clare, and 5½ miles N.W. by N. of Sudbury, has in its parish 2292A. 2R. 36P. of land, having a good mixed soil, rising in bold undulations, and extending southward to the Stour, and eastward to one of the tributary streams of that river. It had 1470 inhabitants in 1831, but they had decreased to 1366 in 1841, owing to the "declining state of the *silk and wool weaving.*" Here is a silk throwsting mill, employing about 60 hands, and some of the inhabitants are employed in weaving silk and velvet for the Sudbury manufacturers. Part of the parish is still in large *open fields.* Edmund Stedman, Esq., is lord of the manor, but the soil belongs chiefly to Samuel Bell, Alex. Duff, and G. W. Poley, Esqrs., Capt. Lungley, Messrs. T. Pung, Wm. Death, and J. E. Hale; and a few smaller owners. The copyholds are subject to arbitrary fines. Odo, Earl of Champagne, held the manor at the Domesday Survey, though the See of Ely had possessions here as early as the time of Edward the Confessor. The village has several good inns and retail shops, and has a *fair* for pedlery and toys on the 24th of June. The *Church* (St. Mary) is a large and handsome Gothic structure, with a tower and six bells, and the *rectory*, valued in K.B. at £30. 0s. 0½d., and in 1835 at £582, is in the patronage of the Bishop of Ely, and incumbency of the Rev. George Coldham, M.A., who has a commodious residence. In the time of Edward the Confessor, a *college of priests*, invested with numerous privileges, was founded here, and they flourished till the reign of Henry III., but what became of them afterwards is not recorded. Kirby says some rents are paid out of this lordship to the Bishop of Ely, by tenants who were formerly exempt from serving on juries, except at Ely. Here is a *Baptist*, and also an *Independent Chapel ;* and a *National School*, established in 1840, for about 70 boys and 30 girls. In 1670, *Thos. Hammond* left a field of 9A. called New Croft, for the relief of six old men of Glemsford. It is now let for about £12 a year. The poor parishioners have about £25. 12s. divided among them at Christmas, under the name of *Doles*, and arising as follows :—£4 from the rents of the Town Field and Workhouse Pasture; £15s. 15s. in six rent-charges, left by various donors ; £7. 7s. from *Poley's Charity*, (see Boxsted ;) and £2. 10s. from the charity of JOHN CORDER, who, in 1636, left his house and 18A. of land at Lawshall, to provide for distributions of bread among the poor of the following parishes, in the proportions named,—20s. each to St. Gregory's, St. Peter's, and All Saints, in Sudbury ; 40s. each to Melford, Lavenham, Lawshall, Glemsford, Shimpling, and the two parishes of Bury St. Edmund's ; and 20s. each to Stanstead, Hartest, Cockfield, Alpheton, and Stanningfield. This charity estate is now let for £30 a year. In 1828, Mr. Ezra Dalton was one of the acting trustees. The old *School House*, in Glemsford churchyard, is now partly occupied by paupers, and partly let for 50s. a year, which is carried to the churchwarden's account. The *Bible Meadow*, half an acre, let for 25s. a year, was left by Edm. Boldero, D.D., in 1699, to provide bibles, &c. for the poor of Glemsford.

Andrews John, beerhouse keeper
Beeton Joseph, carrier to Bury, Wed
Bigg Joseph, butcher
Bouttell Wm. corn miller
Bulmer Wm. hairdresser
Byford Edward. thatcher
Coldham Rev. Geo. M.A. *Rectory*
Copsey Ann, National schoolmrs
Duff Alexander, silk throwster
Freestone My. Ann, schoolmistress
Goody Jeremiah, cart owner
Grigley Daniel, parish clerk
Grimwood Mr Robert
King Geo. sexton & Natl. schoolmr
Mann Wm. soap boiler & tallow chdlr
Neave Wm. collar & harness maker
Rice Jacob, plumber and glazier
Russell Mr William
Shepherd John, plumber ank glazier
Wyatt Mr John Storey

INNS AND TAVERNS.

Black Lion, Wm. Cross
Cock, John Shepherd
Crown, Wm. Golding
Greyhound, Thomas Bowyer (and butcher)

Blacksmiths.

Albon George
Downs Walter
Hanstead Wm.
Smith Wm.

Bricklayers.

Debenham Wm.
Scott Wm.

FARMERS.

Beeton Wm.
Bigg Chas. *Court farm*
Bigg John
Bigg Isaac
Duff Alexander
Golding Wm.
Goody Edward
Mann Wm.
Morley Corben, (grazier) *Lodge farm*
Shepherd Ambs.
Smith Alfred & Thomas
Sparke Josiah, *Mill Hill*

Joiners.

Adams Thos. (& machine mkr)
Pettit Richard
Smith Wm.
Twinn Jepth. (& millwright)

Maltsters.

Shepard John
Smith Alfred
Sparke Josiah

Shoemakers.

Copsey Joseph
Golding Philip
Watkinson Fras.

Shopkeepers.

Allen James
Boreham Stepn.
Goody Thomas, (& beerhouse)
Griggs Alice
Leeks Robert
Mann George
Mortlock Hanh.
Ranson John

Tailors.

Bavis Joseph
Bradman Chas.
Bradman James
Braybrook Thos.
King Mary

Wheelwrights.

Adams Thomas
Curtis Charles
Hartley James
Spencer Henry

GROTON, a pleasant village, nearly 6 miles E. of Sudbury, and W. of Hadleigh, has in its parish 1571A. 2R. 22P. of land, and 624 inhabitants, but the dwellings of some of them form part of the village of Boxford. The parish comprises about 130A. of woodland, and 39A. 33P. of common. It was anciently held by the Abbot of Bury, and was given at the dissolution to Adam Winthorp, Esq., of whose family it was purchased in the reign of Charles I., by Thomas Waring. Sir J. R. Rowley is now lord of the manor of Groton, but part of the parish is in several other *manors*, the largest of which is Castlings Hall, of which H. Green, Esq., is lord. The soil is all freehold, except about 60 acres, and the other principal proprietors are Isaac Strutt, Esq., Rev. G. A. Dawson, and Messrs. J. Vince and F. Benyon. The *Church* (St. Bartholomew) is a neat fabric, with a tower and five bells. Its Registers have been preserved since 1562. The *rectory*, valued in K.B. at £8. 1s. 8d., has 37A. 3R. 24P. of glebe, and a yearly modus of £457, awarded in 1838. J. W. Willett, Esq., and others are patrons, and the Rev. John Hallifax, M.A., of Edwardstone, is the incumbent. Four tenements called *Almshouses*, with a small garden, were purchased with £20 in 1702, and are occupied by poor persons placed in them by the parish officers. The sum of £10, left by *John Doggett*, in 1671, for the poor of Groton, was laid out in the 1st of Charles I., in the purchase of 1A. 1R. 28P. of land called Powers, now let for £1. 15s. a year, which is distributed in bread. About 1650, *Wm. Moore* left for the poor of Boxford and Groton, 16A. of copyhold land in Hadleigh Hamlet, now let for £22 a year.

GROTON PARISH.
(See also Boxford.)

Ardley James, tailor
Baldwin James, shoemaker
Bare George, beerhouse keeper
Cook Arthur, wheelwright
Cook Stephen, maltster
Cook Thomas, maltster
Dawson Rev Geo. Augustus, M.A.
    vicar of Edwardstone
Grist Thomas, shopkeeper
Marsh Joseph, baker
Marsh Philip, glover
Rudley Charles, shoemaker

Steed Joshua, plumber and glazier
Stevens Samuel, blacksmith & vict.
    Fox and Hounds
Studd Rev. Hy. || Wynne Miss M.A.
Strutt Isaac, Esq. *Groton Place*
Swan Francis, wheelwright
Tricker James, harness maker
Waters Wm. shoemaker

FARMERS.—(* *are Owners.*)

Cook Thomas || Manning John
Simpson Wm. || Spraggins Ruffell
Strutt Walter, *Groton Place*
*Vince John, *Groton Hall*
Waters Robert || Waters Wm.

HARTEST, a pleasant village, in the bosom of a deep valley, 8 miles N. by W. of Sudbury, and 7 miles N.E. of Clare, has in its parish 812 souls, and 1964A. 28P. of land, rising in bold undulations, and bounded on the east and west by two rivulets. It anciently belonged to the convent of Ely, and afterwards to the see of Ely, until the 4th of Elizabeth. G. W. Poley, Esq., is now lord of the manor, but a great part of the soil belongs to Thos. Hallifax, Esq., Col. Acklom, Mr. R. Spencer, and several smaller owners. The *Church* (All Saints) is an ancient Gothic fabric, with a tower and five bells, and the benefice is a *rectory*, valued in K.B. at £29. 14s. 2d., and in 1835, at £652, with the rectory of Boxtead annexed to it, in the patronage of the Crown and incumbency of the Rev. J. Maddy, D.D., of Stansfield. The tithes were commuted, in 1839, for a yearly modus of £611, including the quota on 25A. 2R. 29P. of glebe. In 1721, THOMAS SPARKE left to the rector of Hartest and certain trustees, a farm, in this parish, of 39A. 3R. 21P., for charitable uses. The farm is let for £50 a year, out of which the following payments are made, agreeable to the donor's will, viz.,—20s. per annum each to *Rede, Brockley,* and *Hartest,* for the ministers and churchwardens of those parishes, as a remuneration for their trouble in examining the accounts of this charity at Easter; and £6 a year for schooling poor children of Brockley. The residue, after payment of a quit-rent, &c., is applied in sending poor children of Hartest to school. In 1808, the Rev. W. W. Poley and others were appointed as new trustees. In 1646, THOMAS WRIGHT left two cottages for the residence of two poor widows not chargeable to the parish; and for their reparation, he charged an adjoining tenement, called *Penns,* with the yearly payment of 10s. The poor of Hartest have about 25s. yearly from *Corder's Charity* (see Glemsford,) and a fifth part of *Poley's Charity* (see Boxted.)

Albon Richard, blacksmith
Baynton Mr Stephen, *Mount*
Boreham Geo. saddler & harness mkr
Bray Wm. corn miller || Case Mr Jno
Butts Rev Edward Drury, M.A.
    curate, Rectory
Cadge George, builder & wheelwgt
Cawston John, plumber and glazier
Crisp Samuel, *free school master*
Death Ellen, boarding & day school

Everitt Frederick, farrier
Jageman Wm. bricklayer
King George, surgeon
Leadbeater Hy. Esq. *Hartest Lodge*
Maxim Joseph, vict. Bell
Maxim Wm. vict. Crown
Mears Rev Henry, curate of Rede,
    Stow Hill
Ranson Wm. plumber and glazier
Sadler James, shopkeeper

Turner Rt. butcher & cattle dealer
Turpin James, baker
Whindread Wm. beerhouse keeper

FARMERS.
* are Owners.
Abbott Robert,
  Rivett's Hall
Bradenham Jno.
Bray Wm.
Cawston Alfred,
  (and butcher)
Clarke John
Coe George

Debenham Jas.
*Dickerson Jno.
Griggs James
Harvey James
Broom, Brick hs
Haywood Robert
Jackson James
Nice Jno. *Cook's farm*

Payne Samuel,
  (and maltster)
Spencer Robert
Grocers & Drprs.
Bocock James
Bannock Thos.
Shoemakers.
Adams John
Debenham Jas.
Debenham Noah
Kimmes John
Smith Samuel

Tailors.
Kent Richard
Sturgeon George
CARRIERS.
Henry Knopp, to
Bury, M. Wed.
and Sat., & to
Sudbury, Thurs
Isaac Snazell, to
Bury, W. & Sat.
and to Sudbury,
Mon. & Friday

LAVENHAM, an ancient town, which formerly had a weekly market, is pleasantly situated on the crown and declivity of an eminence, on the western side of one of the sources of the river Brett, 7 miles N.E. by N. of Sudbury, 9 miles N.W. by W. of Hadleigh, and 11 miles S.S.E. of Bury St. Edmund's. Its parish contains 1871 inhabitants, and 2812A. 1R. 20P. of land. It was one of the 221 lordships given by William the Conqueror to Robert Mallet, but he forfeited it in the 2nd of Henry I., who gave it to Aubrey de Vere, in whose posterity it remained till sold by Edward, Earl of Oxford, in the reign of Elizabeth, to Paul D'Ewes, Esq. It afterwards passed to the Moores. The Earls of Oxford had a large *park* here, comprising nearly half the parish. The Rev. James Pye, M.A., is now lord of the *manor*, but the soil belongs chiefly to Wm. and Isaac Strutt, Esqs., Sir Hyde Parker, Bart., Mr. G. Mumford, Rev. Joseph Fenn, Mrs. Death, — Montrou, Esq., of London, J. Outhwaite, Esq., of London, Mr. Geo. Andrews, and several resident owners. G. R. Pye, Esq., solicitor, is the manor steward. The copyholds are subject to arbitrary fines, and the custom of Borough English; but part of the parish is freehold, and there is a small manor belonging to the rectory. The town has a spacious *Market Place*, with an ancient cross in the centre, but the market, formerly held on Tuesday, was discontinued in the latter part of last century. A *horse fair* is still held here on Shrove Tuesday, and a *fair for butter, cheese, &c.*, on the 10th of October and two following days. Lavenham is a *polling place* for the Western Division of Suffolk, and was once famous for its manufacture of *blue cloth, serges, &c.*, for the better regulation of which, three *guilds*, or companies, of St. Peter, the Holy Trinity, and Corpus Christie, were established, and it was governed by six capital burgesses, who were chosen for life, and had the appointment of inferior officers. For many years after the decline of its blue cloth trade, Lavenham retained a considerable share in the manufacture of *serges, shalloons, says, stuffs, calimancoes, hempen cloth*, and *fine worsted yarn*, and had a *wool hall*, which, being commodiously situated for the traders of the adjacent parts of the county, was much frequented. The town has still two *woolstaplers* and a *silk mill*, and many of its inhabitants are employed in spinning fine *worsted yarn* on the domestic wheel and distaff, and in making *straw plat*. THOS. SPRING, commonly called the *rich clothier*, died here in 1510, and acquired his immense wealth from the trade of Lavenham, and from him descended Wm. Spring, Esq., of Pakenham, who was created a baronet by Charles I. RICHARD DE LANHAM, or *Lavenham*,

was born here, and took his name from the place. He was a learned divine, and was beheaded with Archbishop Sudbury, by the followers of Wat Tyler, in 1381. Sir THOMAS COOKE, lord mayor of London in 1462, was the son of Robert Cooke, of Lavenham, and was arraigned under Edward IV. for lending money to the house of Lancaster, for which he suffered a long imprisonment, and was heavily fined. His daughter married Wm. Cicil, Lord Burleigh, an ancestor of the present Marquis of Exeter. *Robert de Vere*, in the 18th of Edward I., obtained a charter for Lavenham ; and 'Robert, his son, procured another in the 3rd of Edward III., authorising his tenants here to pass toll-free throughout all England ; which grant was confirmed by Queen Elizabeth, in the 27th year of her reign, but the privilege is now obsolete. The present estimated gross yearly rental of the parish is £5204. 2s. 10d. The *Church* (St. Peter) is one of the handsomest in the county, and was erected on the site of the ancient fabric in the 15th and early part of the 16th centuries, chiefly at the cost of the Earl of Oxford and the wealthy family of Spring, whose arms are to be seen in many parts of the building. It is in the later style of English architecture, and is constructed of freestone, curiously ornamented with flint. It is 156 feet long, and 68 broad. The tower, admirable both for strength and beauty, is 141 feet high and 42 in diameter, and contains eight bells, of which the tenor weighs 23 cwt., and was cast in 1625. In the interior, the roof is richly carved, and two pews formerly belonging to the Earls of Oxford and the Springs, though now somewhat decayed, are highly finished pieces of Gothic work, in the elaborate style of Henry VIII.'s chapel, at Westminster. In the windows are considerable remains of ancient stained glass ; and the porch is of highly ornamented architecture, adorned with armorial bearings. On the left side of the altar is an elegant monument of alabaster and marble, in memory of the *Rev. Henry Copinger*, who was rector here 45 years, and died in 1622. The figures of himself and wife are represented in a kneeling posture in alto-relievo, with an angel standing on each side of them. In the north aisle is a mural monument, upon which are presented a man and woman engraved on brass, kneeling before a table, and three sons and three daughters behind them, and a long inscription below them, in memory of Allan Dister, a clothier, who died in 1534. In the chancel is an old grave-stone, which formerly had a Saxon inscription, at present completely defaced. In the vestry, and over the north and south chapels, are memorials of the Springs, the eminent clothiers who flourished here till the 16th century. The benefice is a *rectory*, valued in K.B. at £20. 2s. 11d., and in 1835 at £658, in the patronage of Gonville and Caius College, Cambridge, and incumbency of the Rev. Richard Johnson, M.A., who has a commodious residence and 144 acres of glebe. The tithes were commuted in 1842 for a yearly modus of £850, including the quota on the glebe, and subject to the parochial rates. The Independents and Wesleyans have chapels here, and the former have had a congregation in the parish since 1697. The town has two public *schools* and a number of valuable *charities*.

LAVENHAM GRAMMAR SCHOOL appears to to have existed at an early period, but there are no traces of its original institution. It was endowed in 1647, by Rd. Peacock, with a yearly rent-charge of £5 out of land in Great and Little Wald-

ingfield, for the education of five poor children to be nominated by the headbc-rough, churchwardens, and overseers. In 1699, the school was rebuilt by sub-scription. The only other endowment is an annuity of £16, out of the manor of Greys, in Great Cornard and Newton, conveyed to 24 trustees in 1699, by Richd. Coleman, to fulfil the intentions of his uncle, *Edward Coleman*, and other per-sons who had contributed towards rebuilding the school premises, which now consist of a house for the master, a school-room, a stable, garden, and 1¼A. of land, worth altogether about £24 a year. The master takes boarders, and teaches five free scholars. The OLD TOWN LANDS ESTATE is under the management of trustees, and is partly settled by sundry ancient deeds, and by usage, for the relief of the poor, and for repairing the almshouses of the town ; and part thereof was devised by *Wm. Lummas*, in 1573, for the poor. It is partly copyhold, and consists of a house, barn, cottage, and 103A. of land, mostly in Brent Eleigh, let for about 170*l.* a year ; a close of 1A. 3R. 9P. in Lavenham, let for 10*l.* ; five closes in Lavenham, left by Wm. Lummas, and comprising 13A. 0R. 5P., let for about 15*l.* ; a cottage and part of the workhouse, let for 4*l.* ; and upwards of 30 cot-tages, or *almshouses*, in and near Church street, occupied rent-free by poor people placed in them by the overseers. The annual rents, amounting to about 200*l.*, are applied in repairing the cottages or almshouses, in the purchase of hempen cloth for shirts, &c., given to the poor, and in occasional donations of money. The *Bell Rope Land*, 1R. 34P., is let for 7s. 6d. a year, which is applied with the church-rates. In 1621, *Henry Copinger* left a tenement and 5A. 2R. 6P. of land, near the church-yard, for the relief of four of the most aged and needy parishion-ers. The tenement fell down some years ago, and the land is let for 25*l.* 10s. a year, which is divided by the rector among four aged poor persons. The parish has 2*l.* 10s. a year from *Corder's Charity*, as noticed with Glemsford. In 1655, ISAAC CREME bequeathed 12A. of copyhold land, called Goymes, and the sum of 500*l.* to be invested in the purchase of other land ; and he directed the yearly proceeds of the whole to be applied by the trustees, towards the maintenance of 24 aged poor parishioners of Lavenham. The 500*l.*, with 70*l* derived from rent and interest, was laid out in the purchase of 44A. 2R. 13P. of freehold land, in Lavenham. In 1823, Creme's charity estate was let on an eight years' lease,—the copyhold land to Mr. Hitchcock, for 12*l.* 10s., and the freehold to Mr. G. Mum-ford, for 48*l.* 15s. per annum ; but in 1828, the Charity Commissioners considered these rents as much below the real value of the estate, which is now worth more than 100*l.* per annum. In 1806, HENRY STEWARD bequeathed a clear legacy of 1796*l.* 1s. 8d. three per cent. consols, to trustees appointed by the minister and churchwardens of Lavenham, in trust, to pay the yearly dividends to the said minister and churchwardens, to be by them applied for the benefit of the poor of Lavenham, in such manner as they should think proper. The dividends (53*l.* 17s. 6d. a year,) are paid towards the support of the *Boys' and Girls' National Schools*, built in 1839, and now affording instruction to about 70 boys and 80 girls, as day scholars, and about 280 Sunday scholars. The cost of the building was 303*l.*, of which 100*l.* was given by the National School Society.

LAVENHAM.

POST-OFFICE at Mary Ann East's, High st.—Letters are received and despatched at 8 mg. & 6 evg

Marked 1, *are in Church street ;* 2, *Market place ;* 3, *Prentice street ;* 4, *Shilling street ;* 5, *Water street ; and the rest in High street, or where specified*

4 Barber Wm. surgeon
Branwhite Miss Ann
2 Branwhite Brook Thomas, gent
Cadman Rev Wm., M.A., *curate*
2 Death Mrs Eliz ‖ East Mrs M. A.
5 Gillingham Benj. straw plat and hat manfr. and leather cutter
1 Hayward George, organist

Johnson Rev Richd., M.A., *Rectory*
Keeble John, veterinary surgeon
King Wm. gentleman
Lee Robert, corn miller
5 Mills Wm. overseer
Millis Rev John (Indt.) Barnes st
Mumford Mrs Frances
2 Peck Wm. gentleman
5 Poulton Joseph, *silk throwster*
Pye George Richard, solicitor
Rust Charles, chemist, druggist, and British wine dealer
Spark James, coach maker
Spring Saml. cabinet mkr. & upholstr
Watts Charles, brazier and tinner
Webber Wm. watchmaker

HOTELS, INNS, AND TAVERNS.
3 Anchor, John Ranson
2 Angel, Thomas Woolard
Black Lion, Westropp Thos. Turner
1 Cock, Henry Death
Greyhound, James Ambrose
One Bell, Wm. Smith
Swan Inn, Wm. Stutter
2 Three Blackbirds, Ann Johnson
2 White Horse, George Deacon

Academies.
* take Boarders.
*Andrews Mary Ann
Hayward Thos.
*Mills Sar. Ann
* Pughe John, *Grammar Schl*
1 Ranson Wm. & My. *Natl. Schl*
Ray Mary
Watts Elizabeth
Bakers, &c.
2 Burch Joseph
Clover Charles
5 Griss Henry
1 Knights Jnthn.
4 Meeking Saml.
Blacksmiths.
5 Lungley Roger
Stribling John
Welton Wm.
Boot & Shoe Mkrs.
Ambrose James
1 East Wm.
King Charles
Mills John
Petley John

5 Smith John
Snell John
Bricklayers and Plasterers.
5 Mills Thomas
5 Turner Samuel
Butchers.
2 Green John
5 Gurling Wm.
Mattham Wm.
Coopers.
5 Ranson Edw.
Walby James
FARMERS.
(* are Owners.)
Andrews Robt.
Bigg Samuel
Branwhite Thos., *Slough Farm*
4 Death Wm.
Herring John, (steward,) *Bright's Farm*
*Howard Robert, *Lavenham Hall*
Lord Adam, *Lodge Farm*
*Meeking Samuel

Mills Sarah, *Nether Hall*
*Mumford Geo., *Hill Farm*
Richardson Jph., *Priory Farm*
Skeet Samuel
Scott George, *Park Farm*
Glass, China, &c. Dealers.
2 Bobby Wm.
5 Price Benj. Pole
Grocers & Drprs.
2 Bobby Wm. (& British wine dlr)
Catling Samuel
5 Price B. P. (and agent to Suffolk Fire Office)
Hair Dressers.
2 Bulmer Henry
Ginn John
Ironmonger.
Ray Dnl. (& wood shovel manfr)
Joiners, &c.
2 Coote Wm.
4 Goold Wm.
5 King Charles
Maltsters.
Ablitt Alfred
3 Baker John
East Robert
Milliners, &c.
Hart Ann
Hayward Sarah

Painters, Plumbers, & Glaziers.
Abbott Wm.
Clements Chas.
5 Partridge Rt.
Saddlers, &c.
Bullivant Thos.
Making Abraham
Whiting Henry
Tailors.
Making Westropp Wm.
Pritchard Edwd.
Rushbrook John
Scarffe Daniel
1 Stribling Chas.
Willis John
Wheelwright.
Hoggar Jemima
Woolstaplers.
3 Hitchcock Ths.
Turner Ths. & Son
Worsted & Poplin Yarn Manfrs.
3 Hitchcock Ths.
Meeking Samuel
Turner Ths. & Son

CARRIERS.
Deacon John, to Ipswich, Mon. and Clare, Wed
Springett Jno. to Bury, Wed. & Sat., and Ipswich, M. & Th

LAWSHALL, a scattered village, 6 miles S. of Bury St. Edmund's, and 10 miles N. of Sudbury, has in its parish 925 souls, and 2906A. 2R. 25P. of land, extending westward to the Brockley rivulet, and now valued, with the buildings, at the gross yearly rental of £4337. 4s. 6d. The Dowager Lady Middleton is lady of the *manor,* but the greater part of the soil belongs to Sir W. F. Middleton, Thos. Hallifax, Esq., and the Hunt, Bigsby, Walton, Nunn, and other families. Most of the parish is freehold, and the remainder copyhold, partly subject to arbitrary, and partly certain fines. Alfwinus, the son of Bricius, gave this lordship and manor, in the year 1022, to Ramsey Abbey, in Huntingdonshire; and at the dissolution, it was granted, with the advowson of the church, to John Rither. The *Church* (All Saints) is an ancient structure, with a tower and five bells; and the benefice is a rectory, valued in K.B. at £20. 2s. 8½d., and in 1835, at £454. N. Lee Acton, Esq., is patron, and the Rev. N. Colvile, D.D., is the incumbent, and has a commodious residence, and about 38A. of glebe.

The tithes were commuted, in 1839, for a yearly modus of £746. 3s. 1d. The *Town Lands* have been vested in trust, from an early period, for the relief of the poor and the repairs of the highways, and comprise about 11A., and a cottage, let for £15. 11s. a year. About 8A. of the land is in Shimpling. There is also a piece of land near Lawshall church, on which the school is built, but it is uncertain whether it was part of the town estate. In 1628, *Thomas Stevens* left 40s. a year for the poor, and 6s. 8d. a year for the minister of Lawshall, out of an estate at Edwardstone. The poor have also about £2 a year from Corder's Charity. The income from these various sources, except 6s. 8d. for the minister, is laid out by the rector in providing clothing for the Sunday scholars and coals for the poor. The *School* was built, about 1820, by Mrs. Barrington Purvis, at the cost of more than £500, and is conducted on the national system.

Adams James, beerhouse keeper
Albon Edmund, carpenter
Armstrong Robert, beerhouse kpr
Ashfield Thos. wheelwright & vict., *Harrow*
Coe Walter, veterinary surgeon
Colvile Rev Nathl., D.D., *Rectory*
Green John, grocer
Last James, National schoolmaster
Matthews Mrs. National schoolmrs
Mortlock Michael, blacksmith
Osborn Richard, shoemaker
Rogers Maria, grocer
Russell John, vict. *Swan*
Spark James, corn miller

FARMERS.
Blythe —
Brown Roger
Dutton James
Good Daniel
Last George
Mayston T.
Nunn James
Patrick Thomas
Payne Jno. *Haningfield Hall*
Payne Wm.&Jas.
Pearson Henry, *Pooley*
Phillipstone Ths.

Proctor Robert
Reeman Jno. and Jas. *Lawshall Hall*
Smith Jonathan
Smith Thomas
Snell William, *Cooper's farm*
Sparke John
Symonds James
Talbott Thomas
Taylor Jacob
Walleker Wm.
Whymark John
Wright Sush.

MELFORD, (LONG) the largest and one of the handsomest villages in Suffolk, is picturesquely seated on the north side of the vale of the river Stour, on the banks of one of its tributary streams, 3 miles N. by W. of Sudbury, 7 miles E. of Clare, and 13 miles S. of Bury St. Edmund's. It consists chiefly of one street, about a mile in length, with a green at the north end of it, where *fairs* are held on Whit-Tuesday, Wednesday, and Thursday; the two former days are for pleasure, pedlery, &c., and the last day is a large cattle mart. It has several good inns and retail shops, three corn mills, six malting establishments, and a foundry; and in its vicinity are several handsome seats. Its parish contains 2597 inhabitants, 5186A. 1R. 12P. of fertile land, and a number of scattered farm-houses and neat mansions. Some of the inhabitants are *silk weavers*, employed by the Sudbury manufacturers. *Petty Sessions* are held at the Bell Inn, once a fortnight. Sir Hyde Parker, Bart., is lord of the manor, for which he holds a court baron yearly; but a great part of the parish belongs to E. S. Bence, Esq., C. Westropp, Esq., Messrs. D. Mills and E. Chenery, and several smaller owners. The copyholds are subject to fines, twice the amount of the quit rents. MELFORD HALL, in a fine deer park, on the banks of the rivulet on the east side of the village, is the seat of *Sir Hyde Parker, Bart.*, whose baronetcy was created in 1681. It is an old spacious brick mansion, in the style of the age of Elizabeth, with four small round towers in front. It was formerly one of the

pleasure houses of the abbot of Bury, but after the dissolution it was granted, in the 37th of Henry VIII., with the manor and advowson, to *Sir Wm. Cordell.* To this grant, Queen Mary, in the first year of her reign, added the lands of the hospital of St. Saviour, without the north gate of Bury, which Sir William settled on the hospital erected by him at Melford. Dying without issue, his estates devolved on his sister, whose daughter carried them in marriage to Sir John Savage, whose grandson was advanced to the dignity of Earl Rivers. Melford Hall belonged to the widow of the third Earl, during the civil wars in the reign of Charles I., when Fuller says it became " the first fruits of plunder in England." The loss of the countess in plate, furniture, money, &c., at this and her other seat at St. Osyth, in Essex, was estimated at £100,000. The first Earl Rivers mortgaged his Melford estate to Sir John Cordell, and it was afterwards sold to Sir Robert Cordell, who, being created a baronet in 1660, made it his seat. On the failure of male issue in his family, the estate devolved to that of Firebrace, and in the middle of last century it was the seat of Sir Cordell Firebrace, one of the parliamentary representatives of this county. It soon afterwards passed to the Parker family. KENTWELL HALL, another fine old mansion, in a well wooded park, a little north of the village, was long the seat of the Cloptons, who acquired the estate by the marriage of *Sir Thos. Clopton,* with the heiress of Wm. Mylde, or Meld, who died in the 48th of Henry III. The heiress of the Cloptons married Sir Simonds D'Ewes, whose daughter carried the estate in marriage to Sir Thos. Darcy, and died in 1661. The estate was afterwards the seat and property of *Sir Thos. Robinson,* who was created a baronet in 1681, but his heirs sold it to John Moore, Esq., of London, from whose family it passed to E. S. Bence, Esq., who now resides at the hall. MELFORD PLACE, the seat and property of Charles Westropp, Esq., is an ancient mansion, with pleasant grounds, at the south end of the village. It was formerly more extensive than it is now, and was long the residence of the Martyn family, one of whom was lord mayor of London in 1567. *Roger Martyn,* of this place, was created a *baronet* in 1667, but his family became extinct about the close of last century, and the estate passed to the Spaldings, and from the latter to its present owner. The Abbot of Bury obtained a charter for a yearly fair, and a weekly *market* on Thursday, in the 19th of Henry III., but the latter has long been obsolete. BRIDGE STREET, a hamlet on both sides of the rivulet, about 2 miles N. of the village, is partly in Alpheton parish. The CHURCH (Holy Trinity) is a beautiful specimen of the architecture of the fifteenth century, about 180 feet long, exclusive of the school at the end, and the small square tower, which is of more modern erection than the body of the structure. It contains many neat monuments of the Martyn, Clopton, Cordell, and other families, formerly seated here. At the upper end of the north aisle, is an altar tomb, bearing the recumbent effigy of Wm. Clopton, Esq., who died in 1446. On the right of the altar, is the splendid monument of *Sir Wm. Cordell,* speaker of the House of Commons, a member of Queen Mary's privy council, and founder of Melford Hospital. On the outside of the pew formerly belonging to the Martyns, are many grotesque heads, carved in oak; and some ancient stones in the floor, at the east end of the chancel, cover the re-

mains of various members of that family. The font has a cover, curiously carved, with a pinnacle and a cross on the top; and on the spot whence it was removed to its present situation, is a raised stone, in the form of a lozenge, with a black cross upon it. The north window still contains some painted glass, with figures and Latin inscriptions, now in a mutilated condition. The *rectory*, valued in K.B. at £28. 2s. 6d., has a good residence, and 150A. 3R. 22P. of glebe, but its value in 1835 was not returned to the Church Commissioners. John Cobbold, Esq., is patron, and the Rev. E. Cobbold incumbent. Here is an *Independent Chapel*, erected about 1724, and also a Wesleyan meeting-house. The parish has a richly endowed Hospital, a National School, two school endowments, and several other charities. Several Roman urns were dug up in a gravel pit in the parish, about thirty years ago; and in a farm yard on Cranmer Green, is a *petrifying spring*.

The *Church and Poor's Estate* comprises a cottage, barn, and about 18A. of land, let for £33 a year, which is applied in equal moieties with the church and poor rates, the property being given for these uses by *William Skeyne*, in 1518. Four cottages, occupied as *almshouses* by poor persons, are repaired at the parish expense, and were given by Sir Roger Martyn. In 1495, *John Hill* gave his quit-rents and woods in the manor of Bower Hall, in Pentlow, Essex, to the poor of Melford, and they now yield £12. 4s. per annum. Since 1694, the income of this charity, and a yearly payment of £2. 8s. 1d. out of the Exchequer, under a grant from Edward VI., have been applied towards the support of the *Parish School*, adjoining the church, at which 12 poor boys, nominated by the church-wardens, are instructed as *free scholars*, along with others on the national system. In 1713, *John Moore* left £300, the interest thereof to be paid to a *school-mistress*, for teaching 10 poor boys and 10 girls of Melford, under the direction of the Governors of Trinity Hospital, and the minister and churchwardens. This charity now consists of £321 old South Sea Annuities, yielding £9 per annum. *Doles*, amounting to £15 a year, are distributed among the poor parishioners at Easter, and arise as follows:—£2. 10s. from *Corder's Charity* (see Glemsford;)— 30s. out of land at Mendlesham, left by *Rd. Smith*, in 1560;—£2 out of an estate at Reydon, left by *John Mayor, D.D.*;—£3 out of the poor rates, for a cottage and garden, given by one *Chaplin*; and £6 out of the poor rates, as the rent of a building long used as the workhouse, but purchased with £100, given by *John Moor*, in 1713. In 1836, *Mrs Harriet Oliver* left the dividends of £4000 three per cent. consols, to be distributed in coal among the poor parishioners. TRINITY HOSPITAL, for a warden, 12 poor men and two poor women, was founded by *Sir Wm. Cordell, Kt.*, in 1580, under letters patent of Queen Elizabeth, which places the institution under the visitatorial power of the Bishop of Norwich for the time being; consequently, the Charity Commissioners did not inquire into it. The hospital consists of a quadrangle, three sides of which are occupied by the 12 brethren, and the fourth by the warden and two sisters. The whole is kept in excellent repair, and the yearly income, amounting in 1836 to £1066. 12s. 10d., is applied, after the payment of incidental expenses, in maintaining and clothing the inmates, who must be old and decayed housekeepers of Melford; or, when such cannot be found, persons of a similar description are to be taken from Shimpling. As already noticed, the endowment consists of lands, &c., formerly belonging to St. Saviour's Hospital, at Bury.

MELFORD (LONG.)

Post Office at Charlotte Catchpole's. Letters desp. at ½ past 6 evening

Abbott Miss Hannah
Almack Richd. solicitor and clerk to the magistrates
Bence Edw. Starkie, Esq. *Kentwell Hall*
Blunden Robt. farrier
Blunden Thomas, auctioneer, *Cranmer House*
Brewster Miss Elizabeth
Button Wm. corn dealer
Castley Thos. Esq. *Rose Cottage*
Churchyard John, hair seating mfr
Cole Sarah, chemist and druggist
Constable Timothy, gardener, &c.
Cresswell Mrs Jane

Downs Wm. whitesmith
Drew Thos. gentleman
Drury Charles, rope and net maker
Eldridge Mrs. Westgate terrace
Faulkner Rev Hy. B., M.A. Westgate House
Gilbert Mr George
Gordon Rt. Esq. *Hill Cottage*
Green George, registrar
Groom Wm. hair dresser
Halstead Miss Bethell
Hanwell Mrs Maria
Harris Robert Esq.
Havell Wm. Gascoign, hat manfr
Hollis Rev Henry (Independent)
Lanchester Robert, gent
Lorking Thos. bookseller, printer, & binder, and agent to the Norwich Union Insurance Company
Parker Sir Hyde, Bart. *Melford Hall*
Parsonson Mrs Lucy
Parsonson Thos. tinner, &c.
Richold Peter, coach builder
Salter Ezekiah, rope manufacturer
Sargeant James, calf jobber
Scott Mrs Rebecca
Steed Robert, parish clerk
Ward (David,) and Silver (James,) iron and brass founders
Westropp Chas. Esq. *Melford Place*
Westhorpe Mrs Mary
Worship Rev John Lucas, B.A. curate, *Hill House*
Worters Mr Robert

INNS AND TAVERNS.

Black Lion, Wm. Harvey
Bull Inn, Jas. Milam, (and posting)
Cock and Bell, Amor King
George, Wm. Medcalf
Hare, James Harris
Ram, Daniel Gooch
Rose & Crown, Jas. Albon, *Bridge st*
Swan, John Bocking
White Hart, Joseph King

ACADEMIES.
(*take Boarders.*)
*Bird Amelia
Frewer Mary
Martin John
*Rist Susan
*Seggins W. Hy.
Bakers, &c.
Algor John
Baker Henry
Goody Ann
King John, (confectioner)
Mills Wm.
Rogers Stephen
Sharman James
Steward Ann
Beer Houses.
Ambrose Thos.
Cooper Thos.
Harrold John
Rixby Charlotte
Steward Charles
Blacksmiths.
Codling Edw.
Hammond John, Bridge street
Ostler Aaron

Ostler Thos. (agt. to Suffolk Am. Fire Office)

Boot & Shoe Mkrs.
Abrose Thomas
Butcher Charles
Crissell James
Hume John
Long Charles
Payne Wm.
Perry Peter
Steed John
Steed Thos. (and organist)

Bricklayers and Plasterers.
Theobald Clemt.
Fordham Wm.
Green Daniel
Green Wm.

Butchers.
Allen Wm.
Mayhew Chltte.
Ostler Patrick
Steed Henry
Worters Joseph

Coopers.
Prigg Robert
Woodgate Thos.

Corn Millers and Merchants.
Ardley Thos. sen.
Baker John, Hall mill
Ruffell George, *Withendale*

FARMERS.
(* are Owners.)
Bigg Edward
Blunden Thos.
Branwhite Thos. *Lodge Farm*
Bullingbrook Jn.
*Chenery Edw.
Coe Geo. John
Cooper Isaac, *Park Farm*
Death Geo. Ford
King John
*Mills Danl. sen. *Glebe Farm*
*Mills Danl. jun. *Rodbridge*
Ostler Aaron
Ruffell William, *Withendale*

Grocers & Drprs.
Bickmore Peter
Cole Wm. Henry
Hunt Samuel
Ostler Hannah
Woods George

Joiners.
Blunden Thos.
Leekes John
Lyng Wm.
Webb Stephen
Wellum James

Maltsters & Corn Merchants.
Ardley Thos. sen.
Ardley Thos. jun.
Corder Thomas
Gooch Daniel
Harris James
Shepard Jno.; h Glemsford

Milliners.
Frewer Fanny
Whitehead Har.

Painters, Plumbers, & Glaziers.
Coates Thos.
Steed John

Saddler.
Spilling Chas.

Shopkeepers. (See Grocers.)
Farrow Wm.
Theobald Clmt.

Surgeons.
Cream Robert
Jones Robert

Tailors & Drprs.
Cater George
Cowey Wm. Hy.
Edwards Wm.
Jolly Wm.
Spilling Wm.
Taylor Henry

Wheelwrights.
Bullingbrook Jn.
Butcher John
Farrow Wm.

COACHES and CARRIERS to Bury, Sudbury, &c. pass daily
John Cammel Fake's waggon, to Bury, Colchester, &c. Tue. Thu. & S

MILDEN, or *Milding*, is a small scattered village, 4 miles S.S.E. of Lavenham, and has in its parish 1332 acres of land, and 186 inhabitants. It was anciently the demense of Remigius de Milden, and afterwards passed to the Allingtons, who sold it to the Canhams, who were formerly seated at the *Hall*, now a farm-house, belonging to the Rev. Henry Powney. The other principal owners of the parish are, Thos. Brown, Esq., Charles Dawson, Esq., and Mrs. Lewis, and each have the manorial rights of their own estates. The *Church* (St. Peter) is an ancient structure, with a tower at the west end, and the benefice is a rectory, valued in K.B. at £10. 13s. 4d., and now having a yearly modus of £340, awarded in 1841. John Gurdon, Esq., is patron, and the Rev. Nathaniel Wm. Hallward, M.A., is the incumbent, for whom the Rev. N. R. Drake, B.A., officiates. Three cottages at Monks Eleigh, let for £4. 2s. a year, were purchased about 1653, with £20 given for the poor of Milden by *James Allington, Esq.* The poor have also a yearly rent-charge of 20s., left by a person named *Canham.* Two cottages and an orchard, left by the Rev. William Birkett, in 1700, are let for £5s. 2s. a year, and the rents are applied towards the support of a *school* for poor children. DIRECTORY :—Rev. Nathan Richard Drake, B.A., curate, *Rectory*; and Stephen Barnes, Samuel Biggs, Sparrow Biggs, Robert Hawkins, (*Hall;*) Robt. Long, and Timothy Stanton, *farmers.*

MONKS ELEIGH is a pleasant and well-built village, in the vale of the river Brett, nearly 6 miles N.W. of Hadleigh, and 2 miles S.W. of Bildeston. Its parish is a *peculiar* of the Archbishop of Canterbury, and contains 732 souls, and 2099 acres of fertile land. On the river are two corn mills, and in the village is a good inn, and several well-stocked shops. The manor was given, with Hadleigh, to the monks of Canterbury, by *Brithnoth*, Earl of Essex, who was killed by the Danes in 991. After the dissolution, it was given to the Dean and Chapter of Canterbury, to whom it still belongs ; but the soil belongs to Isaac Strutt, Thos. Brown, and Chas. Dawson, Esqrs.; Miss Margt. Blair, Mrs. Hicks, Mr. J. Making, Mr. S. S. Baker, and a few smaller free and copyholders. The *Church* (St. Peter) is a large and handsome structure, with a tower containing six bells, and surmounted by a small wooden spire. The interior was thoroughly repaired in 1838, and most of the sittings are free. The *rectory*, valued in K.B. at £13. 18s. 11½d., and in 1835 at £422, has 16 acres of glebe, a good residence, and a yearly modus of £570, awarded in 1837. The Archbishop of Canterbury is patron, and the Rev. Henry Carrington, M.A., incumbent. The *Church Land*, 2½ acres, anciently appropriated to the repairs of the parish clock, is let for about £6 a year, which is carried to the churchwarden's account. The sums of £10, given by *Francis Causton*, and £20 given by the *Rev. Wm. Moore*, for bread for the poor, were laid out in 1717 in the purchase of Butt-field, 2½ A., which was conveyed, together with two cottages belonging to the poor, to trustees, for distributions of bread on Ash-Wednesday and Christmas-day, among the necessitous parishioners frequenting the church. The cottages are occupied rent-free, and the land is let for £4. 10s. a year. Here is a *National School*, built in 1834, and the shoolmistress has the use of part of the old workhouse, which was divided into three tenements in 1838.

Baker Saml. Scott, veterinary surgeon, and shoeing smith
Baldwin Philip, tanner
Brentford Wm. blacksmith
Carrington Rev Hy. M.A. *Rectory*
Clarke Edmd. Wm. West, parish clerk
Clarke Mary, schoolmistress
Clover Thomas, corn miller
Deaves Samuel, castrator
Fuller Edmund, beerhouse keepe
Gage Wm. butcher & cattle dealer
Garnham Henry, spirit merchant & victualler, *Red Lion*
Harris John, corn miller
Hawkins Robert, ironmonger

Hobart John Rt. animal painter
Raynham Mrs || Mudd Sus. school

FARMERS.
(* *are Owners.*)
*Baker Saml. S.
Blomfield John
Durrant John
Gage Robert
Gage Wm.
*Making Joseph, *Hall*
*Strutt Isaac
Wright Robert

Grocers & Dprs.
Alldis Henry
Barnard Wm.

King John
Joiners, &c.
Hawkins James
Warren Zach. (& beerhouse)
Shoemakers.
Ruffell Wm.
Tricker Zach.
Tailors.
Cardy Wm.
Finch George
Wheelwrights.
Bugg Meschach
Cousens Robert

NAYLAND, or *Neyland*, is a small ancient town, on the north side of the navigable river Stour, 9 miles S.E. by E. Sudbury; 6 miles N. by W. of Colchester; 8 miles S.W. by S. of Hadleigh; and 56 miles N.E. of London. It had formerly a weekly market on Friday, and had a flourishing woollen manufacture, but both are now obsolete. It has still a *fair* for cattle, &c., on the Wednesday after October 2nd, and there are in the town several good inns and retail shops, a large *silk throwsting mill*, a *soap manufactory*, a *brewery*, and several *malt kilns*. It communicates with Essex by a large brick *bridge* of one arch, and its parish contains 1114 inhabitants, and 941A. 1R. 29P. of fertile land. Sir J. R. Rowley, Bart., is lord of the *manor*, and owner of most of the soil, and the remainder belongs to a number of small proprietors. It was one of the manors given to Hubert de Burgh by Henry III., when he created him Earl of Kent, but falling into disgrace with that monarch, he was obliged to part with several of his castles and estates to secure the quiet enjoyment of the rest. In the 13th of Edward III., Nayland was the lordship of Lord Scrope, of Masham, in Yorkshire. In 1628, Richard Weston was created *Baron Weston*, of *Neyland*, and was afterwards raised to the dignity of Earl of Portland; but on the death of the fourth earl, without issue, in 1688, these titles became extinct. The town is well-built, and is about to be lighted with gas, but from its low situation, it is subject to occasional inundations. The *Church* (St. James) is a handsome structure, which had formerly a spire steeple, which, being much decayed, was taken down in 1834, when the present tower was erected at the cost of £500. In the tower are six musical bells, and in the chancel are several neat monuments, one of which is in memory of the Rev. Wm. Jones, M.A., a late rector, and author of the "Catholic Doctrine of the Trinity." Here are also several ancient memorials of persons formerly eminent in the clothing trade. Over the altar is a fine picture of the Redeemer, with a chalice. One Abel, a cloth worker, is said to have built the handsome porch of this church, in the wall of which he has a funeral monument, with the letter A. and the figure of a bell upon it, to signify his name. There are a few brasses on the pavement, and on one of the slabs are the words "Queen of France," but the rest of the inscription is obliterated. The benefice is a perpetual curacy, valued in 1835 at £139, in the patronage of Sir J. R. Rowley, Bart., and incumbency of the Rev. W.

E. Sims, M.A., for whom the Rev. Fredk. Sims officiates. The tithes were commuted in 1839 for the yearly payment of £42. 2s. to the incumbent, and £244. 13s. 9d. to P. P. Mannock, Esq., the impropriator. Here is an *Independent Chapel*, belonging to a congregation, which dates its origin from 1732.

Pursuant to a decree of the Court of Chancery, in 1822, various CHARITY ESTATES AND FUNDS, belonging to Nayland and previously held under ancient deeds, were vested and settled in trustees, upon trust to apply the income in the manner proposed in a scheme approved by one of the Masters in Chancery, and sanctioned by the Court. This *charity trust* produces a yearly income of about £210, and consists of the following parcels of property—viz., 8 tenements, let to the overseers for £20 a year; a messuage, occupied by paupers; a tenement, used as a *National School;* £103. 4s. 3d. three per cent. reduced annuities; £789. 10s. 3d. three per cent. consols; Ridhold farm, 36A. 1R. 38P., and land called Fisher's, 19A. 18P., let together for £89. 4s. a year; land called St. Mary's, 18A. 3R. 3P. let for £40 a year; 17 common-rights on *Nayland fen*, let for about £15; *Lewis Meadow*, 1A. in Wiston, let for £1. 13s.; and 589l. 1s. 5d. three per cent. consols. From this trust, the following yearly sums are paid—viz., 38l. to the *perpetual curate* of Nayland; 6l. 6s. to the *parish clerk;* 15l. for the repairs of the church; 20l. for apprenticing poor children; and the remainder, after payment of taxes, repairs, &c., is applied for the relief of the poor, and the education of 20 poor children. The poor parishioners have also 2l. 10s. yearly from an acre of land, in Lewis Meadow, left by *Abm. Caley*, in 1703, for distributions of bread; and 2l. 10s. yearly, left for the same purpose by *Thos. Love*, in 1564. They have likewise a share of *White's Charity*, as noticed with Holton.

NAYLAND.

Post Office, at Wm. Littlebury's.
Letters are despatched *via* Colchester 7 evening, & received at 7 mg.

Allen Rt. coal dealer; h *Ballingdon*
Alston Samuel, solicitor
Barber Wm. beer seller
Brown & Moy, silk throwsters
Cole Nathl. brazier and ironmonger
Creak Mrs Mary‖Crisp Mrs Susan
Cuddon Jas. brewer & maltster
Eisdell & Warmington, leather cutrs
Faiers Rt.&Hy. coopers&basket mkrs
Garrard Isaac, gentleman
Goodrich James, saddler, &c
Hammond Saml. beerhouse keeper
Johnston Rev John (Independent)
Mills John Wi by, veternry. surgeon
Mitchell Isaac Dagnett, currier
Roberts George, cowkeeper
Ryan Peter, dealer in Irish linens
Rule Emily, milliner, &c
Sargent Joseph, wheelwright
Salmon Mrs. ‖ Scott Mrs Sarah
Scott James, blacksmith
Siggers Jno. fellmonger & grocer
Sims Rev. Frederick, curate
Stammers Wm. corn miller
Storey George, watchmaker
Stow Abm. hair dresser
Taylor Mrs Mary
Wilsmore Sarah, tea dealer
Winny John Triggs, soap boiler

INNS AND TAVERNS.

Anchor, Charles Kirby Bocking
Queen's Head, Thomas Crooks
Vine, John Tilby
White Hart Inn (& excise office)
  John Seabrook Mortimer

Academies.
Barker Thomas
Goodrich Cath.
Paine Sar.&Cath
  National
Stow Mary
Warren Sarah

Bakers, &c.
Carrington Saml.
Mussett Wm.
Roberts Wm.

Boot&Shoe Mkrs.
Borrett Henry
Garrard John
Godden Robert
Hill Thomas
Littlebury Wm.
Prestney Jerh.
Simpson Joseph
Thorp Thomas
Wilby John

Bricklayers.
Eagle Charles
Holmes Samuel

Butchers.
Bacon James
Barnard James

Holton Edward

FARMERS.
Bacon James
Green Thomas
Hawes Mary
Holton Edward
Mortimer Jno. S.
Munnings Wm.
Strutt Thomas
  Grocers & Drprs.
Blyth Mary S.
Leigh Thomas
  Joiners&Buildrs.
Beardwell Wm.
Hale John
Mortimer Jno. S.
Mortimer Hy. G.
Smith John
  Maltsters.
Brown John
Cuddon James
Green Thomas
  Plumbrs. Glazrs.
  & Painters.
Barker Wm.
Button Thomas

Shopkeepers.	Smith Susan	Hammond Thos.	Waggons, to London, from the
Beardwell James	Surgeons.	(& hatter)	White Hart,
Crooks Thomas	Daniell Jer. Geo.	Spyke James	Tues. & Frid ;
Groom Jerh.	and Wm.	Wilson Wm.	& Jno. Parker,
Ladkin Thomas	Fenn Thos. Har-		to Ipswich, Mo.
Roberts Wm.	rold		and Colchester,
Winny Thos. Al-	Tailors.	COACHES.	Wed. Thu. &
sop	Beardwell James	To Colchester &	Saturday
Straw Hat Mkrs.	Branch Robert	Stowmarket, call	
Pite Elizabeth	Elliott Wm.	at the Wht. Hart,	
		morning & evg	

NEWTON-NEAR-SUDBURY, a pleasant village, scattered round a green of 40 acres, 3 miles E. of Sudbury, has in its parish 443 souls, and 2197A. 2R. 32P. of land, in the manors of *Newton Hall and Bottelers.* Earl Howe is lord of the former, and the Rev. T. H. Causton of the latter, but part of the soil belongs to J. Gurdon, H. Green, and E. Stedman, Esqrs., and several smallers owners. *Sackers Green,* 1¼ mile S.W. of the village, is a small hamlet in this parish. The *Church* (All Saints) is an ancient fabric, with a tower and three bells, supposed to have been built by the Botteler family, who were seated here, but went to Ireland at the Reformation. The rectory, valued in K.B. at £17. 13s. 8½d., is in the patronage of St. Peter's College, Cambridge, and incumbency of the Rev. Charles Smith, B.D., who has a good residence, 55A. of glebe, and a yearly modus of £597, awarded in 1840. Here is a *National School,* built in 1836. The poor have four rent-charges amounting to £1. 16s. 8d. yearly, left by Wm. and Edw. Alston, in 1564 and 1591, and Robert and John Plampin, in 1603 and 1618, out of property now belonging to the Alston, Nicholson, and Gurdon families.

Chandler Samuel, parish clerk
Farrow Eliz. vict. Saracen's Head
Glass Wm. blacksmith
Hart James, corn miller
Nicholson James, bricklayer
Smith Rev Chas. B.D. *Rectory*
Vincent Wm. cattle dealer
Ward Abigail, carpenter

FARMERS. (* are Owners.)
*Green Hugh, *Newton Hall*
*Hart Jeremiah || Hart James
Hart Walter || Hart Wm.
Sparrow Wm. || Warren Thomas
Taylor Wm. Bernard
*Tiffen Ths. Layzell, jun. *Siam Hall*

POLSTEAD, a scattered village in a picturesque valley, 4½ miles S.W. of Hadleigh, and 3 miles N.N.E. of Nayland, has in its parish 989 inhabitants, many scattered houses, and 3402A. 1R. 7P of land, mostly a light sand, and including part of *Leaven Heath,* extending 2 miles westward, and now enclosed and cultivated. The manor was anciently held by the Lamburns, and afterwards by the Brands. It passed from the latter, in 1814, to the wife of T. W. Cook, Esq., who died in 1825, after which his widow married Chas. Tyrell, Esq., who now resides at *Polstead Hall,* a handsome brick mansion, on a pleasant eminence, in a park of about 100 acres, well-stocked with deer, and containing some fine old timber. His lady, Mrs. Mary Ann Tyrell, is lady of the manor, but a great part of the soil belongs to Sir J. R. Rowley, Sir B. C. Brodie, J. Gurdon, Esq., Sir H. Peyton, and several smaller free and copyholders. Polstead is remarkable for its cherries. It has a *fair* for toys, &c., on the Wednesday after June 16th. The *Church* (St. Mary) is a neat structure, with a tower containing six bells, and surmounted by a small spire.

The rectory, valued in K.B. at £22, and in 1835 at £627, has a good residence, 17A. of glebe, and a yearly modus of £871, awarded in 1841. F. R. Reynolds, Esq., is patron, and the Rev. James Coyte, M.A., incumbent. The present rateable yearly rental of the parish is £4969. 6s. 3d. There was formerly a *chantry* here of the yearly value of £6. 6s. 0½d.. Mrs. Tyrell supports a *school* for poor girls, and the poor parishioners have, on St. Thomas's day, the interest of £100 left by Geo. Martin, in 1814. The *Red Barn* here, which was burnt down, Dec. 26th, 1842, was the scene of the *murder of Maria Martin*, by her betraying lover *Wm. Corder*, who was executed for the horrid crime on the 10th of August, 1828, after having married another, and for some time eluded retributive justice.

Baylham Wm. shopkeeper
Borham Stannard, corn miller, (steam and water mill)
Coyte Rev James, M.A. *Rectory*
Cream Henry, tailor
Drake John, blacksmith
Epleford Edw. beerhouse keeper
Howes Jonth. vict. Shoulder of Mutton, (and butcher)
Payne Geo. grocer and cabinet mkr.
Pryke Jas. Isaac, plumber, glazier, and victualler, *Cock*
Smith Joseph, shopkeeper
Stow James, schoolmaster
Tyrell Chas. Esq. *Polstead Hall*
Watson Thomas, butcher

FARMERS.
(* are Owners.)
*Bouttell Wm.
Brown Wm.
Cousins John, *Leaven Heath*

Everett Joshua
Everett Isaac, *Jacob's Farm*
Grimwade Rd.
Groves Joseph
Harwood Thos. (& Belstead)
King John
Mudd Robert
Smith Benjamin
Smith Joseph
*Strutt John Chaplin
Taber Wm.
*Tomkins Abm. *Gedding Hall*
*Tomkins John, *Leaven Heath*

Watson Wm. & Thomas
Joiners & Wheelwrights.
Baylham John
Bedford Wm.
Shoemakers.
Chisnall Wm.
Cocksedge Chas.
Groves Joseph
Munson John
Richardson Jph.
Watson Ephraim
CARRIER.
Wm. Mann, to Ipswich, Mon. & Fri. and to Sudbury, Tue. and Saturday

PRESTON, a pleasant village, on the western acclivity of the vale of the small river Brett, 2 miles E. by N. of Lavenham, 4 miles W. by N. of Bildeston, and 9 miles from Hadleigh and Sudbury, has in its parish 406 souls, and 1970 acres of land, now rated at the annual value of £2551. It is in *four manors*, viz., *Preston Hall and Swift's*, of which Sir B. C. Brodie, Bart., is lord ; *Maister's*, of which Mr. Thos. Wright is lord ; and *Mortimer's*, of which Mr. Wm. Makin is lord ; but Sir J. Rudsell, R. W. Shepherd, Esq., and several smaller owners, have estates in the parish. *Priory Farm* formerly belonged to Trinity Priory, Ipswich ; and Preston Hall was long held by the Earls of Oxford ; and in the reigns of James and Charles I., was the seat of *Robert Ryce, Esq.*, a great preserver of the antiquities of this county. The *Church* (St. Mary) is an ancient fabric, with a tower and six bells. It has an organ, which was purchased by subscription in 1834. The *rectory*, valued in K.B. at £5. 6s. 3d., is in the patronage of Emanuel College, Cambridge, and incumbency of the Rev. W. H. Shelford, M.A., who erected a new and handsome *Rectory House* in 1835, and has 6A. of glebe, and a yearly modus of £514. 15s., awarded in 1838, in lieu of tithes. The benefice was originally only a vicarage ; but in 1660, *Robert Ryce, Esq.*, then impropriator, obtained an Act of Parliament for consolidating the appropriate rectory of Preston St. Mary with the vicarage of Preston, and confirming the presentation thereof

to the Master and Fellows of Emanuel College; but by the same Act he charged the incumbent with the yearly payment of £5, to be paid to two neighbouring Justices of the Peace, for apprenticing poor children of Preston. In 1814, *Mary Green* left £200, and directed the interest thereof to be distributed in bread and fuel among poor parishioners. This legacy was invested in the purchase of £289. 12s. 6d. three per cent. consols. Here is a large *National School,* erected in 1843 by subscription and grants from the National Society, the Diocesan Society, and Government.

Amos John, wheelwright
Edgar John, corn miller
Green Henry, corn miller
King Joseph, shoemaker
Sewell James, vict. Six Bells
Shelford Rev Wm. Head, M.A., *Rectory*
Stribling Benjamin, blacksmith

FARMERS. (* *are Owners.*)
*Baldwin Wm. || *Death Susannah
Edgar Johnson, *Down Hall*
*Evered Ann, *Old Parsonage*
*Green Johnny, *Priory Farm*
King Thomas || Makin Hannah
*Makin Wm. *Mortimers*
Osborn Ebenezer, Preston Hall
*Wright Thomas, *Maisters*

SHIMPLING, or *Shimplingthorn,* a small village in a picturesque valley, 7½ miles N. of Sudbury, and 4½ miles W.N.W. of Lavenham, has in its parish 517 souls, and 2698A. 2R. 19P. of land, extending nearly two miles N.E. to the hamlet of *Shimpling street,* and including 90A. of wood. It was given by William the Conqueror to Odo de Campania. CHADACRE HALL, a handsome mansion in a sylvan park, watered by a small rivulet, half a mile N. of the village, is the seat of Thos. Hallifax, Esq., who owns a great part of the parish. The Crown has 440A., and the other principal owners are E. S. Bence, Esq., the Rev. M. C. Bolton, Mr. Arthur Blencowe, and Melford Hospital. Chadacre was formerly the seat of the Plampyns. The *Church* (St. George) is a plain structure, with one side aisle and a tower. The rectory, valued in K.B. at £16. 7s. 1d., has a yearly modus of £600 awarded in 1837, and is in the patronage and incumbency of the Rev. M. C. Bolton.

Bolton Rev. Miles Cooper, *Rectory*
Bruce Thomas, blacksmith
Butcher Joseph, corn miller
Gosling Henry, corn miller, *Shimpling Street*
Hallifax Thos. Esq. *Chadacre Hall*
Hammond Philip, shoemaker
Ruffell Samuel, chief constable, *Shimpling Park*
Vickers Frederick, vict. Bush, *Shimpling Thorn*

FARMERS.
Blencowe Arthur (and auctioneer)
Britton Charles || Jervis James
Cawston Abraham, *Shimpling Hall*
Jarvis James
King Wm. || Playle Frederick
Ruffell Wm. || Simons James
Watkinson George, *Gifford's Hall*
Watkinson Wm. (and maltster)
Watts Wm. *Green Tree*

SOMERTON, a small scattered village, 7 miles N.E. of Clare, and 8 miles N.N.W. of Sudbury, has in its parish 143 souls, and 1040 acres of land. G. W. Poley, Esq., is lord of the manor, which was formerly held by the Burghs and Blundells, but a great part of the soil belongs to Joseph Eaton Hale, Esq., of *Somerton Hall,* (a commodious mansion, with pleasant grounds,) Robert Bevan, Esq., and the Rev. John Maddy, D.D., who enjoys the rectories of Hartest, Boxted, Stansfield, and Somerton. The latter is valued in K.B. at

£6. 16s. 8d., and is in the patronage of the Marquis of Downshire, a descendant of the Blundells. The glebe is 39A. 2R. 11P., and the tithes were commuted in 1839, for a yearly modus of £300. The *Church* (St. Margaret) is a small ancient fabric, with a tower and four bells. The poor parishioners have a fifth part of *Poley's Charity*. (See Boxted.) DIRECTORY:— Joseph Eaton Hale, Esq., *Somerton Hall;* Rev. John Maddy, D.D., *Rectory;* and Wm. Brown, Wm. Cutler, and Henry King, *farmers.*

STANSTEAD, a village on a pleasant eminence, 6 miles N. by W. of Sudbury, has in its parish 387 inhabitants, and 1162A. 1R. 9P. of land, bounded on the east and west by two rivulets, from which it rises in fertile and well-wooded undulations. E. S. Bence, Esq., is lord of the manor, but a great part of the soil belongs to Rt. Mapletoft, Esq., of *Spring Hall,* (a neat mansion nearly a mile N. of the church;) the Rev. H. B. Faulkner, and a few smaller owners. The *Church* (St. James) is a neat edifice, with a tower and six bells, and the benefice is a rectory, valued in K.B. at £10, and now in the patronage and incumbency of the Rev. Samuel Sheen, M.A., who has 24A. of glebe, a commodious residence, enlarged in 1843; and a yearly modus of £277, awarded in 1839. The *Poor's Land* is in three pieces, comprising 4½A., let for £5. 10s. a year, which is distributed among poor parishioners, together with the following *yearly doles,* viz., £7. 7s. from *Poley's Charity,* (see Boxted;) 27s. from *Corder's Charity,* (see Glemsford;) 5s. left by *Jerome Calfe* in 1640, out of land called the Pightle; and 7s. 6d., paid out of the poor rates, as interest of a benefaction of £7. 10s.

Bird Richard, wood dealer
Ellis Frederick Wm. relieving officer and registrar
Golding Wm. shopkeeper
Howard George, shoemaker
Kilbourn Wm. blacksmith
Mapletoft Robert, Esq. *Spring Hall*
Pawsey George, shoemaker
Sheen Rev. Samuel, M.A. *Rectory*

Smith John, jun. maltster
Sparke Wm. corn miller
Watts Jacob Sparrow, vict. White Hart

FARMERS.
Alston Daniel, *Stanstead Hall*
Alston Thomas || Bigg Charles
Bird John || French Stephen
Murton Henry || Smith John

STOKE-BY-NAYLAND is a pleasant and well-built village on a bold eminence north of the vale of the Stour, 2 miles N.E. by N. of Nayland, and 6 miles S.S.W. of Hadleigh. Its parish is extensive, fertile, and picturesque, comprising about 4600 acres of land, and 1362 inhabitants, and including several handsome mansions, many scattered farm houses, most of *Leaven Heath,* now enclosed and extending from 2 to 4 miles west; and the hamlet of *Thorrington Street,* from 1 to 2 miles S.E. of the village. The navigable Stour bounds it on the south, and the Brett on the east, and it is intersected by two rivulets. It is in the *manors* of Gifford's Hall and Tendring Hall, now belonging—the former to P. P. Mannock, Esq., and the latter to Sir J. R. Rowley; but part of the soil belongs to several smaller proprietors, the largest of whom is Isaac Hoy, Esq., of *Stoke Priory,* a handsome mansion, 1 mile W. of the church, erected in 1829, and so called from a monastery which existed here before the Conquest, though but little is known of it afterwards. Three small *fairs* for toys, &c., are held at Stoke on Feb. 25th, Whit-Monday, and May 12th. GIFFORD'S HALL, 2 miles E. of Stoke, and 4 miles N.E. of Nayland, has belonged to

the Mannock family since the time of Henry IV., previous to which it was the seat of the Giffords. It was rebuilt in the reigns of Henry VII. and VIII., and is a spacious mansion in the Tudor style, surrounding a quadrangular court, with a tower gateway entrance. The whole is of brick, the mouldings of the windows, doors, and other ornaments, being of the same material. Opposite the entrance are some ivy-mantled remains of an old *Roman Catholic Chapel,* and at the distance of quarter of a mile is a new one, built in 1827. In the hall is a private chapel and several fine apartments, containing some good paintings, and rich carved work. The grounds descend eastward to the vale of the Brett. Sir Francis Mannock was created a baronet in 1627, but the title is now extinct. The present proprietor, Patrick Power Mannock, Esq., resides generally on the continent, and the hall is now occupied by the Catholic priest. TENDRING HALL, a large and handsome mansion, on a commanding eminence in an extensive and well-wooded park, descending southward nearly to the banks of the Stour, 1½ mile W.N.W. of Nayland, is the seat of *Sir Joshua Ricketts Rowley, Bart.,* a captain in the royal navy. The estate anciently belonged to the Tendring family, one of whom had a grant for a market and fair at Stoke in the 31st of Edward I. About 1421, Alice, the daughter and heiress of Sir Wm. Tendring, carried the estate in marriage to Sir John Howard, Kt., the immediate ancestor of the Dukes of Norfolk. From the Howards it passed to the Lords Windsor, and from them to the Williams. Sir John Williams, Kt., who was lord mayor of London in 1736, built the present mansion, and at his decease, the estate was sold to *Admiral Sir Wm. Rowley, Knt.,* one of the lords of the Admiralty, whose son Joshua gave many proofs of courage in the naval service, and was created a *baronet* in 1786. *Stoke Church* (St. Mary) is a noble structure, with a majestic tower, containing six bells, and rising to the height of 100 feet. The latter may be seen as far off as Harwich, a distance of twenty miles, and the high grounds near the village command a prospect of that harbour. The nave and chancel are divided from the side aisles by two rows of lofty pillars, from which spring finely proportioned arches. Here are many handsome monuments belonging to the Mannock, Rowley, and other families. One bears a recumbent effigy of Anna, Baroness of Windsor, and another is in memory of the first wife of John Howard, duke of Norfolk, who fell in the battle of Bosworth, fighting for Richard III. The benefice, a *vicarage,* valued in K.B. at £19. 0s. 10d., and in 1835 at £278, is in the patronage of Sir J. R. Rowley, Bart., and incumbency of the Rev. C. M. Torlesse, M.A., who has a good residence in the village. P. P. Mannock, Esq., is impropriator of the rectorial tithes of Stoke and Nayland, and the latter place is sometimes called a chapelry to the former. On *Leaven Heath,* near the site of an old burial ground, formerly used by the Society of Friends, a neat *Chapel of Ease* was erected a few years ago by subscription, for the accommodation of the western parts of the parish of Stoke, and it is now under the ministry of the Rev. H. T. Curry, who has a neat house adjoining it. Sir WM. CAPEL, draper, and lord mayor of London in 1503, was a native of Stoke, and ancestor of the present Earl of Essex. It is said that after a splendid entertainment given by him to Henry VII., he concluded the whole with a fire, into which he threw a number

of bonds, given by that king for money borrowed of him. On another occasion, to shew his affection for the same monarch, he dissolved a pearl, which cost some hundreds of pounds, and drank it to the King's health, in a glass of wine. Notwithstanding his loyalty, he was unmercifully fleeced by the avaricious Henry, but contrived to retrieve his affairs by industry and commerce, so that he died wealthy, in age and honor. One of his descendants was created Earl of Essex in 1661. In the 15th of James I., *Lady Ann Windsor* founded a *hospital* here for four poor women of Stoke, and endowed it with a yearly rent-charge of £8 out of the manor of Higham. The hospital is repaired at the expense of the parish. Five small tenements, near the churchyard, were given by *Thomas Pursglove*, in 1675, for the residence of poor parishioners, who are placed therein by the minister and churchwardens. The *Parish Lands* comprise 12A. 33P. in three closes, let for £15. 11s., and about one acre enclosed within the park of Sir J. R. Rowley, who pays for it a yearly rent of 21s. For many years, the rent of these lands has been paid to the minister for preaching every Sunday afternoon. A *National School* in the village, and another on Leaven Heath, are supported by subscription.

STOKE-BY-NAYLAND.

*Marked * are at Leaven Heath; and † in Thorrington Street*

Boggis Mary, Post Office. Letters to Colchester, &c. at 7 evening
Boggis George, saddler, &c.
*Bouttell John, beerhouse keeper
Crooks John, beerhouse and shopr
*Curry Rev Henry Thos. M.A. incumbent of *Leaven Heath*
Daking Robert, corn miller
Hoy Isaac, Esq. *Stoke Priory*
Huff John, vict. *Crown*
†Leving Mrs Mary Catherine, *Thorrington Cottage*
Mannock P. P. Esq. *Gifford's Hall, (abroad)*
North Rev Joseph, (Catholic,) *Gifford's Hall*
Pittock Wm. vict. *Angel*
Pryke Hanh. plumber, glzr. & pntr
Rowley Sir Joshua Ricketts, Bart. *Tendring Hall*
†Scowen Wm. vict. & maltsr. *Rose*
Torlesse Rev Chas. Mortimer, M.A. *Vicarage*

Academies.
*Govmar Edw. Nutton
Hudson My.Ann & Maria, *Hill House*

Simmons Rd. & Lucy, *(free)*
*Sparrow Jerh.

Blacksmiths.
Pittock Ann
Pittock Wm.
†Rouse Edw.

Butchers.
Hewes John, (& baker)
Pryke Henry
Stowe Wm.

FARMERS.
Cook Edward, *Scotland Hall*
Cook Hy. *Nether Hall*
Cook Edward, *Weylands*
*Dyer Thos.
Everard James, *Sheldrakes*
Frost Wm.
Hoy Wm. *Lower House*
Huff John
*Jelly Wm.

Johnson Isaac
Sadler
*Lewis W. P.
†Parson Henry
†Parson Edw.
Stannard Alfred, *Shadlow*
Wright Jacob
Wright Robt.

Grocers &Drprs.
Goddard Denis
Mortimer Saml. (& clothier)

Joiners, &c.
Blundon Thos.
Martin Wm.

Maltsters.
Palmer Jesse
Scowen Wm.

Shoemakers.
Chisnall Ephrm.
†Chisnall Thos.
Chisnall Wm.
Pooley Rd.

Tailors.
Hills Henry
Wilson Thos.

WALDINGFIELD, (GREAT) is a village and parish, 3 miles N.E. of Sudbury, containing 676 souls, 2423A. 2R. 2P. of fertile land, and several scattered houses, one of which is *Babergh Place*, once a seat of the Dawsons, but now occupied by a farmer. John Meadows Rodwell, Esq., is lord of the manors called *Brandeston Hall, Moreves,*

&c., but part of the soil belongs to the Mills, Graham, Pochin, Strutt, Hoy, Syer, Bacon, and a few other families. The *Church* (St. Lawrence) is a handsome structure, in the perpendicular style, with a tower and six bells. It was thoroughly repaired, beautified, and re-pewed, from 1826 to 1829, when 121 additional sittings were obtained. The east window is richly decorated with stained glass. Among the monuments are several belonging to the *Keddingtons*, formerly lords of the manors, which had anciently been held by the Corbonwell and Bouchier families. The *rectory*, valued in K.B. at £21. 6s. 8d., and in 1835 at £589, is in the gift of Clare Hall, Cambridge, and incumbency of the Rev Henry Kirby, M.A., who has a good residence, and 23a.1r.10p. of glebe. The tithes have recently been commuted for a yearly modus of £710 ; and the rector has also £80 a year from the tithes of Chilton. He established a National School here in 1842. The poor parishioners have a share of *Appleton's Charity*, as noticed with Edwardstone ; and here is a clothing club, and a parochial library.

Abery Wm. carpenter
Bruning Isaac, carpenter
Bugg Meschach, wheelwright
Kirby Rev Henry, M.A. *Rectory*
Poole Joshua, bricklayer
Sparrow Mr Joseph
  Beerhouses.
Andrews Saml.
Mayhew John
Mayhew Mary
Upton James
  Blacksmiths.
Goody Charles

Halls Edw.
Halls Wm.
  FARMERS.
(* *are Owners.*)
*Ayres Henry
Bacon Abraham, *Brook House*

*Brand Jno. Sparrow
Cady Geo. *Magna Farm*
Hills Jno. *Manor House*
Hills Thos. *Bergh Place*
Hills Wm.
Osborn John
Parson George
Pearson Chas.

Schofield James
Sergent Wm.
*Strutt Robert, *Bradleys*
Vince Susannah
Wade John Ablett, *Branderton Hall*

WALDINGFIELD, (LITTLE) 4½ miles N.E. of Sudbury, is a village and parish, containing 420 souls, and about 1700 acres of land, all freehold, and mostly a clayey loam. The Rev. B. B. Syer, of Ketton, is lord of the manor, owner of a great part of the soil, impropriator of the rectory, and patron and incumbent of the benefice, which is a discharged *vicarage*, valued in K.B. at £4. 18s. 11½d. In 1839, the great tithes were commuted for £217. 13s., and the small tithes for £146. 2s. per annum. The *Church* (St. Lawrence) is a neat fabric, with a tower and five bells. *Holbrook Hall*, a neat mansion, in a park of 43a., is now unoccupied. It belongs, with a large estate, to Chas. Hanmer, Esq. Mrs. Fowke, Mr. S. W. Sandford, and several smaller owners have estates in the parish. The *Wesleyans* have a chapel here. The poor have about 12 acres of land, left by *John Wincoll*, in 1580, and now let for £20. 10s. a year, which is distributed in January, together with £9, as the rent of a tenement, barn, and 8 acres of land at Washbrook, taken in exchange for land at Chelsworth, which had been purchased with £100 left to the poor by *Joshua Dove*, in 1728. *Mary Williamson*, in 1697, left £100 for apprenticing poor boys of this parish, and it was laid out in the purchase of 9a. 2r. 9p. of land at Felsham, now let for £10 a year. In 1608, *Isaac Appleton* left four tenements, adjoining the churchyard, for the residence of poor parishioners ; and here is another building called the *Pesthouse*, occupied by paupers, and repaired by the parish. The poor have a share of Edward Appleton's charity. (See Edwardstone.)

Cady George, vict. *Swan*
Cousins Edward, carrier to Ipswich,
  Monday, Wednesday, & Friday
Day Cornelius, beerhouse keeper
Fayers John, beerhouse keeper
Mills Thomas, shoemaker
Morley John, shoemaker
Poole John, shopkeeper

Smith Henry, blacksmith
FARMERS.
Brand Ann || Clarke Wm.
Deadman Robert
Sandford Sheppard Wm. *(owner)*
Spraggons Joseph, *Slough Hall*
Vincent John, *Wood Hall*
Wade Hy. Hoe || Vince Abm.

WISTON, sometimes called *Wissington*, is a parish of scattered houses on the north bank of the navigable river Stour, 1½ mile W. of Nayland, containing 252 souls, and about 1170 acres of land, belonging to — Beecroft, Esq., Sir J. R. Rowley, Bart., Charles Reeve, Esq., and a few smaller owners. The *Church* (St. Mary) is an ancient structure of Norman-architecture, with a small tower containing three bells. The organ and a new gallery were erected a few years ago. The Cluniac monks of Thetford had the advowson and appropriation, by gift of Robert, son of Godbold, but they gave them to their cell at Horkesey, in Essex. The vicarage, valued in K.B. at £4. 19s. 4½d., is endowed with the rectorial tithes, and is in the patronage of the Crown, and incumbency of the Rev. Charles Edward Birch, M.A., who has a good residence, and a yearly modus of £420. 18s. 5d., awarded in 1839. The *farmers* are George Holton, *Wiston Grove;* Benj. Keningale, *Wiston Hall;* Daniel Lewis, *Wiston Grange;* and John Rose, *Brook House.*

SUDBURY.

SUDBURY is an ancient borough and well-built market town, pleasantly situated on the east bank of the navigable river *Stour*, which separates it from Essex, and sweeps in a semicircular reach, round the western skirts of the town, and is crossed by a good bridge. It is the capital of the *Archdeaçonry, Deanery*, and *Union*, to which it gives name, and is distant 56 miles N.E. of London; 17 miles S. of Bury St. Edmund's; 22 miles W. by S. of Ipswich; 10½ miles W. of Hadleigh; and 7 miles E.S.E. of Clare. Its *population* amounted, in 1801, to 3283; in 1811, to 3471; in 1821, to 3950; in 1831, to 4677; and in 1841, to 5085 *souls*, living in 1051 *houses*, besides which here were 56 dwellings unoccupied and 9 building, when the census was taken in the latter year. Its *parishes of All Saints, St. Gregory*, and *St. Peter*, comprise about 1250 acres of land, (see page 537,) and were incorporated for the maintenance of their poor, as one township, by an act of Queen Anne, under the management of a number of *"governors and guardians,"* constituted a body corporate, of which the mayor and aldermen are members; but Sudbury now forms one of the members of a large *Union* under the new poor law, as noticed at page 537. Besides the three united parishes, the old borough comprises an *extra-parochial* house and 204 acres of land, on the north side of the town, called *St. Bartholomew*, being the site of a priory, and now the property of the Dean and Chapter of Westminster. By the *Parliamentary and Municipal Reform Acts* of 1832 and 1835, the BOROUGH of SUDBURY has been extended to the township or parochial chapelry of *Ballingdon-cum-*

Brundon, which lies on the opposite side of the Stour, in Hinckford Hundred, Essex, and comprises 730 acres, and 843 inhabitants.   Sudbury gives the title of *baron* to the Duke of Grafton, by creation in 1675.   (Vide page 687.)   It first sent two members to parliament in 1559, and its *government*, previous to 1835, was vested in a mayor, recorder, six aldermen, a bailiff, town clerk, 24 common councilmen, and two serjeants-at mace.   Under the new municipal act, the borough is included in schedule A. amongst boroughs, to have a *commission of the peace* and a *court of quarter sessions ;* and in section I. of that schedule, amongst those the parliamentary boundaries of which are to be taken until altered by parliament.   Under the same act, the *Town Council* now consists of a mayor, four aldermen, and twelve councillors. It is not divided into wards.   The *income* of the corporation, in 1840, arising from rents, tolls, and dues, was £146. 2s. 6d., and the *expenditure* £315. 19s. 10d., of which the principal items were, salaries £96, rents, taxes, &c., £87 ; public works, £33`; and police and constables, £23. 13s.   Prior to the passing of the Reform Act of 1832, the *elective franchise* was enjoyed only by the freemen, of whom there were upwards of 700, but many of them being resident in distant places are now disfranchised.   The number of *voters*, registered in 1841, was 603, consisting of 133 occupiers of houses of the yearly value of £10 or upwards, and 470 freemen.   Some of the latter are also respectable householders, but the poorer part of them are sufficiently numerous to swamp the remainder in a contested election.   In consequence of corrupt practices at the last general election in 1841, the two members then elected were unseated, and proceedings have since been in progress in parliament for the *disfranchisement* of the borough, for which purpose, a bill passed the House of Commons in May, 1843, but on being brought before the Lords on the 19th of that month, it was moved and carried that it should be read " that day six months."   After this, a motion was made in the Commons for the issuing of a new writ, but it was lost by a majority of 113, " for leave to bring in a bill for *effectually* enquiring into the bribery and corruption alleged to exist at Sudbury."   This inquiry is still in progress, (Dec., 1843,) and Sudbury is, in the meantime, virtually disfranchised, but has some hopes of recovering its former privilege, as its corruption has not been greater than that of Stafford and some other boroughs, which have been allowed to retain the franchise, after the grossest cases of bribery had been proved against them.   The *Town Hall* and *Borough Gaol* form a neat and commodious range of buildings, on Market hill, erected about sixteen years ago.   In the former, the quarter and petty sessions, assemblies, and public meetings, are held.   The old Town Hall was taken down in 1843.   The BOROUGH MAGISTRATES are Col. Addison, Alex. Duff, Branwhite Oliver, Wm. Bestoe Smith, and John James, Esqrs.   The TOWN COUNCIL and OFFICERS are Thos. Jones, Esq., *mayor ;* Jas. Manning, Esq., *recorder ;* G. W. Andrews, Thos. Goldsmith, Thos. Fox, and John Purr, Esqrs., *aldermen ;* Messrs.W. Hill, T. Meeking, A. S. Syer, H. T. Jones,W. C. Adams, T. Jones, J. Jones, W. B. Smith, G. Lambert, W. Musgrave, R. G. Tovell, and J. Parsson, *councillors ;* Messrs. Wm. Spooner and J. Bridgman, *assessors ;* Edm. Stedman, Esq., *town clerk* and *clerk to the magistrates ;* Wm. Dowman, Esq., *clerk of the peace and coroner ;* Messrs. B. Pratt and W. Warner, *auditors ;* W. R. Bevan,

Esq., *treasurer ;* S. Scott and G. Herbert, *serjeants-at-mace ;* Mr. Jas.
Parsson, sen., *chief constable and bailiff ;* Jas. French and Thos. Al-
bury, *rangers of the commons and conservators of the river ;* Peter Richards Cross, *gaoler ;* Wm. Strutt, *crier ;* and Mr. Geo. Williams Fulcher, *inspector of corn returns.* On Dec. 3rd, 1836, fifteen CHARITY
TRUSTEES were appointed to manage the numerous charities vested with
the corporation.

Sudbury was incorporated at an early period, and was anciently denominated *South-burgh,* in contradistinction to Norwich, then called
North-burgh. It was one of the first places at which Edward III. settled the Flemings, whom he invited to this country, to instruct his subjects to manufacture their own wool. Various branches of the *woollen
manufacture* continued to flourish here for some centuries, and afforded
subsistence to a great number of the inhabitants, but they declined many
years ago, except that of *bunting,* for ships' flags, of which here are still
four manufacturers. Here are also four large establishments employing a considerable number of hands in the manufacture of *silk, velvet,
satin, &c.* This trade was introduced here in the early part of the present century, by the London mercers, on account of dearness of labour
in Spitalfields. In 1838, there were about 600 silk looms in the town
and neighbourhood, but half of them were out of employment, in consequence of the general depression in that year. The *Stour* was made
navigable to Sudbury in 1706, by a body of *commissioners,* who levy
tolls for the support and improvement of the navigation. Here is a
commodious *quay,* where a number of barges are employed in the transit of corn, malt, coals, &c. The *Town* has two highly respectable
banking houses, several corn mills, and a number of malt-kilns. It is
neat, clean, and well-built, and is *lighted, paved, and watched,* under
the powers of a local act, obtained a few years ago for its improvement.
The *Gas-works* were erected in 1836, at the cost of £5000, raised in
£20 shares. The MARKET, formerly held on Saturday, is now held
on Thursday, and is an extensive mart for corn, sold by sample. The
Corn Exchange, on the Market hill, is an elegant and convenient building, which was erected in 1840, for £1620, but the builder is said to
have lost several hundred pounds by the contract. Three *fairs* are
held here on March 12th, July 10th, and Sept. 4th.

The three PARISH CHURCHES of Sudbury are spacious and handsome structures. ALL SAINTS' has a tower and six bells, and is a
vicarage, valued in K.B. at £4. 11s. 5½d., and in 1835, at £123. J.
Sperling, Esq., is patron and impropriator, and the Rev. T. W. Fowke
incumbent. The trustees of the late Rev. C. Simeon have purchased
the next presentation. *All Saints' Parish* had 1262 inhabitants in
1841, exclusive of the chapelry and township of *Ballingdon-cum-
Brundon,* which was formerly a separate parish, and lies on the opposite
side of the Stour, in Essex, as noticed at page 571. The church,
which stood at Brundon, went to decay many years ago, and the sine-
cure rectory is in the impropriation of Admiral Wyndham, who allows
the vicar of All Saints' a yearly stipend of £13. 6s. 8d., in consideration of which, the inhabitants here have the use of that church. ST.
GREGORY'S and ST. PETER'S, the former having eight, and the latter
six bells, are united *perpetual curacies,* valued, in 1835, at £160, and
now enjoyed by the Rev. Henry Watts Wilkinson. *Sir Lachlan Mac-*

lean, Kt., is patron, and has a considerable estate in the two parishes. He has long been a distinguished physician here, and was knighted in 1812. Here are two *Independent Chapels,* one built in 1839, and the other erected in 1822, in lieu of the old Presbyterian Meeting-house, which was built about 1710, by a congregation formed in 1662. The latter has an endowment for the minister and the support of a school. Here is also an old *Friends' Meeting-house,* and a *Baptist Chapel,* erected in 1834.

SIMON DE SUDBURY, who was Archbishop of Canterbury in 1375, was a native of this town, and was beheaded by the populace in Wat Tyler's insurrection. His family name was Theobald. He built one end of St. Gregory's church, and on the spot where his father's house stood, he founded and endowed a *College* for six secular priests, dedicated to St. Gregory, and valued at the dissolution at £122 per annum. The same prelate, in conjunction with John de Chertsey, is said by Leland to have founded an *Augustine Priory* here, but Weever ascribes it to Baldwin de Shimpling and Mabel, his wife, who were both interred in the priory church. This priory was valued, at the dissolution, at £222. 18s. 3d. per annum. The last remains of it were pulled down in 1821. In the reign of King John, Amicia, Countess of Clare, founded an *Hospital* here, dedicated to Christ and the Virgin Mary; and here was a *Lepers' Hospital,* dedicated to St. Leonard. A chapel, dedicated to *St. Bartholomew,* was built near the former hospital, by Wulfric, master of the mint to King Henry II., and given to the abbot and convent of Westminster, who founded near it a subordinate priory of Benedictine monks. This priory was pulled down in 1779, and its site belongs to the Dean and Chapter of Westminster, as noticed at page 571. THOS. GAINSBOROUGH, one of the most eminent English painters of the 18th century, was born here in 1727, and at a very early age, manifested a remarkable propensity for the art in which he was destined so highly to excel. He fixed his residence in London in 1774, after residing some years at Ipswich and Bath, and was soon afterwards patronised by George III., of whom, as well as of many other members of the royal family, he painted excellent portraits. He died in 1788, and was buried at Kew. His brother, a dissenting minister at Henley-upon-Thames, possessed as strong a genius for mechanics as he had for painting, and one of his sun-dials, of ingenious contrivance, is now in the British Museum. WM. ENFIELD, L.L.D., an eminent Unitarian minister, was born at Sudbury in 1741. He was for some years tutor and lecturer at Warrington Academy, and compiled many useful books, one of which is the "*Speaker,*" composed of pieces for recitation, from the best English authors. He published in quarto, "*Institutes of Natural Philosophy,*" and undertook the arduous task of abridging *Buckler's History of Philosophy,* which appeared in 1791, in two volumes quarto. He died in 1797, at Norwich, where he had been twelve years minister of the Octagon chapel, in that city. The numerous list of subscribers to his posthumous *Sermons,* in 3 vols. 8vo., attest the general estimation in which his writings were held. Sudbury has a DISPENSARY, and other institutions, supported by subscription; several *school endowments,* and many *Charitable Bequests,* for the relief of the poor.

GRAMMAR SCHOOL.—In 1491, *Wm. Wood*, master or warden of the *College of Sudbury*, bequeathed a messuage and croft, and the enclosures adjacent, in **the** lane leading from the house of the *Friars Preachers* to the church of St. Gregory, to sixteen feoffees, in trust that the warden of the said college, and his successors, should hire and place in the said messuage a good and honest man to teach **gram-** mar, and daily teach boys and others resort.ng to him for instruction. On **the** dissolution of the religious houses, the possessions of Sudbury College **became** vested in the Crown; and Henry VIII., by letters patent, in the 36th year of **his** reign, in consideration of £1280, granted to *Sir Thos. Paston, Kt.*, and his **heirs** and assigns, the house and possessions of the said college, and the rectories **of** St. Gregory and St. Peter. Since the date of these letters patent, the **successive** appropriators of the said rectories have appointed the master of the **Grammar** School who has usually been perpetual curate of the parish of St. Gregory. **The** school property derived under William Wood's will, consists of a dwelling-house, school, garden, and 1½A. of pasture ground. In addition to this property, **the** late Rev. W. Finley, who died in 1817, and his predecessors, the masters of **the** school as far as can be traced, received the rents of a farm of 95 acres, at **Maple-** stead, in Essex, now worth £90 a year; but some doubt as to the actual right **of** the masters of the school to this farm, has been raised since that period, in **con-** sequence of there being no means of discovering how such right originated; **and** also because the farm is not specifically described in the conveyance deeds of **the** rectory, &c., as part of the school property, though it is enumerated in the **par-** cels of property, &c., immediately after that clause which gives the right of **ap-** pointing the master of the free school to the impropriate rector. Sir **Lachlan** Maclean, M.D., the present lay rector, and consequently patron of the school, did not appoint a master to the school, after the death of Mr. Finley, in 1817, **till** 1827, when he nominated his son, then a minor, and at college. Since 1817, **Sir** L. Maclean has retained the rents of the farm at Maplestead, but has **expended** about £700 in rebuilding the master's house, and enclosing the school-ground, and has allowed the premises to be occupied at a small rent, by a person **whom** he required to teach six free scholars. The Commissioners, after enquiring **into** the state of this school, in 1828, recommended the aid and directions of a **Court** of Equity for establishing or determining its right to the farm at Maplestead, which is still the subject of a suit in Chancery.

NATIONAL AND CHARITY SCHOOLS, IN NORTH STREET.—In 1724, *Susan Girling* devised to five trustees her messuages, lands, and hereditaments, **in** Hitcham and Wattisham, and her share in a real estate at Preston, on trust, **to** apply the rents and profits in teaching and instructing poor children of **Sudbury,** such as the trustees should think fit. The property described as being at **Hitcham** and Wattisham consists of a house, barn, and 10A. 3R. 29P. of land, in the **pa-** rishes of Hitcham and Brettenham, and is now worth about 20l. a year. **The** real estate at Preston was given up for land at Pentlow, in Essex, let for 7l. **a-** year. In 1747, a *subscription* was entered into for building a school, and **extend-** ing Mrs. Girling's charity; and the money raised was laid out in the **purchase of** premises in North street, which are vested in trust with the perpetual curate **of** St. Peter's; as to part thereof, for the use of a master and mistress, to be **ap-** pointed by Girling's trustees, for teaching poor boys and girls; and the **other** parts to be let, and the rents applied for placing out two or three boys, from **the** school, apprentices to trades in any place except Sudbury. The premises **have** been partly rebuilt, and comprise a house for the master, and a large **school-room** and garden; a house for the mistress, and a school-room for girls; and three **te-** nements, with a quarter of an acre of land, let for 13l. a year. In 1775, the **Rev.** *Wm. Maleham* left 50l. to these schools, and it was laid out in the **purchase of** 60l. 1s. 2d. three per cent. consols. Both schools are now conducted on the **na-** tional system, and they are attended by about 150 boys and 50 girls. Here **is** also an *Infant School*, supported by subscription.

Charity Schools, &c., in All Saints.—In 1722, JOHN FENN left a house in **All** Saints, and two acres of land in Friar's Meadow, in trust, to apply 4l. 10s. **yearly** in schooling poor children of Sudbury, and to pay the residue of the rents to **the** minister of the *Presbyterian Chapel*, towards his maintenance. In 1738, *Thos.* *Gainsborough* left a sufficient sum of money to be laid out for paying 10l. **a-year** to the Presbyterian or Independent minister of Sudbury; 2l. 10s. a year for **sup-** porting the charity school there; and 20s. a-year for the trustees. An **estate** was purchased at Westley field, near Bury St. Edmund's, for the benefit of **the**

minister, subject to the two last named annuities. The schoolmistress receives 8*l*. per annum from the two charities, for which she teaches ten poor children to read. In 1719, JOHN LITTEL conveyed to six trustees a house, stable, and garden, in Sepulchre street, in trust, to apply the rents in schooling three poor children of All Saints parish, and three of Ballingdon hamlet. The premises are let for 10*l*. a-year, out of which the trustees pay 9*l*. to a schoolmaster, for teaching 12 poor children to read. In 1790, the *Rev. Henry Crossman* left the dividends of 300*l*. three per cent. stock towards the support of three *Sunday Schools*, at Sudbury, Little Cornard and Little Bromley ; 5s. to be expended yearly out of the share of each school, in the purchase of the testator's Explanation of the Catechism. In 1712, *John Jessup* left a yearly rent-charge of 20s. out of the Bear public-house, to be distributed one year in Bibles and Common Prayer Books, and another year in the "Whole Duty of Man," among the poor of Sudbury, attending the church.

ST. LEONARD'S HOSPITAL was founded by *John Colneys*, in the reign of Edward III.; and certain statutes were made for its regulation, in 1372, by the Bishop of Norwich, with the consent of the founder, whereby it was provided that it should consist of three infirm or leprous persons,—viz., a master and two fellows,—and that the mayor of Sudbury, and the spiritual father of the church of St. Gregory should be visitors. The estates of the hospital were vested in feoffees in the 24th of Henry VII., but no subsequent feoffment can be found. The hospital is situated near the town, on the road to Long Melford, and contains three separate dwellings, with a garden adjoining. The only endowment consists of nearly five acres of land, in two fields, near the hospital. For a long period before and after 1813, the vacancies in the hospital were not filled up, and the charity was grossly abused. In 1822, there being only one person living in the hospital, (a man named Rayner,) and he being driven to apply for parochial relief, *the governors and guardians of the poor of Sudbury* (who are a body corporate, created by an act of the reign of Anne) prevailed on him and the tenant of the land to execute a deed of feoffment, conveying the hospital and land to them, and they have since let the hospital in tenements to poor persons, at low rents, which, with the rent of the land, they have applied with the poor rates. The income which they derive from the hospital and land is about 18*l*. per annum.

In 1662, RICHARD FIRMAN left 4A. of land at Windmill hill, to the mayor and aldermen, in trust, to divide the rents yearly as follows : one moiety among the poor of St. Peter's, and the other among the poor of All Saints and St. Gregory's parishes. The land is let for 8*l*. per annum. In 1620, MARTIN COLE bequeathed out of Shemford Mills, in Henny, and two meadows in Lamarsh, in Essex, a yearly rent-charge of 14*l*. to certain trustees, upon trust, to pay 10*l*. for linen cloth, and 1*l*. for making it into *shirts and smocks*, to be distributed, on the Monday after Ascension day, among the poor of the three parishes of Sudbury—one-half to those of St. Peter's ; 6s. 8d. each to the ministers of St. Peter's and All Saints, for sermons; 6s. 8d. for the town clerk ; and 2*l*. to be spent in a love-feast, by the two ministers and the corporation, in remembrance of the testator. In 1668, NATHANIEL KING bequeathed to the corporation the George Inn, in Sudbury, in trust, to pay yearly out of the rent thereof, 50s., to be distributed in 6d. loaves to the poor men and women receiving shirts and shifts from Cole's charity ; 2s. to be spent in wine at the love-feast ; and the remainder of the rent to be laid out in *coats of grey cloth*, to be distributed by the churchwardens and overseers of St. Peter's, among the poorest aged men of that parish. The inn is now let for 32*l*. a year, on a 21 years' lease, which will expire in 1847. THOMAS CARTER, in 1706, charged his houses and lands, at Pebmarsh, Gestingthorpe, and Little Maplestead, in Essex, with the yearly payment of 60*l*., to provide 50 coats and 50 cloaks for 50 poor men and 50 poor women of Sudbury, on St. Thomas's day ; 10s. for a sermon at St. Gregory's church ; and 20s. for a love-feast for the minister and trustees, on the day of distribution. The estate charged is now the property of Mr. Carter, of Lowestoft. In 1718, ROGER SCARLIN charged his house and land, at Boxford, with the yearly sum of 10*l*., to be distributed in stockings and shoes among the poor people receiving Carter's charity. In 1724, SUSAN GIRLING devised to five trustees her tenements and gardens in Sudbury, and an acre of land in Friar's meadow, upon trust to provide yearly 50 shirts and 50 shifts, of hempen cloth, for the poor people partaking of Carter's charity ; and to allow 10s. yearly for a dinner for the trustees, on the day of distribution. The tenements having fallen into decay, were let with the land

in 1819, on a 31 years' lease, to R. P. Witts, at the yearly rent of 34*l*., the lessee covenanting to expend 350*l*. on the premises, which has been done. The funds of this charity being more than adequate for its purposes, it has been recommended that the surplus (about 10*l*. a year) should be applied in aid of the charity given for education by the same donor, as already noticed. The recipients of Carter's charity have also divided among them 4*l*. per annum. given by the corporation, perhaps in lieu of several *" lost charities."* About 26s. per annum is distributed in each of the three parishes of Sudbury, among the poor, from *Corder's Charity.* (See Glemsford.) In 1718, *John Cradock* bequeathed to the poor of the parishes of St. Gregory and St. Peter, the interest of 100*l*., which, with some interest thereon, was laid out in the purchase of 200*l*. new four per cent. annuities. The dividends are distributed at Christmas, by the incumbent of St. Gregory's and other trustees. A yearly rent-charge of 7*l*. 16s., left by an unknown donor, out of *Outfield,* near Boxford, is applied in a weekly distribution of 1s. worth of bread in each of the three parishes. The following *yearly rentcharges* are distributed in doles of bread by the mayor and corporation, on Ascension day; viz., 16s., left by *Wm. Alston,* in 1564, out of a house adjoining the Rose and Crown; 30s. left by *Robert Paternoster,* in 1591, out of a farm at Pentlow; 20s. left by *Henry Pilgrome,* in 1592, out of the site of a house adjoining the White Horse; and 20s. left by *Thos. Jervis,* in 1631, out of a timber yard, belonging to Mr. Hawkins. At the same time, 6s. 8d. in money is distributed in each parish from an annuity of twenty shillings charged by an unknown donor on five houses in St. Peter's parish. Several charities, left to Sudbury by persons named Polley, Andrews, Crowe, and Newman, are lost; and nothing has been received for many years from the charity of *John Hunwick,* who, in 1593, gave 300*l*. to the corporation of Colchester, to the intent that they should pay certain annual sums for charitable purposes at Colchester, Malden, and Ipswich, and also 10*l*. once every five years to the Mayor of Sudbury, for the poor there.

Among the provident institutions of Sudbury are several *Friendly Societies* and a *Savings' Bank.* The latter was established in 1822, and had deposits amounting, in 1842, to 20,979*l*., belonging to 611 individuals, 19 charitable societies, and 30 friendly societies. It is open every Tuesday, from eleven to one o'clock, and Mr. B. Pratt is the actuary. Here is a *Mechanics' Institution,* established in 1834, and now having a *Museum,* commenced in 1841.

SUDBURY DIRECTORY.

Post-Office at Mr. Alex. Frost's, Friar street. Letters are despatched at a quarter-past 7 morning and evening, to Colchester, London, &c., and at 20 min. past 6 morning and evening, to Bury, Norfolk, &c.

*Those marked * are in Ballingdon-cum-Brundon, Essex ; 1, are in Borehamgate ; 2, Church street ; 3, Cross street ; 4, Friar street ; 5, Gregory street ; 6, King st. ; 7, Market hill ; 8, North street ; 9, Old Market place ; 10, Quay ; 11, Stour st. ; 12, Wicken end ; and the others in Sepulchre st., or where specified.*

Addison Mrs Anna || Adams Mrs C.
11 Barley John, horse dealer
Barnard Mr Wm. Sepulchre street
4 Barwick James, bird, &c. preserver
Bass Wm. corn mert; h Market hill
Bates David Nicholas, surgeon
* Bear Wm. millwgt. & machine mkr
7 Bevan Wm. Robert, Esq., banker
3 Bonny James, plasterer
7 Brown Stephen, corn merchant
1* Brown James, bankers' clerk
2 Brown Wm. farrier

3 Collins Samuel, lath render
3 Crane Alexander, coach builder
7 Cross Peter Richards, gaoler
Dakin Miss Sarah, Mill hill
4 Dansie Jacob, tea dealer
2 Dupont Alfred, carriers' agent
1 Durrell J. registrar of marriages
3 Elliston Miss Sarah
*Ellison Wm. straw plat manufactr
4 Fenn Richard, grocer, &c
Fowke Rev Thorpe Wm. *Vicarage*
*Fox Thomas, brewer
French Mr Saml. || 8 Fitch Mrs E.
4 Frost Alexander, postmaster
Gainsborough Miss || 8 Godfrey Miss
11 Garnham Joseph, gentleman
Goldsmith Misses Eliz. & Charlotte
4 Green Thomas, road surveyor
*Griffiths Mr John
4 Grubb Jonathan, gentleman
6 Harcourt Henry, gun maker and cutlery dealer
Harvey Wm. govr. Union Workhs
1 Hawkins Wm. & Charles, timber and slate merchants
4 Heard Miss S. || 9 Hodge Miss E.

*Heard Jeremiah, land surveyor
Holman John, gentleman
11 Humphry Wm. Wood, Esq. barristr. & distr. of stamps for Suffolk
4 Hurrell Miss Henriette
Jackson Rev Geo. Henry, (Indept)
11 Jennings Jonth. James, farrier
3 Jones Arthur, appraiser
14 Jones Brayshaw, gentleman
8 Jones Mrs Sarah
4 Keeble Samuel, gentleman
4 King Wm. D. bank agent
8 Lillie Wm. bankers' clerk
9 Ling John, clerk
4 Maclean Lady Lachlan
Mills Rev. Simon, School lane
*Mills and Green, lime burners and brick makers
Murray Charles, surgeon
3 Overall Isaac, fellmonger
4 Parsonson Richard and William, carvers and gilders
Parsson James, sen. chief constable
8 Phillips Mrs Alice
4 Pratt Benj. actuary, Savings' Bank
4 Ransom Robert, solicitor, &c
3 Rae Wm. travelling tea dealer
4 Ray Charles, coal merchant
6 Revell Miss Mary
* Robinson Ling, millwright
8 Rose Mrs || Rogers Mrs Sarah
3 Saxby James, dyer
4 Sayer Meshach, gentleman
1 Scott Joseph, clerk || 11 Sims Mrs
Skrimshire Arthur James, M.D.
*Sparrow Wm. gent. & Mrs Ann
Stedman Edmund, solicitor, town & union clerk, supt. registrar, &c.; house, *Belle vue*
Stedman Robert Frost, solicitor
*Steggles Wm. registrar, &c
Strutt Wm. town crier
4 Syer Abraham Stevens, grocer, &c
4 Thresher Miss Ann
Tiffen Henry, solr ; h Meadow lane
11 Tozer Miss Frances
5 Tull Rev Henry, M.A. curate of St Gregory's and St Peter's
4 Wallis Rev. Wm. (Independent)
4 Warner Wm. inspector of weights and measures
Warner John, gent. Castle end
6 Welham John Wm. grocer, &c
4 Wilkinson Rev. Henry Watts, incbt. of St Gregory's & St Peter's
7 Wright Jas. glass, china, &c. dlr
Wyatt Mrs Elizabeth, Curds lane

BANKERS.
4 Alexanders & Co. (on Barnett, Hoare, and Co.) D. W. King, agt
Oakes, Bevan, Moor & Bevan (on Barclay & Co.) Mill hill

FIRE AND LIFE OFFICES.
4 Atlas, Ransom & Tiffen
9 Clerical & Medical, Hy. Harding
7 County (Fire) and Provident (Life) Henry Steed
7 Essex, Bass & Brown
4 Family Endowment, George Ely
7 Farmers', G. W. Fulcher
6 Globe, Syer, Fenn, and Welham
4 Mercantile, Benjamin Mills
7 National Provident, E. Wright
4 Phœnix and Provident, W. King
4 Royal Exch., Wm. Dowman, sen
4 Suffolk Amicable, W. King
7 Western (Life) S. Joscelyne

INNS AND TAVERNS.
4 Anchor, Alice Must
4 Angel, James Sillitoe
1 Bear, Thomas Mills, jun
7 Black Boy, James Balls
2 Bull, Stepn. Spurgeon (cement dlr)
11 Castle, Wm. Byford
Christopher Inn, Nehemiah Rogers Parsson
7 George, Robert Shelley
8 Green Dragon, Thomas Dixey
8 Horn, Ambrose Sillitoe
*King's Head, Js. Marriott Parsson
8 Lion, Johnson Double
11 Rose, Charles Edey
6 Rose & Crown Inn, & Posting hs. Wm. Baker (and vety. surgeon)
1 Royal Oak, Wm. Gooch
Swan (unoccupied)
Waggon and Horses, Shadrach Clover, Acton green
5 White Horse, John Clarke (and excise office)
*White Hart, George Gall Gross

Academies.	11†Thorn John
(† *take Boarders.*)	8 Tourner W. J.
11 Blackman Rt.	(French)
Grammar School,	Whitford Ann
(in Chancery)	*Attorneys.*
†Harridge Sophia	4 Andrews Geo.
11 † Hasell Jas.	William
(& surveyor)	4 Dowman Wm.
†Hindes Eliza	sen. (and clerk
National, Wm.	of peace, co-
Hodson & Sus.	roner, &c.)
Ginn	4 Dowman Wm.
5 Leggett Cornls.	jun.

8 Gooday John Fras. Sikes
4 Ransom and Tiffen
1 Stedman Edmd. and Son
11 Walsh Francis Eldridge
Auctioneers.
7 Blunden and Rolfe
Hurrell Reymes, Croft green
7 Jocelyne Saml. (& land agent)
Bakers, &c.
4 Berry Wm.
8 Clark George
8 Clark Thos.
3 Cook Thos.
3 Cross Wm.
3 Coates George
Digby William, School lane
*Farrow John
2 Goody Harriet
3 Goody Jph.
8 Goody Robert
4 Hale Wm.
*Hasell Jas.
Jones Alfred
1 King James
8 King Thos.
*Rashbrook Rt.
Sadler Thomas, Mill lane
12 Strutt George
5 Strutt John
Basket Makers.
8 Parsonson Chs.
Parsonson Geo., Acton green
*Parsonson Geo.
1 Parsonson Rd.
Beer Houses.
*Carter Mary
8 Dent Thos.
Elliston Samuel, Plough lane
*King Sarah
4 Sillitoe Thos.
12 Strutt George
Blacksmiths.
Frost Jas.Jail ln
4 Gooch Oliver
*Hale Jas.

* Hawkins Jas. (&*ironfounder*)
12 Shelley Jas.
5 Shelley Saml.
Booksellers, Printers, &c.
8 Fitch Alfred
7 Fulcher Geo. Williams
*Hill William, (printer only)
7 Large Jas. (& portrait pntr.)
Boot&ShoeMkrs.
8 Bonney John
4 Burton Jph. W.
Deeks Hy. Jas.
2 Elliott Thos.
* Ely Thomas
Everard Edmd.
4 Fawx Benj.
2 Golding Geo.
8 Goody Baker
8 Goody Thos.
* Hart Wm.
3 Herbert Wm.
4 Mays John Whitlock
3 Mears Wm.
Sillitoe Jonthn., Acton green
7 Steed Henry
8 Strutt Wm.
Ward Thomas
Wilson John
4 Woolby Wm.
Braziers & Tnrs.
4 Beard Joseph
7 Bowen Wm.
Ixer Rt. Straw ln
Purr John
3 Ravenell Wm.
Worts Mannister
Bricklayers.
3 Cook Thos.
1 Ginn Thos.
Green Abishai Js.
12 Grimwood W. and Son
3 Webb Richd.
Butchers.
7 Bear Eliz.
8 Brown Saml.
3 Collis Jph.
7 Collis Saml.
3 Collis Walter
Frost Jacob

8 Golding Herbt.
2 Joscelyne Isc.
3*Plum Saml.
8 Segers Chas.
8 Ward David
Cabinet Makers.
2 Brand John
7 Joscelyne Sml.
4 Murrells Ambrose
3 Prior John
4 Smith Alfred
*Spring John
Turner William, Way lane
Chemists & Drgs.
4 Ely George
9 Harding Hy.
6 Lowdell Thld.
7 Oxley John Ransome
Coal Merchants.
Allen Rt. Alfred, (brick maker & lime burner,) Grove
4 Jones Hy. Ts.
11 Musgrave W.
10 Ray & Hibble
10 Tovell & Co.
Confectioners.
4 Sillitoe Fras.
7 Wells Thos.
Coopers.
Hitchcock Geo.
*Newton Wm.
8 Rudd Edward
Corn Dealers.
Allen Rt. Alfred, Grove
9 Barker Joseph
7 Bass & Brown
*Hasell James
Corn Millers.
Alston William, Newton road
*Cook Edmd.
Mason Joseph, Sudbury mills
*Orbell John, Brundon mill
Curriers, &c.
*Fox Thos.
8 Lambert Geo.
FARMERS.
12 Dupont Gainsborough

12 Jones Thos.
Meeking Thos. *Wood Hall*

Fruiterers.
(† *are Fishmgrs.*)
†Brock Wm.
†7 Rudd Jonth.
Wheeler Edw.
Furniture Brks.
7 Berry Samuel
8 Frost Mark
Gardeners.
7 Bass & Brown, (seedsmen and florists)
3 Davis Chas.
Davis George, Acton green
4 Ling Samuel
Glovers.
1 Durham Jas.
1 Habberton Ts. Wm.
Grocers.
8 Abrey Henry
9 Barker Jph.
7 Browning Edw.
3 Cook Thos.
8 Cook Wm.
Edwards John
4 Frost Josiah
*Hale Samuel
6 Syer, Fenn, and Welham, (and Stamp office)
8 Westropp Hale William
7 Wright Edw.
Hatters.
8 Burrows Jas.
4 King Wm.
4 Spooner Wm.

Ironmongers.
4 Beard Jph.
7 Bowen Wm.
1 Jones John
Purr John
8 Simpkin Spark
Joiners.
8 Ginn James
8 Jones Wm.
1 Mills Thos. sen.
4 Sillitoe Jas.
8 Sillitoe Andw.
Underwood Edw.

Linen & Woollen Drapers.

8 Boggis Edmd.
7 Bridgman John
*Constable Gdng.
*Cook Wm.
7 Edwards E.
6 Hunter Andw.
4 King Wm.
4 Spooner Wm.

Maltsters.

Allen Rt. Alfred, Grove
11 Byford Wm.
4 Death Robt.
8 Hibble & Higgs
4 Jones Hy. Ts.
11 Musgrave W.

Milliners, &c.

7 Moore Sophia
3 Murray Amelia
Witts Frances
4 Woolby Rbca.

Painters, Plumbers, & Glaziers.

6 Anderton Chas.
Byford James
Jones Jacob
1 Mills Chas.
*Strout John
4 Taylor Jph.

Pawnbroker.

4 Mauldon Jas.

Perfumers and Hair Dressers.

6 Davis John
7 Ely W. Waylen
8 Bulmer John
Rice Geo. Hy.
*Rice Stephen
2 Seagrave Jph.
7 Simkin Wm.

Saddlers, &c.

*King Rebecca
8 Ready Edw.
4 Smith Robt.
7 Westoby John

Shopkeepers.

5 Andrews Thos.
Bacon James
*Green Danl.
8 Ling Wm.
3 Webb Saml.
5 Woods James

SILK MANFRS.

Duff & Peacock, Christopher ln
3 Edmunds John
2 Foot Jph. and Son
Hill James & Co.

Silversmiths.

*Aprile Jph.
7 Debenham Wm.
4 Hills Benj.

Stone Masons.

*Harding Jph.
2 Leaning John

Straw Hat Mkrs.

4 Dansie Jacob
Deeks Jane
8 Mears Susanna
3 Murray Amelia

Surgeons.

Mason Maurice
Murray & Bates
6 Smith William Bestoe

Tailors & Drprs.

5 Andrews Thos.
8 Boreham Thos.
8 Driver Thos.
1 Goldsmith Ts.
8 Hart John
*Hart W. Davis
8 Hitchcock John
4 King Wm.
7 Mills Robt.
5 Parsson John
Pemberton Jph.
7 Ready George
Smith John
*Todd Charles

Turners in Wood.

8 Sillitoe Andw.
4 Sillitoe James
10 Turner Wm.

Watch and Clock Makers.

8 Ambrose Jas. Christopher
6 Dawson Geo.
7 Debenham Wm.
4 Hills Benj.
*Howes Henry

Wheelwrights.

8 Dixey Thos.

COACHES.

To London, ¾ bef. 9 mg., and ¼ bef. 12 noon, from the Rose and Crown; at 4 and ½ past 8 mg. from the Swan; & at 6 mg, from the Christopher Inn.

To Bury, at ½ past 3 aftn. & 7 evng., from the Rose & Crown; at ½ past 6 evg. from the Black Boy and the Swan; and at ½ past 12 noon from the Swan.

To Colchester, the mail, from the Swan at half-past 7 evening.

To Norwich, at ½ past 12 noon, from the Rose and Crown.

CARRIERS.

To London, Wm. Sykes, Sepulchre st. daily; Geo. Whorlow, Church st., Tues. and Fri.; and E. Salter, from the Royal Oak, Sunday, Tue. & Fri.
Bures, (Royal Oak) Layzell Thu. & S.
Bury, T. Elliott, Church st. Wed. and Sat., & W. Ruggles (Black Boy) W.
Cavendish, — Farrance (Golden Lion) Thursday and Saturday.
Clare, Wm. Golding (Golden Lion) & Wm. Elmer (Bear) Tuesday & Sat.
Colchester, D. Bray (Anchor) Friday.
Norwich, *Bury*, &c., W. Sykes, Sepulchre street, daily.
Hartest, I. Snazell (Angel) Mon. & Fri.
Hadleigh, W. Mann (Bear) Tu. & Sat.
Ipswich, W. Ruggles (Black Boy) Mon. and Anthony Ship, Gregory street, Tuesday and Friday

*Farrow Benj.

Wine and Spirit Merchants.

6 Adams Willm, Cole
11 Hasell James
9 Sikes John

Woollen (Bunting) Manufctrs.

8 Hibble Thos.
8 James John
11 Musgrave W.
Ponder Henry, Curds lane

LACKFORD HUNDRED

Is the north-western division of Suffolk, and is of a triangular figure, extending about fifteen miles in length, on each of its three sides, and bounded on the north by Norfolk, on the west by Cambridgeshire, and on the southeast by Blackbourn, Thingoe, and Risbridge Hundreds. It is in the Franchise or *Liberty of St. Edmund, Diocese of Ely, Archdeaconry of Sudbury, and Deanery of Fordham;* and includes the *towns* of Brandon and Mildenhall, and parts of Thetford and Newmarket, near the latter of which it has a small detached member, nearly surrounded by Cambridgeshire.

The village from which it has its name is in the adjoining Hundred of Thingoe. It is watered by the navigable rivers *Lark* and *Little Ouse*, the latter of which separates it from Norfolk, and the former, after crossing it near Icklingham and Mildenhall, flows northward, and forms its western boundary. The north-western part of it, extending from Brandon and Mildenhall to the confluence of the Lark and Little Ouse, is an extensive tract of low *fens*, now well drained and cultivated, and forming part of the great BEDFORD LEVEL, which extends from the sources of the Great Ouse river, in Bedfordshire and Northamptonshire, to Lynn in Norfolk, and has its name from the fourth *Earl of Bedford*, who was the principal undertaker in the stupendous work of draining this immense tract of inundated fens ; for the performance of which, 95,000 acres were allotted to him and the few other " adventurers" who were induced by his spirited example to join in the costly and hazardous enterprise. The work was commenced in 1630, and in 1637 the Earl had expended no less than £100,000. He died in 1641, and the work was resumed by his son in 1649, and finished in 1653. In the reign of Charles II., and during the last and present centuries, the drainage of this extensive level has undergone many improvements, one of the last of which is the new channel of the Great Ouse, near Lynn. Mr. Young observes that there are few instances of such great and sudden improvements as were made during last century in the BURNT FEN of Lackford Hundred, comprising more than 14,000A. Seventy years ago, 500A. of it were let for one guinea a year ; but in 1772, an act was obtained for a separate drainage, and 1s. 6d. per acre levied for the expense of *embankments, pumping mills*, and other requisites. In 1777, the bank broke, and most of the proprietors were ruined. In 1782, the drainage was so much improved that various persons of capital and enterprise began to purchase in this neglected district, but the prices at which the lots were then sold, scarcely exceeded the present annual rental. The surface of the fens, from one foot to six, is the common peat of bogs, with an under stratum of white clay or marl ; but by paring, burning, and draining, they have nearly all been converted into fertile land. The central and eastern parts of Lackford Hundred consist chiefly of *light sandy moor and heath land*, of which many thousand acres are still in open *sheep walks and rabbit warrens*, rising in bold undulations, and resting on a thick stratum of *chalk* and *flint*, the latter of which is got both for building purposes and gun locks, and much of the former is ground to whiting. The whole Hundred comprises seventeen parishes, and parts of two other parishes, of which the following is an enumeration, shewing their territorial extent, the annual value of their lands and buildings, as assessed to the property tax in 1815, and their population in 1801 and 1841.

PARISHES.	Acres.	Rent £.	Populatn. 1801.	1841	PARISHES.	Acres.	Rental £.	Population. 1801.	1841.
†Barton Mills..	1827	2995	305	640	†Mildenhall ‡..	16,000	12,220	2283	3731
*Brandon	6760	4523	1148	2002	Newmarket ⎰ St. Mary ¶ ⎱	250	3836	1307	2143
†Cavenham ..	2630	1178	190	277					
†Elveden......	5555	1641	134	240	*Santon ⎰ Downham. ⎱	3860	1185	57	68
†Eriswell	7000	1839	295	501					
Exning§	5710	6293	566	1259	*Thetford St. ⎰ Cuthbert.. ⎱	**	**	41	58
†Freckenham..	2520	1897	256	495					
†Herringswell	2100	1157	126	219	* St. Mary**..	4480	3000	560	677
†Icklingham ⎰ All Saints & ⎱ St. James.. ⎱	6580	1545	335	254	†Tuddenham ..	2435	1438	268	428
				271	†Wangford	3500	950	43	46
†Lakenheath ..	10,550	4343	745	1579	†Worlington ..	1955	1983	326	351
					Total ..	83,712	52,023	8985	15,239

* The *Poor Law Unions* are described at subsequent pages. Exning and New-

market St. Mary are in *Newmarket Union ;* those marked thus * are in *Thetford Union ;* and those marked thus † are in *Mildenhall Union.*

§ *Exning* includes 182 persons in Newmarket Union Workhouse; and *Mildenhall* 29 persons in Mildenhall Union. The *Thetford Union Workhouse* stands in Norfolk, and had 169 inmates in 1843.

** THETFORD has three parishes, and 3934 inhabitants, most of whom are in the *Norfolk part of the borough.* (See page 707.)

‡ MILDENHALL PARISH is divided into four *hamlets,* viz., *Beck Row,* 744 ; *Holywell Row,* 411 ; *High Town,* 1456; and *West Row,* containing 1120 souls.

¶ NEWMARKET has another parish (All Saints) in *Cambridgeshire,* and contains altogether 2956 *souls,* and 570 *acres.*

☞ CHIEF CONSTABLES. Mr. Thomas Steel, of Tuddenham ; and Mr. Hy. Manning, of Beck-row, Mildenhall.

BARTON MILLS, or *Little Barton,* is a neat and pleasant village, 1 mile S.E. of Mildenhall, on the south bank of the navigable river Lark, where there is a large corn mill and a wharf. Its parish contains 640 souls, and 1826A. 2R. 19P. of land, generally fertile and well cultivated. The Rev. Chas. Jenkins, D.D., is lord of the *manor,* which was given to Bury Abbey by Robt. Hoo ; but a great part of the soil belongs to other proprietors, the largest of whom is W. T. Squire, Esq., of *Barton Place,* a large and handsome mansion in a small park. The *Church* (St. Mary) is a small neat structure, with a tower and three bells, and was thoroughly repaired and repewed in 1839. The *rectory,* valued in K.B. at £14. 15s. 10½d., and in 1835 at £550, is in the patronage of the Crown, and incumbency of the Rev. John Fox, B.A., who has a good residence. The tithes were commuted in 1796, for an allotment of 600A. Here is a *Baptist Chapel,* which was built in 1843, in lieu of an old one. During the great storm of thunder, hail, and rain, on August 9th, 1843, the building of this chapel was advanced so far as to be nearly ready for the roof, when the walls were washed down by the flood ; but they were rebuilt, and the building completed, before the end of the year. In 1692, the *Rev. James Davies* left 14A. of land, in the Turf Fen, at Mildenhall, in trust that the rents should be distributed among the poor of Barton Mills, on St. Stephen's Day and Easter Monday. The land is now let for about £13 a year. In 1732, the *Rev. Thos. Malabar* left a piece of land here to the rector for the time being, subject to the payment of 20s. every Christmas Day, for distribution among the poor.

Archer Wm. carrier, *Barton Hall*
Balls John, carrier, *Grange*
Beard Thos. vict. Dog and Partridge
Blackwall Wm. schoolmaster
Ellington Samuel & Sons, (Richd. & Thos.) corn, coal, and seed merts
Folkes John, corn merchant
Fox Rev John, B.A. *Rectory*
Fuller Philip, corn miller, merchant, and maltster
Hanslip Mr James ‖ Fuller Mrs J.
Hobson Rev Jesse (Baptist)
Howe Edward, tailor
Isaacson Edmund Denton, solicitor
Jolley Johnson, bricklayer, &c.
Muncey Charles, carriers' agent
Muncey Susannah, schoolmistress
Reeve Caroline, vict. Bull Inn, and posting house
Smith Robert, butcher
Squire Capt. Wm. Thomas, *Barton Place*
Vickers Rev Wm. B.A. curate

Beerhouses.
Pryke Thomas
Rose John, *baker*

Blacksmiths.
Sparke Richard, (& bell hanger)
Sparke Rachel

Boot&ShoeMkrs.
Cooper George
Folkes James
Folkes Robert

Howlett Wm.

Carpenters.
Aggus James
Brooks Henry
Secker Wm.

FARMERS.
Chenery Richd. *Hall Farm*
Folkes James
Folkes John
Secker Wm.

Steed Jacob,	Sparke Richard	CARRIERS.—*Deacon, Archer, &*
Lodge	*Wheelwrights.*	*Co.'s Vans and Waggons*, to Lynn
Shopkeepers.	Grinling James	and London daily ; to Holt, M. W.
Clarke George	Kendall Robert	and Fri. ; and to Wells, Mon. and
Daniel		Thurs. ; C. Muncey, agent

BRANDON, a well-built market town, noted for *gun-flints, whiting, rabbit-skins*, and *fur*, is pleasantly situated on the south bank of Little Ouse river, which is navigable for barges, and is crossed by a good bridge, at the junction of roads from Lynn and Swaffham, 6 miles W.N.W. of Thetford, 9 miles N.N.E. of Mildenhall, 16 miles N. by W. of Bury St. Edmund's, and 78 miles N.N.E. of London. Its parish increased its population from 1148 souls, in 1801, to 2002, in 1841, and comprises 6760 acres of land, extending six miles westward, along the south side of the vale, to the *fens*, and including about 4500 acres of light sandy land, which was inclosed under an Act passed in 1807, previous to which it was in open sheep-walks, and a large rabbit warren. Though now enclosed, there are still many rabbits to be seen in the parish ; and on its borders are the extensive *warrens* of Lakenheath, Santon Downham and Elvedon, which supply the Brandon furriers with immense quantities of skins, the dressing of which gives employment to about 200 females. During the late war, and before the invention of percussion caps, great numbers of the inhabitants were employed in preparing *gun-flints* from the prolific beds of that mineral, which lie at various depths below the *chalk stratum* ; but the trad had become nearly obsolete in 1838, when a company was formed in 138 £25 shares, for its revival. The flint found here in large masses is said to be the best in the world for the use of fire-arms ; and Brandon is now the only place in England where gun-flints are made to any considerable extent. Here are three *whiting-mills*, and a large *brewery* ; and several barges ply hence to and from Lynn with corn, coal, &c. The *market*, formerly held on *Friday*, became nearly obsolete in the early part of the present century, but was changed to *Thursday* some years ago, and is now attended by many farmers and corn buyers. *Fairs* for cattle, toys, &c., are held here on Feb. 14th, June 11th, and Nov. 11th ; and another is held at *Broomhill*, on the Norfolk side of the river, on July 7th. This town gave name to the illustrious family of *the Brandon's*, two of whom were Dukes of Suffolk, from 1514 till 1551, when the last of them died without issue ; and the title was conferred on the Greys, and soon afterwards on the Howards. Charles Gerard was created Baron Gerard of Brandon in 1645, and *Viscount Brandon* and Earl of Macclesfield in 1679 ; but on the death of his second son, in 1702, these titles became extinct. In 1711, Queen Anne created the Duke of Hamilton, in Scotland, a peer of England, by the titles of Baron Dutton and *Duke of Brandon*, which are still held by his descendants. *Simon Eyre*, who was Lord Mayor of London in 1445, was a native of Brandon. He erected Leadenhall for a granary or the metropolis, and left 5000 marks for charitable purposes.

The *manor of Brandon*, with the advowson of the church, belonged to the Bishop of Ely till the 4th of Elizabeth, when it was seized by the Crown. It was given by James I. to his second son, Charles, Duke of York; and during the greater part of last century, it was held by the Holts. Edward Bliss, Esq., is now lord of the manor, and resides at

Brandon Park, a handsome mansion, with extensive pleasure-grounds, about a mile south of the town. *Brandon Hall*, an old but neat mansion, half a mile west of the town, is now unoccupied. It is the property of J. Angerstein, Esq., who has a large estate here, and resides at Weeting Hall, on the Norfolk side of the river. J. Brewster, Esq., and many smaller proprietors, have estates in the parish ; and *North Court Lodge*, a little south of Brandon Park, is the pleasant seat of T. C. Kenyon, Esq. The *Church* (St. Peter) is an ancient fabric, with a tower containing five bells, and surmounted by a small leaded spire. The chancel was new-roofed in 1842. The *rectory*, valued in K.B. at £20. 18s. 1½d., and in 1835 at £584, with that of Wangford annexed to it, is in the patronage of T. E. Cartwright, Esq., and incumbency of the Rev. Richard Ward, who has a good residence, and now receives a yearly modus of £800 in lieu of tithes, of which £560 is paid by Brandon, and £240 by Wangford parish. Here is a *Friends' Meeting-House ;* also a *Wesleyan Chapel*, built in 1812 ; and a *Primitive Methodist Chapel*, erected in 1838. The poor parishioners have the benefit of several valuable *Charities*, an endowed *Free School*, and a *National School*.

FREE SCHOOL, &c.—In 1646, *Robert Wright* devised his real estates to John Wright, for six years after his decease, upon trust to employ the rents, after payment of testator's debts, and the legacies, &c., named in his will, in the purchase of lands, to be vested in trust with six or more of the most substantial inhabitants of Brandon, that the rents thereof might be employed, in the first place, in the payment of £30 a year to an able *schoolmaster*, to instruct the youth of *Brandon, Santon-Downham, Wangford*, and *Weeting*, in grammar and other literature ; and that the residue of the rents might be employed towards building and repairing a school-room, and a house for the master ; and the overplus be divided into four equal parts, as follows,—three parts thereof for the poor of Brandon, and one part for the poor of Downham and Wangford. In 1664, the sum of £767. 16s. 3d., derived from this bequest, was laid out as follows :—£600 in the purchase of a yearly rent-charge of £40 out of the impropriate rectory of Downham, and £167. 16s. 3d. in the purchase of a large house, with out-buildings, yards, and a garden, which have ever since been occupied by the schoolmaster, and are worth £20 a year. The school-room is in the house, near which is an allotment of 3A. 2R. 11P., awarded to the school at an enclosure, and now let for £2. 17s. a year. An allotment of 8A., awarded to the school under the Bedford Level Act, is let for about £8 per annum. The estates, &c., belonging to this charity were conveyed to new trustees, in 1825, after an expensive suit in Chancery. They pay the master a yearly salary of £40, for teaching 40 free scholars in the ordinary branches of education taught in English schools, few, if any of them, ever requiring to be taught Latin. Thirty of them are boys of Brandon, four are chosen from Weeting, and the other six from Downham and Wangford. E. Bliss, Esq., F. K. Eagle, Esq., and others, are trustees. The old workhouse was converted into a *National School* in 1843.

The POOR'S ESTATE comprises an *almshouse*, in five tenements, occupied rent-free by seven poor widows ; 2A. 2R. of land, near the almshouse, let for £7 a year ; two allotments, awarded on the enclosure of the *Small and High Fens*, about the year 1678, and containing together 9A. 2R., let for about £13 a year ; 16A., called the Town Meadow, let for £25 a year ; and 5A. 2R. of marsh land, in the Small Fen, purchased, in 1678, with £80 given by *Robert Wright*, and now let for £16. 10s. a year. The rents are distributed among the poor at Christmas. The POOR'S ALLOTMENT consists of 116 acres of steril land, which, under the act of Parliament, passed in 1807, for enclosing the open lands of Brandon, was awarded in trust, that the rents and profits thereof should be laid out in purchasing fuel for distribution among the poor parishioners. In 1826, this allotment was let on a 21 years' lease, at the annual rent of £16, subject to the right of the trustees to take flints from a quarry, which is let at a groundage rent of 5s. for every load of flints taken from it. During the war, the profits of the *flint quarry*

were very considerable, and a fund was in consequence accumulated, part of which, £400, was lent on mortgage of 10½A. of land at Feltwell, in Norfolk, and the other part was laid out in the purchase of £350 three per cent. consols. The interest of the mortgage having fallen in arrear, the trustees, in 1826, entered into possession of the land at Feltwell, which they let for £16. 10s. a year. A balance of £50 was laid out, in 1830, in the purchase of stock. The income derived from the above sources is distributed among the poor of the parish in coals.

In 1675, Ann Curtis gave a cottage, containing five rooms, and a small garden, in trust for the use of the poor of Brandon. These premises are occupied, rent-free, by three poor families, and were rebuilt, in 1840, at the expense of the parish. In 1624, Stephen Ashwell bequeathed to the poor a yearly rent-charge of 30s. out of Maid's Head Close. In 1643, Thomas Baker charged all his lands and messuages in Brandon with the yearly payment of two coombs of good barley, ready ground into meal, for distribution, in equal moieties, among the poor of *Brandon and Westrow*. The estates charged were sold, it is said, free from incumbrance, to the late J. J. Angerstein, Esq., and the two coombs of ground barley have not been paid since about 1806. In 1773, *Mrs. Ann Wilder* left an annuity of 50s. out of an estate at Pulham, to keep three tomb-stones of her family in repair, and the residue not so applied to be distributed among poor widows of Brandon. In 1579, *Edmund Almeare* left £60 to the poor of Brandon, Foulden, Northwold, Feltwell, and Weeting, to be laid out in land, and the rent to be distributed in clothing, in annual succession in each parish. The land purchased consists of 14A. 3R. 22P. at Old Buckenham, in Norfolk, now let for £21 a year.

BRANDON.

Post Office at Mr. Robert Webb's, High street.—Letters received at 5 morning, and despatched at ½-past 8 evening

Marked 1, *reside at the Bridge;* 2, *in Bury road;* 3, *in the Fen;* 4, *Brandon Field;* 5, *in High street;* 6, *Lode street;* 7, *London road;* 8, *Market hill;* 9, *Thetford road; and* 10, *in Town street*

9 Batten Alfred M., coachman
Bliss Edward, Esq., *Brandon Park*
10 Cartwright Rev Chas. Johnson, curate
5 Clark John, bookseller, stationer, and printer
3 Clements Jph. Wm., music teacher
1 Clifton Robert, brewer, maltster, and corn, coal, wine & spirit mert
5 Collins Mr Wm. || 9 Doel Mrs Sus
De Charms Dvd., gent. *Brook Cotg*
8 Farrow Roger, parish clerk
7 Forster Mrs Susan
6 Garner Tyrell, sen. game dealer
5 Garner Tyrell, jun. game dealer
5 Goodrich Mr Robert
10 Gross Charles, gamekeeper
5 Hunt James, John, and Thomas, coach proprietors
5 Hubbard Isaac, sexton
5 Jewell Robert, bookkeeper
7 Kenyon Thomas Cookson, Esq. solicitor, *North Court Lodge*
Ledson Mrs Mary, *Rose Cottage*

5 Morley Henry, poulterer
7 Mouncey Mr Peter
1 Murrell John, lighterman
5 Neale Peter, leather cutter
5 Pearmain Mrs Mary
5 Pepworth Richard, lighterman
Roberts Joseph, surgeon
9 Shorten Mr Samuel
5 Smyth Edward Jas. *conveyancer,* master extraordy. in Chancery, &c
5 Smyth S. E. auctioneer & land agt
9 Snare Miss Elizabeth
7 Snare Thos. mason & bricklayer
9 Stanford Thomas, lighterman
5 Thompson Robert, *surgeon*
5 Tilson James L. bookkeeper
7 Walker Mr Benjamin
5 Ward Rev Richard, *Rectory*
5 Webb James, old clothes dealer
7 Webb Thos. travelling tea dealer
8 Webber Benjamin, postman
5 Willett Alice, china, glass, &c. dlr
10 Wood George, timber merchant
Youngman Alfred, excise office

FIRE AND LIFE OFFICES.

Crown, J. Roberts
1 Farmers' General, Robt. Clifton
5 Farmers', John Spinks
5 Norwich Union, Robert Webb
5 Norwich Equitable, E. J. Smyth
5 Suffolk Amicable, John Clark

INNS AND TAVERNS.

5 Bell Inn, Currey Forster
5 Chequers Inn, Sarah Doubleday
10 Crown, J. Wood

8 Five Bells, Thomas Jacob
8 George Inn, Wm. Buckenham
1 Ram Inn, Stephen Steward
8 Star, Harvey Tilney
5 White Hart and Commercial, James Rudd
10 White Horse, Thomas Newdick
9 White Lion, Wm. Rought

ACADEMIES.
(* take Boarders.)
7 Crowford Petr.
7* Mason Misses
8*Notley Mrs
8*Notley John, Free Gram. Sch.
9 Snare Mary

Bakers, &c.
8 Block Wm. Nelson
5 Evered Wm.
7 Hubbard Leond.
5 Palmer Wm.
5 Upcraft James
8 Webber Benj.

Basket Makers.
5 Daynes John
.5 Daynes Wm.

Beerhouses.
8 Clift Jonathan
7 Cooper John
6 Fendick Robt.
9 Groom Robert
9 Hyam Cornls.
9 Terrington Jph.

Blacksmiths and Trap Mkrs.
6 Fendick Robt.
5 Forster Currey
5 Forster Wm.
7 Palmer Mark
7 Palmer Robert

Boot & Shoe Mkrs.
9 Ager Stephen, (and leather cutter)
9 Clarke John
7 Clarke Joseph
7 Davy Ellis
7 Deresley Thos.
5 Hubbard Eliz.
7 Norman Mattw.
7 Pratt George
5 Upcraft Wm.

Butchers.
7 Willett Robt.
5 Willett Thos. and Son

Cabinet Makers.
7 Green James
5 Ramsey Wm.

Chemists & Drgs.
5 Pigott Rd.(Jno. Spinks, manager)
5 Thompson Fred.

Coopers.
5 Daynes John
5 Daynes Wm.
5 Meadows Rt.

Corn and Coal Merchants.
(* are Maltsters.)
5 Brewster John
8 Buckenham W. (coal only)
1*Clifton Robt.
5*Pepworth Rd. and Son

Corn Miller.
7 Chapman Wm.

FARMERS.
Balding Edward, Church Farm
9 Currey Henry
10 Elmer Wm.
6 Garner Tyrell, senior
Newdick Thos. Mayday Farm
3 Palmer Mattw.

Brick kiln
4 Pryer Wm.
Lime kiln
3 Rolfe Evans, Christmas hill
3 Rolfe John
3 Rolfe Thomas
10 Wood George
3 Wright John, Fen House

Furriers. &c.
7 Currey Ann
2 Dickerson John
9 Malt John
5 Mulley Robt.
9 Porter John

2 Rought Judd
8 Smith John

Gardeners.
9 Carr Thomas, Nursery
5 Holmes Thos.
7 Wharfe Robt.

Grocers, Dprs. & Hatters.
9 Greene Harry
5 Jennings John
5 Smith Rt. (and spirit mercht.)
7 Wabe Susan

Gun Flint Mkrs.
6 Brandon Gun Flint Co., Rt. Clark & John Snare, mangrs.
9 Towler Thos.

Hair Dressers.
5 Clark John
5 Risbrook Chas.

Joiners & Bldrs.
5 Barkway Arthur
7 Bretnall Geo.
2 Garner James
7 Green James

Milliners.
9 Clarke Maria
8 Farrow Hanh.
7 Malt Margta.
7 Wabe Susan

Painters, Plumbers, & Glaziers.
5 Clark Robert
5 Osborn Robert

Saddlers.
5 Armstrong Ed.
5 Diggon Ann

Shopkeepers.
8 Block Wm. Nelson
10 Jacob Isaac
5 Ward George
10 Wood Susan

Straw Hat Mkrs.
5 Harvey Eliz.
5 Mulley Eliz.

Tailors.
9 Baker Wm.
7 Chandler Robt.
1 Mortlock Wm.
7 Webber James
10 Wood John

Watchmakers.
7 Malt James
5 Ray David

Wheelwrights.
2 Talbot Edw.
7 West George

Whiting Mfrs.
9 Dixon John
9 Porter John
9 Tabraham Rt.

COACHES.
From the Chequers, to London, ¼ bef. 12 noon daily; to Wells, M., W., and Fri., 3 aftn.; to Holt and Dereham, Tu., Thu., & Sat., 3 aftn.; to Lynn, Tues. at 8, and Thurs. & Sat., at 9 mg.; and to Bury, Tues., Thurs , and Sat. at 7 evg. (also from the White Hart.)

CARRIERS.
To London, Deacon, Archer, & Co., from the White Hart, Mon., Thurs., and Sat., 6 mg.; Swan & Son, from the Ram, Mon., Wed., & Fri., 11 night; and Hacon & Balls, from the George, Tues. and Fri , 5 morning
To Lynn, Deacon, Archer, & Co., Mon., Wed., & Fri., 12 night; and Thos. Jacob, Mon., & Thurs., 8 mg
To Bury, T. Jacob, Wednesday and Saturday, 6 morning
To Newmarket, the Mail Cart, from the Bell, every evening, at ½ past 8
VESSELS to Lynn twice a week, from Richard Pepworth's wharf

CAVENHAM, a neat and pleasant village, 4½ miles S.E. by S. of Mildenhall, and 7 miles W.N.W. of Bury St. Edmund's, has in its parish 277 souls, and 2630 acres of sandy land, extending northward to the navigable river Lark, and nearly all the property of Harry Spencer Waddington, Esq., one of the parliamentary representatives of the Western Division of Suffolk, who resides at the *Hall*, a handsome mansion, in a small park. He is also impropropriator of the rectory, but W. F. G. Farmer, Esq., is lord of the *manor*, called Shardelowes in Cavenham, anciently the demesne of the Earl of Clare, and afterwards of Viscount Townshend. The *Church* (St. Andrew) has a tower and three bells, and was new-pewed and repaired in 1837. The benefice is a discharged *vicarage*, valued in K.B. at £5. 5s. 10d., and in 1835 at £113. The patronage is in the Crown, and the Rev. C. W. Carwardine is the incumbent, for whom the Rev. Rt. Gwilt officiates. At the enclosure, the vicarial tithes were commuted for an allotment of 350A., now let for £120 per annum. The *Church Land*, belonging to this parish, consists of 6A. in Rickinghall, let for £9, and 7A. in Thelnetham, let for £10. 10s. a year. A benefaction of £10 to the poor of Cavenham left by *W. Firmage*, in 1591, was laid out in the purchase of an acre of land, at Rattlesden, let for £1 a year. An *allotment* of 80A., which was awarded to the poor, on the enclosure of this parish, in lieu of their right of cutting fuel on the heath, is let for £22 a year, which is distributed at Easter, partly in coals.

Barnes John, shoemaker
Clarke Wm. corn miller
Harvey Robert, steward
Howard Stephen, shopkeeper
Jaques Richard, joiner and builder
Ransdale Wm. farmer and beerhs.
Waddington Harry Spencer, Esq. M.P. *Cavenham Hall*
Warner Philip, shopkeeper
Wing Richard and Chas. maltsters
Wing Richard, sen. *Park Farm*
Wing Richard, jun. *Hall Farm*

ELVEDEN, or ELDEN, a small village, 4 miles S.W. of Thetford, has in its parish 240 souls, and 5555 acres of light sandy land, all the property of Wm. Newton, Esq., the lord of the manor, who resides at *Elveden Hall*, a large and handsome mansion, in a small park, adjoining a *rabbit warren* of about 1000 acres. It was anciently appropriated to Bury Abbey, and was given by Henry VIII. to the Duke of Norfolk. It afterwards passed to the Crisps, and from them to the Tyrells. It was the property and seat of the late *Admiral Keppel*, second son of the second Earl of Albemarle of his family, who, after displaying great valour and skill in many naval engagements, was created *Viscount Keppel, of Elveden*, in 1782, but dying without issue in 1796, the title became extinct. His nephew, the present Earl of Albemarle, resided here in the early part of the present century, and for some time had in his own occupation 4000 acres of the parish, which he greatly improved by planting and drill-husbandry, though it consists chiefly of a blowing sand. The *Church* (St. Andrew) is a small thatched fabric, and the living is a *rectory*, valued in K.B. at £12. 17s. 6d., and now having a yearly modus of £300, awarded in 1840. Wm. Newton, Esq., is patron, and the Rev. E. R. Benyon incumbent. The *poor* have 10s. a year from two roods of land given by an unknown donor; and £3 a year out of the rectorial tithes, left by Suckling Jay, Esq., in 1675. *Directory*:—Wm. Newton, Esq., *Elveden Hall ;* Rev. F. C. A. Clifford, curate, *Rectory ;* Cphr. Brown, *shopkeeper ;* Jas. Goddard, con-

stable; Chas. Lusher, vict., *Albemarle Arms;* Wm. Napthen, *baker* and gamekeeper; George Postans, *steward;* Fredk. Chas. Payne, *farmer and warrener;* and Peter Williamson, gent.

ERISWELL, a scattered village on an acclivity, 3 miles N. of Mildenhall, has in its parish 501 souls, and about 7000 acres, mostly a light blowing sand, extending westward to the fens, and eastward to the extensive warren of Lakenheath. The manor was anciently held of the King *in capite* as of the honour of Boulogne, by the Roucestre family, and afterwards by the Tuddenhams. A religious society, called the New England Company, are now lords of the manor and owners of a great part of the soil; and the remainder belongs to Alex. Murray, Esq. (who has a neat seat here,) and several smaller owners. The *Church* (St. Peter) is a small thatched fabric, with a tower and three bells. It had a chantry, of the yearly value of £9. 4s. 6d.; and near the Hall, on the north side of the parish, was a chapel dedicated to *St. Lawrence,* the remains of which is now a dove-cote. The *rectory,* valued in K.B. at £16. 6s. 10d., has 52A. of glebe, and a yearly modus of £640. 18s. 11d., awarded in 1839. Thomas Evans, Esq., is patron, and the Rev. Edward Evans, B.A., incumbent. Here is a *Wesleyan* and also a *Primitive Methodist Chapel,* the former built in 1843. The lords of the manor support a small *Free School.* The Poor's Estate consists of two double cottages, with small gardens, occupied by paupers; an allotment of 14A. 14P., let for £3. 15s., and and 3R. 38P., in Holme and Rowley Croft, let for 20s. a year.

Bangs Fuller, tailor
Fishpool Mary, schoolmistress
Murray Alex. Esq., *Eriswell Cottage*
Newdick Shadrach, corn miller
Rudland John, wheelwright
Rutterford Thos. joiner, builder, & agent to the Royal Exchange Fire and Life Office
Sanders Rev. Bradfield, B.A. curate, *Rectory*
Sutterby Henry, vict. *Bell*
Warren John, farm steward
Wicks John, bricklayer

Woolnough Thomas, butcher and vict. *Chequers*

Blacksmiths.
Ashley John
Pearson John

Boot & Shoe Mkrs.
Neale Robert
Melton Wm.
Woolnough Chs.

FARMERS.
Horrex Jane
Morley Henry
Morley Wm.
Newdick Pp *Hall*

Pearmain John, *Rakeheath*
Pearmain Wm., *High Lodge*
Roberson Thos., *ChamberlainHl*
Rudland Thos.
Turrington Geo.
Woods Ann

Shopkeepers.
Halls James
Sparke Wm.

EXNING is a large and well-built village, pleasantly situated in a small fertile valley, with a rivulet running through it, 2 miles N.W. of Newmarket. Its parish, with St. Mary's, Newmarket, forms a small portion of Suffolk, surrounded by Cambridgeshire, and joined to the rest of this county only by the turnpike road. It contains 1259 souls, and 5710 acres of land. It was formerly a member of Stow Hundred, and had a weekly market, which was removed to Newmarket many years ago. It was the birthplace of Etheldreda, daughter of Anna, queen of the East Angles, whom the Pope canonized for a virgin, though she was married to two husbands. Here, also, Ralph Waher, Earl of East Anglia, planned his conspiracy against William the Conqueror, with the Earls of Hereford and Northumberland, and other persons of high rank. Their design being frustrated, Ralph fled first to France, and then to Denmark, leaving his possessions to the mercy of his ad-

versaries. The manor of Exning was afterwards held by the De Valence family. Lady Cotton, mother of Sir St. Vincent Cotton, Bart., is now lady of the manor, but a great part of the soil belongs to the Bryant and other families, some of whom have neat houses here. The village is shaded with fine poplar trees, producing an agreeable contrast to the monotony of the surrounding country, which in general presents one uniform naked plain, forming part of the fens of the great Bedford Level. The *Church* (St. Martin) is a large and handsome fabric, with a tower and five bells. In the east window are some fragments of stained glass, and near the communion table is a square altar tomb, of coarse grey marble, formerly adorned with brasses, which have been torn away. The Dean and Chapter of Canterbury are appropriators of the rectory, and patrons of the *vicarage*, valued in K.B. at £13. 7s. 6d., and in 1835 at £311. The Rev. Thomas F. Debdin, D.D., is the incumbent. The tithes were commuted for allotments of land, at the enclosure, in 1807. The vicar's allotment is 240A. The *Wesleyans* have a chapel here, built in 1834. The *Church Estate*, consisting of a barn and 40A. of land, given by a Mr. Lacey, is let at £62. 10s. per annum. Adjoining it are three roods of land, let for 26s. a-year, and given to the poor parishioners by *John Fabian ;* and 5A., let for £6. 4s. a year, and bequeathed by one *Morden*, for distributions of bread among poor widows. The rectory (now held on lease by Mr. Bryant, of Newmarket,) is charged with the customary payment of *ten coombs of rye*, yearly, or the value thereof, for distribution among the poor of Exning, who have also a yearly rent-charge of 5s., left by the *Rev. John Lawrence ;* and a share of Shepherd's Charity. In 1739, *Samuel Shepherd* gave two yearly rent-charges of £20 each for the poor of Exning and Bottisham ; but in lieu of them, the two parishes have a farm of about 62A. of land, in Exning and Burwell, now yielding a clear yearly income of about £54, which is equally divided between the two parishes, and distributed among the poor, in sums of from 2s. to 8s.

Archer Robert, corn miller, *Exning Mills*
Avis Thomas, banker's clerk
Bryant Robert Wrightson, Esquire, banker, *Exning Lodge*
Clark Frederick Rust, tailor
Crack Thomas, bricklayer
Fison Misses Mary and Ann
Hammond William, gentleman
Heffer James, butcher and drover
Isaacson Mrs Jane
Miller Benj. brewer & coal mercht
Pettit Charles, baker
Pettit Wm. wheelwright
Sturgeon George, farm steward
Wake James, carpenter
Webb John, blacksmith
Webb John, constable

Whiting Rev. Robt. curate, *Vicarage*

INNS AND TAVERNS.
Wheat Sheaf, Wm. Hassall
White Horse, Wm. Pettit
White Swan, Ambrose Frost
   Beer Houses.
Warren R. *brewer*
Webb Pp. *butcher*
Boot & Shoe Mkrs.
Frost Ambrose
Parr Wm.
   FARMERS.
   * *are Owners.*
Bryant Misses
*Bryant Wm. ; h Newmarket
Bunn Harry
*Fison Wm.

*Martin Richd.
Rutter Thomas
*Stigwood Wm., *Rose Hall*
*Westley Wm. *Shopkeepers.*
Knowlden Decimus
Parr Wm., *Post Office*
Payne George
Pettit Eliz.
Warren Robert

FRECKENHAM, a pleasant village in the vale of a rivulet which bounds it from Cambridgeshire, nearly 4 miles S.W. of Mildenhall, is a *peculiar* of the Bishop of Rochester, and its parish contains 495 souls

and 2520 acres of land.   Nathl. Barnardiston, Esq., is lord of the manor, which was formerly held by the Clarkes, but a great part of the soil belongs to P. Bennett, Esq., Clare Hall, Cambridge, Mr. C. Youngman, Miss Pate, and several smaller proprietors.   The *Church* (St. Andrew) is a thatched fabric, with a tower and five bells, and the benefice is a vicarage and rectory united, valued in K.B. at £16. 11s. 4d., and in 1835 at £600.   It is in the patronage of Peter house, Cambridge, and incumbency of the Rev. G.B. Paley, B.D., who has a neat residence.   The tithes were commuted at the enclosure, in 1815, for allotments of land.   Here is a small *Baptist Chapel,* and a *National School,* erected in 1839.   In 1710, *Katherine Shore* left a cottage and about 9A. of land, (now let for £24 a year,) and directed the rents to be laid out yearly in stuff gowns, for poor women of this parish.   Two yearly payments, called *Herring money,* one 2s. 6d., and the other 7s. 6d., are charged on lands belonging to Mr. Palmer and Mr. Dennis.

Baker John, baker
Browne James, shoemaker
Dorling Samuel, bricklayer & vict.
   Golden Bear
Mortlock Jas. shoemkr & schoolmr
Norman Samuel, carpenter
Paley Rev.Geo.Barber,B.D. *Rectory*
Pate Miss and Isaacson Miss
Pettit Simon, corn miller
Reeve Jas beerhouse & shopkpr
Robins Richard, brickmaker

Taylor Robert, carpenter
Tolworthy Chas. blacksmith
Tolworthy John, shopkeeper
Youngman Charles, gentleman
      FARMERS.
Barrett Wm. || Barrett James
Knight Robert
Leonard Joseph
Westropp Wm., *Hall*
Rumbelow Norman & John, millers
Wiseman Henry (& butcher)

   HERRINGSWELL, a small village in the vale of a rivulet, 3½ miles S. of Mildenhall, and 6 miles N.E. by E. of Newmarket, has in its parish 219 souls, and 2100 acres of sandy freehold land, belonging to *John Turner Hales, Esq.,* (who has a pleasant seat here,) except about 150 acres, belonging to Geo. Mure, Esq., of *Herringswell House.* The manor formerly belonged to Bury Abbey, and afterwards to the Holden family.   The *Church* (St. Ethelbert) is a small thatched edifice, with a tower and three bells.   The living is a discharged *rectory,* valued in K.B. at £9. 9s. 9½d., and in 1835 at £200.   The tithes were commuted at the enclosure for an allotment of 360 acres.   J. T. Hales, Esq., is *patron ;* the Rev. Robert Hales, *incumbent ;* and the Rev. Hy. Raymond Smythies, *curate.*   The latter resides at the *Rectory ;* and the *farmers* are Wm. Hensby and Joseph Tubbs, *Hall.*

   ICKLINGHAM ST. JAMES and ALL SAINTS are two adjoining villages and united parishes, on the north side of the small but navigable river Lark, from 3 to 4 miles E.S.E. of Mildenhall, and 8 miles N.W. of Bury St. Edmund's.   They maintain their poor conjointly as one township, and contain 525 souls, and 6580 acres of land, mostly a light sand, and extending northward to the large warrens of Lakenheath and Elveden   The houses are many of them neat and commodious, and are pleasantly ranged about a mile in length, near the north bank of the river.   Robert Gwilt, Esq., is lord of the manor of St. James ; and the Rev. Daniel Gwilt, M.A., is lord of All Saints manor ; but part of the soil belongs to John Gwilt, Esq., and a few smaller owners. The Gwilt family have for a long period been seated here, and held the former manor, and the greater part of the soil in the two parishes ; but

in Kirby's time, the Earl of Essex was lord of All Saints manor. The consolidated *rectories* of All Saints and St. James, valued in K.B., the former at £12. 17s. 6d., and the latter at £11. 11s. 5d., are in the patronage and incumbency of the Rev. Danl. Gwilt, M.A. The advowson and the manor of St. James belonged to Bury Abbey, and were granted by Henry VIII. to Anthony Rous. The tithes were commuted in 1839 for a yearly modus of £564. 10s. The *two churches* are neat but ancient structures, each having towers, and St. James' having one, and All Saints' three bells. In the latter, within the rails of the communion table, and about the chancel, is a considerable quantity of Roman bricks or tiles, which were ploughed up in a neighbouring field, about 35 years ago, and placed here for their preservation. They are of different shapes, slightly traced with the figures of animals, flowers, human faces, &c. ; some few of them are vitrified. Icklingham is supposed by some to have been the ancient Roman station, *Combretonium*, or, according to Horsley, *Comboritum.* Here, at any rate, says the author of a Tour through England, ascribed to the pen of Samuel Richardson, are vestiges of a settlement, which seems to have extended half a mile in length, at a small distance from the river. On the west side of the ruins is a square encampment, which appears to have contained about 25 acres, and is now called Kentfield, said to be a corruptior of Campfield. The vallum is visible all round it, except where the moorish ground has brought it to decay. *Coins* and *fibulæ* have often been found here, especially in a ploughed field, half a mile northwest of the village, and also in the moors, when dug for the purpose of being fenced and drained. Many years since, an ancient leaden cistern, containing sixteen gallons, and ornamented as with hoops, was likewise discovered by a ploughman, who struck his share against the edge of it. Westward of the camp, upon Warren hill, are three large barrows, each encompassed by a ditch. On the estate of J. Gwilt, Esq., a gold coin, several kitchen utensils, and a buck's head and horns, were dug up a few years ago. Here is a small *Wesleyan Chapel.* In the 19th of Henry VII., *Alice Dix* gave for the poor of these parishes a cottage, barn, and 251½ acres of land, now let for only £45 a-year, which is distributed in hempen cloth. In 1706, John King left for the working poor of Icklingham a yearly rent-charge of 20s., out of lands now belonging to the Gwilt family.

ICKLINGHAM.

*Marked * are in St. James' ; and the rest in All Saints'*

*Benstead Jas. miller & schoolmstr
*Burt Charles, furrier
Clarke John, corn miller
Gwilt Rev. Danl. M.A., rector
*Gwilt Mrs Charlotte
Gwilt John, Esquire
*GwiltRev.Rt. curate of Cavnham
Harvey Henry, shoemaker
Hunt Henry, rabbit merchant
Jaggard John, shoemaker
*Levett Benjamin, butcher

*Nayler Sarah, vict. Red Lion
*Nunn Thomas, cart owner
Rumbelow Philip, blacksmith
*Tayler Simon, farm steward
*Wing Richd. & Chas. maltsters

FARMERS.

King Francis, *Wither Hill*
Mainprice Wm.||Newdick John

SHOPKEEPERS.

*King Henry || Johnson Mary
*Ward Thomas || Levett Charles

CARRIER.

Robert Firman, to London, Thursday

LAKENHEATH is a large village, on a sandy acclivity, on the eastern margin of the fens, about 2 miles S. of the Little Ouse river, and 5 miles W.S.W. of Brandon, and N. of Mildenhall. Its parish increased its population from 745 souls, in 1801, to 1579, in 1841, and comprises 10,550 acres of land, including a large portion of fen on the west, and an extensive tract of light sandy land on the east and south, including a rabbit warren of 2400 acres, and another of 250 acres. The Prior and Convent of Ely had a grant for a *market* and *fair* here, in 1309. The former had been established many years earlier, but has long been obsolete ; and we find that, in the reign of John, the abbot of Bury held an inquisition to try by jury whether the lately erected market at *Laking* was not detrimental to the town and market of Bury. A *fair* for cattle, &c., is still held here on the Thursday after Midsummer day ; and a few farmers and corn buyers meet every Monday, at the Bell Inn. The Dean and Chapter of Ely have been appropriators of the *rectory*, patrons of the *vicarage*, and lords of the *manor*, since the dissolution of the monasteries ; but a great part of the soil belongs to Wm. Eagle, Esq., of *Lakenheath Cottage ;* Thos. Waddelow, Esq., of *Undley Hall,* (1 mile W. of the village,) Messrs. E. and R. Gathercole, J. and T. Howard, A. Willett, Thomas Payne, and several smaller owners. The *vicarage*, valued in K.B. at £4. 18s. 9½d., and in 1835 at £136, is discharged from the payment of first fruits and tenths, and enjoyed by the Rev. John Butts. The *Church* (St. Mary) is a large structure, with a tower and five bells ; and here are three places of worship belonging to the *Baptists, Wesleyans,* and *Huntingdonians.* UNDLEY, a hamlet in the fen part of this parish, is a *curacy* annexed to the vicarage. The parish has two *school endowments,* and several *charity estates,* as noticed below.

The POOR'S ESTATE consists of the following allotments, awarded under various enclosure acts, in lieu of lands derived from the bequests of *John Styward* and a *Mr. Hanslip,* in the reign of Elizabeth, viz. 4A. 1R. 6P. in Holmsley Field, let for £6. 6s. ; 10A. 2P., in Hockwell, let for £20 ; and 11A. 2P. in Feltwell, in Norfolk, let for £14. 10s. a year. The rents are distributed among the poor, by the churchwardens and overseers, twice a-year, together with a yearly rentcharge of 12s., given by an unknown donor out of a house belonging to Mr. Rolfe. The POOR'S TURF LAND consists of 154A. of fen, awarded under the Bedford Level Act, in the 15th of Charles II., for the use of the poor parishioners, among whom it is parcelled out for the purpose of digging turf for fuel. In 1762, *John Hanslip* granted for the benefit of 60 poor families of Lakenheath, a yearly rentcharge of £6, out of his estate at Mildenhall, now the property of Mr. Howard. In 1744, *Geo. Goward* gave to the churchwardens and overseers of Lakenheath, and other trustees, 18A. of arable land, at Soham, in Cambridgeshire, upon trust, to pay yearly £6 to Soham, and £6 to Lakenheath, for a monthly distribution of 10s. worth of bread in each of those parishes ; and to employ the residue of the rents in paying a *schoolmaster,* for teaching poor boys of Lakenheath reading, writing, and arithmetic. The land is let for about £60 a-year, so that the schoolmaster has upwards of £40 yearly, for which he instructs 30 *free scholars.* In 1756, *John Evans* and *Robert Kitchener* gave 13A. of land in *Mildenhall Fen,* to provide for the education of poor children of Lakenheath, and it is now let for £10 a-year. The rent is paid to the schoolmaster for teaching seven other free scholars. In 1798, *the Rev. John Barnes* gave 12A. of land at Mildenhall, in trust for a distribution of 10s. worth of bread among the poor of Lakenheath, on the first Sunday of every month, and to apply the residue of the rent to the relief of poor widows.

LAKENHEATH.

Bangs Lieutenant William
Barker Rev Samuel, curate

Brown John, thatcher
Clarke Henry, hair dresser
Cooper Edw. cabinet maker & turner

Death Walter, schoolmaster
Eagle Wm. Esq. *Lakenhealh Cottage*
Flack Joseph, *warrener*
Gathercole Evans, gentleman
Ginger Capt. Joseph
Green Mrs Mary
Lowe Thomas, saddler
Mears Isaac, gentleman
Morley Mary Ann, ironmonger
Morley Wm. gentleman
Newton Wm. gentleman
Pawsey George, farrier
Scott Mr Joseph
Waddelow Thos. Esq. *Undley Hall*

INNS AND TAVERNS.
Anchor, Wm. Witham
Bell, Wm. Fincham
Bull, John Pigott
Green Dragon, C. King
Plough, Wm. Ramsdale
Redmoor Houses, John Mott

Beerhouses.
Allsop Robert
Brown Robert
Norton Edward
Place Elizabeth
Rolph James
Rowe George

Bakers.
Burgess Wm.
Gathercole John

Blacksmiths.
Brown Henry
Newton Thomas
Palmer Samuel
Seaman David

Boot & Shoe Mkrs.
Cash George
Cash Robert
Foster John
Hardy Wm.

Pigott John
Bricklayers.
Rolph Charles
Rolph James
Butchers.
Cash Joseph
Harwin Henry
Corn Millers.
Newdick Charles
Scott Joseph

FARMERS.
Allsop Robert
Bangs Ann
Cash Charles
Cash Roper
Cash Samuel
Coleman Edward
Coleman James
Coleman Wm.
Francis John
Gathercole Rd.
Harding George
Hensby Wm.
Howard James
and Thomas
Morley Rebecca
Newton Thomas
Palmer John
Palmer John, jun.
Palmer Richard
Payne Thomas

Peachey Edward
and John
Peachey Roper
Phipps Thomas,
(warrener)
Rolph Charles
Rolph John
Rowe George
Taylor Wm.
Tuffs Peter
Grocers & Dprs.
Chapman Joseph
Morley Joseph
Smith & House-
hold, (agts. to
the London In-
surance Co.)
Tailors.
Tuck Henry
Yellop James
Wheelwrights.
Fincham Lot
Presland John
Presland Thomas
Siser James
CARRIERS.
Joshua Bland, to
Lynn, Sat.
J. Pigott and
M. Benson, to
Bury, W. & S.

MILDENHALL is a pleasant and well-built market-town, in the vale of the small but navigable river Lark, 9½ miles N.E. of Newmarket, and S.S.W. of Brandon; 12 miles S.W. by W. of Thetford, and N.W. by W. of Bury St. Edmunds; and 70 miles N.E. by N. of London. It has been greatly improved by the erection of new houses during the last ten years; and its three principal thoroughfares, High street, Mill street, and the Market-place, are spacious and well paved and lighted, and contain several good inns, and many well-stocked shops. It is a *polling-place* for the Western division of Suffolk; and *Petty Sessions* are held at the Bell Inn every alternate Friday. The *Market* held every Friday, is now of trifling consequence, only a few farmers and buyers meeting at the Bell and White Hart Inns alternately. A large *fair*, for the sale of wood brought from the woodland districts, is held on the 10th of October; and on the two following days, for pleasure. The parish of Mildenhall is the largest in Suffolk, and increased its population from 2283 souls, in 1801, to 3731, in 1841; but only 1500 of them reside in the town. It extends over 15,990 *acres*, of which 8540 acres are low, but now fertile and well-drained *fens;* and 7450 acres are *skirt lands* and *high lands*, consisting of arable, pasture, and heath, of most variable quality, a large portion being a light sand, extending northward to the large warren of Lakenheath. It is divided into four HAMLETS, of which the following are the names, with their population in 1841 :—*High Town*, 1456; *Beck Row*, 744; *Holywell*

Row, 411; and *West Row*, 1120. The latter is 2½ miles W., Holywell Row 2 miles N., and Beck Row 3 miles N. by W. of the town. Near Beck Row is an assemblage of houses, called *Wild street*. Gas Works were erected at Mildenhall in 1840, by Mr. G. Malam; but they now belong to 44 proprietors of 210 £5 shares. A *silk and worsted manufactory*, which formerly flourished in the town, was converted into cottages some years ago.

Mildenhall Union, formed by the New Poor Law Commissioners in 1835, comprises 13 *parishes*, viz., Mildenhall, Eriswell, Icklingham, Lakenheath, Wangford, Barton Mills, Cavenham, Elveden, Freckenham, Herringswell, Kentford, Tuddenham, and Worlington, which comprise an *area* of 95 square miles, and 9184 *inhabitants*. The average annual expenditure of these parishes, for the support of their poor, during the three years preceding the formation of the Union, was £5978; but in 1838, it amounted only to £4175; and in 1840, to £4026. 19s. The old Workhouse at Mildenhall, was altered and enlarged in 1836, at the expense of the Union. It has room for 110 paupers, but has seldom more than from 20 to 50 inmates. The *board* consists of 16 *guardians*, four chosen for Mildenhall, and one for each of the other parishes. Geo. Gataker, Esq., is *chairman* ; Wm. Newton, Esq., *vice-chairman* ; W. Isaacson, Esq., *union clerk* and *superintendent registrar* ; Thos. Cross, *master of the Workhouse* ; the Rev. J. H. Raven, *chaplain* ; and Mr. Thos. Robinson, *relieving officer* and *registrar of marriages*. The latter is registrar of births and deaths for Lakenheath District ; and Mr. Cawston, for Worlington District.

The *Manor of Mildenhall*, with the rectory, was given to Bury Abbey, by Edward the Confessor, "that the monks might eat *wheaten*, and not as they did before, *barley bread*." In the 4th and 5th of Philip and Mary, it was granted to Thos. Reeve and Chpr. Ballett; and in the 33rd of Elizabeth, to Francis Gaudy and Edward Latimer, who transferred it in 1609, to Henry, afterwards *Sir Henry Warner*, who was descended from the royal family of Sweden. The Warners were seated at *Wammill Hall*, about a mile west of the town, now a farmhouse, bearing evident marks of being once a stately mansion, and now belonging to *Sir H. E. Bunbury, Bart.*, the present lord of the manor, and owner of a great part of the parish, who resides at Barton Hall, as noticed at page 303, and whose family derived this and other estates by marrying the heiress of the *Hanmers*. These families were long seated in the noble mansion a little north of the church, now the *Manor House*, but occupied only by a gardener. *Sir Thos. Hanmer*, who was speaker of the House of Commons in the reign of Queen Anne, resided here, and died in 1746. Contiguous to his house, he had a very fine *bowling green*, and he was one of the last gentlemen of fashion in this county, who amused himself with the diversion of bowling. The late Sir Thomas Charles Bunbury, Bart., one of the representatives of this county in parliament, resided here occasionally. Another mansion here, built in the reign of Elizabeth, was the seat of the knightly family of North. It has a gallery running the whole length of the front, and its apartments are numerous, but of small dimensions. Mildenhall has furnished London with two *lord mayors*, viz., Henry Barton, in 1428; and *Wm. Gregory*, who held the office in 1451. The town suffered by *fire* in 1507, when it is said 37 houses and many outbuildings were destroyed, in the space of two hours. The *Fen Land* in the parish forms part of the Bedford Level, noticed at page 581, and is divided into two districts, one of which, containing about 3000 acres, is called the *Burnt Fen First District*, and consists of those lands which were allotted to the "*adventurers*," who, in the time of

Charles II., executed the drainage act. The other portion is called *Mildenhall Fen*, or *Burnt Fen Second District*, and comprises 5640A., allotted to the owners of the adjacent lands. For improving the drainage of both these fen districts, *acts of parliament* were passed in the 33rd George II. ; 13th, 37th, and 47th of George III. ; 4th of George IV. ; and 6th and 7th of Victoria. There are now upon them two steam engines, and several wind-mill *pumps*. An act for *enclosing the open fields, wastes, &c.*, in the higher parts of the parish, was obtained in 1807, and the award was executed May 1st, 1812 ; but about 1250 acres still form an open *rabbit warren*. MILDENHALL DROVE, running from Beck Row across the fens to Littleport, in the Isle of Ely, was converted into a good *turnpike road*, in 1828, under an act of the 9th of George IV. Part of the parish belongs to various owners, some of whom have neat houses here.

The CHURCH *(St. Andrew)* is a large and handsome fabric, with a rich roof of carved wood work. It consists of a spacious nave, two side aisles, a proportionate chancel, a neat Gothic porch, and a tower 112 feet high, containing six bells, and formerly surmounted by a leaded spire, which was taken down about 14 years ago. In the chancel, are many *monuments* of the Warner, North, Hanmer, Bunbury, Wichforde, and other families. One of them bears recumbent effigies of Sir Henry North and his lady, with six of their children kneeling by their side. Sir H. E. Bunbury, Bart., is impropriator of the rectory, and patron of the *vicarage*, valued in K.B. at £22. 18s. 1½d., and in 1835 at £369. The Rev. Henry Geo. Phillips, M.A., of Welnetham, is the incumbent, and the Rev. J. H. Raven, M.A., is the curate. There are four *Wesleyan Chapels* in the parish ; one in the town, built in 1839 ; one in Beck Row, built in 1829 ; one on the Burnt Fen, erected in 1839 ; and another at West Row, built in 1840. The *Baptists* have a chapel at West Row, erected in 1809, at the cost of £1000 ; and there is an old *Friends' Meetinghouse* at Holywell Row, but it is not often used. The late T. C. Bunbury erected a *Free School* in the town in 1817, and his successor, the present baronet, allows the mistress the use of a cottage, and a yearly salary of £30, for teaching about 60 poor children.

The following POOR'S LANDS are under the management of the churchwardens, viz., the site of a tenement, let for 11s. ; 13A. 21P. in Westrow Fen, allotted to the poor at the enclosure, in the time of Charles II., and now let for £5. 8s. ; 27A. 3R 8P. in Westrow Fen, let for £11, and given in exchange for a tenement and land given by *Wm. Betts*, for the relief of poor children of High town hamlet, except 10s. a year for a sermon ; an allotment of 100 acres, in *Great Delf*, or *Mildenhall Common*, awarded at the enclosure in the 47th of George III., for the purpose of cutting fuel, or otherwise for the use and benefit of the poor parishioners, and now partly let for £40. 10s., and partly used for cutting turf ; 11A. 2R. 16P. in *Holywell Fen*, which is let at a small rent, subject to the right of the poor of Holywell, of cutting turf ; 4A. 2R. 46P. of fen land near *Coldham Hills*, let for £5, and mostly given by an unknown donor, and partly allotted at the enclosure ; 6A. 2R. 18P. in *Peterborough Field*, let for £8, allotted at the enclosure, in lieu of commonrights and old poor's land ; and an allotment of 1A. 23P., which had been held from the time of the enclosure till 1830, by James Williamson and Edmund Bacon, rent free, in consideration of their fencing it and bringing it into cultivation. They afterwards refused to give it up. Part of the above-named allotments were awarded in satisfaction of the following donations, viz., a yearly rent-charge of 30s., given to the poor by one *Fairweather*, together with a piece of land for the church ; 4 acres of land, purchased with the benefactions of *Richd. Taylor* and *Mr. Pope* ; a piece of land given by James Downing, for the poor of

Holywell row ; and land purchased with £60, given by *Elizabeth Coe* and the *Rev. John Hunt.* The rent of the above-named poor's lands amount to about £72 per annum, and are distributed among the poor parishioners, together with the following yearly *rent-charges,* viz., 40s. out of land at Glemsford, left by *John Allen ;* 40s. given by *Edmund Bright,* out of land at Coldham Hills ; 30s. out of land in Beck row, given by *Jeremiah Haske* and an unknown donor; and 20s. given by *Richard Suckerman,* out of a *dolver* in the Hay-land. In 1677, *Alice Boyder* gave out of a tenement in Holywell row, (now belonging to Mr. Wing,) two yearly rent-charges, viz., 10s. for a sermon, and 20s. for the poor on Maunday Thursday. In 1710, *Catherine Shore* left 7A. 2R. 18P. of land in West row, and directed the rent to be applied yearly in providing stuff gowns for poor women, on August 30th. This land is occupied as garden ground, at the yearly rent of £18. 15s. There is a dolver of 16A. 1R. 19P. in Westrow Fen, which is considered as belonging to this charity, but the rent, £3. 5s. a year, is distributed with the income arising from the poor's lands. In 1724, *John Abbott* charged his lands in Mildenhall Fen with the yearly paymeat of £5, for the following uses in High Town, viz., £3 to provide gowns and coats for three poor widows, and £2 for schooling two poor boys. The property charged with this annuity belongs to the *New England Company* for the propagation of the Gospel in America. HANMER'S ALMSHOUSE, for four aged people, was founded by Sir Thomas Hanmer, who endowed it in 1723 with two yearly rent-charges, viz, 40s. for repairing the building, and £38 to provide for each of the poor almspeople a weekly stipend of 2s. 6d. ; and the yearly allowance of 40s. for clothing, and 20s. for fuel. Sir H. E. Bunbury, Bart., is now owner of the estate charged with these annuities. The *Poor's Houses* consist of six cottages, with gardens, occupied by six poor families. They were given by an unknown donor, and are repaired at the expense of the parish. The poor of Westrow hamlet have a coomb of barley meal yearly from *Baker's Charity.* (See Brandon.)

MILDENHALL PARISH.

POST OFFICE at Mr. Charles Brown's, Mill street.—Letters are received and despatched at 4 morning and ½ past 9 evening, by mail cart, from Lynn and Newmarket.

Those marked 1, are in Beck row ; 2, Bridewell st ; 3, Burnt Fen ; 4, Cake st ; 5, Church yard ; 6, Cock lane ; 7, High st ; 8, Holywell rd ; 9, Holywell row ; 10, Kiln st ; 11, Mill st ; 12, Market lane ; 13, Market place ; 14, Pound street ; 15, West row ; and 16, in Wild street.

6 Andrews Joseph, gent. Cottage
13 Andrews Mrs Sarah
12 Bland G., wine, spirit, ale, and porter merchant
2 Bond Mr Robert ‖ 13 Buck Mrs
7 Chifney Thomas Jacob, gent
4 Cook Mr John
5 Cross Thos. master of Workhouse
6 Curling Edward, land agent
2 Coverdale Mrs Elizabeth
11 Damant Samuel, gentleman
7 Eagle Fuller, parish clerk
15 Evered Mr John
2 Fenn John, gardener, *Great House*
1⅔Ford Jephthah Rumbelow, farrier
12 Garvey Emma, coal dealer
2 Gataker George, Esq
13 Gataker Thomas, Esq
7 Godfrey Isaac, gentleman
11 Goodrich Robert, banker's clerk
8 Grieves Wm. horse breaker
13 Haylock David, land surveyor

7 Hills Mr Rd ‖ 11 Hills Mrs Eliz
13 Hills Mr Thos ‖ 11 Last Mrs H.
11 Howes Mark, mangr. Gas Works
11 Isaacson Wotton, solicr., Union clerk, superintndt. registrar, clerk to Commissioners of Taxes, &c
King John, sluice man, *Cowgrove*
Last John, gamekeeper, *Planting*
14 Lucas Charles J. excise officer
10 Morley Frederick, letter carrier
10 Mower Richard, coal dealer
11 Murrells Mr John, *Bridge House*
10 Newton Rev Thos. (Wesleyan)
6 Norman James, game dealer
11 Owers Samuel, miller & maltster
13 Parkinson John, mason
5 Peachey John, sexton
15 Peachey Samuel, thatcher
11 Petley John, veterinary surgeon
13 Playford Saml. printer, dep. regr. & inspector of weights & measures
14 Pope Wm. D. attorney's clerk

8 Raven Rev Jno. Hardy, M.A. curate
10 Robinson Thos. relieving officer and registrar
2 Ward Jno. gent||6 Webb Mrs Jane
11 Webb Wm. dyer, Bridge House
7 Young Wm. Hy. architect & survr
11 Young Wm. gentleman

BANKS.

7 Oakes, Bevan, & Co. (on Barclay and Co.) Thomas Chifney, *agent*
11 Suffolk Banking Co. (on London and Westminster Bank,) Edmund Denton Isaacson, *agent*
7 Worlledge & Le Blanc (on Barclay and Co.) James Read, *agent*

FIRE & LIFE OFFICES.

Crown Life, A. S. Gedge
Farmers', E. Curling
Norwich Equitable, G. Fletcher
7 Norwich Union, W. Isaacson & Sons
7 Suffolk Amicable, James Read

INNS AND TAVERNS.

7 Bell Inn, (posting,) George Gooch
1 Bird in Hand, Robert Hills
15 Ferry House, Jph. Adams Godfrey
9 Greyhound, Wm. Haylock
10 Half Moon, Edward Musk
10 Maid's Head, Clarke Rampling
3 Pig and Whistle, John Cox
3 Plough & Duck, Robert Gatten
7 Ram, Robert Blade
4 Royal Oak, James Cook
11 Ship, Robert Frost
7 Tiger's Head, Francis Hammond
7 White Hart, (posting,) Sar Simpson
15 White Horse, Charles Peachey

Academies.	*Basket Makers.*
* take *Boarders.*	11 Ashen Charles
2*Bond Ths. Wm.	7 Fletcher Wm.
14 Hills Jacob	5 Naylor Thos.
13 Lucas Ann	*Beerhouses.*
5 Roper Lucy	15 Balls Thomas
2*Ward Miss E.	2 Coe George
& Bond Mrs M.	1 Fuller Robert
Attorneys.	15 Girdlestone H.
11 Isaacson Wotton and Sons	1 Hills James
	9 Lofts John
7 Read James	8 Mortlock Micl.
Auctioneers.	15 Morley Taylor
12 Bland George	Munson J. Mays
11 Rolfe John	Munson Richard
Bakers, &c.	2 Wiseman Geo.
* *Confectioners.*	*Boat Builders.*
12*Barrett Edw.	Chapman Dixie, Wammill
7*Doughty John	Garner John, Bridge
6 Doughty Wm.	
13 Pettit James	

Blacksmiths.
1 Cousins John
15 Ford Charles
15 Ford Jno. Wm.
4 Ford Pp. & Jesse
14 Ford Robert
15 Martin Josiah
10 Morter Chas.
7 Sparke Rd. (& bellhanger)
6 Sterling John
Booksellers, &c.
11 Damant Jas.
7 Foyster Chas. (printer, &c.)
13 Haylock Dvd.
13 Playford Saml. (printer only)
7 Winner John
Boot & Shoe Mkrs.
7 Abbott James
1 Andrews David
15 Ayers Robert
2 Bird Robert
14 Bretnall Jno.
2 Cornell John
11 Davis John
7 Doughty Hy.
1 Hills Thomas
8 Mortlock Michl.
9 Orders James
15 Shackel Prmn.
10 Southgate Isc.
11 Tuck Thos.
Braziers and Ironmongers.
7 Bates Abraham Isaac
Clarke Gardener
13 Dyson John
Bricklayers.
9 Haylock Abm.
8 Morley Jas. Edw
15 Palmer Chas.
9 Rickwood Zach.
6 Webb Chas. & Saml. (& brick & tile makers)
Butchers.
11 Towler Robt.
11 Tyler Henry
12 Webb Wm.
2 Wiseman Geo.
Chemists and Druggists.
13 Lucas Thomas Burton

7 Smith Samuel Fuller
Coach Maker.
6 Stribling Nathl.
Coopers.
13 Dye Nathl.
11 Goodrich Jno.
FARMERS.
15 Avis Adam
15 Avis Adam, jn
1 Britwell John
3 Burgess James
3 Burgess Roger
Butcher James, Weston ditch
1 Carpenter Ths.
Carpenter Wm., Common
16 Childerstone Edward
9 Childerstone Frs
9 Childerstone Hy
9 Childerstone Isc
9 Childerstone Js.
Aspal Hall
9 Childerstone Jonathan
16 Childerstone Thomas
3 Clarke Thos.
16 Clements Rd.
15 Cowell Edwd.
1 Cowell Thos.
15 Curtis Charles
3 Edwards Frdk.
3 Flanders Wm.
15 Flatt Joseph
15 Fletcher Isaac
15 Fletcher Robt.
15 Fletcher Wm.
9 Forster John Clements
15 Gittus Robert
11 Goodrich Jno.
2 Halls John
Halls Richard, Common
Hardy William, *Peter's House*
13 Hills Wm. Jas.
15 Jaggard Robt.
15 Jest Wm.
Leonard Henry, Weston ditch
1 Manning Hy.
10 Morter Chas.
1 Morley Eliz.

7 Morley James, (& corn mert)
Mortlock Robert
15 PaineCharles, Carrols
Paine William, Wammill Hall
Peachey Abrm., Kenny Hill
16 PeacheyEdw.
Peachey George, Common
1 Peachey John
4PeacheyReubn.
Phillips William, Burcham Hill
15 Rolfe Robert
Saunders Henry
3 Seaber James
3 Seaber John, FrieslandHouse
3 Seaber Robert Fison
3 Shillito Stephen Tymm
3 Smith Wm.
16 Sucker James
9 Wing Charles
16 Wing Chas.
1 Wing George
9 Wing Henry
16 Wing James
15YoungmanChs

Furniture Brkrs.
13Clarke Gardnr.
13 Moore Jno. (& cabinet maker)

Gardeners, &c.
15 Avis John
15 Batley Eliz.
15 Burgess Jas.
15 EllingtonEbr.
15 Ellington Jno.
15 Parker Wm.

15 Rolfe John
2 Watson Esther

Grocers & Drprs.
7 Avey Chas. (& British wine dlr)
7 Chifney James
7 Large Fras. (& leather cutter)
7 Staples Wm. (British wine dlr.) Stamp off.
Wing Wm.& Jno. (& tal. chndlrs)

Hair Dressers.
14 DockingChas.
13 Graham Robt.
6 Hills John

Joiners.
15 Bacon Henry
15 Burgess Geo.
15 Clarke Edwd.
15 Clarke Richd.
1 Cowell Thos.
7 Hammond Frs.
15 Leonard Thos.
2 WilliamsDavid
7YoungWm.Hy.

Lime Burners.
15 Robins Richd.
6 WebbChs.& Sl.

Milliners, &c.
11 Ashen Mary and Ann
7 Avey Charlotte
10 Burnett Mary

Painters, Plumbers, & Glaziers.
11 Damant Jas.
14 Hills Chas.
11 Rolfe Samuel

Saddlers, &c.
6 MerringtonRd.
13 Peachey Rd.
11 Rolfe John

Shopkeepers.
10 Bangs Fuller
2 Coe George
1 Halls Samuel
15 Girdlestone Horatio
15 Horn Robert
15 King James
2 Morley Wm.
15 Place John
15 RumbelowJph
2 Wiseman Geo.

Straw Hat Mfrs.
14 Ashen Mary
7 Avey Charlotte
13 Scates Martha
6 Watson Chltte.

Surgeons.
11 AdrichPelhm.
11 Gedge Arthur Stedman
6 Robinson John Wadham

Wilde George Reynolds

Tailors.
13 BrightwellJn.
11 Brown Chas.
7 Doughty Robt.
13 Graham Robt. (clothes broker)
15 MorleyTaylor
14 Morley James
13 Morley Wm.
13 Scates Chas.
12 WindettArthr.

Watch & Clock Makers.
7 Eagle Fuller
13 Harris Henry

Wheelwrights.
15 Benstead Jno.
16 Leonard Chas.
15 Phillips John
6 StriblingNathl.

COACH, from the White Hart, to London, 12 noon, & to Holt, 2 aft
Mail Carts, to London, 10 night; to Stoke, 10 mg ; & to Thetford, 4 mg
CARRIERS.
Hacon & Balls' Vans, from the Bell, to London, Tues. & Fri. ; and to Brandon, Watton, &c., Monday and Thursday, 8 morning
Deacon, Archer, & Co.'s Vans, &c., from the White Hart, to London and Lynn daily, and to Holt, Wells, &c. Mon. Wed. and Fri
Geo. Coe & Jas. Morley, from Bridewell street, to Bury, Wed. & Sat. and to Ely, Thursday morning
Wm. Powell, Market place, to Bury, Wednesday and Saturday
BARGES from the Bridge daily, to Bury and Lynn

NEWMARKET.   *(See page* 712.)

SANTON DOWNHAM is a sandy parish of 3860 acres, and 68 inhabitants, on the south side of the Little Ouse, opposite Santon, on the Norfolk side of the river, 2 miles E. by N. of Brandon, and nearly 5 miles N.W. of Thetford.   The *Hall,* a handsome mansion in a small park, near the river, is the seat of Lord William Powlett, the lord of the manor, owner of the parish, impropriator, and patron of the *Church,* (St. Mary,) which is a perpetual curacy, valued in 1835 at £59, and now enjoyed by the Rev. W. E. Sims, for whom the Rev. Hy. Sims officiates.   The manor was given by Wm. the Conqueror to Bury Abbey, and by Henry VIII. to Sir Thos. Kitson, but part of the parish

was held by Ixworth Priory, and granted at the dissolution to Richd. Codington, and Elizabeth his wife. It is remarkable for an *inundation of sand*, which, in 1668, threatened to overwhelm the whole parish. The sand was blown for several years by frequent strong winds of long continuance, from the hills of Lakenheath, distant about five miles to the south-west. It buried and destroyed several houses and cottages, and so choked the navigation of the river that a vessel with two loads weight, found as much difficulty in passing as it had done before with ten. Mr. Wright, who occupied the largest farm house, had all his avenues blocked up, so that there was no access to his dwelling but over the tops of two walls, 8 or 9 feet high; and at one time, the sand filled his yard, and was blown up to the eaves of his out-buildings. For several years, he raised furze edges, set upon one another as fast as they were levelled by the sand. By this experiment, he raised banks near twenty yards high, and brought the sand into the compass of 8 or 10 acres; then by laying upon it some hundred loads of earth and dung, he reduced it again to firm land. He then cleared all his walls; and with the assistance of his neighbours, carted away about 1500 loads, and cut a passage to his house through the main body of the sand. The parish was enclosed about 40 years ago, except 700A. still forming an open warren and sheep walk. DIRECTORY : Lord Wm. Powlett, *Santon Downham Hall;* Edward Butter, *gardener;* Jas. Pollard, *house steward;* Jas. Marsh, *gamekeeper;* Fredk. Phillips, *farm steward;* Robt. Edwards, farmer ; and Thos. Parrott, farmer, *Warren Lodge.*

THETFORD. (*See page* 706.)

TUDDENHAM, a pleasant village on an acclivity near a rivulet, 3 miles S.S.E. of Mildenhall, has in its parish 428 souls, and 2435 acres, extending eastward to the river Lark. The Marquis of Bristol and M. E. Rogers, Esq., are lords of the manors and owners of most of the soil. The *Church* (St. Mary) is a neat structure, with a tower and five bells. The living is a *rectory,* valued in K.B. at £10. 17s. 6d., and in 1835 at £284. The Marquis of Bristol is *patron ;* the Rev. W. Hall, *incumbent;* and the Rev. H. R. Smythies, *curate.* Here is a Baptist Chapel, built in 1843. The *Church Land* is an allotment of 16A. 3R. 29P., awarded at the enclosure in 1796, in lieu of open field land held from time immemorial for the repairs of the church. It is let for about £13 a year. In 1711, *Jane Wotton* left a yearly rent of £6 out of the parsonage of Tuddenham, for distribution among the poor parishioners. The *Free School* was founded by *John Cockerton,* who, in 1723, endowed it with a dwelling-house and 3A. of land, occupied by the schoolmaster, and with a barn, 55A. 2R. 12P. of freehold land, and 36A. 1R. 28P. of copyhold land, let for about £70 a year. The master teaches as free scholars all the poor children of the parish who are sent to him. His house is about to be rebuilt, and the school repaired. Mr. Thos. Steel has a large steam and water corn mill in the parish.

Evered Mr Francis
Finton Walter, tailor
Firman Mary, shopkeeper
Kendall Wm. wheelwright
Nayler James, vict. *White Horse*
Phillips Wm. shoemaker
Reynolds Mrs Sarah
Rumbelow Philip, blacksmith
Sparrow Elias, shoemaker
Sparrow Robert, shopkeeper
Steel Thomas, corn miller
Tyler Peter, butcher & vict. *Anchor*

FARMERS.
Booty John, *Tuddenham Hall*
Steel Thomas || Burt Thomas

Fowler Wm. || Wiseman David
CARRIER, Wm. Craske, to Bury,
Wednesday

WANGFORD parish, 3 miles S.W. of Brandon, has only 46 inhabitants, and 3500 acres of sandy land, all the property of George St.
Vincent Wilson, Esq., and occupied as one farm, by Mr. Robt. Place,
of *Wangford Hall ;* but about 2700 acres from an open rabbit warren,
adjoining that of Lakenheath. The hall, an ancient mansion, was the
seat of Lord Chief Justice Wright, who flourished in the reign of James
II. The manor afterwards belonged to the Holts. The *Church* (St.
Denis) has a tower and two bells, and the rectory, valued in K.B. at
£9. 11s. 10½d., is united with that of Brandon. (See page 584.)

WORLINGTON, a neat and pleasant village on the south bank of
the navigable river Lark, 1 mile W.S.W. of Mildenhall, has in its parish 1955 acres of land, and 351 souls. Geo. Gataker and P. H. Ho-
neywood, Esqrs., are lords of the manors, but part of the parish belongs
to Sir John Rae Reid, Bart, and several other proprietors. The soil
is sandy, but generally fertile. The *Church* (All Saints) has a tower
and three bells, and the living is a *rectory,* valued in K.B. at £19. 6s.
8d., and in 1835 at £197. The Hon. Thos. Windsor is patron, and
the Rev. Jas. Gibson, B.A., incumbent. The tithes were commuted
at the enclosure in 1790, for an allotment of 291 acres. An *Infant
School* was built here in 1840. In 1620, *John Mortiock* left for the
poor parishioners a yearly rent-charge of 30s. out of land now belonging to Mr. Godfrey. They have also a yearly rent-charge of 24s. out of
the rectorial tithes of Stow Upland, left by Thos. Blackerly, in 1688
and the interest of £50 given by an unknown donor, and now secured
on the tolls of the Thetford and Newmarket turnpike. John Hastings,
Earl of Pembroke, died seized of this manor in the 49th of Edward III.
It afterwards passed to the Earl of Oxford, and was carried by his
heiress in marriage to Lord Sandys, who sold it to Geo. Montgomery,
Esq., one of the representatives of Ipswich, in Parliament, in 1754.

Barton Ann, vict. *Bell*
Cawston John, valuer and registrar
Cawston Wm. Westerman, tithe ap-
portioner and general agent
Chapman Frederick, blacksmith
Cooper Frederick, seed merchant
Goodchild, Wm. vict. *Chequers*
Harlock Wm. and John, maltsters
Lindsell John, shopkeeper
Middleditch Jeremiah, shoemaker
Parker Mark, gardener & seedsman
Poulter John, wheelwright
Poulter Wm. carpenter & dep. regr.

Scarlin James, M. gentleman
Smith Caroline, schoolmistress
Turner James, shopkeeper
Waller Rev Wm. B.A. *curate*
Wing Richard & Charles, maltsters
FARMERS.
Booty Mary || Chapman Edward
Godfrey James || Godfrey Edward
Norman Wm. || Poulter Edward
CARRIERS, Jas. Turner, to Bury,
Wed. ; Wm. Chapman, *(mail
cart)* to Soham, 6 morning

☞ *Lackford Hundred continued at page* 706.

THINGOE HUNDRED,

Is a fertile district, of an irregular oval figure, about 9 miles in its greatest breadth, and 11 in length, including the Borough of *Bury-St.-Edmund's*, which lies within its limits, but is a separate jurisdiction. It is bounded by the Hundreds of Lackford, Blackbourn, Thedwestry, Babergh, and Risbridge. The *River Lark* rises within its limits, and is navigable from Fornham-All-Saints, near Bury, to the Ouse, which runs to Lynn, and communicates with the canals of Cambridge, Bedford, and other counties. It is in the *Franchise of St. Edmund's*, in the *Deanery of Thingoe, Archdeaconry of Sudbury*, and *Diocese of Ely*. The Borough of Bury forms a separate *Union* under the New Poor Law ; and *Thingoe Union* comprises all the eighteen parishes in Thingoe Hundred, of which the following is an enumeration, shewing their territorial extent, the annual value of their lands and buildings, as assessed to the property tax, in 1815, and their population in 1801 and 1841 :—

PARISHES.	Acr.	Rntl £.	Populatn 1801	1841	PARISHES.	Acres.	Rental £.	Population 1801	1841
Barrow............	2810	3726	614	995	Rede	1310	1292	161	241
Brockley	1080	1450	253	380	Risby	2620	2500	266	360
Chevington	2240	2681	445	624	Saxham (Great) ..	1670	2301	226	271
Flempton ...•....	720	1049	99	210	Saxham (Little) ..	1300	1727	194	230
Fornham (All Saints)	2200	2119	236	336	Westley	680	974	88	144
Hargrave ......} * Southwell Park..}	1870	2159	324	457 16	Whepstead	3450	3421	546	681
Hawstead ......} * Hardwick, Ex. P}	1980	3560	392	457 19	TOTAL, THINGOE,	31,850	38,528	4,982	6,672
Hengrave..........	1000	1712	196	228	BOROUGH OF				
Horningsheath ..} + Horsecroft......}	1780	2458	543	575 34	*Bury St. Edmund's* St. James'Parish}	3040	13,026	3,565	6.269
Ickworth	1350	2074	67	62	St. Mary'sParish}			4,090	6,269
Lackford	2470	1642	162	193					
+Nowton	1320	1683	170	159	TOTAL, BURY,⸹	3,040	13.026	7,655	12,538

* *Southwell Park* and *Hardwick*, are *Extra Parochial.*

⸹ The Return of St. Mary's, in Bury, includes 106 persons in Thingoe Union Workhouse; 93 in the County Goal and House of Correction; 58 in Suffolk General Hospital; and 93 in Bury St.-Edmund's Workhouse.

† *Horsecroft Hamlet* is partly in Nowton parish, in which 12 of its inhabitants reside.

☞ The CHIEF CONSTABLES of Thingoe Hundred are—Mr. James Payne, of Whepstead ; and Mr. J. R. Kerry, of Little Saxham.

THINGOE UNION, formed under the New Poor Law, comprises an area of 133 square miles, and 46 parishes, of which 15 are in Thedwestry Hundred, 10 in Blackbourn Hundred, 3 in Risbridge Hundred, and 18 constitute the Hundred of Thingoe, just described. It had 18,031 inhabitants in 1841. The average annual expenditure of the district for the support of the poor, during the three years before the formation of the Union, was £13,538; but in 1838, the expenditure was only £9,026; and in 1840, £9,657 4s. The number of paupers relieved in the last quarter of 1842, was 2,056, of whom 206 were in-door poor. The WORKHOUSE stands within the Borough of Bury-St.-Edmund's, near the Suffolk General Hospital, and is a large brick building, which was finished in 1836, at the cost of about £5,000, and has room for 250 paupers, and had 160 inmates in March 1843. Mr. Jas. Thos. Burbridge is *Master of the Workhouse ;* and

James Sparke, Esq., is *Clerk to the Board of Guardians.*   One Guardian is returned for each parish; and the Rev.W. J. S. Casborne is the *Chairman.*

BURY-ST.-EDMUND'S UNION comprises only the Borough, the extent and population of which are already stated in the preceding Table.   Its *Workhouse,* in College-street, was built many years ago, and has room for 200 inmates, and had about 170 in March 1843; but its average number is about 100.   Its expenditure for the support of the poor, in 1837, was £6,627.   Six Guardians are elected for each of its two parishes.   John Cambridge, Esq., is the *Union Clerk ;* and Mr. Thomas Legge is *Master of the Workhouse.*   The two parishes of Bury were united for the support of their poor, by an Act of Parliament passed in 1746.

BURY ST. EDMUND'S,

An ancient borough, the capital of the Western Division of Suffolk, and of the Franchise or Liberty of St. Edmund, and one of the most pleasing and interesting market towns in England, is seated in the centre of a richly cultivated country, upon a bold acclivity, skirted on the north and east by the river Lark and one of its tributary streams, which unite in the grounds of the once splendid Abbey, of which here are still extensive and beautiful remains.   The streets are broad, well paved, and contain many handsome houses and public-buildings, and intersect each other at right angles.   The town is so pleasantly situated, commands such extensive prospects, and the air is so salubrious, that it has been called the Montpellier of England.   On all sides of it, within the distance of a few miles, are the beautiful *parks* and *mansions* of some of the most wealthy nobility and gentry of the county.   The Lark is *navigable* for small craft to Fornham, about a mile below the town, which is approached by excellent turnpike roads, and is distant 14 miles E. of Newmarket; 12 miles S. of Thetford; 26 miles N.W. by W. of Ipswich; 16 miles N. of Sudbury; 13½ W.N.W. of Stowmarket ; 29 miles E.N.E. of Cambridge; 43 miles S.W. by S. of Norwich ; 42 miles S. by E. of Lynn; and 71 miles N.E. of London.

The *Town,* with its suburbs, is about a mile and a half in length, and a mile and a quarter in breadth, and nearly in the centre of the BOROUGH, which is of an irregular circular figure, about three miles in diameter, and divided into the two *parishes of St. Mary* and *St. James,* which comprise 3,040 acres, and increased their *population* from 7,655 in 1801, to 7,986 in 1811; 9,999 in 1821; 11,436 in 1831; and 12,538 in 1841 ; when an equal number was returned for each parish as has been seen at page 601.   These parishes are nearly of equal extent, and have their beautiful *Churches* in the same Church yard, which is entered through an ancient gate-tower, said to be one of the finest Norman Towers in Europe, and formerly the grand portal of the magnificent Abbey Church, in which was the celebrated shrine of *St. Edmund the king and martyr,* from whom the burgh or town had its present name.   *Markets* are held here every Wednesday and Saturday ; the former is an extensive corn and cattle mart, and both are abundantly supplied with provisions.   The *Corn Exchange* is a large and commodious building, erected in 1836.   The *Shambles,* opposite the old market cross, are of free stone, and were fin-

ished in 1761, George, the second Earl of Bristol giving £400 towards their completion. Three annual *fairs* are held here on Easter Tuesday and two following days, for cattle, &c.; on October 2nd and several following days, for toys, fancy articles, pleasure, &c.; and on December 1st, for cattle, cheese, &c. The October fair was established some years ago in lieu of *St. Matthew's Fair*, which was held by charter granted to the Abbot in 1272, and usually continued for three weeks from the 18th of September. It was one of the most frequented and fashionable marts in the kingdom, especially in monastic times, when the Abbot kept an open table for the nobility and gentry who visited it, and persons of inferior rank were entertained by the monks in the refectory. The booths of manufacturers, dealers, showmen, &c., occupied the spacious area called the Angel Hill, and all the avenues leading to the Abbot's palace. Among the distinguished personages who visited it in the 15th century, were the Duke of Suffolk, and his royal consort, Mary Tudor, Queen-dowager of France, who had a magnificent tent erected on the fair-ground for themselves and their splendid retinue. The Easter fair was granted by James I., who, in the 6th year of his reign, granted the other fairs and markets in fee-farm, to the Corporation, who receive the tolls, and have power to extend the fairs to any length of time they think proper. That held December 1st, is now the principal fair. Extensive wool fairs were formerly held here, and great quantities were stored in the buildings still called the *Wool-Halls*.

Here are now two *woolstaplers*, a number of extensive *corn merchants and maltsters*, four breweries, several corn mills, two foundries, two tanneries, several curriers and leather dressers, a parchment manufactory, and nine master coach builders. There are in the principal streets many well stocked shops, and commodious inns and taverns.

The LARK, or *Burn*, a small river which flows southward from Bury to the Ouse, in Norfolk, was made navigable as high as Fornham-All-Saints about a mile below the town, under the powers of an Act of Parliament passed in the 11th and 12th of William and Mary, (A. D. 1698.) This Act was amended by another passed in 1817, which placed the *navigation* under the management of about eighty *commissioners*, of whom fifty new ones were appointed in 1843, to fill up the vacancies occasioned by death. From some misunderstanding between the corporation and the first proprietors, respecting the right to construct wharfs and erect warehouses within the borough, the navigation has never been extended to the town. By virtue of the two acts of parliament and the will of the late Susanna Palmer, her nephew, Sir Thomas Gery Cullum, Bart., of Hardwick House, and the other proprietors of the navigation, are entitled to certain tolls on all coals and goods conveyed on any part of the river between Mildenhall and Bury. Of late years, very large sums have been expended in improving the navigation, and the *tolls* have been reduced from 7s. and 8s. to 4s. 6d. and 5s. per ton; in consequence of which, there is now a much greater traffic on the river to and from Lynn and other places, than formerly; and it is hoped that some arrangement will, ere long, be made with the present corporation, for the extension of the navigation up to the town, which would be of con-

siderable benefit to the inhabitants.   John Greene, Esq. is clerk to the commissioners.   About thirty years ago it was in contemplation to cut a canal from Bury to the river Stour, near Manningtree, but the project was abandoned, in consequence of the opposition of the proprietors of the Lark navigation and a few of the principal land owners, though the intended line was surveyed by Mr. Rennie.   In 1841, an Act was obtained for a *Railway* from Bury to join the Eastern Counties Railway at Kelvedon, in Essex, a distance of about thirty miles; but very little has yet been done in this undertaking, which will complete the route by rails from London to Bury.

An Act for better paving, lighting, cleansing, watching, and otherwise *improving the town of Bury St. Edmund's*, was passed in 1811, and it was amended by another Act passed in 1820.   Under these Acts, the town has been greatly improved, and is now well paved and lighted, and nearly all the streets have flagged causeways in place of the rough pebbled footpaths which existed in most of them till 1811. The *Gas Works* were erected in 1824, at the cost of about £12,000, and are the property of six shareholders.

The BOROUGH sent members to parliament in the 30th of Edw. I., but not afterwards till the 18th of James I., since which time it has regularly returned two representatives.   James I., in the 4th year of his reign, granted the borough a *charter of incorporation.* Two years afterwards, he gave the corporation the reversion of the houses, tithes, and glebes, called Almoner's Barns, and of the fairs and markets, gaol, toll house, &c.   In the 12th year of his reign, he granted them another charter, enlarging their former privileges, &c. and giving them the churches, libraries, bells, rectories, and profits of the said churches, not previously granted to them.   In the same charter, he confirmed to them and other principal inhabitants, as trustees, all the lands and possessions given by former benefactions, and forming a large portion of the numerous charities comprised in what is called the *Guildhall Feoffment*, now yielding an annual income of more than £2,100, as will be seen at a subsequent page.   Under these charters, the *government of the borough* was vested in an alderman, 12 capital burgesses, and 24 common councilmen, and with them rested solely the right of electing the representatives of the borough. They had a recorder, and held quarter sessions, &c.   The alderman, chosen annually from the six capital burgesses, acted as chief magistrate, and six others were assistant justices, and one held the office of coroner.   Under the *Municipal Act* of 1835, the borough has been divided into *three wards*, and placed under the government of a *mayor, recorder, six aldermen, eighteen councillors*, and a commission of the peace, consisting of about *fifteen magistrates;* of whom, with their officers, a list will be given at a subsequent page.   Under the Reform Act of 1832, the right of electing two parliamentary representatives for the borough, is vested in the male occupiers of houses in the borough, of the yearly value of £10 or upwards.   The number of *voters* is now about 700; but there are in the borough about 850 houses of the yearly value of £10 or upwards; and about 200 of them are let at from £20 to £40; and 60 at above £40 per annum.

ANCIENT HISTORY: — Bury St. Edmund's dates its origin from a very remote period, but antiquaries differ much in their

opinions respecting the precise time in which the site of the town began to be inhabited. Some writers, among whom are Camden, Batteley, and Gale, have supposed that it was the Roman Station, denominated *Villa Faustini* · but there being no *data* to support this conjecture, other intelligent writers have questioned its probability; indeed, not a solitary Roman remain has ever been found here. It is generally agreed that it was occupied by the Saxons, under the name of *Beoderic's-worth,* that is, the seat, mansion, or residence of Beoderic; but how long it bore that name is another point on which authors are at variance. Sigbert, the fifth monarch of East Anglia, having embraced *Christianity* in France, whither he had been banished by his half-brother and predecessor, Erpenwald, founded here, about the year 638, a Christian church and monastery, which was called the *Monastery of St. Mary at Beodericworth.* Abbo Floriacencis, a monk, who came here from Fleury, in France, says the town had this name from *Beoderic,* a distinguished Saxon, who, at his death, bequeathed it to *Edmund, the king and martyr,* from whom it was afterwards called *St. Edmund's Bury.* This celebrated monarch of East Anglia succeeded his uncle Offa, in 855. The events of his life, as recorded by monkish writers, are either a tissue of fictions, or are so distorted by them, that it is impossible to distinguish truth from falsehood. Abbo Floriacencis was his first biographer. Coming about 985, on a visit to St. Dunstan, archbishop of Canterbury, he undertook to write the life of the saint from the narrative given from memory by that prelate, who had heard the circumstances related to king Athelstan by a very old man, that had been one of Edmund's officers. The particulars of Edmund's life, previously to his elevation to the throne, are recorded by Galfridus de Fontibus; and the relations of these writers form the ground work of the histories of all succeeding biographers. According to these then, Edmund was the son of Alkmund, a Saxon prince, distinguished for valour, wisdom, and piety. Being upon a pilgrimage at Rome, while performing his devotions, the sun was observed to shine with uncommon brilliance on Alkmund's breast. This was hailed as a happy omen by a prophetess; she promised Alkmund a son, whose fame should extend over the whole world. The prince returned home, and the same year, his queen, Siware, made him a joyful father. In Nuremberg, his capital, Edmund is said to have been born in the year 841. Offa at this time swayed the sceptre of the East Angles, and having no children, he resolved to make a pilgrimage to Jerusalem, there to supplicate the blessing of an heir. On his way to the Holy Land, he visited his kinsman Alkmund, and was captivated by the engaging manners, and amiable qualities of the youthful Edmund. On his departure, he presented to the prince a valuable ring, as a pledge of attachment and regard. Offa, having performed at Jerusalem the religious exercises which were the object of his pilgrimage, was taken ill on his return, and feeling his dissolution approaching, he convoked his council, to whom he earnestly recommended his young relation as his successor. After the celebration of the funeral rites, Offa's nobles hastened to Saxony, and in compliance with the royal mandate, acquainted Edmund with the dying wishes of their master. Alkmund, with the approbation of his assembled bishops and nobles,

gave his concurrence to this arrangement, and Edmund, taking leave of his parents, amidst their tears and blessings set sail for his new dominions. No sooner did he reach the shore, than he threw himself on his knees to thank heaven for past mercies, and to implore its future protection. Five springs of fresh water immediately burst from the dry and sandy soil; on which spot he afterwards built, in commemoration of this event, the town of Hunstanton, in Norfolk.

Edmund did not assume the regal dignity immediately on his arrival, but spent the following year in studious retirement at Attleborough. " It might now be expected," observes Yates, the historian of Bury, " that under such circumstances, his counsellors should direct his young mind to anticipate the cares of royalty : to examine the laws of the state he was about to govern; and to make himself acquainted with the customs, manners, and interests of the people whose happiness was shortly to be intrusted to him."

The genius of the age, however, gave a very different turn to Edmund's studies : he employed the period of his seclusion in committing the psalter to memory.* From this retirement he was drawn, to be invested with the insignia of sovereignty, and was crowned at Bury,† by Humbert, bishop of Elmham, on the 25th December, 855, having then completed the 15th year of his age.

Edmund's biographers, having now seated him on the throne, proceed to record his virtues as a sovereign in a strain of the most pompous panegyric. No facts, however, are adduced to justify these lavish encomiums. The truth seems to be, that Edmund's years, and his natural disposition were such, as to enable the monks and ecclesiastics (from which class of persons he derived all his posthumous celebrity) to govern him with ease. Piety, candour, gentleness, and humility, formed the distinguishing features of his character, and the possession of these insured to him the reputation of all other good qualities. However they might have befitted a cowl, they were certainly not calculated to support the dignity of a crown, in the disastrous times in which Edmund lived. The commencement of his misfortunes is enveloped in the same obscurity as the other events of his life. Most of our ancient annalists and general historians ascribe the invasion of the Danes, who about this period began to make descents on the coasts of this island, and who at length deprived Edmund of his kingdom and his life, to the following circumstances:—

Lodbrog, king of Denmark, was very fond of hawking ; and one day, while enjoying that sport, his favourite bird happened to fall into the sea. The monarch, anxious to save the hawk, leaped into the first boat that presented itself, and put off to his assistance. A sudden storm arose, and carried him,

* The book used on this occasion, was said to have been preserved at the abbey at Bury with religious veneration. A very curious ancient psalter, still to be seen in the library of St. James's church, is thought by some antiquaries to be this very book. *Yates'His.* p.30

† From the uncertain orthography of ancient writers, different places have been mentioned as the scene of this ceremony. Camden is of opinion that it was performed at Bourn, in Lincolnshire ; Matthew of Westminster, says, " at the royal town called Bures," and Galfridus de Fontibus expressly tells us that " Edmund was consecrated and anointed king at Burum, a royal town, the boundary of Essex and Suffolk, situated upon the Stour." This evidently denotes the village of Bures; but as nothing, either in history, or its present appearance, can justify this spot in claiming the distinction of a royal town, we are inclined to follow those authorities which fix the solemnity of Edmund's coronation at Bury, a place which previously held an eminent rank in the kingdom.

after encountering imminent dangers, up the mouth of the Yare, as far as Reedham in Norfolk. The inhabitants of the country, having discovered the stranger, conducted him to Edmund, who then kept his court at Caistor, only ten miles distant. The king received him with great kindness and respect, entertained him in a manner suitable to his rank, and directed Bern, his own falconer, to accompany his guest, whenever he chose to take his favourite diversion. The skill and success of the royal visitor in hawking, excited Edmund's admiration, and inflamed Bern with such jealousy, that one day, when they were sporting together in the woods, he seized the opportunity, murdered him, and buried the body. Lodbrog's absence for three days occasioned considerable alarm. His favorite greyhound was observed to come home for food, fawning upon the king and his courtiers whenever he was compelled to visit them, and to retire as soon as he had satisfied his wants. On the fourth day he was followed by some of them, whom he conducted to the murdered body of his master. Edmund instituted an inquiry into the affair, when, from the ferocity of the dog to Bern, and other circumstances, the murderer was discovered, and condemned by the king to be turned adrift alone, without oars or sails, in the same boat which brought Lodbrog to East Anglia. This boat was wafted in safety to the Danish coast, where it was known to be the same in which Lodbrog left the country. Bern was seized, carried to Inguar and Hubba, the sons of the king, and questioned by them concerning their father. The villain replied, that Lodbrog had been cast upon the shore of England, and there put to death by Edmund's command. Inflamed with rage, the sons resolved on revenge, and speedily raised an army of 20,000 men to invade his dominions.[*]

This armament, which is said to have sailed from Denmark in 865, is reported by some historians to have been driven by contrary winds to Berwick-upon-Tweed. After committing the greatest cruelties in this part of the country, the Danes again embarked, but seem each succeeding spring to have renewed their descents. In 869, these ruthless barbarians proceeded southward from Yorkshire, in a torrent which destroyed every vestige of civilization. In 870, they appear to have reached East Anglia, where Inguar gained possession of *Thetford*, king Edmund's capital. The latter collected his forces and marched to oppose the invaders. The hostile armies met near Thetford, and after an engagement maintained for a whole day, with the most determined courage and great slaughter on both sides, victory remained undecided. The pious king, to use the language of the monkish writers, was so extremely affected by the death of so many martyrs, who had shed their blood in defence of the Christian faith, and the miserable end of so many unconverted infidels, that he retired in the night to Eglesdene. Hither he was soon followed by an embassy from Inguar, who was, soon after the battle, joined by his brother Hubba, with ten thousand fresh troops. The Danish chieftain proposed, that he should become his vassal, and divide with him his treasures and dominions. Bishop Humbert earnestly recommended his compliance; but Edmund returned for answer, that he would never submit to a pagan. At the same time, out of tenderness for his subjects, he resolved to make no farther resistance, and accordingly surrendered without a struggle to the superior force sent against him by Inguar and Hubba. Still refusing to accede to the terms of the con-

---

[*] Turner, in his *History of the Anglo-Saxons*, (vol. II. p. 107,) enters into an examination of this story respecting Lodbrog, and the result of his researches establishes the fictitious character of this narrative of the cause of the Danish invasion.

querors, he was bound to a tree, his body was pierced with arrows, and his head cut off, and thrown contemptuously into the thickest part of a neighbouring wood. His faithful friend, bishop Humbert, suffered at the same time with his royal master. The Danes having entirely laid waste this part of the country, soon proceeded in quest of scenes better calculated to gratify their love of plunder. Released from the terror their presence inspired, the East Angles, prompted by affection to their late sovereign, assembled to pay the last duties to his remains. The body was soon discovered and conveyed to Hoxne, but the head could no where be found. His faithful subjects then divided themselves into small parties, to explore the adjacent wood. Here some of them, being separated from their companions, cried out, " Where are you?" The head immediately replied " Here! here ! here !" If their astonishment was excited by this obliging information so miraculously conveyed, it was not likely to be abated by what followed. On coming to the spot whence the voice proceeded, they found a wolf, holding the head between his fore-feet. The animal politely delivered up his charge, which, the moment it came in contact with the body, returned so exactly to its former place, that the juncture was not visible except when closely examined. The wolf remained a harmless spectator of the scene, and as we are informed by all the ancient historians, after gravely attending the funeral at Hoxne, peaceably retired to his native woods. This happened about forty days after the death of the saint.

These *legendary tales* might perhaps be deemed too frivolous for notice ; but, being intimately connected with the prosperity of Bury, and indeed inseparably interwoven with the history of that place, they could not with propriety be omitted in this account. The arms of the town still commemorate the brute protector of the royal martyr's head, which also furnished ancient artists with a favorite subject for the exercise of their talents. For thirty-three years the body of the king, buried in the earth, lay neglected in the obscure chapel of Hoxne. At length the interference of ecclesiastics, who in those days were capable of guiding the public feeling as they pleased, and perhaps also that reverence which unfortunate royalty seldom fails to inspire, occasioned the circulation of reports, that various miracles had been performed at Edmund's grave. All ranks now concurred to testify their respect for his memory ; a large church was constructed of wood at Beodericworth, and thither the body, found perfect and uncorrupted, and with the head re-united to it, was removed in 903.†
Some ecclesiastics immediately devoted themselves to the monastic life under the protection of the royal saint and martyr ; their number increased, and about 925, they were incorporated into a *college of priests*. The inhabitants, perceiving the advantages likely to accrue to themselves from the increasing celebrity of St. Edmund's relics, chose him for their titular saint, and began to call the place after his name. The monks neglected no opportunity of blazoning the extra-

---

† The incorruption of the body was attested by a female devotee named Oswina, who declared, that she had long lived in seclusion near the town ; that for several preceding years she had annually cut the hair and pared the nails of the saint, and had preserved these sacred relics with religious veneration. A list of six other witnesses of this fact is given in Leland's Collectanea, vol. I. page 222.

ordinary miracles performed by the agency of the sacred body, the fame of which procured the convent numerous oblations and benefactions.

King Athelstan appears to have been the first royal benefactor. Besides other donations, he presented to the church of St. Edmund, a copy of the Evangelists, a gift of such value in those days, that the donor offered it upon the altar *pro remedio animæ suæ*, for the benefit of his soul. But more substantial favors were bestowed upon this establishment by *Edmund, son of Edward the Elder,* who may indeed be considered as having laid the foundation of its future wealth and splendor. He gave the monks a jurisdiction over the whole town, and one mile round it, confirming this and other privileges by a royal grant or charter in 945. This example was imitated by succeeding sovereigns, and other persons of distinction, through whose liberality many considerable manors in the neighbourhood of Bury were soon added to the possessions of the monastery. About this time commenced the disputes between the seculars or established clergy of the country, and the monks or regulars. The latter, by the appearance of superior sanctity, contrived to render themselves highly popular; and by their artifices at length dispossessed the former of their most valuable establishments. The increasing fame and wealth of the convent of St. Edmund had not escaped the notice of the monks, who gained over the bishop of the diocese; and in 990 procured the appointment of Ailwin, one of their number, to be the guardian of the body of the saint, with which the secular priests were pronounced unworthy to be entrusted, "on account of their insolence and irregularity."

Sweyn, king of Denmark, having invaded England, and laid waste the whole of East-Anglia, burnt and plundered Bury in 1010: but previously to this, Ailwin, fearful lest his sacred charge should suffer insult and injury from the Danes, conveyed it to London. Here it remained three years, during which numberless miracles were performed by its operation. The bishop of London, observing the rich offerings that were presented at the shrine of the saint, is said to have conceived a vehement desire to take the custody of it into his own hands; and went with three assistants to remove it privately from the little church of St. Gregory, in which it had been placed. In this attempt, however, he was completely foiled by the good saint, who had no inclination to go with him; so that his shrine remained as fast "as a great hill of stone," and his body as immoveable "as a mountain," till Ailwin arrived, when the martyr quietly suffered himself to be removed to his former residence. Sweyn having gained undisputed possession of this part of the island, in 1014, levied a general and heavy contribution on his new subjects. From this tax the monks claimed an exemption for their possessions, and deputed Ailwin to remonstrate in their behalf with the king. His mission, however, procured no relief. Sweyn's sudden death happening very soon afterwards, it was represented as a punishment inflicted by the angry saint. Being surrounded one evening, we are told, by his nobles and officers, he all at once exclaimed: "I am struck by St. Edmund!" and though the hand which inflicted the wound was not seen, he languished only till the next morning, and then expired in

torments of body which could only be exceeded by the horrors of his mind. The report of this miraculous interposition was highly advantageous to the convent; the people imposed on themselves a voluntary tax of four-pence for every carucate of land in the diocese, which they offered to the honour of the saint and martyr, as an acknowledgment of their gratitude and devotion.

Canute, the son of the successor of Sweyn, is said to have been so terrified by the vengeance of Edmund, that to expiate his father's crimes, and propitiate the angry saint, he took the monastery of Bury under his especial protection. Such was the ascendancy which the regulars had gained over the mind of this monarch, that Ailwin, who in 1020, was consecrated bishop of Elmham, availed himself of it to eject the secular clergy from this convent, and to supply their places with twelve Benedictine monks, whom, with Uvius their prior, he removed hither from the monastery at *Elmham*, in *Norfolk*, from which place the *See* was afterwards removed to Norwich, though attempts were made to fix it at *Bury*. At the same time, bishop Ailwin exempted the convent, and all within its jurisdiction, from episcopal authority, which was to be exercised by the abbot only, and four crosses were erected to fix with accuracy the boundary of his jurisdiction. The following year the bishop laid the foundation of a magnificent church, the expenses of which were defrayed by the voluntary tax upon land above-mentioned, and by the contributions of the pious.

These proceedings of Ailwin were not only ratified by Canute, but he issued a royal charter, confirming all former grants and privileges to the abbot and convent, and conferring several new ones. Of these, the most important was the right of reserving for their own use that proportion of the tax called *Danegeld*, levied upon the inhabitants of the town. These gifts were settled on the abbey with a fearful curse; on such as should molest the monks in the possession of them ; and the charter, signed by the king, queen, and archbishops, was attested by thirty-two nobles, prelates and abbots. In 1032, the new church being finished, was consecrated by Athelnorh, archbishop of Canterbury. The body of the royal martyr was deposited in a splendid shrine, adorned with jewels and costly ornaments ; and Canute himself repairing hither to perform his devotions, offered his crown at the tomb of the saint.

The mistaken piety of succeeding monarchs augmented the fame, the importance, and the wealth of the abbey of Bury ; but to none was it more indebted than to *Edward the Confessor*. This monarch granted to the abbot and convent the town of Mildenhall, with its produce and inhabitants, the royalties of eight Hundreds, together with the half hundred of Thingoe, and also those of all the villages situated in those eight Hundreds and a half which they previously possessed. He likewise conferred the privilege of coining at a mint established within the precinct of the monastery. Edward often paid his devotions in person at the shrine of the royal martyr, and so great was his veneration for him, that he was accustomed to perform the last mile of the journey on foot, like a common pilgrim.

The establishment had now attained such wealth and splendour, that the monks resolved to provide a still more magnificent receptacle

for the body of their saint than any in which it had hitherto been deposited. The third church, built by Ailwin, being mostly of wood, was demolished, and another was erected of hewn stone, under the auspices of abbot Baldwin. The materials for this structure were brought by the permission of William the Conqueror, free of expense, from the quarries of Barnack, in Northamptonshire; and it was in a state of sufficient forwardness to receive the sacred remains in 1095. This was the last removal, as the church now erected continued to exist till the period of the dissolution. The plan, execution, and embellishments of this structure, corresponded with the princely revenues of the establishment to which it belonged. Leland, who saw it in all its glory, in speaking of this town, describes it in the following terms:—A city more neatly seated the sun never saw, so curiously doth it hang upon a gentle descent, with a little river on the east side; nor a monastery more noble, whether one considers its endowments, largeness, or unparalleled magnificence. One might even think the monastery alone a city; so many gates it has, some whereof are brass: so many towers; and a church, than which nothing can be more magnificent; as appendages to which there are three more of admirable beauty and workmanship in the same church-yard."

The ABBEY CHURCH, or *church of St. Edmund*, was 505 feet in length, the transept 212, and the west front 240. The latter had two large side chapels, St. Faith's and St. Catherine's, one on the north-west, and the other on the south-west, and at each end an octagon tower thirty feet each way. The shrine of the saint was preserved in a semicircular chapel at the east end; and on the north side of the choir was that of St. Mary, eighty feet long, and forty-two broad; and St. Mary in cryptis was 100 feet in length, eighty in breadth, and supported by twenty-four pillars. Besides the dome, there was a high west tower over the middle aisle, and the whole fabric is supposed to have been equal in some respects in grandeur to St. Peter's at Rome. As to its height, no data are left to enable us to form an opinion. The ABBEY was governed by an *abbot*, who had several great officers under him, as a *prior*, *sub-prior*, *sacrist*, and *others ;* and in its most prosperous state there were eighty monks, fifteen chaplains, and one hundred and eleven servants, attending within its walls. It had three grand gates for entrance; and its lofty walls enclosed three other churches, besides the abbey church, several chapels, cloisters, and offices of every kind. Among other privileges conferred on this abbey, we find that Edward the Confessor granted to abbot Baldwin the liberty of coinage, which was confirmed by William the Conqueror. Stephen, in his seventeenth year, gave authority for two additional *mints* to be set up in Bury. Stow informs us, that there was one in the town in John's time. Edward I. and II. also had mints at Bury; and some of their pennies coined here are yet extant. The *abbot of Bury* enjoyed all the spiritual and temporal privileges of the mitred abbots; and in addition to them, some very important exclusive immunities. Of the latter kind, was the exemption from the ecclesiastical authority of the diocesan, so that none but the Roman pontiff, or his legate, could exercise any spiritual power within the limits of the abbot's jurisdiction. This privilege often involved him in violent disputes. As early as the reign of

William the Conqueror, we find the abbot Baldwin engaged in a controversy on this subject with Herfast, bishop of North Elmham, who had announced his intention of removing the See to Bury.* The abbot, alarmed at this threatened invasion of the privileges of his convent, applied to the king, and by his advice, repaired to Rome, where pope Alexander II., not only confirmed its former immunities and exemptions, by a bull dated at the Lateran, 6th Calend. Novemb. A. D. 1071., but also presented him with a porphyry altar for his church, with this extraordinary privilege, that if all the rest of the kingdom were under excommunication, mass might be there celebrated, unless expressly and by name prohibited by his holiness. These favors only served to redouble the bishop's exertions to carry his point, and he resolved to try what the seductive eloquence of gold would effect; while the monks, on the other hand, had recourse to still more persuasive means. The issue of this affair is thus related by archdeacon Herman, who himself bore a part in the transaction. "The bishop riding one day, and conversing on the injuries which he meditated against the monastery, was struck upon the eyes by a branch, and a violent and painful suffusion of blood occasioned immediate blindness; St. Edmund thus avenging himself, and punishing the temerity of the invaders of his rights. The prelate long remained entirely blind, and could obtain no relief. Coming in one morning, and commisserating his condition, I said to him: "My lord Bishop, your endeavors are useless, no collirium will avail; you should seek the favor of God and St. Edmund. Hasten to abbot Baldwin, that his prayers to God and the saint may provide an efficacious medicine! This counsel, at first despised, was at length assented to. I undertook the embassy, and executed it on the same day, the festival of St. Simon and St. Jude. The abbot benignantly granted the request; and the feeble bishop came to the monastery: Being graciouly received by the abbot, and admonished to reflect, that as offences against God and St. Edmund were diminished, the medicine to be applied would more certainly alleviate his sufferings; they proceeded into the church, where, in the presence of the elder brethren, and certain peers of the realm, Hugo de Montfort, Roger Bigod, Richard, the son of Gilbert, &c., the bishop declared the cause of his misfortune; recited the injuries he had conceived against this holy place; confessed himself culpable; condemned his advisers under an anathema; and bound himself by a vow to reject such counsels. He then advanced with sighs and tears to the foot of the altar; placed on it the pastoral staff; prostrated himself before God and St. Edmund; performed his devotions, and received absolution from the abbot and brethren. Then having made trial of the abbot's medicine, and as I saw, by the application of cauteries and colliriums, assisted by the prayers of the brethren, in a short time he returned perfectly healed; only a small obscurity remained in the pupil of one eye as a memorial of his audacity." A few years afterwards, however, this prelate, forgetful of his professions, renewed the contest, which was not terminated till the king convoked a council at Winchester, in which the subject was

* The *See* was removed from *North Elmham* to *Thetford*, in 1070; and from Thetford to *Norwich*, in 1094. A few years ago, Bury, and the western parts of Suffolk, were added to the *Diocese of Ely*, as already noticed.

fully discussed, and the claims of the abbot admitted by that august assembly. William at the same time granted a charter, confirming all those of his predecessors, and subscribed by himself, his queen, his three sons, two archbishops, thirteen bishops, and twenty abbots and nobles.

In 1345, a contention not less violent, commenced on the same account, between the abbot, and William Bateman, bishop of Norwich, who claimed a right of subjecting the convent to ecclesiastical visitation. King Edward III., by letters-patent, determined in favor of the abbey, and commanded the bishop to desist from his attempt to violate its privileges. The prelate, however, disregarded this mandate, and excommunicated the messenger who served it upon him. The abbot now had recourse to the law; a jury returned a verdict in his favor, and sentenced the bishop to pay thirty talents, or £10,000, the penalty attached to his offence by the charter of Hardicanute. In subseqent proceedings this judgment was affirmed; but though the bishop's temporalities were decreed to be held in the king's hands till the fine should be paid, and a day was appointed to seize his body, he found means of delay till the 25th of Sept. 1347, when the archbishop summoned a council at St. Paul's to decide the matter, and a compromise was concluded between the contending parties. The bishop engaged not to molest the monastery in the enjoyment of its privileges, and on this condition was restored to his ecclesiastical authority and temporalities. The abbot of Bury was a *spiritual parliamentary baron;* he held synods in his own chapter-house, and appointed the parochial clergy of the town. His temporal were not less important than his ecclesiastical prerogatives. He possessed the power of trying and determining by his high-steward all causes within the franchise or liberty, which extended, as already noticed, over eight Hundreds and a half; and in the town, and a mile round, he had the authority of chief magistrate, and of inflicting capital punishment. No officer of the king could, without his permission, hold a court, or execute any office in Bury. As *lord of the town,* he claimed the right of appointing the *alderman,* though it was afterwards agreed that the other burgesses composing the corporation should enjoy the privilege of electing that officer, who, however, was expected to receive the abbot's confirmation, and to take oath that he would do nothing that might injure the abbot and convent, but would be ready to defend them in all their rights and customs.

The supreme authority exercised over the town by the abbot, was a cause of frequent dissention between him and the inhabitants, which sometimes terminated in the most violent outrages. The most remarkable of these *disputes* occurred in 1327, when the townsmen, headed by their alderman and chief burgesses, and having collected 20,000 persons from the neighbouring towns and villages, made an attack upon the monastery and its possessions, and threatened the total destruction of the establishment. Having demolished the gates, doors, and windows, and beaten and wounded the monks and servants, they broke open the chests and coffers, out of which they took great quantities of rich plate, books, vestments, aud other valuables, besides five hundred pounds in ready money, and three thousand florins. They also carried away three charters of Canute, four of Hardicanute.

one of Edward the Confessor, two of Henry I., three of Henry III., twelve papal bulls, with several deeds, written obligations and acknowledgments for money due to the convent. Great part of the monastery was reduced to ashes, and many of the manors and granges belonging to it in Bury and its vicinity, shared the same fate. The abbot being at this time in London, the rioters seized and confined Peter Clopton, the prior, and about twenty of the monks, whom they afterwards compelled, in the name of the whole chapter of the convent, to execute, under the apitular seal, a deed, constituting the burgesses a guild or corporation. They also forced them to sign an obligation for the payment of ten thousand pounds to certain of the townsmen, to discharge them from all debts due to the monastery, and to engage not to proceed against them at law for any damage done to the monastery. The king being informed of these transactions, a military force was sent to suppress the disturbance. The alderman and twenty-four of the burgesses were imprisoned; thirty carts full of the *rioters* were taken prisoners to Norwich; nineteen of the most notorious offenders were executed, and one was pressed to death, because he refused to put himself upon his trial. Thirty-two parochial clergymen were convicted as abettors. The enquiries that arose out of this affair occupied near five years, the final decision being given by king Edward III. in council, in 1332. The justices commissioned to investigate the amount of the damages sustained by the abbey, had estimated them at the enormous sum of £140,000, but at the king's request, the abbot remitted to the offenders £122,333 6s. 8d., and at length forgave them the remainder, on condition of their future good behavior. All the deeds and charters taken from the monastery were to be restored; all the instruments and obligations obtained by force, were declared null and void, and were to be delivered up to the abbot. Fox states, that Berton, the alderman, thirty-two priests, thirteen women, and 138 other persons of the town, were outlawed; and that some of these afterwards surprised the abbot at the manor of Chevington. Having bound and shaved him, they conveyed him to London, and thence over the sea into Brabant, where they kept him a prisoner. He was at length rescued by his friends, who had discovered the place of his confinement.

The *Abbey of St. Edmund's Bury* remained 519 years in the possession of the *Benedictine monks*, and during that time was governed by thirty-three abbots. Its regular revenues consisted of fifty-two knight's fees and three-quarters, together with the royalties of the eight Hundreds and a half, and were valued at the dissolution by the commissioners at £2,336 16s. The *income of the abbey* must, however, have been most materially under-rated; and besidss this, the monks possessed many sources of revenue which could never be accurately ascertained. An intelligent writer of the last century calculated that all the possessions and perquisites of this abbey, would at that time (1725) be worth not less than £200,000 per annum; and from the astonishing increase in the value of landed property and agricultural produce, since that period, it may safely be assumed that at this time they would yield a yearly income of at least double the above amount.

When *Henry VIII.* resolved to replenish his exhausted treasury, by seizing the possessions of the monastic establishments, the abbey of Bury was included in the general destruction. Some ineffectual struggles were made by the abbot and convent, to avert the impending blow. In 1536, they settled upon secretary Cromwell and his son, an annuity of £10, payable out of the rents of the manor of Harlowe, in Essex. But neither this pension, nor the full acknowledgment of the king's supreme ecclesiastical authority, availed them any thing. On the 4th of November, 1539, the abbot and his brethren, were compelled to surrender the monastery and all its possessions to his majesty ; and were driven from their splendid mansion and ample revenue, to subsist upon a scanty stipend. The official report of the commissioners appointed to visit this abbey at the dissolution, states that they found here " a riche shryne which was very comberous to deface. We have taken," they continue, " in the seyd monastery, in gold and silver, 5,000 markes and above, besyds as well a riche crosse with emerelds, as also dyvers and sundry stones of great value; and yet we have left the churche, abbott, and convent, very well furneshed with plate of sylver necessary for the same." In another report signed "John Ap Rice," and dated " from Burie, 5th Nov. 1539," he says: " As touching the convent we could geate little or no complaints amonge theym, although we did use moche diligens in oure examinacion; and therby with some other arguments gathered of their examinacions formerly, I believe and suppose they shoulde had confedered and compacted befoure our comyng, that they shoulde disclose nothynge ; and yet it is confessed and proved, that there was here such frequence of women comyng, and reassorting to this monasterie, as to no place more. Amongest the reliques we founde moche vanitie and supersticion—as the coles that St. Lawrence was tosted withal ; the paryng of St. Edmund's naylls, St. Thomas of Canterpenneknyff and his bootes, and divers skulls for the head-ache ; peces of the Holie Cross able to make a hole crosse ; of other reliques for rayne, and certaine other supersticious usages, for avoiding of weeds growing in corn, &c." Among the many superstitious practices, and flagrant impostures carried on at this monastery, was the singular ceremony of the *procession of the white bull.* The sacrist of the monastery, as often as he let the lands near the town called *Haberdon,* annexed this condition, that the tenant should provide a white bull, whenever a matron of rank, or any other should come out of devotion, or in consequence of a vow, to make the oblations of the white bull, as they were denominated, at the shrine of St. Edmund. On this occasion, the animal adorned with ribbons and garlands, was brought to the south gate of the monastery and led along Church-gate, Guildhall, and Abbey-gate streets, to the great west gate, the lady all the while keeping close to him, and the monks and people forming a numerous cavalcade. Here the procession ended ; the animal was conducted back to his pasture, while the lady repaired to St. Edmund's shrine to make her oblations, as a certain consequence of which, she was soon to become a mother. As foreign ladies, desirous of issue, might have found it inconvenient to repair hither in person, to assist at these ceremonies, it was stated that they were certain to prove equally efficacious if performed by proxy.

LYDGATE, a MONK OF BURY, was highly distinguished for learning and poetical genius. He appears to have risen to his highest point of eminence in 1430. He was ordained a Subdeacon in 1389, Deacon in 1393, and Priest in 1397. He had travelled into France and Italy, and returned a complete master of the languages of both countries. His models were Dante, Boccacio, Alain, Chartier, Chaucer, and Ocleve. Warton says that he is the first English writer whose style is clothed with that perspicuity, in which English phraseology appears at this day to an English reader, and that to enumerate his various pieces, would be to give a catalogue of a little library; that no poet seems to have possessed greater versatility of talents; and that whether his subject be the life of a hermit or a hero, ludicrous or legendary, religious or romantic, he moves with equal ease in every mode of composition. He was not only the poet of his monastery of Bury, but of the world at large. If a disguising was intended by the company of Goldsmiths, a mask before the King at Eltham, a may-game for the Sheriffs, a mumming for the Lord Mayor, a procession for the Corpus Christi festival, or a carol for the Coronation, on all occasions Lydgate was applied to for the hymn or ballad; and the learned Whethamstede, Abbot of St. Albans, employed him about the year 1430, to give the *Latin legend of St. Alban's in English verse*. The St. Alban's Chronicler adds, that Whethamstede paid him 100 shillings for the translation, writing, and illuminating his MS., and placed it before St. Alban's Altar, having expended on the binding and other ornaments, above three pounds. A copy is preserved in Trinity College, Oxford, and another in Lincoln Cathedral. In the British Museum a most splendid copy is shewn on vellum, which was undoubtedly a present to King Henry VI. Besides the decoration of illuminated initials, and 120 pictures of various sizes, executed with the most delicate pencil, exhibiting the habits, weapons, architecture, and many other curious particulars belonging to the age of the illuminator, there are also two exquisite portraits of the King, one of *William Curteis*, Abbot of Bury, and one of *Lydgate* himself, kneeling before the shrine of St. Edmund. Curteis was Abbot from 1429 to 1445. Lydgate's principal poems are the "Fall of Princes," the "Siege of Thebes," the "Destruction of Troy," the "Life of St. Edmund," and "The Pilgrim," which last-named work is in Stowe Library, (Press 2, No. 100.) and has never been printed. His *Troye Boke* was first printed at the command of Hen. VIII., by Pynson, 1513. Among the decorations in the title page are soldiers firing great guns at the walls of Troy! Lydgate began this poem in 1413, the last year of Hen. IV., (at the request of that Prince) and finished it in 1420. Pitts and Weever place Lydgate's death in 1440, and Grainger follows them; but it is evident, from his works that he lived in 1446. In the Harleian copy of his Chronicle of English Kings, No. 2251, one stanza proves that he survived in 1461.

Before the dissolution, Bury also contained an establishment of *Grey Friars*, or *Franciscans*. About 1255 or '6, some brethren of this order came to the town during a vacancy in the abbacy, and having procured a situation in the north part of Bury, began to perform religious exercises. The Benedictine monks, indignant at this intrusion, and finding remonstrance of no effect, demolished the buildings and expelled the friars, who applied to the court of Rome for redress: when Pope Alexander IV. reproved the monks, and ordered the friars to be put in possession of an estate in the west part of Bury. The Benedictines still continued firm in their resistance to this encroachment on their privileges; so that king Henry III., who with many of his nobility had espoused the cause of the Franciscans, was obliged to send down his chief justice to Bury, and to establish them by force.

Upon this, they lost no time in constructing suitable religious edifices. The Pope soon after dying, the Benedictines renewed their aplication to his successor, and seconding it with an argument which seldom failed of persuading the papal court, Urban IV. revoked the bulls of his predecessor, commanded the Franciscans to demolish their buildings, and on pain of excommunication, to leave Bury within one month. They had not courage to withstand this injunction; but publicly renouncing all right and title to their estate in the town, the abbot and convent assigned them part of the monastic possessions in Babberwell, where they erected a Friary.

At the Reformation, there were in Bury five hospitals, viz.: St. Saviour's at Northgate; St. Peter's at Risby-gate; St. John's at Southgate; and St. Stephen's and St. Nicholas' at Eastgate; and a college called *Jesus College*, in College-street, founded in the reign of Edward IV., for a warden and six associate priests, and now forming part of the Workhouse. Here were also about forty *churches, chapels, and oratories*, of which only the two parish churches of St. Mary and St. James are now standing entire, near the tower and ruins of the Abbey-Church, and the site of St. Margaret's Church. The names and situations of fifteen of the chapels are still known, though the buildings of many of them have long been demolished, viz.: St. Mary's, at Eastgate-bridge; "Our Lady's," at Westgate; Stone Chapel, at Risby-gate; St. Michael's, in the Infirmary; St. Andrew's, in the cemetery of the monks; St. John's-on-the-hill; St. John's-ad-fontem; St. Anne's-in-cryptis; St. Thomas's, at Northgate; St. Lawrence's, in the court-yard; St. Gile's, near the nave of the abbey-church; St. Petronell's, within the Southgate; St. Botolph's, in Southgate-street; St. Edmund's, or Round Chapel, in the church-yard; and St. Denis's. There was also a *hermitage* at the Westgate, now used as a cow-house. Though Bury was never encompassed by a wall, it had five GATES, which were all standing in 1766; but were soon afterwards taken down by order of the Corporation, for the more convenient passage of carriages, &c. Before the Reformation, there was either an hospital, or some religious foundation at each of these gates, where the alms of passengers were collected. Near the site of the North-Gate, are some remains of *St. Saviour's Hospital*, which was of such magnitude, that a *parliament* was assembled in it, in 1446. In this hospital, Humphrey, the virtuous Duke of Gloucester, is supposed to have been murdered. About a quarter of a mile beyond the East-Gate, stood *St. Nicholas's Hospital*, the remains of which have been converted into a farm-house, near which is the hospital chapel, now used as a barn and stable. On the North side of the road between East bridge and this hospital, a few fragments of old walls mark the site of *St. Stephen's Hospital*. Just without the South-Gate, stood *St. Petronell's Chapel* and *St. John's Hospital*, the sites of which are now occupied by modern houses. Close to the site of Risby-Gate, are the remains of the chantry called *Stone Chapel*, converted into a public house, bearing the sign of the Cock;—the flint walls of which have been much admired. Near the road beyond Risbygate, is St. Peter's Barn, enclosed by walls built with the ruins of *St. Peter's Hospital*, which was founded for the reception of infirm and leperous priests.

The ABBEY-GATE, one of the principal ornaments of Bury, was the grand entrance to St. Edmund's Abbey, and opened into the great court yard, in front of the abbot's palace.   Such is the excellence of its materials and workmanship, that it is still in good preservation, though it stood many years roofless and neglected.   Upon the destruction of the original entrance to the abbey, in the violent assault of the townsmen, in 1327, this gate was erected upon a plan, combining elegance with utility.   Its height is 72 feet, but it formerly had turrets at the angles rising 14 feet higher.   Two of its sides are each 62 feet broad, and the other 40.   The architecture is of the best period of the Gothic style.   The embellishments, arranged with taste, and executed with precision, are much more numerous than in edifices of an earlier date, but not in such profusion as in the later and more florid style.   The west front, facing the Angel-Hill, is divided into two horizontal compartments, by an ornamented band, and perpendicularly into three, consisting of a centre and two turriated projecting wings.   The whole is superbly ornamented with devices, and niches for statues.   The heads or groined work, forming the canopies to the niches are elegant ; and the pilasters of those in the centre and in both wings, terminate in well-wrought pinnacles. The spandrils of the arch, above the gateway, are adorned with two quatre-foil bosses or medallions ; and over them, near the top of the building, are two others, each representing two interlaced triangles. The pillars of the gateway are composed of clustered cylinders; the capitals are simple, and chiefly the Gothic wreath.   The counterarch of the entrance is surmounted by an undulated arch or pediment, springing from the external capitals.   Below the embattled band, which divides the building horizontally, is a cavetto moulding ornamented with several figures, most of which are defaced ; but a lion, a dragon, and a bull worried by dogs, may still be distinguished.   In the wall and arch is a groove for the reception of a portcullis.   In the south-west and north-west angles were circular staircases, one of which is yet so perfect, that it is possible, with care, to ascend to the *platform*, which runs round the top of the building, and has five embrasures at either end, and seven on each side.   The area is unequally divided by a stone partition, and its arch was furnished with inner gates of brass, the hinges of which still remain.   The entrances to the stair-cases are in the inner division of the area, so that, if an enemy had forced the portcullis, and obtained possession of the anti-gateway, the defendants would still have commanded the access to the upper part of the fortress, whence they might have greatly annoyed the assailants.   All these precautions, as well as the want of windows next the town, indicate the anxiety of the monks to prevent a repetition of those outrages which occasioned the necessity for erecting this elegant but embattled tower-gateway.   The Eastern or interior front is also richly adorned with niches and light and elegant tracery, and with the arms of Edward the Confessor; Thomas de Brotherton, earl of Norfolk ; and John Holland, duke of Exeter.   This division of the tower has a large and handsome window, which lighted a room 28 feet square, of which there are still vestiges of the floor, roof, and fire-place.   This gate, as already noticed, opens into the *abbey-grounds*, which adjoin the church-yard,

and comprise about 14 acres, still surrounded with the ancient lofty wall, and containing some massive detached fragments of the monastic edifices, near which is a beautiful Botanic Garden of five acres, formed in 1820.

NORMAN TOWER.—This celebrated Tower, erected in the reign of William the Conqueror, as the grand portal or gate-tower of the magnificent Church of Abbot Baldwin, and now forming the grand entrance to the Churchyard of the beautiful Churches of St. Mary and St. James, to the latter of which it serves as the Bell Tower, has been pronounced by competent authorities—foreign as well as English—to be the finest building of its kind and period extant in Europe. The structure is still entire in its main features, and its minor details are not obliterated, although somewhat impaired by age, and more by neglect and injudicious reparation. Within the present century some extensive fissures and settlements have appeared, and these having been treated only by the useless and mischievous applications of cementing and wedging the cracks, and blocking up the arches, the walls have been thrown so much out of the perpendicular, and various parts of the fabric have been so much disturbed, that unless effectual measures of repair be promptly adopted, there is great danger that this unique specimen of Norman architecture may fall into ruin. To prevent this threatened disaster, the parishioners have recently consulted Mr. Cottingham, the architect, so well known for his skilful restoration and repair of Armagh and Hereford Cathedrals and St. Alban's Abbey, who, after a careful examination of the Tower, made an elaborate report of its condition and of the necessary repairs; in which he says that the building is still sufficiently substantial to be rendered perfectly sound and durable for centuries, and that by the introduction of iron chain ties and a better mode of supporting the bells, all danger from the vibration of ringing may be removed. The cost of repairing and securing the tower, including the substantial and accurate restoration of the defective mouldings and ornaments, Mr. Cottingham estimated at £2,370, for raising which, a public subscription has been opened, which amounted to £1,400 in June 1843, when a committee of the principal subscribers resolved " that notice be given for Tenders to be sent in for the Restoration of the Tower, on the plan of Mr. Cottingham; the work to be carried into execution in such portions as may be found advisable, according to the amount of the subscriptions from time to time received." It would be very desirable to remove the two houses which are built against the tower and hide some of its most beautiful features; but this would incur a heavy additional expense; towards which several gentlemen have offered liberal contributions, should this ulterior object be undertaken. The height of the tower is 82 feet 3 inches, and its form is quadrangular. It has a large semicircular-headed arch, admitting the free passage of carriages, &c.; and the three tiers of windows above are also of the Saxon form; but the whole was evidently erected at a period when the round arch, originally introduced into this country by Saxon Pilgrims from Rome, had, in the master hands of the Norman architects, left the debased trammels of Roman imitation, and established a style of architecture in which the semicircular arch was made to combine in perfect harmony with every element of construction. At the basement it measures 40 feet from east to west, including the porch attached to the western entrance; and 37 feet 6 inches from north to south. The walls are 5 feet 10 inches thick from the top of the foundation to the rising plate of the roof, and are faced with plain ashlar, about eight inches thick inside and outside, and the core filled up with rubble work, consisting of flints and stone chippings, grouted with lime and sand. There is a circular stone stair case at the north west angle, and a postern doorway has been discovered in the north wall. The chamber over the

gateway is 23 feet 8 inches square, as also are the third and fourth stories. The latter contains a fine peal of ten bells, and is lighted by twelve windows, three on each side, as also is the third story. Two basso relievos which were some time ago taken out of the turret panels on each side of the archway in the western front, formed no part of the original design. One represented mankind under the dominion of Satan, and the other was emblematical of the deliverance of man from his bondage. The *porch* attached to the western front "has three shafts on each side in square recesses, with bases and capitals, supporting a plain impost, above which a series of plain cable mouldings form the arch, which is covered with a stone pentice roof, having a twisted cable barge moulding to defend the scale ornament which adorns the gable over the arch; it is supported on each side by a delicately panelled turret, which terminates with a pyramidical stone roof, rising a little above the first string course. The jaumbs of the doors are composed of three slender cluster columns with plain bases, carved capitals and moulded imposts; the capitals have, undoubtedly, a conventional meaning; that on the south side represents two lions splitting the jaws of a dragon; the north side capital represents a naked human figure seated between two dragons. The arch above the caps is composed of a semicable moulding on each side with a plain soffit: there was originally a very flat second arch within the jaumbs and soffit, inserted for the doors to shut against; this was probably richly carved with appropriate devices. The second, third, and fourth stories are flanked with small projecting buttresses, enriched between with semicircular arches, supported by small columns in alto-relievo: there are eight windows in this front, and a number of circular and semicircular moulded borders, forming panels which are enriched with a kind of reticulatum or net work, formed by cutting the stones in a diagonal direction into a series of meshes and other device, giving it the appearance of mosaic. The columns in the third story rest upon the backs of lions and chimera, just above the nebule string. The four eyelet windows up the staircase, at the north west angle are pointed, the heads are each cut out of a solid stone. The embattled coping on the top of the tower has every appearance of being the original finish, if so, it gives additional value to the work, as it is perhaps the earliest specimen of embrasure work in existence." About 25 years ago, a portion of the archway on the eastern side fell down, soon after the ringers had finished a peal on the bells, and was very injudiciously repaired; and at the same time the windows in the third story, and some of those in the bell chamber, were improperly bricked up, and thus an additional weight was thrown upon the weakened arch. It is hoped that the repairs and renovations now (Sept. 1843,) in operation, will restore the strength and beauty of this unique specimen of pure Norman architecture, which has weathered the storms of nearly eight centuries.

The *remains of the west end of St. Edmund's Church*, which bound the church yard on one side, now exhibit a singular and motley appearance. One of the octagon towers which formerly terminated either end, is still standing, and has been converted into a stable. Three arches, once the entrances to the three aisles, have been filled up with modern buildings and converted into as many neat houses. The intermediate portions of the original massive wall, which is supposed to have been once faced with marble, present a rugged spectacle, caused by the ravages of three centuries. On the north side of the churchyard is a large house which was the seat of J. Benjafield, Esq. who, about forty years ago, enclosed within his grounds, part of the ruins of the conventual church and a corner of the churchyard, which he planted with trees and shrubs, for the purpose of hiding his mansion from the public gaze, and shutting from his view the numerous mementos of perishable humanity. This desecration of the sanctuary of the dead was improperly permitted by the Corporation. Among the distinguished

persons interred in the conventual church were Alan Fergaunt, earl of Richmond; Thomas de Brotherton, earl of Norfolk, half brother to king Edward II.; Thomas Beaufort, duke of Exeter, uncle to king Henry V.; Mary, widow of Louis XII. of France, and sister to Henry VIII., whose remains were afterwards removed to St. Mary's church; Sir William Elmham, Sir William Spencer, and Sir William Tresil, knights. Many inhabitants of the monastery, remarkable for their learning and piety, were also buried here; but of these none was more celebrated than John Lydgate, already noticed at page 616. In 1772, some labourers being employed in breaking up a part of the ruins of this church, discovered a leaden coffin, which had been inclosed in an oak case, then quite decayed. It contained an embalmed body, as fresh and entire as at the time of interment, surrounded by a kind of pickle, and the face covered with a cerecloth. The features, the nails of the fingers and toes, and the hair, which was brown, with some mixture of grey, appeared as perfect as ever. A surgeon hearing of this discovery, went to examine the body, and made an incision on the breast; the flesh cut as firm as that of a living subject, and there was even an appearance of blood. The skull was sawed in pieces, and the brain, though wasted, was inclosed in its proper membrane. At this time the corpse was not in the least offensive, but on being exposed to the air it soon became putrid. The labourers, for the sake of the lead, removed the body from its receptacle, and threw it among the rubbish. It was found that the corpse which had been treated with such indecency, was the remains of Thomas Beaufort, duke of Exeter, and son of John of Gaunt, duke of Lancaster, who, at the battle of Agincourt led the rear-guard of the English army, and afterwards bravely defended Harfleur against the French. He died at East Greenwich in 1427, and was, in compliance with his will, interred in the abbey church of Bury St. Edmund's, near his duchess, at the entrance of the chapel of Our Lady, close to the wall on the north side of the choir. His mangled remains were enclosed in a strong oak coffin, and re-interred at the foot of the large north-east pillar, which formerly assisted to support the belfry. In 1783, on breaking up some foundations in the north wall of St. Edmund's church, near the chapter house, were found four *antique heads,* cut out of single blocks of freestone, and somewhat larger than the natural proportion. On the subject of these heads, Mr. Yates quotes the various opinions of antiquaries, who he says have viewed them, but how any person with his eyes open, could take them for " Roman divinities," or for " the decorations of some temple, the ruins of which, might afterwards be employed in constructing the church," it is scarcely possible to conceive. Nothing can be more evident, even from the inspection of the engraving given in his own work, than that two of these were representations of St. Edmund's head, accompanied by the leg of its brute protector. It is more than probable, that the other two, though without that striking appendage, were rude memorials of the same subject.

In February 1560, queen Elizabeth, by letters patent under the great seal, granted to John Eyre, esq. in consideration of the sum of £4121 19s. 4d. paid by him, all the site, circuit, and precinct of the late monastery of Bury St. Edmund's, then recently dissolved, besides other premises and lands in the neighbourhood, formerly belonging to the abbot and convent. They afterwards passed into the hands of various purchasers, till in 1720, they were conveyed for the sum of £2800 to the use of Major Richardson Pack. That gentleman soon afterwards assigned the premises to Sir Jermyn Davers, in whose family they continued till it became extinct a few years since, by the death of Sir Charles Davers, bart.

Royal Visits, Rebellions, &c.—Bury has been honoured with the visits of many royal and noble personages, who were drawn hither

by motives of piety, or by the fame and splendour of St. Edmund's Abbey. Besides these circumstances of local interest, the town and its immediate vicinity have been the theatre of important national events. It has been observed, that Bury was frequently honoured with the presence of king Edward the Confessor, who was perhaps the most eminent of the benefactors of the convent, and some of the fruits of whose liberality are still enjoyed by the town. In 1132, Henry I. returning to England, after his interview at Chartres with Pope Innocent III., was overtaken by a violent tempest. Considering it as a judgment of Providence for his sins, he made in the hour of danger a solemn vow to amend his life; in pursuance of which, as soon as he had landed, he repaired to Bury to perform his devotions at the shrine of St. Edmund. Soon after the treaty concluded by king Stephen, with Henry, son of the Empress Maud, by which the latter was acknowledged his successor, Stephen's son, Eustace, came to Bury, and demanded of the abbot and convent considerable supplies of money and provisions, to enable him to assert his claim to the throne. On the refusal of the abbot to comply with this requisition, the prince ordered the granaries of the monastery to be plundered, and many of the farms belonging to it to be ravaged and burned. In the midst of these violent proceedings, he was seized with a fever, and expired at Bury, on St. Lawrence's day, 1153, in the eighteenth year of his age. During the unnatural contest in which Henry II. was engaged with his sons, instigated by their mother, and aided by the king of France, a considerable army was assembled at Bury, by Richard de Lucy, lord chief justice; Humphrey de Bohun, high constable; Reginald, earl of Cornwall, and other noblemen, to support the cause of their rightful sovereign. Robert de Bellomont, earl of Leicester, the general of the rebellious princes, having landed with a large body of Flemings at Walton in this county, proceeded to Framlingham Castle, where he was received by Hugh Bigod, earl of Norfolk, who had espoused the same cause. Here he was joined by a reinforcement of foreign troops; and after ravaging the adjacent country, he set out for Leicestershire with his Flemings, who, as we are told by an old writer, thought England their own; for when they came into any large plain, where they rested, taking one another by the hand, and leading a dance, they would sing in their native language: " Hop, hop, Wilkine, hop Wilkine; England is mine and thine." Their mirth, however, was soon converted into mourning; for on their way they were met by the royal army at Fornham St. Geneveve, where, on the 27th of October, 1173, a bloody engagement took place, and terminated in their total defeat. Ten thousand of their number, according to some writers, were killed; but others assert, that five thousand were slain, and the same number taken prisoners. Among the last, were the Earl of Leicester and his Countess, with many other persons of distinction. In this engagement, the sacred standard of St. Edmund was borne before the royal army, which now made Bury its head quarters

After this *victory* the royal general marched against the Earl of Norfolk, who withdrew to France; but returning soon afterwards with an army of Flemings, he took the city of Norwich, which he plundered and burned. The king, who was in Normandy, being

informed of these proceedings, hastened back to England, and assembling his troops on all sides, ordered their rendezvous at Bury. With this army Henry marched to chastise the Earl; and having demolished his castles at Ipswich and Walton, advanced towards his other places of strength at Framlingham and Bungay; but the Earl, finding that any farther opposition would be unavailing, submitted to the king, and thus terminated this disgraceful contest. In this reign the JEWS, who had established themselves, among other places, in this town, when they first came into England under William the Conqueror, were very numerous at Bury, where they had a regular place for divine worship, denominated the *synagogue of Moses*. In 1179, having, as it is said, murdered a boy of this town, named Robert, in derision of Christ's crucifixion, and committed the like offences in other parts of England, they were banished the kingdom; but they probably found means to make their peace in some places: for it appears that about ten years afterwards, in the second year of the reign of Richard I., they had, by their excessive usury, rendered themselves so odious to the nation, that the people rose with one accord to destroy them. Among the rest, many of those who inhabited Bury were surprised and put to death; and such as escaped by the assistance of the abbot Sampson, were expelled the town, and never permitted to return. *Richard I.*, previously to his departure for the Holy Land, paid a devotional visit to the convent and shrine of St. Edmund, when the abbot requested permission to accompany him in his intended *crusade*, as the bishop of Norwich had already obtained leave to attend the king; but it was not deemed expedient that the abbot should be absent at the same time, and his petition was consequently rejected. On the return of that monarch from Palestine, he offered up the rich standard of Isaac, king of Cyprus, at the shrine of St. Edmund.

To Bury belongs, if not in a superior, at least in an equal degree with Runimede, the honor of that celebrated charter, by which the rights and liberties of Englishmen are secured. It is not generally known, perhaps, that the foundation of *Magna Charta*, is a charter of Henry I., which had fallen into oblivion as early as the time of king John. A copy of it having fallen into the hands of Stephen Langton, archbishop of Canterbury, was by him communicated to the principal nobles of the kingdom, a meeting of whom was convened at Bury to deliberate on the subject. Upon this occasion, each of the persons present went to the high altar of the church of St. Edmund, in which the assembly was held, and there swore, that if the king should refuse to abolish the arbitrary Norman laws, and restore those enacted by Edward the Confessor, they would make war upon him until he complied. The king, on his return from Poitou, in 1214, met his barons at Bury, and with the utmost solemnity confirmed this celebrated deed; binding himself by a public oath to regulate his administration by the grand principles which it established. *Henry III.*, paid several visits to Bury. In the year 1272, he held a parliament here, and by its advice proceeded to Norwich, to punish the authors of a violent insurrection against the prior and monks of that city. Having accomplished the object of his journey, he returned to Bury, where he was seized with the disorder, which soon afterwards

terminated his reign and life. In 1296, *Edward I.* held a parliament at Bury, for the purpose of demanding an aid of the clergy and people. The former, however, fortified with a papal constitution, refused to contribute any thing; and continuing firm in this determination, the king seized all the revenues of the church, and among the rest, confiscated the goods of the abbot and convent, together with all their manors and the borough of Bury. These disputes lasted upwards of two years, till the clergy were at length compelled to submit, and to grant the king a subsidy of one fifteenth, or, according to some accounts, one tenth, of their goods and rents. In the reign of *Edward II.*, his queen Isabella, being dissatisfied with the conduct of the Spencers, who were then the favourites of that imbecile monarch, obtained the assistance of the prince of Hainault, and landed with a force of 2,700 men, furnished by him at Orwell haven; on which she marched to this town, where she continued some time to refresh her troops, and collect her adherents. It is scarcely necessary to add, that the consequence of this measure was the deposition of the misguided monarch. *Edward III.*, and his grandson *Richard II.*, also visited Bury, and paid their adoration at the shrine of St. Edmund. During the reign of the latter, Bury experienced the mischievous effects of that spirit of rebellion which pervaded various parts of the kingdom, in opposition to the *poll-tax,* which pressed heavily on the poor. In 1381, soon after the insurrection of the Kentish men, under *Wat Tyler,* the people of Norfolk and Suffolk rose in great numbers, and under the conduct of *Jack Straw,* committed excessive devastations. Proceeding in a body of not less than 50,000 men, to Cavendish, they there plundered and burned the house of Sir John de Cavendish, the lord chief-justice, whom they seized and carried to Bury; here they struck off his head, and placed it on the pillory. The mob are supposed to have been the more exasperated against Sir John, because it was his son who despatched Wat Tyler in Smithfield. They then attacked the abbey. Sir John Cambridge, the prior, endeavored to escape by flight, but being taken and executed near Mildenhall, his head was set up near that of the lord chief-justice. Sir John Lakenhythe, the keeper of the barony, shared the same fate. The insurgents then plundered the abbey, carrying off jewels to a considerable amount, and doing much mischief to the buildings. They were, however, soon dispersed by Henry le Spencer, the martial bishop of Norwich,* who meeting them at Barton Mills, with a very inferior force, gave them so severe a check, that they were glad to return to their homes.

In 1433, *Henry VI.*, then only 12 years old, celebrated Christmas at the monastery of Bury, where he resided till St. George's day following. Previously to his departure, the King, the duke of Gloucester, and several of his noble attendants, were solemnly admitted members of the community. In 1446, a *parliament* was held here,

---

* This prelate was bred to the profession of arms, and highly distinguished himself in Italy, in the wars of Pope Adrian, a native of England, with the duke of Milan. The Pope, to reward his services, conferred on him the bishopric of Norwich, in 1370. Having, under a commission from Pope Urban VI. but against the will of the King, raised an army, and landed in the Netherlands, to chastise the schismatics of that country; he was deprived, for two years, of his temporalities, to which he was, however, restored in 1385 by the parliament, on account of his eminent services in suppressing this rebellion.

at which that monarch presided in person. This parliament was convened under the influence of Cardinal de Beaufort, the inveterate enemy of *Humphrey, Duke of Gloucester*, the king's uncle, and the popular and beloved regent of England; and there is but too much reason to believe, that the real purpose of this meeting was, to afford an opportunity for his destruction. Hume observes, that it assembled, not at London, which was supposed to be too well affected to the duke, but at St. Edmund's Bury, where his enemies expected him to be entirely at their mercy. Their plan was but too successful; on the second day of the sessions he was arrested, all his servants were taken from him, and his retinue sent to different prisons. Preparations were made for bringing him to a public trial; but his enemies, dreading the effect of the innocence and virtues of *the good duke*, as he was emphatically styled, had recourse to a more certain method of ridding themselves of him than by impeachment. The morning after his apprehension, the duke was found lifeless in his bed, and though an apoplexy was declared to have been the cause of his death, yet all impartial persons ascribe it to violence. Pitts relates, that he was smothered with bolsters, and a traditional opinion prevails, that this atrocity was perpetrated in an apartment of St. Saviour's hospital, then an appendage to the monastery, by William de la Pole, marquis of Suffolk. The duke's body was conveyed to St. Alban's and there interred. Another parliament met at Bury, in 1448; and in 1486, the town was honoured with the presence of Henry VII., in his progress through Norfolk and Suffolk. In 1526, an alarming *insurrection* of the people of Lavenham, Hadleigh, Sudbury, and the adjacent country, was quelled by the dukes of Norfolk and Suffolk, who met for that purpose at Bury, whither many of the ringleaders were brought, and appeared before those noblemen in their shirts, and with halters about their necks, when they received the royal pardon. On the death of Edward VI., 1553, John Dudley, *Duke of Northumberland*, having procured *Lady Jane Grey* to be declared the heir to the Crown, to the exclusion of the princesses Mary and Elizabeth, daughters of Henry VIII., marched with an army into Suffolk, to suppress any attempt that might be made to oppose his plans, and made Bury the rendezvous of his troops. Here he waited for reinforcements; Mary was meanwhile proclaimed Queen by the council, who ordered the Duke to return to Cambridge. On the way he was deserted by most of his men, and thus terminated this ill-judged enterprise. During the reign of *Queen Mary*, Bury witnessed several of those horrible scenes, which then disgraced various parts of the kingdom. James Abbes was here *burned for a heretic*, on the 2d of August, 1555; Roger Clarke, of Mendlesham, in 1556; and Roger Bernard, Adam Forster, and Robert Lawson, on the 30th June, the same year. In like manner, John Cooke, Robert Miles, Alexander Lane, and James Ashley, suffered for the same cause, shortly before the Queen's last illness; and Philip Humphrey, and John and Henry David, brothers, were here brought to the stake only a fortnight anterior to Mary's death. Similar cruelties were perpetrated at Ipswich and other places. (See page 58.) *Queen Elizabeth* re-established the Protestant religion, and in her journey through Nor-

folk and Suffolk, in 1578, paid a visit to this town, where she arrived on the 7th of August, as appears from the register of St James's parish.

" In the year 1608, April 11, being Monday, the quarter-sessions was held at St. Edmund's Bury, and by negligence, an out-malt-house was set on fire; from whence, in a most strange and sudden manner, through fierce winds, the fire came to the farthest side of the town, and as it went left some streets and houses safe and untouched. The flame flew clean over many houses, and did great spoil to many fair buildings farthest off; and ceased not till it had consumed one hundred and sixty dwelling houses, besides others; and in damage of wares and household stuff to the full value of sixty thousand pounds." To this destructive *fire*, thus described by Stow, however terrible and distressful in itself, the present regularity of the streets, is no doubt to be attributed. King James, who was a great benefactor to the town, contributed vast quantities of timber toward rebuilding it. In 1636, the *plague* raged here with such violence, and so depopulated the town, that grass grew in the streets. Four hundred families lay sick of that distemper at the same time, and were maintained at the public charge, which is said to have amounted to £200 a week.

In the 17th century, when the example of the weak, though learn-ed, James I., had excited the popular zeal against the imaginary crime of WITCHCRAFT, Bury exhibited some most disgraceful instances of the effect of his persecuting spirit. One Matthew Hopkins, of Manningtree in Essex, who styled himself, *Witch-finder general*, and had twenty shillings allowed him for every town he visited, was, with some others, commissioned by parliament in 1644, and the two following years, to perform a circuit for the discovery of witches. By virtue of his commission, they went from place to place, through many parts of Essex, Suffolk, Norfolk, and Huntingdonshire, and caused sixteen persons to be hanged at Yarmouth, forty at Bury, and others in different parts of the county, to the amount of sixty persons. Among the victims sacrificed by this wretch and his associates, were doubtless Mr Lawes, an innocent, aged clergyman, of Brandeston, a cooper and his wife, and fifteen other women, who were all condemned and executed at one time at Bury. Hopkins used many arts to extort confession from suspected persons, and when these failed, he had recourse to swimming them, which was done by tying their thumbs and great toes together, and then throw-ing them into the water. If they floated, they were guilty of the crime of witchcraft, but their sinking was a proof of their innocence. This method he pursued, till some gentlemen, indignant at his bar-barity, tied his own thumbs and toes, as he had been accustomed to tie those of other persons, and when put into the water, he himself swam as many had done before him. By this expedient the country was soon cleared of him, and this circumstance is alluded to by But-ler in his Hudibras, as also is that of a lady here, flogging her hus-band at the bed-post, because he had forsaken the cause of Crom-well. Bury witnessed another execution for witchcraft, on the 17th March, 1664, when two poor widows, whose only guilt probably con-

sisted, either in the deformity of their bodies, or the weakness of their understandings, were tried before that learned judge, Sir Matthew Hale, and sentenced to die. This extraordinary trial was published, as an appeal to the world, by Sir Matthew, who, so far from being satisfied with the evidence, was extremely doubtful concerning it, and proceeded with such extreme caution, that he forbore to sum it up, leaving the matter to the jury, with a prayer to God, to direct their hearts in so important an affair. Similar barbarities were practiced at Ipswich, under the same delusion. (See page 59.)

WORTHIES :—The Abbey and town of Bury have produced many men distinguished for learning and piety. Among these may be mentioned the following :—JOHN LYDGATE, the monk, is already noticed at page 616. JOHN DE NORWOLD, who was educated here, was at length chosen abbot, and went to Rome to be confirmed in that dignity by the pope. He wrote much on other subjects, but was principally concerned in the great controversy between Robert Grostest, and Pope Innocent IV. None of his writings are now extant, but his *Annals of England.* He died, and was interred in his monastery, in 1280. JOHN EVERSDEN, a monk, excelled in the belles lettres, and was considered a good poet and orator, and a faithful historian. He wrote several things which acquired considerable celebrity, and died in 1336. ROGER, surnamed the *Computist*, was remarkable for his monastic virtues, and extraordinary learning. In his more advanced age he was chosen prior, after which, he wrote *An Exposition of all the difficult words through the Bible ; Comments on the Gospels*, and other works. He flourished about 1360. BOSTON OF BURY, was a native of this town, and a monk in the monastery here. He travelled over almost all England, to inspect the libraries, and compiled an alphabetical catalogue of all the books which they contained. To render the work the more complete, he gave a concise account of each author's life, and the opinions of the most learned men of his time respecting his writings, noting in what place and library, each book was to be found. He also wrote the following works : *Of the original Progress and Success of Religious Orders, and other Monastical affairs ; A Catalogue of Ecclesiastical writers ; The Mirror of Conventuals*, and *State of his own Monastery*, besides other books. He flourished about 1410. EDMUND BROMFIELD, was a man of such erudition, that Leland is of opinion, that in this respect, none of the monks of this monastery ever surpassed him. He is said to have gone through his studies in England, and then to have repaired to Rome, where he displayed such abilities, that he was chosen professor, and styled by the doctors there, Count Palatine of the University. He was appointed bishop of Llandaff by the pope, in 1389 ; and dying in 1391, was interred in his own cathedral. RICHARD DE AUNGERVYLE, better known by the name of De Bury, from this his native place, was born in 1281, and educated at the University of Oxford. On finishing his studies, he entered into the order of Benedictines, and became tutor to the prince of Wales, afterwards king Edward III. On his pupil's accession to the throne, he was first appointed cofferer, afterwards treasurer of the wardrobe, archdeacon of Northampton, prebendary of Lincoln, Sarum, and Lichfield, keeper of the privy seal, dean of Wells, and lastly, was promoted to the See of Durham. He likewise held the offices of lord high-chancellor and treasurer ; and discharged two important embassies at the court of France. Learned himself, he was a patron of learning, and corresponded with some of the greatest geniuses of the age, particularly with the celebrated Petrarch. The public library which he founded at Oxford, on the spot where now stands Trinity College, was a noble instance of his munificence. This establishment continued till the general dissolution of

the monasteries by Henry VIII., when the books were dispersed into different repositories. This prelate likewise wrote a book, entitled *Philobiblos*, for the regulation of his library; and a M.S. copy of this performance is still preserved in the Cottonian collection. He died in 1345, and was interred at Durham. STEPHEN GARDINER, who is said to have been the natural son of Richard Woodvill, brother to Elizabeth, the queen of Edward IV., was born at Bury in 1483, and educated at Trinity-hall, Cambridge. On leaving the University, he was taken into the family of Cardinal Wolsey, by whom he was recommended to Henry VIII., and from this time he rose with rapid steps to the first dignities both in the church and state. His talents were confessedly great; and it cannot be denied that he exerted them with zeal in promoting the views of his benefactor. He had a considerable share in effecting the king's divorce from Catharine of Arragon; he assisted him in throwing off the papal yoke; he himself abjured the pope's supremacy; and wrote a book in behalf of the king, entitled : *De vera et falsa obedientia*. For these services he was elevated to the See of Winchester; but opposing the Reformation, in the succeeding reign, he was thrown into prison, where he continued several years, till Queen Mary, on her accession to the throne, not only released him, and restored him to his bishopric, but also invested him with the office of lord high-chancellor. Being now in fact entrusted with the chief direction of affairs, he employed his power in some cases for the most salutary ends; and in others abused it to the most pernicious purposes. He drew up the marriage articles between Queen Mary and Philip II. of Spain, with the strictest regard to the interests of England. He opposed, but in vain, the coming of Cardinal Pole into the kingdom. He preserved inviolate the privileges of the University of Cambridge, of which he was chancellor, and defeated every scheme for extending the royal prerogative beyond its due limits. It must be acknowledged, however, that he had a principal share in reconciling the English nation to the see of Rome; and what has fixed a much fouler stain upon his memory, that he was deeply implicated in the cruel persecution carried on against the Protestants: though his guilt in this respect is far from being so great as is commonly imagined, Bonner, bishop of London, having been the chief author of those barbarities. Previously to his death which happened on November 13, 1555, he is said to have manifested the deepest remorse for this part of his conduct, and to have frequently exclaimed : *Erravi cum Petro, sed non flevi cum Petro*. Besides the book above mentioned, he wrote a retraction of that work, several sermons, and other treatises; and is supposed to have been the author of *The necessary Doctrine and Erudition of a Christian*, a piece commonly ascribed to Henry VIII. WM. CLAGGETT, an eminent divine of the seventeenth century, was born in this town in 1646, and educated at Cambridge. His first station in the church was that of minister in this his native place; and he died in March, 1688, lecturer of St. Michael Bassishaw, London, and chaplain in ordinary to his majesty. He was author of a great number of theological tracts, and of four volumes of sermons published after his death. NICHOLAS, brother of this divine, was also born at Bury in 1654, and educated at Cambridge, where he took his degree of D.D. 1704. He was preacher of St. Mary's in this town, and rector of Hitcham. He died in 1727. His son, Nicholas, became bishop of Exeter. JOHN BATTELY, D.D., was born at Bury in 1647, and educated at Trinity College, Cambridge. He became chaplain to archbishop Sancroft, who gave him the rectory of Adisham, in Kent, and the archdeaconry of Canterbury. He was the author of a brief account, in Latin, of the Antiquities of St. Edmund's Bury, and died in 1708. The late REV. DR. MALKIN, who was long master of the Grammar school, is well known to

the literary world by several publications of considerable merit. A handsome monument has recently been erected here in memory of him and his distinguished sons, at the expense of gentlemen who had been his pupils.

PARISH CHURCHES AND CHURCHYARD :—The ABBEY GATE which led to the once-splendid monastery of St. Edmund, and the venerable NORMAN TOWER, which was the gate tower of the magnificent church built by abbot Baldwin, are already noticed at pages 618 to 621, with the other conventual remains. The *Norman Tower*, or *Church-Gate*, now forms the grand entrance into the CHURCHYARD, which comprises about five acres, and contains the two parish churches of Bury, dedicated to *St. Mary* and *St James*, besides which, it formerly contained the Abbey Church, (see page 611,) and another dedicated to St. Margaret, the site of which is occupied by the Shire-Hall. The Churchyard is crossed by two spacious walks which have rows of lofty trees on each side, and round its margin are several neat houses, with pleasant gardens and shrubberies; Clopton's Hospital, the Shire-Hall, and some remains of the west-end of the abbey church. (See page 620.) The memorials for the dead are very numerous, and near the centre is a small plot of ground enclosed with high iron railing, and planted with shrubs and trees. This cemetery belongs to the corporation, but was enclosed and planted by John Spink, Esq., banker, who died in 1794, and lies buried in it, under a plain marble tablet. In the same enclosure is an inscription, in memory of Mary Haselton, who was killed by lightning, when in the act of prayer, repeating her vespers, on the 16th of August, 1785, aged nine years. In the shady avenue between the two churches, " an atrocious attempt was made, in 1721, by *Arundel Coke, Esq.*, barrister, with the assistance of one Woodbourne, a hired assassin, to murder his brother-in-law, *Edward Crisp, Esq*, in the hope of possessing his property. He had invited him, and his wife, and family to supper, and at night, on pretence of going to see a mutual friend, he led him into the churchyard, where, on a signal given, Woodbourne rushed upon Mr. Crisp, and cut his head and face in a terrible manner, with a hedging-bill. Leaving him on the ground for dead, Coke returned to the company as if nothing had happened. Mr. Crisp, however, was not killed, and on recovering himself, mustered sufficient strength to crawl back to the house of his inhuman relative, where his appearance, so cruelly mangled and covered with blood, excited the utmost horror and amazement, and confounded the author of the barbarous deed. It was not long before he was discovered, and with his accomplice brought to trial, on the statute for defacing and dismembering, called the Coventry Act. Mr. Crisp having survived this outrage, Coke was so good a lawyer, and so hardened a villain, as to hope to save himself by pleading that he intended not to deface, but to kill. This justification, little inferior in atrocity to the crime itself, availed him nothing, and sentence of death was passed upon him, and the partner of his guilt. Shortly before the day appointed for his execution, the unhappy convict requested of the high sheriff for the county, Sir Jasper Cullum, that if he thought there were no hopes of pardon, he might suffer early in the morning, to avoid the crowd likely to be collected by such a spectacle. His desire was complied with.

St. Mary's Church was first erected in 1005, but was rebuilt in its present form between the years 1424 and 1433. It is a spacious and handsome structure, with a square tower, and is 139 feet long, and 67½ broad, exclusive of the chancel which measures 74 feet by 68. It is divided into three aisles by two rows of slender and elegant columns. The roof of the nave, constructed in France, and put together after it was brought to England, is much admired for its lightness and elegance, but has been found to be in such a decayed and dangerous state, that it is now (Sept. 1843) undergoing repairs, which it is estimated will cost about £1500; and the organ has been taken down and the nave closed till the work is completed. The repairs will be executed under the direction of Mr. Cottingham, without removing any of the timber; viz. by splicing the principals, and securing the hammer beams to them by cast iron shoes, strongly bolted on each side, and taking a solid bearing upon the wall, where the plate and the ends of many of the timbers are entirely rotted away. This is the finest "open roof" in Suffolk, and the beautifully carved angles on the under side of the hammer beams, fortunately, from their height, escaped the fury of the puritanical zealots of the 17th century. The north porch, especially the *cul de lampe*, is of curious workmanship. Before the Reformation, St. Mary's was distinguished for its numerous altars, images, and pictures; and part of "Our Lady's" altar may still be seen against the south wall. At the dissolution of the abbey, this church, as well as St. James's, was included in the general system of plunder, both of them being stripped of plate and other ornaments, then valued at about £480. Both likewise contained numerous inscriptions and effigies in brass, but these were nearly all torn off by the churchwardens in 1644, and sold for their private emolument; so that the ancient monuments are now much defaced. On the north side of the communion table, in St. Mary's, is a plain altar monument, in memory of Mary Tudor, third daughter of Henry VII., who had been compelled to marry the infirm Louis XII. of France, and after his death, was espoused by the Duke of Suffolk. She was first interred, as already noticed, in the abbey church; but her remains were removed hither after the dissolution of the monastery: Her tomb continued without any external memorial, till 1758, when it was repaired at the expense of Dr. Symonds, and a marble tablet inserted, bearing an appropriate inscription. In the middle of the chancel lies interred John Reeve, the last abbot, who had an annuity of 500 marks allowed him after the dissolution, and retired to a large house at the south-west corner of Crown-street, where he died in the following year. His gravestone was of grey marble, but was taken up about 1744, to make room for one in memory of one Sutton, the purser of a ship, who was buried in the same grave. At the east end of the south aisle is a well executed altar monument, in memory of *John Baret*, who died in 1463, from starvation, as tradition says, in consequence of having endeavoured to fast forty successive days and nights. Here are also stately altar tombs covering the remains of *Sir Robt. Drury*, who was privy councellor to Henry VII. and VIII., and died about 1533; *Roger Drury, Esq.*, who died in 1472, and *Sir Wm. Carew*, who died in 1501. These tombs bear recumbent effigies, and are enclosed with

wooden railing. At the east end of the north aisle is a brass plate on which is engraved the effigy of John Finers, archdeacon of Sudbury, who died in 1497; and in the vestry is another brass, on which is pourtrayed the effigies of *John Smyth*, the great benefactor of Bury, and his wife. This church sustained considerable injury from lightning, on the 11th of August, 1766, when a fissure was made in the wall, several large stones of which were driven into the interior, and so tremendous was the explosion of the electric fluid, that the destruction of the whole edifice was apprehended. It has 3,000 sittings, of which 500 are free. The benefice is a *Donative*, valued in 1835, at £110, in the patronage of John Fitz-Gerald, jun. Esq., and incumbency of the Rev. C. J. P. Eyre, M. A. The Rev Thos. Hickman, M. A. is *curate;* Mr. Wm. Crack, *clerk;* and Mr. John Clark, *sexton.*

St. James' Church was originally built about the year 1200, by Abbot Sampson, who was dissuaded by his brethren of the abbey from his intention of going on a pilgrimage to the shrine of St. James, at Compostella, in Spain, and in compliance with their recommendation, founded this church, in honour of that saint at Bury. The present structure, though far advanced in 1500, was not finished till the Reformation, when Edward VI. gave £200 to complete it, as appears from an inscription over the inside of the west door. It is a fine Gothic structure of freestone, to which the Norman Tower at the entrance to the churchyard serves as the bell tower. (See p. 619.) The nave and aisles are 137 feet in length, and 69 in breadth; and the chancel 56 feet 8, by 27 feet 5 inches. The west end is particularly beautiful, and the windows are numerous, large and handsome, and were originally adorned with painted glass, some fragments of which still remain. The chancel was rebuilt in 1711. St. James's, like St. Mary's, appears to have been formerly in high estimation for its numerous altars and chapels. Against the wall in the south aisle, are two elegant monuments enclosed with iron railing,—one to the Rt. Hon. James Reynolds, chief baron of the Exchequer, who died in 1738; and the other to Mary his wife. He is represented sitting in his robes of justice; on each side is a weeping figure, and above his coat of arms, with other embellishments. The church was thoroughly repaired in 1820, when a new gallery was added. It has about 2,000 sittings, of which 250 are free. The benefice is a *Donative*, valued in 1835, at £106, and is in the patronage of the Corporation of Bury, and incumbency of the Rev. George John Haggitt, M.A. The Rev. H. T. C. Cooper, is the *curate;* Mr. S. Keeling, *clerk;* and Mr. G. Stearn, *sexton.*

St. John's Church. in St. John's street, is an elegant structure, built by subscription, and consecrated Oct. 21st, 1841, as a district church, or chapel of ease for the two parishes, the encreasing population of which had long felt the want of additional church accommodation. It is in the decorated style of architecture which prevailed in the 14th century; and has a highly enriched tower at the west end, surmounted by a lofty but slender spire. It has 850 sittings, half of which are free, and cost about £6,100,—including £1,400 paid for the purchase of the site and parsonage house; £109 for repairing the latter; £386 for enclosing the grounds, and other incidental expenses. The Church Building Society gave £400; the

Trustees of the Guildhall Feoffment £300 ; Lord Calthorpe, the Duke of Grafton, and Lady Hervey, each £200; C. D. Leech, £210; A. J. Brooke, Esq., Rt. Bevan, Esq., Rev. Sir, T. G. Cullum, Bart., W. Dalton, Esq., Rev. H. Hasted, Rev. G. J. Haggitt, Earl Jermyn, the Bishop of London, H. J. Oakes, Esq., Dr. Smith, and H. Wilson, Esq., each £100, and the remainder was contributed in smaller sums by a numerous list of subscribers resident in the town and neighbourhood. The Communion Plate was presented by the Marchioness of Bristol, and the Organ by the Rev. J. D. Hustler. The church is dedicated to St. John the Evangelist, and is a *perpetual curacy*, endowed by the Marquis of Bristol and Earl Jermyn, with £100 per annum, out of lands at Little Saxham. The Bishop of Ely is patron ; and the Rev. Robt. Rashdall, M.A., incumbent. The population of that portion of the borough within the district of this church, is about 3,000. Mr. W. Fordham is the *clerk and sexton.*

St. Mary's Church Estate comprises 1A. 1R. of land, called Turret Close, let for £7, and given by an unknown donor; and 4A. in Babwell Fen, given by John Perfey, for repairing and ringing the bells, and now let for £12 a year. Out of the revenues of the *Guildhall Feoffment*, the following yearly sums are paid to *each* of the churches of *St. Mary and St. James*, viz :—£100 towards lighting, warming, and repairing the buildings ; £50 to each incumbent to provide themselves with houses for their respective habitations ; and £40 to each of the two readers or curates. From the same trust, £50 is paid yearly to the clergyman who preaches the *Wednesday Lecture*, pursuant to the bequest of Fras. Pynner, jun.; and £10 to the minister who officiates as chaplain at the gaol, pursuant to the gift of Margaret Odeham.

CHAPELS :—The *Catholic Chapel*, in Westgate-street, is a small neat building, erected in 1838, and now under the pastoral care of the Rev. H. Brigham. The *Presbyterian Chapel*, in Churchgate-street, has 700 sittings, and was built in 1711, by a congregation formed in 1689, and now having an endowment of £90 per annum. The *Independent Chapel*, in Whiting-street, erected in 1646, and rebuilt in 1804, has more than 900 sittings, and an endowment of £30 per annum. There is also a chapel in Northgate-street, belonging to the Independents, built in 1828, and having 400 sittings. The *Particular Baptists* have two chapels here,—one in Garland-street, built in 1834, at the cost of £1,400, and having 1,000 sittings ; and the other in Westgate-street, erected in 1840, at the cost of £800, and having 500 sittings. The *Society of Friends* have an old meeting-house in Long Brackland; the *Wesleyans* have a small chapel in St. Mary's-square, built in 1811 ; and the *Primitive Methodists* have one in Garland-street, erected in 1820.

Sunday Schools, and *Bible, Tract*, Missionary, and other Institutions, for the propagation of *Religious Knowledge*, are liberally supported here, by the Church and the Dissenting congregations; as also are various Charitable Institutions for the relief of the indigent. The borough also derives from posthumous charity, several thousands per annum, as will be seen in the following account of its *eleemosynary institutions and bequests*, for the solace of age and poverty, the instruction of the poor, and the general weal of the inhabitants.

THE GUILDHALL FEOFFMENT comprises numerous houses, tenements, building sites, farms, &c. let to about 66 tenants, at rents amounting to about £2,111 per annum, and vested with the Guildhall Feoffees of Bury St. Edmund's, in trust, for the public use and benefit of the inhabitants of the town, and for specific charitable purposes, under the settlements and donations comprised in the following summary, and purchases made by the Feoffees at different times. *John,* otherwise *Jankyn Smyth, Esq.,* having settled in Feoffees sundry messuages and lands in Bury, Barton, Fornham-All-Saints, Nowton, and Rougham, by his Will, in 1473, directed them with the rents and profits thereof to keep his anniversary in St. Mary's church, and pay the sum usually paid by the inhabitants of Bury, to every new Abbot of Bury St. Edmund's, on his election, and to apply the surplus rents towards payment of the fifteenths, tenths, taxes, and other burthens imposed on the burgesses; and he directed, that when the feoffees should be reduced to fourteen, the premises should be vested in the surviving feoffees and others of the most substantial inhabitants of Bury, to be elected by the alderman and burgesses, or in their default, by the remaining feoffees, so as to make up the number of 24; and that four of them should be annually chosen to receive the rents and profits of the premises, and render an account thereof yearly: By subsequent wills, he devised his manor of Bretts, in Hepworth, and other estates, for establishing a chantry, the support of a chantry priest, and the sustentation of a college of priests, at Bury; but these being declared superstitious uses, the manor and estates were forfeited to the Crown at the Reformation. In 1477, *Margaret Odeham* devised to the same feoffees, a house in Skinner-row, Bury, and lands in Bury, Barton, Nowton, Horningsheath, and Westley, in trust, after her decease, for the observance of certain superstitious ceremonies in St. James's church, saying mass to the prisoners in Bury gaol, and for finding seven faggots of wood weekly, from Hallowmas to Easter, for the prisoners in the long ward of the gaol; and she directed that the residue of the profits of the lands should be dealt in alms, except 2s. to be given yearly to the brethren of the Candlemas Guild. By a codicil, dated 1479, she gave two tenements in Churchgate-street, for keeping her anniversary, and paying 20s. a year to be distributed in bread to poor people at the Guildhall, to pray for her soul; and by another codicil, dated 1483, she gave her tenements in the Market-stead, Skinner-row, and the Fishmarket, for helping to pay taxes, talliages, and other charges on the town, and for helping the poor inhabitants, at the discretion of the feoffees. That portion of the property which became forfeited to the Crown, as given for superstitious uses, was re-purchased by the feoffees in the reign of Edward VI. In 1483, *Edmund King* left five tenements in High-street,—four of them to be occupied, rent free, by poor people, and the other to be let, and the rent to be applied in repairing the premises. Many other tenements were given to be used as *almshouses,* viz: four in Garland-street, given in 1558, by *Thomas Browse;* two in Little Brackland, given in 1495, by *Margaret Drury;* several in Crown-street, given in 1564, by *Bartw. Brokesby;* six in College-street, given in 1571, by *Wm. Barnaby;* four in Westgate, given in 1635, by *John Hill;* and several others given by *John Ashwell* and others. The *Pest-Houses,* now used as almshouses, were built by the feoffees, about 1665. *Sir John Frenze,* priest, in 1494, gave two pightles of land in Bury-field, for the benefit of the sick lepers in the hospital without Risbygate, now an almshouse. *Adam Newhawe* is said to have given 51A. of land, in 1496, for superstitious and charitable uses, and it is supposed to be included in that part of the Guildhall Feoffment, called the Town Estate, as also are lands in the South and East fields, given by *Wm. Fiske,* in 1499, to the brethren of the Candlemas Guild, to provide a cope for every new abbot, and to pay the task of the town in the manner directed by the will of John

Smyth. In 1503, *John Salter* left a tenement in Northgate, and two acres of land in Risbygate-field, for the same uses as are described in the will of John Smyth. In the reign of Edward VI., the parishioners sold the plate and jewels belonging to the churches of St. Mary and St. James, for the purpose of raising a fund for the future repairs of those buildings. The produce of this sale was £480, which was laid out in the purchase of part of the estates which had been given by John Smyth and Margaret Odeham, for superstitious uses, and the estates which had belonged to dissolved chantries and guilds. The property thus purchased forms the chief part of that portion of the Guildhall Feoffment, called the *Town Estate*, and was vested in trust, that the rents and profits thereof might be applied for the reparation and support of the two parish churches, the payment of taxes and fifteenths, and the relief of poor, lame, and impotent parishioners, and of prisoners in the borough gaol, at the discretion of the feoffees ; of whom, 12 were to be of St. Mary's, and 12 of St. James's parish. In 1557 and 1584, *Catherine Caye* left land and tenements, and *Wm. Markent* £60, for the poor of Bury. In 1556, *Wm. Tassell* left various premises in Bury, (now let for more than £400 per annum,) upon trust, for the payment of 40s. a year towards repairing the two parish churches, and for the payment of levies for setting out soldiers, and taxes and impositions charged on the town, and such like uses as were declared by the will of John Smyth. By letters patent, in the 11th of Elizabeth, (1569) her Majesty, in consideration of £118 11s., granted to *E. Grymston* and *W. Le Grys*, a messuage and premises in Eastgate-street, late belonging to the Guilds of St. Thomas, the Assumption, and St. Peter ; certain messuages and lands in Hepworth, Barningham, and Weston, late belonging to John Smyth's chantry, and a messuage in Bury, called the Guildhall, which had long been appropriated to the common use of the burgesses. All these premises are described in the deed as having been *suppressed* or *concealed*, and withheld from the Crown; and by an indenture of bargain and sale, dated the day following, Grymston and Le Grys conveyed them to Sir Nicholas Bacon and the other feoffees of the Town Lands. In 1572, *Edmund Jermyn* left a yearly rent charge of £40 out of the manor of Torksey, in Lincolnshire, for the relief of the poor of Bury, and it was resolved by the feoffees, in 1611, that this annuity should be employed in clothing and apprenticing poor children and orphans. In 1578, *Thos. Badbye* gave the *Shire House*, in trust, for the use of the Sessions and Assizes, and the public meetings of the inhabitants. In 1587, *Thos. Bright* left a portion of the tithes of Foxearth, in Essex, in trust, to pay 40s. a year towards the reparation of the two parish Churches, 20s. a year to the prisoners in the gaol, and to employ the remainder in such godly uses as should be thought fit by the feoffees. He also left £300 to be employed as a stock for the poor, and in 1612, it was laid out in obtaining a grant or release from the Crown of a fee farm rent, payable by the feoffees out of certain property, out of which they agreed hereafter to distribute £23 yearly in clothing among the poor. In 1604, *Richard Walker* gave for the benefit of the town, £20 and a house in Churchgate. In 1605, *Peter Kembold* gave £100 for the relief of the poor of the North and East Wards. In 1610, *Eustace Darcy* gave, for the common use of the town, a toft and barn in Northgate. In 1612, *James Baxter* gave an acre of land in Spyntlemill-Field, that the rents thereof might be employed in that part of St. James's Church, called the Library. In the 13th of Charles I., *Thomas Bright, jun.*, gave two messuages in the fish or meat market, (afterwards burnt down) in trust, to apply the rents yearly as follows: £5 in apprenticing poor children; 40s. for repairing St. Mary's and St. James's Churches ; 20s. for the poor in the gaol, and the remainder for the repairs of St. Mary's or other public or charitable uses. About the same time, *Peter Ling* left two houses in Short-Brackland, and

another in Westgate, in trust, to employ the rents in clothing the poor of the two parishes. In 1622, *Lady Kytson*, (see Hengrave,) left an annuity of £10 out of the manor of Lackford, for the relief of the aged poor of Bury. In 1626, the feoffees purchased a farm of 95A. at Bradfield, with money arising from the sale of other land, and £200 given by *Stephen Ashwell*, for clothing the poor. They also purchased in the same year, tenements called *Moyse Hall*, now partly used as a police station. In 1631, *Edward Darby* gave £300 to secure the yearly payment of £17 6s. 8d. for a distribution of 10s. worth of bread once a fortnight, among 65 poor people of St. James's parish, and the payment of 3s. 4d. to the minister, at each distribution, for catechising the recipients. This legacy was laid out in the purchase of 44A. of land at Canewden, which was afterwards sold, and the money laid out in land at Hepworth. In 1631, *John Sharpe* gave £200, in trust, to apply the yearly interest as follows: 20s. each to the town and county gaols, for the poor prisoners there; 10s. to the poor in the Bridewell; 10s. to the poor in the Spittle House, and the remainder to be distributed among the poor of the North and East Wards. *Lady Carey* gave £100, for the relief of five poor widows, and it was laid out in 1636, in the purchase of a tenement and land called Jeckes, in Hepworth. In 1637, *Edward Bourne* left £20 to be employed in buying wool to be wrought into cloth by the inmates of the Workhouse and Bridewell, for clothing the poor. He also left three tenements in Westgate, two to be occupied, rent free, by poor people, and the other to be let, and the rent applied in repairing the buildings. He likewise bequeathed 8A. of land at Hepworth, to his son and heirs for 15 years, and directed that it should afterwards be vested with the feoffees for apprenticing poor boys. In 1640, *Fras. Pynner* left a brewhouse in Whiting-street, (since converted into several dwellings) to the intent that £5 should be yearly bestowed in shirts and smocks for the poor of St. Mary's; that 2s. should be given monthly in bread; that the minister should have 20s. yearly for his trouble; and that the remainder of the rents should be applied in repairing the premises, and in buying horn books and primers for poor children. In 1654, *Anthony Smith* settled a messuage in the Meat Market, for clothing poor people of the two parishes. *Martha Cobb* gave £100 for the benefit of five poor widows, and it was laid out in 1697 in the purchase of land at Pakenham.

From the intermixture of property acquired under so many different sources as those just enumerated, it has become impossible to determine what portions of the income ought in strictness to be applied specifically to each of the several purposes of the trust; and this difficulty has been greatly increased by various enclosures and exchanges. The following list of the property, now held by the feoffees, shews the names of the tenants, and the amount of the rents in 1838.

GUILDHALL FEOFFMENT RENTAL, in 1838.

Tenants.	Property.	A. R. P.	Situate.	£.	s.	d.
Allen W.	Farm	101 3 34	Hepworth	150	0	0
Bullen Jon.	House		Abbeygate B.	30	0	0
Betts Sam.	House		Churchgate st.	8	0	0
Boldero M.	Farm	131 2 38	Drinkstone	190	0	0
Boldero & Beeton	Farm	94 1 24	By, Wes. & For.	141	0	0
Bridgman T.	Angel Inn		Angel hill & lane ⎰	325	0	0
——————	Paddock	3 37	& Bridewell lane ⎱			
Bridgman John	Stables		St. Andrew's st.	21	0	0
Bridgman & Palmer	Farm	159 3 35	Bury & Nowton	278	17	6
Barker William	Ground rent.		Northgate street	0	0	8
Blomfield J.	Do.		Walnuttree close	0	2	6
Braddock H.	Ground	0 0 8	80, Southgate st.	1	10	0

Tenants.	Property.	A.	R.	P.	Situate.	£.	s.	d.
Bristol Marquis of.	Ground				Sparrow hill	0	2	0
Brown Susan	House				17, Guildhall st...	3	0	0
Brown John......	House				Lane Northg. st...	4	4	0
Calfe J. and W. ..	2 tenements.				17, 18 Raing. st. ...	21	0	0
Cawston George ..	Ground			4	Eastgate Bridge ..	0	5	0
Coldham James ..	Grd. rent ..				Barrow.........	0	13	4
Cooke John	Farm	69	2	5	Bradfield	95	0	0
Coote Widow	Tenement ..				9, Angel hill	4	0	0
County Magistrates,	Shire hall ..				Bury	10	10	0
Darkins John	House				Lane Northg. st...	4	4	0
Deck John	Ground				Burman's lane	0	0	6
Greene Edward ..	Ho. & land ..	2	0	16	Westgate street ..	10	0	0
Greengrass G.	House				10, Angel lane	5	0	0
Gooday W.	Ground				Westgate st.	0	5	0
Gooch Widow	Tenement ..				72, St. Andw. st. ..	6	0	0
Hobbs Ephraim ..	Ho. & Gd...	0	2	16	Tay Fen	18	0	0
Holden Thomas ..	Land	1	0	0	Hepworth	2	0	0
Hume Sir A.	Rent charge.				Torksey	40	0	0
Jackson Widow ..	Ground				Friar's lane	0	5	0
Kemp Chas.......	Tenement ..				71, St. Andw. st. ..	6	0	0
Kent Sir C.	Rent charge.				Lackford	10	0	0
Last James	House				Traverse	20	0	0
Lockwood E.	Ground				Bridewell lane	0	2	6
Long Geo.	Farm	120	3	15	Hepworth........	160	0	0
Mallows Geo.	Farm	90	2	39	Hepworth........	90	0	0
Mapletoft R.	Farm	41	1	37	Shimpling Stansted.	45	0	0
Mathews Ed.	House				Angel Hill	16	0	0
Middleditch Ch. ..	Land	4	0	5	Nomans Meadows...	16	0	0
Mower John......	Ground			7	12,Long Brackland.	0	5	0
Norfolk Duke of ..	Ground	28	2	38	Fornham St.Martin.	50	0	0
Nunn F.	Land	19	0	7	Horringer	28	10	0
Nunn J. Exec.....	Land	22	0	20	Bury	38	10	0
Oakes H. J.	End of Guild hall				Bury	0	5	0
Orbell John	Tithes				Foxearth	50	0	0
Pattle T.	Stable				St. Andrews st. ..	5	0	0
Payne Noah	Land	9	0	25	Nomans Meadows ..	31	10	0
Peck Peter	Ho.& shop ..				Traverse	20	0	0
Ranson John	Ho. & Grd...				Garland street ..	6	0	0
Reynolds Widow..	House				16, Guildhill st. ..	3	10	0
Robinson H.......	Ground	0	0	1	Southgate street ..	0	1	0
Stave W.	House				Lane Northgate st...	4	4	0
Sidney T.	House				Northgate street	6	6	0
Skipper Lydia	House				11, Angel Lane ..	5	0	0
Sore John........	House				24,Churchgate st. ..	8	0	0
Steel John	Ground				Skinner street	0	5	0
Steggles William..	House				10,Whiting street ..	50	0	0
Do.	House				61,Churchgate st. ..	12	0	0
Do.	2 tenements ..				14&15,ButterMkt..	15	0	0
Do.	Sta. & P. ..	1	0	0	Risbygate street ..	8	0	0
Do.	Ground	0	0	15	Garland street ..	0	3	4
Surveyors........	Ground	0	0	6	St. Andrew's street ..	0	5	0
Savings Bank					Guild Hall	15	0	0
Walton James	Farm	9	3	12	Hepworth	20	0	0
Winn Geo.	Ground				Near Guildhall ..	0	5	0

Total, per Annum, £2,111　1　4

The premises which the Feoffees have to keep in repair are the Guildhall Hall-keeper's-house, Shire-Hall, Bridewell, three Schools, 22 public and private pumps, five wells, many *almshouses*, and all the houses, buildings, &c., let to their numerous tenants. The ALMSHOUSES, are occupied by poor people, but they have no endowment, and their number has recently been reduced from 105 to about 75;—several having been pulled down to make room for the new schools.

The present *Feoffees or Trustees of the Guildhall Feoffment*, are the Rev. H. Hasted, J. Symonds, W. Dalton, G. Moor, H. Le Grice, Rev. T. West, Col. Ray, Dr. Bayne, H. J. Oakes, H. Braddock, S. Adams, G. Portway, Dr. Probart, G. Creed, J. Pace, D. Wright, J. Borton, J. Worlledge, R. Harvey, C. C. Smith, J. Watson, G. Paul, Rev. J. Edwards, T. R. Robinson, G. Brown, Rev. G. J. Haggitt, Wm. Buck, and J. Deck. In 1810, the old trustees being reduced to two, new ones were appointed to make up the number 28, under an order of the Court of Chancery. In 1839, three several schemes for the future application of the income of the Guildhall Feoffment, were proposed for the sanction of the Court of Chancery,—one by some of the principal burgesses; one by 4 old and 8 new trustees; and the other by eleven of the new trustees. Each of these schemes professed to have regard to the sources of income, and the uses and purposes stated in the feoffment deed, of 1810, but they differed considerably with respect to the portions to be allowed for the education of the poor, the support of the two parish churches, and the erection and endowment of a new church or chapel-of-ease. The *scheme* which was ultimately sanctioned by the Court of Chancery, has in view the settlement of those party disputes, between churchmen and dissenters, which had for some time wasted the charity funds, in expensively prolonged litigation. It came into operation in 1843, and its substance is as follows :—That the yearly sums, already named at page 632, shall be paid to the churches of St. Mary and St. James, for the reparation of the buildings, and the use of the incumbents and curates; that £300 per annum shall be paid to the Corporation, and applied with the Borough Rates; that £120 shall be contributed yearly to the Suffolk General Hospital in Bury; that £65 per annum, being the proceeds of property left by *Fras. Pynner* and *Anthony Smith*, shall be distributed among the poor in bread, clothing, &c., as directed by their wills; that £100 per annum shall be distributed in coals, clothing, &c., among poor burgesses not receiving parochial relief; that other doles shall be distributed yearly, according to the wills of Lady Carey, Edw. Bourne, Edw. Darby, Margt. Odeham, and others, as already noticed; and that *three* SCHOOLS shall be erected and supported by the Feoffees, and be open to the children of parents of all religious denominations, and be called " *The Guildhall Commercial School;*" " *The Guildhall School for Poor Girls,*" and " *The Guildhall School for Poor Boys,*" and that the sum of £1,650 should be expended in their erection, according to the specification and estimate of Mr. Jas. Emerson. These schools have recently been finished, and are handsome and commodious structures, in the Gothic style; and are conducted as follows :—

The COMMERCIAL SCHOOL, in College-street, affords instruction to 150 boys in English and other living languages, in writing, arithmetic, geography, history, and so much of the mathematics and dead languages as may be practicable or useful. The master must be a member of the Church of England, and has a salary of £150 per annum, and 5s. quarterly from each boy. The trustees may allow as much as £70 yearly to assistant masters, and £10 for coals, &c. The POOR GIRLS' SCHOOL affords instruction to 150 girls in reading, writing, arithmetic, knitting, sewing, cleaning, washing, &c., and has a *laundry* attached to it. The mistress is

provided with a dwelling-house, and has a yearly salary of £40, and one penny weekly from each scholar. The assistant mistress resides in the same house, and has a salary of £30 per annum. The trustees allow £30 for monitors, rewards, and for supplying the school with stationery, coals, &c. The POOR BOYS' SCHOOL, in Bridewell-lane, affords instruction to 300 boys in reading, writing, arithmetic, the outlines of geography and history; and in manual occupations, particularly in *garden husbandry;* and for that purpose, the trustees are empowered to rent land not exceeding the yearly rent of £15, and to pay £20 per annum to a person for teaching the boys garden husbandry. The master is provided with a dwelling-house, and has a yearly salary of £70, and one penny weekly from each boy. The yearly sum of £30 is allowed for monitors, rewards, stationery, coals, &c. Besides these three schools, supported out of the ample revenue of the Guildhall Feoffment, for the education of 600 children, the borough has an endowed Free Grammar School, and several schools for the poor, supported by subscription. The *Lancasterian School* was established in 1811, for the instruction of 200 boys, but has been discontinued since the establishment of the Guildhall schools. The *National,* or *Central Schools* of the Society for the education of the poor in the principles of the Established Church, in the archdeaconry of Sudbury, were founded about the same year, and are now attended by about 200 boys, and 150 girls. A new school for the girls, and also an *Infant School,* were built in 1842. The *School of Industry,* for poor girls, is supported by subscription, and was established many years ago.

FREE GRAMMAR SCHOOL:—By Letters Patent, in the 4th year of his reign, Edward VI. ordained that there should be a grammar school at Bury St. Edmund's, to be called the Free Grammar School of King Edward the 6th; to consist of a master, and usher, under the control of 16 governors, who should be a body corporate, and have the management of the possessions, revenues, and goods of the school; and his Majesty thereby granted to the governors the then late chantry in Kyrketon, alias, Shotley, with the lands thereunto belonging in Kyrketon, Shotley, and Chelymton; and the then late chantry called Clopton's Chantry, in Melford, with the lands thereunto belonging in Melford, Waldingfield, Semer, and Carsey; and also the manor of Collingham-Hall, late belonging to Frey Chantry, in London. These possessions were then of the yearly value of £21 8s., and were to be held by the governors, of the manor of East-Greenwich, rendering to the King a yearly rent of £1 8s. The governors were empowered, with the advice of the bishop of Norwich, to make statutes and ordinances, for the government of the master, usher, and scholars. All the estates and property mentioned in the letters patent, except a farm at Waldingfield, have been sold at different times, and other estates, &c. purchased in lieu thereof. The school property now consists of a farm of 81A. at Great Waldingfield, let for £115 a year; a house, two barns, and 113A. of land at Bury, let for £201 per annum; £3,191 15s. 11d. three per cent. Consols, yielding £95 15s. a year; and the school premises, consisting of a large house and garden occupied by the master, and the school and play-ground. By the statutes made in 1809, it is provided that he should be of the degree of Master of Arts, at the least; and that he should have a yearly salary of £60, and the usher £30; that these salaries might be encreased at the pleasure of the governors; that the school should be free to all the sons of inhabitants of Bury, who should have learnt the rudiments of the Latin Grammar, and be able to write; except the admission fees of 21s. each to the master and usher, and the yearly payment on Maundy Thursday of one guinea each, by those instructed in Latin only, and two guineas by those instructed in Greek also; that whatever system of education should be

adopted, the free scholars should enjoy all the advantages thereof; that the master might take other scholars and boarders, on terms to be agreed upon by him and the governors; and that he should not have any benefice or cure that might hinder his regular and constant care of the school. In 1828, on the appointment of the late master, (Rev. John Edwards, M.A.) the system of education used in the great public schools, was introduced, and since then, the governors have allowed the master a yearly salary of £112 10s., and £52 10s. a year for every assistant he employs in addition to the usher, whose salary of £30 is augmented by the master, out of the payments made by the free scholars, or royalists, as they are called, from the school being of royal foundation. The school has been long in high repute, and has generally upwards of 100 scholars, nearly half of whom are " royalists." In the 11th of Elizabeth, *Edward Hewer* bequeathed three messuages in Botolph-lane, near Billingsgate, London, to the governors of this school, in trust, for the maintenance of four scholars to be sent hence to the University of Oxford or Cambridge. The property is let for about £100 a year, and the rent is divided equally among four *Exhibitioners* appointed by the governors, and recommended, upon oath, by the master. These exhibitions are given to such candidates as are the best scholars, and are held for four years. In 1670, *John Sudbury*, D.D., dean of Durham, conveyed to ten trustees, 81A. of land in Hepworth, Barningham, and Stanton, upon trust, to apply £30 a year in apprenticing three or more poor children to freemen and inhabitants of Bury, and to employ the residue of the rents for the benefit of the free grammar school, or towards the maintenance of such poor scholars as should be sent from thence to the University of Cambridge. The estate now consists of only 77A. 3R. 21P. of land, let for £100 a year; but the trustees are also possessed of about £250 new four per cent. Annuities. They pay £37 10s. a year towards the support of two Exhibitioners at the University, and apply the remainder of the income, after paying incidental expences, in apprentice fees, of from £10 to £15 given with poor boys of Bury. The two Exhibitioners are chosen from the free scholars; but when there is not one of that class, on a vacancy, to take the exhibition, one of the boys not on the foundation is elected to receive it.

JOHN SUTTON, in 1696, bequeathed, after the death of his two sisters, a yearly rent charge of £32, out of his estates in Brockley and Whepstead, for the relief of six poor men of Bury; and in case of the failure of issue male of his nephew, Thomas Sutton, he devised the said estates, and also the Chequers Inn, Holborn, London, in trust, to pay the above annuity; also £30 a year towards the maintenance of six other poor men, (two to be of the parish of Brockley;) and £30 a year towards the maintenance and education of six poor boys of Bury, in the free school. This charity was for some years withheld, but by a decree of the Court of Exchequer, the trustees, in satisfaction thereof, obtained possession of a house and 120A. of land at Brockley, now let for £100 per annum, subject to a deduction of about £12 a year for land tax, quit rents, &c. They are also possessed of £500 old South Sea Annuities, purchased with unapplied income. They allow yearly, £6 each to ten poor men of Bury, and two of Brockley, besides coals to the value of 30s. a-piece; but the testator's charity, for six poor free scholars, has never been carried into effect, though the funds are now sufficient to afford the application of at least £20 a year for education. The Rev. Sir T. G. Cullum, and others, are trustees

DOROTHY CALTHORPE, in 1693, left £500 to the alderman and two ministers of Bury, in trust, to be invested for *apprenticing poor boys.* Of this legacy, the corporation received only £379, of which they laid out £318 in the purchase of the Chequers Inn, in Bury, and retained the remaining £61 on bond, at five per cent. interest. In 1813, the premises formerly

called the Chequers, having fallen into decay, were let for £30 per annum, on a lease for 28 years, to Wm. Steggles, who covenanted to lay out £300 in repairs within the first three years of the term. This lease has now expired, and the premises are worth upwards of £50 a year. The corporation apply the income with other funds appropriated to apprenticing poor children brought up at the charity schools.

JACOB JOHNSON, in 1708, bequeathed to twelve of the principal burgesses of Bury, three houses in Loom's lane, in trust, for the residence of three poor widows of St. James's parish ; and to provide for their reparation he left another house in the same lane, now let for £4 10s. a year. He charged his house near the Market-cross, (now belonging to Mr. Dalton,) with the yearly payment of £6, for apprenticing two poor boys of Bury, and left two yearly rent charges of £15 each, out of his estates at Rattlesden and Horningsheath, to provide eight poor men and eight poor women of the two parishes of Bury , with blue gowns or coats, and with 5s. each in money, on the 21st of December, yearly ; also to find three gowns once in two years, for the three widows in his almshouses, and to pay yearly 20s. to the lecturer, 5s. to the reader, 2s. 6d. to the clerk, and 2s. 6d. to the sexton of St. James's, for divine service on Innocent's day. By codicil, he directed the surplus of the said rent charges to be employed for the instruction of poor children in reading and writing; but the whole is absorbed by the before-mentioned distributions, and incidental expences. About 15 years ago, the three almshouses were repaired at the cost of about £80

A yearly rent charge of £6, left by *Edward Badby*, is paid out of two houses in Muston and School-hall-street, (belonging to the corporation,) and is divided equally among four poor men and two poor women. The trustees of *Sir Robert Drury's Charity*, (vide Hawstead,) erected an *almshouse* at Bury, about 25 years ago, for the residence of two poor women, each of whom has an annuity of £5. In 1659, *Thomas Sache* left a messuage in Westgate-street, in trust, to apply the rents thereof for the relief of four poor widows,—two of Bury, and two of Horningsheath. The premises were rebuilt in 1819, and are now let as two cottages, at rents amounting to £12 a year. In 1674, *Wm. Granger* left to four trustees, a yearly rent charge of £2 10s. out of his tenement and land in Bradfield-St.-Clare, in trust, to pay yearly 20s. each to two poor men of St. Mary's parish, and 10s. to a poor woman of St. James's. The trustees have for a long period been in possession of the property charged with this annuity, and it now lets for £6 15s. per annum, which is distributed among poor men and widows. O. R. Oakes and Mr. James Mathew were the surviving trustees in 1830, and were also trustees of a yearly rent charge of £11, left by *John Clarke*, in 1681, out of a house in Guildhall-street, to provide a dinner and 10s. a-piece for 20 poor widows of Bury, on the 5th of November. The house charged is now the property of Mr. Smith, surgeon. In 1709, *Wm. Cooke* left two houses in Long Brackland, now let for £10 a year, and 10A. of land at Hargrave, now let for £8 a year, in trust, that the rents should be laid out yearly on Nov. 5th, in clothing four poor old men of Bury. In 1819, Robt. Pawsey, Wm. Buck, Thos. Robinson, and C. D. Leech, were appointed as new trustees of this charity. In 1708, the REV. DR. JOHN BATTELEY left his estate at Chevington, to be applied after the death of his wife, towards the relief of such poor inhabitants of Bury, as are of honest fame, and are members of the Church of England. The testator's widow died in 1741. The estate consists of a house, out-buildings, and 46A. 1R. 21P. of land, let for £26 a year ; which, after deducting about £2 for incidental expences, is divided between two poor men. Messrs. James, O. R., and H. J. Oakes, and others, were appointed trustees of this charity in 1825. *Sir John James*, in 1740, left £1,000 for charitable uses in Bury ; and by a de-

tree of the Court of Chancery, in 1745, it was vested in the purchase of £1,000 Old South Sea Annuities, the dividends thereof to be applied in providing medical and surgical aid for the lame and sick working poor of the borough. The income, £30 a year, is divided among three surgeons. Sir T. G. Cullum, J. and O. R. Oakes, C. Blomfield, and J. Borton, were appointed trustees in 1828. The dividends of £2,282 three per cent. Consols, purchased with the bequest of *Mrs. Chamberlayne* and the *Rev. A. Upcher*, in 1769, are distributed in quarterly sums of 5s. each, among 68 poor women of Bury, by the ministers of the two parishes. In 1814, *Mrs. Mary Green* left £300, (now £304 15s. 3d. new Four per Cents.) in trust, to distribute the dividends yearly, among 12 aged poor parishioners of St. Mary's; £500, (now £724 4. 8d. three per cent. Consols,) in trust, to distribute the yearly dividends in coals, among the poor in the *almshouses* in Westgate-street, Southgate-street, Bridewell-lane, and College-street; and £300, (now £434 10s. three per cent. Consols,) in trust, to divide the yearly dividends among 12 poor persons of St. James's parish, of the age of 70.

CLOPTON'S ASYLUM:—In 1730, Poley Clopton, M. D., devised unto thirteen trustees, so much of his estates as should be of the yearly value of £300, upon trust, that they should erect a convenient house in Bury, for the reception and maintenance of six poor men and six poor women of Bury, of the age of 60 or upwards; half of them from each parish. In pursuance of this bequest, two farms at Stisted, and a farm at Liston and Foxearth, in Essex, were conveyed to the trustees, in 1733, and the charity was established by a decree of the Court of Chancery, in 1736, which requires that the almspeople shall be such as have not received parochial relief. The three farms comprise 562 acres, and are let for £640 a year. The trusteess have also £500 three per cent. Reduced Annuities, and £2,000 three per cent. Consols, so that the yearly income of the charity is £715. Some years ago, they expended several hundred pounds in erecting a new house on the estate at Stisted. The hospital, or asylum, is situated near the church-yard, and has a garden of nearly half an acre. The establishment consists of 12 almspeople, a matron or housekeeper, a butler, and occasional nurses. All of them, except the nurses, are completely clothed and maintained and provided with medical assistance, at the expence of the charity, and have likewise a quarterly allowance of about 26s. each. The Rev. Sir T. G. Cullum, H. J. & O. R. Oakes, Esqrs., and others, are trustees.

Charities belonging to St. Mary's Parish :—The poor have the following yearly doles,—a rent charge of £4 out of two houses in Abbeygate-street, given by *Edm. Bright*, and one of 10s. out of premises in Westgate, given by Agatha Borradale, for distributions of six penny loaves among the poor in the almshouses; a rent charge of £2 12s. out of premises in Hatter-street, given by *Wm. Cropley*, and about £2 per annum from *Corder's Charity*. (See Glemsford.) In 1653, *Jasper Sharp* left £300 to the corporation, in trust, to apply the yearly proceeds thereof for the catechising and relief of poor parishioners. The corporation pay £15 yearly as the interest of this legacy, and £11 of it is distributed in doles of bread, every alternate Thursday, among poor people attending the church, and the other £4 is paid to the minister for catechising the recipients. In 1718, *Thos. Fletcher* left six tenements in Whiting-street, in trust, to pay £5 a year for the education of poor children, and to distribute the remainder of the rents on Christmas day, in sums of 10s. each among poor widows and widowers. The tenements are now worth about £25 a year, of which £10 is paid in equal portions to the National and another charity school. Sir T. G. Cullum, Rev. T. G. Cullum, and O. R. Oakes, and T. Robinson, Esqrs., were appointed trustees in 1810. *John Alvis* left £200 in 1823, to be invested in the funds, and the yearly dividends to be distributed by the minister and churchwar-

dens, among the poor people living in and near Southgate-street. This legacy was laid out in the purchase of £177 5s. 11d. new four and a half per cent. Stock. The *poor of St. James's parish* have a yearly rent charge of £2, left by *Holofernes Allen*, out of land at Chevington, and a house in Risbygate, for a distribution of bread; and a yearly rent charge of £2 12s. out of a house in Hatter-street, left by *Wm. Cropley*, for poor widows. In 1817, *John Gibbon* left a messuage in the Butter Market, to provide coats and gowns for the most poor and aged men and women of St. James's parish that frequent the church. The house has been much improved since 1825, and is now let for about £30 a year. The rent is distributed in clothing on the feast of St. John the Evangelist. The Rev. H. Hasted and others, are trustees.

The SUFFOLK GENERAL HOSPITAL, is a large and commodious structure, with pleasant grounds, near the bottom of Westgate-street, and was established by subscription, in 1826, for the benevolent purpose of affording medical and surgical aid to the sick, lame, and infirm poor, both as *in* and *out* patients; and of providing food, lodgings, &c. for the former, of whom it has sometimes as many as 50 at one time, and from 300 to 400 in the course of a year. It is older and larger than the East Suffolk Hospital at Ipswich, (see page 84,) and arose from very feeble means, but the great necessity for such an institution was soon acknowledged by a numerous list of subscribers and benefactors resident in all parts of the county. Part of the hospital was originally a *Military Depôt*, which was erected here in the early part of the present century. For some years before 1826, there had been a Dispensary in Bury, for the relief of out-patients, and since that year the dividends of £750 three per cent. consols, which belonged to it, have been added to the funds of this hospital, the annual *expenditure* of which is about £1,700, and its *income*, from annual subscriptions, is about £900, and from the dividends of stock and money at interest, about £680 per annum. But of the stock belonging to the institution, £2,719 5s. 10d. 3½ per cent. Reduced Annuities, have been given and accumulated for the purpose of raising a sufficient fund for the establishment of a *Fever Ward*. The occasional *donations* to the hospital, average about £200 per annum, and it has derived no less than £7,914 from the profits of five *Bazaars*, held in 1827, 1830, 1833, 1836, and 1839. The Marquis of Bristol has, in three donations, given to this excellent charity, £1,996 in the 3 and 3½ per cent. Stocks. The late Dr. Goodwyn bequeathed to it £1,000, and the late Rev. Dr. Pettiward, £540; Mrs. Smith, £410; and Sir Wm. Parker, £536; and in its list of donations and legacies are many sums of £100 and upwards. The number of patients admitted in 1842, was 397 *in*, and 1,496 *out*-patients, and the total number to whom it has extended its healing benefits since its first institution, is upwards of 18,000, of whom more than 12,000 were cured. The Duke of Grafton is *president* of the institution; the Duke of Rutland, the Marquis of Bristol and others, are *vice-presidents;* the Rev. Lord Arthur Hervey, is *chaplain;* Drs. Probart, Ranking, and Hake, are the *physicians;* Messrs. C. Smith, G. Creed, and W. Image, *surgeons;* Mr. S. Newham, *house-surgeon and secretary;* and Mrs. Woodroffe, *matron.*

Among the *provident institutions* of the town are several Friendly Societies, and *Lodges of Druids, Odd Fellows, and Free Masons.* One

of the latter is the *Royal Edmund Lodge*, which meets at the Angel Inn, every Monday after full moon. The WEST SUFFOLK FRIENDLY SOCIETY numbers among its insuring members, 440 males, and 52 females, and has an insuring fund of more than £1,700, and an honorary fund of £400. The SAVINGS' BANK here was established in 1816, and on the 20th of Nov. 1842, had a surplus fund of £2,120, and deposits amounting to £61,119, belonging to 1,602 individual depositors, 44 Charitable Institutions, and 20 Friendly Societies. It is open every Saturday from twelve till one o'clock, at the Guildhall. The Duke of Grafton and the Marquis of Bristol are its presidents, and a number of the principal gentlemen of the town and neighbourhood are its directors and trustees.

The PUBLIC LIBRARY, formed in 1806, by the union of two libraries, one instituted in 1790, and the other in 1795, is in Abbeygate-street, and has now a valuable collection of about 3,000 volumes. Here is also a *Mechanics' Institution*, which was established in 1824, and has a library of 2,400 vols. Two *Newspapers* are published here, viz : the " Bury and Suffolk Herald," every Wednesday, and the " Bury Post and East Anglian," every Tuesday evening. The former was established about 1821, and the latter in 1782. The ASSEMBLY ROOMS, on Angel-hill, form a spacious and handsome building, comprising a spacious and elegant ball-room, a subscription *news-room*, billiard-room, supper-room, &c. Near the Corn Exchange is the Old Theatre, which was, about 25 years ago, converted by the Corporation into a large and handsome *Concert Room, News Room*, &c. Part of it is now occupied by the Mechanics' Institution. It stands on the site of the Old Market Cross, and was erected in 1780. The present THEATRE, in Westgate-street, is a commodious structure, which was built in 1818, upon a plan and under the direction of Wm. Wilkins, Esq. It is fitted up with taste and elegance. The BOTANIC GARDEN, near the Abbey Ruins, was established in the year 1820, by its present superintendent, N. S. H. Hodson, Esq., whose love for the science induced him to remove his private collection for the establishment of this beautiful garden, under the patronage of the nobility, gentry, and other principal inhabitants of the town and neighbourhood. It occupies about five acres, and is laid out with such taste, that it excites the admiration of all visitors. The salubrity of the air, and the aspect of the grounds are highly favourable to the growth of the more rare species of hardy plants, which are here cultivated with the greatest success. Strangers have access by means of a subscriber, or by personal application to the superintendent, or to Mr. Turner, the curator.

The GUILDHALL, in the street to which it gives name, is vested with the Trustees of the Guildhall Feoffment, (see page 637,) who hold it and keep it in repair, for the use of the corporation, the borough magistrates, &c. It was erected at a very early period, but has been enlarged and modernised, except the ancient porch of flint, brick, and stone, which still retains its pristine appearance. In the council chamber are several fine portraits; one of Admiral Hervey, by Sir Joshua Reynolds. *Petty Sessions* are held here every Thursday. The SHIRE HALL, which fronts the Churchyard, stands on the site of St. Margaret's Church, which was given, under the name of

the Shire House, by *Thomas Badby*, in 1578, for the use of the assizes and sessions, and the public meetings of the inhabitants; and vested with the Trustees of the Guildhall Feoffment, by whom it is kept in repair. It was rebuilt nearly forty years ago, and was re-modelled, repaired, and the two courts newly fitted up in an elegant style, in 1841. The front is adorned with a handsome portico and eight fluted columns. *Suffolk Lent Assizes* are held here, but since 1839, the Summer Assizes have been held at Ipswich. (See page 67.) *Quarter Sessions*, both for the county and borough, are held here in the usual sessions weeks of January, April, June, and October; and the *Clerk of the Peace, for Suffolk*, (J. H. Borton, Esq.,) and the *Deputy Registrar of the Archdeaconry of Sudbury*, (P. J. Case, Esq.,) have their offices in the town.

The COUNTY GAOL and HOUSE of CORRECTION, which serve also for the *Borough* and the *Liberty of St. Edmund*, form extensive piles of buildings, within a large enclosure, on Southgate-green, about a mile from the centre of the town. The *Gaol*, which has a neat stone front, wrought in rustic, was finished in 1805, and enlarged in 1819, for the purpose of affording a better classification of the prisoners, and a hospital and baths for the sick. It consists chiefly of four wings, 69 feet by 32;—three of these are divided by a partition wall along the centre, and the fourth is parted into three divisions; by which means the different classes of prisoners are cut off from all communication with each other. The gaoler's house is an irregular octagon building, in the centre, raised six steps above the level of the other buildings, and so placed that it commands inspection of all the court yards, as well as the entrance to the gaol. The chapel is in an upper room, and stone galleries lead to it from the various wings. The gaol enclosure is of an octagon form, 292 feet in diameter. The entrance is in the turnkey's lodge, on the leaded flat of which, executions are performed. The *House of Correction* stands in the centre of an enclosure of about an acre, adjoining, and consolidated with the gaol. It is a large square building, having a house in the centre for the principal turnkey. Here is the first *Tread Mill* of the kind ever erected, in which from 80 to 100 men can work at one time, in four different rooms, according to their classes in the prison. They are employed in grinding corn, &c., and have two-fifths of their earnings. Nield, who wrote about 30 years ago, speaks highly of the accommodations and regulations of this prison, and says,—"in the appointment of *gaoler*, I consider the county particularly fortunate in their choice of *Mr. John Orridge*, who, to great abilities, unites firmness and humanity in the discharge of his important trust." The prisoners for the Borough of Bury, are sent here in accordance with an agreement made between the County and Borough Magistrates, in 1770, for a period of 99 years. The *Borough Bridewell*, now used partly as a *Police Station*, is in the Corn-market, on what is called Hog-hill. It was anciently a Jewish synagogue, called Moyse-Hall, and its circular-headed windows are supposed to be nearly as old as the Norman Conquest. Prisoners are only confined here until they have been examined by the magistrates.

The MARQUIS OF BRISTOL is *lord,* or *hereditary High Steward of the Borough and Liberty;* and his eldest son, Earl Jermyn, and Lord Charles Fitzroy, are the present *Parliamentary Representatives of the Borough.*— (See page 604.) They are both privy councillors, and have served in six parliaments.

The BOROUGH MAGISTRATES are the Mayor, and James D. Merest, Thomas Robinson, F. G. Probart, M. D., John Ridley, Fras. K. Eagle, Charles Jas. Fox Bunbury, Henry Braddock, H. J. Oakes, George Moore, Henry le Grice, Wm. Dalton, T. G. Hake, M. D., Philip Ray, John Worlledge, and John Greene, Esqrs.; some of whom are also County Magistrates. Messrs. F. Wing and Richard Durrant are their *clerks.*

Harry Wayman. Esq., is *coroner* for the Borough and Liberty, and also *clerk* to the *County Magistrates,* who hold *Petty Sessions* here, for Thingoe and Thedwestry Hundreds.

CORPORATION AND OFFICERS, (1843.)

Mayor, Major Bullock. || *Recorder,* William Gurdon, Esq. ALDERMEN :—Henry Braddock and Peter Macintyre, Esqrs , for the *East Ward;*—John Pace and H. J. Oakes, Esq., for the *North Ward;*—and George Creed and John Greene, Esq., for the *West Ward.*

COUNCILLORS.

East Ward.	North Ward.	West Ward.
James Harvey	William Groom	William Frewer
George Thompson	James Lee	John Steele
J. P. Everard	Charles Le Blanc	John Trevethan
H. Prigg	J. B. Burrell	John Andrews
Thomas De Carle.	Thomas Bullen	Thomas Bridgman
F. E. Browne	Major Bullock	Frederick Nunn

TOWN CLERK, Joseph Hanby Holmes, Esq.
Mayor's Assessors, Messrs. John Battley, jun., and William Frewer, jun.
Auditors, Messrs. Jas. Button and John Battley.
Serjeants-at-Mace, J. Fowler, H. Howe, H. Smith and R. Simper.
Town Criers, R. M. Leech and James Gray.
Beadles, R. M. Leech and H. Smith.
GAOLER, Mr. John Orridge. — *Bridewell Keeper,* Mr. R. M. Leech.
Inspector of Weights and Measures, John Nixon.
Corn Inspector, Mr. J. Adkin.
Superintendent of Police, Richd. Caney
Crier of the Courts, and *Guild-hall Keeper,* James Ward.

BURY ST. EDMUND'S UNION is already noticed at page 602. Frederick Wing, Esq., is *Superintendent Registrar;* John Cambridge, Esq., *Clerk to the Board of Guardians;* and Mr. Thos. Legge, *Master of the Workhouse.*

The TRUSTEES OF THE GUILDHALL FEOFFMENT are inserted at page 637. John Jackson, Esq., is their *clerk,,* and John Haddock, Esq., *treasurer.*

John Greene, Esq., is Clerk to the *Commissioners of the River Lark Navigation.* (See page 603.)

St. Edmund's Hill, one mile E. of the town, but within the bounds of the borough, is a handsome seat, which was built in 1773, by the late John Symonds, Esq., who was recorder of the borough, and professor of modern history in Cambridge University. Few spots in Suffolk, command so extensive and pleasing a prospect as this mansion, which was lately occupied by Henry Francklyn, Esq.

LIST OF STREETS, LANES, &c., IN BURY.

Abbeygate street, 1 Meat market
Abbey Ruins, Church yard
Albert's buildings, 31 Westgate road
Angel hill, 30 Abbeygate street
Angel lane, 37 Abbeygate street
Bakers' lane, 24 Southgate street
Battley's place, Westgate road
Baxter st. (High & Low) Brentgovel st
Brentgovel street, 10 Corn market
Brackland, (see Long & Short)
Bridewell lane, 39 Churchgate street
Burman's lane, ——————
Butter market, 8 Abbeygate street
Butts road, 18 Westgate road
Canon place, 17 Short Brackland
Cattle market, St. Andrew street
Chalk lane, 56 Field lane
Chequer square, 35 Church gate
Churchgate street, 12 Guildhall st
Church row, 61 St. John's street
Church walk, 55 Bridewell lane
Church yard, 1 Crown street
College street, 49 Churchgate street
Corn hill, 18 Butter market
Corn market, 14 Meat market
Cotton lane, 4 Muston street
Cricketers' row, 23 Field lane
Crown street, 28 Angel hill
Eastgate street, 21 Muston street
Elephant court, 28 Whiting street
Field lane, 56 St. Andrew street
Friars' lane, 12 Westgate street
Garland street, 20 Brentgovel street
Guildhall street, 1 Meat market
Hatter street, 145 Abbeygate street
Hog lane, 29 Guildhall street
Honey hill, 9 Crown street
Hospital road, 32 Westgate street
Long Brackland, 51 St. John's street
Looms lane, 20 Brentgovel street

Mainwater lane, 109 Southgate street
Market place, Corn Exchange, &c.
Meat market, 1 Abbeygate street
Mill lane, Field lane
Mill place, Mill lane
Muston street, 14 Angel hill
Northgate street & road,14 Angel hill
Paradise place, 53 Risbygate street
Pig lane, 34 Churchgate street
Prospect row, 98 Field lane
Providence court, Schoolhall street
Prussia lane, 1 Southgate street
Pump lane, 63 Garland street
Raingate court & square,58 Raingt st
Raingate street, 6 Schoolhall street
Risbygate street, 40 Brentgovel st
Salem place, Field lane
St. Andrew street, Risbygate street
St. Edmund's Hill, Botesdale road
St. John's street, 6 Brentgovel street
St. Mary's square, Sparhawk street
Schoolhall lane, 56 Garland street
Schoolhall street, Honey hill
Shambles, Meat market
Short Brackland, 10 Brentgovel st
Skinner lane, Corn hill
Southgate green, 71 Southgate st
Southgate street, 7 St. Mary's square
Sparhawk street, 6 Honey hill
Swan court, 41 Risbygate street
Tay-fen road, Northgate road
Traverse, 6 Abbeygate street
Turkey court, Field lane
Union terrace, Hospital road
Victoria place, 40 Northgate street
Well street, 14 Brentgovel street
Westgate road, 32 Westgate street
Westgate street, 10 St. Mary's square
Whiting street, 75 Abbeygate street
Woolhall street, 3 Meat market

BURY ST. EDMUND'S DIRECTORY.

Post-Office, 2 Hatter-street; Mr. John Deck, *Postmaster.* The Box closes for London, Sudbury, Colchester, Essex, Ipswich. Bungay, Norwich, Yarmouth, &c., at 8 evening; but letters are taken in till 9, on the payment of the usual fees, as the London Mail is not despatched till half-past 9 evening; and the other Mails till early in the morning.

Miscellany of Gentry, Clergy, Partners in Firms, and others, not arranged in the Classification of Trades and Professions.

Adams Charles, gentleman, 10 Well st
Adkin Jno.*corn inspector,* Brentgovel st
Andrews John, tailor; h 21 St.Andrew street

Baker Mrs. S., 13 Risbygate street
Ballingall Rev. Thos. (Wes.) 4 Hospital road
Barham Mrs. Mary, 82 Southgate st

Barker Wm. joint proprietor of the Bury Post, 18 Northgate street
Barnard Miss Sarah, 73 Whiting st
Bramwell Rev.F.H.Turnor,1 Meat mkt
Barton Hy. gentleman,16 St.John's st
Battley Mr. John, 61 Guildhall st
Baxter Mrs. Mary, 25 Brentgovel st
Bidwell Mrs. Eliz. 6 St. Mary's sq.
Belden John, last, boot tree and kitt tool maker, 7 Honey hill
Belgrave Mrs. F., 52 Westgate street
Bellamy Mr. John, 118 Northgate st
Berkley Mrs. M. E.,114 Northgate st
Beeton George, spirit merchant, 10 St. Mary's square
Bird Mrs. Mary, 4 Risbygate street
Bland Mrs. E. 88 Northgate street
Blake George, gent. Chapel House
Blomfield Mrs. —. —. Angel hill
Blyth Jas. shopman, 79 Whiting st
Botwright John, bath keeper, 12 Angel hill
Bowen George, traveller, North gate
Bramly Rev. Thomas Jennings, 3 Angel hill
Brand George, gentleman, 8 Hog lane
Bridge Misses, 18 Whiting street
Bridgman Mr. George, 5 St. Andw. st
Briggs Hy. cart owner, 37 Canon pl
Briggs John, ostler, Pig lane
Brooks Mrs. H. B. 58 Westgate st
Brooks Mrs. Sarah, 34 Churchgate st
Brown Mr. Henry, 20 St. John's st
Bullen Mrs. Ann Mary, 10 Angel hill
Bullock Major Hy. R. 5 Westgt. st
Burbidge Jas.Thos.,master of Thingoe Union Workhouse
Burland J. B., *willow square maker,* Mill place
Bushell Miss Mary,40 Whiting street
Button Jas. bank clerk, 11 Risbygt
Cambridge Robt. gent. 43 College st
Caney Richd. police supt.,11 Corn mkt
Cartwright Rev. John, South gt. green
Case Pp. Jas., solr. & dept. regr. of the Archdeaconry of Sudbury, 87 Whiting street
Cawston Geo.timber mert.;h.Eastgt st
Chapman John,gent., 70St. John's st
Chilton Wm. John, gent. 2 Union ter
Clarke Mrs. Eliz., 20 Meat market
Clark Geo. tailor; h. 86 St. John's st
Clark Jas. relvg. officer,24 Whiting st
Clark John, sexton, 31 Churchgt. st
Clark Rev. Robt., 30 Risbygate st
Clark Wm.bookkeeper, 68 Westgt. rd
Cobbin Misses M. & E.,30St.Andrew st

Cole Miss Susan, 8 Northgate street
Cook Mr. Benjamin, Salem cottage
Cooke Mr. John, 111 Northgate st
Cooke Wm. gentleman, 1 St.Mary's sq
Conran Capt. James, 19 Whiting st
Cooper Geo. gentleman, 3 Union ter
Cooper Mrs. Snsan, 61 Garland st
Cornish Chas. thatcher, Butts road
Cowgill Wm. excise, 9 Brentgovel st
Cozens John, keeper, Shirehall
Crack Wm. ch. clerk, 10 Honey hill
Creed Misses E. & E.,23 Guildhall st
Croft John, land agent, &c.; h 28 Angel hill
Cullum Rev.SirThomas Gery, Bart, *Hardwick House*
Dalton Wm. Esq. 110 Northgate st
Daniel Geo. coachman, Northgate rd
Davey Mr. Geo., 16 Westgate road
Debenham Saml.travllr. 34 Abbeygt.st
Deck John, post master, auctioneer, &c.; h 15 Churchgate street
Dewhirst Rev. Charles. (Indt.) 56 Risbygate street
Dingle John, Esq., 11 Northgate st
Double Mr. G. 29 Whiting street
Durrant Augustine, carrier and brick maker, Southgate road
Eagle Fras. King, Esq., barrster, 19 Crown street
Eaton Thos. willow cutter, Mill place
Elliot Rev. Jph. (Indt.) Butter mkt
Elvin Rev. C. (Bapt.) Whiting street
Emerson Jas. jun., builder; h 27 Well street
English Geo. news agent, 16 Churchgate street
Ewer Chas. soda water manufacturer, 31 Abbeygate street
Eyre Rev. Charles J. P.; M. A.,incbt. of St. Mary's, 11 Guildhall st
Everett Mrs. Sarah, 24 Well street
Fairweather Alexander, Esq., bank manager, 8 Meat market
Fennell Samuel gent. 2 St. Mary's sq
Finch Eliza, (lodgs.) 70 Whiting st.
Ford Fras. (lodgs.) 55 Church street
Fordham Wm. clerk, 62 St. John's st
Foyster Chas.timber mert.;h Eastgt.st
Frewer Wm. jun., plumber, &c.; h 21 Southgate street
Frost Danl. post office clrk., 1 Crown st
Frost Mrs. Eliz. 69 Westgate road
Frost Mr. John, Cottage mill
Frost Jph. cow kpr., 61 Westgt. street
Fulcher Isaac, cowkpr., *Tay fen road*
Gallant Mr. Wm., 2 Church row

Gallant Mrs. 10 Westgate street
Gardener Mrs. Hannah, 2 Churchgt.st
Garrod Jas. carrier, 2 Risbygate st
Garthwaite Mr. Wm., 31 Risbygt. st
Gedge Johnson, editor & joint propr. of the Bury Post; h 23 Hatter st
Gilson Thos. cowkpr., 43 Whiting st
Girling Mr. Thos., 89 Northgate st
Girton Wm. atty.'s clerk, 30 West st
Goldsmith Cassius, architect, 12 Crown street
Goldson Misses, *Castle*
Goulden Mrs. Frances,1 Honey hill
Gould Edwin, bank clerk, 26 Well st
Gould Mrs. M. S., 4 Angel hill
Gray Thos. crier, 20 Garland street
Greene Hy. John, gent., 91 North-gate street
Greene John, solicitor & clerk to the River Lark commissioners, *Abbey Ruins*
Grief Mrs. Sarah, 19 Low Baxter st
Groom Miss Mary, 86 Whiting st
Gross Wm. suptdt., *Gas Works*
Gudgeon Mrs. Eliz., 31 Crown street
Gudgeon Mrs. Penelope,5 Paradise pl
Haddock Jno, accountant & Borough Treasurer, 30 Guildhall st.
Haggitt Rev. Geo. John, M. A., in-cmbt. of St. James', St. Mary's sq
Harrison Chas. farmer,Eastgt. grange
Harrison Misses, 4 St. Mary's square
Harrison R. millwright, Westgate rd
Harrold Wm. joiner, 78 Whiting st
Hasted Rev. Hy. M. A., 107 Northgt. st
Harvey Benj. gent., Westgate road
Harvey Rt. gent., 24 Westgate street
Haydon Wm. excise, 49 Guildhall st
Head Frederick, gent., 24 Well street
Hearn Mrs. Mary, 99 Southgate street
Hickman Rev. Thos., 50 Westgt. st
Hickman Rev. Thomas, jun., M. A., curate of St. Mary's, 50 Westgt. st
Higgs Thomas. gent., *Tay fen road*
Hill John, gent.,54 Churchgate st
Hine Chas. B., hardware dealer; h 31 St. Andrew st
Hodson N. S. H. Esq.,supt. of *Botanic Garden ;* h 15 Westgate street
Holdrich John, gent. 8 Union terrace
Holmes Joseph Hanby, solr. & *town clerk ;* h St. Mary's square
Houghton Jno. gent. 70 Guildhall st
Howard Mr. Wm. 19 Northgate st
Howe Mrs.Eleanor,34 Long Brackland
Hubbard Captain Wm. 18 Northgt. st
Hubbard Mrs. — 14 Crown street

Hubbard Sar.matron,Clopton's Asylum
Husler Mrs. Ann, 45 College street
Ion Mrs. Sarah, 64 Risbygate street
Iron Joseph, printer, 9 Honey hill
Jackson William, bookseller; h 1 Crown street
Jackson John, solr. 8 Hatter street
Jannings Chas. gent. 23 St. Andw. st
Jenkins Jas. clerk, 15 Southgate st
Jennings Benj. mert. 73 Guildhall st
Jewers Eliz. lodgings, 4 Westgate st
Johnson Cphr. gent. 67 Southgate st
Johnson John, architect, 136 South-gate street
Jones Evan, gentleman, 4 Union ter
Keeling R. S. bank clerk, 82 Risby-gate street
King Mrs. Lucy, Crown street
Last Robert Mason, clerk, 20 Guild-hall street
Last Wm. horse clipper, 56 Eastgate
Lathbury Mrs. Mary, 2 Angel hill
Lee James, measure, hoop, & shovel maker, 27 Risbygate street
Le Blanc Charles, Esq., banker, 12 Meat market
Leech Miss —. 23 Crown street
Leech Robert Moody, Bridewell keeper
Legge Thos. master of Bury Union Workhouse, College street
Leonard John William, clerk, 13 Churchgate street
Lenny John Grimsby, land agent ; h *Wrentham*
Lock Jas. woolstapler ; h Wool hall
Lock Mrs. Sarah, 2 Field lane
Lockwood Edw. gent. 1 Muston st
Lockwood John, wine, &c. merchant; h Southgate green
Lockwood Mrs. Mary Ann, 54 Whit-ing street
Lumley Thomas, Esq., 9 Crown st
Macintyre Patrick, editor of the Herald, 36 Crown street
Main Mrs. Elizabeth, 20 Well street
Major W. sub-editor of the Herald, 55 Churchgate street
Mallett Mrs. Thomasin, 72 Southgt. st
Mallows Geo.Wm.gent. 99 Risbygate st
Marriott Mr. Benj. 8 Southgate
Meekin Mr. Wm. 103 Southgate st
Middleditch Mrs. Eliz. 24 Crown st
Miller Mrs. Eliz. 20 Low Baxter st
Miller D. gentleman, 14 Garland st
Miller James, gent. 13 Crown street
Miller Miss Lucy, 25 Crown street
Mills John, supt. Assembly Rooms

Mills Mrs. Susan, 9 Angel hill
Moor Geo. Esq.,banker, 9 Butter mkt
Mortlock Pp. bee hive mkr. Chalk ln
Mothersole T. printer, 24 Northgate
Mostran W. J. carrier's agent, 32 Butter market
Munro Mrs. Mary, 5 Northgate st
Naylor John, mercht; h 3 Meat mkt
Newell Mr. John, 7 Southgate street
Newman Alex. coachmn. 3H.Baxter st
Newson Henry, auctioneer, &c; h 2 Hatter street
Nicholls Jno. Cphr. foreman, 3 Westgt
Norman Benj. manager, 21 College st
North Mrs. Rebecca, 72 Whiting st
Nunn Edmund, permit writer, 24 Butter market
Nunn Fredk. farmer, 25 Westgate
Nunn Sturley, solr. registrar of Thingoe Union, 1 Whiting st.; h *Ixworth.*
Oakes Henry James, Esq., county treasurer, Corn market; h *Newton*
Orridge John, govr. *County Gaol*
Palfrey William, Woolstapler; h 1 Meat market
Palmer Geo. farmer, Southgt. cotg
Parker Mr. Charles, 69 Risbygate
Parr Edward, superviser, 24 Well st
Pate Miss E. L. 8 Guildhall street
Paul Miss Esther, 3 St. Mary's sq
Payne John Harvey, gent. 22Hatter st
Payne Mrs. M. 40 Crown street
Pearson G. W. foreman, 72 Guildhall street
Pearson Mrs. My. 51 Short Brackland
Pearson Mrs. Sarah, 68 St. Andw. st
Pechey Elisha, gas fitter, 9 St. John's st
Petre Hon. Chas. 106 Northgate st
Pettit Mary, lodgings, 31 Whiting st
Pledger George, farmer, Southgate
Poole Mrs. Ann, 5 Whiting street
Portway George, gent. 63 Garland st
Pryke Mrs. Christna. 26 Whiting st
Punshon George, French polisher, 172 Eastgate street
Ranson Mrs. Elizabeth, 71 Whiting st
Ranson Hy. printer, 12 Whiting st
Rashdall Rev. Robert, M.A. incbt. of St. John's, 54 St. John's street
Ray Mr. John, 94 Northgate street
Reach Thos. bank clerk, 54 Risbygt
Read Mr. Stephen, 5 Union terrace
Rece Henry, gent. 95 Risbygate st
Reeve Mrs. Sarah, 31 Westgate road
Reffell Samuel, pipe maker, 12 High Baxter street
Richardson Mrs. Eliz. 36 Guildhall st

Richer Thos. bookkpr. 1 Westgate st
Riddle John, coachman, 15 St. John's street
Ridley Frederick, currier; h 68 Guildhall street
Ridley John, gent. 15 Low Baxter st
Ridley Thomas, grocer; h 13 Low Baxter street
Roberts Wm. gent. 83 Whiting street
Robinson Mrs. Eliz. 15 Garland st
Robinson Thomas, Esq. 17 Westgate st
Robinson Rt. gent. Southgate road
Rowles Richard, smith, 69 Whiting st
Rutter Samuel, lodgs. 13 Whiting st
Sale Saml. cabt. mkr.; h 84 Risbygt
Sams Miss Frances, 58 Whiting st
Sams Wm. Hy. sol.; h 1 Whiting st
Sawyer James, gent. 82 Whiting st
Scotchmer John, millwt. 50 Westgt st
Scaber Mrs. Ann, Botanic garden
Sendall Rev. S. 26 Crown street
Shadbolt Jph. *clerk of markets*,Risbygt
Simpson Misses M.,S.,& S., Angel hill
Smith Charles Case, surgeon; h 81 Guildhall street
Smith Mr. John, 50 Short Brackland
Smith Mr. John, 19 Westgate road
Smith Mrs. Susan, 6 Sparhawk street
Smythies Walter Tyson, solr.; h 1 Crown street
Soame Mrs. Eliz. 108 Northgate st
Sparham Mr. John, 15 High Baxter st
Sparke Jas. solr. & clerk of Thingoe Union; h 7 Hatter st
Sparke Mr. Gregory, 23 Whiting st
Spink Mr. G. F. 10 Union terrace
Stearn George, sexton, 29 Churchgt. t
Stebbings John, cowkpr. 9 Hatter st
Steele Miss Eliz. 15 Risbygate st
Steele Robert, gent. 69 Risbygate st
Steele Thomas, gent. 33 Risbygate st
Steggall Mrs. Rebecca, 84 Whiting st
Steggall Mr. Wm. 60 Churchgate st
Steward Mr. John & Jas. 9 Hatter st
Stewart Mr. Hy. 92 Northgate st
Stutter William Edw., printer, 62 Guildhall street
Sutton Mrs. A. M., 1 Union terrace
Symonds John. gent., 12 Brentgovel st
Thomas Mrs. Ann C., Schoolhall st
Thompson Edw. regr., 1 Church walk
Thompson John, gent., 1 Looms lane
Thompson Mrs. Mary Ann, 119 Northgate street
Thurlow Miss Mary. 26 Church st
Todd Mrs. Ann, 21 St. John's street
Trevethan Mrs. Ann, 36 Whiting st

Trevethan John, builder, Westgate rd
Turner Hy. curator, *Botanic Garden*
Twill Mrs. Cath., 76 Whiting street
Tyson Geo. solr.'s clerk, 23 Well st
Wismara John, barometer & looking glass manufacturer, 94 St. John's st
Wakeford Jno. 64 Whiting street
Walden Mr Jas., 51 Field lane
Walford Mrs. Rebecca, 25 Northgt. st
Walsham Sir John Jas., Bart., 24 Angel hill, (& *Knill court*, Herefordshire
Ward Hy. law stationer, & dep. crier of the courts, 66 Westgate road
Ward Jas. crier of the courts, & Guildhall keeper, 80 Whiting st
Ward John, paving rate collector, 81 Risbygate street
Wastell Misses F. & S., Southgt. gn
Watson George gent., 19 Eastgate st
Wayman Harry, solr., coroner & clerk to county magistrates, Abbey ruins
Weellam Samuel, gent., 39 Crown st
Wenn George, bank manager, 10 Meat market
West Rev. Thos., B. A., chaplain to gaol, 9 Westgate street
Whatton John, gent., Northgate road
Wheeler Mrs. Eliza, 102 Risbygt. st
Wheeler Geo. agent; h 5 St. John's st
Whitaker Geo. Rt., paving rate collector, 24 Westgate road
Wick Wm. waiter; h Pig lane
Wilkinson Chas. John, gent., 18 Brentgovel st
Williams William, horse breaker, 2 Eastgate street
Williams Mr. William, Hospital road
Wilson Pp. cowkpr., 10 Short Brackland
Wing Fredk. solr., clerk to magistrates, & supt. registrar of Bury Union, 8 Whiting street
Wing Hy. surgn.; h 66 Guildhall st
Wood Mrs. Ann, 66 Whiting street
Wollaston Chas. Esq., *vice-admiral of the Blue*, 116 Northgate street
Woodroffe Mrs., matron, Gnrl. Hospital
Wright Mrs. Ann, 1 Field lane
Wright Mr. A. 14 Church walk
Wright Mrs. Ann Maria, 21 Field ln
Wright John, cowkpr. 51 Bridewell ln
Young Hy. S., bank clerk, 6 Risbygt. rd

ACADEMIES.
(*Marked * take Boarders.*)
Adams Frederick, 130 Southgate st
Aldham Alfred, 3 College street
Anthony Bernard, (teacher of *French*) 16 Hatter street

Armstrong Thomas, 66 Whiting st
*Baker Miss Eliz. 18 Guildhall st
*Bevil Miss My. Ann, 7 Northgt. st
*Burroughs Charles, 2 Mustow st
*Chapman Ann, 1 Risbygate street
*Chapman Dd. (Catholic) 9 Risbygt. st
Cronin Mary Ann, 9 Meat market
*De Carle Jane, 7 Sparhawk street
Fordham Jane, 62 St. John's street
Free Grammar, Rev. John William Donaldson, M.A., *head master;* Rev. J. E. Kemp, M.A., *second;* & Rev. H. Corles, *third master;* 12 Northgate street
Guildhall Feoffment Schools, R. Craske, College st., & William Hy. Fuller, Bridewell lane
* Guy Miss Eliz., 8 St. Mary's sq
Howell James, 25 Whiting street
* Jay Mrs. Maria, 52 Southgate st
Kemp Elizabeth, Sparhawk street
Lease Charles, 46 Garland street
* Lockwood Rev. Charles B.; M. A., 1 Low Baxter street
Lofts John, 53 Whiting street
National, Thos. Stowe, Field lane; and Eliz. Petch, Sparhawk street
Newman Miss Eliz. 2 Looms lane
School of Industry, Mary Williams, Hospital road
* Thompson Rev. Henry Thomas, M. A., Northgate road
Smith Harriet, 5 Churchgate street
Stutter Frances, 14 Brentgovel street
Thomas Charles, (drawing master) Schoolhall street
Winkfield Sarah Ann, 11 Westgate st

ALE & PORTER MERCHANTS.
Clay Eliz. and Son, 43 Guildhall st
Hunter John, 21 Abbeygate street
Wigg Goddard, 16 Meat market

ATTORNEYS.
Adams H. 38 Abbeygate street
Blake Jas. Hy., 69 Risbygate street
Borton Jas. (and proctor) 4 Hatter st
Borton John Hy., (clerk of the peace) Angel hill
Cambridge John, (& union clerk) 40 Brentgovel street
Case Edward, 21 Hatter street
Case Philip Jas., (notary & dep. registrar of the archdeaconry of Sudbury,) 87 Whiting street
Durrant Richard, 6 Hatter street
Hinnell Charles, (and vestry clerk,) 7 Brentgovel street

lon John Watling, 2 Hatter street; h 64 Risbygate street

Jackson, Sparke, & Holmes, 8 Hatter st

Jay Samuel John, 37 Crown st

Leech Chas. Denton & Son, Crown st

Le Grice Henry, 21 Butter market

Le Blanc Charles, 12 Meat market

Nunn and Sams, 1 Whiting street

Salmon Wm. 77 Guildhall street

Wayman, Greene, & Smythies, Abbey ruins

Wing Frederick, (supt. registrar,) 18 Hatter street

Young Samuel D. 18 Brentgovel st

AUCTIONEERS, &c.

Bullen Thos. George, 20 Butter mkt

Cooke Robert, 16 Eastgate street

Daines John Benj., 44 College st

Deck & Newson, 2 Hatter street, and Thetford

Hunter John & Son, 24 Abbeygate st

Lock Nathl. 4 St. Andrew street

Norfolk Thomas, Chequer square

BAKERS & FLOUR DEALERS.

Abbott Samuel, Schoolhall lane

Bacon Samuel, 22 Brentgovel street

Baker Hannah, 2 Whiting street

Bateman Wm. 39 Canon place

Bennet Benjamin, 63 Southgate st

Billinghirst William, 10 Eastgate

Botwright John, 12 Angel hill

Bowley Edward William, 10 Hatter st

Candler Wm. 108 Southgate street

Chapman Robert, 1 Corn hill

Chinery Harriet, 30 Whiting st

Crack John, 6 Crown street

Crick Thomas, 38 Angel lane

Cullum Charles, 6 St. Andrew st

Cullum Charles, 43 Westgate road

Death Daniel, 128 Southgate street

Death Henry, 81 St. John's street

Debenham Samuel, 14 Corn market

Gale Joel, 31 Guildhall street

Golding John, 34 Risbygate street

Harvey Rt. & Son, 45 Guildhall st

Head Charles, 4 Northgate street

Head Samuel, 81 Field lane

Jackson George, 14 Prospect row

Limmer James, 62 Field lane

Limmer John Davy, 91 Risbygate st

Lock James, 65 St. Andrew street

Lockwood James, 19 Church walk

Pawsey William, 58 Churchgate st

Pryke John, 31 St. Andrew street

Ranson John Eagle, 36 Northgate st

Robinson Samuel, 52 Eastgate street

Robinson William, 39 College street

Simkin John, 18 Raingate street

Smith James, 38 Westgate street

Stebbins John, 66 Northgate street

Sturgeon James, 26 Guildhall street

Tracy Mary, 2 Schoolhall street

Warren Mary, 32 Churchgate street

Watson William, 11 Schoolhall st

Wells Samuel, 19 Long Brackland

Westrup C. 25 Angel hill

Winkup Thomas, 8 Brentgovel street

Wright David, 37 St. John's street

Wright Richard, 5 Risbygate street

BANKERS.

National Provincial Bank of England, Meat market, (on Hanburys & Co.,) Alexander Fairweather, Esq., manager

Oakes, Bevan, Moor, and Bevan, Bury & Suffolk Bank, 9 Butter market (draw on Barclay & Co.)

Suffolk Banking Co., 10 Meat market (on London & Westm. Bank,) George Wenn, manager

Worlledge & Le Blanc, 11 Meat market, (on Barclay & Co.)

Savings' Bank, Guildhall, open Sat. from 12 till 1.; Thomas Reach and William Williams, clerks

BASKET MAKERS.

Bradbrook James, 35 Risbygate st

Cook Jacob, 29 St. John's street

Harrold Mrs. Susan, 78 Whiting st

Harrold Thos. 56 Churchgate street

Major William, 6 Traverse

BIRD, &c. PRESERVERS

Bilson William, 90 Whiting street

Head Hy. William, 9 Abbeygate st

BLACKSMITHS.

Bernard Benjamin, St Andrew st

Bowle Henry, Northgate road

Cotton Richard, 21 Angel lane

Crick Robert, 113 Southgate street

Downes Benjamin, 13 High Baxter st

Farrant George, 4 Muston street

Mortlock Henry, St. Andrew street

Neave Thomas, 55 Bridewell lane

Smith Henry, 22 Westgate street

Welton Charles, Butts road

Weldhen Robert Stockdale, 83 South gate street

Tweed William, Church row

BOOKSELLERS, PRINTERS, STATIONERS, &c.

Marked * are Binders, & † Printers only

Banyard J. S., 55 Westgate street

† Birchinall Edw. 20 Churchgate st

Cole Alfred, 53 Abbeygate street

† Frost Frances, 19 Hatter street
Fuller William Henry, 5 Abbeygt. st
† Gedge and Barker, 26 Hatter street
† Gross Samuel, 4 Bridewell lane
Jackson and Frost, 1 Crown street
Lankester Frederick, (and periodical
    publisher,) 17 Abbeygate street
Paul Geo. (and print.) Angel hill
Pechey Robert J., 3 Brentgovel st
Robinson John, 2 Market hill
* Spencer Charles, 48 Church street
† Thompson Geo. (& print., patent
    medicine, &c.) 45 Abbeygate st

BOOT & SHOE MAKERS

Adams John, 37 Risbygate street
Allen Thomas, 36 Long Brackland
Barrett Michael, 23 Church walk
Barrett James, 36 Brentgovel street
Barton John, 41 Churchgate street
Barton Robert, 3 Westgate street
Bloomfield Daniel, 157 Eastgate st
Botevyle Edward, 30 Whiting street
Bowers George, 77 Whiting street
Britton John, 89 St. John's street
Browne Frederick Hy. 37 Abbeygate st
Byatt Thomas, St. Andrew street
Clark Francis, 120 Northgate st
Clark Robert, 21 Churchgate street
Clark and Syrett, 46 Abbeygate st
Clark Thomas, 60 Northgate street
Clark William, 7 Butter market
Cobbell Robert, 29 Risbygate street
Cobbing James, 26 Abbeygate street
Cooper John A., 18 Low Baxter st
Cooper Maria, 42 Abbeygate street
Curry James, 1 Well street
Dallison William, 5 Eastgate street
Downing John, 35 Whiting street
Fordham Wm. 60 St. John's street
Fuller Andrew, 60 Long Brackland
Goodwin James, 21 Mustow street
Graves Edward, 35 College street
Graves James, 27 Abbey gate street
Gurney Frederick, 49 Guildhall street
Harvey John, *Tay-fen road*
Head Henry William, 9 Abbeygt. st
Head Richard, 27 Hatter street
Head Samuel, 2 College street
Houghton William, 15 Butter mkt
Howe John, 35 Westgate road
Howlett William, 56 Whiting st
Hughes Thomas, 43 Churchgate st
Humphrey William, 18 Church row
Hurst William, 77 Risbygate street
Irons Charles, 83 Risbygate street
Kemp Benjamin, 52 Northgate st
Lockwood Henry, 85 St. John's st

Moyse William, 49 St. Andrew st
Moyse Mary, Tay-fen road
Perfect Epton, 31 Southgate street
Prigg John, 15 Guildhall street
Quant Hy. & Son, 29 Abbeygate st
Reach Thomas, 59 Southgate street
Rist John, 23 Mustow street
Ringwood William, 55 Southgate st
Robinson Robert, 69 Bridewell lane
Robinson William, 47 Westgate road
Saunders William, 56 Guildhall st
Saunders Stephen, Butts road
Scotchmer Thomas, 18 Garland st
Scott Stphn. (boot mkr.) 47 Abbeygt. st
Smith William Henry, 5 Cotton lane
Syrett Abraham, 1 Southgate street
Tollady Dollar, 43 Abbeygate street
Tunbridge Wm. 52 Raingate street
Ward William, Friar's lane
White Charles, St. Andrew street
White William, Turkey court
Whiting Elizabeth, 9 Westgate road
Whiting William, 5 Schoolhall st
Wright James, 16 Risbygate street
Wright William, 12 Hatter street

BRAZIERS AND TINNERS.

Ashen Charles, 30 Southgate street
Beard Charles, 7 Corn market
Bradbrook John, 2 St. John's street
Bradbrook Thomas, 66 St. Andrew st
Brand Mark, 152 Eastgate street
Goldsmith David, 4 Corn market
Groom William, 7 Meat market
Lowes William, 6 Honey hill
Munro Alexander, (& zinc worker,)
    30 Mustow street
Thompson Sarah Ann, 10 Field lane

BREWERS.

Braddock Henry, 107 Southgate st
Clarke John, 74 Risbygate street
Greene Edward, Westgate street
Waldwine James, 28 St. John's st

BRICKLAYERS & BUILDERS.

Austin & Golden, 101 Field lane
Carliell Charles, 15 Crown street
Darkin John, 14 Westgate road
Deasley John, Raingate street
Dudley William, 80 Guildhall street
Emerson James & Son, (& surveyors)
    22 Well street
Footer William, 5 Sparhawk street
Fuller George, 18 Eastgate street
Harden Thomas, 15 Westgate road
Harvey Abraham, 3 Hog lane
Jarrold Francis, 66 Risbygate street
King Hy. Wm. 10 Garland street
Kerridge George, 32 Churchgate st

Lomax George, 72 St. John's street
Reed Henry, 103 Northgate street
Robinson Jas. 90 Long Brackland
Steggles Susan (& Woolpit brick & tile dealer,) 17 Whiting street
Steggles Thomas, 104 Northgate st
Trevethan John, (& brick maker,) 71 Guildhall street
Wade Robert, 32 Risbygate street
Warren William, 37 St. Andrew st
Wright Reuben, Field lane

BRUSH MAKER.

Norman Rt. B. 40 Churchgate street

BUTCHERS.

Baynham Samuel, 3 St. John's street
Betts Samuel, 25 Churchgate street
Bird Jas. 1 Shambles; h 58 St. Andw. st
Clarke Isc. 5 Shambles; h 40 St. Andw. st
Cowlin Arthur, 11 Westgate road
Farrow Isaac, 6 Shambles
Flack Abraham, 2 Traverse
Gocher Thomas, Angel hill
Goldsmith Mary, (pork) 17 Butter mkt
Hammond Thomas, 33 St. John's st
Harrold Henry, Brentgovel street
Harrold Thomas, 4 Field lane
Head John, 72 Northgate street
Jarman Isaac, (pork) 11 Southgate st
King Thomas, 13 Hatter street
Mullinger Henry, 2 Shambles
Nunn Frederick, 3 Shambles
Potter Amos, 4 Shambles
Ransom Joseph, 7 Shambles
Shillito James, 7 Traverse
Suttle Robert, 46 Guildhall street
Webb John, 45 Long Brackland
Wheeler Maria, 10 Brentgovel street

CABINET MKRS. & UPHOLSTRS.

(Marked * are Appraisers.)

Bradbury John, 104 Risbygate street
Buck William, 59 Churchgate street
*Bullen Thos. George, 20 Butter mkt
*Fenton Thomas, 6 Meat market
*Hunter John & Son, 24 Abbeygt. st
Matthews Edw. John, 27 Angel hill
Sale Wm. & Saml. 6 Guildhall st
Simper Robert, 42 Guildhall street
Walford Thomas, 22 Southgate street

CARVERS AND GILDERS.

Ladbrook Robert, 42 College street
Matthews Edw. John, 27 Angel hill
Wismara John, 94 St. John's street

CHEMISTS AND DRUGGISTS.

Dakin William, 31 Abbeygate street
Dalton Charles, 56 Abbeygate street
Hadfield F. B., Butter market
Mayhew Anthony, 52 Abbeygate st

Nunn John Vincent, 12 Abbeygate s
Paine William, 19 Meat market
Sabine John, 8 Corn market
Steggles Edward, Chequer square
Whitaker George Rt. 24 Westgt. st
Wigg Thomas Carter, (wholesale & retail,) 29 Butter market

CLOTHES BROKERS.

Blomfield Mary Ann, 20 Mustow st
Child George, 58 College street
Dallaway Thomas, 170 Eastgate st
Scotchmer Hannah, 4 Northgate st
Spall Edward, 29 Guildhall street
Trotman Hannah, 41 Risbygate st
Whiting Elizabeth, 15 Angel hill

COACH BUILDERS.

Crane Francis, 16 Angel hill
Crane Thomas, 22 Mustow street
De Carle Thomas, 1 Sparhawk street
Frost & Clarke, 10 Crown street
Hardy William, 24 Brentgovel street
Howe James, 10 Risbygate street
Porter Robert, Bridewell lane ; h Eastgate street
Spall Edward, St. Andrew street

COACH, &c. OWNERS.

Beeton Joseph, 18 Well street
Burrell Thomas, College street
Cole Stephen, 10 Guildhall street
Edwards John, 53 Risbygate street
Hayward Samuel, Eastgate cottage
Mason Ambrose, 28 Crown street
Palmer John, 85 Southgate street
Pledger George, Southgate cottage
Syrett Wm. (mail cart) 50 Guildhall st
Wiggins Joseph, 34 Churchgate st

COAL MERCHANTS.

(See Corn, &c. Merchants.)

Braddock Henry, 107 Southgate
Maulkin Robert, 10 St. Mary's sq
Mc Leroth Hannah, 64 Guildhall st
Ridley John, jun., 39 Eastgate street

CONFECTIONERS, &c.

Ballan Charles, 10 Hatter street
Bateman William, 39 Canon place
Caney Richard, 11 Corn market
Chapman Robert, 1 Corn hill
Death Henry, 81 St. John's street
Debenham Saml. sen. 14 Corn mkt
Debenham Samuel, 36 Abbeygate st
Harvey Rt. & Son, 45 Guildhall st
Kirrage George, 32 Churchgate st
Pead James, 30 Garland street
Sturgeon James, 26 Guildhall street
Steel L. 42 Churchgate street
Stutter Ann, 15 Abbeygate street
Tayler Letitia, Angel lane

Westrup Charlotte, 25 Angel hill

COOPERS.

Cooper John, St. Andrew street; h 3 Guildhall street
Howe George, 85 Northgate street
Howe John, 114 Southgate street
Lee James, (measure, hoop, & shovel maker,) 27 Risbygate street
Sore Samuel, 60 St. Andrew street

CORK CUTTERS.

Baxter William, 89 Whiting street
Ward Edward, 19 Westgate street

CORN, &c. MERCHANTS.

*Marked * are also Coal Merchants.*

Backhouse James, 9 Brentgovel st
*Cooper Isaac, 17 St. John's street
*Fenton William, 71 Southgate st
*Goldin Ann, 110 Southgate street
*Guy John Hayward, 12 Risbygt. st
Lease Edward Eugene, 53 St. John's st
Lock William, 96 Risbygate street
*Nayler & Jennings, 3 Meat mkt
Rolfe James, 72 St. Andrew street
*Steggles Humphrey, 51 Churchgt st
*Thompson Geo. & Edw. 2 Church walk
*Underwood John, 17 Risbygate st

CORN MILLERS.

Cockrill William, West Mill
Cooke John, Steam Mill, 32 Southgt. st
Cooke Robert, (seed) 16 Eastgate st
Limmer James, *West Mills*
Plumb William, Southgate Mill
Wright Samuel, Southgate Mill

CURRIERS & LTHER. CUTTERS.

Adams & Ridley, 55 St. Andrew st
Brett John, 63 Whiting street
Elven Cornelius, 4 Whiting street
Everard John Potter, 28 Southgate street
Frost John, 5 Crown street

CUTLERS. (WORKING)

Baxter Samuel, 35 Brentgovel street
Bryant John, 8 Traverse

DRAPERS & TEA DEALERS, (TRAVELLING)

Edgar James, 68 Risbygate street
Edgar Robert, Hospital road
Gibbon Thomas, 2 Westgate street
Harrold Samuel, 30 Churchgate st
Holmes William, 23 Northgate street
Kirrage James, 9 Union terrace
McDowall Robert, 78 Whiting street
Rae John, 19 Risbygate street
Reach William, 16 Well street

DYERS.

Cobb M. 34 Crown street
Sexton William Watling, 2 Crown st

EATING HOUSES.

Frost Elizabeth, 95 St. John's street
Gathercole John, 2 Well street
Ward John, 96 St. John's street

ENGRAVERS & COPPER-PLATE PRINTERS.

Birchinall Edward, 20 Churchgate st
Lankester Frederic, 17 Abbeygate st

FELLMONGERS.

Head Edward, 106 Southgate street
Hobbs E. (parchment mfr.) Northgt

FISHMONGERS.

Clarke John Wm. 54 Abbeygate st
Mountain Robert, 60 Abbeygate st

FIRE AND LIFE OFFICES.

Hand-in-Hand, F. Lankester, 17 Abbeygate street
Essex, G. J. Oliver, 11 Abbeygate st
London, Edinbro', & Dublin, (Life) W. Salmon, 77 Guildhall st
Norwich Equitable, Wm. Paine, 19 Meat market
Norwich Union, Edw. Lock, 1 Mustow st
Pelican & Phœnix, T. G. Bullen, 20 Butter market
Promoter (Life) Rd. Durrant, 6 Hatter street
Protector (Fire) G. Wigg, 16 Meat mkt
Royal Exchange, John Haddock, 30 Guildhall street
Suffolk & General Country, Gedge & Barker, 20 Hatter st
Sun, Deck & Newson, 2 Hatter street

FRUITERERS.

Balls John, 8 Risbygate street
Caney Richard, 11 Corn market
Mostran Wm. James, 32 Butter mkt
Peck Peter, 4 Traverse

FURNITURE BROKERS.

Cotton Robert, 13 Prospect row
Creamer John, 32 Northgate street
Crick Robert, 131 Southgate street
Dalling Edw. 89 Southgate street
Davey Thomas, 68 St. John's street
Doe John, 18 Angel hill
Fenton Thomas, 6 & 7 Meat market
Ong Joseph, 17 Eastgate street
Scotchmer George, 37 Risbygate st
Walliker George, 17 Westgate street
Walliker Samuel, 13 Corn market
Whiting Elizabeth, 15 Angel hill

GARDENERS, &c.

Clarke Alexander, 58 Northgate st
Jacob Maurice, 31 Long Brackland
Lomax John, 12 Long Brackland
Lord Wm. (nurseryman & florist) 83 Northgate street

Pettit Robt. (florist & nurseryman)
Cotton lane
Staff David, Northgate road
Steed B. 171 Eastgate street

GLASS, CHINA, & EARTHEN-
WARE DEALERS.

Bowers Wm. 26 Butter market
Gutteridge Thos. 10 Short Brackland
Grayston Eliza, 14 Butter market
Major William, 6 Traverse
Thompson John, jun. 14 Meat mkt

GLOVERS.
(See also Hosiers, &c.)

Gallant Thomas, 10 Southgate street
Harrold Wm. Henry, 41 Abbeygt. st
Perfect Epton, 31 Southgate street
Ranson John, 3 Eastgate street

GROCERS AND TEA DEALERS
Marked * are Tallow Chandlers.

Adams Martha, 3 Hatter street
Bedells Samuel, 6 Corn market
Child George, 58 College street
Child William, 102 Southgate street
High James, 28 Abbeygate street
King George, 6 Brentgovel street
Lanham George, 18 Westgate road
Mann William, 105 Risbygate street
Melton Alfred, 3 Abbeygate street
Oliver George John, 11 Abbeygate st
Pattley Thomas, 1 Traverse
*Pyman Jonathan, 51 Guildhall st
Ramsey John, 79 Guildhall street
*Ridley Thos. & Son, (& soap mfrs.)
36 Abbeygate street
Roberts Luke, 1 Butter market
Steel John, (& stamp office) 13 Butter
market
Tricker Ann, 37 Brentgovel street
Tricker Mary, 97 Risbygate street
Tricker Wm. Hy. 12 Guildhall st
Ward William, 14 Angel hill
Waterfall Jno. Seymour, 30 Butter mkt
*Watson John, 27 Churchgate street

GUN MAKERS.
Bilson William, 90 Whiting street
Norfolk Thomas, 26 Angel hill
Parker Benjamin, Chalk lane
Young William, 17 Meat market

HAIR DRESSERS.
Marked * are Perfumers.

Algar George, 38 Northgate street
Blake Charles Boyd, 50 Eastgate st
Carter Wm. 91 St. John's street
*Clark James Wm. 31 Churchgate st
Clark Rd. John, 10 Sparhawk street
Folkerd Samuel, 33 Westgate street
Galer George, 40 Canon place

*Nice George, 18 Abbeygate street
Sore John, sen. 24 Churchgate st
Sore John, 33 Guildhall street
Southgate William, Bridewell lane
*Veres Robert, 1 Abbeygate street
Wakefield James, 9 Southgate street
Winkup Thomas, 10 Corn market

HARDWARE DEALERS.
Cooper Wm. 5 Brentgovel street
Downes John, 10 St. John's street
Hine Thos. & Son, (Birmingham, Shef-
field, & Manchester warehouse) 50
Abbeygate street
Leech Thomas, 25 Hatter street

HATTERS.
Marked * are Hat Manufacturers.

*Armstrong Elizabeth, 25 Meat mkt
Clark John, 2 Crown street
Creamer John, 32 Northgate street
Cutter Henry, 20 Abbeygate st
Hemsted Charles, 10 Meat market
*Lockwood Charles, 11 St. John's st
Sawer Everard, 15 Corn market
*Scholes John, 6 Butter market
*Wallworth Smith, (& cap mfr.) 11
Butter market

HORSE & GIG LETTERS.
(See also Coach Owners.)

Brazier Charles, 27 Northgate street
Burrell Thomas, College street
Crane Charles, 16 Angel hill
Clement Samuel, Churchgate street
Gilson Thomas, Whiting street
Holden James, 64 Guildhall street
Kemp Robert, 10 High Baxter street
Meggs Thomas, 28 Well street

HOSIERS & HABERDASHERS.
(See also Linen & Woollen Drapers.)

Bullen Jonathan, 55 Abbeygate street
Cooper William, 5 Brentgovel st
Craske Robert, 33 Butter market
Harrold Samuel, 30 Churchgate st
Hine Thomas & Son, 50 Abbeygt. st
Hoy James, (laceman, glover, &c.) 37
Abbeygate street
Leech Thomas, 25 Hatter street
Melton Alfred, 3 Abbeygate street
Parker Benj. Dowman, 5 Butter mkt
Portway George, 60 Abbeygate st
Pryor Jane, 24 Meat market
Reeve Sarah, 1 Guildhall street
Smith Wm. Hy. 24 Butter market

INNS AND TAVERNS.
Angel Inn, (Posting & Coml. hs.)
Thomas Bridgman, Angel hill
Angel & Crown, Henry Brewster, 37
College street

Bell Inn, (Posting & Coml. hs.) John Bridgman, 3 Corn market

BlackBoy, Jas. Holden,64 Guildhall st

Bull, Philip Miller, 17 Angel hill

Bushel, Jas. Waldwine,28St.John's st

Castle, Wm. Hayles, 21 Corn mkt

Chequers, Michl. Down, 40Risbygt.st

Coach & Horses, Robert Watson, 9 Schoolhall street

Cock, Thos. Bishop, Risbygate st

Cricketers'Inn,Thos.Lofts,25 Field ln

Dog & Partridge,MaryAnnRisbrook, 21 Crown street

Dolphin, Robert Wheeler, 59 Short Brackland

Fleece, Robert Storey,50Churchgt. st

Fox, Walter Burroughs, 1 Eastgate st

George, Jph. Mayhew, 37 Westgate rd

Globe Inn, (Posting&Coml. hs.) Fras. Clark, Angel hill

Greyhound, Robert Bollingbroke, 29 Eastgate street

Griffin, Geo. Andrews, 9 Corn mkt

Half Moon, (Posting & Coml. hs.) Henry Gardener, 28 Butter mkt

Hare & Hound, Ann Middleditch, 22 Risbygate street

King of Prussia, Abraham Syrett, 1 Southgate street

King's Arms, Jonathan Armes, 23 Brentgovel street

King'sHead,Jno.Adkin,4Brentgovelst

Magpie, John Lofts, Church yard

Marquis Cornwallis, Robert Sewell, 80 St. John's street

Masons' Arms, Mary Borrett, 14 Whiting street

Plough, Thos. Bruce, 84 Southgt. st

Queen's Head, John Cocksedge, 39 Churchgate street

Railway Tavern, Joseph Wiggins, 34 Churchgate street

Ram, Edward Cox, 25 Eastgate st

Rising Sun, Sarah Last, 93 Risbygt. st

Saracen's Head, Mary Ann Gardener, 60 Guildhall street

Seven Stars, Charles Downes, 35 Long Brackland

Six Bells,Sml. Clements,Churchgt. st

Spread Eagle, Jas. Newell,Westgt. rd

Star, Mrs. Boldero, 12 Mustow street

Suffolk Hotel, (Posting hs.) Henry Everard, 35 Butter market

Swan, Geo. Howe, 85 Northgate st

Sword in Hand,Rt.Reeve,66Southgt.st

Three Bulls, Sml. Mower,21 Meat mkt

ThreeCrowns,Jas.Wright,6Southgt.st

Three Goats' Heads, Henry Lockwood, 14 Guildhall street

Three Horse Shoes, George Downes, 65 Northgate street

Three Kings' Heads, Henry Rudland, 13 Meat market

Three Tuns,JohnChatten,35Crown st

Tollgate, John Rudland, Northgt. rd

TwoBrewers,John Green,27Westgt.st

Unicorn, Rd. Steed, 72 Eastgate st

Waggon, Rt. Jeffes, 3 Risbygate st

WhiteHart,Js.Cotterell,35Southgt. st

White Horse, Ann Bradbrook, 19 Butter market

WhiteLion,SethRolfe,11Brentgovelst

Woolpack, John Knights, 2 Meat mkt

BEER HOUSES.

Billinghurst William, 56 Garland st

Blake William, St. Andrew street

Boyden Joseph, 83 Long Brackland

Brett, George, 34 Northgate street

Clarke Joseph, 55 Risbygate street

Clarke Thomas, 63 Guildhall street

Dooley John, 2 Cotton lane

Edwards Robert, 28 Union terrace

Francis Robert, 53 Long Brackland

Freeman Henry, 16 College street

Hammond Thomas, 33 St. John's st

Head Thomas, 34 Whiting street

Haynard Charles, 40 Prospect row

Lomax John, 12 Long Brackland

Meggs Thomas, 28 Well street

Payne William, 23 Field lane

Stebbings Matthias, Southgate green

Suttle George, 54 Guildhall street

Suttle John, 6 Church row

Warren George, 37 Bridewell lane

Watling Richard, 12 Southgate st

IRON & BRASS FOUNDERS.

Cornish John & Son, 62 Westgate st

Pritty & Hodgson, 63 Abbeygate st

IRONMONGERS.

Beard Charles, 7 Corn market

Goldsmith David, 4 Corn market

Groom William, (& oil, white & red lead, &c. dealer,) 7 Meat market

Pritty & Hodgson, 63 Abbeygate st

Ridley John, jun., (*iron merchant,*) 39 Eastgate street

JOINERS AND BUILDERS.

Austin & Golden, 101 Field lane

Billinghurst William, 56 Garland st

Brewster John, 21 Southgate street

Bull Benjamin, 16 Mustow street

Carliell Charles, 15 Crown street

Chapman Thomas, 83 St. John's st

Darkin John, 14 Westgate road

Emerson Jas. & Son, 22 Well street
Frost Henry, 4 College street
Garwood Ephraim, 6 Hog lane
Last Thomas, St. Andrew street
Miller James, 2 Low Baxter street
Pawsey Robert, 37 Whiting street
Pettit Edward, 42 Whiting street
Plumpton Charles, 54 St. Andrew st
Reed Henry, 103 Northgate street
Trevethan John, 71 Guildhall street
Watson Robert, 9 Schoolhall street
Wright Reuben, Salem place
LIBRARIES.
Lankester Frederic, 17 Abbeygate st
Machanics',Market hill,H.Turner, lib
Public Library, 5 Abbeygate street;
  William Fuller, librarian
Paul George, Angel hill
Robinson John, 2 Market hill
LIME BURNERS.
Jarrold Fras. 66 Risbygate street
Taylor James, 39 Southgate street
Warren William, 37 St. Andrew st
LINEN & WOOLLEN DRAPERS.
Burrell Joseph Brook, 8 Abbeygt. st
Clayton E. E., 12 Butter market
Fyson George, 30 Abbeygate street
Harvey James, 40 Abbeygate street
Hilder Alfred, 35 Abbeygate street
Hemsted Charles, 18 Meat market
Mountain Henry, 19 Corn hill
Jannings William, 48 Abbeygate st
Parker Benjamin D., 5 Butter mkt
Pickering William, 32 Abbeygt. st
Portway Geo. jun., 60 Abbeygate st
Richardson& Bonfellow,27Butter mkt
Roper Henry, 23 Butter market
WilliamsThos. Gardener, 5 Corn mkt
MACHINE MAKERS
Cornish John & Son, 62 Whiting st
Rackham Henry, 38 St. John's street
Smith Henry, 22 Westgate road
MALTSTERS.
Braddock Henry, 107 Southgate st
Cooper Isaac, 17 St John's street
Clarke John, 74 Risbygate street
Fenton William, 71 Southgate street
Goldin Ann, 110 Southgate street
Green Edward, Westgate street
Guy John Hayward, 12 Risbygate st
Lease Edward E.,53 St. John's st
Lee James, 27 Risbygate street
Maulkin Robert, 10 St. Mary's sq
Mc Leroth Hannah, 64 Guildhall st
Steggles Humphrey, 51 Churchgt.st
MILLINERS, &c.
Adcock Alice, 16 Crown street

Allen Mary, 93 Northgate street
Baxter Eliza, 89 Whiting street
Bethen Mrs. 75 St. John's street
Blomfield Mary Ann, 20 Mustow st
Boyd Mary, 50 Eastgate street
Burton Mary, 17 Crown street
Bradbrook Maria, 26 Mustow street
Byford Elizabeth, 10 Churchgate st
Challener Sarah, 38 Crown street
Child Maria, 3 College street
Clark and Syrett, 46 Abbeygate st.
Cobbing Elizabeth, 57 Guildhall st.
Coe Sophia, 8 Low Baxter street
Devereux C. 31 Risbygate street
Dickerson Mrs. 49 Abbeygate street
Drew Miss Harriet, 39 Abbeygate st
Godbold K., Whiting street
Hand Charlotte, 13 Angel hill
Harvey Eliza, 12 Eastgate street
Kersey Caroline, 1 Churchgate st
King Eliza, 10 Garland street
Lowrie Hannah, 38 Abbeygate st
Melton Mrs. 3 Abbeygate street
Mountain Elizabeth, 22 Butter mkt
Mudd Dorothy, 6 Sparhawk street
Newman Mary, 33 Long Brackland
Pearce S. B., 24 St. John's street
Pearson C. 72 Guildhall street
Priest Mary Ann, 4 Crown st
Pryor Jane, 24 Meat market
Scholes Mary Ann, 19 St. John's st
Sore Martha, 33 Guildhall street
Smith Susan, 3 Butter market
Sparke Mary Ann, 8 Southgate st
Stebbings Eliza, 45 Churchgate st
Steel Elizabeth, 43 Canon place
Stocking Frances, 59 Abbeygate st
Stutter Jane, 62 Guildhall st
Walton Elizabeth, 39 Guildhall st
Watson Elizabeth, 13 Guildhall st
Wilson Sarah, 78 Guildhall street
Turner Eliza, 7 Crown street
MUSIC DEALERS, &c.
*Those marked * are Dealers, and the*
  others Teachers only.
Harrington Philip, 4 Crown street
*Last James, 23 Meat market
Nunn Robert, Churchyard
Nunn William, 33 Crown street
*Paul George, Angel hill ;
*Reeve John, 61 Abbeygate st
*Thompson George, 45 Abbeygate st
Watson John, 13 Guildhall st
NEWSPAPERS.
Bury & Suffolk Herald, (Wednesday
  morning,) Samuel Gross, 4 Bride-
  well lane

Bury Post & East Anglian, (Tuesday evening,) Gedge & Barker, 2 Hatter st

OIL CLOTH MAKERS.

Hook John, 13 St. John's street
Partridge Richard, 100 Southgate st
Wigg Goddard, 16 Meat market

PAINTERS, PLUMBERS, AND GLAZIERS.
(Also Paper Hangers.)

Buckel Elizabeth, 74 Whiting street
Coe Frederick, 25 Guildhall street
Coe William, 8 Low Baxter street
Daines John Benj. (window glass, oil, and colour dealer,) 2 Butter mkt
Darkin William, 104 Southgate st
Elmer James, 17 Brentgovel street
Frewer Wm. & Son, 49 Meat market
Goodwin George, 117 Northgate st
Hayhoe James, 19 Well street
Kitson George, 18 Corn market
Spanton William, 16 Westgate st
Spanton Wm. jun. 3 Whiting street
Stebbings Noel, 45 Churchgate st
Thompson Mary, 14 Brentgovel st
Whitaker Thomas, 16 Whiting st
Wicks George, 104 Risbygate street
Wright George, 37 Guildhall street

PARCHMENT MANUFACTURER
Hobbs E. (& leather dresser) Northgt

PATTEN AND CLOG MAKERS.
Norman Rt. Briten, 40 Churchgate st
Smith Wm. Henry, 24 Butter market

PAWNBROKERS.
Haddock John, 30 Guildhall street
Last Thomas, 24 Guildhall street
Weston Robert, 22 Meat Market

PHYSICIANS
Hake Thos. Gordon, 10 Northgate st
Probart Fras. George, 12 Westgt. st
Rankin Wm. H. 6 Whiting street
Smith Thomas, 7 St. Mary's square

PLASTERERS AND SLATERS.
Burroughs John, 17 St. Andrew st. N.
Deasley John, Raingate street
Earl Samuel, 59 Guildhall street
Footer William, 5 Sparhawk street
Kemp Nathaniel, 39 Westgate road

REGISTER OFFICE
(For Servants : established 1800.*)*
Norfolk Thomas, (& general agent,) Chequer square

ROPE MAKERS.
Parr David, 97 Field lane
Partridge Richard, 100 Southgate st

SADDLERS, &c.
Brown John, 16 Abbeygate st
Goodrich Thomas, 6 Abbeygate st

Hales John, 6 Eastgate street
Haslop Thomas, 12 Corn market
Lowe & Mann, 3 St. Andrew st. N.
Miller William, 23 Angel hill
Partridge Richard, 100 Southgate st
Sheppeard Edmund, 16 Butter mkt
Smith John, 49 Churchgate street
Watson John, 93 St. John's street

SEED MERCHANTS.
Cooper Isaac, 17 St. John's street
Grayston Matthew, 17 Corn hill
Nayler & Jennings, 3 Meat market
Rolfe James, 72 St. Andrew street
Steggles Humphrey, 51 Churchgt. st

SHERIFF'S OFFICERS.
Clarke Francis, 120 Northgate street
Lock Joseph, 7 Union terrace
Uttin John, St. Andrew street

SHOPKEEPERS.
Anderson Eliza, Mill place
Barfield Asher, 46 Westgate street
Barham Sarah, 56 Southgate street
Barton John, 41 Churchgate street
Bridge Benjamin, 71 Short Brackland
Bridge Thomas, 44 Canon place
Bird Ann, 140 Eastgate street
Bird John, 21 College street
Brewster John, 21 Southgate street
Brewster Robert, 40 Westgate road
Brydges William, 60 Southgate street
Calfe Samuel, 6 Schoolhall street
Cattermole James, 60 Field lane
Clarke Thomas, 63 Guildhall street
Clark Samuel, 78 Long Brackland
Collings Robert, 6 College street
Calver Robert, 4 High Baxter street
Day Robert, 3 Southgate street
Fowler James, 16 Church row
Green Mary, 61 St. Andrew street
Griffin Margaret, 92 Long Brackland
Hogg Frederick, 25 Southgate st
Howe Susan, 44 Guildhall street
Lock James, 6 Union terrace
Lockwood George, 35 Northgate st
Lockwood Thomas, 41 Northgate st
Lofts John, 26 Long Brackland
Mc Cann Honoria, 2 Garland street
Nickerson John, 75 Long Brackland
Nunn James, 126 Southgate street
Pendred Samuel, Swan court
Payne Noah, 37 Westgate street
Pryor Hannah, 20 St Andrew street
Ranson Charles, 39 Long Brackland
Ranson James, 73 Whiting street
Rose John, 8 St. John's street
Rolfe Charles, 28 Eastgate street
Snelling John, 18 Southgate street

Sparke John, Tay-fen road
Theobald Frederick, 37 Well street
Thompson George, 2 Church walk
Turner James, 48 Field lane
Turner Robert, 13 Mustow street
Viney James, 78 Raingate street
Watling Richard, 122 Southgate st
Winn George, 15 Eastgate street
Wright Reuben, 98 Field lane
Young William, 85 Risbygate st

SILVERSMITHS & JEWELLERS.
Glew Ann, 44 Abbeygate street
Last William Nelson, 11 Butter mkt
Place John, 19 Abbeygate street
Thompson John, jun., 14 Meat mkt
Vale John, 14 Abbeygate street
Weston Thomas, Northgate street

STAY MAKERS.
Adcock Alice, 16 Crown street
Adams Lucy, 130 Southgate street
Byford Elizabeth, 10 Churchgate st
Coates Mary Jane, 20 Westgt. st
Drew Harriet, (French stay & corset)
    Abbeygate street
Levett Eliza, 67 Westgate road
Lusher Mary Ann, 21 Westgate st
Neal Elizabeth, 24 Hatter street
Plowman Sarah, 19 Brentgovel st
Smith Harriet, 5 Churchgate street
Wakeford Ann, 69 Whiting street

STONE AND MARBLE MASONS,
    AND STATUARIES.
De Carle Benjamin, 1 Sparhawk st
Emerson James & Son, 22 Well st.
Reed Henry, 95 Northgate street
Steggles Susan, 17 Whiting street

STRAW HAT MAKERS.
Armes Lucy, 19 College street
Balls James, 87 Short Brackland
Bradbrook Elizabeth, 35 Risbygate st
Clarke Mary, 7 Butter market
Clarke Mary Ann, 21 Churchgate st
Clarke & Syrett, 46 Abbeygate st
Cooper Maria, 42 Abbeygate street
Coe Martha, 40 Westgate street
Cornish L., Butts road
Garves Eliza, 18 College street
Hagreen James, (and furrier) 7 Ab-
    beygate street
Hammond Robert, 20 College street
Jacob Harriet, 23 St. John's street
King Caroline, 10 Garland street
Nunn Elizabeth, 2 Guildhall street
Rushbrook Emma, 28 Guildhall st
Saunders Sarah Ann, 58 Guildhall st
Spinks Harriet, 7 Risbygate street
Tollady Mary Ann, 43 Abbeygt. st

Walton C. 39 Guildhall street

SURGEONS
Coe Thomas, 14 Churchgate street
Creed George, 74 Guildhall street
Dalton John, 85 Whiting street
Dalton Rowland, 88 Whiting street
Day Robert, 75 Guildhall street
Hubbard George, 98 Risbygate st
Image William, 5 Schoolhall street
Macintyre Patrick, 36 Crown street
Newham Samuel, *General Hospital*
Smith & Wing, 81 Guildhall street
Tracy John, (*dentist*) 34 Abbeygate st

SURVEYORS, (LAND, &c.)
*Marked * are Building Surveyors.*
*Deck & Newson, 2 Hatter street
*Dudley William, 80 Guildhall street
*Leach Robert, 105 Northgate street
Lenny & Croft, 28 Angel hill (*& Wren-
    tham*)
Payne Richard, 69 Guildhall street
*Trevethan John, 71 Guildhall st.

TAILORS.
*Marked * are Drapers also, and †
    Clothes dealers.*
*Andrews John & Son, 58 Abbey
    gate street
Ayton Abraham, 8 Churchgate st
Banyard James, 64 Westgate road
Bentley John Artiss, 73 Northgate st
*Best John, 12 Churchgate street
Betts John, 28 Churchgate street
Byford George, jun. 10 Churchgt. st
Byford George, 47 Churchgate st
†Chapman William, 18 Butter mkt
*Clark James William & Son, 20
    Corn hill
*Clark John, 3 Crown street
†Creamer John, 32 Northgate street
*Greaves Robert, 30 Abbeygate st
†Hyam Lawrence, 31 Butter market
Keeling Samuel, 122 Northgate st
Last John, 2 Southgate street
†Major Henry, 5 Traverse
*Moor Wm. Pawsey, 20 Hatter st
Nice William, 28 Whiting street
*Norfolk James P. 9 Meat market
*Prigg Henry, 45 Abbeygate street
Robins John, 29 St. Andrew street
Rowse David, 9 Churchgate street
*Salmon William, 14 Hatter street
†Sawer Everard, 15 Corn market
Sparke James, 8 Southgate street
Whitehead Benj. 14 Long Brackland
Winkup Joseph, 26 Brentgovel st
Winn Samuel, 14 Eastgate street
Woolley Michael, 7 Low Baxter st

TANNERS.
Everard John Potter, 28 Southgt. st
Ridley John, jun., 39 Eastgate street

TEA DEALERS.
(See also Grocers, &c.)
Banks Robert, Royal Suffolk Tea Establishment, 25 Abbeygate street
Battley John, 30 Crown street
Denovan John, 57 Abbeygate street
Jackson & Frost, 1 Crown street
Waterfall John S. 30 Butter market
Ward John, 81 Risbygate street
Young James, 8 Butter market
Youngman George, 16 Corn market

TIMBER MERCHANTS.
Brown Wm. & Co. 8 Sparhawk st
Bull Benjamin, 16 Mustow street
Cawston & Foyster, 8 Eastgate st
Lee James, 27 Risbygate street
Trevethan John, 71 Guildhall street

TOBACCONISTS.
Lamb Samuel, 10 Abbeygate street
Rolfe Harriet, 73 St. Andrew street
Sexton Wm. Watling, 2 Crown st
Young James, 8 Butter market

TURNERS. (WOOD, &c.)
Bentley Thomas, 17 High Baxter st
Cox William, 34 Guildhall street
Hunter Wm. Thos. 12 Honey hill
Kemp Robert Day, 84 St. John's st
Pettit John, 44 Churchgate street
Walton William, 39 Guildhall street

VETERINARY SURGEONS.
Cotton Richard, 14 Angel hill
Dunnett Daniel, 9 St. Andrew street
Neave Thomas, 55 Bridewell lane
Taylor Robert, 50 Eastgate street

WATCH & CLOCK MAKERS.
Fenton Simeon, 2 Traverse
Fuller Thomas, 3 Churchgate street
Garrod Robert, 55 Guildhall street
Hart Martin, 90 St. John's street
Last Wm.(& chronometer)10Butr.mkt
Pace John, 19 Abbeygate street
Ray David, 25 Hatter street
Ray William, 2 Brentgovel street
Smith Francis; 11 St. John's street
Swift John, 4 Guildhall street
Tollady Dollar, 3 Northgate street
Vale John, 14 Abbeygate street
Weston Thomas, Northgate street

WHEELWRIGHTS.
Clarke William, 74 Risbygate street
Coates James, 20 Westgate road
Edwards John, Mainwater lane
Ellis George, 75 Southgate street
Manning John, 58 Northgate street

Mayhew George, St. Andrew street, N·
Spall Edward, St. Andrew street

WHITESMITHS, &c.
Beard Charles, 7 Corn market
Child Joseph, 3 College street
Cornish John & Son, 62 Westgate st
Crowe James, 23 Butter market
Goldsmith David, 4 Corn market
Syrett Robert, 61 Whiting street
Thompson William, 18 Mustow st

WINE & SPIRIT MERCHANTS.
Braddock Henry, 107 Southgate st
Clay Eliz. & Son, 43 Guildhall st
Cooper Jonathan, 6 Northgate street
Hunter John, 21 Abbeygate street
Lockwood John & Co. 54 Whiting st
Maulkin Robt. 10 St. Mary's square
M'Leroth Hannah, 64 Guildhall st.
Simpson Wm. Kent, 25 Butter mkt.
Worlledge & Le Blanc, St. Andrew st

WOOLSTAPLERS.
Head Edward, 106 Southgate street
Lock and Palfrey, Woolhall st. and St. Andrew street.

COACHES.
From the Angel Inn.
To *London*, at 7 morning; to *Cambridge*, at a ¼ before 3 aftern. & to *Ipswich*, at 2 aftern., daily, except Sun. Also the Hope, to *Yarmouth*, every Mon. Wed. & Fri. at 8 morn.

From the Bell Hotel.
To *London*, at 7 and ½ past 11 morning; to *Ipswich*, at 9 morning; and to *Cambridge*, at 11 morning, daily. Also, the Original Hope to *Lynn*, every Tues. at a ¼ before 6, and every Thu. & Sat. at a ¼ bef. 7 mg.

From the Suffolk Hotel.
MAILS, to *London*, at 9 evening; to *Sudbury, Colchester*, &c. at ½ past 5 morning; and to *Norwich*,&c. at 4 morning, daily.
Coaches, to *London*, ¼ past 9 morning, daily; to *Yarmouth*, Tues. Thurs. & Sat. at 9 morning; to *Thetford*, every Wednesday at 5 afternoon, & to *Lynn*, Tues. ¼ before 6, & Thu. & Sat. ¼ before 7 morning.

From the Railway Tavern.
To *London*, at half-past 6 &11 morn., & ½ past 2 aftern.; & to *Diss*, &c. ½ past 2 aftn. daily, except Sunday.
MAIL CARTS, at 5 morning to Ipswich, from 50 Guildhall st., & to Yarmouth, from the Suffolk Hotel.

CARRIERS.

DEACON & Co., 2 Well-st., to London, Sun.Wed.& Fri. morngs. at 8, and Thurs. at 6 evening; and to *Norwich*, &c. every Tues. Thu. & Sat. even. at 7. J. Gathercole, *agent.*

A. DURRANT & Co., 28 Well-street, to *Cambridge,Lincolnshire,*&all parts of the north and west, every Monday and Thursday, at 11 morning.

JAMES GARROD, St. Andrew st., to *Ipswich,* &c. every Sunday, Mond. Wed. & Thurs. at 12 night.

HACON AND BALLS, 32 Butter-mkt. *fly vans* to *Newmarket* & *London,* Monday, Tuesday, and Saturday evenings. W. J. Mostran, *agent.*

WILLIAM SYKES, 100, Risbygate-st., to *London*, every morning at 9; to *Norwich* (*via* Thetford), every Mon. Wed. & Fri., and (*via* Diss) every Tues. & Sat. at 10 morn.; and to *Kenninghall* every Wednesday, at 12 noon. George Wheeler, *agent.*

CARRIERS FROM THE INNS.

Marked 1 *put up at the Bell,* 2 *Black Boy,* 3 *Castle,* 4 *Cock,* 5 *Dog and Partridge,* 6 *Griffin,* 7 *Half Moon,* 8 *King's Arms,* 9 *King's Head,* 10 *Masons' Arms,* 11 *Queen's Head,* 12 *Rising Sun,* 13 *Suffolk Hotel,* 14 *Star,* 15 *Three Goats' Heads,* 16 *Three Kings,* 17 *Waggon,* 18 *White Horse,* 19 *White Lion, and* 20 *at the Wool Pack.*

They generally arrive on Wednesday and Saturday morning, and depart about 4 in the afternoon.

| PLACES. | CARRIERS. |

Alpheton, 13 Elliott; 20 Goshawk
Ampton, 19 Harvey
Ashfield, 7 Robert Lock
Bacton, 7 Lock & Baker; & 8 Green
Badwell Ash, 7 Jas. Goodall &R.Lock
Bardwell, 14 Cage
Barningham, 19 Cleares
Barnham, 3 Fisk; and 9 Davey
Barrow, 16 C. Bird; and 9 Rosbrook
Barton, (Great) 4 Bishop
Barton Mills, 16 Coe; 20 Morley
Beyton, 20 Tudor; and Brown, from 123 Eastgate, daily
Bildeston, 5 Emmerson
Botesdale, 6 Nunn; 19 Bidwell
Boxford, 7 Ruggles

Bradfield, 7 Ruggles; 12 Elliott
Bradley, 3 James Fitch
Branson, 19 J. Bland; 7 Malt; 4 Jacobs; and 16 Ashman
Brent Eleigh, 20 Southgate
Brockley, 17 W. Pawsey
Buckenham, (New & Old) 3 Fisk
Cambridge, 9 Forman; 3 Smith; and 20 Osborn
Cavendish, 3 Wm. Golding; 2 Elmer
Cavenham, 6 John Marshall
Chedburgh, 15 Robert Savage
Chevington, 15 Robert Savage
Chippenham, 20 Audus
Clare, 7 Gridley; 3 Goulden
Cockfield, 3 Osborne; 20 Gladwell
Colchester, 19 Springett
Coldham, 5 George Farrow
Coney Weston, 19 Brothers
Cotton, 8 Green
Cowling, 7 Rowling & Bevis
Culford, Skinner, 7 Garland street
Denham, 17 Pattle
Denston, 15 Robert Savage
Depden, 2 Geo. Ashman & Mrs. Prike
Dereham, 20 Wolsey
Downham, 4 T. Jacobs
Drinkstone, 7 Mansfield
Elmswell, 3 George Beeton
Ely, 3 Smith; 16 Coe; 20 Staples
Fakenham, 4 Peter Firman
Feltwell, 19 Bland; 4 T. Jacobs
Finningham, 3 James Hales
Flempton, 6 J. Marshall; & 20 Morley
Fordham, 9 Ling
Gayley, 20 Osborn
Gislingham, 7 Goodall
Glemsford, 15 Joseph Beeton
Hargrave, 2 W. Payne; 20 Whitred
Hartest, 4 Henry Knop
Haughley, 10 John Firman
Haverhill, 3 Wm. Golding
Hawkeden, 2 W. Payne; 7 Gridley; & W. Taylor, from Saracen's Head
Howstead, 5 George Farrow
Hengrave, 6 Marshall; & 20 Morley
Hepworth, 17 Bales
Hessett, 7 George Hubbard
Honington, 5 J. Balaam
Hopton, 3 James Fisk, Mon. & Thurs.
Hundon, 15 Thomas Jolley
Icklingham, 10 Allsop; 6 Pigott
Ixworth, 3 Fisk; 17 Bales
Lackford, 20 Morley; 16 Coe
Lakenheath, 9 Newdick; 6 Pigott
Langham, 7 Palmer
Lavenham, 20 Southgate

Lawshall, 5 George Farrow
Linton, 3 James Fitch
Livermere, 5 Balaam
Lynn, 19 Bland; 4 T. Jacobs; and 20 Stewart
Melford, 20 Goshawk; 13 Elliott
Mildenhall, 20 Morley & Turner; 16 Cole; 7 Powell; 6 Pigott
Nayland, 20 Southgate
NeedhamMarket (seeGarrod'sWagn.)
Newmarket, 20 Osborne; 3 Smith; 9 Firman
Norton, 3 Stiff; 19 Diggans
Nowton, J. Gill, Bridewell lane, daily
Pakenham, 14 Leeder; 7 Goodall
Polstead, 20 Southgate
Rattlesden, 10 Ramsbottom
Redgrave, 6 Clarke
Rickinghall, 19 Bidwell; 6 Clarke
Risby, 12 Adkin
Rougham, Brown, 123 Eastgate
Shimpling, 5 Mary Sparke
Sicklesmere, 20 Gladwell
Soham, 20 Morley; 16 Coe
Somerton, 1 Callis
Stansfield, 7 Gridley

Stanton, 17 Bales
Stoke-by-Clare, 20 Elmer; 3 Golding
Stoke-Ferry, 4 T. Jacobs; 20 Steward
Stow-Langtoft, 4 Wm. Lambert
Stowmarket, 20 Turner; & Garrod's Waggon, from St. Andrew street
Sudbury, 7 Wm. Ruggles; 13 Elliott
Swaffnam, 7 Malt
Thetford, 20 Wolsey; 3 Stones; 19 Bland; 4 Jacobs
Thurston, 17 Pawsey; 4 Knight; & Brown, from 123 Eastgate
Tostock, 3 Flatt; 10 Firman
Tuddenham, 4 Leonard; 17 Craske
Walsham-le-Willows, 9 Fenn; 7 Goodall
Westhorpe, 3 J. Hales
Weston Market, 19 Cleares
Wetherden, 10 Firman
Whepstead, 2 Clarke; 4 Knop
Wickhambrook, 17 Pettit; 7 Simpson & Bevis; 15 Brown
Woolpit, 4 J. Nunn; 11 Wilden
Worlington, 16 Coe; 20 Turner
Wyverstone, 7 Lock & Baker

THINGOE HUNDRED.

A statistical description of this *Hundred and Union*, is already inserted at page 601, to which add, Mr. Sturley Nunn, of Ixworth, *Superintendent Registrar.*

BARROW, a large and well-built village, 6 miles W. of Bury St. Edmund's, contains 995 souls, and about 3,000 acres of land, including a large *Green*, and about 500 acres of waste, which it is now in contemplation to enclose and cultivate. Here is a pleasure *fair* on May 1st. The Marquis of Bristol is lord of the manor, but part of the parish is in Wm. Mills, Esqr.'s small manor of *Wolfe-Hall*, about a mile S. of the village; and H. Coldham, Mr. B. Cornell, and several smaller owners have estates here. Barrow was the seat and lordship of the Countess of Gloucester, in the reign of Edward I., and was afterwards held by Badlesmere, who was hanged in the 16th of Edward II., for taking part with the Earl of Lancaster. It was subsequently the property of the *Tibetots*, who had a large mansion here, of which there are still some traces. On the south side of the parish, the Bury and Newmarket turnpike is cut through a large *tumulus*, in which human bones have often been found. The *Church*, (All Saints) is a large ancient structure, with a tower, containing five bells. The *rectory*, valued in K. B. at £23 9s. 9½d., has now a yearly modus of £820, awarded in 1840, in lieu of tithes. It is in the gift of the Masters and Fellows of St. John's College, Cambridge, and incumbency of the Rev. A. J. Carrighan, B. A. The *Rev. Dr. Philip Francis*, the translator of Horace, was rector here, as also was the late

Rev. George Ashby, an industrious antiquary, whose extensive collection of manuscripts, &c., relating to this county, passed to various hands after his death, in 1808. Here is a small *Independent Chapel*, built in 1836, at the cost of £200. In the 12th of Elizabeth, the *Rev. John Crosier* enfeoffed to certain trustees, all his lands and tenements in Bury St, Edmund's, in trust, after his death, to employ the rents in repairing the church and highways of Barrow, except £2 6s. 8d. to be yearly distributed among the poor parishioners. This trust property consists of a barn and 13A. of land, let for £36 a year. The *Town Estate* consists of two tenements, occupied rent free, by poor persons, and a house and 14A.1R. of land let for £21 a year. It was vested in trustees, in the reign of Henry VIII., in trust, for the payment of the king's taxes and other charges to which the parish might be liable: but for the last fifty years, the rent has been applied in paying a *schoolmaster*, for the education of 24 poor children, nominated by the rector and churchwardens. The poor have distributed among them yearly, about £20, from *Daynes' Charity*, as noted with Moulton. They have also three *yearly rent charges* of 20s. each, given in the early part of the 17th century, by Thomas Carlow, Wm. Smith, and H. & F. F. Allen.

Barker William Searle, surgeon
Carrighan Rev. Arthur J., B. D., *Rectory*
Charles Rev. Samuel, B. A., curate
Chambers Mrs. Ann, *Barrow Cottage*
Codd Frederick, tailor and draper
Cooper Edw. plumber, glazier, &c.
Death Wm. baker and confectioner
Fenton Fredk. bricklayer and builder
Freeman Misses Mary Ann & Eliz.
Freeman Sarah, milliner
King Mrs. Lucy
Lockwood Samuel, vict. *Red Lion*
Pooley Abraham, farrier
Woods Joseph, carpenter

Academies.
Chambers Misses
Goold Sar.(*free*)
Tayler Charles
Beer Houses.
Edmundson John
Evered James

Blacksmiths.
Bailey John
Frost William
Boot & Shoe Mkrs.
Barkham Edw.
Brand William
Frost Robert
Lydle John

Payne William
BUTCHERS.
Shillito James
Underwood Thos.
Collar & Harness Makers.
Hunt Charles
Rosbrooke Maria
Corn Millers.
Drinkmilk John, New Mill
Hempstead John, Old Mill
FARMERS.
(* *are Owners.*)
*Cornell Benj.
Dearsley Thos.
Evered John
*Fenton James
Halls William, *Wolfe Hall*
*Hunt Richard

*Jarvis Richard
Pask Stephen
Rosbrooke Wm
Shillito Stephen
Tymm, *Barrow Hall*
Spencer Abraham
Grocers, Drapers, and Hatters.
Crown John
Halls Robert
Shopkeepers.
Scott Joseph
Slarke Thomas
Wheelwrights.
Fenton Robert
Hale John
CARRIERS.
To Bury, W. Rosbrooke, dailey,& C. Bird, Wed. & Sat.

BROCKLEY, a scattered village, on the banks of a rivulet, 6½ miles S. by W. of Bury St. Edmund's, has in its parish 380 souls, and about 1500 acres of land, rising in bold undulations. Fras. Capper Brooke, Esq., is lord of the manor, and the other principal owners of the soil are the Rev. J. D. Sprigge, Rev. H. Hasted, and Messrs. J. Langham, G. Garnham, and J. Pawsey, The *Church*, (St. Andrew) has a tower and three bells, and contains a handsome monument of the Sprigge family, and a fine painting of Our Saviour and the Doctors in the Temple. The *rectory*, valued in K. B. at £10 4s. 2d., and in 1835, at £330, is in the patronage and incumbency of the Rev. J. D. Sprigge, B. C. L., who is now (1843) erecting a new *Rectory House*

in lieu of the old one, which was burnt to the ground on the 6th of April, 1841, with nearly all its furniture, &c. Under *Sir Robert Drury's Charity*, (see Hawstead,) the poor of Brockley have divided among them £4 per annum, and a poor widow of the parish is placed in the almshouse at Hawstead, and receives £5 a year. *Sir Robert Jervis*, at some date unknown, gave about 7A. of land at Wickham-brook, for the poor of the parishes of Whepstead, Brockley, and Hargrave, in the proportions of four-ninths to each of the two former parishes, and one-ninth to the latter. It is now let for £8 2s. per annum. The *Town and Poor's Estate* was vested in feoffees long before 1700, for the public use and benefit of the parish, and consists of a house and two cottages, occupied rent free by poor parishioners, and 23A. of land, called Shortnecks, Woodcrofts, and Ediths, let for £31 a year, and given at an early period, partly for the poor and partly for superstitious uses. Most of the rent is destributed among the poor parishioners about Christmas and Lady-day. From *Sutton's Charity*, (see page 639,) two poor men of Brockley receive £6 a year, and coats occasionally. From *Sparke's Charity*, (see Hartest,) Brockley has £6 a year for schooling five poor children.

Avey Charles, vict. *Fox & Hounds*
Brewster Charles, carpenter
Cooper Mary, blacksmith
Garwood Jonathan, shopkeeper
Pawsey Henry, schoolmaster
Pawsey William, beerhousekeeper
Sprigge Rev. Jas. Dewhurst, B.C.L., *Rectory*

Sparke William, corn miller

FARMERS. (*are Owners.*)

Brand William, Brockley Hall
*Bulls Mary
Cooper Elizabeth
*Creaton James
Marsh Thomas

Mudd Arthur
Murton John
*Pawsey John
Pettit Henry
Smith David
Wallis John

CHEVINGTON, a large scattered village, on a picturesque acclivity, 6 miles S.W. of Bury, has in its parish 624 souls, and 2,429 acres of land. At the request of Abbot Baldwin, this manor was given to Bury Abbey. At the dissolution, it was granted to Sir Thos. Kitson. It has long been held by the family of the Marquis of Bristol, its present lord; and the other principal owners of the soil, are the Rev. J., & Misses E. & F. White, Dr. Colvile, J. Worlledge, Esq., and Mr. J. Kemp. The *Hall* is an ancient moated house, occupied by a farmer. The *Church*, (All Saints) is a neat fabric with a tower and five bells, and was thoroughly repaired and new pewed in 1833. The *rectory*, valued in K.B. at £16 3s. 9d. has a yearly modus of £587 10s. awarded in 1838, in lieu of tithes. The Rev. John White, M.A., is patron and incumbent, and has a commodious residence. The Methodists have a small chapel here. The *Poor's Estate*, purchased with benefaction money, comprises a double cottage and shop, with yards, gardens, and 34 roods of land, let for £9 a year; and an allotment, of 6A. 2R. 24P. awarded at the *enclosure* in 1816, and now let for £10 a year. The rents, after deducting for land tax and repairs, are distributed among the poor at Christmas. The sum of £50, given by *Dr. Henry Paman*, was expended in enclosing the poor's allotment. The poor of Chevington have a coat or gown, and an annuity of 40s. from *Lady Kitson's Charity*. (See Hengrave.)

Allen Wm. gent. *Holly Bush Green*
Bridge Elias, carpenter
Edwards Wm. wheelwright, &c.
Fenton Samuel, bricklayer & builder

Mayhew James, blacksmith
Paine Mary, shopkeeper
Parker Wm. shoe mkr. & schoolmstr.
Rolfe Robert, gentleman

Simkin James, beer house
Simkin John, thatcher
White Rev. John, M.A., *Rectory*
White Misses Elizabeth & Frances
Witham James, shopkeeper
Wright Christopher, butcher
FARMERS.
Adams Shadrack, *Hill House*
Argent Robert
Brewster Samuel, *College Farm*
Finch James, *Holly Bush Green*

Gossick James, *Horse Pool*
Jennison William, *Chevington Lodge*
Kemp John, *Chevington Hall*
Kemp John, (& maltster)
Rolfe William R. (& corn miller)
Rolfe William, || Smith Robert
Simkin Robert J. (& vety. surgeon,)
  Garrod's Farm
Simkin Robert, *Hole Farm*
Truggitt — *Broad Green*
Webb John, (cattle dlr.) *Moat Farm*

FLEMPTON, a small pleasant village in the vale of the Lark, 5 miles N.W. of Bury St. Edmund's, has in its parish 210 souls, and 720 acres of land, nearly all the property of Sir Thos. Gage, Bart., the lord of the manor, which formerly belonged to Bury Abbey, and was granted at the dissolution to Sir Thos. Kitson. The *Church*, (St. Catherine) is a small neat structure, which was repaired and partly rebuilt in 1839, at the cost of £2,000, after being long in a ruinous condition. The *rectory*, valued in K.B. at £5, has that of Hengrave annexed to it, and the joint benefices are now worth about £400 per annum. The Rev. Richard Samuel Dixon is patron and incumbent. The *Poor's Land* consists of 3 roods, in Rattlesden, let for 30s., and purchased with £10 left by *Wm. Firmage*, in 1599; and about 3 roods in Flempton Field, let for about 25s. per annum. The poor have also a coat or gown yearly, and an annuity of £2 from *Lady Kitson's Charity.* (See Hengrave.) In 1817, the *Rev.* — *Carter* left £200 three per cent. Consols, in trust, to pay one-third of the dividends to the parish-clerk, and to apply the remainder in schooling poor children.

Ashen William, tailor
Blyth Robert, wheelwright, &c.
Chenery John, shoemaker
Cooke John, farmer, *Flempton Hall*
Dixon Rev. Richard Samuel, *Rectory*

Frost George, beer seller
Herrington William, shopkeeper
Partridge James, parish clerk
Petch Edward, blacksmith
Wood Robert, corn miller

FORNHAM-ALL-SAINTS, a pleasant village with several neat houses, on the south western bank of the small river Lark, opposite the other two Fornhams, 2½ miles N.W. by N. of Bury St. Edmund's, has in its parish 336 souls, and about 2,000 acres of land. A battle is said to have been fought here by Edward, son of king Alfred, with Ethelwald, his uncle's son, over whom he gained a complete victory. Sir Thos. Gage, Bart., is lord of the manor, but part of the soil belongs to the Rev. Sir T. G. Cullum, Bart., on whose estate, at the south-east angle of the parish, 1 mile N. of Bury, is a commodious *Wharf*, at the termination of the *Lark Navigation.* (See page 603.) Penelope, *Countess Rivers*, left, out of lands in this parish, a yearly rent charge of £8, that a sermon might be preached against popery, four times a year at Bury. This lady had the good fortune to marry in succession, three gentlemen who had been her suitors at the same time, but had children only by her second husband, Sir John Gage, of Firle, in Essex. The *Church*, (All Saints) is a neat structure with a tower and five bells. The *rectory*, valued in K. B. at £19 10s. 5d. has that of Westley annexed to it, and the united benefices are now worth about £770 per annum; the tithes of Fornham having been commuted for

£444, and those of Westley for £329 per annum. The patronage is in Clare Hall, Cambridge, and the Rev. Richard Haggitt, M. A., is the incumbent. For *a distribution of coals*, the poor have the following *yearly doles*, viz :—28s. from an acre of land purchased with £10 given by *Wm. Firmage*, in 1599; £3 given by *Lady Kitson*, out of the manor of Lackford; 30s. left by *Thos. Mannock*, out of 10A. of land ; and 20s. out of an estate at Risby, given by *Robert Booty*. From Lady Kitson's charity, the poor of Fornham have a gown and coat yearly. (See Hengrave.) They have likewise an *allotment* of 16A. awarded at the enclosure, in lieu of their right of getting furze. This allotment is let for £24 a year, which is distributed in fuel. For a *distribution of bread*, they have the dividends of £61 10s. 9d. three per cent. Consols, purchased with £50 left by *John Spink*, in 1822 ; and the interest of £10 given by Mrs. Gould, widow of a late rector.

Bailey Mr. James	Hammond Miss My. ‖ Stutter Miss
Brown John, farmer	Howe George, shopkeeper
Cooke Charles, blacksmith	Kerrison Wm. vict. *Three Kings*
Corsbie Mr. John, and Mrs. Ann	Merest James D., Esq., tithe commis-
Durrant Thos. shoemaker & shopr	sioner, *Priory*
Edwards Jph. wheelwright & smith	Nichols Geo. coal agent & wharfinger
Grimwood William, shopkeeper	Wiseman Geo. regr. & relvg. officer
Haggitt Rev. Richard, M. A. *Rectory*	Witt Edward, Esq. farmer, *Hall*

HARGRAVE, a scattered village and parish, 6 miles S. W. of Bury St. Edmund's, comprises about 1800 acres of land, and 573 souls, including an *extra parochial* farm, called SOUTHWELL PARK, which has 330 acres, and 16 inhabitants, and belongs to the Rev. Sir Robt. Affleck, Bart. The Marquis of Bristol is lord of the manor of Hargrave, which was held by Bury Abbey, and afterwards by the Kitsons and Gages. The Steward, Phillips, Harvey, Nunn, Clay, Fenton, and other families, have estates here. The *Church* has a tower and three bells, and the benefice is a rectory, valued in K. B. at £4 11s 8d., and in 1835 at £188. The Rev. John White, M. A., is patron and incumbent. The poor have about £20 a year from *Dayne's Charity*, (see Moulton ;) 18s. a year from *Jervis's Charity*, (see Brockley ;) 20s. and a coat or gown yearly, from *Lady Kitson's Charity*, (see Hengrave ;) and an ancient yearly rent charge of 3s. 4d. given by one *Kirk*, out of a farm here belonging to J. Heathcote, Esq. Two small cottages, on the village Green, have long been held by the churchwardens for the use of the poor.

Marked 1 *live at Bird's end*, 2 *on Hargrave Green*, & 3 *on Knowl Green.*

Bonnett Joseph, bricklayer	Decks John, *Willows*	*Steward Giles, (& brick maker,) Grove*
2 Chaplin William, blacksmith	2 *Fenton John	3 Turner Henry
Nunn S. & H. milliners, &c.	Finch William, *Hargrave Hall*	Suttle John
2 Pask John, shopkeeper	Finch Samuel, *Southwell Park*	*Shoemakers.*
Ruse Stephen, corn miller	3 *Harvey Robert	2 Hammond Wm
Simkin Thos. thatcher	Newbury Richard, *Frogs-end*	1 Mortlock John
Tricker Mrs. Jessey King	2 *Nunn Francis	Plummer Henry
Wingrove Chas. coal dlr. & vict. Bull	1 Phillips Chas.	
Carpenters.	2 Silverstone Thos	
2 Gooch John	1 Phillips Charles	3 Spencer Wm.
2 Gooch Wm. (& shopkeeper)	FARMERS. *(* are Owners)* 3 Calver James	———

HAWSTEAD, a pleasant scattered village, on one of the sources of the river Lark, 3 miles S. of Bury St. Edmund's, has in its parish 2,237 acres of fertile land, and 476 souls, including the detached extra parochial part of the HARDWICK estate, which has 19 inhabitants, and about 114 acres, and is distant only one mile south of Bury, and encompassed by that borough and the parishes of Nowton and Horningsheath. HARDWICK HOUSE, with the extra parochial demesne, on which it stands, has for a long period been annexed to the parish and manor of Hawstead, and is the pleasant seat of the *Rev. Sir Thomas Gery Cullum, Bart.*, lord of the manor, and owner of a great part of the parish, the rest of which belongs to Sir Thos. Hammond, Bart., H. Metcalfe, Esq., J. H. Powell, Esq., Messrs. W. Bigsby, J. Smith, and C. Johnson, and several smaller owners. Hardwick House is a large and commodious mansion, and is picturesquely situated in a beautiful park, upon the very line that divides the open and woodland country; commanding, from its elevated site, pleasing views of Bury and the surrounding country. It was given by King Stephen to Bury Abbey, and tradition reports that it was the dairy and occasional retreat of the abbot. No part of the present building, however, is of any considerable antiquity. It was purchased in 1610, by Sir Robert Drury, who removed to it from the ancient manor house called HAWSTEAD PLACE, which is now a farm house, and was formerly an extensive mansion, on a commanding eminence, forming a quadrangle, 202 by 211 feet within; but was partly taken down, and its furniture, paintings, and ornaments, removed to Hardwick. Between the two porches stands an uncouth figure of Hercules, which formerly discharged by the natural passage, into a carved stone basin, a continual stream of water, supplied by leaden pipes, from a pond, at the distance of near half a mile. From the date on the pedestal, this was probably one of the embellishments bestowed upon the place against the visit of Queen Elizabeth, in 1578, when she slept here one night, and is said to have knighted the owner on the occasion of his restoring her silver handled fan, which she had dropped into the moat. HAWSTEAD HOUSE, the seat of Henry Metcalfe, Esq., is a large and handsome mansion, which has pleasant grounds, and was rebuilt in 1783, of Woolpit brick, by the late Christopher Metcalfe, Esq.,

Hawstead, is called *Haldsted*, in Domesday Book; and is estimated at 13 carucates. The bounds of its parish pass through the north and south doors of the church of the adjacent parish of Nowton, and on its western limit there was, some years ago, a majestic tree, called the *gospel oak*, under which the clergyman used to stop in the annual perambulation, to repeat some prayer for the occasion. Hawstead was given in the reign of Edward the Confessor, to Bury Abbey; and the abbot afterwards granted lands here to several families, one of whom took the name of the place. The Fitz-Eustace family, for a long period held the manor, which afterwards passed to the Clopton's, who, in 1504, gave it to the Drurys in exchange for the manors of Hensted and Blomstons. *Sir Robert Drury*, the last male heir of his distinguished family, left three sisters, to one of whom, married to Sir Wm. Wray, the estate devolved. By the widow of this lady's only surviving son, *Sir Christopher Wray,* the manor of

Hawstead, with the Hardwick estate, was sold in 1656, for £17,697, to *Thomas Cullum, Esq.*, who was created a *baronet* in 1660. The present worthy baronet is the only male heir and representative of the family, consequently at his decease, the baronetcy will become extinct. *The Rev. Sir John Cullum*, the late baronet, was rector of Hawstead, and published the History and Antiquities of the parish in 1784. He was also author of a brief account of Little Sax-ham Church, and Bury St. Edmund's, inserted with views, in the Antiquarian Repertory. Hawstead CHURCH, (All Saints) was rebuilt about the middle of the 15th century, and has undergone many repairs and improvements. It is constructed of freestone and flints, broken into smooth faces, which, by the contrast of their colour, produce a pleasing effect. The square steeple, which contains three bells, is 63 feet high, and the lower part of it, as well as the porches, parapets, and buttresses, has the flints beautifully inlaid in a variety of patterns. The walls, for about two feet above the ground, are of freestone, and project all round in the manner of a buttress. In 1780, the thatched roof was exchanged for tiles. The nave and chancel are parted by a wooden screen of Gothic work, on which hangs one of the small bells, rung in Catholic times, at the consecration and elevation of the host. The church has many headless figures of saints and angels, mutilated in Cromwell's time, and its windows still retain several coats of arms of the Drurys and Cloptons, of whom here are several monuments. Within an arched recess, in the chancel wall, lies a cross legged figure, in stone, supposed to have represented one of the Fitz-Eustaces, who were lords here in the reigns of Henry III. and Edward I. In the middle of the floor is a flat slab of Sussex marble, which, by its escutcheons in brass, appears to cover the remains of Roger Drury, who died in 1500. On a flat stone, in front of the communion table, is the figure of a lady in brass, with a head dress of the age of Henry VII. On an altar tomb, are inlaid in brass, the figures of Sir Wm. Drury, kt., his two wives, and 17 children. In the chancel is a fine marble bust of another Sir Wm. Drury, kt., who was elected one of the knights of the shire, in 1585, and again in 1589, and was killed in a duel in France. In the south-east corner of the chancel is an elegant mural monument of painted alabaster, in memory of Elizabeth, daughter of Sir Robt. Drury, who died in 1610, aged 15. Under an ornamental arch, lies the figure of a young female, as large as life, with her head reclining on her left hand; and above is an emblematical figure surrounded with a glory, and scattering flowers on the figure below. Opposite, is a noble mural monument, in honour of her father, of whom it bears a spirited bust in a marble frame, over the arch. This Sir Robert accompanied the Earl of Essex, to the unsuccessful siege of Rohan, in 1591, where he was knighted at the early age of 16. The *Drury family*, which so long flourished here, produced many persons distinguished in their time, but the most celebrated was Sir William, who passed his youth in the French wars, his maturer years in Scotland, and his old age in Ireland, where he was appointed lord president of the province of Munster, in 1575, and lord chief justice of Ireland, in 1578, but died in the same year, when proceeding to reduce the rebellious Earl of Desmond. Here are also several elegant monuments of the *Cullum*

family, one of which is of white hard plaster, painted and gilt, in honour of the first baronet, who purchased the estate, after amassing a large fortune as a draper in London. The *rectory*, valued in K.B. at £11 16s. 10½d., has a yearly modus of £581, awarded in 1843, in lieu of tithes. The Rev. Sir Thos. Gery Cullum, Bart., is the patron, and the Rev. Edward Gosling, now in his 80th year, has been the incumbent more than half a century. The *Rev. Joseph Hall*, afterwards bishop of Exeter and Norwich, was presented to this rectory in 1601.

An ALMSHOUSE, for six poor unmarried women, was founded at Hardwick, in 1616, by *Sir Robert Drury, kt.*, who charged the manor of *Hawstead Hall-cum-Buckenhams*, with a yearly rent charge of £52, to be applied as follows, viz: £5 to each of the six almswomen, £22 to the poor of the following parishes, viz: £6 to Hawstead; £5 to Whepstead; £4 to Brockley; £4 to Chedburgh; and £3 to Rede. The founder directed that the six almswomen should be selected as follows; one from each of the parishes of Hawstead, Whepstead, and Brockley; one from Chedburgh or Rede; and two from Bury St. Edmund's. Sir Thos. G. Cullum, Bart., as lord of the manor, pays the rent charge of £52. The *Almshouse*, at Hardwick, having fallen into decay, was taken down about 1820, and in lieu thereof, an almshouse for two poor women was purchased at Bury, and another for four poor women was purchased at Hawstead. The TOWN ESTATE comprises the *Church-house*, occupied by paupers, and three cottages and about eleven acres of land let for £21 a year, of which £2 16s. belongs to the poor, and the remainder to the church. The poor of Hawstead have also a yearly rent charge of £5 10s., left by *Sir Thos. Cullum*, for a weekly distribution of bread in 1662, and now paid by the Draper's Company, London. Lady Cullum supports a school here for 25 poor children.

HAWSTEAD.

Cullum Rev. Sir Thomas Gery, Bart., *Hardwick House*
Bligh Rev. Thomas, curate, *Rectory*
Arnold Elizabeth, schoolmistress
Clarke William, & Musk J. shoemkrs
Metcalfe Henry, Esq., *Hawstead House*
Mortlock Michael, blacksmith
Pawsey Richard, butcher
Pryke William, wheelwright, &c.

FARMERS.
Bigsby William, *Hawstead Green*
Buck Samuel, *Hawstead Lodge*
Catchpole Robert, *Pinfer-end*
Payne Samuel, *Hawstead Place*

HENGRAVE, a neat and pleasent village, on the north-western side of the vale of the river Lark, 4 miles W. of Bury St. Edmund's, has in its parish 228 souls, and about 1,000 acres of land, all the property and manor of Sir Thomas Gage, Bart. of HENGRAVE HALL, a fine old mansion, standing in a beautiful *Park* of 275 acres. This mansion affords an unique specimen of ancient domestic architecture, and was built in 1534, by Sir Thomas Kitson. It is of brick and stone, and was once more extensive than at present; some parts at the north and north-east angle being taken away in 1775. The building, which is still large, encloses a quadrangular court, and the apartments open into a gallery, the windows of which overlook the court. They formerly contained a profusion of stained glass, and the bay-window, in the hall, still retains some fine specimens, and is very splendid in its mullions, fan-tracery, pendant, and spandrils; all of which resemble the highly florid example in Henry VII.th's chapel. The form of the turrets, on each side of the entrance, and at the corners of the building, as also of the two small turreted columns at the door, bear a striking resemblance to Moorish minarets, or

the cupolas of Indian edifices. For some time this mansion was the abode of a sisterhood of expatriated *nuns*, of Bruges, to whom the late Sir Thomas Gage liberally afforded an asylum, but when the decree in favour of emigrants was issued in France, in the early part of the present century, they availed themselves of the permission to return to their own country. It is now occupied by Henry Browning, Esq., and is but seldom visited by its present owner. In the reign of Edward I., Hengrave belonged to *Edmund de Hengrave,* a celebrated lawyer; and in 1375, to Thomas Hethe. In the 1st of Richard III., the manor was granted to Henry Lord Grey, but afterwards devolved to the Crown, of which it was purchased in the reign of Henry VIII. by *Sir Thomas Kitson,* who built the hall, and made it his family seat. He was succeeded by his son Thomas, who dying in 1602, the estate devolved by marriage, to Thomas Lord Darcy, whose second daughter conveyed Hengrave in marriage to *Sir John Gage, of Firle, Sussex.* In 1662, Edward Gage, Esq., of Hengrave, was created a *baronet.* The Church stands near the hall, and is a small ancient structure, with a round tower. It has neither pews nor pulpit, and has not been used for divine service during the last century; the *rectory,* valued in K. B. at £9 7s. 1d. being consolidated with Flempton, where there is a church which serves both parishes. Here are however several neat monuments. One is a fine marble tomb, in memory of *Sir Thomas Kitson,* the founder of the hall, and has effigies of himself and one of his wives. He came from the obscure village of Yelland, in Lancashire, and having obtained immense wealth by commercial speculations, in the cloth trade, purchased this and many other estates, and received the honour of knighthood. The Almshouses here consist of four tenements, for as many poor parishioners, and were erected and endowed with an annuity of £10, by Sir Thomas Kitson, whose relict, *Lady Eliz. Kitson,* in 1662, in lieu of the said annuity, charged the manor of Lackford with the yearly payment of £30, for equal division among the almspeople, and with £4 a year to provide 12 gowns for 12 of the most aged poor of Hengrave, Flempton, Lackford, Chevington, Risby, Westley, and the three Fornhams. She also charged the manor of Lackford with the following yearly payments, for the relief of the poor, of the respective parishes, viz:—£10 to Bury St. Edmund's; £3 to Fornham-All-Saints; £2 each to Fornham St Martin, Flempton, Chevington, and Risby; £1 each to Hargrave, Westley, and Fornham-St.-Genevieve; £5 to Lackford; and £3 to St. James', Clerkenwell, Middlesex. The almspeople, at Hengrave, are appointed by *Sir Thomas Gage,* as owner of Hengrave Hall, and one of the trustees of this charity.

Browning Henry, Esq. *Hengrave Hall*
Foreman Edward, gamekeeper
Gill Mrs. Mary, *Hengrave Cottage*
Horrex Robert, shopkeeper
Luggar Edw. farmer, *Stanchells*
Orman John, land agent
Pask William, shoemaker
Raynbird Robert, farmer, *Grange*
Steel John, miller and farmer
Wright James, swine dealer

HORNINGSHEATH, commonly called HORRINGER, is a neat and pleasant village, 2 miles W. S. W. of Bury, on the east side of the extensive and beautiful park of Ickworth. Its parish contains 597 souls, and 1,780 acres of fertile and well wooded land, including the greater part of HORSECROFT *hamlet,* which is a mile E.

of the village, and has 22 inhabitants in this, and 12 in Nowton parish. Horningsheath was formerly in two parishes, but they were consolidated in 1548, after the church of Little Horningsheath had been demolished. The manor was held by Bury Abbey, and the abbot used Little Horningsheath Hall as one of his pleasure houses. The manor and advowson were afterwards held by the Davers, and are now held by the Marquis of Bristol, together with a great part of the soil ; but *Horsecroft* is mostly the property of Wm. Bacon Wigson, Esq.; and A. J. Brooke, Esq., of *Brook House*, (a handsome mansion here,) J. F. Dove, Esq., of *Hopleys Cottage*, (half a mile east of the village,) G Brown, Esq., and several smaller owners have estates in Horningsheath. Among the large *Oaks* in the parish, is one girt by a bench, on which 20 men may sit. The Church (St. Leonard,) is a small neat structure with a tower and six bells, and was new pewed in 1818, at the cost of A. J. Brooke, Esq. The organ was given by the rector, in 1816. The rectory, valued in K. B. at £13 3s. 8½d., has now a yearly modus of £500, awarded in 1840, in lieu of tithes. The Marquis of Bristol is patron, and the Rev. Henry Hasted, M. A., of Bury, is the incumbent. The *Free School* was built by the Marquis of Bristol, and is attended by from 40 to 50 poor children, who are nominated by the rector, and are instructed by a schoolmistress, in reading and writing, and the girls also in knitting and sewing. The mistress has the use of a small garden, and receives about £16 a year from the *Hon. Wm. Hervey's Charity*, (see Chedburgh ;) a yearly rent charge of £6, left by *Samuel Batteley*, in 1714, out of land at Denston ; and £6 4s. as the rent of two cottages left by *Wm. Godfrey*, in 1724. A few poor boys are educated by subscription, at another school. Two poor widows of the parish have £6 yearly from *Sache's* Charity. (See page 640.) A double cottage has belonged to the poor parishioners from time immemorial, and is occupied rent free, as also is a cottage with a garden attached to it, left by *Ann Corder*, in 1591. The Town Estate consists of four tenements, built by the Marquis of Bristol, on the site of the Guildhall and Town House, and now let for £4 a year, which is distributed among the poor in coals; and 2A. 1R. of land, let for £3 a year, which is applied in apprenticing poor boys, and repairing the poor's cottages. Two *lamb fairs* were formerly held here, upon the Sheep green, but only one is now held, on Sept. 4th.

Bevan George, Esq.
Brooke Arthur John, Esq. *Brook House*
Cooper William, corn & hay dealer
Dove John Fowler, Esq. *Hopleys Cottage*
Edwards John, carpenter and parish clerk
Edwards William, wheelwright, &c.
Game Benjamin, beer house keeper
Hall Rev. William, curate
Mison Samuel, vict. *Red House*
Partridge Letitia, schoolmistress
Scarlin Jas. gent. || Read Mrs. Ann
Sturgeon Mrs. Ann
Tayler James, lime burner

Turner Thomas, land agent to the Marquis of Bristol, *Little Horningsheath Hall*
Wigson Wm. Bacon, Esq. *Horsecroft*
Wright James, schoolmaster
Wright John, shoemaker

BLACKSMITHS.
Farrant George
Pryke Thomas

FARMERS.
Bidwell Woodward, *Great Hall*
Chandler Henry
Gardiner Wm.
Kemp John

Sturgeon John
Wigson Wm. B.

Shopkeepers.
Hammond My. A.
Smith Rose Ann
Tweed George

Tailors.
Cornell John
Sanders George

ICKWORTH parish, from 3 to 5 miles S.W. by W. of Bury St. Edmund's, contains only 62 souls, and 1257 acres, all in ICKWORTH PARK, which is eleven miles in circumference, and comprises no less than 1,800a., of which nearly 300a. are in the adjoining parish of Horningsheath. Ickworth formerly belonged to the Abbey of Bury, by the gift of Theodred, Bishop of London. The whole parish has long been converted into a park, in which stands the magnificent residence of the noble family of Hervey, who acquired this estate by marriage with that of Drury. John Hervey was created a peer of the realm, by Queen Anne, in 1703, by the title of *Baron Hervey, of Ickworth ;* and in 1714, was raised to the dignity of *Earl of Bristol.* Frederick Wm. Hervey, F.R.S., the present and fifth earl, was created MARQUIS OF BRISTOL AND EARL JERMYN, in 1826. He was born in 1769, and married in 1798, Elizabeth, daughter of Lord Templetown. He is Hereditary High Steward of Bury St. Edmund's, and his eldest son, the Rt. Hon. Fredk. Wm. Hervey, EARL JERMYN, is one of the parliamentary representatives of that borough, and married a daughter of the Duke of Rutland. *Ickworth Park* may vie with any in the kingdom, in beauty or extent. It is stocked with about 700 head of fine deer, and its gardens occupy $5\frac{1}{2}$ acres, and have near them a fine sheet of water. The *Old Mansion* of the noble proprietor, is not remarkable, but not far from it stands the *New Mansion,* planned upon a very extensive scale, by the late Earl of Bristol, who was also Bishop of Derry, partly for the purpose of depositing in it the various works of art which he had collected during a long residence in Italy. Only the external parts of the grand centre, and the foundations of the wings were completed in 1798, when the late Earl's collections fell into the hands of the French, and he himself was confined by the republicans in the castle of Milan. This event seems to have occasioned him to abandon his design of returning to England, and he continued to reside in Italy, till his death in 1803, when he is said to have left all his personal property to strangers, including such collections as he had made in the last years of his life. His successor, the present noble owner, for some years deliberated on the propriety of pulling down the shell, which his father had erected, rather than incur the immense expence of completing it, and of adding the two extensive wings which formed part of the plan. However, about 15 years ago, he determined to carry out his father's design, and having finished the centre, proceeded with the erection of the wings, which are each more than fifty yards in length, and upon which he still expends large sums yearly. This mansion house, whether from the grandeur of its scale, or the singularity of its design, is one of the most remarkable structures of modern architecture. About 1792, the late Earl laid the foundations of the mansion, on a plan suggested by himself, with the assistance of Francis Sandys, Esq., the architect ; but as already noticed, he did not live to see its completion. It is of tile and brick stuccoed, and consists of an oval centre, connected with wings, by extensive corridors, and faced by a portico on the north side. The whole stands upon a basement containing the offices. The extreme length of the building is 625 feet. The centre, crowned with a dome, rises 105 feet, the diameter being 120 feet north and south, and 106 feet east and west. The corridors

are quadrants of circles, and intersect the centre, so as to leave two-thirds of its largest diameter in advance on the south or principal front. The centre is composed of two orders—the Ionic and Corinthian, and three-quarter columns support the entablatures. The lower entablature is plain, the space immediately below it being enriched with a series of subjects modelled in relief. The upper entablature has its frieze filled with reliefs. On the summit of the dome is a ballustrade concealing the flues. The portico is supported by four columns, with a pediment of the Ionic order. The *south front*, with its noble terrace, is full of grandeur. The reliefs, which are various in their nature, are all modelled after Flaxman's designs, from the Iliad and Odyssey, excepting that in the centre over the entrance within the portico, which was designed by Lady Caroline Wharncliffe. The whole of the reliefs of the lower circle, and part of the upper, were modelled by Carabello and Casimir Donta, two brothers from the Milanese district; and the rest were executed by Coade. The interior is now splendidly furnished, and contains many large and elegant apartments. The CHURCH is a small neat structure, standing in the Park, at a short distance from the two mansions. The benefice is a discharged rectory, valued in K. B. at £7 11s. 5d., and in 1835, at £238, with that of Chedburgh annexed to it. The Marquis of Bristol is patron, and one of his sons, the Rt. Hon. and Rev. Lord Arthur Hervey, is the incumbent. An elegant monumental stone column, 200 feet high, was erected in the Park, a few years ago, in memory of Frederick Augustus, the late Earl of Bristol and Bishop of Derry. In the 12th of James I., Elizabeth Hervey charged her lands here and in Horningsheath with a yearly rent charge of £2, for the poor of Ickworth.

Most Noble Frederick William Hervey, F.R.S., MARQUIS OF BRISTOL, *Earl Jermyn, and Baron Hervey,* Ickworth Park

Rt. Hon. Frederick William Hervey, *Earl Jermyn,* M. P.

Hon & Rev. Lord Arthur Hervey, rector, *Old Mansion*

Hon & Rev. Lord Charles Hervey

Anderson William. *gardener*

Bilson William, *park keeper*

Howe Mr. James

LACKFORD, a small scattered village on the south side of the river Lark, 6 miles N.W. of Bury St. Edmund's, has in its parish 193 souls, and 2,200 acres of land. Though in Thingoe, it gives name to the adjoining Hundred. Its name is no doubt a corruption of Lark-ford; but the river is now crossed here by a good bridge, and is navigable from the Ouse to the vicinity of Bury. (See page 603.) Sir Charles Egleton Kent, Bart., of Grantham-House, Lincolnshire, is lord of the manor, owner of the soil, and patron of the *rectory,* valued in K. B. at £19 10s. 5d., and in 1835, at £271, and now enjoyed by the Rev. Thomas Ellis Rogers. The *Church* (St. Lawrence) is a small thatched fabric, and was in the patronage of Bury Abbey. The poor parishioners have 1A. of land at Rattlesden, let for 20s., and purchased with £10 left by Wm. Firmage, in 1599;—5A. in the same parish, let for £3 10s., and purchased with £30 left by the *Rev. Edward Kirke,* in 1613; and the dividends of £153 6s. 8d. Old South Sea Annuities, given by *John Booty,* in 1771. They have also £5 a year out of the manor of Lackford, pursuant to the bequest of *Lady Elizabeth Kitson.* (See Hengrave). The income

from these sources is distributed among the poor parishioners in fuel. The principal residents are the Rector, and John Muskett, farmer, *Lackford Hall*, and Henry Roper, farmer, *Brook Farm.*

NOWTON, a small village, pleasantly situated on an eminence, 2 miles S. by E. of Bury St. Edmund's, has in its parish 159 inhabitants, and 1,320 acres of land, exclusive of a portion of *Horsecroft* hamlet, which is mostly in Horningsheath parish. (See page 670.) H. J. Oakes, Esq., of *Nowton Court*, (a large handsome mansion), is lord of the manor; but a great part of the soil belongs to the Marquis of Bristol, and a few small owners. The *Church* (St. Peter) is a neat structure with six bells, and was enlarged and repewed in 1843, at the cost of H. J. Oakes, Esq. Two of its windows are beautifully decorated with stained glass. The *rectory*, valued in K. B. at £5 19s. 4½d., and in 1835, at £314, is in the patronage of the Marquis of Bristol, and incumbency of the Rev. M. Wilkinson, for whom the Rev. H. A. Oakes, of Rougham, officiates. Mrs. Oakes supports a small school here for the instruction of poor children; and the parish has 2A. of *Poor's Land* in Bury Field, purchased with £20 benefaction money, and now let for £2 14s. a year. *Directory :—* Maria Blomfield, *schoolmistress ;* John Brewer, gamekeeper ; Robert Buck, farmer, *Nowton Hall ;* Joseph De Carle, registrar & relieving officer ; Isaac Hynard, *shopkeeper ;* Wm. Marshall, farmer ; Henry James Oakes, Esq., banker, *Nowton Court ;* & Mrs. Martha Vardy.

REDE, or *Reed*, a village and parish, near the source of a rivulet, 7 miles S. S.W. of Bury, contains 241 souls, and about 1,300 acres of land. The Marquis of Bristol is lord of the manor ; but a great part of the soil belongs to the Rev. H. Hasted, Mr. Thomas Murrills, and a few smaller owners. The *Church* (All Saints) is a small edifice with a tower and three bells. The living is a discharged rectory, valued in K. B. at £2 18s. 1½d., and now having a yearly modus of £286, awarded in 1841, in lieu of tithes. The patronage is in the Crown, and the Rev. John Latey is the incumbent, for whom the Rev. Henry Mears officiates. As noticed with Hawstead, the poor of Rede have £3 a year from *Sir Robert Drury's Charity,* and one of the poor parishioners is placed in the almshouse at Hawstead, and has a yearly stipend of £5. They have also £1 3s. 4d. yearly, in *three rent charges*, left by Robert Sparrowe, Samuel Bird, and R. Kedington. In 1721, *Thomas Sparke* left 11A. of land called Great and Little Stubbing, in trust, to apply the rents in schooling poor children of Rede, and in buying them books. This land is copyhold of the manor of Brockley Hall, and is let for £12 a year, but is subject to a quit-rent of £1 10s. 1d. The rent is applied towards the support of a *National School*, to which about £7 a year is paid from the *Hon. Wm. Hervey's Charity.* (See Chedburgh.) A new school room was built by subscription in 1843.

Eliot Samuel, shopkeeper	Fayers George
Fayers Ann, schoolmistress	*Murrills Thomas, *Downings*
Frost Charles, blacksmith	Pearson Isaac & Thos. *Pickards Hall*
Paxman Robert, wheelwright	Rollinson George, *Kell Farm*
FARMERS. (*are Owners.)	Rollinson John, *Rede Hall*
*Eliot John ‖ Evered Joseph	

RISBY, a small village, pleasantly situated nearly 4 miles W. by N. of Bury St. Edmund's, has in its parish 360 souls, and 2,620 acres of land, having a light mixed soil. Edward the Confessor gave the manor of Risby to Bury Abbey, and it was granted in the 31st of Henry VIII., to Sir Thos. Kitson. Sir Thomas Gage is now lord of the manor, but part of the parish belongs to the Rev. J. D. Wastel, J. Cottingham, Esq., and a few smaller owners. The *Church*, (St. Giles) is a small ancient structure, with a round tower, and a curiously carved screen. It was new pewed and repaired in 1842, at the cost of £260; and a new vestry was built in 1843. The *rectory*, valued in K.B. at £19 10s. 5d., and in 1835, at £750, with that of Fornham-St.-Genevieve consolidated with it, is in the patronage of the Crown, and incumbency of the Rev. S. H. Alderson, M.A., who has a commodious Rectory House, built in 1839. The tithes of Risby were commuted in 1839 for £575 6s. 8d. per annum, and those of Fornham-St.-Genevieve, for £140. *Risby Poor's Estate* consists of a house and 19A. of land at Needham-street, in Gazeley, let for £14 12s. a year. It was given before the reign of Henry VIII., for the purpose of easing the poor parishioners of the town charges, &c. that might be imposed upon them. For many years no part of the rent has been applied to the payment of taxes, but the whole has been distributed yearly among the poor; who have also £1 13s. 6d. yearly from land purchased with £10 given by *Wm. Firmage*, in 1599; £2 a year from *Lady Kitson's Charity*, (see Hengrave;) £8 10s. 4d. yearly from £212 19s. 1d. new four per cent. Annuities, purchased with £200 left by *Launcelot Danby*, in 1812; and £1 16s. 10d. a year from £61 10s. 9d. three per cent.Consols, purchased with £50 left by *John Spink*, in 1822. DIRECTORY—Rev. Samuel Hurry Alderson, *Rectory;* Wm. Adkin and Zach. Fenton, *shopkeepers;* Wm. and Thos. Orrage, *blacksmiths ;* Hannah Smith, *beerseller ;* George Smith, bricklayer; Mrs. Amy Sutton; Rev. John Daniel Wastel; Wm. Cook, farmer, *Risby Hall ;* John Cottingham, farmer, *Risby Place* Robt. Kemball, farmer; and John Denton Paine, farmer, *Quays.*

SAXHAM, (GREAT) a small scattered village, 5 miles W. by S. of Bury St. Edmund's, has in its parish 271 souls, and 1,417 acres of land, now valued at £1,674 2s. 6d. per annum. It belonged to Bury Abbey, and was granted in the 33rd of Henry VIII., to Sir Richard Long and his wife. For several descents it was held by the Eldred family, one of whom (John,) built a mansion here, which was called Nutmeg Hall, in the reign of James I. In 1641, his son, Revet Eldred, was created a *baronet;* and in 1750, one of his descendants sold the estate to Hutchinson Mure, Esq., who greatly improved and embellished the domain. The old *Hall* was accidentally burnt down in 1779, and a new one erected north-west of it, from a plan by Mr. Adam. This modern mansion is a large and handsome building, in a beautiful park, and is the seat of William Mills, Esq., lord of the manor, owner of the soil, and patron of the *rectory*, valued in K. B. at £11 13s. 11½d., and now enjoyed by the Rev. Thomas Mills, who has a yearly modus of £369, awarded in 1839, in lieu of tithes. The *Church*, (St. Andrew) an ancient structure in the park, has a tower and three bells, and two beautiful painted windows, inserted by the late T.

Mills, Esq., in 1815. In the chancel is a bust of John Eldred, who travelled to the Holy Land, Babylon, &c., and died in 1632, aged 80 years. Under this bust is a raised monument, with a black marble slab, on which, neatly inlaid in brass, is the figure of a man, with a ruff and furred gown, well engraved, with the arms of Eldred, Revet, and a long inscription. The parish has a barn, two cottages, and about 12A. of land at Whepstead, let for £11 10s. a year, and purchased with the following benefactions, viz:—£100 given by *Lady Ann Eldred*, £50 given by the *Rev. Samuel Edwards*, and £10 given by *John Potter*, to purchase lands for the equal benefit of the minister and the poor. An allotment of about two acres of land, at Fornham-All-Saints, was awarded in lieu of other land left to the poor of Risby, by the *Rev. Ralph Weld*, and is now let for £4 a year. The poor have also two yearly rent charges of £2 each, given by *Holofernes Allen*, in 1605 and 1610; one of £1 3s. 4d., given by *Edmund Friend*, in 1604, and another of 6s. 8d. left by *Simon Pitts*, in 1641.

Borley Robert, vict. *White Horse*
Cockrill Robert, farmer
Frost John, butcher
Dennis William, farmer, *Cobs-Hall*
Hammond Fras. wheelwright, &c.
Mills William, Esq. *Saxham Hall*

Robinson Daniel, horse dealer
Scholefield Rev. Richard, curate
Syer William, blacksmith
Taylor William, shopkeeper
Silverstone Samuel, land agent

SAXHAM, (LITTLE) 4 miles W. of Bury St. Edmund's, is a small scattered village, and parish, containing 230 souls, and about 1,200 acres of fertile land, all the property and manor of the Marquis of Bristol, who is also patron of the *rectory*, valued in K. B. at £8. 11s. 5½d., and in 1835, at £300. The Rev. P. Wakeham is the incumbent. The *Church* (St. Nicholas) is an ancient fabric with a round tower, and contains elegant altar monuments and recumbent effigies of Lord Crofts and his lady. The Lucas, and after them the Crofts family, were seated here for a long period. Several of the latter received the honour of knighthood; and one of them, *Sir Thomas Crofts*, was high sheriff of Suffolk in the 36th of Elizabeth. His grandson, Wm. Crofts, was a great sufferer for his loyalty to the Stuart family, and in consideration of his services, Charles II. created him a peer of the realm in 1658, by the title of *Baron Crofts, of Saxham*, which became extinct on his death, without issue, in 1677. The *Hall*, to which Lord Crofts added a grand apartment for the reception of Charles II., was probably built in the reign of Henry VII. It was pulled down in 1771, when much of its painted glass was inserted in the windows of the church. A yearly rent charge of £4 16s. is paid by the Marquis of Bristol, out of his estates in this parish, in satisfaction of bequests to the poor, amounting to about £90, and left by Wm. Firmage, Lord Crofts, and Wm. and Anthony Crofts, Esqrs. This rent charge is distributed in coals and flour, among the poor of the parish, together with the dividends of £289 12s. 6d. three per cent. Consols, purchased with £200 left by *Mrs. Mary Green*, in 1814. DIRECTORY—Rev. Henry Ashington, *curate ;* Mr. Thos. Rodwell, *Honey-Hill ;* Elizabeth Cornell, farmer ; Jas. Rodwell Kerry, farmer, *Honey-Hill :* and Catherine Jane Stutter, farmer.

WESTLEY, a small parish, 2 miles W. of Bury St. Edmund's, has 144 souls, a few cottages, and 1,234 acres of land, all in *one farm*, occupied by Mr. Walter Burrell, of *Westley Hall.* The Marquis of Bristol and Mr. James Lee are lords of the manors, but part of the soil belongs to Mr. W. Burrell, and a few smaller owners. It formerly belonged to Bury Abbey, by gift of Bishop Afric, and was granted in the 31st of Henry VIII. to Sir Thos. Kitson. The old Church (St. Thomas-a-Becket) is in ruins, but a new one was erected in 1836, at the cost of £1,400, of patent cement stone, and dedicated to St. Mary. It has a small spire and about 100 sittings. The Marquis of Bristol gave the site and £600. The rectory, valued in K. B. at £9 15s. 5d., is consolidated with that of Fornham-All-Saints, as already noticed at page 665. The poor parishioners have 20s. a year from Lady Kitson's charity. (See Hengrave.)

WHEPSTEAD, a large but widely scattered village, from 4 to 5 miles S. of Bury St. Edmund's, has in its picturesque parish 681 inhabitants, and about 3,000 acres of fertile land. Sir Thomas Hammond, Bart., of *Plumpton House*, a large mansion with pleasant grounds, is lord of the manor, but a great part of the soil belongs to the Marquis of Bristol, and the Worledge, Jackson, Cocksedge, Image, Ince, Sprigge, Chapman, and other families. The manor was held by Bury Abbey, by gift of Theodred, bishop of London; and was granted to Sir Wm. Drury in the 31st of Henry VIII. It afterwards passed through various families to the late Major General Hammond, who repaired and modernized Plumpton House, in the early part of the present century, and whose descendant, the present owner, has recently been created a baronet. The *Church* is a neat structure with a tower containing five bells, and formerly surmounted by a spire, which was blown down by a high wind, at Oliver Cromwell's death, as also was that at Dalham. It has a handsomely painted east window, and a good organ, purchased in 1812. The *rectory*, valued in K. B. at £14 4s. 2., and in 1835, at £468, is in the patronage and incumbency of the Rev. Thomas Image, M. A., who has a neat residence. The tithes were commuted in 1843. The *Church Estate* consists of a cottage, a garden, and 3R. 38P. of land in this parish, let for £14 a year; 12A. 28P. of tithe free land, at Thurston, let for £15 a year; and a house, a barn, and 6A. of land at Hawstead, let for £10 a year. The rents are expended in the service of the church. The land at Thurston was received in 1809, in exchange for land at Rougham; and that at Hawstead, was obtained in 1814, in exchange for land at Whepstead. A poor widow of this parish is placed in the almshouse at Hawstead, and has a yearly stipend of £5 from the charity of *Sir Robt. Drury*, who also left the yearly sum of £5 to be distributed among the poor of Whepstead, at Christmas, as noticed with Hawstead. They have also about £3 12s. yearly from *Jervis's Charity*, (see Brockley;) and the interest of £200 left by *John Wilson Allen, Esq.*, in 1825. For *schooling* poor children of Whepstead, and providing them with books, *Thomas Sparke*, in 1721, devised a copyhold farm of 24A. 2R. 13P., now let for £21 a year, out of which about £3 is required yearly for repairs, and £1 is paid to the minister and churchwardens, for their trouble in managing the

charity. The *school* is kept in a cottage which was purchased by the trustees, and 10 poor children are taught as free-scholars

Bowers John, beer hs. & shopkeeper
Borroughs John, carpenter
Curry James, vict. *White Horse*
Grimwood Henry, wheelwright
Hammond Sir Thomas, Baronet, *Plumpton House*
Image Rev. Thos., M. A. *Rectory*
King James Edward, *Mellon Green*
Musk John, shoemaker
Pask James, schoolmaster
Pawsey James, parish clerk
Payne Wm. shoemaker & shopkeeper
Rutter Joseph, baker and grocer
Wade John, wheelwright
Webb George, blacksmith
Wells Simon, beer house keeper
Wright James, butcher
        FARMERS.   (* *are Owners.*)
Bigsby William, *Whepstead Hall*
*Bigsby Thomas, (*and corn miller*)

Bradley Alexander, *Tuffields*
Dennis Jonathan, *Riches farm*
*Drinkmilk Mary, *Tuffields*
Goldsmith George, *Sparkes*
Hall Thomas, *Menston Hall*
Hammond Robert ‖ Crack John
Holden Robert *Vincents' farm*
Hustler Mrs., *Malting*
Langham Jph. ‖ Hustler Charles
Lee James, *Doveden Hall*
Payne Abraham ‖ Maid Thomas
Payne James, *Mickley Green*
*Reynolds John, *Waste*
*Reynolds Isaac, (& farrier) *Mellon Green*
Snell John, *High Green*
Vickers James, *Limbers*
Wallace Walter, *Dodds farm*
Watkinson Geo. *Stone-Cross green*
Webb Mary, *Chapman farm*

BLACKBOURN HUNDRED,

In the north-western part of Suffolk, in the *Deanery of Blackbourn,* Archdeaconry of Sudbury, and Diocese of Ely, is about 15 miles in length from east to west, and from 7 to 10 in breadth. It is bounded on the north by the *Little Ouse* river, which separates it from Norfolk; on the east by Hartismere Hundred; on the south by Stow, Thedwestry, and Thingoe Hundreds; and on the west by Lackford Hundred. It was granted as parcel of the *Franchise or Liberty of St. Edmund,* in the 3rd of Elizabeth, to Sir Nicholas Bacon, kt.; and was purchased of the Bacon family, by Lord Chief Justice Holt. George St. Vincent Wilson, Esq., is now lord of the Hundred, for which he holds a *general yearly court,* at the Cock Inn, Stanton, according to ancient custom, on the Tuesday after the feast of St. Faith, where all persons owing suit and service, and quit rents; and all persons claiming to be enrolled for any lands or tenements, in the Hundred, are summoned to attend before Thos. E. Wallace, Esq., the *steward.* It is intersected by the river Thet and several smaller streams, flowing northward to the Little Ouse. The western, and some other parts of it, have a light sandy soil, resting on a substratum of chalk, and having several extensive open sheep walks; and other parts of it rise in bold undulations, and have a strong loamy soil, with some rich marshes in the vale of the Little Ouse. The navigable river Lark forms a part of its western boundary, and the Little Ouse is navigable to Thetford, near its north-west angle. The following enumeration of its 34 parishes, shews their territorial extent; the annual value of their lands and buildings, as assessed to the property tax, in 1815, and their population in 1801, and 1841.

PARISHES.	Acr.	Rntl £.	Populatn 1801	1841	PARISHES.	Acres.	Rental £.	Population. 1801	1841
*Ashfield (Great)..	2030	1901	270	396	*Norton	2450	2778	533	879
*Badwell Ash....	1860	2044	348	458	*Rickinghall Infr ..	1966	2107	427	432
†Bardwell	3142	2972	556	826	Rushforth (part) ? ..	1000	500	30	34
Barnham ...•....	5184	1254	303	412	Sapiston	1155	1053	207	255
Barningham	1555	2380	316	508	+Stanton-All-Snts.)	3254	3828	728	1029
+Culford	2490	1674	244	352	and St.John Bapt.∫				
*Elmswell	2021	2293	451	671	*Stowlangtoft	1358	1034	162	183
Euston ‡ ......}	3780	1592	198	255	+Stow West......)	3050	1156	168	273
Rymer, Ex.pa.∫				15	Chimney Mills‡ ∫				6
Fakenham Magna	2155	1137	157	213	Thelnetham........	1721	1999	444	561
Hepworth	1640	2226	449	582	+Thorpe-by-Ixworth	1000	1163	122	142
*Hinderclay......	1400	1803	335	387	†Troston	1770	1323	247	409
Honington	1204	1500	176	273	*Walsham-le-Wilws.	2760	3661	993	1265
Hopton..........	1322	1389	433	623	*Wattisfield........	1600	2187	520	601
*Hunston	1120	986	143	162	Weston (Coney)	1321	1685	198	244
+Ingham	1809	1450	160	208	Weston-Market	1090	1363	273	330
†Ixworth	2213	2495	827	1064	+Wordwell	2120	853	40	66
Knettishall	1025	1086	49	79					
*Langham ,......	1270	1103	207	293	TOTAL	66,272	59,343	10,803	14,658
+Livermere Parva.	1433	1368	89	172					

UNIONS.—The eleven parishes marked thus * are in *Stow-Union*, (see page 265:) the ten marked thus † are in *Thingoe Union*, (see page 601:) and the other thirteen are in *Thetford Union*.

‡ Euston includes the hamlet of *Little Fakenham*.

? Rushford parish is mostly in Norfolk.

CHIEF CONSTABLES:—Messrs Chas. Thos. Mathew, of Stowlangtoft, and John Woodard, of Stanton Park.

ASHFIELD, (GREAT) a small scattered village, 8 miles N. W. of Stowmarket, and 5 miles E. S. E. of Ixworth, has in its parish 396 souls, and about 2,030 acres of land. ASHFIELD LODGE, a neat mansion with pleasant grounds, is the seat of *Lord Thurlow*, the lord of the manor, owner of most of the soil, impropriator, and patron of the *Church*, (All Saints) a small ancient fabric, with a tower and five bells. The benefice is a perpetual curacy, valued at £65, and now enjoyed by the Rev. John Steggall. But here is also an endowed *lectureship*, of which the Rev. Thos. B. Norgate is incumbent. In 1620, NICHOLAS FYRMAGE gave his land in Hackford, and £300 to be laid out in land, " to a preaching minister of God's word, for a Sunday sermon in the forenoon, to be preached in the parish church of *Ashfield Magna*," viz. to the preacher 8s. for every sermon; to 12 of the poorest householders in the parish 2s. each, every quarter in the year; 2s. to the sexton every quarter, for ringing the great bell to every sermon; and 2s. a year to find bell ropes. By an Inquisition taken of this charity, in the 21st of James 1st, it was found that the rectory and parsonage of Ashfield Magna had, time out of mind, been an impropriation, and that there was no certain maintenance for a preaching minister, the curate having only £20, raised by the voluntary gifts of the parishioners, and the impropriator. The Commissioners of this enquiry decreed that the property, left by Nicholas Fyrmage, should be conveyed to trustees, who should have the nomination and appointment of an able man to preach, as directed by the testator. The £300 was laid out in the purchase of about 40 acres of land, called Hoo-Wood, in Stow-upland and Stow-market, now let for £54 a year. The property at Hackford consists of a farm house, cottage, and 27A. 3R. 23P. of land, let for £44 a year. The income from

these sources, (£98 per ann.) after paying 8s. a year to the sexton, and 2s. for bell ropes, is divided into *five parts*, of which four are paid to the lecturer, and one part is distributed among about 13 poor house-holders. Until 1813, it was usual for the trustees to appoint the per-petual curate to the lectureship; but after that year, they appointed other clergymen. In 1827, the present incumbent curate, considering himself entitled to the lectureship, prohibited the Rev. T. B. Norgate from performing duty in the church, as lecturer, and application was made to the Court of Chancery, which confirmed the appointment of the trustees. In the 13th of Charles I., WM. CLARKE left a yearly rent charge of 20s. out of 4A. called *Wrong Haunt*, for apprenticing poor children of Ashfield. The *Church Lands*, 1A. 3R. 16P., are let for £5 4s. a year, which is carried to the churchwarden's account. *Two Cottages*, adjoining the church-yard, are occupied rent free, by poor persons, and repaired by the parish.

Ashfield is remarkable for being the birth place of that distinguished lawyer, the late LORD THURLOW, and his brother, late *Bishop of Dur-ham*. Their father, the Rev. Thos. Thurlow, was incumbent here, and mar-ried Miss Eliza Smith, the sole heiress of the Smiths, who had long held the manor, and were seated at the old mansion called *Lee*, now Lee farm. Edward, his eldest son, was born in 1735, and at the proper age was sent to Caius College, Cambridge, but did not obtain a degree. On leaving the University, he entered himself of the Inner Temple, was called to the bar and remained unemployed, and unknown, until his abilities were called into action in the Douglas cause; soon after which, he attained such professional distinction, that he was appointed solicitor-general in 1770; attorney-gene-ral, in the following year; and lord chancellor in 1778. On the latter oc-casion, he was elevated to the peerage, by the title of *Baron Thurlow of Ashfield*. In 1786, he obtained the lucrative appointment of teller of the Exchequer; and in 1792 was created *Baron Thurlow of Thurlow*, with remainder failing his male issue, to his brothers, and their male issue. The most re-markable period of his life was the epoch of his majesty's illness, in 1788, and '89. His integrity then shone conspicuous; and in one of his speeches on the regency question, he said, "When I forsake my king in the hour of his distress, may God forsake me." He retired into private life in 1793. His talents, even out of his profession, were so splendid, that Dr. Johnson said, "I would prepare myself for no man in England, but Lord Thurlow; when I am about to meet him, I should wish to know a day before." His lordship, who was never married, died at Brighton, in 1806. His next brother, *Thomas Thurlow*, who embraced the clerical profession, was elevated to the See of Rochester, in 1779, but was translated to Durham, in 1787, and died in 1791. Edward, his eldest son, succeeded, on his uncle's demise, to the title of *Baron Thurlow of Thurlow*, and died 1829, when he was succeeded by the *Rt. Hon. Edward Thomas Hovell Thurlow*, the present Lord Thurlow.

Lord Thurlow, *Ashfield Lodge*
Calver Edward, blacksmith
Elmer Thomas, corn miller
Jackaman Wm., vict. *Thurlow Arms*
Norgate Rev. Thomas, B. lecturer
Peach James, blicklayer
Peach Sarah, schoolmistress
Plummer John & Wm. carpenters
Plummer Elizabeth, shopkeeper
Redit John, blacksmith
Redit Nathaniel, wheelwright

FARMERS.

Barrell Joseph
Bennett John
Boldero Geo. (& brickmaker)
Booty William
Easlea John, *Lee*
Firman Robert
Hunt Richard
Larter William

Parker Robert, *Reed Hall*
Pattle Zachariah
Rice James
Wakeley Mrs. —
Waller William
SHOEMAKERS.
Bloomfield David, (& shopkeeper)
Faires William
Seaton Samuel

BADWELL-ASH, or *Little Ashfield*, is a neat village, 4 miles E. by S. of Ixworth, and its parish contains 458 souls, and 1,860 acres of land. In the 9th of Edward I., it was the lordship of Wm. Creketote, and it was afterwards held, together with Great Ashfield, by the prior and monks of Ixworth. At the dissolution, it was granted to Richd. Codington. It is now in two manors-Badwell Ash and Shackerland, belonging to Miss R. Clough; but a great part of the soil is the property of Lord Thurlow, the Rev. T. B. Norgate, and the Mayhew, Baker, Moss, Wilson, Parker, and a few other families. The *Church*, (St. Mary) is a perpetual curacy, valued at £69. Miss R. Clough is patroness,andtheRev.Thos.BurroughsNorgate,incumbent. The*Town Estate* has been vested from a nearly period, in trust, for the reparation of the church and the relief of the poor, at the discretion of the trustees and the churchwardens. It consists of the Town House, occupied rent free, by poor families, and about 11A. of land, let for £12 3s. 6d. a year, which is wholly applied in the service of the church. For a distribution of bread at the church, the poor have a yearly rent charge of 24s., left by Thos. Blackerby, in the 13th of Charles 2nd., out of the tithes of Stow-upland. The late *Thos. Richer, Esq.*, of this parish, left £400 to the Suffolk General Hospital, in 1843.

Cullum John, shoemaker
Drake Thomas, baker
Fake Samuel, wheelwright
Faires Henry, shoemaker
Green Henry, corn miller
Hovell Miss Mary, *Green*
Hubbard Chas. carpenter & *par. clerk*
Hunt Robert, shopkeeper
Kinsey Simon, vict. *White Horse*
Parker Mrs. Eliz. || Moss Mrs. My.
Richer Mrs. Sar. || Pratt Mrs. Eliz.
Thrower Samuel, blacksmith
Thrower Elizabeth, shopkeeper
Warren Reuben, bricklayer
FARMERS.
Day Edward, *Green*
Easlea Edward, *Chapel farm*
Easlea Thomas, *Street farm*
Francis Thomas, *Shackerland Hall*
Mayhew George, *Tiptodds*
Moss Alex. || Parker Saml.
*Carrier,*Jas.Goodall,toBury,wed.&sat.

BARDWELL, a large well-built, pleasant and healthy village, on the east bank of the river Thet, 2½ miles N. of Ixworth, and 8 miles N.E. of Bury St. Edmund's, and S.S.E. of Thetford, has in its parish 826 inhabitants, 3,142 acres of land, and the small hamlet of *Bowbeck*, 1½ mile N. of the church It gave name to the ancient family of *Berdwell*, who were seated here as early as the Norman Conquest. Sir Wm. Berdwell, a celebrated soldier, whose effigy, in painted glass, still remains in the north-window of the church, died seised of the manor of Bardwell Hall, in 1434. It afterwards passed to the Reads, one of whom married the daughter and heiress of Wm. Crofts. The parish is in *three manors*, of which the following are the names and lords:—*Bardwell Hall*, Sir H. C. Blake; *Wicks Hall*, the Earl of Albemarle; and *Wyken Hall*, the Duke of Grafton; but part of the soil belongs to Thos. Hallifax, Esq., J. Jeffes, Esq., Messrs. R. Grimwood, J. Debenham, J. Cocksedge, P. Sharman, and a few smaller owners. The *Church*, (St. Peter) is a handsome structure, with a lofty tower containing six bells, and surmounted by a short spire. It has several elegant monuments of the Read and Crofts families, and. two of its windows are decorated with stained glass. It was repaired at the cost of £200, in 1842; and in the following year, an organ, which cost £70, was given by the Rev. Henry Adams,

B. D., who now enjoys the *rectory*, valued in K.B. at £7 17s. 1d., and in 1835 at £597. The patronage is in St. John's College, Oxford, and the tithes were commuted in 1839, for a yearly modus of £788. Here is a neat *Baptist Chapel*, built in 1824, and also a small *Wesleyan Chapel*.

The *Town Estate* is appropriated, under sundry ancient deeds, and a decree of the Court of Chancery made in 1639, to the service of the church and the good of the parish, "in such things as should be most needful." The estate is vested with 24 feoffees, and consists of the Guildhall, now in 12 tenements, occupied by the poor parishioners, rent free ; four cottages, let at small rents, and 66A. 1R. 2P. of land. The rents produce £142 16s. per annum, and are applied in repairing the church, the Guildhall, and the four cottages; in payment of the churchwarden's expenses, and the wages of the parish clerk and sexton, and an allowance of £25 a year for schooling poor children. The surplus is divided among the poor of the parish. The yearly sum of £5, paid by the Duke of Grafton, as interest of £100 derived from an exchange of part of the trust land in 1709, is applied with the rents of the town estate. In 1677, *Thos. Reade* left £50 for schooling poor children, and it was laid out with £10 given by Sir C. C. Reade, in the purchase of 4½A. of land in Stanton, let for £6, which, with the annuity of £25 from the town estate, is paid to two schoolmistresses, for teaching about 70 children to read, and the girls to sew. Another *Free-School*, for 24 poor children, is supported by Mrs. Adams. In the 12th of Charles II., *Robert Garrard* left £20 for the relief of 10 poor widows, and it was laid out in the purchase of 2A. 3R. 16P. of land, now let for £5 a year, which is distributed at Christmas, with an annuity of 3s. 4d. left by *John Green*, in 1595, out of Guttrage's Acre, in Ixworth Thorpe. In 1822, *John Jeffes* charged his estate at Bardwell, with the yearly payment of £3, to provide a dinner on Christmas-day for 10 poor men and 10 poor women. On the *enclosure* of Bardwell-Heath, an *Allotment* of 25A. 26P. was awarded to the poor parishioners, in lieu of their right of cutting fuel; and also an allotment of 2A. 3R. 25P. on Bardwell Green. These allotments are now let for £59 11s. per annum, which is distributed in coals, &c.

BARDWELL.

Adams Rev. Henry B. D., *Rectory*
Booty John, gent. Bardwell Green
Browning John, blacksmith
Clarke Mrs Margaret
Cocksedge John, bricklayer
Coe James, gamekeeper
Death James, butcher
Fuller William, vict. *Green Man*
Noble Charles, vict. *Six Bells.*

Academies.
Addison Susan
Browning Mary
Simpson Ann
   Beer Houses.
Firman Peter
Watson Thomas

Carpenters.
Benham Thomas,
   (& wheelwright)
Fuller William
Palfrey James
   Corn Millers.
Addison John

Beard   Robert,
   Steam Mill

FARMERS
* *are Owners.*

Addison George
Beard Robert
Bobby   John,
   Place farm
Cocksedge John
Collis Edward
Cooper Benjamin,
   Heath
Cooper William,
   Barningham Park
Death James

*Debenham Jas.,
   Littlemoor Hall
*Grimwood Robt.
Jewers Francis,
   Bardwell Hall
Pelham Ambrose
Simpson   John,
   Wyken Hall
Grocers & Drapers
Botwright Thos.
Pettit William

   Shoemakers.
Blishard Richard
Palfrey John
Plummer George
Sone Jonathan

BARNHAM, a pleasant village, 2½ miles S. of Thetford, and 9 miles N. of Bury St. Edmund's, has in its parish 412 souls, and 5,184 acres of land, including a large portion of sandy heath, forming an open sheep walk. The Duke of Grafton is owner of the soil and lord of the manor, which was formerly in two parishes, and had two

churches, but that dedicated to *St. Martin*, has been in ruins more than a century. The other *Church*, (St. Gregory) is a neat structure, with a tower and four bells. The consolidated *rectories* of St. Gregory and St. Martin, valued in K.B. at £7 11s. 10½d. and £8 5s. 5d., are united with that of Euston, in the patronage of the Duke of Grafton, and incumbency of the Rev. J. D. Hustler, M.A. The tithes of Barnham have been commuted for about £400, and those of Euston for £296 12s. 6d. per annum. Between these parishes and Thetford, is a row of 10 or 11 *tumuli*, supposed to mark the scene of the sanguinary engagement between king Edmund and the Danes, in 870. (See page 607.) The Duke of Grafton and the rector support a small *school*, for the education of poor children. The *Poor's Land* is held on leases for nearly a thousand years, granted in 1736, and now held, one rood by the rector for 10s., and 3A. by the Duke of Grafton for £2 per annum.

Baker John, corn miller
Banham Edward, parish clerk
Banham Mary, schoolmistress
Chadd Misses M. & M. || Cooper Mrs. E.
Davey Mr. Wm. *Barnham Cottage*
Davey Thomas, carpenter
Deeks Edw. vict. *Grafton Arms*
Debenham Edmund, shoemaker
Edwards John, beer seller

Grieve Rev. John, M. A. curate
Juler John, shopkeeper
Lusher Thomas, blacksmith
Wade John, gentleman
FARMERS.
Cooper William, *Hill House*
Edwards Frederick, *West farm*
Johnson William, North farm
Nunn John

BARNINGHAM, a scattered village and parish, 6 miles **W. of** Botesdale, and N. N. E. of Ixworth, has 508 inhabitants, and 1,555 acres of fertile land. John Thurston, Esq., is lord of the manor, but a great part of the soil belongs to R. Bevan, Esq., T. Thornhill, Esq., Caius College, Cambridge, and a few smaller owners. *Barningham Park* estate is mostly in Bardwell parish, adjoining Euston Park, and is the property of the Duke of Grafton, whose family purchased it of the *Sheltons*, formerly seated there. The *Church*, (St. Andrew) is a neat edifice with a tower and three bells. The benefice is a discharged *rectory*, valued in K. B. at £31 9s. 0½d., and united with Coney Weston, in the patronage and incumbency of the Rev. Geo. Hunt, M. A. The tithes of the two parishes were commuted in 1843, for a yearly modus of £967. Here is a *Wesleyan Chapel*, built in 1811. The *Town Estate* consists of several tenements, occupied by poor families, rent free; and 17A. 3R. 34P. of land let for £34 18s. per annum, which is applied in the service of the church and the payment of salaries to the parish clerk and constable, except 21s. a year which is distributed in bread among the poor, as the rent of about half an acre, purchased with £10 given by *Wm. Fuller*, in 1622. The *Poor's Allotment* consists of 20A. let for £21 a year, and was awarded to the poor in lieu of their right of cutting fuel on the open lands. The rents are distributed in coals.

Bloomfield Elias, shoemaker
Buckel Ann & Son, blacksmiths
Catton Charles Walton, machine maker, wheelwright, & blacksmith
Cook Robert, vict., *Swan Inn*
Fison Thomas, corn miller & merchant, Steam mill

Frost John, bricklayer
Frost Mary, beer seller
Hunt Rev. George, M.A., *Rectory*
Keen Hannah, schoolmistress
Nickerson James, butcher & shopkpr
Ruddock Edward, stone mason
Stimson Robert, beer seller

Sturgeon James, gamekeeper
Tydeman Martin, shoemaker
Wells Rev. Wm., M.A., curate
Whitehead Philip, manager
Wiseman George, gentleman

FARMERS.

Bishop Joseph
Downing George
Fison Thomas
Mullenger John
Sare Robert

Wright Dd. *Hall*

Grocers & Drapers.
Bishop Joseph(& tailor)
Tydeman Zebdh.

CONEY-WESTON, a village, 6 miles N.N.E. of Ixworth, and 5 miles W.N.W. of Botesdale, and S. by W. of East Harling, has in its parish 244 souls, and 1,321a. 1r. 1p. of land. The *Hall*, a neat mansion in a pleasant park, near a small rivulet, is the seat of Edward Bridgman, Esq., lord of the manor, and owner of all the parish, except a farm of 600a. belonging to T. Thornhill, Esq. The manor formerly belonged to Bury Abbey. The *Church*, (St. Mary) is a small thatched structure, and the rectory, valued in K.B. at £13 0s. 4d., is consolidated with Barningham. The tithes here were commuted in 1843, for a yearly modus of £433 19s. The *Town Estate* comprises two cottages occupied by paupers, and 8a. of land let for £10 12s. a year, and partly lying in Barningham parish. The rent is applied in the reparation of the church, and when any surplus remains, it is added to the poor rates. A benefaction of £10, given by R. *Firmage*, in 1611, for the poor of this parish, was laid out in the purchase of land at Rattlesden, now let for £1 10s. 6d. per annum. The poor parishioners have also 10a. of *fen-land*, awarded to them, at an enclosure about 70 years ago, and now let for £5 a year, subject to the right of the poor to enter and cut turf for fuel. DIRECTORY— Edward Bridgman, Esq., *Coney-Weston Hall;* David Bloomfield, *shopkeeper;* Fras. Bloomfield, *shoemaker;* Robt. Calver, farmer, *Heath;* Wm. Wiseman, *Street farm;* and Rev. Garrod Wade, *Lodge.*

CULFORD, a small scattered village, on a pleasant acclivity, on the north side of the vale of the Lark, 4 miles N.N.W. of Bury St. Edmund's, has in its parish 352 souls, and about 2,500 acres of land, including a great portion of the large open *Heath*, extending more than four miles northward. It was formerly the lordship of Bury Abbey, by gift of Thurketel Tyreing. The Rev. Edward Richard Benyon, M.A., of *Culford Hall*, is lord of the manor, and owns and occupies the chief part of the soil. The *Hall* is a large and handsome mansion, in a beautiful park of 500 acres, on the west side of the village, extending to the river Lark, and having a fine sheet of water, and extensive gardens. It was built in 1591, by *Sir Nicholas Bacon*, the first baronet of England, eldest son of the lord-keeper, and half brother of the lord-chancellor; and was given by him with an estate of £1,000 per annum. to his seventh son, Nathaniel, who married Jane Meautys, widow of Sir Wm. Cornwallis, to whose family the estate afterwards passed. Culford Hall was the principal seat of the late *Marquis Cornwallis*, who sold nearly all his estates in this county, before his death in 1823. (See page 325.) The Rev. E. R. Benyon owns above 10,680 acres in this and the parishes of Ingham, West Stow, Wordwell, and Timworth, most of which formed part of the estates of the Cornwallis family. *Culford Church*, (St. Mary) is a small neat structure, which was built by Sir Stephen Fox, whose daughter was wife of the third Lord Cornwallis. It contains a handsome monument and bust of Sir Nathaniel Bacon, with a long in-

scription in memory of his wife, giving her a high character as having saved from ruin, two ancient families, into which she had married. The benefice is a *discharged rectory*, valued in K.B. at £8, and united with Ingham and Timworth, in the patronage and incumbency of the Rev. E. R. Benyon, M.A., who erected a small *chapel-of-ease* in 1841, on the Heath, in the northern part of the parish. The value of the joint benefices was estimated at £549 per annum, in 1835, but as the rector is lord of the manors, and owner of nearly all the three parishes, the tithes are compounded in the rent.

Benyon Rev. Edward Richard, M.A., *Culford Hall*
Gifford George, farm steward
Isley James, carpenter
McDonald Hugh, gardener
Mitchell Joseph, farmer, *Heath*
Petch James, shoemaker
Solly Thomas, land agent

ELMSWELL, a large neat village, pleasantly situated nearly 4 miles N. W. of Stowmarket, and 8 miles E. of Bury St. Edmund's, has in its parish 671 souls, and 2,021 acres of land. The manor was given by King Edward, to Bury Abbey, and was one of the country seats of the abbot. It was granted in the 8th of James I., to Robert Gardiner, and afterwards passed to the Chapmans and Giffords. Miss Gifford is now lady of the manor, but a great part of the soil belongs to Lord George Seymour, Miss Smith, Rev. J. T. Lawton, and the Sparke, Long, Pilbrow, Sturgeon, Pattle, Bennett, Catchpole, and a few other families. The *Church* (St. John) stands on a commanding eminence, and has a very handsome tower. It contains an elegant mural monument in memory of *Sir Robt. Gardiner, Kt.*, who was chief justice of Ireland eighteen years, and died in 1619, aged 80. The figure of Sir Robert, nearly as large as life, and well executed, is in a recumbent posture, and his son is represented as kneeling at his feet. The *rectory*, valued in K. B. at £11 7s. 1d., has now a yearly modus of about £500, awarded in lieu of tithes, in 1843. The Rev. Joseph Thos. Lawton is patron and incumbent, and supports a school for the instruction of the poor. Here is a *Wesleyan Chapel*, built in 1818.

Sir Robert Gardiner, Kt., by deed, in the 12th of James Ist., reciting that he had erected an ALMSHOUSE, at Elmswell, containing five rooms, with a yard and garden containing half an acre; and that he had placed in each of four of the rooms one poor widow, and in the fifth, being larger than the rest, two poor widows; he thereby appointed that the almshouse should be used for the habitation of six poor aged widows, three from Elmswell, and three from Woolpit; and that the successive owners of the manor of Elmswell should keep the buildings in good repair; and he hereby appointed six persons as governors, who should, with the ministers of Elmswell and Woolpit, with the consent of the owner of the mansion house of Elmswell, have the nomination and power of displacing the almswomen, each of whom he endowed by the same deed, with an annuity of £3 10s., and a gown of blue cloth or stuff, yearly; and to provide for these allowances, he gave a yearly rent charge of £16, out of his lands in Thelnetham, and another of £10 out of the manors of Elmswell and Woolpit; the former of which he also charged with the delivery of one load of fire-wood, yearly, for each almswoman. By his will, he afterwards gave £100 to purchase lands for the almspeople, and £30 to purchase lands for the poor of the parish. With these legacies, about 14A. of land was purchased at Combs, now let for £15 a year; three-fourths of which are divided among the almswomen, and the remainder

among poor parishioners. The fire-wood is supplied out of the East wood, now belonging to Lord Thurlow. A weekly stipend of 2s. 6d. is now paid to each almswoman. The *Church Land*, about 26A., and the *Poor's Land*, about 21A., lying in Elmswell and Woolpit, were vested in trust with 12 feoffees, in 1706, and are now let for upwards of £84 per annum. The rent of the latter is distributed among the poor, in sums varying from 6s. to 20s.

ELMSWELL.

Baker George Randall, beer seller
Bridges Mrs. Mary ‖ Cooke Mrs. S.
Browne Mrs., *New Building*
Copping Mr. Wm. ‖ Rowe Mr. Jno.
Cuthbert John, wheelwright
Fakes Robert, cutler & grinder
Lawton Rev. Jph. Thomas, *Rectory*
Mathew Miss Rebecca, schoolmistress
Pattle Mr. Danl. Moss, quarter master
Robinson John, joiner, &c.
Smith William, vict. *Red Lion*
Spencer William, blacksmith
Warren Nathan, woodman

BAKERS.
Mulley George
Wright William

Boot & Shoe Mkrs.
Clarke David
Mulley John

Wright William
BRICKLAYERS.
Mulley William
Sayer William
Butchers.
Graham Ireland

Robinson Charles
FARMERS.
Beeton John
Bridges Denis
Bridges William, *Marsh*
Catchpole Thos., (*& maltster*)
Fisher Henry
Goldsmith Wm.
Graham Ireland
Howlett John
Jackson Isaac
Kitchen Hannah, *Elmswell Hall*
Lawton John
Lord Walter
Lord William
Sturgeon Joseph
Wright David

Wright Reubin
Wright Robert
Gardeners & Nurserymen.
Fenton Edw.
Fenton Zach.
Welham Nunn
Grocers & Drapers.
Mulley John
Wright Robert, (& broker)
TAILORS.
Bull John, (and draper)
Mulley Reubin
Sayer Reubin

Carrier to Bury.
John Beeton, wednesday

EUSTON, a neat village, is pleasantly situated on the east bank of the southern Thet, near the confluence of that river with the Little Ouse, which separates it from Norfolk; 4 miles S.E. of Thetford, and 10 miles N. by E. of Bury St. Edmund's. Its parish contains 270 inhabitants, and 3,780 acres of land, including part of the farm of RYMER HOUSE, which is 4 miles S. of Thetford, and comprises 15 souls, and about 70 acres of *Extra parochial* land, and about 550 acres lying in five different parishes. Euston also comprises LITTLE FAKENHAM, which has a small hamlet on the banks of the Thet, 1½ mile S. of the Church, and was formerly a separate parish, but nearly the whole of it was enclosed in Euston Park, more than a century ago, and not a vestige of its Church (St. Andrew) was remaining in Kirby's time. The Duke of Grafton is lord of the manor, owner of the soil, and occupier of nearly all the parish. He resides generally at EUSTON HALL, a large mansion of red brick, delightfully situated a little south of the village, in the northern part of a beautiful *Park* of more than 1,400 acres, extending more than two miles along the east bank of the river Thet, richly clothed with wood, and stocked with about 700 head of deer. The mansion is surrounded by trees of uncommon growth, and near it the Thet is crossed by a neat wooden bridge, leading to the entrance Lodge on the western side of the river. The scenery around it combines the most delightful assemblage of picturesque objects, and is justly celebrated by Bloomfield, in his "Farmer's Boy." The gardens are extensive, and around them, "woods and groves in solemn grandeur rise." On an elevated situation, in the park, stands the *Temple*, an elegant structure built by the second Duke of Grafton, in 1746, in the Grecian style, and consisting

of an upper and lower apartment, commanding extensive prospects. This building was intended for a banquetting house, and was constructed from a design by the celebrated Kent. *Fakenham Wood*, in the southern part of the park, is one of the largest in the county, covering no less than 314 acres, and abounding in luxuriant timber. *Euston* was anciently the lordship of a family of its own name, from whom it descended to the *Pattishalls*, and from them to *Sir Henry Bennet*, who, for his adherence to the house of Stuart, was appointed secretary of state by Charles II., and created *Lord Arlington, Viscount Thetford*, and *Earl of Arlington.* He built Euston Hall, and left an only daughter, who carried his estates in marriage to *Henry Fitzroy*, one of the natural sons of Charles II., by the Duchess of Cleveland, who was created by his father *Earl of Euston, and Duke of Grafton*, in 1675, and died in 1690. He was succeeded by his son Charles, who died in 1757, and was succeeded by his grandson, Augustus Henry, the late duke, who died in 1811. The present *Most Noble George Henry Fitzroy*, K. G., *Duke of Grafton, Earl of Arlington, Earl of Euston, Viscount Thetford, Viscount Ipswich, Baron Arlington, and Baron Sudbury*, is son of the late duke, and was born in 1760, and married a daughter of the second Earl of Waldegrave. He is *Lord Lieutenant, Vice-Admiral*, and *Custos Rotulorum* of the county of Suffolk, and hereditary Ranger of Whittlebury Forest, in Northamptonshire, where he has another seat called Wakefield Lodge. His eldest son, the *Rt. Hon. Charles Fitzroy, Earl of Euston*, was born in 1791. *Euston Church* (St. Genevieve) stands in the park, near the hall, and is a neat structure with a tower and five bells. The *rectory*, valued in K.B. at £13 7s. 11d., has those of Fakenham Parva and Barnham consolidated with it, in the patronage of the Duke of Grafton, and incumbency of the Rev. James D. Hustler, M.A. The tithes of the two parishes have been commuted for a yearly modus of £696 12s. 6d. (see page 683.) The patron and incumbent support a *school* here for the instruction of poor children.

The Most Noble *Duke of Grafton*; the Right Hon. *Earl of Euston* ; and *Lord Charles Fitzroy, M. P.*, Euston Hall	Baker William, house steward
	Bell Francis, farmer
	Gayford Geo. farmer, *Rymer House*
	Pretty Richard, vict. *Fox*
Hustler Rev. Jas. D., M. A., *Rectory*	Wylie Jas. gardener, *Little Fakenham*
Cooper Geo. Kersey, Esq., land agent to the Duke of Grafton	Carr George, park-keeper
	Tweed James, stud-groom

FAKENHAM MAGNA, a small village in the valley near the south end of Euston Park, 5½ miles S. S. E. of Thetford, and 9 miles N. N. E. of Bury St. Edmund's, has in its parish 213 souls, and 2,155 acres of land, including an old wood of 314 acres. The Duke of Grafton is owner of the soil and lord of the manor, which was anciently held by Gundred de Warren, and afterwards passed to the Nevills, and from them to the Crown. Henry VI. granted "*Fakenham Aspes*" to Reginald de Weste, from whose family it passed to the Talmaches, Taylors, and Sparrows, and from the latter to the first Duke of Grafton. This parish furnished the scenes of several of the poems of *Robert Bloomfield*. In the village opposite the church is a cottage, in which the poet's mother was born. A moated eminence here is supposed to be the site of a mansion destroyed by fire, and

near the inner margin still exist several decayed trees, the remains of a circle of elms, which, according to the poet's tale of the *"Broken Crutch,"* once completely surrounded the mansion. The *Church* (St. Peter) is a small fabric with a tower and three bells. The benefice is a discharged rectory, valued in K. B. at £11 0s. 5d., and now having a yearly modus of £271 15s. 9d., awarded in lieu of tithes, in 1837. The Duke of Grafton is patron, and the Rev. Augustus Fitzroy, M.A., incumbent. They support a *National School*, built in 1827. DIRECTORY, — George Boggis, shoemaker; Peter Firman, pork butcher; Rev A. Fitzroy, M. A., *Rectory ;* Emma Nicholls, schoolmistress; Jacob Moss, thatcher; Samuel Kersey, farmer; and Thos. Kersey, farmer, *Fakenham Hall.*

HEPWORTH, a pleasant village nearly 5 miles N. E. by N. of Ixworth, and W. by S. of Botesdale, has in its parish 582 souls, and 1,640 acres of strong loamy land, lying in two manors, called *Reeve's Hall* and *North Hall.* Thos. Thornhill, Esq. is lord of the former, and the Rev. Thos. Methwold, of the latter; but part of the soil belongs to the Guildhall Feoffment of Bury St. Edmund's, and the Allen, Wright, Randall, and a few other families. Gilbert de Blund held both manors at the Domesday Survey. The *Church* (St. Peter) has a tower and five bells, and the benefice is a discharged rectory, valued in K. B. at £13 17s. 3½d., and in 1835 at £498. The patronage is in King's College, Cambridge; and the Rev. E. R. Payne is the incumbent. The Primitive Methodists have a small chapel here. The *Town Estate* has been long vested in trust, for the common use and profit of the parishioners, and consists of a house and 44A. of land, let for about £63 a year, of which £1 17s. is distributed in clothing, on account of *Asty's charity,* and the remainder is applied in the service of the church; but if any surplus remains it is added to the poor rates. About 17 acres are old enclosure, and the rest was allotted at the *enclosure* of the common and open lands, in 1817. A yearly rent charge of 20s., out of an estate here, now belonging to Mr. Nunn, was left by *Wm. Brundish,* for distribution in clothing. The following benefactions for the poor, viz :—£10 given by *Wm. Asty,* £14 by *Catherine Asty,* and £10 by *John Reeve,* were laid out in 1711, in the purchase of a house and half an acre of garden ground, which are occupied, rent-free, by poor families. The *Poor's Allotment,* 14A. 0R. 23P., was awarded to the poor parishioners, at the enclosure, in lieu of their right of cutting fuel on the commons. It is let for about £34 a year, and the rent is distributed in coals, &c.

Bishop Wm. maltster & corn mert.
Borrows Mary, shopkeeper
Clarke Wm. vict. *Duke of Marlbro'*
Cotton Peter, beer housekeeper
Good Thomas, wheelwright
Mullenger Henry, grocer, draper, and butcher
Payne Rev. Edward R. *Rectory*
Rainbird William, beer house
Seaman John, blacksmith

FARMERS.

Allen William || Bishop Samuel
Buckley William || Clears Robert
James Henry, *Reeve's Hall*
Long George || Olden Thomas
Nunn John ; Thomas; & Mrs. P.
Wright, David || Walton James

HINDERCLAY, a scattered village, 2½ miles W. by N. of Botesdale, and 8 miles N.E. of Ixworth, has in its parish 387 souls, and about 1,400 acres of land ; formerly the lordship and demesne of the

Abbot of Bury St. Edmund's, by gift of Earl Ulfketel. It afterwards passed to the Bacons and Holts. George St. Vincent Wilson, Esq. is now lord of the manor, but a great part of the soil belongs to C. Heigham, Esq., T. Thornhill, Esq., and the Lock, Knott, Mark, Gobbett, Woolsey, and other families. The *Church* (St. Mary) is a neat structure with a tower and six bells. It was thatched till 1842, when it was covered with blue slate. The living is a discharged rectory, valued in K.B. at £9 19s. 4½d., and in 1835 at £408. The tithes were commuted in 1843, for a yearly rent of about £400. Geo.St.VincentWilson, Esq., is patron, and the Rev.Thos.Wilson, incumbent. The *Wesleyans* have a small chapel here. *Mr. Thos. Taylor*, of this parish, is now (1843) a hundred and one years of age, and enjoys all his faculties. The *Town Estate*, nearly 8A., is let for about £20 a year, and the rent is applied in the service of the Church. A small school for poor children is supported by the rector.

Crack Joseph, tailor
Doe Thomas, carpenter
Dover Mr. John ‖ Taylor Thomas
Flowerdew John Symonds,land agent, Hinderclay Hall
Fortis George, parish clerk
Gardener Alfred, bricklayer
Lock Joseph, corn miller
Mark Henry, vict., *Six Bells*
Martin George, carpenter
Wilson Rev. Thomas, *Rectory*

FARMERS.
Flowerdew J. S.
Gobbett William
Kerridge Abm.
Kerridge Charles
Kerridge Samuel
King Cphr.
Knott John
Lock Joseph
Mudd Thomas
Robinson T. jun.

Robinson T. sen.
Wesby Mrs
Wilson Rudd
Woolsey George

Shoemakers.
Cracknell John
Fox William
Gobbett William
Kerridge Edward
Robinson Samuel

HONINGTON, a neat village, pleasantly situated in the vale of a small river, nearly 3 miles N.W. of Ixworth, and 7 miles N.N.E. of Bury St. Edmund's, has in its parish 273 souls, and 1,203A. 3R. 3P. of land. The Duke of Grafton is lord of the manor, but part of the soil belongs to Col. Rushbrooke, Dr. Probart, Mr. Edw. Mothersole, and a few smaller owners. ROBERT BLOOMFIELD, one of the simplest and most captivating of our pastoral poets, was born here in 1766. His father was a tailor, but died before he was a year old. His mother kept a small school here, and married a second husband, but being poor, and having a large family, she sent Robert to his eldest brother, a journeyman shoemaker, in London, where he learnt and followed the same trade; and during his leisure hours, found time to cultivate his mind, and in his garret, among six or seven other workmen, he composed the *Farmer's Boy*, after his return from a visit to his native village, in 1786, previous to which he had written several short poems, which had obtained places in the London Magazine. He afterwards published his "*Wild Flowers*," a work containing a collection of poetical tales. His last production was "Hazlewood Hall," a village drama. He was patronized by the Duke of Grafton, who bestowed on him a small annuity, and made him an undersealer in the sealing office. This situation he was forced to resign on account of ill-health. He then worked again as a shoemaker, but in the latter part of his life, he entered into the book trade, and became a bankrupt. Before his death, in 1823, he was reduced to such a state of nervous irritability, that fears were entertained of his becoming insane. During the harvest of 1782, the village of Honington suffered

severely by an accidental fire, which destroyed the parsonage and five or six other houses. The cottage in which Bloomfield's mother lived, was in the line of the flames, but was preserved by the exertions of the neighbours, and has since been improved into a neat and comfortable dwelling. The *Church* (All Saints) is a small thatched structure with a tower and three bells. The benefice is a discharged rectory, valued in K.B. at £7 13s. 4d., and now having a yearly modus of £333, awarded in 1839, in lieu of tithes. The patronage is in the Crown, and the Rev. W. R Mahon, is the incumbent. The poor parishioners have 48A. 2R. of land, let for £63 18s., for distributions of wood, coals, and bread, viz:—7A. 2R., in *Quake-Fen*, given at an early period, by an unknown donor; 16A. at Ixworth, given by John, Bishop of Lincoln, in 1633; and 25A. allotted to the poor at the enclosure, in 1799, in lieu of their right of cutting furze on the common.

Balaam John, shoemaker
Barrow Rev. G. S., incbt. of Sapiston
Crosby Charles, baker
Elmer William, blacksmith
Goodchild Philemon, corn miller
Major William, wheelwright

Pawley William, shoemaker
Woollard Ann, vict. *Fox*

FARMERS.
Hayward Thomas
Mothersole Edm.
Roper Henry

Rose Charles
Grocers & Drapers.
Hailstone Richd.
Sparrow Edmund

HOPTON, a large, pleasant and well-built village, in the vale of the Little Ouse, 5 miles W.N.W. of Botesdale, and 8 miles N.N.E. of Ixworth, has in its parish 623 inhabitants, and 1,321A. 3R. 22P. of fertile land. Thos. Thornhill, Esq., is lord of the manor, formerly held by Bury Abbey; but part of the soil belongs to J. Goodrich, Esq., and several smaller owners. The *Church* (All Saints) is a neat structure with a tower and six bells. The living is a discharged rectory, valued in K.B. at £13 5s., and in 1835 at £284. The patronage is in the Crown, and the Rev. Henry Dawson is the incumbent. The *Wesleyans* have a commodious chapel here, built in 1836.

Beart Mrs. Esther
Brooke Robert, miller and baker
Button Mrs. Isabella, corn and seed merchant, and maltster
Calver George, clock & watch maker
Clarke Henry, land agent, appraiser, agent to the Suffolk fire office, &c.
Cooper John, blacksmith
Dawson Rev. Henry, *Rectory*
Eacock Robt., veterinary surgeon
Fowell Fredk. solicitor, and agent to the Norwich Union fire office
Good James, wheelwright
Goodrich John, Esq.
Jaques Stephen, gardener
Meadows Ephraim, cooper
Morgan Charles, surgeon
Milston John, machine maker
Norton George, thatcher
Read Henry, parish clerk
Reed John, cook and confectioner
Rye Sarah, toy dealer

Taylor Mr. Charles
Walton James, plumber and glazier
Wilson Charles, schoolmaster
Wood John, gentleman
Woollard George, butcher
   Inns and Taverns.
Chequers, John Pawley, (& portrait painter)
Greyhound, William Olley
Vine, Charlotte Boggis

Boot & Shoe Mkrs.
Bennett James
Farr John
Goodchild Robert
Inman Charles
Partins Leonard
Walker William
   Bricklayers.
Cox Thomas
Lock John
Lock Joseph
Ruddock John

Carpenters, &c.
Brooke Joseph (& builder)
Stevens James
Thurlow Clemt.
Collar & Harness Makers.
Griss John
Tricker William
   FARMERS.
Beales John
Bunn Jno. Phillips

Button Isabella	Scott Wm. (and	*Tailors.*	CARRIERS.
Muston James	British winedlr.)	Abbott George	Jas. Fisk, to *Nor-*
Robinson Thos.		Brooke Charles	*wich*, Mon. and
Taylor William	*Shopkeepers*	Shrimpton Stpn.	Thurs.; and to
Woollard George	Carley Ann	(& auctioneer)	*Bury* Wed.&Sat.
Grocers & Drapers	Peach Wm. (and	Stevens Richard	Charles Brock, to
Deeks George	baker)		*Diss*, Friday

HUNSTON, a small village nearly 3 miles S. E. of Ixworth, and 8 miles E. N. E. of Bury St. Edmund's, and N. W. of Stowmarket, has in its parish 162 souls, and 1,120 acres of fertile land, of which about 150A. belong to Mr. Spenceley Ellis, and the remainder, with the manor, is the property of John Henry Heigham, Esq., of *Hunston Hall*, who, for his services as chairman of the Board of Guardians of Stow Union, had several valuable pieces of plate presented to him in 1843, as noticed at page 266. The Hall is a commodious old mansion, with tasteful pleasure grounds. The manor and rectory were appropriated to Ixworth Priory, and were granted in the 30th of Henry VIII., to Rd. Codington and his wife Elizabeth. J. H. Heigham, Esq., is now impropriator of the rectory, and patron of the *Church*, (St. Michael) which is a perpetual curacy, valued in 1835 at £55, and now enjoyed by the Rev. Henry Ray. In 1723, *Mary Page* gave 10A. of land, called Denby's, in trust, to employ the rents yearly as follows, viz:—£2 to the minister of Hunston, for catechising the children and youth of the parish; £2 for schooling three poor children; 11s. 10d. towards finding them clothes and books; and 10s. to be distributed among poor parishioners. She also directed that each child, on leaving school, should be presented with a copy of the Whole Duty of Man. At the *enclosure*, 2R. 31P. was allotted to this charity land, and the whole is now let for about £10 a year, of which £3 15s. is paid to a schoolmistress for teaching six children. DIRECTORY—John Henry Heigham, Esq., *Hunston Hall;* Spenceley Ellis, *land owner & farmer;* Robt. Avey, gamekeeper; Robert Clark, shoemaker; Amy Fuller, cowkeeper; and Samuel Parker, *farmer.*

INGHAM, a pleasant village on the Thetford road, 4 miles N. of Bury St. Edmund's, has in its parish 208 souls, and 1,808A. 3R. 27P. of land, nearly all the property and manor of the Rev. Edward Richd. Benyon, M.A., of Culford Hall, who is also patron and incumbent of the *Church*, (St. Bartholomew) which is a *rectory*, valued in K.B. at £12 16s. 0½d., and in 1835 at £549, with those of Culford and Timworth annexed to it. (See pages 317 and 684.) Ingham was anciently held by a family of its own name, and was granted in the 31st of Henry VIII., to Sir Nicholas Bacon. It was sold, with other estates in this neighbourhood, by the last Marquis Cornwallis. The *Poor's Land*, given at an early period, by unknown donors, consists of 9A., let for £5 8s. per annum, which is distributed among the poor parishioners, together with the dividends of £100 South Sea Annuities, given by John Booty, in 1771. DIRECTORY—Chas. Barfield, tailor and shopkeeper; John Wm. Cooper, farmer and land agent, *Neville House;* Jas. Cotterell, vict., *Griffin;* George Foreman, shopkeeper; John Goldsmith, shoemaker; Rev. Abm. Peat, *curate;* John Worlledge, Esq., *(banker, &c. at Bury.)*

IXWORTH is a small, but neat and well-built town, which has been much improved during the present century, by the rebuilding of many of the old houses, and is pleasantly situated in the vale of the small river Thet, on the Norwich road, 6½ miles N.E. of Bury St. Edmund's; 11 miles N.W. of Stowmarket; 9 miles W.S.W. of Botesdale; and 10 miles S.S.E. of Thetford. It had a *market* on Friday, which has long been obsolete, as also have its two fairs, formerly held on May-day and Oct 18th. It has, however, a sort of *pleasure fair* on Whitmonday, and *petty sessions* weekly. It consists chiefly of one long street, and encreased its population from 827 souls, in 1801, to 1,064 in 1841. Its parish comprises 2,212A. 2R. 7P. of fertile land, of which about 200 acres belong to James Matthews, Esq., and the greater part of the remainder is the property of Richd. Norton Cartwright, Esq., the lord of the manor, who resides at IXWORTH ABBEY, a neat mansion with extensive gardens and pleasure grounds, built by the Norton family, on the site of a PRIORY founded by Gilbert-de-Blund or Blount, about the year 1100, for canons regular of the Augustine order. This Priory, dedicated to the Virgin Mary, stood on a gentle acclivity near the church and the river, and received many benefactions, being valued, at its suppression, at £280 9s. 5d., according to Speed; but Dugdale says only at £168 19s. 7d. It was granted, with the manor, by Henry VIII., to Richd. Codington and his wife Elizabeth, in exchange for the manor of Nonesuch, in Surrey, as appears by their monument in the church. It afterwards passed to the family of Fiennes, and from them to the Nortons, from whom it descended to the present proprietor. Roman coins and pottery have often been found at Ixworth; and a few years ago, the remains of a *Roman Villa* were discovered about half a mile S.E. of the High-street. Mr. J. Warren has a small collection of coins and antiquities, most of which were found in the town and neighbourhood. The *Church* (St. Mary) is a neat structure, with several handsome monuments, a tower, and six bells. R. N. Cartwright, Esq., is impropriator, and also patron of the perpetual curacy, valued in 1835 at £101, and enjoyed by the Rev. Edward Cornish Wells, M.A., who has a commodious Parsonage House, built in 1839. Here is a *Wesleyan Chapel*, built in 1831; and a *Baptist Chapel*, formed out of a barn some years ago.

About 1A. 2R. of land, in Pakenham, has belonged to Ixworth church from a very early period, and is now let for £1 5s. a year. A Close of 7A., let for £6 a year, was awarded at the *enclosure* of Ixworth, in the 43rd of George III., in lieu of other lands belonging to the church and poor; to the intent that one half of the rent should be applied to the use of the church, and the other half to the use of the poor, in respect of the benefactions of Widow Danby and Thos. and Benj. Kettleborough. A legacy of £10, left to the poor, by *Wm. Firmage*, in 1599, was laid out in the purchase of 1A. 2R. 32P. of land in Rattlesden, now let for £1 5s. a year. Benefactions to the poor, of £50, given by *Sir Robert Gardiner*, and £20 given by *Ann and Wm. Webb*, were vested in the purchase of a yearly rent charge of £4 10s. out of 9A. of land, called Mansfield Closes, now belonging to the Boldero family. The *Groat Money*, which is of unknown origin, consists of a yearly rent charge of 20s., paid out of land at *Foulslough*, in Ixworth, and distributed in groats among the poor, on Michaelmas day. The *manor of Ixworth* has, from an early period, been charged with the yearly distri-

bution among the poor of £5 in money, and £9 worth of wood for firing. In 1789, *Wm. Varey, Esq.,* left £1,000 three per cent. Consols, in trust, to pay one half of the yearly dividends to a man and woman, for keeping Sunday Schools, and to distribute the remainder among such of the working poor of the parish, as do not receive parochial relief. The poor parishioners have also £7 10s. yearly, from *Cooke's Charity,* (see Pakenham.) A *National School* was built here in 1840, and is attended by about 80 scholars. There are in the town several *Friendly Societies,* and a *Lodge of Odd Fellows,* belonging to the Manchester Union.

IXWORTH DIRECTORY.

Post Office, at Mr. Joseph Warren's, High street. Letters received and despatched at 6 morning and 8 evening. The Box closes at 7 evng.

Bantick Wolfran, hawker
Boggis William, parish clerk
Booty John, jun., wine & spirit merchant
Brittain Mary, cowkeeper
Cartwright Richard Norton, Esq., *Ixworth Abbey*
Caudwell Mrs. Elizabeth
Clark Jas. registrar & relieving officer
Cocksedge William, gamekeeper
Cooper Henry Ralph, surgeon
Doe William, carpenter
Eaton Mrs. Ann || Clayton Mrs. A.
Fermor Mrs. Catherine
George Henry Thomas, excise officer
Goldsmith James, hawker
Goldsmith John, gentleman
Howes James, carpenter
Keeble Mrs. L. || Kitchen Mrs. H.
Lanchester Mrs. Margaret
Leman Mrs. Mary || Wheeler Mrs. C.
Lowe John, gentleman, *Cross House*
Mahon Rev. W. R. rector of Honington
Matthews James, Esq.
Nixon John, inspector of weights & measures
Nixon William, fruiterer & thatcher
Nunn Sturley, solr. & superintendent registrar of *Thingoe Union*
Rose Peter, *butler* at the Abbey
Sams William Henry, solicitor
Smith Rev. Charles, (Baptist)
Smith Mr. George, & Mrs. Mary
Spurling William, gardener, Abbey
Sutton Stephen, policeman
Warren Joseph, clock & watch maker, & dealer in old coins and other antiquities
Wells Rev. Edw. Cornish, M.A., incbt. of Ixworth, *Parsonage*

Academies.
Cooke Misses
Minns Maria
Attorneys.
Nunn & Sams, (agents to the Sun fire office)
Auctioneer.
Gifford Edw. (& general agent)
Bakers, &c.
Craske Robert
Jarman John
Richer Mary Ann
Turner Thomas
Blacksmiths.
Bailey William
Smith George
Boot & Shoemakers.
Harrald Henry
Haunton Thomas
Hull Charles
Rye Zachariah
Wells Lewis
Bricklayers, &c.
Howe Frederick
Sharpe Francis
Sharpe Henry
Sutton Stephen
Butchers.
Bantock John
Reeve Samuel
Woollard Joseph
Cabinet Makers &c.
Battley Frederick
Candler William
Chemist & Druggist
Harvey Chas. (& British wine dlr.)
Coopers.
Daynes Thos. (& basket maker)
Meadows William
Corn Miller.
Potter John
FARMERS.
Balls Jerh. *Heath*

Booty John, sen.
Cockerill Charles
Dover Mary
Easlea John
Goldsmith Thos., *Dairy Farm*
Gooch James
Harrison Joseph, *Stack-ings*
King John, *Heath*
Parr Charles
Pickering Thos.
Reeve Joseph
Sharpe Henry
Gardeners.
Goddard Charles
Sharpe Charles
Grocers & Drapers.
Botwright James
Goldsmith Frances Mary
Wiseman James
Hair Dressers.
Brows William
Durrant James

INNS.
Greyhound, John Nixon
Pickerel, Edward Brown
Woolpack, Henry Clemence
Beer Houses.
Bantock Charles
Caudwell Edward
Howard Thos. M.
Ironmonger.
Howard John
Joiner.
Read John, builder & surveyor
Milliners, &c.
Bailey Eliza
Pitts Hannah
Rowley Sophia
Rush Elizabeth

Savage Eliza
Sutton Susan
Wright Susan
Painters,Plumbers
& Glaziers.
Boyce William
Miller Hannah
Saddler, &c.
Dring John
Straw Hat Makers
Goldsmith Susan
Sutton Susan

SURGEONS.
Barsham&Cooper
Green William
Stedman Foster
TAILORS, &c.
Brook Benjamin
Cracknell Charles
Rush Henry

Wheelwright.
Howard John

COACHES.

To *London,* &c., 20 min. before 7 and a ¼ before 11 morng.; to *Bury,* ¼ past 1 aftn.; to *Diss,* &c., ¼ past 3 aftn.; and to Norwich, 4 aftn. daily; and to *Yarmouth,* Mon. Wed. & Fri. at 2 aftn.,and Tues. Thu. & Sat. at

a ¼ past 10 morng.; to *Bury,* Mon. W. & Fri. 2 aftn.; to *Cambridge,* Tues. Thu. & Sat. 2 aftn.; and to *Botesdale,* every Wed. 6 evening. *Mail Cart,* to Bury, 8 evening; and to Scole, 6 morning, daily.

CARRIERS.

John Rowley, to *Ipswich,* Mon. & Thurs., and to Thetford, Wed. & Sat. 7 morng. Also Lambert, from the Greyhound, to *Ipswich,* Thursday, 1 afternoon. *Fisk's Van,* to Norwich, Wed. & Sat. 12 night; and to *Bury,* Wed. 10 morng., and Sat. 3 afternoon, from the Greyhound. *Sykes' Van,* to London, Bury, &c., from the Greyhound, Tues.& Thurs. 7 morng.; and to *Norwich,* 3 aftn.

KNETTISHALL parish, in the vale of the Little Ouse, 4½ miles S. by W. of East Harling, and 8 miles N.N.E. of Ixworth, has only 79 souls, and 1,025 acres of land, including 320 acres of open heath, and 85A. of plantations. Thomas Thornhill, Esq., owns nearly all the soil, and is lord of the manor, and patron of the *Church,* (All Saints) which is an ancient thatched fabric, with a tower and three bells. The living is a discharged rectory, valued in K.B. at £6 7s. 11d., and now enjoyed by the Rev. Wm. Darby, M.A., who has 27A. 6P. of glebe, and a yearly modus of £120, awarded in lieu of tithes, in 1840. Here is a *brick yard,* under the management of John Bolling-broke. Mr. George Matthew occupies *Knettishall Hall,* and farms nearly all the parish, which anciently belonged to the Harlings, and afterwards to the Lovel and Cavendish families.

LANGHAM, a pleasant village, 3 miles E. of Ixworth, has in its parish 293 souls, and 1,270A. of fertile land. Joseph Wilson, Esq., owns most of the soil, and is lord of the manor, which was anciently held by the Cricketotes, and lately by the *Blakes,* one of whom was created a *baronet,* in 1772, and resided at *Langham Hall,* a neat mansion, in a small park, now unoccupied. The present baronet resides with his son, at Great Barton Vicarage. The *Church* (St. Mary) is a *rectory,* valued in K.B. at £5 16s. 10½d., and now having a yearly modus of £280, awarded in 1842, in lieu of tithes. The patronage is in the Crown, and the Rev. Edward Thurlow is the incumbent. Mr. Wilson supports a school here for poor children. In 1630, *John Jolly* left £100 to be laid out in lands, the rents and profits thereof to be distributed among the poor of Langham, on Christmas-day and Midsummer-day. The legacy was laid out in the purchase of a house, occupied rent free, by poor persons, and 12A. 3R. 13P. of land, let for £11 12s. a year, and partly intermixed with land belonging to Mr. Booty. The *Church Lands,* &c., comprise a house, let for £2, and about 8A. of land, let for £11 15s. 6d. a year, and partly intermixed with land belonging to Sir J. Blake and other proprietors.

Directory—George Morley, *gardener ;* Jas. Rosier, *blacksmith ;* Robt. Sadler, *shopkeeper;* Charlotte Tuck, *schoolmistress ;* and Henry Barfield, John Burrell, *Hall ;* Henry Golding, *(Hillwater,)* and James Larter, *farmers.*

LIVERMERE-PARVA parish, 4 miles W. by N. of Ixworth, and 5½ miles N. by E. of Bury St. Edmund's, contains 172 souls, one farm house, 24 cottages, and 1,433 acres of land, a large portion of which is in LIVERMERE PARK, which comprises about 550 acres, and is partly in Great Livermere. The handsome mansion in this park is a sporting seat of Sir Wm. F. F. Middleton, Bart., the lord of the manor, and owner of both parishes. It was built by Mr. Coke, who left it to the second Duke of Grafton, who resided here several years. In the latter part of last century, it was the property of Baptist Lee, Esq., who obtained a prize of £30,000 in the state lottery, and greatly improved the mansion and park, as also did his son, the late Nathaniel Lee Acton, Esq. The *Church* (St. Peter) is a small neat structure in the park. The benefice is a rectory, valued in K.B. at £6 2s. 11d., and consolidated with that of Great Livermere, as already noticed at page 310. The sum of £10, left to the poor of Little Livermere, by *Wm. Firmage,* in 1559, was laid out in 1622, in the purchase of 1A. 2R. 36P. of land at Chevington, now let for 20s. a year, which is distributed in clothing. The principal inhabitants are Thos. Meadows Rodwell, *farmer ;* and John Cutting, *park-keeper.*

MARKET-WESTON, a pleasant village, near the source of the Little Ouse, 7 miles N.E. by N. of Ixworth, and 4½ miles W.N.W. of Botesdale, has in its parish 330 souls, and 1,090 acres of land. It has a pleasure fair on Sept. 28th, but no market. It was anciently the lordship of Hugh Hovell, and afterwards descended to the Bokenhams, and from them to the Tyrrels. John Thurston, Esq., is now lord of the manor, and owner of nearly all the parish. He occupies a neat mansion here called the *Lodge,* but lets the *Hall* to John Josselyn, Esq. The *Church* (St. Mary) has a tower and five bells, and the benefice is a discharged rectory, valued in K. B. at £8 19s. 7d., and now having a yearly modus of £330, awarded in 1840, in lieu of tithes. The Rev. Hy. Thos. Wilkinson is the incumbent. The *Town Estate* consists of the Town House and garden, occupied rent-free, by poor families, and 12A. 2R. of land let for about £15 a year, which is applied in the service of the church, according to ancient usage. The poor parishioners have half an acre of land in Hopton, let for 10s. a year ; and 26A. 22P. of *fen-land,* and 16A. of *furze-land,* allotted to them at the *enclosure* in 1816, for their use to cut turf and furze thereon. They have also a yearly rent charge of 6s. 8d., called *Asty's Dole,* paid out of land belonging to J. Thurston, Esq.

Baker Henry, vict., *Mill Inn*
Bailey Humphrey, gardener
Cooper Joseph, shoemaker
Crack Henry, shoemaker
Day George, blacksmith & shopkpr.
Flotman Richard, corn miller
Good Thomas, wheelwright
Golson James, farmer
Grimsey John & Robert, farmers
Josselyn John, Esq., *Hall*
Mellersh William, land agent
Pake Abraham, blacksmith
Ringer William, gentleman
Smith Ellis, blacksmith
Thurston John, Esq. *Weston Lodge*
Wilkinson Rev. Henry Thos., *Rectory*

NORTON, a large and well built village, pleasantly situated on the eastern acclivity of a fertile valley, 3 miles S. S. E. of Ixworth, and 7 miles E. N .E. of Bury St. Edmund's, has in its parish 879 souls, 2,449A. 2R. 3P. of land, lying in the manors of *Norton Hall* and *Little Haugh*. R. Woodward, Esq. is lord of the former, and Rt. Braddock, Esq. of the latter; but a great part of the soil belongs to the Wilson, Long, Day, Hustler, Sparke, Cocksedge, Plummer, Casborne, Smith, and a few other families. Norton Hall is occupied by a farmer, and *Little Haugh Hall*, by Peter Huddleston, Esq. The latter was a seat of the Milesons, from whom it descended to Mileson Edgar, Esq., who sold it to Alderman Macro, of Bury, from whose family it passed to the Braddocks. Henry VIII. was induced by a credulous kind of avarice, to dig for gold in this parish, but was disappointed in his search. The *Church* (St. Andrew) is a neat structure with a tower and two bells. The *rectory*, valued in K. B. at £14 3s. 9d., and in 1835 at £458, has now a yearly modus of £611, awarded in 1839,in lieu of tithes. It is in the patronage of St.Peter's College, Cambridge, and incumbency of the Rev. Aldersey Dicken, D. D., who has a neat Rectory House. Here is a *Wesleyan*, and also a *Baptist Chapel;* the latter built in 1843, by Mr. S. Hustler, at the cost of £700, with a house for the minister. A *National School* was built here in 1839, and has about 60 scholars. At the Dog Inn is a Lodge of *Odd Fellows*, belonging to the Manchester Union. The *Poor's Estate* comprises a cottage, occupied rent-free, by poor widows; and 13A. 3R. 7P. of land, let for £26 a year, and allotted at the enclosure, in lieu of other land,which had been purchased with various benefactions, in trust, to pay 12s. to the minister, for a sermon on September 19th, and 1s. to the parish clerk, on the same day; and to distribute the remainder of the rents among the poor. In 1650, *John Fiske*, pursuant to the will of his father, settled 2½A. of land in Ixworth, in trust, that the rents thereof should be distributed in weekly doles of bread, among the poor of Norton. This land is now worth about £5 per annum. In 1773, *Wm. Stanniforth*, in fulfilment of the charitable intention of his father-in-law, the Rev. Cox Maers, D.D., gave £600 three per cent. Consols, in trust, to provide yearly, 12 poor men with coats, and 12 poor women with stuff gowns and petticoats. The dividends were not received from 1796 to 1820, and in the latter year, the arrears, and the original stock were laid out in the purchase of £724 8s. 8d. three per cent. Reduced Annuities.

Barsham Thomas, surgeon
Clarke Wm. gent. || Burt Mrs.
Cocksedge Thomas, jun., collar and harness maker
Cooper Rev. Joshua, (Baptist)
Dicken Rev. Aldersey, D.D., *Rectory*
Fuller Ann, schoolmistress
Huddleston Peter, Esq. *Little Haugh Hall*
Jolley John, cooper
Last Samuel, rake maker
Pizzy William, veterinary surgeon
Sealey Elijah, carpenter
Smith William, maltster & vict. *Dog*

Tuck James, baker

Beer Houses.
Gipps Thomas
Tuck Jonathan

Blacksmiths
Collings Charles
Downing Henry
Goold William
Morley Isaac

Boot & Shoe Makers
Drake Joseph
Faires Thomas
Pollard Samuel
Mothersole Wm.

Bricklayers.
Galland William
Stiff David

Corn Millers.
Jannings William
Page John Herbert

FARMERS.
Bantock Henry
Barrett Benjamin
Burt Arthur
Cocksedge Thos.
Cornish Robert

Craske Samuel	*Crowley Hall*	Stiff Robert	*Tailors.*
Day Henry	Miller William,	White Edward	Balls Jonathan
Finbow George	*Norton Hall*	*Grocers & Drapers.*	Craske——
Gipps John	Rice Frederick	Bowen John	*Wheelwrights.*
Golding Cardwell	Rust John Baines	Branch John Gil-	Goold William
Holmes Mark	Shipp Thomas (&	bert	Jolley Robert
Howlett John,	owner)	Galland Mary	Morley Isaac

RICKINGHALL INFERIOR, 8 miles N. E. of Ixworth, and 7 miles W. S. W. of Diss, is a large village, which forms a western suburb of the town of Botesdale, (see page 323,) and lies north of Rickinghall Superior. Its parish has 432 souls, and 1,966 acres of fertile land. It was anciently the lordship and demesne of Ulfketel, Earl of East Anglia, who gave it to the monks of Bury. It was granted by Henry VIII., to Sir Nicholas Bacon, whose family sold it to the Holts. G. St. Vincent Wilson, Esq., is now lord of the manor, owner of a great part of the soil, and patron of the *Church*, (St. Mary) which has a round tower and three bells. The benefice is a rectory, valued in K. B. at £16 5s. 2½d., and in 1835 at £850, with that of Rickinghall Superior annexed to it. The Rev. Thos. Peyton Slapp, of Old Buckenham, Norfolk, is the incumbent, and has now a yearly modus of £1,052, in lieu of the tithes of the two parishes, as noticed at page 343. There is a parsonage house in each parish, and the glebe comprises 47A. T. Thornhill, Esq., Messrs. J. & B. Smith, T. Norton, and several smaller owners, have estates here. An *allotment* of 9A. was awarded on an enclosure, in lieu of land, held from ancient time, for the general use of the parish, and of 1R. 12P. which had been devised by Joseph Barnes, in 1731, for the relief of the poor. The allotment is let for £25 8s. a year, of which 10s. is given to the poor, and the remainder is applied in repairing the church, or similar purposes. The poor have also 10s. a year as interest of £10 left by *John Brown*, in 1731, and £7 17s. 6d. yearly from 2A. 3R. 2P. of land allotted to this parish as its share of *Rookwood's charity*, (See page 344.)

Amys Mrs. Frances, *Cottage*
Boston Robert, tailor
Burroughs Rev. Thos., curate, *Rectory*
Daines John, plumber & glazier
Debenham Mary, grocer & draper
Dobson Elizabeth, confectioner
Golding Rev. Josiah, crt. of Wattisfield
Greengrass Wm. veterinary surgeon
King Joseph, shoemaker
Norman Mrs.
Patrick Thos. grocer & blacksmith
Phillips James, vict., Bell
Robinson Thomas, gentleman
Steggall John, bricklayer
Warren David, blacksmith

White Charles, relieving officer
Wiseman John, corn miller
   FARMERS. *(* are Owners.)*
Baker William, *Broom Hill*
Chaplin Jonas, *White House*
Eavis Jacob, *West street*
Flowerdew Richard, *West Hall*
Goldsmith George
Martin Nathaniel, *Hallwood Green*
*Norton Thomas, *Hill House*
*Smith James || Nunn John
   CARRIERS.
Jas. Nunn, to Bury, Wed. & Saturday
John Spalding, to Ipswich, Tues. &
  Fri. and to Hopton, Mon. & Thurs

RUSHFORD, a small village on the Norfolk side of the Little Ouse river, 4 miles E. S. E. of Thetford, has in its parish 172 inhabitants, and 2,100 acres of land, of which 34 souls, and about 1,000 acres of land, forming *Rushford Lodge estate*, are in Blackbourn Hundred, Suffolk, and all the rest is in the Guiltcross Hundred, Norfolk,

where the *Church* (St. John) is situated, and also SHADWELL LODGE, the elegant seat of *Sir Robt. Jacob Buxton, Bart.*, and his mother, *Lady Buxton.* All the parish belongs to Sir Robert, and he is impropriator of the tithes, and patron of the *curacy*, which was certified at £16, and was augmented with £200 of Queen Anne's Bounty, in 1793, and is now enjoyed by the Rev. Robt. Ward. The church was appropriated to a *College*, founded here by Sir Edward Gonoville, in 1342, for a master and six priests. The *farmers* are John Cooke, *College Farm*, Norfolk; and Robert Ringer, *Rushford Lodge*, Suffolk. The latter was the seat of T. Crookenden, Esq., who sold the estate some years ago, to the late Sir Robt. Buxton, who died in 1842.

SAPISTON, a small scattered village, in the vale of the southern Thet, 3 miles N. by W. of Ixworth, has in its parish 255 souls, and 1,155 acres of fertile land, all the property and manor of the Duke of Grafton. At the Domesday Survey, it was the lordship of Gilbert de Blund, who gave it to the priory which he founded at Ixworth. After the Dissolution, it was granted to Richard and Elizabeth Codington. *Robert Bloomfield*, the poet, commenced his career here as a farmer's boy. (See page 689.) The *Church* (St. Andrew) is an ancient thatched fabric. The Duke of Grafton is impropriator of the tithes, and patron of the perpetual curacy, which is valued at £78, and enjoyed by the Rev. G. S. Barrow. The Duke built a *National School* here, in 1841, and it is now attended by about 50 poor children.

Balam Jph. carrier to Bury, wed.&sat.
Crich Jeffery, vict. *George*
Jacob Edmund, corn miller
Major William, blacksmith
Mayes George, gamekeeper
Prigg Mary Ann, schoolmistress

FARMERS.

Crich Jeffery, (and *cattle dealer*)
Farrow John Ray, *Triangle farm*
Farrow John, *Grove farm*
Gates John, *Sapiston Grange*

STANTON-*All-Saints, and St. John the Baptist*, are two adjoining villages and united parishes, pleasantly situated on the Norwich road, 9 miles N.E. by E. of Bury St. Edmund's, and 3 miles N.E. of Ixworth, and containing 1,029 inhabitants, 3,254 acres of fertile land, the small hamlet of *Upthorpe*, 1½ mile S.E., and several scattered farm houses. Though there are still two churches, Stanton may be considered as one well built village, in which are several good Inns, retail shops, and corn mills. It has a fair for pleasure and pedlery on Whitmonday. Edward the Confessor gave the manor and advowson of All Saints to Bury Abbey, and they were granted in the 31st of Henry VIII., to Sir Thos. Jermyn, Kt. The two rectories were consolidated in 1457, and since the reign of Elizabeth, the two parishes have maintained their poor conjointly. R. E. Lofft, Esq. is now lord of the manor, and owns a great part of the soil, but Mrs. Vautier owns *Stanton Park*, now a large farm, half a mile S. of the village, and here are several smaller owners. *All Saints* and *St. John's Churches* are neat structures, and each has a tower and four bells. The consolidated rectories are discharged from the payment of first fruits and tenths, and rated in K.B., the former at £9 6s. 0½d., and the latter at £9 4s. 9½d. R. E. Lofft, Esq. is patron, and the Rev. George Bidwell is the incumbent, and has a commodious residence, and a yearly modus of £977 2s. 7d., awarded in 1839 The *Wesleyans*

have a chapel here, built in 1839. The *Church Land,* about 12A., let for £20 a year, is vested in trust, for repairing and maintaining the two churches. The *Town House,* purchased in 1779, is occupied by poor people, rent free, as also is a cottage and small piece of land, given to the parish, in 1813, by Phillis Clarke, in consideration of the relief afforded her from the poor rates. For a yearly distribution among the poor, *Catherine Tricker,* in 1605, left £20, and it was laid out in the purchase of an acre of land, now let for £2 per annum. The sum of £10 left to the poor, by *Wm. Firmage,* in 1611, was laid out in the purchase of 1A. 2R. 32P. of land, at Rattlesden, now let for £1 11s. a year. The *Poor's Allotment* comprises 54A. awarded at the enclosure of the commons, and now let for about £90 a year, which is distributed among poor parishioners, in coals.

Baker Thomas, parish clerk
Bidwell Rev. George, *Rectory*
Bowen John, gentleman
Clarke Susan, collar & harness mkr.
Coke William, vict. Rose & Crown
Greeu George, gardener
Howe Mr. Robt. || Jarman Mrs. Sar.
Miller John, maltster
Oxborrow Sheppard, farrier
Robinson Benj. vict. *Cock Inn*
Sturgeon Thomas, gamekeeper
Youngman Benj., vict. *George Inn.*

Beer Houses.
Brewington John
Davey Thomas
Sturgeon John
Academies
(**take Boarders.*)
*Howe Miss S.
*Kent Miss E.
*Raynham Thos.
Sturgeon Henry
Bakers.
Baker Geo. M.
Cutting Samuel
Davey Thomas
Blacksmiths.
Brewington John

Calver George
Hayward Henry
Boot & Shoe Mkrs.
Blishard Wm.
Johnson Wm.
Lucas William
Sare Jonathan
Bricklayers.
Fordham Robert
Millican Pettit
Millican Philip
Carpenters, &c.
Hailstone Henry
PooleyThomas (& lime burner)

Corn Millers.
Markham John
Rollinson Geo.
Trudgett Wm.
Wells Samuel
FARMERS.
(**are at Upthorpe*)
*Avey Thomas
Baker Thomas
*Bradley Francis
Bradley Robert
*Chapman Rt.
Cobb Charles
Downing Robert
Easlea Wm.,*Dale Farm*
Harrison Jonthn.
Howe John
Howe Robert
Marsh Thos.
Pooley Thos.
Ruse Mrs., *Hall*
Spalding Abhm.
Stebbing James
Taylor Daniel, *Wrens-Hall*

Taylor William, *Manor House.*
Woodard John, *Stanton Park*
GROCERS *and Drapers.*
Farrow John
Fisk Edmund *(& tailor.)*
Keeble Jonas
Kent Mary
Kinsey Henry, *(and tailor)*
Taylor Baker
SURGEONS.
Kent Jas. Hy.
Kent John
Wheelwrights.
Good David
Nickerson John
CARRIER.
David Beeton, to Bury,Wed.&Sat. *Post to Ixworth.*
Edm.Carman,at 6 morng. & evng

STOWLANGTOFT is a small neat village, in a pleasant valley, near the confluence of a small rivulet with the southern Thet, 2½ miles S.S.E. of Ixworth, and 6½ miles E.N.E. of Bury St. Edmund's. Its parish contains 163 souls, and 1,358A. 1R. 6P. of land, all the property and manor of Henry Wilson, Esq., who resides at the *Hall,* a large and handsome mansion, with neat pleasure grounds, anciently the seat of the Langtofts, and afterwards of the families of Peche and D'Ewes. One of the latter was Sir Simonds D'Ewes, a learned antiquary of the 17th century. The Hall was partly rebuilt in 1782, by Sir Walter Rawlinson, who inherited the estate from his father, Sir Thomas, who was Lord Mayor of London, in 1754, and purchased this parish in 1760, of the Norton family. The *Church* (St. George) is a neat structure with a tower and three bells, and stands within a

double trenched camp. It is said to have been built in 1370, by Robert Dacy, of Ashfield; and in a field about half a mile from it, a pot full of *Roman coins* of the lower empire, was found in 1764. In Red Castle farm, in the adjoining parish of Pakenham, a fine *tesselated pavement* was discovered about thirty years ago. The *rectory*, valued in K.B. at £8 7s. 8½d., has a good residence, 65A. 2R. 9P. of glebe, and a yearly modus of £243 17s. 6d., awarded in 1843, in lieu of tithes. H. Wilson, Esq. is patron, and the Rev. Samuel Rickards, M.A. is the incumbent. Here is an *Almshouse*, occupied by four poor widows, and about an acre of land, partly occupied as gardens, by the almswomen, and partly let for 21s. a year, which is carried to the poor rates, out of which the almshouse is repaired. The donor is unknown. A small *free school* is supported by Mr. Wilson. DIRECTORY—Henry Wilson, Esq., *Hall*; Rev. S. Rickards, M.A., *Rectory*; Chas. Dennis, farm bailiff; Thos. Green, farmer, *Bridge*; Chas. Thos. Mathew, farmer, *Street*; and Eliz. Tuck, shopkeeper and lime burner.

STOW, (WEST) a small scattered village and parish, in the vale of the river Lark, 5 miles N.W. by N. of Bury St. Edmund's, has in its parish 279 souls, and 3,050 acres of fertile land, including *Chimney Mills*, an extra-parochial place of 20 acres, having a large mill on the river, and a house with 6 inhabitants. The village adjoins the extensive park of Culford Hall, the seat of the Rev. E. R. Benyon, M.A., the lord of the manor and owner of all the parish. He has a great part of the parish in his own occupation, and is patron of the *Church*, (St. Mary) which is a discharged *rectory*, valued in K.B. at £9 17s. 3d., and in 1835 at £302, with that of Wordwell annexed to it, in the incumbency of the Rev. Thomas Hubbard. The manor passed to its present owner from the late Richd. Benyon De Beauvoir, Esq. WEST STOW HALL, now a farm house, has been much reduced in size. It formerly surrounded a quadrangular court, and was moated, and well adapted by its interior arrangement to baronial customs and festivities. It is supposed to have been built about the beginning of the 16th century, and it formerly contained a large collection of armour. Its enbattled pediments, diamond shaped tracery, and finial statues, are curious and unusual appendages in buildings of this order. The Crofts held the manor in the reign of Edward III., and it was afterwards held by the Abbots of Bury. After the Dissolution, it passed successively to the Kitsons, Bacons, Progers, and Fowkes; and was one of the estates sold by the late Marquis Cornwallis. The sum of £10 left to the poor parishioners, by *Wm. Firmage*, in 1599, was laid out in the purchase of 3A. 3R of land, at Rattlesden, now let for £3 a year, which is distributed at Christmas. The *Church Land* comprises one acre, in the In-field, worth only 5s. a year, and 2A. in Culpho Field, let for £1 10s., a year. DIRECTORY—Rev. Thos. Hubbard, *Rectory*; Wm. Day, corn miller, *Chimney Mills*; Wm. Bilham, farmer, *Hall*; Wm. Foulger, farm bailiff, *North Stow*; Geo. Fenner, blacksmith and beer seller; and Jas. Murrell, shoemaker.

THELNETHAM, a scattered village on the south side of the vale, and near the source of the Little Ouse river, 3 miles N.W. of Botesdale, and 5½ miles S. by W. of Kenninghall, has in its parish

561 souls, and 1,780 acres of strong loamy land. The manor of Thelnetham was anciently held by a family of its own name, and now belongs to John Thruston, Esq., but part of the soil is the property of Thos. Thornhill, Esq., Mrs. F. Mallows, and the Nunn, Button, and other families. Sir E. Kerrison is lord of the manor called Eye-Thelnetham. The *Church* (St. Nicholas) is a neat fabric with a tower and five bells. The living is a discharged rectory, valued in K.B. at £16 18s. 4d., and in 1835 at £508. The Rev. Samuel Colby, of Norfolk, is patron and incumbent, and the Rev. E. H. Sawbridge is the curate, and has purchased the next presentation. The *Town Estate*, 28A. 1R. 34P., was awarded on an enclosure in 1821, in lieu of other lands, which had been held from an early period, in trust, for the use of the church and poor. It is now let for about £32 a year, and the surplus of the rent, after paying the churchwarden's expenses, is carried to the poor rates. A benefaction of £10 given to the poor of this parish, was laid out in the purchase of 1A. 2R. 31P. of land, in Rattlesden, now let for £1 12s. a year. The *Poor's Allotment*, awarded at the enclosure, comprises 40A., on which the poor get turf, &c., for fuel.

Baldry Joseph, shoemaker
Baldry Samuel, vict., *White Horse*
Bloomfield Geo. millwright & engineer
Button Mrs. Harriet
Button Richard, corn miller
Button Mrs. Rebecca
Cooke Thomas, butcher
Death Charles, shopkeeper & tailor
Hubbard Charles, shoemaker
Jarrett Robert, shoemaker
Kerry Oliver, wheelwright
Luffington Richard, surgeon
Palmer Lucy, schoolmistress
Sawbridge Rev. Edw. Henry, curate, *Rectory*

Webster John, tailor
Welton Edward, blacksmith

FARMERS.
Baldry Samuel
Bishop Samuel
Button Richard
Buxton John
Cooke   William, (*land agent*)
Cutler John, *Malting Lodge*
Houchin Francis

Kerry James
Long George
Nunn Thomas
Ong Samuel
Pollard Harriet
Sare Thomas
Welton Edward
Woolsey Daniel, *Playford*

THORPE-BY-IXWORTH, sometimes called *Ixworth-Thorpe*, is a small village and parish, 1½ mile N. W. of Ixworth, containing 142 souls, and about 1,000 acres of land, all the property and manor of Sir Charles Montolieu Lamb, Bart., who is also impropriator of the tithes, and patron of the *Church*, (All-Saints) which is a *donative*, valued at only £20, and enjoyed by the Rev. Joseph Haddock, for whom the Rev. E. E. Wells officiates. The manor was held by Ixworth Priory, and was granted at the Dissolution, to Richd. and Eliz. Codington. The Town Estate, which comprises a cottage, barn, and 21A. 1R. 37P. of land in this parish and in Troston and Honington, is vested in trust, for the reparation of the church and the relief of the poor. It is intermixed with property of Sir C. M. Lamb, who pays for it a yearly rent of £20. *John Wright*, in 1674, bequeathed £20 for the relief of poor widows of this parish, and it was laid out, with £10 belonging to the parish, in the purchase of 5A. of land at Hopton, now let for £7 7s. a year. The FARMERS are—Thomas Cooke, *Upper Farm ;* Peter Day, *Red House ;* and John Martin Debenham, *Lower Farm.* The other principal parishioners are Charles Crosby, *beer seller ;* and Samuel Crosby, *shopr. & gamekeeper.*

TROSTON, a neat and pleasant village, $2\frac{1}{2}$ miles N.W. of Ixworth, and $6\frac{1}{2}$ miles N. N. E. of Bury St. Edmund's, has in its parish 409 souls, and 1,776 acres of land, including a sandy moor of 400A., covered with ling and furze. It formerly belonged to Bury Abbey, and afterwards to the Maddocks and Brundish families. Robert Evelyn Lofft, Esq., is now lord of the manor, but part of the soil belongs to Mr. Chas. Wayman, and a few smaller owners. *Troston Hall*, the beautiful seat of R. E. Lofft, Esq., was greatly improved by the late *Capel Lofft, Esq.*, a learned barrister, an eminent writer on legal, political, and other subjects, and a warm patron of literary talents. To gratify his own peculiar taste, he inscribed almost every tree in his garden and pleasure grounds, either to names of classical celebrity, or to such as are venerable for the virtues of the persons who bore them. A laurel bears the name of Howard, to commemorate that philanthropist's visit to Troston, in 1786, and a large elm is denominated *Evelyn*, after the celebrated antiquary and planter. Troston was purchased in 1680, by *Robt. Maddocks, Esq.*, whose father was descended from the family formerly possessed of the sovereignty of Wales, and left that principality at the age of 13, on foot, friendless, and alone, in search of employment. Having arrived in London, he repaired to Cheapside, where, observing a merchant soil his shoe, in crossing the street, he immediately ran and brushed off the dirt. The merchant, struck with the boy's attention, enquired into his situation, and having heard his story, took him into his service. After some time, he was employed in the counting-house; and in the sequel, became a partner in the firm, and acquired a considerable fortune. At Troston Hall, was born, in 1713, *Edward Capel*, (maternal uncle of the late Mr. Lofft,) a writer, distinguished by his commentaries on Shakespear, and by his beautiful edition of the works of the immortal dramatist, in 10 volumes octavo. He held the office of deputy inspector of plays, to which is attached a salary of £200 per annum. The *Church* (St. Mary) is a neat thatched fabric with a tower and three bells, and contains several neat monuments. The living is a discharged rectory, valued in K. B. at £10 4s. 7d., and now having a yearly modus of £332, awarded in 1842, in lieu of tithes. The patronage is in the Crown, and the Rev. R. J. Buller, B. A., is the incumbent. The *Wesleyans* have a small chapel here. In the 18th of Charles II., £20 given to the poor by *Thos. Lamb*, and £14, given by other donors, were invested in the purchase of a yearly rent charge of 34s. out of land now belonging to Rt. E. Lofft, Esq. This annuity is distributed in blankets. The *Poor's Allotment*, 14A. 1R. 31P., was awarded at the enclosure, in 1806, and is now let for £22 a year, which is distributed among the poor of the parish, in coals. The *Church Land*, 1A. 22P. was allotted at the enclosure, in lieu of the old Church Land, and is let for 21s. a year.

Blake John, tailor
Buller Rev. Reginald John, B. A., *Rectory*
Downs Thomas, blacksmith
Fuller John, corn miller
Girkin John, flour dealer
Gladwell George, shopkeeper
Jacob George, vict. *Bull*
Lofft Robert Evelyn, Esq., *Hall*
Pleasance William, gamekeeper
Richardson Charles, gentleman
Richardson Capt. Frederick
Vincent Rd. painter and glazier
Yeomans Robert, carpenter

FARMERS.	Stennett Richard	Shoemakers.	CARRIER.
Fisk Isaac, *Hall*	Wayman Charles	Girkin Wm.& Rt.	James Frost, to
Mathew Robert	(*owner*)	Meadows Wm.	Bury,Wed.&Sat
Roiser Thomas			

WALSHAM-LE-WILLOWS is a large neat village, pleasantly situated 5 miles E. of Ixworth, and S. W. by W. of Botesdale, and 11 miles from Bury, Diss, Stowmarket, and Thetford. It has in its parish 1,265 souls, and 2,760 acres of land, varying from a rich clay, to a light sand and mixed loam. Gilbert-de-Blund had the lordship in the Conqueror's time, and gave part of the parish to Ixworth priory, but after the Dissolution, the rectory and the lands called East-House, were granted to Richd. and Eliz. Codington, and afterwards passed to the Holts. Another large estate here, was held by Wm.-de-la-Pole, Duke of Suffolk, in Henry VIth's reign, and was granted in the 6th of Henry VIII. to George, Earl of Shrewsbury. It afterwards passed to the Hunts, who held it in Kirby's time. Jas. B. Powell, Esq. is now lord of the manor, but a great part of the parish belongs to H. J. and T. H. Wilkinson, S. Golding, and J. Fisher, Esqrs., who have handsome mansions here; J. E. Munro, Esq., Rev. T. B. Syer, Jas. H. Amys, Esq., Rev. James Pye, Miss Lloyd, and many smaller owners, some of whom reside in the parish, in neat and commodious dwellings. The *Church* (St. Mary) is a large and handsome structure, with a tower containing six bells, and surmounted by a small spire. It contains several elegant monuments belonging to the Hunt and Wilkinson families. The interior was cleaned and beautified in 1843, when, on washing off the whitewash on the south side, some fine ancient paintings were discovered upon the wall. A small organ was erected by subscription in 1842, at the cost of £80. The tithes belong mostly to the principal land owners, and were commuted in 1843. Samuel Golding, Esq. is patron of the *perpetual curacy,* which was certified at £12, and valued in 1835, at £93. The Rev. Thomas Lawton is the incumbent. The *Baptist, Independents,* and *Wesleyans* have chapels in the village. The *Town Estate* has, from an early period, been vested in trust, for the benefit of the parishioners, and comprises the Guildhall and Town House, occupied rent-free, by poor families, and 57A. 3R. 24P. of land, let for £85 per annum, all in this parish, except 3A. 2R. in Badwell Ash and Stanton. The rents are applied (after paying the taxes, &c.) in payment of the churchwardens' expenses, and the expense of collecting the lord's quit and free rents; in paying the salary of the parish-clerk; in repairing bridges; and in providing clothing for poor women, and coals for poor housekeepers. The poor parishioners have also £3 15s. 2d. a year from 3A. of land forming part of *Rookwood's Charity.* (See Rickinghall Superior.) A school is supported by subscription, except the payment of one penny per week by each scholar.

Burcham Charles Manby, relieving officer, and registrar of Births, Deaths, and Marriages
Burwood Elizabeth, milliner
Burwood Thomas, tailor's foreman
Chapman Charles, baker & confectnr.
Clarke Richard, thatcher
Clarke Samuel, thatcher
Death Mary Ann, milliner
Drake Henry, plumber & glazier
Gittus James, book-keeper
Golding and King, *solicitors*
Golding Samuel, Esq., solicitor
Hayward William, farm bailiff

Howe Charles, bricklayer
King John Wardle, solicitor
Lake Ann, vict., *Blue Boar*
Last Wm., watch, clock, & gun mkr.
Meadows Mr. William
Meadows Zachariah, cooper
Miller John, sen., gentleman
Miller John, jun., corn merchant, maltster, & ale and porter brewer
Mulley Caleb, thatcher
Nunn James, drillman
Osborne George, hair dresser
Pearson Edward, vict., *Black Swan*
Pearson George, cattle dealer
Pollard Wm., gardener & nurserymn.
Prentice Samuel, gentleman
Seaman John, wheelwright
Spink Ann, straw hat maker
Vautier Mrs., gentlewoman
Vincent Samuel, veterinary surgeon
Wakeham Mrs. Jane
Warren Nathaniel, attorney's clerk
Wilkinson Hooper John, Esq., *Walsham House*
Wilkinson Capt. Thos. H., *West-street*

Academies.

Burcham Chltte.
Lock William
Pyatt John

Beer Houses.

Callow Robert
Clarke John
Day William

Blacksmiths.

Baker George
Smith George

Youngman John

Carpenters, &c.

Day William
Jaggard Henry
Jaggard William, (& baker)
Jeffery William

Corn Millers.

Darby William
Plummer Fredk.

FARMERS.

(* are Owners.)

Baker James
Buckel John, *Fishpond*
Cornell William, (& maltster)
Darby William
*Elliott John
Finch George
*Fisher John, *Walsham Hall*
*Gapp Richard
Goddard Jane, *West-street*
Thurston William

Boot & Shoe Makers.

Baker John
Colson Edward
Pallent Robert
Read Charles
Read Emmerson
Spink Robert

Butchers.

Colson Alfred
Lake Thomas

*Hatten Rt. Hayward
Hunt Thomas
Matthews George, *West-street*
Moore John, *West-street*
Nunn Samuel
Plummer Henry
Plummer John
Proctor John

Simpson Zach.
Thurston   John, *High Hall*
West   Soloman, *Harts Hall*
Whitbread John, *Crown land*
Youngman John

Grocers & Drapers.

Death Charles
Newson Geo. Robt. (& British Wine dealer)
Pollard Henry
Proctor Ann

Rope Makers.

Pamment Isaac
Pollard William

Saddlers.

Boggis John
Scarfe George

SURGEONS.

Freeman Wm. A.
Kent Walton

Tailors.

Clarke Rainbird
Cornell James
Death Charles

CARRIERS.

George Firman, to Ipswich, thurs.
Jas. Fenn & Geo. Finch, to Bury, wed. & saturdy.

WATTISFIELD, a pleasant village on the Bury road, 3 miles W.S.W. of Botesdale, and 6 miles N.E. by E. of Ixworth, has in its parish 601 souls, and about 1,600a. of fertile land, under which is a bed of fine clay, of which, excellent *bricks, tiles,* and *brown earthenware* are manufactured. It was one of the lordships belonging to the Abbot of Bury, and in Kirby's time was held by the Tompson and Moody families. J. B. Powell, Esq., is now lord of the manor, but a great part of the soil belongs to George Mallows, Esq. (who has a handsome seat here,) and several smaller owners. The *Church* (St. Margaret) is a neat fabric with a tower and five bells; and the benefice is a discharged rectory, valued in K.B. at £8 11s. 8d., and in 1835, at £336. Mrs. Morgan is patroness, and her husband, the Rev. R. Morgan, is the incumbent, but does not reside here. In the village is an *Independent Chapel,* built in 1678, by a congregation which was formed at Market Weston, in 1654. It has a small endowment, and seat room for 700 hearers. Here is also a small *Wesleyan Chapel,* built in 1835. The *Town Estate* has been vested in trust, from a very remote period, for the general benefit of the parish, and comprises

a house and one rood of land, occupied rent free, by poor persons, and 54A. 1R. 2P. of land, let for £71 17s. per annum; but of this 2A. 1R. 36P. is "*Poor's Land*," purchased in 1647, with £30 given by Robt. Mallows and Nicholas Lock   The rents are applied in the first instance, in defraying the churchwardens' expenses, and the salaries of the parish clerk and constable; and the surplus is laid out in coals, which are sold at reduced prices, to the poor parishioners. In the 4th of Charles Ist., *Sir Nicholas Bacon* left £33 6s. 8d. to be laid out in lands, and the rents thereof to be applied in repairing *Wattisfield Causeway*, which now forms part of the turnpike road. The 4A. of land, purchased with this legacy, is vested with the surveyors of the highways, and the rent is carried to their accounts.

Buck Sarah, vict., *Black Swan*
Bullock John, shoemaker
Carter Nathaniel, vict., *White Swan*
Cooke Thomas, shoemaker
Cone Saml., grocer, draper and tailor
Doe John, corn miller
Farrow Josiah, cattle dealer
Garthwaite Rev. Wm.,(Indept. Min.)
Golding Rev. Thomas, *curate*
Green Mrs. Elizabeth Ann
Hammond Jesse, shopkeeper
Harrison Thos., brown earthenware manufacturer
Howard Edmund, shoemaker
Howe Roger, brick and tile maker
Kerry Charles, wheelwright
Knight James, baker, &c.

Mallows George, Esq.
Mallows Mrs. Sophia
Nunn John, grocer and draper
Parker Henry, blacksmith
Sill Edmund, gardener and beer seller
Sparke Wm., bricklayer & carpenter
Watson Thos., brown earthenware mfr.

FARMERS.

Beart Lucy, *owner*
Casson John
Clamp George, *Hill Green*
Doe James
Driver William, *Pot kiln*
Farrow William, (& maltster)
Harrison Thomas
Hunt Thomas
Kelton Benjamin
Manning Isaac
Nunn Enoch
Sill Edmund
Youngman Henry, *Hall*
Youngman John

WORDWELL parish, 5 miles N.N.W. of Bury St. Edmund's, comprises 2,120 acres of fertile land, but has only 66 inhabitants. It was one of the estates sold by the last Marquis Cornwallis, and was anciently the property of a family of its own name. It adjoins the extensive park of Culford Hall, the seat of the Rev. E. R. Benyon, the present lord of the manor, who owns all the parish, and has nearly the whole of it in his own occupation. He is also patron and incumbent of the *Church*, (All Saints) which is a rectory, united with that of West Stow. (See page 700.) There are only a few cottages in the parish, occupied by labourers, and Charles Petch, blacksmith and beer seller.

LACKFORD HUNDRED.

(*Continued from page* 600.)

(*For Description, Parishes, Population, &c. Vide page* 581.)

THETFORD BOROUGH.

Thetford is an ancient *borough* and *market-town*, partly in Lackford Hundred, Suffolk, and mostly in *Shropham Hundred, Norfolk,* being chiefly on the north side of the navigable Little Ouse river, 12 miles N. of Bury St. Edmund's, 6 miles E. S. E. of Brandon, 28 miles S.S.E. of Lynn, 28 miles S. W. by W. of Norwich, and 80 miles N. N. E. of London. It was once an important *city,* being the *capital of East Anglia*, in the Saxon era, and the *see* of the bishopric of Norfolk and Suffolk, from the year 1070 to 1096, as has been seen in the general survey of the latter county, at pages 13 to 36. It also shared with Norwich, as the capital of Norfolk, till 1833, when the Lent Assizes, which had previously been held here, were removed to Norwich. The town has been much improved during the last ten years, and its Market-place and principal streets are wide and spacious, containing many good inns, well stocked shops, and neat houses. Many of the latter are separated by gardens and small pastures. Its principal *trade* is the importation of coal, timber, &c., and the exportation of *corn, wool,* and other agricultural produce; but there are here four large *breweries,* three *foundries* and *agricultural machine manufactories,* a *tannery,* two *brick and tile yards,* several *malt and lime kilns,* several *corn mills,* and an extensive *paper mill;* the latter employing about 50 persons in the manufacture of the finer sorts of paper. In 1841, a steam mill was built here for sawing timber, and crushing bones and oil cake. The *Market* is held every Saturday, and the *Shambles,* which stood on the site of the Red-Lion Inn, were taken down and rebuilt on their present site, in 1837, and form a neat building, covered with cast-iron, and having a portico and handsome palisades in front. The *Fairs* are May 14th, and August 2nd and 16th for sheep; Sept. 25th for cattle, pedlery, &c., and in July, or early in August for wool. *Horse Races* were held here from an early period, till 1620, when they occasioned such tumults, that they were suppressed by the privy council. They were revived in 1833, but discontinued about four years ago. The town has its name from the small river *Thet,* which falls into the Little Ouse, on the south side of the town, where there is a *chalybeate spring,* which supplied a Bath House, erected by subscription, about ten years ago, but converted into cottages in 1838. In the vicinity have been found various extraneous *fossils,* particularly large cockle shells, or *cardii,* and button fish, or *eschintæ.* A petrified curlew, and a perfect nautilus were found here many years ago. The *fisheries* in the rivers within the limits of the borough, are noticed as early as the reign of Henry I., as abounding in pike, pickerel, eels, salmon, chub, perch, carp, tench, dace, &c. In 1715, a sturgeon, weighing 13st. 10lbs., was taken out of the mill pool.

The *Borough* increased its *population* from 2,246 souls in 1801, to 3,934 souls in 1841, and comprises 6,976A. 1R. 24P. of land, divided into three PARISHES, of which the following are the names, areas, and number of inhabitants, viz.:—*St. Peter's,* 2,281 acres, and 1,184 souls; *St. Cuthbert's,* 215 acres, and 1,543 souls; and *St. Mary's,*

4,480 acres, and 1,207 souls.   St Peter's is wholly in Norfolk; but all
the land in St. Cuthbert's and St. Mary's, except about fifty acres, is
in Suffolk, as also are 58 inhabitants of the former, and 677 of the
latter parish.   The return for St. Cuthbert's includes *Ford Place*, an
extra parochial house and estate.   Lord Asburton, and Sir R. J. Buxton, Bart., own the greater part of the enclosed lands, and the former
is lord of the *manor*; but there are in the borough, three open commons, and a rabbit warren of 2,913 acres ;—the *soil* being generally a
light sand, resting on chalk and flint.   At an enclosure in 1804, 55a.
were allotted to the poor for fuel.   The surrounding country is generally in large corn fields and extensive open sheep walks, and the air
is highly salubrious, as is shewn by the longevity of the inhabitants.
John Jackson, the oldest man in the town, is 97 years of age, and Mrs.
Tyrrell, of the Black Horse, is upwards of 90.

THETFORD UNION, formed by the new poor law commissioners in 1835, comprises
the three parishes of Thetford, the parishes of Santon Downham, Brandon, Barnham,
Fakenham Magna, Euston, Honnington, Sapiston, Coney Weston, Barningham, Weston
Market, Hepworth, Thelnetham, Hopton, and Knettishall, in Blackbourn and Lackford
Hundreds, *Suffolk*, (see pages 581 and 679.) and the parishes of Kilverstone, Croxton,
East Wretham, West Wretham, Brettenham, Rushford, Methwold, Northwold, Santon,
Hockwold-cum-Wilton, Feltwell, Mundford, Lynford, West Tofts, Sturston, Cranwich,
and Weeting-cum-Broomhill, *in Norfolk*.   These 34 parishes comprise an *area* of 180
square miles, and a *population* of 17,542 souls, of whom 11,051 are in Norfolk, and 6,491 in
Suffolk,   Their average annual *expenditure* for the support of their poor, during the three
years preceding the formation of the Union, was £10,408, but in 1838 it amounted only
to £6,188, and in 1840 to £6,953 18s.   The UNION WORKHOUSE, erected in 1836, at
the cost of about £5000, stands in St. Mary's parish, Thetford, but within the bounds of
Suffolk, about half a mile from the Town, on the Bury road.   It is an extensive brick
building, and its boundary walls enclose three acres of land.   It has room for 300 inmates,
but has seldom half that number, having only 83 in July 1841, and 110 in Sept. 1843.   The
Board consists of 43 *Guardians*, and C. Fison, Esq. is *chairman*, and R. Webb, Esq., *vice-
chairman*.   Wm. Clarke, Esq. is *union-clerk and superintendent registrar*, C. W. Hotson,
Esq., *auditor*, and Mr. John Lucas, *master of the Workhouse*.   The relieving officers and
district registrars are, Mr. Denny Smith for *Thetford District*, and Mr. John Sharpe for
Methwold District.

Thetford, according to some authors, was first a British city, and afterwards a Roman station ; but the arguments adduced in support of these
conjectures, are not very conclusive.   Camden and Plot place the *Sitomagus*
of the Itinerary here ; but Gale and Horsley contend that that station was
at Woolpit, in Suffolk.   At the east end of the town is a large entrenched
mount, about 100 feet in height, 984 in circumference at the base, and 338
in diameter at the base, and 81 at the summit, which is dished or hollowed
out to the depth of 12 feet below the outer surface.   The slope of the mount
is extremely steep, forming an angle with the plain of the horizon of more
than forty degrees ; and yet no traces remain of any path or steps for the
purpose of carrying up machines, or any weighty ammunition.   It has been
surrounded by a double rampart, with an outward ditch, the sides of which
were protected by the horns and bones of the animals slaughtered for the
use of the garrison, but these have been much injured by time and the de-
predations of man.   On the east side is a large area, 300 feet square, evidently intended for parading the troops.   The remaining parts of the ramparts
are about 20 feet high, and the ditch from 60 to 70 feet wide.   These once
formidable works, commonly called the *Castle Hills*, are composed of a
mixture of mould and clunch ; and on the top of the great mound or keep,
are many tumuli.   They were undoubtedly raised for the defence of the
town during the predatory incursions of the Danes, who overthrew the Saxons in a dreadful battle fought at Snare-hill, near Thetford, in 870, when
Edmund, King of East Anglia, surrendered to the marauders, who cut off
his head, and after plundering and butchering many of the inhabitants of
Thetford, reduced the city to ashes.   In 1004, Sweyne, King of Denmark,

invaded East Anglia, and among other places, burnt this. In 1010, Ulfketel, the Saxon earl, suffered a complete defeat, and Thetford was again
destroyed. After the truce which was concluded between Edmund Ironside
and Canute, this town, like a phœnix, arose from its ashes. In the time of
Edward the Confessor, there were in the borough 944 burgesses, all of whom
except 36, could put themselves under the protection of whom they pleased,
without the royal license, providing they paid all the customs, heriots ex-
cepted. In the time of the Conqueror, the burgesses were reduced to 720,
and Bishop Herfast removed the episcopal see from North Elmham to Thetford, whence, however, it was transferred to Norwich in the following reign.
From numerous coins in the cabinets of the curious, it is evident there was a
mint here, from the reign of Athelstan to that of King John. The manor
house, the ancient seat of the Earls Warren, became a royal palace, when
the manor passed to the Crown as part of the Duchy of Lancaster. The
mansion, now called the *King's House*, was rebuilt in the reign of Elizabeth,
and given by James I. to Sir P. Wodehouse, whose descendants were long
seated here. It was modernized by the late T. Wright, Esq., and is now
the property of James Cole, Esq. Queen Elizabeth, Henry I. and II., and
James I., occasionally resided here; but the latter, being offended at the
remonstrance of a farmer over whose grounds he had been hunting, sold the
manor-house to Sir P. Wodehouse. Though an ancient borough by prescription, Thetford is comparatively a modern CORPORATION. In the
Conqueror's time, the town was governed by a *prœpositus*, and other inferior
officers, generally nominated by the Crown; but in 1573, Queen Elizabeth
granted the burgesses a charter, by which a mayor, ten aldermen, twenty
common councilmen, a recorder, town clerk, sword-bearer, and two sergeants-
at-mace, constituted the corporate body and their officers, till the passing
of the Municipal Reform act of 1835. The mayor, during his mayoralty,
was clerk of the markets, and in the following year officiated as coroner. The
same charter also granted them permission to send two burgesses to Parliament, " provided they were discreet and honest men, and were elected at the
expense of the borough." This charter was surrendered to Charles II., and
an imperfect one obtained in its place; but this was rescinded in 1692, and
the original charter restored. The town was governed by the latter till the
passing of the *Corporation Reform Bill*, in 1835, under which the *Town
Council* consists of a Mayor, four Aldermen, and twelve Councillors; and a
Commission of the Peace has since been granted, on the petitition of the
burgesses. The *income of the old corporation*, in 1833 was £1,054, of which
£955 was derived from the *navigation of the Little Ouse*, from Thetford to
White-house ferry, formed under acts of the 22nd of Charles II., and 50th
of George III. This navigation had been mismanaged and neglected till
1827, when it was put into the hands of a superintendent, and a debt of
£4,200 incurried in improving it by the formation of sluices, &c. The income of the new corporation, in 1840, was only £656 16s. 8d., of which
£510 arose from borough rates; £47 15s. from rents, and £38 8s. 10d.
from tolls and dues. The expenditure, in the same year, was £598 7s. 1d.
Quarter Sessions are held for the borough before the Recorder, the Mayor,
and the Magistrates. The number of *voters* is about 300, nearly half of
whom exercise their elective franchise as householders, and the rest as
freemen. The present *Members of Parliament* for the borough are the
Hon. W. B. Baring, and Sir Jas. Flower, Bart. There was a return of
writs and gaol delivery here as early as the reign of Edward I. The *Guild
Hall*, in which the Lent Assizes were held till their removal to Norwich, in
1833, is a fine old building, with commodious court rooms, &c. It was
enlarged and repaired in 1800, and the *gaol* in 1816. The *sword and
mace* berne before the mayor, were presented by Sir J. Williams, Kt., in
1678. The CORPORATE BODY and Officers, (1843,) are as ollows:—

Mayor, L. S. Bidwell, Esq. || *Recorder*, T. J. Birch, Esq.
Magistrates, Hy. W. Bailey, James Fison, Richard Munn, and Leonard Shelford Bidwell, Esquires.
Aldermen, Richard Munn, Shelford Clarke Bidwell, L. S. Bidwell, and William Watts Wickes, Esqrs.
Coroner, Robert Eagle Clarke, Esquire.
Councillors, Messrs. Edw. Palmer, Geo. Tyrrell, Henry Roberts Tyrrell, Henry Green, Robert Snare, jun., Philip Jas. Cowell, Michael Frost West, Robt. Edwards, Wm. Whistler, John Simpson Spendlove, Wallis Rogers, and George Kingdon.
Town Clerk and Clerk of the Peace, Wm. Clarke, Esq. (and Clerk to the Magistrates for Guiltcross & Shropham Hundreds, Norfolk ; & to *Comssrs. of Taxes.*)
Clerk to the Borough Magistrates, Robert Willan, Esq.
Treasurer, B. Faux, Esq. || *Auditors*, Messrs. J. Brett & W. Johnson.
Gaoler & Chief Constable, Mr. Philip Penn Wilson.
Beadle & Crier, Wm. Boldrick.

The Rev. Robert Ward is *chaplain*, and H. W. Bailey, Esq., *surgeon to the gaol;* Wm. Clarke, jun. Esq , is *sub-distributor of stamps ;* and Mr. George Green, *corn inspector.*

A neat cast iron BRIDGE crosses the Little Ouse, and connects the Norfolk and Suffolk parts of the town. It was built by the Corporation, in 1829, in lieu of the old wooden bridge, erected in 1794. As already noticed, the *Little Ouse* was made navigable from White House, near Brandon, to Thetford, under an act passed in the reign of Charles II. It opens a water communication, by small craft, from hence to Lynn, Wisbech, &c. On the 9th of August, 1843, this town, like many other places in the neighbourhood, suffered severely from a dreadful STORM of thunder, lightning, hail, rain, and wind. For about twenty-five minutes, between six and seven in the evening, rain and hail descended in torrents, and most of the windows that faced the hurricane were broken. Many of the cellars were filled with water, and some of the warehouses and shops were inundated to the depth of two feet. When the coach came in from Lynn, the horses, in passing through Bridge street, were up to their chests in water. In various parts of the town, walls were thrown down by the immense weight of water pressing against them ; and in the surrounding country, the gardens and corn fields sustained great injury. Many of the hailstones, or rather pieces of ice, were upwards of 1¼ inch square, and after the storm, more than 100 sparrows were picked up dead in the garden of W. Clarke, Esq. Similar storms happened in the preceding and in the same month, in various parts of the kingdom.

CHURCHES AND MONASTERIES.—The ruins of ecclesiastical and other buildings, in various parts of Thetford, furnish a few slight evidences of its ancient splendour. It had at one time 20 churches and 8 monasteries, besides other religious and charitable foundations, and was called by the learned of the monkish ages, " *Hierapolis et Monachopolis.*" Of these ecclesiastical edifices, the names only of many of them remain, and the sites of others are marked only by a few dilapidated walls. Most of the monastic institutions were granted at the dissolution, to Richard Fulmerston, Esq., and the Duke of Norfolk. The *Nunnery* was founded originally for monks, as a cell to Bury Abbey, in the reign of Canute ; but in 1176, the monks being reduced to two, it was re-founded for a convent of nuns, who removed hither from Lynn. Some of its remains may be seen in the outbuildings of a farm-house. The *Priory*, or *Abbey*, first erected on the Suffolk side of the town, in the churchyard of the cathedral, was removed to a more convenient situation on the margin of the river. It was founded by Roger Bigod, for Cluniac monks, in 1104. The ancient gateway, of freestone and black flint, with part of the church, &c. still remains. Its revenues were valued at the dissolution at £312. 11s. 4½d. ; the Nunnery at £50. 9s. 8d. ;

and the *Monastery of St. Sepulchre*, at £82. 6s. The latter was founded by Earl Warren and Surrey, in 1109, for Augustine canons; and the porter's gate and part of the church still remain, in Canon's close,—the latter converted into a barn. The *Austin Friary* was founded by John of Gaunt, Duke of Lancaster, in 1387, for mendicants, and its site is still called the priory close. On removing the foundations of the friary church, the remains of Lady Todenham and Lady Hengrave were discovered and re-intered near the same spot, under a handsome altar tomb, erected in 1807, by Geo. Beauchamp, Esq. The latter lady died in 1402, and the former in 1412. The *Maison de Dieu*, which stood at the corner of Canon's close, was founded by Wm. Rufus and Earl Warren, for two chaplains and three poor men, who were to be fed, clothed, and lodged, and have water for washing the pilgrims' feet. Here were four *Hospitals* for lepers, &c., dedicated to St. John, St. Mary and St. Julian, St. Mary Magdalen, and St. Margaret, but no vestiges of them now remain. Of the 20 churches, only three are now standing, and they give name to the three parishes. The first church here, dedicated to *St. Mary*, was rebuilt by Bishop Herfast, as the cathedral, and is supposed to have stood on the site of the free school. It had four churches appendant to it. The tower of *St. Nicholas*, and some small fragments of a few of the other ancient churches, are still extant. St. Mary's, formerly called *St. Mary the Less*, is the only church in the Suffolk part of the town, and its parish comprises 4480 acres, and 1142 souls. It is a large thatched fabric, with a square tower and six bells. The interior is neatly pewed, and has several marble monuments—one to the memory of Sir Rd. Fulmerston. The benefice is a *perpetual curacy*, valued in K.B. at £1. 13s. 6½d., and in 1835 at £83. It was augmented in 1722-3, with £200 given by Henry Campion, Esq., and £200 of Queen Anne's Bounty. The Duke of Norfolk is patron, and the Rev. Wm. Collett, incumbent. St. Peter's is a large and handsome church, chiefly of flint, and consisting of a nave, chancel, side aisle, and tower. The latter, containing eight bells, was rebuilt in 1789, when a great part of the body was also rebuilt. The battlements on the south side, and the buttresses, are decorated with ornaments and large letters, inlaid in flint work. The living is a rectory, valued in K.B. at £5. 1s. 5½d., and in 1835 at £55. It was augmented in 1726 with £200 royal bounty, and £200 given by Hy. Campion, Esq.; and in 1814, with a parliamentary grant of £1200. It is united with the *perpetual curacy of St Cuthbert's*, in the patronage of the Duke of Norfolk, and incumbency of the Rev. Thomas Sworde. The latter benefice was valued in 1835 at £50, and was augmented with £1600 of Queen Anne's Bounty, in 1811 and 1813. St. Cuthbert's Church is a small fabric, with a tower and five bells. The other places of worship in the town are a *Friends' Meeting House;* a *Wesleyan Chapel*, built in 1830; an *Independent Chapel*, erected in 1817; a handsome *Catholic Chapel*, built in 1826; and a *Primitive Methodist Chapel*, erected in 1838.

The Free Grammar School and Hospital, in St. Mary's parish, on the Suffolk side of the river, were founded in 1666, by *Sir Richd. Fulmerston*, who endowed them with part of the possessions of the dissolved monasteries, some of which had previously been employed for similar uses. The endowment now yields about £508 per annum, and the founder bequeathed it in trust to his heirs, for the support of a schoolmaster and usher, and a preacher or master of the hospital, and four almspeople, namely, two poor men and two poor women. After the trust had been for some time grossly abused, it was transferred to the Corporation. The school is open to all the boys of the borough, free of expense, both for English and classics. About one-half of the endowment goes to the master and usher. The four almspeople have each a weekly stipend of 5s.,

and the master or preacher of the hospital has a yearly salary of £75, besides £20 in lieu of a residence. The number of free scholars varies from 30 to 40. Here are *National Schools*, built by subscription in 1825, and now attended by about 70 boys and 70 girls; a *Spinning, Knitting, and Reading School*, supported by subscription, for about 30 poor girls; a school connected with the British and Foreign School Society; and an *Infant School*, built in 1836. *Sunday Schools* are attached to all the churches and chapels. HARBORD'S HOSPITAL, in Magdalen street, was founded by Sir Charles Harbord, for the residence of six poor aged men. They were endowed for 99 years with £30 per annum, but this ceased many years ago. In 1701, SIR JOSEPH WILKINSON, then recorder of the borough, bequeathed to the Corporation, in trust for *apprenticing poor children* at Thetford, a house and land at Tuddenham, now let for £308 per annum, which is dispensed in apprentice fees of from £20 to £25. The BENEFACTIONS for distribution among the poor of Thetford, are £1000 three per cent. stock, left by *Peter Sterne, Esq.*, in 1817, and the following *yearly rentcharges*, viz., £16 left by *Sir Edwin Rich,* in 1675; £8. 10s. by Thomas Duke of Norfolk; £3 by Mrs. Eadon; 20s. by Sir J. Wodehouse, in 1751; £4, by Alderman Barnham, out of the Red Lion Inn; £12. 10s , by Hy. Smith, in 1627; and 20s., left by Samuel Snelling. There are in the town several *Lodges of Odd Fellows*, of the London and Manchester Unions, and also several Friendly Societies, and other provident institutions.

Among the WORTHIES born at Thetford are *Thos. Martin*, F.A.S., author of the History of Thetford, born in 1696, and died 1771; and *Thomas Paine*, author of " The Rights of Man," " Common Sense," " The Age of Reason," and other political works, which, being written in a peculiarly popular style, with much freedom of thought and expression, and published at a time when the French Revolution had excited an extraordinary ferment in the public mind, they were eminently calculated to produce a revolution in this kingdom, and were consequently suppressed by Government. Paine died in America in 1800, but his bones were afterwards brought to England by the late Wm. Cobbett. The late *E. H. Barker, Esq.*, of Thetford, was author of " Parriana," or notices of the Rev. Saml. Parr, L.L.D., and also re-edited an edition of " Lempriere's Classical Dictionary." On the 12th of August, 1555, Thos. Cobbe, Roger Coe, and James Abbes, three *martyrs* to the Reformed religion, were burnt at Thetford, after undergoing a mock trial, before Michael Dunning, the bloody chancellor of Norwich. *Assemblies* are occasionally held in the town; but the small *Theatre*, which used to reap a good harvest during the assize week, has been but little used since the removal of the assizes to Norwich, in 1833.

THETFORD DIRECTORY.

POST OFFICE : Mr Wm. Christopher, *postmaster*, King street. Letters despatched to London, &c., at 8 evening; to East Harling, &c. 20 min. past 6 mg; to Watton, &c. 6 mg; & to Newmarket, &c. at ½ p. 8 nt.

MARKED 1, *reside in Back street* ; 2, *Bury road,* (*in* SUFFOLK ;) 3, *Botany Bay Lane* ; 4, *Bridge Street;* 5, *Chapel Street;* 6, *Croxton Road* ; 7, *Earls Lane* ; 8, *Gaol Street;* 9, *Guildhall Street;* 10, *Great Magdalen Street* ; 11, *King Street* ; 12, *Little Magdalen Street* ; 13, *London Road,* (*in* SUFFOLK ;) 14, *Market Place;* 15, *Oldman's Lane* ; 16, *Old Market Place;* 17, *Water Lane* ; 18, *White Hart Street* ; 19, *Raymond Street* ; *and* 20, *in Well Street.*

Ashby Rev.John (Indt) Norwich rd
Buckley John, fellmonger & glover, Common

12 Barker Mrs Ann Elizabeth
10 Barton Miss Sarah
1 Best Henry, Esq. *Prospect House*

8 Bidwell Thomas, Esquire
7 Boldrick Wm. town crier
2 Burrell James, iron founder, &c
10 Burton John P., supervisor
10 Churchard Thomas, letter carrier
10 Clarke James, carrier
13 Clarke Rt. Eagle, Esq., coroner
13 Clarke Wm. Esq. solicitor, town clerk, union clerk, supt. regr. &c
13 Clarke Wm. jun. sub-distributor of stamps
4 Clarke Wm. bookkeeper
2 Coburn Isaac, tea dealer
18 Cole John, bookkeeper
2 CollettRev.Wm. inct. of St.Mary's
12 Cooke Miss Elizabeth
12 Cooke John, dyer
1 Cronchey Mrs Margaret
Debenham Alfd. clerk, *Ford Cottage*
9 Dent Miss Mary
9 Duly Daniel, solicitor's clerk
Elsey Mrs. Norwich road
4 Faux J. B. Esq. bank manager
20 Faux Mrs Susan
Featherston Thos. gent. *Abbey*
4 Fison Jas. & Sons, bone and cake crushers & timber sawers, *Steam Mill*
13 Gates Rev. Robert (Catholic)
16 Gates Mrs Susan
2 Gifford Mrs Sarah
19 Gill Mrs Eliz. || 17 Godfrey Mrs
16 Gill Eliz. fishmonger
17 Godfrey Simon and George, boat builders and owners
11 Green George, corn inspector
11 Guest Mrs Mary D.
11 Hall Thomas, ironmonger, &c
9 Hailstone James, attorney's clerk
19 Harvey Wm. brush maker, &c
10 Harvey Miss Mary
12 Hawks Jas. clerk of St. Mary's
13 Hobbins Mr William
9 Humphrey Mr Jonathan
11 Hunt Edward, carriers' agent
2 Jackson Oliver, (P. Meth. Min.)
12 Jones Rev Thomas Lewis
2 Kemp John, gentleman
2 Lucas Jno. govrnr. Union Workhs
2 Mann David, manager
9 Mann Mr James
Marsham Miss S. V., *New place*
11 Methold Rev. Thomas, rector of *Kilverstone*
1 Neale Miss Mary Ann
12 Newbury Mr George
1 Norman Mr William

2 Palmer Mrs Susan
13 Pollard Mrs. || 13 Pratt MissMy.
19 Price George, excise officer
2 Ray Robert, excise officer
13 Rumball Mrs F.
12 Sayer Richd. Edw. bank clerk
3 Sims Rev. Henry, curate
12 Smith Denny, registrar, &c
12 Spalding Thomas, foreman
11 Steggall Mrs Ann
15 Stone Wm. carrier
18 Sworde Rev. Thomas, rector of St. Peter's
9 Stokes Joseph, cork cutter
10 Thrower Jas. hay & straw dealer
9 Tyler John Clement, mayor's officer
Vipon Mrs Mary, Ford place
11 Whistler John, game dealer
11 Whistler Wm. game dealer, and clerk of St.Peter's & St. Cuthbert's
16 Wilson Philip Penn, gaoler and chief constable
10 Woods Mr William
11 Young Andrew, Esquire
10 Youngman David, traveller

BANKS.

4 Harvey & Hudson, (on Hankey & Co ;) J. B. Faux, *manager*
4 Oakes, Bevan, & Co., (on Barclay & Co ;) John Juler, agent

FIRE AND LIFE OFFICES.

18 Family Endowment, G. Faux
13 Guardian, Wm. Clarke
11 NorwichEquitable,Wm.R. Green
Norwich Union, Wm. Catton
4 Farmers' & General, J. Cronshey
4 Royal Exchange, John Juler
4 Suffolk Amicable, Henry Brown
13 Sun, Henry Newson
13 Union, John Houchen, junior

INNS AND TAVERNS.

4 Anchor, Wm. Johnson
14 Angel, Wm. Gunstone
Bell Inn, Robt. Edwards (posting)
10 Black Horse, My. Tyrrell & Son
11 Chequers, Frederick Cooper
9 Dog & Partridge, Peter Fitch
16 Dolphin, Wm. Boyce
18 Fleece, John Golding
14 Green Dragon, Wm. Bullen
Half Moon, Hy.Moore, Mundford rd
15 Horse Shoe, Samuel Burt
11 King's Arms, Mary Goodbody
18 King's Head, Isaac Gray
14 Red Lion, Chas. Dewing Tyler
1 Rose and Crnwn, Jas. Pooley
16 Spread Eagle, Thomas Pentney

2 Star, Wm. Smith
2 Trowel & Hammer, John Carter
White Hart Inn, Chas. Balaam
19 White Horse, Daniel Davy

Academies.
(* take boarders.)
7 Bundy J.
9* Cross Mary
13 *Free Gramr.*
  Rev R. Ward,
  & J. P. Cowen
9 Gates John
2 Hayward Eliz.
* Kingdon John
6 *National*, J. J.
  Cobb & Maria
  Kingdon
4 Pecher E.
* Rogers Misses.
  King's Houses
9 *Spinning &c.* S.
  Miller

ATTORNEYS.
13 Clarke Wm.
18 Faux Gregory
13 Houchen Jno.
  jun.
4 Willan Robert
Auctioneers, &c.
11 Christopher W
13 Deck & Newson
11 Green Geo.

BAKERS, &c.
2 Clarke Susan
19 Craske Edmd.
18 Handcock J.A
9 Harrold Ann
16 Jones Wm.
Johnson Sarah
11 Oldman Stphn
15 Oldman Wm.
2 Palmer Jas.
10 Rogers Mary
1 Stearne Susan
10 Traise John
Basket Makers.
20 Reynolds Jno.
  and Robert
Beer Houses.
7 Basham Geo.
2 Cary John
7 Francis Frnces.
1 Fuller Jn. Avis.
9 Hammond Jno.
10 Howard Chas.
12 Jay Wm.

Largent William
  Mundford rd
1 Meek Wm.
2 Parlett Fras.
6 Rudland Thos.
Skippins Thomas
  Norwich road
2 Spalding John
8 Whistler Hy.
1 Wing Isaac
Blacksmiths.
18 Arbon John
19 Booth Geo.
Booth Rd.
1 Chamberlain J.
16 Gill Rt. and
  bell hanger
10 Howard C.
11 Howard Jph.
1 King Thos.
1 Rushbrooke J.
*Booksellers and
Printers.*
14 Carley Robt.
17 Fleet James
  (binder only)
11 Priest Thos.
Boot & Shoe Mkrs.
Archer John
18 Car Isaac
10 Churchard Rt.
12 Davy Geo.
9 Fletcher John
18 Frost Edw.
12 Foulger Jno.
14 Howard Jacob
15 Pallant Wm.
1 Payman John
10 Pechey Jph.
9 Stearne Brnd.
12 West Michl.
Braziers & Tinrs.
8 Clarke J.& Son
9 Diver John
*Brewers and
Maltsters.*
16 Bidwell Lnd.
  Shelford
5 Branford J.W.
10 Tyrrell Mary
  and Son
19 Wickes Wm.
  Watts

Bricklayers.
16 Boyce Wm.
15 Huggins Rt.
12 Nunn Edw.
1 Norman Wm.
12 Palmer Jph.
2 Palmer James
10 Palmer John
2 Porter Robert
18 Snare Robt.
Brick & Tile Mkrs
6 Snare Rt. sen.
Tyrrell Hy. Rbt.
  Mundford rd.
BUTCHERS.
1 Allison Philip
16 Boyce James
10 Flack Nathan.
14 Fuller Geo.
1 Fuller John
10 Whisker Ths.
14 Webster Ths.
18 Wright Wm.
*Cabinet Makers
& Upholsterers.*
2 Atkins Wm.
9 Battle John
4 Browne Jn. B.
11 Oldham John
  (and appraiser.)
Chemists & Drgts
4 Cronshey Jas.
11 Nye Charles
*China, Glass &c.,
Dealers.*
11 Catton M.& A.
10 Scales T. jun.
Coach Makers.
2 Huggins Geo.
13 Palmer Afd.
Confectioners.
14 Bond Wm.
18 Edward Jas.
  (& toy dealer.)
11 Pratt Sarah
10 Traise John
Coopers.
2 Parlett Fras.
12 Thompson G
*Corn and Coal
Merchants.*
(*are Maltsters.)
16* Bidwell Lnd.
  Shelford
5* Branford J.W.
4* Fison Jas. and
  Sons. Steam mill

5 Gill John Withers & Garner
  (& boat ownrs.)
8* Tyrrell Henry
  Roberts
Corn Millers.
10 Flack N.
Gill J. W. & G.
  Water mill
3 Green Henry
15 Oldman Wm.
6 Oldman W. jun.
CURRIERS, &c.
18 Frost Edw.
14 Howard Jacob
Skippins Thomas
  Norwich road
*Earthenware
Manfrs. (Brown
ware.)*
Scales T. sen. &
  jun. Croxton rd

FARMERS.
2 Bartlett Henry
  Canons' warren
Featherston T.A
3 Green Hy.
2 Hipperson Jno.
  Thetford place
Turner Harrison
  Norwich road
18 Tyrrell H. R.
10 Tyrrell Walter
Gardeners, &c.
2 Sparrow Thos.
  Nursery
13 Stebbing Jph.

*Grocers & Drprs.
(* Hatters also.)*
18* Gayford Fdk.
11* Green Geo.
10 Hammond
  Sophia
12 Hill Chas.
9 Hill Mary
4* Juler John
16 Kingdon Geo.
5 Richardson Ts.
14* Rogers Wallis
18 Spurgeon Simeon
Hair Dressers.
18 Christopher B.
10 Storkey Wm.

714

THETFORD DIRECTORY.

Iron and Brass Founders & Agl. machine mkrs.
Burrell Chas. St. Nicholas lane
11 Burrell & Hall *(& engineers.)*
13 Palmer Edw.
Ironmongers.
14 Bond Wm. (& gun maker.)
4 Brown Hy.
11 Burrell & Hall
Joiners, &c.
9 Battle John
12 Betts Wm.
10 Coats Wm.
19 Hambling Js.
16 Johnson John
12 Palmer Jph.
1 Smith James
12 Thompson G.
14 Tyler C. D.
18 Tyrrell Geo.
Lime Burners.
12 Palmer Jph.
2 Porter Robt.
12 Thompson G.
Linen & Woollen
DRAPERS. (See *Grocers, &c.*)
9 Neobard John
11 Scott John
Milliners.
7 Brock M.&Ann
20 Brown J.
11 Clarke Har.
2 Cummings M.
12 Davy Mary
11 Howard Eliz.
18 Nunn Sophia
10 Newell Elnr.
11 Pennington S.
27 Petch Sarah
12 Tyler Eliz.
PAPER MFRS.
Munn Rd. & Co. *Ouse mill*
Plumbers, Glaz. and Painters.
16 Browne Peter
11 Norman Sarah
9 Pretty John
Rope Makers.
12 Cock John
Noble William, Common

Saddlers.
18 Abel Samuel
10 Barnard Jno.
4 Catton Wm.
6 Codling John
Shopkeepers.
16 Basham Geo.
Booth Rd. Norwich road
12 Burgess Eliz.
18 Edwards Jas.
2 Gunstone Dd.
15 Nunn Mary
Stone Masons.
1 Knowles Hy.
10 Snare Rt. sen.
Straw Hat Mkrs.
17 Dickman M.A
18 Garner Ann
11 Howard Har.
12 Hurrell Har.
18 Tyler Har.
Surgeons.
14 Bailey Henry Woodruffe
11 Best Hy. W.
13 Firth Charles Edward
Tailors
(* *Drapers also.*)
2 Baker Noah
4* Brett John
11* Carley Php.
11* Christopher William
1 Ellis Philip
7 Farrow Benj.
2 Hayward John
Jackson Evan, Norwich road
11* Meadows J.
9* Neobard Jno.
19 Sewell Wm.
9 Smith Wm.
12* Towell Geo.
Tanner.
5 Frost Edward, (fell-monger & wool mercht.)
Timber Merchts.
4 Brown Hy.
17 Godfrey Simon & Geo.(& boat builders)
10 Hollingsworth Richard
12 Thompson G.

18 Tyrrell Geo.
Vetrinry. Surgns
11 Howard Jph.
4 Parry Thomas
Watch Makers.
12 Branch Chas.
11 Carley Jonthn.
4 Spendlove John Simpson
13 Zippel Chas. (Ger. clock)
Wheelwrights.
20 Howard John
2 Huggins Geo.

1 King Thos.
12 Thompson G.
Wine and Spirit Merchants.
16 Bidwell Lend. Shelford
13 Clay Rt. Ts.
11 Cole Jas. jun. (& ale) King's House
5 Gill J. Withers & Garner
19 Wickes Wm. Watts

COACHES.

From the Bell Inn.
To London, ¼ before 6 mg., ½ before 11 morning, and at 11 night
To Bury, ½ past 10 mg ; to Cambridge, 2 aftn ; to Norwich, ¼ before 4 mg ; and at 1 and 3 aftn—daily, except Sunday. Also, to Bury, Wed. 10 mg ; & Tue. Thu. & Sat. 8 evg ; and to Lynn, Tues. at 7, & Thu. & Sat. at 8 morning
From the White Hart.
Mail, to Bury, Newmarket, &c. at 8 night ; and to Norwich, 6 morning
From the King's Head.
To Lynn, Tues. 7, & Thu. & Sat. at 8 mg ; & to Bury, same evenings, at 8
VESSELS to Lynn weekly : J. W. & G. Gill, and S. and G. Godfrey, *owners and wharfingers*

CARRIERS.

Deacon, Mack, & Co.'s Vans, &c., to London, &c. 2 mg ; and to Norwich, &c. 11 night, daily (except Sunday ;) Edward Hunt, *agent*, King street
W. Fowell's Van, from Gaol street to London, Monday, 12 noon
To Bury, Abm. Wolsey, Magdalen st Wed ; G. Ashburn (Green Dragon,) Wed and Sat ; and Wm. Stone, Oldman's lane, Wednesday & Saturday
To Dereham, &c. Abm. Wolsey, Magdalen street, Monday and Thursday
To Diss, Thomas Miller, Oldman's lane, Friday morning
To Ipswich, G. Lambert, Green Dragon, Monday
To Ixworth, John Rowley (Chequers) Wednesday & Saturday, 2 afternoon
To Lynn, Rd. Steward, Mundford rd. Mon. & Thu. 9 morning ; & to Bury, Wednesday and Saturday
To Norwich, Jas. Clarke, Gt Magdalen st. Mon. & Thu. 3 afternoon ; & to Brandon, Wed. & Sat. 2 aftn

NEWMARKET, one of the most fashionable schools of the turf in the annals of *horse racing*, is a handsome market town, with several elegant houses and public buildings, pleasantly situated on the gentle declivity of an eminence, mostly in Suffolk, and partly in Cambridgeshire, 13 miles W. of Bury St. Edmund's, 13 miles N.E. of Cambridge, and 61 miles N.N.E. of London. It increased its population from 1792 souls in 1801, to 2956 in 1841. It is in two parishes, viz., *All Saints*, which has 320 acres, and 714 souls, and is in Cheveley Hundred, Cambridgeshire; and *St. Mary's*, which has 250 acres, and 2134 souls, and is in Lackford Hundred, Suffolk, forming, with Exning, a detached member of the latter county, as noticed at page 588. The Duke of Rutland is lord of the *manor*, but part of the soil and most of the buildings belong to other proprietors. The *market*, held every Tuesday, has a commodious *Corn-Exchange*, which is well attended by growers and buyers; and here are two annual *fairs* for horses, sheep, &c., held on Whit-Tuesday, and Nov. 8th. *Petty Sessions* are held here every Tuesday. The town is a great thoroughfare, and its principal street is a about a mile in length. Most of the houses are modern and well built; and many of those which have been erected as the occasional residences of the nobility who attend the races, are extremely handsome. The inns and hotels are numerous, and are proverbial for the excellence of their accommodations. The *New Rooms*, erected about 70 years ago, form a large and elegant stone building, belonging to the Jockey Club, and comprising coffee, dining, card, billiard, betting, and news rooms, all handsomely furnished, and provided with every accommodation for the gentlemen of the turf, when they meet to ratify their agreements or settle matches. The *Gas Works* were erected in 1839, at the cost of £3000, raised in 300 £10 shares. The trade of the town depends almost exclusively on affairs connected with the turf, for which it has long been celebrated.

The RACE COURSE, one of the finest in the kingdom, is on the fine sandy heath on the north-west side of the town, in Suffolk, partly in St. Mary's, but mostly in Exning parish. Here are *seven racing weeks* yearly, but the races held in Easter week, and in the month of October, are the principal. The diversion of horse-racing, though undoubtedly practised in this country at the time of the Roman invasion, does not appear to have made much progress till the accession of James I., who introduced it from Scotland, where it came into vogue from the spirit and swiftness of the Spanish horses which had been thrown ashore on the coast of Galloway, when the vessels of the Armada were wrecked. From this period it became more fashionable, and Newmarket had probably some kind of a racing establishment as early as the reign of this sporting monarch, who erected a house here, which was destroyed in the civil wars, but was rebuilt by that distinguished patron of the turf, Charles II., and is still dignified with the name of *Palace*, being occasionally visited by royalty, but occupied by Mr. W. Edwards, the noted trainer. The idea of improving the breed of horses, has in a certain degree induced the legislature to encourage this species of gambling; and even the throne seems to sanction its continuance, for, in addition to the plates given by the nobility, the Sovereign has for many years given two annually at Newmarket, and several at other places. A gentleman who visited the October races here in the reign of Queen Anne, said he saw "a great concourse of the nobility and gentry from London and all parts of England, but they were all so intent, so eager, so

busy upon the sharping part of the sport," that they seemed to him "just so many horse coursers in Smithfield; descending, the highest of them, from their high dignity and quality to the picking of another's pockets." He was so sick of the jockeying party, that he left the crowd about the posts to observe the horses; "how the creatures yielded to all the arts and management of their masters; how they took their airings in sport, and played with their daily heats which they run over the course before the grand day, but how, as knowing the difference equally with the riders, they would exert their utmost strength as much as at the time of the race itself, and that to such an extremity that one or two of them died in the stable when they came to be rubbed after the first heat." The sport gives employment here to many *trainers*, jockeys, and grooms, who, in fine weather, may be daily seen exercising their racers upon the heath. In March, 1683, when Charles II. and other members of the Royal family, with a large concourse of nobility and gentry, had assembled to witness the races, a *fire* broke out and consumed the greater part of the town. It has been supposed that the defeat of the Ryehouse plot, may be attributed to this accident, as it occasioned the company to depart much earlier than had been calculated upon by the conspirators. Charles I. passed through the town a prisoner in 1647. Newmarket gave birth to *Thomas Merks*, bishop of Carlisle, who became famous from his steady adherence to Richard II., for which he was degraded to be titular bishop of Samos. Several coins of Trajan, one of Faustina, and one of Maximianus Herculius, were found near the heath about eighty years ago. About two miles west of the town, is the *Devil's Ditch*, consisting of a deep ditch and elevated vallum, running seven miles in a direct line to the fens of Ely, and supposed to have been cut by the Saxons or Danes. The two *Parish Churches* are neat structures, each having a tower containing five bells, and surmounted by a small spire. *St. Mary's*, as already noticed, is in Suffolk, and is a *discharged rectory*, valued in K.B. at £4. 15s. 2½d., and in 1835 at £375, with the vicarage of Wood Ditton, in Cambridgeshire, annexed to it. The Duke of Rutland is patron, and the Rev. P. Wilson, incumbent. The tithes were commuted in 1813. *All Saints Church* is in Cambridgeshire, and is a *perpetual curacy*, valued in 1835 at only £37. It is in the patronage of the Bishop of Norwich, and incumbency of the Rev. Wm. Taylor. On the south side of the town are two *Chapels*, one belong to the *Independents*, and the other to the *Wesleyans*. The former was built in 1796, and the latter in 1841. The town has a school endowment, and several charities for the poor.

RICHARD PICKLES, at some date unknown, charged his house (formerly the Greyhound, and now belonging to three proprietors,) with certain distributions of beef, bread, fish, &c., in lieu of which a yearly rent-charge of £13. 5s. has long been paid, and is dispensed as follows:—£3. 17s. 6d. for a distribution of bread and meat among the poor of St. Mary's parish; £10. 11s. for a distribution of bread, meat, &c., among the poor of All Saints; and 16s. 6d. to the clerk of All Saints. In 1591, SAMUEL HUDSON left for the poor of Newmarket, a yearly rent-charge of 20s., out of half an acre of land, and a house, formerly the Feathers Inn, and now the Post-office. From a distant period, all that has been derived from this charity is 13s. 4d. yearly. *Lord Allington* left two yearly rent-charges, viz., 13s. 4d. for the poor of St. Mary's, and 6s. 8d. for the poor of All Saints, out of the lordship of Newmarket. The poor of St. Mary's have 13s. 4d., left by *John Muckham* and *Walter Pratt*, out of the manor farm (now belonging to Mr. Bryant;) 15s. per annum as the rent of land at Exning, given by *Mary Buck*; 30s. a year out of the Greyhound Inn, left by *John Archer*; and the interest of £40, left by *Abraham Goodall*, in 1735. Two tenements and half an acre of garden ground, in Black Bear lane, are supposed to have been derived from the bequests of *Robert and Thomas Row*, and are occupied by poor families, except part of the land, which is let for 21s. a year. A yearly payment of £50 (subject to a deduction of £8. 15s. for office fees,) is made out of the Exchequer, under a donation of QUEEN ANNE, for the support of *Charity Schools*, at

Newmarket. It is paid to a master and mistress for teaching 21 boys and 21 girls. They are taught at the *National School,* which was built by subscription in 1820, and now affords instruction to about 90 other scholars, for small weekly payments.

NEWMARKET UNION, formed by the New Poor Law Commissioners, in 1836, comprises the two parishes of Newmarket, the six parishes of Dalham, Gazeley, Lidgate, Moulton, Ousden, and Exning, *in Suffolk ;* and the twenty-one parishes of Ashley, Boro' Green, Bottisham, Brinkley, Burwell, Cheveley, Chippenham, Dullingham, Fordham, Isleham, Kennet, Kirtling, Landwade, Soham, Snailwell, Stetchworth, Swaffham Priory, Swaffham Bulbeck, Westley, Wicken, and Wood-Ditton, *in Cambridgeshire.* These 29 parishes comprise an area of 150 square miles, and a population of 27,383 souls, of whom 6029 are in Suffolk, and 21,354 in Cambridgeshire. The WORKHOUSE stands half a mile north of the town, in Exning parish, and was built, in 1836, at the cost of £6909. It is a spacious building of white brick, having room for 380 inmates. The number in the house in July, 1841, was 182 ; and in September, 1843, 169. The average annual *expenditure* of the 29 parishes for the support of their poor, during the three years preceding the formation of the Union, was £18,191 ; but in 1838, it was only £11,511, and in 1840, £15,062. 11s. The total number of in and out-door poor relieved in the last quarter of 1842, was 2770. Thirty-six *guardians* are elected yearly, and J. P. Allix, Esq., is *chairman,* and William Bryant, Esq., *vice-chairman* of the Board. Wm. Parr Isaacson, Esq., is *Union clerk* and *superintendent registrar ;* W. Bryant, jun., Esq., *treasurer ;* Richard Faircloth, Esq., *surgeon ;* Rev. Robert Whiting, *chaplain ;* Henry Rance, Esq., *auditor ;* Mr. Edward Miller, *master of the Workhouse ;* and Mr. Chas. Clarke, *relieving officer and registrar.* PETTY SESSIONS are held every Tuesday, by the Suffolk magistrates, at the offices of Messrs. Isaacson and Gillson ; and by the Cambridgeshire magistrates, at the Kingston Room.

NEWMARKET DIRECTORY.

POST OFFICE, High street :—Mr. Wm. Le Pla, *postmaster.* Letters despatched to London, Cambridge, and the North, South, and West, at 20 minutes past 11 night; and to Lynn, Norwich, Bury St. Edmund's, &c., at 3 morning.

Those marked 1, *reside in Albert street ;* 2, *Albion street ;* 3, *Bury road ;* 4, *Cheveley road ;* 5, *Exning road;* 7, *Kingston square ;* 8, *Mill Hill;* 9, *Market lane ;* 10, *Market place ;* 11, *Rutland lane ;* 12, *Sandpit lane ;* 13, *Sun lane ;* 14, *Wellington street ; and the rest in* HIGH STREET, *or where specified. Those with an* * *prefixed are in Cambridgeshire, and all the others are in Suffolk.*

14 Andrews Fuller, sheriff's officer
4*Arnull Mrs Lucy
13*Ashford Thomas, clerk and sexton of All Saints
Aylieff Jph. excise officer, Heath
1*Balls Benjamin, carrier
13*Barber Mrs Jane
12 Barker Mrs Mary
9 Blackwin Martin Chas. bottle mert
8 Bonnett James, coachman
BottomChas.Jno.&Wm.coach proprs
Bottom Mrs Mary Ann
3 Brown Wm. farmer
Bryant Wm. Esq. banker, &c
Burchley Mrs Ann
Carey Richard, Esq.
Chapman Mr Thomas
4 Chifney Mr Wm.
Clarke Chas. relieving officer & regr

8 Clark John Francis, architect, &c
13*Cope Rev James (Independent)
*Cocken Mr Wm.
*Crockford Wm. Esq
Cross Wm. coachman
4*Edwards Mrs Mary
Feist E. attorney's clerk
1*Ford George, Esq
Frye Charles, banker's clerk
8 Frye F. R. organist, regr. of marriages, and clerk to the Provident Medical Society
Gillson George, solicitor
Goodhough Mrs Sophia
Goodisson Mrs Hannah
9 Granger Sar. eating house keeper
10 Greata Mrs Ann
1*Groves Charles, foreman
* Hall Henry, artist

*Hacon John, currier
Hammond Chas. Eaton, Esq. banker
8 High Philip, gentleman
*Hilton Wm. bankers' clerk
2 Hodgson Thomas, brewer
Howlett James Barber, solr.'s clerk
Isaacson Wm. Parr, solr. union clerk, supt. regr. & clerk to magistrates
13*Jacob John, fruiterer
Jeffrey Richard S. constable
5 Leech Wm. poor rate collector
Le Pla Wm. postmaster
*Lushington Charles, Esq
1*Manning Jas. clerk to Jockey Club
8 Manning John, clerk of St. Mary's
5 Miller Edwd. govr. *Union Workhs*
1*Neale Mrs Ann
*Norton Mrs Mary
1*Paler John, foreman
*Pars Albertus Thomas, *News room*
1*Perren Mr John || Pavis Mrs E.
8 Perren Thos. clerk of race course
*Piper Stephen, Esq
10 Porter Mr Wm.
8 Prickett John, excise officer
8 Prince Mr John
Ratliffe Wm. gentleman
*Robson Martha (lodgings)
13*Smallman Fras. gent. *Nunnery*
South Misses Sophia and Mary
13 Stevens Hy. Rowe, registrar of Cheveley district
1 Stofer Mr Isaac
8 Stofer Mr Isaac || Taylor Mrs My.
1*Taylor Rev Wm. inc. of All Saints
1*Turner Mr John
Wallis Thomas, coachman
*Wetherby Edward, Esq.
*Wheatley Mr Wm.
5 Wilkinson James, gas manager
Wilson Rev Plumpton, B.A. rector of St. Mary's

HOTELS, INNS, AND TAVERNS.

Black Bear, Samuel John James
Black Bull, Thomas Smith
*Black Horse, Wm. Barrett
Bushel and Wine Vaults, John Mainprice
Crown, Francis Linch Bloss
9 Dolphin, James Howlett
8 Five Bells, Robert Hassall
Golden Lion, Ralph Westley
Greyhound, (posting,) Wm. Jarvis
Grosvenor's Arms, Robt. Parkinson
Half Moon, Francis Day
*Horse and Groom, Charles Rayner
1*Horse Shoes, Stephen Goodall

9 Lamb, John Frost
8 Queen Victoria, Jas. Fras. Deeks
*Rising Sun, John Ashford
*Rutland Arms, (posting) Thomas Sabin
2 Sir John Barleycorn, Dvd. B. Coe
*Star, Family and Commercial Hotel, John Snell
10 Three Tuns, James Clark
2 Two Old Brewers, Oliver Hitchen
Waggon and Horses, John Martin
14 Wellington, Mary Murrells
8 Wheat Sheaf, Samuel Speechly
White Hart, (coml. & posting house,) Charles Bottom
White Lion, Philip Arber
10 Woolpack, Thomas Hills

BANKERS.

Bryant Robert & Son, (on Hanbury and Co.)
Eaton, Hammond, & Co. (on Cocke and Co.)
Savings' Bank, Richard Bayley, sec.

FIRE AND LIFE OFFICES.

Alfred, W. P. Isaacson
Atlas, Soloman Payne
Crown, Robert James Peck
Farmers, Charles Chapman
Free Masons', Robert Rogers
Medical and Invalid, G. B. Porter
National Mercantile, Hy. Hassell
Norwich Union, Wm. Newman
Pelican & Phœnix, A. T. Pars
Suffolk and General, Richard Bayley

ACADEMIES.

Butt C.
8 Culmer Geo.
8 Feist Charles
8 Frye E. F. (prepy. boarding,)
Berners House
*Henderson Eliz.
8 Jeffs Eliz.
Manning John
5 Medbury John
8 Prince Nancy
8 Swindell John

Attorneys.

Isaacson & Gillson
*Kitchener Wm. Cripps
2 Phillips Chas.

Auctioneers.

Chapman Chas.
10 Stamford Simeon

Bakers.

8 Allen Geo.
10 Andrews Fny.
* Clark Wm.
*Claxton Thos.
*Kelleway Thos.
Newman John
8 Pond Ann

Basket Makers.

10 Cole John
9 Jarvis Robt.

Blacksmiths.

Barrow Wm. and Richard
10 King Luke & Son
*Kerry Mary
13 * Stevens Hy. Rowe

Booksellers, Printers, &c.

Rogers & Clark
10 Simpson Allen,

(and news agt.
and librarian)
Boot&ShoeMkrs.
9 Ashman Chas.
2 Craske Edw.
11*DanielsChas.
1*Harris Saml.
9 Haylock John
8 Howlett Saml.
14 Pettit Thos.
1*Prigg Thos.
13*Purkis Jas.
6*Rayner Robt.
13*Soggott Hy.
2 Utton Thos.
13*Waters Thos.
Braziers.
8 Scott Mary Ann
10 Stamford Simeon
Brewers.
Moody Tyrell
2 Phillips Chas.
Bricklayers.
Bouttell Wm.
13*Bye Stephen
8 Clark John
9 Hitchen Wm.
Butchers.
Bloom Wm.
14 Gent Wm.
Goodchild Wm.
10 Holmes Chas,
10 Holmes John
10 Reed Thos.
10 WisemanNorman
*Cabinet Makers
and Upholsterers.*
8 Chapman John
Hull Hy. & Son
Newman Wm.
*Chemists, Drugs.
& TeaDealers.*
Dunning Thos.
*Martin Joseph,
(& hatter)
Rogers Robt.
Coach Makers.
*Hunnybun and
Venden
Confectioners.
*Derisley Mary
10 Porter Wm.
(& tobacconist)
*Spicer Joseph

Coopers.
1*Franks Thos.
4*Franks Wm.
9 Jarvis Robert
Corn Merchants.
Bloss Fdk. Linch
10 Cole Robert
Corn Miller.
5 Halls Joseph
Curriers, &c.
*Everard John
Potter
Holland Horatio
Fishmongers.
14 Brown Rt. (&
game, &c. dlr.)
Furniture Brkrs.
Brasher Joseph
Hull Hy. & Son
Grocers, &c.
Bayley Rd.&Son
Hurley Wm.
Porter G. Brooks
10 Wiles Stephen
Hair Dressers.
10 Miller James
14 Stebbing Chs.
10 Symonds Ths.
Hatters.
*Hassell Henry,
(manufactr.)
Hassell Joseph
Ironmongers.
14 Adlard Chas.
(& patten mfr)
Brasher Joseph
8 Cross My. Ann
10 Paul & Brown
Rowling George
Jockeys.
See also Trainers.
8 Boyce Wm.
7*Chapell James
5 Edwards Edw.
4*Flatman John
3 Pettit George
8 Robinson Jas.
8 Robinson John
Wakefield Chpr.
Joiners.
8 Frost Charles
*Parkinson John
7*Ruse John
11*Westley Sml.
*Linen & Woollen
Drapers.*
1*Andrews Hy.

Hurley Wm.
Pask Thos.
Porter G. Brooks
Pratt James
10 Wiles Stephen
MachineMakers.
2 Cohen Jacob,
(wire worker &
cutler)
1*Holmes Abm.
Maltsters.
1 Bryant Wm.
4*Dobede John
2 Phillips Chas.
Moody Tyrell
Milliners.
1*Arnull Susan
8 Gossling Mary
*Jennings S. M.
8 Sadler Chltte.
*Wiles Ellen
Painters, Plumbers, & Glaziers.
Clark Thomas
Kent Samuel
*Payne Solomon
Saddlers & Harness Makers.
Boyce Charles
*HollandHoratio
*Turner Jph.
*Westley Wm.
Shopkeepers.
8 Chapman Thos.
9 Frost Charles
8 Hilton Mary
9 Le Pla Saml.
8 Mendham Ths.
Stone Masons.
Arber Philip
*ParkinsonRobt.
(and statuary)
Straw Hat Mkrs.
8 Argent Martha
1*Balls Eliz.
*Jennings Susan
Mary
14 Munnings E.
2 Utton Susnh.
Surgeons.
*Faircloth Rd.
Fyson Robert
*Page Fredk.
Peck Rt. James
and Son

Tailors.
14 Avis William,
(hatter and
clothes dealer)
10 Bradfer Jas.
Clark My. Ann
2 Folkes Joseph
Hassell Joseph,
*(leathr breeches,
&c.)*
14 Husband Ths.
14 Horsley Rt.
9 Le Pla Samuel
10 Sydenham Jn.
10 Thorns Hy.
*Wickes James
TRAINERS
of Race Horses.
*Arnull Wm.
Berresford Wm.
4*BlossFdk.Chs.
4*Boyce Richard
Dixon
4*Boyce Rd. jun.
4*Chifney Saml.
Cooper Wm.
12 Edwards Geo.
11*EdwardsWm.
Palace
12 Haylock Wm.
4 *Howe John
3 Meynell Capt.
Edw. Fras.
3 Pettit Robert
*Risdall Willm.,
Crockford wall
12 RobinsonJohn
Rogers Joseph
Stephenson Chpr.
Stephenson Rt.
Vety. Surgeons.
Barrow Wm. &
Richard
*KerryMy.(John
Wells, *mangr*)
5 Leech Joseph
13 Stephens Hy.
Rowe
*Watch and Clock
Makers.*
10 Harris Wm.
Hull Robert
Kates James, (&
glass, &c. dlr)
Wheelwrights.
8 DeeksJas.Fras.
Hyde James

Whitesmiths.
1*Pond Chas.
Rowling Geo.
8 Scott My. Ann

Wine and Spirit Merchants.
*FlemingRichd., (wine)
10 Mainprice Jn.
2 Phillips Chas.

COACHES.
From the White Hart.
To *Bury*, 5 aftn.; to *Cambridge*, at ¼ bef. 1, and at 4 aftn.; to *Dereham*, ¼ past 1 aftn.; to *Ipswich*, ½ p. 11 mg.; to *Norwich*, ½ p. 1, and at 2 aftn.; and to *London*, at 1, ½ p. 1, and at 2 aftn., *daily*; and on Mon. Wed. and Fri., at 8 mg. Also, to *Fakenham*, Mon. Wed. and Fri., at ¼ p. 1 aftn.; to *Holt*, Tue. Thu. and Sat., ¼ p. 1 aftn.; to *Thetford*, Tu. Thu. and Sat., at ½ p. 8 night; and to *Yarmouth*, Mon. Wed. and Fri., at 20 minutes past 11 morning
From the Half Moon.
To *London*, ¼ p. 11 night; to *Norwich*, 3 mg.; and Mail Carts, to Huntingdon, ¼ p. 11 night; and to Stoke, 3 morning
From the Greyhound.
To *London*, at 11 mg.; and to *Bury*, 2 aftn., daily, except Sunday
CARRIERS.
Hacon and Balls' Vans, &c., to London, and all parts of Suffolk and Norfolk, daily, except Sat. and Sun., from High street

FROM THE INNS.
Marked 1, *use the Golden Lion ; 2, Horse and Groom ; 3, Star ; 4, Waggon and Horses ; 5, White Lion ; and 6, the Crown.*
To *Bury*, J. Osborn, (High st.) W. and Sat.; 3 H. Watts, Tues.; 5 A. Durrant, Tuesday and Saturday
Cambridge and Ely, 4 W. Swan and Sons, Mon. Wed. and Fri.; Thomas Smith, (Bull,) Sat.; 5 A. Durrant, Monday and Friday
Gazeley, 6 Joseph Osborn, Tuesday
Haverhill, 3 J. Cornell, Tuesday
Icklingham, 4 R. Firman, Saturday and Thursday
London, (see Hacon & Balls,) 4 J. Clements, Tues. and Fri.; 1 Deacon, Mack, & Co., daily; 4 W. Swan & Sons, M. W. and Fri.; 4 Robt. Firman, Tu. and Friday; and 4 W Fowell, Monday
Lynn, 1 Deacon, Mack, and Co., daily, except Monday
Norwich, 4 W. Swan & Sons, Mon. Wed. and Fri.; 1 Deacon, Mack, and Co., daily, except Monday
Soham, 4 J. Clements, M. and Th.; 3 E. Staples, Tues. and Sat.; and W. Bullen, (Black Horse,) Tues. and Sat.
Thetford, 4 W. Fowell, Friday
Thurlow, 3 G. Brand, Tuesday
Wickhambrook, 3 Joseph Rowling, Tuesday and Friday

RISBRIDGE HUNDRED

Is the south-western division of Suffolk, and is of an irregular figure, extending 15 miles from north to south, and varying from 9 to less than 4 miles in breadth.   It is bounded, on the west, by Cambridgeshire ; on the south, by Essex ; on the east, by Babergh and Thingoe Hundreds ; and on the north, by Lackford Hundred and a small part of Cambridgeshire.   It is in the *Franchise or Liberty of St. Edmund*, and in the *Archdeaconry of Sudbury, Deanery of Clare*, and *Diocese of Ely*.   It is bounded on the south by the river *Stour*, and intersected by several smaller streams.   It is generally a fertile district, varying from a clayey to a good mixed soil, and comprising many neat villages and handsome seats, and the two small market towns of *Clare* and *Haverhill*, at the latter of which, *silk*, *drabbett*, and *straw plat*, are manufactured.   It contains one Extra-parochial place, 30 *parishes*, and several hamlets, of which the following is an enumeration, shewing their *territorial extent*, the *annual value* of their lands and buildings, as assessed to the property tax in 1815, and their *population* in 1801 and 1841.

PARISHES.	Acrs.	Rental.	Populatn. 1801.	1841.	PARISHES.	Acres.	Rental. £.	Population 1801.	1841.
Barnardiston ⎞	1000			207	Hundon	4000	5294	824	1095
Risbridge- ⎬		1094	142		Kedington‡ ..	1600	1576	467	628
Monks ‡.. ⎠	85			10	§Kentford	800	620	120	152
Bradley Great	2204	2049	395	544	*Lidgate......	1957	1438	323	450
Bradley Little	958	985	48	33	*Moulton	3073	1542	249	379
†Chedburgh ..	508	645	179	284	*Ousden	1490	1348	274	340
Clare ......⎞	2179	3417	1100	1550	Poslingford ..	2300	2782	253	343
Chilton Ham. ⎠				150	Stansfield	1850	2311	376	510
Cowling	3000	3593	570	882	Stoke-by-Clare	2330	3116	687	868
*Dalham....⎞	2070	1951	428	394	Stradishall	1400	1524	460	379
Dunstall Grn ⎠				204	Thurlow Great	1928	2098	299	431
Denston	1230	1450	277	339	Thurlow Little	1357	1643	348	422
†Denham	1990	1239	141	182	Wixoe	600	712	130	164
†Depden	1523	1824	240	345	Wickhambrook	4000	4204	1002	1623
*Gazely. with ⎞	2270			445	Withersfield ..	2059	2346	424	640
‡Higham Gn. ⎬	2500	2640	523	370	Wratting Great	1330	1206	260	355
& Needham ⎠	900			45	Wratting Little	950	856	107	239
Haverhill‡	1817	2485	1104	2152					
§Hawkedon ..	1210	1658	237	339	Total	58,468	59,646	11,987	17,493

‡ *Risbridge-Monks* is Extra-parochial. HAVERHILL is partly in *Essex,* and contains altogether 2465 acres, and 2451 souls, including 106 in Risbridge Union Workhouse. KEDINGTON is partly in *Essex,* and its entire parish contains 2400 acres, and 710 souls. *Higham Green Hamlet* is in Lackford Hundred.

POOR LAW UNIONS.—§*Hawkedon* is in *Sudbury Union ;* and *Kentford* is in *Mildenhall Union.* The five parishes marked thus * are in *Newmarket Union ;* the three marked thus † are in *Thingoe Union ;* and the other twenty parishes are in *Risbridge Union.*

☞ CHIEF CONSTABLE, Mr. John Isaacson, of Clare.

RISBRIDGE UNION comprises, besides the 20 parishes noticed above, *six parishes in Essex,* viz., Ashen, Birdbrook, Bumpstead-Steeple, Bumpstead-Helions, Ovington, and Sturmer. These 26 parishes contain a population of 17,440 souls, of whom 13,565 are in Suffolk, and 3875 in Essex. The WORK-HOUSE is at *Haverhill,* and was built many years ago, for the use of that parish only, but was enlarged in 1836, at the cost of £800, for the accommodation of the in-door paupers of this Union. It has room for 280 inmates, but had only 106 in July, 1841, and 134 in Nov. 1843. The Board consists of 28 *Guardians,* of whom two each are chosen for Clare and Haverhill, and one for each of the other parishes. J. H. Jardine, Esq., of Clare, is *Union Clerk and Superintendent Registrar ;* Mr. Frederick Laws, *master of the Workhouse ;* Mr. Charles Punchard, *auditor ;* and Mr. T. B. Brook, of Kedington, is *registrar of marriages* for the whole Union. The latter is registrar of births and deaths, and relieving officer for *Haverhill District ;* and Mr. Thomas Jolley for *Clare District.* Mr. J. P. Brown is registrar, and Mr. D. Slater, relieving officer, for *Wickambrook District.*

BARNARDISTON, a scattered village, about 5 miles N.W. of Clare, and N.E. by E. of Haverhill, has in its parish 1130 acres of fertile land, and 217 inhabitants, including MONKS-RISBRIDGE, an *Extra-parochial* farm of 85 acres, and 10 souls, 1½ mile N. of the village, belonging to Wm. Turner, Esq., and occupied by Mr. Simon Golding. *Barnardiston* gave name to a family whose several branches had seats at Kedington, Brightwell, Wyverston, and other places. They held the *manor* till the latter part of last century, but it is now held by Mark Teverson, Esq. A large portion of the soil belongs to other proprietors, some of whom are residents. Monks-Risbridge was given by Thomas de Woodstock, Earl of Buckingham and Duke of Gloucester, (sixth son of Edward III.) to Pleshy College, in Essex. The

Church (All Saints) is a neat fabric, with a tower and five bells. The rectory, valued in K.B. at £7. 10s. 5d., and in 1835 at £191, is in the patronage and incumbency of the Rev. Val. Ellis, for whom the Rev. Wm. Syer officiates. The poor parishioners have nearly an acre of land let for 20s. a-year; and they ought to have a share of *Vernon's Gift,* as noticed with Great Wratting.

Jarvis James, vict. Red Lion
Ling John, beerhouse & shopkeeper
    FARMERS. (* *are Owners.*)
*Ambrose Thos. *Barnardiston Hs*
Chapman Jacob, Clare Charity fm.
*Chapman Wm. ‖Baldry John
Golding Simon, *Monks Risbridge*
*Purkis Joseph‖Pearl Edw. *Hall*
*Teverson Henry, *Francis Farm*

BRADLEY (GREAT), a scattered village, near a small rivulet, 6 miles N. of Haverhill, and 8 miles S. of Newmarket, has in its parish 2204 acres of land, and 544 souls. It had formerly a fair, on September 29th, and was anciently held by the Somerie family, barons Dudley. Lord Dacre is now lord of the manor and patron of the *Church,* (Saint Mary,) which is a neat structure, with a tower and three bells, and was new pewed in 1841. The rectory, valued in K.B. at £17. 1s. 5½d., and in 1835 at £407, is enjoyed by the Rev. Wm. Parr Wilder, who has 52A. of glebe, and a yearly modus of £600, awarded in 1843. A large portion of the parish belongs to St. John's College, Cambridge, C. Lamprell, Esq., Mrs. Soame, Mr. D. R. Haylock, and several smaller proprietors. The present assessed yearly rental of the parish is £2242.

Barker Wm. wheelwright & vict., Fox and Goose
Crick Edward, cooper
Danby Philip, joiner and builder
Lawrence James, tailor
Nice Hanslip, corn miller
Packman Wm. beerhouse keeper
Pettit Mr Richard
Plumb Stephen, shopkeeper
Potter Samuel, shoemaker
Rowling Ambrose, bricklayer
Simperingham Mrs Margaret
Wakeling Joseph, blacksmith
    FARMERS.
Bailey Samuel ‖ Dowson John
Day Wm. (and corn merchant)
Haylock Daniel Robinson
Josling John, steward to St. John's College
Long Hanslip
Nice Wm. (& brick & tile maker)
Smith Geo. (and corn merchant)

BRADLEY (LITTLE) is a small parish, 1 mile S. of Great Bradley, and 5½ miles N. by E. of Haverhill, containing only 33 inhabitants, and 957A. 3R. 24P. of fertile land, all the property of Wm. and Charles Lamprell, Esqrs., who have neat mansions here, and have nearly all the parish in their own occupation. They are also patrons of the *Church* (All Saints,) which has a round tower, and contains a curious monumental brass in memory of John Daye, the printer, who died in 1584, at Walden, in Essex. The living is a discharged *rectory,* valued in K.B. at £5. 0s. 10d., and now enjoyed by the Rev. Charles Lamprell, jun., who has a yearly modus of £250, awarded, in 1841, in lieu of tithes. DIRECTORY:—Charles Lamprell, Esq., *Bradley Place ;* Wm. Lamprell, Esq., maltster, *Hall ;* Richard Hayward, *carpenter ;* and Thomas Smee, vict., *Royal Oak.*

CHEDBURGH, a pleasant village, near the source of a rivulet, 7½ miles S.W. of Bury, and 10 miles N.N.E. of Clare, has in its small parish 284 souls, and 508 acres of land. Two small portions belong to Mr. Thos. Green and Mr. Wm. Rutter, and the remainder to the

Marquis of Bristol, who is lord of the manor, and patron of the *Church* (All Saints,) which has a spire steeple, and is a discharged rectory, valued in K.B. at £4. 2s. 8½d., and now having 28A. of glebe, and a yearly modus of £150, awarded in 1839. Until about seven years ago, it was united with Ickworth. The Rev. George Ingram is the present incumbent.

The poor parishioners have £4 a year from *Sir Robert Drury's Charity*, and a poor widow of Chedworth and Rede alternately, is entitled to be placed in the almshouse founded by him at Hawstead. (See page 669.) The donations of *Henry and Oliver Sparrow*, for the rector and poor, were laid out, in the 8th of James I., in the purchase of 3A. 2R. of land at Langham, now let for £3. 10s. a year, of which the rector retains two-thirds, and distributes the remainder among poor parishioners, together with a yearly rent-charge of 10s., left by Anthony Sparrow, out of a mill at Stanstead. In 1815, the Hon. WM. HERVEY left £180, long annuities, to nine annuitants, in sums of £20 each, and after their decease, to his nephew, the Earl of Bristol (now Marquis of Bristol,) in trust, for any object of charity he might think proper. After the payment of legacy duty, this bequest was reduced to £162 *a year*, long annuities, which were afterwards sold, and the proceeds laid out in the purchase of £4185. 10s., three per cents. reduced annuities, now vested in trust, subject to the annuities payable to the surviving annuitants, for the education of such poor children of Chedburgh, Horningsheath, Ickworth, and the adjoining parishes, as the trustees think proper objects of charity, in the then schools of Chedburgh and Horningsheath, or elsewhere. In 1830, two of the nine annuitants were dead, and their shares had become available to this charity. The trustees in that year paid £16. 10s. for the teaching of 12 children in *Chedburgh School*, which was built at the expense of the Marquis of Bristol, and applied the remainder of the income towards the support of schools at Rede and Horningsheath.

CHEDBURGH.

Bullock Ann, farmer, *Hall*
Ellington Cornelius, schoolmaster
Elsden John, hoop maker
Frost George, shopkeeper
Ingram Rev George, *Rectory*
Gooch James, farmer
Green Thomas, farmer and owner
King James, blacksmith
Orriss Christopher, shoemaker
Porter Mrs Susan
Porter George, thatcher
Pryke Robert, cooper
Ransom Samuel, vict. Queen's Head
Rutter Wm. grocer and draper
Rutter Wm. farmer and owner
Thompson John, vict. Marquis Cornwallis
Watkinson Wm. corn miller

CLARE, a small market town of great antiquity, with many neat houses, good inns, and well-stocked shops, is situated on a pleasant acclivity, on the north side of the river Stour, which separates it from Essex, 15 miles S.S.W. of Bury St. Edmund's, 8 miles E. of Haverhill, and 55½ miles N.N.E. of London. Its *parish* had 1170 inhabitants in 1811, and 1700 in 1841, and comprises 2178A. 3R. 35P. of fertile land, including CHILTON, a hamlet of 150 souls, more than a mile N. of the town, and *Chilton Hall*, the seat and property of Mrs. Territt. Clare is celebrated for the remains of a *castle and priory*, and some of its female inhabitants are employed in the manufacture of *Tuscan straw-plat*. The streets, though spacious, are neither paved nor lighted; but they are well supplied with water, and the approaches to the town have been much improved during the last ten years, and the Market-place considerably enlarged by the removal of many unsightly buildings. The old *Market Cross* was taken down in 1838, and a handsome and commodious *Corn Exchange*, 64 feet long, and 36 broad, was erected by Mr. James Fenner, at the cost of £400, in the centre of the Market-place. The *market*, formerly held on Friday, is now held on Monday;

and here are two annual *fairs*, for toys, pedlery, &c., on Easter Tuesday and July 26th. *Petty Sessions* are held at the Half Moon Inn every fourth Monday. Courts Baron and Customary are held yearly for the *manors of Erbury* and *Stoke-with-Chilton*, of which J.ʲP. Elwes, Esq., is lord, and for the *Honour of Clare*, which belongs to the Crown, as part of the Duchy of Lancaster. But a great part of the parish belongs to Mrs. Territt, of Chilton Hall; Mrs. Barker, of Clare Priory; Thos. Weston, Esq. ; and the Cooke, Jones, and other families. Clare derived considerable importance, during the Saxon Heptarchy, from being on the frontier of the kingdom of East Anglia ; and after the Norman Conquest, it was distinguished for having given the title of *Earl* to Richard Fitz-Gilbert (a kinsman of the Conqueror,) whose grand-son took the name of *De Clare.* This was one of the 95 lordships in this county given by the Conqueror to Richard, the *first Earl of Clare ;* but the Honour of Clare comprised also many other parishes, in the counties of Essex, Surrey, Middlesex, and Hertford. The title and honour remained in his family till the death of Gilbert de Clare, Earl of Clare, Hertford, and Gloucester, in 1313, without issue. *Lionel Plantagenet,* third son of Edward III., having become possessed of the Honour of Clare, by marrying the heiress of the last Earl, was created, in 1362, *Duke of Clarence.* This title was forfeited, in 1477, by the attainder of George Plantagenet, and was not revived till 1789, when George III. created his third son, William Henry, Duke of Clarence and St. Andrews, and Earl of Munster, in Ireland. He succeeded to the Crown as Wm. IV., in 1830, and died in 1837, when the title of Duke of Clarence became extinct, but may be revived in some of the future princes of the blood royal.

CLARE CASTLE, which was anciently the baronial residence of the Earls of Clare, and of which some interesting ruins and vestiges still remain, stood on the south side of the town, and was not inferior in grandeur to any of the feudal mansions in the kingdom. The site of the whole fortification, which may be distinctly traced, contains an area of 30 acres, once surrounded by a deep fosse, and divided into an outer and inner ward or bayley, the latter of which was enclosed with a wall. On the summit of a steep hill, about 100 feet high, of no great circumference at the base, and probably of artificial formation, stand the remains of the once formidable keep, which was a massive circular tower, built of flints, strongly cemented with mortar, and strengthened with buttresses. Part of the wall on one side, is standing nearly to the height of the original elevation. A narrow path, winding round the hill, leads to this relic of the Saxon era, which forms a highly picturesque object, the sides of the mound being covered with trees and shrubs. A fragment of wall, built of flints, like the keep, runs down the hill along the north side of the area of the castle ; and a small portion is still standing on the opposite side. Though this once magnificent castle was undoubtedly founded early in the time of the Heptarchy, it is not noticed in history till Egbert had assumed the sovereignty of England. Early in the tenth century, Earl Aluric, son of Withgar, held this fortress, and founded in its precincts a church dedicated to St. John the Baptist, and endowed it with several prebends, which were given by Gilbert de Clare, in 1090, to the monks of Bec, in Normandy. On the south-west side of the town, near the precints

of the castle, are the remains of CLARE PRIORY, founded in 1248, by Richard de Clare, Earl of Clare, Gloucester and Hertford, for canons regular of St. Augustine, as a cell to the abbey of Bec, in Normandy; but it was made indigenous by Richard II., in the 19th year of his reign, and by him given as a cell to St. Peter's, at Westminster. Richard de Clare gave to this priory the hermitage of Standune, that divine service might be there celebrated for him and his. This and other donations and endowments were confirmed by the Archbishop of Canterbury and the Pope. Edmund, Earl of March, heir of the founders, converted this priory into a college, consisting of a dean and secular canons, in the 7th of Henry V. It was valued at the dissolution, at £324. 4s. 1d., and granted to Richard Friend. A large portion of the *Priory* has nearly ever since that period been occupied as a private dwelling, and is now the seat of Mrs. Barker, whose family have long held it. Though it has undergone considerable repairs and alterations, it retains much of its original character. It is two stories high, exclusive of the attics in the roof, and its walls are supported by buttresses. It has tasteful and well-wooded pleasure-grounds, and at a short distance is an ancient barn, which is all that remains of the priory church, in which was interred Joan of Acres, the second daughter of Edward I., and wife of Gilbert de Clare, after whose death she married Ralph de Morthermer, who had been servant to the earl, and was afterwards created Baron Morthermer. She died here in 1305, and her funeral was attended by most of the English nobility. Many other distinguished persons were buried here. To the north-west of the town are evident marks of a *Roman camp*.

The *Parish Church* (St. Peter and St. Paul) is a large handsome and ancient fabric, chiefly in the decorated style of English architecture, with a square tower, containing eight bells, and of an earlier date than the body. The interior, which has been improved by the heightening of the nave and the addition of side aisles, is richly ornamented. From 1834 to 1836, the whole edifice was repaired and internally beautified, and 640 additional sittings provided by means of a new gallery, making the whole number 1190, of which 774 are free, partly in consideration of a grant of £300 from the Incorporated Society for building and enlarging churches. The repairs and the new gallery cost about £1000. A large brass eagle on a pedestal, with wings expanded, forms the reading desk. The font is octagonal, and elegantly designed in the later English style. In the chancel is said to have been interred Lionel, Duke of Clarence, who died at Piedmont, in 1368, but there is no monument to his memory. The benefice is a *discharged vicarage*, valued in K.B. at £4. 18s. 9d., and in 1835 at £195. The Queen, as Duchess of Lancaster, is patroness, and the Rev. Geo. Wightman, D.D., is the incumbent. Here is an *Independent Chapel*, which was rebuilt in 1841, at the cost of £700, and a *Baptist Chapel*, rebuilt in 1823. The former sect originated here in 1700, and the latter in 1803. Sunday schools are connected with the church and chapels; and here are several *Almshouses*, an *Infant School*, established in 1843; a small *Free School*, and a number of *Charities* for the relief of the poor parishioners, as noticed below.

The *Church Estate* consists of 22½A. of land, five cottages, with gardens and a barn, now let for about £114 per annum, which is applied in the service of the

church, together with two rent-charges of 2s. each, given by unknown donors, for ringing the bells on Nov. 5th. The ALMSHOUSES consist of four cottages, near the church-yard, left by Wm. Cadge, Esq,, and occupied by eight widows; and two cottages near the Common Pasture, occupied by poor families. The POOR's LAND consists of 3A. in Bridewell Meadow, given for finding fuel for the almshouses, and now let (with a cottage belonging to the church) for £20 a year; and 11A. 2R. called Goose croft, let for £32 a year, which is distributed in bread among the poor of Clare and Chilton. About 2½A. of this land was purchased with £50 belonging to the parishioners, in 1723, but it is not known how the remainder was acquired. The poor of Chilton hamlet have, by ancient custom, 6s. 8d. yearly from land called Collins. In 1668, WM. CADGE left, out of his estate in Barnardiston, a yearly rent-charge of £25, to be applied by the vicar, churchwardens, and overseers of Clare, as follows:—£10 thereof for schooling 10 poor boys, and £15 for clothing eight poor widows in the above-named almshouses. The annuity having fallen greatly into arrear, the churchwardens, in 1735, entered into possession of the estate, which they still retain. It consists of a cottage, barn, stable, and 55A. 1R. 8P. of land, let for £74 a year, out of which £10 is paid to a *schoolmaster*, for teaching 10 poor children reading, writing, and accounts; £15 is laid out in clothing the eight almswomen, and the remainder is carried to the churchwardens' accounts. The COMMON PASTURE, comprising 62 acres of land, formerly called *Houndwall and Erbury-Garden*, was granted by Philip and Mary, in the first and second year of their reign, for the use of such inhabitants of the borough of Clare, as do not occupy more than 15 acres, to depasture their kine and horses upon. It pays £3. 6s. 8d. towards the yearly *fee farm rent* of £31. 13s. 4d., payable to the Crown out of the demesne land of the *manor of Erbury*, which is parcel of the honour of Clare. By a decree of the Court of Chancery, in 1610, the feoffees and the parishioners had to pay £200 for the perpetuation of this grant. The feoffees meet at Easter, when the Common Pasture is let in gates for 40 cows, to such persons as do not occupy 15 acres of land; and in addition, the vicar has the depasturing of two cows. The sum paid yearly for each cow is 25s., and the income arising from this source, after paying the fee-farm rent of £3. 6s. 8d., and £2 a year to the pinder, is distributed among such poor parishioners as have no cows upon the land. The eight almswomen have each a weekly stipend of 2s., and a gown and 30 bushels of coal yearly. Here is a *Protestant Association*, established in 1838, and an *Horticultural Society*, founded in 1841.

CLARE DIRECTORY.

10 Andrews Charles, gentleman
2 Armstead John Barron, gent.
Atterton George, gardener
Baker Lieut. Col. George, *Priory*
Barker Mrs Caroline, *Priory*
10 Blackman Mrs
2 Bradford Saml. tea dealer, *(tvlng)*
10 Cadge Mrs Elizabeth
10 Callice Wm. attorney's clerk
3 Choat Mr John
3 Dallison Mrs Sarah
2 Draper Richard, coachman
5 Farrand Joseph Harvey, confectioner and dealer in fancy goods
2 Fenner Mrs Caroline
9 Fenner Mrs Sarah, organist
5 Garnham Richard, gentleman
10 Garred Mrs Elizabeth
5 Goodchild Mrs Eliz. & 7 Mrs Sar.
7 Gunn Mr Robert
9 Halls James, clog & patten mkr.
7 Hammond Geo. basket maker and corn dealer
7 Harris Rev Saml. Link, (Indpt.)
9 Horrex Mr James
2 Hyde Major Thomas
9 Ince Wm. umbrella and Tuscan plat manufacturer
5 Isaacson John, chief constable
5 Isaacson and Tattersall, auctioneers and estate agents
3 Jennings Rev Daniel, (Baptist)
2 Jolley Thos. regr. & relvg. officer
10 Lester John, traveller
5 Linton Joseph, sen. parish clerk
7 Mathew Mrs Charlotte

2 Pearsons Richard, gardener
7 Pearsons Thomas, rate collector
10 Pemberton Rev Jeremiah
2 Perkins John, coal dealer
7 Pomfrett Miss Hannah
2 Potter Miss My.||9 Ridley Mrs
5 Robinson Mrs Frances
10 Rocket Mr Thomas
1 0 Rumbelow John, excise officer
5 Snell Wm. gentleman
4 Sounby Mrs J.
7 Stammers Mary, clothes dealer
10 Suttle Samuel, *coach maker*
5 Tattersall Edmund, auctioneer
Territt Mrs Anne Catherine, *Chilton Hall*
2 Territt Mrs Fanny
2 Wightman Rev Geo. D.D., vicar

ACADEMIES.
(*Marked * take Boarders.*)
9*Brown Miss Sar. & Miss Durrant
2*Free Grammar School, Lewis Briveau, Grove House
10*Fuller Hy. Wm. *Clare House*
1 Horrex Walter || 3 Brown Ann
3*Howard Miss Ann
9 Steed Miss Frances

ATTORNEYS.
9 Arden George, (*attends Monday*)
2 Jardine John Hy. (*atts. Mond.*)
10 Sams Wm. Henry
10 Stevens Saville Warner, (clerk to the Magistrates)

FIRE & LIFE OFFICES.
10 Clerical & Medical, J.B.Andrews
2 Crown, George Martin
5 Essex Economic, J. H. Farrand
9 Farmers', James Fenner
7 Norwich Equitable, Chs. Dewhirst
10 Norwich Union, J. R. Ray
9 Western (Life,) John Smoothy
5 Royal Exchange, John Isaacson

INNS & TAVERNS.
9 Bear and Crown, Sar. Bridgman
9 Bell, Micha Mellor
2 Cock, Susan Shilly
10 Cricketers' Arms, Rd. Linsell
7 Half Moon & Commercial,Wright Gittus
7 Swan, John English
4 White Hart, Henry Mason

Bakers & Flour Dealers.
10 Dyson John
9 Flanders John
1 Lewis Samuel
7 Pearsons Geo.
5 Sargent John
6 Taylor John

BANK.
(*open Monday*)
9 Oakes, Bevan

and Co. ; J. Fenner, *agent*
Beerhouses.
1 Jarvis Sus.
4 Rivett John
Blacksmiths.
4 Bowyer Saml.
9 Ellington Wm.
5 Jarvis John
2 Sparks Eliz.
Bookseller, Printer, &c.
7 Burch John (& toy dealer)
Boot&ShoeMkrs.
7 Cooper Peter
10 Crow Josiah
10 Crow Lot
5 Cutts and Son
7 Glazin Thos.
1 Jarvis Charles
1 Shilly Samuel
1 Shilly Thomas
10 Steed John
10 SwayneS.&E.
8 Taylor Joseph
2 Walliker Sar.
Bricklayers.
6 Boreham Jas.
10 Chandler Frs.
6 Ellingham Jas.
1 Howe John
7 Perry Wm.
10 Taylor Abm.
4 Webb Henry
2 Webb Wm.
Butchers.
9 AmbroseMatw.
7 Goodchild Ths.
10 Newman Rt.
Cabinet Makers & Upholsterers.
8 Dyson Wm.
9 Holmes Michl.
10 Mortlock Chs.
2PaineJohnHart
9 Smoothy John
Chemists&Dgsts.
10 Andrews Jno.
Betts,(*stamps*)
7 Dewhirst Chs.
9 Fenner James, (vety. surgeon & fancy repry.)
Coopers.
9 Elger James
9 Atterton Chas.

Corn Millers.
10 Clark Joseph
10 Gayfer Thos.
Ray Chas. *Water Mill*
Currier.
2 RobinsonCrnls.
FARMERS.
10 Brown Mary Ann
4 Coe Samuel
4 Dennis Thos.
1 GoldingHenry, (& *auctioneer*)
1 Goodchild Ths.
Heigham Capt. Ths. *Houghton Hall*
7 Ince John, Church Farm
10 Jones Chas.
4 Lees John Tnd.
4 Suttle Wm.
4 Turner, Hy.{W.
Peacock'sFarm
3 Viall King
Grocers & Lprs.
9 Goody Samuel
10 Parry Benj.
Pearson
10 Ray Jas.Reynolds & Sons
7Smith Geo.Fdk.
Hair Dressers.
9 Parry George
7 Sparge Richd.
Ironmongers and Whitesmiths.
10 Scarff Wm.
7 Wade Thos. & Chs. (machine mkrs. oil & colourmen, &c.)
Joiners.
2 Ambrose Jph.
9 Flanders John
8 Ives James
4 Ives Robert
10 Martin Jph.
7 Parry Wm. (& surveyor)
Maltsters.
10 Gayfer Thos.
Ray Chas. *Water mill*
Milliners.
9 Atterton Eliza

5 Baker Chltte.
10 Bell Eliz.
7 Deeks Eliz.
7 French My. A.
7 HammondHar.
10 Lambert Sph.
2 Robinson M.
Millwrights.
3 Ager Absalom
1 Ager Abner
6 Ager John
Painters, Plumbers, & Glaziers.
7 Hailey Thos.
2 Robinson Thos.
Saddlers & Harness Makers.
2 Foulger Boanerges
10 Hewson Ths.
10 Hewson Wm.
Shopkeepers.
1 Eagle Martha
2 Foulger Boanerges

4 Mason Henry
4 Suttle Wm.
6 Taylor John
Straw Hat Mkrs.
10 Crow Mary
7 HammondHar.
9 Ince Sarah
1 Turner My. A.
Surgeons.
10 Barnes John
2 Martin George
Taitors.
(* are Drapers.)
7*Alston Stephen
(and hatter)
9*Bloomfield W.
10 French Jph.
10 Ives Thomas
10* Jolley Jas.
5 Linton John
9*Robinson Wm.
(and glover)
Watch & Clock Makers.
7 HammondHar.

9 Mortlock Jas.
8 Mortlock Wm.
9 Palmer Walter

COACHES

To *London,* from the Half Moon daily, except Sunday, at $\frac{1}{2}$ past 6 and $\frac{1}{2}$ past 7 morning; and Monday at $\frac{1}{2}$ past 5 morning.

CARRIERS.

To *London,* John Jarvis, Church st. Mon. and Thu. 7 evg.; and John Potts, Church st., Tues. 3 aftn.

Bury, J. Golding, Common street, and Wm. Elmer, Bridewell street, Wed.; and to *Colchester & Nayland,* Tue. and Fri.; *Sudbury,* Saturday; and *Haverhall,* Tuesday and Thursday.

Ipswich and *Lavenham,* (from Bear and Crown,) John Dakin, Wed.; *Linton,* (from the Swan,) Chalk's Van, Mon., Wed., and Fri.

Wickhambrook and *Haverhill,* John Jarvis, Church street

Wheelwrights.
10 Hills Esther
2 Hills John
4 Potter George

COWLING, or *Cowlinge,* a pleasant scattered village, 8 miles N.N.W. of Clare, N.N.E. of Haverhill, and S.S.E. of Newmarket, has in its parish 882 souls, and about 3000 acres of fertile clayey land, mostly freehold. Mrs. F. A. Osborne is lady of the manor, and owner of a great part of the soil, and until lately resided at BRANCHES PARK, a large handsome mansion, with extensive pleasure grounds, nearly a mile W. of the church, formerly the seat of the Dickens family, but now unoccupied. The manor was the seat and property of Wm. Long Espec, Earl of Salisbury and Somerset, son of Henry II. by fair Rosamond. J. Tillbrook, gent., Mr. H. Andrews, and eight resident occupiers, have estates in the parish. *(See Farmers.)* Two large sheep and cattle *fairs* are held here yearly, on July 31st and Octr. 17th. The *Church* (St. Margaret) is a neat structure, with a brick tower containing five bells. The Master and Fellows of Trinity Hall, Cambridge, are appropriators of the rectory, and patrons of the perpetual curacy, by gift of Sir John and Sir Thomas Shardelowe, in 1333. The curacy is worth only about £100 per annum, and is enjoyed by the Rev. Horatio Saml. Banks. The rectorial tithes produce upwards of £700 per annum. The *Independents* have a chapel here, built about five years ago. Ten acres of land are held by the *parish clerk,* as annexed to his office, but the donor is unknown. For a distribution of sheets and blankets, the poor parishioners have £20 a year from *Deyne's Charity.* (See Moulton.)

Deacon Golding, vict. *Green Man*
Drake Wm. butcher
Erratt Edward, schoolmaster
French John, beerhouse keeper
Haylock Edward, bricklayer
Tillbrook John, gentleman

Blacksmiths.
Chapman Jas.
Chapman Wm.
Piper Samuel
Boot&ShoeMkrs.
Deacon Golding

Marsh George
Potter Chas.
Snazell Wm.
FARMERS.
(* are Owners.)
Baldry David

Blizard George
*Cater Wm.
*Chapman Wm.
Drake Wm.
Eagle John
*Gifford Daniel, *Lamb fair gn*
*Gooch John
*Gooch Jno. jun.

* Pond Samuel, *Hobbles green*
Rutter John
Shepherd & Bird
*Slater Chltte.
Tillbrook Thos.
*Webb George
Webb Rd. (cattle dealer,) *Hall*
Woollard Edw.

Wright ——
Shopkeepers.
Bailey John
Eagle J .(*joiner,*)
Post-office
GoochJohn,(*corn miller*)
Rutter MaryAnn
Tailors.
Hammond Jas.

Smith Chas.
Wheelwrights.
Chapman Wm.
Clark Thomas
CARRIER.
Thomas Bevis, to Bury, Wed., & Newmarket, Tuesday

DALHAM, a neat and pleasant village, in the vale of a small rivulet, nearly 6 miles E.S.E. of Newmarket, and 9 miles W. of Bury St. Edmund's, has in its parish 2070 acres of fertile land, and 598 souls, of whom 204 are in the hamlet of *Dunstall Green*, more than a mile S.E. of the church. Dalham was the lordship of Walter de Norwich, a parliamentary baron in the reign of Edward II. On the death of his great-grandson, it passed to William de Ufford, Earl of Suffolk. It afterwards passed to the Estotevilles, who sold it to Dr. Simon Patrick, Bishop of Ely, whose son disposed of it to Gilbert Affleck, Esq., whose family has since been seated here, and was elevated to a baronetage in 1782. The *Rev. Sir Robert Affleck, Bart.*, is now lord of the manor, and owner of nearly all the parish. He supports a small free-school, and resides at *Dalham Hall*, a large red brick mansion in a beautiful park, a little north of the village. The offices below are arched, and above them a noble gallery, 24 feet wide, runs quite through the building, which was erected about the year 1705, by Dr. Patrick, Bishop of Ely. The *Church* (St. Mary) is a neat structure, with a tower containing five bells, and formerly surmounted with a spire, which was blown down by the high wind at Oliver Cromwell's death. The rectory, valued in K.B. at £15. 10s. 5d., and in 1835 at £419, is in the gift of the Rev. Sir Rt. Affleck, and incumbency of the Rev. James Danby Affleck. The tithes were commuted at the enclosure, about 25 years ago.

*Marked * are at Dunstall Green, and the others in Dalham*
Affleck Rev Sir Robert, Bart. *Dalham Hall*
Affleck Rev James Danby, *Rectory*
Bosanquet Rev Edwin, *curate of Denham*
Dunning John, vict. *King's Head*
Fitch John, gamekeeper
Fyson Wm. baker and shopkeeper
*Herbert Benj. farrier
Marrow John, glazier, &c.
Murray Mrs Mary
Norman James, shopkeeper
Plummer Gilbert, bricklayer

Plummer John, carpenter
Plummer John, bricklayer
Ruffell Wm. miller and maltster
*Sealey Timothy, shoemaker
*Sparrow James, shoemaker
*Swann Wm. beerhs. and shopkeeper
Tabram John, blacksmith
Thompson Mr Daniel
Watkinson James, shoemaker
FARMERS.
*Andrews James
Dearsley Thos.
Fitch Chas. *agent*
Garrad Edw.
*Gillings Wm.
Moore Jeremiah
Moore Thomas
Ruffell Wm.
*Sargent Fredk.
*Snape Charles
*Webb James

DENHAM, a small scattered village, nearly 7 miles W.S.W. of Bury St. Edmund's, has in its parish 182 souls, and 1990 acres of land, having a good mixed soil. Wm. Francis Gamuel Farmer, Esq., is impropriator, owner of the soil, lord of the manor, and patron of the *Church*, (St. Mary,) which has a singularly constructed tower, and is

a perpetual curacy, endowed with a yearly stipend of £100, and now enjoyed by the Rev. R. Stephen Stevens, of South Petherwin, Cornwall, for whom the Rev. Edward Bosanquet, of Dalham, officiates. In Edward the Third's time, Denham belonged to the Hethe family. It was afterwards appropriated to some monastic institution, and was granted at the dissolution to *Sir Edward Lukemore*, of whose son and great-grandson there are handsome monuments in the church, the latter bearing a fine recumbent effigy. The heiress of the Lukemores carried the estate in marriage to the first Lord Viscount Townshend, who died in 1687, and it belonged to his family in Kirby's time. The *Hall*, which was the seat of the Lukemores, is now a moated farmhouse. On a farm called Denham Castle, is a moated eminence, supposed to have been occupied by the Saxons or Danes. In 1662, *Lady Mary Townshend* left £100, to be laid out in lands, and the profits thereof to be applied in apprenticing poor orphan children of this parish. The estate purchased consists of a house and about 8a. 1r. 8p. of land, at Cowling, let for £14 a year, which is given partly in apprentice fees and partly in blankets. The poor parishioners have £2 a year out of Denham Hall estate, given by one of the *Townshend* family.

Barrow Joseph, blacksmith
Drake Maria, vict. *Plough*
Robinson Francis, gamekeeper
Walker John, carpenter & wheelgt
FARMERS.
Halls Fredk. Edwin, *Abbot's Hall*

Halls Elizabeth, *Denham Castle*
Halls James, *Denham end Lodge*
Halls Joseph, *Denham Hall*
Sparrow James

DENSTON, or DENERDISTON, a pleasant village in the vale of a rivulet, 6 miles N. of Clare, has in its parish 339 souls, and 1230 acres of strong fertile land. DENSTON HALL, a large neat mansion in a small park, on the south side of the village, is occupied by Samuel Yate Benyon, Esq., but belongs with the manor and nearly all the soil to the Misses Walpole, for their lives, after which the estate will pass to Wm. Pigott, Esq., now only eight years of age, and for whom Earl Powis is trustee. Here was a *college* or chantry, endowed with £22. 8s. 9d. per annum, and granted, with a manor called *Beaumonds*, in the second of Edward VI., to Thomas and John Smith, who sold it to Wm. Bird. In 1764, John Robinson was seated here, and owned the estate. The *Church* (St. Nicholas) is a large ancient structure, and the living is a perpetual curacy, valued in 1835 at only £51, and now enjoyed by the Rev. Wm. Suttaby, M.A. Misses Walpole are patrons and appropriators, and support a small *free school* here. The poor have two annuities of 13s. 4d. each; one given by an unknown donor, and the other by Anthony Sparrow. (See Wickhambrook.)

Benyon Samuel Yate, Esq. *Denston Hall*
Coote Mary, shopkeeper
Hinds George, vict. *Plumbers' Arms*, and Post-office
Pryke George, butcher
Pryke Susan, schoolmistress
Raymond Henry, cooper
Webb Thomas, veterinary surgeon

Went Henry, shopkeeper
FARMERS.
Brown John, *Water lane*
Gooch Nathan, *Church Farm*
Metcalf Hy. (steward,) *Gomers*
Rutter Richard, *Elm Farm*
Westrup John and Peacock George, *Sheepcote*

DEPDEN, a scattered village, 9 miles N. by E. of Clare, and S.W. of Bury St. Edmund's, has in its fertile parish 345 souls, and 1523 acres of land. The *Hall*, now a farm-house, was formerly the seat of the Coels, Thornhills, and Mures. Wm. Adair, Esq., is now lord of the manor ; but a great part of the parish belongs to the Marquis of Bristol, H. J. Oakes, Esq., Mr. George Steel, Mr. Wm. Isaacson, and a few smaller owners. The *Church* (St. Mary) is a small neat fabric, with a tower and three bells, and was new roofed in 1843, at the cost of £150. The living is a rectory, valued in K.B. at £10. 11s. 5½d., and now having 23A. of glebe, and a yearly modus of £455, awarded in 1842, in lieu of tithes. The patronage is in the Crown, and the Rev. Martin Lloyd is the non-resident incumbent. *Dr. Anthony Sparrow*, bishop of Norwich from 1676, till his death, in 1685, was born here. The poor parishioners have a cottage, and 3½A. of land, at Hargrave, given by Dr. Macro, in 1733, and now let for £10 per annum. They have also £2 yearly from *Sparrow's Charity*, as noticed with Wickhambrook.

Ashman George, beerhouse keeper
Bull George, shopkeeper
Manning Robert, blacksmith
Pryke James, shopkeeper
Shaw John, wheelwright
Waller Rev Rt. P. *curate*, Rectory

FARMERS.

Deadman Mrs || Pratt Catherine
Green James, *Depden Hall*
Green Richard (and miller)
Isaacson Wm. || Paine Edward
Ransom Jas. || Steel George, *Elms*
CARRIERS *to Bury*, Wed. and Sat., Geo. Ashman and Mrs Pryke

GAZELEY, a neat and pleasant village, 5 miles E. by S. of Newmarket, and 9 miles W. of Bury St. Edmund's, has in its parish 5670A., and 860 inhabitants, but is divided into three *hamlets*, viz., GAZELEY, containing 2270 acres, and 445 souls; HIGHAM GREEN, containing 2500 acres, and 370 souls; and NEEDHAM, containing 900 acres, and 45 souls. *Higham Green* is in Lackford Hundred, and has a scattered village, 2 miles N.E. of Gazeley, and 7 miles W. of Bury; and its soil belongs Robt. Bartley, Esq., Henry Le Grice, Esq., Mrs. Holmes, Mr. Thos. Cornell, and a few smaller owners. *Needham* hamlet, one mile N. of Gazeley, belongs to Chas. Eaton Hammond, Esq., and has only seven cottages and *Needham Hall*, the latter now a farm-house, occupied by Mr. Henry Webb. W. F. G. Farmer, Esq., is lord of the *manor of Gazeley*; but a great part of the soil belongs to the Rev. Sir Robt. Affleck, (impropriator of the rectory,) C. E. Hammond, Esq., Mr. T. C. Burroughes, Mr. Cracknell, Mr. J. Steel, and a few smaller owners. The open fields, &c., were enclosed in 1840. The *Church* (All Saints) is a neat structure, with a tower and six bells, and was appropriated to one of the prebendaries of Stoke College, near Clare. The rectory was granted, in the 9th of James I., to Fras. Moore and Fras. Phillips. The *vicarage*, valued in K.B. at £10. 10s. 5d., is discharged from the payment of first-fruits and tenths, and has the rectory of Kentford annexed to it. It has about 4A. of glebe, and a yearly modus of £456, awarded in 1841, of which £180 is in lieu of Kentford tithes. The patronage is in Trinity College, Cambridge, and the Rev. George Howes is the non-resident incumbent. Here is a *National School*, built in 1843 ; and at *Higham Green*, is a small *Free School*, built by R. Bartley, Esq., in 1833 ; and a *Baptist Chapel*, erected in

1836, by Mr. Sabine. The poor parishioners have two yearly *rent-charges*, for distributions of red herrings; viz., 7s. 6d., given by George Warren, in 1683; and 10s., given by Simon Pratt, in 1641. They are payable out of land here, belonging to C. E. Hammond, Esq., of New-market. At the Chequers Inn, a lodge of Odd Fellows was opened in Oct., 1843. *Desning Hall* and *Lodge* are two farm-houses.

*Marked * are in Higham Green; and the others at Gazeley, or where specified.*

Barnes John, millwright
Birch Rev Wm. curate, *Vicarage*
Chambers Fredk. vict. *Chequers*
*Cooke James, vict. *Lamb*
Drake Edward, butcher
French Wm. shoemaker
Layton John, collar & harness mkr
Plummer James, bricklayer
Symonds Henry, gentleman
Willis John, tailor
Willis Miss, *National School*

Blacksmiths.
Norton James
Sutton George
Corn Millers.
Death Wm.

*Ray Thos. Reynolds (& maltster)

FARMERS.
Burroughes Tho-mas Cook
*Cornell Thomas
Death Wm.
*Ellis Joseph, *Higham Hall*
*Fyson Edward
*Fyson William, *Higham Lodge*
King Henry
King Jas. *Desning Hall*
Moore James, steward, *Desning Lodge*
Moore John
Norman Wm.
*Ray Thos. R.
Webb Henry, *Needham Hall*

Wilson John
Shopkeepers.
*Baker John
Bradley George
*Osborne Ambrs.
Wilson John, (& draper and agt. to Suffolk Fire Office)
Wheelwrights.
Rush Rd. Haynes
Whitmore Thos.
CARRIER.
Jph. Osborne, to Bury, Mon.; Cambridge, — Sat.; & New-market, Tues.

HAVERHILL is an ancient market-town and parish, 8 miles W· of Clare, and 54 miles N.N.E. of London, mostly in Risbridge Hundred, Suffolk, and partly in Hinckford Hundred, Essex. It had 1308 inhabitants in 1801, and 2451 in 1841, including 106 paupers in *Ris-bridge Union Workhouse*, which is already noticed at page 721. It comprises 2465 acres of land, of which 648 acres, and 229 of its inhabitants, are in Essex, and form that part of the town and parish called *Haverhill Hamlet.* The town consists chiefly of one broad street, about a mile in length; and many of its old thatched houses have given place to neat slated buildings, during the last twenty years. It was formerly noted for checks, cottons, and fustians, and has now a *silk mill*, employing about 70 hands, and several manufacturers of *drabbetts*. Many females are here employed in making up the latter article into *smock-frocks*; and many others in the town and neighbourhood are engaged in making *Tuscan straw-plat*, which was first introduced by Mr. John Parry. Here are about 330 *weavers* employed on drabbetts, and 70 on silk, which is here woven into umbrella and parasol fabrics. The linen and cotton yarns of which the drabbetts are woven, are mostly brought from Leeds and Stockport. The *market*, formerly held on Wednesday, was changed to Friday many years ago, and is well supplied with corn and provisions. The Market Place is spacious, and had an ancient market-house or cross, which was taken down about twelve years ago. A house, on one side of it, was converted into a *Corn Exchange*, in 1839. *Fairs* are held here on May 12th, for cattle, &c.; and Oct. 10th, for pedlery, pleasure, &c. Sir George Howland Willoughby Beaumont, Bart., of Cole-Orton, Leicestershire, is lord of the *manor of Haverhill*, which was anciently held by the noble families of Stafford and Grey; but a great part of the parish belongs to J. Spir-

ling, Esq.; Queen's College, Cambridge; and several smaller proprietors. The *Church* (St. Mary) is a large ancient structure, with a tower and five bells. It has a good organ, and about a thousand sittings. It was appropriated to Castleacre Priory, in Norfolk; and the rectory and advowson were granted, in the 29th of Henry VIII., to Thomas, Lord Cromwell. J. Spirling, Esq., is now impropriator of the rectory; and Sir G. H. W. Beaumont is patron of the discharged *vicarage*, which is valued in K.B. at £6. 5s., and is enjoyed by the Rev. Robert Roberts, M.A., who has now a yearly modus of £220, awarded in 1841. A chapel, called " *Le Nether Chirche*," anciently stood near the homestead of the chapel-farm, about a mile N. of the town; and a little to the west are some vestiges of a castle. There are in the town, a *Friend's Meeting-house*, a *Baptist Chapel*, a *Presbyterian Chapel*, built in 1707, and rebuilt in 1843; and an *Independent Chapel*, erected in 1839, at the cost of £1000. The church and chapels have each a *Sunday School*, and here is also a *National School*. The SAVINGS' BANK, for Haverhill and its vicinity, was established in 1836. It is open every Friday, at the Post Office, and, in Nov., 1842, had deposits amounting to about £4600. The Rev. Wm. Mayd, of Withersfield, is the secretary and treasurer. The INFIRMARY, for the relief of the lame and sick poor of Risbridge Union, stands near the Workhouse, and was built in 1840, at the cost of £2200. It had 15 in-patients in July, 1841; and 8 in Nov., 1843. S. S. G. Eastcott is the surgeon. In the town are several *Friendly Societies* and other provident institutions. *Dr. Samuel Ward*, a celebrated divine of the 17th century, was born here. He was master of Sidney College, Cambridge, and accompanied Bishop Carlton, Dean Hall, and Dr. Davenant, to the synod of Dort. Imprisonment and ill-usage, during the civil wars between Charles I. and the Parliament, occasioned his death, in 1643. His father was vicar here, and lies buried in the chancel.

HAVERHILL.

POST OFFICE at Mr Jno. Turner's. Letters are despatched at 4 aftn. and received at 9 and 11 morning.

Marked 1, *reside in Baker's row;* 2, *Bull lane;* 3, *Burton-end;* 4, *Chantry croft;* 5, *Haverhill Hamlet, in Essex;* 6, *High street;* 7, *Market place;* 8, *Pea market hill; and* 9, *in Withersfield road.*

2 Adcock MrsSus.|| 6 Basham Mrs S.
1 Basham Wm. gent'eman
7 Boreham Wm. Wakelin, gent.
6 Brainsford Rev. Charles, (Indpt.)
1 Chater John and Son, gardeners and nurserymen
4 Clare Wm. millwright
3 Cole Joseph, cart owner
1 Crick John, farrier
4 Copsey Mr Samuel
5 Davies Rev. Jas. (Presbyn. min.)
1 Elliston James, fellmonger, leather cutter, and glover

6 Hall John, brick and tile maker
6 Hall Jas. gent || Frost Mrs Ann
8 Havers Henry, hop and tea mert.
6 Hinds Thomas, traveller
1 Laws Fredk. govr. *Workhouse*
3 Oakes, Bevan, and Co. bankers, (& Sudbury, &c) Jph. Boreham, *agt.*
6 Page Edward, confectioner. &c
5 Roberts Rev. Robert, M.A. vicar, *Manor House*
7 Skipper Henry, excise officer
4 Suckling James, rope maker
4 Underwood Mr Robert
5 Walton Mrs Mary Ann
2 Webb Mr Barnabas & Mrs Mtbl.
3 Wright Ellington, traveller
7 Wright Isaac, gentleman
6 Wright John, traveller

FIRE AND LIFE OFFICES.

6 Atlas, Wm. Burleigh
6 Crown, Henry Martin
7 Norwich Union, John Turner

7 Suffolk and General, Charles Kitching and Isaac Wright
6 Sun, Henry Wyld Jackson

INNS AND TAVERNS.
7 Bell, Elias Ellis
2 Bull, (unoccupied)
7 Greyhound, Martha Scotcher
1 Queen's Head, John Price
6 Ram, Wm. Woolard
9 Rose and Crown, Daniel Gilby
5 Weavers' Arms, James Backler

Academies.
(*take Boarders.*)
6*Dean Eliz. and Bridgman Mra
6 Dearsley Wltr.
7*Dix Elizabeth
6*Gibling Sarah
9 Hall Harriet

Attorneys.
6 Burleigh Wm.
6 Jackson Hy. W.

Bakers, &c.
6 Brown Wm.
4 Bridge Joseph
6 Crick Mary
8 Crick Thomas
9 Radford John
6 Turner Thos.
6 Woolard Thos.

Beerhouses.
6 Backler Geo.
1 Bigmore Saml.
5 Bush Wm.
3 Campion Wm.
6 Cracknell Jas.
7 Crick John
5 Frost James
4 Mason Thomas
9 Scott Charles

Blacksmiths.
2 Frost John
6 Page Edwd. (& whitesmith)
4 Spicer Eliz.
6 Spicer James
2 Williams Rd.

Booksellers and Printers.
1 Bigmore Saml. jun. (&orgnst.)
6 Dearsley Wltr.

Boot & Shoe Mkrs.
1 Albon Wm.
8 Hickford Wm.
8 Mizen Wm.
5 Starns Henry

1 Suckling John
1 Suckling Saml.
7 Turner John
6 Turner Thos.

Braziers & Tinrs.
7 Dix John
1 Fairweather W

Bricklayers and Plasterers.
6 Arber John
6 Backler Geo.
6 Scotcher Jas.

Butchers.
6 Berry James
6 Freeston Sus.
6 Siggs Cook

Cabinet Makers.
1 Jolly Hy. (and bellhanger)
6 Sizer Jonathan

Chemist & Drgt.
7 Kitching Chas.

Coach Maker and Wheelwright.
6 Barker Daniel

Coopers.
7 Crick John
6 Lee Joshua (& turner)

Corn and Flour Dealers.
1 Snape Charles
7 Snape My. Ann

Corn Millers.
3 Brown James, *New Mill*
4 Major Cornls.
Ruffel Richard, *Old Mill*

DRABBETT *and Smock Frk. Mfrs.*
7 Gurton Daniel and Son
6 Nott Joseph
7 Pearce & Chater
6 Sizer Martha

6 Webb Stephen

FARMERS.
Brook Thos. *Hall*
Cross Philip, *Hazel Stubb*
Diggins John, *Chapel Farm*
Harrison Thos.
Osborne James, *Haverhill place*
Richardson Jesse, *Hanchet*
Robinson George, *Moor Hall*
5 Scotcher John, *Manor Farm*
1 Snape William (bailiff)
Unwin Joseph, *Hazel Stubb*

Glass, China, &c Dealers.
7 Dix John (and furniture bkr.)
7 Hagger Josiah
6 Palmer Harriet

Grocers & Drprs.
7 Dennis Wm.
7 Dix John, Stamp Office
1 Lawrence Jno.
7 Pearce & Chater
6 Peck James

Hair Dressers.
1 Heckford John
6 Kiddle Henry

Ironmongers.
7 Dix John
1 Fairweather W
6 Smoothy Geo.

Joiners & Bldrs.
6 Butcher Rt.
1 Hall Charles
6 Hall Wm.
8 Hepler Edwd.
4 Mason Thomas

Maltsters.
3 Boreham Jph. (& brewer & spirit mert.)

4 Good Charles
6 Purkis John

Milliners.
8 Burleigh S.
6 Howe Eliz.
4 Kemball Sarah
7 Killingback Elz
1 Scotcher My. A.

Painters, Plumbers, & Glaziers.
6 Brown Wm.
7 Finch Elijah
1 Pate Wm.
1 Wiles Edward

Saddlers & Harness Makers.
4 Bridge Hovell
4 Bridge Joseph
7 Hagger Josiah

Shopkeepers.
6 Banks Jane
4 Bridge Joseph
7 Cracknell Jas.

SILK MANFR.
5 Roberts Richd.

Straw Hat Mkrs.
7 Ellis Ann Maria (and draper)
6 Hinds Mary

Straw Plat Mfrs.
7 Chapmau John
7 Parry John
6 Spencer Margt.

Surgeons.
6 Eastcott Sandford Saml. Geo.
6 Martin Henry
6 Robinson Thos.

Tailors & Drprs.
4 Ellis James
7 Ellis Thomas
7 Fairweather W.
6 Howes George (clothes broker)
6 Lock George

Watch & Clock Makers.
6 Carter Wm.
6 Palmer Har.
6 Wham George

COACHES.
To London, Mon. Wed. and Fri. at ½ past 10 mg. from the Bell; and Mon. Wed. and Fri. at 3 aftn., and Tu. Thu. and Sat. at 12 noon, from the Greyhound.

CARRIERS.

To *London*, Jno. Jarvis, (Bell,) Tu. and Sat.; Wm. Cockerton, (Greyhound,) Thurs.; and Wm. Clarke, (Queen's Head,) daily, except Sund. *Bury*, Jas. Cracknell, High st. Wed

Cambridge and *Newmarket*, Jas. Cornell, Pea market hill, Tuesday. *Clare*, Wm. Elmer, Mon. & Thu. and J. Jarvis, Tu. and Sat. from the Bell; and J. Golding, Monday, from the Ram.

HAWKEDON, a scattered village on a pleasant acilivity, near a rivulet, 6 mile N.N.E. of Clare, and 9 miles S.S.W. of Bury St. Edmund's, has in its parish 339 souls and 1210 acres of land. It is in two manors, viz., *Hawkedon Hall*, (a neat mansion,) the seat and pro- perty of J. Frost, Esq.; and *Thurston Hall*, of which H. J. Oakes, Esq., is lord. *Swan Hall*, another ancient mansion, now a farm-house, belongs, with a large estate, to G. W. Poley, Esq., and was formerly a seat of the Abbot family. J. H. Frere, Esq., Jno. Hammond, Esq., the Rev. J. Maddy, the Rev. A. A. Colvile, and several smaller owners have estates in the parish. The *Church* is an ancient structure, with a tower and five bells, and the living is a rectory, valued in K.B. at £7. 10s., and in 1835, at £275, but now having 45A. acres of glebe, and a yearly modus of £400, awarded in 1841. Henry James Oakes, Esq., is patron, and the Rev. George John Haggitt, M.A., of Bury, is the incumbent. The poor have nearly 2A. of land at Stansfield, let for 30s. a year, and given by a Mr. Shaw. They have also 10s. a year, from *Anthony Sparrow's Charity*, (see Wickhambrook,) and 20s. a year, given by a *Mr. Ray*, out of a farm at Denston.

Adams John, shopkeeper
Frost Jno. Esq. *Hawkedon Hall*
Game James, shoemaker
Hanbury Rev. Arthur D. C. L. curate
Ward Susan, vict. *Queen's Head*
Webb John, blacksmith

FARMERS.

Brown Thos. || Hibble James

Hammond James, *Langley farm*
Moore Simon, *Swan Hall*
Mortlock Thomas, *Gallowgate*
Sparrow George, *Hungerdown Hall*
Tilbrook Wm. *Chrislands*
Wiseman Jas. *Thurston Hall*
CARRIER, Wm. Taylor, to Bury Tu. Wed. and Sat.

HUNDON, a large village pleasantly situated, 3½ miles N.N.W. of Clare, and 6 miles E.N.E. of Haverhall, has in its fertile parish 1095 inhabitants, about 4000 acres of land, the small hamlets of *Worsted Green* and *Scotch Green*, and many scattered houses. Sir Robt. Harland, Bart., is lord of the manor of *Hundon with Chilburn*, and owns about half of the parish. The remainder belongs to Jesus' College, Cambridge, the Deanery of St. Paul's, Mrs. F. Territt, Mrs. A. C. Territt. S. Ware, Esq., Mrs. Webb, Mrs. Crown, several smaller owners, and the nine persons marked thus * in the subjoined list of farmers. The manor belonged to the Earl of Clarence, in the reign of Edward III., and was afterwards held by the Vernons. *Great Park, Estry Park*, and *Broxley Park*, are three estates in this parish, which were held by Stoke priory, near Clare, and were sold, in the 3rd of Edward VI., to Sir John Cheke. In 1687, more than 200 *Saxon coins* were discovered by the sexton, while digging a grave in the church-yard. They were of the value of 4d. each, and of various mints. The *Church* (All Saints) is a large neat fabric, with a tower and six bells. It was new leaded in 1843, and has undergone many repairs during the last six years. In a building attached to it is a noble pyramid of marble, in memory of Arethusa, wife of James Vernon, Esq., and daughter of Lord Clifford,

who died in 1728. The appropriation and advowson were held by Stoke priory. The great tithes are now held by Sir Robert Harland. The benefice is a discharged *vicarage*, valued in K.B. at £7. 13s. 4d., and in 1835, at £201. The patronage is in Jesus College, Cambridge, and the Rev. Robert Wilson Stoddart, M.A., is the incumbent. A *fair* for pedlery, &c., is held here on Holy Thursday.

Hundon Charity Estate comprises a messuage occupied by paupers; a house divided into two tenements, used as a school and an almshouse for aged poor; and a farm of 113A., partly in Barnardiston, and now let for £120 a year. It is held in trust, as declared by a decree in Chancery, for the repair of the church and causeways in the parish; the relief of the poor; and other charitable uses, at the discretion of the trustees. A portion of the income is distributed in blankets, clothing, bread, or money, among the poor parishioners, who have also 40s. a year, out of premises in Wood-street, left by *Wm. Rich*, in 1690, for distributions of bread at Hallowmass and Christmas. In 1737, *James Vernon*, who had contributed largely towards the erection of workhouses in Hundon, Wickhambrook, and Stradishall, gave a yearly rent-charge of £32, out of his farms at Wickhambrook, in trust to pay to the churchwardens of Hundon £22 thereof, for the following uses, viz., £10 for the master of the parish-workhouse; 5s. each for the vicar and two churchwardens, and the remainder for the schooling of poor children, except what may be necessary for repairing the donor's monument. He gave the other £10 of the annuity of £32, to the parish of Wickhambrook, and left a yearly rent-charge of £10 out of lands at Stradishall, for the master of the workhouse in that parish. For £10 a year received from this charity, a schoolmaster in Hundon teaches 16 poor children.

HUNDON.

Bradman Wm. tailor
Crown Hannah, vict. *Red Lion*
Gibbons John, cattle dealer
Goodchild Wm. butcher
Green George, vict. *Rose and Crown*
Missen John, parish clerk
Nock Thomas, carpenter
Rutter Thomas, glover, &c.
Savage Mary, vict. *Cock*
Stoddart Rev. R. Wilson, M.A. *vicar*
Wade David, schoolmaster
Whiting Wm. collar & harness mkr.
Wade Andrew, vict. *Plough*

Beer Houses.
Rogers Thomas
Savage Abraham

Bakers.
Chapman Wm.
Stiff James

Blacksmiths.
Crown Hannah
Eldred George
Rivett Henry

Boot & Shoe Mkrs.

Bowers Wm.
Green George
Parmenter Geo.
Potter Daniel
Savage Josiah

Bricklayers.
Burrows Robert
Casbolt Thomas

Corn Millers.
Deeks George
Ruse John

FARMERS.
(*are owners.*)
* Baldry George
Brown George
* Carbolt Thos.
* Choat William
   Worsted green
Cuthbert Thomas
Deeks Charles
* Deeks George
Deeks Matthew
* Deeks Susan,
   Wash farm
Deeks John
* Eagle Samuel
Frost Charles
Golding William,
   Worsted green
Goodchild Wm.
Hammond Hy.
   Scotch green
Howe S. maltster,
   Hall
Leech Wm. *Estry Lodge*

* Potter Dd. & Rt.
   Scotch green
* Savage Abrm.
Silverstone Jas.
Snell John Fras.
   Great Lodge
Taylor Wm.
Teverson Chas.
   Broxley Lodge
Unwin Ralph
Wade Noah
   Shopkeepers.
Medcalfe George
Ruse Thomas
Savage Charles
Savage Josiah
Savage Abrm.
Wade Wm.
   Wheelwrights.
Pulham Mattw.
Savage Charles
   CARRIER.
Thos. Jolley, to
   Bury, Wed.

KEDINGTON, now corruptly called KETTON, is a large scattered village, near one of the tributary streams of the river Stour, 5 miles W.N.W. of Clare, and 2½ miles E.N.E. of Haverhill. Its parish contains 2400 acres of fertile land, and 710 souls, of which about 800 acres and 82 souls are in Hinckford Hundred, *Essex*, and the remainder in Risbridge Hundred, Suffolk. At the Domesday survey, it was the lordship of Ralph Baynard; but being forfeited in the reign of

Henry I., it was given to Richard Fitz-Gilbert, progenitor of the earls of Clare. It afterwards passed to the *Barnardistons,* who were long seated at the *Hall,* which was a large and handsome mansion, but was taken down many years ago. Sir Thos. Barnardiston, of Kedington, was created a *baronet* in 1663, but the title has been many years extinct. In the reign of Queen Anne, two baronets of this family, Sir Samuel and Sir Thomas, sat at the same time in Parliament. This family is also remarkable for having given rise to the appellation of *Roundhead,* during the civil commotions in the reign of Charles I. " The London apprentices," says Rapin, " wore the hair of the head cut round ; and the Queen, observing out of a window Samuel Barnardiston among them, cried out, ' See what a handsome *round-head* is there.' " Hence came the name, which was first publicly used by Captain Hyde. Kedington has a *fair* for pedlery, &c., on June 29th. The parish is all freehold, and belongs to the Rev. B. B. Syer, Sir J. R. Rowley, Mr. B. Gooch, Mr. Hammond, the seven resident occupiers marked thus * in the subjoined list of farmers, and a few smaller owners. The *Church* (St. Peter and St. Paul) is a neat structure, with a tower and five bells, and contains several monuments of the Barnardistons, of whom there are also some memorials in stained glass in the windows. The *rectory* is valued in K.B. at £16. 8s. 6¼d., and in 1835, at £498, but now having a yearly modus of £701. 18s., awarded in 1840, including the quota on the glebe (about 100A.,) and subject to rates and taxes. The Rev. B. B. Syer is patron and incumbent. The celebrated *Archbishop Tillotson* was rector here at the time of the Commonwealth. A farm of 34A. 3R. 34P., at Sturmer, in Essex, belongs jointly to the parishes of Sturmer and Kedington, and is vested in twelve feoffees, pursuant to ancient deeds, in trust to apply the rents and profits, in equal moieties, for the repairs of the churches, and the relief of the poor of the two parishes. It is let for £35 per annum, so that Kedington receives £17. 10s. yearly, and one moiety thereof is applied in the service of the church, and the other for educating and apprenticing poor children. About 3 acres, called *Town Land and Rope Acre,* are held by the churchwardens of Kedington for the repairs of the church, and are let for about £3. 10s. per annum. For the same purpose, they have three rent-charges, amounting to 25s. 4d. per annum, left by persons named Bateman, Fairclough, and an unknown donor. Thirteen poor widows of Kedington have divided among them, 4s. 3d. yearly, given by one *Bateman,* out of an estate here belonging to Mr. Mathew.

Bowyer Edward, butcher
Bowyer John, blacksmith
Bowyer James, pig jobber
Bowyer Samuel, pig jobber
Brook Thomas Barsham, registrar of births, deaths, and marriages, and relieving officer
Cornwell Frederick, shoemaker
Deeks James, wheelwright
Deeks Joseph, bricklayer
Diver John, wheelwright
Garwood John, blacksmith & beerhs

Golding Henry, gentleman
Goodchild Wm. gent. *Dane House*
Ling John, shoemaker & vict. Bell
Martin Thomas, baker
Pettit Wyatt John, cabinet maker
Price John, brewer and maltster
Price Charlotte, beer house
Price Wm.P.vict. Barnardiston Arms
Punchard Charles, corn miller, *Water Mill*
Syer Rev Barrington Bloomfield, *Rectory*

Syer Rev Wm. Henry, curate

FARMERS.
(* are Owners.)
Bowyer Henry,
(and butcher)
*Chapman Wm.

*Goodchild John,
(and maltster)
*Martin Joseph
*Price John
Price Walter

*Purkis Henry
*Rumball James,
(& corn miller)
*Rumball Robert
Teverson Henry

Shopkeepers.
Callow Thos. (and baker)
Cornwell Charles
Cornwell James,
(& shoemaker)

KENTFORD, a small village and parish, on the Bury road, 4½ miles E. of Newmarket, contains 152 souls, and about 800 acres of fertile land, belonging to Mr. J. Wellsman, Mr. Samuel Clark Jonas, and a few smaller owners; but W. F. G. Farmer, Esq., is lord of the manor. The *Church* (St. Mary) is a small fabric, with a tower and three bells. The *rectory*, valued in K.B. at £7. 3s. 4d., is consolidated with the vicarage of Gazeley, as already noticed at page 731. The tithes here were commuted, in 1843, for a yearly modus of £180. On the enclosure of the open fields, &c., in this parish, under an act passed in 1826, several parcels of old poor's land were exchanged for three allotments in Worlington Field, containing together 17A. 1R. 17P. They are let by the rector and churchwardens, who distribute the rents yearly among the deserving poor of the parish.

Avey Richard, vict. Cock
Fletcher George, gentleman
Fletcher John, schoolmaster
Gillson Henry, shopkeeper
Hills Rev — (Independent minister)

Poulter James, blacksmith
Ruse Robert, farmer
Wilson Elijah, poulterer
Wellsman John, owner and farmer
Fox & Bull Inn (unoccupied)

LIDGATE, a pleasant scattered village, near the source of a rivulet, 7 miles S.E. of Newmarket, and 10 miles W.S.W. of Bury St. Edmund's, has in its parish 459 souls, and 1957 acres of land. Near the church is a moated mound, on which there are still some traces of a *castle*, though the foundations have been nearly all dug up for the reparation of the roads. The inhabitants usually call it *King John's Castle*, but its origin is unknown. The parish gave birth and name to *John Lydgate*, the learned monk of Bury, noticed at page 616. In the 49th of Edward III., it was the lordship of John Hastings, Earl of Pembroke, and it afterwards passed to the Jermyns, Davers, and Seymours. The Conqueror is said to have given it to one of his followers called *Reynold sans Nase*, from having lost his nose in battle. The Duke of Rutland is now lord of the manor, but the soil belongs to T. J. Ireland, Esq., Col. Wollaston, Mrs. F. A. Osborne, N. W. Bromley, Esq., and several smaller owners. The *Church* (St. Mary) is a neat edifice, with a tower and five bells, and the living is a *rectory*, valued in K.B. at £15. 10s. 5d., and now having 54A. of glebe, and a yearly modus of £480, awarded in 1817. The Rev. John Wm. Travis is incumbent, and the Duke of Rutland patron, but the next presentation has been purchased by Mrs. Jackson, of Doncaster. A handsome new *Rectory House* was built in 1842. The *Independents* have a preaching room here. A *National School* was built by subscription in 1835, at the cost of £160, and it is attended by about 60 day, and 100 Sunday scholars. At the *enclosure* in 1814, an allotment of 7A. 2R. 12P. was awarded, in lieu of land appropriated from ancient time to the payment of the clerk's wages, and to the repairs of the church. It is let, together with 2A. 2R. 12P., allotted to the poor, and the rent, about £15 a year, is applied as follows:—£2 to the parish clerk, £6 to

the National School, and the remainder towards the repairs of the church and the relief of the poor.

Bailey James, cattle dealer
Bell Sampson, vict. Oak
Charvill Joshua, shopkeeper, and *carrier to Bury, Wednesday*
Day John, bricklayer
Dowding Rev Chas. curate, *Rectory*
Hammond Philip, collar maker
Longster James, National schoolmr
Pawsey Rt. grocer,draper,& shoemkr
Pryke Thomas, shoemaker

Ransom Gooch, blacksmith, and parish clerk
Silverston James, surgeon
Turner Thomas, wheelwright, &c

FARMERS.
Baldry James
Bell Sampson
Carsboult John
Day Jno.& Robt.
Dobitz George, *(owner)*

Harvey Richard
Pask Simon (and beer house)
Pawsey George, *Hall*
Phillips Charles and Wm.

MOULTON, a neat village, on the banks of a rivulet, 3½ miles E. of Newmarket, and 10 miles W. of Bury, has in its parish 379 souls, and 3073A. 1R. 17P. of sandy land. It is a *peculiar* of the Archbishop of Canterbury, under the jurisdiction of the Dean of Bocking. John Agnerus had a grant for a market here, in the 26th of Edward I. The *manor* afterwards passed to the Chyverston, Lutterell, and other families. It is now held by the Duke of Rutland ; but a great part of the soil belongs to Trinity Hall, Cambridge ; H. and E. Hammond, Esqs.; W. Webber, Esq., of *Fidget Hall ;* Mr. W. Davison, and a few smaller owners. The *Church* (St. Peter) is an ancient structure, with a tower and five bells ; and the benefice is a *rectory and vicarage* united, valued in 1835 at £477, and in K.B., the former at £13. 6s. 8d., and the latter at £4. 7s. 8½d. About 20 years ago, the Rev. Edward Wilson endowed it with a farm of 217A. 2R. 8P.; besides which it has 169A. 2R. 14P. of glebe. The open fields, &c., were enclosed in 1839 ; and in 1840, the tithes were commuted for a yearly modus of £397. 10s., including the quota on the rectorial land. The patronage is in Christ College, Cambridge ; and the Rev. G. H. Greenall, M.A., is the incumbent. Here is a small *Independent Chapel*, built about 16 years ago. On *Folly Heath*, is an ancient pyramidal building, which may be seen at the distance of 20 miles, and is said to have been built by one of the Earls of Orford. Moulton *Town Estate* is vested with the churchwardens, for the reparation of the church and bridges of the parish, and consists of 4A. at Freckenham, let for £10 a year ; and 13A. in the open fields of Moulton, let for £9 a year. The poor parishioners have 5A. at Newmarket, called *Fuel Land*, and let for £20 a year to Mr. Crockford, forming part of his garden and pleasure-grounds. The donor is unknown, and the rent is distributed in money or turf among poor families. In 1755, Mr. Worthington left £12 for the poor, and it is vested with the rector, at interest of 10s. per annum. In the 35th of Elizabeth, *Wm. Deynes* left a farm of 75A. 2R. 20P. at Cowling, in trust for the relief of the needy poor of Moulton, Barrow, Cowling, and Hargrave. It is now let for about £80 a year, of which each of the four parishes receives £20 for distribution among the poor. A yearly rent-charge of 7s. 6d., called *Herring Money*, is paid out of an estate belonging to E. Hammond, Esq., and distributed among the poor of Moulton ; but the donor is unknown.

Bailey James, shoemaker
Barnes Wm. shopkeeper

Fyson Richard, shopkeeper
Goer Wm. gentleman

Greenall Rev. George Hutton, M.A. *Rectory*
Leach Reuben, tailor
Moule Joseph, shoemaker
Poulter James, blacksmith
Tweed Benj. carpenter and vict. King's Head
Watt Rev. Robert, M.A. curate
Webber Wm. Esq., *Fidget Hall*

Wellsman John, maltster
FARMERS.
Fletcher John
Gardner Thomas, *French Hall*
Hammond Ellen, *Heath*
Holder James, *Moulton End*
Staples Wm. *Moulton Hall*
Woods John, *Trinity Hall Farm*

OUSDEN, a scattered village, 7 miles S.E. by E. of Newmarket, and 10 miles W.S.W. of Bury, has in its parish 340 souls, and 1490 acres of land, having a fertile mixed soil. *Ousden Hall*, a handsome mansion, with pleasant grounds, is the seat of T. J. Ireland, Esq., the lord of the manor, and owner of nearly all the soil. The *Church* (St. Peter) is a small structure, with a tower and five bells; and the living is a *rectory*, valued in K.B. at £10. 3s. 9d., and in 1835 at £285. T. J. Ireland, Esq., is patron, and the Rev. C. H. Bennet incumbent. The tithes were commuted at the enclosure, about 25 years ago, for an allotment of 350 acres. The Moseleys were formerly seated here, and were lords of the manor, which was held by the late Rev. J. T. Hand. The *Town Estate* consists of a cottage, called the *Town House*, occupied rent-free by poor persons; and about 3a. of land, let for £4. 10s. a year, which is applied in the service of the church. In 1593, *Wm. Deynes* left a yearly rent-charge of 13s. 4d. out of land at Barrow, for the poor of Ousden. In 1743, *Richard Moseley* charged a farm here with the yearly payment of £10, for schooling 20 poor children of this parish.

Anderson Isaac, *Boarding school*
Bennet Rev Chpr. Hand, *Rectory*
Clarke John, gentleman
Cruthe Wm. shopkeeper
Everitt Thomas, shoemaker
Goldstone Hannah, schoolmistress
Hoy George, tailor and draper
Ireland Thos. Jas. Esq. *Ousden Hall*

Moore Mrs. *corn miller*
Peachey Robert, blacksmith
Reynolds Wm. vict. *Fox*
Seagrott Wm. gamekeeper
Tweed Wm. wheelwright
Woollard Thomas, *(miller)*
FARMERS.—Andrews Thomas
Jillings Wm. || Snape Reuben

POSLINGFORD, a small pleasant village, 2½ miles N. by E. of Clare, has in its parish 343 souls, and 2500 acres of land, including several scattered houses, and the small hamlet of CHIPLEY, which had a small abbey or priory, 1½ mile N.W. of Poslingford, founded at an early period, and annexed to Stoke College in 1468. The *Abbey Farm* has an ancient house, and belongs to Sir Robert Harland. *Poslingford Park*, 1 mile N. of the village, has a handsome mansion, and is the seat and property of Lieut.-Col. Thos. Weston; but Samuel Ware, Esq., is lord of the manor; and the Rev. J. W. Stribling, J. Snell, T. Wade, and a few smaller owners, have estates in the parish. The land is all freehold, and was anciently the lordship of Ralph Baynard. The *Church* is a small ancient structure, with a tower and five bells, and was repaired in 1839, when a small gallery was erected. It was appropriated to Dunmow Priory, Essex, and granted, in the 28th of Henry VIII., to Robert, Earl of Sussex. Lieut.-Col. T. Weston is impropriator of the rectory, and patron of the discharged *vicarage*, which is valued in K.B. at £6. 10s., and is now enjoyed by the Rev. Wm. L. Suttaby, M.A., who has 9a. of glebe, and a yearly modus of

£100, awarded in 1841, when the rectorial tithes were commuted for £199 per annum. The *Church and Poor's Estate* comprises 7A. 3R. of land, which has been held from ancient time for the reparation of the church, and the relief of the poor; and two cottages, with gardens, purchased in 1675, with £6 belonging to the poor, and £6 given by the inhabitants. The land and cottages are let for about £18 a year, which is mostly expended in the service of the church. The *Poor's Cottage*, is in two tenements occupied by persons put in by the overseers. In 1668, *Wm. Cadge* charged a farm called Lynns with the payment of 20s. a year, for distribution among the poor of Poslingford.

Codling Frederick, blacksmith
Fitch Thos. grocer and draper
Suttaby Rev Wm. Leonard, M.A. *Vicarage*
Weston Lieut.-Col. Thomas, *Poslingford Park*

FARMERS.

Ambrose John, *New House*
Boreham Joseph, *Bulley Green*

Fisher James, *Clopton Hall*
Hale John & Chas. *Poslingford Hall*
Hunt Sarah, *Wentford House*
Raymond John
Robinson Thos. (steward) *Chipley Abbey*
Rutter George, *Flax Farm*
Wade Thomas, *Hills Farm*
Ward Robt. (and beerhouse keeper)

STANSFIELD, a pleasant village, near a small rivulet, 5½ miles N. by E. of Clare, has in its parish 510 souls, and 1850 acres of freehold land, including the hamlet of *Assington Green*, and many scattered houses. The lordship is in the Crown, but the soils belongs to G. W. Poley, Esq., J. and W. Sworde, Esqrs., S. Ware, Esq., Dr. Probart, Rev. N. Colvile, and the Cooper, Pratt, Everard, Pigott, Rutter, Taber, Bridgman, and other families. The Kedingtons were formerly seated here. The *Church* (All Saints) is a neat structure, with a tower and five bells, and the benefice is a rectory, valued in K.B. at £10. 9s. 4½d., and in 1835 at £395. The patronage is in the Crown, and the Rev. John Maddy, D.D., of Somerton, is the incumbent. The glebe is 76A., and the tithes were commuted in 1838 for a yearly modus of £500. Here is a neat *Independent Chapel*, with a house for the minister, erected in 1833 at the cost of £850. The chapel was built by subscription, and the house at the cost of the minister, the Rev. John Rutter. Day and Sunday Schools are attached to the church and the chapel. The *Church Land*, about 2A., is let for £8 a year. The poor parishioners have the following *yearly doles*, viz., 20s. out of Cordell Hall, given by *Robt. Kedington* and others; 13s. 4d. from *Anthony Sparrow's Charity*, (see Wickhambrook;) 6s. 8d. given by an unknown donor out of Cook's Farm; and about £2. 12s. from a double cottage, given by the Rev. R. Shaw for the use of poor widows.

Carter Henry, watch maker
Claydon John, shopkeeper
Cornell John, wheelgt. & beerhs. kpr.
Frost Thomas, beer seller
Golding Wm. shoemaker
Gridley Daniel, shopkeeper and *carrier to Bury*, Wed.
Maddy Rev Joseph, M.A. curate, *Rectory*
Powles Mary, schoolmistress
Rannow John, grocer and draper
Ransom Wm. blacksmith

Rutter Rev John, (Independent)
Sargeant Mary, schoolmistress
Spurling John, wheelwright
Webb Edw. Hy. vict. & shoemaker
Webb Thomas, blacksmith

FARMERS.

Balls John, *Assington Green*
Bridgman James, (*owner*)
Dunning Benjamin
Everard Wm. (*& miller*) Church cot.
Granger Wm. *Hole farm*
Pratt John, (owner,) *Purton Hall*

Prewer John, *Assington Green*
Foreman John, (bailiff,) *Gatesbury*
Rutter John, *Raymond's farm*
Sargeant Joseph, *Assington Green*

Slater Martin, *Cordell Hall*
Spencer Robert, *Stansfield Hall*
Woolard John

STOKE-BY-CLARE, a large and well-built village, pleasantly situated on the north bank of the river Stour, 2¼ miles W.S.W. of Clare, and 7 miles E.S.E. of Haverhill, has in its parish 868 souls, and 2329A. 1R. 22P. of fertile land. It has a small *fair* for pedlery, &c., on Whit-Monday. As noticed at page 724, a Benedictine Priory, which had been founded at Clare Castle, was translated to Stoke, but about 1415, Edmund Mortimer, Earl of March, having augmented its revenues, obtained the king's permission to change the institution into a *College*, consisting of a dean and six secular canons. At the dissolution, it was valued at £324. 4s. 1d. per annum, and granted to Sir John Cheke and Walter Mildmay, from whom it passed to the Triggs. It afterwards passed with the manor to *Sir Gervase Elwes*, who was created a baronet in 1660, and died in 1705, but the title became extinct on the death of his grandson, Sir Hervey Elwes, in 1763. From this distinguished *miser*, the estate passed to his worthy successor, John Elwes, Esq., as afterwards noticed. On the death of the last named miser, in 1789, it passed to the late J. H. T. Elwes, Esq., from whom it came to John Payne Elwes, Esq., the present lord of the *manor of Stoke-with-Chilton,* and owner of the fine old family mansion, called *Stoke College,* now occupied by Charles Gonne, Esq. But part of the soil belongs to Mrs. Payne, Mrs. Jardine, Messrs. J. A. Fitch, W. Walford, and D. Pannell, and a few smaller owners. All the parish is freehold, except a small farm belonging to Mrs. Payne. The *Church* (St. Augustine) is a neat structure, with a tower and six bells, and was appropriated to Stoke College. The benefice is a perpetual curacy, valued in 1835 at £130, and now having 59A. of glebe, a yearly modus of £117. 1s. 6d., awarded in 1841, and a yearly rent-charge of £30, left by Sir Gervase Elwes in 1678. Lady Rush is patroness, and the Rev. Henry Griffin, M.A., incumbent. Here is a small *Chapel* used by the Baptists and Independents.

In 1681, *Mary Barnes* left £225 to be laid out in the purchase of land, the rents and profits thereof to be employed in apprenticing poor children of Stoke parish. The land purchased comprises 10A. 2R. 22P., let for £31. 10s. a year, which is dispensed by the churchwardens and overseers in apprentice fees. In 1526, *Richard Brown* directed an ALMSHOUSE to be erected at Stoke for six poor people, to each of whom he left 6s. 8d. yearly, charged on his estate, called Stowers, at Ashen, in Essex, which he also charged with the expense of repairing the almshouse. J. P. Elwes, Esq., owns this estate, and pays 40s. to the almspeople, and 10s. a year for repairs. The poor of Stoke have had from time immemorial 1A. 1R. 17P. of land in Wixoe, and it is now let for £4. 10s. a year, which is divided among the almspeople and other poor parishioners, together with a yearly rent-charge of 20s., left by *Wm. Bendlow* in the 19th Elizabeth, out of a farm, called Glyns, in Finchingfield, Essex. A cottage occupied by two aged parishioners was given by *Ralph Turner*, who endowed it in 1599 with an annuity of 6s. 8d., out of Huddes Gap, now belonging to the Rev. M. J. Brunwin, of Blackwater, Essex, who also pays 20s. a year for the poor out of Tenter Croft, pursuant to the bequest of *Thos. Edwards,* in 1653. The yearly sum of 40s. is paid by ancient custom out of the Town Close, and is distributed among the poor on Plough Monday. In 1678, *Sir Gervase Elwes,* to the end that the office of *schoolmaster and perpetual curate* of Stoke might continue for ever in some good Protestant divine, charged his mansion house and estate at Stoke with a yearly rent-charge of £30, but there is no free school here, except a Sunday School supported by subscription.

In the annals of avarice, there is not a more celebrated name than that of Elwes. *Sir Gervase Elwes,* of Stoke, who died in 1705, involved, as far as they would go, all his estates, so that his grandson and successor, SIR HERVEY ELWES, found that he was nominally possessed of some thousands a-year, but had really only a clear income of about £100 per annum. He declared, on his arrival at the family seat of Stoke, that he would never leave it till he had entirely cleared the paternal estate, and he lived not only to do that, but to amass above £100,000 in addition. The accumulation of money was the only passion and employment of the long life of Sir Hervey, who, though given over in his youth for a consumption, attained to the age of upwards of eighty years. To avoid the expense of company, he doomed himself, for about sixty years, to the strictest solitude ; scarcely knew the indulgence of fire and candle, and resided in a mansion where the wind entered at every broken casement, and the rain descended through the roof. His household consisted of one man and two maids ; and such was the systematic economy which governed his whole establishment, that the annual expenditure of Sir Harvey, though worth at least £250,000, amounted to only £110. Among the few acquaintances he had (says Mr. Topham,) was an occasional club at his own village of Stoke, and there were members of it two baronets besides himself, *Sir Cordell Firebrace* and *Sir John Barnardiston.* However rich they were, the reckoning was always an object of their investigation. As they were one day settling this difficult point, an odd fellow, who was a member, called out to a friend who was passing, " For Heaven's sake, step up stairs and assist the poor ! Here are three baronets, worth a million of money, quarrelling about a farthing !" On the death of Sir Hervey, in 1763, he lay in state, such as it was, at Stoke ; and some of his tenants observed with more humour than decency, that it was well he could not see it. His immense property devolved to his nephew, *John Meggot,* who, by his will, was ordered to assume the name and arms of Elwes. This was the celebrated JOHN ELWES, Esq., whose mother had been left a widow by a rich brewer, with a fortune of one hundred thousand pounds, and starved herself to death. He proved himself a worthy heir to her and Sir Hervey. During the life of his miserly uncle, he often visited him at Stoke, and ingratiated himself into his favour by always changing his dress for one of a humbler description before he reached the mansion. After his uncle's death, he settled at Stoke, and for some time kept a pack of hounds and a few hunters, at the cost of about £300 a-year. After a residence of nearly 14 years at Stoke, he was chosen to represent Berkshire in Parliament, on which occasion he removed to his seat at Marcham, in that county. He now relinquished the keeping of horses and dogs ; and no man could be more attentive to his senatorial duties than Mr. Elwes. In travelling, he rode on horseback, avoiding all turnpikes and public-houses, carrying in his pockets crusts of bread, hard boiled eggs, &c., for his own refreshment, and allowing his horse to feast on the grass which fringed the sides of the roads. On his retirement from public life, to avoid the expense of a contested election, he was desirous of visiting his seat at Stoke, where he had not been for some years. When he reached this place, once the seat of more active scenes, somewhat resembling hospitality, and where his fox-hounds had diffused something like vivacity around, he remarked that he had formerly expended a great deal of money very foolishly, but that a man grows wiser in time. During his last residence at Stoke, the mansion was suffered to fall into decay for want of repairs. If a window was broken, there was to be no repair but that of a little brown paper, or piecing in a bit of broken glass, which had at length been done so frequently, and in so many shapes, that it would have puzzled a mathematician to say what figure they described. To save fire, he would walk about the remains of an old greenhouse, or sit with a servant in the kitchen. During the harvest, he would amuse himself with going into the fields to glean the corn on the grounds of his own tenants ; and they used to leave a little more than common, to please the old gentleman, who was as eager after it as any pauper in the parish. In the advance of the season, his morning employment was to pick up any stray chips, bones, and other things to carry to the fire, in his pocket; and he was one day surprised by a neighbouring gentleman in the act of pulling down a crow's nest, for that purpose. On the gentleman wondering why he gave himself this trouble, " Oh, Sir ! replied old Elwes, " it is really a shame that these creatures should do so— do but see what waste they make ! they don't care how extravagant they are." His food and dress were of the meanest description. He once eat a moor hen,

that had been brought out of the river by a rat; and he wore a wig that had been picked up in the rut of a lane. But with all his meanness, he sometimes displayed a real generosity of spirit, and occasionally became the dupe of artful adventurers. He once embarked and sacrificed £25,000 in an iron work in America, of which he knew nothing. He was also an occasional gambler, strict in the payment of his losses, but never asking for his winnings if they were withheld; and several instances are recorded of his voluntarily advancing large sums to assist his friends in their difficulties. He died in 1789, and bequeathed his real and personal estates, to the value of half a million, to his two natural sons, George and John, the latter of whom succeeded to the Stoke estate.

STOKE-BY-CLARE.

Bard John, wheelwright
Bridge Thomas Little, gentleman
Bruster Thos. miller & schoolmaster
Chapman John, tailor
Crown John, surgeon
Doe Robert, shoemaker
Dyke Rev. Wm. cu ate
Eldred Daniel D. joiner and vict. Red Lion
Emberson Cornls. baker & beer hs
Farrant Thos. baker & beer house
Fitch Joshua A. corn miller
Gonne Chas. Esq. *Stoke College*
Gowers Mary, bricklayer
Hale Elizabeth, shopkeeper
Jardine John Hy. solicitor, & clerk & supt. regr. of Risbridge Union

Ling David, butcher
Reeve Wm. tailor
Rogers Hannah, baker & shopkpr
Rogers Wm. parish clerk
Sparks Wm. blacksmith
Stribling John, blacksmith
Tatum Wm. lime burner
Turner John, beerhouse & shopkpr
Turner Samuel, gardener
Wright Ebenz. joiner & vict. *George*

FARMERS.

Andrews Robert
Canham Abm. (& brickmaker)
Deeks Charles
Farrant Thomas
Pannell Daniel, *Beyton End*
Tattersall Edm.
Turner Ann
Viall King, *Chapel Street*
Walford Walter, *Moor Hall*

STRADISHALL, a pleasant village near the source of a rivulet, 5½ miles N.W. of Clare, has in its parish 379 souls, and 1400 acres of strong clayey land, mostly belonging to and occupied by Wm. Rayner, Esq., of *Stradishall Place*, a neat mansion near the church. The remainder belongs to Misses Walpole, and Messrs. Joseph Cooke, J. W. Dennis, and Joseph Wallis. The *Church* (St. Margaret) is an ancient fabric, with a tower and five bells; and the living is a rectory, valued in K.B. at £9. 11s., and now having 52A. of glebe, and a yearly modus of £400, awarded in 1840. Sir R. Harland is patron ; and the Rev. Charles Jenkin, D.D., incumbent. The old Workhouse was converted into a *Wesleyan Chapel*, in 1843, at the expense of W. Rayner, Esq. In 1573, *John Hoult* left a house for the residence of two of the poorest men and women of Stradishall, and charged his mansion-house with the yearly payment of £3 for distribution among the occupants of the said house, and the other poor of the parish. By a decree of the Court of Chancery, for establishing this charity, in the 26th of Elizabeth, it was ordered that the inmates of the *almshouse* should be appointed by six of the principal parishioners, and that £33, being the amount of eleven years' arrears of the annuity, should be laid out in land, the rents thereof to be bestowed in the repairs of the almshouse, and the relief of the poor parishioners. This sum of £33 was laid out, with £20 given to the poor by *Ann Smythe*, in the purchase of 5A. 2R. of land, at Wickhambrook, now let for £7 a year, which is distributed in bread or money. The *almshouse* fell down about 1813, and the annuity of £3 was suffered to accumulate till a few years ago, for the purpose of rebuilding it. For the support of a *workhouse*, this parish has £10 a year from *Vernon's Charity*. (See Hundon.)

Chapman John, shopkeeper
Clarke Joseph, shopkeeper
Cooke Joseph, *Moat Farm*

Denniss James Wing, *Hill Farm*
Goodison Robert, farm steward
Ive Wm. wheelwright

Jenkin Rev. Charles, D.D. *Rectory*
Pettit James, tailor, Haw bush
Rayner Wm. Esq. *Stradishall Place*
Seabrook Richard, shoemaker

Seabrook Saml. vict. Fox Hounds
Wallis Joseph, corn miller
Webb Thomas, maltster

THURLOW, (GREAT) is a pleasant village in the vale of a rivulet, adjoining Little Thurlow on the south, and 4 miles N.N.E. of Haverhill, and 8 miles N.W. by W. of Clare. Its parish contains 431 souls, and 1928 acres of fertile land. Lady Harland is lady of the manor, and owner of a great part of the soil, and the remainder belongs to W. H. Crawford, Esq., and the Jonas, Traylen, Golding, Snazell, and a few other families. Here was a small *Hospital*, or free chapel, dedicated to St. James, founded in the reign of Richard II., and subordinate to the foreign hospital of Hautpays, or *de alto passu*. In the reign of Edward IV., it was valued at £3 per annum, and granted to the Maison de Dieu, in Cambridge, now part of King's College. The lordship formerly belonged to John King, Esq., then to the Waldegraves, and afterwards to Sir Cordel Firebrace, Bart., who sold it to James Vernon, Esq. Lady Harland, its present possessor, is the heiress of the Vernons, and wife of Sir Rt. Harland, Bart. The Vernons were long seated at the *Hall*, a neat mansion in a pleasant park, now occupied only in the shooting season, by Joseph Alfred Hardcastle, Esq. The *Church* (All Saints) is an ancient fabric, with a tower and five bells. The *vicarage*, valued in K.B. at £10. 11s. 5½d., is endowed with the great tithes, and has now a yearly modus of £518, awarded in 1840. Lady Harland is patroness, and the Rev. Wm. Wayman, M.A., incumbent. Here is a small *Independent Chapel*, built in 1835. The poor parishioners participate in some of the *charities*, noticed with Little Thurlow and Great Wratting. A *fair* for sheep and toys is held here on October 10th. The *Thurlow family* derive their name, and the title of *baron*, from this parish, as noticed at page 680.

Brand George, poulterer
Bridgman Samuel, blacksmith
Chapman John, wheelwright
Daniels James, grocer and draper
Farrow Robert, beerhouse keeper
Gardner Thos. miller and maltster
Kettle John, tailor
Maulkin Robert, gentleman
Payne John, bricklayer
Rollinson Thos. saddler, &c
Rose Richd. vict. *Crown*
Selbie Rev Wm. (Independent)
Snazell Wm. joiner and builder
Talbot Samuel, baker

Thompson Samuel, joiner
Wayman Rev Wm. M.A. *Vicarage*
Woolard Samuel, shoemaker
FARMERS. († *are Owners*.)
Bridgman George, and maltster
†Golding Geo. || Gardner Thos.
†Jonas Samuel, *West end*
Pearl James, *Harlica*
Pearl Rands, *Wadgells*
†Snazell William
†Traylen Lucy and ChristopherJph.
  Sawley Green
Wakelin Barsham, *Westend*

THURLOW, (LITTLE) a neat village, adjoining that of Great Thurlow, 4½ miles N. by E. of Haverhill, has in its parish 422 souls, and 1357 acres of strong fertile land. Mrs. Soame, of Bury, is lady of the manor, and owner of most of the soil, and the remainder belongs to the Rev. Wm. Chafy, D.D., and a few smaller owners. The HALL, now a farm-house, on the west side of the vale, was built in the reign of Elizabeth, by Sir Stephen Soame, Knight, who had been lord mayor of London, and founded the school and almshouse here, as afterwards noticed. There is a monument to his memory in the *Church*, (St. Peter,) which has a tower and five bells, and was new pewed and repaired in 1843. The *rectory*, valued in K.B. at £7. 10s. 5d., and in 1835, at £401, is in the patronage of Mrs. Soame, and incumbency of the Rev. Thomas Crick, B.D., for whom the Rev. Fredk. Crick, M.A., officiates. The present estimated yearly rental of the parish is £1859. 18s. 6d.

Soame's Almshouse and School:—In the 15th of James I., *Sir Stephen Soame, Knt.*, by his will declared that an ALMSHOUSE, which he had built in Little Thurlow, should be for the habitation of eight poor unmarried persons, men and women, of the age of 64 years or upwards, and who should have been resident 24 years in Little Thurlow; but if so many could not be found here, he directed that the remainder might be chosen from Great Thurlow, or Wratting. He also ordered that the ninth room in the middle of the almshouse should be occupied by a person who should read prayers to the rest of the almspeople. He willed that his executors should purchase a yearly rent-charge of £30, to provide for the weekly payment of 14d. a week to each of the nine almspeople, and to supply them with eight loads of good faggots yearly, and with a gown each once in two years. And after reciting that he had built a SCHOOLHOUSE here, he declared that it should be employed as a *free school* for the parishes of Little and Great Thurlow, Great and Little Bradley, Wratting, Ketton, Hundon, and other parishes in Suffolk; and that the children should be taught by the master and usher in the English and Latin tongues, writing, and cyphering. By a codicil dated March 2nd, 1618, the testator charged the manor of Carlton, in Cambridgeshire, with the yearly rent-charges of £30 for the almshouse, and £30 for the school; and of the latter he directed £20 to be paid to the master, and £10 to the usher. By an indenture in the 1st of Queen Anne, the manor of Carlton was also charged with providing the faggots and gowns for the use of the almspeople, who are appointed by the owner of the said manor, and the minister and churchwardens of Little Thurlow. The school has attached to it apartments and a garden for the use of the master, who receives £30 a year, and teaches reading, writing, and arithmetic gratuitously to about 12 poor children nominated by the rector and churchwardens. No usher has been appointed for many years, and the salary of the usher was not paid till a few years ago, when the present owner of the manor of Carlton agreed to add it to the master's annuity. The POOR'S ESTATE, given by *Josiah Houghton*, in 1693, consists of about 3A. of land, let for £5 a year, and the Town House, which is partly occupied by paupers, and partly let to three tenants at rents amounting to £4 a year. The rents are carried to the poor-rates, but they ought to be distributed among such poor inhabitants as do not receive parochial relief.

THURLOW (LITTLE.)

Baker Benjamin, surgeon
Betts Benjamin, wheelwright
Choat Mr Simon || Collins Mr Rd.
Crick Rev. Frederick, M.A. curate, *Rectory*
Daniels James, grocer and draper
Dearsley Joseph, corn miller
Dench Capt. T. || Farrow Hy. farrier
French John, schoolmaster
Lee Joshua, turner and shovel mkr
Neave Ezra, collar and harness mkr
Sargeant John, beerhouse keeper
Smith Joseph, tailor

Sparrow Thomas, vict. Cock
Trudgett George, butcher
Vince Wm. grocer and draper
Wakelin James, blacksmith
Webb John, butcher
Webb Wm. Henry, vetrny. surgeon

FARMERS.
Bailey Samuel
Goodchild Jph.
Howard Mary
Osborne Alice
Osborne Wm.

Shoemakers.
Fitch James

Fitch Joseph
Webb Henry

CARRIERS.
Wm. Cockerton, to London, Wed.
James Fitch, to Cambridge, Sat. and Bury, Wed.

WIXOE, or *Whixoe*, a small village and parish on the north bank of the river Stour, 4 miles W.S.W. of Clare, and E.S.E. of Haverhill, has only 164 souls, and about 600 acres of land. J. P. Elwes, Esq., is lord of the manor, but part of the soil belongs to Mrs. Jardine and J. Nottidge, Esq., who have neat houses here. The *Church* is a small ancient structure, and the benefice is a discharged rectory, valued in K.B. at £5. 13s. 1½d., and in 1835, at £180. J. P. Elwes, Esq., is patron, and the Rev. Frederick Elwes, B.A., incumbent. The latter has a neat residence, and the other principal inhabitants are Joshua A. Fitch, corn miller and farmer, *Water Mill;* Mrs. Elizabeth Jardine; Joshua Nottidge, Esq., *Rose Hill;* and Mrs. Elizabeth Payne, *Water Hall.*

WICKHAMBROOK, a large scattered village, in the pleasant vale of a rivulet, 7 miles N. of Clare, and 11 miles S.W. of Bury St. Edmund's,

has in its extensive parish 1623 inhabitants, and about 4000 acres of fertile clayey land, including many widely scattered farm houses, and the *hamlets of Ashfield Green*, half a mile N.E.; *Genesis Green*, 2 miles N.; part of *Boyden End*, 2 miles N.W.; and *Clopton*, half a mile E. of the village. It is in three MANORS, viz., *Badmondisfield Hall*, formerly held by the Somersets, Norths, and Warners, and now by Nathaniel Warner Bromley, Esq.; *Gaines Hall*, held by Mrs. Sparke; and *Clopton Hall*, anciently appropriated to Stoke College, and now forming part of the charity estates belonging to Thaxted, in Essex, left by Lord Wm. Maynard. Wm. Rayner, Esq., owns about one-third of the parish, and here are several smaller proprietors. (See list of Farmers.) *Gifford's Hall*, now a farm house, one mile S.E. of the village, belongs to Mr. Chinery, and was formerly held by the Owers family. *Wickham House* was formerly the seat of Major Robert Sparrow, and is now occupied by Mr. G. H. Sparrow. *Petty Sessions* are held at the White Horse every fourth Friday; and the neighbouring farmers and buyers hold a monthly meeting at the same Inn every fourth Thursday. The *Church* (All Saints) is a neat structure, with a tower and five bells, and the living is a vicarage, valued in K.B. at £8. 6s. 10½d., and in 1835, at £210, but now having a yearly modus of £350 awarded in 1840. The patronage is in the Crown, and the Rev. Charles Borton is the incumbent. The rectorial tithes belong to N. W. Bromley, Esq., and three other impropriators. There was anciently a *free chapel*, dedicated to St. Mary, at Badmondisfield, in the patronage of the Hastings and Grey families; but it was granted in 1583, to Wm. Mansey, of London, and no traces of it are now extant. In the village is a neat *Independent Chapel*, belonging to a congregation formed in 1734. Two *schools* are partly supported by subscription. A tenement and about 15A. of land are vested in trust as declared by ancient deeds, for the relief of the poor and the reparation of the church, and are now let for £15 a year, of which £2. 5s. belongs to the church, and the remainder to the poor. It is not known how the property was acquired, except 4A. purchased with the benefaction of Thomas Heigham. In 1785, *Anne Warner* left £400 three per cent. reduced annuities, in trust to distribute the dividends thereof on Christmas-day, among the poor parishioners, who have also the dividends of £250 three per cent. stock, bequeathed in 1818 by *Elizabeth Chinery*, for distributions of hempen cloth. They have likewise three rent-charges, amounting to £2. 10s. per annum, given by *Dr. Palmer, Charles Owers*, and *Benjamin French*. The sum of £10 a year, towards the support of the poor, is received from *Vernon's Charity*. (See Hundon.) ANTHONY SPARROW, in 1615, charged the Stansfield Mill Farm with the yearly payment of £8, for the relief of the poor of the following parishes, viz., £2 to be distributed in Depden; 13s. 4d. in each of the parishes of Stansfield, Denston and Rede; 10s. in Chedburgh and Hawkedon; and £3 to be divided among the six inmates of the *Almshouse*, which he had built at Wickhambrook. Attached to this almshouse is about 1R. 20P. of garden ground.

Borton Rev Charles, *Vicarage*
Brown John, P. regr., vestry clerk, and beerhouse keeper
Chapman Joseph, vict. *Crown*
Coleman Rev Henry, (1ndpt. min.)
Cross Miss, schoolmistress
Dunthorn and Stutter, surgeons
Garrod James, cooper
Gudgeon John, vict.*White Horse Inn*
Marrow Ann, plumber and glazier
Rannow Mrs Ann, *Thorn Cottage*

Slater Daniel, relieving officer
Smith James, schoolmaster
Smith John, parish clerk
Smith Thomas, beerhouse keeper
Blacksmiths.
Crick Alfred
Hinds Elizabeth
Simpson Robert
Boot & Shoe Mkrs.
Chapman George
Edgley John
Hargent John
King Robert
Parry —
Pryke George
Pryke Thomas
Pryke Thos. jun.

Bricklayers.
Parker John
Smith James
Butchers.
Death Robert
Kemball James
Corn Millers.
Chapman John
Woollard Joseph
FARMERS.
(* *are Owners.*)
Ayton — Barber's *Farm*
Crick John
Everard George, *Clopton*
Frost Jno. Rookery
*Frost Jas. *Boyden-End*
Frost Sarah, *Boyden-End*

* Fuller Bnj. *Badmondisfield*
Fuller Wm. *Hole Farm*
Goldsmith Geo. *Genesis green*
*Isaacson Mrs. *Gaines Hall*
Johnson Stephen *Bromley*
Pask James
*Pawsey George, *Atterton green*
Peacock Wm. *Ashfield-Place*
Peacock George
Pearl Henry, (& *maltster*)
*Pryke James, *Ashfield green*
*Pryke John, *Ashfield Hall*

Rowling Joseph, *Baxter green*
Rutter John, (& glover)
Saville John, *Clopton Hall*
Saville Wm. *Gifford's Hall*
Shave Simeon
Sparrow George Hibble, *Wickham House*
Spencer Wm.
Smith Mrs. *Ashfield green*
Wing Wm. *ditto*
Wakelin John, *Genesis green*
Woollard Joseph, *Parkgate*
Shopkeepers.
Brewster John, (& joiner)

Tyson Richard
Hockley Wm.
Marrow Josiah
Pattle Thos. (& baker)

Tailors.
French James
Pymer Benjamin

Wheelwrights.
Claydon John
Crick Alfred

CARRIERS
To *Bury, Wed. & Sat.*
Brown Henry
Simpson Thomas
Whitred James
To *Clare, Tues. and Thursday.*
Jarvis John

WITHERSFIELD, a scattered village, 2 miles N.W. of Haverhill, has in its parish 640 souls, and 2059 acres of fertile land, having a heavy mixed soil, and bounded on the west by Cambridgeshire. Thos. Duffield, Esq., is lord of the manor, and owner of a great part of the land. Bethnal Green Free School and Hospital, founded in 1722 by Thos. Parmiter, has an estate here, and other parts of the parish belong to Lord Thurlow and several smaller proprietors. The *Church* (St. Mary) has a tower and five bells, and the living is a *rectory*, valued in K.B. at £9. 17s. 2d., and in 1835 at £465, but now having, besides 41A. of glebe, a yearly modus of £590, awarded in 1841. Thos. Duffield, Esq., is patron, and the Rev. Wm. Mayd, M.A., incumbent. There is a cottage, in four tenements, in this parish, occupied rent-free by poor persons ; and a blacksmith's shop, let for £2 a year, which is applied in repairing the cottage. It is unknown how the premises became appropriated to the poor.

Barnet Miss Charlotte
Betts David, wheelwright
Bigmore John, vict. White Horse
Choat Thomas, carpenter
Claydon Thomas, blacksmith
Furbank Henry, shoemaker
Mayd Rev Wm. M.A. *Rectory*
Moore David, shopkeeper
Nunn Wm. shopkeeper & beer seller
Pearl John, corn miller

Trudgett John, butcher
Webb Thomas, bricklayer
FARMERS.
Bailey Wm.
Chinery Robert
Claydon Wm.
Lawrence Edw.
Olley Frederick
Rollinson Joseph

Smoothy Joseph, *Hall*
Surridge James, *Charity Farm*
CARRIER.
Jas. Bradman to Ipswich, Wed.

WRATTING, (GREAT) a pleasant village in the vale of a rivulet, 2½ miles N.E. of Haverhill, and six miles W.N.W. of Clare, has in its parish 355 souls, and 1329A. 3R. 12P. of land, having a good mixed soil. Lord Thurlow is lord of the manor, but part of the soil belongs to F. and G. Gibson, Esqrs., J. Spirling, Esq., Misses French, and a few smaller owners. The *Church* (St. Mary) is a small structure, with a tower and one bell. The rectory, valued in K.B. at £8, has that of Little Wratting annexed to it, and the joint benefices were valued in 1835 at £450 ; but the tithes here were commuted in 1841 for £341, and those of Little Wratting for £250

per annum. The Rev. Thos. B. Syer, B.A., is patron and incumbent. The *Church Land*, 2½A., is let for £5. 5s. a year, which is applied in repairing the church. Two tenements are occupied rent-free by poor persons placed in them by the churchwardens and overseers. In 1747, *Jas. Vernon* left his messuage here, called Weathercock Farm, to be used as a *Workhouse* for the parishes of Great Wratting, Great Thurlow, Chilbourn, and Barnardiston, and he endowed it with a yearly rent-charge of £10, out of lands now belonging to Sir Robt. Harland. The messuage ceased to be used as a workhouse many years ago, and only a small part of it now remains, which is occupied rent-free by a poor family. In consequence of the disuse of the workhouse, the annuity is not paid.

Barrett Wm. vict. *Bell*
Howard Wm. vict. *Red Lion*
Ling Jacob, blacksmith
Marsh Thomas, shopkeeper
Mitson Thos. and Wm. shoemakers
Syer Rev Thos. B., B.A., *Rectory*

FARMERS.
Burroughes Lot || Garrod Simon
Golding George
Hymus Stephen, *Hill Farm*
Jannings John, *Wratting Hall*
Taylor Wm.

WRATTING (LITTLE) is a small village in a pleasant valley, 2 miles N.E. of Haverhill, and adjoins Great Wratting on the south. It has in its parish 239 souls, and 950 acres of fertile land, all freehold, and belonging to Mrs. Lucy Bird, Mrs. Frost, Wm. Margetts, Esq., Mrs. C. Jardine, and a few smaller proprietors. The *Church* is a small ancient structure, and the benefice is a *rectory*, valued in K.B. at £4. 19s. 9½d., and united with that of Great Wratting, as noticed above. The principal inhabitants are Edwin Binks, *shopkeeper ;* John Goodchild, farmer, *Wash ;* Mrs. Caroline Jardine ; Wm. Owers, *Hill-farm ;* and Charles Punchard, corn miller and farmer, *Blunts Hall.*

[*END OF SUFFOLK.*]

DISS, a pleasant and well-built market town, *in Norfolk*, in the Hundred to which it gives name, is situated on rising ground, near a fine *lake* or mere, on the north side of the vale of the Waveney, 23 miles N. of Ipswich. Its parish has 3195 acres of land, and 3205 inhabitants, including the hamlets of *Heywood, Walcot Green,* and *Westby Green.* The market is on Friday, and here is a large *stock fair* on Nov. 8th, and a *lamb fair* on the first Friday in July. The history of this improving town will be found in our Norfolk Work.

POST OFFICE, Crown street ; Mr. Southby Williams, *postmaster.* Letters despatched to London, &c., at ½ past 7 evening ; to Bury, &c., at ½ past 5 evening ; and to Norwich, &c., at ½ past 6 morning

In the following DIRECTORY OF DISS, *those marked* 1, *reside in Brook street ;* 2, *Chapel street ;* 3, *Cherry Tree lane ;* 4, *Church street ;* 5, *Cock street ;* 6, *Cock street green ;* 7, *Crown street ;* 8, *Half-Moon street ;* 9, *Heywood ;* 10, *Market place ;* 11, *Mere street ;* 12, *Mount street ;* 13, *Scole road ;* 14, *Shelfanger road ;* 15, *Walcot green ;* 16, *Westby green ; and* 17, *in St. Nicholas street.*

12 Baldwin Wm. clog, &c. maker
7 Bardwell Miss Harriet
12 Barkway John, clog, &c. maker
12 Browne George Fredk. solicitor
6 Bryant Edmund, clothes dealer
Buckingham Jas. chimney sweep
Button Mr Wm. Fredk., Mere st
6 Calver, James, bookkeeper
11 Clarke Hy. fishmonger
Clarke Miss E. S. Mount street
6 Colman Thos. corn inspector & regr
Cross Miss Mary Ann
Couzens Mrs Mary, Church street
13 Curtis Isaac, horse letter
Darby Mrs Eliz. Market hill
Eaton Mrs Sarah, Mount street
6 Farrow Samuel, chief constable
13 Field Joseph, Independent min.
10 Fincham Robt. Esq., banker
6 Garrard Mrs Dinah
7 Harrison Wm. house, &c. agent
Holmes John, dyer, Mere street
11 Jeffery John, umbrella maker
3 Lewis Rev John Philip, (Baptist)
17 Long John, music teacher
13 Manning Rev Wm. M.A. rector
13 Manning Miss Frances
Marsh Mrs Sarah, Mere street
13 Medley Rev G. B., B.A curate
Mines Edw. Esq. Mere street
12 Morris Rev Thos Brooke, rector
   of Shelfanger
Moore James, gent. Mount street
Nice Robert, postman, Crown street
Parley Mrs Mary Ann, Crown st
2 Parr Robert, sexton and organist
17 Rayner Robt. hay and straw dlr
12 Redgrave John, solicitors' clerk
4 Rix John B. bankers' clerk
10 Simpson Zach. bankers' clerk
13 Smith Mark, botanist
Spurdens Robt. postman
12 Taylor Mrs Elizabeth
12 Thorn John, excise officer
Watson Mrs Eliz. Mount street
7 Williams Mr Southby, postmaster
   and news agent
12 Womack Miss Mary Ann
   BANKERS.
10 Oakes, Fincham, and Co. (draw
   on Barclay and Co.)
10 Taylor and Dyson, (draw on Bar.
   netts and Co.)
   FIRE AND LIFE OFFICES.
10 Family Endowment, J. U. Eldridge
7 Norwich Equitable, J. Crowe
10 Pelican, Robert Fincham

4 Suffolk Amicable, J. B. Rix
HOTELS, INNS, AND TAVERNS.
7 Bee Hive, James Brooks
10 Bell, Charles Ayton
3 Cherry Tree, Charles Crowe
6 Cock, Jonthn. Payne, (& millwgt)
11 Cross Keys, Benj. Berrett
7 Crown & Commercial, Robert B.
   Winkup
4 Dolphin, Nathl. Garrett
7 Greyhound, John Chapman
8 Half-Moon, Timy. Buckingham
10 King's Head Inn, (posting,) Jane
   Maplestone
12 Saracen's Head, Fras. Edwards
14 Ship, Philip Goold
10 Star, Robert Moye
Sun, Philip Rayner, Mere street
7 Two Brewers, John Shaw
13 White Hart, Michael Rowell
10 White Horse, Samuel Stowers

Academies.
Cuthbert Cornls.
   & Eliz. *Natl. Sch*
6 Harme Edwd.
4 Nunn Edward
   Cooke *(classl. &c)*
4 Tripp Eliza
12 Whitby Saml.
   James
Attorneys.
11 Brook John
   Calver
12 Heffill Henry
12 Muskett Jno.
   (coroner, and
   commissnr. for
   takg. acknow-
   ledgments of
   married wo-
   men)
17 Norton Edw.
11 Taylor Thos.
   Lombe
12 Wallace and
   Brown
Auctioneers.
17 Alger Cleer S.
   (& land survr.)
11 Elliott Wm.
   Waller, (and
   Thelveton)
11 Gostling Thos.
Bakers, &c.
11 Baxter Mrgt.
4 Cattermole Isc.
Driver Harriet

6 Frost John
10 Juby Thomas
12 Scrivener Rd.
17 Scrivener Ths.
6 Whiting Robt.
Basket Maker.
11 Berrett Benj.
Beer Houses.
11 Barrett Philip
7 Church Sarah
13 Easto Richd.
Ellis James
6 Ford David
16 Levi Samuel
9 Moore Eliz.
13 Payne John
Blacksmiths.
11 Goold Philip
3 Hayward Hy.
12 Reeve Abslm.
2 Slack Richard
12 Towell Wm.
Booksellers,
Printers, &c.
11 Abbott Edw.
11 Gostling Ths.
17 Pittuck John
   Samuel
Boot & Shoe Mkrs.
13 Barker Ebzr.
10 Bloomfield W.
4 Bloomfield Jas.
13 Freeman Wm.
11 Hammond Wm
7 Hayward Thos.
7 Knowles Saml.

7 Le Good Eliz.
4 Ready Richd.
Braziers & Tinrs.
11 Brook Samuel
11 Bryant Robt.
13 Smith Samuel
Brewers and Maltsters.
7 Cuthbert Hy.
6 Farrow Chas.
7 Taylor & Dyson
Brush Manfrs.
7 Aldrich Robert
7 Barkham Thos.
7 Broad George
Bricklayers.
7 Downing Robt.
7 Garrard Robt.
13 Houchen Geo.
12 Hubbard Spha.
7 Rout John
12 Welham Hy.
Butchers.
10 Baker George
7 Browning My.
10 Loocock Jas.
11 Plummer Jno.
7 Robinson Jas.
13 Rowell Michl.
3 Sandy Samuel
10 Tyrrell Geo.
Cabinet Makers.
10 Barkham Ths.
12 Battel Wm.
7 Harrison Wm.
7 Parker John
Chemists and Druggists.
11 Cupiss Fras.
(oil & colourman, vety. surgeon, & propr. of the constitution horse balls)
10 Eldridge Jas. Upton
Coach Makers.
11 Garrett Nathan and Son
7 Lait Thomas
11 Lait Charles
Confectioners.
11 Alger James
10 Browning Sml.
11 Baxter Ann
11 Berrett Php.

11 Leeder Simon
6 Whiting Wm.
Coopers.
11 Berrett Benj.
7 Burch Thomas
Corn and Coal Merchants.
4 Baker George
13 Chaplyn Wm.
11 Cutting John
6 Levick Wm.
(and maltster)
Corn Millers.
13 Chaplyn Wm.
3 Cornell Samuel
9 Ellis Stimson
13 Jay Thomas
11 Leathers Chs. Jay
6 Pike Henry
13 Rush Thomas
Curriers, &c.
4 Baldwin John
10 Leech John
FARMERS.
(* are Owners.)
9 Booty Rhoda
13*Calver Enoch
9 Chapman Geo.
9 Coe Charles
9*Corey John
9 Ellis Stimson
13*Ellis Robert
9 Ellis Henry
9 Esling John
*Fincham Jas.
9 Fisher Ann
12 Fulcher Hy.
9 Fordham John
9 Grant John
9 Johnson Chas.
9*Murton Robt.
9 Marton Rt. jun
9 Newdick Wm.
9*Palmer Geo.
13 Payne Nunn
9*Smith Edmd.
9*Smith Shldrk.
9 Smith John
9 Stollery Chas.
9*Surling Wm.
9 Tacon Joseph
*Wallace T. E.
9 Wells Fredk.
Gardeners, &c.
2 Cornell Wm.
13 Goldsmith Mk.

7 Gooderam Ed.
7 Parker Richd.
6 Parker Richd.
Glass and China Dealers.
17 Alger Charles
10 Corey John Sandel
11 Gostling Thos.
Glover, &c.
17 Nice James
Grocers & Tea Dealers.
17 Aldrich Robt.
17 Alger Chas.
10 Browning Sml.
11 Burrows Gibson
13 Chaplyn Wm.
6 Cotman Thos.
10 Corey John S.
7 Crowe James
17 Read John
3 Sandy Samuel
7 Spelman Geo.
4 Witting Chas.
Gunsmith.
11 Mallett John
Hair Dressers.
10 Burrows Bendley
10 Haunton Rt.
6 Sandy Stephen
12 Whitehead Rt.
Hosier & Worsted Manufacturer.
17 Leech Thos.
Iron Founders & Machine Mkrs.
12 Swootman Wm
10 Whaite John and Thomas
Iron Merchant.
11 Brook Saml.
Ironmongers.
11 Brook Saml.
7 Lines John
10 Whaite John and Thos. (and gas fitters)
Joiners & Buildrs.
12 Angold Henry
2 Atkins George and Son
11 Cobb Samuel
6 Farrow Jph.

Linen Manfr.
11 Warne Hy.
Linen & Woollen Drapers.
10 Blake Jno. G.
17 Bobby Wm. and Son
10 Bulwer Wm.
10 Cracknell Jno. Smith
7 Debenham Edw
17 Eglinton Slmn.
10 Hall Wm.
Milliners, &c.
12 Elsey Jane
12 Jolley Ann
7 Turner Eliz.
Painters, Plumbers, & Glaziers.
12 Aldrich John
11 Cobb Samuel, (and builder)
11 Coe Charles
12 Hunting Wm.
10 Whaite J. & T.
Porter Merchts.
11 Berrett Philip
11 Berrett Thos.
Saddlers.
17 Church Wm.
7 Terry James
7 Walne Mlndr.
Stone Masons.
4 Alger Charles
7 Farrow Thos. (& timber mert)
Straw Hat Mkrs.
12 Martin J.
12 Youels Har.
Surgeons.
7 Harrison Php.
11 Haydon Hy. Phippard
12 Mines Wm.
7 Ward Henry
Tailors.
7 Andrews Wm.
12 Bailey Mark
7 Bond George
11 Cooper David
11 Bryant Danl.
17 Eglinton Slmn.
7 Goold Philip
7 Hague Wm.
7 Lait Thos jun
17 Stannard Rt.
13 Trudgill Chs.

Turners (Wood)
7 Meadows Rt.
3 Tipple George

Watchmkrs. &c.
6 Dove John
10 Marsh Wm.
10 Scrivener Edward Keer
11 Taylor Denis

COACHES to London and Norwich daily, from the Crown; and to Yarmouth, Cambridge, &c., from the King's Head

CARRIERS.

To *London*, from the Crown, Noller's Vans, Tues. and Fri. ; and to *Nor-*

Wheelwrights.
13 Everett Robt. (& millwright)
12 Kerry Jonth.
Nicholson Teigh

Wine and Spirit Merchants.
7 Cuthbert Hy.
10 Browning Sml.
6 Farrow Chas.
7 Taylor & Dyson

wich, Mon. and Thursday. Also, Sykes' Waggon from the Sun
To *London*, Deacon and Co., from the King's Head, Mon. and Fri. ; and to *Bury*, Tues. and Saturday Bury St Edmund's. (See London)
To *Bungay*, Neeve, from the Duke's Head, Monday and Friday
To *Ipswich*, from Scole road, Robt. Websdell, Mon. and Thurs. ; and Richard Easto and John Cutting, daily ; and to *Norwich*, Tue. & Fri.
To *New Buckenham*, J. Hughes, from the Bell, Thursday Norwich. (See London & Ipswich)
To *Thetford*, T. Miller, from the Star, Friday

HARLESTON, a small market town, in Earsham Hundred, *Norfolk*, on the north side of the vale of the Waveney, 8 miles W.S.W. of Bungay, and nearly 10 miles E. by N. of Diss, is mostly in the parish of Redenhall-with-Harleston, and partly in that of Mendham. It has about 1700 inhabitants, and its history will be found in our Norfolk Work. The *Market* is held on Wednesday ; and the *Fairs* on July 5th, Sept. 9th, and Dec. 1st. The *Post Office* is at Mr. James Caley's; and letters are despatched at 8 evening. In the following *Directory*, those marked 1, are in *Redenhall village* ; and 2, in the *Mendham part of the town.*

Asten Jno. jun. corn merchant
Balls Jabez, auctioneer
Beaumont Mrs. Broad street
Blomfield Mr James
Brooks Thomas, patten maker
Bryant Sarah and Martha, milliners
Cann Wm. bankers' clerk
Chappell Geo. Wm. assistant magistrates' clerk
Chappell Mr Samuel, senior
Chilvers Samuel, glover
Cole Rev. Stephen Martin, curate of Mendham
Donnison Rev. J. W. S., curate
Etheridge Mrs Har. and Mrs Sar.
Gedney Mrs My. || Fox Mrs Eliz.
Gilbert Mrs J. medicine vendor
Gilbert Thos. coach builder
Godbolt John, parish clerk
Green Miss Mary Eliza
Habberton Miss Sarah
Harris Wm. dyer
Hart Robert, gentleman
Harvey Robt. corn & flour dealer, Chapel plain
Hazard Wm. solr. & magistrates' clk
Hart Rt. gent || Heyman Mrs Mary
Holmes Wm. Sancroft, Esq., & Mrs Hannah, *Gaudy Hall*

2 Jenner Lieutenant
Laidler Stephen (Indept. minister)
Metcalfe Rev. Wallace, M.A. curate
Oldershaw Ven. John, B.D., archdeacon of Norfolk, and rector of Redenhall: h *Starston*
Norman Wm. gentleman
Parker Mr John, Broad street
Palmer Ellen and Sophia, milliners
Pooley James Henry, drawing mstr
Priest Richd. gent. & Miss Sarah
Prime Henry, carrier to Norwich
Sewell Ann, sub-distributor of stamps
Sharman Samuel, agent
Simons Mr Charles || Smith Mr Wm.
Swallow John, servants' regr. office
Turner Mrs Elizabeth
Whaite Miss S. & Woods Mrs M.
2 Wilson Robert, bleacher
2 Woodward Rev. B. B. (Indepndt.)
Vipond Mr John

BANKERS.

East of England Banking Co. (on London and Westminster,) Wm. Cann, agent
Gurneys & Co. (on Barclay & Co.,) Wm. Hazard, agent

Norfolk & Norwich Joint Stock Co. (on Masterman & Co.,) George Carthew, agent

FIRE AND LIFE OFFICES.
Atlas, Edward Grimwade
Norwich Equitable, James Musket
Norwich Union, Samuel Carman
Royal Exchange, James Caley
Suffolk, James Barnaby

INNS AND TAVERNS.
Cardinal's Hat, Rt. Read Bloomfield
2 Cherry Tree, Robert Borrett
Crown, Wm. Feek
Duke William, James Riches
Grapes Tap, John Reeve
Green Dragon, Benj. Kerridge
Horse Shoes, Robert Rayner
2 Magpie Inn, Thomas Edwards
Red Lion, Robert Bullock
Royal Oak, James Sheldrake
Swan Inn, Jonthn. Nobbs (posting)
Two Brewers, Robert Mason
Yew Tree, John Dunn

Academies.
Devereux Agnes
Elliot Sarah
Parker My. Ann
Pooley Ann Lyd.
Priest Sarah
1 Robinson Wm.

Attorneys.
2 Barnaby Jas.
Carthew George
Hazard & Jeffes
Bakers & Flour Dealers.
Lillistone Wm.
Gobbett Jonth.
Smith Henry
Wilson Chpr.
Wilson John
Wilson Wm.
Beer Houses.
Bear John
Gibbs Henry
Mason Lydia
Blacksmiths.
Colls John
Smith Verdon
Booksellers, Printers, &c.
Cann Robert
Grimwade Edw.
Boot & Shoe Mkrs.
Agar John

Aldis Thomas
Barber Thomas
Baxter Wm.
Colling John
Freston Henry
Freston Wm.
Hurry Joshua
Pritty Robert
Rodwell Wm.
Rodwell Charles
Warne John

Braziers & Tinrs.
Abbott Rhoda
Chatton Robert
Mason Robert
Bricklayers.
1 Godbolt John
Hales Robert
Pedgrift James
Pedgrift Samuel
Pedgrift Wm.
Butchers.
Dunham John
Grice Benjamin
Hall John
Shipston Pleasne.
Watson Sarah
Cabinet Makers
Barley John
Tillett Fredk.

Chemists & Dgts.
Grimwade Edw. (& colourman)
Musket James
Coach Makers.
Freston Jonth.
Gilbert Thomas
Confectioners.
Feltham Wm.
Lillistone Wm.
Coopers.
Hart Jonathan
Woolnough Wm.
Corn Millers.
1 Asten Robert
1 Barber Wm.
Curriers.
2 Aldis Thomas
Hughman Jph. (& brewer)
2 Mason Cornls.
FARMERS.
1 Aldous John
Aldous James
Burleigh John
2 Cooper Arthur
Dordery Wm.
1 Fisher James
1 Gedney John
1 Hart Henry
Hudson Henry
Lombard
Kersey Edw. A., *Shotford Hall*
2 Mayhew Elias
1 Moore Jas Vinct
1 Murrell James
1 Parker James, *Redenhall Ldg*
Parker Nathl.
2 Rackham Robt.
2 Riches Fras.
2 Sheppard Ann
Glass, China, &c. Dealers.
Humphreys Eliz.
Seman Thomas
Grocers & Draprs
Aldis Jas. Lines
Favour Robert
2 Francis James
Pratt Jonathan
Burford
Prentice Samuel
Smith and Buck
Snell Frank

Smith Saml (*draper only*)
Watling Chpr.
Woolnough Mark
Hair Dressers.
Colby Wm.
Colby Wm. jun.
Ironmongers.
Brown & Clowes
Caley James
Chappell Samuel, (& gunsmith)
Crow Wm.
Joiners, &c.
Foulger Wm.
Francis Robert
Hammond Chas.
Hammond Robt.
Nash Richard
Rayner Robert
Sheppard Chas.
Wilton Charles, (wheelwright)
Plumbers, Glaz. and Painters.
Chappell James
Caley James
Hawke James
Wigg Robert
Saddlers.
Freston Charles
Goggs Charles
Wright John
Surgeons.
2 Bunn Wm.
Crisp Benj. John (& registrar)
Priest Richard
Tailors & Drprs.
Allured Wm.
Blomfield John
Chatton Robert
2 Freston Richd.
Mayhew John
Squire George
Swallow Thomas
Titlow Samuel
Veterinary Surgeons.
Roulfe Richard
Terry Wm.
Watch Makers.
Brown John
Carman Saml. (& corn inspector)
Feltham Wm.

Wine, Spirit, Ale	Cann & Hodgson	COACHES,
& Porter Merts.	Corbould Pelham	To *Norwich*, Ipswich, Bungay, &c.
Aldous James	(& maltster)	daily. Also, *carriers' waggons* & vans several times a-week, from the inns.

EAST HARLING is a small market town, in Guiltcross Hundred, *Norfolk*, 9 miles E. by. N. of Thetford, and 21 miles S.W. of Norwich. Its parish has 2568A. 3R. 17P. of land, and contains 1062 inhabitants. The *market* is held on Tuesday, and three *fairs* for cattle, &c., are held on May 1st, the first Tuesday after Sept. 12th, and on Oct. 24th. The *history* of this town will be found in our Norfolk Work, and the following are its principal inhabitants. POST OFFICE, at Mr. Chas. Kerrison's. Letters despatched at ¼ before 8 morning, and at ½ past 5 evening.

Atmore Richard, gentleman
Bailey Wm. cabinet maker
Barber John, national schoolmaster
Cooke George Sparham, wine and spirit merchant
Doynes Thos. cooper and basket mkr
Everett John and Robt. gentlemen
Gant Mr Wm. || Hubbard Mr Abm.
Jary Thomas, corn miller
Lanchester Wm. patten maker
Milner John, saddler
Postle Tolver, surgeon
Read Frederick, corn chandler
Rush Henry, veterinary surgeon
Rust Robert, horsebreaker
Smith John, baker
Warren Mr Wm. || Sparrow Mrs
Whewell Wm. earthenware dealer
Whitrod John, watchmaker and ironmonger
Wilkinson Rev Thos. B. *Rectory*
Willingham Mrs Susan

INNS AND TAVERNS.
Bull, John Pearl
Nag's Head, Wm. Watson
Queen's Head, Wm. Jolley
Swan, Edward Wiseman Betts
White Hart, John Eagling
 COACH, to Norwich, from the
Swan, Mon. Wed. and Sat. at 7 mg
 CARRIER, James Fisk, to Bury,

Sat., and Norwich, Thurs., from the Nag's Head
 Beerhouses.
Barrett Joseph
Smith Richard
 Blacksmiths.
Jolley Wm.
Loveday John (& ironfounder)
Peake Geo. & Sl.
Pearl John (and ironmonger)
 Boot & Shoe Mkrs.
Barnard Rt. Jno.
Gregory Wm.
Knights John
Pull Robert
Squire James
 Bricklayers.
Clarke Robert
Kerrison Charles and Son
Kerrison C. jun.
Kerrison George
Kerrison Solomon
 Butchers.
Woodcock Geo.
Wright Thomas
 FARMERS.
Bartlett Robert
Cooke Robert

Goddard Thomas
Jary Thomas
Harrold Philip
Kerrison George
Palmer George
West Robert
 Grocers & Drprs.
Drake Elizabeth
Everett John, jun. (and chandler)
Gallant James
Lark Jas. B.
Youels Wm.
 Plumbers, Glaziers, &c.
Allen Amos
Watson Wm.
 Tailors.
Barrett Joseph
Cracknell Wm. (and draper and hatter)
Minet James
Mounseer Leond.
Rust Robert
Youels James
 Wheelwrights.
Le Gryse Thos.
Loveday John

KENNINGHALL, in Guiltcross Hundred, *Norfolk*, is a small, ancient market-town, nearly 3 miles E. of East Harling. Its parish has 3516A. 3R. 27P. of land, and 1389 souls. A large *stock market* is held here every Monday; and *fairs*, on July 18th, for cattle ; and on Sept. 30th, for sheep. The history of Kenninghall will be found in the Norfolk Work, and the following are its principal inhabitants. *Post Office*, at Mr. Samuel Fisher's ; letters despatched at 4 afternoon.

Barham Eliz. and Dinah, milliners
Bond Wm. poulterer
Briggs John, gardener
Calver Daniel, solicitor, stamp distr. ;

 and coroner for the Liberty of the Duke of Norfolk
Carter Wm. gentleman
Clarke Saml. turner & patten maker

Davy Robert, watchmaker
Dent Peter, surgeon
Dixon Zach. brazier and ironmonger
Howell Rev. Henry (Baptist)
Humphrey Jonathan, gentleman
Humphrey T. J. brick & tile maker
Kent Geo. regr. and relvg. officer
Killett Rev. Wm. B.A. vicar
Linstead George, saddler
Morley James, parish clerk
Rackham Thomas, master of Guilt-cross Union *Workhouse*
Sayer George, cabinet maker
Turner Mr Charles || Reeve Mrs
Turner Thomas, supt. registrar
Wells Saml. and Robt. brewers and maltsters

INNS AND TAVERNS.

Crown, James Collings
George, Matthew Wilde (& painter, glazier, &c.)
Red Lion, Robert Cook
White Horse, Richard Holmes

Academies.	*Blacksmiths.*
Ellis Misses	Barker Thomas
Harvey Robt (& bookbinder)	Collings James
	Wade John
Webster —	Wade Nathaniel
Bakers.	*Boot & Shoe Mkrs.*
Ashton John	Fisher Samuel
Long Zachariah	Horne John
Beerhouses.	Horne J. jun. (& currier)
Jackson Robert	
Mallett Henry, (and gardener)	Moyse George
	Rush Thomas
Wells Samuel & Robert	Smith Robert
	Smith Thomas

Bricklayers.
Barham Robert
Osborne George
Butchers.
Cross Wm.
Huggins Wm.
Coopers.
Daines Robert
Davy Robert
Corn Millers.
Cook Robert
Reeve James
Wells Wm.
FARMERS.
Avis Ann
Barham Robert
Bilham Stephen
Burlingham Jas.
Cooke Nathaniel, *Grange*
Coulson John
Cracknell W.
Fincham John
Green John
Harvey George
Holmes Mary
Humphrey T. J.
Osborne George
Reeve Samuel
Ruffell F. J.
Spurling Daniel
Wells John
West Wm.
Weston John
Wrentham John
Youels James
Youels Robert

Grocers & Drprs.
Betts Chas. (and wine mercht.)
Bryant Rd. (and merchant)
Rivett Robert (& brush maker)
Wells Sl. & Rt.
Tailors.
Buxton James
Coe Robert
Cooke Thomas
Thurlow John
Turner James
Wheelwrights.
Clarke Thos. sen. and jun.
Garrett Benj.
Lawrence Stphn.
Wheal John
COACH, — to Norwich, Mon. Wed. and Sat. 7 morning
CARRIERS, to *Norwich,* J. Fisk, M. & Thu.; and J. Bowen, Tu. & Fri.
To *Bury,* W. Sykes, Thu.; & J. Fisk, W. and Sat.
R. Clark, to *Diss,* Fri.; and *Thetford,* Sat.

BURY ST. EDMUND'S.

(ALTERATIONS since the Directory at pages 646 to 662, was printed.)

Arnold John, vict. Unicorn, 72 Eastgt
Barton Rt. shoemaker, 15 Guildhall st
Betts Wm. confectioner, 69 St. John st
Blake Jas. Hy. solicitor, 124 Northgate
Boby Robert, ironmonger, 7 Meat mkt
Chapman Ann. school, 6 Angel hill
Clark Frederick, vict. White Hart, 35 Southgate
Claxton Jno. coal dealer, 11 Whiting st
Cole Alfred, bookseller, 26 Butter mkt
Fairweather Alex. gent. 69 Risbygate
Fake Thos. joiner, 38 Westgate road
Foster Wm. vict. Magpie, Church yard
Goodchild Mrs Susan, 22 Angel hill
Groom Mrs Elizabeth, 73 Guildhall st
Hake Thos. G., M.D. 74 Guildhall st
Hodgkinson Rev Geo. C. second master of the *Grammar School*
Lenny & Croft, surveyors, 82 Whiting st
Limmer Lionel, eatinghouse, 39 Brentgovel street
Muskett John, Esq. Church yard
New Manchester Warehouse, 20 Abbeygate street
Parish Wm. horse dealer, 12 Whiting st
Plummer Rt. and Rd. grocers and tea dealers, 104 Risbygate
Portway George, Esq. manager of the National Provincial Bank of England, Meat market
Powell Wm. vict. Three Crowns, 6 Southgate
Rose Hy. shopkeeper, 12 Guildhall st
Salmon John, dyer, 1 Risbygate
Sore Samuel, cooper, 2 Abbeygate
Steggles Wm. builder, 10 Whiting st
Stutter Wm. Edw. printer and bookseller, 62 Guildhall street
Tricker Mary, grocer, 3 Abbeygate
Wade Mrs A. school, 10 Whiting st
Walford Thomas, shopr. 22 Southgate
Wallworth Smith, hat mfr. 53 Abbeygt
Wright Jas. vict. Two Brewers, Westgt

BRANDON.

(Alterations.—See page 585.)

Hyam Cornelius, vict. *Five Bells*
Jacob Thomas, vict. *White Lion*
Rix Wm. vict. *White Hart*
Rought Wm. shoemaker
Snare Thomas, gentleman
Rogers — Esq. *Brandon Hall*
Towell Samuel, tailor and draper

CORRECTIONS, &c.

Arcedeckne A. Esq. is in a few places misprinted *Archdeckne*
Crook Jph. auctioneer, &c. Old Butter market, *Ipswich*
Capon Samuel, cattle dealer, *Stratford St. Andrew*

Hutchinson James, gardener, *Ampton Hall*
Page 86, line 13, for Blything, read Bosmere and Claydon Hundred
Page 94, Peecock John, (not Peacock)
,,   Shreiber W. F. (not Shriber)
Page 141. The Rev R. Jones, of Upton, near Wisbech, is now *vicar of Bawdsey*
Pages 146 and '7, Rev C. G. Watson (not Walton)
Page 202.   PETER ISAAC THELLUSON, ESQ. died in 1797; and it was his eldest son, of the same name, who was created *Lord Rendlesham.* He was born at Paris, in 1735, and settled in London as a merchant, with a fortune of £10,000. He was naturalized by Act of Parliament, 1762. After providing for his three sons and three daughters, he left about £600,000 in trust for *accumulation* during the lives of his three sons, and the lives of their sons, born at the time of his decease, or in due time afterwards. This singular trust is contingent on the lives of nine persons, the last of whom, it is calculated, may survive till 1870. After the death of the survivor, the accumulated property will go to the eldest male lineal descendants of the testator's three sons, or the survivor of them; and should there. be no male heirs, (which is not likely to happen,) the estates are to be applied to the use of the *Sinking Fund*, in such manner as may be determined by Act of Parliament.
Page 245, for BESTED, read BESTED.
Page 308. The *Right Hon. John Thos. Manners Sutton*, LORD MANNERS, who purchased the Fornham estate, is a peer of the realm, and not a son of the Duke of Rutland. His father was Lord Chancellor of Ireland, and was created a baron in 1807.
Page 309. The Corporation of Ipswich (not Bury) were patrons of *Gedding Rectory ;* but they sold the advowson in September, 1843.
Page 661, third line, second column, for Branson, read *Brandon*
Wm. Woods Page, Esq., formerly of Woodbridge, and for 28 years a magistrate of Suffolk, died in London in July, 1843, aged 77, and was buried at *Clopton.*
A *Floating Light* was placed, Dec. 12, 1843, in the Cockle Gat, at the north entrance into *Yarmouth Roads.*

ROBERT LEADER, PRINTER, INDEPENDENT-OFFICE, SHEFFIELD.